INTERNATIONAL HANDBOOK OF CONTEMPORARY DEVELOPMENTS IN SOCIOLOGY

INTERNATIONAL HANDBOOK OF CONTEMPORARY DEVELOPMENTS IN SOCIOLOGY

EDITED BY

Raj P. Mohan & Arthur S. Wilke

GREENWOOD PRESS
Westport, Connecticut

Library of Congress Cataloging-in-Publication Data

International handbook of contemporary developments in sociology /
   edited by Raj P. Mohan and Arthur S. Wilke.
      p. cm.
   Includes bibliographical references and index.
   ISBN 0–313–26719–7 (alk. paper)
     1. Sociology—History—Handbooks, manuals, etc. 2. Sociology—
Study and teaching—Handbooks, manuals, etc. 3. Sociology—
Research—Handbooks, manuals, etc. I. Mohan, Raj P. II. Wilke,
Arthur S.
HM19.I59   1994
301'.09—dc20   93-37504

British Library Cataloguing in Publication Data is available.

Library of Congress Catalog Card Number: 93–37504
ISBN: 0–313–26719–7

First published in 1994

Greenwood Press, 88 Post Road West, Westport, CT 06881
An imprint of Greenwood Publishing Group, Inc.

Printed in the United States of America

The paper used in this book complies with the
Permanent Paper Standard issued by the National
Information Standards Organization (Z39.48–1984).

10 9 8 7 6 5 4 3 2 1

Contents

Part IV. Sociology in Southern Europe

Part V. Sociology in Africa and the Middle East

Part VI. Sociology in the East

Preface

This handbook is envisioned as a reference book, assembled to provide the reader ready access to some of the major trends and literature dealing with sociology found in various nations throughout the world. The work provides sociologists a snapshot of various national constituencies of sociologists and their work. It also provides some initial clues on similarities and differences in various national sociologies. Its value resides in that in one project one can find a reasonable sampling of dominant ideas and works in sociology. For those concerned about broader questions such as the nature of culture in an emerging information-dominated, postmodern age, a work of this kind dealing with sociology is valuable. Sociology has long been a self-conscious activity, hospitable to epistemological issues. Studying sociology provides important clues to disciplinary contributions to cultural life.

This handbook was commended in that it had been nearly a generation since the last compilation had been undertaken by Raj P. Mohan and Don Martindale. Our intent has been to update the 1975 volume and provide greater coverage. In addition, the project was organized to elicit somewhat more systematic and even contributions. While we have been somewhat more successful, this volume reveals some unevenness, in part due to the differing strengths of various national sociologies.

The scope of this volume is, for the most part, limited to developments of the past twenty years. We provided each contributor with some general guidelines for what we wished to see in each chapter. Our major interests were to highlight the dominant ideas or theories, methods, and substantive findings which characterized a nation's sociological work, primarily since the mid-1970s. In addition, we were interested to see what other institutionalizing forces might be at work shaping the discipline. Contributors have variously complied with our request, though most have made a major effort to comply with it. While we are appreciative of the efforts of those who have contributed to this project, we did experience one surprising thing: the immense number of things sociologists, like many other disciplinary practitioners, do. In some instances this meant that those whom we initially contacted were unable to work this project into their schedules. They exhibit what Kenneth J. Gergin[1] describes as identifying attributes of "saturated selves."

And there is a lingering impression that just as the liberal nation-state faces significant challenges, some sociologists are not as enthusiastic with a project of this nature. Whether other constraints or properties of contemporary academic and scholarly work could account for this has not been explored.

The organization of the text proceeds in terms of continents. In turn, each surveyed nation is given a separate chapter. Extensive treatment of U.S. sociology has been included because of the dominant position the nation's sociologists enjoy among the world's sociologists. The United States hosts a large population of sociologists and predominates in the sheer volume of work. The additional emphasis on U.S. sociology was undertaken to develop surveys and critiques, especially in the theoretical and substantive domains. If the post–cold war climate prevails with economic stagnation, it may be that sociology in the United States will continue to be seriously challenged. There are some indications that sociology programs in the United States will face challenges or limitations imposed by financial duress as well as by disciplines such as management studies and communications which routinely have incorporated sociological work into their disciplinary canons. While the 1970s witnessed what seemed to be a theoretical impossibility, stagnation, the late 1980s and 1990s reveal that the material conditions for knowledge workers may be undergoing significant challenge. Education is no longer as privileged as it once was. Our contributors were not asked to assess the role of sociology in education, a worthwhile but difficult task in its own right. And new economic and technical developments which come under the title of "information revolution" seem poised to redefine many features of scholarly work, and there have been other developments such as postmodernism which not only challenge the traditional, logical, positivist-informed epistemology but also promote new combinations of literary texts and observer subjectivity, creating what at the moment is this generation's avant-garde. We have not entertained these topics, anticipating that the contours of these developments, if they proceed, will be clearer for those reviewing sociology in the next generation. In this survey of developments in world sociology, the organizational frameworks for the disciplines identified for several generations remain dominant.

The present handbook offers, as elaborated and developed by leading researchers, portraits of sociology in the United States and abroad. One can make the argument why some countries are left out while others are included. Initial efforts were made to invite leading sociologists from many more countries than are included here. The contributions were not forthcoming from many countries, for reasons too numerous to list. However, every effort has been made to include the best possible contributions we could gather. Editing a volume of this nature takes much more out of the editors and the contributors than writing one. In our view, this is a labor of love and we hope the results justify it.

Sociology emerged in the wake of two major developments: a general shift in the meaning of knowledge and the growth and diffusion of the nation-state. By the beginning of the eighteenth century in Europe a decisive shift in the meaning of knowledge was apparent. Attention veered away from an emphasis on self-knowledge and toward knowledge as skill, *techne,* but with some modification. From ancient times *techne* was shrouded in "the mystery of a craft skill," a tightly controlled system of induction and practice of how-to knowledge. The eighteenth century witnessed the wedding of *techne* "with logy, organized, systematic, purposeful knowledge."[2]

With the proliferation of organized technical knowledge/technology, crafts receded. Meanwhile the division between knowledge and "reality" increased. By the nineteenth century clear philosophic distinctions were being made between reality, the province of metaphysics, and knowledge, the focus of epistemology. Epistemological concerns were further amplified with the growth of what today are recognized as academic disciplines. In much disciplinary work epistemological concerns dominated: "claims to knowledge . . . were increasingly justified solely on intradisciplinary grounds" with some concern for interdisciplinary import.[3]

Sociology became a self-referencing, disciplining activity during the nineteenth century, one in which epistemological concerns were central. Sociology confronted but then joined the proliferation in the disciplinary division of labor. Sociology as envisioned by Auguste Comte (1798–1857) was to be a regal discipline, standing at the apex of various disciplinary pursuits. Sociology was to give place and purpose to the other, necessary but lesser, disciplinary pursuits. Buttressing Comte's proposal was an epistemological program in which he advanced a philosophy of historical ideas or knowledge. This historical portrait traced types of ideas along a natural evolutionary path. Dubbed the "law of three stages," knowledge and human history were subsequently conflated, portrayed as proceeding from a theological state to a metaphysical state to a positivistic one. In his fashioning of sociology as the crowning disciplinary achievement, Comte's work further provided an interdisciplinary rationale for the dividing intellectual, disciplinary landscape. It was joined by other work such as that of

John Stuart Mill (1806–1873) in promoting the building of interdisciplinary epistemological bridges. Mill outlined transcending rules of discourse, logic. Subsequently this contribution was wedded to the positivist program, which asked for clear, unambiguous claims to be grounded in empirical observations of natural things. In the twentieth century concerns for precise discourse and observation were formally recognized with the emergence of logical positivism. Such epistemological preoccupation was very attractive to those in the behavioral and social studies, providing some general normative guidance not only in how to undertake scientific investigations of the human condition but in how to affirm the identity of "scientists" on those doing such studies. Various disciplines, ranging from philosophy to sociology, embraced the requirements for knowledge, abiding by the rules of logical discourse and support in empirical verification. These were further enshrined in disciplinary subfields such as the philosophy of science and sociological research methods.

During the past generation, logical positivist concerns in various disciplines, including sociology, have receded. Residues nevertheless remain, often canonized in procedures for conducting and reporting research. These techniques remain in force in part because they are augmented by a close affiliation with state data, a topic addressed below.

Although the portrayal of sociology as the regal science was not sustained, the epistemological mission of sociology was evidenced in the next generation of sociologists after Comte, most notably in the personage of Emile Durkheim (1858–1917). Durkheim sought to sustain the interdisciplinary relevance of knowledge activities in a Kantian way, proposing that there were discoverable universal cognitive categories or cultural forms in all social orders. If a scientific sociology confirmed cognitive universals, sociology's position as a subject having interdisciplinary relevance was supported. Durkheim, however, did not intensely pursue concerns about contemporary knowledge. This was a task for the twentieth-century writer Karl Mannheim (1893–1947), a central figure in establishing the sociology of knowledge. Mannheim's attention to knowledge challenged the notion of underlying cultural universals. For him, most epistemological concerns were seen to be anchored in the structures and activities of specific social orders with the exception of the physical sciences. The physical sciences, reflecting a logical positivist view, were treated as a privileged, transcendent, universal system of knowledge. It is a view which more recent sociologies of science informed by a social constructionist perspective have challenged.[4] Nevertheless, Mannheim's work continued the concern that sociology address the epistemological issues in a transcendental fashion.

Added to the preoccupation with epistemological concerns in sociology was the formal recognition of applied knowledge, of *techne*. Disciplinary sociology was increasingly portrayed, following Lester F. Ward (1841–1913), as divided between pure and applied pursuits. While concerns for pure sociology led to preoccupations with ideas, many of which supported the history and legitimacy of the nation-state and have informed theoretical discourse, applied sociological concerns sought a place in the modern liberal state, as they frequently do today. This close connection with the state was recognized by Mohan and Martindale in their 1975 edition of the *Handbook of Contemporary Developments in World Sociology,* when they noted that sociology was "one of the nation-state's distinctive intellectual enterprises . . . becoming a world-wide discipline with the diffusion of the nation-state." With the diffusion of the nation-state, they further noted, sociology exhibited "tendencies toward the universalization of its methods, but a particularization in its problems and substantive concerns as its resources have been brought to bear on the problems peculiar to a given nation-state."[5]

The universalization of sociological methods was aided not only by epistemological considerations but by practical ones involved in statecraft. With the nationalization of space, key measures of activities of concern for overseeing political regimes, state-istics, became institutionalized. This resulted in data which could serve as comparative indicators on how regimes were doing. A number of things ensued from the collection and use of data based on demographic, ecological, and economic units of observation: large, diverse populations of often anonymous people could be efficiently monitored; tactical and strategic assessments regarding resources could be fostered; and narratives for national and international legitimacy could be fashioned about these raw materials.

The narratives surrounding the development and comparisons of various nations, often informed by historical and statistical data, constitute a type of bureaucratic propaganda[6] for which there are differing constituencies. Sociology continues to provide a place for constructing and disseminating some of these narratives. Through sociologists' embrace of philosophies of history, often in the form of "theories" of social and cultural change, combined with efforts to distinguish state-relevant applied knowledge from popular beliefs, the discipline has contributed to the promotion of the liberal state, a state to which the fate of sociology is closely aligned. Many contradictions inherent in the legal order of the liberal state are continually played out in terms of disputes of unresolved contradictions such as the emphasis on determinant rules versus ad hoc standards, the "notion that values or desires are arbitrary, subjective, individual and individuating while facts or reason are objective," and "the commitment to an intentionalistic discourse, in which human action is seen as the product of a self-determining individual will, and deterministic discourse . . . viewing subjects' conduct as an expected outcome of existing structures."[7]

At times there is a call for toleration or simply a recognition that sociology is composed of multiple paradigms,[8] leaving unaddressed the fundamental intellectual contradictions inherent in law and social theory.

As the twentieth century closes, the nation-state is undergoing significant transformation and challenge. Where it has an entrenched history and
presence, in North America and Europe, there is growing attention to
transnational, global concerns. Meanwhile, some former East European
countries as well as some in Central Africa are realigning along tribal and
ethnic lines. The Mideast reveals a shifting set of alliances in which the-
ocratic and secular forces are confronting each other within countries and
internationally. And in Asia a rapidly changing face of economic development reveals that nation-building may be reaching a new plateau.

As the nation-state undergoes transformation, sociology is also challenged. In the United States a growing appeal to the internationalization
of the discipline is now being made.[9] Meanwhile, assemblages such as the
Twelfth World Congress of Sociology in Madrid, Spain, in 1990, grapple
with metaphors to give expression to the tensions of universal and local
concerns. The Twelfth Congress's theme was "Sociology for One World:
Unity and Diversity," which, Arthur Meier noted, meant that attention be
directed "not simply upon one agreed world but rather on the rich and
contradictory strands making up the world—a whole and in its multifaceted aspects." This will result, as Meier envisioned it, in establishing a
global society which "would transcend conventional boundaries especially
those between nation-states, and eventually break down walls between
closed settings."[10] Meier's views highlight one of the intractable problems
of the liberal state written largely onto an international canvas: an appeal
to a rule-based system versus an appeal to a situational-standard approach.
Instead of probing this contradictory stance, which is manifested in multiple arenas, there is at once an appeal to diversity and to unity, leaving
the resulting contradiction unresolved. Like Comte, Meier makes the appeal that sociology will somehow serve as an epistemological referee if not
a moving agent in transforming the world or, perhaps simultaneously, be
an appropriate forum for diversity. The result: a global synthesis with tolerance for differences. This normative appeal, anchored in the contradictions of the liberal state, simply transports these concerns to a purportedly
larger arena. If a global state does not ensue, a critical question is, Will
sociology as it has developed under the aegis of the nation-state continue
to flourish?

Appeals to unity, diversity, and tolerance make up a congeries of claims
and sentiments well entrenched in sociology and many other disciplines.
These contradictory threads of thought and sentiment are sustained by
older spatio-temporal models of social life, coincident with the geopolitical
identity of the state, one more akin to the world of the eighteenth and
nineteenth centuries. Given that in those times spatial separation was pronounced and that available technology did not immediately bridge distinctions, sociologists could address the world much like incidental tourists,
assured that the world afar was different from the domestic situation. This

aided in promoting an appeal for the development of a transcendent discourse or discipline. Differences observed on the face of the earth were to be appreciated. This appreciation was part of a political cultural attack on domestic ethnocentric thought and action as well as a vehicle for providing the necessary variability for the development, possibly, of universal laws of collective life following logical and scientific procedures for data collection, analysis, and applied efforts such as "socio-cultural development."

The vision of variable sociocultural life reflecting different temporal orderings and being arrayed differentially in space is charming. Yet it is a vision which is at odds with other experiences of sociocultural life. This can be illustrated by the film *Scenes from a Mall.* In the film, Bette Midler and Woody Allen play a professional, urban, middle-class California couple. They are encapsulated in a lifeway which doesn't celebrate diversity but rather reduces it to some consumer choices in a common setting, the shopping mall. Not foreignness, but residues of international settings are rendered into commodities—food, entertainment, and other products. Here all the elements, in commodity form, are present which international sociologists such as Meier wish to consider only in nationally proscribed settings. More critically, the mall is a machine, one which fashions an extensive, dynamic, complex culture.[11] Various diverse residues are available with immense individual possibilities in patterns of acquisition. In the movie, the characters played by Midler and Allen use the mall as a stage for playing out the dramas of their lives. In the course of one afternoon the couple engage in intense personal conflicts and reconciliations. At one point they go to a movie in the mall, where they find fewer intrusions than at their home for engaging in erotic intimacy. The mall exhibits unity and diversity; however, the spatial and temporal markers long associated with portraying social life in global, nation-state configurations are collapsed. The foreign is domesticated, constrained as a consumer preference. The contradictions of the liberal state pale next to the engulfing experiences of the mall. As sociologists continue to seek order and diversity in dominant nation-state settings, they may be ignoring the drama of events which are dynamic and captivating. That the mall may not be a uniform experience is unquestioned. However, many of the commodities exhibited there are found in some fashion throughout the world. This is dramatized in the film *The Gods Must Be Crazy,* a parable of acculturation. An empty popular soft drink bottle drops from the sky. The movie details a sequence of transforming results which are set in motion. But unlike the movie, the soft drink or its portrait in the lives of more and more people reveals how ubiquitous such things are. And the popular dramas and narratives ensuing from their presence reveal a more fluid set of sociocultural conditions than are portrayed, for example, in Comte's "law of three stages."

NOTES

1. Kenneth J. Gergin, *The Saturated Self: Dilemmas of Identity in Contemporary Life* (New York: Basic Books, 1991).

2. Peter F. Drucker, "The Rise of the Knowledge Society," *The Wilson Quarterly* 17 (Spring 1993), pp. 56–57.

3. Steve Fuller, *Social Epistemology* (Bloomington, IN: Indiana University Press, 1988), p. 5.

4. Ibid., p. 4. Fuller proposes to wed the philosophic and sociological studies of knowledge into an approach he calls social epistemology.

5. Raj P. Mohan and Don Martindale, Preface to *Handbook of Contemporary Developments in World Sociology* (Westport, CT: Greenwood Press, 1975), pp. ix–x. This handbook was the outgrowth and expansion of articles originally appearing in the *International Journal of Contemporary Sociology*.

6. See David Altheide, *Bureaucratic Propaganda* (Boston: Beacon Press, 1980).

7. Mark Kelman, *A Guide to Critical Legal Studies* (Cambridge, MA, and London: Harvard University Press, 1987), p. 3.

8. George Ritzer, *Sociology: A Multiple Paradigm Science* (Boston: Allyn and Bacon, 1974).

9. J. Michael Armer, "Parochial Content Reported in U.S. Undergraduate Sociology," *Footnotes* 21, no. 2 (February 1993), p. 8. And introductory texts are increasingly exhibiting what is dubbed a "global perspective."

10. Arthur Meier, *Program,* Twelfth World Congress of Sociology, Madrid, Spain (1990), p. xiii.

11. This portrait of the mall was advanced by Sean Fisher.

Acknowledgments

This project would not have been completed without the help of several colleagues: Professor Erik Allardt, Kansler, Åbo Akademi, who helped in securing the essay on Russian sociology; Professor Aleksander Gella, who assisted in obtaining the essay on Polish sociology; Professor S. N. Eisenstadt, who directed us to the authors of the chapter on sociology in Israel; and Dr. M'hammed Sabour, for his efforts in putting us in touch with Professor Pierre Ansart and his contribution on the French sociological debate.

At Greenwood Press we appreciate the efforts of the following: Dr. Jim Sabin, Executive Vice President, for initiating the project; Dr. George Butler, Acquisition Editor, for pushing us to complete the project and for offering various constructive critiques; Maureen Melino, Coordinating Editor, for help with the logistics of all the details; and Sasha Kintzler, Production Editor, for producing the volume.

We want to acknowledge and appreciate Professor Ari Antikainen and Dr. M'hammed Sabour at the University of Joensuu for bringing different perspectives to our professional lives and for taking over the management and publication of the *International Journal of Contemporary Sociology.* The 1975 edition of the *Handbook of Contemporary Developments in World Sociology* (edited by Raj P. Mohan and Don Martindale) was an outgrowth of a special issue of the journal. Friends like Ari Antikainen, Mikko Salo, M'hammed Sabour, and Yrjö-Paavo Häyrynen at the University of Joensuu; Erik Allardt at the Åbo Akademi; and supportive colleagues at Auburn have helped to sustain interest in the international development of sociology which continues with this *Handbook.*

We also thank Wendy Leprettre for typing parts of the manuscript and

Penny Kirkley and Rebecca Gregory for assistance received in working on what seemed to be neverending correspondence.

Finally, we thank our families for providing the space between the life of the mind and various distractions of routines and everyday life. Without this, completion of this task would have been more daunting.

Part I

Sociology in Western and Northern Europe

Seventeenth-century Europe exhibited significant changes. Populations were growing and being redistributed in space. With changes in organizational and spatial arrangements of larger concentrations of anonymous people, older ways of surveillance were less valuable. For various monarchs, those changes posed new challenges for maintaining domination.

The intellectual reflection of these changes came with Rationalists, who at once critiqued ancient institutions and advanced a view that human beings should be examined in a universal, natural philosophic way. From this perspective, all people were considered pretty much the same. More critically, if genius was to be manifested, it would require an understanding of the anonymous average person. This portrait by the Rationalists found ready audiences among the monarchs of the age.

Rationalist doctrines continued to expand and became codified. Enlightenments in various nations and aspiring nations—France, England, Scotland, and Germany—contributed a set of doctrines, which laid the foundation for the rise of sociology. Among these doctrines were these: (1) humans, like other forms of organic and inorganic life, obeyed natural laws; (2) intelligence came about through the mastery of natural laws; (3) the human and nonhuman worlds could be guided by intelligent (i.e., rational) beings; and (4) intelligent guidance of these worlds would result in continual progress.

With the consolidation of monarchies came a growing awareness of discrepancies. Domination by monarchies increasingly seemed at odds with assumptions about the nature of people, the use of intelligence to guide human conduct, and the ever-present promise of progress for all. Discontent ranging from utopist longings to revolutionary fervor became prominent. In an effort to redeem Enlightenment sentiment from the hands of despotic control, a new chartering idea, a transcending idea, came to the forefront: the modern idea of society. If monarchs had failed and if revolutionaries had failed, it may very well have been due to their inability to understand the total social collective. What was needed was to recognize that the collective was the appropriate unit of analysis, a unit which could be studied by the adaptation of positive methods of science. With this, sociology and its project were conceived. Without demonstrating the efficacy of this approach, the sociological promise later embraced evolutionary notions and biological analogies.

Sociological interest was, as it is today, often nation-specific. It was sustained by a continual reflection on its own conceptual apparatus and changes in particular nation-states. In most instances the promise was continually renewed; sociology would emerge only if better fact-finding techniques could be found and standards of judgment regarding concepts and facts could be established. For sociologists anchored in national settings this program was continually strained. Many nation-states did not remain stable entities. Wars and revolutions complicated the concerns of the fledgling sociologists. For Europe this frequently meant that sociological concerns became narrow or even nonexistent.

In Part I we see that sociology has reemerged in post–World War II Europe, although it remains subject to the changing fate of national political and economic developments. This epoch reveals revitalized intellectual efforts in many nations. These efforts, however, are tempered by strains which affect national political economies. If the movement toward a European economic union proceeds, it can be anticipated that the identity as well as focal concerns of European sociology may be redirected. In many countries sociology has been battered by economic austerity. How those in the discipline will respond to the homogenization of the political economic life on the one hand and resistant, balkanized developments on the other is unclear. It is likely that another revisiting of this terrain a generation from now will reveal significant transformations. But for the moment, our attention focuses on more recent developments.

Being reconstituted after World War II, French sociology became organized around several dominant voices, which emerged in the 1960s. Pierre Ansart identifies four major approaches or paradigms and their leading exemplars, three of which are holistic in character and one of which is individualistic. The holistic are represented by Pierre Bourdieu, Alain Touraine, and Michel Crozier. The individualist is represented by Raymond Boudon. Bourdieu's work, labeled genetic structuralism, seeks to find patterns to cultural objects and social relationships. Touraine's dynamic structuralism seeks to uncover the dynamics of collective action underlying many features of social life. And Crozier, who sees organizational change issuing from crises, not smooth, seamless transformations, focuses on power relationships and individual strategies. Raymond Boudon, a methodological individualist, is noted for his qualitative methods and for advancing arguments analogous to the common reconstituted polemic in which Weber is positioned in opposition to Marx.

Whereas in the United States nonsociological French writers such as the late Michel Foucault have penetrated sociology from literature, Ansart's portrait suggests that French sociology is a somewhat more insular, bounded activity than its U.S. counterpart.

Steven Yearley highlights how Thatcherism in Britain was a focused attack on sociology, something parallel to what happened in the same era in both the United States and the former Soviet Union. The attack was a part of general efforts at retrenchment directed at Britain's university system. After the first volleys, however, sociology enjoyed a renaissance, in part due to market factors; it is a cheap discipline to deliver in educational settings and one that responded to growing student demand. Yearley notes that among the strong or traditional subfields in British sociology are stratification, education, crime and deviance, and medicine. There is an emerging interest in the environment, and British science studies and conversational analyses are becoming major areas of interest. Sociological theory appears dominated by metatheoretical concerns, not logical empiricist ones. Meanwhile, postmodernist thought is making its appearance in sociological circles.

The outline for Belgian sociology, Liliane Voyé and Karel Dobbelaere report, was laid out in the 1950s and 1960s. Exhibiting a convergence of Anglo-Saxon, French, and German influences, sociology there is developing along institutional and thematic lines (e.g., industry and labor, law, poverty, religion, politics, education, and the like). Theoretical concerns also reflect a strong metatheoretical bent, with postmodernism and emotions appearing to be emergent concerns.

In the Netherlands, sociology experienced a reversal around 1980, parallelling, claim Henk A. Becker and Frans L. Leeuw, trends elsewhere in the world. Contributing to this decline are changes in the Dutch academic environment. After advancing a brief history of Dutch sociology, the authors highlight the current status of the field. Anchored in a policy realm, Dutch sociology has had a large policy component dealing with knowledge transfer. This augments interest in social change. Among the other specialties which are reviewed are social stratification, education, organizations, the labor market, and population studies. Historical work, rational-choice, and interpretive sociology are reported as dominating the theory domain. Methodologically, attention has been directed at data collection and analysis. In the latter case, qualitative procedures are stressed.

In Switzerland, reports Jacques Coenen-Huther, 1971 marked the first meeting in the modern epoch of the Swiss Sociological Association. Coenen-Huther reviews the institutional landscape of the nation's sociological establishment, highlighting how major schools and leading persons dominate the intellectual landscape. The portrait which is drawn reveals that features of the discipline are subordinate to institutional dominance, something which might be accounted for given the recent development of sociology and the small, homogeneous nature of Switzerland.

After a brief history of sociology in Germany, Walter L. Bühl claims that sociological thought there parallels that found in the United States, especially in the area of action theory and interpretive sociology, the latter of which is seen as stagnating. Bühl suggests that the influences of Jurgen Habermas and Niklas Luhmann are not well integrated into sociological thought. The residues of Marxism and Leninism which dominated the former German Democratic Republic are reported to be negative, inasmuch as historical materialism was the stultifying hegemonic doctrine of that regime. Methodology is similarly a contested terrain. In substantive research areas Bühl also sees a relative decline, with a preoccupation with an "academic science" approach to the world and substantial introversion. Attention to an external world seems less and less compelling, claims Bühl, to German sociologists.

Christian Fleck reviews the emergence of sociology in Austria. He highlights that in the interwar years there was a flourishing of sociological writing; however, it was anchored in individual scholarly activity. It did not have an institutional locus. Of late there have been some efforts to institutionalize sociology, but these developments are still in comparative infancy.

Sociology was established in Sweden in 1947, reports Richard Swedberg. Though there are three generations of sociologists, one commonality is that sociology in Sweden has not been preoccupied with classical literature. Instead, a neopositivistic, statistical focus predominates. With the 1970s, political relevancy emerged as a concern. Today sociology is found in five universities with interests ranging from the philosophy of science to deviance. The current generation of sociologists is, Swedberg reports, interested in the welfare state and the sociology of work, while sustaining resistance to the domination of quantitative methods.

Established as an academic discipline in ten colleges and universities, Finnish sociology, Erik Allardt writes, is now treated as a basic social science. Structurally, academic interests are divided between sociology and social policy. Although the United States was a source of some original concerns for Finnish sociologists, there is a growing independence. Methodologically, quantitative concerns dominate. Of late sociology has become more pluralistic. Citing the collaborative work of Ellsworth Fuhrman and Erkki Kaukonen, Allardt reports that there is an emergent sociological interest in lifeways and everyday culture. A variety of subfields, consistent with those found in a number of countries, shows vitality.

In Denmark the institutionalization of sociology began after World War II. Since then, a battle for greater inclusion of sociology in Danish education has been periodically waged. As within many countries, Marxism has found some reception. Of late, note Heine Andersen,

Britt-Mari Blegvad, and Mogens Blegvad, differentiation and fragmentation have come to characterize sociology. As in other Scandinavian countries, one type of sociological attention has focused on social welfare concerns. Among the other areas of identifiable interests are labor markets and working conditions, political sociology, medical sociology, criminology, and the sociology of law.

1

Contemporary Sociology in Austria

Christian Fleck

GRÜNDERZEIT—COGNITIVE FOUNDATIONS

Sociology in Austria[1] can look back on a very long tradition, which was, however, not without discontinuities and deep-reaching lines of fault. If we disregard historical reports and other literary descriptions of social conditions, as well as contributions to *Polizeywissenschaft,* which can be seen as the basis for an understanding of the Josephinian and *Vormärz* administration, the first important representative of a sociology that did not as yet call itself such must be Lorenz von Stein (1815–1890), who was a professor of political economy at the University of Vienna for 30 years. He directed his interest in social sciences toward the so-called social question, (i.e., toward the emergence of a new social class in the aftermath of industrial development). His emphasis on labor as the driving force behind social integration and conflict between social classes make Stein the pioneer of the non-Marxist analysis of society in the German-speaking world. He did not, however, attempt to establish sociology as a new scientific discipline; his argument with sociopolitical issues and the social movement took place within the context of political science and economy which, according to Stein, are based on an idealistic philosophy. This makes Stein one of the founders of *Kathedersozialismus* (i.e., the paternalistic conception of the new social problem of the working class and the labor movement).

The first person in Austria to speak out in favor of the creation of sociology as a discipline, who endeavored to found such a faculty, was the Polish-born Ludwig Gumplowicz (1838–1909), who was a professor of public law at the University of Graz from 1876 onwards. Gumplowicz viewed sociology *naturalistically* as an exact science whose obligation it was to discover the laws of society. He also viewed it as *holistic,* since society was composed of different social groups, and as *conflictual,* since these social groupings, or aggregates, were at odds with each other.[2] There was an extraordinarily lively response to Gumplowicz's theory, even during his lifetime. Not only did he have students and followers in various countries and his works translated into all major languages, but the international scientific community also acknowledged him and his theory.

While it is possible to approve of Gumplowicz's theory insofar as it could have been the basis for a university discipline, the conditions under which he was working clearly demonstrate why this never came about. First, there is Gumplowicz's multiple marginality: he was a Pole by birth, working at a German-speaking university, which was also a provincial university, and hence had little prestige within Austria; he was a Jew and agnostic in a German nationalistic, anti-Semitic, and Catholic environment; he was a "sociologist" among law professors, and finally he led a secluded life, doing little to rally students and followers around him.

It is also worth considering Jerzy Szacki's comment: "Gumplowicz was too radical for the conservatives and too conservative for the radicals."[3] Another reason for his theory's not being overall positively received, especially later on, was the fact that he used the term "race" at the core of his argument. He viewed "race" in the cultural, anthropological context of "ethnic," rather than as a biological term; however, this does not prevent those reading and interpreting his theory, even today, from classifying Gumplowicz alongside racist social Darwinists. Among Gumplowicz's followers were the Austrian scholar and Field Marshall Lieutenant Gustav Ratzenhofer (1842–1904), Franz Oppenheimer in Germany, the Italian Franco Savorgnan, and the American Lester Ward.[4]

FIRST ATTEMPTS AT INSTITUTIONALIZATION

Sociology reached its first peak between the turn of the century and World War I, due, no doubt, to the intellectual impetus stimulated by Gumplowicz's work. This was manifested most clearly by the creation of Sociological Societies in Vienna (1907) and Graz (1908). In 1909 sociology for the first time took on an institutional form in the German-speaking world with the founding of the German Sociology Society, even before the advent of the German Empire. The equivalent Austrian institution was, however, not as strong as its German counterpart in that the applicants had fewer ties with the academic world. It was therefore not possible to establish a sociology faculty in the form of university chairs and courses of studies, which had been the initial intention.

The most important representatives of this founding generation are the philosopher Wilhelm Jerusalem (1854–1923), Rudolf Eisler (1873–1926),

Max Adler (1873–1937), the later State Chancellor and Federal President Karl Renner (1870–1950), and the independent scholar ("Privatgelehrter") Rudolf Goldscheid (1870–1931). Loosely affiliated to this learned society were Eugen Ehrlich (1862–1922), a professor of Roman law at Czernowitz; Hans Kelsen (1881–1973), a professor of public law at the University of Vienna; and the medievalist Ludo Moritz Hartmann (1865–1924).[5] The following points are useful indicators to any intellectual common ground between the representatives of this founding generation: there were philosophical similarities between the early Austrian sociologists and Ernst Mach (1838–1916),[6] an outstanding natural scientist, philosopher, and theorist of science, even though some showed a tendency toward neo-Kantianism in their thinking.[7] The evolutionist train of thought originating from Darwin and Spencer, and the then very popular Ernst Haeckel and Wilhelm Ostwald, is regarded as extremely relevant for the social sciences, even though none of the above-mentioned representatives shared the Darwinians' conviction of the survival of the economically fittest. Sociopolitically, the early Austrian sociologists belonged to the reformist wing of the enlightened bourgeoisie, and some were (or later were) party supporters or sympathizers of the social democratic labor movement.[8]

Among the lasting intellectual accomplishments of the members of this founding generation, although little attention was paid to them, are the contributions to sociology of knowledge,[9] sociology of law,[10] Marxist sociology,[11] and state and financial sociology.[12] A striking feature and even a peculiarity of the development of sociology in Austria is the early appearance of such specialization in sociological research. However, this generation failed to produce large, systematic, informative works as their contemporaries did in Europe and the United States.[13] The early specialization can be viewed in correlation with the high rate of development in neighboring disciplines: economy, philosophy, and psychology at the turn of the century have for a long time aroused the interest of histories of ideas.[14] The early cognitive differentiation is one of the reasons why none of the above-mentioned Austrian sociologists were able to establish sociology as a university discipline.

We must also mention the authors of the first sociological overviews and textbooks,[15] as well as the editors and translators responsible for making the works of Durkheim, Tarde, and William James, among others, accessible to a broad public shortly after their original publication.[16]

CLOSED UNIVERSITY AND UNATTACHED CREATIVITY

Attempts to institutionalize the teaching and research of sociology, that is, the establishment of an academic sociology, were not crowned with success. The outbreak of World War I, the ensuing fall of the Habsburg

Monarchy, and the difficulties encountered in the reconstruction of the democratic republic after the so-called Austrian Revolution[17] created conditions in the 1920s and 1930s which were even more unfavorable to the institutionalization of sociology than before:

1. The chronic lack of university funding and the stronger emerging anti-Semitism, primarily among the ranks of the more educated classes, who faced the threat of impoverishment and social degradation, restricted the possible development of new disciplines, among them sociology.

2. The number of potential professional sociologists was diminished in the postwar period by two mobility processes: on the one hand, some scholars who had published scientific articles before 1914 assumed political posts (Otto Bauer, Michael Hainisch, Rudolf Hilferding, Karl Renner, and, temporarily, Joseph Schumpeter), without, as was requisite during the Habsburg Monarchy for those holding professor ministerial posts, having university positions, to which they could have returned after their political careers. On the other hand, outstanding social scientists emigrated or did not return to Austria (Carl Grünberg, Hans Kelsen, Emil Lederer, Jacob Moreno, Karl Pribram, and Joseph Schumpeter).

3. The few university positions available were taken up by right-wing intellectuals, of whom Othmar Spann (1878–1950) immediately became the leader. In the tradition of the German romantic movement (Adam Müller, 1779–1829) and of Albert Schäffle's organicism (1831–1903), his ensuing thinking can justifiably be described as "anti-sociology." Through Spann's skillful personnel policy, competing sociologists were kept away from or ousted from the universities. This applied equally to the "old"-liberal theorists, who, in the tradition of the Austrian School of Economics (Carl Menger), were also dealing with sociological issues,[18] such as Ludwig Mises (1881–1973), a bourgeois Republican who was denied access to the most prestigious university of the time in Vienna, as was Schumpeter (1883–1950), or those who were squeezed out (Kelsen); and to left-wingers, who were denied the possibility of receiving their postdoctoral lecturing qualification, with the exception of Max Adler.[19] The academic sociology of the First Republic was the domain of semifascist social theorists.

Despite these unfavorable political and institutional circumstances, sociology developed during this period to an intellectual peak unmatched in Austria since.[20]

The studies of Alfred Schütz (1899–1959)[21] and Felix Kaufmann (1895–1949)[22] emerged from Ludwig Mises' private seminar. These two, especially Schütz, after emigrating to the United States, greatly influenced phenomenological sociology and ethnomethodology. However, in the course of the transatlantic process of approval, it was forgotten that the ideological basis of Schütz's radical thinking was rooted in the liberalism of the end of the nineteenth century, and that his theory was supposed to be the sociophilosophical backing for Mises' anti-statist program.[23]

Several social scientific authors belonged to the neopositivistic Vienna circle: after the circle organizer, Otto Neurath (1882–1945), there was Edgar Zilsel (1891–1944). While the former programmatically pleaded for the unity of social and natural sciences, Zilsel, during his years in Vienna, presented sketches of a sociological history of science, which he extended during his few years of emigration to the United States.[24] The underlying assumption of the German Positivism Debate of the 1960s,[25] that positivism also signifies political conservatism, is not borne out by a closer investigation of this school of thought. The thinkers of this school, who were also active in the field of natural science, were convinced that it was worth "forming thinking tools for everyday use, for the everyday use of scholars, but also for the use of everyone somehow involved in the conscious forming of life. The intensity of life, which is visible in the attempts to reform the order of society and science, flows through the movement of the scientific conception of the world."[26]

Many sociological articles were printed in the theoretically sophisticated magazines of the labor movement, and social democratic publishers published several socially critical articles.[27] One of the few links between the intellectual world of the labor movement and institutionalized science could be found under the patronage of Karl and Charlotte Bühler (1879–1963 and 1893–1974, respectively), who were professors of empirical psychology at the University of Vienna from 1923. Assistance from the Rockefeller Foundation (which also sponsored Ludwig Mises' Austrian Institute for Economic Research) enabled in particular Charlotte Bühler, who was working on child development and family psychology, to support younger researchers in the field of social psychology. Thanks to the Bühlers the young Paul Lazarsfeld (1901–1976) was given the possibility of establishing a Research Group for Industrial Psychology. The most prominent work of this group of young, left-wing graduate students was the investigation of the effects of long-term unemployment: *Die Arbeitslosen von Marienthal* became one of the classics of empirical social research.[28]

The cognitive productiveness of the interwar years was matched by institutional stagnation: it can even be said that ground that had already been covered was lost again, such as in the fields of academic publishing and, of course, in the world of paid university positions.

This phase, which lasted only fifteen years, came to an end with political changes: the transition to a corporate state in 1933–1934 and the *Anschluss* of Austria to Nazi Germany in 1938. Almost all sociologists were forced to emigrate, most of them because of their Jewish ancestry, and some of them for political reasons.[29]

LONG PERIOD OF SLACK AND LATE NORMALIZATION

After the fall of Austrofascism and National Socialism, it took sociology in Austria almost two decades to recover. For many years the Catholic thinker August M. Knoll (1900–1963), a social philosopher trained by

Spann, Johann Mokre (1901–1981), a member of the Catholic wing in Graz after returning from emigration in the States, and Johannes Messner (1891–1984), who worked at the Catholic theology department of the University of Vienna, were the only sociologists in Austria, assuming one adopts an extremely broad definition of the term *sociology*. Messner endeavored to establish a social theory based on natural law, Mokre hardly distinguished himself as a prolific writer, but Knoll emerged in later years as a knowledgeable critic of ideology, especially of Catholic natural law and ecclesiastical history.[30] The early attempt at carrying out a sociological analysis of the Nazi concentration camps through Benedikt Kautsky (1894–1960), on the other hand, remained an episode, because its author did not hold a university position and was prevented from carrying out scientific work by his participation in the trade union program for adult education.[31]

It was only the founding of the Institute for Advanced Studies (IHS) in Vienna in 1963, financed by the Ford Foundation and energetically pushed forward by Oscar Morgenstern and Lazarsfeld, that led to a reconstruction of sociology in Austria.[32] This period also saw the founding of commercial opinion research institutes, most of which sympathized with political parties,[33] as well as the founding of the first social science specialist journal: *Die Meinung*[34] was primarily committed to the field of public opinion research and Lazarsfeld also had a hand in its founding. It was only in 1966 that the universities followed suit, after a recommendation by the Organization for Economic Cooperation and Development (OECD), with the establishment of sociology as a course of studies.

Since then it can be said that a sociological education is available in Austria on a university and extra-university level. The clear division between these two sectors is also reflected by research efforts and publications. The extra-university research's stronger ties with the political world correspond to a greater extra-scientific research significance (even if only temporarily). Apart from a few exceptions, the majority of this research is pure contract research and rather insignificant. On the other hand, university research is earmarked by its tendency toward complacency, and its results can seldom be regarded as important after a certain amount of time.

The cohort effect can also partly explain the development of sociology in Austria over the past two decades. The creation of university chairs, almost all of which were filled at the same time, preceded the introduction of sociology as a course of studies (in Vienna and Linz in 1966 and in Salzburg and Graz in 1984). More than half of the full professors still lecturing today were appointed in the 1960s. None of these professors were able to establish a good, stable rapport with their students, partly due to the politically turbulent years of the student movement and uprisings in West Europe, which also left its mark on Austria. The results of

this anomaly are the publication of numerous, rather unprofessional research reports by the younger generation and the retreat to the ivory
tower of artistic complacency on the part of the spurned professors.[35] (The
above-average number of textbooks produced by Austrian sociology professors is not necessarily an indication of their pedagogical ethos.)

The IHS was temporarily an exception in this respect: the usual practice
in the first half of the 1970s—engaging excellent foreign researchers as
guest lecturers and employing them as project supervisors—collapsed in a
few noteworthy empirical studies.[36] This development came to an end with
the waning of the Austrian social democratic enthusiasm for reform toward the end of the 1970s, and especially after the recent worldwide economic crisis: the transformation of the IHS from a multidisciplinary basic
research institute into an institute for economic prognoses and applied
research—in connection with this Anatol Rapoport was fired as director
in 1984 under undignified circumstances—also put an end to this innovation.

The high degree of specialization[37] is of particular importance, since the
small number of researchers into particular topics prevented an exchange
of ideas.[38] Even the founding of the *Österreichische Zeitschrift für Soziologie* did little to change the undeveloped desire for discussion.[39]

In relation to this, it must be said that there are hardly any sociologists
who deal with questions of *sociological theory* on a general level; the pre-
destined (through their position) university sociologists hardly distinguish
themselves with relevant publications.[40] Together with the lack of continuous research in the field of sociology is the purely rhetorical reference to
the modern authors and theories: in the late 1960s it was the theory emanating from the Frankfurt School, which was followed in the early 1970s
by structuralist French-originating neo-Marxism, after which theoretical
references multiplied: the spectrum stretches from Luhmann through Habermas to Bourdieu.

There is more continuity, while still mantaining an internationally respectable level, in the field of methodology. Since 1972 Kurt Holm has
been lecturing at the University of Linz; he and his collaborators have
published numerous works concerning the techniques and methods of
quantitative social research.[41] Authors of methodological works were also
to be found elsewhere.[42]

There is no room to mention all the works in the subfields of sociology
here. After referring to research institutes, I will restrict myself to a few
examples, which will presumably still be worthy of discussion in a few
years' time. The *sociology of the life-cycle* goes back a very long way, to
which Leopold Rosenmayr, the doyen of academic sociology, was committed from the very beginning. During his forty-year career Rosenmayr
carried out research into succeeding life-cycles. He has most recently been
examining the process of age.[43] Thematically assignable to this field is also

an extensive literature study on the use of autobiographical documents in different human and social sciences by Sigrid Paul, from which thoughts about biographical methods in sociology originate.[44]

Another field, which has been studied for years, is that of *deviant behavior*. Research into this is being carried out at the Institute for Legal and Criminal Sociology, which was founded in connection with the reform of criminal law, and at the Ludwig Boltzmann Institute for Research into Drug Abuse, both of which are located in Vienna.[45] Works based on the observation of marginal groups were published by Roland Girtler,[46] and a theoretically more critical study is Peter Strasser's discussion of the history and tradition of criminology.[47]

Following the emerging unemployment of the 1980s, attempts at research into this were relatively quickly established; these were primarily initiated and financed by the Federal Ministry for Social Affairs. As well as empirical studies,[48] there are attempts at interdisciplinary research[49] and international cooperation.[50]

Extensive reports on the situation of the family and of women in Austria appear regularly, which are also organized and financed by the state.[51] The last group especially can be viewed in relation with emerging feminist women studies.[52]

There is no doubt that there is a lack of research in Austria carried out in many fields abroad and that research results presented by Austrian sociologists only seldom receive international recognition. On the other hand, after many years, sociology, which was primarily in the hands of independent scholars during the interwar period, such as Schütz, Kaufmann, Neurath, Zilsel, and Lazarsfeld, has become professionalized and will therefore be in a better position to weather the coming storms. Or so one hopes.

NOTES

1. For the period before 1918 I am limiting myself to the development of sociology in the German-speaking part of the Habsburg Empire. Second, only those who are working or who have worked in Austria are mentioned.

2. Ludwig Gumplowicz, *Der Rassenkampf* (Innsbruck: Wagner, 1983; new edition 1926, reprinted Aalen: Scientia, 1973); Gumplowicz, trans. Fredrick W. Moore, *The Outlines of Sociology* (Philadelphia: American Academy of Political and Social Science, 1899; first in German, 1885; new edition, ed. with an introduction and notes by Irving L. Horowitz, New Brunswick: Transaction Books, 1980). See Gerald Mozetic, "Ein unzeitgemäßer Soziologe: Ludwig Gumplowicz," *Kölner Zeitschrift für Soziologie und Sozialpsychologie* 37 (1985), 621–647.

3. Jerzy Szacki, *History of Sociological Thought* (London: Greenwood Press, 1979), 285f.

4. See Mozetic, "Ein unzeitgemäßer Soziologe"; *The Ward-Gumplowicz Correspondence: 1897–1909,* trans. and with an introduction by Alexander Gella, pref-

ace by Irving L. Horowitz (New York: Essay Press, 1971); Dieter Haselbach, *Franz Oppenheimer* (Opladen: Westdeutscher Verlag, 1985).

5. For more details see Christian Fleck, *Rund um "Marienthal"* (Vienna: Gesellschaftskritik, 1990).

6. See Rudolf Haller and Fritz Stadler, eds., *Ernst Mach* (Vienna: Hölder-Pichler-Tempsky, 1988).

7. See Max Adler, *Kausalität und Teleologie im Streite um die Wissenschaft* (Vienna: Volksbuchhandlung, 1904), and Rudolf Eisler, *Kant-Lexikon* (Berlin: Mittler, 1930).

8. See Ingrid Belke, *Die sozialreformerischen Ideen von Josef Popper-Lynkeus (1838–1921) im Zusammenhang mit allgemeinen Reformbestrebungen des Wiener Bürgertums um die Jahrhundertwende* (Tübingen: Mohr, 1978), and Friedrich Stadler, "Spätaufklärung und Sozialdemokratie in Wien 1919–1938," in Friedrich Kadrnoska, ed., *Aufbruch und Untergang* (Vienna: Europa, 1981), 441–473.

9. See Wilhelm Jerusalem, "Die Soziologie des Erkennens," *Gedanken und Denker* (Vienna: Braumüller, 1925 [first 1902]; Jerusalem, "Die soziologische Bedingtheit des Denkens und der Denkformen" (first 1924), in Volker Meja and Nico Stehr, eds., *Der Streit um die Wissenssoziologie* (Frankfurt: Suhrkamp, 1982), vol. 1, 27–56. (See, for a short overview of Jerusalem's sociological approach, the last chapter concerning sociology and philosophy of history in Jerusalem, trans. Charles F. Sanders, *An Introduction to Philosophy* [New York: Macmillan, 1932], 311–517.)

10. Eugen Ehrlich, *Fundamental Principles of the Sociology of Law* (first in German 1913), trans. Walter L. Moll, introduction by Roscoe Pound (Cambridge, Mass.: Harvard University Press, 1936); Karl Renner, *The Institutions of Private Law and Their Social Functions* (first in German 1904), trans. Agnes Schwarzschild, ed. with an introduction and notes by O. Kahn-Freund (London: Routledge & Kegan, 1949).

11. See, as an overview, Tom Bottomore and Patrick Goode, eds., *Austro-Marxism,* introduction by Tom Bottomore (London: Oxford University Press, 1978); and Gerald Mozetic, *Die Gesellschaftstheorie des Austromarxismus* (Darmstadt: Wissenschaftliche Buchgesellschaft, 1987).

12. Rudolf Goldscheid, "Staatssozialismus oder Staatskapitalismus" (1917), in Rudolf Goldscheid and Joseph Schumpeter, *Die Finanzkrise des Steurstaates,* ed. Rudolf Hickel (Frankfurt: Suhrkamp, 1976), 40–252.

13. Attempts at such "grand systems" were made by insignificant authors; those worthy of mention are Albert Schäffle, *Bau und Leben des sozialen Körpers* (Tübingen: Laupp, 1875–1878); Gustav Ratzenhofer, *Soziologie* (Leipzig: Brockhaus, 1907); and Ratzenhofer, *Die Soziologische Erkenntnis: Sociological Knowledge: The Positive Philosophy of Social Life* (Salem: Ayer, 1975).

14. See Allan Janik and Stephen Toulmin, *Wittgenstein's Vienna* (New York: Simon and Schuster, 1973); William M. Johnston, *The Austrian Mind* (Berkeley: University of California Press, 1972); Carl E. Schorske, *Fin-de-siecle Vienna* (New York: Alfred A. Knopf, 1980).

15. Gumplowicz, op. cit., Ratzenhofer, op. cit., Jerusalem, op. cit.; Rudolf Eisler, *Soziologie* (Leipzig: Weber, 1903); and Albert Schäffle, *Abriß der Soziologie* (Tübingen: Laupp, 1906).

16. *Philosophisch-soziologische Bücherei* (34 vols.), editor: Rudolf Eisler (Leipzig: Kröner, 1907–1915). This is all the more remarkable since the scientific community was then very small and it was taken for granted that everyone spoke French and English. See Fleck, *Rund um "Marienthal."*

17. Otto Bauer, *Die Österreichische Revolution* (Vienna: Volksbuchhandlung, 1923), see also Bottomore and Goode, eds., *Austro-Marxism.*

18. For example, Friedrich Wieser, *Das Gesetz der Macht* (Vienna: Springer, 1926).

19. He also remained a nonappointed university lecturer during his lifetime.

20. Compare biographical articles in the *International Social Science Encyclopedia:* the Austrians, who found recognition, were working in the interwar period or before in Austria. See Christian Fleck, "Vertrieben und vergessen. Ein Überblick über die aus Österreich emigrierten Soziologen," in Josef Langer, ed., *Geschichte der österreichischen Soziologie* (Vienna: Gesellschaftskritik, 1988), 257–278.

21. Alfred Schütz, *Der sinnhafte Aufbau der sozialen Welt* (Vienna: Springer, 1930). See also Ingeborg Helling, "Strömungen des methodologischen Individualismus—Alfred Schütz, Felix Kaufmann und der Mises-Kreis," in Langer, ed., *Geschichte der österreichischen Soziologie,* 185–201.

22. Felix von Kaufmann, *Methodenlehre der Sozialwissenschaften* (Vienna: J. Springer, 1936); Helling, "Strömungen des methodologischen Individualismus," H. G. Zilian, *Klarheit und Methode* (Amsterdam: Rodopi, 1990).

23. Ethnomethodology "can be understood as a philosophically radicalized version of the type of unreflexive sociology (Gouldner)," Kurt H. Wolff, "Phenomenology and Sociology," in Tom Bottomore and Robert Nisbet, eds., *A History of Sociological Analysis* (New York: Basic Books, 1978), 532. For the economics, see, for example, Ludwig Mises, *Human Action* (Chicago: Contemporary Books, 3rd ed., 1966; first edition, 1949); see Helling, "Strömungen des methodologischen Individualismus"; Claus-Dieter Krohn, "Die Emigration der Österreichischen Schule der Nationalökonomie in die USA," in Friedrich Stadler, ed., *Vertriebene Vernunft* (Vienna: Jugend & Volk, 1988), 2:402–415.

24. Edgar Zilsel, *Die sozialen Ursprünge der neuzeitlichen Wissenschaft,* ed. and trans. Wolfgang Krohn (Frankfurt: Suhrkamp, 1976).

25. Theodor W. Adorno et al., *The Positivist Dispute in German Sociology* (London: Heinemann, 1976 [German edition, 1969]).

26. Otto Neurath, "Wissenschaftliche Weltauffassung. Der Wiener Kreis," in *Gesammelte philosophische und methodologische Schriften,* ed. Rudolf Haller and Heiner Rutte (Vienna: Hölder-Pichler-Tempsky, 1981), Bd. 1, 304. Neurath sharpened the intentions of the Vienna circle even more when he noticed in a review of Rudolf Carnap's "Logischem Aufbau der Welt": "Antimetaphysicians (strengthen) the force of the proletariat" (Neurath, Bd. 1, 338).

27. Some of the authors were Alexander Gerschenkron, Marie Jahoda, Paul F. Lazarsfeld, Käthe Leichter, and Karl Polanyi; see Fleck, *Rund um "Marienthal."*

28. Leipzig: Hirzel, 1933 (English trans.: Marie Jahoda, Paul F. Lazarsfeld, and Hans Zeisel, *Marienthal: The Sociography of an Unemployed Community.* London: Tavistock, 1972). In addition: Paul F. Lazarsfeld et al., *Jugend und Beruf* (Jena: Fischer, 1931); in comparison with the background, see Fleck, *Rund um "Marienthal."*

29. See Friedrich Stadler, ed., *Vertriebene Vernunft*, 2 vols. (Vienna: Jugend und Volk, 1987 and 1988).

30. August M. Knoll, *Katholische Kirche und scholastisches Naturrecht* (Neuwied: Luchterhand, 1968 [first edition 1962]; Knoll, *Zins und Gnade* (Neiwied: Luchterhand, 1967); see also, Christian Fleck, "Soziologie in Österreich nach 1945," in Christoph Cobet, ed., *Einführung in Fragen an die Soziologie in Deutschland nach Hitler* (Frankfurt: Cobet, 1988), 123–147.

31. Bendikt Kautsky, *Teufel und Verdammte* (Zürich: Gutenberg, 1946). Later on, through his role as co-editor of Karl Marx's works, Kautsky paved the way for a Marx renaissance in the German-speaking world.

32. For example, Adolf Kozlik, *Wie wird wer Akademiker?* (Vienna: Europa, 1965).

33. Since 1953 the Catholic church has had a polling institute.

34. Founded in 1961, entitled *Journal für angewandte Sozialforschung* in 1968, *Journal für Sozialforschung* in 1980, since 1984 divided into *Journal für Sozialforschung* and *SWS-Journal.*

35. In relation to this it is worth remembering that also younger academics have emigrated abroad, not always of their own free will. Worthy of mention are Ernst Topitsch (1962 to Heidelberg), Judith Janoska-Bendl (1967 to Darmstadt), Henrik Kreutz (1974 to Hannover), Hermann Strasser (1977 to Duisburg), Karin Knorr-Cetina (1980 to Bielefeld); it must also be mentioned that many Austrians qualified as university lecturers in the Federal Republic of Germany because they encountered difficulties in Austria.

36. The project on Austria's health care system was supervised by Frieder Naschold: Frieder Naschold et al., eds., *Systemanalyse des Gesundheitwesens in Österreich,* 2nd ed. (Vienna: Montan, 1978); the project on social reporting, social structure, social mobility, and inequality was advised by Wolfgang Zapf, John Goldthorpe, and Robert W. Hodge, among others: Josef Bucek and Marina Fischer-Kowalski, eds., *Lebensverhältnisse in Österreich* (Frankfurt: Campus, 1980); Max Haller, *Klassenbildung und soziale Schichtung in Österreich* (Frankfurt: Campus, 1982); inspired by Paul F. Lazarsfeld: Karin Knorr, Max Haller, and Hans Georg Zilian, *Sozialwissenschaftliche Forschung in Österreich* (Vienna: Jugend und Volk, 1981); other projects, which were only presented as project reports, were advised by Otis D. Duncan and Wolf-Dieter Narr, among others.

37. Mainly in the form of institutes organized by the Ludwig Boltzmann Society, which, however, do not have continuous, communicative links with each other; there were Ludwig Boltzmann Institutes for, among others, medical sociology, research on drug abuse, social gerontology, and life-cycle research; the Institute for Criminal Sociology was dropped from the Society after ten years of very successful activity and has since been reestablished as the Institute for Legal and Criminal Sociology. Further research institutes are financed by the Austrian Academy for Science (Institute for Socioeconomic Development Research), UNESCO (European Center for Research into Social Sciences and Documentation), the UN (European Center for Social Welfare), municipalities, parties, trade unions, or boards.

38. It is worth considering that there are strong ties with West German sociology.

39. An exception was the number of plaintive reactions by the guild to a publicly

reported criticism of the science minister: Herta Firnberg, "Zur Rolle der Sozial-wissenschaften in der österreichischen Wissenschaftspolitik: Das Anwendungsde-fizit der Soziologie," *Österreichische Zeitschrift für Soziologie* 3, 1 (1978), 4–10, and the replies in this and the following journals.

40. Exceptions are Judith Janoska-Bendl, *Methodologische Aspekte des Ideal-typus* (Berlin: Duncker & Humblot, 1965); Heinz Steinert, *Strategien sozialen Han-delns* (Munich: Juventa, 1972); Johann A. Schülein, *Theorie der Institution* (Opladen: Westdeutscher Verlag, 1987); Andreas Balog, *Rekonstruktion von Handlungen* (Opladen: Westdeutscher Verlag, 1989); Helmut Kuzmics, *Der Preis der Zivilisation* (Frankfurt: Campus, 1989); Helga Nowotny, *Eigenzeit* (Frankfurt: Suhrkamp, 1989); examples from neighboring disciplines are Elisabeth List, *All-tagsrationalität und soziologischer Diskurs* (Frankfurt: Campus, 1983), and Peter Koller, *Neue Theorien des Sozialkontrakts* (Berlin: Duncker & Humblot, 1987).

41. See especially Kurt Holm, ed., *Die Befragung,* 6 vols. (Munich: Francke, 1975–1979); Gerhard Arminger, *Faktorenanalyse* (Stuttgart: Teubner, 1979); Her-mann Denz, *Analyse latenter Strukturen* (Munich: Francke, 1982); Johann Bacher, "Einführung in die Clusteranalyse mit SPSS-X für Historiker und Sozialwissen-schaftler," *Historical Social Research* 14, 2 (1989), 6–167.

42. Henrik Kreutz, *Soziologie der empirischen Sozialforschung* (Stuttgart: Enke, 1972); Kreutz is also the senior editor of the journal *Angewandte Sozialforschung* 1 (1969 ff.). Heinz Steinert not only received recognition through having edited the first reader on interactionism in German (Heinz Steinert, ed., *Symbolische Interaktion* [Stuttgart: Klett, 1973]), but also published, alongside his works on social deviance, essays on methodological questions: e.g., Heinz Steinert, "Das Interview als soziale Interaktion," in Heiner Meulemann and Karl-Heinz Reu-band, eds., *Soziale Realität im Interview* (Frankfurt: Campus, 1984), 17–60.

43. Leopold Rosenmayr, "Jugend," in Rene König, ed., *Handbuch der empir-ischen Sozialforschung,* 2nd ed., vol. 6 (Stuttgart: Enke, 1969); Rosenmayr, "Alter, Familie," in König, vol. 7, 1969; Leopold Rosenmayr and Hilde Rosenmayr, *Der alte Mensch in der Gesellschaft* (Reinbek: Rowohlt, 1978); Leopold Rosenmayr, *Die Kräfte des Alters* (Vienna: Edition Atelier, 1990). Also concerning youth: Hen-rik Kreutz, *Soziologie der Jugend* (Munich: Juventa, 1974); concerning old age: Anton Amann, *Die vielen Gesichter des Alters* (Vienna: Verlag der österrei-chischen Staatsdruckerei, 1989). Since 1980 Rosenmayr has also been the director of the Ludwig Boltzmann Institute for Social Gerontology and Life-Cycle Re-search in Vienna.

44. Sigrid Paul, *Begegnungen,* 2 vols. (Hohenschäftlarn: Renner, 1979).

45. The journal *Kriminalsoziologische Bibliografie* (1974ff.) continuously re-ports on the studies; compare the two "Festschriften": 9 (1982), 36/37, and 14 (1987), 56/57. Also from this institute are Arno Pilgram, . . . *endet mit dem Tode* (Vienna: Gesellschaftskritik, 1989); and Gerhard Hanak et al., *Ärgernisse und Le-benskatastrophen* (Bielefeld: AJZ, 1989).

46. Roland Girtler, *Vagabunden in der Großstadt* (Stuttgart: Enke, 1980); Gir-tler, *Der Strich,* 2nd ed. (Munich: Heyne, 1987); Girtler, *Wilderer* (Linz: Landes-verlag, 1988).

47. Peter Strasser, *Verbrechermenschen* (Frankfurt: Campus, 1984).

48. See Federal Ministry for Employment and Social Affairs, *Forschungsberi-*

chte aus Sozial—und Arbeitsmarktpolitik, and H. G. Zilian and Christian Fleck, *Die verborgenen Kosten der Arbeitslosigkeit* (Frankfurt: Anton Hain, 1990).

49. Since 1986, under the co-direction of the two economists Kurt Rothschild and Gunter Tichy and financed by the National Research Fund, research efforts have been channeled into the dynamics of unemployment and employment, which sociologists are also researching. See Kurt W. Rothschild and Gunter Tichy, eds., *Arbeitslosigkeit und Arbeitsangebot in Österreich* (Vienna: Springer, 1987); Manfred Prisching, *Arbeitslosenprotest und Resignation in der Wirtshaftskrise* (Frankfurt: Campus, 1988).

50. Egon Matzner et al., eds., *Arbeit für alle ist möglich* (Berlin: edition sigma, 1988); Matzner et al., *Beschäftigungsrisiko Innovation* (Berlin: edition sigma, 1988); Georg Vobruba, ed., *Strukturwandel der Sozialpolitik* (Frankfurt: Suhrkamp, 1990).

51. *Frauenbericht* 1975, 1985, 1990. *Familienbericht* 1979 and 1990.

52. For (feminist) women's studies in Austria, see Helga Nowotny and Karl Hausen, eds., *Wie männlich ist die Wissenschaft?* (Frankfurt: Suhrkamp, 1986); Elisabeth List, "Helden im Wissenschaftsspiel. Geschlechtsspezifische Implikationen der Wissenschaftskultur," in Beate Frakele et al., eds., *Über Frauenleben, Männerwelt und Wissenschaft* (Vienna: Gesellschaftskritik, 1987), 18–33.

2

Contemporary Sociology in Belgium

Liliane Voyé and Karel Dobbelaere

INTRODUCTION: THE EMERGENCE AND ESTABLISHMENT OF SOCIOLOGY IN BELGIUM[1]

In 1835, the Belgian Adolphe Quételet published his *Sur l'homme et le développement de ses facultés ou essai de physique sociale.*[2] Since Quételet systematically statistically analyzed human, political, and social phenomena and, particularly, social problems, looking, for example, for the impact of sex, age, education, and professional status on the propensity for criminal behavior, we may consider him to be the first Belgian sociologist. Indirectly, he also led Auguste Comte to coin the term *sociology.* Indeed, Comte objected to the grounding of a science of society, which he also called *"physique sociale,"* on the statistical method and advocated the historical method. Consequently, a couple of years after the publication of Quételet's book, Comte coined the term *sociology* to designate his concept of a science of society.[3]

The first work in the line of Comte but also of Herbert Spencer appearing in Belgium was Guillaume de Greef's *Introduction à la sociologie.*[4] In de Greef's opinion, sociology was not a purely theoretical field developing a systematic theory but also an applied science that provided a necessary basis for social policy. This need for an analysis of factual data as a basis for social policy was strongly felt in Belgian university circles at the end of the last century. The relationship between theory, research, and policy would have a great impact on the shaping of sociology in Belgium.

The first courses in sociology were taught at the Université Libre de Bruxelles. The Universitas Catholica Lovaniensis also stressed the need for the direct observation of facts and the need for a comparative study of institutions but did not incorporate sociology into the curriculum of its Ecole des Sciences Politiques et Sociales (founded in 1892). It was also at the Université Libre de Bruxelles that the first sociological research institute was established by the Belgian industrialist Ernest Solvay: the Institut de Sociologie Solvay. E. Waxweiler directed the institute, and, in 1906, he published his *Esquisse d'une sociologie.*[5] It presents a nominal view of society (society is nothing more than an association of individuals) and may be considered anti-Durkheimian.

At first, sociology was clearly a product of a Francophone free-thinking milieu associated with the Université Libre de Bruxelles. It is only in the thirties that sociology was introduced by the other Belgian universities. This was not easy in the Universitas Catholica Lovaniensis since sociology was thought to be a product of the positivistic Durkheimian school, which was considered to be anticlerical and opposed to the traditional philosophy and ethics. It was Canon J. Leclercq who introduced sociology in his course on moral philosophy, which was subtitled "An Attempt to Introduce Sociology." For a long time, sociology was part of curricula in philosophy, law, or social and political sciences. Only in the early sixties were the first degrees in sociology offered in the Universities of Bruxelles/Brussel and Louvain/Leuven.

In the early 1950s, the Société Belge de Sociologie was established by the professors teaching sociology at the Universities of Bruxelles/Brussel, Louvain/Leuven, Ghent, and Liège. This society was an academic, predominantly Francophone, and closed association. Its members were mostly interested in theoretical, philosophical, and epistemological discussions. Two of its eminent members published theoretical treatises, J. Haesaert (Ghent) a *Sociologie générale*[6] and H. Janne (Brussels) his *Le système social: Essai de théorie générale.*[7] Pierre de Bie (Louvain) studied the history and development of sociology in Belgium, and René Clemens (Liège) stimulated the interaction between theory and research. A typical study in this vein was *L'assimilation culturelle des immigrants en Belgique, Italiens et Polonais dans le région Liègeoise.*[8]

It was only in 1955 that another major research institute was established in addition to the Institut Solvay: the Centrum voor Sociale Studies/Centre d'Etudes Sociales. Upon the division of the Universitas Catholica Lovaniensis into two independant universities—one French speaking and one Dutch speaking—the Center was split into the Centre de Recherches Sociologiques, which has published the first purely sociological review *Recherches Sociologiques* since 1970, and the Sociologisch Onderzoeksinstituut. On the Dutch-speaking side, an interuniversity sociological review was founded in 1979: *Het Tijdschrift voor Sociologie.* With these research institutes, a new type of sociologist emerged: the professional researcher. On the Flemish side, they organized themselves and established their own organization, the Organisatie voor Vlaamse Sociologen (1962). Later, with the development of sociological research and the extension of the teaching of sociology, the two existing associations disappeared and, in 1975, two new ones emerged, again along linguistic lines: the Association des Sociologues Belges de Langue Française and the Vereniging voor Sociologie.

Sociological research, unlike the situation in some other countries, is nearly exclusively located in university centers. This research is funded by the universities themselves, the National Fund for Scientific Research, and the Fund for Collective Fundamental Research. Policy research is commissioned by, among others, the government, political parties, and trade unions. A National Research Program on the Social Sciences (1975–1981) and some foundations also sponsor applied sociological research.

Consequently, sociological research has flourished from the sixties on along the lines set in the mid-fifties. Its development prefigured the curricula in sociology that were established in the sixties and seventies: domain specific (industry, labor, family and population, religion, culture, urban and rural, etc.), research oriented, and applied. A detailed description of the fifties and sixties, the emerging research, and later on, the establishment of the sociological curricula, is given in P. de Bie's study that was published in the previous edition of this handbook.[9] We will turn now to a description of Belgian sociological production in the late seventies and the eighties.

THEORY AND METHODOLOGY

Janne's *Le Système Social* is still one of the most important theoretical works.[10] The author intended to reaffirm the global society—considered as an organic, open, and dynamic system that produces a socio-material and a psychosocial reality—as the object of general sociology.

More recently, Jozef C. Verhoeven and Martin Ruebens (KUL)[11] have concerned themselves with metatheoretical questions that sustain metatheoretical pluralism in sociology. On the basis of critical study of the sociological literature and interviews with theoretically oriented sociologists, they search for the basic assumptions and the methodology of the different theoretical models. They analyze, in particular, interpretative sociology, symbolic interactionism, phenomenological sociology, ethnomethodology, and "frame analysis," in order to confront these action theories with system theories, and to evaluate the extent to which the two perspectives may be bridged.[12] The core of the theoretical work of Antonio Piaser (UCL) proposes a systematization of the general epistemology and a reconstruction of the most prevalent quantitative and qualitative methods in sociology. On this basis, he analyzes long-term changes in Belgian capitalism and the transformations of economic and social politics, the technological evolution, and the changes in politics and trade unionism.[13]

The work of Claude Javeau (ULB) is most of all a theoretical reflection on the foundations of sociology, the historical genesis of the discipline, and general epistemology and methodology, in an attempt to reconcile determinism and voluntarism. Javeau is also interested in the sociology of everyday life. In a constructivistic perspective, he gives specific attention to phenomena such as death and rituals. Comprehensively oriented as in the German tradition, he is also strongly influenced by the phenomenology of Alfred Schutz.[14]

In a Weberian perspective. Jean Remy, Liliane Voyé, and Emile Servais (UCL) intended in their book *Produire ou reproduire?* to show how the practices of everyday life, in their ambiguities, work to stabilize an established model of society and, at the same time, to produce an alternative one. They contribute to the theory of ideology on the basis of the analysis of social movements and on the elaboration of the concept of transaction in its cultural dimensions. They are particularly interested in the present pluralistic society, with its internal differentiation, complexity of social positions, and transformation of the hierarchy of its subsystems.[15]

From an ideological point of view, Jan Lauwers (UIA) analyzes secularization theories. He considers them to be "social action theories" used by (anti-) secularizers to change the relationship between religion and society. Such an approach stresses the study of secularization theories from the perspective of the sociology of knowledge.[16] Karel Dobbelaere (KUL), on the other hand, distinguishes different levels in secularization theories: the societal, the subsystem, and the individual. This may allow, in his opinion, the development of an empirically founded theory based on the analysis of processes such as functional differentiation, rationalization, and "Vergesellschaftung." He also shows the convergences and divergences between secularization theories based on different paradigms.[17]

As far as methodology is concerned, we have to distinguish between quantitative and qualitative or "clinical" methods. In the first sequence, it is particularly interesting to point to the work of J. Bonmariage, E. Legros, J. Marquet, and their team (UCL); the first of them is the founder of the BASS (Belgian Archives for Social Sciences), which not only collects data on various topics but also and primarily refines mathematical and data-processing tools for the specificity of the sociological point of view. Jaak Billiet and Geert Loosveldt (KUL) have done experimental research to evaluate the improvement of data collection, especially in survey research. They have analyzed question-wording effects and effects of interviewer training on the improvement of the quality of responses and also the practicability of measuring the intensity of attitudes. Their aim is to formulate well-founded guidelines about wording survey questions and to explain response effects.[18] Mark Swyngedouw has sought to improve the estimation of shifts and party preferences in successive elections; and Paul Houben, also at the KUL, elaborated mathematical models to test the effect of ideological factors on public expenditures and the explanatory value of coalition theories.[19]

The qualitative or "clinical" methods have also undergone important developments, especially at the UCL and the ULg. Among them, we may particularly mention the method of "life stories," which is used by Bernadette Bawin (ULg) in family sociology[20] and by Robert Williame (UCL) in historical sociology.[21] The latter intends to reconstruct the "collective memories" of industrialization in Belgium. An original method of content analysis was developed by Jean-Pierre Hiernaux and Jean Remy (UCL) to elucidate the unconscious logic according to which an actor guides his practices.[22] Michel Molitor (UCL) uses "collective hermeneutics," a specific methodology aiming at bringing out the conscience structures of the actors and their social dynamics.[23] The method of scenarios is used especially by Jean Remy and Liliane Voyé (UCL) in urban sociology to help decision making in town planning. Impact studies have been developed by the same two authors and by other researchers of the same group, D. Bodson and A. Wallemacq (UCL), to evaluate such things as the various incidences that the implantation of "*grands équipements*" (large equipment) has on a region, before and after the fact.[24]

LABOR PROCESSES, NEW TECHNOLOGIES, AND ORGANIZATIONS

The sociology of labor and industry has been from the outset a quantitatively well-developed subdiscipline. However, since this field is very problem oriented, the topics have changed and with them the types of research. High on the research agenda are the new technologies and their effects on information and bargaining structures; the effects of the implementation of new technologies on the labor process, human resources management, flexibility and new forms of work; and types of unemployment, studied from the theoretical point of view of the dual labor market theory and the ensuing need for occupational resettlement and refresher courses. Such studies were done at the KUL in the Department of Sociology and the Higher Institute of Labor (HIVA), a joint venture of the Catholic University of Leuven and the Christian Workers Association (ACW), by Jan Bundervoet, Albert Martens, and Peter Van der Hallen.[25] A special foundation, *Stichting Technologie Vlaanderen,* also promotes multidisciplinary research on the new technologies in which these sociologists cooperate along with sociologists of other Flemish universities, such as A. Mok (UIA) and J. Vilrokx (VUB). The types of research used are based on statistical analysis, survey research, case studies, and action research. Vilrokx's study group has conducted many studies, pertaining to collective bargaining and technology agreements, sectorial developments, collective behavior in industry, and so forth. The Relative Autonomization

Tendency in/of Organizations (RATO) is used as a theoretical and empirical framework for these research activities.[26] At the Department of Sociology of the KUL, the organizational structure, ideology, and actions of the Belgian trade unions are also studied.

On the French-speaking side, we note the studies of François Pichault and Michel De Coster (ULg), who are especially interested in the social and organizational aspects of technological innovation and in the conflicts that occur within technical configurations.[27] They have founded a research center (LENTIC) especially for this problem area. Work changes are also central for Michel Molitor (UCL). In a comparative international perspective, he focuses his research on the new cultural models of work emerging in the developed societies, specifically in those that industrialized very early and have to confront new social regulations and new collective identities operating in work.[28] And there are also the comparative studies that are done by Marcel Bolle de Bal (ULB): he has set out to discern how remuneration is or is not linked to performance and to see what the strategies of social actors are in this regard.[29] Considering, too, the new conditions of the labor market, Jacques Delcourt (UCL) is analyzing the links between it and the school system. He is also interested in the new conditions of work (e.g., "flexibility") and in the rights of the workers.[30]

Some connections with this field are to be found in other research directed to the understanding of the new forms of organization. This line is represented at the ULg by Olgierd Kuty, who is analyzing the new forms of work organization in relation to the restructuring of the welfare state. He is also interested in the hospital as an organization and in home care.[31] Alain Eraly (ULB) is studying the rationalization and the structuring of organizations in line with the work of Anthony Giddens. He is trying to integrate the contributions of the classic works on organizations into a reconceptualization of organizations as social formations. He intends to go beyond the dualism of structure and human action, by taking into account the cognitive processes of the social actors and the spatial and temporal dimensions of the organization.[32]

SOCIOLOGY OF THE WELFARE STATE

Research on the welfare state is being conducted at the UFSIA.[33] According to Herman Deleeck, the large increase in the volume of social transfers and public services (social security, education, housing, health care, cultural facilities) has produced a general rise in the standard of living, but participation in the welfare state has remained unequal. This Deleeck explains by the "Matthew effect": within the welfare state, because of sociocultural and sociopolitical factors, social benefits tend to flow to the higher and middle classes more than to the lower ones. His center has developed its own poverty standard, which is of the so-called subjective type. This allows him to construct an instrument to evaluate the extent and the distribution of poverty and the adequacy of social security. This instrument is now being applied in other European countries, thus permitting comparative studies. Jan Vranken has extended the analysis of poverty and the poor into the migrant world. In the Center for Social Policy (KUL), Frans Lammertyn and Edward Leemans guide studies on social problems: social inequality and education, poverty, the elderly, the handicapped, and so on. Lammertyn also directs research on the welfare policies of national and regional authorities, the structure and activities of welfare organizations, and the professionalization of this field.[34] We also must mention, at the UCL, the work of Jacques Delcourt, who is studying social justice and social policies.[35] This question is also being explored by Antonio Piaser, who proposes pedagogic cards to evaluate these social policies.

SOCIOLOGY OF LAW

The sociology of law is approached from a broad point of view at the Facultés Universitaires St. Louis (Brussels): their Center for Sociological Studies (directed by Jean Remy and Luc Van Campenhoudt) is interested in the modes of production, interpretation, application, and transformation of norms, particularly when there is social change, crisis, innovation, or transition. Thus, they have studied the impact of the "trade union of the magistrature" on the transformation of the world of the judiciary. They are also interested in other kinds of norms, such as linguistic (B. Wynants) and sexual ones (M. Hubert).[36]

At the University of Antwerp, Jean Van Houtte (UFSIA) directs socio-legal studies on institutions of family law.[37] Two such institutions were studied with the assumption that the law lags behind social evolution: the maintenance obligation between elderly parents in need and their children and between husband and wife. Following a legal reform of the rights and duties between spouses, studies were done to evaluate how successful the reform was. Finally, the paradigm of "social engineering" was applied to the new adoption legislation. After several institutions of family law were analyzed, a more synthetic research project, "Family and Law," is now being conducted. At the same center, Francis Van Loon has studied the so-called litigation explosion.[38] He has examined the evolution of the activities of civil courts since 1830, considering the type of conflicts, parties involved, duration, and development of the case, results, and so forth. In Leuven (KUL) Luc Huyse has focused his research on the legal profession and on the political role of the courts.[39]

Working with a combination of survey research, qualitative interviewing, and statistical and historical data, Lode Van Outrive and associates (KUL) have developed the sociology of the administration of justice.[40] It includes studies of police and intelligence systems, penitentiary systems, the privatization of order maintenance and investigation, victimization, and alternatives to repressive penal administration of justice. They use an interactionist approach combined with a more structuralist and critical sociology.

POLITICS

Political sociology is a well-developed field in Belgium. For several years, André-Paul Frognier (UCL) has been conducting research on the question of legitimacy as a central dimension in the relationship between the governed and the governors.[41] Referring to the Parsonian theoretical frame of the "social medias," he intends to elaborate an operational theory of the thresholds of legitimacy in the political system and thus to be able to interpret or predict crises and instability. Frognier is also interested in comparing the relationships between the decisional structures of politics and the "mass" or "citizen politics." So doing, he focuses particularly on the Belgian situation and the evolution of the "pillars." His interest in Belgian politics has also led him to study a panel on the evolution of national feelings. Finally, Frognier studies comparatively the structures and the working of the West European governments. At the University of Antwerp, Guido Dierickx focuses primarily on the relevance of political culture and ideology in political decision making and this in a comparative perspective.[42] This has led him to promote and participate in research projects about the role of European Parliaments in managing social conflict, the political culture of senior civil servants, and the ideological factor in macroeconomic policy making. On the level of theory, he is mainly interested in the comparison between various paradigms as applied to sociological and politological research. At the UCL, the Groupe de Sociologie Wallonne conducts research into local public administration and public services.

At the KUL, Wilfried Dewachter heads a research group that concentrates on empirical research on Belgian and European elections (campaign costs, elections as a process of power achievement, and the electoral demonstration of the law of weak parliamentary institutions); political parties and decision making, with an analysis of "particracy"; cabinet stability and power hierarchies and elites.[43] Currently, he is working on a general analysis of political decision making in Belgium. At the same university, Luc Huyse is also interested in political conflicts based on religion, language, and social class and the process of consociational decision making as a technique for the accommodation of such conflicts in Belgium.[44]

The recent emergence of the ecology parties prompted researchers to study their electoral successes, the relationships between contemporary social movements and these parties, the organizational practices of these parties, and the political beliefs and careers of the activists involved.[45] In the perspective of sociolinguistics, Albert Verdoodt (UCL) studies the link between political power and languages, especially in reference to regional and minority languages.[46]

SOCIOLOGY OF RELIGIONS

A link between political sociology and the sociology of religion is made by studies on pillarization. Jaak Billiet and Karel Dobbelaere (KUL) have tried to explain the survival of the Catholic pillar notwithstanding the profound religious changes of the late sixties and early seventies. They stress the emergence of a new collective consciousness, that is, sociocultural Christianity, and selective internal social control.[47] Liliane Voye (UCL) added to these the appeal of the "private character" of the Christian pillar, in a period in which the public sphere is under heavy criticism, and its multiclass character.[48] The link between the corporate and the political channel of the Christian pillar has been studied especially by Billiet. More recently, a comparative macrosociological analysis was carried out by S. Hellemans (KUL) that linked pillarization and studies on social movements.

In the field of religion Dobbelaere has linked macrosociological (functional differentiation, rationalization, and *Vergesellschaftung*) to microsociological trends (compartmentalization and individualization) in order to explain the decline of church religiosity and the emergence of a *"Catholicism à la carte."* He has also stressed the impact of a changing church policy in the recent decade.[49] Elaborating on these trends, he and Voyé (UCL) extended their explanation by referring to hypotheses inferred from theories on postmodernity.[50] Voyé works most of all at the UCL with Jean Remy. They are interested in Catholicism in Belgium: the confrontation of Catholicism with modernity; religion and the linguistical conflict; the image non-Catholics have of the Catholics, and so forth. Remy includes this in his study of the general question of symbolism, and Voyé, for her part, is interested in the redefinition of the sacred and in institutional aspects of the Catholic church.[51]

We also have to mention the work of Michel Voisin (ULg) on sectarian movements and utopian communities and the work of Dobbelaere with Bryan R. Wilson on the Moonies and on Jehovah's Witnesses.[52]

In the field of the sociology of religions, the work of François Houtart and Geneviève Lemercinier (UCL) is very specific. They have two orientations: first of all, they are concerned with the evaluation of the role of religions in the reproduction of societies; in this perspective, they have made historical studies, especially in Asia and in Latin America. Second, they try to understand the religious aspect of the culture, using factor analysis of correspondence.[53]

SOCIOLOGY OF EDUCATION

In the field of the sociology of education, important work is being done by Anne Van Haecht (ULB).[54] She wrote a sociohistorical study on the high schools in Belgium and a trend report on studies in the field of the sociology of education published in French. She has also analyzed the purposes and the effects of the "enseignement rénové," a profound reform of the conception and methodology of education progressively generalized in the Belgian high schools. In the same field, some research considers the differentiations appearing in the Belgian school network at different levels. Jean-Emile Charlier (UCL-FUCAM), for instance, studies the images existing in public opinion about different high schools and the various "rites" that schools and pupils create and diffuse in the school surroundings.[55] Ch. Maroy (Fac. ND Namur) is interested in the multiplication of training cycles outside the school and in the development of permanent education. These scholars stress the rapprochement of the sociology of education with the sociology of the family and the sociology of work, since there is an effect of family education on school results and on the level of unemployment.

In two Flemish universities, teams are doing research in the field of education. Herman Brutsaert (RUG) has done a longitudinal study on the Belgian educational reforms and their impact on the pupils by means of a comparative contextual analysis. He also studied self-esteem: for girls it depends upon the emotional support they receive from their immediate surroundings during puberty, for boys it is more dependent upon their sense of mastery. However, in early adolescence, the self-esteem of girls is also based on their sense of mastery.[56] In his studies on educational reform. Jozef C. Verhoeven (KUL) stresses that the changing curricula prescribed by the government have less effect than does the educational training of the teachers. The local autonomy of school authorities also seems to be very important in promoting educational reform.[57]

SOCIOLOGY OF THE FAMILY

In the Flemish part of Belgium, sociology of the family and population is well developed at the VUB and the KUL. Ron Lesthaeghe and associates have studied the relationship between changes in patterns and tempo of family formation (unmarried cohabitation, marriage, divorce, postdivorce cohabitation, martial and extramarital fertility) in Western Europe since the 1960s and alterations within various ideational dimensions (i.e., changes in meaning systems and value systems). They have also promoted research on nuptiality and reproduction in sub-Saharan Africa.[58] Wilfried Dumon and Koen Matthijs have done a panel study on some consequences of divorce, especially the new housing situations, arrangements concerning the custody of children and maintenance obligations, the emotional processing of divorce, the consequences for children, and the problems of complex stepfamilies. They also study migration and publish an annual overview of sociological articles published in international journals. Finally, in line with the "Social Indicator Movement," Matthijs has set up a statistical databank and has developed an instrument to measure "life satisfaction," also based on family indicators, and Dumon has studied the politics and programs of family policy.[59]

In the French part of Belgium Bernadette Bawin (ULg) is most of all interested in the mechanisms of continuity and ruptures and in the incidences of the latter. Her findings show that there exist various types of conjugal and parental behavior according to different moments in the family cycle. Bawin has also investigated the question of economic survival of women after divorce in an effort to understand why maintenance obligations are so often not met.[60]

SOCIOLOGY OF CULTURE AND VALUES

It is social change that is the focus of Rudolf Rezsohazy's studies (UCL). In this perspective, he worked out a method of continuous observation and organized recurrent and standardized inquiries on the evolution of values, behavior, youth, family, and couples, "revisiting" each of these subjects every five years.[61]

Jan Lauwers (UIA) is studying cultural integration resulting from tension between socialized individuals and mobilizing organizations, without losing sight of the overarching and integrating role of the community (territory, family, and religion).[62] At the KUL, Frans Van Mechelen and Urbain Claeys have organized empirical research on sports, leisure time, social tourism, voluntary associations, and housing.[63] The last of these was also developed in Antwerp by Luc Goossens.[64] At the VUB, Micheline Scheys is doing research on lifestyle, viewed as a series of symbols actors use to present themselves, in order to study the rise of individualism.[65] In his analysis of culture, C. L. Kruithof (RUG) makes an interpretative analysis of "marginal men" (e.g., the executioner) and sociologically marginal subjects (e.g., shame and humiliation). Through these studies of marginal phenomena he tries to understand the surrounding culture and society.[66]

In order to understand modern society and culture, Mark Elchardus, Ignace Glorieux, and other members of the VUB *Tempus Omnia Revelat* research group view the study of time as essential. At the structural level, time is viewed as a concept that expresses the temporal organization of systems. It is based on two dimensions. The specific way in which these dimensions are dealt with in art, science, ritual, and belief is studied on the symbolic level of analysis. The concepts of time and attitudes toward timc are studied on the individual, subjective level. On the organizational level, attention is devoted to the way in which structural dimensions, symbolic practices, and subjective beliefs become institutionalized. Here special attention is devoted to the conflicts between the temporalities of different spheres of action and their consequences for the quality of life. These studies are based on literary analysis, historical work, ethnographic observation, and time-budget analysis.[67] The problem of time also emerges in the work of Anne Wallemacq, whose approach stresses the role of perceptions in the construction of reality.[68]

In the sociology of the arts, the Centre de Sociologie du Théâtre (ULB), directed by Roger Deldime, must be mentioned. It is a multidisciplinary center, working on artistic creation, audiences, and the reception of shows. This center has gradually given up a sociographical analysis of the public and favors a psychosociological study of spectator behavior.[69] At the ULB also, there is a center for the sociology of the arts. It operates under the direction of Claude Javeau and its main promoter is Daniel Vandergucht. They are interested in the meaning of works of art and in the "spirit of the times" artists pretend to express through their work.[70]

URBAN, RURAL, AND REGIONAL SOCIOLOGY

Rural sociology was a topic in Belgian sociology very early on. G. Hoyois, at the UCL, was well known in this field. He was succeeded by Jean Remy, who broadened the topic and founded the Centre de Sociologie Urbaine et Rurale. Urban society has been at the heart of the work of Remy and Voyé for about twenty years. They are interested in the understanding of the role space has in defining the possibilities of different social actors. They have also planned a number of new towns, which has permitted them to construct "scenarios of social life"—a methodological tool that allows them to anticipate the organization of space according to different types of populations and the uses they make of equipments and services it offers. They have also published a book on different kinds of violence in towns, trying to explain them not only as forms of deviance but also as a result of cultural clashes and forms of town planning.[71] At the same Centre Daniel Bodson is most of all interested in an epistemological approach to rurality, since he considers that most of the research conducted in this field is commissioned by political or religious interest groups that criticize industrial and urban society.[72] A similar approach is used by Marc Mormont and Catherine Mougenot at the FUL.[73] The transformation of urban spaces and forms also interests Nicole Delruelle (ULB), who links them to societal changes. With the Centre de Sociologie Générale et de Méthodologie, she is studying Brussels from this point of view.[74] At the ULB too, Jacques Malengreau studies the social groupings

of farmers, especially the social political structures that organize their relations with the environment and with production.[75]

At the junction of economy and sociology, Michel Quévit (UCL) directs
the Groupe de Recherches Interdisciplinaires en Développement Régional
(RIDER). This center is interested in exploring the processes of technological innovation in enterprises and the effect the local environment has
on their capacity for innovation. It also tries to determine the potential of
technical, economic, and human development of the French-speaking region of Belgium in the perspective of the Unified Market of 1992. In the
same perspective, the RIDER helps to harmonize the interstate norms:
laws, state aid, and so forth.[76]

MEDICAL SOCIOLOGY

At the KUL, Yvo Nuyens directs research in medical sociology on the
organization of health care, primary health care, the medical profession,
professionals and volunteers in health care, the psychiatric discourse,
health economics, trade unions in health care, and self-help in health and
social welfare.[77] E. Van Hove's work has been in empirical and applied
research in health and social-services planning (UIA). Projects have been
carried out in the planning of psychiatric services and the introduction of
information technology in psychiatric hospitals, organization studies of social services, comparative studies of health-care systems and the integrated
development of poverty areas in urban settings. The applied research of
Fred Louckx (VUB) is twofold: he studied the health situation of and the
organization of health care for underserved groups (migrants, unemployed, terminal patients, and political refugees) and also manpower planning (especially nurses), preventive strategies in primary health care, and
information systems in health care.[78] Similar topics are discussed in the
works of Olgierd Kuty (ULg), who is also interested in analyzing the
health practices of elderly people and scientific innovations in medicine.[79]

COMMUNICATION

The studies of Yves Winkin (ULg) concern communication considered
as an interactive practice and as a profession (publisher, journalist, public
relations, etc.). He is also interested in the history of ideas, people, and
institutions, which, in the United States, has given the status of scientific
matter to interpersonal communication. The concepts he uses are those of
"structural" sociologists, like Pierre Bourdieu, and action theorists, like
Erving Goffman. To study the rites of interaction, he employs ethnographical methods, and to reconstitute an intellectual field he works as a social
historian.[80] At the same university, François Pichault and Michel De Coster study the socioeconomic implications of new media in the field of com-

munication. In this line, Pichault, with G. Tremblay (Université du Québec à Montréal), founded an international review: *Technologies de l'Information et Société.*[81]

In several books and articles on mass communication and communication theory, Guido Fauconnier (KUL) has developed an integrated view of two fundamentally different research traditions in his field: the rather empirical one and the more philosophical one. He has also contributed to the development of a scientific foundation of communication modalities, such as public relations and advertising. During the last ten years, he has initiated and developed research activities on new media and new information technologies.[82]

OTHER DEVELOPMENTS

Apart from new methodological, theoretical, and substantial questions already discussed above, other new questions have emerged. However, mostly, the old questions have required a new theoretical and methodological approach, notably migration, the elderly, poverty, and tourism.

The topic of the immigrants is well developed in Belgium: the demographic aspects of these populations, their place in the job market, the secularization of their children, the politics of the Belgium institutions regarding different migrant groups, and so forth (Michel Voisin, ULg; W. Dumon and Albert Martens, KUL). Analyzing these questions for a long time. Albert Bastenier and Felice Dassetto (UCL) have added a new concern: they try to understand how migrants' communities, and especially the Muslim communities, are functioning internally as well as in their relations with the Belgian populations and institutions.[83]

Marguerite Lisein-Norman (ULB) has conducted studies on women, especially on their conditions of work in an industrial milieu and in reference to the new technologies.[84] The Groupe de Sociologie Wallonne (UCL) is also interested in women's problems, specifically in the questions of equality of social opportunities and of violence against women.[85] At the KUL, UIA, and VUB, sociologists also participate in interdisciplinary groups called women's or gender studies.

Questions concerning ageing are becoming important subjects of sociological research in Belgium. This is the case with the work of France Govaerts (ULB) and of Olgierd Kuty (ULg). The former shows that cultural, social, and economic interventions may transform the process of ageing, which was previously defined as "natural."[86] The latter analyzes health practices of old people and also does action research to develop programs preparing for retirement. This last concern is at the heart of the work of the Groupe de Sociologie Wallonne (UCL—J. Lefèvre and A. Garcia), which has created a "university for the elderly," which is flourishing.

Jean-Pierre Hiernaux (UCL) has published many studies about the relations between school and work to explore the problem of youth unemployment. However, in recent years, his main topic has been poverty, as
he is the coordinator of the European program against poverty. In this
capacity, he is in charge of the definition of the experimentation in and
the evaluation of new social action to reduce poverty and to confront its
new forms.[87]

The cultural, economic, and social importance of tourism and the need
for a contextual approach to this phenomenon has, in this last few years,
stimulated a new trend of research and the start, in 1990, of an M.A.
program in tourism at the UCL (Daniel Bodson and Liliane Voyé).[88]

Two new themes have emerged recently: "postmodernity" and "existential sociology." Voyé (UCL) is interested in postmodernity considered
as a new cultural environment and in the changes it introduces in different
aspects of life, whether it be religion or economy, architecture and town
planning, or the evaluation of the welfare state and civil society.[89] Rudi
Laermans (KUL) situates "the social logic of postmodernity" (social fragmentation, a flowing "sociality") within the broader perspective of modernization theory. He also analyzes how the current shift toward a
postmodern culture is reflected in the growing domination of a consumer
culture within the youth culture, the contemporary body culture, and personal lifestyles in general.[90] Ch. Delhaye (KUL) uses a related approach
in her research on the evolution of fashion consciousness within different
postwar generations of young women.

From a very different point of view, Marcel Bolle de Bal (ULB) endeavors to conceptualize an "existential sociology," taking into account
the person with his affectivity and his emotions. His main themes are
reliance, maieutic intervention, socioanalysis, and existential self-
management. Also concerned with the reintroduction of the personal dimensions into the interpretation of the social, P. Ninane (UCL) uses
various philosophical concepts, such as imagery, representation, affectivity,
intentionality, reason, consciousness, unconsciousness, and so on. He interprets social conduct such as the collective imagery, the rationalistic and
the hedonistic culture, and the power of institutions in reference to the
subject.[91]

CONCLUSIONS

At the juncture point of Latin and Germanic cultures, Belgian sociology
links the Anglo-Saxon, French, and German contributions to the field. In
general, Belgian sociologists have a good knowledge of the theoretical
approaches of these three sources. However, each Belgian sociologist is
also marked by the specificity of one of them. Some adopt more or less
the literary form, typical of French sociology, corrected by more economic

training. Others are closer to the empirical Anglo-Saxon approach; still others join with the philosophical German tradition.

A second characteristic of Belgian sociology is its concern for practical applications, which is reflected in the development of particular subfields and their contributions to social policies and decision making. This interest in subfields and practical applications also has repercussions on theoretical and methodological developments.

NOTES

1. Pierre de Bie, *Les premiers essais de Sociologie en Belgique à la fin du XIXe siècle* (Louvain: Warny, 1944); Pierre de Bie, "Sociology in Belgium: Teaching and Research," *Contemporary Sociology in Western Europe and in America* (Roma: Luigi Sturzo Instituto, 1967), 133–152; Pierre de Bie, *Naissance et premiers développements de la sociologie en Belgique* (Bruxelles: CIACO, 1988); Wilfried Dumon, "Sociologie in Belgie," in L. Rademaker, ed., *Sociologische grondbegrippen: Theorie en analyse* (Utrecht: Spectrum, 1981), 166–178.

2. Paris: Bachelier, 1835.

3. B. C. van Houten, "Saint-Simon en Comte," in L. Rademaker and E. Petersma, eds., *Hoofdfiguren uit de sociologie: I. Klassieken* (Utrecht: Spectrum, 1974), 34–35.

4. Guillaume de Greef, *Introduction à la sociologie* (Bruxelles: G. Mayolez, 1886).

5. Bruxelles: Misch et Thron, 1906.

6. Bruxelles: Erasme, 1956.

7. Bruxelles: Université Libre, 1968.

8. René Clémens et al. *L'assimilation culturelle des immigrants en Belgique. Italiens et Polonais dans la région liégeoise* (Liège: Vaillant-Carmanne, 1953).

9. Pierre de Bie, "Contemporary Sociology in Belgium," in Raj P. Mohan and Don Martindale, eds., *Handbook of Contemporary Developments in World Sociology* (Westport, Conn.: Greenwood Press, 1975), 31–45.

10. Janne, *Le systéme social.*

11. Abbreviations used for the different Belgian universities:

FAC. N.D. Namur: Facultés Notre Dame de la Paix à Namur

FUCAM: Faculté Universitaire Catholique de Mons

FUL: Fondation Universitaire Luxembourgeoise

KUL: Katholieke Universiteit Leuven

RUG: Rijksuniversiteit Gent

UCL: Université Catholique de Louvain

UFSIA: Universitaire Faculteiten Sint Ignatius te Antwerpen

UIA: Universitaire Instelling Antwerpen

ULB: Université Libre de Bruxelles

ULg: Université de l'Etat à Liége

VUB: Vrije Universiteit Brussel

12. Jozef C. Verhoeven, "Goffman's Frame Analysis and Modern Microsociological Paradigms," in Horst J. Helle and S. N. Eisenstadt, eds., *Micro-Sociological Theory* (London: Sage, 1985), 71–100; Jozef C. Verhoeven, "Phenomenological 'Verstehen' and Interactionist 'Sympathetic Understanding': Similarities and Differences," in Horst J. Helle, ed., *Interpretative Sociology. Essays on Verstehen and Pragmatism* (Berlin: Duncker and Humblot, 1990); Martin Ruebens, "The Social Study of Science and the Problem of Order: A View from Ethnomethodology," in Helle, ed., *Interpretative Sociology;* Martin Ruebens, *Sociologie van het alledaagse leven: Een grondslagendebat tussen handelingstheorie en systeemtheorie* (Leuven: Acco, 1990).

13. Antonio Piaser, *Méthodologie et épistémologie en sociologie* (Louvain-la-Neuve: CIACO, 1984); Antonio Piaser, *Les mouvements longs du capitalisme belge* (Bruxelles: Vie Ouvrière, 1986).

14. Claude Javeau, *Leçons de sociologie* (Paris: Méridiens-Klincksieck, 1987); Claude Javeau, *Mourir* (Bruxelles: Eperonniers, 1988); Claude Javeau, *Le petit murmure et le bruit du monde* (Bruxelles: Eperonniers, 1985).

15. Jean Remy, Liliane Voyé, and Emile Servais, *Produire ou reproduire?* (Bruxelles: Vie Ouvrière, vol. 1, 1978, and vol. 2, 1980).

16. Jan Lauwers, *Secularisatietheorieen. Een studie over de toekomst-kansen van de godsdienstsociologie* (Leuven: Universitaire Pers, 1974).

17. Karel Dobbelaere, "Secularization: A Multi-Dimenstional Concept," *Current Sociology* 29, 2 (1981), 1–213; Karel Dobbelaere. "The Secularization of Society? Some Methodological Suggestions," in Jeffrey K. Hadden and Ansome Shupe, eds., *Secularization and Fundamentalism Reconsidered. Religion and the Political Order,* vol. 3, (New York: Paragon House, 1989), 27–44: Karel Dobbelaere, "Secularization Theories and Sociological Paradigms: A Reformulation of the Private-Public Dichotomy and the Problem of Societal Integration," *Sociological Analysis* 46, 4 (1985); 377–387.

18. Jaak Billiet and Geert Loosveldt, "Improvement of the Quality of Responses to Factual Survey Questions by Interviewer Training," *Public Opinion Quarterly* 52, 3 (1988), 190–211; Lina Waterplas, Jaak Billet, and Geert Loosveldt, "De verbieden versus niet toelaten asymmetrie. Een stabiel formuleringseffect in survey onderzoek," *Mens en Matschappij* 63, 4 (1988), 399–418; Jaak Billet, "Wat te doen? Beschouwingen over het nut van pasklare voorschriften voor the ontwerpen van survey-vragen," in Johannes Van de Zouwen and Wil Dijkstra, eds, *Sociaal-wetenchappelijk onderzoek met vragenlijsten* (Amsterdam: VU-uitgeverij, 1989), 35–52.

19. Mark Swyngedouw, *De keuze van de kiezer: Naar een verbetering van de schattingen van verschuivingen en partijvoorkeur bij opeenvolgende verkiezingen* (Rotterdam: Erasmus Universiteit and Leuven: SOI, 1990); Paul Houben, *Formele beslissingsmodellen en speltheorie* (Leuven: Departtment Sociologie, 1988), 5 vols.

20. Bernadette Bawin. *Familles, mariage, divorce* (Bruxelles: Mardaga, 1988).

21. Robert Williame, "Pour une micro-sociologie historique: La méthodologie des récits de vie," in Hubert Gérard and Michel Loriaux, eds, *Au-delà du quantitatif* (Louvain-la-Neuve: CIACO, 1988), 179–248.

22. Jean-Pierre Hiernaux, *L'institution culturelle* (Louvain-la-Neuve: Institut des

Sciences Politiques et Sociales, 1975), Jean Remy. "Mythe de la collectivité: dialectique du soi et du social. Une méthode d'analyse de contenu et son propos interprétatif," Gérard and Loriaux, eds., *Au-delà du quantitatif,* 249–280.

23. Michel Molitor, "L'hermeneutique collective," Gérard and Loriaux, eds. *Au-delà du quantitatif,* 281–300.

24. Jean Remy and Liliane Voyé, *Scenarios de vie sociale* (Louvain-la-Neuve: Centre de Sociologie Urbaine et Rurale, 1969).

25. Albert Martens et al., *Na de bedrijfssluiting* (Leuven: Sociologisch Onderzoekinstituut, 1979); Jan Huys and Peter Van der Hallen, *Les accords de technologie en Belgique* (Brussel: Commission des Communautés Européennes, 1986); Albert Martens, ed., *Nieuwe technologieen: de dans met de Silicon-duivel* (Leuven: Acco, 1985); Jan Bundervoet and Geert Van Hootegem, *Nieuwe technologieen, nieuwe vormen van arbeidsorganisatie, nieuwe vormen van arbeidverhoudingen?* (Brussel: Diensten voor programmatie wetenschapsbeleid, 1987).

26. Jacques Vilrokx, *Self-Employment in Europe as a Form of Relative Autonomy* (Brussels: European Commission/FAST [FOP157], 1987); Jacques Vilrokx, "Relative Autonomy and New Forms of Work Organization," in E. Poutsma and A. Walravens, eds., *Technology and Small Enterprises: Technology, Autonomy and Industrial Organisation* (Delft: Delft University Press, 1989), 213–227.

27. François Pichault, *Le conflit informatique* (Bruxelles: de Boeck-Wesmael, 1990); Michel De Coster, *Sociologie du travail et gestion du personnel* (Bruxelles: Labor, 1987).

28. Michel Molitor, "Les jeunes et le transitoire. Les nouveaux contextes de la socialisation," in Christian Lalive d'Epinay and Roger Sue, eds., *Chomage, marginalité, créativité* (Genève: Université de Genève, 1987), 49–64.

29. Marcel Bolle de Bal, *Les doubles jeux de la participation. Rémunération, performance et culture* (Maestricht: Presses Universitaires Européennes, 1990).

30. Jacques Delcourt, "Flexibility: A Source of New Rights for Workers?," in Georges Spyropoulos, ed., *Trade Unions Today and Tomorrow* (Maestricht: Presses Universitaires Européennes, 1987), 145–167; Jacques Delcourt, "Travail et emploi. Contextes et lignes de développement," *Cahiers de l'Institut des Sciences du Travail* 24 (1989), 1–19.

31. Olgierd Kuty. "Le paradigme de négociation," *Sociologie du Travail* (1976), 157–175; Olgierd Kuty, "L'espace interorganisationnel et la post-sociale démocratie," *Recherches Sociologiques* (1987), 29–42.

32. Alain Eraly, *La structuration de l'entreprise: la rationalité en action* (Bruxelles: ULB, 1988).

33. H. Deleeck, B. Cantillon, and J. Huybrechs, *Het Matteuseffekt. De ongelijke verdeling der sociale overheidsuitgaven in Belgie* (Antwerpen: Kluwer, 1983); Herman Deleeck, "Social Expenditure and the Efficiency of Social Policies in Europe," in Jacques Van Damme, ed., *New Dimensions in European Social Policy* (Kent: Croom Helm Ltd., 1985), 39–74; Herman Deleeck, "The Adequacy of the Social Security System in Belgium, 1976–1985," *Journal of Social Policy* 18, 1 (1989), 91–117; Herman Deleeck and Bea Cantillon, "Prestations non contributives et revenu minimum garanti: approche comparative." *EISS Yearbook 1985, Balance Development of Long-Term Benefits, Proceedings of the European Institute for Social Security* (Deventer: Kluwer, 1987), 273–304; Jan Vranken, "Non-income

Dimensions of Poverty. An Analysis of the Nine National Reports on Poverty," in Giovanni Sarpellon, ed., *Understanding Poverty* (Milano: Angeli, 1984), 292–328; Jan Vranken, "Industrial Rights," in Z. Layton-Henry, ed., *The Political Rights of Migrant Workers in Western Europe.* Sage Modern Politics Series 25 (London: Sage, 1990), 47–73.

34. Luc Bijnens, Edward Leemans, and Frans Lammertyn, *Opvangstructuren voor gehandicapten, Cijfers en tendensen.* National Onderzoeksprogramma in de Sociale Wetenschappen, vol. 22B. (Brussel: Ministerie van Wetenchapsbeleid, 1981); Frans Lammertyn. "Sociale ongelijkheid en universiteit," *Onze Alma Mater* 41, 3 (1987), 151–185; Frans Lammertyn, Dirk Luyten, Christine Delhaye, and Hilde De Wit, *Les avants droit au minimex en Belgique* (Leuven: Departement Sociologie–K. U. Leuven, 1987).

35. Jacques Delcourt, "Les justifications économiques et sociales de l'Etat Social," in Jacques Etienne and Pierre Watté, eds, *La souveraineté en question. Etats-Nations/Etat de droit* (Louvain-la-Neuve: CIACO, 1988), 53–74.

36. Michel Molitor, Jean Remy, and Luc Van Campenhoudt, eds., *Le mouvement et la forme: Essai sur le changement social en hommage à Maurice Chaumont* (Bruxelles: Facultés Universitaires St. Louis, 1989); Raymond Quivy, Danièle Ruquoy, and Luc Van Campenhoudt, *Malaise à l'école. Les difficultés de l'action collective* (Bruxelles: Facultés Universitaires St. Louis, 1989).

37. Jean Van Houtte, "Sociological Research on Family Law," in Jean Van Houtte, ed., *Sociology of Law and Legal Anthropology in Dutch Speaking Countries* (Dordrecht: Martinus Nijhoff, 1985), 45–57; Jean Van Houtte, "Pour une sociologie des institutions du droit de la famille," *Revue de l'Institut de Sociologie,* vol. 1–2 (1985), 147–178; Jean Van Houtte. "The Socio-legal Approach to the Institutions of Family Law," in Joginder S. Gandhi, ed., *Law and Social Change* (Jaipur: Rawat Pub., 1989), 116–127.

38. Francis Van Loon and Etienne Langerwerf, "Prozesshäufigkeiten und Prozessmuster in Belgien," in Erhard Blankenburg, ed, *Prozessflut? Indikatorenvergleich von Rechtskulturen auf den Europaischen Kontinent* (Koln: Bundesanzeiger, 1989), 231–255.

39. Luc Huyse, *De kleur van het recht* (Leuven: Kritak, 1989); Luc Huyse, "Legal Experts in Belgium," in Richard L. Abel and Philip S. Lewis, eds., *Lawyers in Society, The Civil Law World* (Berkeley: University of California Press, 1988), 225–257.

40. Lode Van Outrive and Cyrille Fijnaut, "Police and the Organisation of Prevention," in Maurice Punch, ed., *Control in the Police Organisation* (Cambridge: MIT Press, 1983), 76–101; Lode Van Outrive, "Die Bedingungen fur einen neuen interdisziplinaren Ansatz in der Kriminologie," in J. J. Savelberg, ed., *DFG-Kolloquium Zukunftperspektiven der Kriminologie* (Stuttgart: F. Enke Verlag, 1989), 163–178; Lode Van Outrive, "Dossier: La recherche sur la police," *Sûreté du Québec* 16, 8 (1986), 13–21; Lode Van Outrive, "Travail au noir et position socio-économique," *Déviance et Société* 13, 4 (1989), 281–300.

41. André-Paul Frognier, "Belgium: A Complex Cabinet in a Fragmented Policy," in Jean Bondel and Ferdinand Muller-Romel, eds. *Cabinets in Western Europe* (London: Macmillan, 1988), 68–86; André-Paul Frognier, "Le systéme belge de gouvernement: la gestion complexe d'une société divisée," *Diagnostics: Enjeux politiques et sociaux en Belgique* (Louvain-la-Neuve: Ecole de Sociologie de Lou-

vain, 1989), 31–52; André-Paul Frognier, "The Mixed Nature of Belgian Cabinets Between Majority Rule and Consociationalism," *European Journal of Political Research* 16, 2 (1988). André-Paul Frognier and Pascale Delfosse, "Etat libéral et formation des partis politiques en Belgique," *Recherches Sociologiques* 19, 1 (1988), 59–81.

42. Jeffrey Obler, Jurg Steiner, and Guido Dierickx, *Decision-Making in Smaller Democracies: The Consociational "Burden,"* Sage Comparative Politics Series 6 (London: Sage, 1977); Guido Dierickx, "Ideological Oppositions and Consociational Attitudes in the Belgian Parliament," *Legislative Quarterly* 3, 1 (1978), 133–160; Guido Dierickx and André-Paul Frognier, "L'espace idéologique au parlement Belge. Une approche comparative," *Res Publica* 12, 1–2 (1980), 151–176; Guido Dierickx, "The Management of Subcultural Conflict: The Issue of Education in Belgium (1950–1975)," *Acta Politica* 19, 1 (1984), 85–95; Guido Dierickx, "De sociologen en de verzuiling," *Tijdschrift voor Sociologie* 7, 3 (1986), 509–549.

43. Wilfried Dewachter. "The General Elections as a Process of Power–Achievement in the Belgian Political System," *Res Publica* 10, 3 (1967), 369–411; Wilfried Dewachter and Edi Clijsters, "Belgium: Political Stability Despite Coalition Crises," in Erik C. Browne and John Dreijmanis, eds., *Government Coalitions in Werstern Democracies* (New York: Longman, 1982), 187–216; Wilfried Dewachter, "Crises macro-sociales et stabilité de l'élite. Etude de l'élite belge face aux perturbations sociales dans la période 1919–1981," *Res Publica* 24, 2 (1982), 305–325; Wilfried Dewachter, "Changes in a Particratie: The Belgian Party System from 1944 to 1986," in Hans Daalder, ed., *Party Systems in Denmark, Austria, Switzerland, the Netherlands and Belgium* (London: Printer, 1987), 285–363.

44. Luc Huyse, *Passiviteit, pacificatie en verzuiling in de Belgische politiek* (Antwerpen: Standaard Wetenschappelijke Uitgeverij, 1970); Luc Huyse, "Political Conflict in Bicultural Belgium," in Arend Lijphart, ed., *Conflict and Coexistence in Belgium* (Berkeley: University of Berkeley Press, 1981), 107–126.

45. Kris Deschouwer and Patrick-Edward Stouthuysen. "L'électorat d'Agalev," CRISP, Courrier Hedomadaire, 1061, 1984; Herbert Kitschelt and Staf Hellemans, *Beyond the European Left: Ideology and Political Action in the Belgian Ecology Parties* (Durham/London: Duke University Press, 1990).

46. Albert Verdoodt, *The Written Languages of the World: A Survey of the Degree and Modes of Uses, 3, Western Europe* (Québec: Presses de l'Université Laval, 1990).

47. Karel Dobbelaere and Jaak Billiet, "Les changements internes au pilier Catholique en Flandre: d'un Catholicisme d'Eglise à une Chrétienté Socioculturelle," *Recherches Sociologiques* 14, 4 (1983), 141–184; Karel Dobbelaere, "Contradictions between Expressive and Strategic Language in Policy Documents of Catholic Hospitals and Welfare Organizations: Trials instead of Liturgies as Means of Social Control," *The Annual Review of the Social Sciences of Religion* 6 (1982), 107–131; Jaak Billiet, "On Belgian Pillarization: Changing Perspectives," in M.C.P.M. Van Schendelen, ed., *Consociationalism, Pillarization and Conflict Management in the Low Countries* (Boom: Meppel, 1984), 117–128; Jaak Billiet and Karel Dobbelaere, "Vers une désinstitutionalisation du pilier catholique?," in Liliane Voyé, Karel Dobbelaere, Jean Remy, and Jaak Billiet, eds., *La Belgique et ses Dieux* (Louvain: Cabay, Recherches Sociologiques), 119–152.

48. Liliane Voyé. "Du monopole religieux à la connivence culturelle," *L'Année Sociologique* 38 (1988), 135–167.

49. Karel Dobbelaere, "Secularization, Pillarization, Religious Involvement and Religious Change in the Low Countries," in Thomas M. Ganon, ed., *World Catholicism in Transition* (New York: Macmillan, 1988), 80–115.

50. Karel Dobbelaere and Liliane Voyé, "From Pillar to Post-Modernity: The Changing Situation of Religion in Belgium," *Sociological Analysis,* 1990. Karel Dobbelaere and Liliane Voyé, "Western European Catholicism since Vatican II," in Helen R. Ebough, ed., *Vatican II and American Catholicism* (Greenwich, Conn.: Jai Press, 1990).

51. Jean Remy, "Le Catholicisme en Belgique: similitude et différence entre la Flandre et la Wallonie," in Rudolf Rezsohazy, ed., *Diagnostics: enjeux politiques et sociaux en Belgique* (Louvain-la-Neuve: CIACO, 1989); Jean Remy, "Revalorisation de la religion populaire et recomposition du champ religieux," *Recherches Sociologiques* 18, 2 (1987), 163–183; Jean Remy, "Le défi de la modernité: stratégie de la hiérarchie catholique aux 19è et 20è siècles et idée de chrétienté," *Social Compass* 34, 3 (1987), 151–173; Liliane Voyé, "Approche méthodologique du sacré," in M. Cloet and F. Daelemans, eds., *Religion, mentalité et vie quotidienne* (Bruxelles: Archives et Bibliothèques de Belgique, 1988), 255–277.

52. Michel Voisin, "Communautés utopiques et structures sociales: le cas de la Belgique francophone," *Revue Française de Sociologie* 12, 2 (1977), 271–300; Michel Voisin, ed., "Les lendemains de l'utopie communautaire," *Recherches Sociologiques* 1 (1979); Karel Dobbelaere and Bryan R. Wilson, "Jehovah's Witnesses in a Catholic Country: A Survey of Nine Belgian Congregations," *Archives de Sciences Sociales des Religions* 50, 1 (1980), 89–110; Bryan R. Wilson and Karel Dobbelaere, "Unificationism: A Study of the Moonies in Belgium," *The British Journal of Sociology* 38, 2 (1987), 184–198.

53. François Houtart, *Religion and Ideology in Sri Lanka* (Colombo: Hansa Publishers, 1974); François Houtart and Geneviève Lemercinier, *The Great Asiatic Religions and Their Social Functions* (Louvain-la-Neuve: Centre de Recherches Socio-religieuses, 1980); François Houtart and Geneviève Lemercinier, *Genesis and Institutionalization of Indian Catholicism* (Louvain-la-Neuve: Centre de Recherches Socio-religieuses, 1981); Geneviève Lemercinier. *Religion and Ideology in Kerala* (Louvain-la-Neuve: Centre de Recherches Socio-religieuses, 1983).

54. Anne Van Haecht, *L'enseignement rénové. De l'origine à l'éclipse* (Bruxelles: ULB, 1985); Anne Van Haecht, *L'école à l'épreuve de la sociologie. Questions à la sociologie de l'éducation* (Bruxelles: De Boeck-Wesmael).

55. Jean-Emile Charlier, *Les logiques internes des districts scolaires. Rites et images d'écoles secondaires* (Louvain-la-Neuve: UCL, 1988).

56. Herman Brutsaert, "Type of High School System and Subjective School Outcomes," *International Journal of Comparative Sociology* 23, 1–2 (1982), 88–98; Herman Brutsaert, *Gelijke kansen en leerlinggerichtheid in het secundair onderwiis* (Leuven/Amerfoort: Acco, 1986); Herman Brutsaert, "Changing Sources of Self Esteem among Girls and Boys in Secondary Schools," *Urban Education* 24, 4 (1990), 432–439.

57. Jozef C. Verhoeven, "Belgium: Linguistic Communalism. Bureaucratisation and Democratisation," in Hans Daalder and Edward Shils, eds., *Universities, Politicians and Bureaucrats* (Cambridge: Cambridge University Press, 1982), 125–171.

58. Ron Lesthaeghe and Johan Surkyn, "Cultural Dynamics and Economic Theories of Fertility Change," *Population and Development Review* 14, 1 (1988), 1–54; Ron Lesthaeghe, ed., *Social Organization and Reproduction in Sub-Saharan Africa* (Berkeley: University of California Press, 1989).

59. Joan Aldous and Wilfried Dumon, eds., *The Politics and Programs of Family Policy* (Leuven: University Press Leuven, 1980); Wilfried Dumon et al., *Gezinswetenschappelijke Documentatie Jaarboek* (Leuven: Universitaire Pers Leuven, 1990), Wilfried Dumon et al., *OCDE-Système d'observation permanente des migrations—Belgique* (Leuven: Department sociologie, [yearly]; Koen Matthijs, *Echtscheiding als sociaal proces* (Leuven: Departement sociologie, 1990); Koen Matthijs, *Belgoscopie* (Tielt: Lannoo, 1988).

60. Bernadette Bawin, ed., *La dynamisque familiale et les constructions sociales du temps* (Liège: Département des Sciences Sociales ULg, 1988); Bernadette Bawin et al., *La problématique socio-économique des créances alimentaires en Belgique* (Bruxelles: Inbel, 1989).

61. Rudolf Rezsohazy, "Ways of Life and Social Change: Methodology of a Recurrent Investigation," in Alexander Szalai and Frank M. Andrews, eds., *The Quality of Life, Comparative Studies* (London: Sage, 1980); Rudolf Rezsohazy, "Recent Social Developments and Changes in Attitudes to Time." *International Social Sciences Journal* 107 (1986), 33–48; Rudolf Rezsohazy and Jan Kerkhofs, eds., *L'univers des Belges, Valeurs anciennes et valeurs nouvelles dans les années 80* (Louvain-la-Neuve: CIACO, 1984).

62. Jan Lauwers and Jef Van Lint, *Burgers in de weer De mobilisatie rond een milieuproject* (Leuven: Acco, 1979); Jan Lauwers, "Les Belges et le travail," in Rudolf Rezsohazy and Jan Kerkhofs, eds., *L'univers des Belges,* 189–215; Jan Lauwers, *Op zoek naar welzijn* (Leuven: Acco, 1987).

63. Frans Van Mechelen, "The Influence of Housing on the Socialization of the Children and on Their Cultural Identity," *Cahiers Familles dans le Monde* 18 (1985), 9–13; Frans Van Mechelen, "Urbanisme et logement familial," *Cahiers Familles dans le Monde* 26 (1986), 25–33; Frans Van Mechelen, "From Homelessness to Family Housing," *Cahiers Familles dans le Monde* 30 (1988), 237–254; Urbain Claeys, "Evolution of the Concept of Sport and the Participation/Nonparticipation Phenomenon," *Sociology of Sport Journal* 2, 3 (1985), 233–240; Urbain Claeys, "Violencia e Fair Play no desporto: causas e medidas," *Desporto e Sociedad* 2, 1 (1986), 1–13.

64. Luc Goossens, "Belgium," in Hans Kroes, Frits Ymkers, and André Mulder, eds., *Between Owner-Occupation and Rented Sector: Housing in Ten European Countries* (De Bilt: The Netherlands Christian Institute for Social Housing, 1988), 215–241.

65. Micheline Scheys, "The Power of Life Style," *Society and Leisure* 10, 2 (1987), 249–266.

66. C. L. Kruithof, *Verschijnselen aan de rand: een bundel cultuursociologische opstellen* (Zeist: Kerckelbosch, 1989).

67. Mark Elchardus, "The Rediscovery of Chronos: The New Role of Time in Sociological Theory," *International Sociology* 3, 1 (1988), 35–59; Mark Elchardus and Ignace Glorieux, "Signification du temps et temps de la signification," in Daniel Mercure and Anne Wallemacq, eds., *Les Temps sociaux* (Bruxelles: De Boeck-Wesmael, 1988), 97–118; Mark Elchardus, "The Temporalities of Exchange, The

Case of Self-Organization for Societal Governance," in Bernd Marien, ed., *Generalized Political Exchange* (Frankfurt/New York: Campus/Westview, 1990).

68. Daniel Mercure, and Anne Wallemacq, eds., *Les temps sociaux;* Anne Wallemacq, *Le temps: contribution à une sociologie de la perception* (Bruxelles: De Boeck-Wesmael, 1990).

69. Roger Deldime, *La mémoire du jeune spectateur* (Bruxelles-Paris: De Boeck-Wesmael/Ed. Universitaires, 1988); Roger Deldime, ed., *Acts of the First World Congress of Sociology of Theatre* (Roma: Bulzoni, 1988).

70. Daniel Vandergucht, "La notion d'art comme paradigme central de la sociologie de l'art," *Cahiers du Séminaire* (Bruxelles: Institut de Sociologie).

71. Jean Remy and Liliane Voyé. *La ville et l'urbanisation* (Gembloux: Duculot, 1974); Jean Remy and Liliane Voyé, *Ville, ordre et violence* (Paris: PUF, 1981).

72. Daniel Bodson. *Les villageois ou: rien n'est jamais égal par ailleurs* (Bruxelles; De Boeck-Weśmael, 1990).

73. Catherine Mougenot and Marc Mormont, *L'invention du rural, L'héritage des mouvements ruraux* (Bruxelles: Vie ouvrière, 1988); Marc Mormont, "Rural Nature and Urban Natures," *Sociologia Ruralis* 27, 1 (1987), 3–20; Catherine Mougenot, "Histoire de la catégorie rurale et représentation de l'espace en Belgique," *Recherches Sociologiques* 3 (1989), 311–329.

74. Nicole Delruelle, *Sociologie urbaine et changements sociaux* (Bruxelles: ULB, 1990).

75. Jacques Malengreau, "Barrio y Campo: divisions et remembrements parentaux du territoire dans les Andes septentrionales du Pérou," *L'Ethnographie* (Paris) 85, 1 (1989), 89–112.

76. Michel Quévit and Roberto Camagni, eds., *Politiques d'innovation au niveau local* (Paris: ERESA, 1990); Michel Quévit et al., *Les conséquences socio-économiques de l'achèvement du Marché intérieur pour les régions de tradition industrielle de la Communauté Européenne* (Bruxelles: CCE, DGXVI, 1989); Michel Quévit, *The Regional Implications of Industrial Restructuring* (Paris: OECD, 1989).

77. Yvo Nuyens, *De eerste lijn is krom* (Deventer: Van Loghum Slaterus, 1980); Yvo Nuyens, ed., *Sociologie en gezondheidszorg,* vols. 1 and 2 (Antwerpen: Van Loghum Slaterus, 1982); Jan Branckaerts, Yvo Nuyens, et al., *Het zachte verzet* (Deventer: Van Loghum Slaterus, 1982); Rita Schepers, "The Legal and Institutional Development of the Belgian Medical Profession in the Nineteenth Century," *Sociology of Health and Illness* 7. 3 (1985), 314–342.

78. Erwin Bosman and Fred Louckx, *Une politique de la santé en l'an 2000 D'un système de soins sectoriel à une politique de la santé intégrée* (Brussel: VUB, Faculteit Geneeskunde en Farmacie, 1988).

79. Olgierd Kuty, "Les innovations scientifiques dans le champ de la santé," *Sciences Sociales et Santé* (1983), 119–74; Olgierd Kuty. "La population des soins et services à domicile," *Revue Belge de Sécurité Sociale,* 1989.

80. Yves Winkin, ed., *La nouvelle communication* (Paris: Seuil, 1981); Yves Winkin, ed., *Erving Goffman: Les moments et leurs hommes* (Paris: Seuil, 1988).

81. Michel De Coster and François Pichault, *Le loisir en quatre dimensions, De la critique des théories à la définition d'une sociologie* (Bruxelles: Labor, 1985).

82. Guido Fauconnier, *Mass Media and Society* (Leuven: Leuven University

Press, 1982); Guido Fauconnier, *Some Aspects of the Theory of Communication* (Pretoria: Arcadia, 1987).

83. Felice Dassetto and Albert Bastenier, *L'Islam transplanté, Vie et organisation de minorités musulmanes de Belgique* (Bruxelles: EPO, 1984); Felice Dassetto and Albert Bastenier, *Europa Nuova frontiera dell' Islam* (Roma: EL, 1988).

84. Marguerite Lisein-Norman, "Les parents pauvres du pouvoir public," *Revue Nouvelle* 1 (1990), 67–78.

85. Groupe de Sociologie Wallonne, "The Changing Role of Women in Belgium: An Overview on Research," in Werner Ritcher, ed., *Changing Role of Women in Society. A Documentation of Current Research* (Oxford: Pergamon Press, 1989); Groupe de Sociologie Wallonne, "The Poverty of Women in Belgium," *The Feminisation of Poverty and Labour Markets* (Sheffield: Sheffield City Polytechnic, 1990).

86. France Govaerts, "Temps social, personnes âgées et identité," *Gérontologie et société* 25 (1983); France Govaerts, "Belgium: Old Trends, New Contradictions," in Anna Olszewska, ed., *Leisure and Life-Style. A Comparative Analysis of Free Time* (London: Sage, 1989).

87. Jean-Pierre Hiernaux, "Les laissés pour compte de la comptétition économique," *Enfance et adolescence dans la société d'aujourd'hui* (Bordeaux: OREAG, 1989), 1–16; Jean-Pierre Hiernaux, Agnés Ganty, et al., *Selection, Elimination and Marginalization in Schemes for the Young Unemployed* (Koln: ISG, 1987); Jean-Pierre Hiernaux, *Lutter contre la pauvreté en Europe. Acquis et perspectives de l'échange transnational des experiences de terrain* (Koln: ISG, 1989).

88. Daniel Bodson, "Les composantes émergentes et les motivations de la demande touristique. Quelques réflexions théoriques," *Sociologia Urbana e Rurale* 10, 26 (1988), 69–75; Liliane Voyé. "L'Italie vue du Nord," *Sociologia Urbane e Rurale* 10, 26 (1988), 77–86.

89. Liliane Voyé, "Du modernisme au postmodernisme: le monument architectural," in Françoise Bradfer, ed., *Le Corbusier la modernité et après* (Louvain-la-Neuve: Unité d'architecture UCL, 1987), 166–172; Liliane Voyé, "Les images de la ville. Questions au post-modernisme." *Espace et Société*.

90. Rudi Laermans, "Moderne kritiek en postmoderne retoriek Kanttekeningen bij het (post)modernisme-debat," *Streven* 54 (1987), 6409–17 and 7505–14; Rudi Laermans, *Beyond the Sign, City-Culture, Mass Media and Modernity,* Penn-Congress, "The Clash of Values. Cultural Literacy in the Media-Age." Louvain, 3–5 August 1989; Rudi Laermans, *De stijl van de jeugd. Opstellen over jeugd in Vlaanderen en elders* Leuven: Kritak, 1991.

91. Marcel Bolle de Bal, *La tentation communautaire Les paradoxes de la reliance et de la contreculture* (Bruxelles: ULB, 1985); Marcel Bolle de Bal, "La sociologie . . . et la personne? Ou: J'ai même rencontré un sociologue heureux." *Bulletin de l'AISLF* 3 (1986), 115–148.

3

Contemporary Sociology in Britain

Steven Yearley

INTRODUCTION

An axiom of the sociology of knowledge is that no body of knowledge develops independently of the social circumstances in which it is produced. This axiom is thoroughly borne out by U.K.[1] sociology in the period 1975–1991. Probably the dominant influence on the discipline and profession of sociology during this period has been the long-standing conservative government headed, until late 1990, by Margaret Thatcher. Her premiership was important for sociology in many ways. Thus, she developed a particular political ideology—stressing individual responsibility and, as she famously put it, "Victorian values"—whose progress sociologists were keen to chart. Equally, social scientists analyzed the social changes which her government's policies brought to the United Kingdom. For example, her emphasis on people's right to buy their own properties fed a vast demand for housing in some regions; this in turn resulted in rapid house-price rises in certain geographical areas, affecting geographical mobility and the effective distribution of wealth. Her emphasis on workplace productivity and on the restriction of trades union power led to some far-reaching changes in industrial relations (especially in the mining, newspaper, and broadcasting industries) and to sharp but regionally concentrated increases in unemployment.

But, on top of these influences, Mrs. Thatcher's administrations had a direct impact on the discipline of sociology, a subject for which she displayed little personal sympathy. She argued that sociologists tended to concentrate their analysis on a level of reality—"society"—which did not in truth exist. She appeared to dismiss sociology as an intellectual excuse for all manner of unwanted interference in the operation of the market, as a source of justifications which people could call on to avoid taking responsibility for their actions, and as a self-serving rationale for the expansion of unproductive social "service" professions. Occasional sociologists who were outspokenly critical of the Marxist assumptions of many of their colleagues and who wrote in praise of the vitality of free-market capitalism were lionized, but such sociologists were far from numerous.[2]

These strongly antipathetic views were shared in Mrs. Thatcher's many cabinets and resulted in a direct confrontation with the discipline's principal source of financial support, the Social Science Research Council (SSRC). In the United Kingdom during the period to be reviewed here, research money flowed to the higher education sector though grants to institutions (partly for teaching and partly for research) and through research grants supplied through the various research councils, including the Medical Research Council and the Science and Engineering Research Council. The SSRC was faced with two sorts of threats. The first was that its income was squeezed relative to the other research councils. At a time of restraint in public expenditure the overall research budget had to be reined in; the government chose to do this, not by making equal restrictions across the board but by sacrificing social research to other forms, forms which could more easily trumpet their economic and practical value. Between 1981 and 1985 the council's share of the research budget fell by nearly a sixth (from almost 5 percent of the total to just over 4) with the diverted money helping to fund selective expansion in the other sciences.[3] The second challenge was even more direct. The then Secretary of State for Education, Sir Keith Joseph, insisted that the SSRC change its name to eliminate the reference to science since, in his view, the SSRC's client disciplines did not enjoy the status of sciences. The SSRC duly became the Economic and Social Research Council (ESRC).

The same public expenditure restraint which had affected the research budgets also left its mark on general funding for the universities. In the early and mid-1980s U.K. universities experienced successive rationalizations and appointment freezes; even the elite institutions such as Cambridge and Oxford operated registers of suspended posts. If a university had to cut, say, forty posts, the idea was that until forty people left—in whatever discipline—no new posts would be created. On the forty-first departure the first new appointment would be made, although not necessarily by filling the post which had first become vacant. Sociologists were, generally speaking, low on universities' lists of priorities; accordingly, when sociologists left (which they had the self-preservational sense not to do frequently), they were not speedily replaced. Consequently, throughout the United Kingdom, departments full of sociologists tended to carry on with little change, with few new appointments and with jobs available only in short-term, nontenurable research posts.

These apparently unfavorable changes overtaking the profession came to be reversed to a significant extent later in the 1980s, not because the government changed its ideological spots, but because of the implementation of another aspect of conservative philosophy. As part of continuing pressure on public expenditure levels, statutory bodies were encouraged to increase their productivity. In the case of universities this meant both that they should process more students and that they should deliver more of the other "goods" they offered to dispense, such as research. Initially, attempts were made to adjust these changes in productivity to the government's conception of utility. The authorities had, for example, a high regard for information technology, the physical sciences, and the traditional humanities. Efforts could be made to expand the prestige and attractions of such subjects. But this thinking ran counter to another principle, which is that the market should handle questions of distribution and provision. Once customer (i.e., student) demand was substituted for governmental preference, the social sciences began to fare better. They were cheap courses to offer; staff-student ratios were more favorable (in financial terms) than in the laboratory sciences; and there was strong demand. Moreover, unlike the humanities, the social sciences did at least have a corresponding research council so that sociology departments could generate external revenue rather more easily than could, say, their colleagues in classics.

The ironical renaissance of sociology was assisted by one further development. My account so far has concentrated on the universities. But the higher education sector contains approximately equal numbers of students working in polytechnics. These institutions tended not to have large traditional humanities departments. Neither did they have medical schools and other high-status, but costly departments. Often their strength lay in the social sciences which, as with the universities, they could cheaply and plentifully supply. The government had an admiration for the productivity—at least in terms of teaching—of these polytechnics, and during the 1980s these institutions took the opportunity increasingly to professionalize themselves. Polytechnic departments found that, given the scarcity of university posts, good young academics with a commitment to research could be appointed. Given that polytechnics shared the universities' entitlement to apply to the research councils, it was not surprising that their research output and publishing productivity increased. Within sociology, the country's professional association—the BSA (British Sociological Association)—witnessed greater participation from polytechnic-based academics. Indeed by 1990, its executive contained more polytechnic staff than university employees. This rise in the fortunes of the polytechnics was consolidated when the government announced that from 1992, all polytechnics would be free to redesignate themselves as universities. In this way the discipline of sociology will in the 1990s be even more firmly established in the United Kingdom's university sector.

REVIEWING THE STATE OF PLAY

These changing fortunes have made the period under review a difficult and uncertain time for sociologists—a discipline, according to A. H. Halsey, "unloved in a cold climate."[4] A number of intellectual responses have emerged during this period which can be related in distinct ways to the changing external circumstances, not only of governmental philosophy, two economic recessions, and the social changes associated with the government's characteristic policies, but also with other events such as growing European federalism, the collapse of state socialist regimes, and the increasing acknowledgment of environmental problems.

The reviewer of this period in U.K. sociology has a great deal to encompass since he or she must try somehow to take into account the work of a discipline represented in the great majority of the around one hundred universities and polytechnics, as well as in government departments and social research companies. Luckily, my job is eased by two publications prepared by eminent social scientists: one a study commissioned by the ESRC in 1986, published the following year, *Horizons and Opportunities in the Social Sciences;* the other a whole issue of the *British Journal of Sociology* in 1989 dedicated to an overview of the "current state of British sociology."[5] The latter also contains an account of the University Grants Committee's (UGC) subject review of sociology, a review published that same year.[6]

These reviews endorse the general picture of the discipline's fate presented above. Additionally, the authors of the article on the UGC's evaluation exercise note that university sociology departments tended to report

that they were now more active—if also harder pressed—than ever. Certainly, nostalgia for any past "golden age" was little in evidence; and the material we saw pointed to the 1980s as a period of high productivity, in research no less than in teaching.[7]

As well as using these reviews to assess the mood of sociology in Britain, it is interesting to juxtapose the judgments they offer about the spread and quality of work within the discipline. Treating all the papers in the *British Journal of Sociology*'s review issue together, both it and the ESRC—as would be expected—spot weaknesses as well as strengths in British sociology. But it is the differences in the details of their evaluations which are revealing. According to the ESRC report, "UK sociology is generally well respected abroad and seen as outstanding in some areas. . . . Britain is a leading force in such areas as historical sociology, theoretical sociology and studies of stratification."[8] The principal weakness cited lies in quantitative sociology. The authors in the *British Journal of Sociology* review agree that studies of stratification remain a strength and they

generally concur about the British lack of numerical flair (a trend con-
fessed in Jackson's forerunner to this article).[9] However, more striking
than the agreements are the diverging interpretations. The authors offering a general overview in the *British Journal of Sociology*—Martin Bulmer, Norman Dennis and, to some extent, A. H. Halsey—are wistful and
reproachful. For them, British sociological theory, despite the appearance
of productivity, has become preoccupied with Marxist themes and with
philosophical intrigue, sometimes dedicated to the protection of Marxist
assumptions against troublesome rebuttals at the hands of empirical evidence; other theorists have dwelt on whimsical interactionist studies, car-
icatured by Dennis as finally giving "due attention . . . to such activities as
the art of walking."[10] By contrast, the ESRC's panel sees British theory
as a highlight; theory was also given a flattering description by the reviewers on the UGC assessment panel and received respectful mention from
Halsey.[11]

The evaluation of U.K. sociological theory is an important issue which
I shall return to later. For the moment, however, let us turn to the subfields
and chart their development. This approach will turn out to be justified
since in many cases it is through work in these fields that theoretical analysis has advanced.

BRITISH DEVELOPMENTS IN MAJOR SUBFIELDS

The *British Journal of Sociology* review devotes only three of its seven
articles to accounts of subfields: women's studies, social mobility, and the
sociology of religion. It is not obvious that these are the particular specialties in which British sociology has either been concentrated or excels.
The sociology of religion, for example, is peculiar because it is rather
poorly represented within British sociology but features particularly eminent and productive academics. There are other specialties—for example,
the sociology of education, studies of crime and deviance or medical sociology—which have more exponents, attract larger numbers of students,
and win bigger grants. Moreover, precisely because of the secularization
of mainstream English/British society (more of which later)—the reality
of which is stoutly defended in the overview by Roy Wallis and Steve
Bruce[12]—the social importance of their subject matter is arguably decreasing. By contrast, the social importance of crime and deviance is easily
argued for, especially during a period of conservative government when
the authorities are traditionally seen as particularly tough on crime and
when, therefore, there is political sensitivity to increases in crime.

Recent years have seen a growth in interest in two types of criminological work: first, on the victims of crime, and second, ethnographic and
observational work on the lifeworlds of both criminals and police. The
increase in victim studies has compensated for an aspect of crime which

was too little studied in the past—although no doubt part of their recent appeal has been that they allow authors to comment on issues of "law and order."[13] Such research can be developed to argue, for example, that society is more lawless than official figures lead us to believe since victims report only a proportion of crimes. Victims may not report robberies or assaults or—probably most notoriously—sexual assaults. Such a view functions to throw doubt on official assurances about the effectiveness of governmental measures.

This work has been complemented by highly popular accounts of the curious and intriguing lifeworld of the professional criminal.[14] These have been matched by accounts of the (sometimes very closely related) police world.[15] An understanding of the background assumptions, everyday reasoning, and occupational culture of the police has been made more topical both by concern over the police treatment of minorities—highlighted during episodes of unrest in English cities in the early 1980s—and by worries provoked late in the 1980s when a series of prosecutions of people, mostly on terrorist offenses stemming from the ethnic conflict in Northern Ireland, were overturned. In a series of reviews, police officers and forensic scientists were found to have been slipshod or economical with the truth, to have falsified evidence, or to have extracted forced confessions. The ubiquity of informal procedures in police life meant that at one level these findings were not surprising to sociologists, but commentators were left wondering about the dividing line between malpractice and necessary informality. In 1991 the problem was perceived to be so grave that a Royal Commission was appointed to examine the matter; this was the first such Commission since the Conservatives had come to power and was established after Margaret Thatcher had been replaced as prime minister. Significantly, a sociologist (also a titled and highly successful businessman), W. G. Runciman, was appointed to chair it.[16]

The sociology of health and illness also showed strong development with the growth of specialist publications and an active stream within the British Sociological Association. Interactionist studies have taken root strongly in this area with Goffmanesque work on patient-doctor-family interactions, most regularly associated with P. M. Strong, standing out.[17] Here again distinctive features of conservative policy were a stimulus to publication since the government was intent on introducing market-style disciplines to the health service. The government's political opponents argued that the encouragement given to "opting out" was tantamount to the privatization of health care which, in their view, would have the effect of increasing inequalities in health provision. These changes also provided a growing need for the services of health economists whose attempts to apply a mathematical logic to the organization of health care would become the subject of sociological scrutiny; the study of this managerial technique could readily be accommodated alongside the analysis of other medical technologies within the umbrella of the "political economy of health."[18] Finally, medical sociology has received a stimulus from the disturbing rise in HIV infection; sociologists—more easily in many cases than their medically trained colleagues—have been able to investigate the cultures in which HIV infection initially took hold.[19]

These and other important subfields have grown in the last fifteen years, but they have generally grown in a way that resembles their growth in other countries' sociological communities. British victim studies are in most respects like those in the United States. Some issues, usually matters of policy or politics, do lend work in these subfields a particular salience (as with police "discretion") or give them a unique focus (the political economy of health when hospitals opt out), but these research areas are not usually quintessentially British.

The most significant area where this is true is in women's studies. Women's studies have had a major impact on British sociology, giving rise to or being associated with studies of women in the workplace, women in professions, the domestic division of labor, domestic violence, studies of reproduction and of reproductive technology, of women as carers and as patients within the health service, and many other areas.[20] It has also led to popular and sustained challenges to common sociological practices, for example, by asking about the suitability of accepted methodologies for the study of women's lives, about the way women are treated in work on stratification, and—at an epistemological level—about the applicability of the customary sociological concepts to the description of women's social action. For example, what does the "sociology of leisure" mean for many women when their lives are not arranged in a way that allows them to separate a leisure time in the usual sense.[21]

These are all areas of practical and intellectual significance. For example, the debate about the methodological treatment of women in stratification studies has generated a prolonged and sophisticated controversy. In part the issues are practical, with established statisticians arguing that the admitted exceptional cases are not statistically significant while others claim that stratification procedures deny the reality of increasingly numerous dual income households.[22] However, as Pamela Abbott notes,

Most of those involved in the debate surrounding the incorporation of women into social class analysis are concerned primarily with how to place households or individuals in a system of social stratification, rather than with questions of class orientation and class action.[23]

The debate has more profound implications for sociology if it is accepted that women may have a distinctive class imagery from that of men. Not only may women have been methodologically excluded from determining the ascribed class of their households, but the very definitions of class in everyday use may diverge from the perceived reality of half the population. Such questions evidently go right to the heart of sociology.

Still, in an important sense, these issues and studies are not particularly British. Women's studies networks are often international, and the theoretical perspectives and epistemological and methodological critiques have often been developed in the United States. As with the sociology of health and illness, there are definite national issues which seize U.K. researchers' attention. Thus the U.K. women's movement has faced a less concerted opposition about pro-choice politics than have their sister organizations in the United States. The U.K. movement has been able to call on the legislative force of the European Parliament to back suggested reforms. But there has not developed a particular, British school of women's studies, and indeed the very strong institutionalization of the specialty in North America is likely to ensure that country's continued preeminence.

The last area I shall consider in this way, although there are other candidates,[24] displays the pattern very clearly; it is the sociology of the environment. Widespread, sustained, and institutionalized environmental awareness and anxiety came later to Britain than to most Western countries. Following general ecological concern at the end of the 1960s, many policy innovations were adopted in the United States including the establishment of an Environmental Protection Agency. The regulatory successes achieved by this body were to some extent reversed under President Reagan, who often presented environmental activists as the enemies of American enterprise and as the cause of economic difficulties. In Northern Europe and Scandinavia this reversal did not take place, and in many respects these countries have set the pace for reform, whether in relation to alternative energy, the development of recycling infrastructures, or pollution limitation. British interest in ecological issues grew rapidly at the end of the 1980s with huge increases in the membership of environmental organizations and a surprise polling of nearly 15 percent for the (hitherto largely unsuccessful) Green party in the 1989 European elections. But British sociologists have been poorly positioned to build on this popular interest.

In 1991 Howard Newby, one of the foremost figures in rural sociology and currently chairman of the ESRC, took the British sociological community to task over this neglect. He argued that social scientists had allowed the natural sciences to make the running on the analysis of environmental problems as though such problems were susceptible to a technical fix. But any solution to, for example, problems of global warming is more likely to result from socioeconomic changes than from radical advances in, say, nuclear fusion technology. Worse still for the BSA, the elements of a social science response which Newby could detect came from geography and economics, not sociology. Against its pragmatic interests and contrary to its intellectual potential, sociology had ignored this challenge. Newby saw no defense for this neglect:

A consideration of the environment, and particularly of the concept of sustainable development, raises precisely the same kind of fundamental questions about the organisation of society that faced the early founders of the discipline when they encountered the rise of industrialism, capitalism and liberal democracy. But our syllabuses and textbooks remain silent and the research cupboard is almost bare.[25]

Newby located the roots of this neglect in sociology's reluctance to accord the natural world a direct explanatory role in social change. It has virtually become a defining characteristic of sociology that it regards all natural causes as mediated by culture; it is thus contrary to the sociological paradigm to view ecological transformations as an independent source of major social developments. Stephen Cotgrove, a pioneer in this field in British sociology, additionally wishes to lay blame on the dominance of neo-Marxism which, he suggests,

has seen concern with the environment as a middle-class preoccupation, and has attributed environmental problems to the exploitative and predatory nature of the capitalist mode of production, rather than to any inherent characteristics of industrialisation.[26]

Currently, official interest in the environment is strong and the ESRC has responded with a targeted research program, "Global Environmental Change"; to date sociologists have done poorly in terms of funding received from this program. There are signs that British sociologists are beginning to respond to the opportunities in this area but they, like the British government, have been left behind by many of their Continental and North American counterparts. In the near future, however, we can anticipate an upturn in British sociologists' interest in environmental issues, beginning—I suspect—with further work on green social movements and on environmental issues in the sociology of development.[27]

DEVELOPMENTS IN CHARACTERISTICALLY BRITISH SUBFIELDS

While in many areas British scholarship has mirrored the development of sociological subfields as they have progressed elsewhere, there are a few areas where British work appears rather distinct or peculiarly advanced. Naturally, this distinction is not clear-cut; nearly all subfields have a characteristic British element since they have developed in response to social and policy trends in the United Kingdom. Still, this rough distinction proves helpful for presentational purposes.

The first area is one designated as special in the ESRC report: science studies. Science studies include both science policy studies and the sociology of science, in both of which Britain is strong although only the latter concerns us here. British work in the sociology of science has developed, as the ESRC report says, to a state of "international pre-eminence" in large measure by basing research in this subfield on the sociology of scientific knowledge.[28] Dating more or less from the beginning of this review period (1975), science studiers have adduced philosophical and sociological arguments to claim that sociological analysis can extend into the study of cognitive developments in the natural sciences. In other words, they have claimed that there is an irremovable social component in the interpretation of scientific data and in the evaluation of competing theories. In the late 1970s this epistemological audacity set British work apart.

Different analysts have sought to develop this basic insight in different ways. Thus David Bloor has adopted a Durkheimian approach to the social analysis of scientific thought, while Barry Barnes and Donald MacKenzie, also both at Edinburgh, have tried to relate cognitive strategies to actors' economic and political interests; H. M. Collins has adopted a more interactionist orientation, while others, Michael Mulkay and Steve Woolgar, for example, have taken more ethnomethodological and linguistically radical approaches.[29] Accordingly it is not possible to speak of a single British school, but there is a more or less shared research program which allows these researchers to form a recognizable community.

The development of this strain of work has been facilitated by the way in which the ESRC, as the supporter of many science studies, has seen the appeal of marketing this "cognitive product" to the other Research Councils. The other councils are, potentially at least, clear customers for science studies research; they of all people should want to know how science works. The anomalous character of science studies was recognized by the ESRC when it agreed to the formation of the Science Policy Support Group, a semi-autonomous policy analysis agency handling much of the ESRC's science studies budget. The sociology of science also benefited from another ESRC initiative, this time the Program on Information and Communication Technologies (PICT), which included in its large-scale funding two centers (Edinburgh and Brunel, West London) with strong commitments to this style of work in the sociology of science and technology. PICT was an unusual form of research funding since it brought long-term jobs to universities; it accordingly served to differentially expand sociology in, among other areas, science studies.

A second area in which British sociology experienced a characteristic development was in relation to the "linguistic turn" taken by sociology around 1980. Although based on U.S. work in ethnomethodology and conversation analysis (and aided by the presence in Britain of Jefferson), a small number of conversation analysts developed their work in a specialized way. Much American conversation analysis (CA) had used rather exotic or extraordinary kinds of talk (calls to help lines and so on) as the basis for seeking out universal features of conversation. Once a number of these supposedly universal characteristics had been identified, it was then feasible to reverse this procedure and to study how talk was adapted for use in special contexts, for example, in classrooms, in court, between doctors and patients, between parents and children, or in political speeches.[30] In each of these cases, it turned out to be possible to explain many of the characteristics of the talk in terms of the special job at hand and the special dictates of the occasion. For example, talk on the radio has to be designed to be "overheard." Such design features account for and are reflected in the character of the talk.

This development—which although not unique to the United Kingdom was especially marked here[31]—had interesting implications for divisions within sociology. Previously ethnomethodologists had boasted of their "indifference" to conventional sociology, but on these occasions it seemed that the two enterprises were becoming more similar. Thus, CA-inspired studies were able to give alternative accounts of features of social spaces—such as courtrooms—which had previously been interpreted in terms of status, power, or ideology. On the other hand, some of the epistemological loftiness of CA was taken from it when exponents had to acknowledge the role of context and, in particular, when they had to spell out what features of "context" they saw as significant. Analyses of political speeches could not be contributions to political sociology.

This relaxation of the methodological limitations usually imposed on themselves by conversation analysts (limitations which in any case had often provoked epistemological criticism) led to further innovative developments. Science studiers were able to benefit from an analysis of scientists' Nobel speeches undertaken in analytic terms borrowed from CA.[32] And CA exponents were offered research positions at Xerox's Europarc in Cambridge (although this industry interest in ethnography and ethnomethodological work had been pioneered in the United States). Although some leading figures have left the British academic world, this research area is still developing with new book-length publications due in 1992. Additionally, other approaches to the sociology of language—whether sociolinguistic, semiological, or Foucault-inspired—have contributed to the high profile of language studies in British sociology.[33]

The final example to be cited in this section was also one nominated by the ESRC: stratification. In his essay for the review issue of the *British Journal of Sociology,* G. Payne helpfully divides work on social mobility into five kinds: developments in mobility itself, increases in the sophistication of the measures used, analyses of the connection between social mobility and class, work on issues associated with mobility such as industrial change or educational policy, and—finally—international comparisons of mobility rates.[34]

Payne places developments in the study of mobility clearly within this review period since it was only after 1975 that new, better data on the United Kingdom were published indicating "greater fluidity, over 'long distances,' from low in the class hierarchy to its upper reaches." Furthermore, it was only at this time that specialist work on mobility became available "to a much wider group of other sociologists."[35] These studies revealed high rates of upward mobility (with the changing occupational and class structure) but suggested that mobility rates themselves were not increasing greatly over time; if society was more open than had been thought, its openness was not growing. By 1988 Marshall and his colleagues were able to publish their work on *Social Class in Modern Britain,* addressing the third of Payne's categories. Building on increased knowledge of mobility and greater methodological sophistication, these sociologists felt able to conclude that

data from our own survey confirm that class solidarities retain an importance that undermines recent accounts of the alleged demise of class consciousness and class politics, and associated rise of aggressive consumerism. Social class is to the fore among conceptions of collective identity. . . . Class politics is far from exhausted.[36]

Culturally, politically, and in terms of values, Britain is still a class society. From this conclusion they are able to propose that Labour's run of electoral failures in the 1980s derived from "a political rather than a sociological source."[37] On this view, Labour has been let down, not by being beached by changes in class alignment, but by a failure to appeal across the whole spectrum of its potential supporters.

These insights are supported by work in Payne's fifth category: international comparisons. According to Payne, British work here has not been at the forefront in these international studies although individuals have made outstanding contributions. Such work indicates that the British relative mobility measure is unremarkable but that the "occupational distinctiveness of Britain is its low proportion of employment in agriculture, and the high proportion in the industrial manual sector."[38] The significance of this is that deindustrialization—closely associated with Mrs. Thatcher's assault on unproductive workplaces in the early 1980s—will accordingly have a particularly strong impact in Britain.[39]

BRITISH SOCIOLOGY AND THE UNITED KINGDOM

Up to this point the identity of "British" sociology has been taken for granted, but even in the material covered so far, there have been grounds for doubting the suitability of this term. Thus, as Payne notes, the comparative mobility data on Britain are really data on England and Wales. There had been a separate Scottish mobility study. The study of deindustrialization and manual labor cited at the end of the last section was allied to a later publication, *Redundancy and Recession in South Wales.*[40] The general trend toward secularization described earlier applies only in a very moderated sense to Northern Ireland. Again, the question of the informal procedures adopted by police officers has a special salience in relation to political terrorism, itself chiefly practiced in Northern Ireland. How much then is British sociology an admixture of the separate sociologies of the countries of the United Kingdom?

Sociologists in the United Kingdom have admittedly paid some attention to these issues. Thus, the sociological distinctness of Scotland has been strongly debated. On the one hand, Kendrick, Bechhofer, and McCrone argue that industrial and occupational change in Scotland should not be interpreted in terms of a special relationship of dependency on England or in terms of a core-periphery model. Scotland can usefully be treated as similar to regions of England. Tony Dickson retorts that "Scotland is different, OK."[41] The political culture of Scotland is distinct; the Scots' response to the "Thatcherite" political ideology was different from that of the English. In the late 1970s Nairn wrote *The Break-up of Britain,* and the exploration of national identity, national culture, and nationalist politics has grown since that time.[42] But we are still awaiting publication of the first "sociology of Scotland" book and students at Scottish universities have to learn their sociology—although not of course their history—from books dealing with the English class structure, English criminals, and English workers.[43]

The Welsh situation is in many respects similar although Welsh nationalism is more strongly rooted in a language movement, a factor which has received recognition in, for example, the provision of a Welsh-language channel as one of the four television services. Still, for administrative purposes Wales is routinely handled as part of "England and Wales" so that statistical and other forms of official information on Wales are highly integrated into that concerning the core. There is no "sociology of Wales" book although a yearbook series draws together social and economic research on Wales.[44]

Finally there is Northern Ireland. By any criteria this is an exceptional region and one which ought to excite the interest of sociologists. The political and policy-related literature is extensive and growing; sociological analyses are comparatively outnumbered. Thus, a recent ESRC-related collection of studies on Northern Ireland's "social and economic life" had no substantive chapters contributed by sociologists and only one, by a social anthropologist, on a sociological theme: informal work and the black economy.[45] Sociologists in Northern Ireland have produced influential work on, for instance, the sociology of education, on equal opportunities and fair employment, and on regional development policy, but this work has largely supplied a local audience and has not generally appeared in the mainstream sociology journals.[46] Other researchers have published on "regular" sociological topics but ones whose importance is heightened in some way by the "troubles," such as the media, policing, and youth lifestyles.[47] But what, for many observers, is the distinctive sociological question about Northern Ireland—the connection between ethnicity, religion, and class—has received few systematic answers. Steve Bruce and the late Roy Wallis, whose review chapter on the sociology of religion was mentioned earlier, made an important, although controversial, contribution to the analysis of Loyalism by asking about the continuation of religious belief in Northern Ireland. They proposed that

in the absence of a clear national consciousness, an identity formulated in terms of evangelical Protestantism is ultimately the only viable one for defending the continued social and cultural autonomy and dominance of Ulster loyalists, even for many working-class Protestants who have long since ceased to be religiously observant.[48]

Thus, for them, the Northern Ireland conflict is a religious conflict. Not exclusively a religious conflict, of course, but a conflict with an ineliminably religious component. Recent work by John Fulton has offered a largely complementary analysis of the role of Roman Catholicism in Irish nationalism.[49]

As an Englishman myself, I am aware of the risks I run in aiming to represent sociological work carried on in the other countries of the United Kingdom. There are bound to be omissions in the above statements and, naturally, sociologists in Scotland, Wales, and Northern Ireland have contributed to the overall strength of "British" sociology; to take just one example, Edinburgh is probably the United Kingdom's leading center for the sociology of science and technology. Still, in this section I have indicated that within British sociology there are distinct national sociologies and distinct intellectual challenges to the discipline of sociology. The trend is toward growing self-awareness and self-confidence in these sociologies.

THE MEANING OF THEORY IN BRITISH SOCIOLOGY

When British and U.S. sociologists meet they commonly fail to understand each other's interpretation of "theory." For Americans, or so it seems to me, "theory" normally refers to propositions of a higher order or abstract kind which can be tested through empirical inquiry of some specifiable kind, often involving a data set. British sociologists may share this view or they may take theory to be something yet more abstract, having to do with social ontology, semiology, or issues in hermeneutics. In his review for the *British Journal of Sociology* Martin Bulmer is critical of this tendency within British sociology. He detects a dearth of "incisive general formulations with explanatory power" and laments the

great proliferation, particularly in British sociology book publishing, of what may be called tertiary or quaternary literature, essays and commentary in which the author dilates upon what others have said previously about a phenomenon ... or about a body of thought.[50]

In the material reviewed so far there is a great deal to set against the gloomy prospect offered by Bulmer. There is plentiful theoretical interpretation which advances empirical understanding. Choosing a small number of examples from the foregoing, we find that theory and empirical research can be linked in a number of ways. Thus, explicit epistemological theorizing helped to create the space for the numerous case studies in the sociology of science by undermining philosophical limitations on the sociological bailiwick.[51] In the case of the sociology of religion, Weberian notions of ethnic honor helped analysts explain why "Paisley's religious rhetoric and style succeed among a population [Northern Irish Protestants] which has slid ever closer to the northern European norm of religious indifference."[52] In the case of the sociology of language, quite abstruse theoretical considerations led to insightful, yet readily understood analyses of political rhetoric. Finally, Newby offered a challenge to sociologists to develop a theoretical interpretation of modern industrial capitalism which would give due acknowledgment to the significance of ecological changes.

In these cases the connections between theory and empirical work are not always straightforward. Theory sometimes "informs" empirical practice in an indirect way rather than fitting, even loosely, into the pattern implied by the hypothetical-deductive model.

It could still be argued, however, that these cases do not address the role played in British sociology by "grand theory" of the grandest sort. I will finish this chapter by looking briefly at one grand theoretical view which is overtaking the British sociological community with epidemic speed: postmodernism.

It is currently virtually impossible to avoid new publications on postmodernism; publishers' catalogs arrive weekly announcing new twists on postmodernity. And of all the isms affecting sociology in the last fifteen years, postmodernism offers itself as the obvious candidate for the theoretical interpretation of the whole period since David Harvey, in his authoritative and widely read analysis, dates the transition from modernism to postmodernism around 1972.[53]

The core of the argument advanced by Harvey and others is that the postmodern aesthetic, eschewing the formal rules of modernism and celebrating diversity and change, has an elective affinity with recent, "post-Fordist" capitalism. The new conditions of production emphasize flexibility, both in production processes—where information technology has allowed smart machines to produce small runs of customized goods—and in the status of workers—where big firms have developed a core of key workers and have come to supplement this by subcontracting to small firms and the self-employed and by taking on casual, part-time, and temporary workers. Thus, as the slogan has it, postmodernism is the cultural logic of "late" capitalism.

Numerous authors have, it seems, struggled to make theoretical discussion of these issues as obscure as possible, and Bulmer's point about the growth of a "tertiary or quaternary literature" is sadly justified here. All the same, discussion of postmodernism allows us to draw together the results from various strands in British sociology: work on "casualization" in the labor force and on unemployment, studies of the changing nature of work and on the black economy, work on the political economy of information technology, and work on industrial change and on the "labor process."[54]

One could waste several lifetimes unprofitably reading British books on social theory, but no discerning sociologist will do so, nor will she or he encourage it in their students. Grand theory can play a synthesizing role in British sociology even if the connection between theory and empirical practice is indirect and poorly understood. Bad "theory" books are, in my view, merely a tax on this ill-understood benefit; better still they are a tax it's easy to avoid.

NOTES

1. I have used the term "U.K." rather than "British" in most places in this chapter since there is some ambiguity about the meaning of "British": the "U.K." clearly consists of Great Britain (Wales, Scotland, and England) plus Northern Ireland. This is not a merely semantic point since, as I shall stress later on, it is unclear how well "British" sociology represents the social experience of the whole United Kingdom.

2. Apart from philosophers and economists who held strong views on the failings of sociology, Marsland was the principal academic to make his name in this fashion; see David Marsland, *Seeds of Bankruptcy: Sociological Bias against Business and Freedom* (London: Claridge, 1988).

3. Discussed in Steven Yearley, *Science, Technology and Social Change* (London: Unwin Hyman, 1988), 82–84.

4. A. H. Halsey, "A Turning of the Tide? The Prospects for Sociology in Britain," *British Journal of Sociology* 40, 3 (1989), 353.

5. Ibid., and ESRC, *Horizons and Opportunities in the Social Sciences* (London: ESRC, 1987). Although the reviews I cite here have aided me in overcoming

some of the difficulty in summarizing fifteen years of British sociology, they do not help me with my other problem: adequately representing all the relevant publications. Since I cannot hope to be comprehensive in my listings, I have decided to be merely indicative. My apologies go out to the many authors whose work I have omitted.

6. The UGC was the statutory agency standing between government and the universities, responsible for allocating governmental funds to particular institutions. The report is discussed in John Westergaard and Ray Pahl, "Looking Backwards and Forwards: The UGC's Review of Sociology," *British Journal of Sociology* 40, 3 (1989), 374–92.

7. Ibid., 380.

8. ESRC, *Horizons and Opportunities,* 1.

9. John A. Jackson, "Sociology in Contemporary Britain," in Raj P. Mohan and Don Martindale, eds., *Handbook of Contemporary Developments in World Sociology* (Westport, Conn.: Greenwood Press, 1975), 26.

10. Norman Dennis, "Sociology and the Spirit of Sixty-eight," *British Journal of Sociology* 40, 3 (1989), 429; and Martin Bulmer, "Theory and Method in Recent British Sociology," *British Journal of Sociology* 40, 3 (1989), 393–417.

11. ESRC, *Horizons and Opportunities,* 1; Westergaard and Pahl, "Looking Backwards and Forwards," 381; and Halsey, "A Turning of the Tide?," 354.

12. See Roy Wallis and Steve Bruce. "Religion: The British Contribution," *British Journal of Sociology* 40, 3 (1989), 493–501, and the further references to their work cited there.

13. See Trevor Jones, Brian MacLean, and Jock Young, *The Islington Crime Survey: Crime, Victimization and Policing in Inner-City London* (Aldershot: Gower, 1986), which, interestingly, has a Foreword by a prominent Labour Shadow Cabinet Member, Gerald Kaufman MP.

14. For examples, see Laurie Taylor, *In the Underworld* (Oxford: Blackwell, 1984); Dick Hobbs, *Doing the Business* (Oxford: Oxford University Press, 1988); and Janet Foster, *Villains: Crime and Community in the Inner City* (London: Routledge, 1990).

15. Again, for example, Simon Holdaway, *Inside the British Police* (Oxford: Blackwell, 1983), and Nigel Fielding, *Joining Forces* (London: Routledge, 1988).

16. W. G. Runciman is best known recently for *A Treatise on Social Theory,* vol. 1: *The Methodology of Social Theory* and vol. 2: *Substantive Social Theory* (Cambridge: Cambridge University Press, 1983, 1989).

17. P. M. Strong, *The Ceremonial Order of the Clinic* (London: Routledge and Kegan Paul, 1979).

18. On health economics see Malcolm Ashmore, Michael Mulkay, and Trevor Pinch, *Health and Efficiency: A Sociology of Health Economics* (Milton Keynes: Open University Press, 1989); more generally see Lesley Doyal with Imogen Pennell, *The Political Economy of Health* (London: Pluto, 1979).

19. See A.P.M. Coxon, "The Effect of Age and Relationship on Gay Men's Sexual Behaviour," *SIGMA Working Paper 13* (London: SIGMA, 1991), one of the reports, using confidential diary data, from the London-based SIGMA study.

20. The potential list of references here is truly vast. For an overview see Ann Oakley, "Women's Studies in British Sociology: To End at Our Beginning?," *British Journal of Sociology* 40, 3 (1989), 442–70. On the topic areas listed, see, for

example, S. Walby, *Patriarchy at Work: Patriarchal and Capitalist Relations in Employment* (Cambridge: Polity, 1986), and M. Stanworth, ed., *Reproductive Tech nologies: Gender, Motherhood and Medicine* (Cambridge: Polity, 1987).

21. This point is developed in R. Deem, *All Work and No Play? The Sociology of Women and Leisure* (Milton Keynes: Open University Press, 1986). Some of the concrete methodological issues are also examined in Hilary Graham, "Do Her Answers Fit His Questions? Women and the Survey Method," in Eva Gamarni kow et al., eds., *The Public and the Private* (London: Heinemann, 1983), 132–46.

22. See Oakley, "Women's Studies in British Sociology," 453–54. Also see G. Payne and P. Abbott, eds., *The Social Mobility of Women* (Basingstoke: Falmer, 1990).

23. Pamela Abbott, "Women's Social Class Identification: Does Husband's Oc cupation Make a Difference?," *Sociology* 21, 1 (1987), 92.

24. Several other candidates are listed in the UGC review: ethnic relations, education, ageing, and political and urban sociology, although for the last two the review observes that "most research on these subjects now goes on in departments and centres of politics, planning and geography." Westergaard and Pahl, "Looking Backwards and Forwards," 381.

25. Howard Newby, "One World, Two Cultures: Sociology and the Environ ment," a lecture to the BSA printed in the BSA bulletin *Network* 50 (1991), 6. A similar argument is made in Steven Yearley, *The Green Case: A Sociology of Environmental Issues, Arguments and Politics* (London: HarperCollins, 1991), 184– 86.

26. Stephen Cotgrove replied to Newby in a note in *Network* 51 1991, 5. Cot grove is well known for the research reported in his *Catastrophe or Cornucopia: The Environment, Politics and the Future* (Chichester: Wiley, 1982).

27. On development, see the work of Michael Redclift, including *Development and the Environmental Crisis: Red or Green Alternatives?* (London: Routledge, 1991 [latest reprint]).

28. ESRC, *Horizons and Opportunities, 1.*

29. Just some examples: David Bloor, *Knowledge and Social Imagery,* revised edition (Chicago: Chicago University Press, 1991); Barry Barnes and Donald MacKenzie, "On the Role of Interests in Scientific Change," in Roy Wallis, ed., *On the Margins of Science* (Keele; University of Keele Press, 1979), 49–66; H. M. Collins, *Changing Order: Replication and Induction in Scientific Practice* (London: Sage, 1985); Michael Mulkay, *Sociology of Science: A Sociological Pilgrimage* (Mil ton Keynes: Open University Press, 1991); and Steve Woolgar, *Science: The Very Idea* (Chichester: Ellis Horwood, 1988).

30. For example: J. M. Atkinson, *Our Masters' Voices: The Language and Body Language of Politics* (London: Methuen, 1984); J. M. Atkinson and Paul Drew, *Order in Court* (London: Macmillan, 1979); and C. C. Heath, "The opening se quence in doctor-patient interaction," in P. Atkinson and C. C. Heath, eds., *Med ical Work: Realities and Routines* (Farnborough: Gower, 1981), 71–90. The strategy adopted in such studies is discussed in John C. Heritage, "Ethnomethodology," in Anthony Giddens and Jonathan H. Turner, eds., *Social Theory Today* (Cambridge: Polity, 1987), 257.

31. Thus, work in the United States on classroom talk and, particularly, on male-female interaction (a comparatively neglected issue in the United Kingdom) would

readily fit into this category; see the special issue of *Sociological Inquiry* 50, 3–4 (1980).

32. Michael Mulkay, "The Ultimate Compliment: A Sociological Analysis of Ceremonial Discourse," *Sociology* 18, 4 (1984), 531–49.

33. For an early attempt to bring a lot of this material together, see David Silverman and Brian Torode, *The Material Word: Some Theories of Language and Its Limits* (London: Routledge and Kegan Paul, 1980).

34. G. Payne, "Social mobility," *British Journal of Sociology* 40, 3 (1989), 472–73.

35. Ibid., 475.

36. G. Marshall, D. Rose, H. Newby, and C. Vogler, *Social Class in Modern Britain* (London: Unwin Hyman, 1989), 267.

37. Ibid., 273.

38. Payne, "Social Mobility," 486.

39. Ibid., 487; see also C. C. Harris et al., "Redundancy in steel," in B. Roberts, R. Finnegan, and D. Gallie, eds., *New Approaches to Economic Life* (Manchester; Manchester University Press, 1985).

40. C. C. Harris, *Redundancy and Recession in South Wales* (Oxford: Blackwell, 1987).

41. S. Kendrick, F. Bechhofer, and D. McCrone, "Is Scotland Different? Industrial and Occupational Change in Scotland and Britain," in H. Newby et al., eds., *Restructuring Capital: Recession and Reorganization in Industrial Society* (London: Macmillan, 1985), 63–102; and Tony Dickson, "Scotland is different, OK?," in David McCrone et al., eds., *The Making of Scotland: Nation, Culture and Social Change* (Edinburgh: Edinburgh University Press, 1989), 53–69.

42. T. Nairn, *The Break-Up of Britain* (London: Verso, 1977).

43. David McCrone, *Understanding Scotland: The Sociology of a Stateless Nation* (London: Routledge, 1992). The point about the courses offered at Scottish universities was drawn to my attention by Steve Bruce.

44. Edited by G. Rees and G. Day, the yearbook is entitled *Contemporary Wales: An Annual Review of Economic and Social Research* (Cardiff: University of Wales Press, 1987 on).

45. Richard Jenkins, ed., *Northern Ireland: Studies in Social and Economic Life* (Aldershot: Avebury, 1989). The chapter in question is by Leo Howe; see also his *Being Unemployed in Northern Ireland: An Ethnographic Study* (Cambridge: Cambridge University Press, 1990).

46. Again, a small number of examples (selected at great peril of upsetting my colleagues): R. D. Osborne, R. J. Cormack, and R. L. Miller, eds., *Education and Policy in Northern Ireland* (Belfast: Policy Research Institute, 1987); R. J. Cormack and R. D. Osborne, eds., *Discrimination and Public Policy in Northern Ireland* (Oxford: Clarendon, 1991); and Liam O'Dowd, "Trends and Potential of the Service Sector in Northern Ireland," in Paul Teague, ed., *Beyond the Rhetoric: Politics, the Economy and Social Policy in Northern Ireland* (London: Lawrence and Wishart, 1987), 183–210.

47. As in the last note: Bill Rolston, ed., *The Media and Northern Ireland. Covering the Troubles* (London: Macmillan 1991); John Brewer with Kathleen Magee, *Inside the RUC: Routine Policing in a Divided Society* (Oxford: Clarendon, 1991);

and Richard Jenkins, *Lads, Kids and Ordinary Citizens* (London: Routledge and Kegan Paul, 1983).

48. Roy Wallis, Steve Bruce, and David Taylor, "Ethnicity and Evangelicalism: Ian Paisley and Protestant Politics in Ulster," *Comparative Studies in Society and History* 29, 2 (1987), 310. These arguments are developed in Steve Bruce, *God Save Ulster!: The Religion and Politics of Paisleyism* (Oxford: Oxford University Press, 1986).

49. John Fulton, *The Tragedy of Belief: Division, Politics and Religion in Ireland* (Oxford: Clarendon Press, 1991).

50. Bulmer, "Theory and Method," 396.

51. Rationalist philosophers of science had argued that sociological interest in scientific knowledge had to be limited to explaining error; true beliefs were self-explanatory. This view is countered in Bloor, *Knowledge and Social Imagery,* ch. 1.

52. Wallis, Bruce, and Taylor, "Ethnicity and Evangelicalism," 310.

53. David Harvey, *The Condition of Postmodernity* (Oxford: Blackwell, 1990); for humorously precise dating of the commencement of postmodernism, see pages 38–39.

54. Once again, sampling from a vast literature, see R. E. Pahl, *Divisions of Labour* (Oxford: Blackwell, 1984), as well as his edited collection (admittedly far from all British), *On Work: Historical, Comparative and Theoretical Approaches* (Oxford: Blackwell, 1988). See, too, Anna Pollert, *Girls, Wives, Factory Lives* (London: Macmillan, 1981); Kevin Robins and Frank Webster, *Information Technology: Post-industrial Society or Capitalist Control?* (Norwood, N.J.: Ablex, 1986); and for a recent overview, Keith Grint, *The Sociology of Work* (Cambridge: Polity, 1991).

4

Contemporary Sociology in Denmark

Heine Andersen, Britt–Mari Blegvad, and
Mogens Blegvad

I. THE INTRODUCTION, INSTITUTIONALIZATION, AND DEVELOPMENT OF SOCIOLOGY*

It is not always easy, or even meaningful, to date the beginning of sociology in a country. In the case of Denmark one might point to 1897, the year when an ad hominem chair in philosophy and sociology was created for Claudis Wilkens (1844–1929) at the University of Copenhagen, the only university in the country at that time.[1] By training, he was a philosopher but had written on social and economic questions. In particular, in 1881 he had published the first textbook of sociology in Danish. Its title, *Samfundslegemets Grundlove. Et Grundrids af Sociologien* (The Fundamental Laws of the Social Body. An Outline of Sociology), shows the influence of Schaeffle. An evolutionist tendency also makes itself strongly felt in its contents. Wilkens's teaching and writings seem, however, to have had little impact.

Another Danish philosopher, C. N. Starke (1858–1926), won some international acclaim for his book on the primitive family, which was published in German in 1888 and in English and French translations in 1889 and 1890, respectively. Starke was elected a member of *L'Institut International de Sociologie,* but did not do any further work in sociology. He went into politics as one of the founders of the Danish single-tax party, conducted a progressive school, and finally became professor of philosophy.

*Authors are listed in alphabetical order. Their individual contributions to this chapter are as follows: Sections I, II, and V are written by Mogens Blegvad; Section III is contributed by Heine Andersen; and Section IV is written by Britt-Mari Blegvad.

The next phase in the story of attempts at establishing sociology in the country belongs to the period between the two World Wars. In 1924 a philosopher, Svend Ranulf (1894–1953), obtained a doctoral degree for a dissertation on Greek philosophy in which he applied Levy-Bruhl's theory of primitive and semi-primitive logic. Ranulf used the right to lecture as a "private docent" at the university which the degree gave him, to introduce the French sociologists to the few who attended his lectures. If and when sociology was introduced as an academic subject, he hoped to obtain a teaching position at the university and sought to qualify himself by historical studies of morality in its social setting (*The Jealousy of the Gods and the Origin of Penal Law in Athens, 1933–34, Moral Indignation and Middle Class Psychology, 1938*). These studies, published in English, did not pass unnoticed outside of Denmark. David Riesman, among others, refers to them, and the latter work was republished in the United States in 1964.

As a matter of fact, around 1930 there was some interest in introducing sociology at the university, but for various reasons, among them the economic crisis, nothing happened. In addition to Ranulf, another Dane, not a philosopher but an economist, Joseph Davidsonhn (1894–1943), was interested in obtaining a teaching position and had qualified himself by publishing *Om Betingelserne og de naermeste Opgaver for en eksakt Sociologi* (The Conditions and the Proximate Tasks for an Exact Sociology), for which he obtained a doctoral degree in 1923. Like Ranulf, for a while, he taught as a "private docent" and published a couple of other books in sociology. Although quite original in their concepts, his works show a strong affiliation with the French school. Finally, it should be mentioned that around 1930 one of the professors of economics, Axel Nielsen (1880–1951), taught an elementary course in sociology to students of economics who were interested.

In 1933 Theodor Geiger (1891–1952) came to Denmark as a refugee from Nazi Germany.[2] He had taught sociology at the Technische Hochschule in Braunschweig and knew Denmark and the Danish language from previous visits. He was given the opportunity to work in Copenhagen (at the semiprivate Institute of History and Economics), and in 1938 he was appointed to a new chair in sociology, created at the University of Aarhus (which had been established in the year 1929), in competition with Ranulf. However, Ranulf was appointed professor of philosophy at that university the following year.

There is reason to regard Geiger's appointment as a turning point. He was, however, not allowed to work at the university during the Occupation and spent the years 1943–1945 in Sweden. Before he died in 1952, on his way back from a year's teaching in Canada, he initiated and carried out important research (i.e., on social stratification and mobility) and trained at least one able assistant, Torben Agersnap (b. 1922). As early as 1939

Geiger published a comprehensive sociological textbook in Danish, *Sociologi, Grundrids og Hovedproblemer* (Sociology, Outline and Main Problems) and succeeded in creating a small research institute. He was active in organizing sociological associations on international (ISA), Scandinavian, and national (Dansk sociologisk Selskab) levels. After his death, his chair and the institute were abolished. Agersnap left for Copenhagen, where he was able to build up what is now the Department of Organizational Studies and the Sociology of Work, at the Handelshojskole (Business School).

In 1948 the Minister of Education gave the University of Copenhagen the opportunity to establish a chair in sociology. The Faculty of Law and Economics appointed a committee, in which the Faculty of Humanities was represented, to evaluate the applicants. After the committee had reported to the Faculty of Law and Economics, it was decided to appoint none of the applicants, but to look for an American sociologist who would be willing to come as a visiting professor to initiate the subject. A search revealed that Kare Svalastoga (b. 1914), a Norwegian historian who had studied sociology at the University of Washington, Seattle, had just obtained his Ph.D. and was interested in coming to Denmark. He started teaching in 1950, and in 1955, following a competition, he was appointed professor of sociology. What was at first merely a section of the Department of Economics became an independent department, and degrees in sociology at various levels were gradually introduced. Together, with his assistants, Svalastoga embarked on extensive studies of stratification and mobility. He retired in 1984, but no successor was appointed. At that time a large number of sociologists had graduated from the department. In 1965 they had formed a union (*Dansk Sociologforening*) that gradually took over the functions of Dansk sociologisk Selskab, which was dissolved a few years later. For a period a Swedish sociologist, Joachim Isreal (b. 1920), functioned as a second professor of sociology in Copenhagen.

In 1958 a governmental Institute of Social Research was established. It employs psychologists and economists as well as sociologists and does research in applied social science, particularly for the Ministry of Social Affairs. The initiative which led to its establishment came from Henning Friis (b. 1914), and economist by training. Friis had worked in the said ministry as secretary for the Youth Commission after World War II, and had administered an extensive program of investigations of the conditions of young people in Denmark. In 1948 Friis was appointed social-scientific consultant to the Ministry of Social Affairs, but soon found that the tasks he was asked to take on required a permanent institute with a professional staff and a network of lay interviewers throughout the country. In 1953 a commission was appointed to discuss the establishment of such an institute. In vain Svalastoga, who was a member, argued that it would be superfluous since a university department could do the work. Henning Friis became the first director of the institute. He retired in 1979. For some years he served as chairman of Dansk sociologisk Sclskab and was very active in international organizations within sociology and social research (i.e., as a member of the Executive Council of ISA, 1959–1966). After his retirement he has been the scientific director of a study of future social trends in Denmark (Egmont Fondens Fremtidsstudie), which has published four volumes (1984–1985).

Around 1960, when a commission on reform of secondary education proposed the establishment of social-scientific branches in the Danish gymnasium, Friis successfully argued that sociology should be taught in these branches. A need for including sociology in the university education of social science teachers for the gymnasium then arose. In Copenhagen this led to the creation of a chair within the Faculty of Humanities. In order to distinguish it from Svalastoga's chair within the Faculty of Law and Economics, it was called a chair in cultural sociology. This name well matched the interests of the man called in 1964 to fill the chair, Verner Goldschmidt (1916–1982). Goldschmidt, a lawyer by training, had for many years worked in Greenland on problems arising from the encounter of Eskimo culture with Danish civilization and was particularly interested in questions about cultural conflicts. He was able to build up a department and a system of degrees characterized by the integration of social anthropology and social psychology with sociology in the curriculum and research. In 1969 a second chair in cultural sociology was established for Torben Monberg (b. 1929), who had a degree in the history of religion and had done research in the British Solomon Islands. The department had studied immigrants in Denmark, and Goldschmidt had studied the United Nations peace force on Cyprus.

At the University of Aarhus, the teaching of sociology was resumed in connection with the introduction of a degree in political science in 1958. However, even after a chair in sociology had been established, it was still considered mostly as an adjunct to this subject. The incumbent is Ole Borre (b. 1932), an economist by training.

The department that Torben Agersnap has built up at the Copenhagen Business School, an institution of higher education charged with research and given the right to confer doctoral degrees, has grown from a very modest beginning in 1953 into a large unit with a scientific staff of more than thirty persons, of whom a number are sociologists. Its range of research is wider than suggested by its name (see above), and it has become one of the major centers for training and research in sociology in the country.

It has been comparatively unaffected by the events which shook the universities around 1970 and led to a permanent crisis in a number of departments, including those of sociology, and also by the economics stringency of the late 1970s and 1980s which hit the universities hard. In the late 1960s several factors including a far too rapid expansion had led to a growing dissatisfaction and unrest among the students and younger teachers at practically all institutions of higher education. Disruption and violence broke out in 1968. As a consequence a new law concerning the governing structure of universities was introduced. It gave the students more power than similar reforms in other countries. The "revolution" had a strong ideological aspect; various branches of Marxism came for a period to dominate many university departments, including the Department of Sociology and the Department of Cultural Sociology in Copenhagen. The professors who did not join the Marxist wave became isolated and some, including Goldschmidt and Monberg, preferred to leave.

Although the wave has now subsided, conditions in the two departments for a long time were such that the authorities finally lost their patience and tried to close them down and start over again with advice and help from outside the country. Although it proved impossible to dismiss the teachers, the two departments were merged and a process of reform not yet completed was initiated.

II. METHODOLOGICAL AND THEORETICAL TRENDS IN DANISH SOCIOLOGY

Although Geiger and Ranulf both died in the early 1950s, it may be worth mentioning that their methodological positions were so different that they criticized each other vehemently in writing. Ranulf in 1946 published a textbook of social scientific methodology (*Socialvidenskabelig Methodelaere*) in which he not only propounded an extremely positivistic philosophy of social science[3] but also accused Geiger of maintaining a position not far removed from the German metaphysics which, according to Ranulf, had paved the way for Nazism. Geiger retaliated with a pamphlet (*Ranulf ctr. Geiger,* 1946) in which he rebutted these accusations and debated a number of main questions in sociological methodology. Geiger's conception of social science at that time was a behavioristically tinged empiricism, which many would call a kind of positivism, using this label in the broader sense in which it later came to be applied. Ranulf, on the other hand, was a positivist in the original Comtean sense. Geiger admitted in his pamphlet that previously he had a more Husserlian position, but maintained that by now he considered the concepts that seek to express the essence of social phenomena only as provisional and liable to be modified in the light of experience. The correct method is not the deductive, but the hypothetical-deductive method. Ranulf, on the other hand, seemed to favor a purely inductive method.

Seen in the light of later developments, this debate signified a conflict between two kinds of what came to be called positivism: a more radical kind, represented by Ranulf, and a more moderate one, represented by

Geiger. For quite a time such a conflict characterized Danish sociology. Svalastoga also advocated an extreme positivism, although of a Lundbergian, rather than of a Comtean stamp, while others maintained an eclectic empiricism. While Svalastoga and his pupils recognized only work with hard data and quantitative methods as scientific, the Department of Cultural Sociology accepted qualitative methods and soft data and was influenced to some extent by the type of phenomenology which dominated the Department of Psychology. Goldschmidt had worked closely with one of the professors of psychology, Franz From (b. 1914), in the Greenland investigations.

The picture changed radically with the advent of Marxism as the dominating orientation around 1970. Not only the position of Svalastoga and his pupils, but also that of Goldschmidt, was rejected by what has come to be called the 1968 generation. The theoretical and methodological debate for a period became dominated by various branches of Marxism, imported mostly from Germany. Although the Frankfurt School attracted a lot of attention, "Kapitallogik" also gained devoted followers. Also with the Marxist wave came a growing interest in what may be called interpretive ("verstehende") sociology, including hermeneutics and ethnomethodology. The present-day dividing lines run mostly between these interpretive positions on the one hand, and on the other what may be called mainstream empiricism as represented by the work of the Institute of Social Research.

Since Geiger, it cannot be maintained that Danish sociology has produced comprehensive theoretical presentations of such a quality and originality that they merit the attention of scholars from other countries. Various factors have contributed to making the development of sociology in Denmark a conflict-ridden, not too straightforward and successful one. But nevertheless many valuable studies of specific topics have been made as appears from the following.

III. CURRENT TRENDS WITHIN SUBFIELDS OF DANISH SOCIOLOGICAL RESEARCH

An examination of some of the subfields of Danish sociological research reveals that two features have been conspicuous in the last ten to fifteen years: a significant differentiation and fragmentation, and a shift toward attaching greater importance to applied research. These tendencies are partly caused by the specific institutional and historical conditions of Danish sociology, and partly by the general tendencies embedded in the government policy on research and education since the seventies.

Denmark has only two institutes of sociology, both located at the University of Copenhagen. From the early seventies and throughout the eighties, the research environment of both institutes was subject to strong theoretical influence by the current debates between the different Marxist schools. Furthermore, from the middle of the seventies, government policy on education and research resulted in a receding intake of new students and recruitment of researchers. This development reached its peak some years ago, when the Ministry of Education decided to close down both institutes in preparation for a fundamental restructuring of the discipline. Hence, Danish sociology is currently in a serious institutional crisis.

In spite of this situation, sociological research has expanded and proved very innovative; however, the major part of this development has taken place within other milieux rather than in the purely sociological ones, that is, milieux affiliated with other established disciplines such as political sociology, medicine, criminology, technology, and so forth, and partly milieux within institutes for applied research, and new interdisciplinary environments at the new university centers, established during the seventies and aiming at specific types of vocational training.

This has resulted in the current boundaries between sociological research and other related disciplines, and between various traditional subdisciplines within sociology being rather blurred. This development has led to a shift toward emphasizing applied research at the expense of basic research.

Although, to some extent, the same trends can be found in other countries, they are probably most pronounced in Denmark. One of the results has been that sociological research in Denmark has been subject to considerable differentiation and fragmentation. Methodologically, the discipline has also become more differentiated, as hermeneutic and qualitative methods have gained ground, for example.

When it is necessary to select and to delimit the fields, the described trends make it very difficult to give an account of the development within different subfields. The following presentation is, therefore, extremely selective. As the most important fields of sociological research, we have selected welfare and living conditions, political sociology, labor market relations and working conditions, medical sociology, and criminology.

Research on Welfare and Living Conditions

While studies of the population's living conditions[4] can be traced back to the birth of sociology, modern welfare research was introduced in the late sixties to study the emergence of the welfare state and its social reforms, ensuring social security and welfare. During the sixties many countries undertook to work out statistical indicators and time series aiming at illuminating welfare conditions. In an attempt to develop more coherent and sociologically based welfare concepts and methods, the Scandinavian countries launched a number of large-scale surveys mapping out living conditions and their distribution. This research has primarily been empirically based, but it has continuously been accompanied by discourses on theoretical and operational definitions of the core concepts: living conditions, welfare, and poverty.

In 1976 Erik Jorgen Hansen at the Danish National Institute of Social Research conducted a pioneer study within Danish welfare research.[5] The study was carried out as a panel survey, and the population of the 1976 study was reinterviewed in 1986.

In many ways the study was a continuation of previous Scandinavian welfare studies, especially the Swedish studies, the principal architect being Sten Johanson. The welfare concept applied is based on the assumption that individual welfare is determined by the social, economic, and physical conditions for utilizing individual resources (abilities, knowledge, physical, and psychical resources). This leads to a fairly objective welfare concept based on a catalog of social components and standards for living conditions, prearranged by the researcher to comprise physical and psychical health conditions, education, social relationships, influence on daily life matters, housing conditions, employment, working environment, and economic conditions. Furthermore, attempts were made to lay down objective norms for what could be labeled good and poor living conditions respectively.

As could be expected, the study revealed that components of living conditions were extremely unequally distributed on a number of background variables such as gender, age, and social stratum.

The study was repeated in 1986, reinterviewing 86 percent of the original population, and the results were in many ways both interesting and rather surprising. A major conclusion was that, in general, economic recession and growing unemployment had not resulted in poorer living conditions; on the contrary, living conditions seemed to have improved. However, the one very conspicuous exception was the working conditions. The study showed that in 1986 an increasing number of women were exposed to increased deprivation in working conditions by way of growing psychical strain, risking industrial injury and occupational accidents, or their work did not provide them with sufficient challenges enabling them to utilize their skills and qualities. One of the primary reasons for this situation is that the majority of women entering the labor market during the period from 1976 to 1986 undertook unskilled work (i.e., within the health and social sector).

Another significant result from the study was that, in general, the distribution of living conditions on social strata did not seem to have changed during the ten-year period. Class differences seem to be relatively robust properties even in such a modern welfare state as the Danish.

Danish welfare studies have, like other Scandinavian welfare studies, given rise to rather intensive debates among researchers, politicians, and the public in general. The sociological debate primarily concerned the con-

cept of welfare, which has been criticized for being too empirical, for focusing too much on the individual, and for being too strongly based on
pragmatic policy information. Criticism has been directed toward a lacking
theoretical fundament of the empirical surveys, which can explain the social mechanisms determining living conditions and inequality. Furthermore, the concept is criticized for not taking into consideration that
different historical periods are characterized by different forms of life and
social norms. Hence, welfare is a heterogeneous, standardizable concept.[6]

During recent years, the welfare studies have been followed up by research applying qualitative methods for analyzing especially the living conditions of deprived groups of people and their way of coping with daily
living problems. The studies have been especially inspired by Peter Townsend's studies.[7]

John Andersen and Jorgen Elm Larsen have carried out a study that in
many ways breaks with previous practices.[8] This study tries to uncover the
structural causes and social effects of modern poverty, by using a relative
poverty concept and by combining quantitative and qualitative methods.
It also analyzes and assesses the consequences of the welfare policy implemented. The general conclusion of the study is that in Denmark relative
poverty is far more widespread than previously suggested by welfare research. The pursued welfare policy has not adequately prevented the risk
of poverty; which people are struck by more lasting effects of poverty
depends on a number of specific conditions such as material and social
resources, possibilities of support from social relationships, possibilities of
exploiting subsistence economy, and so forth.

Labor Market and Working Life

Labor market relations is another field of study that Danish sociologists
have been increasingly attracted to during recent years.[9] The Danish labor
market is very organized and is comprised of strong central organizations
and a well-institutionalized structure. During the last decades, the labor
market has been subject to important structural changes: (1) the public
sector and the private service sector have expanded at the expense of
industry and agriculture; and (2) the educational level has been improved
and there has been an influx of women to the labor market. The recent
economic recession has made the labor market an increasingly important
factor in economic policy, not only in relation to income development but
also in relation to structural conditions such as mobility and flexibility.

The growing importance of institutional and structural conditions has
led to a search for alternatives to the idealized neoclassic theory of economics, assuming the existence of perfect market mechanisms. A core example of this is sociological studies of segmentation and flexibility in the
labor market, of which one of the most comprehensive Danish studies was

implemented by Thomas P. Boje.[10] The main objective of the study was to investigate the segmentation of the Danish labor market and assess the applicability of the theories of segmentation, using empirical data based on M. J. Piore's works on the theory of segmentation. The study employed register data covering a test sample of the total Danish labor market in the years 1980 and 1981. The database contained information on variables concerning firms as well as employees. It was thus possible to map out in detail the mobility within the given period.

The study confirmed that the Danish labor market was characterized by strong trends toward segmentation. The most evident submarkets were made up by (1) the public sector, especially white-collar workers and academics; (2) skilled and unskilled workers in the iron and steel industry and in the building and construction industry; (3) white-collar workers within trade, insurance, and production; and (4) a submarket for unskilled women within industry, trade, and service. The study suggested that institutional conditions and education played a more important role in Denmark than in the United States. Furthermore, it revealed a more complex picture than that implied by the dual labor market theory.

During the 1980s a number of rather large-scale studies on labor market organizations and institutions were completed. The Danish labor market was strongly organized and centralized, and increasing attempts have been made to persuade the organizations to commit themselves to the government's general economic policy and to adapt wage formation to this.

Jesper Due and Jorgen Steen Madsen have carried out a six-year longitudinal case study on the wage formation in the public labor market.[11] In Denmark, public wages are negotiated between, on the one side, the Ministry of Finance and the municipalities, and on the other, a few central labor market organizations. The study employed both documentary data and interviews with key persons among top negotiators in collective bargaining, and supplied in-depth analyses of the development of the bargaining mechanism and, especially, the important role that informal social relations play during the course of bargaining. One of the conclusions was that the employees' organizations play a leading role in current changes within the public sector, but their structure was actually hampering the very same changes.

The growth in the service industry and the public sector has increased the importance of white-collar organizations. Traditionally, these organizations have often been analyzed by comparing them with the organizations for manual workers. However, many groups of white-collar workers find themselves in the intermediate position between manual workers and professionals. This was the point of view in Steen Scheuer's study of a selection of white-collar unions in Denmark.[12]

The study departed from the concept that two dimensions were decisive in the understanding of the organizational processes characterizing such unions: the degree of professionalism and the degree of collectivism. When these variables were dichotomized, four types of white-collar unions emerged: skill-based collectivism, professionalism, collectivism, and service unionism. The study employed the methodology of both surveys and qualitative interviews with union leaders. The results showed that organizations could be typologized according to these dimensions, and significant, identified differences could be explained theoretically. One of the major results of the survey was that professionalism and collectivism were seen as important variables for the understanding of white-collar unions. Collective strategies are prevalent among groups of unskilled or semiskilled workers, while organizations characterized by professionalism give high priority to education.

Other important studies focus on the sociological and psychological aspects of unemployment.[13]

Political Sociology

The structure of the Danish political system has undergone important changes during the last two decades. Most conspicuous is the rather dramatic change in the Danish party structure since the beginning of the seventies. Also, during the same period a range of new social movements, grassroot movements, have emerged trying to gain influence on the decision-making processes. The third most important process has been Denmark's membership in the EEC.

Due to election by proportional representation, the political system in Denmark consisted of several parties. Up to the seventies, the system was relatively stable, being dominated by four traditional parties. In 1973 the country experienced a landslide election, bringing three new parties into Parliament, collectively representing more than 25 percent of the votes. Although these parties no longer represent such a large number of votes, they still maintain an influential position in Parliament.

This situation and the subsequent shift in voters' preferences have had an important impact on political sociological research during the last ten to fifteen years.[14] Themes such as class voting, contra issue voting, dealignment and realignment, and the role of the media have been subject to several major surveys, including panel surveys that have supplied important data on the behavior of voters. Ole Borre[15] has summarized the results from several of these studies and has found distinct indications of dealignment from the beginning of the seventies, followed by a period which seemed to be characterized by realignment. Class voting is decreasing, but at the same time the parties seem to be reestablishing relatively stable voter bases. Ole Tonsgaard has shown that during the same period the attitudinal pattern of the voters has changed; previously the traditional left-right dimension was decisive of party identification, while the current attitudinal pattern is multidimensional.[16]

Other problems related to this process were the voters' trust in or alienation from the political system, their level of activity, and their degree of interest in politics. Here, the studies showed that though the first part of the seventies was characterized by a growing mistrust in the political system, the voters gradually regained trust in the political system. On the other hand, nothing indicates that the voters have become more actively involved in politics. Only the electorate voting for new parties seems to actively follow election campaigns in the mass media.[17]

As to the influence of the mass media in general, several studies were implemented during the period from 1971 to 1987. Until 1988 Denmark had only one television channel (state run), which might lead to the assumption that TV played an important role in the election results. On the basis of surveys and content analyses of parliamentary elections and elections to the Parliament of the EEC, Karen Siune concludes, however, that TV plays a role primarily in setting the agenda, influencing opinions, and bringing persons into focus.[18] The studies indicated that journalists played a considerable steering role in these matters.

Another new element in the political pattern, which has been the object of several studies, is the new grassroots movements that emerged during the sixties.[19] Peter Gundelach's study of approximately 100 organizations of this type revealed characteristic features. They are segmental; their boundaries are blurred; a majority of the members are recruited from the middle class; and they are primarily oriented toward collective consumption. The societal background is a dissolution of previous distinctions between market and state, resulting in new types of conflicts that are not directly related to the traditional class structure. Departing from Ronald Inglehardt's thesis on a shift from materialistic to postmaterialistic values, Gundelach explains the overrepresentation of the middle class by referring to the extension of postmaterialistic values among this class.[20]

In a comparative study of Scandinavian grassroots movements, Lise Togeby[21] tests the thesis of the special importance of postmaterialistic values in the emergence of grassroots movements and their recruiting basis. To some extent her findings confirm the hypothesis, but there are also indications of an inverted causal relation—that the very mobilization of grassroots movements creates changes in postmaterialistic values.

Medical Sociology

Denmark is famous for its well-developed and relatively well-functioning public health service. During recent years, however, this sector has faced stagnation in resources. This development has been accompanied by expanding sociological research into the field of health, both as to how sociological factors affect health conditions and how the health service operates.[22]

Lars Iversen has conducted a number of studies on how unemployment affects health. The closing down of two Danish shipyards provided rather unique data for studying the effects of unemployment. The design of the study was longitudinal, and a control group made it possible to control the sequence in time and direction of the causal relation. The study showed that unemployment is very likely to cause psychosomatic as well as mental health problems. On the other hand, nothing indicated that unemployment gave rise to increased consumption of alcohol.[23] This study has been supplemented with a statistical survey on unemployment and mortality in the period from 1970 to 1980 based on census data. The survey showed that the mortality rate of the unemployed increased considerably, which is interpreted as an expression of both health-related selection and increased susceptibility associated with the psychosocial stress of unemployment.[24]

The influence of the working environment on health has been elucidated by a number of major studies. The most comprehensive one comprised a sample of 3,000 female workers within seven branches that traditionally have been dominated by women.[25] The study showed that the women were primarily occupied with monotonous piecework and were exposed to harmful effects from the environment. The major symptoms were stress and pains in the back, arms, and legs.

The functions of the health service and its relationship to the population have also been the object of several studies. Laila Launso and Hanne Marie Jensen conducted one of the major studies comparing primary health care with alternative (unauthorized) types of treatment, largely applying qualitative methods.[26]

One of the central questions concerned what information the health workers possessed about the individual users of health care, and what their "paradigm" was. Alternative health workers were asked the same question. The paradigm of the authorized health workers, "the clinical paradigm," was found to be expert-dominated, based on a theoretical understanding of disease, and the user was defined as being a passive recipient. In contrast, the "alternative paradigm" of the unauthorized health workers (who have increased in number) was democratic in structure and was based on a practical concept of disease. Another study found that, to a large degree, lay concepts and strategies for handling symptoms of disease were built on everyday experiences and experiments over a long period of time, rather than on medical expert knowledge and research.[27]

Criminology

Sociological studies have played an important role to criminological research in Denmark during recent years.[28] Societal attitudes and reactions to crime have been treated by Flemming Balvig, who conducted his first theoretical and empirical study of how the population, the authorities, and the media perceived of crime in the middle of the seventies.[29] From the beginning of the seventies, fear of crime became an increasingly important issue on the criminal political agenda. On the basis of a "moral-panic-model" the study dealt with the population's experiences with and knowledge about the extent of crime; the development and causes of crime; and the role that interest groups, authorities, and the media played in forming opinions on crime. The moral-panic-model implies that fear of crime is assumed not to be rational but influenced by the media and secondary sources rather than by people's own experiences and knowledge. Moreover, fear of crime is reinforced among persons occupying a peripheral and powerless position in the social structure. These factors form part of a self-increasing circuit, and the model proved very useful for interpreting the empirical results from the study in the middle of the seventies.

However, the model seems less applicable to the recent development in Denmark. In a study from 1990, Balvig reassesses the model on the background of results from a series of subsequent studies.[30] Since Balvig's 1978 study, the population's fear of crime has decreased in spite of growing criminality. Using analyses of the extension of fear of crime among different population groups and changes in this fear, Balvig advances the thesis that the social structure has changed qualitatively, resulting in different opinions on and reactions to crime which no longer comply with the moral-panic-model. Society has become segregated along the center-periphery dimension and increasingly individualized with different consequences to the center and periphery respectively. The center is shielded from the periphery, and the center is populated by people to whom concrete experience and rational knowledge play an important role, while the population of the periphery adhere to a more fatalistic attitude.

Drug abuse is another issue on the political agenda brought about by the social development since the late sixties because of the emergence of new kinds of drugs and new groups of drug addicts. Jacob Hilden Winsloew analyzed and summarized his own findings and those of others in a thesis from 1984.[31] The thesis addressed the historical development of drug abuse, its extension, and the creation of new drug addict cultures, as well as society's attitude toward and reaction to drug abuse. It focused especially on the system of control and treatment of addicts and its latent effects. The Danish treatment of addicts involves both medical care and social workers. Winsloew demonstrates that both types of treatment contain a number of dysfunctional properties such as goal displacement, insufficient fulfillment of goals, exclusion of clients, and so forth.

Studies of crime and social change, and of the imprisonment process, as well as a comparative study of the historical development of crime in Denmark and other countries, should also be mentioned.[32]

IV. SOCIOLOGY OF LAW IN DENMARK

Introduction

Traditionally sociology of law in Scandinavia covers a broad field of quantitative fact-finding related to legal theories as well as sociological and psychological research in legal institutions (Thorstein Eckhoff, 1960, on Scandinavian research, which both then and now includes Danish research).

There is an overlap between what is going on in sociology of law and criminology, especially as this field acquired the status of a separate science around 1920 in Denmark.[33] In the last part of this section, we will return to this demarcation for a brief discussion of its relevance today.

Phase One: Founding Fathers

It took some time before an interest in sociology of law developed.[34] A strong beginning was made by the first sociology professor in Sweden, Uppsala, Torgny T. Segerstedt. His work was based on his interest in the concepts of social norms, social control, and uniform behavior.

In 1945, Segerstedt and associates did a study on what he called "the common man's attitude towards legal rules" which resulted in general observations about differences between rural and urban populations, between sexes, and between different classes.[35]

This general theme was then taken up again in the middle of the sixties by the Danish psychologist Berl Kutchinsky, and a comparative European project, Knowledge and Opinion about Law, the so-called KOL studies, emerged. The main topic was the ordinary citizen's sense of justice (1966).[36]

Parallel to this development Theodor Geiger[37] started a discussion of the nature of sociology of law. For him the essential point was how law as a subject was treated. Eventually these points were taken up twenty years later in a debate by the Danish lawyer and philosopher Alf Ross. The main task of the doctrinal law is to state what is "valid law" or "law in force" in a given community.[38]

Phase Two: The Greenland Studies and Law and Dispute Treatment

This debate was used as a theoretical foundation for Verner Goldschmidt's[39] sociological studies on official behavior in the field of law enforcement. The decision-makers have the special function of solving conflicts and using sanctions whenever the norms of the system have been violated.

Goldschmidt's main point is, however, that a violation of a norm is not always a sufficient condition for sanction behavior. Differences in personality between agents working in the same environment may produce differences in behavior.

Parallel to this study, Goldschmidt, Torben Agersnap, and Agnete Weis Bentzon studied the Greenlanders' perception of the existing sanction system. The sanctions used were completely different from those of Denmark. Imprisonment was unknown as a sanction; the local courts used fines. Moreover, individual sanctions of an educational nature were applied, such as a further education in a foster family.

In 1950, Goldschmidt prepared a bill which codified formerly valid Greenland law and was accepted by the authorities both in Greenland and in Denmark. The law comprised a sanction system which strongly differed from the Danish and other Scandinavian criminal codes. For example, the concept of punishment was not used. What social consequences would such a sanction system evoke? Ten years later a study of this system was in fact carried out by Verner Goldschmidt.

His report shows that the conservation of the Greenland sanction system, which had been attempted by mean of the codification referred to above, had failed, and he gave as a reason that Greenland had undergone a tremendous economic and social development during this period. From being a colony, the country in 1953 had become a part of Denmark.[40]

Goldschmidt's work and the theoretical discussions which followed, as well as Eckhoff's paper "The Mediator, the Judge and the Administrator," which appeared in 1966, have strongly influenced yet another field of empirical research around which much of the current debate is centered: law and dispute treatment.

Eckhoff refers to Aubert's distinction between two types of conflict— competition and descensus—in which the essential elements are opposing interest and disagreements. For Eckhoff the essential element is the tension arising from the competing interests of the actors involved, rather than from third-party intervention. He discusses the roles of these parties and emphasizes that the judge, by a secondary set of norms, is singled out as the proper person to settle disputes brought before him.[41]

Eckhoff uses a functional approach when making his analysis. A similar approach is taken by Agnete Weis Bentzon in her discussion of the judicial system and its function in West Greenland. Her problem is this: Can social scientific methods answer the question of whether West Greenland ought to be served by lay judges or by legally trained personnel?[42]

All the foregoing studies in this section used models developed within the framework of social psychological or ethnographical theories rather than models from jurisprudence. There is, however, one example—a comparative Scandinavian study on the use and nonuse of civil litigation— when treating commercial conflicts.[43] The study showed that commercial arbitration could be regarded as a functional alternative to litigation in certain areas where complicated legal and technical problems were at stake and the expert element was important for the decision making.

Discretion was used to a great extent, and arbitration aimed at reaching compromises rather than Zero-all solutions.[44] The activities followed three lines: discussions on the nature and the systematic position of sociology of law, presentations of earlier and current models used, and discussions about current projects. A result of this work was a special issue of *Acta Sociologica: Contributions to the Sociology of Law* in which Aubert Bentzon, Eckhoff, Goldschmidt, Kutschinsky, and Blegvad made contributions.[45] But by the end of the sixties the interest in this type of cooperation faded.

Phase Three: From Vacuum to Theoretizing

The end of the sixties did not have room for empirical and/or theoretical studies. The political dimensions became the focus of the debate, and Marxism and critical studies gave new perspectives.

However, by the middle of the seventies Goldschmidt finished a study on primary sanction behavior by the Danish members of the United Nations peace corps.[46] As in Greenland, he found that as a rule it was the lower ranks of an authoritative system—here the peace corps—which got the best results from their interventions. Quick, direct actions turned out to be advantageous.

This became a theme he also discussed in the press in relation to squatters (B-Z's) and occupiers of Christinia (a part of Copenhagen). Slowly sociology of law as a discipline got its new bearings.

The large, rather permanent sociology of law groups have been replaced by a loose, open system of shifting parties which sometimes join their forces for a specific cause like the book published in honor of Verner Goldschmidt (1988),[47] or a discussion initiated by a Scandinavian group[48] of Teubner's article of reflexive law. A third endeavor was the establishment of a periodical, *Retfaerd* (Justice), which is run by a board recruited from the Scandinavian countries.

Most of the recent publications do not use sociolegal models in the sense put forward by Eckhoff. Balvig[49] is perhaps one of the exceptions in establishing this mix of fact-finding and relating it to legal theories as well as sociological and psychological research in legal institutions, as Eckhoff says in his 1960 definition.

The fact that Eckhoff enlarged his perspective on law was evident in his 1976 article on law and politics: "I will distinguish between questions concerning whether activities 1) have had political consequences, 2) have their origin in political considerations or motives, and 3) whether these activities are connected to societal conditions under debate" (p. 19).[50]

He, as well as other researchers within the field, has accepted this perspective as crucial. One finds this in the debate established by the lawyer and philosopher Dalberg-Larsen[51] on the constitutional state, the welfare state, and the role of law; in works by the lawyer Stig Joergensen on the dilemma of democracy;[52] in the lawyer Ole Krarup's study of the role of labor legislation, where he places it between legal dogmatics and social theory.[53] Different views of political influence on law and gender problems are put forward by, on the one side, the lawyer Inger Koch-Nielsen in her more psychologically influenced studies on divorce[54] and its consequences and, on the other side, by the lawyer Hanne Petersen's important writings about labor legislation, the state, and women.[55] The common perspective here is that law is unsatisfactory as it starts for women from questionable perspectives. The lawyer Agnete Weis Bentzon has continued her work on the public administration of justice, again with a focus on the role of lay judges in countries like Greenland which are in transition from colonial to home rule status.[56] Finally, law and economics have been introduced as a mix by a lawyer. Blegvad has used both organizational and sociological perspectives on her continuing studies of dispute treatment and norm generation.[57] Here the political perspective is placed on the microlevel of the worker and the consumer in different studies of their voice.

The examples indicate that sociolegal studies need access to all types of experts. The pluralistic background of the development of sociology of law in Denmark may be an advantage from this viewpoint. Granted, our opinion holds that we can expect a continuing rather broad debate in Denmark.

Compared to the other Scandinavian countries, Denmark has been slow in accepting sociology as an independent science and in recognizing sociologists as forming a socially useful profession. A number of, partially coincidental, factors are responsible for this backwardness. Nevertheless, a not inconsiderable amount of research, mostly in the applied fields, has been carried out through the years. And the future looks more promising, in particular since a committee headed by Torben Agersnap is hard at work reorganizing the department of sociology at the University of Copenhagen.

NOTES

1. The main accounts of the history of sociology in Denmark are Jesper Due and Jorgen Steen Madsen, *Slip sociologien los* (Kobenhavn: Hans Reitzel 1983), 113–135; Mogens Blegvad, "Sociology and Philosophy—Some Reflections Occasioned by the paper presented by Harld Hoffding at the First Meeting of the Society for Philosophy and Psychology," *Danish Yearbook of Philosophy* 13

(1976), 221–241; and Preben Wolf, "Sociologiens historie ved Kobenhavns Universitet," *Sociolognyt* nr. 92 (Dec. 1984), 2–12. In addition, one may refer to the biographies of Joseph Davidsohn, Henning Friis, Theodor Geiger, Verner Goldschmidt, Torben Monberg, Svend Ranulf, Kare Svalastoga, C. N. Starcke, and Claudius Wilkens in *Dansk Biografisk Leksikon,* Tredie udgave, red. Sv. Cedergreen Bech. Bind 1–16 (Kobenhavn: Gyldendal, 1979–84).

2. Bibliographies of the works by Theodor Geiger may be found in *Acta sociologica* 1 (1956), 80–84 (the whole issue is dedicated to the memory of Geiger) and in Renate Mayntz, ed., *Theodor Geiger on Social Order and Mass Society* (Chicago: University of Chicago Press, 1969), 239–242.

3. Even the philosopher Jorgen Jorgensen, who was considered a logical positivist and who, as a member of the Copenhagen committee, had voted for Ranulf to become professor of sociology, was dissatisfied with this work. See his critical paper in *Socialt Tidsskrift* 23 (1946), 249–260.

4. Much of this section is based on information provided by John Andersen and Erik Jorgen Hansen, whom I thank for their cooperation.

5. The most important publications are Erik Jorgen Hansen, *Fordeling af levevilkarene* (Copenhagen: The Danish National Institute of Social Research, 1978–80); Erik Jorgen Hansen, *The Distribution of the Living Conditions in Denmark* (Copenhagen: The Danish National Institute of Social Research, 1982); Erik Jorgen Hansen, *Danskernes levekar—1986 sammenholdt med 1976* (Copenhagen: Hans Reitzels Forlag, 1986); and Erik Jorgen Hansen, *Generationer og Livsforlob i Danmark* (Copenhagen: Hans Reitzels Forlag, 1988). Results from the last two books are summarized in Erik Jorgen Hansen, "The Female Factor in the Changing Living Conditions," in E. J. Hansen et al., eds., *Scandinavian Trends in Living Conditions* (New York: M. E. Sharpe, 1991).

6. Peter Abrahamson, ed., *Welfare Stats in Crisis: The Crumbling of the Scandinavian Model?* (Copenhagen: Forlaget Sociologi, 1988); and Jan Peter Henriksen, "Some Perspectives on Scandinavian Welfare Research," *Acta Sociologica* 30, 3/4 (1987), 379–392.

7. See, among others, Peter Townsend, *Poverty in United Kingdom* (Hammondworth; Penguin, 1979).

8. John Andersen and Jorgen Elm Larsen, *Fattigdom i velfaerdstaten* (Copenhagen: Samfundslitteratur, 1989). Other studies of poverty that should be mentioned are Mogens Holm, ed., *Det splittede samfund. Om fattigdom og dualisering i velfaerdssamfundet* (Copenhagen: Samfundslitteratur, 1989); Iver Hornemann Moller, *Samfundet polariseres* (Aalborg: Aalborg Universitetsforlag); Finn Kenneth Hansen, *Materielle og sociale afsavn i samfundet* (Copenhagen: The Danish National Institute of Social Research, 1989), reviewed in Helge Hvid, "Ulighed, fattigdom og socialpolitik," *Dansk Sociologi* 1 (1990), 56–69.

9. We thank Thomas P. Boje and Reinhard Lund for fruitful discussions on this section.

10. Thomas P. Boje, "Segmentation and Mobility: An Analysis of Labour Market Flows on the Danish Labour Market," *Acta Sociologica* 29, 2 (1987), 171–178; and Thomas P. Boje, *Mobilitets-og beskaeftigelsesmonstre pa det danske arbejdsmarked 1980–81* (Roskilde: Roskilde University Centre, 1987).

11. Jesper Due and Jorgen Steen Madsen, *Nar der slas som i* (Copenhagen: Jurist-og Okonomforbundets Forlag, 1988).

12. Steen Scheuer, *Fagforeninger mellem kollektiv og profession* (Copenhagen: Nyt fra Samfundsvidenskaberne, 1985); and Steen Scheuer "Social Structure and Union Character," *Acta Sociologica* 29, 1 (1986), 45–50.

13. See articles by Rune Larsson, Reinhard Lund, Jorgen Moller, Soren Winter, Birte Bech Jorgensen, and Charlotte Block, in Peder J. Pedersen and Reinhard Lund, eds., *Unemployment. Theory, Policy and Structure* (New York: Walter de Gruyter, 1987).

14. We thank Ole Borre and Peter Gundelach for their proposals for this section.

15. Ole Borre, "Traek af den danske vaelgeradfaerd 1971–84," in Joergen Elklit and Ole Tonsgaard, eds., *Valg og vaelgeradfaerd. Studier i dansk politik* (Aarhus: Forlaget Politica, 1984), 148–166.

16. Ole Tonsgaard, "Hoejre og venstre i dansk politik," in Joergen Elklit and Ole Tonsgaard, eds., *To folketingsvalg* (Aarhus: Forlaget Politica, 1989), 107–134.

17. Ole Borre, "Traek af den danske vaelgeradfaerd 1971–84."

18. Karen Siune, "Bestemmer TV valgresultatet?," in Joergen Elklit and Ole Tonsgaard, eds., *Valg og vaelgeradfaerd. Studier i dansk politik* (Aarhus: Forlaget Politica, 1984), 132–147; Karen Siune, "EF-valg: Vaelgerpavirkning og vaelgerraektioner," op. cit., 353–368; Karen Siune, "Valgkampene og vaelgerne," in Joergen Elklit and Ole Tonsgaard, eds., *To folketingsvalg* (Aarhus: Forlaget Politica, 1989).

19. Peter Gundelach, *Graesroedder er seje* (Aarhus: Forlaget Politica, 1980); Peter Gundelach, "Grass-roots: Organizations, Societal Control and Dissolution of Norms," *Acta Sociologica* 25, supplement (1982), 57–66; Peter Gundelach, *Sociale beaegelser og samfundsaendringer* (Aarhus: Forlaget Politica, 1988); Leif Thomsen, *Den autoritaere by. Storbykrise, bykampe, sociale bevaegelser og lokal magt* (Copenhagen: Akademisk Forlag, 1981); and Lise Togeby, *Ens og forskellig* (Aarhus: Forlaget Politica, 1980).

20. Ronald Inglehardt, *The Silent Revolution* (Princeton: Princeton University Press, 1977).

21. Togeby, *Ens og forskellig,* 85–104.

22. Lars Iversen and Dorte Gannik have contributed to this section.

23. Lars Iversen and Svend Sabro, "Plant Closures, Unemployment and Health: Danish Experiences from the Declining Ship-Building Industry," in D. Schwefel, P-G. Svensson, Zollner, eds., *Unemployment, Social Vulnerability, and Health in Europe* (Berlin: Springer Verlag, 1987), 31–47.

24. Lars Iversen, O. Andersen, P. K. Andersen, K. Christoffersen and N. Keiding, "Unemployment and Mortality in Denmark, 1970–80." *British Medical Journal* 5 (1987), 85–92.

25. Tage Soendergaard Kristensen, *Kvinders arbejdsmiljoe* (Copenhagen: Fremad, 1978).

26. Laila Launso, "Integrated Medicine—a Challenge to the Health Care System," *Acta Sociologica* 32, 3 (1989), 237–251; and Laila Launso and Hanne Marie Jensen, *Sundhedsarbejde pa tvaers* (Copenhagen: Institute of Social Medicine, 1980).

27. Dorte Gannik and Marianne Jespersen, "Lay Concepts and Strategies for Handling Symptoms of Disease," *Scandinavian Journal of Primary Health Care* (1984), 67–76.

28. We thank Flemming Balvig for supplying information for this section.

29. Flemming Balvig, *Angst for Kriminalitet* (Copenhagen: Gyldendal, 1978).

30. Flemming Balvig, "Fear of Crime in Scandinavia—New Reality, New Theory?," in A. Snare, ed., *Violence in Scandinavia. Scandinavian Studies in Criminology* (Oslo: Norwegian University Press, 1990).

31. Jacob Hilden Windsloew, *Narreskibet* (Copenhagen: SocPol, 1984). Some of the results are summarized in Jacob Hilden Windsloew, "Drug Abuse Treatment as a Cause of Excess Mortality among Danish Drug Abusers," in Per Stangeland, ed. *Drugs and Drug Control. Scandinavian Studies in Criminology* (Oslo: Norwegian University Press, 1987), 87–100.

32. Flemming Balvig, *The Snow-White Image. The Hidden Reality of Crime in Switzerland* (Oslo: Norwegian University Press, 1988); Flemming Balvig, *Den tyvagtige dansker* (Copenhagen: Borgen, 1987); and Ulla Bondesen, *Prison and Prisoners* (Rutgers, N.J.: Transaction, 1990).

33. See also in the previous text—Section III: Criminology.

34. The section is based on five articles which may be regarded as a continuing evaluation of Scandinavian sociology of law: Thorstein Eckhoff, "Sociology of law in Scandinavia," *Scandinavian Studies in Law* (1960), 31–58; Britt-Mari Blegvad, "The System Position of Sociology of Law in Current Scandinavian Research," in Britt-Mari Blegvad, ed., *Contribution to the Sociology of Law, Acta Sociologica,* vol. 10, fasc. 1–2 (Copenhagen, 1966); Britt-Mari Blegvad, "The Consumer and the Scandinavian Sociology of Law," *Archiv fur Rechts—und Sozialphilosophie,* vol. 1971, 57/1, and "Sociology of Law in Denmark, Its Origin, Development and Present Perspective."

35. Torgny Segerstedt, G. Karlsson, and B. Rundbald, "A Research into the General Sense of Justice," *Theoria* (1949), 15.

36. Berl Kutschinsky, "Knowledge and Attitudes Regarding Legal Phenomena in Denmark," in N. Christie, ed., *Scandinavian Studies in Criminology* 2, (1966).

37. Theodor Geiger, "Vorstudien zu einer Soziologie des Rechts," *Acta Jutlandia* (Kobenhavn, 1947). See also in sections I and II of the text.

38. Alf Ross, *On Law and Justice* (London, 1958).

39. Agnete Weis Bentzon, "Verner Goldschmidt," in Henning Sorensen and Egil Fivelsdal, eds., *From Marx to Habermas* (Nyt fra Samfundsviden-skaberne, 1988).

40. Verner Goldschmidt, "The Greenland Criminal Code and Its Sociological Background," *Acta Sociologica,* vol. 1, fasc. 4; and Verner Goldschmidt, "New Trends on the Studies in the Society of Greenland. A Miscellany in Honour of Birket Schmidt," "Folk", (Copenhagen, 1966).

41. Britt-Mari Blegvad, ed., *Contributions of Sociology of Law, Acta Sociologica,* vol. 10, fasc, 102 (Copenhagen, 1966). Eckhoff's paper in *Acta Sociologica* might, by the way, be mentioned as one of the (few) examples of Scandinavian sociolegal analysis which has influenced American sociolegal theory.

42. Agnete Weis Bentzon, "The Structure of the Judicial System and Its Function in a Developing Society," in Britt-Mari Blegvad, ed., *Contributions to the Sociology to the Sociology of Law, Acta Sociologica,* vol. 10, fasc. 1–2 (Copenhagen, 1966).

43. Britt-Mari Blegvad, "A Case-study of Inter-organizational conflict," in Nils Christie, ed., *Scandinavian Studies in Criminology* 2 (1968).

44. Britt-Mari Blegvad, P. Bolding, Ole lando, *Arbitration as a Means of Solving Conflicts* (Copenhagen, 1973).

45. *Acta Sociologica,* vol. 10, fasc. 1–2 (1966), edited by Britt-Mari Persson Blegvad.

46. Verner Goldschmidt, "Primary Sanction Behaviour," in Britt-Mari Blegvad, ed., *Contribution to the Sociology of Law, Acta Sociologica,* vol. 10, fasc. 1–2 (Copenhagen, 1966).

47. Agnete Weis Bentzon, "Verner Goldschmidt," 163.

48. Asmund Born, et al., eds., *Refleksiv ret. Reflexive Law.*

49. See also in the previous text—Section III: Criminology.

50. T. Eckhoff, "Juss og politikk" (Law and politics), in *Kritisk Juss* (1976), 18–60.

51. J. Dalberg-Larsen, *The Welfare State and Its Law* (Berlin and Vilseck: Verlag Dr. Tesdorf).

52. Stig Joergensen, *Demokratiets Dilemma* (The Dilemma of Democracy. (Arhus: Juridisk Bogformidling, 1981).

53. Ole Krarup, *Arbejdsretten* (Labour Law). (Copenhagen: Hans Reitzels Forlag, 1980).

54. Inger Koch-Nielsen, *Skilsmisser* (Divorces). SFI, Publikation 118 (1982).

55. Hanne Petersen, "A Feminist Perspective on Industrial Relations in the Public Sector," Kobenhavns universitet, 1986.

56. Agnete Weis Bentzon, *Forholdet mellen den statslige lovgivning og de folkelige retsopfattelser* (Relationship between Government Legislation and Legislation and Popular Ideas). (Institut for Nordisk Ratt, 1988).

57. Britt-Mari Blegvad, "Commercial Relations, Contract and Court in Denmark—a Discussion of Macaulay's Contracting Theory," *Law and Society Review,* no. 2 (1990).

5

The Development and Present State of Sociology in Finland

Erik Allardt

EARLY HISTORY: SOCIAL CHANGE AND THE RISE OF SOCIOLOGICAL INQUIRY

Sociology was academically established comparatively early in Finland. The first teacher of sociology at the University of Helsinki was appointed in 1890. The 1890s was a period of intensive economic and social development in Finland. Due to its forests and the greatly increased demand for paper products on the world market, Finland was quickly drawn into the world economy. The economic breakthrough was followed by bustling cultural activity, social innovations, and rapid development of Finnish scientific life. Particularly two schools of social science research rose to eminence and influence. The first and internationally known of these two traditions was ethnosociological in content and founded by Edward Westermarck. The other school centered on descriptions of social problems and their structural origins in the Finnish society.

Westermarck and his pupils concentrated on the evolution of social institutions. His own main works, *The History of Human Marriage*[1] and *The Origin and Development of the Moral Ideas,*[2] not only were pieces of meticulous empirical research but exerted in their days also an influence on British cultural climate and life. During several decades Edward Westermarck held simultaneously professorships both at the London School of Economics and at Finnish universities. Westermarck's ethnosociological school was empirical in orientation in the style of British social and cultural anthropology. Fieldwork was done by Westermarck[3] in Morocco, by Rafael Karsten[4] in South America, and by Gunnar Landtman[5] in New Guinea. Their work was by no means untheoretical and devoid of general social science interest. In his book on the origin of the moral ideas, Westermarck analyzed the very foundation of the social order,[6] and Landtman's[7] main theme was the sources and origin of social inequality. A work with direct focus on the state and politics was Rudolf Holsti's doctoral dissertation, "The Relation of War to the Origin of State."[8] Holsti was not only Westermarck's student but also Finland's foreign minister during 1919–1922 and 1936–1938. Another work with interest for the study of political systems was Rafael Karsten's[9] work on the Inca state.

The members of the school of structural social research were more numerous than the adherents of the Westermarckian tradition. Their main focus was the rural proletariat, which had grown large by the end of the nineteenth century, and their inspiration came from the German historical school of political economy with Gustav Schmoller as the foremost representative. The German focus on the "labor question" was in Finland transformed to an emphasis on the "agrarian question." Despite the obvious national orientation and the lack of more intensive international contacts, the Finnish school of structural social research was intellectually rich and powerful. Its influence on later Finnish sociology has, in fact, been stronger than that of Edward Westermarck and his disciples. The school of structural social research also had a considerable influence on some large-scale social reforms in Finnish society. A great number of studies on Finnish society were conducted by the members of the school of structural research.[10] Aksel Warén's study of the tenant farmers,[11] Eino Kuusi's[12] descriptions of seasonal unemployment, and Jaakko Forsman's[13] analysis of why socialism spread in the Finnish countryside are examples of studies with lasting sociological and political interest.

Compared to the bustling first decades of the twentieth century the period between the two World Wars represents a time of tranquility if not downright intellectual poverty for the development of Finnish social science. The fate of the two traditions of sociology discussed above is revealing. Both traditions lost their momentum, but for different reasons.

Finland's declaration of independence on December 6, 1917, was followed in January–May 1918 by a civil war between whites and reds. Unlike in the neighboring Russia, in Finland the whites won a complete victory. The 1920s and 1930s became a period of national consolidation as regards both cultural life and economic development. In the humanities academic subjects which supposedly could strengthen national solidarity and integration, such as history and folklore, were supported and flourished. A socially critical school such as the school of structural social research could not develop further in a climate with a basically right-wing orientation. Analysts of the welfare policies in Finland have pointed out how the winners of the civil war pursued an antireformist policy as regards the industrial working class, but nevertheless succeeded in mitigating the conflicts between the landowning farmers and the landless rural population.[14] A contributing fact in the decline of the school was that due to land reforms its main object of study, the landless population, had ceased to exist.

The reasons for the decline of the research tradition of Edward Westermarck were quite different. The school was, as already mentioned, strongly international in its orientation, but in the early 1920s it had lost much of its international and cultural importance. Edward Westermarck was a late representative of ethnological evolutionism. After World War I new orientations such as functionalism as represented by Bronislaw Malinowski, Westermarck's successor at the London School of Economics, began to replace it as a salient theoretical orientation. The lost momentum was reflected in Finland in the fact that the internationally famous members of the Westermarckian school had already taken their Ph.D.s before World War I and that the recruitment of new disciples in the 1920s and 1930s clearly declined. There were some important individual exceptions, but they all represented new developments. Two of them become professors at the two universities, a Finnish-language one and a Swedish-language one, in the city of Turku. Uno Harva was professor of sociology at the University of Turku, whereas K. Rob. V. Wikman became professor at the Swedish-language Åbo Academy. Both of them were oriented toward phenomena and studies related to their own society and culture. Harva was a specialist of religion and social relationships among the Fenno-Ugric peoples[15] and Wikman's main study focused on marriage and family patterns in the Swedish-speaking populations in Sweden, Finland, and the Baltic countries.[16] A third sociologist trained in the Westermarckian tradition but departing on new paths was Hilma Granqvist, who specialized in family life and training of children among the Arabs. She received very little academic recognition in Finland beyond her Ph.D. thesis,[17] but she had a good international reputation in her field of study.

Also the tradition of structural social research was represented by some outstanding individuals who followed new paths. Eino Kuusi wrote useful and thorough presentations on social policy as it had developed in the European countries.[18] Of particular importance for the development of sociology was Heikki Waris, who was professor of social policy at the University of Helsinki between 1948 and 1969. Although it was presented in the department of history, his doctoral dissertation was the first sociological treatise in the modern sense of the word, and it was also the first one influenced by American sociology. It was a study of the rise of the working-class community and suburbs in Helsinki at the end of the nineteenth century.[19] Heikki Waris had studied at the University of Chicago, and his treatise also bore clear marks of influence from the Chicago school of the 1920s.

Related to the concerns of the school of structural social research there was a tradition for study of criminality and drinking of alcoholic beverages. The latter interest was strongly spurred by the temperance movement,

which in all the Scandinavian countries had considerable political importance and backing. A pathbreaking study of the so-called alcohol question
was Matti Helenius-Seppälä's doctoral dissertation, presented at the University of Copenhagen in 1902.[20] In Finland the foremost bearer of the
European criminological traditions was Veli Verkko, who in 1947 became
the first professor of sociology at the University of Helsinki after sociology
had been redefined to deal also with industrial society. Internationally he
became known particularly for his studies of crimes against life and their
relationship to drinking habits.[21]

INSTITUTIONALIZATION OF SOCIOLOGY

Despite the existence of chairs in sociology prior to World War II, it
seems correct to say that sociology had to be established anew in the
postwar years. Previous teaching in sociology had mainly been based on
ethnological descriptions and studies of non-European cultures, whereas
the industrial and particularly the Finnish society now came into the focus
of attention. American sociology with its strong empirical bent was supposed to be the model to be followed. The same patterns prevailed in all
Scandinavian countries. When sociology in its present form was established at the Scandinavian universities after World War II, it developed
in an academic milieu with a positivistic orientation. The quest for middle-
range theories and precise measurement methods had a positive appeal in
the postwar situation with its wariness of big theories and metaphysical
speculations.

One important part of the institutionalization was the development and
creation of a national sociological association. It bears the name of Westermarck Society, and it was founded in November 1940. Its aim was declared to be "the furthering of sociological and philosophical research." It
was assumed that a principal activity of the Society would be to cherish
the memory and work of Edward Westermarck (1862–1939). In reality the
society developed into the national sociological association.

The Westermarck Society represents Finland on the Council of the International Sociological Association. It organizes meetings and an annual
national convention. One of the activities of the Westermarck Society has
been to publish bibliographies of Finnish sociology. The first covered the
years 1945–1959,[22] the second the decade of 1960–1969,[23] the third the
years 1970–1979,[24] and the fourth the five-year period 1980–1984.[25] The
bibliographies provide an excellent source for describing the development
of Finnish sociology after World War II.

The bibliography for the years 1945–1959 reveals that it took some time
before the new sociology could get off the ground. The Finnish sociological
literature of the second half of the 1940s was still almost entirely based
on work and ideas prevailing before World War II. The largest fields for

the whole fifteen-year period according to the bibliography are social anthropology, urban and rural sociology, criminology and deviant behavior,
and the study of alcohol consumption and drinking. All of them were
already important before the reorientation of academic sociology. Yet in
the 1940s some new important works were published. Of particular importance was Heikki Waris's comprehensive book on the structure of
Finnish society, used as a basic textbook for many decades.[26] Veli Verkko
continued his studies based on interpretations of criminal statistics.[27] The
first doctoral thesis reflecting a new orientation and produced by Knut
Pipping,[28] a member of the postwar generation, was based on personal
war experiences and analyzed a machine-gun company as a social unit.

Yet, the second half of the 1940s was in Finland still a passive period
as regards sociological publication activities. Some of the initial difficulties
of the new sociology were definitely related to Finland's economic difficulties in the postwar situation. It is revealing to make comparisons with
Norway, where sociology rapidly grew rich and active in the immediate
postwar period. Norway had been on the winning side in the war, and
leading American sociologists showed keen interest in visiting Norway. In
Finland the time from 1945 until the so-called Korean boom around 1952
was a period of political readjustment, economic sparsity, and national
concentration on paying the economically demanding war reparations to
the Soviet Union. Foreign books could not be bought, foreign contacts
were sparse, and travel to other countries rare. Yet, there was a very
strong urge to gather knowledge about American sociology in particular,
and many ingenious devices were used in getting new information about
scientific developments.

The bibliography also reveals the dependence on the fashions of American sociology. In the 1940s and early 1950s American sociology had a
strong social psychological bent. It was a time of group dynamics and small
group research. In the Finnish bibliography this is reflected by the fact
that items classified as social psychology are comparatively much more
numerous than in the later bibliographies. New fields developing in the
1950s were the study of norms and roles, political sociology, and industrial
sociology.

During the 1950s an increasing number of sociological dissertations were
presented by the postwar academic generation and written in the style of
modern sociology. At the end of the 1950s the first modern Finnish textbook of sociology was published. The book,[29] its new editions, and their
Swedish translations[30] were used for many decades as introductory texts
both in Finland and Sweden. A useful introductory text in the methods of
sociology was published in 1962.[31]

Journals and monograph series were published and developed in the
1950s and 1960s. A joint Scandinavian journal *Acta Sociologica* was started
in 1955 and became an important outlet for studies all over Scandinavia.

The Westermarck Society had already started its own monograph series, Transactions of the Westermarck Society, in 1947, but it became a truly important publication outlet in the 1960s. Some of the Transactions of the 1960s received international recognition such as the volume *Cleavages, Ideologies and Party Systems* containing important contributions by well-known political sociologists such as S. M. Lipset, Juan Linz, S. N. Eisenstadt, Stein Rokkan, and others.[32] A domestic journal *Sosiologia* with papers in Finnish and occasionally also in Swedish started in 1962. It became a success from the start, and it is not only read by sociologists but also observed by mass media in general.

By 1990 sociology was a well-established academic discipline in Finland. It is represented in ten universities and colleges, and it is considered among the basic social sciences in the faculties of social science all over the country.

A Finnish specialty also in comparison with the other Scandinavian countries has been the division of sociology into two different and separate academic disciplines, sociology and social policy. There are chairs and departments in both sociology and social policy at all social science faculties at Finnish universities. Social policy as an academic subject was planned and conceived to focus systematically on the development, prerequisites, and effects of social legislation, social security reforms, and welfare provisions. With the institutionalization of the welfare state the difference between sociology and social policy as academic disciplines has become obscure and difficult to observe. In sociology the welfare institutions have to be analyzed on par with other societal institutions. It is still practical and fruitful to have special chairs for social policy and social administration, but the rationale for treating sociology and social policy as different subjects has more or less ceased to exist.

TRENDS IN THEORY AND METHODOLOGY BEFORE 1970

The last years of the 1960s formed a watershed in the theoretical and methodological development. The student revolt at the end of the 1960s (often dated to 1968 due to the events in Paris in May of that year) was not as violent in Finland and the other Scandinavian countries as in many Continental countries, or in the United States and Japan. The student revolt did, however, occur also in Finland, and it had profound effects on the development of sociology.[33,34] At any rate, the developments before and after 1970 differ clearly from each other.

Before the end of the 1960s there was comparatively little interest in grand theory in Finnish sociology. Theoretical interests and orientations were by no means nonexistent, but under the influence of American sociology, there was a strong orientation toward middle-range theories.

In Finnish sociology there has always been, as already indicated, a strong interest in macrosociological analyses of social structure and change. These studies were for the most part untheoretical and descriptive, but they were nevertheless guided by some general notions about master processes of structural change, industrialization, and modernization. General descriptive outlines of social change in the Finnish society were published by Heikki Waris both in 1948[35] and in 1968.[36] A more quantitative approach was used by Paavo Seppänen.[37] He collected time series data for more than 100 variables for every year between 1911 and 1961 and submitted the data to factor analysis in various ways.

In the bibliography of Finnish sociology for the years 1945–1959 there were only a few items under the heading of political sociology. During the 1960s political sociology became an important field and was closely related to the interest in macrosociology. As was the case internationally, Finnish political sociology in the 1960s focused on the relationship between social class and political behavior. In the 1960s there were several studies of the basic cleavages and conflicts in Finnish politics.[38,39,40] Some studies dealt with the differences in the social background of Backwoods and Industrial Communism, which in the postwar decades was a very salient division in Finnish political radicalism.[41] Also, attitudinal studies of conditions for democratic and nonauthoritarian behavior were conducted.[42]

Among other studies with a macrosociological bent was Elina Haavio-Mannila's study of village fights in traditional Finnish rural society.[43] It was one of the few Finnish studies containing an application of functional analysis. It indicated that village fights were frequent in those parts of Finland in which the village was the key unit in the social structure, and that the institutionalized village fights deteriorated to fights with knives and drunken brawls when land ownership was restricted in such a fashion that economic cooperation within the village was no longer necessary.

In addition to the above-mentioned studies that applied theoretical ideas in an instrumental and practical manner, there were a few studies presenting theoretical ideas which became applied outside the domain originally studied. The theories and categories of Emile Durkheim were used by Erik Allardt in analyses of political radicalism and patterns of modernization.[44,45] The theoretical framework developed led to international discussions,[46] and it was domestically applied in a number of studies in other fields of sociology. Among these was Veronica Stolte Heiskanen's work on the prerequisites for different kinds of kinship structures and patterns of personal influence within families.[47]

Another theoretical development with general effects was the studies of power and influence conducted by the social psychologists Kullervo Rainio[48] and Antti Eskola.[49] The book on social psychology by Antti Eskola published in Finnish in 1971[50] and then translated to Swedish, Norwegian,

Danish, and Dutch[51] became widely acclaimed as a very useful text in the field.

In the 1960s and 1970s Finnish sociologists tended to be very quantitative in their methodological approaches. Quantitative methods were of course used everywhere, but in Finland the quantitative methodology had some special features. Foreigners were often astonished by the fact that Finnish sociologists at that period frequently used factor analysis of some variety in their studies. Factor analysis became a sort of standard method in Finnish studies. Yrjö Ahmavaara, a theoretical physicist turned behavioral scientist, invented transformation analysis, by which factor matrices obtained from different populations could be quantitatively and mathematically compared.[52] The use of factor analysis in sociological analyses contained many pitfalls, but it led to a general interest in the development of multivariate statistical methods.

One particular methodological problem that attracted great attention among Finnish sociologists was that of contextual analysis in the sense of Paul Lazarsfeld. The importance of using variables denoting both individual and collective properties was emphasized.[53,54] Later, when Tapani Valkonen made this problem the object of several interrelated studies, the problem appeared more complicated and multifaceted than had been assumed.[55,56]

Mathematical models for theory building were rarely used by Finnish sociologists. An exception was a stochastic model for social contacts developed by Kullervo Rainio, professor of social psychology at the University of Helsinki.[57]

Another side of the preference for quantitative analysis was that methods of qualitative analysis such as participant observation only rarely were used. There were some exceptions such as the already mentioned study by Knut Pipping on the social life in a machine-gun company.[58]

RECENT THEORETICAL AND METHODOLOGICAL TRENDS

As already emphasized, the student revolt at the end of the 1960s had despite its nonviolent character some profound effects on sociology in Finland. This is not astonishing considering that sociology students were strongly mobilized by the revolt and that in Finland as in many other countries several leaders of the protests were students in sociology. The revolt introduced a new interest in Marxism and in conflict-oriented perspectives generally.

Yet the effects of the student revolt and its aftermath on Finnish sociology are hard to pinpoint because they were both penetrating and small. The effects were small in terms of substance: most types of now ongoing research have their roots in work in progress when the student revolt came. Yet the changes were profound as regards some general and international orientations.

The dependence on American sociology began to weaken. It did not disappear, but the earlier tendency to take American sociology as a given model more or less disappeared. Citation studies have also shown that the number of references to American sources decreased.[59]

At the same time, Finnish sociology became more pluralistic in its emphases and orientations. Marxist approaches, traditional American sociology, and influences from new schools such as the French semiotics, offshoots from the critical Frankfurt school, and rational choice models exist side by side.

It was said that the student revolt brought Marxism back into sociology. This was, as we know, an international phenomenon, but it meant slightly different things in different countries. In Finland it meant that many sociologists indicated some interest in Marxist ideas and thoughts but that only a very few confined themselves to Marxism. In most cases it really meant a pluralistic orientation. Only a few serious studies of Marxist theoretical thought have appeared. One of those is Jukka Gronow's doctoral dissertation presented at the University of Helsinki, on the relationship between the ideas of Kautsky and Marx.[60] Another study was Seppo Toiviainen's analysis of the young Lucács.[61]

The new popularity of Marxism in the early 1970s also increased the interest in other founding fathers and classical writers of sociology such as Max Weber, Emile Durkheim, and Georg Simmel. Small informal reading groups scrutinizing Max Weber's main works sprang up. Translations of the classical works of sociology began to appear. Emile Durkheim's main works were translated into Finnish by Seppo Randell, professor of sociology at the University of Tampere, ending his work in 1990 by the publication of a translation of the book on the division of labor.[62]

The strong interest in Marxist theory in the early 1970s faded away toward the end of the 1970s. It is still difficult to assess the importance of the Marxist revival and its fading away almost within a decade. In the beginning of the 1970s professors and teachers lost much of their authority unless they were willing to go along with the new trends and fashions. By the 1990s some of this authority had been restored but, as said, the situation is more pluralistic than it was in the 1960s when the leftist-oriented activism began to emerge. The increased pluralism and the tolerance for different paradigms and approaches also had their liabilities. Particularly in the 1980s a loss of community could be observed among the sociologists. In the first postwar decades the sociologists formed an academic community with shared knowledge, common aims, and a basic agreement about what constitutes good sociology. The 1980s was characterized by the tendency to form factions that used a language of their own and tended to develop their own particularistic code systems. By 1990 a greater unity could again be observed although the situation still was diffuse and difficult to penetrate.

In the 1970s some large-scale analyses of the predicament of Finnish society were inspired by Marxism. One study focused on the economic bases of the steering mechanisms in Finnish society. This study was commissioned by the Finnish Social Science Research Council in order to analyze the conditions of equality and democracy in Finnish society.[63] At the same time the Social Science Research Council commissioned a parallel study by political scientists with a supposedly different and less leftist frame of reference.[64] Both studies presented important information without being dogmatically confined to their assumed ideological commitments. In the early 1970s the commissioning of the two studies created a vivid and at times stormy debate in the Finnish mass media. A theoretically more astute but also more systematically Marxist research program was carried out under the title of *The Finnish Capitalism* with Pekka Kosonen as its major editor.[65] Pekka Kosonen later continued his analyses by combining the Marxist perspective with other approaches in interesting and revealing comparative analyses of the predicament of the Scandinavian welfare state.[66]

Ellsworth Fuhrman, an American specialist in the sociology of science, and his Finnish assistant, Erkki Kaukonen, analyzing Finnish sociology, conclude that in the mid-70s the large projects on Finnish capitalism caught public interest but that by the end of the 1970s these projects were no longer part of public debate. They also speak of two other important developments in the 1970s.[67] One was a strong new interest in studies of the welfare state, an interest which almost simultaneously proliferated in all the Scandinavian countries in the 1970s. The new interest led to very concrete and empirical studies, but they did have a clear background in democratic theory.

As a political model the Scandinavian welfare state was already being discussed in the 1930s. In comparison with the economists, sociologists were late in focusing their interest on the special forms and attributes of the Scandinavian welfare state. This lag was probably due to a strong dependence on American sources in the formative years of Scandinavian sociology. At any rate, toward the end of the 1960s and the beginning of the 1970s, an emerging and rapidly enlarging interest developed in welfare research. This new interest was related to the social indicator movement, which grew strong in the international social science community toward the end of the 1960s. The Scandinavian interest in social indicators was definitely focused on the question of how people live in a welfare state. A strong tradition arose of conducting surveys of how well individuals actually fare in the Scandinavian states. This research tradition has recently been well described in *The Scandinavian Model: Welfare States and*

Welfare Research, edited by Robert Erikson, Erik Jørgen Hansen, Stein Ringen, and Hannu Uusitalo.[68] Typical of Scandinavian surveys of citizen well-being has been their attempt to capture comprehensively most aspects of people's level of living, the reliance on objective rather than on subjective attitudinal indicators, and an interest in the problem of inequality. A Finnish contribution was the comparative study of the level of well-being in Denmark, Finland, Norway, and Sweden conducted by the Research Group for Comparative Sociology at the University of Helsinki in the first half of the 1970s.[69] It was influenced by the first Swedish Level of Living Survey, but it also very clearly departed from the Swedish model by introducing measures of the quality of life and subjective attitudinal indicators.[70]

Whereas the welfare studies in the 1970s were based on measuring the level of welfare and well-being by social indicators, the research interest in Finland, as in the other Scandinavian countries, turned in the 1980s toward an interest into the institutional buildup of the welfare state. Several large-scale comparative projects were developed. An excellent chapter on Finland was written by Matti Alestalo and Hannu Uusitalo in a large report on the West European welfare states after World War II, edited and led by Peter Flora from Mannheim.[71] Also other Finnish sociologists such as Kyösti Raunio contributed with substantial reports about the predicament of the welfare state.[72]

A distinguishing feature of the Finnish as well as the other Scandinavian studies of well-being and the welfare state is that they clearly relate social policies to the overall social structure and to the political system. Conventional research on social policy often concentrated solely on descriptions of the policy measures, but the new type of welfare research presents social policy in a general societal context. Thereby the welfare studies have contributed decisively to another and very important theoretical development, namely, to an increasing attempt to combine a structural and an institutional approach. There is a new interest in analyzing how the welfare state and its institutional arrangements mold the class structure and social stratification in society. This is very evident in Matti Alestalo's study of the development of the Finnish class structure with the illuminating title *Structural Change, Classes and the State.*[73] Pekka Kosonen's studies of the Scandinavian welfare states share the same feature in combining institutional and structural analysis.[74]

The second new feature of Finnish sociology in the 1970s mentioned by Fuhrman and Kaukonen was an increasing interest in studies of ways of life and the everyday culture. In this field there has been an emphasis on problems of the individual, subjectivity, and everyday life. Important studies in the field have often been led and initiated by J. P. Roos.[75,76] An influential monograph in the field was written by Matti Kortteinen on the life in a Helsinki suburb.[77] The way of life studies have been related to a general new interest in the study of culture and cultural habits in modern urban conditions.[78] The writings of the French sociologist Pierre Bourdieu have exerted a crucial influence on the way of life studies.[79]

Fuhrman and Kaukonen emphasize perceptively some of the positive side-effects of the way of life studies. They indicate how the new orientation enlarged the methodological arsenal of Finnish sociologists to include qualitative methods, and they hint at the possibility that it also helped some of the Marxists out of the deadlock in which they had been led by a dogmatic adherence to Marxism.

In the 1970s and 1980s the use of qualitative methods certainly strongly increased and became used in many empirical sociological studies. Yet the technique in itself—in other words, the rules for collecting data by observation, by qualitative interviews, by participatory techniques, and so forth—hardly implied anything that had not been known and taught before. The novelty in the popularity of qualitative methods was related to semiotics and to the ways of describing and interpreting the cultural meanings of social action, habits, and institutions. Furthermore, the rules for interpreting and the methods for establishing cultural meanings are not found in textbooks, but rather they are seen in empirical studies of specific social phenomena. They often deal with trivial, everyday phenomena. Good examples of such studies are one about the meaning of drinking in local pubs[80] and another one about the semiotics of sex and gender.[81]

Simultaneously with the increased talk about qualitative methods, the quantitative methodology has less ostensibly but also rapidly developed. New multivariate techniques have become widely used. In particular there has existed a need for methods simultaneously enabling conclusions about causal mechanisms and accounting for a great number of explanatory or independent variables. An illuminating example is a methodological solution by Tapani Valkonen and Tuija Martelin in combining the conventional method of elaboration in explanatory survey research, a causal ordering of the independent variables, and log-linear regression analysis.[82]

CURRENT RESEARCH IN PROMINENT SUBFIELDS

By the 1990s there existed in Finland sociological studies in practically all subfields of sociology. They cannot all be mentioned here, and it seems reasonable to focus particularly on studies representing a clear continuation of already strong fields, on one hand, and on studies from newly emerged and strengthened fields on the other.

Macrosociology, including analyses of the welfare state, studies of social stratification, and political sociology, has continued to be a major orientation. In the field of welfare studies Hannu Uusitalo's study of the effects of the welfare state and structural change on the income distribution in Finland during the years 1966–1985 is worth a special mention.[83] In political sociology the major recent work is Risto Alapuro's book *State and Revolution in Finland* analyzing the state formation, national integration, and class struggles by which present-day Finland was formed.[84] An important and well-edited textbook currently in its second edition by Tapani Valkonen and others presents the basic social formations and structural divisions in Finnish society.[85]

The study of social stratification has grown and become differentiated by many different approaches. An international research project with ten participant countries, led by Erik Olin Wright, also included Finland and has resulted in several interesting publications. On the basis of comparative data of the project, Raimo Blom[86] and Markku Kivinen[87] have initiated discussions of both intercountry variations and recent thorough changes of the class structure in modern nations. Likewise, on the basis of comparative data Seppo Pöntinen has published several studies on social mobility, among them his doctoral dissertation about social mobility in the Scandinavian welfare states.[88] On the whole the comparative aspect has become a strong element in Finnish stratification studies. Some of the comparative analyses describe the rise and decline of different sectors and occupational groups. Timo Toivonen studied the development of the proportions of entrepreneurs in Denmark, Finland, and Sweden from 1930 onwards for five decades.[89] A very crucial phenomenon in present-day Scandinavian societies has been the rapid rise of public employment. It has been studied by Matti Alestalo and some of his Scandinavian colleagues. Some of their results appeared in a 1990 joint Scandinavian publication, edited by the Norwegian Jon Eivind Kolberg, on the predicament of the Nordic welfare state.[90]

Some new fields with a macrosociological bent came into existence or were revived in the 1970s and 1980s. One was the sociology of language and sociolinguistics. Most studies have dealt with either the Swedish-speaking minority in Finland or the Finnish-speaking minority in Sweden, but also some theoretical and comparative studies were published. Tom Sandlund discussed the relationship between language and class in his dissertation of 1976,[91] and Erik Allardt conducted a comparative study of the ethnic revival and the territorial linguistic minorities in Western Europe.[92] Two very interesting studies on language change were published in the late 1980s. One was Marjut Aikio's study of language shifts between the Sami language and Finnish in Finnish Lapland,[93] and the other was Marika Tandefelt's study of language shifts from Swedish to Finnish in the Helsinki region.[94] Analyses of the formation of ethnic identities in many different groups have been conducted by Karmela Liebkind.[95]

As in other West European countries the study of sex and gender became an important field of study toward the end of the 1960s. So-called women's studies were already actively pursued in Finland on behalf of the Finnish women's movement at the turn of the century. Women's studies

as part of sociology did not, however, become important until the revival
of the women's movement in the 1960s and 1970s. One very well written
study in the field of social history on the battle over sexual morality at the
turn of the century was published by Armas Nieminen in 1951.[96] In the
1960s the field was revived by Elina Haavio-Mannila with a book published in 1968 about Finnish men and women.[97] She continued the work
with a long range of studies conducted both by herself and by colleagues
from other Scandinavian societies.[98] An interesting comparison of the
women's movement from different periods was made by Riitta Jallinoja.[99]
Initially the revival of the study of sex and gender led to studies of sex
roles and to statistical analyses of equality between men and women in
the working life, in education, and in politics. In the 1980s there was a
new orientation toward a study of the total gender system which defines
and regulates identities of men and women in different realms of society.[100]
Several sociology departments such as the ones at the University of Helsinki, Åbo Academy, University of Tampere, and University of Jyväskylä
have active research groups for the study of the gender system. A large-
scale new research program on the gender system in the welfare system
began in 1990 by support from the Social Science Research Council and
the Academy of Finland under the supervision of Liisa Rantalaiho and
Raija Julkunen.

In the 1950s and 1960s Finnish sociologists often conducted social ecological studies based on data about the smallest administrative unit in
Finnish society, the communes, and on the use of multivariate techniques
such as factor analysis.[101,102] Geographical and structural differentiation on
the basis of ecological data was easy to study because of the availability
of statistical data for long periods. In the last decades the problems of
geographical and ecological differentiation have focused on the center-
periphery distinction and the social life and problems in peripheries. The
methodology has been qualitative, and based on observations and unstruc-
tured interviews. A good example is provided by Pertti Rannikko's study
of the decline of peripheral villages in eastern Finland.[103] Another study
is Kirsti Suolinna and Kaisa Sinikara's descriptive but revealing analysis
of a peripheral village dominated by a religious revival movement.[104]

The social and human aspects of threats against nature and the ecological balance have naturally caught the interest of sociologists. By the year
1990 very few studies had been published. Liisa Uusitalo has published
studies of the environmental impacts of consumption patterns,[105] Timo
Järvikoski has studied the effects of water regulation measures on the local
community,[106] and Ilmo Massa has edited a thought-provoking reader on
the relationships between energy production-consumption and cultural development.[107] Sociologists have been active within many government commissions and committees dealing with protecting the environment,
planning sustainable development and developing methods for future

studies, and assessing technology. More massive contributions both by sociologists and for the benefit of general sociology are probably yet to come.

The study of alcohol consumption and drinking has been an important subfield in Finnish sociology. The State Alcohol Monopoly established in 1950 a research program and a research institute which was to become the most important sociological research unit outside the universities. Its importance was based both on the fact that the Alcohol Monopoly had more money at its disposal than other research units and a skillful and enlightened leadership. In particular its development was influenced by sociologically trained administrators such as Pekka Kuusi,[108] who was to become managing director of the Alcohol Monopoly, and by the longtime director of the institute, Kettil Bruun.[109] The Research Institute for Alcohol Studies has become an international leader in its field with highly acclaimed studies of the measurement and precise recording of drinking habits,[110] thorough studies of international consumption patterns,[111] and studies of the systems of control of the use of alcohol and drugs.[112]

Some subfields have emerged and been considerably strengthened in the last decades. Of these fields the sociology of health and medicine, sociology of work, and sociology of science are worth a special mention. In medical sociology Elianne Riska has conducted and published several studies of ideologies and paradigms in health education and health policy.[113] Of great importance for the development of the field was the research activities of the Research Institute for Social Security at the National Social Insurance Institution.[114] An extra impetus to the field came from demography, which in 1977 was made part of the Sociology Department at the University of Helsinki, and its leading researcher, Tapani Valkonen, whose demographic research on socioeconomic mortality differences has been of interest in the field of public health.[115]

Another field which particularly in the 1980s grew in strength was industrial sociology and sociology of work. This was for a long time an undeveloped part of Finnish sociology, and the number of studies in the field remained clearly smaller than, for instance, in Norway and Sweden. The growth of engagement in industrial sociology has occurred in many sociology departments,[116,117] but the field gained particular strength at the University of Tampere with the appointment of Antti Kasvio[118] and Liisa Rantalaiho[119] as professors in the field of the study of the working life.

The increased activities in science policy and planning of higher education stimulated growth of and an interest in the sociology of science. Societal use of science and technology has been analyzed by Veronica Stolte Heiskanen from different angles.[120] She started in 1989 a new international journal, *Science Studies,* with both international and Finnish contributions. One of its first most interesting Finnish contributions analyzed the societal background of the present tendency for support of science and technology in Finland.[121] In a long, stretched country with many small universities it became interesting and important to analyze the social functions of the regional universities.[122]

NOTES

1. Edward Westermarck, *The History of Human Marriage* (London, 1891; 5th ed. rewritten in 3 vols., London: Macmillan & Co, 1921).

2. Edward Westermarck, *The Origin and Development of the Moral Ideas,* 3 vols. (London: Macmillan & Co., 1906–1908).

3. Edward Westermarck, *Ritual and Belief in Morocco I–II* (London: Macmillan & Co., 1926).

4. Rafael Karsten, *The Civilization of the South American Indians* (London: Kegan Paul, 1926).

5. Gunnar Landtman, *The Kiwai Papuans of British New Guinea* (London: Kegan Paul, 1927).

6. Knut Pipping, "Who Reads Westermarck Today?," *The British Journal of Sociology* 35 (1984), 315–332.

7. Gunnar Landtman, *The Origin of the Inequality of the Social Classes* (London: Kegan Paul, 1938).

8. Rudolf Holsti, "The Relation of War to the Origin of State," Ph.D. diss., Helsinki, 1913.

9. Rafael Karsten, *La civilisation de l'empire Inca. Un état totalitaire du passe* (Paris: Payot, 1952; 2nd ed., 1957).

10. Risto Alapuro et al., *Suomalaisen sosiologian juuret* (The Roots of Finnish Sociology) (Porvoo-Helsinki: WSOY, 1973), 84–110.

11. Aksel Warén, *Torpparioloista Suomessa* (The Finnish Tenant Farmers) (Helsinki, 1898).

12. Eino Kuusi, *Talvityöttömyys, sen esiintyminen, syyt ja ehkäisytoimenpiteet Suomen suurimmissa kaupungeissa* (Winter Unemployment, Existence, Causes, and Methods of Prevention in the Largest Cities of Finland) (Helsinki, 1914).

13. Jaakko Forsman, *Mistä syystä sosialismi levisi Suomen maalaisväestön keskuuteen* (Why Did Socialism Spread in the Finnish Countryside) (Helsinki, 1935).

14. Matti Alestalo and Hannu Uusitalo, "Finland," in Peter Flora, ed., *Growth to Limits. The Western European Welfare States Since World War II* (Berlin–New York: Walter de Gruyter, 1986), 199–292.

15. Uno Harva, *Altain suvun uskonnot* (The Religions of the People of Altai) (Porvoo: WSOY, 1933).

16. K. Rob. V. Wikman, *Die Einleitung der Ehe. Ein vergleichende ethnosoziologische Untersuchung über die Vorstufe der Ehe in den Sitten der Schwedischen Volkstums* (Åbo: Acta Academiae Aboensis, Humaniora, 1937).

17. Hilma Granqvist, *Marriage Conditions in a Palestinian Village 1* (Helsingfors: Societas Scientiarum Fennica. Commentationes Humanarum Litterarum, 1931).

18. Eino Kuusi, *Sosiaalipolitiikka I–II* (Social Policy) (Helsinki: WSOY, 1931).

19. Heikki Waris, *Työläisyhteiskunnan syntyminen Helsingin Pitkänsillan po-*

hjoispuolelle I, with an English Summary: The Rise of a Workingman's Community on the North Side of the Long Bridge in Helsinki I (Helsinki: Historiallisia tutkimuksia, 1932).

20. Matti Helenius-Seppälä, "Alkoholikysymys, Sosioloogis-tilastotieteellinen tutkimus" (The Alcohol Question, A Sociological-statistical Study), Ph.D. diss., Helsinki, 1902.

21. Veli Verkko, *Verbrechen wider das Leben und Körperverletzungsverbrechen. Eine statistisch-methodologische Untersuchung I,* Helsinki, 1937.

22. Tor W. Holm and Erkki J. Immonen, *Bibliography of Finnish Sociology 1945–1959* (Åbo; Transactions of the Westermarck Society, 1966).

23. Sisko Lamminen in collaboration with Majlis Tullander, *Bibliography of Finnish Sociology 1960–69* (Helsinki: Transactions of the Westermarck Society, 1973).

24. Terttu Turunen-Noro, *Bibliography of Finnish Sociology 1970–79* (Helsinki: Transactions of the Westermarck Society, 1985).

25. Maria Forsman, *Bibliography of Finnish Sociology 1980–84* (Helsinki; Transactions of the Westermarck Society, 1989).

26. Heikki Waris, *Suomalaisen yhteiskunnan rakenne* (The Structure of Finnish Society) (Porvoo: WSOY, 1948).

27. Veli Verkko, *Homicides and Suicides in Finland and Their Dependence on National Character* (Kobenhavn: G.E.C. Gads forlag, 1951).

28. Knut Pipping, *Kompaniet som samhälle,* with an English Summary: The Social Life of a Machine Gun Company (Åbo: Acta Academiae Aboensis, Humaniora, 1947).

29. Erik Allardt and Yrjö Littunen, *Sosiologia* (Sociology) (Porvoo: WSOY, 1958).

30. Erik Allardt and Yrjö Littunen, *Sociologi* (Uppsala: Almqvist & Wiksell, 1962).

31. Antti Eskola, *Sosiologian tutkimusmenetelmät I* (The Research Methods of Sociology I) (Porvoo: WSOY, 1962).

32. Erik Allardt and Yrjö Littunen, eds., *Cleavages, Ideologies and Party Systems. Contributions to Comparative Political Sociology* (Turku: Transactions of the Westermarck Society, 1964).

33. Veronica Stolte Heiskanen, "The Role of Centre-Periphery Relations in the Utilisation of the Social Sciences," *International Sociology* 2 (1987), 189–203.

34. Ellsworth Fuhrman and Erkki Kaukonen, "On the Circulation and Legitimation of Social Science Knowledge: The Case of Finnish Sociology," *Social Epistemology* 2 (1988), 43–59.

35. Heikki Waris, *Suomalaisen yhteiskunnan rakenne.*

36. Heikki Waris, *Muuttuva suomalainen yhteiskunta* (Changing Finnish Society) (Porvoo: WSOY, 1968).

37. Paavo Seppänen, "Dimensions and Phases of Change in Finnish Society," *International Journal of Politics* 4 (1974), 222–253.

38. Antti Eskola, *Maalaiset ja kaupunkilaiset* (Rural and Urban People) (Rauma: Kirjayhtymä, 1963).

39. Antti Eskola, "Perceptions of the Basic Cleavages of Finnish Society," *Journal of Peace Research* 7 (1970), 259–266.

40. Erik Allardt and Pertti Pesonen, "Cleavages in Finnish Politics," in Stein

Rokkan and S. M. Lipset, eds., *Party Systems and Voter Alignments: Crossnational Perspectives* (New York: The Free Press, 1967), 325–366.

41. Erik Allardt, "Social Sources of Finnish Communism: Traditional and Emerging Radicalism," *International Journal of Comparative Sociology* 5 (1964), 49–72.

42. Yrjö Littunen, *Sosiaalinen sidonnaisuus* (Socially Closed Minds) (Porvoo-Helsinki: WSOY, 1962).

43. Elina Haavio-Mannila, *Kylätappelut,* with an English Summary: Village Fights (Porvoo-Helsinki: WSOY, 1958).

44. Erik Allardt, "Emile Durkheim—Sein Beitrag zur politischen Soziologie," *Kölner Zeitschrift für Soziologie und Sozial-Psychologie* 20 (1968), 1–16.

45. Erik Allardt, "Types of Protests and Alienation," in Erik Allardt and Stein Rokkan, eds., *Mass Politics. Studies in Political Sociology* (New York: The Free Press, 1970), 45–63.

46. Bernard Lacroix, *Durkheim et le politique* (Montréal: Presses de L'Université Montréal, 1981).

47. Veronica Stolte Heiskanen, *Social Structure, Family Patterns and Interpersonal Influence* (Turku: Transactions of the Westermarck Society, 1967).

48. Kullervo Rainio, *A Stochastic Model of Social Interaction* (Turku: Transactions of the Westermarck Society, 1961).

49. Antti Eskola, *Social Influence and Power in Two-Person Groups* (Turku: Transactions of the Westermarck Society, 1961).

50. Antti Eskola, *Sosiaalipsykologia* (Social Psychology) (Helsinki: Tammi, 1971).

51. Antti Eskola, *Sociale Psychologie: enn maatschhappij-kritische benadering* (Rotterdam: Kooyker, 1976).

52. Yrjö Ahmavaara, *Transformation Analysis of Factorial Data* (Helsinki: Annales Academiae Scientiarum Fennica, 1954).

53. Erik Allardt, "Yksilö ja yhteisömuuttujat sosiaalitutkimuksessa," with an English Summary: Individual and Contextual Variables in Social Research, *Politiikka* 5 (1965), 51–60.

54. Ilkka Heiskanen, *Theoretical Approaches and Scientific Strategies in Administrative and Organizational Research: A Methodological Study* (Helsinki: Commentationes Humanarum Litterarum, 1967).

55. Tapani Valkonen, "Individual and Structural Effects in Ecological Research," in Mattei Dogan and Stein Rokkan, eds., *Quantitative Ecological Analysis in the Social Sciences* (Cambridge, Mass.: MIT Press, 1969), 53–68.

56. Tapani Valkonen, "Community Context and Politicization of Individuals," *Acta Sociologica* 12 (1969), 144–155.

57. Kullervo Rainio, *Stochastic Field Theory of Behavior* (Helsinki: Commentationes Scientiarum Socialium, 1986).

58. Knut Pipping, *Kompaniet som samhälle.*

59. Pertti Rautio and Pertti Suhonen, *Yhteiskuntatieteiden tietovirrat ja suomalainen tutkija* (The Flow of Information in the Social Sciences, and the Finnish Researcher) (Helsinki: Suomen Akatemian julkaisuja, 1981).

60. Jukka Gronow, *On the Formation of Marxism. Karl Kautsky's Theory of Capitalism, the Marxism of the Second International and Karl Marx's Critique of Political Economy* (Helsinki: Societas Scientiarum Fennica, 1986).

61. Seppo Toiviainen, *Nuori Lucács: kriittinen esitys Georg Lukásin varhaisesta ajattelusta ja toiminnasta (1906–1929)* (Young Lucács: A Critical Presentation of the Early Thoughts and Actions of Georg Lucács) (Helsinki Kansankulttuuri, 1977).

62. Emile Durkheim, *Työnjako* (Translation from French of *De la division du travail* by Seppo Randell) (Helsinki: Tammi, 1990).

63. Jukka Gronow, Pertti Klemola, and Juha Partanen, *Tandem, tasa-arvon ja demokratian tutkimus* (Tandem, The Study of Equality and Democracy) (Juva: WSOY, 1977).

64. Tuomo Martikainen and Risto Yrjönen, "Central Government Politics and Control Strategies in the Production and Distribution of Public Services: An Evaluation Study," *Scandinavian Political Studies* 11 (1976), 93–112.

65. Pekka Kosonen et al., *Suomalainen kapitalismi* (Finnish Capitalism) (Jyväskylä, 1979).

66. Pekka Kosonen, *Hyvinvointivaltion haasteet ja pohjoismaiset mallit* (Challenges Facing the Welfare State and the Nordic Models) (Tampere: Vastapaino, 1987).

67. Ellsworth Fuhrman and Erkki Kaukonen, "On the Circulation and Legitimation of Social Science Knowledge," 51.

68. Robert Erikson, Erik Jørgen Hansen, Stein Ringen, and Hannu Uusitalo, eds., *The Scandinavian Model. Welfare States and Welfare Research* (Armonk and London: M. E. Sharpe, 1987).

69. Erik Allardt and Hannu Uusitalo, "Dimensions of Welfare in a Comparative Study of the Scandinavian Societies," *Scandinavian Political Studies* 7 (1972), 9–27.

70. Erik Allardt, "Having, Loving, Being: An Alternative to the Swedish Model of Welfare Research," in Martha C. Nussbaum and Amartya Sen, eds., *The Quality of Life* (Oxford: Clarendon Press, 1993).

71. Matti Alestalo and Hannu Uusitalo, "Finland."

72. Kyösti Raunio, *Hyvinvointi ja taloudelliset muutokset* (Welfare and Economic Change) (Turku: Sosiaalipoliittisen yhdistyksen tutkimuksia, 1983).

73. Matti Alestalo, *Structural Change, Classes and the State. Finland in an Historical and Comparative Perspective* (Helsinki: Research Group for Comparative Sociology, 1986).

74. Pekka Kosonen et al., *Suomalainen kapitalismi.*

75. J. P. Roos and Barbara Roos, "Ways of Life, Subjective and Objective. Studies on the Way of Life in Social Change," *Research Project on "The Way of Life in Social Change," University of Helsinki—Academy of Finland, Research Reports,* no. 11, 1981.

76. J. P. Roos and Keijo Rahkonen, "In Search of the Finnish New Middle Class," *Acta Sociologica* 28 (1985), 257–274.

77. Matti Kortteinen, *Lähiö. Tutkimus elämäntapojen muutoksesta* (The Suburb. A Study of the Change of the Way of Life) (Keuruu: Otava, 1982).

78. Katarina Eskola and Erkki Vainikkala, eds., "The Production and Reception of Literature. A Seminar Report," *The University of Jyväskylä, Publications of the Research Unit for Contemporary Culture,* no. 8, 1988.

79. Pekka Sulkunen, "Society Made Visible—On the Cultural Sociology of Pierre Bourdieu," *Acta Sociologica* 251 (1982), 103–115.

80. Pertti Alasuutari, "The Male Suburban Pub-goer and the Meaning Structure of Drinking," *Acta Sociologica* 28 (1985), 87–98.

81. Risto Heiskala, "Sex and Gender in the Semiotic Perspective. Male and Female Cultural Identities in Finnish Cultural Products from the 1950's to the 1980's," *Acta Sociologica* 30 (1987), 207–212.

82. Tapani Valkonen and Tuija Martelin, "Occupational Class and Suicide: An Example of the Elaboration of a Relationship" (Helsinki: Department of Sociology, Research Reports, 1987).

83. Hannu Uusitalo, *Income Distribution in Finland. The Effects of the Welfare State and the Structural Changes in Society on Income Distribution in Finland in 1966–1985* (Helsinki: Central Statistical Office of Finland, 1989).

84. Risto Alapuro, *State and Revolution in Finland* (Berkeley–Los Angeles–London: University of California Press, 1988).

85. Tapani Valkonen, Risto Alapuro, Matti Alestalo, Riitta Jallinoja, and Tom Sandlund, *Suomalaiset. Yhteiskunnan rakenne teollistumisen aikana* (The Finns. The Structure of the Society during Industrialization), 2nd ed. (Juva: WSOY, 1985).

86. Raimo Blom, "The Relevance of Class Theory," *Acta Sociologica* 28 (1985), 71–92.

87. Markku Kivinen, *The New Middle Classes and the Labour Process, Class Criteria Revisited* (Helsinki: Department of Sociology, Research Reports, 1989).

88. Seppo Pöntinen, *Social Mobility and Social Structure. A Comparison of Scandinavian Countries* (Helsinki: Commentationes Scientiarum Socialium, 1983).

89. Timo Toivonen, "The Entrepeneurs in Denmark, Finland and Sweden 1930–1970," *Acta Sociologica* 28 (1985), 193–206.

90. Matti Alestalo, Sven Bislev, and Bengt Furuåker, "Public Employment and Class Formation," in Jon Eivind Kolberg, ed., *Between Work and Social Citizenship* (Armonk and New York: M. E. Sharpe, 1990).

91. Tom Sandlund, *Social Classes, Ethnic Groups and Capitalist Development—An Outline of a Theory* (Åbo: Svenska Litterarursällskapet i Finland, 1976).

92. Erik Allardt, *Implications of the Ethnic Revival in Modern, Industrialized Society. A Comparative Study of the Linguistic Minorities in Western Europe* (Helsinki-Helsingfors: Commentationes Scientiarum Socialium, 1979).

93. Marjut Aikio, *Saamelaiset kielenvaihdon kierteessä* (The Same People in the Turmoil of Language Shift) (Mänttä: SKS, 1988).

94. Marika Tandefelt, *Mellan två språk* (Between Two Languages) (Uppsala: Acta Universitatis Uppsaliensis, Studies Multiethnica Upsaliensis, 1988).

95. Karmela Liebkind, ed., *New Identities in Europe. Immigrant Ancestry and the Ethnic Identity of Youth* (Aldershot: Gower Press, 1989).

96. Armas Nieminen, *Taistelu sukupuolimoraalista*, with an English Summary: The Battle over Sexual Morality. Problems of Marriage and Sex in Finland appr. from 1860 to 1920 (Helsinki: WSOY, 1951).

97. Elina Haavio-Mannila, *Suomalainen nainen ja mies* (The Finnish Man and Woman) (Porvoo-Helsinki: WSOY, 1968).

98. Elina Haavio-Mannila, "Convergences between East and West: Tradition and Modernity of Sex Roles in Sweden, Finland and the Soviet Union," *Acta Sociologica* 14 (1971), 114–125.

99. Riitta Jallinoja, *Suomalaisen naisliikkeen taistelukaudet* (The Battle Periods of the Finnish Feminist Movement) (Juva: WSOY, 1983).

100. Aino Saarinen, "Feminist Research: In Search of a New Paradigm," *Acta Sociologica* 31 (1988), 35–52.

101. Olavi Riihinen, *Teollistuvan yhteiskunnan alueellinen erilaistuneisuus* (The Inner Differentiation of Society in the Process of Industrialization) (Helsinki, 1965).

102. Paavo Piepponen, "Suomen kuntien sosiaalisen rakenteen perustekijät," with an English Summary: Dimensions of Ecological Differentiation in Finnish Communes, *Yearbook of Population Research in Finland* (1961–1962), 34–46.

103. Pertti Rannikko, *Metsätyö—Pienviljelijäkylä. Tutkimus erään yhdyskunta-tyypin noususta ja tuhosta* (Forestry—Small Farmer's Village. A Study of the Rise and Fall of a Type of Community) (Joensuu: University of Joensuu, Publications in Social Sciences, 1989).

104. Kirsti Suolinna and Kaisa Sinikara, *Juhonkylä. Tutkimus pohjoissuomala-isesta laestadiolaiskylästä* (Juhonkylä, A Northern Finnish Village Dominated by Laestadianism) (Helsinki: SKS, 1986).

105. Liisa Uusitalo, *Environmental Impacts of Consumption Patterns* (Shaftes-bury, Dorset: Gower, 1986).

106. Timo Järvikoski, *Vesien säännöstely ja paikallisyhteisö* (Water Regulation and the Local Community), Research Reports, Institute of Sociology (Turku: University of Turku, 1979).

107. Ilmo Massa, ed., *Energia, kulttuuri ja tulevaisuus* (Energy, Culture and the Future) (Porvoo: SKS, 1982).

108. Pekka Kuusi, *Alcohol Sales Experiment in Rural Finland* (Helsinki: The Finnish Foundation for Alcohol Studies, 1957).

109. Kettil Bruun, *Drinking Behavior in Small Groups: An Experimental Study* (Helsinki: The Finnish Foundation for Alcohol Studies, 1959).

110. Klaus Mäkelä, "Unrecorded Consumption of Alcohol in Finland 1950–1957," Helsinki: *Alkoholipoliittisen tutkimuslaitoksen tutkimusseloste,* 1979.

111. Pekka Sulkunen, "Individual Consumption in Capitalism. An Exercise in the Logic of Capital," *Acta Sociologica* 21 (1978), 35–46.

112. Kettil Bruun, Lynn Pan, and Ingemar Rexed, *The Gentlemen's Club: In-ternational Control of Drugs and Alcohol* (Chicago and London: The University of Chicago Press, 1975).

113. Elianne Riska, "Health Education and Its Ideological Content," *Acta So-ciologica* 25 (1982), 41–46.

114. Tapani Purola, Esko Kalima, and Kauko Nyman, *Health Services Use and Health Status under National Sickness Insurance. An Evaluative Survey of Finland* (Helsinki: Publications of the Social Insurance Institution, 1974).

115. Tapani Valkonen, "Socioeconomic Mortality Differentials in Finland," in Måten Lagergren, ed., *Hälsa för alla i Norden år 2000* (Göteborg: Nordic School of Public Health, 1983).

116. Pertti Koistinen and Kyösti Urponen, eds., *New Technologies and Societal Development* (Joensuu: Research Reports in Social Policy and Sociology, 1984).

117. Heikki Leimu, *Työntekijän työasema ja työpaikkaliikkuvuus erikokoisissa teollisuuyrityksissä,* with an English Summary: Blue-Collar Work Position and

Workplace Mobility in Small and Large Industrial Firms) (Turku: Turun yliopiston julkaisuja, 1983).

118. Antti Kasvio, *Teollisuus ja elämäntapa,* with an English Summary: Industrial Work and the Way of Life (Tampere: Acta Universitatis Tamperensis, 1982).

119. Liisa Rantalaiho, "Finnish Women in Working Life," in Sirkku Kuusava, ed., *Vocation: Women* (Tampere: The National Council of Women in Finland, 1988).

120. Veronica Stolte Heiskanen, "Societal Use of Scientific and Technical Research. Existing and Alternative Models," in Jacques Richardson, ed., *Models of Reality: Shaping Thought and Action* (Mt. Airy, Md.: Lomond Publ., 1984).

121. Marja Alestalo, "Government Policy and the Demands for Economic Innovations: A Historical Example of a European Periphery," *Science Studies* 1 (1988), 25–34.

122. Ari Antikainen, *The Regional University* (Joensuu: Publications of the University of Joensuu, 1980).

6

The Sociological Debate in France
(1960–1991)

Pierre Ansart

Sociological research in France between 1960 and 1991 was marked by wide-ranging debates about theory which raised a number of fundamental questions. Successively (and in some cases simultaneously), phenomenology, structuralism, dynamism, ethnomethodology, and methodological individualism divided researchers and brought about the formation of rival schools in constant discussion with one another. Far from remaining at the level of abstraction, these theories oriented research, raised varying hypotheses, and served as guides for divergent schools. One may therefore consider them in a sense as concurrent "paradigms."[1]

Within the scope of the present chapter, I review the main theoretical currents in France from 1960 to the present and the areas of research associated most closely with them. I would also like to cite as influences those intellectual traditions dating from Auguste Comte, Alexis de Tocqueville, or Emile Durkheim which have been extended by these paradigms and to suggest how nineteenth-century traditions of these researchers have been reconsidered and transformed through multiple exchanges between their German, English, and in particular their American colleagues.

And in conclusion I would like to advance and verify a hypothesis in these pages. It seems to me that the root of these theoretical oppositions lies, at least in part, in the very complexity, contradictions, and strong transformation of social relationships and society itself of the present period. In the attempt to take into consideration the essential dimensions of these shifting relationships, sociologists may have been led to stress varying dimensions of contemporary societies in flux in the time period under discussion.

I will outline in succession four paradigms which seem to me to sum-marize clearly the scope of the contemporary debate in French sociology. They are genetic structuralism (Pierre Bourdieu), dynamic structuralism (Georges Balandier, Alain Touraine), the strategic approach (Michel Crozier), and methodological individualism (Raymond Boudon).[2]

GENETIC STRUCTURALISM

One might characterize the research of Pierre Bourdieu as work whose sources lie in a double tradition with one strand which could be described as social class theory and the other deriving from Durkheim. Although he does not follow the political conclusions of Proudhon and Marx, Bourdieu renews the attempt to reformulate the division into classes of the entire social construct. He takes as his goal the analysis of new forms taken by present class antagonisms. Like Durkheim, he repudiates the philosophy of history and the historicism of Marx and tries to show that social phenomena really possess an objective reality that normally passes unnoticed by common opinion and that he is capable of revealing the directions of society in the strong transformation of social relationships.

Yet this sociological tradition from the past has been profoundly re-thought and reorganized through the structuralism of the 1960s. The an-thropological work of Claude Lévi-Strauss of that period proposed an ambitious analytical model intended to reveal the relationships between social structures and symbolical structures in social systems and their rules of transformation. By taking into consideration these analytical methods which had shown their efficacy in linguistics and ethnology, Bourdieu pro-posed to analyze the multiple relationships between objective structures and symbolic structures within contemporary French society.

The main objective of Bourdieu's research is twofold—whether it is concerned with cultural behaviors[3] or professional behavior.[4] On the one hand, he wishes to analyze objective structures, the division into social classes, and the "system of positions." On the other hand, he analyzes individual behaviors and their representations in order to bring out the relationships between the objective system of positions and the behaviors or representations of agents. Choosing to study an example as simple as the practice of photography, Bourdieu and his colleagues show how greatly the uses of photography vary from one class to another and how the relations of determination between social positions and cultural be-haviors bear out each other in this example. Thus, we can see that farmers do not engage in photography and, in fact, consider it to be a foolish pastime whereas the members of the urban lower classes engage in it frequently. One should note that members of this class take pictures for utilitarian and family purposes. It is only the members of the middle clas-ses and, more specifically, those involved with technology, who make photography an art and take photographs for aesthetic reasons, while for the most part the other members of the middle class (i.e., white-collar workers or members of the liberal professions) consider photography to be a waste of time.

The relationships between objective structures (the distribution of the members of society into classes) and behaviors validate each other (although not without a considerable degree of subtlety in other areas), in the ways people go to museums, for example,[5] in the attitudes of different students,[6] or in the access of students to major graduate schools.[7]

Other "systems of positions" are revealed in another form in institutions like the university. Within the university system one may indeed demonstrate the growth of two essential systems. One is internal and particular to institutional function, and the other is exterior. The former (proper to internal function) distributes positions of power involving decision making and prestige (presidents, deans, etc.) to submissive positions without prestige. A second structure, which is, for the most part, exterior, distributes positions of authority and prestige gained from outside the internal structure through scientific publications and by other obligations to the scientific community. These two systems of positioning determine differing attitudes, judgments, and motivations as well as generating types of conflict peculiar to academics at the university level.[8]

There exist still other systems of positions that may be observed in entities as broad and complex as a political system or an intellectual field. Bourdieu proposes the use of the word "field" (Fr. "champ") to designate not only those persons engaging in the area or activity, for example, those involved in the production of culture, but more precisely the system of positions and powers that structures the relations between agents of intellectual production. Among such persons one would include not only those artists and writers who are competing for cultural legitimacy but also an ensemble of institutions (i.e., publishing houses, academic societies, literary and artistic circles and groups), participating in the competition normally pertaining to this field (or "champ"), which define authorities and hierarchies.

And so, although not without calling upon a demanding objective construction (Fr. "construction d'objet"),[9] Bourdieu sets out to reveal social structures that can be taken as determinative of the attitudes, aspirations, and behaviors of agents. It is therefore at this point that the question arises of knowing how this determination shows itself in contradictions and in the strong transformation of social relationships.

In order to answer that question, Bourdieu stresses above all that every individual receives inclinations and tendencies of behavior, whether it be from his or her milieu or from family models of perception which are then interiorized or "incorporated." Once socialized in this way the individual tends to reproduce these acquired inclinations and these schema of perception, evaluation, and action. It is the concept of *habitus,* then, that shapes this double process of interiorization and exteriorization through which, even as they pursue their own objectives, individuals reproduce interiorized models and in this way participate seemingly spontaneously in their reproduction at the societal level.

Bourdieu therefore strives to reject as invalid oppositions which he believes to be artificial, such as those between freedom and determinism, and domination and submission. For him, social agents are not determined mechanically. They may receive from their milieu a "cultural capital" or a linguistic capital, for example, which engages them in the social system. And it is through this received capital that they will pursue strategies and direct struggles involving competition and "distinction."[10] By the same token, wielding power obviously separates the dominant from the dominated. But the symbolic violence inherent in this relationship is maintained to a certain degree by the *habitus* (habits) of class, and it is through them that this symbolic violence works itself out in individuals who accept it unconsciously as given.

Bourdieu has applied these general principles to areas as diverse as education, student milieus, the university system, cultural behaviors, and linguistic exchanges with an admirable display of analytical skills.[11]

Moreover, through his empirical research, he has contributed significantly to work on problems of theory and methodology.[12]

DYNAMIC SOCIOLOGY

The numerous works associated with this second school raise very different questions about according central importance to the study of social structures and their reproduction. This research places at the heart of its investigation questions of social change, development, and mutation. Research projects in dynamic sociology have as their goal to describe and explain these phenomena by postulating that modern society is essentially characterized by these transformations.[13]

Such projects thus renew the major tradition of social thought today which has continued to inquire through diverse forms into change and the dynamic of change whether it be through the work of Saint-Simon, Auguste Comte, Marx, or Herbert Spencer in the past. This sociology draws its major themes more directly from the historical experience of the twentieth century, from the military upheavals of World War II, and the processes of decolonization, technological change, and the demographic explosion.[14]

The revision of the relationship between ethnology and sociology con-

stituted an important moment in the development of this "dynamic sociology," to use the term coined by Georges Balandier. It is true that far
from conceiving traditional and modern societies as being radically opposed, the anthropologists associated with this school have tended to stress
the great degree to which so-called traditional societies previously considered to have been relatively tranquil and immutable were in fact racked
by tensions, contradictions, and renewals just as modern societies are.
Along with English anthropologists (E.E. Evans-Pritchard and M. Fortes),
the theorists who stressed these similarities revealed to what degree political systems are, at the same time, both generalized and diverse in ancient African societies, for example.

This reversed perspective (obviously diametrically opposed to the dynamic hypothesized by structural anthropology) produced a dramatic increase in the links between this new anthropology and sociology. That is
why Balandier insisted strongly on the value of making a "detour" through
those so-called traditional primitive societies to seek to discover social,
symbolical, and political relationships in them and to compare them to
relationships in industrial societies.[15] In the case of power relationships,
for example, or in the case of conflictual relationships between sexes and
generations, it would be instructive to examine the kinds of tension and
conflict that exist in order to understand more clearly certain contemporary phenomena.[16]

For Alain Touraine, when looking beyond these permanent dynamics,
it is essential to delineate very clearly the distance between nineteenth-
century industrialized society and present-day society. Taking up the analyses of Daniel Bell and Jurgen Habermas, Touraine characterizes
industrial society (as did Marx before him) by the effects and uncontrolled
development of the forces of production. Touraine contrasts to that society
produced by the Industrial Revolution the model of post-industrial society
which is characterized not by the forces of production, but by the decision-
making, programation, compromises, and communications required of individuals and groups by numerous projects involving organization and
development.[17] Instead of reproducing itself, according to this paradigm,
post-industrial society keeps producing itself or, one might say that it
keeps "making or creating itself."[18]

If this were true, the concerns of sociology would not be limited merely
to the study of social "facts" as Durkheim wished. Nor would they be
confined to analyzing ways structures as functions recompose themselves,
as Talcott Parsons suggested. But they would rather extend further and
require examination of the dynamics, the processes, and the conflicts that
can continue to transform contemporary societies. Instead of studying
structures and stabilities, it would be more appropriate to follow this paradigm to analyze actions, systems of action, and their transformations.

According to Touraine, the analysis of what he proposes to call the "historicity" of a society, that is, the study of its creativity and autotrans-formation, would constitute an essential objective for dynamic sociology. Unlike the concept prevalent in the sociology of the nineteenth century, this "historicity" would not simply involve economic and technological development. Instead, it would combine work in which the sciences and the social sciences play an essential role. In this view, investment, in all its forms, is no longer a simple condition of reproduction but rather the major source of change. The representation of the future which Touraine calls "the cultural model,"[19] and which is founded on a relative social consensus leading to "development" and "expansion" whose broad out-lines are accepted by a large majority, constitute for Touraine an essential component in this ongoing production of society.

This paradigm of society in a permanent state of transformation where a massive part of production is withdrawn from consumption and invested is divided, by necessity, into a governing, dominant class on the one hand, and the remaining, dominated classes on the other. But contrary to the theories of Marx, this multiform conflict no longer opposes the possessors of the means of production and the salaried workers. It opposes instead the group of leaders who are actively involved in political and economic decision making and the dominated lower classes.

One therefore commonly encounters a central conflict at the heart of this "system of historical action," which Touraine analyzes as a "double dialectic" between social classes. The ruling class inevitably possesses two opposite yet complementary characteristics. It manages investment to con-form to the common cultural model. But at the same time it orients it in the direction of its own private interests and in a direction that will rein-force its own power. Therefore, the dominated class in this conflict has two dimensions as well. It is submissive to the expropriation of dominance and takes a defensive, protective attitude toward itself and its type of life. What is more, different movements issuing from this dominated class will attempt to oppose its own objectives to the appropriation of the dominant class. Ecological movements may serve in the whole as an example of such initiatives.

The study of "social movements" therefore constitutes a prime area for sociological research for these investigators. Touraine uses this term not to describe those movements related uniquely to the defense of pressure groups which lead to limited conflicts and compromises, but to include collective actions intended to control collective orientations and their modifications. Thus, during the period from 1960 to 1980 it was of major concern to determine whether social struggles such as the move toward self-expression by students, women, and militant ecologists were likely to become "social movements" capable of shaping a cultural and political orientation.

By investigating the role of sociology in these conflicts, Touraine has developed a thesis that runs counter to the tradition of Max Weber which postulates that the role of sociologists is limited to that of neutral observer. Touraine believes that it is possible to create situations in which sociologists intervene directly. He believes that in such situations the sociologist working in groups may intervene to help these relatively inchoate groups to coalesce if they are capable of doing so into a social movement. This sociological intervention would have as its goal the stimulation of such groups to become more conscious of their identity, of their opposition to the existing order, and of their own social agenda. This enterprise would not necessarily be successful. It could succeed only if the potential of the group were strong enough and had some chance of transforming scattered initiatives into a social movement.[20]

THE STRATEGIC APPROACH

The two paradigms that have been outlined retain the hypothesis of the division of modern societies into classes and the notion that it is possible to have knowledge of a social totality. By contrast, the two paradigms that follow question the validity of that possibility and concentrate for that reason on the study of action, agents, and their strategies. Speaking in the broadest terms, one might say that as they abandon the focus on social class theory of Proudhon and Marx, these paradigms see themselves as following resolutely in the actionalist tradition of Weber.

For Michel Crozier and his colleagues, not only are industrial and administrative organizations simply the major area that is particularly appropriate for studies of society, but they also constitute the basic, essential phenomenon of the contemporary world. Thus, for them, the sociology of organizations should be approached in terms of the crucial role played by organizations, and as the introduction to a general knowledge of contemporary societies which may and can lead to the formulation of a diagnosis of their crisis.

This paradigm therefore follows a tradition very different from the two discussed previously. It finds its sources in the individualist, liberal tradition, in the comparative observations of de Tocqueville, and in the insights of Weber on bureaucracy. But these studies of bureaucratic functions and dysfunctions, of negotiations and conflicts in businesses, and of the attitudes and behaviors of different categories of personnel are more directly inspired by the vast body of research on organizations begun before 1940 founded on the theses of F. W. Taylor, H. Fayol, and E. Mayo and continued after 1945 in the work of Robert Merton, Alvin Gouldner, George Homans, P. Selznick, and J. G. March and H. A. Simon.

A second theoretical contribution to this approach should also be mentioned. I refer to systematism as it was formulated from initial work by L. von Bertalanffy. The goal of the systematic approach is to reconsider whole systems rather than their parts, to investigate dynamic interactions instead of causalities, and complexity instead of simplicity. This approach has been applied in order to consider organizations as integrated systems.

The approach of Michel Crozier, who first studied the bureaucratic phenomenon (1963)[21] and then the general theory of modern organizations, is very representative of this kind of work.

Crozier's studies of enterprises in the public sector were intended to analyze the extent of the frustrations, dissatisfactions, waste, and inability to adapt produced by a bureaucratic system. The spread of impersonal rules may seem to rationalize activities when in fact it distracts those in a position to act from the concerns they should have with results and efficiency. Centralization of decision making encourages leaders of systems to seek greater stability and to maintain hierarchies. The isolation of each category from the others in fact restricts each agent to that agent's own group and therefore encourages each group to defend itself against the others. While such a system multiplies conflicts between the different categories of personnel, it does nothing to use these conflicts to improve function or efficiency. Thus one may observe the formation of what Merton and Gouldner have described as "vicious circles." One might consider, for example, the cycle of the dissatisfaction of those who carry out instructions which provoke authoritarian reactions by those in positions of leadership, which, in turn, reinforce the dissatisfaction that existed already.

In the 1970s Michel Crozier and his colleagues suggested that this kind of bureaucratic system was characteristic of most French enterprises. They found it to be especially characteristic of administration.[22] A system of this kind would, by its very nature, encounter great difficulties if it were faced with the necessity of transforming itself to adapt to changes. Such a system was thought to be condemned to evolve through successive crises rather than through progressive adjustments. The crisis faced by French universities in 1968 served as a good example of this kind of crisis that occurs in an excessively bureaucratized organization.

But the example of the French universities as a system is only one particular model of organization. In their earlier work, Michel Crozier and Erhard Friedberg tried to propose a general organizational model which would reveal organizations' essential characteristics.[23] In the first place they stress the fact that despite the commonly held illusion which makes them seem to be realities or natural givens, organizations are, in fact, "social constructs" which are never completed. Instead they are always in a state of tension and are constantly striving to bring about collective action.

It would follow from this dynamic concept that two essential dimensions will therefore characterize any organization: power relationships and individual strategies. Power relationships are inevitable and permanent since the organization is striving to achieve common objectives and can do so only through the imposition of rules, norms, and constraints. Whatever forms the exercise of power may take—from the most highly bureaucratized organizations to the most interactive forms where negotiation plays a role, it is impossible to avoid the imposition of constraints and the restrictions of freedom. But in any organization, contrary to the imagery of permanent dominance, power is the subject of a continuing process of transaction—between individuals and between categories. Each of these individuals and categories has a margin for resistance as well as a margin for action and initiative. Power is exercised through formal and informal relationships, between agents who all possess a certain degree of freedom despite the fact that they are not equals.

Disagreeing with functionalist conceptions which would reduce agents to being simply agents or decision-makers, Crozier insists upon the importance of this margin of independence possessed by every participant in the regulated game which makes up an organization. Each participant (Fr. "acteur") pursues his or her own interests and therefore follows his or her own strategy, which evolves as a function of that agent's personal history and awareness of responsibility. In this regard Crozier returns to the debate over the "limited rationality" of those who act. He rejects both the illusion of complete rationality and the illusion of total constraint. In his view each participant is, in fact, an agent who acts within a system of which he or she is only partially aware.

This permanent presence of power relationships makes organizations places of continual conflicts. Inevitably, freedom is limited. Frustrations are widespread. The efforts of each person to maintain or increase his or her margins of initiative and to limit zones of uncertainty are pervasive as well. By the same token, in power relationships where some degree of arbitrariness must remain, there are permanent conflicts; they cannot be totally eliminated. They serve only to reinforce the affective dimensions of these power relationships. And so frustrations, dissatisfactions, aspirations, attachments to the enterprise, and disappointments with it are all part of the daily life of organizations and contribute to their dynamic.

The strategic approach has therefore engaged in a vigorous critique of public or private bureaucracies and articulated a carefully thought-out examination of the general conditions of the industrial and administrative dynamic. When dealing with public administration, Crozier and his colleagues have been extremely critical of examples of state centralization.[24] They have criticized their cost and their dysfunctional aspects. They have advocated vigorously the decentralization of structures and decision-making bodies. As for organizations themselves, while not advocating radical reforms of an ideological nature, they have attempted to institute progressive reforms, including the participation of those involved, in order to obtain more effective management and to achieve better ways of resolving conflicts. This is the way in which this organizational sociology has

participated directly in the modernization of businesses and public administration in France and in Europe during this period.

METHODOLOGICAL INDIVIDUALISM

In order to review the liveliness of the sociological debate in the period
under consideration, it is essential to underscore the central position occupied by methodological individualism. This approach (represented in
France, particularly by the work of Raymond Boudon and François Bourricaud) engages in a vigorous critique of the positions we have just described, and especially in a critique of genetic structuralism.

As we observed, genetic structuralism takes as its point of departure
positions occupied within social space, that is to say, the position of classes.
It examines the ways in which agents are determined by these positions
and structures within this frame of reference. In the tradition of Marx and
Durkheim it is posited that the objective givens of class positions determine behaviors and that the task of the sociologist is to seek out these
determinative factors and, insofar as that is possible, to discover the reg-
ulative social behaviors that flow from them.

Methodological individualism raises a double objection to these principles. The first centers on the very existence of deterministic factors and
of laws of behavior. Advocates of this approach would claim that so-called
sociological laws, whether one means by that term either very general laws
like the law of evolution or more specific ones like those governing development, have been increasingly invalidated by more probing research.
Their second objection involves the very notion of individual behavior
itself, which they feel cannot be completely reduced to deterministic factors. And so, methodological individualism restates, in a way, the objections that Max Weber raised to Marxist doctrine, and it follows the
tradition in sociology which challenges the existence of universal determining factors, either in sociology or in history.

This criticism is directed in part toward Durkheim's work. Raymond
Boudon admits that in many passages in *Suicide,* for instance, Durkheim
was willing to recognize the place of choices and of individual decisions
and aspirations. But Boudon stresses that the main thrust of the work of
this founder of sociology remained, nevertheless, oriented toward science
and objectivity.[25] Methodological individualism, therefore, follows the
other tradition informed by Weber's criticism of historical determinism,
the Austrian marginalist school (Carl Menger), the logical criticism of C.
G. Hempel, K. Popper, and the American sociologists of the individualist
school.

Clearly the principles of methodological individualism are diametrically
opposed to sociological objectivism. By the qualifier "methodological"
they stress the fact that they propose in principle and by method to find

how a social phenomenon results as a consequence or as the creation of the actions of individuals.[26] The proper concern of individualist methodology is therefore the analysis of a social phenomenon or a relationship seen as the effect of the logic governing the individuals concerned.

Instead of placing the description of social "facts" at the center of their analyses, these sociologists feel it is far more suitable to study how and why individual actions come together to cause a social phenomenon to appear. They advocate study of a collective act, for example. It follows that the notion of "emergence" becomes centrally important to this paradigm. It is therefore essential to them to analyze what a social entity is made up of. The example of collective action is therefore particularly revealing since it is possible to verify that in many situations in which one would expect that a collective action would take place, since such action would correspond to the interests of the individuals concerned, no collective action does, in fact, emerge.[27] The notion of "perverse effect," that is to say, situations in which phenomena occur which are not only unintentional on the actors' part, but even harmful to their interests, also lend credence to this paradigm since they suggest that when dealing with human phenomena it would be illusory to believe that the consequences of actions correspond to the conscious intentions of those performing them.

In this theoretical approach the study of interactions is extremely important provided, of course, that such interactions are analyzed as phenomena arising from individual behaviors. Boudon insists on that fact that all interactions, even those defined in their broad outlines by an institution, are in fact, reinterpreted by their actors and re-created by them with a margin of freedom, of acceptance or rejection which make them distinct and particularized.

The debate between microsociology and macrosociology is therefore joined once again. Boudon resolves it in a systematic way by bringing to bear an answer at the same time to the question of the choice of quantitative and qualitative methods. At the level of empirical research and the assemblage of givens, this individualistic approach stresses to the maximum the importance of qualitative materials (interviews, participatory observation, the restitution of interactions, and so on). On this level the thrust of research is directed toward the understanding of attitudes, of interpretations, and of individual choices since these decisions lie at the heart of interaction. The study of the structures of interaction constitutes another level of observation requiring its own methods. Game theory contributes to these methods by permitting the formalization of conducts and norms. In such analytical frameworks it is possible to reveal both the constraints upon individual actions and the choices made by individuals facing those constraints. Boudon carries his analysis further by showing that the individualistic approach in no way excludes quantitative research or the mathematical analysis of givens.[28] And in fact in his work the observation of individual behaviors through questionnaires, for example, does in fact yield materials which lend themselves to mathematical treatment as well as to the search for causalities consistent with what Durkheim taught in *Suicide*. The temptation to be avoided, however, at all levels of analysis would be to generalize the results to an inappropriate degree, and to transform conclusions which may only be provisional, explicative models valid only for the particular field studied into general laws and rules. Whatever the regulations revealed through statistic analysis may be, it is essential to keep in mind that we are dealing with quantified aggregates and not with laws determining the choices and actions of individuals.

Let us recall two examples of this kind of research. For his book *The Inequality of Opportunity*,[29] Boudon had done research which shows that children of underprivileged families have, on the average, scholastic results inferior to those of families that are better off. Boudon polemicizes on that subject against a number of theories of social classes which hypothesize the existence of a mechanical relationship between membership in a certain social class and failure to perform well in school. According to Boudon and the principles of methodological individualism, it would be necessary to investigate the goals and choices of the parents of these children. If one were to do so, one would discover that parents belonging to the lower classes do not hold extended years of study in much esteem. They favor instead short apprenticeships and so do not orient their children toward the pursuit of those academic degrees that require long periods of study.

In his book *Ideology*,[30] Boudon reexamines a problem studied and developed traditionally by the Marxists. Here again he criticizes the classical or structural approach, which presupposes a determinative relationship between a symbolic system and ideology and individual behaviors. Methodological individualism raises a number of quite different questions. It might prove fruitful to analyze why individuals adhere to one ideology instead of another, or to investigate from what social position they adhere to it and to see what daily experience or interests they seek to pursue through this choice, or perhaps to seek to reveal what uses they derive from it. Perhaps it would be possible to understand and explain the success of clichés in this way.

For Boudon the aim of this individualistic sociology is to rethink all the problems derived from sociology as a whole, whether they are related to work or to questions of political sociology. He stresses that although these conceptions do not maintain direct links to liberal ideology they are, nevertheless, a part of a liberal and individualistic outlook. In conclusion, we may well inquire about the liveliness of these debates and raise the question of the reasons underlying the oppositions we have been discussing.

These disagreements and their intensity are less surprising if we consider the history of French sociology as I have tried to do briefly here. Since the days of Auguste Comte or Emile Durkheim, French sociology has been characterized by lively theoretical oppositions which have continued to stimulate research. By the end of the nineteenth century it was already possible to discern three major theoretical tendencies in French sociology. One was the school of social class theory illustrated by Saint-Simon and Proudhon. Then, too, there was Durkheim's school. And finally, an individualist tendency emerged, illustrated as early as 1840 by Alexis de Tocqueville. Moreover, these contrasting currents were not unrelated to opposing political positions, and one can still find these political oppositions in French sociological debates today. More generally, these differing sociologies prolong a dual tradition which is philosophical and political by nature and which maximizes interest in questions of a general nature and the political stakes involved with them.

One must also add, nevertheless, that the four paradigms we have discussed are also related to different dimensions of French society and more generally to European societies. Thus genetic structuralism, which gives a special place to the study of social reproductions, class division, and the central importance of institutional structures, reveals with great pertinence all aspects of repetition and the mechanism of reproduction that is part of contemporary society. So the debate is not only an academic one between genetic structuralism and dynamic sociology which tends to emphasize all of the elements of change included in all contemporary societies. The same opposing interpretations of the very facts themselves are to be found in the successive orientations of Michel Crozier. In the final analysis, it is possible to distinguish operating through individualist sociology those same effective transformations which involve both the economy and mentalities in France and in Europe.

That is why it would be erroneous, in my view, to see only scientific or academic quarrels in these debates, for they are as meaningful as the upheavals that are currently questioning all European societies and not French society alone.

NOTES

This chapter was translated from French by Robert M. Henkels, Professor of French, Auburn University.

1. C. F. Thomas Kuhn, *The Structure of Scientific Revolution* (Chicago: University of Chicago Press, 1962).

2. I developed these four studies further in *Les Sociologies contemporaines* (Paris: Editions du Seuil, 1990).

3. Pierre Bourdieu, Luc Boltanski, Robert Castel, Jean-Claude Chamboredon, *Un art moyen, essai sur les usages sociaux de la photographie* (Paris: Editions de Minuit, 1965).

4. Pierre Bourdieu, *Homo academicus* (Paris: Editions de Minuit, 1984).

5. Pierre Bourdieu and André Darbel, *L'Armour de l'art, les musées et leur public* (Paris: Editions de Minuit, 1966).

6. Pierre Bourdieu and Jean-Claude Passeron, *Les Héritiers, les étudiants et leurs études* (Paris: Editions de Minuit, 1964).

7. Pierre Bourdieu, *La Noblesse d'Etat: Grandes Ecoles et esprit de corps* (Paris: Editions de Minuit, 1989).

8. Pierre Bourdieu, *Homo Academicus.*

9. Pierre Bourdieu, Jean-Claude Passeron, and Jean-Claude Chamboredon, *Le Métier de sociologue, préalables épistémologiques* (Paris: Mouton-Bordas, 1968).

10. Pierre Bourdieu, *La Distinction, critiqeu sociale du judgement* (Paris: Editions de Minuit, 1973).

11. Pierre Bourdieu, *Ce que parler veut dire, l'économie des échanges linguistiques* (Paris: Fayard, 1982).

12. Pierre Bourdieu, Passeron, and Chamboredon, *Le Métier de sociologue;* P. Bourdieu, *Le Sens pratique* (Paris: Editions de Minuit, 1980); P. Bourdieu, *Choses dites* (Paris: Editions de Minuit, 1987); P. Bourdieu with Loïc J. D. Wacquant, *Réponses* (Paris: Editions du Seuil, 1992).

13. In addition to works by Georges Belandier and Alain Touraine, many sociologists associated with this theoretical approach could and should be cited, such as Marc Augé, Cornélius Castoriadis, Jean Duvignaud, Eugéne Enriquez, and Edgar Morin.

14. Georges Balandier, *Afrique ambiguë* (Paris: Plon, 1957).

15. Georges Balandier, *Le Détour: Pouvoir et modernité* (Paris: Fayard, 1985).

16. Georges Balandier, *Anthropo-logiques* (Paris: Presses Universitaires de France, 1974).

17. Alain Touraine, *La Société post-industrielle* (Paris: Denoël, 1969).

18. Ibid.

19. Alain Touraine, *Production de la société* (Paris: Editions du Seuil, 1973).

20. Alain Touraine, *La Voix et le regard* (Paris: Editions du Seuil, 1978).

21. Michel Crozier, *Le Phénomène bureaucratique* (Paris: Editions du Seuil, 1963).

22. Michel Crozier, *La Société bloquée* (Paris: Editions du Seuil, 1970).

23. Michel Crozier and Erhard Friedberg, *L'Acteur et le système, les contraintes de l'action collective* (Paris: Editions du Seuil, 1977).

24. Michel Crozier, *Etat modeste, Etat moderne, Stratégie pour un autre changement* (Paris: Fayard, 1987).

25. Raymond Boudon, *La Crise de la sociologie* (Paris: Droz, 1971).

26. Raymond Boudon and François Bourricaud, *Dictionnaire critique de la sociologie* (Paris: Presses Universitaires de France, 1982).

27. Raymond Boudon, *L'Analyse mathématique des faits sociaux* (Paris: Plon, 1979).

28. Ibid.

29. Raymond Boudon, *L'inégalité des chances; la mobilité sociale dans les sociétés industrielles* (Paris: Colin, 1973).

30. Raymond Boudon, *L'Idéologie ou l'origine des idées recues* (Paris: Fayard, 1986).

7

Contemporary Sociology in Germany

Walter L. Bühl

THE RECENT HISTORY OF GERMAN SOCIOLOGY

"German Sociology" or "Sociology in Germany"? Certainly, all the determined empirical sociologists would like to entitle the history of their discipline "From German Sociology to Sociology in Germany."[1] Although this would be a correct description of the main trend in mainstream sociology since 1955, there is nevertheless a distinctive "German sociology" or there are "typical German" characteristics, which are not only a subject of the exterior view but an acute problem of professionalization in the interior view. Currently, sociology in Germany is deeply divided: whereas in the professional self-conception of most German sociologists today sociology is an empirical science without exceptional national ties, it has in fact been fully institutionalized only as an academic "cultural science," or part of the humanities. But in this respect it is "typically German," even if it makes universal claims (e.g., about "enlightenment" or "emancipation").[2] Only this heavy speculative sociology is discussed by the German cultural intelligentsia in the journals and in the media. Unfortunately, also abroad only this "German" sociology attracts attention,[3] whereas the majority of professional sociologists are absorbed in international academic cooperation and division of labor without mention. Nevertheless, even the "internationalists" are forced to spend much time criticizing this kind of sociology methodologically and chasing breathlessly after its fashionable suggestions and untenable assertions.

But even in its foundation period, German sociology was repeatedly divided. At the first session of the Deutsche Gesellschaft für Soziologie, DGS (German Sociological Association, founded 1909) in Frankfurt in

1910, a fundamental conflict arose between those who wanted to see sociology as a "natural science" like all other sciences (as did Ferdinand Tönnies, Georg Simmel, Leopold von Wiese) and those who defined it as "cultural science" (as did Werner Sombart and Max Weber).[4] In addition to this scientific rift, the time between the wars was dominated by the grim political opposition between the Left- and Right-Hegelians, that is, the Marxists and the Conservatives.[5] With the foundation of the Institute for Social Research at the University of Frankfurt in 1924 (with Carl Grünberg, Friedrich Pollock, and Max Horkheimer), with the Zeitschrift für Sozialforschung, which stood directly opposed to the Research Institute for Social Sciences at the University of Cologne, founded in 1919 (with Leopold von Wiese and Max Scheler) and with Kölner Vierteljahreshefte für Soziologie, strangely enough on the one hand "Marxism" was fused with "cultural science," and "conservativism" with "natural science" on the other.[6] Nevertheless, on both sides the first specialist sociologies emerged, and the first empirical and methodological founded studies were written. But the first imposing *Handwörterbuch der Soziologie,* edited by Alfred Vierkandt in 1931, appeared outside these opposing schools. As far as the sociology of the Third Reich (1933–1945) is concerned, a fierce controversy broke out as late as 1980, as to whether German sociology was dead at the moment of seizure of power ("the melodies were played to the end," Helmut Schelsky) or it was "beheaded" by the emigration of two-thirds of the recognized sociologists (René König).[7] In this controversy a third split comes to light, the split between the emigrants and those who stayed at home, or the internationalists and the nationalists.

In the postwar period, however, these rifts were hidden as long as nearly all German sociology was oriented toward American sociology.[8] This was due partly to the leading role of the repatriates; practically all the available sociological literature was American, and some of the first postwar generation of German sociologists received their professional training in the United States. With the American foundations of the Sozialforschungsstelle in Dortmund 1946 and the Institut für Sozialwissenschaftliche Forschung in Darmstadt 1949, with the UNESCO-Institut für Sozialforschung in Cologne 1951 and the foundation of some private institutions of survey research for the first time in history, the professionalization of sociology in Germany started on the basis of empirical social research. In 1955 there existed again twelve chairs of sociology, just as in 1932. But at that time the sociologists did not succeed in incorporating greater research institutions into the universities. And so, in effect, sociology has been reinstitutionalized, once again, apart from empirical social research and within the context of the humanities at the universities.

This one-sided academic setting brought about three strongly personal schools of German sociology in the sixties, forming groups around Helmut Schelsky, René König, and Theodor W. Adorno. Schelsky, at first in Hamburg, then in Münster (later on in Bielefeld), reigned over the Sozialfor-schungsstelle Dortmund and the *Soziale Welt*. König had some research groups in Köln at his disposal; he was the omnipotent editor of the *Kölner Zeitschrift für Soziologie und Sozialpsychologie* and was supported by the Westdeutsche Verlag. Adorno, Horkheimer, and Habermas were the exponents of the Frankfurt School and reached a large public through great numbers of the "suhrkamp taschenbuch wissenschaft" (stw). Of the disciples of Schelsky and König, twenty-five of each attained a professorship between 1974 and 1979, and twelve of the Frankfurt School.[9] But the ideological cohesion and attraction was greatest among the Frankfurt School, whereas the dissertations at König or Schelsky were rather heterogeneous.

Not until the great masters left the academic scene, about 1975, did a multiparadigmatic state of sociological theory develop, which is not so much attached to particular persons, institutions, or publishers. But at the same time sociology seems to have become irrelevant, or only tired. At the time of the Social-Liberal coalitions (till the change of chancellorship from Willy Brandt to Helmut Schmidt), sociology had a phase of great awakening and took part in all great reform projects (education, university, public health service, administrative reform), in the newly established conflict and peace research, development aid, industrial and technology politics—at any rate it produced thousands of expert opinions and proposals; but in the final stages of this coalition sociology was regarded as rather disturbing, and the Conservative governments led by the CDU (Christian Democratic Union) since 1982 have preferred the more abstract and less obliging advice of some philosophers and historians.[10] Since then the discipline diversified in an impressive manner; now there is a great variety of specialties, of theoretical perspectives and (self-made) traditions; but at the same time sociology is overcome with self-doubt, self-restraint, and self-denunciation.[11] In fact, sociology is struck with a crisis of identity and shows obvious signs of disintegration. Many no longer take any notice of what others are doing; others prefer to speak of "social sciences" but not of "sociology"; in any case the scientific community of sociologists hardly functions as a monitor of the quality and further development of this discipline.[12] Apart from the replacement rate in teaching and research, there is no job market for sociologists as such. Empirical research depends largely on financing from outside. The permanent problem of teaching is to convey knowledge to heterogeneous students with low vocational motivation.[13] Besides this, the German sociologists are split in a generation gap: an abrupt transition from a period of excessive personal and institutional expansion in the seventies to a lasting stagnation in the eighties has brought about a situation in which not so old "archons" block the careers of young (or not so young) sociologists for years.[14]

INSTITUTIONAL DEVELOPMENT

As the main focus of German sociology is in the academic setting, the statistics of students and professors will give a first impression of the discipline. In the winter semester 1987–1988 the former Federal Republic of Germany (BRD) had 1,409,000 students in all, of which 39,000 studied political and social sciences, this is 2.7 percent (of which about one-third counts for political science and two-thirds for sociology).[15] For these students there were 2,124 academic teachers, of which 824 were professors. Not only the quantitative relation of teachers and students (1:47) but also the financial expenditure proves sociology to be an inexpensive mass course (0.83 percent of the total financial expenditure).[16] However, the universities are financed totally by the states (Länder), and there are no tuition fees. Sociology as a university discipline has about 500 professors and 1,000 other senior teaching and research positions.[17] The Deutsche Gesellschaft für Soziologie includes about 1,000 members, of which about 430 are professors.[18] The centers of sociological study are Berlin, Bielefeld, and Frankfurt. The circumstances in the former German Democratic Republic (DDR) are quite different. Here, all sociological research was concentrated in the institutions of the Academy of Sciences, and sociology was fully identified with the political dogma of Marxism-Leninism. Now it is one of the most important tasks to reestablish sociology as a university discipline and to put the available personnel—insofar as the necessary professional abilities are there—back into the universities. At present, in the whole of Germany there are about 15,000 sociologists working in a professional position, but recently the labor market for sociologists has narrowed.

Social research is pursued and financed partly by public organizations and public spending, partly by commercial enterprises. The commercial research is for the most part survey research. In 1989 there were 165 full-service opinion research institutions in Germany, but frequently small enterprises with six to twenty employees. The largest opinion research institute is INFRATEST with 600 employees. The enterprises united in the Study Group of German Market Research Institutes (ADM) carry out mainly survey research, and they produce nearly 3,000 data sets per year; the institutes united in the Study Group of Social Science Institutes (ASI) in addition perform observations and tests, and they deliver 1,000 data sets per year. All together they make a turnover of DM 2,000 million per year.[19] In 1987 also DM 7,288 million of public funds was spent on scientific research in all, but only DM 933 million of this went toward the social sciences and humanities (12.8 percent). With this money, all in all, 20,574 scientists were financed, of which 3,406 were in the social sciences or humanities (16.5 percent).[20] Public spending finances research institutes like the Max-Planck-Institut für Gesellschaftsforschung (Social Research) in Cologne, or Bildungsforschung (Educational Research) in Berlin, the German Youth Institute in Munich, the Institute for the Labor Market and Occupational Research in Nuremberg, the Federal Institute of Vocational Training in Berlin, the Social Science Research Center in Berlin, and the University Information System in Hannover. The Deutsche Forschungsgemeinschaft (DFG, German Research Association), which is a self-governing organization without political instructions, administered DM 1,086 million in 1988, promoting above all individual projects at university institutes. Of this sum DM 51.3 million (4.7 percent) was spent on the social sciences, that is, for 873 (5.7 percent) salaries and scholarships. The DFG attempts to concentrate a part of its resources in Focus Research Programs, in 1989, for example, for "Social Politics" at the University of Frankfurt (DM 5,422 million), "Status Passages and Risk Situations in the Course of Life" at the University of Bremen (DM 1,547 million), or "Developmental Perspectives of Work" at the University of Munich (DM 1,729 million).[21]

The dissolution of the academy system of the former GDR and the return of these scientists to the university demand more than proportional resources and new scientific tasks for the new "Länder." Out of 24,000 members of the Academy of Sciences, 90 percent were natural scientists, 10 percent social scientists in the widest sense of the term, but only 210 members (about 70 at the universities, 140 at the institutions of the academy) were commendable sociologists.[22] On the part of the social science institutions, all party-linked institutions (like the Academy for Social Science at the Central Committee of the SED, Socialist Unity Party) have been dissolved; other institutions (like the Central Institute for Youth Research in Leipzig, Institute for Sociology and Social Politics in Berlin, and Center for Social Science Information in Berlin) are to be preserved in cooperation with West German institutions. But first and foremost, at all East German universities new sociological institutes have to be rebuilt because the university system has been criminally neglected compared with the academy system. So first of all a "University Replacement Program" will have to manage the structural, instrumental, and personnel requirements for the restructuring of the universities. The Max-Planck-Gesellschaft is trying to preserve 1,000 academic jobs by founding new institutes in the new "Länder," but only 170 of these will be for social sciences and humanities.[23] In 1991 the DFG established a Focus Research Program for "Social and Political Change in the Course of German Integration," but 20 percent of the regular applications for individual research projects already come from the new "Länder." Only in connection with the rebuilding of social science teaching and research at the universities can one also expect a sound development of the commercial social research.

Whereas the publication organs of the former GDR made hardly any contribution to the scientific development of sociology, a whole range of German-language journals of sociology is currently available: *Kölner Zeitschrift für Soziologie und Sozialpsychologie,* refounded 1949, a theoretical and empirical comprehensive journal, interested in the further development of the discipline; *Soziale Welt,* edited by the Study Group of Social Science Institutes, founded 1949, a journal for the analysis of German social structure, of industrial and occupational sociology, recently also for the sociology of technology and the environment; *Archives Européennes de Sociologie,* since 1949, with essays in comparative European sociology in English, French, and German; *Sociologia Internationalis,* since 1962, with contributions in comparative cultural and historical sociology, mainly in English and German; *Zeitschrift für Soziologie,* edited by the Faculty of Sociology at the University of Bielefeld since 1972; *Annali di Sociologia/ Soziologisches Jahrbuch,* edited since 1985, now by a Italian-German Association of Sociology; *Berliner Journal für Soziologie,* since 1991; *Sociologus,* a ethnosociological journal since 1950; *Angewandte Sozialforschung* since 1972, *Analyse und Kritik* since 1972 too. But also the *Schweizerische Zeitschrift für Soziologie/Revue Suisse de Sociologie,* founded 1975, and the *Österreichische Zeitschrift für Soziologie,* established 1976, or *Journal für Sozialforschung,* founded 1960 by Paul F. Lazarsfeld, or *SWS-Rundschau,* a journal for survey research (since 1960) are open for German contributions. For the neighboring disciplines some journals like the demographic journal *Zeitschrift für Bevölkerungswissenschaft* branched off in 1974, *Psychosozial* in 1977, and *Familiendynamik* in 1975. Political sociological contributions are also published in political science journals like *Politische Vierteljahresschrift* or *Zeitschrift für Politik.* Social history has a long tradition with *Vierteljahresschrift für Sozial- und Wirtschaftsgeschichte,* founded 1914, and now completed with *Geschichte und Gesellschaft* (1974) and *1999: Zeitschrift für Sozialgeschichte des 20. und 21. Jahrhunderts* (1985), or the Austrian *Geschichte und Gegenwart* (1981). Last but not least, there are review journals such as *Soziologische Revue* and *Sozialwissenschaftliche Literaturumschau,* both since 1977, and a communication journal of the DGS, *Soziologie,* with irregular publication. Naturally, the greater social research institutes all have their own communication journals, such as *ZUMA-Nachrichten, ZA-Information* (Zentralarchiv), *WZB-Mitteilungen* (Wissenschaftszentrum Berlin), *BISS Public* (Berliner Institut für Sozialwissenschaftliche Studien).

STRUCTURE OF PARADIGMS

As a result of a free scientific exchange in the Western world, the structure of sociological paradigms in Germany is nearly the same as in America. Often there are international research groups which pursue common projects and organize common conferences and publications. But there are some characteristics, already typical at the beginning of the century, returning in the seventies, above all the notorious philosophical or metaphysical shift in German sociology. One of the more estimable features of the philosophical shift is the highly systematic (sometimes oversystematic) working out and also connection of most of the paradigms. Something less estimable is the inevitable reference to the "classics," in the first instance "German classics" like Karl Marx, Max Weber, Georg Simmel, or Alfred Schütz, but also George Herbert Mead, Talcott Parsons, or Erving Goffman, who are elevated to the nobility of world classics in retrospect to the German classics. In connection with the expensive "complete editions" of their works (Max Weber since 1984, Georg Simmel since 1989), which will require decades, the editorial and interpretative preoccupation with the classics is built up to the standing of genuine sociological research ("Max-Weber Research").[24] The strong emphasis on the classics rests on the view that sociology will never reach the status of an intercultural objectivizable and cumulative theory anyway, and that there is therefore no other choice but to orient oneself toward the changeable stars of our history.[25] But if, as Weber says, "everlasting youthfulness" is granted to sociology,[26] would it not be logically more consistent to search for new concepts and more suitable explanations in historically new situations? The overvaluation of classics has to be seen in the context of the revival of the humanities and cultural sciences in the eighties.[27]

The "philosophical shift" has still less valuable implications for the scientific development of sociology if it degenerates into "social metaphysics" or "parasociology," which is in the service of immediate legitimation or delegitimation of the political system. If sociology as a science is not held in high esteem (much less than the economic or political sciences, not to speak of jurisprudence or medicine), this parasociology nevertheless gets the widest publicity and the support of many journalists and the mass media. It is this kind of sociology which provides material for the speakers of commerce, politics, and cultural industry, and this in turn influences the sociological community itself, which tries to strengthen its reputation by great rhetoric and not so much by unspectacular scientific work. Just as in the seventies,[28] the public scene is dominated by two "schools," the (self-appointed) "critical theory" of the Frankfurt School, and a Liberal-Conservative counterschool—although Jürgen Habermas and Niklas Luhmann took over from Theodor W. Adorno and Helmut Schelsky. Even though Luhmann has replaced the old general formula of "reduction of complexity" with "autopoiesis of the social system," or Habermas changed his formula (take Mead for Marx) of the "emancipation of the human genus" into "intersubjectivity" and "communication," the dichotomization and reification of fundamental sociological concepts remains the same: "subject" and "system," "consensus" and "dissension," (primary) "life-world" and (secondary, inhuman) "system," "action theory" and "systems theory" are confronting one another like knights in a tournament.[29]

Though many German sociologists consider the occupation with this kind of speculative theory as a mere waste of time (and call it "Luhmasiologie"), they are deeply occupied with it, not only because hundreds of students taking their doctorates write erudite treatises pro and con and thousands of students picked up the one or the other jargon, but also because the intellectual public in Germany (and even more so abroad) identifies "German sociology" with these authors. As the obligatory Festschriften demonstrate, the radiation into the humanities of theology and literary studies, pedagogy and communication theory and, of course, philosophy is much greater than the effect within the discipline.[30] The amazing thing is that these very difficult texts (if not esoteric, as in the case of Luhmann) find so great a readership. This is explainable only by the fact that the discussion has two levels—and in ordinary life the lower level defines the context of meaning. At the upper level all seems to be a matter of highbrow philosophy (found especially in German idealism), but at the lower level Habermas is simply identified with a socialist welfare state and Luhmann with a radical economic liberalism and the "capitalist system." Naturally, both adversaries refuse to descend to this level, but these political identifications cannot be shaken off by even the most ambitious theory constructions.

The "philosophical turn" really ended in catastrophe where—as in the former GDR with Marxism-Leninism—it was directly linked to the doctrine of a one-party state. There it suffocated or was at least adulterated— with all its great resources in a centrally and hierarchically organized academy system—all empirical research (in official statistics as in field research, analysis, and theoretical interpretation).[31] In a state which was usurped by a dictatorial party, the so-called historical materialism only served as a means of selection in academic occupations, especially in the humanities and social sciences.[32] As a result, opportunism and orthodoxy were promoted but creativity and spontaneous development dreaded. The principal contents of the social science journals in the GDR seem to have been Marxist catechesis and the censure of Western thought, while the government lacked the most necessary figures about public opinion, the change of social structure, and even about the state of the economy. Not even between East and West German Marxists was there meaningful scientific cooperation, although there were enough eager Marxists in the West, and the members of the Academy of Sciences strove for political and scientific recognition all over the world.[33] During the seventies Marxist sociology was (in network expansion, institutionalization, and theoretical pretension) without doubt the most comprehensive paradigm, and at all West German universities large and very agile Marxist Groups carried on their excesses, but in the eighties it was without import—because the central dirigisme of the planned economy failed almost totally in the development of a technically advanced and dynamic industrial society. With the considerable gap in welfare and capability of development between FRG and GDR being felt more strongly each year, the doctrine of "Histomat" lost all credibility in the East and all utopian attraction in the West.[34]

If one considers those paradigms which have been empirically fruitful and brought forth methodological innovations, the last thirty years are characterized by a sequence of four dominant paradigms, namely, structural-functional analysis, critical theory, systems theory, and the rational-choice approach, while the "interpretative" or "verstehen" paradigms of symbolic interactionism, phenomenological sociology, and ethnomethodology were of course differentiated and advanced, but were never taken up by the mainstream. According to an analysis of the three most important journals of sociology (*Kölner Zeitschrift, Soziale Welt,* and *Zeitschrift für Soziologie*) structural-functional analysis in the spirit of Parsons and/or Merton was the absolutely dominant paradigm in the sixties.[35] The intellectual center (with René König, Erwin Scheuch, and Renate Mayntz) and the organizational medium (with *Kölner Zeitschrift*) was Cologne. Although the representatives of this paradigm made every effort to comprehend the processes of the industrialization and development of developing countries, of nation-building and revolution, criticism spread that it was not really able to explain social change.

Beginning with the student unrest in 1968, this criticism became political and was directed against the American or capitalistic hegemonial model in the world and particularly in West Germany. The center of this fervent criticism was the Frankfurt School (with Theodor W. Adorno, Herbert Marcuse, and Jürgen Habermas). The "Positivism Controversy"[36] manifested a deep cleavage between the empirical-scientific sociologists on the one side and the dialectical-critical on the other. Though the term "critical theory" was meant as a code word for "Marxist theory,"[37] yet the essential aim was an up-to-date revision of the economistic-mechanistic Marxism of the GDR-Academy. Therefore, the emphasis was on (extraeconomic) "interaction" and "equal communication" which are to be realized even in a highly technical and abstract "system," particularly in the "life world."[38] Under the leadership of Habermas, who was (in tandem with Carl F. von Weizsäcker) director of the Max-Planck-Gesellschaft for the Investigation of the Scientific-Technical World (at Starnberg near Munich), this criticism was to have been transformed into an interdisciplinary research program. But with its speculative and ideological preoccupation with "capitalism critique,"[39] it was—in terms of sociology as an empirical science, not in terms of political influence—a failure.[40] The end of the hegemony of "critical theory" is marked by the dissolution of the Starnberg Institute in 1985. Reestablished in Cologne, now as the Max-Planck-Institute for Social Research and under the direction of Renate Mayntz und Fritz Scharpf, it has

a strong organizational and systems theoretical orientation and tries hard
to approach the methods and mathematical models of the natural sciences.[41]

It is ironic that critical theory in company with functionalism and structuralism has fallen into the same postmodernistic process of corruption.
The great promise that functionalism would advance the development of
society in all social-organizational and sociotechnical aspects has been unfulfilled, as has the hope that critical theory would contribute with its
"emancipative" concepts to a really "enlightened" social politics. In the
meantime even the rationality of science, especially of the social sciences,
is questioned.[42] Although Habermas holds fast to the "unfinished project
of modernity" and defends it programmatically against the French poststructuralists (such as Michel Foucault, Jean-François Lyotard, or Jacques
Derrida),[43] nevertheless he too has lost the "metanarration" of the moral
evolution of society (constructed in the seventies with the help of Jean
Piaget's "genetical structuralism"),[44] just as Luhmann has. The glorification of reason as a general and uniform human potentiality is meaningless
if the inevitable antagonisms (Lyotard: Le Différend, 1983) cannot be denied, not only in cultural values and political interests but also in the social
nature of man.[45] Also the neofunctionalist renovation program of Jeffrey
C. Alexander has not been accomplished, that is, the program of a historical functionalism which combines processes of institutionalization with
those of individualization, and which can grasp not only equilibrium but
also development and decay.[46] Instead, "postfunctionalism" has arrived,
either in the shape of "post-Parsonianism" with a combination of Parsons's action theory and systems theory,[47] or as "postfunctionalism" (and
perhaps also "poststructuralism") of Niklas Luhmann which knows no
"functional requisites" or "functional equivalents" any more but only
"self-reference," "self-organization," and "autopoiesis." In a somewhat
mystic way, complex systems regulate themselves, and there is no need or
no possibility to define or to control specified functions, and any attempt
at system integration is in vain.[48] Presumably falsely founded on the "biology of cognition" and a new brand of constructivism (with H. R. Maturana, F. Varela, and E. von Glasersfeld), all specifically sociological
problems are passed over. Nevertheless, Luhmann represents today—together with some students and colleagues at the University of Bielefeld—
the most appealing paradigm in German sociology.

In spite of terminological similarities, Luhmann's "systems theory" is
not identical[49] with usual systems theory originating in "general systems
theory" and linked with names as E. Laszlo, J. W. Forrester, D. Meadows,
K. W. Deutsch, A. Etzioni, or K. Boulding. Naturally, this systems theory
is interdisciplinary and international and shows no special German characteristics. It seems to have been its natural science or mathematical orientation which has heavily blocked its access to German sociology (and

political sciences). After the exhaustion of the sociological behaviorism (including "exchange theory") of George C. Homans and Peter Blau, which was broadly accepted in Western Germany going along with the expansion of market economy,[50] there opened two possibilities of joining natural and social sciences in the seventies, namely, (human) ethology and sociobiology. Ethology, in Germany hastily associated with Konrad Lorenz (Nobel Prize for medicine and physiology 1973, then director of the Max-Planck-Institute for Behavioral Physiology), could not be made fruitful for sociology because ethology itself purported to be an ersatz or short-circuited sociology.[51] At this time ethology was the opinion leader of conservative social and cultural critics, whereas sociology was generally discredited and pushed into the left corner. Ethology competed with sociobiology, which explains human social behavior, even at the level of genetic selection.[52] But there were high barriers of misunderstanding from the beginning.[53] While there was a great discussion of the science-theoretical and ethical implications, the impact on sociological theory was negligible. The weaknesses of both attempts at integration were their atomism and reductionism, which hindered a meaningful connection of genetic and cultural evolution, of behavior and action, of extensional coordination of behavior and intensional meaning. This was not made feasible until the concept of the "living system" as a multicentered and multilevel system was introduced.[54] But the response of German sociology was only modest.[55] Now—subsequent to the nonlinear thermodynamics of Ilya Prigogine (Nobel Prize for chemistry 1977)[56]—efforts are concentrated upon modeling a nonlinear theory of complex and dynamic social systems (including fluctuations and chaotic motions, cycles, turbulences, and catastrophes). Yet until now the empirical relevance of these attempts has only been demonstrated in future research, in management research, and in "systems therapy."[57]

Nothwithstanding the great German tradition of action theory (Karl Marx, Max Weber, Georg Simmel, Arnold Gehlen, Alfred Schütz, and Jürgen Habermas), it never succeeded as a dominant paradigm. The lack of a macrosociological dimension was too obvious, as was the often false conclusions drawn from individual action (or only the intention of action) concerning collective phenomena or system states. But also in the area of microsociology any conception of action (or ideal-typical distinction between different forms of action, e.g., "instrumental," "strategic," and "communicative" action, as with Habermas)[58] is laden with hardly objectifiable concepts of "meaning," "value," or "motivation."[59] So in spite of the notorious narrowness of utilitarianism, there seems to be no other solution than to conceptualize preferences in subjective utilities and to define the action problem as a decision problem of utility maximization.[60] Anyway, this is the starting point of the rational-choice approach which today enjoys great esteem within the range of action theory. The one-sidedness or shallowness of this approach can be corrected by the systematic connection of "action" with "situations" or "frames" and the systemic or ecological "constraints."[61] The best solution seems to be a "deep explanation" which connects several levels, namely, the "selection of action" with the "logics of the situation" and the "problem of aggregation."[62] This form of action theory seems most apt in those spheres of action in which the actors (individuals or collectivities) are free to decide without grave normative obligations and situational constraints. But the rational-choice approach is far from presenting a new universal sociological theory. The most difficult problem is the "aggregation problem"—because only few collective phenomena, system states or process connections, functional interdependences and integrations are explainable by the mere addition of individual decisions or effects. The great hopes that synergetics could give a simple solution have to be buried, or are to be restricted to processes of individual migration (of persons, votes, goods, or payments).[63] To be able to explain changes in social structure or in a collective value system, revolutions and reforms, one also needs a two-level explanation which combines the individual and collective levels, instrumental and value-oriented action, external criteria (like efficiency) and internal criteria (like identity).[64] Actually it has become apparent once more that the transfer of natural science models to sociological problems is very difficult or at least impractical.[65]

So from this side there are hardly compelling arguments rejecting the interpretative paradigms as "unscientific." Also the great undertaking to overcome the multiparadigmatic state and to find a universalistic foundation of sociology by a comprehensive comparison of all sociological theories[66] must be considered a failure. But despite the common name, the interpretative approaches form no consistent paradigm. Despite some endeavors to unite "phenomenological sociology," "symbolic interactionism," and "ethnomethodology" in the broader perspective of "hermeneutics"[67] or "pragmatism,"[68] they differ widely in theoretical and methodological implications as in institutional network and mutual citations. There are only some epistemological essentials in common. First, all these approaches proceed from "symbols" or "symbolic forms" (E. Cassirer), from meanings and mental constructs, myths and rites. Second, it is the task of the sociologist to develop his/her (secondary) scientific constructs and models out of the first-order constructs of his/her fellows. Third, all have the conviction that there is no ahistorical or definitive knowledge. But in the last analysis, this is not an inadmissible conflict with the ahistorical or generalist theories which in fact can only be considered scientific if and insofar as they are designed for falsification and revision.

Phenomenology as a philosophy (with Edmund Husserl, Max Scheler, and Adolf Reinach) originated in Germany, but not until the (American) popularizing work of (the Germans) Peter Berger and Thomas Luckmann[69] was phenomenology admitted to sociology, the works of Alfred Schütz being returned to Germany and rescued from oblivion. However, as a result of the odd mixture of Marx and Mead, Schütz and Goffman, phenomenological sociology has been leveled down to a mere "sociology of everyday life"[70] without any methodological means aside from introspection. Nevertheless, in respect to sociology, it was a decided improvement compared with the "monadological" constructions of Schütz's "transcendental phenomenology," when the approach was enlarged to include a constitutional analysis of "inter-subjectivity" and a structural analysis of the corresponding "milieux."[71] But Husserl's (or more so Scheler's) concept of "life world" means more than "everyday life," namely, also the world of "extraordinary" borderline situations of sickness and death, love and desire, hope and anxiety, loneliness and communion. To be consistent, "transcendental phenomenology of consciousness" has to be developed further to a "structural phenomenology" and finally to a "depth phenomenology," that is, a phenomenological sociology which is apt to combine the deepest behavioral and biosocial foundations with the highest mental and sociocultural achievements of mankind, and which grasps the connection of the microsociological constitution with macrosociological and historical structures.[72]

In contrast to phenomenological sociology, ethnomethodology in Germany—but also in American sociology[73]—has lost its impulse and its integrative power. Since the first reception in the seventies,[74] when ethnomethodology behaved like a rebellious movement confronting all commercial and public social research without exception, no work of theoretical importance has been published any more (apart from a lot of meager dissertations). Admittedly, the ethnomethodological analysis pushed forward from everyday life and conversation analysis into the area of the professions, administrations, clinics, social welfare, and laboratories,[75] but the advocates of this paradigm themselves feel compelled to defend their work against the criticism of being esoteric and practically irrelevant.[76] In fact, especially in connection with a "radical constructivism" and the "strong program" in the sociology of science, ethnomethodology shows stark subversive and denunciatory features.[77] Forgetting the principle of "referential reflexivity,"[78] too many ethnomethodologists arrogantly tend to ignore their own role in the broader scientific and political discourse—which is more and more characterized and confined by a fashionable relativism and even hostility toward science and industrial society.

Neither can one deny a certain stagnation of symbolic interactionism. Owing to its close relation to everyday social life and its good didactic preparation,[79] this paradigm is of overriding importance in academic teaching (and examinations), but in social research Goffman's presidential address at the ASA congress 1982 seems to have been the last word not only in the United States but also in Germany.[80] This may be partly due to the belated reception of George Herbert Mead and also of Erving Goffman (and the reintegration of Georg Simmel in this tradition),[81] but it is partly due to the complete absorption of Mead by the Habermas-Luhmann controversy.[82] This highly ideological controversy with its metaphysical dichotomies tends to a grave misjudgment of symbolic interactionism which, as the exact opposite, focuses on social processes, joint acts, and institutional interconnections—to overcome the separation of microsociology and macrosociology, of "self" and "system." Whereas the conceptions and results of symbolic interactionism are assimilated so well into the areas of group sociology, communication, socialization, and self-identity that their origin falls into oblivion,[83] the contribution of symbolic interactionism to macrosociology in the realm of democracy, economic associations, churches, states, and international relations has yet to be discovered.[84]

All in all, the increase in the number of sociologists has been accompanied by a sizable differentiation of paradigms, under which the dominant paradigms come into and go out of fashion, but the marginal paradigms show greater continuity. On the negative side, none of the existing paradigms is capable of integrating all sociological theory.[85] In Germany the rift between natural sciences and cultural sciences seems extremely deep and, contrary to the abstract program of "micro-macro link,"[86] the antagonism between "subject" and "system" remains a matter of worldview. All these differences are not justifiable in scientific terms—because in the meantime irreversibility, nonlinearity, and historicity have found their way in the natural sciences; and the humanities are concerned with the foundations of cognitive biology, brain research, and artificial intelligence. They are only an inheritance of the "two cultures" to which the social sciences could not add a third. The rather "academic" idea of "interdisciplinarity" was also doomed to failure; instead there is a great demand for "multidisciplinarity" and the cooperation of different disciplines for effective problem solutions.[87] Perhaps there are only two strategies of combining several paradigms and methods, namely, the path of a multilevel systems theory, and the path of historical sociology. Systems theory should try to combine the behavioral and the mental level, actor and environment, linear and nonlinear dynamics.[88] Historical sociology would combine different forms of explanation at different levels (individuals, institutions, collectivities, systems) and in different phases of development or social change (in the processes of institutionalization and deinstitutionalization, in system-building and catastrophe).[89] But, incidentally, even in Germany the classification and analysis of paradigms is regarded as an academic exercise whereas actual social research makes use of different explanations and methods at any time, modifying and combining them for its own purposes, depending on the perceived structure of problems.

METHODOLOGICAL DEVELOPMENTS

Unlike the seventies, when the "Positivismusstreit" dominated the academic scene and the "methods of empirical social research" were rather simple and did not require a high degree of specialization, today the methodology of social research is fully institutionalized not only as a part of the university curriculum but also outside the university in the form of counselling centers and information offices. Today not only are the methods of social research a great specialty in themselves, but the social researchers of the "third generation" are split into different methodological directions and special approaches which have only little to do with each other.[90] There is an increasing dualism between a highly reflective "academic methodology" and a methodologically "cheap" commercial social research (predominating in opinion and market research).[91] While on the one hand social research is devoted to "computerization" and the execution of elegant models, without paying attention to the quality and relevance of the underlying data, so on the other hand there is daily publicized data which is highly dramatized by the media, without contributing the least to consistent long-term social research.[92] In this manner the exploration of factual social behavior is replaced by self-made opinion constructs, deprived of any prognostic or explanative value. In 1974 as in 1989 there is no established methodological "professional culture" in Germany which would force all those who make statements on social and political problems to be concerned with the procedures and results of empirical research.[93] On the other hand, methodologically conscious social researchers may be accused of selecting only those problems which conform to their refined methods, or breaking off their work before the macrosociological consequences are clear enough.[94]

The "crisis of quantitative social research," which was and is a "crisis of complexity," has not yet been overcome—though today it is on a higher level. Already in the seventies, when most sociologists operated with single variables, correlating them directly with the help of electromechanical sorting machines, it was clear that "multi-collinearity" is the normal case and that only a small part of the variation could be explained by the dependent variables.[95] In the meantime, it is plain enough that many factors have only weak effects, but that nearly all are correlated with one another, and that most factor correlations can only be detected indirectly. Now, increasingly, social research is confronted with the problem of "non-linearity" concerning the really critical variables, that is, data and single factors cannot simply be "aggregated" any longer, because "ecological" and "synergetic" effects make themselves felt. In this case, it is not enough to carry on working with the conventional means of statistical mathematics; now fundamental new models of data processing are necessary which transcend the imagination of mechanics or statistical thermodynamics.

Above all, this is the task of mathematical model-building, at least at the qualitative level. At first different topological situations and typical forms of dynamics have to be designed (with the help of decision, game, catastrophe, or fluctuations theory)—indeed different "logics of behavior." Only afterwards will it be possible to develop quantitative models. Yet it is exactly in this direction of mathematical modeling that several seemingly fruitful developments began to emerge over the last fifteen years. After the repeated breakdown of some premature overgeneralizations of a particular model, a conjoint theory of nonlinear dynamics seems to be emerging.[96]

Abandoning the general implication of linearity, neither can time sequences continue to be regarded as reversible, and from microdata (e.g., individual attitudes, motivations, calculations) one cannot infer macrodata (e.g., birth rates, social mobility, value changes, system states), and vice versa. Diachronic courses of events are no longer (on the assumption of linearity) deducible from synchronic comparisons, that is, one needs individual "real-time" data. Whereas in 1974 the problems of data collection seemed to lose their significance, and everyone believed it was enough to confine oneself to data analysis, the situation has now turned around: the computerized data processing programs are elaborated far beyond the "measuring level" of the collected data. Slowly we begin to realize that the necessary data for the diagnosis of societal transformations are still missing and are not to be collected by our offices of statistics (or made anonymous and "timeless" for data protection). In this way perhaps some progress was made in the last ten years: First, the opinion polls (in connection with voting research, social indicators, quality-of-life research, life-events research) have been compiled as continual series of repetitive investigations.[97] Second, by means of personal longitudinal data of national representative samples for the first time a real connection between microlevel and macrolevel has been established.[98] Third, network studies of decision structures in communities and corporations have made it possible to connect different research procedures and levels of analysis.[99] Fourth, international comparative analyses of social structure have been linked to the analysis of historical sequences—to avoid the comparison of incomparable system states and the subsequent derivation of false prognoses.[100]

At the organizational center of these endeavors are ZUMA (Center for Surveys, Methodology, and Analysis) at the University of Mannheim, which is also in charge of the General Social Survey and ALLBUS (a biannual survey for Germany); the Zentralarchiv (Central Archive for Social Research) which collects and provides the data of all social research investigations in Germany and has been doing so now for thirty years; and the Informationszentrum (Information Center for the Social Sciences) which registers regularly all social science projects. Since 1987 these three institutions have been united in GESIS (Federation for Social Sciences Infrastructure Facilities). The aims of this umbrella organization are the provision of research data free of charge for all researchers from the universities or from private and commercial research institutes, mutual information, and advice in all methodological problems. The fact that all these data are collected and prepared by the research institutes themselves may have the advantage of averting any political disposal on the one hand, and of building up broad competences in many small institutes on the other hand; but the disadvantage may be general political irrelevance.

Concerning the methods of social research themselves, they are characterized today by a great flexibility of application. In the past, quantitative and qualitative methods confronted one another irreconcilably—the ones associated with positivism, the others with the interpretative paradigms—but now there are indications of a pragmatic integration. The first period of "qualitative social research" in the seventies was caused by the breakdown of the ambitious social reform movement and the retreat of social research to a subject-centered perspective in which the prime concern was the situation of marginal groups and deviants. At this time, these attempts were extremely heterogeneous theoretically as well as methodologically (and politically). Most researchers were interested only in the description of the situation and in data collection, but not in methodological reflection; so the results were hardly generalizable.[101] In a second period in the eighties social researchers thought more about the applicability of quantitative as well as qualitative methods.[102] Following the invention or further development of qualitative methods (like narrative interview, life history method, text analysis and context analysis, conversation analysis, group discussion, or participant observation),[103] and finally the codification of these methods in textbooks,[104] both—quantitative and qualitative—methods seem complementary to one another, even if focus and costs may differ. At the beginning of the nineties there were signs of integration even inside the same research project—where qualitative methods are especially apt for "explorative pilot studies," for the analysis and evaluation of case studies or for the selection of samples; and quantitative methods for the explication of the structural contexts, respectively, the generalization and validation of the overall results.[105]

RESEARCH SITUATION AND SOCIETAL RELEVANCE

In the last twenty years, despite considerable increase in the number of professors and assistants at the university (though this increase has not been in step with the increase of student numbers) and despite a remarkable expansion of commercial social research and a rising tide of publications, the research situation has not improved in comparison with 1974, rather deteriorated insofar as the universities are absorbed more and more by teaching and examining. So in the future the German university will not be a good place for research. On the other hand, the activities of the commercial research institutes are beyond the control of the scientific community.[106] If the main task today is—as it has been requested repeatedly for two decades[107]—to capture the dynamics and long-term developments of a complex and transnational society, then the contemporary research structure is ill-adapted. Insofar as some small research groups have been able to establish themselves at the university (with the help of DFG or subsidies from a third party), they are working from grant to grant, and they can deal only with small-scale or partial tasks. Quite similar is the situation of research institutes outside the university, which on average are too small to devote themselves to larger and long-term tasks. Studies of greater caliber can be carried out only within the framework of DFG-financed Special Research Areas at the universities. But even this special research often exists in the twilight world between university and commercial institutes, without gaining access to really relevant empirical research. Also the large, newly established Science Center at Berlin (with eighty-six social scientists) depends on very divergent political considerations on the one hand, and on the acquisition of (private and public) research assignments with permanently changing interests and problems on the other hand. Within this very fragmented research structure four main trends have emerged between 1974 and 1990.

Without doubt the overwhelming tendency is that of dissociating the social sciences toward an academic science with a literary-speculative orientation on the one hand and an exclusively practically oriented empirical science on the other hand. In this manner, sociology will be consolidated only as an academic subject and a literary genre, and the separation from empirical research will increase further. This danger results not only from the lack of communication and exchange of personnel between university and commercial research, but also from the increasing dependence of research resources upon impositions and constraints.

A second tendency is the "introversion" of the academic studies, turning away from the great problems of our time. Not that there has been no great pressure of problems, but these seem not to be problems of the kind sociologists like.[108] This escape from reality may be covered up scientifically in one way or the other: sociology can be stylized into a "reflexive science" which is concerned only with "observations of observations." Or sociologists indulge in value judgments and moral advice without having sufficient authority. Or there is the possibility of a backward-looking sociology, that is, to interpret the "classics" and annotate their works endlessly. Or one can avoid the really difficult problems if one is devoted exclusively to the cultivation of scientific orchids. In fact, the teaching subjects at German universities in 1984 are overcrowded with theoretical paradigms, whereas topicality and international format are lacking.[109]

While lectures and courses in methodology are among the most frequently chosen subjects, the empirical references are weak. The differentiation and specialization of sociology under the reign of (political and) scientific pluralism has favored the segmentation, if not "chaotization," of the discipline.[110] The unity of the discipline has been lost even at the university. And in spite of a lot of common subjects and methods, the neighboring disciplines (like psychology, history, or political science) are beginning to remove themselves from sociology.

The academization of the university is contrasted by the flatness of the utility-oriented social research, the results of which—even in the case of public bodies—are made available only selectively (or in highly aggregated form) to the scientific public. Here methods, concepts, and theories are normally only used as tools which are not refined and developed further. So social research in its entirety falls into a vicious circle: compared with the economic and political sciences, sociology is in a marginal position; but with restricted means, it can deal with only restricted problems, which are far from the really critical problems of social change and are in odd contrast to the great expectations of the public. From the point of view of usual science policy and compared with the natural sciences, sociology is a soft or underdeveloped science, but in the terms of applied research, it is not practical enough. So in both senses, a broad and systematic advancement of social research seems not to be justified.

Sociology, which was in the seventies defined by German sociologists as a "crisis science" and a "critical science," has fallen in a critical situation itself. If one observes the accounts at the congresses of the DGS, one cannot help saying that German sociology has lost its critical or missionary impetus; but also as a practical science, it has not been able to come up to the expectations which the professionalization debate of the seventies had formulated.[111] In place of innovations or at least alarming theses, disruption and mutual misunderstanding prevail.[112] Certainly, the procreation of new specialties continues, and the congresses burst with countless sections and ad-hoc meetings, but in spite of the publicly demonstrated seriousness and topicality,[113] a marked loss of political or societal relevance cannot be denied. In any case, it is more than "depolitization" or "normalization," if so important specialties as political sociology and sociology of development have nearly disappeared from the discussion, whereas cultural sociology—not without reason suppressed or forgotten for forty years—is rewakening and penetrating all other specialties.

The sociology of development had its bloom of youth in the sixties and seventies, when the missionary zeal of German sociology was projected into the Third World (while Germany was divided and was unable to move in a stagnating West European integration). But soon after the appearance (1969) of a special edition of the *Kölner Zeitschrift*,[114] representing the international state of the art, developmental sociology continued to supply inexhaustible food for dissertations, though the sparse research was dispersed over a lot of disconnected petty regional problems. With the German Sociological Meeting 1990 in Frankfurt ("The Modernization of Modern Societies") the sociology of development has returned home from afar. Now such immense problems as the reconstruction of the GDR, West European economic and political integration or East European developmental aid await solutions. And even "ethnosociology," always linked to sociology of development, but never seriously accepted in Germany, has become indigenous in the form of the problems of "guest workers," "right of asylum," and the "multicultural society."[115]

Most perplexing is the decay of political sociology.[116] In the conference papers of the Sociological Meeting 1986 the name of political sociology has disappeared. Although it is an important teaching and examination subject, for many years no new textbook of political sociology has been published. In Germany political sociology was introduced as a "sociology of democracy,"[117] and that it remained, but in the end only "political culture" was discussed (until it was incorporated into the vocabulary of the politicians).[118] With the growing practice of democracy and with the institutionalization of survey and voting research, however, this form of political sociology, which was mainly a sociology of the political institutions (parties, unions, government, bureaucracy, public opinion),[119] receded into the background, or (cooperating with political sciences, administration sciences, public law) it has become interdisciplinary—as it was previously. Beginning with the protest generation of 1968, anti-institutional themes like "postmaterialist value change" or "social movements"[120] have captured scientific interest. The guild of German sociologists (apart from some individual exceptions) neither succeeded in incorporating these themes nor was able to depart from German introspection into the realm of international and transnational relations.

Transmuted past recognition is the sociology of science to which a promising special edition of *Kölner Zeitschrift* was dedicated as late as 1975.[121] Under the now interdisciplinary heading "science research," problems of "technology assessment" are in fact discussed.[122] What today goes by the name "sociology of science" are only fragments left over by the "ethnomethodologization" of science and the "strong program" imported from Cambridge,[123] or there are grandiose reflections about the "autopoiesis" of science[124] which prevent any attempt at control and—in consequence—analysis. The "sociology of technics" has become again (as with Arnold Gehlen[125] and Helmut Schelsky in the fifties and sixties) a strongly philosophical or cultural-anthropological subject, however now without any faith in the progress of mankind and, on the contrary, firmly in the context of ecological risks and dangers.[126]

In full accordance with the AGIL scheme of Parsons, cultural sociology was—after economic sociology, political sociology, and the analysis of so-

cial structure—the last specialty which entered the scene. Cultural sociology was a typical German creation, arising as a kind of compensation
for the injuries of the lost war and the treaty of Versailles 1919. Hence it
was essentially "cultural critique" or "civilization critique" (confronting
Western industrialism). With its idealistic glorification of "high culture"
and its dichotomic conceptual structure ("spirit" vs. "power," "ideal-
factors" vs. "real-factors," etc.), moreover deeply infected with grand historical speculations, it never found empirical ground and remained
methodologically feeble. By means of a special edition (1986) of the *Kölner Zeitschrift*[127] and the establishment of a section of the DGS, a serious
attempt was made to find the right track. But the danger of a renewed
"culture-critical" trend cannot be ruled out, now perhaps in connection
with a powerful "alternative movement." Let us hope that the discovery
of "everyday culture" and that many good investigations of "popular culture" will open the view for the multilayered and processual features of
culture.[128] Up to now the functional interdependencies between culture
and politics, culture and economics, culture and technics are so obvious
that there will be no "special world" for culture from now on. Also the
methods of cultural analysis (e.g., with ethnomethodology and hermeneutic text analysis, with reception research and cultural statistics) are sufficiently developed to block the way to mere speculation.

It is no wonder that in accordance with this shift of the main focus,
sociologists have to complain about general "political irrelevance."[129] But
one must distinguish at least three spheres of influence with very different
impact. An area in which sociology still has great influence, even though
more indirectly, is public opinion. This was already the great lament in
the days of Helmut Schelsky who—in 1974 in the face of the socially
critical left (the Marxists and the Frankfurt School)—feared a new "class
rule of the meaning communicators," and especially of sociologists.[130] Ten
years later Friedrich H. Tenbruck claimed a nearly perfect "social scien-
tification of everyday life," according to which all people define their own
self, all their social relations and experiences in terms of role theory or
reference group theory or the trendy social criticism of sociologists.[131] And
also today the brand-new "jargon of authenticity"—to be read in literary
journals and to be heard in jubilees—is delivered more often than not by
sociologists (now, e.g., by Habermas and Luhmann), less by political scientists or philosophers. Amazingly enough, particularly in public discourse, which develops a momentum of its own and is difficult to see
through, again and again sociological definitions and explanations win
public recognition.[132]

Quite another thing is the application of sociological knowledge to the
social services professions such as organizing employment, youth and social work, vocational training, or adult education. It was here that the
greatest impact was once expected, but the sociologists had to learn that

a mere application is out of the question; on the contrary, the scientific knowledge offered is selected and used according to the professions' own institutional and strategic purposes.[133] A special weakness of sociology, compared with economics, medicine, or pedagogy, is that it has no institutional access to one of the social professions, and consequently no control over the application of its research results. So sociology gains access only indirectly through the infiltration of the neighboring disciplines, and, to be precise, not through well-tried problem solutions but through labeling the social problems.[134] But in doing so, the accent of labeling has shifted in the last decades: whereas in the sixties a general belief in social progress and in systematic planning prevailed, in the seventies only partial aspects were treated (and declared problems of special or marginal groups), but in the eighties the problems are usually labeled as "personal problems" not of interest to or the responsibility of society.

By far the least influence of sociology is in political consultation or political planning on the level of government or the great corporate actors (like corporations, banks, parties, associations). To be sure, in a complex and extensively decentralized market economy and in a pluralist society, it would be a great mistake to assume an obsolete "technocratic" model of social control and political steering, in which the social sciences would have the best knowledge for government, and the politicians had only to accept and "implement" it. But without any institutionalized and continually working consultation or planning organization not even the necessary data can be obtained.[135] The terrible vision of "technocracy" arouses political suspicion where the private actors (multinational corporations, the German Federal Bank, commercial economic advisers, research institutes, or foundations) have better data and make better forecasts and calculations than the public actors. It is no little tragedy that in the old FRG a sufficient scientific capacity is available, but in the former GDR a centralist-technocratic regime—though of course without a really scientific basis of social research—has failed totally, and so nearly all confidence in the social sciences is lost. Today German sociologists are under the impression that a "gigantic social experiment" is unfolding before their eyes, but one which they cannot influence, one which they can face only as a "forum of reflection."[136]

NOTES

1. Erwin K. Scheuch, "Von der Deutschen Soziologie zur Soziologie in der Bundesrepublik Deutschland," *Österreichische Zeitschrift für Soziologie* 15 (1990), 30–50.

2. "Emancipation" is the leitmotiv of Jürgen Habermas from *Theorie und Praxis* (Neuwied: Luchterhand, 1960), to *Der philosophische Diskurs der Moderne* (Frankfurt: Suhrkamp, 1985); Niklas Luhmann has published five collections of his

essays under the title *Soziologische Aufklärung* (Opladen: Westdeutscher Verlag, 1970, 1975, 1981, 1987, 1990).

3. Some German emigrants to the United States (or Canada) are very busy confirming this cliché. See Volker Meja, D. Misgeld, and Nico Stehr, eds., *Modern German Sociology* (New York: Columbia University Press, 1987).

4. Dirk Käsler, "Der Streit um die Bestimmung der Soziologie auf den Deutschen Soiologentagen 1910 bis 1930," in M. R. Lepsius, ed., *Soziologie in Deutschland und Österreich 1918 bis 1945* (Opladen: Westdeutscher Verlag, 1981), 207.

5. René König, *Soziologie in Deutschland* (München: Hanser, 1987), 230–257.

6. Helmut Dubiel, "Dialektische Wissenschaftskritik und interdisziplinäre Sozialforschung," *Kölner Zeitschrift für Soziologie und Sozialpsychologie* 26 (1974), 237–266; Heine von Alemann, "Geschichte und Arbeitsweise des Forschungsinstituts für Sozialwissenschaften in Köln 1919–1934," in Wolf Lepenies, ed., *Geschichte der Soziologie* (Frankfurt: Suhrkamp, 1981), vol. 2, 349–389.

7. R. König, *Soziologie in Deutschand,* 388 ff.; H. Schelsky, "Zur Entstehungsgeschichte der bundesdeutschen Soziologie," *Kölner Zeitschrift für Soziologie und Sozialpsychologie* 32 (1980), 417–456.

8. For the postwar situation see Ilona Spinner, "The Development of West German Sociology Since 1945," in Raj P. Mohan and Don Martindale, eds., *Handbook of Contemporary Developments in Sociology* (Westport, Conn.: Greenwood Press, 1975), 69–81.

9. Heinz Sahner, *Theorie und Forschung* (Opladen: Westdeutscher Verlag, 1982), 76.

10. Michael S. Freund, "Zur Berg- und Talfahrt der Sozialwissenschaften in Deutschland," *Soziologie* 1987/2, 159.

11. Johannes Weiß, "Die Normalität als Krise," *Soziale Welt* 40 (1989), 124–132.

12. Ralf Dahrendorf, "Einführung in die Soziologie," *Soziale Welt* 40 (1989), 3.

13. Friedrich Fürstenberg, "Soziologie—die fragwürdige Profession," *Soziale Welt* 40 (1989), 326.

14. Cf. "Heskemer Protestation," *Zeitschrift für Soziologie* 19 (1990), 223–225.

15. *Statistisches Jahrbuch für die Bundesrepublik Deutschland* (Stuttgart: Metzler-Poeschel, 1989), 352.

16. This shows also the statistics of examinations (l.c., 356): Compared with 2,553 passed examinations in the whole year 1987 and a period of study of 10–12 semesters, this makes about 1,265 examinations per semester or a chance of success less than 40 percent.

17. Ludger Viehoff, "Zur Entwichlung der Soziologie an den Hochschulen der Bundesrepublik Deutschland von 1960 bis 1981," *Zeitschrift für Soziologie* 13 (1984), 264–272, counted in 1981 a total of 1,290 persons: 212 full professors, 213 other professors, 245 assistants, and 620 other research personnel.

18. List of members of the DGS, August 1991. The DGS admits only members who have graduated with a Ph.D. and have produced relevant publications.

19. E. K. Scheuch, "Von der Pioniertat zur Institution—Beobachtungen zur Entwicklung der empirischen Sozialforschung," in D. Franke and J. Scharioth,

eds., *40 Jahre Markt- und Socialforschung in der Bundesrepublik Deutschland* (München: Oldenbourg, 1990), 58f.

20. *Statistisches Jahrbuch 1989 für die Bundesrepublik Deutschland,* l.c., 362.

21. Deutsche Forschungsgemeinschaft *Tätigkeitsbericht 1989* (Bonn 1989), 170.

22. M. R. Lepsius, "Zur Entwicklung der Soziologoie in den neuen Bundesländern," *Kölner Zeitschrift für Soziologie und Sozialpsychologie* 43 (1991), 139.

23. Hans F. Zacher, "Wissenschaft und Forschung im vereinten Deutschland," *MPG-Spiegel* 1991/5, 25.

24. See Johannes Weiß, ed., *Max Weber heute* (Frankfurt: Suhrkamp, 1989); Heinz-Jürgen Dahme and Otthein Rammstedt, eds., *Georg Simmel und die Moderne* (Frankfurt: Suhrkamp, 1984); Hans Joas, *Praktische Intersubjektivität (G. H. Mead)* (Frankfurt: Suhrkamp, 1980).

25. Friedrich H. Tenbruck, "The Significance of the Classics and the Nature of Theory," in Horst J. Helle, ed., *Verstehen and Pragmatism* (Frankfurt: Lang, 1991), 17–23.

26. Max Weber, "Die 'Objektivität' sozialwissenschaftlicher Erkenntnis" (1904), in M. Weber, *Soziologie, Weltgeschichtliche Analysen, Politik,* ed. by Johannes Winckelmann (Stuttgart: Kröner, 1956), 251.

27. See Wolfgang Frühwald, ed., *Geisteswissenschaften heute: Eine Denkschrift* (Frankfurt: Suhrkamp, 1991); Peter Weingart, ed., *Die sog. Geisteswissenschaften (1954–87)* (Frankfurt: Suhrkamp, 1991).

28. See W. L. Bühl, "Theorie und Paratheorie," in G. Albrecht, H. Daheim, and F. Sack, eds., *Soziologie—Festschrift für R. König* (Köln: Westdeutscher Verlag, 1973), 48–67.

29. William Rasch, "Theories of Complexity, Complexities of Theory: Habermas, Luhmann, and the Study of Social Systems," *German Studies Review* 14 (1991), 65–83.

30. Dirk Baecker, ed., *Theori als Passion: Niklas Luhmann zum 60. Geburtstag* (Frankfurt: Suhrkamp, 1987); Axel Honneth, ed., *Zwischenbetrachtungen im Prozeß der Aufklärung: Jürgen Habermas zum 60. Geburtstag* (Frankfurt: Suhrkamp, 1989).

31. Artur Meier, "Die Revolution entläßt ihre Theoretiker," in Bernd Giesen and Claus Leggewie, eds., *Experiment Vereinigung* (Berlin: Rotbuch, 1991), 28–37; Frank Adler and Rolf Reißig, "Sozialwissenschaftliche Forschung als Modernisierungs—Ferment des Realsozialismus—eine gescheiterte Illusion," *BISS Public,* 1991, 5–37.

32. Ulrich Hedtke, "Marx als Thema der Sozialphilosophie—eine Problemskizze," *Berliner Journal für Soziologie* 1 (1991), 211–218.

33. Ansgar Weymann, "Eine deutsche Ideologie," in Giesen and Leggewie, eds., *Experiment Vereinigung,* l.c., 52–58; Johannes Weiß, "Kompetenz, Kontrolle, Korruption," ibid., 59–67.

34. Wolfgang Zapf, "Der Untergang der DDR und die soziologische Theorie der Modernisierung," in Giesen and Leggewie, eds., l.c., 38–51.

35. Heinz Sahner, "Trends in German Post-War Sociology" (Arbeitsbericht 7), Hochschule Lüneburg, 1985, 9.

36. Theodor W. Adorno, ed., *Der Positivismusstreit in der deutschen Soziologie* (Neuwied: Luchterhand, 1969).

37. Rolf Wiggershaus, *Die Frankfurter Schule* (München: dtv, 1989), 13.

38. See Habermas, *Theorie des kommunikativen Handelns* (Frankfurt: Suhrkamp, 1981).

39. See Habermas, *Legitimationsprobleme im Spätkapitalismus* (Frankfurt: Suhrkamp, 1973); Claus Offe, *Strukturprobleme des kapitalistischen Staates* (Frankfurt: Suhrkamp, 1972); Klaus Eder, *Geschichte als Lernprozeß* (Frankfurt: Suhrkamp, 1985).

40. Hans-Joachim Giegel, "Die Architektonik der Kritischen Theorie," *Berliner Journal für Soziologie* 1 (1991), 225–230.

41. See Renate Mayntz and Birgitta Nedelmann, "Eigendynamische soziale Prozesse," *Kölner Zeitschrift für Soziologie und Sozialpsychologie* 39 (1987), 648–668; Renate Mayntz, B. Rosewitz, U. Schimank, and R. Stichweh, *Differenzierung und Verselbständigung: Zur Entwicklung gesellschaftlicher Teilsysteme* (Frankfurt: Campus, 1988); R. Mayntz/T. P. Hughes, eds., *The Development of Large Technical Systems* (Frankfurt: Campus, 1988).

42. Ulrich Beck and W. Bonß, *Weder Sozialtechnologie noch Aufklärung?* (Frankfurt: Suhrkamp, 1989); W. Bonß and H. Hartmann, eds., *Entzauberte Wissenschaft* (Special Number 3 of *Soziale Welt)* (Göttingen: Schwarz, 1985). For the political sciences see Klaus von Beyme, *Theorie der Politik im 20. Jahrhundert: Von der Moderne zur Postmoderne* (Frankfurt: Suhrkamp, 1991).

43. J. Habermas, *Der philosophische Diskurs der Moderne* (Frankfurt: Suhrkamp, 1985); Manfred Frank, *Was ist Neostrukturalismus?* (Frankfurt: Suhrkamp, 1984); M. Frank, *Die Grenzen der Verständigung* (Frankfurt: Suhrkamp, 1988).

44. J. Habermas, "Zum Thema: Geschichte und Evolution," *Geschichte und Gesellschaft* 2 (1976), 310–357; N. Luhmann, "Evolution und Geschichte," ibid., 284–309.

45. Bernhard Waldenfels, "Zeitgenössische Philosophie diesseits und jenseits des Rheins," *Spuren* 30/31 (1989), 48–52.

46. Jeffrey C. Alexander, "Introduction," in Alexander, ed., *Neo-Functionalism* (London: Sage, 1985), 7–18.

47. See Richard Mümch, *Die Kultur der Moderne,* 2 vols. (Frankfurt: Suhrkamp, 1986); Hans Haferkamp, *Soziales Handeln* (Opladen: Westdeutscher Verlag, 1987); Michael Schmid, *Sozialtheorie und Soziales System* (München: Universität der Bundeswehr, 1989).

48. N. Luhmann, *Die Wissenschaft der Gesellschaft* (Frankfurt: Suhrkamp, 1990), 627 ff.; Luhmann, "Die Autopoiesis des Bewußtseins," *Soziale Welt* 36 (1985), 402–446.

49. See Johannes Berger, "Wie systemisch ist die Theorie sozialer Systeme?" in H. Haferkamp and M. Schmid, eds., *Sinn, Kommunikation und soziale Differenzierung* (Frankfurt: Suhrkamp, 1987), 129–152.

50. Hans J. Hummell, "Psychologische Ansätze zu einer Theorie sozialen Verlaltens," in R. König, ed., *Handbuch der empirischen Sozialforschung,* vol. 2 (Stuttgart: Enke, 1969), 1157–1277; Karl-Dieter Opp, *Verhaltenstheoretische Soziologie* (Reinbek: Rowohlt, Rowohlt, 1972).

51. See Konrad Lorenz, *Das sogenannte Böse* (Wien: Schoeler, 1963); *Die acht Todsünden der zivilisierten Menschheit* (München: Piper, 1973); *Der Abbau des Menschlichen* (München: Piper, 1983).

52. See Edward O. Wilson, *Sociobiology* (Cambridge: Harvard University Press, 1975); *On Human Nature* (Cambridge: Harvard University Press, 1978);

Richard Dawkins, *The Selfish Gene* (New York: Oxford University Press, 1976); Wolfgang Wickler and Uta Seibt, *Das Prinzip Eigennutz* (Hamburg: Hoffman & Dampe, 1977).

53. Heiner Flohr and Wolfgang Tönnesmann, "Die Bedeutung der Life Schiences für die Politikwissenschaft," in Flohr and Tönnesmann, eds., *Politik und Biologie* (Berlin: Parey, 1983).

54. James G. Miller, *Living Systems* (New York: McGraw-Hill, 1978); Kenneth E. Boulding, *Ecodynamics* (London: Sage, 1978).

55. Dieter Claessens, *Das Konkrete und das Abstrakte: Soziologische Skizzen zur Anthropologie* (Frankfurt: Suhrkamp, 1980); W. L. Bühl, *Struktur und Dynamik des menschlichen Sozialverhaltens* (Tübingen: Mohr, 1982).

56. Ilya Prigogine and Isabelle Stengers, *Dialog mit der Natur* (München: Piper, 1981); Grégoire Nicolis and I. Prigogine, *Die Erforschung des Komplexen* (München: Piper, 1987); Bernd Martens, *Differentialgleichungen und dynamische Systeme in den Sozialwissenschaften* (München: Profil, 1984); Feliz Geyer and J. van der Zouwen, eds., *Sociocybernetic Paradoxes* (London: Sage, 1986); W. L. Bühl, *Sozialer Wandel im Ungleichgesicht* (Stuttgart: Enke, 1990).

57. Ervin Laszlo, *Global denken* (Rosenhaim: Horizonte Verlag, 1989); Philipp Herder-Dorneich, *Systemdynamik* (Baden-Baden: Nomos, 1988); Hans Ulrich and Gilbert J. G. Probst, *Anleitung zum ganzheitlichen Denken und Handeln* (Bern: Haupt, 1988); Dietrich Dörner, *Die Logik des Mißlingens* (Reinbek: Rowohlt, 1989); Paul F. Dell, *Klinische Erkenntnis* (Dortmund: Verlag modernes Lernen, 1986); Hans R. Fischer, ed., *Autopoiesis* (Heidelberg: Auer, 1991).

58. Andreas Dorschel, "Handlungstypen und Kriterien," *Zeitschrift für philosophische Forschung* 44 (1990), 220–252.

59. Hartmut Esser, "Rational Choice," *Berliner Journal für Soziologie* 1 (1991), 231–243; Helmut Wiesenthal, "Rational Choice," *Zeitschrift für Soziologie* 16 (1987), 434–449; Rolf Ziegler, "Norm, Sanktion, Rolle," *Kölner Zeitschrift für Soziologie und Sozial-psychologie* 36 (1984), 433–463.

60. H. Esser, "Habits, Frames and Rational Choice," *Zeitschrift für Soziologie* 19 (1990), 231–247.

61. Uwe Schimank, "Gesellschaftliche Systeme als Akteurfiktionen," *Kölner Zeitschrift für Soziologie und Sozialpsychologie* 40 (1988), 619–638.

62. H. Esser, "Habits, Frames and Rational Choice," l.c., 231 f.

63. Hermann Haken, "Can Synergetics Be of Use to Management Theory?" in H. Ulrich and G. J. B. Probst, eds., *Self-Organization and Management of Social Systems* (Berlin: Springer, 1984), 33–41; Peter Weise, "Der synergetische Ansatz zur Analyse der gesellschaftlichen Selbstorganisation," *Ökonomie und Gesellschaft* 8 (1990), 12–64.

64. Ralph H. Turner, "The Use and Misuse of Rational Models in Collective Behavior and Social Psychology," *Archives européennes de sociologie* 32 (1991), 89f.

65. Renate Mayntz, "The Influence of Natural Science Theories on Contemporary Social Science," *MPIFG Discussion Paper* 90/7; Klaus von Bayme, "Ein Paradigmenwechsel aus dem Geist der Naturwissenschaften," in *Journal für Sozialforschung* 31 (1991), 3–24.

66. M. Rainer Lepsius, ed., *Zwischenbilanz der Soziologie* (Stuttgart: Enke, 1976), 14–82.

67. Hans-Georg Soeffner, *Auslegung des Alltags—der Alltag der Auslegung* (Frankfurt: Suhrkamp, 1989); Soeffner, "Verstehende Soziologie und sozialwissenschaftliche Hermeneutik," *Berliner Journal für Soziologie* 1 (1991), 263–269.

68. H. J. Helle, "Epistemological Affinities between Verstehen and Pragmatism," in Helle, ed., *Verstehen and Pragmatism,* l.c., 1–16.

69. P. Berger and T. Luckmann, *Die gesellschaftliche Konstruktion der Wirklichkeit* (Frankfurt: Fischer, 1969 [am. 1966]).

70. Werner Bergmann, "Lebenswelt, Lebenswelt des Alltags oder Alltagswelt?" *Kölner Zeitschrift für Soziologie und Sozialpsychologie* 33 (1981), 50–72; Kurt Hammerich and Michael Klein, eds., *Materialien zur Soziologie des Alltags* (Köln: Westdeutscher Verlag, 1978); H. G. Soeffner, ed., *Kultur und Alltag* (Göttingen: Schwarz, 1988).

71. Richard Grathoff and Bernhard Waldenfels, eds., *Sozialität und Intersubjektivität* (München: Fink, 1983); B. Waldenfels, *In den Netzen der Lebenswelt* (Frankfurt: Suhrkamp, 1985); Ilja Srubar, *Kosmion (A. Schütz)* (Frankfurt: Suhrkamp, 1988); R. Grathoff, *Milieu und Lebenswelt* (Frankfurt: Suhrkamp, 1989).

72. Heinrich Rombach, "Das Tao der Phänomenologie," *Philosophisches Jahrbuch* 98 (1991), 1–17; W. L. Bühl, "Phenomenological Reduction, Functional Insight, and Intuition of Essences," in H. J. Helle, ed., *Verstehen and Pragmatism,* l.c., 79–105.

73. Douglas W. Maynard and S. E. Clayman, "The Diversity of Ethnomethodology," *Annual Review of Sociology* 17 (1991), 411.

74. Elmar Weingarten, F. Sack, J. Schenkein, eds., *Ethnomethodologie* (Frankfurt: Suhrkamp, 1976); Stephan Wolff, *Der rhetorische Charakter sozialer Ordnung* (Berlin: Duncker & Humblot, 1976).

75. Stephan Wolff, *Produktion von Fürsorglichkeit* (Bielefeld: AJZ-Verlag, 1983); Ernst von Kardoff and Elmar Koenen, *Psyche in schlechter Gesellschaft* (München: Urban & Schwarzenberg, 1981); Karin Knorr-Cetina, *Die Fabrikation von Erkenntnis* (Frankfurt: Suhrkamp, 1984).

76. S. Wolff, "Das Gespräch als Handlungsinstrument," *Kölner Zeitschrift für Soziologie und Sozialpsychologie* 38 (1986), 55–84.

77. Robert Nola, "The Strong Programme for the Sociology of Science, Reflexivity and Relativism," *Inquiry* 33 (1990), 273–296.

78. Melvin Pollner, "Left of Ethnomethodology: The Rise and Decline of Radical Reflexivity," *American Sociological Review* 56 (1991), 372.

79. See Herbert Blumer, "Der methodologische Standort des Symbolischen Interaktion ismus," in Arbeitsgruppe Bielefelder Soziologen, ed., *Alltagswissen, Interaktion und gesellschaftliche Wirklichkeit* (Reinbek: Rowohlt, 1973), 80–147; Horst J. Helle, *Verstehende Soziologie und Theorie der Symbolischen Interaktion* (Stuttgart: Teubner, 1977/1992).

80. Erving Goffman, "The Interaction Order," *American Sociological Review* 48 (1983), 1–17.

81. Hans Joas, *Praktische Intersubjektivität* (Frankfurt: Suhrkamp, 1989); H. Joas, "Symbolischer Interaktionismus," *Kölner Zeitschrift für Soziologie und Sozialpsychologie* 40 (1988), 417–446; Robert Hettlage and Karl Lenz, eds., *Erving Goffman—ein soziologischer Klassiker der zweiten Generation* (Bern: Haupt, 1990).

82. See Hans Haferkamp, "Interaction Theory in the Federal Republic of Germany," *Symbolic Interaction* 10 (1987), 143–165; H. Haferkamp, "Autopoietisches soziales System oder konstruktives soziales Handeln?" in H. Haferkamp and M. Schmid, eds., *Sinn, Kommunikation und soziale Differenzierung* (Frankfurt: Suhrkamp, 1987), 51–88.

83. Johann A. Schülein, "Funktion und Strukturwandel subjekttheoretischer Konzepte in der Mikrosoziologie," *Österreichische Zeitschrift für Soziologie* 14 (1989), 64–79; Hans Geser, "Die kommunikative Mehrebenenstruktur elementarer Interaktionen," *Kölner Zeitschrift für Soziologie und Sozialpsychologie* 42 (1990), 207–231; Andreas Balo, "Multiples Selbst und Lebensentwurf," *Österreichische Zeitschrift für Soziologie* 15 (1990), 71–87.

84. Ludwig Nieder, "George Herbert Meads Analyse sozialer Prozesse: Makrosoziologische Aspekte seines Denkens," Ph.D. Universität München, 1992.

85. But this is also a problem of American sociology; see Jonathan H. Turner, "The Disintegration of American Sociology," *Sociological Perspectives* 32 (1989), 419–433.

86. Jeffrey C. Alexander, B. Giesen, R. Münch, and N. J. Smelser, eds., *The Micro-Macro Link* (Berkeley: University of California Press, 1987).

87. See Jürgen Kocka, ed., *Interdisziplinarität* (Frankfurt: Suhrkamp, 1987).

88. See Jürgen Friedrich and E. Sens, "Systemtheorie und Theorie der Gesellschaft," *Kölner Zeitschrift für Soziologie und Sozialpsychologie* 28 (1976), 27–47; Niklas Luhmann, "Neuere Entwicklungen in der Systemtheorie," *Merkur* 42 (1988), 292–300; W. L. Bühl, "Entwicklungslinien einer soziologischen Systemtheorie," *Annali di Sociologia* 5 (1989/II), 13–46.

89. M. Rainer Lepsius, *Interessen, Ideen und Institutionen* (Opladen: Westdeutscher Verlag, 1990); Erwin K. Scheuch, "Quantitative Analysis of Historical Material as the Basis for a New Cooperation Between History and Sociology," in Jerome M. Clubb and E. K. Scheuch, eds., *Historical Social Research* (Stuttgart: Klett, 1980), 25–46; Heinrich Best, "Historische Sozialforschung als Erweiterung der Soziologie," *Kölner Zeitschrift für Soziologie und Sozialpsychologie* 42 (1990), 1–14.

90. Karl U. Mayer, "Empirische Sozialstrukturanalyse und Theorien der Gesellschaftlichen Entwicklung," *Soziale Welt* 40 (1989), 301.

91. E. K. Scheuch, "Von der Pioniertat zur Institution," l.c., 59.

92. Peter Atteslander, "Soziologie—eine freundliche Wissenschaft?" *Soziale Welt* 40 (1989), 284–296.

93. E. K. Scheuch, "Forschungstechniken als Teil der Soziologie heute," in M. R. Lepsius, ed., *Zwischenbilanz der Soziologie* (Stuttgart: Enke, 1976), 113.

94. K. U. Mayer, "Empirische Sozialstrukturanalyse...," l.c., 299.

95. E. K. Scheuch, "Forschungstechniken...," l.c., 111.

96. R. H. Abraham, "Complex Dynamics and the Social Sciences," *World Futures* 23 (1987), 1–10.

97. Max Kaase and H. D. Klingemann, *Wahlen und politisches System* (Opladen: Westdeutscher Verlag, 1983); Gerhard Franz, "Zeitreihenanalysen zu Wirtschaftsentwicklung, Zufriedenheit und Reegierungsvertrauen in der BRD," *Zeitschrift für Soziologie* 14 (1985), 64–88; Heiner Meulemann and W. Wiese, "Bildungsexpansion und Bildungschance," *Zeitschrift für Sozialisationsforschung und Erziehungssoziologie* 4 (1984), 287–306; K. U. Mayer and H. -P. Blossfeld, "Die

gesellschaftliche Konstruktion sozialer Ungleichheit," in P. A. Berger and S. Hradil, eds., *Ungleichheit und Lebenslauf* (Special Edition No. 7 of *Soziale Welt*), 1989, 297–318.

98. Karl M. Bolte, "Feststellungen und Überlegungen zum Stand bevölkerungs wissenschaft," *Soziale welt* 7 (1981), 401–432; Johann Handl, *Berufsmuster und Heiratschancen von Frauen* (Frankfurt: Campus, 1988); Gerd Wagner and H. J. Hoffman-Nowotny, "Gesamtgesellschaftliche Determinanten des Individualisierungsprozesses und seine Konsequenzen für Ehe und Familie," *Annali di Sociologia* 6 (1990), 26–43; Ansgar Weymann, ed., *Handlungsspielräume* (Stuttgart: Enke, 1989); K. U. Mayer, "Lebensverläufe und Sozialer Wandel," *Kölner Zeitschrift für Soziologie und Sozialpsychologie* (Special Edition 31), 1990, 7–21.

99. Franz-U. Pappi and P. Kappelhoff, "Lokale Eliten," *Zeitschrift für Soziologie* 13 (1984), 87–117; Rolf Ziegler, "Das Netzwerk der Personen- und Kapitalverflechtungen deutscher und österreichischer Wirtschaftsunternehmen," *Kölner Zeitschrift für Soziologie und Sozialpsychologie* 36 (1984), 586–614.

100. Max Haller and W. Müller, eds., *Beschäftigungssystem im gesellschaftlichen Wandel* (Frankfurt: Campus, 1983); Walter Müller, A. Willms-Herget, and J. Handl, *Strukturwandel der Frauenarbeit 1880–1989* (Frankfurt: Campus, 1983).

101. Christian Lüders and J. Reichertz, "Wissenschaftliche Praxis ist, wenn alles funktioniert und keiner weiß warum," *Sozialwissenschaftliche Literaturrundschau* 9 (1986), 90–102.

102. T. P. Wilson, "Qualitative oder quantitative Methoden in der Sozialforschung," *Kölner Zeitschrift für Soziologie und Sozialpsychologie* 34 (1982), 487–508; C. Hopf, "Nichtstandardisierte Erhebungsverfahren in der Sozialforschung," in Max Kaase and M. Küchler, eds., *Herausforderung der empirischen Sozialforschung* (Mannheim: ZUMA, 1985), 86–108.

103. See Gerhard Kleining, "Textanalyse als Heuristik," *Angewandte Sozialforschung* 16 (1990/91), 23–29; Bettina Knauth, W. Krooner, and S. Wolff, "Konversationsanalyse von Texten," ibid., 31–43; Christian Spengler, "Zur Methode der Kontextanalyse," *Familiendynamik* 16 (1991), 255–273.

104. Siegfried Lamnek, *Qualitative Sozialforschung,* vols. 1/2 (München: Psychologische Verlagsunion, 1988/89).

105. Hans-J. Freter, B. Hollstein, and M. Werle, "Integration qualitativer und quantitativer Verfahrensweisen," *ZUMA-Nachrichten* 29 (1991), 98–114.

106. Burkart Lutz, "Zur Lage der soziologischen Forschung in der Bundesrepublik," *Soziologie* 1975/1, 88.

107. M. R. Lepsius, *Zwischenbilanz der Soziologie,* 1976, l.c., 410; B. Lutz, "Zur gesellschaftlichen Entwicklung der Soziologie," in B. Lutz, ed., *Soziologie und gesellschaftliche Entwicklung* (Frankfurt: Campus, 1985), 19f.

108. M. R. Lepsius, "Die Soziologie und die Kriterien sozialer Rationalität," *Soziale Welt* 40 (1989), 215.

109. Heinz Hartmann, "Mängel im soziologischen Lehrangebot," *Soziale Welt* 40 (1989), 222 ff.

110. Joachim Matthes, "Soziologie ohne Soziologen? Zur Lage des Soziologiestudiums in der Bundesrepublik," *Zeitschrift für Soziologie* 2 (1973), 48.

111. H. J. Krymanski, "Zehn Jahre Kontingenz: Zum 22. Deutschen Soziologentag," *Düsseldorf Debatte* 1984/3, 58–60.

112. H. Bollinger and M. S. Rerrich, "Im Westen nichts Neues: Eindrücke vom 22. Deutschen Soziologentag in Dortmund," *Soziale Welt* 36 (1985), 128–137.

113. Arndt Sorge, "Technik, sozialer Wandel und soziologisches Beharrungsvermögen," *Soziale Welt* 31 (1986), 487–497.

114. René König, ed., *Entwicklungssoziologie* (Opladen: Westdeutscher Verlag, 1969).

115. E. K. Francis, *Interethnic Relations* (New York: Elsevier, 1976); Robert Hettlage, ed., *Zwischenwelten der Gastarbeiter* (special edition of *Schweizerische Zeitschrift für Soziologie* 10) 1984; Peter Waldmann, *Ethnischer Radikalmus* (Opladen: Westdeutscher Verlag, 1989); Claus Leggewie, *Multikulti* (Berlin: Rotbuch, 1991).

116. However not only in Germany, also in the United States. See William Buxton, "The Decay of Political Sociology," in W. Buxton, *Talcott Parsons and the Capitalist Nation-State* (Toronto: University of Toronto Press, 1985), 11236–60.

117. S. M. Lipset, *Soziologie der Demokratie* (*Political Man,* 1960) (Neuwied: Luchterhand, 1962).

118. F. U. Pappi, *Wahlverhalten und politische Kultur* (Meisenheim: Hain, 1971); S. Greiffenhagen and R. Prätorius, eds., *Handwörterbuch zur politischen Kultur der Bundesrepublik Deutschland* (Opladen: Westdeutscher Verlag, 1981).

119. See Kurt Lenk, *Politische Soziologie* (Stuttgart: Kohlhammer, 1982).

120. See Helmut Klages and P. Kmieciak, eds., *Wertwandel und gesellschaftlicher Wandel* (Frankfurt: Campus, 1979); Otthein Rammstedt, *Soziale Bewegungen* (Frankfurt: Suhrkamp, 1978); Joachim Raschke, *Soziale Bewegungen* (Frankfurt: Campus, 1985).

121. Nico Stehr and R. König, eds., *Wissenschaftssoziologie* (Opladen: Westdeutscher Verlag, 1975).

122. See Rodrigo Jokisch, ed., *Techniksoziologie* (Frankfurt: Suhrkamp, 1982); Walter Bungard and H. Lenk, eds., *Technikbewertung* (Frankfurt: Suhrkamp, 1988).

123. For the international scene see Mario Bunge, "A Critical Examination of the New Sociology of Science," *Philosophy of the Social Sciences* 21 (1991), 524–560. On the German side, see Karin D. Knorr-Cetina, *The Manufacture of Knowledge* (New York: Oxford University Press, 1981); Jürgen Klüver, *Die Konstruktion der sozialen Realität Wissenschaft* (Braunschweig: Vieweg, 1988).

124. Niklas Luhmann, *Die Wissenschaft der Gesellschaft* (Frankfurt: Suhrkamp, 1988). An attempt of a more empirical application is: Wolfgang Krohn and G. Küppers, *Die Selbstorganisation der Wissenschaft* (Frankfurt: Suhrkamp, 1989).

125. Arnold Gehlen, *Die Seele im technischen Zeitalter* (Reinbek: Rowohlt, 1957).

126. Ulrich Beck, *Risikogesellschaft* (Frankfurt: Suhrkamp, 1986); *Gegengifte* (Frankfurt: Suhrkamp, 1988).

127. Special edition no. 27, ed. by Friedhelm Neidhardt, R. M. Lepsius, and J. Weiß, *Kultur und Gesellschaft* (Opladen: Westdeutscher Verlag, 1986).

128. Hans Haferkamp, ed., *Sozialstruktur und Kultur* (Frankfurt: Suhrkamp, 1990); Wolfgang Lipp, ed., *Kulturtypen, Kulturcharakter* (Berlin: Reimer, 1987).

129. Joachim Matthes, "Soziologie—Schlüsselwissenschaft des 20. Jahrhunderts?" in J. Matthes, ed., *Lebenswelt und soziale Probleme* (Frankfurt: Campus, 1981), 15–27.

130. Helmut Schelsky, *Die Arbeit tun die anderen: Klassen kampf und Priester-herrschaft der Intellektuellen* (Opladen: Westdeutscher Verlag, 1975), 167 ff., 233.

131. Friedrich H. Tenbruck, *Die unbewältigten Sozialwissenschaften, oder die Abschaffung des Menschen* (Graz: Styria, 1984), 30 ff.

132. Christoph Lau, "Die Definition gesellschaftlicher Probleme durch die Sozialwissenschaften," *Soziale Welt* 40 (1989), 393.

133. U. Beck and W. Bonß, "Zum Strukturwandel von Sozialwissenschaft und Praxis," *Soziale Welt* 40 (1989), 200 ff. U. Beck, ed., *Soziologie und Praxis* (special edition no. 1 of *Soziale Welt*) 1982.

134. Ansgar Weymann and M. Wingens, "Die Versozialwissenschaftlichung der Bildungs- und Arbeitsmarktpolitik," in U. Beck and W. Bonß, eds., l.c., 176–301.

135. Helmut Klages, ed., *Arbeitsperspektiven angewandter Sozialforschung* (Opladen: Westdeutscher Verlag, 1985); W. L. Bühl, "Zwischen Offenheit und Richtungslosigkeit: Zur Situation der Zukunftsplanung in der Bundesrepublik Deutschland," *Der Staat* 28 (1989), 525–556.

136. Bernd Giesen and Claus Leggewie, "Sozialwissenschaften vis-à-vis," in B. Giesen and C. Leggewie, eds., l.c., 7–18.

8

Contemporary Sociology in the Netherlands

Henk A. Becker and Frans L. Leeuw

INTRODUCTION

In our opinion contemporary sociology, in general as well as in the Netherlands, begins in the early eighties.[1] In those years five publications on the state of the art in sociology were issued that avoided discussions of a crisis in the discipline almost completely. They focused instead on the achievements in sociology.[2] These state-of-the-art publications came from a wide range of countries and sociological traditions. Their authors evidently acted on their own, without previous knowledge of each other's ideas.

Do these state-of-the-art publications issued in the early eighties indeed mirror a major shift in the discipline? Assessments published at the end of the eighties and in the early nineties confirm the hypothesis of a trend reversal around 1980, both in the Netherlands and abroad.[3] A number of developments has triggered this reversal. The growth of knowledge has been stimulated in particular by opportunities offered by data archives and improved techniques for data analysis. Explanatory analyses have profited from theoretical models adopted from psychology and economics. Historical analysis has been strengthened by the elaboration and application of figurational frames of reference. These achievements have also elucidated the limits to sociological knowledge: on the one hand, limits related to the imperfect state of knowledge in contemporary sociology, and on the other hand, limits related to our knowledge in general.[4]

The trend reversal in sociology in the early eighties has been triggered by developments external to the discipline as well. The large number of students of the early seventies dropped considerably in later years. In the second half of the decade the majority of sociologists working at universities have taken advantage of the decrease of the teaching load by investing time in research. This strategy contributed to the trend reversal at the beginning of the eighties. Alongside the shifts in academic sociology in this country we see a continuous contribution to the discipline by research institutes independent of universities.

In the Netherlands, as in Western countries in general, a major economic crisis started in the mid-seventies. In the early eighties the Netherlands adopted drastic deregulation policies in order to stimulate an economic revival. In the course of these policies the Dutch government has cut back its expenditures, including drastic retrenchments of the universities. As a result of these cutbacks a number of faculties of sociology have been forced to close down. Some others have had to merge, and all had to reduce their staff. The retrenchments have been accompanied by external evaluations and by selective funding of faculties and research teams that were able to meet the evaluation criteria. The overall picture of Dutch sociology in the eighties and early nineties has been positive, however. Sociologists have fought a heavy battle, they have been quite successful, and their discipline has started its comeback.

In the years of deregulation politics and retrenchments in universities, Dutch sociologists have had to defend their identity and their contribution to science and society time and again. An effective line of defense has been a better presentation of sociology as a discipline. A lot of sociologists have learned to present their discipline by stating the major problems dealt with in sociology and to relate their own research problems to them. The first problem relates to cohesion and to continuity in society. How can we explain the existence of society? The second problem points at inequality and conflict. How are controversies resolved? The third problem deals with rationalization and modernization. How is social change coped with? Each of these three classical problems in sociology is related to a fourth classical problem dealing with opportunities for interventions. Is planned change feasible, and what would be its consequences (looking at intended and unintended effects of interventions)? An additional advantage of presenting sociology this way is that it clarifies the borderlines with related disciplines. Sociology is the one and only discipline dealing with this set of four problems.[5] We will return to this issue later on.

In this chapter we will first present a short history of sociology in the Netherlands. Next we will give an overview of the institutionalization of contemporary sociology in this country. Following this, recent trends in theory, methods, knowledge transfer, and application will be dealt with. We will continue by looking at current trends in a number of subfields. Finally an epilogue will be presented.

A SHORT HISTORY OF DUTCH SOCIOLOGY

On the one hand, we are talking about sociology in a small Western country, mainly shaped by ideas and methods coming from countries prominent in the discipline: the United States, England, France, and Germany. From the beginning Dutch sociologists have traveled widely, and colleagues from other countries have discovered that Holland is "right in the middle" between the centers of international sociology. Sociologists in the Netherlands take part in sociology as an international discipline. In this sense, there is no typically Dutch sociology. On the other hand, there are sociological achievements that are typically Dutch. This applies to research on problems specific to this country: human settlement in areas reclaimed from the sea, and ecclesiastical segregation (polarization) in the Netherlands after World War II, to give some examples. This also applies to original contributions of Dutch sociologists to the body of knowledge of the discipline. In this respect it does make sense to speak of "Dutch sociology." We will use both terms, Dutch sociology and sociology in the Netherlands, as interchangeable.

The Period of the Pioneers

The founding fathers of Dutch sociology were historians and economists in the late nineteenth century, primarily interested in solutions to the pressing social problems of their times.[6] In the early twentieth century Steinmetz, trained in law and having defended a doctoral thesis in ethnology, became "the father of Dutch sociology." He developed a type of research that became famous as "the Amsterdam school." This school, which had to provide the empirical basis for sociology, existed from 1925 to 1940. It has often been compared with the Chicago School, and indeed both schools followed about the same approach. Steinmetz abhorred idle speculation and for that reason emphasized the importance of empirical fact-finding. The type of social research he advocated, "sociography," did not show much theoretical sophistication. It is also argued that Steinmetz's explanatory framework boils down to a crude kind of social Darwinism.[7]

Sociography in the Netherlands dealt with a wide array of subjects: rural, urban, religious, and industrial problems, to give some examples. For instance, Ter Veen, one of its members, studied the new polders and advised policymakers about the migration of farmers from their home villages to the new dwellings. The link between sociography and theory-related sociology has remained weak. Sociography has stimulated sociology in another way, however. It has been the learning environment for a number of young sociologists that received their academic training during and shortly after World War II. Among others, E. G. Van Doorn,

Groenman, C. J. Lammers, and P. Thoenes later on became key figures in Dutch sociology.

Growth and Establishment of Sociology (1945–1968)

In the years following World War II, at all universities in the Netherlands professors of sociology were appointed and sociological institutes were established.[8] The number of first-year students grew from 94 in 1954–1955 to 225 in 1959–1960 and 954 in 1969–1970.[9] Historical accounts of Dutch sociology in this period can be found elsewhere.[10] This gives us a free hand to concentrate on a limited number of achievements.

At this stage in the development of Dutch sociology F. Van Heek, professor of empirical sociology at the University of Leiden, became a prominent figure. His research program on stratification and social mobility was guided by a sequence of questions:

1. What does the ladder of occupational prestige for the Netherlands look like?
2. How many males have high, intermediate, and low prestige jobs, and did these numbers change in the course of time?
3. How much father-son mobility occurs along the ladder of occupational prestige, and did this mobility increase or decrease?
4. What explains differences in mobility among Dutchmen, and what accounts for differences in mobility between the Netherlands and other countries?[11]

In 1968 Van Heek and his team published the results of a major research project on "hidden talent" in Dutch society. The Leiden research group focused on social class, participation in secondary and higher education, and educational aptitude. They noted that "a boy from an upper class family and living in a middle-sized or a large town has a twenty times higher chance of becoming a university student than a boy of the same age from a lower-class family living in a rural area." Van Heek's team analyzed educational mobility in the Netherlands and specified inadequacies in the educational system. They concluded that the "waste of talent" they identified could best be reduced by providing specialized educational facilities for children from working-class families whose educational aptitude was adequate, but had not been able to develop in the existing educational system.[12]

I. Gadourek, who had written his dissertation under the supervision of Van Heek, continued the Leiden research tradition of large, professionally conducted social surveys at the University of Groningen. In 1963 he published "Hazardous Habits and Human Well-being," focusing on smoking cigarettes and drinking alcohol.[13] Gadourek inter alia predicted an ongoing emancipation of women, including more participation of women in the labor market. He also predicted an increase of cigarette smoking among women, stimulated by the stress of having to compete with male colleagues, followed by an increase in the incidence of lung cancer among women. These research outcomes have stimulated campaigns to make women aware of the risks involved in smoking cigarettes. The prediction did not turn out to be self-denying, however. Ultimately the percentage of women who smoked became about the same as that among men, and the percentage of women having lung cancer follows this trend.

At Leiden University, later at the Rotterdam School of Economics, Van Doorn specialized in critical reflection on social change, taking consequences for policymaking into account. He focused on the dynamics of the welfare state. Van Doorn founded the Rotterdam School of policy-oriented research and reflection on planned social change. The Rotterdam School has led to a considerable number of research projects, oriented to an enhancement of knowledge in the discipline and to the elucidation of practical problems.[14] The Rotterdam School did acquire a strong position in this period. In the next period all faculties of sociology in the country have followed the Rotterdam example by establishing sections of policy-oriented research and teaching.

Characteristic for this period is the success of *Modern Sociology,* an introduction to the discipline published by J. A. A. van Doorn and C. J. Lammers in 1959. This book is an offspring of the mainstream at that time: the analytical tradition in sociology.[15]

Turbulence and Perseverance (1968–1979)

While sociology in the Netherlands was searching for an identity of its own and trying to build up a research tradition and establish links with policymakers in government and industry, elsewhere a number of controversies emerged and gradually became aggravated. The controversies grew into a revolt of sociology marginals against sociology mainliners, in the Netherlands just as in other Western countries.[16] The attacks on analytical sociology focused on the reprimand that accomplishments in this tradition did not meet its own standards.[17] Authors prepared to defend analytical sociology pointed out that the subject matter of sociology contained a relatively large amount of "noise," and for that reason standards common to all empirical disciplines could only be met to a limited degree.[18] Neither the mainliners nor the marginals succeeded in winning the battle. Ultimately, each of the traditions decided to spend its energy on meeting its own standards as far as possible. As a result of this about 1975 the acute turbulence slowed down, and the analytical, historical, and interpretative traditions in sociology actively began to consolidate their positions.

In the first place this resulted in a new start in theory formation. In 1976 Arts, Lindenberg, and Wippler edited a volume on explanation in sociology, taking psychological explanation as an example.[19] Since that time explanatory sociology has prospered in this country. One of the important developments has been the integration of micro and macro (a.o. institutional) factors in theory and empirical research, while another concerns the explanation of the emergence, maintenance, and effects of social institutions.[20]

Second, the use of theory in the historical and interpretative tradition acquired a new vitality. At Amsterdam University Norbert Elias inspired sociologists like Goudsblom to apply figurational frames of reference to historical phenomena. At Erasmus University C. J. M. Schuyt published *Law, Order, and Civil Disobedience,* taking a sociological and phenomenological approach.[21] Van Doorn continued his critical reflection on social change initiated in the former period.

Third, the years between 1968 and 1979 were used to apply and improve sociological research methodology, related to both disciplinary and policy research. A. J. A. Felling at Nijmegen University applied and further developed network analysis.[22] At Utrecht University P. G. Swanborn elaborated research methodology in general, and H. A. Becker used and improved methods for applied social research, in particular simulation and scenario models.[23]

Fourth, sociological knowledge has been enhanced in subfields in the discipline. At Utrecht University, P. Thoenes and his team explored sociological aspects of the welfare state.[24] Developments in a number of other subfields will be discussed in a later section.

R. K. Merton in 1976 published a critical evaluation of sociology that applies to the Netherlands as well. He stressed that the discipline has to deal with two kinds of "crises." In the first place, a chronic ambiguity as a consequence of the fact that sociologists alternate "between phases of extravagant optimism and extravagant pessimism . . . about their capacity . . . to find abiding solutions to the problems of human society and the problems of human sociology, that is, solutions to the major social problems and the major cognitive ones."[25] In the late sixties and early seventies, according to Merton, an acute crisis was superimposed upon the latent ambivalence in sociology. Merton also diagnosed the competition between paradigms in the seventies as "social rather than cognitive competition."[26] Marginals first claimed that sociology was in a crisis, and next used this diagnosis as an argument to push the solution to the crisis they had to offer.

INSTITUTIONALIZATION

Since 1980 sociology in the Netherlands has been confronted with a continuous flow of governmental budget cuts, major governmental interventions, and a number of minor restructurings of teaching and research arrangements. The sheer number of changes in so short a period has been a severe handicap for the development of the discipline. On the other hand some of the government interventions have had positive (side-) effects. We shall sketch a number of these interventions.

Government officials in the early 1980s believed that the social sciences were fragmented and lacked cognitive coherence, while also the quality and the efficiency of research and teaching programs were considered too low and hence had to be increased. A third background of the policy interventions dealt with the strongly increased public spendings on higher education, while finally it was believed that the earlier interventions applied during the 1970s, which were based mainly on pro-rated budget cuts, had not been effective. The Ministry of Education and Sciences therefore launched several retrenchment policies. The first major governmental intervention came in 1983. The operation Division of Labour and Concentration in Higher Education (TVC) forced the sociological department at Leeuwarden, associated with the University of Groningen, to close its doors.

The second major operation, Growth and Retrenchments of Universities and Academic Hospitals (SKG),[27] in 1986 forced the sociology departments at Amsterdam Free University and Wageningen Agricultural University to close their doors. It also forced the sociology department at Leiden University to close down and to merge with the sociology department at Erasmus University, Rotterdam. Also, systematic peer review evaluations (by "visitation committees" and inspection teams) were carried out[28] with the result of a rank-ordering of all sociology departments and units by using performance indicators. Examples of these indicators are publication productivity data, the number of the (tenured) teaching and research staff with a Ph.D., and the capacity of obtaining grants and subsidies for fundamental and applied research.

It should be stressed that not all interventions focused only on reduction of funds for training and research in the social sciences. Several also implied an increased level of funding as well as establishing better facilities for (empirical) research. Examples are new funding on behalf of women's studies, demography, labor studies, and policy and program evaluation, while also extra money has been allocated in the field of computerization and social information. Another example is the Pioneer Program. This program provides financial support to young scientists who are able to do advanced research. In 1991 and in 1992 sociologists have acquired these prestigious grants.[29]

Apart from these activities, one policy measure, implemented during 1983–1984, aimed at establishing centers of excellence of (post-)graduate teaching programs and advanced (fundamental) social research. It concerned a financial incentive that could be obtained for a period of six years by submitting a proposal for the establishment of such a center. In the early 1990s, results from an evaluation study on the effects of this measure became available.[30] Originally, thirty-three proposals for the establishment of centers of excellence were submitted by Faculties of Social Sciences. Thirteen of them were nominated. However, only four were awarded a subsidy by the Ministry of Education and Sciences. Two of these groups came from sociology. Seven years after the implementation, one of the questions of the evaluation was to find out if there indeed were established "centers of excellence." It turned out that only two groups had realized the two conditions required to be characterized as centers of excellence (i.e., a postgraduate teaching and training system and an advanced research program). Both groups, one at the Catholic University of Nijmegen and focusing on mathematical cognitive modeling, the other focusing on explanatory sociology and affiliated with the Universities of Groningen and Utrecht [Interuniversity Center for Theory and Methodology within the Social Sciences, ICS], however, had not received the extra government subsidy, although both groups were nominated.

The Teaching of Sociology

In 1991 six universities offered M.A. courses in sociology: Groningen, Utrecht, Amsterdam, Rotterdam (Erasmus), Brabant, and Nijmegen. They prepared graduates primarily for two sectors of the labor market: employment as assistants to policymakers and employment in social research. The first year of the sociology curriculum is almost the same in the six universities. In the second, third, and fourth year of the sociology curriculum, the departments of Groningen, Utrecht, Brabant, and Nijmegen university offer programs that are almost identical. The second year involves a disciplinary introduction. The third and fourth years bring teaching focused on either policymaking or sociological research. The department at Amsterdam University focuses on two areas: policymaking and organizations, and historical and cultural developments. The department at Rotterdam primarily focuses on policy items.

In Table 8.1 we give an overview of the teaching programs in the second, third, and fourth year of the sociology curriculum. The universities offer three years of about forty weeks each; each week yields one credit point.

The number of first-year students in sociology was 562 in 1989–1990. In 1990–1991 it increased to 606. Further growth of the number of first-year students in sociology is expected, primarily as a result of an inflow of students that have graduated from polytechnics.[31] Besides students majoring in sociology, we find students majoring in integrated social science courses. At the University of Utrecht, for instance, in 1991 about 1,500 students started on a General Social Science course, an integration mainly of sociology and psychology.

Table 8.1
MA Programs and Credit Points in Sociology at Six Universities in the Netherlands

	RUG	RUU	UvA	EUR	KUB	KUN
general and theoretical sociology	32	16	35	15	36	36
specialisation in sociology	42	56	28	62	52	34
research methodology	20	16	28	22	12	28
miscellaneous courses	8	4	-	13	10	8
free choice in courses	24	32	35	15	20	20

RUG = University of Groningen
RUU = University of Utrecht
UvA = University of Amsterdam
EUR = Erasmus University at Rotterdam
KUB = Catholic University of Brabant, at Tilburg
KUN = Catholic University of Nijmegen

Source: P.G. Swanborn (1991), *De Sociologie-Opleidingen, Argumenten en Feiten,* Utrecht, 46.

In 1991 the position of sociology graduates on the labor market has been relatively strong. About 6 percent of the sociology graduates were registered as looking for employment at that time. That percentage is one of the lowest in the social sciences. It is about the same as that for all academics looking for jobs. The unemployment of sociology graduates is mainly the problem of a hard core of older sociologists who graduated in the late seventies and early eighties and have been unemployed since those times.[32]

Institutionalization in a Broader Perspective

Naturally contemporary sociology in the Netherlands is shaped outside universities too. One of the major institutions active in this respect is the

Social and Cultural Planning Bureau (SCP). In 1974 the Social and Cultural Planning Bureau published its first Social and Cultural Report (SCR). Since then, SCRs have appeared every two years. These publications are to provide facts and figures as well as interpretations for informative purposes and to contribute to government policy; to promote the rationality of government policy and to contain suggestions for the efficiency of government policy.[33]

With respect to the sociological relevance of the Social and Cultural Reports, Ester and Nauta made the following observation: "In actual practice, [in SRCs] growing use is made of whatever social science theories and research results are available. There is an extensive recourse to theories on social stratification, social mobility, the diffusion and adoption of social change, collective goods, social participation and so on. . . . However, the most common form of academic presentation (formal specification of problems posed, review of theories, testing the hypotheses) is frequently not explicitly adhered to, although explicit attention is devoted to operationalization problems." The Social and Cultural Planning Bureau has also analyzed processes of social change; it has simulated the consequences of public policy in the Netherlands; and it is involved in productivity studies pertaining to public sector activities carried out by the police, prisons, schools, and medical organizations.[34]

Next we want to mention the Netherlands Interdisciplinary Demographic Institute (NIDI) at the Hague. In NIDI among others demographers, sociologists, and economists cooperate. As an example of interdisciplinary research at NIDI that is relevant to sociology we take a long-term project measuring every three to four years the attitudes of the Dutch population regarding demographic developments, their causes and policies. In the subsection on the sociology of population we will return to research carried out by NIDI.

The Netherlands Sociological and Anthropological Association (NSAV) acts as the professional association of sociologists in this country. This association organizes conferences and workshops, for instance, on the state of the art in sociology, and offers prizes for the best article published by a sociologist in a scientific journal, the best essay written by a young sociologist, and the best essay on an issue relevant to sociology written by a pupil in secondary education.[35] The NSAV, steadily growing in membership, represents Dutch sociologists in the International Sociological Association.

Because of increasing international relationships, Dutch sociologists participate in numerous European and international scientific associations and research institutes. As a result, institutionalization of sociology in the Netherlands is closely linked to the international institutionalization of sociology.

RECENT TRENDS IN THEORY, METHODS, KNOWLEDGE TRANSFER, AND APPLICATION

The core of sociology consists of theoretical sociology, methods in sociology, and the transfer and application of sociological knowledge. In Dutch sociology in the eighties each of these three areas showed new developments. We will concentrate our attention on a selection of elements in these three areas. Later on we will elaborate upon some of these elements.[36]

Theory

In the seventies theory formation and theory testing in sociology, in the Netherlands and elsewhere, showed little progress.[37] The first signs of a change for the better can be detected in the late seventies. According to Wippler, the structural-individualistic approach in Dutch sociology defined itself in this period as a research program on the road toward an explanatory social science. The core around which research activities had to be centered consisted of

the task of explaining social phenomena. By explanation is meant a deductive argument showing how a statement describing the phenomenon to be explained follows logically from general propositions and descriptions of specific conditions. The deductive system explaining a social phenomenon may then be called a theory of this phenomenon. Therefore, aiming at the explanation of social phenomena is synonymous with aiming at a further development of theoretical sociology.[38]

In 1980 Tazelaar applied this approach to patterns of mental incongruity in labor market processes.[39] A major event was the publication in 1983 of *Models in Sociology*. In this volume theoretical sociologists looked at both psychological and economic models for explanatory paradigms to be applied in their discipline. Applications were reported, coming inter alia from the sociology of education, medical sociology, the sociology of work and organizations, and the sociology of population.[40] An important other aspect in the role of theories in research is the following. While in the early 1970s relatively little emphasis was given to the use of explanatory theories when doing (field) research, in the 1980s a development took place stressing explicit use of one or even several (competing) explanatory theories. Often from these theories problem-specific propositions are deduced. Apart from that, attention has been given to a metaprojection comparing explanatory theories as such.[41]

In the eighties and early nineties Dutch sociologists, Lindenberg in particular, stressed that a new integration was taking place of the socioeconomic sciences, especially sociology and economics. He quotes Swedberg, who set out

to find out exactly what is going on at the moment at the interface of economics and sociology. What is happening is very significant: the border line between two of the major social sciences is being redrawn, thereby providing new perspectives on a whole range of very important problems both in the economy and in society at large.[42]

Lindenberg lists substantive work done on syntheses in five major areas: theory of action, theory of resources, theory of labor markets, theory of organizations, and theory of households.[43] Lindenberg writes as a member of the analytical tradition in sociology, utilizing rational choice theory as an approach to explanation in sociology and related social sciences.

In the eighties other traditions in the discipline were active in theory formation as well. Wilterdink states that in the historical approach in sociology in the Netherlands, the work of Norbert Elias has been the dominating influence. Figurational sociology dominates historical sociology in the Netherlands to such an extent that the two overlap considerably. According to Wilterdink, in figurational sociology the assumption of various relatively autonomous social processes can lead to an increasing refinement of explanations, but also to a loss of consistency and parsimony. If the nature of the causal connections among social processes is assumed to vary according to the specific case studied, no cumulation of insight on the level of general theory is to be expected. If, however, this goal is not abandoned, one should look for general theoretical principles that are applicable to different social processes and can explain their interconnections. Several general sociological concepts (such as power, interdependence, competition, and conflict) may be and have been used for this purpose. They are applicable as analytical instruments, and can help us formulate theoretical propositions on high levels of abstraction.[44]

One general model that has recently come to play an important role in historical sociology is a brand of rational choice theory. The basic proposition of this brand of rational choice theory is that the individual's behavior is a function of his self-interest, given constraints. In his book *In Care of the State,* a comparative study of the "sociogenese of the welfare state" in Europe and the United States,[45] De Swaan uses this brand of rational choice theory to analyze the problems, or "dilemmas," of collective action that established citizens encountered when confronted with the poor, the sick, and the unemployed. De Swaan combines this with the concept of interdependence: it is precisely because the privileged and the underprivileged strata were interdependent that the former had an interest in supporting the latter. M. H. D. van Leeuwen follows a similar line of thought in his study on assistance to the poor in Amsterdam (1800–1850).[46]

In the formation of social care institutions as an attempt to solve the problems of collective action, the relations of interdependence and, as a consequence, the problems of collective action changed. In other words, the figuration of relations of interdependence has to be brought into the analysis of collective action, and both should be viewed in a dynamic perspective.

In the third major tradition in the discipline, interpretative sociology, theory formation in the eighties and early nineties has led to reflection on the welfare state and its main problem areas. C. J. M. Schuyt analyzed the core of the welfare state, and Engbersen and Van der Veen looked at modern poverty. Methodology in interpretative sociology has been improved by, among others, Wester.[47]

Methods

In writing about "methodological achievements in Dutch sociology," one faces two problems. First, research methodology is obviously a multidisciplinary endeavor. Many of the methods currently used by sociologists were developed by scientists working in other disciplines, especially biologists, psychometrists, econometricians, epidemiologists, and political scientists. On the other hand, some of the methods developed by sociologists are used in other disciplines as well. Second, research aimed at the development of research methodology or methods research is internationally oriented: there is hardly any research in this field that is typically Dutch. However, quite a few Dutch social scientists are active in the part of the international, multidisciplinary methods research that is relevant for sociology.[48]

The Dutch contribution to research methodology is in the first place related to methods of data collection. We will give an example. In close cooperation with the Netherlands Institute for Opinion Research (NIPO), Saris and his colleagues developed a new type of survey research, which they called "tele-interviewing." Members of a panel use the keyboard of their home computer to answer questions which are transmitted every week via a modem to their computer. With the same modem, their responses are transmitted to the central computer of the research institute. Tele-interviewing leads to a considerable decrease in the amount of time needed for data collection: it is possible to conduct a full-fledged survey (including the descriptive statistical analysis of the data) within a few days. Dutch sociologists have also contributed to methods of data collection by analyzing the quality of data collected by questionnaires. They have measured the effects of the wording of the question on responses, and they have analyzed the information distortion in interviews due to inadequacies in the interaction process between the interviewer and the respondent.

This type of research resulted in several guidelines for improving the quality of survey data.[49]

In data collection we also find that not only data at one point in time but also longitudinal data and life course data are collected.

The second category of contributions lies in the domain of data analysis. For instance, at the Universities of Nijmegen and Rotterdam, computer programs have been written for qualitative analysis of large portions of text, such as verbatim protocols of open interviews. Dutch sociologists constructed procedures for the transformation of verbal theories into formal models, known as computer-assisted theory construction. In interpretative sociology a method has been developed, based on principles of conversation analysis, and designed for the structural analysis of conversations, for example, consultations of general practitioners.[50]

Knowledge Transfer and Application

In terms of scope, the concept of knowledge transfer is broader than the concept of application. Results from applied or policy research can be transferred to the lay public and to other audiences, but that is also possible with respect to findings and conclusions produced by discipline-oriented or fundamental research. Examples are the transfer and diffusion of findings from sociological dissertations to larger audiences.

In the Netherlands, the relevance of practical applications of social (policy) research was already acknowledged more than sixty years ago. Later on, in the 1970s, practical contributions of sociology were most often seen in conjunction with the idea that societies could be systematically changed by implementing policy programs. Policy was conceptualized as planned social change. During the 1970s, there was a sharp rise in the number of sociologists active in this field. Indicators included the growing government budgets for commissioning applied research (annually around U.S. $100 million), the foundation of profit and nonprofit research institutes, and the establishment of university subdepartments specialized in policy research and analysis.

When the confidence in planned social change lost ground in the early 1980s, policy research nevertheless preserved its position. In order to realize budget cuts as well as policy changes, including policy termination, the government needed adequate information. It also needed adequate information to help it develop new policy approaches such as privatization. Moreover, applied research was called for to promote the efficiency and effectiveness of governmental organizations. Among others, Parliament also became more involved in policy evaluation research.

Central government earmarked this type of research as a special field of interest during the latter part of the 1980s. Also, organizations that till the 1980s were not (at all) involved in carrying out this type of research such as the National Audit Office of the Netherlands got strongly involved in these activities. Approximately 25 percent of its audit and research staff now has a degree in one of the social sciences and is being "trained-on-the-job" in the field of policy research.[51]

With regard to university-based research, data about the early 1990s indicate that at least 30 percent of this research is commissioned and financed by the central government. Generally it is considered that social policy research is a core business of applied sociologists. We therefore focus on the question of what have been the most important characteristics of this type of research during the 1980s.

Social policy research is concerned with the development, implementation, and evaluation of policies by local and central government and by large social agencies and organizations. In the eighties and early nineties, several articles were published on the state of the art of policy research.[52] In this chapter we restrict ourselves to three topics of study that have played a major role in this field of study during the 1980s:

• evaluation research
• research in the field of policy theories, and
• the social policy research paradigm.

Evaluation Research

As J. M. Hutjes[53] has argued, the need for information on the effects of policy interventions within society gave the initial impetus to the almost stormy development of evaluation research within Dutch (applied) sociology. In his earlier review of Dutch sociology Van Doorn[54] remarked that "for sociology, evaluation research is very important: [in this type of investigation] the sociologist studies in detail the results policies have achieved in order to convert the objective findings into new policies." Fran L. Leeuw has worked out how many proposals for evaluation research submitted by sociologists have been honored by the National Committee on Program and Policy Evaluation Research (CPE). This committee carried out its activities between 1986 and 1992, and one of its main tasks was to encourage quality and quantity of policy and program evaluation in the Netherlands. Data are available for the 1986–1989 period. During this period twenty-two proposals were honored by CPE. Nine of them were submitted by sociologists. It concerns evaluation research in such divergent fields as mental health, minority questions, and higher education policies. When one takes into account that the recruitment area of CPE not only covers the social and behavioral sciences but also economics, Dutch sociology did not come off badly.

Research on Policy Theories

Policies are based on assumptions, either implicitly or explicitly. Since the late seventies a number of Dutch sociologists and policy scientists[55] have been addressing the question how theories that underlie policies can be reconstructed and evaluated. These theories are referred to in the literature in a variety of ways. Some authors refer to "theories-in-use," others to "policy impact models," or practitioners' "theories-in-use." H. T. Chen[56] referred to action theory and conceptual theories underlying policy programs. A policy theory is a system of social and behavioral assumptions that underlie a public policy which have been reformulated in the form of propositions. These propositions reflect beliefs of policymakers about the cognitions, attitudes, and behaviors of a policy's target groups: the people whom the policy is to affect. But they also refer to more structural factors on which policymakers have been making assumptions.

Identifying policymakers' policy assumptions and reconstructing them in terms of policy theories is an important task. But more important is the fact these reconstructions allow one to compare these assumptions with the state of the art in research fields. By confronting policy theories with research evidence, we may observe the level of use or underuse of scientific research made by policymakers. These comparisons first shed light on the question how well-founded a public policy is and what its chance of success is. This facilitates assessing future consequences of policy. Moreover, this type of sociological study comes close to one of the important societal functions of sociology, debunking or demystifying common (non)sense social knowledge.

The reconstruction and evaluation of policy theories also allow for policy advice. When important research evidence was used in the policymaking process, researchers engaged in the analysis of policy theories are able to inform public policy officials and motivate them to use research evidence henceforward.

The Social Policy Research Paradigm

The "social policy research paradigm" indicates that social policy research is in need of a special, professional paradigm. The founder and supporter of this idea has been Mark van de Vall.[57] The starting point of his line of thought is the "advisement model" of policy research. When sociologists apply this model, they not only provide policymakers with methodologically sound diagnoses of problems, they also advise the client system with regard to the diffusion of research findings, the development of policy measures aimed at reducing policy problems and the implementation of these measures. Within the advisement model, the professional role of the social policy researcher consists of a wider range of tasks and activities than the role played within the "enlightenment model."[58] The most important elements of the professional paradigm are the following[59]:

—To a certain extent, policy researchers need to identify themselves with the core goals of the client. A reasonable level of "going native" is essential.

—Social policy research not only devotes attention to research itself but also to the development and implementation of policies, integrated within a model of planned social change.

—Van de Vall claims that there are important differences between methods and techniques including statistical analyses and discipline-oriented sociological research. This is also considered to be the case with regard to the function of sociological theories. "While discipline-oriented research is nomothetical in nature, social policy research above all is ideographically oriented."[60]

The idea of a professional paradigm of social policy research was originally based on a metastudy of 120 Dutch social policy research projects in the fields of industry, labor unions, regional planning, and health and welfare. These projects were carried out in the late 1960s and early 1970s. Second, the idea is grounded on national and international publications by other applied researchers.

Predominantly in the early 1980s, Van de Vall's claims were under discussion, while most often attention was paid to methodological aspects of the social policy research paradigm. Instead of discussing critique and rejoinder item by item,[61] we earlier concluded that as yet, no systematic data are available to answer the question, To what extent are client groups of social policy research satisfied with the approach and its subsequent results? Nor is information available ascertaining the empirical content of the assumption that results and policy advice produced by investigators following the professional paradigm guidelines, are indeed more often used by policymakers than results produced by other types of policy research. Finally, the original material Van de Vall's claims are based on (the analysis of 120 social policy research projects) must be considered outdated.

CURRENT TRENDS IN A NUMBER OF SUBFIELDS

The four core problems in sociology mentioned in the introduction have had their impact on the main subfields in the discipline. To the Dutch population the late sixties, the seventies, and the eighties were a period of ongoing social change. This sense of turmoil has stimulated many Dutch sociologists to analyze their society in terms of discontinuity and threatened coherence. In the second place, social inequality has fascinated sociologists also because there was a political debate on the degree of inequality that society could or should cope with. In educational, occupational, and organizational sociology both opportunities and inequality have been recurring themes. Studies of interventions in social systems have gained a prominent position too, mainly because insights were needed into the strong and weak points of policy systems and into the effects and side-effects of policy instruments.

Sociological Aspects of Social Change

In 1982 Gadourek, at Groningen University, published "Social Change as Redefinition of Roles", a milestone in the analysis of dynamics in Dutch society. Gadourek focused on changes in value orientations during the seventies. In 1975, Gadourek carried out interviews among a representative sample of the Dutch population, and in 1977 he interviewed the same individuals again. He also analyzed secondary data, and he made a comparison with his own research from earlier periods. Gadourek finds a relatively large continuity of value orientations, but also some shifts. His data show a gradually softening of role prescriptions until the middle of the decade, and afterwards a slow turning of the trend toward a retightening of role prescription, especially with regard to ideas related to elitism and redistribution of scarce goods. In other words, on the basis of his data he is able to pinpoint the end of the cultural revolution. This reversal of trends, however, was not a general phenomenon. For example, the softening of sexual standards was going on steadily throughout the entire period. At the beginning of the seventies, it was absolutely unthinkable that young people who lived together without being married could participate in orthodox ecclesiastical life. By the end of the decade, however, this has been largely accepted. Gadourek has chosen for a structuralist approach. This means that he assigns little explanatory value to manipulation of value orientations by the government or similar corporate actors. Gadourek's research has been followed by a number of sequel projects, inter alia on the changes in value orientations with regard to power sharing.[62]

Researchers at Nijmegen Catholic University interviewed a cross-section of the Dutch population in order to test the thesis of Inglehart that there was a shift from a materialist to a postmaterialist generation. Felling, Peters, and Schreuder concluded that instead there has been a shift from bourgeois to nonbourgeois value orientations. Individuals born after 1949 appreciate hedonism more than those born earlier, and familiarism less. Like Inglehart, Felling, Peters, and Schreuder used a model of two generations.[63]

Since 1978 researchers at Brabant Catholic University have been participating in the work of the European Value Systems Group. In 1981, fieldwork was carried out in the Netherlands and eight further European Economic Community countries. In this study too, the Inglehart thesis was reinvestigated. Halman and others came to the conclusion that the outcomes of their research did support the Inglehart thesis, but not impressively. In 1990, the survey was replicated.[64]

In 1985 Becker, at Utrecht University, developed a model with four generations. The model specifies the Prewar generation (born about 1910–1930), the Silent generation (born about 1930–1940), the Protest generation (born about 1940–1955) and the Lost generation (born about 1955–1970). Characteristic of this model is that it presents a pattern of generations whose members differ not only regarding value orientations, but also on life courses (inter alia level of education, career, fertility, and income) and behavioral patterns. On a systems level differences in generational culture are taken into account. Hypotheses derived from the thesis on the pattern of four generations have been tested in a dozen research projects.[65]

Next we turn to the systems level. In the eighties the welfare state in the Netherlands started to stagnate. Van Doorn and Schuyt tried to diagnose this deterioration and to find out whether new configurations were emerging. They analyzed to what extent citizens were treated according to their legal rights and to rules of social justice.[66] Could new ways of cooperation between the state on the one hand and private organizations and social networks on the other hand prevent social conflict? Is the welfare state in this country strong enough to integrate the flow of immigrants? Research into contemporary types of poverty made clear that relatively large numbers of citizens had been forced into a permanent position of economic and social marginality.[67]

Stratification, Social Mobility, and Social Justice

Mobility questions were out of favor in the 1970s. They became one of Dutch sociology's growth industries in the 1980s.[68] Van Heek's sequence of questions was completed by Ganzeboom, De Graaf, and Ultee. Recycling Van Heek's scale for occupational prestige and Van Tulder's mobility table, Ganzeboom and De Graaf demonstrated that father-son mobility increased between 1954 and 1977.[69] Another study observed that the father-child educational mobility had increased from 1891 to 1960.[70] In addition, the research group answered the last question in Van Heek's sequence. One study involving nine EEC countries and another including thirty-five nations all over the world addressed the questions of why societies vary in father-son mobility and whether social democracy makes greater mobility of this kind.[71] On the basis of crossings of husband's and wife's education for twenty-three industrial nations, another study raised a different subquestion of the openness problem, that of why countries differ in educational heterogamy.[72] By combining data on father-son mobility with data on educational heterogamy, the later study also dealt with the issue of whether more father-son mobility in a country goes together with more educational heterogamy (as Lipset maintained in the 1950s) or whether father-son inheritance and educational homogamy are compensatory strategies of reproduction (Bourdieu's counterargument in the 1970s).

Yet another study of this research group addressed an explanatory question on a neglected aspect of openness. In the 1980s, the question of whether the unemployed constitute an underclass came to be of growing political significance. Ultee, Dessens, and Jansen restated this question as a mobility problem: Does a higher rate of unemployed in a country make for less mobility from employment to unemployment and from unemployment to employment? Data for fourteen Western industrial countries were compared.[73]

In the eighties and beyond the analysis of social mobility has been closely linked to research on social justice. W. A. Arts has evaluated income policy, using the concept of distributive justice as a frame of reference.[74] P. L. J. Hermkens has been the first in this country to study judgments on the fairness of incomes by using the vignette technique.[75]

Sociology of Education

Inspired primarily by the work of Van Heek and his Leiden School, sociologists in this country have concentrated on the study of educational opportunities, educational careers, and the transition from school to work. What are the impacts of financial and cultural resources on educational careers?[76] Also the effects of teacher expectations have been studied, leading to the conclusion that these expectations, influenced by the socioeconomic status of the students, lead to unequal educational opportunities for students with the same learning abilities.[77] Comparative analyses into the processes of status attainment and educational mobility in the Netherlands, Hungary, and Poland led to the conclusion that differences between the countries were related to differences in the level and speed of industrialization, not to differences in the political system.[78]

Also attention has been paid to questions high on the political and social agenda in the Netherlands. An example here is a study into the question if, and to what extent, the belief is empirically true that female labor force participation has a negative effect on the school achievement of children. The belief could not be empirically validated.

Sociology of Organizations and Social Networks

In 1983 Lammers published a comparative analysis of the sociological study of organizations.[79] His book reviews a large number of theories and empirical findings about organizations, coming from sociologists both in the Netherlands and in other countries. Lammers was not able to provide a general theory. Some years later an explanatory framework was presented, based on rational choice theory. Following this tradition in the first place, cooperation in organizations has been studied.[80] In 1988, Weesie presented reputation as a mechanism of stable cooperation, explicitly linking it to network analysis. He demonstrated that reputation effects (depending on network density) could compensate for short time horizons (a short "shadow of the future") and vice versa.[81] Subsequently this analysis was extended.[82] In the second place, structural change in organizations was studied. For instance, R. S. Batenburg traced the process of structural change in organizations due to the introduction of computer technology.[83] An effort at modeling organizational decision making can be found in the work of Masuch. Using computer simulation, he constructed a model for the bounded rationality aspects of decision making.[84] Theories on the workings of specific organizations are another aspect of achievement in this subfield. Perhaps the most prominent example is the field of health care systems.[85]

Labor Market

Contributions to the theory of labor markets primarily relate to institutional aspects, wages, allocation, participation, reentry, job search, and careers.[86] We will first give some examples of research regarding job search and careers, looking at discrimination between men and women. Sanders studied differences in first job between female and male graduates of a "masculine" advanced vocational course, using a life-perspective theory.[87] Many women show a life perspective that is oriented partially toward the home and partially toward gainful employment and, as a consequence, is incompatible with career orientation. Selectors assume women have this dual life perspective, therefore making discrimination on a societal level also based on this duality. The macro-effect that even higher educated women have less attractive positions is a combination of job choice and statistical discrimination, both based on the same mechanism. However, if women definitely do have a career life perspective, they can break through the statistical discrimination and signal the difference. Empirical testing confirmed the theory. H. A. Becker and A. M. G. Beekes analyzed the careers of male and female academics at Dutch universities.[88] Next we give some examples of research related to job search in general. Sprengers used the theory of mental incongruity to study unemployment duration. He applied the method of decreasing abstractions.[89] E. A. W. Boxman studied the effects of networks of personal relations on labor market outcomes.[90]

Sociology of Population

The relationship between demography and sociology is manyfold. First, sociology is one of the constituent disciplines of the "interdiscipline" demography. Theories on determinants of social behavior can be incorporated within demographic research, making it possible to answer Vance's classical question "Is theory for demographers?" affirmatively.[91] Second, in many sociological research activities attention is paid to demography, in terms of concepts and methodology used and variables analyzed. Third, some of the interesting specialties within sociology, such as medical sociology, pay attention to issues which are also considered to be of interest for demographers. Examples refer to determinants of morbidity and mortality questions ("social inequality to death") and to the influence of the medical system on morbidity.[92]

During the 1950s and 1960s this interest was often restricted to the use of demographic background variables in surveys, without always knowing whether or not these variables could be helpful in explaining research findings. Starting in the 1980s, joint ventures between demography and other social and behavioral sciences were developed that are of a more theoretical nature.

Before answering the question what some of the major developments since the 1970s have been with regard to social demography, we'll first mention one of these joint ventures. The example is related to research carried out by the Netherlands Interdisciplinary Demographic Institute (NIDI).[93] In this project every three to four years attitudes of the Dutch population are measured dealing with demographic developments and their causes, while also attention is paid to the questions to what extent population policy measures are socially acceptable and are able to influence demographic behavior. These (quasi-)longitudinal studies have three cornerstones. The first refers to public opinion surveys with regard to demographic issues. The main problem with these studies is their lack of theory. The second cornerstone refers to social-psychological studies on determinants of cognitions and attitudes as (co-)determinants of demographic behavior, while the third cornerstone deals with the hypothetical-question-survey methodology.[94] In this type of survey respondents are confronted with policy measures that have not yet been implemented in a country, but are discussed in governmental, scientific, and/or parliamentary circles.

In the NIDI project attention is focused on population policies like family founding loans, child and family allowances, and child care arrangements. The theoretical framework, originally spelled out by Rozendal and others, (1985), has been validated and expanded in later rounds of data collection and analysis, while also measurements have been improved over the years. The first of these surveys was carried out in 1983, the second in 1986, and the third in 1990. Comparative analyses took place including survey data from Italy and Germany.[95] The case study illustrates that during the 1980s (social) demography had come a rather long way from the descriptive (sociographic) type of investigations that during the 1950s and 1960s formed the bread and butter of Dutch social demography.[96]

In his "Developments in Dutch Demography," Van Nimwegen concluded that during the 1960s demography developed rather well. However, his data on the distribution of Dutch publications on topics like theory construction within demography, demographic and economic interrelationships, and methodology show that in those years not too many activities were taking place.[97] Moreover, most of the studies were published in Dutch. Although there had been an increase in the number of studies published between 1945 and 1954 (291) compared to the 1975–1979 period (829), the proportion of studies published in other languages fell from 20 percent to somewhat over 10 percent. Several years later, J. H. Jansen and F. L. Leeuw in their study on publication and citation behavior of Dutch demographic researchers showed that even 92 percent was published in Dutch.[98] In this overview Van Nimwegen also found that the level of institution building was rather limited. Starting in the middle of the 1970s, however, the National Program for Demographic Research focused on coordination and programming of research activities with an emphasis on applied studies. In total over four million guilders were spent on this national program, which was positively evaluated. In 1983 a Committee on Programming Demographic Research was installed that continued to be active with regard to coordination and institution building.

Sociology of Policy Systems

Till approximately the early 1960s an important specialty in Dutch sociology had been "administrative sociology." Attention was paid to questions dealing with the culture and structure of the Dutch civil service, as well as to the analysis of the state structure and processes of policymaking and implementation. In the eighties and early nineties, apart from sociologists who had taken up a career as social policy researchers, there was only a limited number of university-based sociologists active in this branch of the discipline, largely because the administrative and policy sciences as specialties had taken over large parts of this field of study. Classical, Weberian types of questions, dealing among other things with the explanation of the development of bureaucracy during this century, were still referred to in introductory sociology textbooks, but the larger portion of the sociologists that studied public policy in the 1980s instead focused on items such as futures research, ex ante impact assessments, scenario building, and testing and evaluation research, including effectiveness investigations.[99] Often using (large-scale) empirical research, sociologists have been active in demystifying statements of policymakers, civil servants, members of parliament, representatives of labor unions, and participants of social movements dealing with questions like the causes of juvenile delinquency, educational attainment in relation to child care, side-effects of the current system of social security, and many other topics.[100]

A recent development is the growing interest of theoretically oriented sociologists in policy and organizational questions.[101] By combining theories from economics and organization science, such as transaction costs theory, agency theory, and network theories, new approaches to classic questions are developed and put to empirical tests. An example is the question of handling noncontractual relationships, originally formatted by MacCauley, while another example refers to the question under which conditions networks between civil servants can be regarded as the "social capital" a government department possesses when trying to reach its goals.[102] This research can be seen as a spin-off from earlier social network studies.[103]

In the sociology of policy systems we also find studies about the dynamics of these systems that try to enhance disciplinary knowledge about these systems and to enlighten practitioners regarding practical problems. As an example we take the ex post evaluation of futures research.[104] Regarding forecasts a theoretical framework that explains forecasting errors has been developed and partially tested.

EPILOGUE

In 1990 at a conference organized by the Netherlands Sociological and Anthropological Association to discuss the achievement of sociology in the Netherlands, the epilogue was held by Esser. Looking from a neighboring country (Germany), but having visited the Netherlands frequently, he characterized the situation aptly as follows:

To the outside observer, present day Dutch sociology has a somewhat unique dual form. It exhibits a singular fragmentation into two different, even conflicting "paradigms": the figurational sociology, especially around the university of Amsterdam, and the explanatory sociology around the universities of Groningen and Utrecht. There are also a host of small groups and activities which, following the tradition of "pragmatic" Dutch sociology, link careful description with theoretical considerations of a "middle range," referred to by Laeyendecker (1990) as "data-oriented social research." These activities include internationally renowned studies on the methods of empirical social research and statistics, as well as numerous other research traditions on contextual analysis, school and education sociology, social classes, religious and political cleavages, questions of the explanatory power of the concept of the "generation," migration and interethnic relationships and so forth.[105]

Esser concluded that the two main paradigms would both profit much from convergence and cooperation. In the early 1990s indeed a shift had taken place toward broader networks and more links between them. Co-operation around the university of Amsterdam had increased, in particular because Schuyt, an important interpretative sociologist, had joined ranks with historical sociologists like Goudsblom and De Swaan. The Amsterdam network had further developed its own branch of policy-oriented social research. The second network, around the Universities of Groningen and Utrecht, had also expanded. The Interuniversity Center of Theory and Methodology in the Social Sciences (ICS), for instance, had been joined by sociologists from the University of Nijmegen. This network also expanded its policy-oriented research activities. De Swaan has tried to decrease the gap between the two networks inter alia by trying to combine the two paradigms in his analysis of the welfare state.[106] In the field of research methodology also, attempts have been made to bridge the gap, by among others Swanborn.[107] Next to these two major networks a number of relatively small research groups are active, each following a course of its own. On the one hand, it seems plausible to expect that this pattern will continue. On the other hand, a further increase of cooperation would broaden the basis for large-scale research and teaching and would provide a better basis for international activities.

These endeavors to further develop sociology and to strengthen its identity are confronted with developments that at first sight indicate a loss of identity of the discipline. Since 1980 increasingly more or less "original" sociological problems have been studied by sociologists as well as by members of other disciplines. Undoubtedly as a result of this the intellectual necessity of continuing sociology as a specific discipline on its own has diminished. Lindenberg for instance—as was concluded—has pointed out that the borderlines between sociology and economics have become less marked. On the other hand, we have to keep in mind that the four major problems addressed by sociologists described at the beginning of this chapter still operate as an integrating framework. If a member of another discipline studies a sociological problem, the results of his or her study enhance the body of knowledge of sociology. Sociology continues as an institution and sociologists go on to live in an institutionalized community. These arguments induce us to conclude that in the decades to come, sociology will continue as a distinct institution. Perhaps in the longer run, an integration of the social sciences into an institution like the "medical sciences" is to be expected. In that case, sociology, in our view, would continue as a core specialty, as epidemiology does now.

Sociology in the Netherlands is more and more combining national and international activities. On the one hand, practical problems of the country itself are tackled, inter alia leading to numerous publications in Dutch. On the other hand, Dutch sociologists participate in social networks and organizations in other countries, in Germany and the United States and in international organizations like ISA. A large number of sociologists publish both in Dutch and in English. In this respect "Dutch sociology" is merging with sociology in general.

NOTES

1. The authors wish to thank Albert Beekes, Geert Dewulf, Jos de Haan, Piet Hermkens, Hein Moors, and Frits Tazelaar for their valuable contributions to this chapter.

2. H. M. Blalock, ed., *Social Theory and Social Research* (Glencoe, Ill.; Free Press, 1980); J. F. Short, ed., *The State of Sociology: Problems and Prospects* (Beverly Hills; Sage, 1981); K. Knorr-Cetina and A. V Cicourel, eds., *Advances in Social Theory and Methodology, Towards an Integration of Micro and Macro-Sociologies* (Boston and London: Routledge and Kegan Paul, 1981); H. A. Becker, "Voortgang en Vooruitgang in dc Sociologie," *Mens en Maatschappij* 56, 2 (1981), 118–153 (Continuity and Progress in Sociology); T. Bottomore, S. Nowak, and M. Sokolowska, eds., *Sociology, the State of the Art* (London and Beverly Hills: Sage, 1982).

3. F. Borgotta and K. S. Cook, eds., *The Future of Sociology* (Newbury Park: Sage, 1988); C.G.A. Bryant and H. A. Becker, *What Has Sociology Achieved?* (London: Macmillan, 1990); H. A. Becker, F. L. Leeuw, and K. Verrips, eds., *In Pursuit of Progress, an Assessment of Achievements in Dutch Sociology* (Amsterdam: SISWO, 1991).

4. R. Boudon, *Theories of Social Change* (London: Polity Press, 1986); S. P. Turner and J. H. Turner, *The Impossible Science, an Institutional Analysis of American Sociology* (Newbury Park: Sage, 1990).

5. The first three questions are often associated with Durkheim, Marx, and Weber; the fourth question has got attention from each of them; see W. Ultee, "How Classical Questions Were Enriched," in H. A. Becker et al., *In Pursuit of Progress.*

6. J. De Bosch Kemper, 1808–1876; H.P.G. Treub, 1834–1917; see J.A.A. van Doorn, *Beeld en Betekenis van de Nederlandse Sociologie* (Image and Relevance of Dutch Sociology) (Utrecht: Bijleveld, 1964).

7. E.g., S. R. Steinmetz, *Inleiding tot de Sociologie* (Introduction to Sociology) (Haarlem: Bohn, 1931). However, H. Flap, "Het betrekkelijke succes van de sociografische beweging," *Sociologische Gids* 30, 1 (1983), 4–17, shows that, although rather implicitly, several sociographic studies were linked with theoretical ideas.

8. Van Doorn, *op.cit.*

9. H. A. Becker and T. J. JJzerman, "De arbeidsmarkt voor Sociologen in Nederland," in L. Rademaker et al., eds., *Sociologie in de Nederlanden* (Deventer: Van Loghum Slaterus, 1979), 127 (The Labor Market for Sociologists in the Netherlands).

10. E.g., Van Doorn, *op.cit.;* M. Gastelaars, *Een Geregeld Leven, Sociologie en Sociale Politiek in Nederland 1925–1969* (Amsterdam: SUA, 1985) (A Disciplined Life).

11. W. Ultee (1991), *op. cit.*

12. F. van Heek et al., *Het Verborgen Talent* (Assen: Van Gorkum, 1968). (Hidden Talent).

13. I. Gadourek, *Riskante Gewoonten en Zorg voor Eigen Welzijn* (Groningen: Wolters, 1963); also *Absences and Well-being of Workers* (Assen: Van Gorkum, 1965).

14. Inter alia; H.A. Becker, *Management als Beroep* (Den Haag: Martinus Nijhoff, 1968) (Management as an Occupation).

15. J.A.A. van Doorn and C. J. Lammers, *Moderne Sociologie, een systematische inleiding* (Utrecht: Spectrum, 1959) (Modern Sociology).

16. I. L. Horowitz, *Professing Sociology: Studied in the Life Cycle of Social Science* (Chicago: Aldine, 1968).

17. E. Topitsch, ed., *Logik der Sozialwissenschaften* (Cologne: Kiepenhever & Witsch, 1968 (Logic of the Social Sciences); T.W. Adorno et al., *Der Positivismusstreit in der deutschen Soziologie* (Darmstadt: Luchterhand, 1972) (The battle about positivism in German sociology); A. W. Gouldner, *The Coming Crisis of Western Sociology* (London: Heinemann, 1970).

18. Inter alia Topitsch, *op. cit.*

19. W. Arts, S. Lindenberg, and R. Wippler, eds., *Gedrag en Structuur,* special issue of *Mens en Maatschappij* (Rotterdam: Rotterdam University Press (Behavior and Structure).

20. M. Hechter, K.-D. Opp, and R. Wippler, eds., *Social Institutions* (New York: Aldine de Gruyter, 1991).

21. C.J.M. Schuyt, *Recht, Orde en Burgerlijke Ongehoorzaamheid* (Rotterdam: Rotterdam University Press, 1972) (Law, Order, and Civil Disobedience).

22. A.J.A. Felling, *Lokale Macht en Netwerken, sociaal netwerk analyse* (Alphen aan den Rijn: Samsom, 1974) (Local power and networks).

23. P. G. Swanborn, *Methoden van sociaal-wetenschappelijk onderzoek* (Boom: Meppel, 1981) (Methods of social research); H. A. Becker, red., *Simulatie in de Sociale Wetenschappen* (Alphen aan den Rijn: Samsom, 1976); H.A. Becker et al., eds., *Handleiding voor het Ontwerpen van Scenario-projecten* (Utrecht: Faculty of Social Sciences (Manual for design of scenario projects).

24. P. Thoenes, *Utopie en ratio* (Meppel: Boom, 1969); policy-oriented sociology at Utrecht University was established by Groenman.

25. R. K. Merton, "Structural: Analysis in Sociology," in R. K. Merton, *Sociological Ambivalence* (New York: Free Press, 1976).

26. Merton, *op. cit.*

27. The SKG operation was preceded by an external evaluation carried out by demographer Dirk J. van de Kaa in 1986.

28. See P.J.J.M. van Loon et al., "Sterkte/Zwakteanalyse sociologie, politicologie en bestuurskunde" (Strength and weakness in sociology, political sciences, and administrative sciences), *Acta Politica* 23 (1968), 21–61.

29. Masuch, University of Amsterdam, on computer simulation of theory formation (1991); Raub and Weessie, University of Utrecht, on cooperation models (1992).

30. C. Remery, F. L. Leeuw, and J. de Haan, *Zwaartepuntvorming in de maatschappijwetenschappen en overheidsbeleid: evaluatie van de TVC-DAS-operatie* (Utrecht: Department of Sociology, ISOR publications, 1992). A "center of excellence" was defined as a group of scholars characterized by advanced (postdoctoral) research and the establishment of an integrated Ph.D. training program.

31. P. G. Swanborn, *De Sociologie-Opleidingen* (Utrecht: Report Department of Education and Sciences, 1991) (Courses in Sociology).

32. J. Dronkers and H. G. Hamaker, "Meer werk voor sociologen, maar minder voor antropologen: de stand van januari 1991," *Sociodrome* (Employment for Sociologists).

33. For instance, H. van Fulpen et al., *Berekend Beleid:* personele inkomensverdeling in 1981, met een micromodel-simulatie van de verdelingseffecten van verschillende overheidsmaatregelen (Simulated Policy, personal distribution of incomes in 1981, with a micromodel-simulation of distribution effects and budgetary effects of a number of governmental interventions) (Rijswijk, 1981); J. W. Becker, *Reacties op Werkloosheid* (Reactions on Unemployment) (Rijswijk, 1989); SCP, Doelmatig dienstverlenen, Rijswijk.

34. P. Ester and A.P.N. Nauta, "A Decade of Social and Cultural Reports in the Netherlands," *The Netherlands Journal of Sociology* 22 (1986), 72–87.

35. NSAV organizes state-of-the-art conferences every four to five years. The outcomes of a conference on this subject held in 1990 have been reported by H. A. Becker, F. L. Leeuw, and K. Verrips, *op.cit.*

36. General sociology consists of the analysis of concepts, the history of sociology, and the study of central problems in the discipline. In the next section we will pay attention to sociological aspects of social chance and to sociological aspects of governmental policymaking, both issues in general sociology. In this overview of contemporary sociology in the Netherlands we will abstain from dealing with developments in the analysis of concepts. The history of the discipline gets attention in each section of this essay.

37. J. Goudsblom, *Sociology in the Balance* (Oxford: Basil Blackwell, 1977); W. C. Ultee, "Groei van de Kennis en Stagnatie in de Sociologie, een aantal regels van de methode en een kritische doorlichting van enkele sociologische tradities" (Growth and stagnation of knowledge), Ph.D. diss., 1977; J.M.M. de Valk, "Contemporary Sociological Theory in the Netherlands," in Raj P. Mohan and Don Martindale, eds., *Handbook of Contemporary Developments in World Sociology* (Westport, Conn.: Greenwood Press, 1975), 47–58.

38. R. Wippler, "The Structural-Individualistic Approach in Dutch Sociology," *The Netherlands' Journal of Sociology* 14 (1978), 139.

39. His theory assumes that action situations are structured in terms of what discrepancies between cohort should be and what is perceived to be the case. F. Tazelaar, *Mentale Incongruenties, Sociale Restricties. Gedrag; een onderzoek naar beroepsparticipatie van gehuwde vrouwelijke academici* (Mental incongruences, social restrictions, behaviors) (Utrecht, 1980).

40. S. Lindenberg and F. N. Stokman, eds., *Modellen in de Sociologie* (Deventer: Van Loghum Slaterus, 1983) (Models in Sociology). This volume was issued in celebration of Gadourek, who had been appointed a professor of sociology at Groningen University twenty-five years before.

41. K.-D. Opp and R. Wippler, eds., *Empirischer Theorievergleich. Erklärungen sozialen Verhaltens in Problemsituationen* (Opladen: Westdeutscher Verlag, 1990) (Empirical comparison of theories).

42. R. Swedberg, *Economics and Sociology, Redefining their Boundaries: Conversations with Economists and Sociologists* (Princeton: Princeton University Press, 1990).

43. S. Lindenberg, "Recent Contributions of Dutch Sociologists, Toward a New Integration of the Socio-economic Sciences, Especially Sociology and Economics," in Henk A. Becker, Frans F. Leeuw, and Kitty Verrips, eds., *op.cit.,* 71–89.

44. N. Wilterdink, "New Views in Historical Sociology," in H. A. Becker, F. L. Leeuw, and K. Verrips, *op.cit.,* 53–70.

45. A. de Swaan, *In Care of the State, Health Care, Education and Welfare in Europe and the USA in the Modern Era* (London: Polity Press, 1988). On rational choice theory and its brands, see H. A. Becker, "Achievement in the Analytical Tradition in Sociology," in Bryant and Becker, *op.cit.*

46. M.H.D. van Leeuwen, *Bijstand in Amsterdam (ca. 1800–1859), armenzorg als beheersingsen overlevingsstrategie* (Amsterdam: Thesis Publishing, 1992) (Poverty Relief in Amsterdam).

47. C.J.M. Schuyt, *Op zoek naar het Hart van de Verzorgingsstaat* (Leiden: Stenfert Kroese, 1991) (Looking for the Heart of the Welfare State); G. Engbersen and R. Van der Veen, *Moderne Armoede, Overleven op het Sociaal Minimum* (Leiden: Stenfert Kroese, 1987) (Modern Poverty, Survival on the Minimal Subsistence Level); on methodology inter alia F. Wester, *Strategieën voor Kwalitatief Onderzoek* (Muiderberg: Coutinho, 1987).

48. The subsection on methods is primarily based on J. van der Zouwen and T. W. Kantebeen, "Progress in Methods of Data Collection and Data Analysis in Dutch Sociology," in H. A. Becker, F. L. Leeuw, and K. Verrips, eds., *op.cit.*

49. See Van der Zouwen and Kantebeen, *op.cit.*

50. See Van der Zouwen and Kantebeen, *op.cit.*

51. F. L. Leeuw, "Regierungspolitik und Policy-forschung in den Niederlanden," *Jahrbuch zur Staats- und Verwaltungsforschung* 3 (1989), 291–314 (Governmental policy and policy research in the Netherlands).

52. J. M. Hutjes, "Policy Research between the Accumulation and Implementation of Knowledge," *Knowledge and Policy* 4, 10–27. Also F. L. Leeuw, *op.cit.,* 291–314.

53. J. M. Hutjes, "Beleidsonderzoek in de jaren tachtig, een poging tot balans," *Sociologisch Jaarboek* 1985, Deventer, 25–42 (Policy research in the 1980s).

54. J.A.A. van Doorn (1964), *op.cit.,* Utrecht.

55. A. Hoogerwerf, "Beleid berust op veronderstellingen: de beleidstheorie," *Acta Politica* 19 (1984), 493–531; F. L. Leeuw and H. van de Graag, "Onderzoek naar beleidstheorieën: uitgangspunten, methodische aspecten en praktische relevantie," *Beleid en Maatschappij* 15 (1988), 1–6; F. L. Leeuw, "Beleistheorieën; veronderstellingen achter beleid," in A. Hoogerwerf, red., *Overheidsbeleid* (Alphen aan den Rijn, 1989), 91–106.

56. H. T. Chen, *Theory-driven evaluations* (Newbury Park, CA: Sage Publications, 1990).

57. M. van de Vall, *Sociaal beleidsonderzoek, een professioneel paradigma* (Alphen aan den Rijn, 1980). M. van de Vall and Herb J. Ulrich, "Trends in Data-Based Sociological Practice," *Knowledge: Creation, Diffusion, Utilization* 8 (1986), 167–184.

58. M. van de Vall, "De waardencontext van sociaal beleidsonderzoek: een theoretisch model," in M. van de Vall and F. L. Leeuw, *Sociaal Beleidsonderzoek* (Den Haag, 1987), 35–36.

59. M. van de Vall (1980), *op.cit.;* M. van de Vall, "De waardencontext van sociaal beleidsonderzoek: een theoretisch model," in M. van de Vall and F. L. Leeuw, (1987), *op.cit.*

60. M. van de Vall (1980), *op.cit.,* 208.

61. M. van de Vall, "Over normalen en revolutionaren, ofwel de strijd om het professionele paradigma van sociaal beleidsonderzoek," Paper presented at the Netherlands Sociological and Anthropological Society Seminar, 18 May 1980; M. van de Vall, "Over een empirische indringer in het heilige huisje der methodologie," *Sociale Wetenschappen* (1981), 24.

62. I. Gadourek, *Social Changes as Redefinition of Roles: A Study of Structural and Cultural Relationships in the Netherlands of the "Seventies"* (Assen: Van Gorkum, 1982).

63. A. Felling, J. Peters, and O. Schreuder, *Burgerlijk en Onburgerlijk Nederland* (Deventer: Van Loghum Slaterus, 1983) (Bourgeois and Nonbourgeois Netherlands).

64. L. Halman, F. Heuks, R. de Moor, and H. Zanders, *Traditie, Secularisatie en Individualisering, een studie naar de waarden van de Nederlanders* (Tilburg: Tilburg University Press, 1987) (Tradition, Secularization, and Individualization).

65. H.A. Becker, ed., *Life Histories and Generations* (Utrecht: ISOR, 1990).

66. J.A.A. van Doorn and C.J.M. Schuyt, eds., *De Stagnerende Verzorgingsstaat* (Meppel; Boom, 1978) (The Stagnating Welfare State).

67. C.J.M. Schuyt (1991), *op.cit.;* G. Engbersen and R. van der Veen (1987), *op.cit.*

68. W. Ultee, *"How Classical Questions Were Enriched;* the relation between problems of general sociology and sociology's specialisms in the Netherlands in the 1980's," in H. A. Becker, F. L. Leeuw, and K. Verrips, *op.cit.;* this section is mainly based on this review. See also W. C. Ultee, "Beyond Stratification and Mobility," in W. Jansen, J. Dronkers, and K. Verrips, eds., *Similar or Different? Continuities in Dutch Research on Social Stratification and Social Mobility* (Amsterdam: Siswo, 1989).

69. H.B.G. Ganzeboom and P.M. de Graaf, "Intergenerational, Occupational Mobility in the Netherlands in 1954 and 1977," in: B.F.M. Bakker, J. Dronkers, and H.B.G. Ganzeboom, eds., *Stratification and Mobility in the Netherlands* (Amsterdam: Siswo, 1984).

70. H.P.M. Ganzeboom and P.M. de Graaf, "Intergenerationele Opleidingsmobiliteit in Nederland van geboortecohorten 1891–1960," *Sociale Wetenschappen* 32 (1989), 263–278.

71. W. Ultee and R. Luyks, "Integrational Standard-of-Living Mobility in Nine EEC Countries," *European Sociological Review* 2 (1986), 191–206; H.B.G. Ganzeboom, R. Luyks, and D. J. Trieman, "Intergenerational Class Mobility in Comparative Perspective," *Research in Social Stratification and Mobility* 9 (1989), 3–84.

72. W. Ultee and R. Luyks, "Educational Heterogamy and Intergenerational Class Mobility in 23 Industrial Nations," *European Sociological Review* 6 (1990), 125–149.

73. W. Ultee, J. Dessens, and W. Jansen, "Why Does Unemployment Come in Couples?" *European Sociological Review* 4 (1988), 111–122.

74. W. A. Arts, *Eerlijk Delen, over verdelende rechtvaardigheid en inkomens-beleid* (Den Haag: VUGA, 1984) (Fair Distribution).

75. P.L.J. Hermkens, *Oordelen over Rechtvaardigheid van Inkomens* (Den Haag: VUGA, 1983) (Judging the fairness of incomes).

76. N.-D. de Graaf, *Postmaterialism and the Stratification Process,* Ph.D. diss. (Utrecht, ISOR, 1988). See also G.W. Meijnen, *Van zes to twaalf, een longitudinaal onderzoek naar de milieu- en schooleffecten van loopbanen in het lager onderwijs* (Den Haag: SVO, 1984).

77. A.A. van der Hoeven-van Doornum, "Effecten van leerlingbeelden en streefniveaus op schoolloopbanen," Ph.D. diss., Nijmegen, 1990.

78. J. L. Peschar, *Zo vader - zo zoon, zo moeder - zo dochter? Vergelijkende analyses naar de processen van statusverweving en onderwijsmobiliteit in Nederland, Hongarije en Polen* (Lisse: Swets & Zeitlinger, 1987); also J. Dronkers, "Een empirisch onderzoek naar de effecten van betaalde beroepsarbeid door vrouwen op de schoolloopbanen van hun kinderen," *Pedagogische Studiën* 64 (1987), 277–284.

79. C. J. Lammers, *Organisaties Vergelijkenderwijs* (Utrecht: Spectrum, 1982).

80. Review: S. Lindenberg, "Recent Contributions of Dutch Sociologists, Toward a Net Integration of the Socio-economic Sciences, Especially Sociology and Economics," in H. A. Becker, F. L. Leeuw and K. Verrips (1991), *op.cit.,* 71–94.

81. J. Weesie, "Mathematical Models for Competition, Cooperation and Social Networks," Ph.D. diss., Utrecht, 1988.

82. J. Weesie, A. Verbeek, and H. Flap, eds., "An Economic Theory of Social Networks," in J. Weesie and H. Flap, eds., *Social Networks through Time* (Utrecht: ISOR, 1991).

83. R. S. Batenburg, "Automatisering in Bedrijf," Ph.D. diss., Groningen, 1991.

84. Inter alia M. Masuch, P. LaPitin, and R. Verhorst, "Kunstmatige Intelligentie in organisaties; een simulatiemodel van organisatorische besluitvorming," *Mens en Maatschappij* 61 (1987), 358–381.

85. On health care delivery organizations, see inter alia: P. P. Groenewegen, *Lokatiekeuze en Huisartsendichtheid* (Utrecht: NIVEL, 1985); Tj. Tijmstra, *Sociologie en Tandheelkunde, resultaten van een gecombineerd sociaal-wetenschappelijk en tandheelkundig onderzoek* (Groningen, 1980).

86. Overview: S. Lindenberg (1991), *op.cit.*

87. K. Sanders, "Vrouwelijke Pioniers; vrouwen en mannen met een 'mannelijke' hogere beroepsopleiding aan het begin van hun loopbaan" (Female Pioneers), Ph.D. diss., Groningen, 1991.

88. H. A. Becker and A.M.G. Beekes, eds., *Loopbanen van mannelijke en vrouwelijke academici aan Nederlandse Universiteiten, een studie naar de ontwikkelingen tussen 1974 en 1986* (Utrecht, ISOR, 1990); A.M.G. Beekes, *De Hordenloop, ontwikkelingen in de achterstand van vrouwelijke op mannelijke academici aan Nederlandse universiteiten in de periode 1960–1985* (Utrecht: ISOR, 1991) (Careers of male and female academics at Dutch universities).

89. M. Sprengers, "Explaining Unemployment Duration, an Integrative Approach," Ph.D. diss., Utrecht, 1992.

90. E.A.W. Boxman, "Contacten en carrière, een empirisch-theoretisch onderzoek naar de relatie tussen sociale netwerken en arbeidsmarktpositie," Thesis, Amsterdam, 1992.

91. R. B. Vance, "Is Theory for Demographers?, *Social Forces* 31 (1952), 9–13.

92. P.P. Groenewegen (1985), *op.cit.*

93. N. van Nimwegen, *Onderzoek naar bevolkingsvraagstukken in de jaren negentig* (Den Haag: NIDI, 1991), (Research on population problems in the 1990s).

94. R. Simon and J. Simon, "Money Incentives and Family Size: A Hypothetical-Question Study," *Public Opinion Quarterly* 38 (1974), 46–61; P.J. Rozendal, H. G. Moors and F. L. Leeuw, *Het bevolkingsvraastuk in de jaren tachtig; opvattingen over beleid* (Den Haag: NIDI, 1985) (The population problem in the 1980s).

95. H. G. Moors, "Attitudes towards Demographic Trends and Population Policy: Italy and the Netherlands in a Comparative Perspective," *Population Research and Policy Review* 9 (1990), 179–194.

96. F. L. Leeuw and A. van Gageldonk, *Differentiatie in sociaal- en geesteswetenschappelijk onderzoek* (Den Haag: Staatsuitgeverij, 1984) (Serie Beleidsgerichte Studies Ministerie van O & W) (Differentiation in the humanities and the social sciences).

97. N. van Nimwegen, "Developments in Dutch Demography," in H. G. Moors, ed., *National Population Bibliography of the Netherlands 1945–1979* (Den Haag, 1981).

98. J. H. Jansen and F. L. Leeuw, "Publikatie- en verwijsgedrag in de Nederlandse demografie,"*Bevolking en Gezin* 23 (1987), 125–142 (Publication and citation behavior in Dutch demography).

99. H. A. Becker and A. Porter, eds., *Impact Assessment Today,* vols. 1–2 (Utrecht, 1986).

100. P. Ester, *Sociologie als ambacht* (Tilburg: Tilburg University Press, 1991) (Sociology as a craft); F. L. Leeuw, "Knowledge Transfer and Application in Dutch Sociology: Some Developments between 1980 and 1990," in H. A. Becker, F. L. Leeuw, and K. Verrips, eds. (1991), *op.cit.*

101. W. Raub and J. Weesie, *The Management of Matches,* Pioneer-proposal, Utrecht University, Department of Sociology, 1991.

102. A. Bulder, H. D. Flap, and F. L. Leeuw, "Netwerken van ambtenaren: het sociaal kapitaal van de overheid," Paper, Vakgroep Sociologie, RU Utrecht, 1992.

103. J. Weesie and H. Flap, eds., *Social Networks through Time* (Utrecht: ISOR, 1990); H. Flap, *Conflict, Loyalty and Violence* (Frankfurt: Peter Lang, 1988).

104. G. Dewulf, *Limits to Forecasting, Towards a Theory of Forecast Errors* (Amsterdam: Thesis Publications, 1991).

105. H. Esser, "Dutch Sociology from the Viewpoint of an Outside Observer," in H. A. Becker, F. L. Leeuw, and K. Verrips, eds. (1991) *op.cit.;* also: L. Laeyendecker, "What Dutch Sociology Has Achieved," in C.G.A. Bryant and H. A. Becker (1990), *op.cit.*

106. De Swaan, *op.cit.*

107. Swanborn, *op.cit.*

9

Contemporary Sociology in Sweden

Richard Swedberg

Swedish sociology is part of Swedish culture and society, so a few general words on Sweden may be useful before we approach our main topic more directly.[1] When one looks at Sweden through social scientific glasses, the following picture emerges.[2] Sweden is a small country on the periphery of Europe. It was hammered into national unity in the 1500s; it became one of the major military powers in Europe in the 1600s; and it was industrialized in the beginning of the twentieth century. Sweden is a homogeneous country with no major linguistic, religious, or ethnic divisions. It has never been occupied by a foreign power and it has not been involved in a war since the 1810s. There was no real feudalism in Sweden and there has been less inequality between the social classes than in most countries. The social structure of Sweden has always been "exceptionally well-balanced," to quote Schumpeter.[3] During much of the twentieth century the employers' organizations and the trade unions have been roughly equal in strength. The Social Democratic party has held political power during most of the post–World War II period. During these years the famous Swedish welfare state was created.

The culture of Sweden is homogeneous and reflects, among other things, that the country has not been urbanized for very long. Sweden is secular, but the Protestant past of the country is obvious in the national importance attached to work. Indeed, work and equality are two key ingredients in Swedish culture. A high value is also placed on what is perceived as "natural" and "normal." Manners, reflecting the popular past, are frank rather than refined. The roles of men and women are distinct and rarely questioned. Silence is more appreciated than verbal dexterity. Science is highly admired (Nobel was a Swede), but there is actually more of a tradition in

Sweden of technology than of high science. Engineering became important to Swedish industry very early and is still integral to the performance of such multinationals as Volvo, Ericsson, and ABB.

How has sociology fared in this environment? Does it reflect the general Swedish climate of conformity and class compromise? Or has it broken away and attached itself to some single aspect of the culture? And how does it relate to the national admiration for engineering and technology? These are some of the questions which may be useful to keep in mind when one takes a closer look at Swedish sociology.

THE PREHISTORY OF SWEDISH SOCIOLOGY

The birth of Swedish sociology is usually set to 1947, when the first chair in sociology was established. This took place at Uppsala University, and the first professor was Torgny Segerstedt, former professor of moral philosophy and ethics. In 1954 a second chair was created at the University of Stockholm, and it was given to Gunnar Boalt. In 1956 a third chair was created at the University of Lund (Gösta Carlsson); in 1960 one in Gothenburg (Edmund Dahlström); and in 1965 one in Umea (Georg Karlsson). Thereby all five major universities of Sweden had a chair in sociology.

What is striking about the establishment of sociology in Sweden is, first of all, that it took place so late. It can be mentioned in this context that the Swedish university system is quite old. The first chair in political science dates, for example, to 1622 and the one in economics to 1741. It may of course be argued that what happened in 1947 and afterwards was more a process of *institutionalizing* than of actually *founding* Swedish sociology. This, however, is not entirely right. Those who claim that there is a long tradition of Swedish sociology usually point out that Carl von Linné made some sharp social observations in his famous travel accounts and that Sweden has the oldest statistical office in the world, founded in 1753. References are also made to people like Anton Nyström (1842–1931), G. H:son Holmberg (1864–1929), and Gustav Steffen (1864–1929). Nyström was a follower of Comte and founded a positivist institute in Stockholm in 1879. It was in all likelihood through Nyström that the term "sociology" was introduced into Swedish language. In any case, the first recorded instance of the term being used is in a lecture series from the 1880s given by one of Nyström's followers, Carl Yngve Sahlin.[4] A certain interest in social science, including sociology, was also transmitted through the labor movement. The syndicalist G. H:son Holmberg wrote, for example, several books explicitly about "sociology." And so did Gustav Steffen, who from 1903 held a chair in "economics and sociology" at the University of Gothenburg. Steffen was inspired by the Social Democratic labor movement in Germany, and he was interested in a mixture of social science and social reforms. Together with August Strindberg, Sweden's foremost author,

Steffen decided at the turn of the century to make a sociological study of the peasants in France. Steffen and Strindberg, however, became enemies during the trip in France, and the whole thing ended up that Strindberg wrote the book himself. It was called *Bland franska bönder (Among French Peasants,* 1889), and it contains an excellent and amusing description of rural France.

Steffen died in 1929, and no one was appointed to replace him. Since he had few followers (Per Nyström was an exception), his influence on Swedish sociology has been minor. Those who argue that Swedish sociology has its roots in the public studies commissioned by the government have more of a case. There is first of all the famous study of emigration from the turn of the century, conducted by Gustav Sundbärg (1857–1914).[5] Sundbärg's collaborator, E. H. Thörnberg (1873–1961), is also often mentioned in this context. Especially his work on social movements, such as *Folkrörelser och samhällsliv* (People's Movements and Social Life, 1943), has been appreciated by later sociologists. Other parliamentary investigations, which may be cited as examples of early Swedish social science, include studies of population, women's work, unemployment, and urbanization.[6]

To claim that Swedish sociology grew out of these parliamentary investigations is, however, to exaggerate their importance. More to the point is the fact that Swedish sociology has often, just like these parliamentary investigations, tried to unite social science with a strong concern for social reforms. "Social engineering" is the term that is used for this mixture of science and politics in Sweden. A particularly good example of this type of work can be found in the writings by Alva Myrdal (1902–1986) and Gunnar Myrdal (1898–1987). The Myrdals clearly deserve a chapter of their own in the history of Swedish sociology.[7] There is, of course, no place here for such an undertaking, but a few words must be said about their contribution.

Gunnar Myrdal's three major works—*The Political Element in the Development of Economic Theory* (1930, tr. 1953), *An American Dilemma* (1944), and *Asian Drama* (1968)—are all of importance to sociology. The first book contains an interesting discussion of the problem of objectivity, which would later result in the well-known pamphlet, *Objectivity in Social Research* (1969). Myrdal's major work in sociology is, however, *An American Dilemma.* This work is undoubtedly also the most famous work in sociology ever written by a Swede.[8] Those who claim that Swedish sociology was created in 1947 by Torgny Segerstedt do well to ponder the fact that Myrdal was already in the late 1930s in the United States, leading a major research project together with people like Samuel Stouffer, Louis Wirth, and E. Franklin Frazier. *An American Dilemma* was very much appreciated by U.S. sociologists. Robert Lynd called it "the most penetrating and important book on our contemporary American civilization that has been written."[9] W.E.B. DuBois described *An American Dilemma* as a "monumental and unrivaled study," and in Howard Odum's opinion it was "the best thing that has been done on the Negro and is likely to be the best for a considerable time to come."[10] *An American Dilemma* was eventually to become a social science classic, and it was cited by the U.S. Supreme Court in the famous 1954 *Brown* decision through which discrimination was outlawed in public schools. Myrdal's basic thesis in his study was that American citizens feel a conflict between their basic morality ("The American Creed") and their actual conduct. This idea has been criticized, among others by Robert Merton, on the ground that a strongly prejudiced person does not necessarily feel the "dilemma" that Myrdal talks about and that "The American Creed" is by no means accepted in all parts of the United States.[11]

Myrdal's third work of interest to sociology—*Asian Drama* (1968)—was to have much less of an impact on sociology than his earlier work on race relations. *Asian Drama* contains nonetheless many interesting sociological observations on the development of Asia, for example, on the role of foreign trade in the creation of inequality between nations and on the role of the state in the Third World. Myrdal's work, however, was part of the modernization literature, which by this time was becoming quite unpopular. For this and other reasons *Asian Drama* has not been given the close reading by sociologists that it no doubt deserves. Ideological reasons, but of a different kind, have also helped to obscure the important sociological contribution by Alva Myrdal. Very early she began to draw attention to the social situation of Swedish women.[12] Her most succinct contribution to the growing literature of gender studies, however, is the pioneering work (written together with Viola Klein), *Women's Two Roles* (1956). The main thesis in this work is that there is a growing conflict in today's society between women's role in the family and at work; and that the two are very difficult to coordinate. Alva Myrdal's work on disarmament, *The Game of Disarmament* (1976), is another untapped source of sociological insights.

Why was sociology so poorly developed in Sweden? The answer has perhaps to do with the fact that Swedish society is such a homogeneous one. To be homogeneous may be useful for a community, but it does not necessarily make for a good sociology. Swedish society reminds in this aspect of Japan, another homogeneous country with a poor tradition of sociology.

THE THREE GENERATIONS OF SWEDISH SOCIOLOGY

Since the establishment in 1947 of sociology there have been three generations of Swedish sociologists. Each of these has its own special profile, both in terms of research interests and social characteristics (see Table

9.1). The first generation, born during the first two decades of the twentieth century, was primarily interested in defining sociology and in carrying out research in accordance with this definition. This was the real pioneering generation in Swedish sociology, and its individual members had all taught themselves what they meant by "sociology." The members of the second generation were typically born in the 1920s and 1930s. They were brought up on the kind of sociology that had been selected by the first generation. Before climbing up in the academic hierarchy, they often worked as assistants to the founders of Swedish sociology, whose pioneer spirit they often came to share. The sense of helping to found sociology is entirely missing among the members of the third generation, which in many ways grew out of the student rebellion in the 1960s. They have typically been taught sociology by the second generation; they were born in the 1940s; and most are still climbing up in the academic hierarchy. Sociology, as it exists today in the Swedish universities, is dominated by a mixture of the second and the third generation. Several members of the second generation have recently been retired, but the second generation still controls much of the resources in Swedish academia.

The people who make up the first generation of Swedish sociology were all very much influenced by moral philosophy and ethics. Segerstedt, for example, was professor of moral philosophy and ethics before becoming professor of sociology. Boalt and Carlsson were well versed in moral philosophy and ethics and also participated in the important social science seminar that was taught in the 1940s by Gunnar Myrdal, Herbert Tingsten, and Einar Tegen at the University of Stockholm.[13] One might think that this background in moral philosophy would have made the early Swedish sociologists prone to ask broad, existential questions and the like. In reality, however, the opposite is true. Through philosophy—especially through the ideas of the important Uppsala philosopher Axel Hägerström—Segerstedt, Boalt, and the others had come to distrust any kind of speculative thinking and to view science in the most positivistic way. Hägerström claimed that no objective values exist, and the motto he had chosen for his philosophy was *"metaphysics must be destroyed."*

Hägerström's influence is also clear in the important report about social science that the Swedish state issued in 1946.[14] The purpose of this report was to evaluate the need for various types of social science in Swedish society and at the universities. The section which deals with sociology says that it is absolutely necessary to introduce sociology into the Swedish universities. Since this part of the report contains an explicit discussion of the kind of sociology that was needed in Sweden (and which was later referred to in various key academic appointments), there is good reason to take a closer look at it. The report, in other words, lays the ideological foundation for Swedish sociology.

In the 1946 report it is said that sociology is needed in modern society,

Table 9.1
The Three Generations of Swedish Sociology

THE FIRST GENERATION

Key Members:

Torgny Segerstedt (1908-), Gunnar Boalt (1910-), Gösta Carlsson (1919-), Bertil Pfannenstil (1909-).

Characteristics:

Self-taught, learned academics from the old, elite-oriented Swedish university system with an interest in strictly positivistic, anti-metaphysical and U.S. inspired sociology. Strong emphasis on methods, social psychology and microoriented social processes.

Major Works:

See especially Gösta Carlsson, *Social Mobility and Class Structure* (1958). See also Torgny Segerstedt, *Social Control as a Sociological Concept* (1948); Torgny Segerstedt and Agne Lundquist, *Människan i Industrisamhället (Man in Industrial Society*, 1952-1955); and Gunnar Boalt, *The Sociology of Research* (1969).

Time Period:

Main impact during 1940s to the early 1960s.

THE SECOND GENERATION

Key Members:

Edmund Dahlström (1922-), Ulf Himmelstrand (1924-), Joachim Israel (1920-), Carl-Gunnar Janson (1926-) Georg Karlsson (1917-), Agne Lundquist (1919-), Walter Korpi (1934-), Bengt Rundblad (1925), Hans Zetterberg (1927-), Bertil Gardell (1927-1987), *Bo Anderson (1931-), Johan Asplund (1937-), Bengt Abrahamsson (1937-), Robert Erikson (1938-), Sten Johansson (1939-), Karl-Gunnar Rosengren (1932-), Rita Liljeström (1928-), Bengt Gesser (1931-), Eckart Kühlhorn (1931).

Characteristics:

Educated by the first generation of Swedish sociologists, these researchers were bred on positivism and "hard data" sociology. In the 1960s and 1970s some rebelled against their background by becoming interested in Marxism; a few also started to use alternative sociological methods. This generation produced the first studies of the Swedish welfare society.

Major Works:

See especially Hans Zetterberg, *On Theory and Verification in Sociology* (1954); Walter Korpi, *The Working Class in Welfare Capitalism*, 1978; tr. 1979); Johan Asplund, *On undran inför samhället (Reflecting on Society*, 1970). See also Ulf Himmelstrand et al., *Beyond Welfare Capitalism* 1981); Joachim Israel, *Alienation* (1968); Carl-Gunnar Janson (ed.), *Det Differentierade samhället (Differentiated Society*, 1968); Sten Johansson, *Om levnadsnivå-undersökningen (About the Level of Living Survey*, 1970); Rita Liljestrom and Edmund Dahlstrom, *Arbetarkvinnor i hem-, arbets- och samhällsliv (Working Women at Home, at Work and in Society*, 1981); Gösta Carlsson et al., *Svensk samhällsstruktur i sociologisk belysning (Swedish Social Structure from a Sociological Viewpoint*, 1959-1969; Bengt Gesser, *Utbildning, jämlikhet, arbetsdelning (Education, Equality, Division of Labor*, 1985); Robert Erikson (and John Goldthorpe), *The Constant Flux* (1992).

Table 9.1 (*continued*)

Time Period:

Active already in the 1950s, this generation came to dominate Swedish sociology in the 1960s and 1970s. During the 1980s several were retired, while others still exert a very important influence on Swedish sociology.

THE THIRD GENERATION

Key Members:

Göran Therborn (1941-), Rune Åberg (1942-), Göran Ahrne (1944); *Ulla Bergryd (1942-), Boel Berner (1945-), *Margareta Bertilsson (1944-), *Thomas Brante (1947-), *Olof Dahlbäck (1944-), *Björn Eriksson (1941), *Ron Eyerman (1942-), *Mats Franzén (1948-), Bengt Furåker (1943-), Peter Hedström (1955-), *Carl le Grand (1947-), *Jan O. Jonsson (1957-), *Lorentz Lyttkens (1947-), *Staffan Marklund (1945-), Thor Norström (1942-), *Gunnar Olofsson (1942-), Sven E. Olsson (1950-), Casten von Otter (1941-), *Joakim Palme (1958-), *Leif G. W. Persson (1945-), *Tomas Peterson (1950-), *Åke Sandberg (1944-), *Anne-Marie Sellerberg (1943-), Sune Sunesson (1944-), *Stefan Svallfors (1957-), *Richard Swedberg (1948-), *Ryszard Szulkin (1950-), *Michael Tåhlin (1957-), *Lars Udéhn (1948-), Håkan Wiberg (1942-), Karin Widerberg (1949-).

Characteristics:

This generation has mainly grown out of the new reformed university system in Sweden. It was educated in the positivistic tradition of Swedish sociology but also formed by the student rebellion of the 1960s. It is often positivistic but also tends toward pluralism in methodological questions and has, besides a well developed interest for Swedish society, also a penchant for topics such as the sociology of science and sociology of culture.

Major Contributions:

See especially Göran Therborn, *Class, Science and Society* (1974) and *Borgarklass och byråkrati i Sverige (Bourgeois Class and Bureaucracy in Sweden,* (1989). See also the two anthologies: Ulla Bergryd (ed.), *Den sociologiska fantasin (The Sociological Imagination,* 1987) and Ulf Himmelstrand and Göran Svensson (eds.), *Sverige—vardag och struktur (Sweden—Everyday Life and Social Structure* (1988) as well as Göran Ahrne,*Vardagsverklighet och struktur (Everyday Life and Structure,* 1981) plus *Agency and Organization* (1990), Boel Berner, *Teknikens värld (The World of Technology,* 1981), Thomas Brante, *Vetenskapens struktur och förändring (The Structure and Change of Science,* 1980), Lars Udéhn, *Methodological Individualism* (1987), Peter Hedström, *Structures of Inequality* (1988), Staffan Marklund, *Paradise Lost?* (1988), Robert Erikson and Rune Åberg (eds.), *Welfare in Transition* (1984), tr. 1987), Richard Swedberg, *Economics and Sociology* (1990), Mats Franzén, *Den folkliga staden (The City of the People,* 1992).

Time Period:

This generation has started to replace the second generation and will dominate Swedish sociology by the mid-90s.

Note: All people in this table (save those with an asterisk before their names) have held or hold the position of what is called "professor" in the Swedish university system (roughly the equivalent of the U.S. "full professor").

not the least for democratic reasons. There exists "a close relationship," according to the report, "between social science and democracy."[15] One form of social science which was particularly necessary, it was continued, was sociology. It could, however, not be any kind of sociology; it had to be a nonspeculative, quantitative sociology. *"What Swedish social science needs is empirical sociology.... What has to be avoided is speculative sociology."*[16] "Speculative sociology" was the kind of sociology "which can be found among many French and German sociologists."[17] "Empirical sociology," on the other hand, was defined as the kind of sociology which has "first and foremost been developed in the U.S."[18] According to Torgny Segerstedt, who formulated the text in the report, by "French and German sociologists" he meant people like Emile Durkheim, Lucien Lévy-Bruhl, Max Weber, and Georg Simmel.[19] By American sociology, he meant the work by George Lundberg, Samuel Stouffer, and similar sociologists.

Swedish sociology, it should be noted, thus opted from the beginning to stay away from classical sociology, as formulated by Weber and Durkheim (and Marx). In practical terms, this meant that these authors were neither taught nor very much read. The emphasis was instead on a very special type of U.S. sociology, mainly a neopositivistic and statistically oriented sociology. Especially the writings of George Lundberg were appreciated. His work was "regarded as the bible" by Swedish sociologists.[20]

The kind of sociology which was produced by the first generation of sociologists (and initially also by the second generation) was first of all methodologically correct. The main idea was to produce hard social science, and various forms of social psychology experiments seemed especially promising in this respect. The doctoral dissertations of such key members as Ulf Himmelstrand and Walter Korpi were, for example, narrowly focused on social attitudes. Much of this work was later to be forgotten, as Himmelstrand, Korpi, and others started to produce a different kind of sociology some years later. The same thing also happened with another type of sociology, which was quite popular in the carly ycars of Swedish sociology, namely community studies.

The second generation of sociologists seemed initially to approve of the same kind of sociology as Segerstedt and others. By the end of the 1960s, however, many signs of discontent were visible. Hans Zetterberg, for example, published an essay in 1966 in which he attacked Swedish sociology for being too oriented toward one specific kind of American sociology, "hard data sociology" as he called it.[21] By being so positivistic and trying to operationalize everything, Swedish sociology ended up proclaiming "rather self-evident truths" and producing reports filled with "mediocre (that is, boring) ideas." Nordic sociology in general, Zetterberg said, reminded him of those soulless international hotels that one finds near any large airport.

Zetterberg's critique had a huge impact since he was one of the stars of Swedish sociology; he had worked with Robert K. Merton and Paul Lazarsfeld, and he was the author of the famous *On Theory and Verification in Sociology* (1954).[22] The discordant note struck by Zetterberg was picked up by Johan Asplund, another talented member of the second generation. Asplund now started a debate in the journal of the Swedish Sociological Association, *Sociologisk forskning* (1964–), about the possibility of producing sociology without using "hard data" (the so-called soft data debate). Using Vilhelm Aubert's *The Hidden Society* as his example, Asplund noted that one could produce very good sociology without any tables or statistics. *"What we need,"* Asplund said, *"is a scientific ideology according to which soft data sociology is as legitimate as hard data sociology."*[23] Some time after Asplund had started up the soft data debate, Joachim Israel also attacked mainstream Swedish sociology. From an epistemological point of view, Israel charged, Swedish sociology was hopelessly naive. It tried to pass itself off as a kind of natural science, and it was always trying to operationalize everything. Swedish sociology, he said, was suffering from a "Lundbergian curse."[24]

These critiques of early Swedish sociology should not be allowed to obscure the fact that some very valuable sociology was produced during these years. Hans Zetterberg's own accomplishments have already been referred to. There is also the work of Gösta Carlsson, who was soon recognized as a major sociological talent. His work from 1958, *Social Mobility and Class Structure,* is generally regarded as a classic in the social stratification literature. Still, there is something to the accusations of Zetterberg and others that something had gone seriously wrong in Swedish sociology. Exactly what this was, however, was harder to say. According to Carl-Gunnar Janson, Swedish sociology lacked "independence."[25] Göran Therborn noted dryly that Swedish sociologists were not original and had no ideas.[26] Erik Allardt suggested that the cause of it all was that Swedish sociologists saw man as a "tabula rasa" and "society" as something which was totally predictable.[27] A particularly interesting and sophisticated diagnosis of Swedish sociology from this period can be found in one of Alvin Gouldner's writings.[28] Gouldner had visited Sweden in 1965 and was a friend of Gunnar Boalt, whose work in the sociology of science he found very valuable. As Gouldner saw it, Swedish culture was Apollonian rather than Dionysian in character: everything had to be in its right place and everything had to be "balanced and orderly." The Swedish academics Gouldner met were formalistic and unwilling to engage in speculations: *"[they] seemed to be engaged in an undeclared war against uncertainty . . . reluctant to play with ideas and reluctant to award those who could and did."*[29] Gouldner summed up his impression of Swedish sociology in the following way:

It seemed to me that Swedish sociology was of one piece with Swedish culture, most particularly with respect to the consensus that was given concerning the importance of using formalized, systematic, and external methodologies. It was my impression that there is no group of sociologists anywhere in the world today who, more than those in Sweden, have a clearer and more agreed-upon view of the standards and values to which good sociology should conform. Swedish sociologists seemed to me to be the people of, by, and for a formal methodology. This methodological drive of the Swedish sociologists appears to be typically Apollonian; to express a quest for something firm, hard-edged, well-boundaried, and clearly structured.[30]

THE TURNING POINT OF 1970

It is sometimes said that Swedish sociology can be divided into two fairly distinct periods: before and after 1970.[31] As we have already seen, there existed already by the late 1960s a considerable discontent with mainstream sociology among the members of the second generation. The student rebellion of a few years later fed straight into this process: it strengthened the desire to bring in something new and it provided an excellent opportunity to do so. Finally, the student rebellion also supplied a fresh legitimation for the new type of Swedish sociology which now emerged: *an activist sociology.*

The student rebellion immediately brought about changes in the small sociological community in Sweden. For one thing, the departments were suddenly swamped by students. During 1967–1970 the number of students at the department of sociology at the University of Stockholm increased threefold, to roughly 2,500. Education had suddenly to be mass-produced, and many new and inexperienced teachers were quickly hired. The students wanted to study Marxism; and especially Louis Althusser, Nicos Poulantzas, and Jürgen Habermas became popular in Sweden. At some departments the students tried to get Mao Tse-tung and similar authors on the reading lists. The student rebellion horrified and alienated some of the older teachers, who either left their jobs or withdrew in silence.

The rebellious students who now swarmed into sociology were primarily interested in a mixture of science and politics. They started up several social science magazines with a left-wing ideology, such as *Häften för Kritiska studier* and *Zenit,* through which a variety of new ideas and thinkers were introduced into Sweden. Especially at the University of Lund there emerged a group of sophisticated left-wing students of sociology. The key figure was Göran Therborn, who in 1966 helped to give a voice to the student movement through *En ny vänster* (A New Left). Therborn was first of all inspired by structuralist Marxism and wrote an important dissertation on the emergence of sociology along Althusserian lines, *Class, Science and Society* (1974). After the mid-1970s Therborn switched to a more open-ended Marxism, now inspired by Poulantzas rather than by Althusser. Like before, however, a steady stream of interesting works poured forth from his pen.

Many of the second-generation sociologists looked on the student rebellion with a certain benevolence. They began to read Marx themselves, and they liked what they read. Joachim Israel, for example, published a book on the concept of alienation in 1968, which was very well received internationally. Ulf Himmelstrand inspired many others to write Marxist sociology and produced himself several studies along these lines (see especially Himmelstrand et al., *Beyond Welfare Capitalism* from 1981). Walter Korpi joined Israel and Himmelstrand in switching over from the old, narrowly positivistic style of Swedish sociology to its new and more political form. In 1978 Korpi published *The Working Class in Welfare Capitalism,* which received the C. Wright Mills Award the next year when it was translated into English. On the basis of a survey study of the members of the Swedish metalworkers' union, Korpi in this work criticized people like Clark Kerr for their unproblematic picture of industrial society. In its stead Korpi proposed a theory that emphasized class conflicts. The same theoretical thrust (including the idea that power can be conceptualized in terms of resources) can be found in Korpi's second major work, *The Democratic Class Struggle* (1981; tr. 1983). In this study Korpi analyzes Swedish politics during the twentieth century while paying special attention to the interactions between unions and employers.

One of the most important accomplishments of people like Himmelstrand and Korpi was that they initiated the sociological study of the Swedish welfare state. In Swedish sociology before the 1960s, it should be noted, very little attention had been paid to broad social and political developments in Swedish society. While Korpi and Himmelstrand have mostly been interested in looking at the welfare state from a broad historical perspective, other sociologists have investigated it from different viewpoints. Especially the work of Sten Johansson and Robert Erikson should be mentioned here. In the late 1960s Johansson conducted a survey study of the "level of living" in Sweden as part of a parliamentary investigation (the so-called LNU-study).[32] This study, which essentially was a kind of "social report" based on various indicators, was immediately recognized by politicians and social scientists as supplying useful information. In 1974 and 1981 it was therefore decided to conduct similar LNU-studies. The Central Statistical Bureau of Sweden (SCB) has also carried out similar studies (the so-called ULF-investigations).[33]

Robert Erikson's doctoral dissertation, "Uppväxtförhållanden och social rörlighet" (Conditions of Upbringing and Social Mobility, 1971), was part of the original LNU-study and constitutes a valuable contribution to the Swedish literature on stratification. Like Johansson (later head of the Central Statistical Bureau of Sweden) and Korpi, Erikson has conducted most of his research on the "level of living" at the Institute for Social Research (Institutet för social forskning = SOFI), which was founded in 1972. The main purpose of this institute, which is an independent administrative unit at the University of Stockholm, is to provide research of relevance for social policy and on the Swedish labor market. The Center for Working Life (Arbetslivscentrum = ALC) is also an independent research institute, where some sociologists work. ALC was founded in 1977 and its main purpose is to study various aspects of work. The creation of SOFI and ALC in the 1970s clearly signals that the Swedish state finds certain types of social research quite useful, especially those relating to work and "the social question."

SWEDISH SOCIOLOGY TODAY

From an organizational viewpoint, contemporary Swedish sociology displays the following characteristics.[34] The core consists of the five departments of sociology at the universities in Stockholm, Gothenburg, Uppsala, Lund, and Umeå. A little more than a hundred sociologists work here. Apart from these five major universities, Sweden also has a number of high schools situated in small towns like Örebro, Karlstad, and Sundsvall. Sociology is taught at many of these as well as at the interdisciplinary University of Linköping. All these institutions typically have a couple of sociologists on their staff. There also exist a few independent research institutes, both academic ones (like SOFI) and commercial ones (like the Swedish Institute for Survey Research, SIFO, which was originally created by Hans Zetterberg). Many sociologists work here as well as at the Central Statistical Bureau of Sweden. All in all, there probably exist something like 200 full-time, professional sociologists in Sweden. The Swedish Sociological Association, it should be added, had about 500 members in 1989. This means that the number of people who identify themselves as sociologists probably is considerably larger than the number of full-time professional sociologists.

In a survey of this type most interest is naturally directed at the sociologists who work at the five major universities, since they produce the lion's share of the academic research. It should first of all be emphasized that the five major departments of sociology are quite different from one another, in intellectual atmosphere as well as in research interests. They are also somewhat isolated from one another; and a Swedish sociologist typically works at the same place as he or she graduated.

From Table 9.2 we can see that fourteen people had the title "professor" in the late 1980s at these five departments.[35] Five of these professorships are chairs in sociology in general ("ämnesprofessurer"), while the others are typically chairs in a certain specialty, say alcohol research or social policy. The highest status is attached to the five general chairs. Still, the fact that there also exist several other chairs means that the structure of Swedish sociology is not as hierarchical today as it was in the 1950s and

Table 9.2
**Sociologists at the Five Major Universities in Sweden as of February
1987**

	Gothenburg	Lund	Stockholm		Umeå	Uppsala	Total
"professorer"	3(1)	4(0)	4(0)		1(0)	2(0)	14(1)
"docenter"	8(3)	9(3)	3(1)		2(0)	8(0)	30(7)
"forskarasst."	1(0)	4(1)	1(0)		4(1)	2(1)	12(3)
"lektorer"	9(1)	12(5)	13(3)		10(2)	6(2)	13(50)
Total	21(5)	29(9)	21(4)		17(3)	18(3)	106(24)

Note: The figure within brackets denotes the number of female sociologists. 3(1), for example, means that one out of three professors is female. The Swedish term "professor" is roughly equivalent to the U.S. full professor; "docent," to associate professor; and "forskarassistent" and "lektor," to assistant professor.
Source: Richard Swedberg, "Den nya kvinnoforskningen och sociologin i Sverige, 1975–1986," in Erik Allardt, Sverre Lysgaard, and Aage Sorensen, *Sociologin i Sverige* (Stockholm: HSFR, 1988). 236.

1960s. There is more room to breathe, in other words, for those on steps 2, 3, and 4 of the academic ladder: "docenter" (or associate professors), "forskarassistenter" (or assistant professors), and "lektorer" (also the assistant professors). It should also be emphasized that since the late 1950s there has existed a huge difference between researchers and teachers at the Swedish universities. Those who are employed as "lektorer" only have time to teach, while those in the other three categories both teach and do research. This system is generally regarded as having had very negative consequences for Swedish academic life and is in principle on its way out. It will in all likelihood, however, last a few decades more.

As is clear from Table 9.2, there are few female sociologists in the Swedish university system. As of 1987 there was only one female professor, Rita Liljeström, and her appointment was financed via a public research institute (HSFR) as opposed to an ordinary university department. In 1989 the chair in general sociology at Uppsala University was offered to Birgitta Nedelman, a German sociologist with some links to Sweden. She, however, soon resigned and was in 1993 replaced by Göran Ahrne. During the intervening period Boel Berner had been offered and accepted a professorship at the University of Linköping, and Karin Widerberg had been appointed to a prestigious chair in Norway. In general, the more one descends the academic hierarchy, the more women there are. Roughly one quarter of the people who earned a doctorate during 1969–1986 were women. On the undergraduate level, however, the majority of the students are female.

As of 1986 there were about 400 Ph.D. students in sociology at the five major universities. Nearly half of these were at the University of Lund, where the department of sociology is very pluralistic and alive. At the University of Umeå, which is situated farthest to the north of the Swedish universities, there were only about 20 Ph.D. students. Somewhere between 10 and 20 doctoral dissertations in sociology are produced every year in Sweden. Since 1969 a student may go straight from a M.A. to a Ph.D. A second doctoral dissertation (the old "licentiatavhandlingen") is, in other words, no longer needed to earn a doctorate. Today's Swedish doctoral dissertation is roughly similar to an American one in depth and length. The old doctoral dissertations were considerably longer and were essentially produced by people who aspired to the position of "professor." The average age of a Swedish doctor in sociology is 35.5 years today. Efforts to push down the age have failed.

Before being accepted as a doctoral candidate, the student has usually studied some sociology. Due to the way that the Swedish university system works, this education is, however, likely to have been of a rather low quality. One important reason for this is that during the 1970s and 1980s most undergraduate education at Swedish universities was offered in the form of so-called lines, which in all brevity meant that traditional academic disciplines were cut up and taught in miniscule bits and pieces. Instead of learning how to handle a discipline in an independent manner, students were in other words spoon-fed knowledge in a few areas. Though the "line" system was formally abolished in the early 1990s, it clearly lives on in the habits of many teachers as well as in newly designed courses.

If we now move from the organization of the sociological profession in Sweden to its intellectual production, the following picture emerges. Swedish sociologists are in general interested in a huge variety of topics. According to a survey of Swedish sociologists, which was conducted in 1986, the three major areas of interest were philosophy of science, political sociology, and sociology of work (Table 9.3).[36] Men and women differed in their interests, with women preferring such topics as medical sociology and minorities while the men chose sociology of work and sociological theory. It also turned out that the five major university towns differed quite a bit from one another. In Gothenburg, for example, sociology of work topped the interest list; in Uppsala, it was philosophy of science; and in Stockholm, political sociology (read: welfare state research). The difference between the five university towns came out even stronger in questions about methodology. In Stockholm the sociologists preferred various types of survey research and regression analysis. In Lund, on the other hand, the sociologists were interested in nonstructured interviews and did not find survey research and regression analysis particularly useful.

In terms of generations, it is clear that the second generation of sociologists still dominates much of Swedish sociology. When sociologists in

Table 9.3
Major Areas of Interest of Swedish Sociologists as of 1986

Areas of Interest	Percentage
philosophy of science	26%
political sociology	25%
sociology of work	19%
social psychology	19%
sociology of culture	19%
medical sociology	18%
sociological theory	17%
sociology of organizations	16%
stratification	16%
deviance	14%

Source: Anders S. Olsson, "Svenska sociologer: en enkätundersökning," in Allardt, Lysgaard, and Sorensen, *Sociologin i Sverige,* 218.

1986 were asked which of their colleagues' work they found to be the most interesting, more than half of the authors that were mentioned came from the second generation (see Table 9.4). The most interesting Swedish sociologist turned out to be Johan Asplund, a sociologist at the University of Lund who is little known outside of Sweden. Asplund is a subtle thinker who is interested in social psychology and the sociology of culture. That Asplund is mainly known and appreciated within the small Swedish sociological community became clear when a search was made in the Social Science Citation Index on Swedish sociologists (see Table 9.5). For the period 1972–1986 Asplund (who writes only in Swedish) was number 21 with only thirty-two citations. Five names, however, appear on both lists. The works of these people were in other words considered interesting and they were also often quoted. These five were Walter Korpi, Göran Therborn, Hans Zetterberg, Joachim Israel, and Edmund Dahlström.

If one takes a closer look at the research that is presently going on in Sweden, it is, for example, clear that the study of the welfare state is very much alive. This is to a large extent due to the activities at the Institute for Social Research, where a series of doctoral dissertations have recently been produced under the guidance of Walter Korpi and Robert Erikson. One of these dissertations at SOFI—*Structures of Inequality* (1988) by Peter Hedström—was also presented at Harvard University and earned

Table 9.4
Most Interesting Swedish Sociologists (1986)

Author	Share
Johan Asplund	32%
Göran Therborn	21%
Joachim Israel	16%
Walter Korpi	10%
Göran Ahrne	9%
Hans Zetterberg	9%
Kaj Håkansson	8%
Edmund Dahlström	8%
Rita Liljeström	7%
Rune Åberg	5%

Note: Sociologists were asked to name the Swedish sociologist whose work they found the most interesting.
Source: Anders S. Olsson, "Svenska sociologer: en enkätundersökning," in Allardt, Lysgaard, and Sorensen, *Sociologin i Sverige,* 226.

the author a professorship at the University of Stockholm at the record young age of thirty-four. A mathematical model which relates organizational levels to earnings is here presented and tested (the reader may also consult a briefer version of Hedström's argument in the 1992 issue of the *American Journal of Sociology*). Robert Erikson has continued his work in stratification research and is the editor (together with Rune Åberg) of an important work on Swedish welfare, which is based on three level-of-living studies, *Welfare in Transition* (1984, tr. 1987). He has also recently published an important work in stratification studies together with John Goldthorpe, *The Constant Flux* (1992).

Walter Korpi has been involved for the past few years in a huge research project on Swedish social policy in a comparative perspective. The basic idea is that by studying the development of social policy during the period 1930–1980 in eighteen OECD countries, it should be possible to clarify what accounts for the differences between these countries in their social security systems.[37] Sven E. Olsson's careful and detailed studies of the Swedish welfare state should also be mentioned in this context as well as a huge project on Swedish enterprises by Carl le Grand, Ryszard Szulkin, and Michael Tåhlin.[38]

Some interesting studies have also been produced at the Center for

Table 9.5
The Ten Most Cited Swedish Sociologists, 1972–1986

Name	Number of quotes
Joachim Israel	406
Göran Therborn	329
Hans Zetterberg	263
Walter Korpi	261
Gösta Carlsson	192
Bertil Gardell	170
Bengt Abrahamsson	162
Robert Erikson	133
Edmund Dahlström	120
Jan Trost	107

Note: A search was made in Social Science Citation Index using a list of 74 Swedish sociologists who had held either the title "docent" or "professor."
Source: Olle Persson, "Svenska sociologers visibilitet på den internationella tidskriftsmarknaden," in Allardt, Lysgaard, and Sorensen, *Sociologin i Sverige,* 258.

Working Life. The Center has for the most part tried to sponsor action research and has unique contacts with unions and enterprises. It published a journal called *Economic and Industrial Democracy* and has many skillful researchers—such as Bengt Abrahamsson, Åke Sandberg, and Casten von Otter—on its staff. The Center has, however, also been much criticized and has recently had to reduce its activities to a minimum.

A special discussion should clearly be devoted to the work of Göran Therborn, who is the most prominent member of the new generation in Swedish sociology. As mentioned earlier, Therborn changed direction in his research around the mid-seventies when he embraced a more open-ended form of Marxism. Results of this new approach can be found in such works as *What Does the Ruling Class Do When It Rules?* (1978) and *The Ideology of Power and the Power of Ideology* (1980). Of particularly great interest is also Therborn's project on Sweden during Social Democracy 1932–1976, which has resulted in several interesting books and articles.[39] A particularly fine example of Therborn's political and historical sociology can be found in *Borgarklass och byråkrati i Sverige* (Bourgeoisie and Bureaucracy in Sweden, 1989). Therborn's most recent project involves the emergence of modernity in Europe.

It is clear that the third generation of Swedish sociologists is very interested in topics such as the welfare state and the sociology of work. This, however, does not exhaust its repertoire. During the last ten to fifteen years, sociology of science, sociology of culture, and sociological theory have also become popular among younger Swedish sociologists. Networks, organization theory, and gender studies are on the current agenda as well. How successful this third generation will ultimately be is, however, very much an open question. It is clear that there exists a strong tradition in Swedish sociology when it comes to methodology, and one can also find some interesting theoretical insights in the Swedish sociological community about the workings of the welfare state. But if this is enough to handle the world of tomorrow—and Sweden of the year 2000 promises to be rather different from the Sweden of today—is a different question.

NOTES

1. Ulf Himmelstrand and Göran Svensson, eds., *Sverige—vardag och struktur* (Stockholm: Nordstedts, 1988), 23–25.

2. There exists a huge literature on Sweden. Good introductory readings are Eli Heckscher, "The Place of Sweden in Modern Economic History," *The Economic History Review* 4, 1 (October 1932), 1–22; Gunnar Myrdal, "Ett bra land som borde kunnat vara mycket bättre," in Jan Herin and Lars Werin, eds., *Ekonomisk debatt och ekonomisk politik* (Stockholm: P.A. Nordstedt & Söners förlag, 1977), 235–248; and Göran Therborn, "Hur det hela började. När och varför det moderna Sverige blev vad det blev," in U. Himmelstrand and G. Svensson, eds., *Sverige—vardag och struktur* (Stockholm: Nordstedts, 1988), 23–53.

3. Joseph A. Schumpeter, *Capitalism, Socialism and Democracy* (New York: Harper & Row, 1950), 325.

4. Torgny Segerstedt, "Svensk sociologi förr och nu," in Katrin Fridjonsdottir, ed., *Om svensk sociologi* (Borås: Carlssons, 1987), 11.

5. See especially Gustav Sundbärg, *Betänkande i utvand-ringsfrågan* (Stockholm: P.A. Nordstedt & söner, 1913).

6. See on this point, as so often when one discusses the early history of Swedish sociology, Anders Gullberg, *Till den svenska sociologins historia* (Stockholm: Häften för Kritiska studier, 1972).

7. This chapter still remains to be written since the Myrdals have never been very popular among Swedish intellectuals. In the meantime, see especially Ron Eyerman, "Rationalizing Intellectuals: Sweden in the 1930s and 1940s," *Theory and Society* 14, 6 (1985), 777–808; and David W. Southern, *Gunnar Myrdal and Black-White Relations—The Use and Abuse of An American Dilemma, 1944–1969* (Baton Rouge: Louisiana State University, 1989).

8. See in this context also the classical works by Herbert Tingsten and Eli Heckscher, especially Tingsten's *Political Behavior* (1937) and *The Swedish Social Democrats* (1941, tr. 1973) and Heckscher's *Mercantilism* (1931, tr. 1935) and *An Economic History of Sweden* (1941, tr. 1963).

9. Lynd's opinion as cited in Walter A. Jackson, "The Making of a Social

Science Classic: Gunnar Myrdal's *An American Dilemma*," *Perspectives in American History* 2 (1985), 258. See also Jackson's *Gunnar Myrdal and America's Conscience: Social Engineering and Racial Liberalism 1938–1987* (Chapel Hill: University of North Carolina Press, 1990).

10. Jackson, *Gunnar Myrdal. . . ,* 259–260.

11. Robert K. Merton, "Discrimination and the American Creed," in R. M. MacIver, ed., *Discrimination and National Welfare* (New York: Harper & Brothers, 1949), 99–126.

12. See, for example, Alva Myrdal, "Den nyare tidens revolution i kvinnans ställning," in A. Myrdal et al., *Kvinnan, familjen och samhället* (Stockholm; Kooperativa Förbundet, 1938), 5–41.

13. See on this point especially Ingemar Nilsson, "Einar Tegen och tidig svensk sociologi," in T. Nybom, ed., *Universitetet och samhälle* (Stockholm: Tiden, 1989), 58–72.

14. *Betänkande angående socialvetenskapernas ställning vid universitet och högskolor m.m.* (SOU 1946:74).

15. Ibid., p. 20.

16. Ibid., p. 81. *Emphasis added.*

17. Ibid., p. 80.

18. Ibid.

19. Information from Segerstedt as supplied to the author on January 19, 1990. Segerstedt also said in this conversation that he later had regretted that he took such an antitheoretical stance in the 1946 report. The reason, he said, was that it was absolutely necessary to highlight the distinct nature of sociology in order to get it accepted as a university topic of its own. The opposition to sociology was very strong at this time in Swedish universities, Segerstedt emphasized.

20. Bertil Pfannenstil, "Från praktisk filosofi till sociologi," in Fridjonsdottir, ed., *Om svensk sociologi,* 28. See also the contributions to this volume by Joachim Israel and Georg Karlsson.

21. Hans Zetterberg, "Traditioner och möjligheter i nordisk sociologi," *Sociologisk forskning* 3, 1 (1966), 1–21.

22. Some time later Zetterberg would be instrumental in bringing out the standard edition of Weber's *Economy and Society* in English. This happened in 1968 and the name of the press was Bedminster Press Incorporated, which Zetterberg had started himself. In 1986 Zetterberg also edited a fine small book of Weber texts in Swedish, *Kapitalismens uppkomst* (The Emergence of Capitalism) (Stockholm: Ratio, 1986).

23. Johan Asplund, "Aubert och mjukdatasociologin," *Sociologisk forskning* 2 (1966), 104. *Emphasis added.*

24. Joachim Israel, "Spridda tankar om sociologisk teori," *Sociologisk forskning* 5, 1 (1968), 85–92. See also Israel's contribution to Fridjonsdottir, ed., *Om svensk sociologi.*

25. Carl-Gunnar Janson, "The Case for a Scandinavian Sociology," *Sociology and Social Research* 58, 3 (1974), 278–285. Mainly interested in research methods and social ecology, Janson's main contribution consists of his project "Metropolitan." This project was started in 1964 and consists of a longitudinal study of 15,000 children born in 1953 in the Stockholm area. The data produced in this project is internationally unique and has been used in a number of studies. For an intro-

duction, see Carl-Gunnar Janson, *Project Metropolitan: A Presentation and Progress Report* (Stockholm: University of Stockholm, 1984).

26. Göran Therborn, "De sociologiska verksamheterna," *Sociologisk forskning* 10 (1973), 21.

27. Erik Allardt, "Om svensk sociologi," *Sociologisk forskning* 10 (1973), 5–20.

28. Alvin W. Gouldner, "Personal Reality, Social Theory and the Tragic Dimension in Science (1969)," in *For Sociology* (London: Allan Lane, 1973), 300–322.

29. Ibid., 313. *Emphasis added.*

30. Ibid., 310–311.

31. See, e.g., Erik Allardt, Sverre Lysgaard, and Aage Sorensen, *Sociologin i Sverige* (Stockholm: HSFR, 1988), 37.

32. Sten Johansson, "The Level of Living Survey: A Presentation," *Acta Sociologica* 3 (1974), 211–219. By "level of living" Johansson essentially means the amount of resources that a person commands in those areas which can be affected by political decisions. These resources include "economic resources," "political resources," "housing," and so on.

33. See Sten Johansson, "Om ULF-projektet—en utvärdering av SCBs undersökningar av levnadsförhållanden i samhället," *Statistisk tidskrift* 1 (1979), 5–16.

34. Unless otherwise stated, the following is based on Allardt, Lysgaard, and Sorensen, *Sociologin i Sverige.*

35. There also exist a number of professorships in special types of sociology outside the departments of sociology at these five universities. These include professorships in the sociology of law, the sociology of religion, and the sociology of literature. There exist in addition two professorships in sociology at SOFI (presently held by Walter Korpi and Robert Erikson) and two at ALC (presently held by Bengt Abrahamsson and Casten von Otter). All in all, there are about twenty professors of sociology in Sweden.

36. It should be noted that only 53 percent of all sociologists returned the questionnaires in this survey.

37. See, e.g., Walter Korpi, "Power, Politics and State Autonomy in the Development of Social Citizenship," *American Sociological Review* 54 (1989), 309–327; and Gösta Esping-Andersen and Walter Korpi, "From Poor Relief to Institutional Welfare States: The Development of the Scandinavian Social Policy," in R. Erikson et al., *The Scandinavian Model* (New York: M. E. Sharpe, 1987), 39–74.

38. See especially Sven E. Olsson, *Social Policy and Welfare State in Sweden* (Lund: Arkiv Förlag 1990) and Carl le Grand, Ryszard Szulkin, and Michael Tåhlin, *Sveriges Arbetsplatser* (The Work Places of Sweden; forthcoming on SNS Förlag).

39. The books are Anders Kjellberg, *Facklig organisation i tolv länder* (The Organization of Workers in Unions in Twelve Countries, 1983); Staffan Marklund, *Klass, stat och socialpolitik* (Class, State and Social Policy, 1982), and Bo Rothstein, *Den socialdemokratiska staten* (The Social Democratic State, 1986). Therborn's own articles include Therborn et al., "Sverige före och efter socialdemokratin," *Arkiv för studier i arbetarrörelsens historia* 15–16 (1979), 3–36; "Den svenska socialdemokratin träder fram," *Arkiv för studier i arbetarrörelsens historia* 27–28 (1987), 1–71; and "Arbetarrörelsen och välfärdsstaten," *Arkiv för studier i arbetarrörelsens historia* 41–42 (1989), 3–51.

10

Contemporary Sociology in Switzerland

Jacques Coenen-Huther

In Switzerland, sociology is a rather young discipline. This is to be understood as younger than in most other West European countries, and
certainly in the two major neighboring countries, France and Germany.
As Professor Mohan put it in a previous edition of this book, "until the
mid-1950s Swiss sociology was virtually nonexistent." Although a professional association had been formed and sociology was being taught at the
university, Swiss sociology had "not yet acquired a national identity of its
own."[1] Of course, there have been sociologists in Switzerland since the
nineteenth century. In Geneva, for example, sociology was introduced at
the university as early as 1886 and the chair was attributed to Louis
Wuarin. In Lausanne, Pareto succeeded as an economist to Walras, the
founder of the "Lausanne School," in 1893. He resigned his function in
1907 to devote himself to sociology.

But there is no continuity between the work of these forefathers and
the emergence of modern sociology in the country. In Switzerland, there
is no indigenous source of inspiration like the Durkheimian school in
France or the Weberian approach in Germany. It means that when modern sociology began to develop, it did not build on a local heritage. Aside
from the strong position of Jean Piaget in Geneva and Lausanne, Swiss
sociologists were very receptive to a variety of foreign influences but could
not integrate them in any regional or national intellectual tradition. Some
authors went so far as to suggest that sociology has long been in a pre-
carious position in Switzerland because it is not a genuine Swiss product.
Referring to the German-speaking part of the country, Peter Gross recently wrote that sociology was introduced there by foreigners, practiced
by foreigners, and promoted mostly by foreigners.[2] Even now, sociology

is not as firmly established in Switzerland as in other West European countries. But this is not only the result of a lack of local traditions; there is still a certain suspicion of sociological viewpoints among policy-makers, in the media, and in the public opinion at large. The process of institutionalization of Swiss sociology has not been completed so far, and more than in other countries, the current position of sociology is the product of the efforts of a limited number of individuals who actively try to create favorable conditions for the discipline as a whole. This means that Swiss sociology can be seen as an interesting case for a sociology of sociology.

Compared with other European countries, Switzerland is a small country with a small population: 6.5 million inhabitants, with an active population of about 3 million people. The small scale of Swiss society becomes obvious if one looks at the major towns in the country. The only big agglomeration to be found is Zurich, but it has no more than 840,000 inhabitants. Following are Geneva, with 380,000 inhabitants, Basel, with 360,000 inhabitants, and Bern, the federal capital, with 300,000 inhabitants. The small size of the country and its towns certainly accounts for the provincial character of Swiss society, which is as such an impediment to the development of sociological thought and its cosmopolitan orientation. The pluricultural character of Swiss society is also worthy of mention since it contributes to its segmentation. About 65 percent of the population speak German, or German dialects. About 18 percent of the population, in the western part of the country, speak French. About 10 percent, in the south and southeast, speak Italian or an Italian dialect. At the national level, there are, however, only two languages which play a significant role: German and French. Since there is no university or other institution of higher education in the Italian-speaking part of the country. Switzerland as a whole can be seen as a German-speaking country with Latin minorities. As far as sociology is concerned, however, it is only in a very limited way that Swiss sociology performs the function of a cultural bridge between the French and the German sociological traditions. With the exception of some individuals, French- and German-speaking sociologists in Switzerland form two distinct scientific communities, with little interest in each other.[3] There is more to it than just a matter of language and communication. The two major language groups are cultural communities with different sensitivities and different attitudes toward a series of societal problems, as was illustrated dramatically on December 6, 1992, by the results of the vote on the European Economic Area.[4]

In 1971, at the first national congress of the modern-day Swiss Sociological Association, the late Peter Heintz, from Zurich, said, "*Man kann die Schweiz als eine soziologische* black box *bezeichnen*" (Switzerland can be described as a sociological black box).[5] By this, Professor Heintz meant that very little sociological knowledge on Switzerland was available, and that sociologists really had to start from scratch. After about twenty years, how did the situation of Swiss sociology evolve? In 1980, the number of Swiss sociologists[6] was evaluated at about 500. In 1983, a mailed questionnaire was sent to all people supposed to have a degree in sociology. At that time, 585 target-persons were located.[7] Such figures, however, were misleading and led to overestimation. Not all persons holding a degree in sociology were professionally active as sociologists. The 1983 survey delivered finally 328 usable questionnaires. Besides, the number of members of the Swiss Sociological Association has long fluctuated between 300 and 350. As a result of recent recruitment efforts among graduate and undergraduate students, it has recently increased to 450. At the end of 1992, the number of Swiss sociologists, active as sociologists, could be roughly estimated at something between 350 and 400 persons. Various European colleagues have tried to present some international comparisons, using the concept of "sociologists' density," that is, the number of sociologists related to the active population. Some years ago, the percentages for the Netherlands, the Federal Republic of Germany, and Switzerland were respectively

0.09 (4,500 sociologists, in an active population of about 5 million);

0.05 (7,500 sociologists, in an active population of about 15 million);

0.0017 (500 sociologists, in an active population of about 3 million).[8]

Where do Swiss sociologists get their training? There are in Switzerland seven universities. In three of them, courses are taught in French (Geneva, Lausanne, and Neuchâtel). In three others, the language is German (Zürich, Bern, and Basel). The seventh one (Fribourg) is a bilingual institution. In all these universities, sociology can be studied, and a degree can be obtained either in sociology or in social sciences, with possibly sociology as a major course. There are also courses in sociology in two federal institutions, Lausanne and Zurich Polytechnics, as well as in St. Gallen School of Economics. The number of students in sociology as well as the total of graduates in sociology show that sociology is more widely accepted as a legitimate discipline in the French-speaking part of Switzerland, the *Suisse romande,* than in the German-language areas. Only 18 percent of the population speak French, but more than 40 percent of graduates in sociology are French speakers. There is also a regular migration from German-speaking sociologists to the French-speaking areas where they find better job opportunities.[9] This certainly has to do with the well-spread conception of sociology as a "critical science," which is better tolerated by the French-speaking Swiss, traditionally exposed to the cultural model of the Paris intellectual, than by the rest of the country.

It was said that sociology is in Switzerland a relatively young discipline, and the indications given by Roger Girod in the 1975 edition of this book testify to that.[10] Let us mention here some other general features:

- In their present form, the departments, institutes, and services where sociology is being practiced are about thirty years old. Most of them were founded or transformed at the beginning of the 1960s.

- In its modern form—at the same time, scientific society and professional association—the bilingual Swiss Sociological Association is twenty years old. It was founded in 1970.

- The trilingual Swiss Journal of Sociology (*Schweizeriche Zeitschrift für Soziologie/Revue suisse de sociologie*) publishes articles and book reviews in German, French, and English. It was founded in 1975 and published its eighteenth volume in 1992. After the first five years of operation, it became obvious that the Editorial Committee found it difficult to sustain regular publication while maintaining an acceptable scientific level. This is not to say that Swiss sociologists do not write good articles, but the pool to be tapped is small and the best articles increasingly found their way to foreign journals in French, German, Italian, or English. Since the beginning of 1992, a new editorial team has been at the helm, implementing a new editorial policy. It is currently trying to give the Swiss Journal of Sociology a more markedly international character and to have it play a role as a bridge between cultures, turning the handicap of pluriculturalism into an asset. It is too early to judge whether this ambitious new policy will be successful or not.

- As for books, efforts to create a sociological series in which Swiss sociologists can publish their works began in 1976 but have foundered several times. Although about twenty books have been published in agreement between the Swiss Sociological Association and various publishing houses, a new start had recently to be made. In 1988, the Swiss Sociological Association created its own publishing house (Seismo Press, Zurich), which works at relatively low costs and manages to publish several books each year. Seismo Press, however, is widely perceived as a German-language publishing house, and finds it difficult to publish and to market books in French. But here again, the best books are published abroad, in France, in Germany, in Italy, and even in the United States.

In 1972, in its "state of the arts" with relation to scientific research, the Swiss Science Council stated that sociology was one of the disciplines of which the development was slow. The Council then advised all relevant agencies to help support the development of sociology.[11] Two years later, the Swiss Sociological Association published its own diagnosis. It came to the conclusion that sociology was considerably less institutionalized in Switzerland than in most other West European countries, that research providing sociological knowledge about Swiss society was almost nonexistent, and that in places other than Geneva and Zurich, sociological institutions did not have sufficient resources to bring about a take-off of sociological research.[12] Of course, this assessment was presented in the hope of mobilizing more resources on behalf of sociology. For this reason, it might have been excessively gloomy. On the whole, however, it seems to reflect quite acurately the situation of Swiss sociology in that time.

Eighteen years later, in March 1990, the Swiss Science Council undertook a new evaluation of the problems and perspectives in the field of social sciences. As a result of this initiative, four coordinated studies were carried out on the situation in four disciplines, sociology being one of them.[13] The report on sociology[14] presents data collected through a questionnaire sent to all professors and to all directors of research units. Although the author of the report is a bright young sociologist himself,[15] he obviously showed a lack of caution in engaging in a study clumsily designed by federal bureaucrats and in paying too little attention to the policy implications of his conclusions. The study was subjected to arbitrary limitations in scope and time, due partly to financial constraints but most of all to the technocratic inspiration of the project. As a consequence, prestigious publications were neglected just because they did not come out during the two-year period taken into account, the presence of Swiss sociologists on the international scene was systematically underestimated, wrong diagnoses were applied to various research institutions on the basis of indicators of dubious value (e.g., interactions among researchers belonging to the same institution), the seminal character of the research work in some fields (e.g., family sociology) was totally overlooked, and the importance of some research units was highly overrated. For all these reasons, the report raised sharp criticisms when it was circulated among sociological circles. After a period of intense discussions behind the scene, the chairman of the Swiss Sociological Association, Professor René Levy, found it necessary to express various reservations in a foreword and to give a more balanced assessment.

Indeed, one can really wonder whether this report on sociology does justice to the achievements of Swiss sociologists during the last twenty years, and whether once again a too negative picture has not been given. As things now stand, however, a diagnosis of relative backwardness of social sciences in general, and sociology in particular, has been spread through the media,[16] with all the risks entailed. Will it be cleverly used by representatives of the various disciplines involved in order to get additional support, or will it be used against them in order to reduce available resources? Only the future will tell.

In the meantime, however, it has to be said that Switzerland is no longer the "sociological black box" it used to be, even if some gaps are still to be filled. Sociological research is being carried on in all the places where sociology is taught. In 1992, the long awaited Center for Information and Documentation in the Social Sciences (SIDOS) was created in Neuchâtel, and it is hoped that it will become a national database favoring the cumulativity of research efforts. Geneva and Zurich are clearly the two poles of development, with Geneva being undoubtedly the busiest center of sociological research in the whole of Switzerland. Lausanne and Bern can be seen as secondary centers. Other places of significance are Basel, Fribourg, Neuchâtel, and St. Gallen. Let us take a systematic overview of sociological activities in all these cities. The extreme decentralization of the country, and the fact that the cantons, much more than the Swiss confederation, are the centers of public life, fully justify a presentation by towns rather than by research topics.[17]

GENEVA

The most active center of sociological research in Geneva is the Department of Sociology of the university. Although the influence of Jean Piaget, combined with other influences, is still pervasive as a general epistemological perspective, there is a wide variety of theoretical and methodological orientations in the department, and six professors promote research in various fields. Roger Girod, the "grand old man" of Geneva sociology, now an honorary professor, has retired from teaching duties but is still active in research. He has specialized in research on social mobility and social inequalities, in relation to education.[18] He has studied the effects of education on professional mobility and found that they were less important than originally thought. Jean Kellerhals, after some research on youth, and on voluntary associations,[19] specialized in family sociology and sociology of small groups, with strong emphasis on typology and on the normative aspects of social interaction.[20] He has trained many young researchers, and the research group he is currently leading has all the makings of a sociological school. At the moment, he has certainly established himself as one of the leading sociologists of family in Europe. Christian Lalive d'Epinay has also become known internationally as a very dynamic president of the International Association of French-speaking Sociologists (AISLF).[21] He began as a sociologist of religion;[22] later on, he also did research on leisure activities,[23] on the changing attitudes of the Swiss population toward work,[24] and nowadays on the elderly.[25] The Interdisciplinary Center for Gerontological Studies created at his initiative and under his leadership has accumulated considerable resources and research opportunities. Patrick de Laubier is a historian of social thought and a specialist on social policy.[26] He is very much interested in current developments in Eastern Europe and the former Soviet Union, as well as in their historical background.[27] Uli Windisch has applied the methods of anthropological research to rural Switzerland[28] and has made use of content analysis to study hostile reactions to foreign residents in the country.[29] He now specializes in sociolinguistics,[30] in the iconography of Swiss myths,[31] and in the language relationships in bilingual areas of Switzerland.[32] Jean Ziegler first specialized in African culture, dealing for example with time perception and sense of history among Black Africans.[33] He later moved away from scholarly work *stricto sensu* and took a militant stance as a radical intellectual, highly critical of the Swiss establishment and committed to solidarity with Third World revolutionaries.[34]

Another important center of sociological research in Geneva is the Service for Sociological Research (SRS) of the Cantonal Education Office, under the direction of Walo Hutmacher. Research in this service focuses on the school system, education, and socialization processes. Most of the projects aim at producing policy-relevant data and research results. On the theoretical level, the influence of Pierre Bourdieu can be perceived.[35]

On a smaller scale, the Sociological Research Unit of the Academic Institutions of Psychiatry, under the direction of Werner Fischer, carries on research in the field of health and mental health. As in the SRS, most of the scientific production of this unit belongs to what economists would call "cameral science." Here also, Bourdieu's influence is quite obvious.

ZURICH

In Zurich, the center of sociological activities is the Institute of Sociology of the university. With only three of its members—Volker Bornschier, Hans Geser, and Hans-Joachim Hoffmann-Nowotny—holding a full professorship, it is smaller than the Department of Sociology of the University of Geneva, but quite active as well. Volker Bornschier, president of the World Society Foundation established by Peter Heintz to promote research on the world-system, has a keen interest in long-range social and economic processes seen in an international comparative perspective.[36] Hans-Joachim Hoffmann-Nowotny has played for two decades a leading role in Zurich in three areas of research: the migrant minorities,[37] the social aspects of demographic processes,[38] and the development of a system of social indicators for Switzerland.[39] Hans Geser, who currently leads research projects on political life at the local level and on trade unions, has also established a reputation of solid scholarship abroad.[40] Among other members of the Zurich Institute, François Höpflinger, *Privat-Dozent,* is quite active in the fields of family sociology[41] and social demography.[42] Still in Zurich, a new professorship in sociology has recently been created at the Polytechnic—the Swiss Federal Institute of Technology (ETH). The first woman professor and the first professor of sociology at the ETH is Marlis Buchmann, former *Privat-Dozent* at the Institute of Sociology of the University of Zurich, the "coming woman" of Swiss sociology whose study on youth has been published in the United States.[43]

In Zurich, more than in Geneva, a unifying theoretical and methodological orientation can be perceived, and that is Peter Heintz's general theory of social dynamics.[44] Although research is being carried on on a wide range of topics, some general characteristics of the research programs of the Institute of Sociology can be mentioned: priority to policy-relevant topics, special attention to the role of macrostructures, preference for research themes which easily lend themselves to the construction of formal models, and emphasis on the international dimension of the phenomena being studied.

In 1974, only three years after the right to vote in federal matters was granted to Swiss women, Thomas Held and René Levy, two young researchers trained by Peter Heintz, made headlines by publishing a study on the position of the woman in Swiss society. This study pointed out some discriminations, and it was the first time that sociological research sparked off a public debate in the country.[45] In that time, the publication of the Held and Levy study came as a scandal. Now, almost twenty years later, various Swiss universities have reached the stage of affirmative action in respect of the status of the woman, women's studies are being taught in various institutions, and a national research program was initiated on the situation of Swiss women.

LAUSANNE

In Lausanne, the two major centers of sociological research are the Faculty of Social and Political Sciences of Lausanne University, and the Department of Architecture of Lausanne Polytechnic.

The most prominent sociologist at the university is Giovanni Busino. In his various publications, he displays a great interest in the historical perspective in the study of social and economic processes. Strongly influenced by the epistemological views of Jean Piaget, he has tried to combine Piaget's theoretical perspective with the teaching of the old "Lausanne School" of Walras and Pareto. In so doing, Busino is one of the few individuals who are trying to establish a connection between modern Swiss sociology and its forerunners. Giovanni Busino is the editor of the *Oeuvres complètes de Vilfredo Pareto*[46] and of the *Cahiers Vilfredo Pareto Revue européenne des sciences sociales*.[47] He has published numerous books in French and Italian.[48]

Although highly controversial at home, Alfred Willener, another sociologist at Lausanne University, has made himself known at the international level by some pioneer research in the field of sociology of work and industrial relations inspired by the French Georges Friedmann.[49] As early as 1957, he was discovered by Ralf Dahrendorf, who quoted heavily from him.[50] He also published in the field of sociology of culture,[51] which later became his main interest.

A relative newcomer at the University of Lausanne, René Levy—who got his education in Zurich, as we have seen—specializes currently in the sociology of work, in cooperation with colleagues from other parts of Switzerland.[52]

Jean-Pierre Keller is a solitary scholar who does not participate very often in activities of the Swiss sociological community. His specialty—sociology of arts—does not bring him very often into the limelight, but his publications always testify to his intellectual brilliancy.[53]

At the Department of Architecture of Lausanne Polytechnic, Michel Bassand, professor of sociology, is co-director of the Institute of Research on the Built Environment (IREC). A successful fund-raiser, Bassand has promoted an amazing number of research projects in the field of urban sociology and environmental planning. Aside from numerous research reports, he is the author or co-author of an impressive series of books.[54]

BERN

The sociological scene in Bern has long been dominated by Walter Ruegg, whose sociology can best be characterized as an attempt to combine a functionalist frame of reference with a phenomenological view on social reality.[55] In addition to his work on general theory, Ruegg has promoted research on the military in Switzerland, and this field of interest has been taken up by some of his followers.

Leading sociologists in Bern are now Claudia Honegger, whose experience abroad has given new impetus to the activities of the Institute of Sociology; Andreas Diekmann, a specialist of quantitative analysis and the uses of mathematics in sociology;[56] Wolf Linder, engaged in various research projects on Swiss political life; Ruth Meyer-Schweizer, active in various fields—sociology of work, culture and values, the Swiss army;[57] and Katharina Ley, known for her contributions to women's studies.[58]

BASEL

Although Basel is on the whole a lively center of cultural and intellectual activities, sociological endeavors at the university have not led so far to the creation of a full department of sociology. The function of director of the seminar for sociology has been held since 1969 by Paul Trappe. Professor Trappe, who is editor of the series Social Strategies and associate editor of the series *Heidelberger Sociologica,* is active in the fields of sociology of law as well as sociology of development.[59] He has been influenced by Theodor Geiger, whose sociology was the topic of his Ph.D. dissertation[60] and of whom he edited the major works.[61]

The lack of suitable job opportunities for sociologists in Basel has prevented some of Paul Trappe's associates from staying in town. Christian Giordano and Robert Hettlage, who have had teaching and research assignments at Basel University, have moved to Germany. Hettlage still holds an academic position in Regensburg. Giordano came back to Switzerland after a stay in Frankfurt.

FRIBOURG

At the University of Fribourg, the dominant figure in social sciences has long been Arthur Utz, who became director of the Institute of Ethics and Social Philosophy in 1946. Professor Utz has shown a special interest in the ideas of Thomas Acquinas that he found suitable for the solution of problems of our time. He has tried to come to a synthesis of Thomist views on natural law and various sociological orientations.[62]

In Fribourg as in Basel, however, the process of institutionalization of sociology has not yet reached the stage of the constitution of a department. A seminar of sociology is under the direction of Professor Riccardo Lucchini, whose theoretical and methodological orientation is a structural-functionalist one. His main fields of interest are political sociology, culture and mass communication, marginality and drugs.[63] Other sociologists who have to be mentioned in Fribourg are Jean Widmer[64] and Christian Giordano, coming back from Germany.[65]

NEUCHÂTEL

More than in any other place in Switzerland, sociology in Neuchâtel has long been a one-man business. For nearly forty years, the chair of sociology at the university was occupied by Maurice Erard, whose priority was in building up a general frame of reference for sociological taxonomy. A follower of Georges Gurvitch, Professor Erard developed a unique "scheme for a pluralistic sociology" inspired by Gurvitch's dialectical sociology.[66] At the moment, it becomes quite clear that Erard's taxonomy has lost any appeal for the new generation of sociologists in Neuchâtel. This second generation, under the leadership of a dynamic young professor, François Hainard,[67] seems to be rather eclectic in its theoretical inspiration and gives priority to policy-relevant research topics, which seems to be a sound strategy of development in a university where the very existence of sociology was menaced when Erard was about to retire.

ST. GALLEN

St. Gallen School of Economics has a high reputation in Switzerland as a school of management. Sociology has long played a very limited role in its activities. During the last decade, however, there has been a process of development, and St. Gallen is becoming a center of sociological research. Professor Peter Gross has returned from the University of Bamberg, Germany, to take over the direction of the seminar of sociology. With a good team of collaborators from Bamberg and from St. Gallen, he is actively promoting research on a wide variety of topics, including work, industrial relations, and the introduction of new technologies in enterprises. In another research unit, the *Forschungsinstitut für Arbeit und Arbeitsrecht,* Emil Walter-Busch is running projects on poverty, on quality of life, on change of values, and on defense of professional interests.[68]

If we take a look at the institutional development of Swiss sociology during the last thirty years, three phases can already be distinguished. The first one (till about 1971) is the time of the pioneers. A handful of sociologists of the first generation, like Roger Girod in Geneva, Peter Heintz in Zurich, or Maurice Erard in Neuchâtel, developed curricula or established departments. They are the ones who made the efforts of their followers possible. The second phase (1971–1982) is marked by the foundation of the modern Swiss Sociological Association. This is the time of an aggressive policy to gain visibility and to promote sociology as an academic discipline and as a profession. The Committee of the Swiss Sociological Association, under the presidency of Walo Hutmacher from Geneva, was very active as a lobbying group. The third phase (since 1982) can be characterized altogether as a time of consolidation on the domestic front, and of international recognition. The activities of the Swiss Sociological Association are less intense than before, but some sociologists have discreetly moved to key positions with federal agencies. Besides, Swiss sociologists get published in France, Germany, Italy, and even the United States.

With the exception of Lausanne and Zurich Polytechnics, high education in Switzerland is under the responsibility of the cantons. The main source of research funds, however, is a federal agency: the Swiss National Funds for Scientific Research. During the last twenty years, the policy of the National Funds toward sociology has been the focus of a recurrent debate among sociologists. In 1974, the Swiss Sociological Association published an ambitious plan for the development of sociological research in Switzerland.[69] In 1981, the Association presented an analysis of the efforts made by the National Funds during a ten-year period.[70] The conclusion was that sociologists had received only 2.6 percent of the subsidies attributed to social sciences and humanities, and only 0.4 percent of the total amount of subsidies. In its memorandum, the Association drew a distinction between "other-determined" and "self-determined" research. Projects conceived and initiated by sociologists were called "self-determined" (*auto-déterminés* or *selbstbestimmt*); projects conceived and initiated by others, and commissioned to sociologists, were called "other-determined" (*hétéro-déterminés* or *fremdbestimmt*). The Association found out that the quantitative relation between funds attributed to "self-determined" and "other-determined" projects was one to three, and announced that it would request a change of policy, such as to reach a 1/1 ratio in a first phase of development, and a 2/1 ratio in a later stage. In 1983, these claims were renewed, and the 1/1 ration was set as a policy goal for the five following years.[71] The discussion, however, went on among sociologists, some of them arguing that unrealistic goals could only lead to self-imposed marginalization and lamenting the "syndrome of complaints" (*Klagensyndrom*) of their colleagues,[72] others pointing out that the development of Swiss sociology was subjected to other conditions than just "more money," and that better defining the identity of the discipline was one of these conditions.[73]

Looking back to the discussions of the 1970s and early 1980s, there is every reason to feel that the time has come for some reappraisal. It seems quite clear now that aiming at a 1/1 ratio (not to speak about the 2/1 ratio) was not very realistic. But the fact that such a goal was set at all can be seen as a result of the late institutionalization of Swiss sociology. As for the very distinction between "self-determined" and "other-determined" research as it was used, it did not rely on a sociological view on the exchange relations between a scientific community—any scientific community—and society at large. Sociological thinking develops in confrontation with a social demand induced by social change, and it can be doubted that a situation such as the one advocated ten years ago by the Swiss Sociological Association would have been stimulating for the further development of sociology. Given the fact that Swiss sociologists have to gain wider acceptance in an unfavorable societal environment, the reasonable option seems to strike a balance between the requirements of "other-determined" projects and the ambitions of "self-determined" development.

During the last ten years, the research funds allocated to sociologists have increased mostly through their participation in the so-called National Programs, that is, policy-oriented research programs to which priority is attributed by a decision of the federal government. It means that "other-determined" research is still the major source of development. Even so, one cannot say that the relative position of sociology, compared with other disciplines, has improved, and this is one of the few undisputed results of the study recently commissioned by the Swiss Science Council.

Two or three years ago, before it became widely recognized that Switzerland would be struck by an economic and budgetary crisis, the policy options of the Swiss National Funds for Scientific Research for the period 1992–1995[74] indicated quite clearly that recent developments in higher education could provide a new, paradoxical rationale for the development of social research in the subsequent years. In all Swiss universities, an extraordinary increase in the numbers of students in the social and economic sciences was observed. Since numerous chairs would have to be created or reattributed, it seemed wise to provide support to young researchers, to help them qualify for the university posts to be filled before the end of this century, and that is what the National Funds was intent to do. In addition to that, a federal program of promotion of lifelong education was supposed to provide a boon for postgraduate studies. At the end of 1992, however, the mood changed rather abruptly while authorities at all levels were slashing into the budgets with seemingly little concern for long-range priorities. It becomes obvious that very much—including the very survival of some research institutions—depends on the speed of the economic recovery. But whatever the scenario, the new trends do not favor sociology as an autonomous discipline. For sociology, the real problem of the 1990s is no longer to avoid participation in "other-determined" ventures, but to resist pressures to be relegated to the role of an ancillary discipline. This certainly will require a new openness to interdisciplinary cooperation, but sociologists will have to be careful of devising strategies of interdisciplinary research, making allowance for the specificity of sociological conceptualization. Swiss sociologists will have to chart a course between the pitfalls of mere data collecting and the dreams of an all-embracing science. The problem of the identity of Swiss sociology will again be on the agenda.

It was mentioned several times before that Swiss society has to be seen as a rather unfavorable environment for the development of sociology as a discipline and as a profession. Is it possible to propose a sociological interpretation for this relative lack of receptivity to sociological viewpoints? I think it is. In an earlier publication in Dutch, I sketched a comparison between the situation of sociology in two small West European countries, Switzerland and the Netherlands.[75] It seems to me that this comparative approach can help to better understand the situation in Switzerland. In various respects, as we shall see, Switzerland and the Netherlands can be put on the two extremes of a scale, with maybe Belgium in an intermediate position.

From the point of view of the sociopolitical system, there is the opposition between a liberal state[76] with laissez-faire policies on the one hand, and a welfare state on the other hand. It has been repeatedly pointed out that a welfare state system induces an institutional growth[77] that creates opportunities for various categories of experts, including sociologists, who are in demand with problem-solving agencies. In Switzerland, such opportunities are still limited. Of course, a slow but gradual expansion of the area of competence of the federal government can be observed, and it can be expected that this evolution—in an "after-crisis" future—will bring some advantages to sociologists in the long term. It means, by the way, that Swiss sociologists could gain from the development of federal bureaucracies, even if they despise them, and that they might increasingly be torn between local attachments and federal rewards. It is not pure chance that the most important sociological research unit in a nonacademic setting, the Service for Sociological Research, is located in Geneva.

According to Swiss standards, Geneva is indeed the canton which looks the most like a small-size welfare state, even in a time of deregulation and reduction of spending.

Of particular relevance for this discussion are the ways to promote special interests and to regulate conflicts. In Switzerland, much more than in the Netherlands and in Belgium, a consensus is permanently being sought in all matters.[78] This reflects in a system of government which, as many fear, could have to be significantly transformed when the time will come—since it will come—to join the European Community. Social and cultural harmony is elevated to an ideological construction, and all that does not fit in the general picture of a harmonious society is mentally suppressed. In this context, sociological thinking has a disturbing effect. As a consequence, the "visibility through the media," singled out as a factor of strategic significance by the Flemish sociologist Wilfried Dumon,[79] is subjected to important limitations.

On the level of attitudes and mentalities, an opposition has also to be mentioned between Switzerland and the Netherlands. Typical for the average Dutch attitude is the group orientation, and the breakdown of the traditional "pillarization" (verzuiling) has not changed much to it. In a book that caused some irritation among Dutch intellectuals a few years ago, Derek Phillips emphasized two factors: first, the reluctance of the Dutch to hold the individual responsible for his actions; and second, the Dutch tendency to consider that all problems are to be solved at a structural level.[80] There is a clear affinity between the Dutch mentality, as described here, and sociological thinking. In Switzerland, and this is very important for our purpose, the dominant attitude is quite the opposite. It puts emphasis on individual responsibility and the freedom to make personal choices. Although this is obviously a sound basis for civic attitudes in small-scale communities, it has rather unpleasant aspects as well; Swiss society displays little tolerance of deviant behavior considered as the direct consequence of free choices.

In brief, compared with other West European countries, Swiss society is characterized by a liberal state with only residual competencies, by consensual decision making at all levels, and by the dominance of the ethos of individual responsibility.[81] This all contributes to create a climate of pre-sociological thinking, inimical to the development of sociology. In neighboring countries, even when sociology has been weakened as an academic discipline in recent years, a sociological vulgate has spread through society. Publicists may poke fun at sociologists for their jargon, but the decision-makers and the media have become used to taking into account the structural variables that have priority in sociological interpretations. In Switzerland, it is less the case: there is still a long way to go.

NOTES

1. Raj P. Mohan and Don Martindale, eds., *Handbook of Contemporary Developments in World Sociology* (Westport, Conn.: Greenwood Press, 1975), 6.

2. Peter Gross, "Enge und Flucht. Soziologische Literatur aus der Schweiz," in *Soziologische Revue* (Munich) 14 (1991), 33–47. French translation under the title "Horizons bornés et évasion. De la production sociologique récente en Suisse alémanique," in *Schweizeriche Zeitschrift für Soziologie-Revue suisse de sociologie* 18, 1 (1992), 129–148.

3. Some years ago, two colleagues from Zurich, Hans Geser and François Höpflinger, presented an analysis of mutual quotations among Swiss sociologists. The results confirmed the importance of the language barrier. German-speaking sociologists cite German-speaking colleagues; French-speaking sociologists cite French-speaking colleagues (Hans Geser and François Höpflinger, *Soziologische Anmerkungen zu einer Diffusionspolitik der Soziologie* [Zurich: Soziologisches Institut, 1974]; "Professionelle Orientierungen in der schweizerischen Soziologie," in G. Hischier et al., *Weltgesellschaft und Sozialstruktur* [Diessenhofen: Rüegger, 609–630].

4. The ratification of the treaty was rejected by a majority of the people and a majority of the cantons, but was approved massively in the French-speaking part of the country.

5. Peter Heintz, "Die Soziologie in der Schweiz," *Cahiers Vilfredo Pareto* 27 (1972).

6. By "Swiss sociologists" we mean here sociologists professionally active in Switzerland, regardless of their citizenship.

7. M. Bürgisser and A. Fritz, *Soziologen in der Schweiz,* Bulletin der Schweizerischen Gesellschaft für Soziologie, Spezial-Nummer (Zurich: Soziologisches Institut, 1983).

8. These are figures for the period 1978–1980, but it can safely be assumed that no significant change in the proportions has occurred in the meantime. See on this K. Weber, "Produktion, Kontrolle, Verteilung und Verwendung soziologischen Wissens," *Schweizerische Zeitschrift für Soziologie/Revue suisse de Sociologie* 6, 3 (1980), 299–307, 304.

9. There is also a constant emigration from German-speaking Swiss sociologists to Germany, where they occupy academic positions in various universities. Let us mention, for example, Karl Ulrich Mayer in Frankfurt, Urs Jaeggi and Martin Kohli in Berlin, Kurt Lüscher and Walter Müller in Constance, and Johannes Siegrist in Augsburg. As Siegrist put it, there were ten years ago more Swiss professors of sociology in German universities than in the whole of Switzerland (see Johannes Siegrist, *Soziologie in der Medizin/La sociologie en Médecine,* Bilingual publication. French version translated from German by Jacques Coenen-Huther [Geneva: Cahiers de l'Institut Sandoz, 1982]). Although a few Swiss sociologists are active in France (e.g., Jean-Claude Thoenig), till very recently the French universities did not offer similar possibilities to the French-speaking Swiss.

10. Roger Girod, "Contemporary Sociology in Switzerland," in Raj P. Mohan

and Don Martindale, eds., *Handbook of Contemporary Developments in World Sociology* (Westport, Conn.: Greenwood Press, 1975), 59–68.

11. Conseil suisse de la Science, *Rapport sur la recherche* (Bern, 1972).

12. Société suisse de Sociologie, "Propositions pour un plan de développement de la recherche sociologique en Suisse," in *Politique de la Science,* Supplément, 3 (Bern, 1974).

13. The three others were the sciences of education, political science, and psychology.

14. Olivier Tschannen, *Enquête sur la situation de la recherche en sciences sociales en Suisse. Rapport pour la sociologie.* Politique de la recherche, 4/1992, Swiss Science Council, Bern.

15. See, from him, Olivier Tschannen, *Les théories de la sécularisation* (Geneva: Droz, 1992).

16. The word "backwardness" might sound severe, but it is to be found in the synthesis report of the study. See Pierre Moessinger, *Enquête sur la situation de la recherche en sciences sociales en Suisse. Rapport de synthèse.* Politique de la recherche, 5/1992, Swiss Science Council, Bern.

17. A presentation by research topics made sense fifteen years ago, when Roger Girod undertook it for an earlier version of this book, since they were fewer activities to be mentioned. Repetition of the same pattern nowadays would create a sense of confusion.

18. Roger Girod, *Mobilité sociale* (Geneva: Droz, 1971); *Inégalité—Inégalités* (Paris: PUF, 1977); *Politiques de l'éducation. L'illusoire et le possible* (Paris: PUF, 1981); *Les inégalités sociales* (Paris: PUF, 1984); *Le savoir réel de l'homme moderne* (Paris: PUF, 1991).

19. Jean Kellerhals, *Les associations dans l'enjeu démocratique* (Lausanne: Payot, 1974).

20. Jean Kellerhals (with collaborators), *Mariages au quotidien* (Lausanne: Favre, 1982); *Microsociologie de la famille* (Paris: PUF, 1984); *Figures de l'équité. La construction des normes de justice dans les groupes* (Paris: PUF, 1988); *Les stratégies éducatives des familles* (Neuchâtel: Delachaux et Niestlé, 1991).

21. He was the president of the Association from 1985 till 1988. He is now one of its honorary presidents.

22. Christian Lalive d'Epinay, *Haven of the Masses: A Study of the Pentecostal Movement in Chile* (London: Lutterworth Press, 1969); *Religion, dynamique sociale et dépendance* (Paris and The Hague: Mouton, 1975).

23. Christian Lalive d'Epinay (and others), *Temps libre. Culture de masse et culture de classe aujourd'hui* (Lausanne: Favre, 1982).

24. *Le mythe du travail en Suisse* (Geneva: Georg, 1988); *Les Suisses et le travail* (Lausanne: Réalités sociales, 1990).

25. Already at the end of the 1970s and the beginning of the 1980s, Christian Lalive d'Epinay led, together with Jean Kellerhals, an important research program on the position of the elderly in modern society (see *Vieillesses. Situations, itinéraires et modes de vie des personnes âgées aujourd'hui* [Saint-Saphorin, Switzerland: Georgi, 1983]). Among his recent publications on the elderly, see *Vieillir ou la vie à inventer* (Paris: L'Harmattan, 1991).

26. Patrick de Laubier, *Idées sociales. Essai sur l'origine des courants sociaux contemporains* (Fribourg: Editions universitaires, 1982); *La politique sociale dans*

les sociétés industrielles, de 1800 à nos jours, 2nd ed. (Paris: Economica, 1984); *La pensée sociale de l'Eglise catholique,* 2nd ed. (Fribourg: Editions universitaires, 1984); *Histoire et sociologie du syndicalisme, XIXème-XXème siècles,* 2nd enlarged ed. (Paris: Masson, 1985); *Une alternative sociologique Aristote-Marx. Essai introductif à la sociologie,* 3d ed. (Fribourg: Editions universitaires, 1987).

27. Patrick de Laubier, *1905: mythe et réalité de la grève générale. Le mythe français et la réalité russe,* 2nd enlarged ed. (Fribourg: Editions universitaires, 1989).

28. Uli Windisch, *Luttes de clans, luttes de classes,* 2nd ed. (Lausanne: L'Age d'Homme, 1987).

29. Uli Windisch, *Xénophobie? Logique de la pensée populaire* (Lausanne: L'Age d'Homme, 1978).

30. Uli Windisch, *Le raisonnement et le parler quotidiens* (Lausanne: L'Age d'Homme, 1985); *Le K.-O. verbal. La communication conflictuelle* (Lausanne: L'Age d'Homme, 1987).

31. Uli Windisch and Florence Cornu, *Tell au quotidien* (Zurich: Editions M, 1988).

32. Uli Windisch (with collaborators), *Les relations quotidiennes entre Romands et Suisses allemands. Les cantons bilingues de Fribourg et du Valais,* 2 vols. (Lausanne: Payot, 1992).

33. Jean Ziegler, *Sociologie de la nouvelle Afrique* (Paris: Gallimard, 1964); *Le pouvoir africain* (Paris: Le Seuil, 1973).

34. Jean Ziegler, *Une Suisse au-dessus de tout soupçon* (Paris: Le Seuil, 1976); *Main basse sur l'Afrique* (Paris: Le Seuil, 1978); *Retournez les fusils! Manuel de sociologie d'opposition* (Paris: Le Seuil, 1980); *La victoire des vaincus* (Paris: Le Seuil, 1988); *La Suisse lave plus blanc* (Paris: Le Seuil, 1990).

35. See Philippe Perrenoud, *La fabrication de l'excellence scolaire: du curriculum aux pratiques d'évaluation* (Geneva: Droz, 1984). An earlier work by another SRS member, Cléopâtre Montandon, also deserves a mention: *Le développement de la science à Genève aux XVIIIe et XIXe siècles* (Vevey, Switzerland: Delta, 1975). This book emerged from a Ph.D. dissertation prepared at Columbia University, under the direction of Robert K. Merton.

36. See, for example, Volker Bornschier, *Westliche Gesellschaft im Wandel* (Frankfurt and New York: Campus Verlag, 1988); Volker Bornschier et al., eds., *Diskontinuität des sozialen Wandels. Entwicklung als Abfolge von Gesellschaftsmodellen und kulturellen Deutungsmustern* (Frankfurt and New York: Campus Verlag, 1990).

37. Hans Joachim Hoffmann-Nowotny, *Soziologie des Fremdarbeiterproblems* (Stuttgart: Enke Verlag, 1973); "Social Integration and Cultural Pluralism: Structural and Cultural Problems of Immigration to European Industrial Countries," in William Alonso, ed., *Population in an Interacting World* (Cambridge, Mass., and London: Harvard University Press, 1987), 149–172; "Paradigmen und Paradigmenwechsel in der sozialwissenschaftlichen Wanderungsforschung. Versuch einer Skizze einer neuen Migrationstheorie," in Gerhard Jantz and Albert Müller, eds., *Migration in der Feudalgesellschaft. Studien zur historischen Sozialwissenschaft,* vol. 8 (Frankfurt and New York: Campus Verlag, 1988), 21–42.

38. Hans Joachim Hoffmann-Nowotny, "Soziologische Aspekte abnehmender demographischer Wachstumsraten," *Schweizerische Zeitschrift für Volkswirtschaft*

und Statistik 111, 4 (1975), 507–515; (with others), *Planspiel Familie* (Diessenhofen, Switzerland: Verlag Rüegger, 1984); "Weibliche Erbstätigkeit und Kinderzahl," in Uta Gerhard and Yvonne Schütze, eds., *Frauensituation. Veränderungen in den letzte zwanzig Jahren* (Frankfurt: Suhrkamp, 1988), 219–250.

39. Hans Joachim Hoffmann-Nowotny, with the collaboration of M. U. Peters and P. G. Zeugin, eds., *Soziale Indikatoren. Internationale Beiträge zu einer neuen praxisorientierten Forschungsrichtung* (Frauenfeld and Stuttgart: Huber Verlag, 1976).

40. Among his recent publications, his article "Kleine Staaten im internationalen System," *Kölner Zeitschrift für Soziologie und Sozialpsychologie* 44 (1992), has attracted the attention of prominent sociologists in Germany.

41. François Höpflinger, *Wandel der Familienbildung in Westeuropa* (Frankfurt and New York: Campus Verlag, 1987).

42. François Höpflinger, *Bevölkerungswandel in der Schweiz* (Chur, Switzerland: Verlag Rüegger, 1986).

43. Marlis Buchmann, *The Script of Life in Modern Society. Entry into Adulthood in a Changing World* (Chicago: University of Chicago Press, 1989).

44. Peter Heintz, ed., *A Macrosociological Theory of Societal Systems, With Special Reference to the International System,* 2 vols. (Bern and Stuttgart: Huber, 1972); *Ungleiche Verteilung, Macht und Legitimität. Möglichkeiten und Grenzen der strukturtheoretischen Analyse* (Diessenhofen, Switzerland: Verlag Rüegger, 1982).

45. Thomas Held and René Levy, *Die Stellung der Frau in Familie und Gesellschaft* (Frauenfeld and Stuttgart: Huber, 1974); French translation: *Femme, Famille et Société* (Vevey, Switzerland: Delta, 1975).

46. Geneva: Droz.

47. Ibid.

48. Among Giovanni Busino's most recent works, let us mention *Per un'altra sociologia* (Turin: Einaudi, 1983); *Pareto, Croce, les socialismes et la sociologie* (Geneva: Droz, 1983); *La permanence du passé. Questions d'histoire de la sociologie et d'épistémologie sociologique* (Geneva: Droz, 1986); *Elites et élitisme* (Paris: PUF, Coll. QSJ?, 1992).

49. Alfred Willener, *Travail, salaire et production,* 2 vols. (Paris and The Hague: Mouton, 1972).

50. Alfred Willener, *Images de la société et classes sociales* (Lausanne: Thèse de sciences sociales, 1957). See, on this, Ralf Dahrendorf, *Soziale Klassen und Klassenkonflikt in der industriellen Gesellschaft,* 1957; English translation: *Class and Class Conflict in an Industrial Society* (London: Routledge and Kegan Paul, 1961, reprinted, 1972).

51. Alfred Willener, *L'image-action de la société ou la politisation culturelle* (Paris: Le Seuil, 1970).

52. René Levy, ed., *La vie au travail et son avenir* (Lausanne: Réalités sociales, 1988).

53. The last one being *La nostalgie des avant-gardes. Essai,* Editions Zoé/Editions de l'Aube, Col. Mondes en cours, 1991.

54. Of which we give a selection here: Michel Bassand and Jean-Pierre Fragnières, *Le pouvoir dans la ville. Essai sur la démocratie urbaine* (Vevey, Switzerland: Delta, 1978); Michel Bassand and M.-C. Brulhardt, *Mobilité spatiale* (St. Saphorin, Switzerland: Georgi, 1980); Michel Bassand, *Villes, régions et sociétés*

(Lausanne: Presses polytechniques romandes, 1981); Michel Bassand (and others), *Les Suisses entre la mobilité et la sédentarité* (Lausanne: Presses polytechniques romandes, 1985); *Innovation et changement social* (Lausanne: Presses polytechniques romandes, 1986); *Les enjeux de l'urbanisation* (Bern: Lang, 1988); *Culture et régions d'Europe* (Lausanne: Presses polytechniques et universitaires romandes, 1990).

55. Walter Ruegg, *Bedrohte Lebensordnung. Studien zur humanistischen Soziologie* (Zurich: Artemis, 1978).

56. See, for example, "Mathematische Soziologie," in G. Reinhold, ed., *Soziologielexikon* (Munich: Oldenbourg, 1991).

57. Among her recent publications are these: Ruth Meyer-Schweizer, "Der Jugendliche und sein Verhältnis zur beruflichen Arbeit," in National Unesco Commission, ed, *Der junge Mensch und die künftige Arbeitswelt* (Bern, 1986), 18–27; "Peut-on parler d'une mutation des valeurs en Suisse?" in Christian Lalive d'Epinay, ed., *Travail, activité, condition humaine à l'aube du XXIe siècle* (Maastricht: Presses Interuniversitaires Européennes, 1989); "Conscientious Objection in Switzerland," in Sozialwissenschaftliches Institut der Bundeswehr, ed., *Forum International 5* (Munich, 1987), 257–282.

58. Katharina Ley, "Swiss Women and the World of Work," in Janet Hilowitz, ed., *Switzerland in Perspective* (Westport, Conn.: Greenwood Press, 1990).

59. Among his numerous publications in these fields, let us quote here two recent works: Paul Trappe, *Kritischer Realismus in der Rechtssoziologie* (Wiesbaden: Franz Steiner, 1983); *Soziale Breitenwirkung einer Entwicklungsintervention "Lac Alaotra—Grenier de Madagascar,"* Social Strategies, vol. 19 (Basel: Karger Libri, 1987).

60. Paul Trappe, "Die Rechtssoziologie Theodor Geigers," Ph.D. diss. University of Mainz, 1959.

61. Paul Trappe, ed., *Theodor Geiger, Arbeiten zur Soziologie,* Soziologische Texte, vol. 7 (Berlin: Duncker und Humblot, 1962); *Theodor Geiger, Vorstudien zu einer Soziologie des Rechts,* Soziologische Texte, vol. 20, 4th ed. (Berlin: Dunker und Humblot, 1987).

62. Among his numerous publications, let us mention Arthur F. Utz, *Zwischen Neoliberalismus und Neomarxismus* (Frankfurt: Athenäum Verlag, 1974); French translation: *Entre le néo-libéralisme et le néo-marxisme* (Paris: Beauschene, 1976).

63. Riccardo Lucchini, *Sociologie du fascisme* (Fribourg: Editions universitaires, 1973); "Mass Media and Personal Influence: Opinion Leaders and Group Structure," *Revista Internacional de Sociologia* 8 (1975); *Drogue et Société* (Fribourg: Editions universitaires, 1985); "Le débat brésilien sur la justice des mineurs," in *Déviance et société* (Geneva) 15, 2 (1991), 175–186.

64. Interested in sociolinguistics and in etnomethodology. See, for example, "Goffman et Garfinkel: cadres et organisation de l'expérience," in *Langage et société* (Paris), no. 59, March 1992.

65. Known for his anthropological orientation. See, for example, "Agrargesellschaft im sozialistischen System: zur Persistenz der Agrarfrage in Polen," in *Schweizerische Zeitschrift für Soziologie-Revue suisse de sociologie* 14, 2 (1988), 177–198.

66. Maurice Erard, "Introduction à une sociologie générale pluraliste," in *Perspectives de la sociologie contemporaine* (Paris: PUF, 1968).

67. For a typical product of this research team, see Pierre Rossel, François Hainard, and Michel Bassand, *Identités, animation territorialisée et gestion des crises* (Lausanne: Editions L'Age d'Homme, 1993).

68. Emil Walter-Busch, *Das Auge der Firma. Mayos Hawthorne-Experimente und die Harvard Business School, 1900–1960* (Stuttgart: Enke Verlag, 1989).

69. Société suisse de Sociologie, "Propositions pour un plan de développement de la recherche sociologique en Suisse," *Politique de la Science,* Supplément, 3 (Bern, 1974).

70. Société suisse de Sociologie, "Mémoire concernant la politique de la science et le développement de la sociologie en Suisse depuis 1970," *Bulletin* 32 (June 1981).

71. Schweizerische Gesellschaft für Soziologie, "Schwergewichte und Prioritäten für die Forschung in der Schweiz in den nächsten 10–15 Jahren," *Bulletin* 43 (February 1984).

72. Emil Walter-Busch, "Die Förderung soziologischer Forschung durch den Schweizerischen Nationalfonds, 1970–1987. Hinweis auf einige Daten sowie Möglichkeiten ihrer Interpretation," *Bulletin* 44 (May 1984).

73. Hans-Peter Meier-Dallach, "Soziologie: vom Klagen zur Forderung," *Bulletin* 45 (September 1984).

74. Schweizerischer Nationalfonds, "Forschungsförderung 1992–1995," *Wissenschaftspolitik* (1990).

75. Jacques Coenen-Huther, "Sociologie in Zwitserland," *Sociodrome* (Amsterdam) 3 (1988), 15–18.

76. The word "liberal" is used here in its European sense, as the context certainly indicates.

77. As far as the United States is concerned, see Alwin W. Gouldner, *The Coming Crisis of Western Sociology* (London: Heinemann, 1972).

78. Guido Dierickx, "Politieke conflictbeheersing in België, Italië en Zwitserland," *Tijdschrift voor Sociologie* 5 451–472.

79. Wilfried Dumon, "Van sociologie als vak naar sociologie als beroep en terug?" Paper presented at the joint Dutch-Flemish Sociological Congress in Amsterdam, April 24–25, 1984.

80. Derek Phillips, *De naakte Nederlander. Kritische overpeinzingen* (Amsterdam: Uitgeverij Bert Bakker, 1985).

81. For a short presentation of Swiss society, in a sociological perspective, see René Levy, *Sozialstruktur der Schweiz* (Zurich: Pro Helvetia, 1982) (French and English translations available). The same author also suggests that the Swiss context produces a rather limited demand for sociological knowledge. See, on this, "Weshalb gibt es (k)eine schweizer Soziologie?" in *Schweizerische Zeitschrift für Soziologie-Revue suisse de sociologie* 15, 3 (1989), 453–487.

Part II

Sociology in the Western Hemisphere

Sociology in the Western Hemisphere is a postcolonial development although the colonial impress had differential impact on North and South America. Portugal and Spain, predominantly Catholic countries, were dominant in the early colonization of South America. France, England, and Holland dominated in North America, and though North America was religiously pluralistic, Protestantism was more influential in civic life than Catholicism.

It has become received wisdom that sociology developed more extensively in North America than South America because the former had developed a large, vibrant middle class, thought to be the foundation of democratic institutions. A democratic nation-state has been seen as a prerequisite for the development of sociology. There seems to be ample evidence that where there are nominally democratic nation-states, sociology flourishes. However, the nature of that democracy is often left unexplicated along with other contradictions of the liberal nation-state.

For the generation of sociologists coming of age immediately after World War II, the notion that the United States was a democratic society, anchored on the contributions of a large, influential middle class, was a popular portrait. This intellectual portrait of history was sustained despite two overwhelming facts: most Americans prior to World War II were clearly anchored in the lower socioeconomic stratum of social life, and the generation of people coming into the expanding middle class of the post–World War II period were often seen exchanging loyalty to large organizations in the private and public sectors for promises of security.[1] If the United States had a middle-class imprint in its communities and institutions, by the twentieth century this was often expressed as a longing, as a "loss" of community.

Why has the middle-class democratic-institution notion persisted? First, academics had a long history of ignoring social stratification, preferring to embrace ideological longings rather than facts.[2] Second, a long history of anti-communism gave prominence to normative democratic thought as popular ideology. Third, the history of ideas became confused with the history of people. Democratic ideas have had a prominent place in civic life, especially in areas attractive to intellectuals, such as the educational establishment. Fourth, given an idealist orientation, there remains a tendency to conflate material accumulation with democracy; the United States, especially immediately after World War II, was outstripping many parts of the world in accumulation, accumulation which engulfed more and more people. Fifth, some facets of civic life, particularly in areas of concern to academics, such as civil liberties, revealed some substantial growth in freedoms. Those citing this often ignore the low rate of political participation in the United States compared with other Western-style democracies. Sixth, given commitments to tolerance, necessary to deal with contradictions in political and intellectual life, tolerance has been raised to the status of a virtue rather than as a source of engaged critical thought.

Among the first generation of post–World War II sociologists to take issue with the notion that the United States was dominated by an active middle-class presence was the late C. Wright Mills (1962). In his book *White Collar,* Mills challenged what was primarily the romantic view of a decisive middle class shaping the personal and community destinies. By mid-century the United States was clearly influenced by dominant corporate and political entities. Instead of the middle class being a locus of independent economic and political power and of civic life generally, most in the middle class were finding their ways into the ranks of large bureaucracies. Fitting in was more the norm than the notion of independent voices guiding and directing community affairs.

Western-style sociology has not flourished in authoritarian settings. However, sociology in the United States was clearly the outgrowth of two non-middle-class forces: philanthropy and the appropriation of the German university model. One of the dominant centers for U.S. sociology, the University of Chicago, was given substantial support by the oil baron John D. Rockefeller. Many other leading centers of U.S. sociology were and continue to be found in large midwestern land grant institutions. These institutions evolved from training grounds for the transformation of an unskilled labor force into one composed of technically proficient people aware of the latest developments in the agricultural sciences and mechanical arts. These institutions, along with many others, eventually became comprehensive universities anchored in the German tradition. It is here that sociology found its home.

Sociology's distinctiveness from social work did not emerge until the 1930s. Its popularity as a university discipline did not appear until the 1960s and 1970s, long after the middle class could be accurately portrayed as an independent, decisive sociocultural force. Meanwhile, the emergence of a large, middle stratum of increasingly affluent consumers in an increasingly bureaucratized social order came in the wake of World War II.

In addition to the institutional location of sociology, primarily in education, which became a large enterprise, the development of sociology was aided by another factor: no significant form of violence, revolution, or war on U.S. territory occurred during the emergence and development of the discipline. Sociology could serve national interests, but sociologists, students, and citizens were not confronted with the challenges faced by their counterparts in nations wracked by revolutions and wars.

By the early 1970s sociology in the United States was at its zenith, as indicated by student enrollments, degrees granted, funding support, and professional memberships. Since that high water mark, the field has languished. Several graduate programs have closed. And generally the field has received a poor press. Though it reflects immense diversity in specific interests, three general concerns, Dennis Wrong recently noted,[3] dominate the discipline: a general body of ideas with numerous variations which often center on a debate as to whether sociology is a positivistic discipline or an interpretive one; a methodological emphasis reflecting a preoccupation with statistical and mathematical concerns; and a social problems concern which garners support for those interested in reform and giving expression to value preferences. And these domains seem to be spinning outward in different, noncomplementary trajectories. The discipline in the United States, like its Canadian counterpart, reveals growing specialization with little general work reaching out to a larger audience of informed nonspecialists. No longer does the discipline resonate to the degree it did in the past with writers who do not possess the credential of sociologist.

The reception and development of sociology in South America has been decidedly different than in North America. The plantation system; the struggle to deal with diverse populations of aristocrats, mestizos, and natives; and an unstable political environment, often ruled by authoritarian figures, resulted in a different kind of interest in social and cultural affairs. In nations which had not developed an extensive infrastructure, the materials for social and cultural analysis were sought elsewhere, often in ethnographic work. And for various peoples the lack of social justice and corruption resulted in a restiveness.

In the twentieth century, many South American countries have witnessed revolutions, an explosive growth in population, mass migrations to urban areas, and continual challenges to development and trade. Whether the current reshaping of the global economy will provide new opportunities for developing independent nations or will fuel the limited interests of elites remains an open question.

Currently there are moves to link Mexico, the United States, and

Canada via the North American Free Trade Agreement (NAFTA). While the merits of this are still being debated, it remains an open question if this kind of economic union, also being developed in Europe, will eventually encompass more of the South American continent.

In this section there are four essays on sociology in the United States. Graham Kinloch explores major debates occurring in the discipline over time, highlighting how these relate to academic institutionalization. Arthur Wilke and Raj Mohan write on theory in U.S. sociology. Often appealed to as a synthesizing and directing activity in the discipline, theory has become a component, one which itself is classified and addressed in a routine fashion, in effect giving emphasis to metatheoretical concerns. Thomas Petee examines the institutionalized nature of sociological methodology and the growth in quantitative techniques. He reviews techniques commonly used in analysis. Raj Mohan and Arthur Wilke's review of selected works in 1975, 1980, 1985, and 1990, appearing in several recognized journals of the discipline, the *American Journal of Sociology, American Sociological Review, Social Forces,* and *Sociological Quarterly,* highlight not only the dominance of quantitative techniques but continual maintenance of rather well-established subdisciplines.

Reflecting the less developed state of sociology in Latin America, Louis Bluhm, a participant observer, struggles to find a means to capture some of the nuances of sociology in the region. Instead of collecting and commenting on collected bibliographic citations, Bluhm sketches a sociology of sociology perspective.

Harley Dickinson and B. Singh Bolaria, using the premise that historically the development of sociology was tied to the development of the nation-state and the national society, focus on Quebec sociology anchored in the use of the French language on the one hand and on the other the development of English Canadian sociology as it relates to the struggles Canada continues to have over its national identity and independence. They provide some thoughts on the future of Canadian sociology.

NOTES

1. Paul Leinberger and Bruce Tucker, *The New Individualists: The Generation after the Organization Man* (New York: HarperCollins, 1991).

2. Barbara Ehrenreich, *Fear of Falling: The Inner Life of the Middle Class* (New York: HarperPerrenial, 1990).

3. Dennis Wrong, "The Present Condition of American Sociology: A Review Article," *Comparative Studies in Sociology and History* 35 (January 1993): 183–96.

11

Expansion and Survival: Canadian Sociology and the Development of the Canadian Nation

Harley D. Dickinson and B. Singh Bolaria

Raj P. Mohan and Don Martindale have noted that historically the development of sociology is related to the development of nation-states and national societies.[1] This observed relationship tends to be characterized by a universalization of sociological methods combined with a particularization of problem definition and substantive concerns as the discipline's resources are developed and applied to "the problems peculiar to the given nation-state."[2] The development of Canadian sociology is no exception to this rule. The obvious implication is that an understanding of Canadian sociology requires an understanding of the structure of Canadian national society and the forces affecting its development. It is not possible here to describe completely the anatomy of Canadian society. There are a number of basic features, however, that are important. These include internal cleavages along racial/ethnic and linguistic dimensions. The most important of these cleavages historically has been and, arguably, continues to be a French-English dualism. Related to this dualism, but not completely congruent, is an extensive regional diversity and disparity. The characteristics mentioned above are related to a historical and contemporary subordination of the Canadian economy as a resource supplying hinterland to various metropolitan centers of dominance.[3]

These factors have rendered the existence and survival of Canada as an independent nation problematic. As a result Canadian sociology has developed around the problems of national existence, survival and unity, rather than around a "social problems" focus characteristic of societies whose national existence is taken for granted.

A dominant strategy for national survival historically has been expansion: geographic, demographic, economic, and political. Indeed, C. B.

MacPherson has argued that the imperatives of expansion and survival have shaped the "patterns of social and historical thought in Canada," as well as "their rates and directions of growth."[4] The role and function of sociology within the general project of national expansion and survival, of course, changed over time, and was realized differently in French and English Canada. In this chapter we outline schematically the development of sociology within the context of Canadian national survival and expansion. In this undertaking we do not provide a comprehensive description of either Canadian national society or Canadian sociology. Our objective is more modest. We wish to draw attention to selected aspects of the nature of Canadian society and some of the often contradictory ways they have intersected with the institutional expansion and survival of Canadian sociology.

The chapter is organized into two main sections. In the first we examine the development of Quebec sociology in relation to the development of Quebec society and Quebec nationalism. In the second section we look at the development of English Canadian sociology in relation to the struggle for Canadian national survival and expansion. The chapter is concluded with a brief discussion of the future of Canadian sociology.

SOCIOLOGY AND FRENCH CANADA

As MacPherson stated, social scientific and historical writing in Canada has been oriented to the two processes of national expansion and survival. These same two impulses characterized both the French and English colonies in North America prior to the British conquest of the French in 1760. Given the diverse nature of the two original colonies, forces and factors that facilitated the survival and expansion of the English colony were not necessarily the same as those that facilitated the expansion and survival of the French colony. Indeed, in many instances they were diametrically opposed.

Thus, following the Conquest, the participation of French Canadians in Canadian nation-building generally has been viewed as a coerced compliance with their own domination by *les Anglais.* Although political association with the English is thought to have imposed restrictions on the full flowering of French Canadian culture, the accommodations made between *les Anglais* and the French Canadian clergy and business class did guarantee the survival of a French-speaking, Roman Catholic society within the context of a predominantly Protestant, English-speaking North America. At the time of Confederation efforts to secure French Canadian compliance emphasized this point by drawing attention to the assimilationist consequences of possible annexation by the United States.

Although there was strong pressure to legislate a unitary state at the time of Confederation, the political reality of the French-English dualism resulted in a federal political structure intended to preserve English economic and political dominance while ensuring French Canadian cultural, linguistic, and religious survival. Stanley B. Ryerson has stated that the constitutional split in powers between federal and provincial governments guaranteed both objectives. "But," he asked, "was it enough to guarantee the right of the French-Canadian nation to *survivance* and *epanouissement,* to survival and full flowering?"[5] Much of French Canadian sociology has attempted to answer that question.

Four main periods of development of French Canadian sociology can be identified. The first spanned the period between Confederation and the end of the Great Depression of the 1930s. The second covered the period between 1940 and 1970. That period roughly corresponded to the modernization of French Canadian society. The third period encompassed the decade of the 1970s. The fourth period began in the early 1980s and continues to the present.

The first period of development of French Canadian sociology roughly corresponded to the period between Confederation (1867) and the end of the Great Depression (1939). The constitutional accord that was Confederation, among other things, guaranteed the survival of a distinct French Canadian community in Quebec. During that period of relative security, sociology, to the extent that it existed, developed around church interests in social problems.[6] The 1891 papal encyclical, *Rerum Novarum,* for example, influenced early French Canadian sociology. Elaborating this point Donald R. Whyte and Frank Vallee stated: "The Roman Catholic Church defined the limits and content of early francophone sociology, and the Catholic Action Movement became the vehicle for a Catholic sociology in Quebec."[7]

La survivance was the orienting theme and objective of French Canadian sociology. Sociological and historical writings of that period contributed to a view of French Canadian society as a relatively homogenous society of rural, Catholic, French-speaking peasants.[8] The principal external threats to the survival of that church-dominated, rural, peasant society were generally seen to be absorption by the processes of societal modernization and capitalist industrialization, and assimilation to either English Canada or the United States. Pierre Trudeau, for example, stated that from the time of the Conquest (1760) the assumption of English policy had been that the French Canadians would be "swamped by immigration" and that they would be assimilated through the processes of democratic rule based on representation by population.[9] He went on to argue, however, that constitutional guarantees and adept use of the machinery of democracy by French Canadian elites helped ensure cultural and national survival.[10]

As real as these external threats were to the survival of a distinct French Canadian national society within North America, the primary structural contradiction that resulted in the transformation and modernization of traditional French Canadian society was internal to that society itself. Specifically it was the limit imposed on its continued expansion by the availability of arable land. This, combined with the dominant system of rural land tenure and distribution, resulted in an ever-increasing surplus population.[11] This contradiction at the heart of rural Quebec society facilitated the rapid transformation of Quebec society through the related processes of capitalist industrialization and urbanization by providing a rapidly growing population available for wage labor functions. That process of societal modernization generally is referred to as the Quiet Revolution, and it corresponds to the second main phase of the development and institutionalization of Quebec sociology.

The second phase spanned the period from 1940 to 1970. During that period sociology began to be differentiated and institutionalized as a distinct discipline in Quebec. This process of institutionalization, of course, continues to the present. Unlike English Canada, the institutionalization of French Canadian sociology proceeded with support of the Quebec societal elites, including the progressive fragment of the Roman Catholic clergy.[12]

The first Francophone department of sociology in Quebec, for example, was established at the Catholic Laval University in Quebec City. Although originally established in 1943 as a joint department, it became indedendent in 1951. The second Francophone sociology department was opened at the University of Montreal in 1955. The third, and most recent department, was opened in 1970 at the University of Quebec at Montreal (UQAM).

The opening of the sociology department at UQAM brought the number of sociology professors in Francophone universities to sixty. By 1982–1983 this number had increased to about seventy-five. Danielle Juteau and Louis Maheu pointed out, however, that the emergence of sociology out of the processes of academic differentiation and specialization also resulted in the differentiation from sociology of a number of other disciplines including criminology, demography, communications, and urban and regional planning, to name a few.[13] As a result, by 1983 more than 40 percent of professors with sociology degrees in Quebec universities were working in departments other than sociology.[14]

Student enrollment and degrees granted tended to increase in the Francophone universities throughout the post–World War II period, up to and in some cases including the early 1980s. At the undergraduate level enrollments in Francophone sociology departments increased steadily, reaching slightly more than 400 in 1972, peaking at more than 1,200 in 1977, and declining steadily since that time to something just over 800 in 1983.[15] This trend was generally followed in terms of undergraduate degrees granted in sociology by Quebec Francophone universities. Juteau and Maheu reported about 110 undergraduate sociology degrees granted in 1975.

The number increased steadily, with only slight variation in 1979–1980, to a high of more than 250 degrees in 1981. This was followed by a dramatic drop in 1982 to about 1975 levels followed by a steady increase to approximately 160 degrees in 1984.

At the graduate level of training in sociology in Quebec Francophone universities, the following patterns were reported by Juteau and Maheu.[16] With regard to master's level enrollments, between 1972 and 1983, with only slight variation in two or three years, the trend was toward a steady increase in numbers; from just under 250 in 1972 to just over 350 in 1983. The number of master's level graduates fluctuated more widely over the 1975 to 1984 time period which Juteau and Maheu reported on, going from about 33 in 1975 to approximately 42 in 1976 then dropping to a low of less than 20 in 1979 and increasing to a high of just under 60 in 1982, after which time the number has dropped steadily to something less than 40 in 1984.

Doctoral level enrollments in Francophone Quebec universities generally followed a similar pattern of steady increase between 1972 and 1976 followed by a slightly modulating enrollment between 1977 and 1981 followed by steady increases between 1980–1981 and 1983–1984. During the 1980–1981 to 1983–1984 time period, for example, the number of Ph.D. level enrollments in Quebec Francophone universities was 438, and the number of doctoral degrees granted was 32.[17] In 1989 the number of doctoral degrees in sociology granted by Francophone Quebec universities was 16, one less than the year previous.[18]

Other indications of the institutionalization of Quebec Francophone sociology are increased levels of research funding and the establishment of professional associations and journals. An additional indicator of professional institutionalization is the fact that between 1972–1973 and 1983–1984 the level of research funding increased from $170,000 to $1,210,000.[19] The main sources of this funding were the FCAR, which organizes and subsidizes Quebec university research, and in recent years the Quebec Ministry of Higher Education and Research. Additionally, the Canadian federal government, through the Social Sciences and Humanities Research Council (SSHRC), supports sociological research in Quebec and throughout Canada.

In terms of autonomous sociological journals, the first French-language sociology journal in Quebec, *Recherches Sociographiques,* was established in 1960 at Laval University. The second, titled *Sociologie et Sociétés,* was established in 1969 at the University of Montreal. The third, and most recent sociological journal, was established in 1983 at UQAM. It is titled *Cahier de Sociologie.* In addition to this there is the bilingual *Canadian Review of Sociology and Anthropology* established in 1964. There also exist other French-language journals which serve as outlets for Francophone sociologists such as *Anthropologie et Société* established in 1977 and the journal of the Quebec Institute of Cultural Studies, titled *Question de Culture,* published since 1981.[20]

The greatly expanded and institutionalized Francophone sociology of the second period, as described above, remained intimately connected with the processes of Quebec nation-building. The imperative had become survival through expansion in the form of modernization and industrialization, however, rather than defensive struggles to ensure the survival of the traditional rural, agricultural way of life. *Rattrapage,* or catching up, was the cry that rallied the new middle classes which were both driving forces behind and beneficiaries of Quebec's modernization.[21] Although initially sponsored by a rationalized church, the new professional middle classes, including sociologists, became increasingly autonomous of the church and other traditional elites, and increasingly oriented to the provincial state.

During that period, Francophone sociologists tended to reject cultural explanations for the retarded development of Quebec society and to see the long period of church domination of Quebec society to be caused by English Canadian domination of the provincial economy. David Nock, for example, stated that in the 1950s and 1960s an increasing number of sociologists became convinced "that it was not only the reactionary ideologies of the elite that had caused French Canada's retardation, but the exploiting role of the English in Quebec."[22]

The view that English domination and exploitation was an important factor in explaining French Canadian "backwardness" was not universally shared among Quebec intellectuals. The other view, represented in the journal *Cité-Libre,* for example, was that the role of the English was inconsequential as an explanation of the nature of French Canadian society. Proponents of that view advocated a general program of catching up via the modernization of Quebec institutions, but rejected the call for Quebec national independence as reactionary at worst and misguided and utopian at best.[23] A commitment to a renewed Canadian federalism was seen as the best political framework to pursue the continued modernization and democratization of Quebec society.

Despite the divergence of diagnosis and political prescription, by the 1970s, many Quebec sociologists were committed to the cause of Quebec separatism. A number of reasons have been suggested for separatism, including the imposition of the War Measures Act in response to the October crisis of 1970,[24] and the politicization that resulted from a number of key strikes.[25] Whatever the combination of reasons, by the 1970s for a growing proportion of the Quebec Francophone new middle class, social and cultural survival and expansion meant the political separation from the rest of Canada and the establishment of an independent Quebec nation. The ideological and political slogan of that period of Quebec nation building was *maîtres chez nous,* a slogan taken from an earlier period and imbued with a separatist meaning. The rise to dominance of the *separatiste* version of Quebec nationalism also marked the beginning of the third period of development of Quebec sociology.

A strong symbiotic relationship developed between Quebec intellectuals, the provincial state, and other modernizing public sector and para–public sector institutions.[26] The modernization of Quebec society was to be achieved in part by the development and application of social scientific knowledge, including sociological knowledge, in the form of social policy. Thus, not only were the newly institutionalized social sciences intended to produce the knowledge required for effective modernization, but they were intended to contribute to the production of the trained labor force required for its effective application, particularly in the areas of education, health care, and social welfare. During this period the Quebec state came to be the master institution of Quebec society, replacing the church.[27] For many, either the Canadian federal state was seen as unnecessary for the realization of Quebeckers' aspirations, or it was seen as an obstacle to the independent expansion and survival of the Quebec nation-state.[28]

Many, including sociologists, saw the election in 1976 of the Parti Quebecois (PQ) as a possible vehicle for achieving both independence and a more thoroughly modernized, democratized, or possibly even socialist society. Marc Renaud, Suzanne Dore, and Deena White, for example, stated,

With the Parti Quebecois in the governing role, an important fraction of the intellectual community in Quebec—of which sociologists were a significant element—in a sense "took power." The nationalist and social democratic movements were fused with legitimate government in one swift and dramatic stroke. Participants in the new State bureaucracy were to a large extent drawn from university departments. Individuals with sociological training took up positions as cabinet ministers, heads of government enterprises, and even as deputy ministers.[29]

By the early 1980s, however, capitalist economic industrialization had brought to the fore issues of class, gender, and racial exploitation and oppression, and the unity of social democratic, *separatiste,* and modernization forces had collapsed. The PQ was unable, for example, to link issues of women's liberation to the *separatiste* cause as indicated by the "Yvettes" movement in opposition to the separatist option in the 1980 referendum.[30] Quebec's economic strategy for resource development also generated increased demand for self-government and brought to the fore Indian demands to settle long-standing land claims. Thus, the modernization of the Quebec economy sharpened a number of contradictions within Quebec society and generated a number of social antagonisms. Within Francophone Quebec sociology this contributed to a reconsideration of the relationships between ethnicity, nation, class, and gender. In particular, the notion of "ethnic class" that had been propounded by

Jacques Dofny and Marcel Rioux,[31] and which clearly had implied an identity between class interests and the struggle for national survival in the face of English Canadian economic exploitation and political oppression, came to be seen as inadequate both as a theoretical basis for understanding Quebec society and as a basis for directing the nationalist (separatist) struggle.

That point was driven home with the failure of the 1980 referendum on Quebec sovereignty to give the Quebec provincial government a mandate to negotiate constitutional separation from the rest of Canada. This political setback for the PQ government and its separatist supporters was followed immediately by an economic blow in the form of the 1981 recession. The recession was accompanied by the adoption of cost control strategies in both federal and provincial government welfare spending in the name of deficit reduction and cost control. At the provincial level this contributed to the breakdown of the social democratic alliance that had helped bring the PQ to power. The 1981 recession and the accompanying fiscal crisis of the Quebec state also highlighted for many the limits of liberal and state reform. The failure of the 1980 referendum contributed to the disorganization of the separatist forces. The 1982 repatriation of the Canadian constitution *without* Quebec as a signatory, however, provided a renewed focus for organization.

The failure of the Meech Lake constitutional accord in the summer of 1990 from the point of view of separatist forces added insult to the injury of the 1982 repatriation, and it has served to reinvigorate the demands for Quebec sovereignty. A new referendum on Quebec independence was planned for October 1992. It is unlikely, however, that even if it is successful and the Quebec state receives a mandate to negotiate political independence from the rest of Canada, that Quebec sociologists will be as unified in their support for, and commitment to, Quebec national sovereignty. The problems of class, gender, race, and other forms of social inequality and injustice remain, and few now believe that separation from the rest of Canada will resolve them. These events have had a number of consequences for Quebec sociology and sociologists.

Many sociologists no longer viewed the Quebec state as the key to societal democratization.[32] Rather, sociologists increasingly began to explore both impediments and imperatives to the further extension of justice and equality to various class and nonclass groupings in Quebec society. An expression of this is the increased interest in the "new social movements" on the part of Quebecois sociologists.[33] An increased empirical interest in the "new social movements" was associated with renewed attempts to theorize the relations between civil society and the state.[34] The practical objective of this theoretical undertaking is to discover organizational bases and strategies outside the state that will facilitate the further democratization of Quebec society and the empowerment of those groups and classes that currently remain relatively powerless in the wake of the Quiet Revolution modernization process. The ideological principle informing the work of Quebec sociologists in the current and fourth period is *la prise en charge communautaire*—empowering the community.[35]

The "community empowerment" strategy is seen as an alternative to the previous statist development strategy of the Left and the current market-oriented strategy proffered by the Right. Substantively the new Quebec sociology is characterized by an interest in a plurality of social issues and social problems.

In this context, Quebec sociologists are taking on more of an oppositional role vis-à-vis the state. This is related, of course, to the "new social movements" focus of attention and community empowerment ideology. The oppositional stance emerging within Quebec sociology also corresponds to a convergence with sociology in English Canada. This may account for an apparent renewal of interest in establishing closer professional relations between the French and English Canadian sociologies.[36]

THE SOCIOLOGY OF ENGLISH CANADA

Like sociology in Quebec, English Canadian sociology emerged in response to, and as part of, the struggles for national survival and expansion. We propose four main periods within which to analyze the development of Canadian national society and Anglophone Canadian sociology. The main referent for the periodization proposed is Canada's relationship to various metropolitan powers, first France, then Great Britain, and most recently the United States. Our first period began with the British conquest of the French in 1760 and ended with Confederation in 1867. Throughout that period Canada was a direct colony of Great Britain. During the second period, which began in 1867, direct colonial dependence on Great Britain decreased, a process that culminated in 1931 with the passage of the Statute of Westminster. That act of the British parliament officially marked the end of Canada's direct colonial status and its membership in the British Commonwealth of Nations, a global trading block within which member nations received preferential terms of trade.[37] Period three, 1931–1960, corresponded to a shift from colonial dependency on Britain to economic integration as a junior partner in the U.S. dominated economy of North America. Although the shift was apparent from at least the time of World War I,[38] the process of continental economic and cultural integration accelerated throughout the interwar years and was clearly established as dominant by the end of World War II. The fourth period, 1960 to present, has been characterized by increased integration of the continental economy and, partly related to that, increased provincial powers vis-à-vis the federal government. In what follows we briefly examine some main dimensions of English Canadian nation-building and the relationship of Anglophone sociology to that process throughout the periods mentioned above.

It was during the period between 1760 and 1867 that the unequal union of French and English in Canada was forged and that English dominance was institutionalized.[39] During that period no Anglophone sociology existed as such. Much of the social analysis and historical writing of that period was informed by theory and methods transferred to Canada from Europe.[40] Substantively, much of it was a celebration of the civilizing consequences of a triumphant British imperialism.[41]

During the period between Confederation and 1931 sociology began to emerge in English Canada, generally not as an independent academic discipline, but as an adjunct to social work programs and "social gospel" inspired reform movements. A number of universities offered sociology courses during that time period, but within the context of a university system with strong ties to the British academic hierarchy, the newly emerging American discipline was greeted with hostility and contempt.[42] Anti-Americanism, in one form or another, has been an element of Canadian nationalism and nation-building since the eighteenth century, and it has influenced the introduction and development of sociology in Anglophone Canada.

During the first several decades of period two, particularly up to World War I, economic, political, geographical, and population expansion of the Canadian nation was seen as imperative not only for Canadian mercantile, financial, and industrial interests, but also to ensure British imperial interests. Continued access to the Orient, which had been threatened since the middle of the nineteenth century by American continental expansion, was a perpetual concern of the British. That combination of interests facilitated Canadian national expansion and survival, but in a position of subordination relative to Britain. The processes and nature of national expansion and development between Confederation and 1931, provided the focus for an emergent Anglophone Canadian sociology in period three.

The first autonomous department of sociology in Canada was established at McGill University in Montreal in 1925. Montreal, at that time, was the undisputed center of dominance in relation to the Canadian economy.[43] As a private university, McGill was controlled by a Board of Governors dominated by the Anglophone industrial, mercantile, and financial elite of Montreal. The Board of Governors, at that time, imbued McGill University with a utilitarian ethos.[44] Thus, the expectation was that sociology, and other social sciences, would contribute to the solution of a range of practical problems associated with industrialization, unemployment, urbanization, immigration, and race and ethnic relations.[45]

Difficulties were created for the nascent sociology department at McGill, in part, because of contradictory interests of the Canadian capitalist class. On the one hand, like large capitalists everywhere, the Anglophone elite was interested in harnessing the social sciences to the tasks of increased worker productivity and efficiency. It was hoped that social science, including sociology, could both discover the individual, social, and cultural impediments to increased productivity and efficiency and devise strategies for their transcendence. Thus, the quest for efficiency and productivity within the context of a capitalist economic system was/is associated with the liberal reformation of social and cultural institutions thought to obstruct individual initiative and productive capacity. The processes of capitalist modernization, on the other hand, delegitimated and threatened the racial, gender, and class base of traditional white, male, Anglo-Saxon, Protestant, domination of Canadian social, political, and cultural institutions. That contradiction was manifested, in part, in the form of uncertainty and conflict over the function of the university in Canadian society; was it to be in the vanguard of capitalist modernization and societal rationalization, or was it to be the guardian of traditional British values and social and cultural institutions?

Sociology in Canada developed in the midst of the contradictory struggles to modernize society and redefine the function of the university in Canadian society.[46] At the political and ideological levels those contradictions were manifested, in part, in the form of contending nationalisms; was Canada to modernize, liberalize, and democratize its societal institutions; that is, should it become Americanized, or should it remain true to the more traditional, conservative, and elitist traditions of British imperialism?

Sociology in Anglophone Canada both manifested and contributed to those struggles. Unlike the institutionalization of Francophone sociology in Quebec, however, the institutionalization of sociology in Anglophone Canada did not receive unambiguous support from the elites of English Canada. Consequently, its institutionalization in Anglophone Canada was slow and halting until the 1960s.

Sociology courses had been taught at McGill, and elsewhere, prior to World War I. It was not until an autonomous department was established in 1925, however, that sociological research into the development of the Canadian national society commenced. Sociological research at McGill generally was financed from grants from large American philanthropies such as the Rockefeller and Ford foundations and the Carnegie Endowment. Indeed, an early social science research project in Canada, which included a specifically sociological component, was funded by a five-year Rockefeller Foundation grant of $110,000. That grant, which was awarded in 1929, established the multidisciplinary Social Science Research Project (SSRP), the purpose of which was to study unemployment and immigrant adjustment in Montreal and other parts of Canada.[47] Another grant was awarded to researchers from several central Canadian universities by the Carnegie Endowment for the Frontiers of Settlement Project. A third major grant was also awarded by the Carnegie Endowment for the study of American-Canadian relations. A fourth grant was awarded in the interwar period by the Rockefeller Foundation for studies of the emergence of protest political parties in western Canada, especially the Social Credit in Alberta.[48]

In 1940 the Canadian Social Science Research Council (CSSRC) was established. The primary functions of the CSSRC were to secure funding and to coordinate national research activities. It received virtually no government financial support between its inception and 1958.[49] Throughout the whole of the third period, the major source of funding was the large American philanthropic foundations. Between 1940 and 1958, for example, the total budget of the CSSRC was $718,850. Of that amount $636,325 was provided by three American philanthropies; the Rockefeller Foundation provided $499,795, the Ford Foundation gave $74,400, and the Carnegie Foundation provided $61,130; the remaining part of the budget during that time period was provided by Canadian Universities and Colleges ($35,225) and various private sources ($47,300).[50] The funds from the Ford and Carnegie foundations were primarily used to cover the operating costs of the CSSRC itself, while funds from the Rockefeller Foundation were distributed to various researchers.[51] Another Ford Foundation grant of $150,000 was spread over a three-year period at the end of the 1950s.[52]

In 1957 the Canadian federal government established the Canada Council and provided it with an operational and research support budget. Although the budget was relatively small, it was crucial for the continued expansion and survival of social research in Canada for two reasons. First, the American philanthropic foundations did not provide funds to support ongoing research. Their strategy was to provide seed money intended to mobilize funds from other private and public sources.[53] Second, government support was crucial to the development of social science research in Canada because of the hostility and lack of moral and material support provided to the social sciences, particularly sociology, within Canadian universities.[54] The provision of even minimal government support helped to establish and legitimate sociology, which was widely seen as an irrelevant Americanism by Anglophone Canadian academic elites.[55]

Despite its hostile reception in Anglophone Canada, sociology slowly differentiated itself and established a distinct professional existence. The creation of a separate sociology section within the Canadian Political Science Association in 1956 was a small step in that process. It was during the first decade or two of the fourth period, 1960 to present, that the institutionalization and legitimization of sociology proceeded apace.

The first bilingual sociological journal, the *Canadian Review of Sociology and Anthropology,* as we have seen, was established in 1964. The following year a separate national professional association was founded, the Canadian Sociology and Anthropology Association. About the same time, the Canada Council for the first time received funding from direct parliamentary appropriation.[56] That, combined with a modest, but steady, increase in the amount available for sociological research and graduate student training over the following years, served to further entrench and legitimate the newly emerging discipline.[57]

The utility of sociological research was also accorded increased recognition as a result of contributions made by sociologists to several important national commissions and inquiries in the 1960s and 1970s.[58] These included the Royal Commission on Health Services (1961–1964), the reports of which contributed to the establishment of a national medical care and hospital services insurance program. Sociologists also contributed to the Royal Commission on Bilingualism and Biculturalism (1963–1967). That Royal Commission was part of the federalist response to the emergent Quebec separatist movement that developed out of the modernization processes of the Quiet Revolution. The recommendations of the "Bi and Bi" Commission had significant consequences for Canadian language and cultural policies. Several of the policy recommendations of sociologists who contributed to the Royal Commission on the Status of Women (1964–1966) also were adopted. Canadian sociologists have made additional significant contributions to policy formation and Canadian nation-building in the form of contributions to "Senate committees on poverty and on aging, and institutional research under independent and quasi-governmental sponsorship," as well as to numerous provincial commissions and task forces.[59]

The increased demand for the research expertise of sociologists for planning and policy formation purposes on the part of both federal and provincial levels of government, as well as by certain elements of the private sector, was accompanied by increased demand for university faculty to satisfy a growing student population. Expansion of Canadian universities during the 1960s was particularly dramatic. Full-time undergraduate enrollment in all disciplines, for example, increased by threefold and graduate enrollments increased by a factor of six.[60] The increase in the number of students during the decade was 10–15 percent annually, and government spending increased by approximately 20 percent per year.[61]

To accommodate expanded numbers of students, both undergraduate and graduate, it was necessary to expand the number of sociology departments and faculty. By 1960 sociology had been established at the departmental level in only a handful of universities in all of Canada.[62] Excluding Francophone Quebec universities twenty-two institutions offered undergraduate degrees in sociology in 1966, by 1969 the number had increased to forty, and in 1990 there were forty-three.[63]

With regard to graduate level training in 1966, nine institutions offered master's level degrees in sociology and/or anthropology. The number had increased to twenty-three institutions by 1969; with some slight fluctuation, the number had increased to twenty-five institutions in 1990.[64]

At the doctoral level of training, five Anglophone institutions offered Ph.D.'s in sociology in 1966, nine in 1969, and by 1990 the number had increased to thirteen.[65]

The average annual growth rate among sociology faculty during the 1960s was 33 percent.[66] In absolute numbers that represented a demand for fifty to sixty Ph.D.'s annually. Only nineteen doctorates in sociology were awarded in Canada, however, in that time period.[67] By 1976 the total number of earned doctorates in sociology from Anglophone Canadian universities had increased to forty; the number peaked at forty-nine in 1978 and again in 1980; by 1989 the number had dropped slightly to forty-three. In that year, for the first time, half the total number of earned doctorates, from both Anglophone and Francophone Canadian universities, were awarded to women.[68] Notwithstanding the fact that more earned doctorates in sociology were awarded to men than to women the following year, thirty-four compared to twenty-five, the trend seems to be in the direction of gender equity in terms of earned doctoral degrees in Canada.[69]

If we look at the gender distribution of sociology degrees in Canada from both Francophone and Anglophone institutions at the baccalaureate and master's level of education, a clear trend toward the feminization of sociology is evident. In 1988, for example, 73.8 percent, or 2,321 baccalaureate degrees in sociology were awarded to women. That was the continuation of a long-term trend. At the master's level, 52.9 percent, or 111 degrees in sociology were awarded to women. That was down from a high of 124 degrees, amounting to 59.3 percent of all master's degrees in sociology, being awarded to women the previous year. Despite that reversal the overall trend is toward the feminization of sociology at both the baccalaureate and master's levels of training.[70]

During the 1960s, however, not enough Canadian or Canadian-trained doctorates in sociology were being produced to satisfy the greatly expanded demand. Americans and American-trained sociologists helped meet the shortfall. By 1970–1971 that resulted in the situation where 40.3 percent of all sociologists and anthropologists were Canadian citizens and 38.5 percent were American.[71] There is reason to believe, however, that a substantial number of Canadian citizens with doctoral degrees in sociology were American trained. In 1965–1966, for example, of the fifty-five Canadian doctoral candidates, eleven were studying in Canada, six in the United Kingdom, and thirty-eight in the United States.[72]

These data suggest an interesting contradiction, namely, that the establishment and expansion of Anglophone Canadian sociology corresponded to an Americanization of the discipline. The Americanization of Anglophone Canadian sociology encompassed both personnel, and perspective and content dimensions. With regard to the second aspect, Nathan Keyfitz, for example, noted that English Canadian sociology and American sociology were indistinguishable in terms of topics studied, style, content, and quality.[73] Similarly, S. D. Clark stated, "A review of the history of the discipline in this country leads to the almost inescapable conclusion that what has developed here is not a Canadian sociology but a sociology that is American."[74] These views were shared by others including Jan J. Loubser,[75] Michale Gurstein,[76] Frank Jones,[77] and Lorne Tepperman.[78] In reaction to the Americanization of Canadian sociology, there emerged what Harry H. Hiller termed the Canadian sociology movement.[79]

THE CANADIAN SOCIOLOGY MOVEMENT

A principal objective of the Canadian sociology movement was to develop a distinctly Canadian perspective and content for Canadian sociology. An essential feature of such a sociology was that it not be American. Indeed, for many the search for a distinct content and perspective for Anglophone Canadian sociology was seen as part of the struggle against American imperialism and a necessary component of the struggle for continued national survival. Hiller, for example, stated that "to the extent that the Canadian sociology movement represents a struggle for differentiation from American sociology, it is co-extensive with the national need for differentiation in general."[80] Others also made this point. Rodney Crook, for example, stated "the problem of a distinct English Canadian sociology is precisely an expression of the problem of Canadian nationhood itself."[81] James Stolzman and Herbert Gamberg stated "the absense of a Canadian sociology is an ideological reflection of the arrested development of Canada's national sovereignty."[82] See also G. B. Rush and others,[83] Dennis Forcese and Stephen Richer,[84] and Paul Lamy[85] for similar comments.

The search for a distinct Anglophone Canadian sociology combined with expansion of the discipline facilitated the establishment of a second English-language general sociology journal, *The Canadian Journal of Sociology,* in 1975. The debate over the need for a Canadian sociology was expanded by the establishment of that journal with the publication of several articles.[86] Several other journals have been established in Canada that serve as outlets for the work of some sociologists. These include *The Journal of Social and Political Theory,* 1977; *Labour/Le Travail,* established in 1976; *Studies in Political Economy,* created in 1979; and the *Journal of Canadian Studies,* established in the mid-1960s. In addition to the journals mentioned above, a number of specialty journals dealing with various substantive topics, such as ethnic relations, marriage, and the family, also exist.

Sociologists in Anglophone Canada have also innovated in developing alternative publication outlets for their original empirical and analytical work. Largely in reaction to the overwhelming use of American textbooks for teaching purposes and the paucity of Canadian research and textbooks, Canadian sociologists, and those committed to the development of a distinctly Canadian sociology, began to publish original research monographs as textbooks. Commenting on Anglophone Canadian sociology in 1978, Tepperman, for example, commented that the most, and generally "the best recent sociological writing has appeared in a textbook format."[87] He carried on to point out that

the textbook format has been used to develop new ideas about Canada while addressing a relatively substantial market of naive readers. No one anticipated the consequences: a broadening of the notion of "textbook" beyond its usual bland, even noxious connotations. In countries like the United States and Britain original and pointed ideas can reach their audience in a monograph with limited circulation. Outside Canada there has been less need, hence less willingness, to teach while innovating. But, in Canada, necessity has been mother to the invention of a new kind of textbook.[88]

Those same structural imperatives have more recently, generally beginning in the mid-1970s, resulted in a further innovation in sociological publishing in English Canada, with the development of textbooks in the form of edited collections of original research and sociological analysis. Not only have these related innovations in teaching and publication contributed to the differentiation of Anglophone Canadian sociology from sociology in other national contexts, but they tend to differentiate sociology from other social sciences in Canada. Part of the motivation for the innovations mentioned above, of course, were derived from the Canadian sociology movement.

Assessments of whether the Canadian sociology movement was successful are mixed, although the majority opinion seems to be that it was a success and that a distinctly Canadian sociological perspective grounded in an indigenous political economy tradition has been developed and, indeed, has probably become the dominant perspective in many Anglophone departments of sociology.[89] Some, however, question that conclusion. Marcel Fournier, for example, concluded his assessment of the development of sociology and sociological theory in Anglophone Canada with the following observation: "Even if there has been a 'Canadianization' movement over the last decade, and in spite of its efforts at renewal, English-Canadian sociology remains greatly influenced by American sociology, both in theoretical and methodological terms."[90] Similarly Clark, in 1975, expressed the opinion that critical sociology associated with the Canadianization movement, particularly various neo-Marxist versions of political economy, was an American import: "One is left with the uneasy feeling . . . that the new left wing sociology that is seeking to establish itself in Canada is very much an American import."[91] He went on to express some skepticism about the capacity of the new critical sociology to have "meaning in terms of Canadian experience."[92]

Others are more certain of the authenticity and success of the Canadianization movement. They point out, however, that it is not unchallenged as a perspective even within academia.[93] Donald R. Whyte, for example, felt that "by articulating an alternative conception of society," Anglophone Canadian sociology has successfully differentiated itself from the dominant form of American sociology of the 1960s. Despite that, he concluded that "it failed to situate that conception in a broad field of practice."[94] In other words, like Clark,[95] he is uncertain of the relevance of Canadianized sociology to the development of Canadian national society.

Several reasons have been suggested for why a Canadianized sociology has been relatively ineffectual in shaping the development of Canadian national society. These include the economic and cultural domination of Canada by the United States, the structurally fragmented nature of Canadian society and politics, and the heterogeneous nature of Anglophone Canadian sociology itself.[96]

SUMMARY AND CONCLUSION

The history of the development of the Canadian national society has been characterized by an ambivalent relationship to the United States. Some have even argued that Canada as a national society only exists as a rejection of, and defense against, America and Americanization.[97] A primary area of concern for anti-American Canadian nationalists has been the American dominance of the Canadian economy. Particular concern was expressed over the extent and consequences of American foreign direct investment in the Canadian economy. The general concern of Canadian nationalists was that foreign direct investment was a form of neo-imperialism that threatened Canadian independence and sovereignty.

Since the 1970s it has become apparent that certain fragments of the Canadian capitalist class have also greatly expanded their direct foreign investment, particularly in the United States, and repatriated control of previously foreign-owned corporations through stock purchases and other means.[98] Although the Canadian and American economies are increasingly integrated, it is not as clear in the post-1970s period that the Canadian capitalist class is completely subordinate in that relationship. This essence of contemporary interdependence between dominant fragments of the Canadian and American capitalist classes was captured by William K. Carroll when he stated, "Canadian monopoloy capital, while presently more independent of singularly American interests than it has been in several decades, is deeply involved in a complex structure of international politico-economic relations in which the largest imperialist power necessarily plays a focal role."[99]

One possible consequence of the current pattern of continental economic integration is that the dominant fragment of the Canadian capitalist class may have contradictory interests with regard to certain forms of Canadian nationalism.[100] In particular, one would expect a Canadian economic elite with extensive foreign direct investments to view protectionist and isolationist forms of anti-American Canadian nationalism as contrary to their interests. Recent research on the political ideology of the Canadian capitalist class supports that view. Michael Ornstein, for example, reported that "business executives were much more favourable to foreign investment than state officials, labour leaders, and the general public."[101] One-half of the business executives responding thought there should be no screening of foreign investment, 65 percent said that foreign investment had "mostly good" effects on the Canadian economy, while only about 17 percent thought the integration of the Canadian and U.S. economies was too great. Interestingly, however, only one in six business executives proclaimed support for closer continental integration.[102]

The active support of organized sectors of the Canadian capitalist class for the Canada-U.S. Free Trade Agreement during the 1988 federal election, and current support for negotiations for the establishment of a U.S.-Mexico-Canada Free Trade Agreement, seems contrary to the opinions of Canadian business executives on continental integration reported by Ornstein. Whatever the reasons for this apparent contradiction, the nature and extent of direct foreign investment by Canadian capitalists, as well as the positive economic consequences of foreign direct investment in Canada, structurally predispose that fragment of the Canadian capitalist class most directly involved to reject the isolationist and protectionist forms of nationalism characteristic of the Canadian sociology movement of the late 1960s and 1970s. To the extent that Anglophone Canadian sociology is imbued with an anti-American vision of Canadian nation-building, it may find itself taking an oppositional stance vis-à-vis the interests of a key fragment of the Canadian capitalist class, and against the Canadian state that has facilitated the pusuit of capitalist-class interests regarding economic development generally and continental integration more particularly.

The oppositional stance of much Anglophone sociology relative to the state was increased throughout the 1980s partly as a result of the restructuring of state expenditures, and the shift from Keynesian economic policy to a version of supply-side economics policy. The Canadian federal state and all the provincial-level states adopted policies of cost control and the privatization of service delivery in the name of deficit reduction. The re-ordering of social institutional arrangements associated with the downsiz-ing and rationalization of the welfare state followed closely on the heels of an economic policy adopted in the 1970s which reduced wage inflation through high levels of unemployment. The developments in Canadian so-ciety resulted in much analytical attention being focused on theories of the state, particularly on the nature and consequences of economy-state relations. In the 1980s, there seemed to be an emergent interest in the new social movements and in the analysis of the state–civil society relation. At the level of policy and practice a primary objective of such theoretical work is to discover the basis for extending social democratic reforms in the face of economic concentration and centralization and state rational-ization and rationing of various welfare services. In this regard there seems to be a substantive and practical convergence between Anglophone and Francophone sociology.

The concentration and centralization of capital within the context of Canadian economic development has reinforced the role of Canada as a supplier of various staples to world markets. This too has had conse-quences for domestic social and political relations. As a consequence of the fact that staples, such as oil and natural gas, pulp and paper, various minerals, water, and hydroelectric power, are natural resources which are geographically concentrated and unevenly distributed, their development for domestic consumption or export has contributed to increased regional disparities and differentiation of regional interests. Politically, this has contributed to a perpetual constitutional crisis that both impedes the de-velopment of national unity, and in some cases, threatens national sur-vival.

The French-English dualism of Canadian society, at least in part, is a reflection of economic regionalism as well as a cultural and linguistic du-alism. Another dimension of the political crisis associated with current resource development practices are renewed and intensified demands by Canadian Indians for settlement of outstanding land claims and, partly related to the desire for control over natural resources, demands for self-government. The patterns of postwar staples development has helped to place these items close to the top of the Canadian political agenda in recent years.

These developments have tended to reinforce the political economic analytical tradition within Anglophone Canadian sociology, as well as to encourage investigations of race and ethnic relations and studies of Ca-nadian regionalism. These tendencies, particularly with regard to race and ethnic relations, have further been encouraged by postwar immi-gration patterns and the adoption of an official policy of multicultura-lism.

Another structural characteristic of the postwar expansion of the Canadian economy has been an expansion of the service sector of the economy and a contraction, both absolute and relative, of the number of persons employed in the goods manufacturing sector. The expansion of the service sector, which is not unique to Canada, has proceeded largely on the basis of increased female participation in the capitalist wage labor force. The extent and nature of this aspect of postwar Canadian economic expansion, especially after 1970, contributed to a renewed feminism. This has had a profound influence on the recent development of both Anglophone and Francophone sociology. The feminist challenge to the content and perspectives of Canadian sociology has resulted in both theoretical and empirical advances in terms of our knowledge about Canadian society and its consequences for individuals.[103] The feminist movement in Anglophone Canada has had strong links to academic feminists.[104] There is every indication these links will be strengthened and extended.

As this brief discussion has tried to illustrate, the restructuring of the world capitalist economy in the postwar period, and the ways in which Canada has been integrated into, and affected by, that process has had consequences for the nature of Canadian society and the role of sociology. One of those consequences has been that Anglophone Canadian sociology, particularly that undertaken from the dominant political economy perspective, has tended to become entrenched in its oppositional stance relative to state policy and dominant patterns of economic development. Currently, however, there are discernible attempts to imbue social science research with a new utilitarianism. These include changes to the level and nature of funding provided to social scientists through the Social Science and Humanities Research Council (SSHRC). SSHRC's plan for the future includes continued identification of areas of strategic national importance for research support, the active encouragement of multidisciplinary research and, within that context, an expanded emphasis on graduate student training.[105] These developments are reminiscent of the objectives that underpinned social science research at McGill, and other centers in Canada and elsewhere, in the 1930s and 1940s.

If these assessments are correct, then it appears that a possible contradiction exists between the nationalist lament and oppositional stance characteristic of sociology and the expectations of current elites for a renewed utilitarianism and expansive nationalism. Some concern has been expressed that the current situation may result in the forcible eviction of the social sciences from the universities.[106] Others are of the opinion that sociology will be rendered irrelevant.[107] Yet others feel that renewal is possible and with it an enhanced capacity for the discipline to more fully realize its emancipatory potential.[108] Current uncertainty about the future of Canadian sociology is at least partly a reflection of uncertainty about the future of Canadian national society.

NOTES

1. Raj P. Mohan and Don Martindale, eds., *Handbook of Contemporary Developments in World Society* (Westport, Conn.: Greenwood Press, 1975), ix.

2. Ibid., x.

3. Alan B. Anderson, Peter A. Sinclair, B. S. Bolaria, and S. Parvez Wakil, "Sociology in Canada: A Developmental Overview," ibid., 159–172.

4. C. B. MacPherson, "The Social Sciences," in Julian Park, ed., *The Culture of Contemporary Canada* (Toronto and Ithaca: The Ryerson Press and Cornell University Press, 1957), 181.

5. Stanley B. Ryerson, *Unequal Union: Roots of Crisis in the Canadas* (Toronto: Progress Books, 1973), 374.

6. See, for example, Anderson et. al., op. cit.; David Nock, "History and the Evolution of French Canadian Sociology," *Insurgent Sociologist* 4, 4 (1974), 15–29; Harry Hiller, *Society and Change: S. D. Clark and the Development of Sociology in Canada* (Toronto: University of Toronto Press, 1982); Donald R. Whyte and Frank Vallee, "The Field of Sociology," in Lorne Tepperman and James Curtis, eds., *Readings in Sociology: An Introduction* (Toronto: McGraw-Hill Ryerson Ltd., 1988).

7. Whyte and Vallee, op. cit., 14.

8. Fernand Dumont and Guy Rocher, "An Introduction to a Sociology of French Canada," in Marcel Rioux and Yves Martin, eds., *French Canadian Society,* vol. 1 (Toronto: McLelland and Stewart, 1964); Phillippe Garique, "French Canada: A Case Study in Sociological Analysis," *Canadian Review of Sociology and Anthropology* 1, 4 (1964), 186–192.

9. Pierre E. Trudeau, *Federalism and the French Canadians* (Toronto: Macmillan of Canada, 1968), 118, note 23.

10. Ibid.

11. Horace Miner, *St. Denis: A French Canadian Parish* (Chicago and London: Pheonix Books; The University of Chicago Press, 1963 [1939]); Everett C. Hughes, *French Canada in Transition* (Chicago: The Chicago University Press, 1943); Hubert Guindon, "Social Unrest, Social Class, and Quebec's Bureaucratic Revolution," in Rioux and Martin, op. cit..

12. Guindon, 1964, op. cit.; Danielle Juteau and Louis Maheu, "Introduction: Sociology and Sociologists in Francophone Quebec: Science and Politics," *Canadian Review of Sociology and Anthropology* 26, 3 (1989), 363–393. Unless otherwise indicated, information about the institutionalization of Francophone Quebecois sociology is from Juteau and Maheu.

13. Juteau and Maheu, ibid., 371.

14. Ibid.

15. Figures derived from ibid., 369, Graph 3.

16. Figures derived from ibid., 368, Graphs 2 and 3.

17. Ibid., 368, Graphs 1 and 2.

18. Statistics Canada, *University Enrollment and Degrees, 1990;* and *1991* (Ottawa: Minister of Supply and Services, 1990 and 1991).

19. Juteau and Maheu, op. cit., 371.

20. Ibid.

21. Hubert Guindon, "Social Unrest, Social Class, and Quebec's Bureaucratic Revolution," in Bernard R. Blishen, Frank E. Jones, Kaspar D. Naegle, and John Porter, eds., *Canadian Society: Sociological Perspectives,* 3rd ed. (Toronto: Macmillan of Canada, 1968); Hubert Guindon, "The Modernization of Quebec and the Legitimacy of the Canadian State," in Daniel Glenday, Hubert Guindon, and Alan Turowetz, eds., *Modernization and the Canadian State* (Toronto: Macmillan of Canada, 1978); Hubert Guindon, "Quebec and the Canadian Question," in James Curtis and Lorne Tepperman, eds., *Images of Canada: The Sociological Tradition* (Scarborough, Ont.: Prentice-Hall Canada Inc., 1990).

22. Nock, op. cit., 24.

23. Trudeau, op. cit.

24. Gerard Pelletier, *The October Crisis* (Toronto/Montreal: McLelland and Stewart, 1971), 155.

25. Guindon, 1978, op. cit.

26. Steven Brooks and Alain G. Gagnon, *Social Scientists and Politics in Canada: Between Clerisy and Vanguard* (Kingston and Montreal: McGill-Queen's University Press, 1988).

27. Raymond Breton, "Quebec Sociology: Agendas from Society or from Sociologists," *Canadian Review of Sociology and Anthropology* 26, 3 (1989), 557–570.

28. Guindon, 1978, op. cit.

29. Marc Renaud, Suzanne Dore, and Deena White, "Sociology and Social Policy: From a Love-Hate Relationship with the State to Cynicism and Pragmatism," *Canadian Review of Sociology and Anthropology* 26, 3 (1989), 431.

30. Michele Jean, Jacqueline Lamothe, Marie Lavigne, and Jennifer Stoddart, "Nationalism and Feminism in Quebec: The 'Yvettes Phenomenon,' " in Roberta Hamilton and Michele Barrett, eds., *The Politics of Diversity: Feminism, Marxism and Nationalism* (London: Verso, 1986), 322–338; Diane Lamoureux, "Nationalism and Feminism in Quebec: An Impossible Attraction," in Heather Jon Maroney and Meg Luxton, eds., *Feminism and Political Economy: Women's Work, Women's Struggles* (Toronto: Methuen, 1987), 51–68.

31. Jacques Dofny and Marcel Rioux, "Social Class in French Canada," in Rioux and Martin, op. cit.

32. Renaud et al., op. cit.

33. Ibid.; William D. Coleman, "The Political Economy of Quebec," in Wallace Clement and Glen Williams, eds., *The New Canadian Political Economy* (Kingston/Montreal/London: McGill-Queen's University Press, 1989).

34. Renaud et al., ibid.

35. Ibid.

36. John D. Jackson, "John Jackson Remembers . . . Celebrating Our History/ Celebons notre heritage," Special 25th Anniversary Edition, *Society/Société: Newsletter of the Canadian Sociological and Anthropological Association* 14, 3 (1990); Guy Rocher, "The Quiet Revolution in Quebec," in James Curtis and Lorne Tepperman, eds., *Images of Canada: The Sociological Tradition* (Scarborough, Ont.: Prentice-Hall Canada, Inc., 1990); Guy Rocher, "The Two Solitudes among Canadian Sociologists," *Society/Société: Newsletter of the Canadian Sociology and Anthropology Association* 14, 3 (1990), 3–4.

37. A. W. Currie, *Canadian Economic Development* (Toronto: Thomas Nelson and Sons, 1942).

38. Donald V. Smiley, ed., *The Rowell/Sirois Report/Book 1* (Toronto: McLelland and Stewart, 1963).

39. Ryerson, op. cit.

40. Hiller, 1982, op. cit.

41. MacPherson, op. cit.

42. S. D. Clark, "Sociology in Canada: An Historical Overview," *Canadian Journal of Sociology* 1, 2 (1975), 225–234.

43. Oswald Hall, "Some Recollections of Sociology in Two Universities: McGill and the University of Toronto," in R. Helmes-Hayes, ed., *A Quarter Century of Sociology at the University of Toronto, 1963–1988: A Commemorative Volume with Essays by S. D. Clark and Oswald Hall* (Toronto: Canadian Scholars Press, 1988); Marlene Shore, *The Science of Social Redemption: McGill, The Chicago School and the Origins of Social Research in Canada* (Toronto/Buffalo/London: The University of Toronto Press, 1987).

44. Robin Ostow, "Everett Hughes: The McGill Years," *Society/Société: Newsletter of the Canadian Sociology and Anthropology Association* 8, 3 (1984), 12–16.

45. Shore, op. cit.

46. A. B. McKillop, *A Disciplined Intelligence: Critical Inquiry and Canadian Thought in the Victorian Era* (Montreal: McGill-Queen's University Press, 1980).

47. Shore, op. cit., 12.

48. Hiller, 1982, op. cit., 17.

49. Ibid., 18.

50. Mabel F. Timlin and Albert Faucher, *The Social Sciences in Canada: Two Studies* (Ottawa: Social Science Research Council of Canada, 1968), 64, Table 9.

51. Hiller, op. cit., 18.

52. Ibid.

53. Ibid.

54. Ibid.; Clark, 1975, op. cit.; Shore, op. cit.; Aileen Ross, "Sociology at McGill in the 1940's," *Society/Société: Newsletter of the Canadian Sociology and Anthropology Association* 8, 1 (1984), 45.

55. S. D. Clark, "The Changing Image of Sociology in English-Speaking Canada," *Canadian Journal of Sociology* 4, (1979), 393–403.

56. Hiller, 1982, op. cit., 26.

57. There has been a leveling off of growth in social sciences research funding since the late 1970s. The Social Sciences and Humanities Research Council (SSHRC), for example, reported in a recent planning document that "in real terms—the budget of the council as we enter the 1990s barely exceeds its budget level for 1979. . . . The SSHRC'S share of the financing provided for the three federal research granting councils (the SSHRC, the Natural Sciences and Engineering Research Council, and the Medical Research Council) has declined from 16 percent in 1978–79, to 12 percent in the last few years. . . . Overall, Canada's investment in research and development, calculated as a percentage of Gross Domestic Product (GDP), has not kept pace with that of its major trading partners. . . . And the relative share of the Canadian R & D pie which has been allocated to the social sciences and humanities has also dropped significantly within the past decade." SSHRC, *A Vision for the Future: A Five Year Strategy from the Social*

Science and Humanities Research Council (Ottawa: Social Sciences and Humanities Research Council, 1990), 5.

58. Whyte and Vallee, 1988, op. cit.; G. N. Ramu and Stuart D. Johnson, "Toward a Canadian Sociology," in G. N. Ramu and Stuart D. Johnson, eds., *Introduction to Canadian Society: Sociological Analysis* (Toronto: Macmillan Company of Canada, 1976); Fred Schindeler and C. Michael Lanphier, "Social Science Research and Participatory Democracy in Canada," in W. E. Mann, ed., *Social and Cultural Change in Canada,* vol. 2 (Vancouver: Copp Clark Publishing, 1970).

59. Whyte and Vallee, 1988, ibid., 15.

60. Hiller, 1982, op. cit., 129.

61. Ibid.

62. Whyte and Vallee, 1988, op. cit., 14.

63. Association of Commonwealth Universities, *Commonwealth Universities Handbook,* vol. 2 (London: Association of Commonwealth Universities, 1966; 1969; and 1990).

64. Ibid.

65. Ibid.

66. Max Von Zur-Mehlen, "The Ph.D. Dilemma in Canada: A Case Study," in Sylvia Ostry, ed., *Canadian Higher Education in the Seventies* (Ottawa: Economic Council of Canada, 1972), 92, cited in Harry H. Hiller, "The Canadian Sociology Movement: Analysis and Assessment," *Canadian Journal of Sociology* 4, 2 (1979), 129.

67. Hiller, 1979, op. cit.

68. Statistics Canada, *University Enrollment and Degrees, 1978; 1980;* and *1982* (Ottawa: Minister of Supply and Services, 1978; 1980; and 1982); Statistics Canada, 1991, op. cit.

69. Statistics Canada, 1991, ibid.

70. Ibid.; Statistics Canada, 1990, op. cit.

71. Abraham Rotstein and Gary Lax, "Faculty Citizenship in Canadian Universities," in Abraham Rotstein and Garry Lax, eds., *Getting It Back: A Program for Canadian Independence* (Toronto: Clarke Irwin, 1974), 199, cited in Hiller, 1979, op. cit., 130.

72. Hiller, 1982, op. cit., 24, Table 5.

73. Nathan Keyfitz, "Sociology and Canadian Society," in T. N. Guinsberg and G. L. Reuber, eds., *Perspectives on the Social Sciences in Canada* (Toronto: University of Toronto Press, 1974).

74. Clark, 1975, op. cit., 225.

75. Jan J. Loubser, ed., *The Future of Canadian Sociology in Canada* (Montreal: Canadian Sociology and Anthropology Society, 1970).

76. Michale Gurstein, "Towards the Nationalization of Canadian Sociology," *Journal of Canadian Studies* 7, 3 (1972), 50–58.

77. Frank Jones, "Current Sociological Research in Canada: Views of a Journal Editor," *Journal of the History of the Behavioural Sciences* 13 (1977).

78. Lorne Tepperman, "Sociology in English-Speaking Canada: The Last Five Years," *Canadian Historical Review* 59, 4 (1978), 435–436.

79. Hiller, 1979, op. cit.; Hiller, 1982, op. cit.; Harry H. Hiller, "Paradigmatic Shifts, Indigenization, and the Development of Sociology in Canada," *Journal of the History of the Behavioural Sciences* 16 (1980) 263–274.

80. Hiller, 1979, ibid., 135.

81. Rodney K. N. Crook, "Teaching and Learning Sociology," in Dennis Forcese and Stephen Richer, eds., *Issues in Canadian Society: An Introduction to Sociology* (Scarborough, Ont.: Prentice-Hall, 1975), 497.

82. James Stolzman and Herbert Gamberg, "The National Question and Canadian Sociology," *Canadian Journal of Sociology* 1, 1 (1975), 99.

83. G. B. Rush, E. Christensen, and J. Malcolmson, "Lament for a Notion: The Development of Social Science in Canada," *Canadian Review of Sociology and Anthropology* 18, 4 (1981), 519–544.

84. Dennis Forcese and Stephen Richer, "Introduction: Social Issues and Canadian Sociology," in Dennis Forcese and Stephen Richer, eds., *Social Issues: Sociological Views of Canada,* 2nd ed. (Scarborough, Ont.: Prentice-Hall Canada Inc., 1988).

85. Paul Lamy, "The Globalization of American Sociology: Excellence or Imperialism," *The American Sociologist* 11, 2 (1976), 104–114.

86. Stolzman and Gamberg, 1975, op. cit.; Lawrence F. Felt, "Nationalism and the Possibility of a Relevant Anglo-Canadian Sociology," *Canadian Journal of Sociology* 1, 3 (1975), 377–385; Dorothy E. Smith, "What It Might Mean to Do a Canadian Sociology: The Everyday World as Problematic," *Canadian Journal of Sociology* 1, 3 (1975), 363–376; I. C. Jarvie, "Nationalism and the Social Sciences," *Canadian Journal of Sociology* 1, 4 (1976), 515–528; Hiller, 1979, op. cit.; Clark, 1975, op. cit.; Clark, 1979, op. cit.; Gwyn Nettler, "Sociologist As Advocate," *Canadian Journal of Sociology* 5, 1 (1980), 31–53.

87. Tepperman, op. cit., 443.

88. Ibid.

89. Patricia Marchak, "Canadian Political Economy," *Canadian Review of Sociology and Anthropology* 22, 5 (1985), 673–709; Raymond A. Morrow, "Critical Theory and Critical Sociology," *Canadian Review of Sociology and Anthropology* 22, 5 (1985), 710–747; R. Jack Richardson and Barry Wellman, "Structural Analysis," *Canadian Review of Sociology and Anthropology* 22, 5 (1985), 771–793; Breton, 1989, op. cit.; Wallace Clement, "Approaches Toward a Canadian Sociology," in Lorne Tepperman and James Curtis, eds., *Readings in Sociology: An Introduction* (Toronto: McGraw-Hill Ryerson, 1989).

90. Marcel Fournier, "Sociological Theory in English Canada: A View from Quebec," *Canadian Review of Sociology and Anthropology* 22, 5 (1985), 802.

91. Clark, 1975, op. cit., 233.

92. Ibid.

93. John D. Jackson, "Introduction [to the Special Issue on the State of the Art and New Directions, vol. 1: Sociology in Anglophone Canada]," *Canadian Review of Sociology and Anthropology* 22, 5, (1985). 615–618; Margrit Eichler, "And the Work Never Ends: Feminist Contributions," *Canadian Review of Sociology and Anthropology* 22, 5 (1985), 610–644; Raymond A. Morrow, "Critical Theory and Critical Sociology," *Canadian Review of Sociology and Anthropology* 22, 5 (1985), 710–747; John O'Neill, "Phenomenological Sociology," *Canadian Review of Sociology and Anthropology* 22, 5 (1985), 748–770.

94. Donald R. Whyte, "Sociology and the Constitution of Society: Canadian Experiences," paper presented at the 25th Annual Meeting of the Canadian So-

ciology and Anthropology Association, University of Victoria, Canada, May–June 1990, 9.

95. Clark, 1975, op. cit.

96. Jackson, 1985, op. cit.; Brooks and Gagnon, 1988, op. cit.; Gordon Laxer, "The Schizophrenic Character of Canadian Political Economy," *Canadian Review of Sociology and Anthropology* 26, 1 (1989), 178–192; Donald Whyte, "Sociology and the Nationalist Challenge in Canada," *Journal of Canadian Studies* 19, 4 (1984/ 85), 106–129; Clement and Williams, 1989, op. cit.

97. Arthur K. Davis, "Canada as Hinterland versus Metropolis," in Curtis and Tepperman, 1990, op. cit.; David Bell and Lorne Tepperman, *The Roots of Disunity: A Look at Canadian Political Culture* (Toronto: McLelland and Stewart, 1979).

98. J. Niosi, "The Canadian Multinationals," in Tepperman and Curtis, 1988, op. cit.; William K. Carroll, "Dependency, Imperialism and the Capitalist Class," in Curtis and Tepperman, 1990, op. cit.

99. Carroll, ibid., 177.

100. Daniel Drache, "The Canadian Bourgeoisie and Its National Consciousness," in Ian Lumsden, ed., *Close to the 49th Parallel: The Americanization of Canada* (Toronto: University of Toronto Press, 1970).

101. Michael Ornstein, "Political Ideology of the Canadian Capitalist Class," *Canadian Review of Sociology and Anthropology* 25, 2 (1986), 200.

102. Ibid.

103. Hamilton and Barrett, 1986, op. cit.; Robert Brym with Bonnie Fox, *From Culture to Power: The Sociology of English Canada* (Toronto: Oxford University Press, 1989); Eichler, op. cit.; *Studies in Political Economy: A Socialist Review, Special Issue on Feminism and Political Economy* 30 (Autumn, 1989); *Canadian Review of Sociology and Anthropology, 25th Anniversary Issue on Feminist Scholarship* 25, 2 (1988).

104. Brym with Fox, op. cit.

105. SSHRC, 1990, op. cit.

106. Marchak, op. cit., 699.

107. Whyte, 1984/5, op. cit.

108. Jackson, 1985, op. cit., 618.

A View of Contemporary Latin American Sociology

Louis H. Bluhm

THE SOCIOLOGY OF SOCIOLOGY

A search of the sociological literature pertaining to Latin America leads one to the conclusion that the standard approach to such a review produces an incomplete understanding of Latin American social thought. The citations available to scholars through the typical search techniques are only the tip of an iceberg. The implication is that even the ability to identify the existence of sociological output is determined by a complex social process; in truth, standard indexes are misleading and do not convey all of the important realities. This observation is not particularly surprising, nor is it especially radical. It would be naive and ethnocentric of the practitioners of sociology to assume that the profession would function in the same way in culturally diverse situations.

Nevertheless, as a preliminary step, a standard search of sociological literature pertaining to Latin America reveals that the articles and books listed touch on virtually every aspect of sociology. While the scope is wide, the depth appears to be restricted. Extensive bodies of work are concentrated in a limited number of areas, such as rural sociology, socioeconomic development, demography, and, to some degree, sociological theory, political sociology, and introspective discussions focusing on the nature of society and of the profession itself. This distribution reflects the consequences of social and cultural factors which have affected the development of the profession for several decades.

Sociology, like other institutions, is molded by the blend of social forces found in the society of which it is part.[1] The profession of sociology and its sociocultural environment are fused to such an extent that it is sometimes difficult to distinguish them conceptually. The types of problems studied by sociologists, the types of methods used, the types of evidence accepted, and the internal organization of the discipline are all subject to variation in different cultural settings. Consequently, it would be virtually impossible to speak of sociology and social thought in Latin America without speaking of the conditions in each of the different Latin American societies—a task which would be too comprehensive and too complex for this chapter. Yet, some common conditions and concerns do exist, which have affected all of Latin American sociology with varying degrees of intensity at one time or another.

In this chapter, the general factors affecting the discipline of sociology in Latin America will be discussed from the perspective of the sociology of sociology, rather than advancing an extensive bibliographic classification of substantive subject matter studied by practitioners in the discipline. The substantive concerns of scholarship are interpreted as indicators of the larger social forces impinging upon the profession. That is to say, the focus of attention of the practitioners of sociology at any given point in time, in any given country, is a reaction, a response to the changing sociocultural environment. Consequently, the future development of sociology in Latin America will most likely depend more on changes at the societal level than on the dynamics of science and the elaboration of theory within the discipline.

Many of the observations included in this chapter are based on a number of years of participant observation. Some of the observations included have been gleaned from "fugitive sociology," that is, observations made by colleagues in informal conversations and discussions, as well as insights communicated in exchanges of personal correspondence. Many of the insights contained in the informal culture of sociology will probably never reach print, nor have all of the observations undergone rigorous scientific tests. Consequently, the database used in this chapter is not perceived as strictly representative; nevertheless, the observations do have heuristic value and add a dimension not found in statistical tables. Most important, the discussion suggests that sociologists can profitably rely on their own sociological imaginations and serve as their own knowledgeable informants as they attempt to understand their own social environments.

Several of the examples are drawn from Brazil, though the principles involved have much broader application than one nation. In many respects, Brazil is a microcosm of the social forces affecting the continent. Most of the problems, the possibilities, and the institutional constraints found in other parts of Latin America are, or have been, exemplified by Brazil. It is a developing nation which is large in size, diversified in culture, and provides ample illustrations of more general conditions found in all, or most, of Latin America.

PROFESSIONAL ORGANIZATION

Cultural Imperialism

One of the most ubiquitous influences affecting the institutional development of sociology in Latin America is the incontestable fact that the countries in the Southern Hemisphere are a collection of diverse, developing nations. These countries are typically characterized by decidedly unequal distributions of wealth, power, and technological expertise, both internally and externally, that is, vis-à-vis the competing international community. The multiple issues implied by this observation cannot be ignored in any discussion of Latin American sociology. Not only are national, regional, and international factors—as well as social dynamics internal to the discipline—interesting in their own right, but the resulting professional structure, in turn, affects individual scholarship.

Few countries in Latin America, if any, have escaped the specter of cultural imperialism emanating from abroad. Both the United States and Europe have had considerable vested interest in the colonization and development of these societies, which, incidentally, also applies to the organization of educational institutions housing such disciplines as sociology. In the countries of Latin America, sociology is, in a sense, a hybrid, having some characteristics in common with both the United States and Europe, but not necessarily an exact copy of either. Traditionally, many intellectuals were trained in Europe. Possibly for that reason, a common organizational model followed in the Latin universities is similar to the European model. That is, a discipline tends to be organized in terms of some variant of a "chair professor" model. An individual who held the chair position, or, if not one individual sometimes a small group of individuals, essentially dominated the departments until death or retirement changed the composition of the faculty.

National Identity

The events related to World War II accelerated a process of social change which shows few signs of slowing even at the close of the century. For example, World War II highlighted the existence of relatively large German ethnic minorities in various Latin American countries, minorities whose loyalty was questioned, minorities which were unintegrated into the social order to the extent that they might only communicate through the German language. This revelation raised the general issue of societal cohesion and solidarity, since the German minority was only one group among many. Some Latin scholars and leaders wondered if the nations on this southern continent were in fact making progress toward nationhood. The issue of how to define national entities, or, perhaps, how to create them, became pertinent. These concerns accelerated the production of studies and novels which explored the concept of national identity.

Institution Building

Partly as a response to the issue of national identity aggravated by World War II, institution-building programs, primarily administered by universities and governmental agencies in the United States and Europe, came into vogue. One significant reason for their emergence, no doubt, is that the period immediately after the war represents the beginning of the cold war, which pitted the capitalist nations led by the United States against the eastern block nations lead by Marxist Russia. At the macro-level, intervention in the less developed nations could be interpreted as part of a global containment policy directed toward the Soviet Union. Even though Marxism had already gained a toehold on the South American continent prior to World War II, it apparently had not been considered a real threat. However, the division of the world into two powerful camps at the close of the war meant that the Marxists in Latin America could serve as a potential fifth column in a grand, geopolitical struggle. Hence, the introduction of institution-building projects along with other large foreign aid projects were motivated by strong political self-interest on the part of the donor nations.

Individuals involved in these institution-building activities, however, sometimes found the traditional social structure in the host country, such as the university organizational structure, resistant to change and innovation. One strategy used in these institution-building efforts was to circumvent parts of the existing system and build parallel institutions. The physical sciences, such as agronomy, probably had less difficulty integrating into the traditional university system than did the social sciences. The nature of the subject matter within the social sciences, however, made them more threatening to existing vested interests, both within and outside the university system. As a result, the perception that these new social sciences posed a threat stimulated a degree of resistance. For this reason, it was convenient and, in a sense, logical to organize new sociology programs in institutes which were adjuncts to the university, but not an integral part of the traditional system. In other words, in those cases in which linkages with existing "chair" departments in the university were difficult to establish, one strategy used was to substitute "research institutes," which were loosely affiliated with the universities in question. Even though these affiliates were not part of the traditional structure, they still might offer academic courses of some sort, depending on the orientation of the institute.

But the nature of the threat posed to vested interests by these changes involved issues related to perspective rather than substance. The transplanted social sciences, including sociology, tended to operate from a different philosophical orientation, from a different frame of reference. That is to say, the social sciences exported to Latin America were pragmatic and applied in their approach; in general, they tended to avoid social criticism and esoteric theoretical studies. Typically, these new programs focused on the short-term, practical problems of society, especially in the realms of production, of economic development, and of providing social infrastructure.

The applied nature of the disciplines involved in these institutional changes created the tendency to perceive these newly introduced institution-building efforts in the social sciences as essentially synonymous with rural sociology, demography, or agricultural economics.[2] However, rather than challenging the traditional, established schools of thought by presenting radically different concepts, grand ideas, or revolutionary theories, it proved to be the applied techniques, the middle-range theoretical perspectives, and the pragmatic orientations of these disciplines which actually posed the major challenge. In short, the strained relationships generated by the newcomers can be perceived, in part, as a difference of opinion concerning the legitimate focus of the discipline and a disagreement, to a large extent, over appropriate procedures and methods.

Compartmentalization

The intervention of development-oriented agencies created different schools of thought which competed with one another for recognition, legitimacy, and power. The structure of the discipline resembled, to some extent, the preparadigm stage of science described by Thomas S. Kuhn in his book *The Structure of Scientific Revolutions.*[3] Clearly, within the academic community, a certain amount of competition and conflict emerged which affected the development of sociology, but not necessarily in the manner which Thomas Kuhn's work might suggest. That is to say, no one paradigm or organizational principle emerged as dominant. Rather, as the subsequent analysis indicates, the divisions of the preparadigm stage became institutionalized and essentially remain permanent fixtures of the academic scene.[4]

One of the justifications used to defend these new programs against their critics was that they were actually money-making enterprises competing for research contracts, an activity for which the traditional chair departments of sociology were not trained nor especially suited. Portraying these institution-building projects as money-making endeavors had certain advantages from the perspective of the institution-building teams. Simply put, the possibility of gaining an economic benefit served as an inducement for the participation of host country counterparts. The strategy also served another purpose in the sense that the external funding removed the host country participants in these new sociology programs from the sphere of power centered in the chair departments, insulating the new breed of academic innovators, to some degree, from economic pressure and criticism. A host country intellectual could hardly be faulted by colleagues for pursuing personal interest and increasing personal income.

An argument could be made that the segmentation of the discipline which resulted from creating parallel organizations had negative consequences for the development of sociology. These divisions and patterns of behavior tended to become institutionalized in the general structure of the profession. Currently, given the manner in which the discipline has evolved, well-trained sociologists, perhaps rural sociologists, working in adjunct research institutes sometimes are not personally acquainted with the faculty in the sociology department at the same university. In this sense, the structural insularity which historically served to protect fledgling organizational innovations has been institutionalized, in some situations, as a compartmentalized system which tends to fragment the subject matter of the discipline and has the potential for inhibiting stimulating interaction within the professional community.

Carpetbagging

Another occasional consequence of institution-building projects has been the perception of intellectual and economic "carpetbagging." In fact, this English term has appeared in the lexicon of some studies of Latin American sociology. Many projects in diverse interest areas over the span of several decades were initiated and put into the field. These institution-building projects—which might or might not involve adjunct institutes separated from the traditional university structure—served as convenient academic outposts for faculty from the United States and other countries. A three- or four-year foreign tour provided the opportunity to gather ample data for publication in various academic outlets. Much of this publication did not occur in the host country, even though some efforts were made to translate some of the material.

The possible inclination of researchers to engage in carpetbagging is understandable given the academic pressure exerted by professional expectations in the sundry universities associated with these projects. For the faculty member from the United States, publication represents one of the major motivations for engaging in research, since a substantial record of publication is essential for promotion and tenure within the university system. For the Latin American sociologists, publication tended to be less important, or, at any rate, opportunities were less available. Consequently, the offer of joint publication, as an incentive for cooperation, tended to be less effective than other inducements. As stated above, one incentive which was in fact viewed favorably by many host country counterparts was financial support. The differing professional environments of the two academic groups, at times, probably congealed into a swap, or at least the appearance of a trade, that is, exchanging financial support for publishable data. The imagery of the faculty member from a foreign university arriving with a well-funded project and leaving with a substantial amount of data readily lends itself to a perception of carpetbagging. These perceptions can be translated into feelings of exploitation and dependency within the Latin American academic community. Perhaps the dependency theories which became popular in sociological theory struck a resonant note because of the dependency relationship experienced by the host country intellectuals. More immediately pertinent for the profession, however, is that the accusation of carpetbagging can lead to a reluctance to engage in joint academic ventures.

Scholarships

Scholarships and fellowships for study in the United States were another major incentive for cooperation with institution-building projects. But these inducements can also lend themselves to an interpretation of carpetbagging. On the surface, it is difficult to argue against the assertion that educating Third World counterparts enhances educational institutions in the Third World host country. Furthermore, educating students from developing countries as sociologists would seem to be a logical mechanism for developing the discipline of sociology by increasing the numbers of practitioners. The potential problem arises, however, in the way fellowships might be used. The use of Third World graduate students, such as Ph.D. candidates, to collect data in developing countries is an efficient, relatively inexpensive method for faculty advisers in the United States and Europe to conduct research by proxy. While there is nothing wrong with this commonly used arrangement, the power differential between a faculty adviser and a graduate student is such that there is always the potential for misunderstanding. In this type of situation, the possibility that research problems might be formulated in terms of the faculty adviser's interests and professional needs rather than those of the host country, or host institution, always exists. The manner in which these scholarships and fellowships were integrated into the institution-building process invites the criticism of carpetbagging. There is no doubt, however, that many students who received graduate education in the United States benefited from the experience, both personally and professionally. Many are now teaching in universities; many hold important posts in their respective societies.

One unforeseen consequence of the scholarship and fellowship opportunities nested within the institution-building efforts resulted from the tendency to educate a given cohort of host country students within a relatively short time span. These students, on their return home, tended to fill the limited number of positions available. Consequently, the potential job market for sociologists tended to become rather restricted in some academic markets. The lack of opportunity perceived by subsequent cohorts of students probably affected the number of new students studying for advanced graduate degrees in sociology. Several decades later, the potential for a mass retirement, or at least a large number of retirements within a limited time frame, now raises the issue of how vacant positions in sociology will be staffed in the foreseeable future. The implication is that the impact of past intervention by such development agencies as USAID and the World Bank is now progressing through the system, affecting the future staffing of sociology positions, the teaching of sociology, and, consequently, the manner in which the discipline of sociology will develop in the Latin American societies.

Funding Sources for Research

One of the most important legacies of the institution-building efforts is found in the ongoing relationship between governments and the practitioners of social science. The early institution-building efforts, which typically utilized the mechanism of external funding, have, in a sense, been replicated, serving as a model for the relationship between academia and political institutions. Today, it appears that many research projects and contracts, even if conducted in more traditional university settings, even if funded by Latin American sources, are pursued by individuals under the auspices of government agencies or other organizations. The notion that social research is a personal business opportunity, that is, an opportunity for consulting, has generally become predominant and continues to be an important idea in the thinking of many individuals. Hence, one of the driving forces for social research activity, besides a personal dedication to knowledge and an individual's curiosity, is the fact that research represents additional income. In other words, government research contracts typically pay the researcher a stipend which is in addition to remuneration received for teaching. The researchers, in general, do not substitute research activities for teaching time within the institutional setting of the university.

One of the results of this system is that governmental agencies and other funding sources have considerable control over the direction of social research conducted by intellectuals. In one sense, this close linkage allows flexibility and a rapid change of priorities in social research, based on perceived national need. This ability to respond rapidly to changing conditions should not be dismissed as inconsequential. The negative aspect of this governmental control, however, is that the definition of what constitutes a researchable problem is, or at least can be, rather biased in the sense that the perceptions and the vested interests of the government tend to be foremost. The situation is made more complex by the fact that the vested interests of a specific bureaucratic structure within the government may be the operative definition of what constitutes national interest in any given branch of the government.

An additional complicating factor within a specific bureaucracy, however, is the existence of a diversity of interests based on personal relationships and patronage. In many cases, especially in situations in which employment opportunity is limited, governmental bureaucracy has become a mechanism, perhaps a major mechanism, for distributing social status. This allocation of social status and respectability is not always based on technical proficiency or merit. Rather, family and friendship ties loom as major criteria in the selection of individuals destined for relatively lucrative bureaucratic posts. The urban, bureaucratic model is in essence similar to the traditional rural pattern of the patron, or "coronelismo." The implication is that loyalty to a particular strongman or patron is of utmost importance in these relationships. This means that the vested interests of a given clique within a specific bureaucracy could, for all practical purposes, become the definition of the national interest in the context of approving the disbursement of research funds. It is conceivable that the government, that is, the vested interests of cliques within the government bureaucracy, could just as easily inhibit timely research to meet changing national needs as they could facilitate them. Whether or not this happens depends on who is defining the national need and who has control of the research funds in any particular context.

The implication is that while the concerns of carpetbagging faculty from the United States and Europe perhaps defined, at one time, researchable issues, the structure has evolved into a system in which the interests of governmental agencies, perhaps defined in part on the basis of pork barrel politics, now influence the definition of researchable problems. In other words, the direction which the discipline of sociology takes in terms of research is determined to a large extent by factors external to the theoretical framework of the discipline itself. The result is that the research enterprise tends to be rather conservative, addressing problems defined by a political process, rather than by theoretical developments.

The fact that research is potentially controlled by cliques which have gained a measure of political control, perhaps momentarily, has some long-term implications. For example, the long-term development of a social research program is difficult under these circumstances. Furthermore, creative, innovative ideas might not be recognized nor appreciated as such by those in the bureaucratic establishment who are interested in short-term political gain. In other words, when proposals are presented for funding, the standards used to judge them will probably have strong political overtones.

In practical terms, these circumstances might actually be beneficial in the debate over the relevance of sociology, providing a type of automatic legitimization of the research conducted by the discipline. This is not a small benefit in situations in which sociology has been attacked from time to time as subversive and anti-establishment. Nevertheless, the fact that research is viewed as an adjunct to the discipline under the paid control of either the government or other funding agencies has profound implications for the profession.

INSTITUTIONAL INFLUENCES

Libraries and Publication Outlets

Another aspect of the academic system which affects the development of sociology is the constraint imposed by an inadequate library system, which translates into a paucity of publication opportunities. The traditional organization of academia emphasizes the libraries of individual scholars rather than those of institutions. University libraries are often inadequate and poorly funded, sometimes smaller in size and poorer in quality than the private collections of faculty. This means that structurally there is a limited market for academic production. For example, the market for professional journals is limited to private scholars who can afford to pay for them and a few libraries which have adequate public funding. Even when publicly funded libraries exist, funding is generally so low that a wide selection of current journals and recent books cannot be purchased. These same conditions contribute to the lack of international journals and books housed in university libraries, which means that it is difficult for Latin American professionals to remain current with developments in sociology in other parts of the world. Perhaps this lack of access to mainstream publications serves to reinforce the tendency of some Latin American sociologists to become preoccupied with classical theory, including Marxist theory. In small part, classical sociology might be attractive because a scholar can invest in a limited number of classical works which then require a substantial investment of time in terms of in-depth study in order to master the material—material which will be subject to limited revision over time.

The lack of publishing opportunities, however, is not necessarily perceived by Latin American sociologists to be a serious weakness in the structure. The partial separation of the teaching of academic subject matter and the research function, especially "applied" research, from salary considerations eliminates one of the cornerstones of sociology as practiced in the United States. Typically, publishing is not a major avenue to promotion or salary increments in the university. In terms of research activities, faculty are paid by an agency to conduct research and to write a research report describing the results. This report might not receive wide distribution even in the existing library system and might be limited to the official use of the agency which has provided the funds for the research. In short, the sociologist in academia in Latin America typically has limited need and limited opportunity to publish.

The implication is that the difficulty of finding an outlet for publication imposes a structural limitation on the motivation to publish. The result is that financial considerations tend to assume a greater importance for the individual in the decision to engage in research. Another facet of the same issue is that the difficulty of gaining access to published material available in the library system imposes economically determined parameters on the content of the ideas used in the research which is actually conducted. These forces tend to be invisible to the casual observer, but they nevertheless influence the quality of scholarly activity.

Research Support Systems

Another factor affecting the development of the discipline is that the faculty involved in research in this system typically do not have enough time to do the work. Complaints of this nature are frequent. The problem is not a lack of effort on the part of intellectuals; Latin American sociologists often have workdays which extend beyond the norms applied to their North American counterparts. However, as stated above, the university system in Latin America typically does not make provisions for buying a block of research time from the portion of time dedicated to teaching. Research activity essentially amounts to an overload, which means that the pressure for time becomes a crucial factor affecting both the way sociology is taught in the classroom and the way sociological research is conducted in the field. Many universities do not have the type of elaborate support system for research which is found in the United States or Europe. Finding interviewers, data-processing facilities, software, and logistical support can become time-consuming, as well as expensive. Fortunately, since research tends to be legitimized by its affiliation with governmental agencies, it is often possible to improvise support, such as transportation or interviewers, with the help of various governmental agencies external to the university. The fact remains, however, that in many cases, there is no structural location where trained personnel and equipment can be retained; typically, each project must re-create every aspect of the endeavor. Consequently, the efficient use of time can be a constraint in sociological research projects, especially since social research in Latin America typically entails extensive fieldwork. For example, technological innovations such as mail questionnaires or telephone interviews are not easily utilized.

Since research is usually defined as outside of the university's main area of interest, there is limited motivation on the part of the university to maintain a support system dedicated to providing the services needed in a large research project. A research institute functioning as an adjunct to the university, if it existed, could provide these services, but with increasing competition for funds, with more and more faculty receiving graduate degrees in a wide range of disciplines abroad, all research is not channeled through research institutes. In fact, research activities have expanded to the point that they have become widely diffused throughout the governmental and university systems which have linkages with international funding agencies.

Dual Career Patterns

As stated above, the lack of a well-organized institutional locus for computers, secretarial assistance, interviewers, and so forth, is a constraint linked to the lack of financial resources channeled to the university system. In part, the lack of financial resources is due to the fact that national economies are not especially robust. Since universities have little interest in providing support services for faculty pursuing part-time employment, the result is that sociological research is hampered. In order to overcome the constraints imposed by weak economic systems, intellectuals often accept part-time, or temporary, positions with governmental agencies. Individuals move back and forth between the public sector and academic institutions with relative ease, sometimes holding two positions at the same time. These blurred boundaries probably make sense, however, in countries which might have a relatively small core of educated individuals available. Trained and educated people tend to be a scarce commodity.

The exchange of personnel between government and academia means that universities sometimes provide income and social position for the political opposition, that is, for those who lose in the patronage shuffle as one political group gains power and ousts the incumbents, either through the electoral process or through a coup. This dual career pattern provides a degree of security as individuals wait for the next change of political power when the new incumbents will again draw from their friends on the university faculty to staff the new administration.

University Faculty: An Anti-Establishment Force

By serving as a haven for those who momentarily might be political outsiders, the university tends to become a source of political and social criticism. Perhaps more accurately, social criticism tends to become concentrated in the social science departments of universities. This situation is probably one of the factors which contribute to the general perception that the universities in Latin America are subversive, anti-establishment institutions and that the social science departments are especially prone to engage in this tendency. Structural influences dictate that the universities will probably contain a relatively large percentage of individuals critical of whatever government is in power. In most cases, participants in the process understand the informal rules of the game and are prepared to accommodate some degree of conflict and criticism, of rhetorical posturing. It is to the self-interest of any political appointee to have a place to go if future changes in political power require it.

The tolerance of criticism has limits, however. If the political system becomes extremely authoritarian, then a purge of political foes in the faculty of the university can occur. For example, a detention center reportedly established on one university campus meant that students and faculty moving from one class to another heard the screams of tortured colleagues emanating from the building. Given the inclination of the social scientist to describe, and perhaps criticize, prevailing social conditions, given the possibility that political ambition might lurk behind the criticism, it is understandable that sociologists in particular have been viewed with suspicion by some of the more authoritarian governments. These conditions have affected the profession of sociology in the past and currently influence practitioners in various countries. For example, after the military took control of the government in Brazil, the profession of sociologist was literally eliminated as an official occupational designation used on national identity cards.

Currently, faculty dissatisfaction is especially focused on salary issues. Salaries of faculty tend to be determined by a political process. University faculty are typically organized into unions or have strong professional lobbies which function to protect the economic interests of both active and retired faculty. Since administrators in Latin American universities, including the rectors of institutions, are often elected, the university community tends to exhibit substantial solidarity, which means that universities can become politicized. Salary complaints are perennial. Strikes are a common weapon used by university faculty to enforce salary demands. For example, in 1991, Brazilian university faculty reportedly engaged in a national strike which lasted for 105 days. The result of these recurring strikes is that teaching and research have been hampered.

SOCIAL CHANGE

The Middle-Class Expansion

The number of faculty at the national level has expanded substantially in the last few decades. In part, this expansion is due to the intervention of development activities, which involve assistance programs not only focusing on educational institutions but also on other areas outside the universities. These multipronged efforts helped to stimulate and enhance the general economy. To some extent, the containment strategy aimed at Marxism in Latin America was presumably based on the notion of building a middle class which would tend to be democratic and conservative, acting as a brake on social movements on both the ultra left and the ultra right. The creation of this middle class was the result of concerted efforts by governments, development agencies, and other financial institutions. The role of the middle class was not the same in all Latin American countries, however.[5] A plausible hypothesis is that a substantial portion of the middle class created in the developing nations of Latin America was built on the basis of credit, that is, international development loans or investment.

The strategy to stimulate the development of a middle class at first appeared to be viable. In the past few years, there has been considerable discussion in the international development community concerning economic miracles perceived to be looming on the southern horizon. But the ideas began to falter with the onset of recent international economic problems. Repayment of debts became difficult. Inflation became rampant. One result was that currencies were devalued—sometimes by as much as a factor of a million within the span of a decade or two.

Latin American colleagues teaching at universities report that the number of sociologists expanded along with the other segments of the middle class. But as economic conditions deteriorated, the newly developed middle class found it increasingly difficult to maintain a middle-class standard of living. In contrast, the social elites were usually able to protect their wealth and privilege during this period. Since the elites were not inclined to share their privileges, and since the middle class began to exert economic pressure through strikes to maintain their standard of living, one of the options open to the system was to extract even more from the lower socioeconomic classes. It could be argued that the creation of the middle class, largely through credit, perhaps amplified the problems of the poor, though the lower socioeconomic class might not understand the obscured connection. The result was that the downwardly mobile social scientists, as members of the strained middle class, as individuals who were already prone to be critical of the system, had a natural ally (or audience) in the lower socioeconomic class, which was receptive to theories proposing the redistribution of wealth and property. In short, social factors interacted with the discipline of sociology, which probably contributed to some extent to the popularity and dissemination of Marxism, neo-Marxism, and dependency theories.

The Institutionalization of Violence

Diverse cultural groups, such as the Portuguese, Spanish, Germans, Italians, Japanese, and indigenous Indian, are prominent in the social environment. In addition, several countries in Latin America have a legacy of slavery which typically depended on African populations. These immi-grants were involved in the exploitation of the agricultural and mineral riches of this vast area—whether peasant families from Europe or elites bent on establishing slavery—and produced a value system oriented to-ward conquest. The worldview which emerged from the frontier experi-ence resulted in a set of norms which involved an acceptance of authoritarianism, exploitation, and a degree of racial prejudice. This ten-dency, at least at the local level, found expression in the "Coronelismo" syndrome and in the institution of "patron" in many Latin nations. In essence, the local strongman has been a prominent fixture of local com-munity life and lingers in both the traditions of the rural communities and in more recent urban society. This cultural heritage tends to produce a social system which blends resourceful individualists and loyal followers into communities which have little desire or need for linkages with the larger society.

One predictable result of the struggle to dominate and subdue natural and social frontiers is the development of a violent element in the cultures of the region, which has found expression through various avenues, such as political revolution, banditry, crime, police assassination squads (the death squads), and the unwillingness of the individual citizen to relinquish the option of personally settling a dispute through violent means. For ex-ample, juries have repeatedly exonerated individuals in murder cases in-volving husbands who have killed wives and lovers. In spite of legal directives to the contrary, the populace tends to feel that a man has a personal right to defend his honor—with violence, if necessary. The pos-session of firearms by private individuals is widespread in some parts of Latin America and probably could not be abolished without traumatic social results. A case in point is the military regime which was established after the coup in Brazil. The military government felt that it was neither necessary nor wise to abolish private ownership of firearms.

Understandably, under these circumstances, intellectuals continue to ponder the question of how nations can be built on a foundation of self-sufficient, diverse communities containing a substantial number of individ-uals willing to resort to culturally condoned violence. In this context, concerns with national solidarity and self-definition are pragmatic con-cerns, not esoteric, academic exercises. Individualism and independence, perhaps partially held in check by authoritarian social structure, are not always useful in the process of nation building. For that reason, the social thinkers who engage in ethnic studies and the novelists who explore the intricate concept of national culture cannot be considered a residue from the past and relegated to a remote, violent historical period. Many of the old, familiar cultural currents still operate in many parts of the region and still dictate intellectual and academic concerns. For example, in recent years, there has been considerable discussion in the mass media and among sociologists regarding the meaning of an increase in lynchings and vigilantism. The perpetrators of lynching or assassination are not simply concentrated in the agencies of repression supported by political establishments. Recently, the perpetrators of this type of violence have been found in the general populace, where citizens in a community sometimes prefer to lynch a person caught in a criminal act than to allow local police to take the criminal into custody. Reportedly, businessmen sometime hire off-duty police to assassinate groups of abandoned children and juveniles who have formed street gangs and who are perceived as a social problem. In essence, the old, authoritarian values of an elitist society, incubated in conquest and exploitation, which at one time helped to organize these societies, have emerged in mass culture contributing to a degree of instability. Sociological research suggests that the trust and confidence necessary for building a society have become a relevant issue.

The authoritarian environment on the continent has influenced the entire range of social thought. From time to time, the social sciences were viewed as stimulating radicalism, and when criticism of the elites and the mass poverty became too strident, authority was sometimes used to stifle sources of dissent—including sociology. The implication is that sociology essentially developed in a hostile and violent environment. At times, even the survival of the discipline was questionable. The central issue is the strategy which sociology might employ. The situation confronting the discipline offers two basic options: (1) sociologists can emphasize a very applied, social engineering approach and hope to avoid confrontation, or (2) they can become even more radical and combative in the face of social problems and violent opposition.

Land Tenure and Agrarian Reform

Population control and economic development are perceived as major areas of concern by the establishment. On the surface, these goals are relatively easy for the conservative branch of sociology to adopt. But the consequences of these social processes energize the more radical branch of sociology as well. Population increase intensifies rural poverty. Migration of surplus population to urban areas poses substantial social problems and exerts pressure on the political system, sparking both organized and unorganized violence in many quarters. While some sociologists worked within the system to stimulate economic development, others questioned the system itself. Hence the power structures of society, their vested interests and values, became foci of study for the more radical branch of sociology, irritating influential elites.

Nevertheless, the more conservative branch of sociology promised to help alleviate urban social problems complicated by excess population and the growth of slums. Authorities attempted to stabilize rural populations by improving the lives of those most likely to migrate, that is, the small landholder or the landless workers. Reaching the "poorest of the poor" became a catchphrase within the international development community. Since the rural poor became a target population, rural institutions became important areas for research. Consequently, research in rural sociology expanded substantially as policy makers, both in Latin America and the United States, looked to rural sociology to make a contribution to the improvement of rural life in Latin America as it had done in the United States during the great economic depression of the 1930s. Various institution-building endeavors were launched which were similar to strategies used in the United States in the 1930s and 1940s. For example, resources were channeled into an extension system which worked to improve farm productivity through the diffusion of innovations.

The substantial number of publications related to these activities indicates that these endeavors were well funded and successful to varying degrees, depending upon the country and the specific project. The rural sociologists of the post–World War II era told stories of making their first trips into the interior using jeeps and sometimes other, more flamboyant means of transportation. At professional meetings, these pioneer sociologists sometimes mused over the extensive changes which had occurred, that is, the increased modernization which they had observed. Some of the rural regions of Latin America were transformed into prototypes of mechanized agriculture found in the United States, Canada, and Europe.

The issue of agrarian reform, that is, providing rural families with enough land to create an economically viable farming unit, remained attractive politically and socially as mass participation in the political process at the national level increased. The problem was that in many parts of Latin America, ownership of land was concentrated in the hands of a few individuals or families, and the traditional power base was synonymous with the landed rural families. These large landholdings, from a practical point of view, represented the only immediate source of land for the landless, with the exception of undeveloped lands or frontier areas.

As an alternative to agrarian reform, some frontier areas were made more available. The Amazon Basin was, for a time, viewed as a panacea for the problems of poverty related to population expansion. Roads were built, typically using development loans, to open some of the inaccessible areas. In the process, however, rural elites were able to gain control of sizable tracts of the Amazonian land and a substantial amount of the resources. Consequently, many aspects of the old social patterns were perpetuated rather than alleviated.

The promise of the frontier was elusive and held substantial ecological dangers. As a result, large landholdings again came under scrutiny and pressure in many parts of the continent. Action was sometimes official, in the form of formal programs which divided large estates into smaller units and made them available to peasants, though not always through direct ownership. Sometimes the pressure was unofficial, in the form of illegal occupation of land by peasants. Upon occasion, these movements were accompanied by violence and murder. More recently, some of these government programs have moved toward complete privatization, that is, creating a system which is based on an open market.

Sociologists tended to serve those who formulated social policy in the sense that land tenure and agrarian reform became accepted topics for research. The notion was that social science might help in organizing these programs to make them work more efficiently. In other words, the role of the social scientist was typically viewed by government as that of social engineer. At the same time, an intellectual countercurrent developed which tended to be Marxist in form. The Marxist branch of sociology gave the ideological justification and the blueprints for action against the establishment when progress in the alleviation of social problems slowed or became nonexistent. Typically, this type of sociology was not sanctioned by those holding power.

Industrial Development

The flow of migrants is especially strong from the impoverished sections of the countryside to the more industrialized, urban areas. In most cases, aid programs and attempts at agrarian reform have not been able to stem the flow of migration. Modification of policy occurs periodically. The effort to raise the standard of living in rural areas has diminished somewhat in favor of efforts aimed at absorbing the excess rural population. This policy urges such action as the development of industries at the source of migration flows and at strategic points along the channel of migration. The intent is to give migrants an early option and thereby entice them to stop and settle before they have made the trek to the large cities.

Again, sociology tended to incorporate these subjects into its domain. For a time, the topic of industrialization served as a magnet for research funds within the discipline. The notion of modernization became popular, in terms of identifying both the factors which caused modernity as well as its impact upon society.

Un-developing Development

One of the more recent trends is the use of sociologists to inhibit some types of socioeconomic development. The use of sociologists to stop development and the exploitation of natural resources marks a change in the traditional role of the social scientist. For example, opening the frontier and exploiting unused land, including settlement in the huge Amazon Basin, became less attractive due to ecological concerns. The negative aspects of stimulating socioeconomic development in such ecosystems as the Amazon have provoked negative responses from some segments of the international community; official policy was modified several times, vacillating as the political climate changed. But in spite of the attempts of national authority to control the penetration of frontier areas, goldminers, farmers, woodcutters, and others, individually or in small groups, continue to circumvent controls. Pushing the frontier into such areas as the Amazon has often been violent. The flow of motivated entrepreneurs into the region who have little regard for national policy or legal institutions is proving to be a difficult force to manage. Further complicating the process, a few individuals, often large landowners, have become powerful in the affairs of these communities, typically at the expense of the workers, the landless, or the indigenous population. These developments have defined current problems for scientific research. For example, there were a number of Fulbright Fellowships available to sociologists to study land tenure and ecological issues in the Amazon in recent announcements.

Social scientists are encouraged and funded to engage in research which might show how these economic activities could be inhibited. As a consequence, social scientists are again turning their attention to different types of land reform, receiving substantial amounts of research funds, but also risking the alienation of powerful elites in the process. Land tenure, the environment, community studies, and aboriginal studies will presumably continue to be emphasized as topics for sociological research for some time to come.

CONCLUSION: A NEW PHASE OF SOCIOLOGICAL DEVELOPMENT

Clearly, changes in the environment of the discipline of sociology have had an impact on the way practitioners pursue their work. For example, Alfonso Trujillo Ferrari has classified the development of sociology in Brazil into three stages: the pre-1928 stage, the 1929–1964 stage, and the post-1964 stage, that is, the post-right-wing coup d'état.[6] This author suggests that these time periods correspond to three different social eras which produced three stages in the development of sociology. The study identifies the first as being concerned with the definition of national culture. The second phase reflected the heavy bourgeois dominance during and after World War II. The third phase began in Brazil with the military coup in 1964.

The issues raised by the author probably are not unique to Brazil, though the specific details and the time references would, perhaps, vary from country to country. More important, the addition of a new, fourth phase might be required with the recent decline of Russian power and the discrediting of Marxist dogma. As stated above, Marxism and dependency theory served as ideological foundations for protest movements and anti-establishment activities throughout the region. But changing world conditions now create the possibility that these interpretations will lose much of their credibility in Latin America or, at the very least, will be scrutinized more carefully in terms of contributions to viable sociological theory.

Presumably, the discontent arising from such factors as continuing social inequalities will be expressed in terms of different, redefined ideological symbols. Marxist-oriented theory presented an explanation for internal social problems, an interpretation of international inequality, and a plan of action. With the decline of the Soviet Union, the political environment, which has had a profound effect on the development of sociology in one form or another in most of the countries of Latin America, has changed abruptly. This challenge to Marxist theories comes not from research conducted within the discipline, but from external world events. Nevertheless, this development leaves a void within sociological theory which must be filled in some fashion. To complicate the problem of sociological theory in Latin America even further, the new plan, the new solution offered by the former Soviet Union, is to embrace a free market, capitalistic economy. This suggestion presumably leaves social thinkers in Latin America in a quandary. What the Soviet Union is now embracing as social policy, the Latin American countries have had in place for some time. The economies in Latin America, which in general are based on some version of capitalism, have not had a history of working exceptionally well. It is, in part, the unimpressive performance of the international capitalist system and the perception of exploitive relationships which legitimized the type of arguments found in Marxist theory in the first place. The experience of Latin American countries, which includes an inflation factor of as much as a million within a twenty-year period, does not produce a high degree of confidence in the social theories now embraced as a panacea by the Soviet nations.

In the past, the threat posed internally by leftist social movements and externally by some countries attempting to export Marxist revolution served as a stimulus and, more importantly, as a justification for various right-wing, repressive political measures. If there is no longer a communist threat, any right-wing, repressive activities against the poor will require a new rationale. On the other hand, since the Soviets are espousing a free market system, leftist movements directed against the establishment in Latin America suffer from ideological abandonment. Since international Marxism has lost much of its potency as a symbol, social relationships of inequality must presumably be recast in terms of revised social theories and ideologies. In other words, the frame of references used by both the left and the right will undoubtedly be ripe for redefinition. Resistance to the establishment, the status quo, will require a new ideological foundation; however, the imposition of repressive, authoritarian regimes designed to protect the vested interests of the elites will also require a new justification. In the years to come, many of these ideological battles will be fought in the social sciences, especially sociology. In the end, both the conservative and the radical branches of sociology might suffer since both could lose their sponsorship.

From time to time, there were attempts to purge critical social thinkers and/or supporters of Marxist theory from the ranks of sociology. These attempts at repression were successful to some degree; thousands of individuals lost their lives, especially during and after political revolutions. One of the lessons learned, however, is that sociological thought and theory are not the exclusive domain of sociologists. Ideas about society continued to percolate through the consciousness of various groups, ideas which were presumably determined by the social dynamics operating in a particular society.[7] One of the most notable intellectual developments was the body of ideas found in liberation theology. The intellectual heritage of liberation theology is complex, but many of the ideas found there have counterparts in sociological theory.[8] The rationale for the resistance of the poor—perhaps even violent resistance—to the powerful social elites was formulated in terms of religious symbols. In some cases, religious leaders emerged as leading social thinkers and activists.

The implications of these converging trends are not entirely clear. Social forces have a profound effect on thought, but sociological thought is not limited to those who label themselves as sociologists. There is a distinction between the content of social thought and the profession of sociology. In the intellectual vacuum that exists now that the Soviet system has grown weaker, the profession of sociology might well lose some of its vitality, perhaps even experience some confusion. But this does not mean that sociological thought will diminish. The new ideological symbols used to represent these old struggles and social forces might become more religious in nature if the profession of sociology is either absorbed into the political system or repressed. In essence, due to changes in social structure in Latin America, viable social thought could find a home in institutions other than sociology, since a substantial portion of the current structure of Latin American sociology seems to be a legacy of post–World War II containment policy.

NOTES

1. Octavio Ianni, "Sociology in Latin America," in *Handbook of Contemporary Developments in World Sociology,* eds. Raj P. Mohan and Don Martindale (Westport, Conn.: Greenwood Press, 1975).

2. David O. Hansen, Ivo Schneider, and Vincent de Paul Vitor, "Rural Sociology in Brazil—Institutional Growth (1965–1977)," *International Review of Modern Sociology* 9,1 (Jan.–June 1979), 31–48.

3. Thomas S. Kuhn, *The Structure of Scientific Revolutions* (Chicago: University of Chicago Press, 1970).

4. James Petras, "The Metamorphosis of Latin America's Intellectuals," *International Journal of Contemporary Sociology* 28, 3–4 (1991), 161–70.

5. Fernando Henrique Cardoso and Enzo Faletto, "Development and Social Change: The Political Role of Middle Classes," in *Dependency and Development in Latin America* (Berkeley: University of California Press, 1979).

6. Alfonso Trujillo Ferrari, "A Expansao da Sociologia no Brasil," *Revista Brasileira de Sociologia* 6, 1–2 (Jan.–Dec. 1980–81), 3–22.

7. Howard S. Becker, "Social Theory in Brazil," *Sociological Theory* 10,1 (Spring 1992), 1–5.

8. Thomas D. Hanks, *God So Loved the Third World* (New York: Orbis Books, 1983).

13

Sociology's Academic Development as Reflected in Journal Debates

Graham C. Kinloch

The academic development of any discipline may be measured by demographic indices such as numbers of college departments, faculty, majors, courses, graduates, professional associations, publishing outlets, and research grants.[1] Other approaches focus on major authors, orientations, types of theory, models, or paradigms over time.

A more dynamic perspective, perhaps, concentrates on the discipline's major debates over time, regarding academic institutionalization as a *process*. Mindful of Kuhn's admonition concerning the significance of inexplicable results and their attempted removal in the development of science (Kuhn, 1970), the discussion to follow presents an analysis of the major topics and criteria of debate published in the *American Journal of Sociology* and *American Sociological Review* from the early 1900s through the 1980s. These dialogues are considered useful indices of changing bodies of ideas (Kuhn, 1970) regarding *both* theory and methodology as the discipline is established and subject to ongoing professionalization. Understanding what academics argue about and the criteria they use provides useful insight into sociology's foundation and changing development. These processes are central to appreciating trends in its current conceptual frameworks.

For purposes of this analysis, all debates and controversies contained in the *American Journal of Sociology* and *American Sociological Review* from the beginning of publication through 1989 were selected for analysis. Each involved a paper or issue critique and the author's response as published in the Letters to the Editor or Debates and Commentary sections. These particular journals were selected since they represent the major publishing outlets in American professional sociology rather than the more regional

Table 13.1
Analytical Categories

Debate Topics	Examples
Professional concerns	Sociology and other sciences, teaching
Theory	Explanatory factors, group fallacy, instincts
Methods	Survey methods
Statistics	Scatter, correlations
Family	Family cycles, sex lives, marital age, dating
Military	Writers' War Board, military service
Science	Power of science
Religion	Protestant Ethic
Education	Educational inbreeding
Industry	Caste and class, managerial succession
Politics	Political morality, political attitudes
Stratification	Status, socioeconomic indices, theories
Demography	Birth rate, cities, urban correlates
Social psychology	Culture and personality, morale, needs, anomie
Race relations	Racial friction, race relations, riots
Social problems	Deviance, crime, delinquency
Social change	Modernization, world economy
Debate Criteria	
Conceptualization	Literature citation, terminology, definitions
Explanation	Obsolete theory, terms, justification
Interpretation	Misinterpretation, moral judgments
Data	Observations, sample, data quality
Measurement	Validity, estimation, operational problems
Analysis	Statistical problems, statistical abuse
Other	Agreement, space limitations, small point

concerns of other publications (e.g., *Social Forces, Pacific Sociological Review, Sociological Quarterly*). Excluded also were book reviews, unanswered critiques, and more recent journals such as *Footnotes, The American Sociologist,* and *Contemporary Sociology,* since these tend to be highly specialized or limited to recent decades.

Each commentary or debate was examined for the topic at issue, critique of that question, and the author's response. This produced a total of 503 debates, starting in 1902 and ending in 1989. These were analyzed by publication decade and classified into major topics, critiques, and responses. Analytical categories were developed inductively from the data and are summarized in Table 13.1. It can be seen that major debate topics consisted of professional matters, theoretical issues, methodological problems, statistical questions, and institutional concerns relating to the family, military, science, religion, education, industry, and political sociology. Stratification and demographic controversies were debated also, along with social psychological problems, race relations, deviance and social problems, and social change. Critiques, on the other hand, focused on conceptual issues, problems of explanation, and interpretation. Methodological critiques were also raised concerning data problems, measurement issues, and data analysis complications. Similar categories were used to classify critique responses and consisted of conceptual defenses, explanatory issues, interpretive reactions, methodological rejoinders, measurement problems, and defenses of the data analysis. The "other" category was reserved for critiques and responses that did not fall into any of the above divisions. These topics, critiques, and responses were analyzed by publication decade.

Using such information, it is possible to examine major debate topics over time, providing insight into the discipline's professional development. It is important to emphasize that such data are subject to several limitations: only two journals are used as sources, disagreements presented in journal articles are not analyzed, critiques without responses are omitted, as are book review controversies, while some time periods contain very little data. Providing these restrictions are kept in mind, it appears reasonable to view these debates as useful indices of changing perspectives.

Table 13.2 presents the major topics of debate for each of the decades with available data. The results show decidedly that professional and theoretical matters figure prominently during the 1900s through the 1930s, moving to a concern with social problems, specifically deviance, during that decade. Military issues come to the fore during the 1940s, along with social psychological matters. Stratification and social psychological concerns prevail during the 1950s, while the following decade highlights major debates over social problems, social psychological and theoretical issues. The 1970s reveal a continuing interest in theoretical matters as well as social problems and social psychological concerns. Finally, the 1980s reveal major controversies over methodological and theoretical matters, as well as contemporary stratification and social problems.

Turning to the specific issues involved in these trends, major controversies move from a concern with establishing and teaching sociology, along with appropriate types of explanation, through an interest in delinquency, crime, race relations in the army, the measurement, types, and effects of stratification, anomie, alienation, prejudice, and mental illness, to the interpretation of theorists, multivariate models, and exchange theory. More recent disputes revolve around mental illness, delinquency, poverty, crime, violence, capital punishment, mobility models, measurement issues, and theoretical arguments over Mead, sociocultural evolution, and sociobiology. From these trends it is evident that once sociology was professionally established, it responded to major social problems in a changing social

Table 13.2
Major Debate Topics over Time

YEARS:	1905-09 %	1910-14 %	1920's %	1930's %	1940's %	1950's %	1960's %	1970's %	1980's %
TOPICS:									
Professional Concerns	30.0	50.0	0.0	0.0	16.6	0.0	2.6	0.5	1.5
Theory	15.0	12.5	66.6	18.7	5.5	6.1	10.2	11.8	14.3
Methods	0.0	12.5	0.0	18.7	0.0	6.1	9.0	5.1	15.8
Statistics	0.0	0.0	33.3	6.2	0.0	12.1	5.1	8.8	0.0
Family	15.0	0.0	0.0	12.5	11.1	12.1	1.3	2.1	3.7
Military	0.0	0.0	0.0	0.0	22.2	3.0	0.0	3.6	0.7
Science	0.0	0.0	0.0	0.0	11.1	0.0	0.0	2.6	0.0
Religion	5.0	0.0	0.0	0.0	0.0	0.0	2.6	3.1	3.0
Education	0.0	0.0	0.0	0.0	0.0	0.0	5.1	3.1	2.2
Industry	0.0	0.0	0.0	12.5	0.0	0.0	5.1	4.1	9.0
Politics	0.0	12.5	0.0	0.0	0.0	9.1	5.1	4.1	9.0
Stratification	10.0	0.0	0.0	0.0	5.5	21.2	9.0	7.2	11.3
Demography	10.0	0.0	0.0	6.2	5.5	9.1	3.8	5.7	3.0
Social Psychology	0.0	0.0	0.0	0.0	22.2	15.1	17.9	11.8	4.5
Race Relations	5.0	0.0	0.0	0.0	0.0	0.0	3.8	8.8	2.2
Social Problems	0.0	0.0	0.0	25.0	0.0	3.0	15.4	12.4	15.8
Social Change	10.0	12.5	0.0	0.0	0.0	3.0	3.8	5.1	3.7
N:	20	8	3	16	18	33	78	194	133

environment undergoing economic depression, war, postwar booms, social problems, and spectacular scientific developments that had a major impact on the profession's research methods. The dynamics of the social context are reflected in the discipline's continuing disagreements.

Table 13.3 presents the major critique and response criteria involved in these debates. Several trends are evident. During the 1900s and 1910s matters of explanation, interpretation, and conceptualization are paramount. The 1920s, however, while lacking in data, disclose similar concerns but an emerging interest in methodological issues also. A focus on theoretical matters continues into the next decade but with increasing evidence of measurement and analysis interests also. Both interpretation and empirical concerns prevail during the 1940s while the next decade reveals a major increase in methodological critiques and responses in the "other" category. Empirical concerns rule the 1960s—a trend continued into the 1970s but with a renewed interest in theoretical matters. Finally, the 1980s highlight criticisms regarding matters of interpretation and analysis in particular, with measurement, explanation, and data issues raised somewhat less often. Responses, on the other hand, display a major emphasis on the critics' perceived misunderstanding, misrepresentation, or misinterpretation of the authors' articles and reaffirmation of their studies' original conclusions. Principally, then, these data indicate an overall decline in theoretical controversy and increase in methodological concerns, while problems of explanation, interpretation, measurement, and analysis remain stable. Discourse generally moves from controversy over what to include in sociological explanation, through discussions of measurement, statistical, and operational problems, to empirical pragmatism (such as data availability) and reaffirmation of one's own conclusions based on the perceived misinterpretation of critics.

Qualitative changes in these debates are illustrated in Table 13.4. As can be seen, controversy begins in 1905 over professional matters such as the position of sociology in relation to the other social sciences, pedagogical aspects of the discipline in the college context, factors behind social conflict, and the complex relationship between ideas and beliefs. Critiques indicate a concern with theoretical matters such as the scope of the discipline and studies using psychic phenomena to explain sociological situations. Responses include a stress on the relevance of historical data, the importance of fieldwork exposure, and a general accent on making sociology as scientific as possible.

The 1910s indicate a continuing concern with professional issues such as teaching matters, theoretical discussions regarding explanation difficulties, methodological questions such as social surveys, and political interests relating to reformism. Critics raise problems relating to loose conceptualizations and lack of scientific explanations, while authors respond that their theories are scientific and that psychic factors are important to an understanding of human behavior.

Table 13.3
Major Debate Criteria over Time

YEARS:	1905-09		1910-14		1920's		1930's		1940's		1950's		1960's		1970's		1980's	
	%		%		%		%		%		%		%		%		%	
	C*	R**	C	R	C	R	C	R	C	R	C	R	C	R	C	R	C	R
CRITERIA																		
Conceptualization	10.0	3.7	44.4	50.0	0.0	0.0	0.0	0.0	9.5	5.3	20.9	15.4	11.0	14.8	8.0	4.0	7.9	6.0
Explanation	30.0	25.9	11.1	25.0	66.6	50.0	33.3	10.5	4.8	5.3	13.9	10.2	18.7	11.1	17.4	23.6	17.7	10.5
Interpretation	40.0	33.3	33.3	25.0	0.0	0.0	23.8	36.8	28.6	42.1	2.3	15.4	9.9	16.0	18.3	27.1	21.3	53.4
Data	10.0	7.4	0.0	0.0	0.0	0.0	4.8	5.3	14.3	10.5	9.3	2.6	9.9	4.9	15.5	11.0	15.2	11.3
Measurement	0.0	7.4	11.1	0.0	33.3	25.0	19.0	15.8	19.0	10.5	18.6	12.8	26.4	17.3	18.3	10.6	17.7	9.0
Analysis	10.0	18.5	0.0	0.0	0.0	25.0	19.0	26.3	14.3	15.8	34.9	15.4	24.1	29.6	22.5	21.1	20.1	9.8
Other	0.0	3.7	0.0	0.0	0.0	0.0	0.0	5.3	9.5	10.5	0.0	28.2	0.0	6.2	0.0	2.5	0.0	0.0
N:	20	27	9	8	3	4	21	19	21	19	43	39	91	81	213	199	164	133

* C = critique
**R = response

Table 13.4
Major Debate Topics and Criteria over Time

YEARS	DEBATE TOPICS	DEBATE CRITERIA
1905-1909	sociology & other sciences, teaching sociology social conflict, value contradictions	scope of sociology, psychic factors* historical data, fieldwork, science**
1910-1914	teaching sociology, social forces, surveys political reform	conceptualization, scientific explanation* scientific theory, psychic factors**
1920's	group fallacy, social psychology, instincts statistical problems, standard deviation	obsolete theory, confused terms, statistical measurement* scientific sociology, cultural factors, statistical scatter**
1930's	measurement in sociology, statistical significance, psychological elements, Lombrosia, methods, strat, social problems	false premises, statistical problems, historical data* misrepresentation, scientific measurement, cultural factors statistical, scientific measurement**
1940's	Writers' War Board, status measurement morale, social psych methods, army race relations, military service, science and power, family cycle	interpretation, methods, measures, objectivity, measurement* scientific knowledge/support, misinterpretation, data availability**
1950's	marital age, dating, stratification culture lage, social psychological issues political attitudes	literature, terminology, validity, ordering, assumptions* validity, misinterpretation, statistical problems, other support**
1960'S	education, stratification, values, demography anomie, social problems, theoretical, methodological, demographic, social psychological issues	measurement, analysis, theory, method/statistical problems* support, data availability, own aims, other support**

Table 13.4 (*continued*)

1970's	theory, social psychology, racial issues social problems, theor/stat interpretation, social problems, social change	interp., logic, methods, inference, logic, data, models* misinterp, empirical support, data support**
1980's	crime, violence, capital punishment, economic inequality, mobility models, measurement, Mead, sociocultural evolution sociobiology	understanding, interpretation, stat/data/explanation probs.* misunderstand, misinterp, irrelev, confused, own logic/data**

* = critique   ** = response

The 1920s display a continuing concern with explanatory problems and the use of instincts by social psychologists to account for behavior. Statistical objections to the use of standard deviations and arguments over the shape of statistical scatter are also raised. Critiques underline obsolete theory and obscure terms, while responders see environment and culture as more important than biological factors and emphasize the need to make sociology more scientific. While issues during this period are particularly scarce, the data indicate the beginnings of a shift from predominantly theoretical and professional concerns toward the more statistical.

The next decade brings increased concern with methodological and statistical questions, including measurement and statistical significance problems involved in sociological research. More specific topics include juvenile delinquency and other types of deviance. Some argue about psychological elements involved in sociological explanation, others raise the issue of the Lombrosian myth, with additional topics including the problems of caste and class in American industry, juvenile delinquency in the family, and social variables behind crime. Critics focus on false premises, statistical problems implicit in the analysis of ecological areas, the relationship between biological and sociocultural elements in sociological explanation, and the importance of historical data. Authors respond that critics have misrepresented their arguments, argue that their studies are scientific and statistical, and emphasize that, in their view, culture determines personality.

The 1940s reflect a major concern with war-related matters relating to author organizations, army race relations, and problems associated with regular military service. Other issues include the measurement of morale, methods used in social psychology, family topics such as Glick's family cycle, and the universal power of science. Critics raise interpretative problems inherent in different levels of analysis, selecting appropriate methods, reified measures, scientific measurement standards, and the need to exclude moral judgments. The authors, in turn, emphasize sound research, scientific knowledge, empirical support for their own conclusions, and the need for "correct" interpretations of their work. They also reaffirm that their data are valid and the best available.

During the next decade debates concentrate on family-related matters such as marital age and dating theories, social stratification in Latin America, socioeconomic indices and functional theories of stratification, the cultural lag problem, social psychological concerns such as complementary needs, and political issues relating to status consistency and political attitudes, Catholic political preferences, and the relationship between power and commitment. Critics point to the relevance of past literature, problems of terminology, data and validity restrictions, the causal ordering of key variables, ignored evidence, and statistical weaknesses involved in data analysis. Responders argue that their work is valid and conclusive, defend their own definitions, and point to support provided by other studies.

A wide range of topics is debated during the 1960s. These vary from educational inbreeding in Texas, occupational classification, the relationship between values and ability, problems in demography, and anomie, to a broad spectrum of social problems such as crime, juvenile delinquency, and mental illness such as schizophrenia. Critics highlight conceptual problems, theoretical defects and misinterpretations, as well as methodological problems such as sample limitations, measurement validity, and statistical tests. Rejoinders concentrate on data availability, support by others, the relative uniqueness of their research aims, and the support they possess for their empirical conclusions.

An even wider range of topics is debated during the next decade; however, major interchanges focus on theoretical and statistical interpretations as well as social problems such as mental illness, race riots, violence, and major social changes involved in modernization and the emerging world economy. Criticisms highlight model logic, data limitations, causal inferences, misinterpretations, data problems, and inaccurate explanations. Respondents continue to emphasize the uniqueness of their explanations, accuse their critics of misunderstanding, and defend their data as the only available and highly supportive of their original conclusions.

We turn finally to the 1980s, with their emphasis on critical social problems such as crime, deviance, and violence. Other leading topics include economic inequality, social mobility, the interpretation of Mead's work, debate regarding sociocultural evolution and sociobiology, and major concern with methodological complexities associated with variable measurement and logical modeling. Dominant critiques focus on interpretative problems such as misunderstanding, mistaken, misinformed, imprecise, and misleading approaches to the research question at hand, and analytical limitations relating to statistical and testing shortcomings. Associated issues regarding logic and measurement design are also raised. Authors largely respond that their critics have misunderstood, misrepresented, misinterpreted, or are mistaken in their evaluations of their studies, arguing instead that the data support their original conclusions.

Examining these debates chronologically, several trends can be delineated: the 1900s through the 1920s indicate a principal concern with professional and theoretical issues involved in the establishment of professional sociology among the social sciences, resulting in debates of interpretative issues and factors to be used in sociological explanation. With further professional development through the 1930s, however, attention shifts to more statistical and methodological matters reflected in critiques of measurement, data, and analysis problems. Such criticisms draw defenses of the authors' own measurement techniques and use of statistics. These concerns continue into the next decade combined with an increasing interest in social problems. Interpretative concerns persist but suggest a progressive interest in empirical explanations involved in variable relationships and associated operational issues. Problems associated with military, family, and stratification-related matters during the postwar years indicate increasing concern with measurement and interpretative issues, evoking defenses of research and design validity as well as data availability. Social problems such as anomie, delinquency, and mental illness are the central issues of the 1960s, combined with a continuing concern with measurement/interpretative matters, defended by a plurality of perspectives and support of those with similar views. The next decade indicates major concern with social problems but theoretical and methodological issues also, producing debates concerning the logic and statistical structure of causal explanations, defended primarily in terms of the authors' reaffirmation of their original conclusions and assumed critics' misunderstanding. Finally, the 1980s display a continuing concern with major social problems as well as theoretical and methodological issues. Studies are criticized primarily for their design and mode of analysis with defensive responses reminiscent of the 1970s.

CONCLUSIONS

From these data it can be seen that the academic development of American sociology reflects a concern with contemporary social problems, a heavy emphasis on attitudes as indicated in the striking development of social psychology, increasing evaluation of knowledge in scientific terms, and emergence of an increasingly egocentric defense of one's own perspective and conclusions. Particularly interesting is the progressive concern with scientific methodology, on the one hand, combined with an expanding egocentric defensiveness. This dualism highlights the discipline's normative character, despite its scientific aspirations.

This analysis suggests that the academic establishment of American sociology moved from its professional foundation through the scientific analysis of social problems to diversified views of these problems and the methods used to study them as the discipline became increasingly specialized. Criteria involved in the scientific understanding of these problems have also changed from a concern with professional boundaries, through the application of the scientific method, to perceived support for one's own point of view and assumed misinterpretation of others when attacked. Professional sociology, following its successful establishment and application of scientific methodology, has simultaneously become an increasingly diversified and egocentric discipline. This is reflected in debate dynamics accentuating defensive critiques and responses based on the scientific rationalization of one's own viewpoint. Regardless of claims to scientific objectivity, professional sociology reveals the degree to which it is based on *egocentric scientism.* Such a defensive attitude clearly detracts from productive dialogue and should be viewed with the skepticism it deserves.

NOTE

1. This discussion is based largely on the author's article, "The Development of American Sociology as Reflected in Journal Debates," published in the *International Journal of Contemporary Sociology,* 21, 1984, pp. 65–81. Thanks are due the editor for permission to use the article in this manner.

REFERENCE

Kuhn, Thomas. 1970. *The Structure of Scientific Revolutions.* Chicago: University of Chicago Press.

14

Contemporary Sociological Methodology in the United States

Thomas A. Petee

INTRODUCTION

Any discussion of research methodology hoping to have a singular focus becomes at once problematic because of the very definition of methodology. As employed in the social sciences, the term "methodology" refers to a number of different aspects of the research process including operationalization of theoretical concepts, measurement, data collection, and data analysis. Typically, a discussion of trends in sociological methodology would take one of two different approaches. On one hand, one could focus on the data collection process, looking at, for example, how frequently survey methodology or field methods are employed in sociological research. On the other hand, one could examine the types of techniques employed in analyzing data. If one were to look at the journal *Sociological Methodology,* for example, the focus is on data analysis. For this chapter, I have chosen to employ the latter approach in examining the trends in sociological methodology in the United States.

The types of methodology employed in American sociological research have drastically changed since the 1960s, becoming increasingly quantitative in orientation. While more qualitative techniques such as observational analysis or case study methods remain a viable part of the discipline's methodology, inferential statistical analysis, aided by the popularity of survey research and by the convenience of secondary data sources, has begun to dominate sociological research in the United States. Moreover, the discipline has gradually moved from a focus on bivariate relationships between variables to the examination of multivariate relationships.[1]

The increased sophistication of statistical analyses in sociological research since the 1960s is not simply a function of an increased understanding by sociologists of the various statistical techniques. It is no mere coincidence that this trend corresponds to the availability of computer facilities and statistical software packages. Until recently, any type of multivariate analysis would entail complicated and cumbersome computations which made statistical analysis a relatively inefficient way to conduct research. Today, however, access to a computer allows researchers with the requisite understanding of statistics to use the most sophisticated techniques in analyzing their data.

This trend was especially evident during the 1970s and 1980s, when most American sociology journals would regularly feature articles using more sophisticated statistical techniques such as multiple regression analysis, log-linear analysis, structural equation modeling, time series analysis, or logistic regression. This has led to charges by some of a quantitative bias, especially in the major American sociology journals. Although some sociologists have lamented the increasing dominance of quantitative methods within the discipline, and have questioned whether statistical methodology has led to any real progress in the field,[2] others have concluded that it is in this area that sociology has made its greatest strides in recent years.[3] While this question is still open to debate, it is hard to argue with the impact that statistical methodology has had on the discipline in terms of the sophistication of sociological analysis in the study of complex social phenomena. One need only look at some of the more recent applications of sociological methodology to appreciate this impact: multiple pathways of causality; modeling change over time; and, examining underlying or "latent" structures, to name only a few. On the other hand, concentration on the technical aspects of methodology has perhaps led to attention being diverted from the importance of the interaction between theory and methods in sociological analysis.

The remainder of this chapter is divided into two sections. The first part provides an overview of some of the more commonly used methods of statistical analysis in American sociology. This section is not intended as a comprehensive discussion of these methods, and as such is not particularly technical. The second part is an examination of the major trends in American sociological methodology in the 1980s by way of a content analysis of three major American sociology journals: *The American Sociological Review, The American Journal of Sociology,* and *Social Forces.*

COMMONLY USED METHODS OF ANALYSIS

As is well documented in most methods or statistics texts, analytic techniques in sociological research are often determined by data constraints. For example, the level of measurement of the dependent variable(s) (i.e., nominal, ordinal, interval, or ratio), the marginal distribution of the variables, or even the type of research design (e.g., cross-sectional or longitudinal) may well dictate the type of statistical technique that is employed in data analysis. However, despite these constraints, some techniques are more popular than others, sometimes leading to charges that sociological research is methods driven. Nonetheless, any review of sociological methodology would be incomplete without a discussion of some of those techniques.

Regression Analysis

The widespread use of *regression analysis* in social science research has been well documented in the methodology literature.[4] Given the versatility and robustness of regression, in its various derivative forms, the popularity of this technique should not be surprising. In many ways *multiple regression analysis,* that is, the use of regression with more than one independent variable, is the foundation for most other multivariate statistical techniques.

In essence, regression analysis describes the relationship between a dependent variable (symbolized with the notation Y) and an independent variable or set of independent variables (symbolized with the notation X_l ... X_k) through the use of an equation for a straight line, assuming that the relationship is a linear one (see Figure 14.1).[5] The relationship between these variables, expressed in the regression equation formula,

$$Y = \alpha + \beta X1 + \ldots \beta Xk$$

specifies the change in the dependent variable corresponding to a unit increase or decrease in the independent variable, where α is the intercept, that is, the value of Y when $X = 0$, and β represents the slope or steepness of the line. There are situations, such as in the physical sciences, where the relationship between the variables will be exact, so that with a unit change in the independent variable, we will see a precise change in the dependent variable each and every time. In the social sciences, however, the relationship between variables is almost always inexact, introducing a certain degree of error into the estimation of the linear equation.[6] Thus the predicted values of Y (symbolized with the notation Y') will typically differ from the actual observed values of Y. The goal of the regression technique is to attempt to find the best fitting line, given the degree of error, which describes the changes in a dependent variable which correspond to variation in an independent variable(s).

Probably the most popular method for estimating the best fitting line is the *ordinary-least-squares* criterion (hereafter OLS), which attempts to

Figure 14.1
The Linear Regression

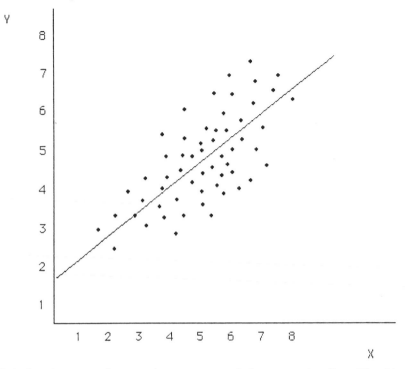

minimize the sum of squared errors around the regression line. The idea behind OLS estimation is that the better the "fit" of the regression line, the smaller the difference between observed and predicted values of Y.[7] However, other estimation techniques exist which have specific applications relevant to the data analysis. For example, the *weighted-least-squares* criterion is commonly used when the regression assumptions of variance homogeneity or independence are problematic.[8] Other estimation techniques include *generalized-least-squares,* which is typically applied in time series analysis, and *instrumental variables, indirect-least-squares,* and *two stage-least-squares,* all of which have applications in structural equation modeling.

Analysis of Variance/Analysis of Covariance

The category of techniques known collectively as *analysis of variance* (hereafter ANOVA) is concerned with analyzing differences in the means of a variable across groups of observations. Essentially, ANOVA attempts to establish whether the difference in the sample means of a dependent variable across categories of an independent variable(s) is due to random variation or is truly different, a concept known as statistical significance.[9] *One-way ANOVA,* involving the use of only one predictor variable, determines the amount of variance in the dependent variable accounted for by the independent variable (*between group variance*) relative to the variance accounted for by random chance (*within group variance*). The resulting *F ratio:*

$$F = \frac{S_{bg}^2}{S_w^2}$$

where s_{bg}^2 is the between group variance and s_w^2 is the within group variance, is then evaluated using the *F sampling distribution.*[10] More complex versions of ANOVA, employing more than one independent variable, additionally test for the existence of interaction effects. In the *Two-way ANOVA,* the contribution of each of the independent variables and the interaction between these variables are assessed by examining the amount of variance explained by these sources relative to unexplained variance (known as *error sum of squares*), with F ratios being calculated for each of these sources. The *N-way ANOVA* is simply an extension of the Two-way ANOVA model with more than two independent variables.

Analysis of covariance (ANCOVA) is typically used when the researcher wishes to examine the relationship between a dependent quantitative variable, one or more quantitative independent variables, and at least one categorical independent variable.[11] In the ANCOVA model, one or more of the independent variables are used solely for the purpose of control. The effect of the variable or variables one wishes to control for, known as the covariate(s), is seen as confounding the relationship between the dependent variable and the independent variable of interest.[12] The purpose of ANCOVA, therefore, is to partial out the effect of the covariate(s) from the dependent variable, thereby increasing the precision of the analysis.[13]

Correlational Analysis

Correlational analysis is a broad class of statistical techniques which examine the relationships that occur between variables. These techniques determine the degree of association, if any, that exists between random variables. Unlike many other multivariate techniques, however, no causal interpretations can be safely made with correlational analysis.[14]

The *product moment correlation coefficient,* sometimes referred to simply as the *correlation coefficient,* has wide applications in the social sciences. This coefficient measures the linear relationship between two normally distributed interval or ratio level variables, with a value of $+1.00$

indicating a perfect positive linear relationship, and a value of −1.00 indicating a perfect inverse (negative) linear relationship. Intermediate values represent varying degrees of the magnitude of the correlation with a value of 0 signifying no relationship. Although other measures of correlation exist, the product moment correlation coefficient is probably the best known.[15]

The concept of correlation is central to many multivariate methods of analysis. In fact, several commonly used multivariate methods employ the correlation coefficient as the focal point of the technique. *Canonical correlation,* for example, is used to determine the degree of correlation between two *derived* variables, or variable sets, each of which consists of a weighted combination of other variables. The squares of the canonical weight can then be used to estimate the relative contribution of each component variable to the derived variable.[16] Other common statistical methods employing the concept of correlation include the *correlation matrix, partial correlation,* and *serial correlation.*

Time Series Analysis

The popularity within the social sciences of longitudinal research designs and demographic data such as the census has led to variations on the regression model which allow researchers to examine the relationship between variables over time. The use of such variables within the standard regression model can result in biased estimation because of the violation of the regression assumption that error terms for succeeding observations are independent of one another.

The function of *time series analysis* is essentially twofold: to describe the relationship between a dependent variable and a set of independent variables, as is the case with multiple regression analysis; and to forecast how the variables of interest will behave in the future.[17] Data are collected over a series of time points with particular attention being paid to the ordering of the time points. This attention to temporal ordering is necessary so as to better estimate the regression equation which might be influenced by the time sequence, and to allow for the inference about probable future behavior.[18] Temporal ordering may be especially important if the variable of interest has been consistently increasing (or decreasing) over time. This has implications not only for estimating the statistical properties of the variable, but also affects the forecasting function.[19] *Event history analysis* is a family of techniques which examine "events," that is, variables which undergo gradual change, over a period of time.[20] Using regression-based techniques, event history analysis identifies a *risk set,* which can be defined as the set of individuals for whom the event might occur at each point in time. From this risk set, a *hazard rate* is calculated by determining the probability that the event will occur for an individual during a particular interval of time.[21] The hazard rate is then treated as a dependent variable within a regression equation, attempting to show how the hazard rate is influenced by a series of explanatory variables over time.[22]

Log-linear Analysis and Logistic Regression

Despite the popularity of OLS regression in sociological research, there are limitations with the procedure which constrain the researcher in the application of this technique. One such limitation is the assumption that the dependent variable is continuous, that is, that it has infinitely varied fractional values. Although OLS regression is a robust enough technique to allow for some flexibility with this assumption, the use of a dichotomous dependent variable presents a serious problem for the researcher. In such a case, OLS regression becomes statistically inefficient, resulting in the possibility of misestimating the effects of independent variables, and leading to serious errors in inference.[23] In the social sciences, this problem becomes particularly perplexing because many variables of interest (i.e., potential dependent variables) for social scientists are operationally dichotomous (e.g., decision-making, attitudinal measures, voting behavior).[24]

Log-linear analysis is one multivariate technique which can be employed with categorical data. There are two different approaches to log-linear modeling: the *general log-linear model,* which is symmetric, that is, it makes no distinction between the dependent and independent variables, and examines the relationship between variables through the analysis of expected cell frequencies; and the *logit model,* which analyzes the expected odds of a dependent variable as a function of a set of independent variables.[25] In the logit model, which has the greatest applicability for sociological research, a distinction is made between *saturated models,* which include the main effects of the independent variables as well as first-order and all higher-order interactions, and other, not *fully saturated models.* In the later case, expected cell frequencies can be estimated, and maximum-likelihood parameter estimates can be computed which can be used to evaluate the "fit" of the model. The goodness of fit is essentially determined by how well the expected cell frequencies approximate the observed data.[26]

Unlike OLS regression, which rests on assumptions pertaining to the linear constancy of change and the distribution of error terms, the *logit model* of *logistic regression* represents the underlying relationship between variables as a logistic function.[27] The dichotomous dependent variable is conceptualized as a probability with the outcome of interest having a probability of 1.0. Thus the probability of the outcome of interest is presented in the logistic equation:

$$P(Y = 1 | X1, \ldots Xk)$$

Figure 14.2
The Sigmoid Curve Representing the Logistic Function

where P(Y = 1) denotes the probability of the outcome of interest, and $X_1, \ldots X_k$ are the independent variables. This logistic function is indicated by a sigmoid, or S-shaped curve (see Figure 14.2), which better portrays the distribution of a probability than does the linear model used in OLS regression.[28] Unlike log-linear analysis, in which all variables should be categorical, logistic regression can be used in situations where the dependent variable is dichotomous, but the explanatory variables are continuous, thus allowing for greater versatility in application.

Factor Analysis

The family of techniques known as *factor analysis* is primarily concerned with reducing a set of variables into a smaller set of *underlying* variables or factors.[29] Factor analysis involves the examination of the intercorrelation among variables, determining if observed correlations can be explained by the existence of some underlying factor.[30] *Exploratory factor analysis* is used when the researcher is unsure as to how many underlying factors exist for a particular set of data. With this orientation, factor analysis is used primarily to determine the minimum number of factors that account for observed covariation in the data. By contrast, *confirmatory factor analysis* is used for testing specific hypotheses concerning the number of underlying factors and which variables correspond to those factors.[31]

Starting with the correlation matrix, factor analysis involves the creation of a *factor matrix,* which demonstrates the relationship between the variables and the underlying factors. The cell entries of this matrix are called *factor loadings,* which are the correlation coefficients between the variables and the underlying factors.[32] Within this matrix certain variables will load high on some factors and low on others.

Using the *principal components technique* of factor extraction, a factor is initially extracted for each of the original set of variables.[33] Each of these initially extracted factors will account for a certain proportion of the variance in the data. The first factor extracted will account for the largest proportion of this variance, and subsequent factors will account for a diminishing proportion of the variation.[34] Each derived factor will have a corresponding *eigenvalue,* which can be interpreted as the equivalent number of variables the factor represents. These eigenvalues are then used to evaluate how many factors should be retained for the final analysis, usually those that account for the variance of a typical variable. The retained factors are then reanalyzed through a process known as factor rotation, which involves the redefining of factors so that the explained variance is redistributed among the final factors.[35] The resulting factors represent a smaller and more efficient set of underlying variables, reducing the redundancy inherent in some data sets.

Path Analysis and Structural Equation Modeling

Causal modeling has become increasingly popular within the social sciences in general and with sociology in particular. The notion of examining the structure of relationships between variables so as to determine causality is intuitively appealing especially in light of the increasingly complex multivariate statistical models employed in sociological research. Within the framework of causal modeling, certain variables are designated as "exogenous" and "endogenous." *Exogenous variables* are those whose variability are assumed to be determined outside of the context of the causal model. In other words, these variables act as the "cause" and never as the "effect" within the model.[36] By contrast, *endogenous variables* are those that are directly or indirectly influenced by other variables within the model, in essence the "effect."[37] Additionally, a distinction is made between *recursive causal models,* in which the causal flow of the model is unidirectional, and *nonrecursive models* (see Figure 14.3), which permit reciprocal relationships among variables.[38]

One method applied to causal modeling is *path analysis,* which uses regression techniques to establish relationships among pairs of variables.

Figure 14.3
Illustration of Recursive and Nonrecursive Causal Models

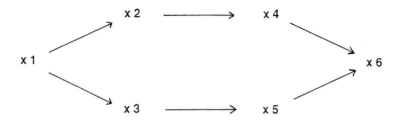

Recursive Causal Model

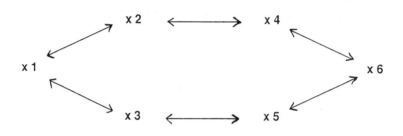

Nonrecursive Causal Model

The resulting standardized regression coefficients, known as *path coeffi-cients,* represent the magnitude of that relationship holding constant the effects of all other variables in the model. Unlike multiple regression anal-ysis, in which a dependent variable is regressed on a set of independent variables within a single regression equation, path analysis may call for several regressions in which each endogenous variable is regressed on the variables presumed to influence it.[39]

Structural equation modeling is the name given to a family of causal modeling techniques which employ such methods as regression, factor analysis, and correlational analysis. Probably the most popular structural equation modeling technique is LISREL (*Li*near *S*tructural *Rel*ations), a program based on maximum-likelihood estimation of parameters.[40] Per-haps the greatest strength of this technique is the ability to model latent variables, that is, constructs which are unobserved. In the social sciences, a single indicator does not always correspond exactly to the variable of theoretical interest, and consequently researchers must often employ multiple indicators in their research in order to measure a complex construct in a valid and reliable manner. The LISREL model allows for the incorporation of both unobserved, latent theoretical concepts and observed indicators within the same structural equation model, something path analysis and other statistical techniques are ill-equipped to do.[41] The LISREL model itself is based upon confirmatory factor analysis techniques which allow for the testing of hypotheses regarding the nature of factors using maximum-likelihood procedures.[42]

TRENDS IN AMERICAN SOCIOLOGICAL METHODOLOGY: 1980–1990

Perhaps the best way to demonstrate the trends in the sociological methodology in the United States is through an examination of articles appearing in what are arguably the three major sociology journals in the United States: *The American Sociological Review* (hereafter *ASR*), *The American Journal of Sociology* (hereafter *AJS*), and *Social Forces*. These journals were analyzed for methodological content at three different points in time: 1980, 1985, and 1990. Five-year time intervals were used primarily to avoid any "masking" of gradual change in journal content which might occur if succeeding years were used in the analysis. Because *Social Forces* and *AJS* do not use the calendar year in sequencing their volumes, each time interval contains portions of two volumes for those journals.[43] Because articles often contained more than one statistical technique, it was decided that only the major statistical application would be enumerated.[44]

Tables 14.1, 14.2, and 14.3 show the relative frequency distribution of articles appearing in the three journals for 1980, 1985, and 1990 respectively. Several trends are apparent from these tables. First of all, regression analysis, in its various forms, is by far the most frequently and consistently used method of analysis for these journals. Although there were fluctuations in the application of this technique across journals and at the different time points, the use of regression analysis was never less than 25 percent of the articles appearing in a journal (low of 25.5 percent for *AJS* in 1980). Moreover, no other statistical technique ever exceeded the relative frequency of usage of regression for any of the three journals at any of the time points.

Second, the popularity of logistic regression/log-linear analysis appears to have increased over time. In 1980, these techniques were used in less than 10 percent of the articles appearing in *ASR* and *Social Forces*. In 1985, and again in 1990, the application of this technique had increased

Table 14.1
Relative Frequency Distribution of Methodological Techniques, 1980

	ASR[1]	AJS[2]	SF[3]
Regression Analysis	40.8%	25.5%	35.1%
Logistic Regression/Log-linear Analysis	6.1%	10.6%	5.3%
Structural Equation Modeling/Path Analysis	12.2%	4.3%	5.3%
Time Series/Event History Analysis	4.1%	4.3%	3.5%
Factor Analysis	4.1%	4.3%	1.8%
Measures of Correlation/Association	2.0%	10.6%	5.3%
Analysis of Variance/Covariance	6.1%	0%	0%
Descriptive Statistics	2.0%	17.0%	21.1%
Nonempirical/Theoretical	18.4%	14.9%	12.3%
Other	4.1%	8.5%	10.5%

1: American Sociological Review
2: The American Journal of Sociology
3: Social Forces

significantly. The increase in 1985 was largely due to the popularity of log-linear analysis, a trend which is concealed by the inclusion of both techniques under one category.[45] The opposite is true for 1990, however, with logistic regression accounting for the higher relative frequency. Neither of these trends should be particularly surprising given developments in the application of these techniques in the social sciences.

Third, there is an increase in the "time series/event history analysis" category in 1990 for *ASR* and *Social Forces*. Again, the cause of this trend is concealed by the inclusion of multiple techniques under one category. The change in 1990 can largely be accounted for by the popularity of event history analysis, and not coincidentally corresponds to the publication of the much heralded *Social Dynamics: Models and Methods* by Nancy Brandon Tuma and Michael Hannan,[46] which represents the definitive text on the technique.[47]

Fourth, there was a decline in the use of correlational analysis as a primary statistical technique between 1980 and 1990. In 1980, use of measures of correlation/association ranged from a low of 2 percent for *ASR* to a high of 10.6 percent for *AJS*. By 1990, none of the articles appearing in the three journals employed correlational analysis as the primary statistical technique. This is not to say, however, that correlational analysis is in

Table 14.2
Relative Frequency Distribution of Methodological Techniques, 1985

	ASR[1]	AJS[2]	SF[3]
Regression Analysis	33.3%	36.1%	42.6%
Logistic Regression/Log-linear Analysis	20.4%	13.9%	14.9%
Structural Equation Modeling/Path Analysis	7.4%	8.3%	8.5%
Time Series/Event History Analysis	7.4%	2.8%	0%
Factor Analysis	0%	2.8%	0%
Measures of Correlation/Association	1.9%	0%	6.4%
Analysis of Variance/Covariance	5.6%	0%	0%
Descriptive Statistics	5.6%	5.6%	6.4%
Nonempirical/Theoretical	16.7%	11.1%	19.1%
Other	1.9%	19.4%	2.1%

1: American Sociological Review
2: The American Journal of Sociology
3: Social Forces

decline. Rather it is just no longer the major methodological focus of articles appearing in these journals.

Finally, and perhaps most intriguing given the supposed quantitative bias of *ASR, AJS,* and *Social Forces,* a relatively sizable proportion of the articles appearing in these journals fell under the category "nonempirical/theoretical." With one exception (*ASR* in 1990), this category accounted for more than 10 percent of all articles. While that proportion may not seem to be particularly high, over the time span of this analysis, that category represents the second highest percentage of articles appearing in the three journals.

In terms of the remaining methodological categories, no clear patterns emerge. For example, while it would appear as though *Social Forces* has published a relatively higher proportion of articles employing descriptive statistics, there is such variation in this proportion over time that it is unclear whether any pattern actually exists. Most of the other techniques show minimal variation in usage.

CONCLUSIONS

The trend in sociological methodology in the United States has been toward quantitative analysis. Increasingly, more sophisticated statistical

Table 14.3
Relative Frequency Distribution of Methodological Techniques, 1990

	ASR[1]	AJS[2]	SF[3]
Regression Analysis	38.8%	32.4%	39.6%
Logistic Regression/Log-linear Analysis	20.4%	14.7%	15.1%
Structural Equation Modeling/Path Analysis	4.1%	5.9%	5.7%
Time Series/Event History Analysis	16.3%	5.9%	11.3%
Factor Analysis	0%	2.9%	3.8%
Measures of Correlation/Association	0%	0%	0%
Analysis of Variance/Covariance	2.0%	0%	0%
Descriptive Statistics	0%	2.9%	13.2%
Nonempirical/Theoretical	4.1%	23.5%	11.3%
Other	12.2%	11.8%	0%

1: American Sociological Review
2: The American Journal of Sociology
3: Social Forces

techniques are employed in articles appearing in most American sociology journals. As David A. Freedman points out, regression modeling in particular has become a dominant paradigm within the discipline.[48] At times this has led to what could almost be called a "fixation" on methodological issues. The content of many of the articles appearing in sociology journals today revolves around a methodological discourse which can be fairly technical. In fact, a sociologist relatively untrained in statistical analysis would likely have a difficult time determining the type of methodology employed in some of the articles analyzed in this chapter.

Unfortunately, this can lead to the perception that the role of theory in sociological analysis is minimal, or certainly downplayed. The interaction between method and theory is critical to the sociological enterprise. While untestable theories are especially problematic to a researcher, atheoretical analysis which is "methods driven" is equally fruitless. In order to employ many of the statistical methods that are popular today, one needs an elaborate theory which specifies the variables in the system and their causal interconnections.[49]

This is not to say, however, that the quantification of American sociology is a bad thing. Sophisticated methodology is necessary in order to test some of the complex theoretical models that interest sociologists today. Certainly great progress has been made in sociological methodology in recent years, but the relevance of that progress is ultimately measured by its impact on the development of sociological theory.

NOTES

1. Elazar J. Pedhazur, *Multiple Regression in Behavioral Research,* 2d ed. (New York: Holt, Rinehart, and Winston, 1982).

2. See Stephen P. Turner, "Underdetermination and the Promise of Statistical Sociology," *Sociological Theory* 5, 2 (1987), 172–184; and Alan Sica, "Hermeneutics and Axiology: The Ethical Content of Interpretation," in Mark L. Wardell and Stephen Turner, eds., *Sociological Theory in Transition* (Boston: Allen and Unwin, 1986), 142–157.

3. See Aage B. Sorensen, "Progress in Studying Change" (Review of *Social Dynamics: Models and Methods,* Nancy Brandon Tuma and Michael T. Hannan), *American Journal of Sociology* 92, 3 (1986), 691–696; and George C. Homans, "Fifty Years of Sociology," *Annual Review of Sociology* 12 (1986), xiii–xxx.

4. See Pedhazur, op. cit.; and David A. Freedman, "Statistical Models and Shoe Leather," *Sociological Methodology* 21 (1991), 291–313.

5. The terms "criterion variable" and "predictor variable" are sometimes used synonymously with "dependent variable" and "independent variable" respectively.

6. Michael S. Lewis-Beck, *Applied Regression: An Introduction,* Sage University Paper Series on Quantitative Applications in the Social Sciences, Series No. 07-022 (Beverly Hills and London: Sage Publications, 1980).

7. David G. Kleinbaum, Lawrence L. Kupper, and Keith E. Muller, *Applied Regression Analysis and Other Multivariate Methods,* 2d ed. (Boston: PWS-Kent Publishing Company, 1988).

8. Ibid.; John Neter, William Wasserman, and Michael H. Kutner, *Applied Linear Statistical Models,* 2d ed. (Homewood, IL: Irwin, 1985).

9. Gudmund R. Iversen and Helmut Norpoth, *Analysis of Variance,* 2d ed., Sage University Paper Series on Quantitative Applications in the Social Sciences, Series No. 07-001 (Newbury Park, CA: Sage Publications, 1987).

10. Ibid.

11. Albert R. Wildt and Olli T. Ahtola, *Analysis of Covariance,* Sage University Paper Series on Quantitative Applications in the Social Sciences, Series No. 07-012 (Beverly Hills and London: Sage Publications, 1978).

12. Ibid.

13. Pedhazur, op. cit.

14. Sam K. Kachigan, *Multivariate Statistical Analysis: A Conceptual Introduction* (New York: Radius Press, 1982).

15. Ibid.

16. Bruce Thompson, *Canonical Correlation Analysis: Uses and Interpretation,* Sage University Paper Series on Quantitative Applications in the Social Sciences, Series No. 07-047 (Beverly Hills and London: Sage Publications, 1984); and Kachigan, op. cit.

17. Charles W. Ostrom, Jr., *Time Series Analysis: Regression Techniques,* Sage

University Paper Series on Quantitative Applications in the Social Sciences, Series No. 07-009 (Beverly Hills and London: Sage Publications, 1978).

18. Ibid.; and Robert S. Pindyck and Daniel L. Rubinfeld, *Econometric Models and Economic Forecasts,* 3rd ed. (New York: McGraw-Hill, Inc., 1991).

19. E. M. Uslaner, "Editor's Introduction," in Charles W. Ostrom, Jr., *Time Series Analysis: Regression Techniques,* Sage University Paper Series on Quantitative Applications in the Social Sciences, Series No. 07-009 (Beverly Hills and London: Sage Publications, 1978), 5–7.

20. Paul D. Allison, *Event History Analysis: Regression for Longitudinal Event Data,* Sage University Paper Series on Quantitative Applications in the Social Sciences, Series No. 07-046 (Newbury Park, CA: Sage Publications, 1984); and Nancy Brandon Tuma and Michael T. Hannan, *Social Dynamics: Models and Methods* (Orlando: Academic Press, 1984).

21. Ibid.

22. There are actually several distinct conceptions of "time" within the various forms of event history analysis. See Douglas A. Wolf, "Simulation Methods for Analyzing Continuous-Time Event-History Models," *Sociological Methodology* 16 (1986), 283–308; and Allison, op. cit.

23. John H. Aldrich and Forrest D. Nelson, *Linear Probability, Logit, and Probit Models,* Sage University Paper Series on Quantitative Applications in the Social Sciences, Series No. 07-045 (Newbury Park, CA: Sage Publications, 1984); and Paul D. Cleary and Ronald Angel, "The Analysis of Relationships Involving Dichotomous Dependent Variables," *Journal of Health and Social Behavior* 25 (September 1984), 334–348.

24. Anthony Walsh, "Teaching Understanding and Interpretation of Logit Regression," *Teaching Sociology* 15 (April 1987), 178–183.

25. David Knoke and Peter J. Burke, *Log-Linear Models,* Sage University Paper Series on Quantitative Applications in the Social Sciences, Series No. 07-020 (Beverly Hills and London: Sage Publications, 1980).

26. Ibid.; and Stephen E. Fienberg, *The Analysis of Cross-Classified Categorical Data,* 2d ed. (Cambridge, MA: The MIT Press, 1980).

27. Although similarities exist, the logit model of logistic regression should not be confused with the logit model of log-linear analysis.

28. Walsh, op. cit.

29. That is, the variables are unobserved, unlike the observed "indicators" which make up the larger set of variables.

30. Jae-On Kim and Charles W. Mueller, *Introduction to Factor Analysis,* Sage University Paper Series on Quantitative Applications in the Social Sciences, Series No. 07-0013 (Beverly Hills and London: Sage Publications, 1978); and Richard L. Gorsuch, *Factor Analysis,* 2d ed. (Hillsdale, NJ: Lawrence Erlbaum Associates, Publishers, 1983).

31. Kim and Mueller, op. cit.

32. Kachigan, op. cit.

33. There are other techniques for factor extraction such as principal axis factoring, alpha factoring, and image factoring, but principal components analysis is the most commonly used technique. See Gorsuch, op. cit.

34. Kachigan, op. cit.; and Jae-On Kim and Charles W. Mueller, *Factor Analysis: Statistical Methods and Practical Issues,* Sage University Paper Series on Quanti-

tative Applications in the Social Sciences, Series No. 07-0014 (Beverly Hills and London: Sage Publications, 1978).

35. Ibid.

36. Pedhazur, op. cit.; and Leslie A. Hayduk, *Structural Equation Modeling with LISREL: Essentials and Advances* (Baltimore, MD: The John Hopkins University Press, 1987).

37. Edongenous variables in a causal model can, however, "cause" other endogenous variables within that model.

38. Pedhazur, op. cit.; William T. Bielby and Robert M. Hauser, "Structural Equation Models," *Annual Review of Sociology* 3 (1977), 137–161; and Herbert B. Asher, *Causal Modeling,* 2d ed., Sage University Paper Series on Quantitative Applications in the Social Sciences, Series No. 07-003 (Beverly Hills and London: Sage Publications, 1983).

39. Ibid.

40. Karl G. Joreskog and Dag Sorbom, *LISREL: Analysis of Linear Structural Relationships by the Method of Maximum Likelihood,* Version VI (Mooresville, IN: Scientific Software, Inc., 1986).

41. Hayduk, op. cit.; and Pedhazur, op. cit.

42. Jöreskog and Sörbom, op. cit.

43. For example, articles appearing in *Social Forces* in 1990 were taken from issues 3 and 4 of volume 68, and issues 1 and 2 of volume 69.

44. For example, a researcher might use factor analysis to construct one or more of the measures employed in the article, present a correlation matrix of the data used in the study, and then perform a multiple regression analysis. In this case, the major analytic focus of the article would be multiple regression, so only that technique would be enumerated.

45. The inclusion of several related statistical techniques under one category was primarily used for presentation purposes.

46. Tuma and Hannan, op. cit.

47. If one factors in lag time between the publication of this text and the impact it would have had on articles appearing in the three journals, the correspondence between the two becomes more clear.

48. Freedman, op. cit.

49. Ibid.

15

The United States: Metatheoretical Concerns

Arthur S. Wilke and Raj P. Mohan

> During normal times the problems are well defined, the techniques are
> established, and the criteria of solution agreed on. In crises or new fields, the
> problems are ill defined and there is no agreement on facts, concepts, tech-
> niques or solution criteria.
>
> —Paul Diesing,
> *How Does Social Science Work?*[1]

> Social science produces a multiple, contradictory truth for out time—that
> is, a set of diversified perspectives and diagnoses of our changing, tangled and
> contradictory society. The truth lives in the practice and understanding of a
> research community, not in particular laws, and when that community peters
> out, its truth passes into history along with the society it tried to understand.
>
> —Paul Diesing,
> *How Does Social Science Work?*

> Indeed, it is our contention that important social scientific debates largely
> consist of arguments over the criteria for evaluation that are immanent in
> different levels of discourse (e.g., criteria about presuppositions, ideologies,
> models, and methods).
>
> —Jeffrey C. Alexander and Paul Colomy,
> "Traditions and Competition"[2]

Sociological theory, like disciplinary sociology in the United States, is
more like an impressionistic painting than a well-defined blueprint. Despite efforts to provide a clear portrait of interhuman affairs and possibly
even more numerous efforts to bring clarity to theoretical portraits, coherence, as the above quotations suggest, is not within the immediate

reach of sociologists. Nevertheless, theory remains one of the staples of sociological practice. More appropriately, the allure of theory remains, an allure contributing less to illumination and explanation of social life and more to efforts to consolidate, assess, and debate theory. It is this tendency to be preoccupied by the metatheoretical impulse which dominates the state of sociological theory in the United States. In this chapter we explore some of the things contributing to this impulse and the way it is manifested. The signature to the times is in the formal recognition of metatheory as an object of study, a development which is consistent with what is occurring in many parts of U.S. academic life, especially those in the humanities.

A part of the strain toward classifying and assessing ideas inheres in the self-consciousness of sociology's epistemological project. The received vision of sociology is that it coincides with and examines modernity.[3] This bears the imprint of Auguste Comte (1798–1857), whose proposal for sociology was seen as an evolutionary adjunct to the modern epoch, one engulfing a philosophy of history marked by the law of three stages: religion, metaphysics, science. By the end of World War II, the Comtean vision was well established. The ideas sociologists used to inform their discourse became more proscribed. Courses in social thought which sampled from a larger universe of ideas became passé.[4] Theory dealt with only modern figures and concerns, meaning ideas whose lineage began in the nineteenth century. This linked sociology to a widespread, academic project of legitimating modernism. In this project, significant effort was made to portray the modern as a break with the past. This was accomplished by not only periodizing ideas into those of the pre-Enlightenment and Enlightenment, but dramatizing that ideas and practices which resisted academic disciplinary practices were manifestations of anti-Enlightenment "tradition."

Because sociology is an academic subject more so than a research subject, the polemic directed against contemporaries manifesting little recognition or appreciation for Enlightenment concerns sustained a form which is reproduced in issues and arguments concerning theory. This was aided substantially in the post–World War II period by the embrace of logical empiricism. At once, logical empiricism[5] seemed to reveal standards of thought which could clearly delineate modern, scientific thought from earlier, archaic kinds. An idealist program of thought, logical empiricism emphasized a critical use of a carefully crafted system of semantics and syntax. Theory was to be treated as a proposition or family of propositions. In the sociological embrace of logical empiricism, constituent elements of propositions, concepts, were operationally defined. Operationally defined items, in turn, made up hypotheses which could be subjected to some type of empirical test. Sociological knowledge was to stand or fall on the results of the empirical test of hypotheses.

The hope was nurtured in the era of logical empiricism that sometime the confirmed hypotheses could be inductively consolidated into some general laws of social life. Once this occurred, the foundation would be set for making sociology truly a deductive science. It is a day which has not yet arrived. Meanwhile, other practices called sociology, ranging from speculative interpretations to outright moralizing, were found among practicing sociologists. These voices, however, were rendered into the margins of the professionalizing discipline.

At the height of the sociological embrace of logical empiricism, there were numerous criticisms and challenges going on in philosophical circles concerning this approach. These did not penetrate the central figures in sociology, and even today many residues traced to logical empiricism are anchored in research methods writings and training. It is this differential response to criticism of logical empiricism which contributes to the different trajectories that works in sociological theory and methods have taken, trajectories which are now institutionalized in the curriculum specialties of theory and methods. Meanwhile, the impress of logical empiricism remains entrenched in another residual form: the form for sociological reporting. These, dissertations, and journal articles continue to be organized around a form which could lead unsuspecting readers, possibly even the writers, into believing that much of the reported work followed a deductive model and that truth claims are decisively established through hypothesis testing. Even within sociology, it seems, cultural lags can be detected. A further attraction of logical empiricism, one which sociology shares with other disciplines, such as philosophy, is that by privileging the logical empiricist notions, of articulating the "real" criteria of science, speakers could at once present themselves as superior in their understanding of science, possibly superior to other scientists, and at the same time subordinate their own activities to an academic hierarchy wherein there was more attention and value accorded the physical sciences. For sociologists, who as a category do not come from the most traditionally competitive stratum of students, the aura of being conversant with "real" science and the critical criteria gave a muscular aura, one which dominated core areas in sociology—theory, methods, statistics. Not only sociologists' activities, but their self-referential identities were at stake. Preoccupation with these concerns takes time. In the temporal constraints of academic life, in a world in which there is a proliferation of texts and claims, the time to carefully reflect on one's own intellectual architecture no less report on the surrounding world is limited. These conditions contribute to an intellectual dissimulation if not exhaustion of insights and concerns.

Until the 1960s logical empiricism dominated central discussions regarding theory and methods in U.S. sociology. A crack in this coherency appeared in the wake of the publication in 1962 of Thomas Kuhn's *The Structure of Scientific Revolutions,*[6] a book which had substantially more impact on theoretical discourse than on methodological discourse. Kuhn challenged the view that scientific ideas were sustained and developed through the procedures derived from logical empiricism. Formulations, he went on, which made up scientific knowledge were not confirmed by the judicial-like empirical test. Those attentive to Kuhn's claims and evidence now became receptive to other critics of logical empiricism. Among those critics were those who had noted that the exemplar of science for logical empiricists, physics, did not seem to conform to what had been the received view of science in many parts of academic life, including sociology.

Instead of a logical-deductive mode of thought, with its a priori determination of terms and rules of syntax, Kuhn suggested that the general defining notions of an area of inquiry were governed by paradigms and research operations. This augured nicely with sociologists since it suggested that science was a social activity. It also provided a warrant for many who either were involved in a different epistemological agenda or who wished to continue to moralize without being held accountable to canons which undertook to carefully patrol distinctions between facts and values. And if one were to embrace the Kuhn thesis, there was a momentary respite. Instead of worrying about the adequacy of scientific discourse and procedures, one might again romp in the world of numerous social actors. It was a promise not fully realized.

The general operations in a scientific field were, according to Kuhn, done through mimicry. Instead of critical ideas and procedures being the hallmarks of scientific endeavor, most research followed, he suggested, previous routines of thought and procedure called paradigms. Revolutionary change in scientific knowledge came about only when inconsistent findings and anomalies began accumulating. Among those most likely to be intolerant of these conditions would be a new generation of researchers. Biology as manifested in the demography of academics seemed to be a more critical arbiter of ideas than reason and observation.

Kuhn's work appeared at the very time when there was an explosive growth on campuses throughout the United States. The demand for academic workers escalated, creating conditions tolerant of those exploring different claims and arguments. At the same time, the highly valued newcomers to the field, among them those receptive to Kuhn's thesis, used works like Kuhn's to express discontent. Kuhn's work addressing paradigm shifts became itself an exemplary of a paradigm shift. The problem with the paradigmatic moves in the discipline is that they engaged in more reflexive talk about sociology and sociologists than describe and narrate about the world of people. In the arena of substantive concerns it wasn't paradigms as much as deep-entrenched political ideological issues which affected what entered into the domain of sociological interest. And from what can be determined, this was not substantially different than what had been occurring since the 1930s.[7]

The embrace of Kuhn's work by a cohort of students and young faculty, though dramatic, manifests anomalies. Kuhn's portrait of paradigm was loosely used. And the embrace involved conflating criticisms of logical empiricism and science. Except for his view that dominant scientific practices exhibited paradigmatic unity and followed a research exemplar, Kuhn portrayed most day-to-day scientific activity as rather pedestrian. This latter view was not received by sociologists attuned to Kuhn's work. Instead, they homed onto the revolutionary thesis of Kuhn's work, committing themselves to making a heroic revolution in the domain of sociology. The heroic imagery, we surmise, was from the way sociological ideas and their authors' personae were fashioned. Biographies, from the reading of conventional portraits of "theorists" and their works, were decisive. Why sociological contextualizing did not emphasize looking at these writers and their work critically remains a puzzle though it is likely that the Comtean aura of sociology as a young science was a factor.

Kuhn's work marked a watershed. It undercut theory work in the logical empiricist tradition such as Hans Zetterberg's program for axiomatic reduction of propositions in his work, *On Theory and Verification in Sociology* (1966 [1954]).[8] Despite this, residues remain. Walter Wallace in *Sociological Theory* (1969) provided a systematic assessment of sociological work which could be classified under the title, sociological theory. His objectives were to identify and define elements which could be made into a propositional sociology. After a generation of effort, Wallace continues to appeal for definitional and classificatory consistency in the field.[9] It is an effort which remains as remote as when he first began his efforts. In part this stems from his own metatheoretical effort of beginning theory work through a systematic reading of ideas, not codifying descriptions.

Logical empiricism did not overwhelm the post-1960s world of U.S. sociological theory. It remained, however, entrenched in the methodological world. There it was reformulated as a vehicle to resuscitate theory. Aiding this was the emergence in the 1960s of computer-aided computation, which paved the way for the extensive use of multivariate data analysis techniques such as multiple regression. Given the existence of large-scale, often secondary data compilations and what in effect is a modelling mechanism in regression analysis, the methodologically inclined undertook a modified logical empiricist agenda. Begun with Hubert Blalock's *Causal Inferences in Nonexperimental Research* (1964 [1961]),[10] the logic of regression model was premiumed. The residue of the logical empiricists' admiration of a physics-fashioned world remained. If one appropriated the logical empiricist agenda, aided by advanced modelling of data relationships, one had at hand a machine, a machine for what became known as theory construction.[11] After a brief flurry through routines such as path analysis, this formal program for theory construction gave way to an often less rigorous research agenda, one in which data handling was premiumed. The promised coherence of theory construction waned. Among the remaining, but unexplored problems with the theory construction project as well as other less precise multivariate modelling techniques are the correspondence and consistency the logic of the techniques has with the logic of some of the informing ideas which come from various historical texts of sociological theory (e.g., Marx, Durkheim, Weber). The hope that the black box of computational magic will overcome logical and observational problems relating to validity and reliability remains unaddressed despite the logical empiricist aura of such activity. The result is a further muddling of theoretical interests and foci.

Linear, multivariate approaches to data handling stress additive models. Their calculations result in weighing the contribution of constituent variables. This weighting can be affected by the nature of the variable (e.g., how skewed the observations) and the number of variables used in a constituent calculation or model. Seldom does such an effort correspond to any of the source ideas found within the domain of sociological "theory."

Failing to model the data in a fashion corresponding to a verbal portrait, multivariate approaches are used to test a family of propositions dealing with a similar topic. The propositions in effect are fragments derived from various texts in the theory domain (e.g., from Durkheim propositions relating things to suicide). Theory texts in effect provide names for variables or, in some instances, concepts for data which must be treated as proxies. Once the variables and accompanying hypotheses are specified, the multivariate analysis constitutes a closed system for testing hypotheses among hypotheses exhibiting a family resemblance (i.e., they all deal with suicide). This becomes at once a system for testing a number of hypotheses while controlling for the effects of other hypothesized and measured relationships. The underlying logic of this exercise is seldom probed. In part because of the problem of data reliability and in part because of a lack of a clear illuminating objective, these findings tend not to promote a cumulative knowledge-building strategy. If they do, the findings are often pedestrian in nature. This results in making novelty an operating condition in multivariate research. One can find a voice by finding some different data, advancing some similar and some different hypotheses, and then questioning, possibly inappropriately, some hypothesized relationships found in a differently specified regression model. This approach works well for data dredgers who mix and match textual claims with various permutations and combinations of variable selection and computation. Aside from ostensible claims, this activity sustains metatheory in that coherence of the activity and the identity of the researchers derives from some abstracted, coherency-conferring clues from sociological literature. In short, multivariate analysts constitute a market for metatheoretical products, those abstracted ideas from various texts which can be mined for concepts or variable labels. Those inducted into this arena soon learn that there are numerous caveats, caveats in the form of assumptions as well as excuses why things don't work out. Among the latter are such notions as inadequate sample; poorly conceived measures; and inadequate operationalization of concepts. Under such a regimen theoretical concerns were left unexamined.

A second path in the wake of Kuhn's work, one finding greater reception among those favoring tasks identified under the title sociological theory, was a compromise position. Exemplifying this is George Ritzer's *Sociology: A Multi-Paradigm Science* (1980 [1975]).[12] Following Kuhn, Ritzer proposed, not unlike logical empiricists, that sociology was not a coherent disciplinary pursuit. Instead, sociology was a pluralistic subject. Embracing the view that paradigm coherence was the critical mark of a true science, Ritzer began his work by isolating three dominant paradigms/ preparadigms and exemplary works/authors—social facts (Emile Durkheim), social definition (Max Weber), and social behavior (B. F. Skinner).

Imbued with a sense of the heroic and not unlike the logical empiricists who had a desire to create a unified science, Ritzer took as his object sociology. Sociology should have an integrated paradigm.[13] Although this would not be a *fait accompli,* Ritzer clearly elevated the status of items previously viewed as preparadigmatic. In his effort he identified subjective and objective attributes of collective and personal life, and highlighted what was becoming a growing metatheoretical concern, the purported interface between immediate, often face-to-face or micro activities and large, abstract, contingent or macro factors surrounding actors.[14]

Ritzer's work was a signature of the late 1970s and 1980s in that there was an acceptance that there were some incommensurate formulations in sociology. The three which gained academic-disciplinary recognition, though at odds with Ritzer's classification, were functionalism, conflict, and symbolic interaction, with the latter being folded into the more generic category of social interaction. These formulations came about because, it was claimed, the logical empirical program of a single, overarching paradigm was not realized. Ritzer added somewhat to the confusion by suggesting that there was something lacking in sociology by not having a single unifying paradigm, but at the same time pointing to some formulations which could be taken either as paradigms (the multiparadigmatic nature of sociology) or as inadequate formulations (the preparadigmatic character of the discipline). Although Ritzer sought to unify, the practice in academic and professional circles was to treat Ritzer's three paradigms as distinct. More critically, what in effect occurred was that Ritzer had simply provided another metatheoretical system, a way of reading some different voices. The value of his work was that he initially reduced the sociological theory domain to three metatheories (also portrayed as perspectives). This simplification aided in closing discourse on a number of observations or formulations. The task was simply to be able to know one's way around these outlines of this classificatory system, know some exemplary writers under each, and be able to engage in the increasingly stylized critique which could be launched against each. Writers such as Ritzer approached similar tasks with the seeming style of a diplomatic representative of state, urging like a sage that integration should proceed. There should be some means to accommodate and integrate disparate voices under the great sociological tent.

A third path in the post-Kuhnian epoch acknowledges what Diesing, who is quoted at the beginning of this chapter, reads as the situation of many social sciences and their theoretical expression; there is immense, incoherent diversity. The task then is, as sociologists Alexander and Colomy who are also quoted above suggest, to probe the underlying logics and expressions of varying sociological discourses. This is unlike the logical empiricist program which imposes, a priori, a fixed model of discourse, discourse analysis, and empirical confirmation. Hence the label of post-positivist which they affix to their work undertakes to capture varying types. The task for those working in the theory domain is not to worry about the external, sensory-experienced or empirical world or building narratives about such circumstances. Instead attention focuses on illuminating narrative elements in things identified as sociological theory. This is unabashedly metatheoretical. One cannot "read" the world until one "reads" the formulations which propose to narrate something about the world.

Since Kuhn's epochal work, metatheoretical efforts have been canonized into classification schemes of theory. In addition, consistent with the direction of such reflexive projects, this has given birth to the continual reading and rereading of texts which are classified as theory and, most recently, a program for reading what Ritzer, in work we take up later, identifies as metatheory or what is more appropriately identified as the metatheory of metatheory.

The three paths following in the wake of Kuhn's formulation—retrenchment of logical empiricist efforts, acknowledgment of pluralisms sprinkled with a hope of integration, and metatheorizing—highlight the irregular contours of sociology and sociological theory. Metatheory, as a postpositivist stance, reveals sociological theory to be at once narrative or an account of consciousness:[15] a developed, often prefigured consciousness of anonymous others examined with contingent conditions (e.g., class, color/race, gender) and a consciousness of being a sociologist embattled in contesting narratives and techniques. In the first instance of prefigured consciousness, theory becomes simply a way of retelling events. In the latter sociological voices are established in reenactment of arguments against disembodied intellectual forms. For example, a sociologist employing a "conflict perspective" may direct the conflict claims against a "functionalist perspective," or in international affairs a proponent of dependency will direct attention against features of modernization "theory."

Theory in such situations is a rhetorical pose, not an illuminating foray either into the world or the intricacies of a carefully crafted intellect.

With concerns directed away from actual efforts at intellectual work or illuminating the world in which people live, much sociology is engulfed in metatheory. This, we anticipate, may rankle some, those who seize upon our attention given over to discourse. When attention is given to the way sociologists express themselves, there is uneasiness. We anticipate that one rebuttal to what we are sketching is to describe our efforts as postmodernist. This conflates reports with advocacies. We focus and report on discourse and discourses on discourse (e.g., metatheory), both empirical exercises. However, it is common for those who become uneasy as the spotlight is turned onto many rather unremarkable activities which come under the rubric of sociology and sociological theory to be confused. Critics are known to conflate observations about discourse with advocacy.[16] Their argument is that focusing on discourse, on narratives, betrays an anti-science position. Such a position, it is claimed, fails to distinguish science from literature. This reveals an embrace of postmodernism. Our preemptory response to such a view is that we are simply reporting, describing, albeit in an abbreviated fashion, a terrain. Failure to distinguish what is being studied from the identity and performances of an observer is nonsensical. To the charge of being anti-science we simply ask: Where is the science? What standards are we to accept a priori? Unless one wishes to carefully explore the epistemological issues relating to science, all we are being subjected to is a stipulation of science. This is not enlightening. Rather, it is simply an unfounded judgment. In asking the question as to what is to be taken as science, we do not rule out the possibility of science, only that saying the term "science" is neither necessary nor sufficient for a definition of science. Instead of expressing, a priori, a preference, we simply wish to see and explore more. Meanwhile, if many features of sociology and its theories are a congeries, fashioned in a haphazard fashion, as pastiche, this might lead those nominally attuned to observation to heuristically place such items under the heading of postmodern (as opposed to modern). It does not indicate that in using such categories and placing observations under them that the observers necessarily endorse postmodernism. To explore boundary features of cells and place some under the category cancer cells does not indicate anything about cell preference on the part of the one employing the classification. Instead, it is proposed, contrary to Alexander's earlier assertion about sociology being connected to modernism, that contemporary sociology like many of its academic counterparts manifests numerous postmodernist attributes. Does this appear to be a trajectory? Our review leads us to say yes. We did not invent metatheorizing based on classifying "theories" as functionalist, conflict, symbolic interactionism. On the other hand, we routinely encounter textbooks and observe interrogations of students and colleagues using such items. Job interviews, including the ones we have participated in, find that theory or more appropriately metatheory is a routinely used and expected self-referencing device. And such classificatory efforts are often far more a mixture of claims, definitions, and biographies than a carefully worked out logic. By contrast, seldom do job interviews, texts, research articles, or student interrogations pose startling questions or observations about the observed world that are expected to challenge or even shatter preexisting narrative forms. This is confirmed in assessments of the nature of sociological work by those who otherwise are critical of postmodernists.[17]

Although developed narratives make up the most specific, intentional definition of theory, in the general area of sociological theory, as we have suggested, numerous things come to be identified as "theory" or "theoretical": metaphors, analogies, terms and definitions, embedded histories of the discipline and intellectual life, heroic images, forms and appraisals of discourse, and what a sociologist is or should be. In short, the "theory" domain is fuzzy. And current efforts to bring clarity seem to be turning further away from developing or imagining narratives about how an external world operates and more into considering how sociologists and their theories work or, more critically, should work. It is a position which existed when logical empiricism was dominant and which exists today, but with less definition.

With the decline of the positivist and logical empiricist auras in sociology, historical reconstructions and apologies for sociology being a "young" discipline become less compelling. Simply the passing of time makes this the case. Disciplinary sociology may be a half-century younger than some disciplines, but after having a disciplinary identity of over a century, we see that harboring the infantile discipline defense is eroding with each passing year.

The question, then, is, given the acknowledged diversity in the discipline, including its theories, how has the field maintained any coherence? There are, we suggest, external and internal elements to disciplinary coherence. These elements, especially the external ones, are not fixed. The external source of coherence for sociology derives from the intellectual-ideological condition known as cold war liberalism. In the wake of the breakup of the Soviet Union and its satellite system, cold war liberalism and its disciplining effects are, we sense, increasingly strained. This is taken up below.

The internal intellectual coherence, whatever there is in sociology, derives from metatheoretical practices, many of which are found in the teaching, reading, and writing of sociology. These practices are fostered by a contingent condition, one to which learning and doing sociology are an integral part, the general cultural process Ben Agger labels "fast capitalism."[18] Fast capitalism, consistent with the general development of a postmodern culture, is characterized by the rapid, large-scale production and accumulation of texts. The demand to produce texts and index available texts directs attention on features of texts. There is little time left for the appreciation of texts, no less determining if the texts are in any critical way linked to the world of living beings. Under these conditions imaginative spaces as might occur with careful reading shrink or become less valued. The world of the signifier and the world signified lose distinction. Metatheory, in its various manifestations, then, is a vehicle to aid the fast identification and fast reading (or abstracting) of texts. At the same time it remains a phenomenally abstract activity, one bearing little relationship to the tasks of empirical research or illuminating its purported object of study—humans in various contexts and contingencies. This folds the domain of disciplinary theory into the realm of literary criticism, promoting texts as the dominant reality. We will return to this later, but first we examine the external intellectual-ideological condition of cold war liberalism, something which may be unravelling in light of current world events.

LIBERALISM, NATIONALISM, AND THE COLD WAR

Since 1945 U.S. sociology has contributed disproportionately to the world literature in sociology. This exceptional production coincided with the growth of U.S. hegemony in world affairs. As cracks appeared in this dominance,[19] the diversity in sociology via contesting metatheories became more prominent. So too did the self-conscious awareness of sociology as a cultural practice in crisis.[20]

Throughout the growth and decline of U.S. hegemony, U.S. sociology continued to primarily focus on domestic matters or fashioned portraits of the world placing the United States, if not at the center, at the cutting edge of contemporary history. This was done with crude comparative measures. More finely grained analyses of foreign settings and peoples became less prominent, led by the withdrawal of such companion disciplines as anthropology from the international arena.

Despite the decline of the United States in various political, economic, and even military spheres, residues of the earlier hegemonic epoch remain in the texts and practices of the discipline. These texts remain wedded to a political philosophic outlook, liberalism. The late C. Wright Mills[21] highlighted the role of liberalism as a defining condition of not only social life but the social sciences. As with any political philosophy, liberalism provides critical assumptions about the nature of people and the world in which they live. It contributes to the assumptions, concepts, and even portraits which become known as theory. In the domain of sociology and sociological theory, U.S. liberalism was manifested in portraits of international and domestic life. The international face of liberalism became ascendent with post–World War II U.S. hegemony. Like dollars, U.S. intellectual products, including sociological ideas and techniques, prolifer-ated throughout the world. One manifestation of this proliferation was applied sociology to aid other nations and people with modernization. American experts were dispatched to aid in international development. Students along with representatives of foreign governments came to the United States to be trained in development strategies. These efforts were not always coordinated nor coherent. They could range from military as-sistance to community development projects, the latter to which sociolo-gists might be attached. With the onset of U.S. involvement in Vietnam (1964–1973), domestic and international opposition mounted over official U.S. efforts to develop and modernize a world which in the vise of su-perpower cold war machinations was identified as the Third World. Coun-tering formulations of development and modernization was the dependency thesis. Unlike proponents of development and modernization, elevated domestically to a portrait of world history and U.S. benevolence, dependency argued that the United States was one of a continual line of central control and influence which emanated outward to the Third World periphery. The fate of Third World countries was not, as development and modernization themes held, a race of time and effort in simply figuring out the fastest way to attach them to the historic train of progress. Un-derdevelopment and undevelopment in dependency formulations were portrayed as products, however unintentional, of imperial, colonializing influences. With the onset of the Vietnam War the United States, with a checkered history of support for national liberation and oppression, was increasingly linked with the latter. And oppositional sentiment sought to highlight that U.S. influence was not just benignly harmful, but malevo-lently so. Despite their differences, the U.S. antagonists—modernists and developmentalists versus *dependenistas*—shared a common outlook. Both embraced a view of the United States as a dominant moral force, the former celebrating its manifestation and the latter suggesting that the moral compass had become defective. *Dependenistas* in academic settings, while romantically attached to wars of national liberation, were like non-violent civil rights advocates in trying to redeem the soul of the country. Despite these apparent differences, the antagonists resonated with themes long found in U.S. cultural history[22] and which had deep-rooted counter-parts in U.S. sociology.[23]

Many involved in U.S. intellectual life were inattentive to their own dependency on U.S. world dominance, world dominance in a bifurcated world of military superpowers. Just as there was an expression of or appeal to moral superiority in viewing U.S. foreign affairs, a domestic counterpart of liberal sentiment ensued. Expressed in a growing attention to social justice, the political philosophy of which this was an element gained per-suasive power because of the cold war. The Soviet Union always provided a convenient counterpart against which to hold up U.S. domestic practices.

And in international affairs the Soviet Union continually looked for ways
to reveal problems with the United States cold war liberalism, then, entailed programs for international involvement and domestic social justice
as a counter to the image of an oppressive, authoritarian Soviet Union.
Much of the fashioning of this image came from rhetorical excesses rather
than well-established evidence. A climate for theory was cultivated. This
was done primarily through a philosophic idealist program wherein ideas
and ideals were treated as the driving force of history. Since most citizens
and intellectuals were immersed far more in ideas and ideals than evidence, this resulted in a consistent practice. The United States was virtu-
ous, the Soviet Union an evil empire.

C. Wright Mills punctured this shroud of thought, although he left himself little room to maneuver. Not only did he view U.S. liberalism, cold
war liberalism, as moribund, he similarly indicted the Soviet Union and
its fatigued expression of socialism. Mills proposed a remedy to what he
saw was an exhaustion of critical intellectual discourse among the superpowers. The remedy was a type of vision in which sociologists and, it
seemed, citizens were to do battle against these repressive and stultifying
forces. Mills's tools remained those of a philosophical idealism: think
straight, he seemed to counsel. This was a particularly vexing position
given that Mills had already highlighted the terrain of a dominant power
elite, ruling a world of anemic middle-class citizens. Mills, however, could
not resist the great sociological move, to call up heroic images, images of
great thinkers who had contributed to his version of an encompassing
sociological imagination. In the ideological climate, Mills was dismissed.
In generous moments he was portrayed as a radical. In less generous ones
he was regarded simply as a pamphleteer without redeeming scholarly
value.[24]

Not only was Mills far from being a major radical, it is now apparent
that his call for the heroic had little salience in a world which he himself
had critically described. In a world dominated by the production of mass
culture, fashioning sociology as yet another body of redemptive and redeeming ideas calls forth an image of life in another epoch, possibly a
premodern one. Mills, concerned about exhausted imaginations, was himself struggling with this problem in another light. Cold war liberalism,
anchored in a nation dominated by pervasive consumerism, created conditions which were difficult not just to describe, but to critically penetrate
and appraise.

Very likely the cold war was a response to possible threats. Domestically, however, empirical evidence about the USSR was limited. And it
was the domestic face of the cold war which had major impact on intellectual efforts. It was an impact characterized by ideological rigidity, car-
icatures rather than evidence. This aided a major structural dynamic of
the period, military Keynesianism. Like World War II, the ensuing cold

war disciplined the U.S. population. As a side benefit it fueled an industrial policy for producing and distributing immense surpluses in the form of military hardware. Associated with the cold war were domestic policies controlling not only political expression but labor force decisions. The dependency of the U.S. economy on military Keynesianism did not become widely apparent until the 1980s when President Ronald Reagan led the last assault in behalf of economic maintenance and recovery through enhanced military spending. The economy seemingly did not decline, but the cost, combined with other deferred financial maneuvers, was astronomical. Meanwhile, the Soviet Union reeled under the weight of its own military machine plus other economic hardships leading to the eventual unravelling of the Soviet Empire. But before this occurred, sociology in both the United States and the Soviet Union was on the wane. In the United States this was aided by Reagan political functionaries who were overtly hostile to sociology on ideological grounds. This was matched by a decline in the public use of sociological discourse. More severe and somewhat parallel to this was the outright banning of sociology in the USSR during the Brezhnev era.

As the U.S. economy became less inclusive, sociologists retreated further into liberal ideologies, a stance that first became highly visible in the 1960s when expansive civil rights efforts and related protests combined with President Johnson's vision of social justice in his formulation of the Great Society. Liberal sentiments, long a staple of U.S. social science, were more prominent with the growing interest in and support for a generic political-cultural activity, that of social problems.[25] Social problems activity is the means for defining, appropriating, and directing critical attention and discourse, one sustaining the liberal ethos in which the state is appealed to as a vehicle by which redress for inequality proceeds.[26] Today, social problems defining and commenting activities are extensive. Among the currently fashionable intertwined social problems concerns dealing with inequality are color with a focus on African Americans, gender with attention riveted on women, and, somewhat less compelling, social class with a focus on poverty. Most other specific social problems topics such as crime, medical delivery, the aged, and the like are fashioned with these concerns as major elements. In the waning of the cold war these liberal residues appear less and less totalizing and more and more as small, but pervasive outputs to scavenge power, power which is often more prominent in battles over academic discourse than in policy or certainly a utopian vision of a socially just social order. The decline in economic fortunes and the loss of the political disciplining force of cold war regimes seems to be unfolding in a series of episodic, balkanized skirmishes, many of which get their most focused expression in academic life. In academic affairs discourse is increasingly patrolled with the aid of sociologists. This further sustains the retreat to fortresses of metatheoretical discourse as a possibility. On one hand notions of class, gender, and race penetrate as metatheoretical concerns, going well beyond simply a set of conceptual concerns. Those retreating to the battlement of metatheory find this effort breached with the fusillades charging sexism and racism. Sexism and racism are portrayed as acts of commission on the content of ideas. This charge often spills over in questioning the identity of a writer or speaker, frequently stipulated as a racist, sexist, or some other despoiling label.

Although these stylized social problems discourses have intensified sensitivities and have directed attention to previously neglected areas of social life, they have not and are not expected to foster critical insight into the discourses and processes in which these and related social problems concerns are pressed.[27] The prominence of social problems can be seen in the incorporation of such issues into even introductory-level texts. The texts and their presentations work less to clarify than to police particular types of discourse. This is done through continual comparisons of unequal portrayals purportedly done to raise consciousness. This social problems mobilization tactic, however, nurtures a pervasive discontent, one expressed in skirmishes over discourse and hypostatized personal-identifying accounts. It does not penetrate into the persistent, even growing divisions fostered by these hypostatized notions. Quickly this leads to questions over the epistemological adequacy of the discipline. Again, the road to metatheory seems to beckon. As laudable as the goals of social problems advocates might be, they are mired in many cliché-driven encounters, fostering a seemingly relevant, but obfuscating discourse. Correspondence notions, so suspect in the evolving tradition of logical empiricism, have returned in these highly stylized social problems arenas. The result: a static, often overly simplistic portrait of the world. This becomes even more premiumed as identities more so than substantive claims are the major concern. The challenges this poses for post–cold war late capitalism and its ossified liberalism remain to be concerns.

Before we leave this topic we enter a caveat. We are mindful that one of the pervasive problems in sociology and numerous disciplines is how to proceed. Social problems advocates and stylizers have found a way to give expression to discontent, to get noticed. The efficacy of this type of discourse relative to outcomes may need assessment. This does not mean we have a covenant with a royal right way to proceed. If anything, we consider the barriers even more pervasive than do those who can announce that all can be explained by class, gender, or race or that once the poor, women, and African-Americans become empowered with a voice, new and liberative conditions will dawn in social life. Such claims, as even social problems advocates recognize, are too sweeping and daunting. They continue the old Enlightenment move of conflating some type of truth-claim or knowledge with domination. That this is at once being criticized and being reproduced by those proclaiming to be interested in the "voices from the margins" is intriguing.

Social problems provides a self-promoting discourse for those previously treated as distant or marginal "others" or their self-appointed representatives. The efforts appeal to state intervention, often in an effort to punish the discourse of actual and hypostatized antagonists. The result: the production of a lexicon of fighting words and the expansion of new symbolic terrains of victimage. This merges with a general movement in which everyone can become a victim. Though unexamined, the terrain relating to freedom and responsibility is being transformed. What the effects of relying principally on discourse as a vehicle of action and understanding is a terrain which we find not well illuminated. Meanwhile, the aura of the postmodern lingers and the road to metatheory seems ever so seductive.

Despite the expansion of social problems discourse in sociology, the discipline has experienced incipient decline, corresponding to the declines of U.S. hegemony and the engine of cold war liberalism. In the exigencies of recent history, many facets of sociology have been eclipsed by a more obtuse, abstract system of thought, economics. With zero-sum[28] cultural and material conditions becoming more manifest, economic assessments proliferate at the expense of sociology, which once could energize the detailing of what is happening in the lives of people in various collective settings. Without state-induced disciplining of the population, sociology is limited as an organized activity to foster discipline, circulate interest, or intervene with respect to opportunities.[29]

Despite sweeping events, sociological practice continues to seek out niches. In sociological theory efforts at disciplinary renewal are made. This follows a long-established tradition, one exhibiting the confidence of those charged with reassembling the broken Humpty-Dumpty. It is this continuing effort to reassemble a plurality of fragmented discourses and practices that directs our attention to the internal dynamics of sociology which is more explicitly captured in the topic of metatheory.

THE PROMINENCE OF FORMALIZED METATHEORY

When sociological theories are connected to specific fact-constructing or fact-gathering activities, they reflect diversity. Based on a variety of logics-in-use,[30] the things called sociological to which the term *theory* is applied are anchored in local[31] and topical[32] practices. The result: numerous definitions, claims, and disputes have become treated as belonging to the domain of sociological theory.

For those crafting disciplinary sociology, numerous fragments of symbolic materials—metaphors, analogies, propositions, definitions—have become the things addressed in theory work as well as in forays into epistemology.[33] Theory workers, theorists, are those who essay, organize, and assess these primarily textual materials. Today, the effort to reassemble the sociological enterprise and its discourses is pursued with increasing intensity.

Much writing and teaching addressing theory is not theory per se, but rather it is about sociological theory. In effect it is metatheoretical. Formally, metatheoretical work is characterized by the categorization of various symbolic elements making up the theory domain. Such categorization is done, according to proponents such as George Ritzer,[34] to aid the understanding, development, and promotion of overarching or simplifying formulations.

Ritzer, following his penchant for reconstructing sociology, examines metatheory, fittingly enough, metatheoretically. It is a project having detractors, though as Ritzer deftly notes detractors who are themselves metatheoreticians.[35] Though metatheorizing is not unique and it is tempting to be dismissive of Ritzer, his effort of subsuming all metatheoretical work as a topic itself is indicative of something more than an idle curiosity or a misplaced effort. He is up to something more than crafting a counterpart to what might be an index and abstract to Cliff Notes.[36]

Ritzer is aware that careful reading of texts is not a common occurrence in sociological and, we note, academic-intellectual practice. He senses, uneasily, that sociological texts are often appraised to the degree that they conform to some received metatheoretical identity (e.g., a conflict perspective, etc.). That he wishes, in his own heroic vein, to transcend this situation with yet another metatheoretical system is puzzling until it is remembered that this fits Ritzer's program to integrate sociological discourse.

Ritzer's work reflects, we suggest, an embedded set of developments in the political economy of culture, one in which the distinctions between texts, the worlds that texts address, and the reflections on texts are collapsing. With the existence of so many texts, constrained by other temporal exigencies on careers (e.g., "publish or perish"), a metatheory serves as a predigested form of literary criticism, a stylized way of doing postured reading and reporting. The battle of texts becomes premiumed. It is a way of appearing to master an extensive literature, a posture more important than being familiar with details and problems or, for that matter, a sympathetic understanding of the authors of texts. Instead of sociological theory being a script portraying and illuminating social life, theory becomes a theory text to be addressed through stylized, often social problems–infused, interpretive frameworks. In the extreme, the boundaries between text and life become so blurred that social life is treated as a text, meaning that all that is needed to describe and understand the world of humans is to launch patrols of certain kinds of textual discourses either found in texts or traced from texts. Theory supplants observation as the source of

Figure 15.1
Types of Metatheorizing for Understanding

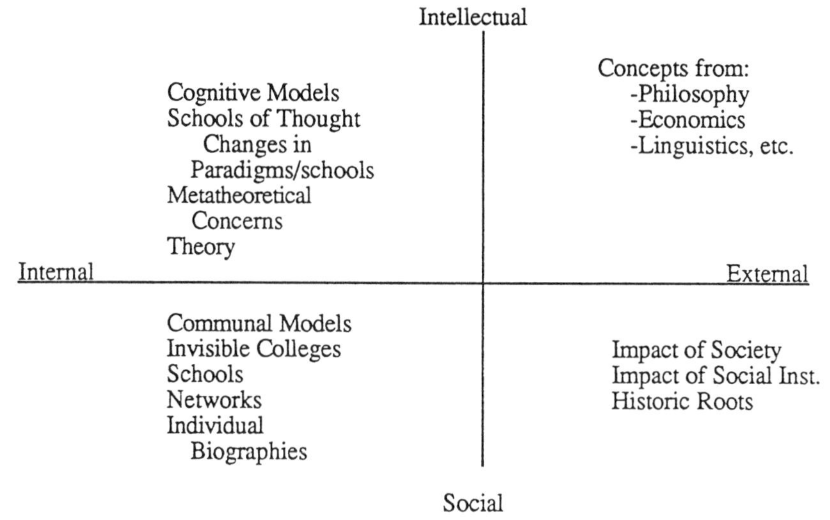

	Intellectual	
		Concepts from:
Cognitive Models		-Philosophy
Schools of Thought		-Economics
Changes in		-Linguistics, etc.
Paradigms/schools		
Metatheoretical		
Concerns		
Theory		
Internal		External
Communal Models		
Invisible Colleges		Impact of Society
Schools		Impact of Social Inst.
Networks		Historic Roots
Individual		
Biographies		
	Social	

Source: George Ritzer, *Metatheorizing in Sociology* (Lexington, MA, and Toronto: Lexington Books, 1991), p. 18.

"facts." Theory holds the promise of penetrating some features of everyday life. In the productionist environment of prestige-seeking academic workers, subtleties are ignored in favor of more generic, stipulated abstract appraisals of textual interpretation. In such an environment, metatheory and the metatheory of metatheory combine to become a giant machine to indiscriminately circulate indistinctness. This indistinctness ensues from the perpetual combinations and permutations of eclectically chosen signifiers.

USING METATHEORY FOR UNDERSTANDING AND IDENTITY

Ritzer maintains that there are several uses to which metatheory can be applied. A major one which has had currency for some time and is manifested in textbooks on sociological theory is what is labeled M_U: metatheoretical efforts to aid in "attaining deeper understanding of sociological theory." Such efforts at classification—schools, types of theories, networks, meeting criteria of science—are in effect reading instructions, a type of imposed literary criticism. See Figure 15.1. In most instances they retain an indexical unit, that of the biography of people identified as theorists. These biographies and their written works become exemplars of "theory." The biographies along with the identification of metatheoretical subcategories are building blocks of sociologists' identities. At appropriate moments the trained sociologist can mention Weber or Marx. In professional presentations, invoking a metatheoretical standard becomes a commonplace: "What kind of sociologist are you?" Answer: "I'm a conflict theorist." These are the face value of cards used in the game of identity-making and conferral. The labels indicate a place in a comfortable universe of discourse and are engaged in with the ease of one who is identified as a fast food or supermarket customer. These are postmodern markers, like the comforting identifying signs of gasoline stations and fast food restaurants. Their ubiquitous and generic quality sustains life in the anonymity of many settings, having a universal currency value. Aside from establishing an identity, these metatheoretical snippets provide a script to establish an identity and foster an appropriate appreciation. If mentioning "functionalism" is not clarifying enough, the name of Talcott Parsons can be invoked. Once done, a plethora of expressive clues for a speaker or writer issues forth to qualify the identities of writers and speakers. Through most of the 1970s and 1980s, the term functionalism and the name Talcott Parsons created predictable discourse and social interaction. The clichés were easy to identify. "Functionalism ignores conflict." "It isn't attentive to change." "Parsons was a 'grand theorist.'" "Parsons's prose is turgid." In most instances these circulating comments provided an account of things not being done, in effect nonsense. However, it is out of such nonsense that some sociological identities are crafted, ones which polemicize and negate these cliché-like, ubiquitous assertions making up some, possibly much, professional talk. Each statement underscoring deficiency rules out one's addressing puzzles about the surrounding world. Once ensnared, the capacity to distinguish in such a fashion, to encounter friction between one's discourse and some kind of describable world, vanishes. Instead shards of biography and bits of definitions and claims predominate.

For those venturing the identity of "theorist," seemingly more meaningful in teaching contexts than in other performances, this is to be taken in one of several ways. One is to be identified as a person immersed in texts. This is to be shrouded with the mysterious mantle of master of a number of seemingly undecipherable texts. Another is to be viewed as a lost soul in the sea of metatheoretical musings and subcategories waiting for a sociological equivalent to Beckett's Godot, preferably an integrating Godot. Theory like the sociology it serves is a distant becoming.

The prominence of metatheoretical systems and biographical reconstructions of sociologists' identities via metatheory is linked to the political condition of sociology, one which Diesing notes exhibits weak internal government but is preoccupied with an extensive, often contentious socialization process.[37]

THE COMMODIFICATION OF TEXTS

Biographies, a staple in metatheoretical summaries, are important for another reason related to the academic workplace. They reaffirm that texts, including theory texts, in sociology are products of authors. Invoking an author is in effect appropriating a discourse,[38] not only demarcating how the text should be approached but also reaffirming that texts are created or authored. Acknowledging authorship is affirming the notion that the text was made, and that its creator or representative has a proprietary interest. This conferral of ownership commodifies discourse. Authored texts are the foundation for establishing symbolic capital,[39] the creation and appropriation of which is a distinguishing feature of many workers whom Barbara Ehrenreich[40] identifies as the "professional middle class." In addition, this type of exercise, one which abstracts the text to authorship and proprietary interests, augurs well with sustaining an abstracted notion of exchange. Texts are looked at less and less for their claims and increasingly for their exchange value: the money or prestige accruing to authorship.[41]

Under developed capitalism, symbolic capital faces the same contradiction inherent in other forms of capital: with greater accumulation the rate of profit declines.[42] Symbolic capital needs to circulate, to be reinvested. As authors and texts multiply, the competition for authorial recognition of texts increases. To counterbalance this competition, a short-term remedy is to "speed up" text production. In a growing number of U.S. academic settings it is no longer sufficient to simply "publish or perish," but "publish at an increasing rate or perish." This exemplifies an aspect of a condition Agger labels "fast capitalism."[43] Under conditions of fast capitalism, authors and texts increasingly accumulate, creating an aura of despairing "noise"[44] for those for whom texts have been a vehicle for distancing themselves from the world which they wish to critique. Under fast capitalism, texts are collected and indexed. Their use in constituting, if not promoting, disparate meanings from the world in which the readers no less than the authors live is neutralized. In Agger's terms, this signals a decline of discourse.[45] For the shards of notions and ideas identified as sociological theory, this means that there is less and less validity to the experiences and concerns of readers-cum-observers-cum-conversationalists. Whatever civilizing[46] function abstracted communication such as theory may have had in directing others' attention to things which were otherwise ignored or to claims by people which were insipid if not simply stupid becomes less likely. Trophies in terms of commodified, not appreciated, texts prevail.

The production of numerous texts of declining value aids the growth of various indexical and classification schemes. One which fast capital competitors in the social sciences like is the *Social Sciences Citation Index*

(*SSCI*). The *Index,* using bibliometric procedures, publishes a ranking of various journals in their contribution to accumulation. Those whose articles are cited more frequently are held to have more impact. Similarly, one can compare individual scholars using the *Index* by comparing the number of citations to their publications in indexed works.[47] Predictably, conditions for comparative levels of assessment[48] are fueled. Despite indexing an impressive array of journals, there is a decidedly Western hegemonic aura to the selection. Accumulation and dominance become the standard-bearers of certified knowledge production and distribution. And consistent with fast capitalism, if the title of an article is not sufficiently precise, its circulation value in the indexing and circulation or recovery process is limited.

Ritzer's program for metatheory, especially efforts to better understand theory texts, confronts the same problem the *SSCI* combats: sheer numbers of items. Ritzer undertakes a nominal classification system which has, to its credit, a more ambitious objective than those who become fixated on impact scores and assessments.[49] It has the advantage that items so hidden under numbers in the *SSCI* are easier to discern.

To confront the rapidity affecting symbolic capital, metatheoreticians seek solace in classifying authors and texts relating to theory. One such ambitious formulation is Don Martindale's *The Nature and Types of Sociological Theory.*[50] Martindale classified a plethora of sociological works in terms of two metatheoretical subcategories: humanistic and scientific. The humanistic subcategory highlighted texts whose antecedents could be traced to pre-Enlightenment figures whereas the scientific highlighted post-Enlightenment texts. Like a classical economist, employing cyclical formulations such as those advanced by Pitirim Sorokin,[51] Martindale could deal with fast capital concerns as having a fateful resolution (i.e., this too shall pass), or he could retreat to a humanistic posture where the antithesis to fast capitalism was done by calling up those authors and works premiuming resistance to the world science and facts through appealing to claims of enduring values. What this ignored was that Martindale's metatheoretical efforts were abstracting and compacting not only the works he labeled scientific, but those he labeled humanistic. To illustrate the problematic, in his effort to address change, Martindale found himself entrapped in his own metatheoretical construct, reading his problems through the abstracted texts which he had previously classified.[52] Meanwhile, the metatheoretical subcategories of humanities and science, though having heuristic value, frequently serve to identify features believed to have produced discourse rather than to aid participation in and use of discourse. This leads to differentiation, not engaged conversation and debate. For example, the "humanist" sociologist through metatheoretically encouraged identity work imposes not only an inability but even an unwillingness to communicate with the "positivist-cum-scientist" sociologist and vice versa. These postures add to discourse as much as someone indicating that she is a "female mathematician" or an "aged poet." And at this level there is little to which one can respond.

EXPLORING RITZER'S METATHEORETICAL PROJECT

Of Ritzer's three types of metatheorizing designed to harness a myriad of claims, we again turn our efforts to his M_u subcategory, metatheorizing to aid understanding. As Figure 15.1 reveals, this is a metatheoretical exercise to classify other metatheoretical efforts which, if we follow Alexander and Colomy, quoted at the beginning of the chapter, becomes a vehicle for M_D metatheorizing for theoretical development and possibly an overarching metatheoretical scheme M_o.

Ritzer's classification of metatheories M_u uses two dichotomies identical to that of Jonathan Cole and Stephen Cole:[53] intellectual emphases versus social contexts and foci on things internal to sociology versus things external. The intellectual pole stresses cognitive attributes identified in sociological theory. The social pole highlights the activities and consequences of features of theory. The internal-external division is self-explanatory.

Although Ritzer's is not the only program in metatheory, his work is the first or among the first to undertake the integrating effort, whereas other works have been content to accept different metatheoretical classifications[54] or uncritically employ them in an effort to unravel the distribution and networks of ideas.[55]

METATHEORY IN PRACTICE

Up to this point we have explored the state of sociology and its moves toward metatheory, highlighting the external conditions in such things as cold war liberalism and a shifting set of markets. We have suggested that this is reflected in sociological practice. We have looked at some of the internal dynamics as it is related to discourse. We now highlight some of the prominent domains of metatheory found in more specific practices internal to the discipline, things associated with sociology curricula and professional literature.

METATHEORY IN SOCIOLOGY CURRICULA

Sociology is saturated with theory or what we highlight as metatheory: categories of biographies, concepts, and claims. Wherever one turns, theory exists. Since the 1970s, introductory texts in sociology have delineated three theory domains—conflict, functionalism, and symbolic interactionism. In some instances these are used to highlight different ways to frame or "explain" sociocultural things. In other instances this introduces students to the multivoiced nature of the field which will be encountered in other courses.

After the introductory-level course many undergraduate texts and courses are laced with theories. Textual representation involves becoming familiar with the claims and counterclaims of various positions. Substantive concerns are shrouded in a terrain of arguments. Students are expected to translate observations into one of these narrative forms. A query might be: how would a conflict theorist look at "x"? A variation in this occurs when students are routinely asked to engage in activities such as comparing and contrasting, for example, the conflict perspective with that of symbolic interactionism.

Because many of the ideas underlying these global categories are tied to biographies of canonical figures in the discipline, a variation of the above question is to ask students to either critique, respond, or identify a debate in claims, for example, about Durkheim, Marx, and Weber. In most instances the understanding of these people's work—just like the more categorical systems of conflict, functionalism, and symbolic interactionism—is derived from secondary sources. Aside from temporal constraints, there is resistance to examining original texts. The conditions for fast capitalism are in place.

In graduate study there is a greater likelihood that original texts will be examined. The categorizations established in the undergraduate curriculum continue, however, to be energized. They take on greater significance in that now two additional elements are added to the repertoire of the student: identity work and induction into an academic style. In both of these metatheory plays a part. Identity work involves situating one's self in a world of texts. Generally, there are two systems of interlaced texts which are to be used: theory-metatheory texts and specialty texts. This established, one can appear, for example, as a symbolic interactionist criminologist. This establishes terms for not only what the person reads and represents, but how that person will be identified in a bureaucratic setting. In many instances, however, these domains are less distinct given the overdetermination of theory-metatheory. That the storehouse of puzzling facts does substantially multiply, the graduate student must work through a maze of commentaries and critiques of theoretical framing combined with some skill in handling data which might be related to the concerns at hand.

The second, intertwined feature of theory-metatheory in graduate study centers on developing a polemical style.[56] Theory-metatheory provides the outlines for an argumentative voice, one which establishes claims or embraces in part at the expense of some actual or hypostatized other. In the first instance the other can be a figure or body of thought (metatheory) which can be critiqued and criticized. The abolition of the other is a stylized approach which serves to establish one's own voice. This rhetorical device establishes the value of one's own work by discrediting others, including the metatheories and assertions that are made. Two factors contribute to this. First, as Diesing notes, in disciplines, such as sociology, which are principally centered in socialization activities, this provides something to do. Second, the polemic, often augmented by a commitment to social problems thought, provides a style by which to engage many contemporary concerns considered of interest and relevance to sociologists. This stylized debunking, fostered in social problems productions, promotes an argumentative frame in which others, often hypostatized others—sociologists or nonsociologists—are savaged. For example, in the arena of AIDS, attention is often directed at the intolerance of fundamentalists in the community despite the fact that this isn't confirmed by survey evidence.[57] But because sociological practice is linked to social problem promotion, the polemic against fundamentalism seems more persuasive than the evidence. Theory and metatheory disputes divert attention from empirical and logical explorations.[58] They also serve as a cultural form for the circulation of polemical stances.

CANONS AND THEORY USE IN PROFESSIONAL LITERATURE

With its overdetermination of theory-metatheory and strong commitment to polemics, sociology has become a highly canonized field. As noted, historical figures and categorized formulations continually surround the expressive practice of sociologists. Strangely, a field which has long claimed a covenant with modernism is one which has, like ancient Roman statuary, built up a diverse army of canonical figures and metatheoretical identifiers serving as critical guides in framing sociological voices.

The late Don Martindale explored canonization in intellectual life. Martindale's sociohistorical work was directed at distinguishing conditions for various forms of community formation. One of the things which provided a clue to the state of communities was the nature and type of manifested intellectual life. In creative epochs, when new, complex human communities emerged, "the sphere for manifestation of individuality is widened and its products are rewarded." Encouragement of creativity declines during the mature phase of a community. "The sphere of social life left open for the free construction of individuals is narrowed, and a restrictive array of intellectual forms is fixed." Whereas in a creative period truth is determined "in terms of standards and criteria established in the proper conduct of the thought processes," in periods of conformity "there is a tendency to establish socially acceptable truth by institutional procedures."[59]

Martindale's formulation can be modified in the wake of contemporary fast capitalism. Fast capitalism is characterized by an immense accumulation of texts. Simple operationalists might suggest this is indicative of a creative, increasingly complex epoch. Creating metatheoretical classifications would seem to suggest that the concern is with thought itself. However, one finds that it isn't thought but an informational, preformed literary criticism model which dominates. The result is that an abstracted reading of texts occurs, a reading which is suffused with a false dialectic. Texts are placed within some type of metatheoretical schema, differences in their content and construction noted by some imposed schema, and then readers—students and faculty—are asked to energize the differences of the metatheoretical systems. Though this is an activity immersing the reader into a type of thought process, it is one which abstracts the abstract. Those entering into the domain of theory in this fashion are in effect confronting, building on Karl Mannheim, a hyperideological system.[60] Mannheim perceptively noted not only that an age of ideology was a defense of an institutional order but that it phenomenally involved discounting intellectual activity by subordinating it to interpretations using attributions and contextual placements. In the metatheoretically saturated practice of sociology this results in hyperideological thought characterized by (a) abstracting elements[61] of different kinds of "theories" (humanistic vs. scientific in an earlier epoch; functionalist-conflict-symbolic interactionist in the current epoch); (b) fashioning the categories into conflicts framed in terms of an attributed philosophy of history (e.g., cyclical, conflict); and (c) indoctrinating and ritually requiring those exposed to metatheoretical categories to participate in a frozen dialectic—a highly stylized set of self-referencing arguments in which the identity of the spokesperson is established simultaneously with a ritual polemic (e.g., symbolic interactionism framed to seemingly negate conflict).

The employment of this pseudo-argumentative style anchored in and reproductive of metatheory is highly ritualized. This occurs, Ritzer unhappily notes,[62] because of the seeming inability of numerous sociologists to read what is presented as sociology if it is not framed in appropriate metatheoretical terms and moves. In short, the very identity of the sociological speaker is constrained to the issuing of limited metatheoretical categories and simulating an argument through a ritual polemic.[63]

Who have become the canonized figures in sociology? A review of textbooks devoted to sociological theory reveals a staple of figures: Auguste Comte, Herbert Spencer, Karl Marx, Emile Durkheim, Vilfredo Pareto, Max Weber, Georg Simmel, George Herbert Mead, and Talcott Parsons. Others in the conflict, phenomenological, and symbolic interactionist traditions are mentioned. And of late one can encounter reviews of works as those by Anthony Giddens, Jürgen Habermas, and Pierre Bourdieu, among others. In some ways these works not only consolidate, but go beyond the canonization of ideas and persons associated with theory. To show this we first reviewed a selection of symposia volumes published since 1945: Harry Elmer Barnes (ed.), *An Introduction to the History of*

Sociology (1948),[64] Robert K. Merton, Leonard Broom, and Leonard S. Cottrell, Jr. (eds.), *Sociology Today: Problems and Prospects* (1959),[65] Joseph S. Rouceck (ed.), *Readings in Contemporary American Sociology* (1961),[66] Robert E. L. Faris (ed.), *Handbook of Modern Sociology* (1964),[67] Paul F. Lazarsfeld, William H. Sewell, and Harold L. Wilensky (eds.), *The Uses of Sociology* (1967),[68] Nicholas C. Mullins, *Theories and Theory Groups in Contemporary American Sociology* (1973),[69] and Neil J. Smelser (ed.), *Handbook of Sociology* (1988).[70] Since these constitute state-of-the-field documents, we were interested to see what the canonical domain was with respect to writers cited in the volumes. Not all are used in the field as theoretical exemplars; however, there is sufficient overlap to suggest that there is a nesting effect. Table 15.1 lists nearly 150 names of writers appearing in at least five of the seven volumes.

Another way to explore the canonization of sociological thought is to view the use of sociological theory. To do this we constructed a list of theorists gleaned from a review of current theory texts.[71] Table 15.2 lists the names of theorists according to degree of frequency of citation in selected volumes—five-year intervals beginning in 1975—in several leading journals in sociology—the *American Journal of Sociology,* the *American Sociological Review,* and *Social Forces.* Among the subcategory of most frequently cited are Peter Berger, Peter Blau, Emile Durkheim, Erving Goffman, George Homans, Karl Marx, Robert Merton, Talcott Parsons, Georg Simmel, and Max Weber. In most instances these names also appeared in Table 15.1. The case of Peter Blau is an anomaly only in that his citations range across a number of different distinct interests from large-scale organization to social stratification and proxies of structural heterogeneity.

In the subcategory of least frequently cited, those who were particularly low in citations were Jean Baudrillard, Pierre Bourdieu, Janet Chafetz, Nancy Chodorow, Auguste Comte, Sigmund Freud, and Dorothy Smith. With the exception of Comte, none of these names appear on Table 15.1. This generally reflects the more recent appearance of some of the writers, particularly women writers. Unlike the women cited in Table 15.1—Jessie Bernard, Beverly Duncan, Mirra Komaravsky, and Helen M. Lynd—later writers such as Chafetz, Chodorow, and Smith are less likely to be linked with a disciplinary specialty and more likely to be involved with issues relating to theory and theory disputation. The relatively low number of citations to Baudrillard and Bourdieu indicates not only their comparatively recent arrival in texts in sociological theory, but possibly a cultural mazeway which is resistant to foreign writers. While Habermas circulates in a wide array of sociological and nonsociological circles, his work similarly does not lend itself to much journal science unless it is connected with the metatheoretical classifications of Marxism and neo-Marxism.

The sample of journal articles was examined to see how the cited authors' works were used. The predominant use of writers and their works appears to be as part of a background or context for the article. This

Table 15.1
Canonized Figures in Sociology: 1948–1988

Theodore Adorno	Neil Gross	Robert E. Park
Gordon Allport	Paul Hatt	Talcott Parsons
Solomon Asch	Amos Hawley	A.R. Radcliff-Brown
Robert Bales	Rudolph Heberle	Walter Reckless
Bernard Barber	August Hollingshead	Robert Redfield
Chester I Barnard	George C. Homans	Frederick Redlich
Aloen Barton	Carl I Hovland	Albert J. Reiss
Raymond Bauer	Everett C. Hughes	David Riesman
Howard S. Becker	Helen Hughes	F J Roethlisberger
Bernard Berelson	Herbert H. Hyman	Edward A. Ross
Jessie Bernard	Alex Inkeles	Peter H. Rossi
Peter Blau	Morris Janowitz	Wilbur Shram
Herbert Blumer	Joseph Kahl	Philip Selznick
Edgar F. Borgatta	Elihu Katz	William H. Sewell
Leonard Broom	Patricia L. Kendall	Clifford R. Shaw
Ernest W. Burgess	Mirra Komaravsky	M. Sherif
Theodore Caplow	Harold Lasswell	Edward Shils
John A. Clausen	Paul F. Lazarsfeld	Georg Simmel
Marshall clinard	Nathan Leites	Herbert A. Simon
James S. Coleman	Daniel Lerner	Richard L Simon
Auguste Comte	Claude Levi-Strauss	Albion W. Small
Charles Cooley	Daniel J. Levinson	Neil Smelser
Leonard S. Cottrell	Marion J. Levy	Pitirim Sorokin
Donald R. Cressey	Kurt Lewin	Herbert Spencer
Robert A. Dahl	Gardner Lindzey	Samuel Stouffer
Kingsley Davis	Ralph Linton	Anselm Strauss
Morton Deutsch	Ronald Lippitt	Fred L. Strodtbeck
John Dewey	Seymour Lipset	Edward A. Suchman
Stuart C. Dodd	Charles P. Loomis	William G. Sumner
John Dollard	George Lundberg	Ed. H. Sutherland
Beverly Duncan	Helen M. Lynd	Guy E. Swanson
Otis D. Duncan	Robert S. Lynd	Gabriel Tarde
H. Warren Dunham	Bron. Malinowski	W. I. Thomas
Emile Durkheim	Karl Mannheim	Ferdinand Tonnies
Friedrich Engels	Karl Marx	Ernst Troeltsch
Erik H. Erikson	William McPhee	Willard Waller
Amitai Etzioni	George Herbert Mead	Lester F. Ward
Robert E. Faris	Roberto Michels	W. Lloyd Warner
Leon Festinger	C. Wright Mills	Max Weber
E. Franklin Frazier	Barr. Moore, Jr.	S. K. Weinberg
Erich Fromm	Wilbert Moore	Pascal Whelpoton
Charles J. Galpin	Jacob L. Moreno	Ralph K. White
Hans H. Gerth	Gunnar Myrdal	William F. White
Franklin H. Gidding	Theodore Newcomb	Harold Wilensky
Erving Goffman	Robert Nisbet	Robin Williams
William J. Goode	William F. Ogburn	Louis Wirth
Alvin W. Gouldner	Vilfredo Pareto	Hans Zetterberg
		Carle C. Zimmerman
		Florian Znaniecki

Source: Works listed in text. Authors in at least five texts.

Table 15.2
Assessing the Use of Identified Theorists in Professional Literature, 1975–1990

More Frequently Cited	Less Frequently Cited
Theodore Adorno	Jeffrey Alexander
Peter Berger	Jean Baudrillard
Peter Blau	Pierre Bourdieu
Herbert Blumer	Janet Chafetz
Randall Collins	Nancy Chodorow
Ralf Dahrendorf	Auguste Comte
Emile Durkheim	Charles H. Cooley
Anthony Giddens	Lewis Coser
Erving Goffman	Michel Foucault
George Homans	Sigmund Freud
Karl Marx	Harold Garfinkel
George Herbert Mead	Jurgen Habermas
Robert K. Merton	Arlie R. Hochschild
C. Wright Mills	Marion J. Levy
Talcott Parsons	Karl Mannheim
Georg Simmel	Herbert Marcuse
Pitirim A. Sorokin	Vilfredo Pareto
Max Weber	Theda Skocpol
	Dorothy Smith
	Herbert Spencer
	Immanuel Wallerstein

Source: Selected issues of the *American Journal of Sociology, American Sociological Review,* and *Social Forces.*

highlights the importance of literature review in the construction of journal articles. Substantially less frequent is the use of an author's work to provide an *ex post factum* portrait of what was being reported on. Less frequent is the use of a writer's work as a source of concepts or propositions, as a source for assumptions about the world, or as a model linking various elements—concepts, claims, and so forth—in some type of coherent whole. This latter effort might require a different type of textual analysis to further validate this conclusion.

This brief exploration in the arena of professional self-referencing as found in the seven symposia volumes and the sample of citations in three leading journals reveals that U.S. sociology has a canonical terrain of writers. Most of the canonical figures are of long standing. This buttresses the finding that most subdisciplinary divisions in sociology have remained intact since the original *Handbook on Contemporary Developments in World Sociology* was published.

SUMMARY

Sociological theory continues to be a central element in sociology curricula and in sociological writing. The nature of it, however, seems encapsulated in ever-expansive metatheoretical systems, systems by which a variety of ideas are abstracted and classified. This activity seems to diverge from research efforts, research efforts retaining elements of logical empiricism. As the examination of journal articles revealed, works associated with those identifiable as "theorists" show that these serve primarily to advance a context or background for a problem. They are not principally sources of concepts and propositions nor, for that matter, is there fundamental effort to fashion somewhat different portrayals of collective life and social action.

Sociological theory is linked with the self-referencing, self-identifying activities of sociology. This activity has been affected by a changing political economic climate, one showing the declining relevance of cold war–inspired disciplining of the citizens and cultural institutions. The effect is a gradual withdrawal of support and interest for the discipline.

Supporting the discipline, it was claimed, was cold war liberalism. Since the heyday of U.S. hegemony, liberalism has retrenched and become a part of the political terrain of the United States, a terrain which finds significant sociological effort focusing on the social problem. This sustains an ideological climate, one emphasizing the part played by class, gender, and race. In many ways these have become superconcepts, transcending any particular theoretical portrait.

With growth in the number of sociologists and, more critically, sociological texts, texts which are portrayed as theoretical or of theoretical import, there continues to be a promotion of metatheoretical formulations. The strain for this derives from several sources, primarily from the problems inherent in fast capitalism. Fast capitalism is manifested in the continual effort to sustain circulation of symbolic capital, but to provide a system for a quick appraisal of the constituent ideas.

What does the future hold for sociology and sociological theory? Sociology can continue to produce the fragmented discourse which Diesing notes at the outset of the chapter. It may find in people such as Ritzer, the grand synthesizer, something which to date has eluded the discipline and which, we anticipate, will continue to do so. Nevertheless, the enticement to continue to produce more metatheory will remain. However, this runs the risk of reducing disciplinary identity, something Giddens[72] sees within the social science domain. The growth of postmodern scholarly pursuits and the attention to the escalation of discourse and meta-analyses have already merged some segments of the humanities with sociology. Meanwhile, on the nation's campuses there is an undercurrent of opposition which argues that the discipline is becoming indistinct from certain subfields of history and historical political economy. Despite the efforts to merge micro and macro concerns, the technology and methodology available to the symbolic capitalizing sociology seem destined to circulate a domain of known facts, addressing them with a social problems discourse.

If, as Agger suggests, fast capitalism continues and there is no sustained resistance, it is possible that theory and metatheory as it has been championed could disappear. In a world of immense, rather unremarkable but widely available, representative data, we speculate, attention may rivet on certain patterns and visualizations of the data, transforming convenient data sources (e.g., census, standardized surveys) into visual arrays which are to be "clarified" by looking for deep, analogic structures, something which is on the computer horizon. With this, any pretense at the logical empiricist program for sociology dissolves, replaced by the search for aesthetically appreciated, computer-aided portraits of data. The resulting aesthetics could eclipse the imaginary space produced by individuals struggling to find a voice in texts, texts which are increasingly abstracted and withdrawn from active thought and contemplation. While this portrait is an imaginative reflection, as postmodernists continually note, the tendency is for life to imitate art, albeit a mass cultural art. A society guided by leaders who envisioned a Star Wars defense system, the Strategic Defense Initiative (SDI), is one in which far less pressing matters such as the future of sociology and sociological theory can be easily engulfed by imaginative constructions.

NOTES

1. Paul Diesing, *How Does Social Science Work?* (Pittsburgh, PA: University of Pittsburgh Press, 1991), pp. 163, 318.

2. Jeffrey C. Alexander and Paul Colomy, "Traditions and Competition: Preface to a Postpositivist Approach to Knowledge Cumulation," in George Ritzer, ed., *Metatheorizing* (Newbury Park, CA: Sage, 1992), p. 34.

3. Jeffrey C. Alexander, *Structure and Meaning: Relinking Classical Sociology* (New York: Columbia University Press, 1989), p. 1.

4. This is captured in works such as Rollin Chambliss, *Social Thought: From Hammurabi to Comte* (New York: Dryden Press, 1954), p. 1: "Some of the wise men of old gave answers to their fundamental questions about man [*sic*] in society, but also to ours."

5. Works in the tradition which were used in sociological training included Herbert Feigl and May Brodbeck, eds., *Readings in the Philosophy of Science* (New York: Appleton-Century-Crofts, 1953); and Ernest Nagel, *The Structure of Science: Problems in the Logic of Scientific Explanation* (New York: Harcourt, Brace & World, 1961). A general history of the discipline highlighting this is Stephen Park Turner and Jonathan H. Turner, *The Impossible Science: An Institutional Analysis of American Sociology* (Newbury Park, CA: Sage, 1990).

6. Thomas S. Kuhn, *The Structure of Scientific Revolutions* (Chicago: University of Chicago Press, 1962).

7. Hans Gerth and Saul Landau, "The Relevance of History to the Sociological Ethos," in Maurice Stein and Arthur Vidich, eds., *Sociology on Trial* (Englewood Cliffs, NJ: Prentice-Hall, 1963), p. 31. The authors noted that U.S. sociologists were

generally ignorant of the "facts" of Naziism during its heyday. With Vietnam dawning, there was concern that this would be repeated. And although there was conflict over Vietnam, with many sociologists and sociology students circulating critical views of U.S. foreign and military policy, it is less clear if substantially new facts concerning the nature and operation of the social world came to the forefront. These activities did pave the way for a reception of the ideas of Karl Marx, which have since become appropriately metatheorized in the "conflict perspective."

8. Hans L. Zetterberg, *On Theory and Verification in Sociology* (New York: Bedminister Press, 1966 [1954]).

9. Walter L. Wallace, ed., *Sociological Theory: An Introduction* (Chicago: Aldine, 1969). Wallace's efforts to link theory in a consistent fashion with methods can be seen in his work *The Logic of Science in Sociology* (Chicago and New York: Aldine-Atherton, 1971). Wallace's most recent effort can be found in his "Toward a Disciplinary Matrix in Sociology," in Neil J. Smelser, ed., *Handbook of Sociology* (Newbury Park, CA: Sage Publications, 1988), pp. 23–76.

10. Hubert M. Blalock, Jr., *Causal Inferences in Nonexperimental Research* (Chapel Hill, NC: University of North Carolina Press, 1964 [1961]).

11. Theory construction veered in two directions, one coming out of multivariate data analysis, path analysis. Cf. H. M. Blalock, Jr., ed., *Causal Models in the Social Sciences* (Chicago: Aldine-Atherton, 1971). The other direction, more consistent with the logical empiricist mode, is illustrated with works such as Jack Gibbs, *Sociological Theory Construction* (Hinsdale, IL: Dryden Press, 1972).

12. George Ritzer, *Sociology: A Multiple Paradigm Science,* rev. ed. (Boston: Allyn and Bacon, 1980 [1975]).

13. George Ritzer, *Toward an Integrated Sociological Paradigm: The Search for an Exemplar and an Image of the Subject Matter* (Boston: Allyn and Bacon, 1981).

14. *Ibid.* Also see Jeffrey C. Alexander, *The Micro-Marco Link* (Berkeley: University of California Press, 1987).

15. Following Sartre, consciousness is simply being conscious of an object. "[C]onsciousness posits and grasps the object in the same act." Jean-Paul Sartre, *The Transcendence of Ego: An Existentialist Theory of Consciousness* (New York: Noonday Press, 1957), pp. 40–41. This is recognized, but in a static fashion, in works such as Alex Inkeles, *What Is Sociology? An Introduction to the Discipline and Profession* (Englewood Cliffs, NJ: Prentice-Hall, 1964), Chapter 1. Inkeles identifies the subject matter of sociology in terms of canonical literature (the founding "fathers"), activity of sociologists, and the objects of consciousness. Theory and the identity of sociologists are intertwined.

16. Stephan Fuchs, *The Professional Quest for Truth: A Theory of Science and Knowledge* (Albany, NY: State University of New York Press, 1992), pp. 168ff.

17. *Ibid.,* Chapter 7.

18. Ben Agger, *Fast Capitalism: A Critical Theory of Significance* (Urbana and Chicago: University of Illinois Press, 1989). How this is reflected in the construction of sociological journal articles is taken up by Agger in *Reading Science: A Literary, Political and Sociological Analysis* (Dix Hills, NY: General Hall, 1989).

19. Aside from the Vietnam War, a major break in the acknowledged dominance and stability of the United States came in President Nixon's first term of office (1969–73) when his administration unilaterally broke the agreement. Instead

of currencies having fixed values relative to each other, the U.S. dollar's value was to be established in open market trading. The effect was to acknowledge that the U.S. dollar was no longer the undisputed currency leader in the world. Domestically, 1973 is conventionally agreed upon as the beginning of changes in the domestic and international stature of the U.S. economy. It is a date which Bowles et al. were among the first to note. Cf. Samuel Bowles, David M. Gordon, and Thomas E. Weisskopf, *Beyond the Waste Land: A Democratic Alternative to Economic Decline* (Garden City, NY: Anchor Books, 1984 [1983]). This also marks the period in which several other things peaked affecting the political economy of sociology: undergraduate enrollments and the granting of Ph.D.'s. This is summarized in Turner and Turner, *The Impossible Science.*

20. See also Alvin W. Gouldner, *The Coming Crisis of Western Sociology* (New York and London: Basic Books, 1970).

21. C. Wright Mills, *The Marxists* (New York: Dell, 1962), pp. 11–12.

22. The moral superiority of the United States has long historic antecedents going back to colonial times and the figure John Winthrop, who portrayed the land as a "city on the hill." Cf. Loren Baritz, *Backfire: A History of How American Culture Led Us into Vietnam and Made Us Fight the Way We Did* (New York: William Morrow, 1985).

23. A secular manifestation, specifically in sociology, is described by Arthur J. Vidich and Stanford M. Lyman, *American Sociology: Worldly Rejections of Religion and Their Directions* (New Haven and London: Yale University Press, 1985).

24. For his assessment of the middle class, see C. Wright Mills, *White Collar: The American Middle Classes* (New York: Oxford University Press, 1956). Among the first to question Mills's project of heroic biography and the sociology of imagination is Norman K. Denzin, "Presidential Address on the Sociological Imagination Revisited," *The Sociological Quarterly* 31, 1 (1990), pp. 1–22. A more biting presentation is Allen Shelton's "Writing McDonald's, Eating the Past: McDonald's as a Postmodern Space," *Studies in Symbolic Interaction* 15, 1 (1993) (forthcoming).

25. Arnold W. Green, *Social Problems: Arena of Conflict* (New York: McGraw-Hill, 1975).

26. Barrington Moore, Jr., *Reflections on the Causes of Human Misery and upon Certain Proposals to Eliminate Them* (Boston: Beacon Press, 1973 [1960, 1972]).

27. See Alan Wolfe, *Whose Keeper? Social Science and Moral Obligation* (Berkeley: University of California Press, 1989). Wolfe proposes that sociology return to concerns of moral philosophy. This proposes another activity rather than critically examining the liberal ethos.

28. Lester C. Thurow, *The Zero-Sum Society: Distribution and the Possibilities for Economic Change* (New York: Basic Books, 1980). The prominence of the economic issues over some of the traditional social problems constituencies was seen in the political campaigns of Democrats Bill Clinton and Paul Tsongas.

29. The growing popularity of Michel Foucault (see Paul Rabinow, ed., *The Foucault Reader* [New York: Pantheon Books, 1984]) has occurred not only when there is a challenge to some of the boundary-maintaining notions attached to the historical portrait of the Enlightenment as a "break" with a repressive, feudal past, but with the decline of such disciplining mechanisms as the draft (submission to involuntary military service). The irony is that as Foucault's work has become

intellectually fashionable, the residues of repression remain primarily in the re-capitulation of intellectual history and in the labyrinth of socialization and bound-ary maintenance rituals found in sociology. For the most part, however, Foucault's work is appreciated in the nexus of humanities and social science less so than in the disciplinary activities which continue to be presented as "scientific."

30. Abraham Kaplan, *The Conduct of Inquiry* (San Francisco: Chandler, 1964). Kaplan distinguishes logic-in-use or how things are actually thought about from reconstructed logic, the rhetorical form in which ideas and results are presented to readers.

31. Clifford Geertz, *Local Knowledge: Further Essays in Interpretive Anthro-pology* (New York: Basic Books, 1983).

32. Leon H. Warshay, *The Current State of Sociological Theory: A Critical In-terpretation* (New York: David McKay, 1975).

33. See Steven Seidman, "The End of Sociological Theory: The Postmodern Hope," *Sociological Theory* 9, 2 (1991), pp. 131–146.

34. Ritzer distinguishes three types of metatheoretical efforts: (1) to gain "deeper understanding of theory"—metatheorizing for understanding (M_U); (2) as "a prelude to theory development" (M_D); and (3) as a "source of overarching theoretical perspectives" (M_o). George Ritzer, *Metatheorizing in Sociology* (Lex-ington, MA: Lexington Books, 1991), p. 6. Only the first will be of immediate interest here. Also see George Ritzer, ed., *Metatheorizing* (Newbury Park, CA: Sage, 1992).

35. Among the works Ritzer notes that exhibit criticisms of metatheoretical ef-forts (of metatheoretical efforts) of the kind he exemplifies are Randall Collins's "Is 1980s Sociology in the Doldrums?" *American Journal of Sociology* 91 (1986), pp. 1335–1336; Theda Skocpol's "The Dead End of Metatheory," *Contemporary Sociology* 16 (1986), pp. 10–12; and Jonathan Turner's *The Structure of Sociolog-ical Theory,* 5th ed. (Belmont, CA: Wadsworth, 1991).

36. Cliff Notes refer to copyrighted, outlined, and digested summaries of texts. They are particularly popular among students of literature.

37. Diesing, op. cit., p. 339.

38. See Rabinow, op. cit.

39. For the idea of symbolic capital see Pierre Bourdieu, *Outline of a Theory of Practice* (Cambridge, UK: Cambridge University Press, 1977 [1972]), pp. 171–183.

40. Barbara Ehrenreich, *Fear of Falling: The Inner Life of the Middle Class* (New York: Harper Perrenial, 1990 [1989]).

41. Alfred Sohn-Rethel, *Intellectual and Manual Labour: A Critique of Episte-mology* (Atlantic Highlands, NJ: Humanities Press, 1983 [1978]).

42. Diesing, op. cit., p. 202.

43. See Ben Agger, *Fast Capitalism: A Critical Theory of Significance* (Urbana and Chicago: University of Illinois Press, 1989).

44. For an effort to sort and identify noise from other communications, see Orrin E. Klapp, *Openings and Closing: Strategies of Information Adaptation in Society* (New York: Cambridge University Press, 1978).

45. Ben Agger, *The Decline of Discourse: Reading, Writing and Resistance in Postmodern Capitalism* (New York: Falmer Press, 1990).

46. The notion of theory as a persuasive, civilizing discourse is hinted at as one

of the affirmative features associated with the growth in manners. See Norbert Elias, *Power and Civility: The Civilizing Process* vol. 2 (New York: Pantheon Books, 1989 [1939]). This should not be, as humanistic voices often do, romanticized. Excessive ritualism can be stifling, as suggested by J. Huizinga's *The Waning of the Middle Ages* (Garden City, NY: Doubleday Anchor Books, 1954 [1924]).

47. The index is published quarterly, with annual compilations, by the Institute for Scientific Information, Philadelphia, PA. Using a fixed time frame, an impact score is the ratio of citations to articles published in a specific journal to all articles published by a specific journal. An impact score of 2.0, high for sociology journals, indicates that on average each published article was cited two times in the universe of indexed journals.

48. See John Thibaut and Harold Kelly, *The Social Psychology of Groups* (New York: John Wiley & Sons, 1959).

49. In one remarkable instance with which the authors are familiar, a coworker was so enamored with citation analysis that he not only directed focus of his work, rather successfully, to subjects having high market biggest impact scores (i.e., most "influence"). As an exemplar of the fast capitalist hustler, he aggressively lobbied along with his lumpenbourgeois gang to grade merit increases exclusively on this criterion. This, he asserted, was a "scientific" measure. Other gang members were so duped that they could meet these standards only be coauthoring with the ring leader or, like Nazi intellectuals, call up past slights, arguing that their past merit had been "stolen." Their reification of the impact measure led to a phenomenal deconstruction of their own text: as social scientists they could only produce a thin narrative, one having psychological (i.e., characterological) attributes, not one which struggled with the complexities of administration and the struggle for inclusive discourse. The lack of subtleness, a signal of bad manners under a civilizing discourse, was administratively tolerated as an expression of (repressive) academic freedom. That the victims did not pursue a libel action seems increasingly regretful.

50. Don Martindale, *The Nature and Types of Sociological Theory,* 2nd ed. (Boston: Houghton Mifflin, 1981). To further amplify a succeeding point, for many graduate students at the University of Minnesota during Martindale's tenure, the first edition of this work and his lectures were considered excellent preparation for comprehensive examinations as well as preparation for teaching theory.

51. See Pitirim A. Sorokin, *Social and Cultural Dynamics,* 4 vols. (New York: American Book Company, 1937–1941). For one of the earliest efforts at metatheorizing, see Pitirim A. Sorokin, *Contemporary Sociological Theories: Through the First Quarter of the Twentieth Century* (New York: Harper Torchbooks 1956 [1928]). The uniqueness of this work is that it directed readers' attention to sociological work undertaken in a variety of national settings. This interest in an international sociology declined precipitously in years after World War II. It was nearly thirty years later when the predecessor of the current volume came on the scene. See Raj P. Mohan and Don Martindale, eds., *Handbook of Contemporary Developments in World Sociology* (Westport, CT: Greenwood Press, 1975).

52. Don Martindale, *Social Life and Cultural Change* (Princeton, NJ: D. Van Nostrand, 1962).

53. Jonathan R. Cole and Stephen Cole, *Social Stratification in Science* (Chicago: University of Chicago Press, 1973).

54. William E. Snizek, Ellsworth R. Fuhrman, and Michael Miller, eds., *Con-*

temporary Issues in Theory and Research (Westport, CT: Greenwood Press, 1979), Part I.

55. An effort to use metatheory (i.e., classifications of theories and emphases), subsuming it under a network analysis via citation analysis, is Nicholas Mullins, *Theories and Theory Groups in Contemporary American Sociology* (New York: Harper & Row, 1973). A content analysis of articles appearing in the *American Sociological Review* assessed with a theory classification was done by Richard H. Wells and J. Steven Picou, *American Sociology: Theoretical and Methodological Structure* (Washington, D.C.: University Press of America, 1981). Although both works are informative, they employ metatheoretical frames which highlight the energy and circulation of this kind of theory activity.

56. Erik Wilke has developed a compelling position on this. We thank him for sharing this point.

57. This was perceptively pointed out to us by Erik Wilke, who was working on the approach to AIDS by sociologists.

58. We are not suggesting by this statement a naive *a priori* regarding logic and empiricism, only the strong tendency to not be concerned about these items in practice. The position of one of the authors, following an ordinary language tradition, is that logic does not always have to follow the rigid form of the philosophy of science regarding necessary and sufficient conditions, but simply considers whether certain language acts—whether of sociologists or those being studied—cohere and are appropriate to what is known about the syntax and semantics one is employing. This position suggests that the empirical is a more problematic condition than operationalists suggest.

59. Martindale, *Social Life and Cultural Change,* p. 498.

60. Karl Mannheim, *Ideology and Utopia: An Introduction to the Sociology of Knowledge,* trans. by Louis Wirth and Edward Shils (New York: Harcourt, Brace, 1936 [1929]).

61. What Ritzer in *Metatheorizing in Sociology* calls M_u metatheorizing for understanding, it is suggested, is primarily a program to assess interpretive contexts and procedures employed in the classifying of texts. M_u is to obtain understanding from texts on texts. Authorship, other than a vague remembrance of a property right, is subordinated to readership. What energizes this abstracted discourse, we suggest, may be profitably explored through forms reinforced in cold war disputes and through textual reproductions of social problems mobilizations.

62. Ritzer, *Metatheorizing in Sociology.*

63. Writers using sociological theories/metatheories are entrapped in establishing an identity through the selection and linkage of texts meeting certain literary criticism standards. The result is that the identity of the speaker is removed from the local arena of observation or "knowledge" and placed into an abstract representation and pseudo-dramatic matrix.

64. Harry Elmer Barnes, ed., *An Introduction to the History of Sociology* (Chicago: University of Chicago Press, 1948).

65. Robert K. Merton, Leonard Broom, and Leonard S. Cottrell, Jr., eds., *Sociology Today: Problems and Prospects* (New York: Basic Books, 1959).

66. Joseph S. Roucek, ed., *Reading in Contemporary American Sociology* (Patterson, NJ: Littlefield, Adams, 1961 [1958]).

67. Robert E.L. Faris, ed., *Handbook of Modern Sociology* (Chicago: Rand McNally, 1964).

68. Paul F. Lazarsfeld, William H. Sewell, and Harold L. Wilensky, eds., *The Uses of Sociology* (New York: Basic Books, 1967).

69. Nicholas C. Mullins, *Theories and Theory Groups in Contemporary American Sociology* (New York: Harper and Row, 1973).

70. Neil J. Smelser, ed., *Handbook of Sociology* (Newbury Park, CA: Sage, 1988).

71. Assistance for this compilation was obtained from Regina Broadway, Katrine Meier, Kris Nelson, Pelagie Nyirahabimana, Robert Taunton, and Derek Windham. We are appreciative of their efforts.

72. Anthony Giddens, *Social Theory and Modern Sociology* (Cambridge, UK: Polity Press, 1987), p. 37.

16

Research Features of U.S. Sociology: Reflections and Dilemmas

Raj P. Mohan and Arthur S. Wilke

The emphasis on specialties, sometimes the specialties themselves, in a discipline rise and fall. This dynamic can be traced to such things as shifts in (1) funding sources; (2) methodological innovations; (3) data availability; (4) changing priorities regarding what are to be considered problems; and (5) researcher interests.

This chapter is a report on a review of some dominant specialty areas within sociology for the years 1975, 1980, 1985, and 1990. The 1975 date was chosen because that was the year the last edition of the *Handbook* was published.[1] Sociology has followed the bureaucratic division of labor. This has not resulted in some optimal efficiency as an application of Adam Smith's (1723–1790) notion of the division of labor suggested. Instead, it reflects, following Emile Durkhiem (1858–1917), the failure to build a moral solidarity appropriate to an increasingly subdivided world. The vision that sociology might somehow provide a unifying vision of collective life and in the process advance a coherent, interdisciplinary, or even trans-disciplinary framework has not materialized. With the establishment of a number of substantive specialties an emergent image of the field is one of a wild forest, not that of a planned garden. It is a situation not unique to sociology. Writing in the *Journal of the American Medical Association,* the Association's vice president of medical education, Carlos J. M. Martini, notes that medicine has witnessed an explosion in specialty areas. Currently, he notes, U.S. medical training programs list 25 physician specialties and 56 subspecialties. Of the latter, 35 have been recognized during the last five years, ranging from addiction treatment to circus medicine.[2]

For those wishing a unified vision of social life, the proliferation of specializations is troubling. A sense of this concern was recently voiced in the *Chronicle of Higher Education.*[3]

Over the last few decades, sociology has grown increasingly diffuse. The sociology of aging to methodology to the sociology of sex and gender; the actual number of specialties in the field goes well beyond that. Such diffusion has caused . . . the perception that sociology is "all over the map" and has no central focus.[4]

In the same article, Richard F. Hamilton opines that

the field has, in a way, fallen apart into a bunch of little segments that are independent, or semiautonomous. . . . They chart their own directions, and they can be their own judges as to what constitutes compelling evidence. That means they can be little baronies or principalities. . . . To the extent that happens . . . it is no longer an integrated field with agreed upon standards.

Neil J. Smelser takes a different position in the same article. He views the history of sociology as one in which there have been paradigm shifts out of which emerged a "peaceful pluralism." "It is not a vigorous or vicious period of polemics, . . . but . . . (one in which it is generally) accepted idea that there is a variety of legitimate approaches and subjects—a kind of catholicism." This results, suggests Smelser, writing in the *Handbook of Sociology,* in "the increased diversity and richness of interpretive frameworks within each subfield," although he concedes that there results a "lesser degree of consensus about what is the central organizing basis for knowledge generated in . . . (a) subfields."[5]

The lingering tensions between central rules of disciplinary discourse and situational standards seem to revolve about sentiments for the former anchored in some forms of theoretical discourse while the situationally responsive approach to diversity resides with specialties. This accommodation, while consistent with the structure and operations of the liberal state, leaves unresolved tensions.

In this chapter, attention is directed at a sample of works in identified subfields. This provides at once a selection of works which have appeared during the past generation and a foundation, if warranted, for further reflection on the contested domain regarding whether sociology should be a unified or a diverse disciplinary pursuit.

THE PROCEDURE

Disciplinary knowledge involves not only a publicly identifiable topic, but, as the above discussion on specialties indicates, an organizational identity. Publicly identified knowledge is based on its categorization and indexing. We chose the *Social Sciences Index* as the vehicle by which to identify publicly classified topics. We began by looking at those topics which were categorized or cross-listed under the headings of "social" or "sociology." Table 16.1 is a list of topics, some of which were cross-references. An inspection of the table reveals that concepts (e.g., alienation, caste, crowds), subfields (e.g., collective behavior, comparative sociology, human ecology, industrial sociology), and schools of thought (e.g., the Chicago School, the Frankfurt School, network analysis, phenomenological sociology) were dominant features of the list.

The indexed items were then compared with the organized specialties recognized by the American Sociological Association (ASA) and published in its *1989 Guide to Graduate Departments*. Table 16.2 lists these items. Although there are a large number of specialties which, in practice, are divided into further subspecialties, there has been a substantial stability in these areas since the ASA published the *1975 Guide*. The 1989 edition has several additions—criminal justice, environmental sociology, the sociologies of language/social linguistics, markets, and mental illness. Several have changed: applied sociology/evaluations research has been redesignated sociological practice, gender was added to the sociology of sex roles specialty and has recently been further specialized in the 1990s as women's studies. Socialization has been dropped.

The items in the *Social Sciences Index* and the corporate specialties in sociology exhibit sufficient correspondence so that we proceeded to compile a list of topics, most of which reflect a generic idea in sociology or a recognized specialty. If an area had ten or more indexed publications for the years 1975, 1980, 1985, and 1990, articles appearing in either the *American Journal of Sociology*, the *American Sociological Review, Social Forces*, or *Sociological Quarterly*, four leading journals in the discipline, would be the ones selected for review. An effort was made to obtain a purposive sample of articles appearing in the four journals.

Table 16.3 summarizes the topics meeting the criteria and those selected for review in this chapter. In several instances very specific concerns (e.g., Marxism, network analysis) or key concepts (e.g., assimilation, division of labor) are included in the list garnered from the *Social Sciences Index*.

Before the review, there are several caveats. First, the reviews are based on journals with a general orientation, not a specialty. For example, crime is covered extensively in a number of specialty journals. Second, the effort is directed at getting a flavor of the research which has been undertaken in these areas.

HUMAN ECOLOGY

The students of human ecology focus on human adaptation as reflected in seeking food and shelter, propagating the species, and controlling technical resources. Parker W. Frisbie and Dudley L. Poston, Jr.[6] test one of

Table 16.1
Topics Related to Sociology Appearing in the *Social Sciences Index:*
1992

Anomie

Art(s) and Society

Assimilation

Biosociology

Caste

Charities

Chicago School of Sociology

Civil Supremacy Over the Military (Military, Civil. . .)

Collective Behavior

Comparative Sociology

Community

Community Life

Crime and Criminals

Cross-Cultural Studies

Crowds

Culture

Demography

Division of Labor

Deviant Behavior

Economic Concepts in Sociology

Economics—Social Aspects

Elites

Equality

Family

Frankfurt School of Sociology

Gerontology

Groups

Health (and Illness), Social Aspects of

Historical Sociology

Human Ecology

Human Settlements

Individualism

Industrial Sociology

Islam and Economics

Recreation

Religion and Sociology

Science, Social Aspects/Sociology of

Sex and Gender

Small Groups

Social

Social Change

Social Contract

Social Control

Social Ethics

Social Institutions

Social Mobility

Social Movements

Social Norms

Social Problems

Social Structure

Social Systems

Socialism

Socialization

Sociobiology

Sociolinguistics

Sociological Jurisprudence

Sociological Research

Solidarity

Sport(s)

Structuralism

Symbolic Interactionism

Technology and Civilization

Typology (Sociology)

Unemployed/Unemployment

War and Society

Women's Studies

Table 16.2
Specialties Recognized by the American Sociological Association

Collective Behavior/Social Movements

Community

Comparative Sociology/Macrosociology

Criminal Justice

Criminology/Delinquency

Cultural Sociology

Demography

Development/Modernization

Deviant Behavior/Social Disorganization

Economy and Society

Education

Environmental Sociology

History of Sociology/Social Thought

Human Ecology

Industrial Sociology

International Development/Third World

Law and Society

Leisure/Sports/Recreation

Marriage and the Family

Methodology: Qualitative Approaches

Mass Communication/Public Opinion

Methodology: Qualitative Approaches

Microcomputing/Computer Application

Military Sociology

Occupations/Professions

Penology/Correction

Political Sociology

Race/Ethnic/Minority Relations

Religion

Rural Sociology

Small Groups

Social Change

Social Control

Social Organization/Formal/Complex

Social Psychology

Socialization

Sociological Practice/Social Policy

Sociology of Aging/Gerontology

Sociology of Art/Literature

Sociology of Knowledge
Sociology of Language/Social Linguistics
Sociology of Markets
Sociology of Mental Health
Sociology of Science
Sociology of Sex and Gender
Sociology of World Conflict
Stratification/Mobility
Theory
Urban Sociology

Table 16.3
Frequent Topics, 1975–1980

Assimilation
Collective Behavior
Crime
Cross-Cultural Studies
Deviant Behavior and Labeling
Division of Labor
Elite
Groups (sociology)
Human Ecology
Marriage and Family
Marxism
Network Analysis
Occupation
Philosophy, Theory*
Religion and Sociology
Social Change
Social Control
Social Movements
Social Structure

Source: *Philosophy Theory is dealt with in a special essay on "The United States: Meta-theoretical Concerns" in this volume by Arthur S. Wilke and Raj P. Mohan.

the basic assumptions of the human ecological theory: that there is a significant relationship between sustenance organization and population growth or decline. They operationalize several components of the sustenance organization and relate these to relative population change between 1960 and 1970 in the nonmetropolitan counties of the United States. They find that population and sustenance affect each other only slightly.

Claude S. Fischer[7] deals with a basic question of the social effects of urbanism. Using Louis Wirth's theory as a backdrop, he develops a model. In this model he reintroduces the variable of size in a manner different from that by Wirth. In addition he reviews most of the relevant literature. He focuses on the unconventionality of urban life and advances four propositions: The more urban a place, (1) the greater its subcultural variety, (2) the more intense its subcultures, (3) the more numerous the sources of diffusion, and (4) the higher the rates of unconventionality.

Marcus Felson and Mauricio Solaun[8] examine the relationship between population density and fertility. To study this hypothesis the authors suggest that people living in crowded apartments and who have no options of moving to another location tend to reduce fertility. They use data from a Colombian public housing project in Cuidad Kennedy in Bogota, Colombia. In this project upper-working-class people were located in apartments while lower-working-class people were given houses with a lot of land. Those in apartments had lower fertility than those in houses, supporting the claim that crowding (density) leads to lower fertility. John R. Logan and M. Semyonov[9] examine the factors in the growth of metropolitan communities using Burgess's concentric zone formulation as a backdrop. They use data on the suburban communities of Nassau-Suffolk (Long Island) SMSA having a 1960 population of over 2,500. This area constitutes one part of the suburban ring around New York City. The authors argue that a fuller explanation of the Burgess ecological life-cycle theory requires addressing additional factors such as initial development patterns, age of the existing housing, social heterogeneity, and the presence of minority and low-income residents. In addition, they argue that incorporation of an area significantly impacts succession. Limiting attention to the effects of distance, as Burgess's theory does, does not effectively address the ecological and sociopolitical factors contributing to suburban growth.

John M. Stahura[10] studies the determinants of short-term changes in suburban age structures with an examination of 816 suburban areas in 1960 and 1970. During the ten-year interval, 100 of the suburban areas were lost because of either annexation or loss in population. The data revealed that the percentage of the population between 0–14 and 25–44 decreased, while the percentage of population between 15–24, 45–64, and 65 and over increased. The data only partially support a structural model of aging. The ecological position of a suburban area within the metropolis can explain to some extent the changes that occur in the structure of suburban populations. Other contributing factors are yet to be explored. David F. Sly and Jeffrey Tayman[11] examine the ecological expansion theory. By using fifty of the largest standard Metropolitan Statistical Areas (SMSAs) in the United States during 1970–1974, the authors found that twenty-six had net migration. This shows that many people are moving from the core of the city to the outer ring, which means that each component part of the SMSAs is increasing its dependence on the ring. The data suggest that SMSAs with out-migration were considerably more expanded than the SMSAs with in-migration. They conclude that the outer rings are becoming metropolitan areas of the city's core.

Glen R. Carroll,[12] in a study of 2,808 American local newspaper organizations for the years 1800–1975, using ecological perspective, finds that despite the high levels of local concentration many small and specialized newspapers function successfully. He divided newspapers into two categories, local and national dailies. These are examined in terms of an ecological niche, a resource space within which a population can exist. Carroll advances a resource-partitioning model to explain the interorganizational relationships between different types of newspaper organizations and concludes that ecological perspective lends itself to new insights in the study of organizations.

SOCIAL CHANGE

Change is the permanent alteration of relationships in a social structure. It can involve replacing of one social unit with another. As Don Martindale noted, social change is the capstone of sociological theory, one which is least understood. Our review of studies of social change starts with a study by Robert M. Hauser and others.[13] Their work reexamines the data on occupational mobility among men in the United States. The data came from the March 1962 *Current Population Survey Supplement,* "Occupational Changes in a Generation," which gathered information on 17,200 male respondents. In addition, they used the 1974 survey of National Opinion Research Center (NORC), 1952–1957 surveys by Survey Research Center at the University of Michigan, the 1962 Occupational Changes in a Generation survey conducted by Bureau of Census, and a 1972 NORC survey. From these data it was found that there is no relationship between father's occupation and the son's occupation over time. Instead of a clear pattern of intergenerational mobility in a stable occupational structure, they found that a changing occupational distribution is the major factor in occupational mobility.

In his venture to find the best corresponding model for American society, Edward A. Tiryakian[14] reviews the works of Karl Marx, Max Weber, and Emile Durkheim. He rejects the Marxian concept of modern society because it is based upon the necessity of revolution and the development of class consciousness among the working class. Following a long line of thinkers, he argues that because of the greater accommodation offered to the American working class by existing institutions, workers in America never developed class consciousness. Durkheim, he argues, does not have a model which fits American society. The concept of anomie as normlessness (not unsatiated desire) in Durkheim is least applicable because American society is least anomic of modern societies. He believes that the Weberian model of modern society with its emphasis on Protestant ethic, a thesis which has been seriously challenged, is of greatest value in interpreting American society. In his cultural interpretation, he draws attention to the Puritan culture and cultural themes: "wilderness" and "voluntarism."

After a twenty-five-year interval, Albert Hunter[15] replicates and tests the loss of community hypothesis of Donald Foley's "Neighbors and Urbanites." The study explores three different aspects of community: local facility use, informal neighboring, and sense of community. The study is based on a survey of residents in the area. Foley's study had 437 respondents while the Hunter survey sample consisted of only 154. In the period under study there was a decline in the use of facilities within the local area. The study also found that there was no decline in informal neighboring. It is a dimension which may have slightly increased, as did the sense of community. The author explains that residents consciously sought out this area, creating an "ecological niche." Furthermore, residents consciously attempted to create a community through an active local community organization.

Martin S. Weinberg and Colin J. Williams[16] examine the relationship between social class position and sexual behavior using the embourgeoisement thesis that the "working class is increasingly adopting middle-class values and behaviors." They use data collected by Alfred C. Kinsey and his associates between 1938 and 1968 as well as more recent data from 1969–1970 collected by the Institute for Sex Research. Their analysis reveals that social class is still an important determinant of sexual behavior and that there has been no embourgeoisement of sexual patterns since 1940. Further, they found that differences still exist in number of partners, the age at first experience, and the sexual activities of middle-class and working-class males. For females there are also differences in age at first experience, reaction to first experience, and frequency of sexual activity.

In their paper "Racial Violence and Socioeconomic Changes among Blacks in the United States," William R. Kelly and David Snyder[17] attempt to determine if there is a relationship between racial violence during the sixties and socioeconomic changes that occurred among blacks in the following years. They analyze the effects between 1960 and 1970 of racial violence frequency and severity of changes in three socioeconomic variables: racial composition of selected occupations, unemployment rates, and nonwhite income. Their results consistently indicate that racial violence had no effect on the three variables and that any relationship between it and socioeconomic items was dependent upon other variables.

Steven F. Messner[18] tests the Durkheimian hypothesis that with greater social development, there is an increase in crime. The author uses per capita Gross Domestic Product, Protestant population, school enrollment ratio, social equality, and homicide rates derived from various international sources on fifty countries to test the Durkheimian model as reinterpreted by Anthony Giddens. He also used additional variables such as urbanism, population growth, population size, and population density in the study. The results show that there is no evidence to support the relationship between homicide and societal development based on greater equality.

By reviewing the extensive literature on state-building and revitalization movements in four Native American societies, the Cherokee, Choctaw, Delaware, and Iroquois during 1795–1860, Duane Champagne[19] found that Choctaw and Cherokee were influenced by state building while Delaware and Iroquois were influenced by revitalization movements. He found the Delaware and Iroquois societies were less structurally differentiated and more influenced by revitalization movement than the Choctaw and Cherokee, societies which were more structurally differentiated and hence influenced by state-building.

In a paper dealing with measurement issues in the study of social change, Stanley Presser[20] examines "whether observed shifts in public opinion based on comparisons between identical items can be affected by the form in which the item is asked . . . and examines whether alternate forms of the same attitude item behave in similar fashion over time."[21] The data used in the study were from the 1976 and 1986 Detroit Area Studies. The data show that the wording of a question made a difference but that the difference was the same over time. The results also indicate that open and closed questions may yield different answers over time.

Laurence R. Iannaccone and Carrie A. Miles[22] study the Mormon church's response to change in women's roles. The authors analyze articles on women in the Mormon church's official periodical from 1950 to 1986. The data show that social change resulted in increased attention that the church gave to the women's roles even though the attention came years later. The study shows that the accommodation by the church of the changing roles of women increased participation among younger members but resulted in decreased participation among older members. In the authors' view the church must maintain a balance between accommodation and resistance to change to be successful.

In this section we omitted three studies because either these are classified under another specialty and are dealt with there or they did not deal with concerns and trends in American sociology.[23,24,25] Three additional studies are classified under Network Analysis section are discussed there.[26,27,28]

SOCIAL CONTROL

Every society develops a set of strategies and techniques for the control of human behavior. As Rousseau had opined: "Everyone is born free but everywhere he is in chains." These are the chains of control which permeate people's lives from birth to death. Social control is an essential strategy for giving shape to social life.

R. K. Hawkes[29] claims that mathematical models provide powerful tools for the evaluation of a verbal theory. To pursue this he elaborates the concepts of norms, deviance, and social control, translating these into mathematical form to develop an elementary theory of relationships between these concepts. He proposes that a simple theory of deviant behavior can be expressed as a linear mathematical model. His equations lend support to his argument.

C. R. Tittle,[30] in his study of deviant behavior, examines the effects of sanctioning drawn from control and labeling perspectives. Drawing on current literature, he finds that the data do not favor the secondary deviance interpretation over deterrence. He finds gross theoretical inadequacy in considering the issue of sanctioning deviant behavior. According to Tittle, there is no clear solution to this problem. He believes that sanctions may either create or deter deviance or both and that a clearer understanding of this issue will require substantive empirical work.

Morris Janowitz[31] examines the concept of social control and its historical usage which is referred to as the capacity of a social group to regulate itself. This paper is based upon the critical reading and rereading of classical and contemporary literature. The study deals with intellectual foundations of the concept of social control, its earlier diffusion and usage, and its transformation into a narrower definition of the processes of developing conformity, and the persistence of the traditional usage since 1945. Janowitz argues that in its original meaning this concept can help in the integration of empirical data with sociological theory. This will aid the linking of the codification of research findings with the question of social values in sociological analysis.

S. R. Burkett and E. L. Jensen[32] examine the effects of formal and informal sanctions on deviant behavior, specifically marijuana use. Their study is based upon the data gathered from 546 white male and 510 white female seniors in three high schools from all white communities in Washington State. The authors classified the sample into three types: "Nonusers" (never tried marijuana), "Experimental Users" (tried at least once or use up to once a month), and "Regular Users" (use more than once a month). Four indices to measure ties to conventional others were attachment to school, attachment to parents, school involvement, and family involvement. The likelihood of apprehension and the extent of interaction with other users were measured by using responses to items: "If I were to use marijuana, I would probably get caught" and how many "close friends" used marijuana. Their findings reveal that the marijuana use was least likely among those who believed that their use would result in apprehension as well as having nonusing peers serving as sources of control. Their findings show that the level of marijuana use varies with belief items and conventional ties.

J. G. Hougland Jr., and Wood[33] explore the effect of the amount and distribution of power, or control, in an organization on the commitment of organization members. They obtained data from fifty-eight randomly selected Protestant churches in Indianapolis, Indiana. They found that the amount of power is a valuable predictor of members' commitments to organizations.

Louise Shelley[34] focuses on the geographical distribution of criminality in the former Soviet Union, a social order in which social control was exercised over the mobility and residence of the population. Increasing urbanization in the Soviet Union was not correlated with higher rates of criminality. Crime rates were higher in the newly established cities of the far eastern and far northern parts of the then USSR and the rapidly developing smaller urban centers, areas in which direct control on mobility or host conditions were least in evidence. The analysis is based on a one and a half year study by the author in the Soviet Union and research from both classified and published works by Soviet criminologists.

R. J. Stevenson[35] focuses on how the U.S. military sanctions norm breakers. Using the data from various previous studies of military strength in World War II, Korea, and Vietnam and the Selective Service System, the author examines the "turning points" in the military organizational reaction to social deviance since World War II. The study finds that official sanctions intensified when the qualifications of those in charge were most problematic.

D. D. Heckathorn[36] examines the conditions under which external sanctions and intragroup normative control, help or retard each other. By constructing a formal model the author concludes that social control which is resultant from the sanctioning of the individuals has its inception in the group control called compliance norms. Under other circumstances intragroup controls work against the external sanction. This results in what he calls opposition norms. How a group responds to sanctions depends upon a number of variables which he discusses in detail.

R. J. Sampson and J. H. Laub[37] reconstructed the longitudinal data from the Gluecks' well-known study of delinquent and nondelinquent males from childhood to the age of thirty-two. Their model shows that antisocial behavior in childhood is predictive of developmental problems in adulthood in a variety of areas, although social bonds within the family and work in adulthood are also explanatory.

SOCIAL MOVEMENTS

Social movements are transforming social actions, ones which can be found in multicultural, multiethnic, multireligious, and technologically advanced societies. The United States hosts social movements which both promote and resist change.

Jack A. Roach and Janet L. Roach[38] challenge the work of Frances Fox Piven and Richard Cloward, activists for the rights of the poor. They show that the four groups used by Piven and Cloward were not comparable; they did not all fall under the category "poor people." The Roaches propose that the poor should mobilize their efforts through labor unions, which have an organizational structure capable of achieving the improvements in their lot. Their arguments are based on the accomplishments of certain trade unions in the elimination of poverty, ignoring the fate of unions and the growth of unemployed and marginally employed poor people.

In a study of members of social movements who engage in litigation, Steven E. Barkan[39] examined the impact that individual cases had on the achievement of movement goals. He sees litigation as a tool to legitimize and publicize a movement's goals and ideals. On the one hand, court cases can be used by government agents and agencies as a means of social control, diverting the attention and resources of the movement. On the other hand, Barakan contends, there are limits to the effectiveness of litigation as a means of achieving movement goals. He also examines the role of the press in determining how a court case affects a social movement. Barakan demonstrates that the trend toward using litigation as a means of furthering the cause and achievement of goals is on the increase and does not show any signs of slowing down.

William Gamson published his *The Strategy of Protest* in 1975, which was based on data on fifty-three social protest groups. In this book he asserts that a protest group's chance of success is strongly influenced by the organization and tactics of the group. Gamson's data was reanalyzed by Jack A. Gladstone,[40] who asserts that the original assumptions were weak because they were frequently based upon spurious zero order correlations. In Gladstone's reanalysis of data he does not find any effect of organizational and tactical parameters. When he introduces additional data on the timing of the social protest group success, using a stochastic model, Gladstone finds that timing of success is substantially independent of the tactics and organization of the protest group. The errors attributed to Gamson were his definition of success of a protest movement, the lack of differentiation between displacement and nondisplacement groups, group pairing, and lack of follow-up of groups whose activities had ceased for a period of time. Gladstone found that the presence of goal displacement and the time in which the movement existed had a significant effect on the success of the movement.

One of the important questions in the study of social movements is why some people get involved in these while others do not. David A. Snow, Louis A. Zurcher, Jr., and Sheldon Ekland-Olson[41] compiled data on the recruitment process. Their data included interviews with the members of the Nichiren Shohu movement and with some Hare Krishnas as well as a sample of students from the University of Texas who completed a questionnaire about involvement in movements. They found that social networks are a key component of differential recruitment in all cases they studied with one exception, the Hare Krishnas. This is also true of political and religious movements. Who is recruited and how the recruitment is done are more a function of the structure of an organization than its worldview. They also contend that structural variables are more compelling in explaining recruitment than a "susceptibility" variable. Networks within a social movement determine whether or not a person who is "susceptible" to the influence of the movement will remain in the movement once he or she is introduced to the movement.

Naomi Rosenthal and others[42] used data derived from historical references to organizational affiliations of women reform leaders in New York State between 1820–1914. Using network analysis they constructed matrices showing the interconnections intensity and directionality between organizations. Their data were based on biographies of those involved in the movements, biographical dictionaries, and books and articles written on the topic of women's social movements and causes. One significant finding is that leaders in one group were also members of other movement groups. Categorizing the ties among groups as weak, moderate, or strong, the authors found that there were few strong ties between groups and many weak ties. The researchers acknowledged their conclusions might not be representative of all social movements.

NETWORK ANALYSIS

Social life is a web or a network both at the micro and the macro levels of societal reality. These networks are the springs of action through which our daily lives are structured and through which meaningful behavior is engaged. Explorations into this aspect of social life have given rise to the subfield of network analysis.

Gwen Moore's[43] study of the integration among U.S. political elites is based on the data taken from the American Leadership Study (1971), a study of 545 top position holders in key institutions of American society. She concludes that there was no segmentation among the elites in different sectors and that the level of integration among the elites was considerable. The existence of a central elite circle allows for easier communication among the larger, dispersed elites and the smaller, more specialized sectors. Thus, a social network exists for a potential ruling elite.

Edward O. Laumann and Peter V. Marsden[44] suggest a theoretical explanation for characterizing oppositional structures in political elites and introduce the concept of the collective actor. They recognize three major components of groups found in a political conflict: degree of cohesion, degree to which a well-defined preference or purpose is shared, and the degree of active participation. They define the collective actor as the set of all members in an entire elite decision-making system. They develop spatial models describing alternative forms of oppositional structures. In order to collect empirical evidence on collective actors, they study two small communities, examining the size of the group, the percentage of possible linkages, and the distance connecting members. To reveal oppositional data they studied five different "impact" issues in each community. Their study found that explicit accounts of preferences in addition to data on linkages.

Peter Killworth and Russell Bernard[45] present a model of the decision-making process. Their model draws on the Small World (SW) technique developed by Stanley Milgram as a means of measuring "chain links" between individuals. They present a practical model of how information travels between links in a Small World. Through an experiment, Killworth and Bernard found that location and occupational position were the two most important factors in SW links. They divided the distances into four categories: town, area, region, and far distance. An almost linear fit was found for the probability of choosing the next link based on either location or occupation.

Ronald S. Burt defines and illustrates a concept of "structural autonomy" based on recent developments in network analysis. Structural autonomy is also based on the ideas of oligopoly in economics and group-affiliation in sociology. The aspects of autonomy concern the relations among actors jointly occupying a status in a system and the manner in which actors jointly occupying a status are related to actors occupying other statuses in their system. Burt[46] used various data on manufacturing industries, using derived equations to define and illustrate "structural autonomy." Seven of Burt's hypotheses were supported: (1) an oligopoly has a positive effect on profits, (2) lack of conflicting group-affiliates constrains autonomy, (3) forming an oligopoly having conflicting group-affiliates leads to increased autonomy, (4) firms in an industry will establish cooperative relations with one another as long as they are not constrained by firms in sectors, (5) firms in a sector having a negative effect on the structural autonomy of firms in an industry will be the object of co-optive positions, and (6–7) firms in a sector which does not constrain the structural autonomy of firms in an industry will be ignored in the industry's co-optive strategies hypothesis. One hypothesis was rejected: an increase in structural autonomy results from mergers. Burt's hypotheses predict how groups are interconnected and what kinds of mutual constraints corporations place on each other because of their network of transactions.

Rodney Stark and William Sims Bainbridge[47] examine the traditional view that recruitment to cults and sects is based on ideology and interpersonal bonds. The long-established, former view is based on the notion that people join religious deviant groups to gain relief from personal kinds of deprivation. A previous study by Stark and John Lofland, however, suggested that interpersonal bonds between members and potential members were the main reason that recruits joined. When interpersonal bonds failed to develop, newcomers did not join. Stark found that the long-standing relationships between the cult members and potential recruits usually existed before recruitment. Thus, recruitment spread through existing social networks. Stark and Bainbridge observed three cults/sects. These were the Doomsday Group, the Ananda Commune Group, and the Mormons. They found evidence that interpersonal bonds and social networks are essential for successful recruitment to deviant religious groups, something upon which conventional religions also heavily depend. Deprivation and ideological capabilities appear to serve only as general contributory factors in the recruitment process.

Myra Marx Ferree[48] conducted a study of working-class women to find whether or not these women were more inclined toward traditional views or more feminist ones. Previous studies suggested that the more conservative working world would call for more women with traditional views than nontraditional ones. Data for this study came from a survey of 135 working-class women in 1974–1975, who were married with their youngest child in the first year of elementary school. The data show that employed women appear to have substantially more feminist views than full-time housewives. One explanation is the involvement in differing social networks in which these women operate. The social networks of the workplace appear to facilitate the spread of movement ideas and values, while the social networks of housewives appear to strengthen the resistance to change.

Jon Miller[49] states that the integration into an interorganizational network of activity of an individual organization member is a good predictor of other work-related behavior. To test this he surveyed professional practitioners in six regional programs in a national project for the deinstitutionalization of status offenders (DSO). The DSO programs emphasize that involvement in a professional resource results in greater community involvement. Each program was required to establish and oversee an interagency service delivery "system" or network as a way of bringing autonomous service delivery resources in the community together. Using data for 360 total subjects from 88 agencies, he performed separate regression analysis on each program, to find that the network location had (a) positive impact on the level of practitioners' contact with non-DSO organizations in four programs and (b) a questionable impact in two programs.

Richard E. Ratcliff[50] explores whether the loan decisions of a bank are influenced by the extent of a bank's centrality to economic and social networks. He argues that capitalist class coordination occurs in which dominant groups exercise influence on banks and corporations. His data include loan portfolio transactions of all seventy-eight commercial banks headquartered in St. Louis County, Missouri, and the economic networks within each bank. The class structure characteristics of banks as reflected in the network linkages of their board of directors is a critical determinant of lending decisions. A bank's linkages with the centers of economic power and upper-class social interaction within the capitalist class, it is found, influence a bank's lending practices within the capitalist class.

Ronald S. Burt[51] and others detail a theory that predicts co-optive uses of corporate directorates from the structure of the market in which they operate. This theory is based on Burt's model of a structural autonomy explained in a previous article (January 1980). Occupants in a structural autonomy enjoy the freedom to pursue their interests in their system within constraints. This freedom ensures low competition among the participants of this structure while causing high competition among the other organizations outside of their group. The analysis is based upon the twenty two-digit SIC industries from establishments in fifty-one manufacturing and nonmanufacturing sectors in 1967.

Three types of market constraints were identified: intra-industry, industry constraint, and industry nonconstraint. Burt and others conclude that the network model of structural autonomy appears to be an accurate predictor where ties occur in the American economy as a co-optive relation. Co-optive relations tend to eliminate market constraints. They further recommend that intra-industry co-optation should be studied separately because of the weak support using directorate ties.

Joseph Galaskiewicz and Karl Krohn[52] examine community structure as a network of interorganizational linkages, focusing on new ways to study the community as a social network while developing a method to measure dimensions of community structure. Their study also examines the perceived influence of organizations in community affairs as a function of the organizations' global positions within the community network. Galaskiewicz and Krohn analyzed the structurally equivalent roles of two communities for three organizational resource networks: money, information, and moral support. This study found several things. First, organizations with the same structure, goals, and activities tended to be positioned in the same space and drew on the same sources, money, and so forth. Second, different types of organizations were in the same social space, only sharing interest in some community event. Third, the two communities shared similar money networks. Fourth, local dependencies within the money network in the two communities were similar. Finally, within the money network, the transmitters of money were generally more influential than the generators of money.

Peter V. Marsden and Karen E. Campbell[53] address the problem of measuring tie strength in a network. Their paper defines tie strength in terms of the time spent in the relationship and the intensity or intimacy measures within the tie. The data they used were drawn from three cross-sectional surveys. In all three studies, respondents were asked to identify their three closest friends and to report characteristics about them. Two types of variables were included in the measurement models the authors formulated: indicators and predictors of tie strength. One fairly clear conclusion: a measure of "closeness," or the emotional intensity of a relationship, is the best indicator of the concept of tie strength. Two measures that had to do with time spent in a relationship, duration and frequency, resulted in overestimates and were not good indicators of tie strength.

Edward O. Laumann and others[54] develop a causal model examining factors in organizational participation in state policy areas. They use five antecedent variables in the model that affect resource exchange networks and locations in communication, including issue interests, monitoring resources, and influence reputation. These variables affect the efforts of the organization in influencing policy decisions. The variables were measured with data collected from interviews. A total of 121 health and energy issues were found in the five-year period. The monitoring capacity was taken solely from the internal staff resources used by each organization. Reputed influence was measured by the number of times the other participants mentioned an organization as especially influential with regard to national health and/or energy policy formulation. The communication network location was identified by asking respondents to identify people in other organizations with whom they frequently discussed policy matters. The resource exchange network location was identified by the informants' responses regarding which organizations their group engaged in other various transactions.

The authors found that organizational interests are a prime factor affecting the breadth of policy-event participation. They also found the absence of any direct effects of resource possession on event participation. Monitoring capability and influence reputation did not directly increase event involvement.

James G. Anderson and Stephen J. Jay[55] examine why social network analysis is of importance in making policy decisions with regard to adoption and utilization of new technology by physicians. Data on referrals, consultations, discussions, and on-call coverage was obtained from interviews and hospital records. A computer-based hospital information system and personal practice characteristics from twenty-four physicians also provided information. The results suggest that the physician's relative position in a network is an important determinant of his/her participation in the diffusion process. This study found that physicians turn mainly to their peers before implementing new procedures and/or technology. Wesley Shrum and others[56] report the findings from a large-scale national network study of two technical systems. The study was designed to explore the relations between communications patterns and research performance. The two types of technical R/D networks systems are distinguished by technology under development for "collective" or "private" goods. Data were collected from 297 individual interviews from 97 organizations involved in nuclear waste and solar cell research. The first difference between the two technical systems is the degree to which national labs dominate the research in nuclear waste and to which private firms dominate solar cell research. Nuclear waste research represents a technical system oriented toward the production of the collective good and is largely dependent on state funds. In the solar cell research area, private good production is accompanied by a greater dispersion of funds, especially among the predominant private firms. Communication patterns among researchers align with the way in which funding and personnel are structured.

David Knoke[57] studies the effects of network interaction on the participation and voting results of citizens. These effects are classified as an "ego-centric network" in which an individual ("ego") dominates and a set of others ("alters") to whom ego is connected to interact. The data were gathered through the General Social Survey of 1987 that focused on the interviewees' perception of their ego-centric networks prediction of involvement in political elections. A total of 1,819 respondents were interviewed. The author concludes that ample evidence exists showing that structural relations are critical in shaping American politics. Increased interaction with others in a person's ego-centric network results in greater political influence. The overall conclusion of the study is that the greater the interaction, the more consistency that exists, and that closer ties will result in a more influential political network of people.

SOCIOLOGY OF OCCUPATIONS

The occupational structure of premodern societies was far simpler than the occupational structure in the modern epoch. With the increasing technology and specialization the occupational structure multiplied, becoming increasingly complex. To detail, understand, and explain attributes such as human capital, perceptions, rewards, mobility, and life chances, the subfield of occupational sociology has emerged. R. M. Stolzenburg[58] reexamines the relationship between schooling and wage earned using the data drawn from 1960 and 1970 U.S. Censuses and from the publications of the U.S. Bureau of Labor Statistics. Specifically he investigates how this relationship pertains to the differences in wages earned between black and white men. Previous research had pointed out the entwinement of racial differences in schooling and earnings. Studies have repeatedly found black men less successful than white men in converting their schooling into profit within their occupations. However, the differences in return from education are not strongly related to racial differences in wages. Using regression analysis Stolzenburg concludes that labor force experience has a bearing on the relationship between schooling and earnings. He then compares the earnings of white and black men in the same occupational categories and concludes that racial differences in the quality of education are not substantially related to racial differences in the earnings of men already within an occupation.

Using a regression analysis of NORC occupation prestige studies from 1947 and responses from 45 occupations, N. D. Glenn[59] calculated a "prestige increment score." He found that white-collar/blue-collar distinctions are increasingly less important. He also found that being white-collar may have made a modest contribution to the prestige of 24 nonmanual occupations in 1947 but such an effect had largely disappeared by 1963. Previous literature suggested that status symbols add to the prestige of an occupation above and beyond that associated with skills, education, and salaries. Glenn found no evidence of this.

The Davis-Moore theory of social stratification views the inequality in the distribution of rewards as linked to the social contribution of occupational positions. According to B. D. Grandjean and F. D. Bean,[60] this theory has been difficult to test empirically due to its analytical deficiencies. They attempt to extend and modify the theory using the concept of distributive justice in order to create testable hypotheses. The concepts of training, the joint determination of rewards, and equal opportunity are also used in the formulation of hypotheses. Using a 1964 Italian national sample of 1,569 male family-heads for data, they found support for a modified Davis-Moore theory.

J. P. Gibbs and D. L. Poston, Jr.,[61] using data from the Bureau of Census published in 1963, detail occupation composition as a way to measure sustenance differentiation. Six different equations are developed. The type of measurement chosen is based upon what researchers believe to be the number of classes and the distribution of individuals in these classes and its predictive accuracy regarding sustenance differentiation. The authors conclude that most forms of occupational differentiation are insightful as they measure the division of labor.

Work on social standing often uses the family as the social unit as well as characteristics of male household heads in establishing a family's social status. The family's social status is then examined for the effect it has on occupational achievement and mobility. Race has also been found to have utility in assigning statuses to households. W. A. Sampson and P. H. Rossi[62] explore the differences between blacks and whites as they relate to family social standing. The authors interviewed 267 respondents in 1972, asking them to assign a social status to several hypothetically created families. The study revealed that both blacks and whites felt that the wife's education and occupation had some effect on social standing and that both viewed occupation as being more important than education in determining social status. The race of the household is important, with white households faring better. Though race is important when viewing the bases on which status is established, overall the author found that race is less important than usually imagined in gaining status.

B. F. Turner and C. B. Turner[63] undertook a study of how sex and race relate to individual perceptions about discrimination in occupational opportunities. They administered a questionnaire to 1,457 white females, 1,429 white males, 70 black females, and 75 black males who were preparing to enter a large university as freshmen. First, they sought to test the hypotheses that whites would perceive less discrimination against blacks than would blacks, and males would perceive less discrimination against females than would women. Second, they maintained that black females perceive more discrimination against them than white women do. Finally, white women perceive less discrimination against women than do black females, black males, and white males. The data supported their hypotheses. White women view little discrimination against themselves because they are not taught by society that they are persons to be discriminated against, which is more the case with black females and black males.

Stolzenburg[64] deals with the question why some workers earn more money than others. To address the question he combines the perspectives of sociologists and economists in explaining wage attainment process. He proposes three hypotheses which link these perspectives into one, highlighting within-occupation earnings differentials. Labor markets are, he argues, fragmented along occupational lines because of differences in the supply and demand of labor, judgments about the value of work, and social organizations among workers in varying occupations. The processes governing wage earnings vary across occupations. Finally, the forces that lead to occupational fragmentation of labor markets also lead to occupational differences in wage earnings. The analysis of the data from 1960 and 1970 U.S. Censuses and from the publications of the U.S. Bureau of Labor Statistics supports his assertions.

Functionalists maintain that occupational prestige hierarchies show the necessity of social stratification in all societies. This view, Roger Penn[65] notes, is given support in Clark Kerr's related convergence thesis that industrialization results in many of the same features, including similar value systems, in all countries. It is also a view embraced by Robert Marsh, who maintains that occupational roles have similar attributes, requirements, and rewards in all societies. Penn uses the original NORC study on occupational prestige as well as a 1966 Czechoslovakian survey to demonstrate that the claims of Kerr and Marsh are false. There are differences in occupational prestige in both countries. His analysis invalidates the convergence thesis, casting doubt on the functionalist argument. The author considers that the theses of Kerr and Marsh do not take into account socialist systems which lack legitimacy. In turn socialism creates an entirely new system of moral worth and a different way of attributing prestige to occupations. For this reason, it is argued, the stratification in these two industrialized societies is different.

A. L. Kallenberg and L. J. Griffin[66] address the differences between class and occupation and their effects on job rewards. They suggest that inequality in job rewards originates from inequality in positions and that class and occupation are important variables in the inequality. They assert that the distinction between the definitions of class and occupation is essential in order to have a clear explanation of their effects on job rewards and their relationship to each other. In this study *class* describes positions defined by ownership and authority whereas *occupation* refers to activities within the division of labor. Using the data from the 1972–1973 Quality of Employment Survey and from an Educational Testing Service administered to the same sample in 1955 and 1970, the authors conclude that class and occupation have independent effects on allocations.

J. N. Baron[67] in his study of occupational mobility across generations reviews Natalie Rogoff's classic study based on the data for Marion County, Indiana, from 1910 to 1940. Rogoff based her study on the continuity and mobility of occupations within families in Marion County. After empirically deriving a structural model from Rogoff's data, he applies it to an intergenerational mobility matrix. The author applies the results of the 1973 Occupational Changes in a Generation II survey. His comparison reinforces the idea that intergenerational mobility exists. However, the study reveals that the patterns of mobility vary between two time periods.

Robert Schoen and Lawrence E. Cohen[68] studied occupational and generational effects on intermarriage among Mexican Americans. Generation and occupation reflect two different aspects of assimilation. *Generation* shows the extent of Americanization of the individual, and *occupation* is a variable which shows the extent of successful assimilation into American economic life. Applying these two variables to intermarriage provides insight into assimilation because it expresses a high degree of social acceptability. It would seem that generation would be more relevant to exogamy than occupation because cultural assimilation seems to move more rapidly than structural assimilation as represented by occupation. By reanalyzing the data from an earlier study by Frank G. Mittlebach and Joan W. Moore, Schoen and Cohen show that their thesis holds. The Mittlebach and Moore study data was based on 7,492 marriage licenses in Los Angeles County in 1963.

Marsden[69] undertakes to clarify the relationship between occupations and mobility. He uses the work of R. Beiger, who argues that the manner in which occupations are aggregated into social classes must be understood before analyzing mobility in social classes. He suggests that occupations should be placed in the same social class if they share the same amount of mobility. This is called the "internal homogeneity" model. The other model examined is the "collapsibility" model in which occupations are grouped together without knowledge of their mobility. Mardsen reformulates both these models in what he calls the latent structure models. Latent structure models allow previously unobserved class variables to be used in analyzing occupational mobility tables. The claim is that these models allow for variables to be marginal and to take into account the imperfections in occupational boundaries. This allows for some occupations to be grouped into more than one class. Previously collected data and Goodman's latent structure model is used to examine both the "internal homogeneity" and the "collapsibility" models as well as to create a new model allowing for marginality.

SOCIOLOGY OF RELIGION

How does society influence religion, its value system, and practices? How does religion influence social organization and institutional role relationships? These are just a few of the questions which the subfield of sociology of religion undertakes to explore and explain.

Ralph Underhill[70] uses George Murdock's Ethnographic Atlas to provide the 91 variables from 1,168 cultures. The research used slavery, economic complexity, political complexity, family organization, population size of local communities, settlement patterns, endogamous castes, and presence of social classes as measures of monotheism. The measures of economic complexity included the presence of hunting, animals, fishing, gathering, crop, agriculture and agricultural intensity, animal husbandry, and milking as indicators. The analysis of the data resulted in several conclusions. He found that economic complexity, the presence of endogamous castes, and political complexity (in that order) were the best indicators of monotheism in a given society. The research also found that political and economic complexity are independent of each other. Contrary to the predictions of Durkheim and Swanson, he found that political complexity did not explain the correlation between economic complexity and monotheism. Finally, he concluded that complexity of a society is a good indicator of monotheism, but it is not the only variable involved.

Conversion is a fairly common occurrence in religious settings. Youth conversions are, however, a challenging condition. To explain conversion Ronald C. Wimberley and others[71] surveyed a Billy Graham crusade at the University of Tennessee football stadium in the spring of 1975. Surveys were placed in randomly selected rows and seat numbers in clusters of six. Researchers collected these surveys before the beginning of the crusade. The surveys collected information on religious background, age of the converts, and the techniques used in the Billy Graham organization to attract and label converts. The data on the participants' background indicated that 91 percent of the respondents were church members, 32 percent higher than the national average of the time, with many of the respondents receiving their tickets to the crusade from their church. Using the data obtained from Graham's organization, Wimberley and others found that 73 percent of the converts were in their teens or younger but they made up only 31 percent of the audience. They noted that massive advertising and the buildup before the crusade may have influenced the decision to convert. The researchers criticized crusaders for not separating the number of converts from those who rededicated themselves to their creed. The conclusions of the study are that to "go forward" at a crusade is to show an alignment with the existing belief and value systems and when many people identify themselves as converts, they are reidentifying themselves as what they already are.

Harold S. Himmelfarb[72] takes typologies on religions to task. He opined that typologies being used are either too vague or not mutually exclusive. Instead, one should study types of religious involvement rather than just involvement in an organized religion. He constructs a typology of religious involvement in which he identifies its four major dimensions and nine subdimensions. The first dimension is supernatural and has three subdimensions: devotional, doctrinal, and experiential. The second is communal, characterized by two subdimensions: affiliation and ideology. The third, composed of intellectual and affectional subdimensions, is called the cultural dimension. The last is called interpersonal, characterized by ethical and moral subdimensions. He believes that these dimensions are universal; however, specific religions might vary on each dimension. To test his typology Himmelfarb selected distinctively Jewish surnames from the Chicago area home directory. He selected Jews because less was known about them than Christians. He supplemented his data with surveys of alumni from two Jewish schools in Chicago to insure that his sample would have subjects with higher education. In all, 1,278 usable responses were gathered, a return rate of 30 percent. During his study he realized that the devotional element of the supernatural dimension was unexpectedly being divided into two new subcategories, namely, daily and weekly rituals. He threw this category out. This deletion left him with eight factors for the study. He employed factor analysis in using an orthogonal rotation.

Though aware that orthogonal rotation gives variables an independence which might not exist in reality, he nevertheless concludes that his typologies are a good measurement of types of religious involvement. He found that religious involvement for American Jews is behavioral rather than ideational. Furthermore, he suggests that studies of religious involvement should use different methods of measurement for Jews and Christians.

Hart M. Nelson and others[73] start by discussing the ideas of Gary Marx. Marx maintains that religion contains a contradiction—it both encourages and discourages civil rights militancy. When black religion focuses on temporal matters it leads to militancy. A focus on eternal matters, however, inhibits militancy. Nelson and his colleagues chose Bowling Green, Kentucky, as the site for their research. This town had recently experienced changes in race relations. They selected 418 households from housing lists. Black interviewers were used. The response rate was 96.9 percent. The study used usual demographic variables like age, sex, education, orthodoxy, sectarianism, and religious associational involvement as indicators of civil rights militancy. The analysis of the data revealed that sectlike religious ideology was inversely related to militancy whereas orthodoxy was positively related. Education, followed by orthodoxy, was the best indicator of militancy. The research also indicated that blacks find the church to be a stimulus for militancy and protest.

Robert H. Lauer[74] undertakes to empirically test the relationship between social and religious mobility. Using a telephone survey of a small midwestern town with little interdenominational movement, he gathered data from 1,270 respondents on social mobility (measured by intergenerational occupational mobility) and religious mobility (measured by intergenerational changes in religious preferences). Denominational prestige was measured using a scale developed by Bruce L. Warren which measured the economic success of different denominations. Episcopals topped the list while Pentecostals were at the bottom. No direct relationship between occupational and religious mobility was noted. The majority of the people changing denominations moved up or left the religion entirely. Education was as strong an indicator of mobility as was occupational mobility. The combination of two had the strongest effect on occupational mobility.

Using data on 2,482 adults collected by Temple University, Charles W. Mueller and Weldon T. Johnson[75] explored the relationship between socioeconomic status and religious participation. Their research found a weak positive relationship between religious affiliations and gender. It showed that low socioeconomic status was associated with lower levels of religious and nonreligious participation. Religious participation was found to be higher for married people with children and single people without children.

Antonio Gramsci argued that dominant groups influence the interests and desires of subordinate groups and was interested in proposing how subordinate groups resist being dominated and struggle to achieve independence. Gramsci believed that class struggles in the West are a "war of position" involving political struggles. Gramsci viewed religions as multiplicities of other contradictory religions that were a "residue of a precapitalist world." Dwight B. Billings[76] uses Gramsci's ideas to account for why labor unions were supported by evangelical Protestant religion in the coal fields of Appalachia but rejected by the same in the mills of North Carolina. Workers in the coal fields viewed their religion as a call to activism. When company ministers disagreed, workers stopped attending their formal churches and produced their own lay ministers. In North Carolina during crisis, religion was used to maintain social order. Ministers were on the payroll of the companies. They were able to influence their parishioners to avoid social unrest and strike. Thirty years later mill workers in North Carolina were still opposed to change. Billings uses a wide variety of sources ranging from oral accounts to previous sociological research.

CONCLUSIONS AND COMMENTARY

Social research presents at times a bewildering diversity. From the time of Comte to the present, there has been an overarching concern that sociology become an integral arm of the state, affecting the nature and direction of political-cum-social affairs. In recent times a more sobering view has emerged, one which questions if such a quest is even feasible. There exists a tension between the sentiments of early sociologists and current practices in which numerous facts are accumulated and relationships are sought and assessed. Rather than contributing to a coherent whole or totalizing view of the world, there continues to be growing series of intellectual fiefdoms which have become circulating machines for various canons of theory and research.

There is something to be said about the mushrooming of specialty areas in sociology. It has some advantages because it brings together scholars and researchers with similar interests to create a body of knowledge. On the other hand, many others remain uninformed about specialties other than their own. This can result in duplication of effort. And as specialty participants become their own referees and reviewers, feeding each other's interest, the resulting polymorphism in research can lead to the avoidance of standards as to what is considered adequate evidence.

Sciences in general and sociology in particular have been engaged in research in little niches or small areas of concern. This has resulted in a plethora of mini hypotheses, propositions, and so forth, with a multitude of people contributing to bodies of "evidence." What is the utility of this multifaceted "evidence"? Little effort is being expended to synthesize this "evidence." Unless this "evidence" can be synthesized, unifying episte-mological concerns remain a distant dream for defining the discipline.

After almost two centuries of struggle to distinguish the subject matter of sociology from other sciences, the metaphysical stage of development, to use Comte's terminology, persists. Some might maintain that sociology has arrived at a positive (scientific) stage. But the evidence is limited. The proliferation of subfields in sociology is extensive. This may be necessary but it seems rather *extensive* more than *intensive*. Research in the subfields tends to say a little about everything, but a sustained probing of the nature and operation of social life remained undeveloped, left often to the spec-ulative preoccupation of theoretical disputants. Much research has pro-duced plausible and probable explanations of "special" phenomena without regard to its place in addressing matters of importance. We do not propose an uncritical holism, but a hand apart from a body has little meaning. For example, the study of suicide as a specialty within social sciences has little meaning if the explanations of it cannot be instructive regarding an extensive field of conduct.

For a generation American sociology has been viewed as being in a crisis. This recognition occurred in the 1960s and 1970s, a time, as Don Martindale observes, which "was a Gilded Age and the research entre-preneurs had been invited to a Great Barbecue at public expense. It re-sulted in an excessive fragmentation of the field into research specialties."[77] But now the Great Barbecue is over. Funding has been steadily declining, and the dream of a consolidated discipline remains il-lusory.

As long as much work does what Pitirim Sorokin called "a painful elab-oration of the obvious," the accumulation of "little facts" in academic sociology having little relationship to each other will continue. The result will continue to be "piece-goods" research, insufficient to make a com-plete garment.

Although predisposed to a normative program, John E. Owen, writing in 1954, described these persistent problems in sociology. "The science," he wrote,

that should ideally be a means of human betterment becomes a mysterious cult ... inaccessible for all but the few initiated. In this connection, witness the use of academic "journals," the pseudoscientific jargon in which sociological conclusions have been couched. ... Along with professional educationalists and psychologists, sociologists tend to resemble medieval scholastics in their use of well-nigh incom-prehensible vocabulary.

This jargon has not only placed sociology outside the grasp of intelligent layman but it has also been a means of shielding its own lack of ideas and intellectual content. ... Sociologists have assured that there are dozens of "facts" to be ac-cumulated and that when sorted and counted these will yield social "laws" which exist independently of the observer.[78]

Since 1954, when John Owen wrote this, the situation has become even more problematic. In 1954, the jargon, which has some boundary-defining function, was limited to specialties in sociology. Today there exists an elaboration of this jargon to disciplinary subspecialties. A good example is the study of social control, which is now fragmented into various subspecialties. Social control evolved from a general concern over the institutionalized means to promote behavioral conformity to a social psychological perspective stressing internalization on controls to an emphasis on formal agencies of social control such as criminal law enforcement.[79] Within these traditions attention has focused on manipulation within a general framework which values Western parliamentary democracy. Recently David Sciulli[80] has undertaken a major critique of these issues and is developing an approach which distinguishes social control from social integration. Social integration involves a general recognition and understanding of shared social duties. Social control emerges when social duties are unrecognized or not understood. Sciulli argues that through this division one may find that the resulting social order is sustained not simply because of social control efforts and their legitimacies, but by general shared notions of social duties. Such notions may be manipulated, as Marxists might contend, or they may simply persist despite the understanding and efforts of those occupying dominating social positions.

Under the guise of various labels—poststructuralism, postmodernism—a second approach to the varieties of sociological research is stressed. Affirmatively, it can be argued that this is symptomatic of a growing pluralism. In a world wherein the state may be less a central agency, or at least holds less promise of being so, intellectual efforts are diverse, challenging, even "wild."[81] This heralds the emergence of marginal voices and a recognition that the Eurocentric view of social life having highly organized and dominating loci of control is crumbling. What this will entail is unclear.

Negatively, the varieties of sociological research as well as other types of intellectual discourse reveal that many Western intellectuals made a bargain with the sovereign, with various agents of the state, and they are losing. The quest to influence social policy, to make society in the image of a politically invoked system of domination, may be less and less a promise for social scientists.

The irony of what is unfolding is that sociology, begun as a conservative intellectual movement, uneasy about the encroachment of a growing political economy, may find that at the time when it came to embrace the sovereign and the belief in redemption through power, these very conditions were eroding. Left with incidental facts and some canonized works, many North American sociologists find themselves not extricated but further enmeshed in the several-centuries-long tension between natural philosophic and moral-empirical philosophic outlooks. The tradition of positivism and much of research methods have premiumed the former, fashioning a view that social science can be the force suggested by the Enlightenment forebears, as a source of judicious social direction. The latter, by contrast, stresses concerns over values and consistency of argumentation. This more dialogic view requires that active intellects situate themselves in an ongoing struggle to sustain and transform discourse. While there is growing sentiment for these views,[82] the structural conditions of most North American intellectuals precludes an effective pursuit of this option.[83] The problems which John Owen and Don Martindale highlighted persist in sociology. The present preoccupation with technique rather than substance has created an image in the mind of the intelligent lay public, one which many disciplines no longer cultivate, that sociology is no more than an academic abstraction. The abandonment of general education and the quest to influence public policy through institutionally legitimate mechanisms remain elusive.

Sociology is not without its achievements: it contains a large body of evidence gained through the efforts of many researchers, and the internationalization of social life will be reflected in the discipline. The XIIth World Congress of Sociology in Madrid, Spain, had "Sociology for One World: Unity and Diversity" as its theme. One hope is that the continuing advancement in research and theory would eventually lead sociology toward maturity and social responsibility for the service of global society or at least a human face in the wake of rapid change.

NOTES

The authors appreciate reference checking by the following: Jonathan Carbonnell, Danette Clifton, Melissa Compher, Ashley Heron, James Keffer, Tracey Loftis, Heather Murphy, Mary Roughton, Joy E. Smith, J. York, and Jonathan Zimlich.

1. See Raj P. Mohan and Don Martindale, eds., *Handbook of Contemporary Developments in World Sociology* (Westport, CT: Greenwood Press, 1975).

2. Brenda Coleman, "Excessive Medical Specialization Drives Health Costs Up, Experts Say," *The Birmingham News,* Thursday, September 3, 1992.

3. Ellen K. Coughlin, "Sociologists Confront Questions about Field's Vitality and Direction," *The Chronicle of Higher Education* 38, 49 (August 12, 1992): A7–A9.

4. Ibid., p. A7.

5. Neil Smelser, ed. *Handbook of Sociology* (Newbury Park, C.A.: Sage Publications, 1988), p. 18.

6. Parker W. Frisbie and Dudley L. Poston, Jr., "Components of Sustenance Organization and Nonmetropolitan Population Change: A Human Ecological Investigation," *American Sociological Review* 40, 6 (1975): 773–84.

7. Claude S. Fischer, "Toward a Subcultural Theory of Urbanism," *American Journal of Sociology* 80, 6 (1975): 1319–41.

8. Marcus Felson and Maurico Solaun, "The Fertility-Inhibiting Effect of Crowded Apartment Living in a Tight Housing Market," *American Journal of Sociology* 80, 6 (1975): 1410–27.

9. John R. Logan and M. Semyonov, "Growth and Succession in Suburban Communities," *The Sociological Quarterly* 21 (1980): 93–105.

10. John M. Stahura, "Ecological Determinants of the Aging of Suburban Population," *The Sociological Quarterly* 21 (1980): 107–18.

11. David F. Sly and Jeffrey Tayman, "Metropolitan Morphology and Population Mobility: The Theory of Ecological Expansion Reexamined," *American Journal of Sociology* 86, 1 (1980): 119–38.

12. Glen R. Carroll, "Concentration and Specialization: Dynamics of Niche Width in Population of Organizations," *American Journal of Sociology* 90, 6 (1985): 1262–83.

13. Robert M. Hauser, John N. Koffel, Harry P. Travis, and Peter J. Dickinson, "Temporal Change in Occupational Mobility: Evidence for Men in the United States," *American Sociological Review* 40 (1975): 279–97.

14. Edward A. Tiryakian, "Neither Marx nor Durkheim . . . Perhaps Weber," *American Journal of Sociology* 81 (1975): 1–33.

15. Albert Hunter, "The Loss of Community: An Empirical Test Through Replication," *American Sociological Review* 40 (1975): 537–52.

16. Martin S. Weinberg and Colin J. Williams, "Sexual Embourgeoisment? Social Class and Sexual Activity: 1938–1970," *American Sociological Review* 45 (1980): 33–48.

17. William R. Kelly and David Snyder, "Racial Violence and Socioeconomic Changes among Blacks in the United States," *Social Forces* 58 (1980): 739–60.

18. Steven F. Messner, "Societal Development, Social Equality and Homicide: A Cross-National Test of a Durkheimian Model," *Social Forces* 61 (1982): 225–40.

19. Duane Champagne, "Social Structure, Revitalization Movements and State Building: Social Change in Four Native American Societies," *American Sociological Review* 48 (1983): 754–63.

20. Stanley Presser, "Measurement Issues in the Study of Social Change," *Social Forces* 68 (1990): 856–68.

21. Ibid., p. 857.

22. Laurence R. Iannaccone and Carrie A. Miles, "Dealing with Social Change: The Mormon Church's Response to Change in Women's Roles," *Social Forces* 68 (1990): 1231–50.

23. An article by William Edgar Maxwell entitled "Modernization and Mobility into the Patrimonial Medical Elite in Thailand," *American Journal of Sociology* 81 (1975): 465–90 has been excluded as it does not deal with the concerns or contribute to trends in American sociology.

24. One of the articles which was indexed under social changes was also indexed under social movements. This is an article by Janet K. Roach and Jack L. Roach entitled: "Turmoil in Command Politics: Organizing the Poor," which appeared in *The Sociological Quarterly* 21 (Spring 1980): 259–70. We discuss this article under the heading of Social Movements.

25. Ben-Yehuda's article entitled "The European Witch Craze of the 14th to 17th Centuries: A Sociologist's Perspective," which appeared in *American Journal*

of Sociology 86 (1980): 1–31, was indexed under social change, but in our view it does not contribute to any trends in research in social change in the United States. We do wish to acknowledge its publication in the *AJS*.

26. Naomi Rosenthal et al., "Social Movements and Network Analysis: A Case Study on Nineteenth-Century Reform in New York State," *American Sociological Review* 90 (1985): 1022–33. Discussed under the section in Network Analysis.

27. Wesley Shrum et al., "The Organization of Technology in Advanced Industrial Society: A Hypothesis on Technical Systems," *Social Forces* 64 (1985): 46–63. Discussed under the section on Network Analysis.

28. David Knoke, "Networks of Political Action: Toward Theory Construction," *Social Forces* 68 (1990): 1041–63. Discussed under the section on Network Analysis.

29. R. K. Hawkes, "Norms, Deviance and Social Control: A Mathematical Elaboration of Concepts," *American Journal of Sociology* 80 (January 1975): 886–908.

30. C. R. Tittle, "Deterrents of Labeling?" *Social Forces* 53 (March 1975): 399–410.

31. Morris Janowitz, "Sociological Theory and Social Control," *American Journal of Sociology* 81 (July 1975): 82–108.

32. S. R. Burkett and E. L. Jensen, "Conventional Ties, Peer Influence, and the Fear of Apprehension: A Study of Adolescent Marijuana Use," *Sociological Quarterly* 16 (Autumn 1975): 522–33.

33. J. G. Hougland, Jr. and James R. Wood, "Control in Organizations and the Commitment of Members," *Social Forces* 59 (Summer 1980): 85–109.

34. Louise Shelley, "Geography of Soviet Criminality," *American Sociological Review* 45 (Fall 1980): 111–22.

35. R. J. Stevenson, "The Officer-Enlisted Distinction and Patterns of Organizational Reaction to Social Deviance in the U.S. Military," *Social Forces* 68 (June 1990): 1191–1209.

36. D. D. Heckathorn, "Collective Sanctions and Compliance Norms: A Formal Theory of Group Mediated Social Control," *American Sociological Review* 55 (1990): 366–84.

37. R. J. Sampson and J. H. Laub, "Crime and Deviance over Life Course: The Salience of Adult Social Bonds," *American Sociological Review* 55 (1990): 609–27.

38. Jack A. Roach and Janet L. Roach, "Turmoil in Command of Politics: Organizing the Poor," *Sociology Quarterly* 21 (Spring 1980): 259–70.

39. Steven E. Barkan, "Political Trials and Resource Mobilization: Towards an Understanding of Social Movement Litigation," *Social Forces* 58 (March 1980): 944–61.

40. Jack A. Gladstone, "The Weakness of Organization: A New Look at Gamson's *The Strategy of Social Protest*," *American Journal of Sociology* 85 (May 1980): 1017–60.

41. David A. Snow, Louis A. Zurcher, Jr., and Sheldon Eckland-Olson, "Social Movements and Network Analysis: A Microstructural Approach to Differential Recruitment," *American Sociological Review* 45 (October 1980): 787–801.

42. Naomi Rosenthal, Meryl Fingrutd, Michele Ethier, Roberta Karant, and David McDonald, "Social Movements and Network Analysis: A Case Study of

Nineteenth-Century Women's Reform in New York State," *American Journal of Sociology* 90:5 (1985): 1022–54.

43. Gwen Moore, "The Structure of a National Elite Network," *American Sociological Review* 44 (1979): 673–91.

44. Edward O. Laumann and Peter V. Marsden, "The Analysis of Oppositional Structures in Political Elites: Identifying Collective Actors," *American Sociological Review* 44 (1979): 713–32.

45. Peter Killworth and Russell Bernard, "Pseudomodel of the Small World Problem," *Social Forces* 58 (1979): 477–505.

46. Ronald S. Burt, "Autonomy in Social Topology," *American Journal of Sociology* 85 (1980): 892–923.

47. Rodney Stark and William Sims Bainbridge, "Networks of Faith: Interpersonal Bonds and Recruitment to Cults and Sects," *American Journal of Sociology* 85 (1980): 1376–95.

48. Myra Marx Ferree, "Working Class Feminism: A Consideration of the Consequences of Employment," *Sociological Quarterly* 21 (1980): 173–184.

49. Jon Miller, "Access to Interorganizational Networks as a Professional Resource," *American Sociological Review* 45 (1980): 479–96.

50. Richard E. Ratcliff, "Banks and Corporate Lending: An Analysis of the Impact of the Internal Structure of the Capitalist Class on the Lending Behavior of Banks," *American Sociological Review* 45 (1980): 553–70.

51. Ronald S. Burt et al., "Testing a Structural Theory of Corporate Cooptation: Interorganizational Directorates Ties as a Strategy for Avoiding Market Constraints on Profits," *American Sociological Review* 45 (1980): 821–41.

52. Joseph Galaskiewicz and Karl Krohn, "Positions, Roles, and Dependencies in an Interorganizational System," *Sociological Quarterly* 25 (1984): 527–50.

53. Peter V. Marsden and Karen E. Campbell, "Measuring Tie Strength," *Social Forces* 63 (1984): 482–501.

54. Edward O. Laumann et al., "An Organizational Approach to State Policy Formation: A Comparative Study of Energy and Health Domains," *American Sociological Review* 50 (1985): 1–19.

55. James G. Anderson and Stephen J. Jay, "The Diffusion of Medical Technology: Social Network Analysis and Policy Research," *Sociological Quarterly* 26 (1985): 49–64.

56. Wesley Shrum et al., "The Organization of Technology in Advanced Industrial Society: A Hypothesis on Technical Systems," *Social Forces* 64 (1985): 46–63.

57. David Knoke, "Networks of Political Action: Toward Theory Construction," *Social Forces* 68 (1990): 1041–63.

58. R. M. Stolzenburg, "Education, Occupation, and Wage Differences between White and Black Men," *American Journal of Sociology* 81 (1975): 299–323.

59. N. D. Glenn, "The Contribution of White Collars to Occupational Prestige," *Sociological Quarterly* 16 (1975): 184–89.

60. B. D. Grandjean and F. D. Bean, "The Davis-Moore Theory and Perceptions of Stratification: Some Relevant Evidence," *Social Forces* 54 (1975): 166–80.

61. J. P. Gibbs and D. L. Poston, Jr., "The Division of Labor: Conceptualization and Related Measures," *Social Forces* 53 (1975): 468–76.

62. W. A. Sampson and P. H. Rossi, "Race and Family Social Standing," *American Sociological Review* 40 (1975): 201–14.

63. B. F. Turner and C. B. Turner, "Race, Sex, and Perception of the Occupational Opportunity Structure among College Students," *Sociological Quarterly* 16 (1975): 345–60.

64. R. M. Stolzenburg, "Occupations, Labor Markets and the Process of Wage of Attainment," *American Sociological Review* 40 (1975): 645–56.

65. Roger Penn, "Occupational Prestige Hierarchies: A Great Empirical Invariant?" *Social Forces* 54 (1975): 352–64.

66. A. L. Kalleberg and L. J. Griffin, "Class, Occupation, and Inequality in Job Rewards," *American Journal of Sociology* 85 (1980): 731–68.

67. J. N. Baron, "Indianapolis and Beyond: A Structural Model of Occupational Mobility Beyond Generations," *American Journal of Sociology* 85 (1980): 815–39.

68. R. Schoen and L. E. Cohen, "Ethnic Endogamy among Mexican American Grooms: A Reanalysis of Generational and Occupational Effects," *American Journal of Sociology* 85 (1980): 359–66.

69. P. V. Marsden, "Latent Structure Models for Relationally Defined Social Classes," *American Journal of Sociology* 90 (1985): 1002–21.

70. Ralph Underhill, "Economic and Political Antecedents of Monotheism: A Cross-Cultural Study," *American Journal of Sociology* 80 (1975): 841–61.

71. Ronald C. Wimberley, Thomas C. Hook, C. M. Lipsey, Donald Clelland, and Marguerite Hay, "Conversion in Billy Graham Crusade: Spontaneous Event or Ritual Performance?" *The Sociological Quarterly* 16 (1975): 162–69.

72. Harold S. Himmelfarb, "Measuring Religious Involvement," *Social Forces* 53 (1975): 606–18.

73. Hart M. Nelson, Thomas W. Madron, and Raytha L. Yokley, "Black Religion's Promethean Motif: Orthodoxy and Militancy," *American Journal of Sociology* 81 (1975): 139–46.

74. Robert H. Lauer, "Occupational and Religious Mobility in a Small City," *The Sociological Quarterly* 16 (1975): 380–92.

75. Charles W. Mueller and Weldon T. Johnson, "Socioeconomic Status and Religious Participation," *American Sociology Review* 40 (1975): 785–800.

76. Dwight B. Billings, "Religion as Opposition: A Gramscian Analysis," *American Journal of Sociology* 96 (1990): 1–27.

77. Don Martindale, "Trends in Sociological Theory Since World War II," in Ulf Himmelstrand, ed., *The Multiparadigmatic Trends in Sociology* (Stockholm: Almqvist and Wiksell International, 1987), p. 53.

78. John E. Owen, "Sociology at Mid-Century," *The Western Humanities Review* 8, no. 1 (Winter 1954): 33–40.

79. See David Sciulli, *Theory of Societal Constitutionalism: Foundations of a Non-Marxist Critical Theory* (Cambridge: Cambridge University Press, 1992).

80. Ibid.

81. See Gilles Deleuze and Felix Guattari, *Anti-Oedipus: Capitalism and Schizophrenia* (New York: Viking, 1977). The notion that instead of central agency and domination, looking for "rhizomic" connections in sociocultural life heralds a methodological strategy emphasizing interpretation over logical-empirical analysis.

82. Alan Wolfe, *America at Century's End* (Berkeley, CA: University of Cali-

fornia Press, 1991). Wolfe makes a direct appeal for sociology to return to a moral philosophic project.

83. Russell Jacoby, *The Last Intellectuals: American Culture in the Age of Academe* (New York: Basic Books, 1987). Jacoby sees the centrality of universities in intellectual life fragmenting public discourse and substituting a growing bureaucratization and narrowing of concerns. The result is an estranging of disciplines such as sociology from a public constituency.

Part III

Sociology in Eastern Europe

Max Weber once observed that the creation of new sociocultural forms and interpretations frequently occurs not in the centers of power and capitals of high cultures but in the hinterlands, particularly in the interstitial or marginal areas between centers of high culture. If we were to phrase Weber's observation in contemporary terms, the centers of power of any given society's Establishment often prohibit serious reflection on underlying presuppositions. However, in marginal areas removed from the centers of Establishment power and possibly subject to the distant influence of more than one Establishment, it may be much easier to bring fundamental assumptions under review. Weber's observations seem to apply to the development of sociology both in the Western Hemisphere and in Eastern Europe.

Sociology arose in Western Europe as a form of collectivism or holism borne by the middle classes in service of consolidating the nation-state around its interests. From the beginning North American sociologists tended to modify the early collectivism sociology received from Europe, giving it a more individualistic or elementaristic thrust. When a variety of elementaristic positions eventually emerged in Europe toward the end of the nineteenth century, these were immediately thrust into a primary position in American sociology and integrated with endemic elementaristic traditions (particularly pragmatism). American sociology was destined to become the most influential in the world.

At the same time that sociology was introduced to the New World, it was diffusing to Eastern Europe. Here again it moved into a marginal area. Eastern Europe was multiethnic, multilinguistic, and culturally transitional to Asia. All the major intellectual traditions of the

West were brought into confrontation and reviewed in the perspective of unique problems. In Russia, for example, such thinkers as Belinsky, Chernichevsky, Peter Kropotkin, Elisee Reclus, Michail Bakunin, P. Ya. Chaadayev, Pobedonoshev, Peter Lavrov, Nikolai Mikhailovsky, G. V. Plekhanov, and Maxim Kovalevsky were variously familiar with the theories of Comte, Spencer, Darwin, Adam Smith, Le Play, Marx, and numerous others.

The tendency to criticize, extend, or refine the Western intellectual traditions runs through the work of these thinkers. Peter Kropotkin in *Mutual Aid* (1902) brought social Darwinism under review; Eugene De Roberty (who, to be sure, belongs to France as well as Russia) proposed to clarify and extend sociological positivism; J. Novikov developed the concept of an intellectual elite as the real directive formed of society; Peter Lavrov was the first to formulate a subjective method for sociology, a method extended by Mikhailovsky. Kovalevsky brought Western sociologists under review, abandoned the notion that it was the task of sociology to find laws for all history, and insisted that a multicausal approach to social life was essential if sociology were to become truly scientific. But above all, the Russian social scientists began to give far more importance to Marxism as a tool for social analysis and social reconstruction than it ever had elsewhere in the West. Thus, while the Western Hemisphere carried out an unparalleled extension of elementaristic perspectives, Eastern Europe became a stronghold of left-wing collectivism.

Ludwik Krzywicki is conventionally viewed as the founder of Polish sociology. He translated Marx's *Das Kapital,* undertook empirical investigations on the status of workmen in Warsaw, and was interested in the flow of ideas in space and time. After World War I, he occupied the first chair of sociology at the Warsaw faculty of law. Krzywicki also became director of the Institute for Social Economy, which researched the peasant economy of Poland.

Though Hegelian and other Western intellectual traditions were popular in Czechoslovakia before then, by general agreement Thomas Garrique Masaryk, later president of the first Czechoslovak republic, was its first important sociologist. Already in the 1880s Masaryk was conducting studies of suicide and codifying sociological methods. Edward Benes, his pupil and collaborator and the successor to Masaryk as president, continued his sociological studies. Emanuel Chalupny was also an active theoretical and empirical researcher of the Masaryk school, developing the theory of civilization and conducting empirical studies of such phenomena as the death sentence, suicides, the operations of the penal code, and educational sociology.

In Hungary, sociology was primarily a social science of the state. Its founders pioneered the sociology of power. The founder of the Hungarian Sociological Society (1900), Agost Pulszky, was a jurist.

Bulgarian sociology emerged after the country's liberation from Ottoman bondage (1878) and was developed in the work of such revolutionary democrats as Lyuben Karavelov, Vassil Levski, and Hrito Botev. Both Hegelian and Marxian traditions were present from an early period, but by relatively even steps in the twentieth century the Marxian tradition became dominant.

In Romania both German and French cultural influences were strong. Among the founders of Romanian sociology were Dobrogeano-Gherta, a socialist theorist and student of the Romanian peasantry who braced the relations between history and sociology and established a logic of the historical sciences, and, particularly, Dimitri Gusti (born 1880), who studied in Germany under Wilhelm Wundt, Georg Simmel, and Gustav Schmoller among others, and who occupied the first chair of sociology and founded the Romanian Social Institute.

Yugoslavian sociology was powerfully influenced by social geography and ethnography. Sociology was established in the universities and found outlets in professional journals before World War I.

The present section adds many details to this quick outline of beginnings: they trace the emergence and dominance of traditional Marxism over the sociology of Russia and the complex fate of sociology in the Iron Curtain countries as its practitioners struggled for autonomy under the domination of the Soviet government after World War II.

This section provides four rich portraits of East European sociology. As the Iron Curtain disintegrates it will provide new challenges, opportunities, and problems and predicaments for social sciences. Sociology will breathe anew as its fate is intimately tied with the development of the nation-states.

Anna Giza-Poleszczuk captures the essence of changes in Polish society and their effect upon the development of sociology in Poland. She discusses in detail how both the empirical and theoretical dimensions of Polish sociology have been influenced by social and political events over the years. Velichko Dobrianov examines the sociological tradition in Bulgarian society and how socialist planning helped advance the discipline. He sees the existence of sociological knowledge in contemporary Bulgaria at two levels: abstract-theoretical and concrete-empirical. At present sociology in Bulgaria is occupied with the study of various problems of society both at the micro and at the macro levels.

The newly won freedom in Hungary and the emergence of parliamentary democracy has opened up new opportunities as well as challenges for Hungarian sociologists. However, with the long historical background which sociology in Hungary enjoys, it will not be difficult to reorient sociological thought to grapple with these challenges. Tibor Huszàr examines the transition from Marxist-oriented sociology toward a rapid institutionalization and professionalization of autonomous sociology.

Gennady S. Batygin and Inna F. Deviatko trace the origins of sociology in Russia through the various historical stages and various influences both internal and external. They also analyze the effects of pre-1988 political reforms by Gorbachev and the confusion which emerged from these in sociology. However, they are hopeful for a diversification of interests and research in sociology through its institutional development during the last few years of the present century.

17

Contemporary Sociology in Bulgaria

Velichko Dobrianov

During the past thirty years there has been a rapid development of sociology in Bulgaria in all fields of the discipline. Briefly outlined, the causes of this phenomenon appear as follows.

First, it was believed that socialist society in principle involves a planned guidance of social processes, which requires not only a general theory but also a huge amount of empirical information. Thanks to its specific subject, which comprises society as an integral system, sociology with its apparatus of concepts and methods of investigation constitutes an irreplaceable social science, the task of which is not only to explain social phenomena and processes but also to help in the making of adequate social decisions.

Second, the rapid advance of the scientific and technological revolution and its penetration into all social activities and relations, including the people's everyday life, accelerates social processes, makes their interrelations more and more vigorous, internationalizes the existing societies, increases the speed of the development of productive forces, and gives rise to a number of social problems. The study of social processes at all levels in their interrelations, from the angle and by the methods of sociology, is an indispensable condition for their macro- and micro-prognostication and for the timely and adequate change in the integral totality of societal relations and social institutions.

Third, the overcoming of certain sectarian and dogmatic attitudes has more and more enhanced the position, importance, and role of sociology in the study and the purposeful guidance of social processes, the widening and deepening of man's outlook.

HISTORICAL PREREQUISITES

Sociology's upsurge in Bulgaria is based on a solid tradition, established in the nineteenth century. To the scholars of a state that celebrated the 1,300th anniversary of its foundation, it appears tempting to look for elements of sociological thought in their nation's remotest part. In fact, the first beginnings of social knowledge—although they were not differentiated in the shape of independent conceptions and were indissolubly linked with various theological, philosophical, and aesthetic views—emerged in Bulgaria as far back as the first centuries of its existence. Attempts at systematizing this knowledge in the form of definite conceptions of social life were made during the Bulgarian Renaissance that occurred around the end of the eighteenth century in a close relation to the struggle for national revival and liberation from Ottoman bondage. Prior to the liberation from Ottoman bondage (1878), Bulgarian sociological thought developed mainly in the works of the revolutionary democrats Lyuben Karavelov,[1] Vassil Levski,[2] and Hristo Botev.[3]

After the liberation, sociology in Bulgaria emerged and made its first successful steps thanks to the rich and varied theoretical activity of Dimitur Blagoev.[4] In the first half of the twentieth century, both general sociology and a number of sector sociological disciplines developed in Bulgaria. The first empirical sociological investigations, connected with the names of Georgi Bakalov,[5] Iliya Yanoulov,[6] and Ivan Hadzhiyski,[7] were also conducted at that time.

In contrast and in opposition to certain prejudices, it should be noted that empirical sociological investigation is not something new in Bulgaria. As far back as the end of the 1890s the *Rabotnicheski Vestnik* daily, the organ of the Bulgarian workers' Social-Democrat party, became the organizer of empirical sociological and other social investigations on the basis of which various theoretical generalizations were made regarding the workers' and trade-union movements. Starting from 1899, over a thirty-year period, the Bulgarian sociologist and jurist Iliya Yanoulov carried out over twenty empirical sociological investigations, while Georgi Bakalov is the first Bulgarian author who (as early as 1903) elaborated a special questionnaire of 105 questions for an empirical sociological investigation of the working class.[8]

By substantiating, in the 1930s, the specific subject of sociology, Todor Pavlov laid the foundations for the gradual formation of sociology as a most general social science which, although it is closely related to and based on philosophy, is not of a philosophical nature. Todor Pavlov, in his capital work *Teoriya Na Otrazhenieto* (Theory of Reflection), substantiated the idea that sociology is an independent and most general, nonphilosophical science of society, the subject matter of which is "the structure and the structural regularity of social reality."[9]

The practical needs of the society and the internal logic of the development of social sciences after the 1944 revolution again focused attention on the subject of sociology and its place within the system of social sciences. In the second part of the 1950s a far-reaching discussion developed in Bulgaria in the course of which two basic views on sociology took shape. The controversy, essentially an argument between philosophers, reflected a natural process of differentiation of sociology from philosophy. An important number of the participants continued to support the view of the identity of sociology and historical materialism, which for its part is a component or aspect of philosophy. Another group substantiated the view that sociology is a most general science of society, which rests on philosophy as its most general methodology but is not identical with and is not a part of philosophy. It has the characteristics of a particular scientific discipline and is of a nonphilosophical nature. This view was thoroughly substantiated by Zhivko Oshavkov and Kiril Vassilev.[10] The predominant characteristic of this discussion was an attempt to interpret the classical heritage of Marxism; that is, the authors supported their theses mainly by invoking one or another statement of the classics of Marxism.

With the advent of the 1960s the discussion about sociology entered a new stage, not only in that it was joined by younger authors but also because now the center of gravity was shifted from general arguments to attempts at a more concrete consideration of sociology's basic theoretical questions, such as its scope, system, and methods. The aim was now set on the development and the further building up of sociology, with a view to giving it all the properties of a harmonious theoretical and empirical scientific discipline, with its own category apparatus and system of methods and its own position and role both within the system of the sciences of society and man and within the realm of social practice.

Three volumes of the *Anthology of Bulgarian Sociological Thought* demonstrate historical development of social thoughts and sociology in Bulgaria.[11] The first volume includes writers from the ninth to the nineteenth centuries; the second, from 1878 to 1944; and the third presents contemporary writers. It is understandable that the anthology includes selected works of selected authors.

THE INSTITUTIONALIZATION OF BULGARIAN SOCIOLOGY

The process of differentiation of sociology as an independent nonphilosophical discipline in Bulgaria has also expressed itself in *The Institutionalization of Sociology in Corresponding Organizational Structures.* In 1959 a group of twenty-four scientific workers of the field of social sciences, mainly philosophers, set up a sociological society in the People's Republic of Bulgaria. In that same year the society became a member of the International Sociological Association. Ten years later, in 1969, it changed its structure and name to Bulgarian Sociological Association, with its seat in Sofia. Nowadays the association unites about 30 sociological societies in district capitals and in other larger towns, as well as more than 1,200 sociologists forming the individual membership. The association engages in intensive activity for the advance of sociology both within the country and on an international scale. Undoubtedly the most important international manifestation so far of the association and of Bulgarian sociologists in general was the organization and holding of the Seventh World Congress of Sociology in Varna in 1970.

In 1962, a group for sociological research was formed in the historical materialism department of the institute of philosophy at the Bulgarian Academy of Sciences. Later on (in 1968) this group became the nucleus of the newly set up institute of sociology at the Bulgarian Academy of Sciences. Although rather young, the institute has affirmed itself as the main theoretical and methodological center regarding the problems of sociology and empirical sociological research in Bulgaria. Its structure comprises different sections, corresponding to the main branches of sociological science, which elaborate the respective topical sociological problems theoretically, and prepare and conduct empirical investigations.

The last decades have been a period of intensive development of sociology, which manifested itself also in the creating of a number of units for applied social investigations, such as the information and sociological center at the central committee of the Bulgarian Communist Party, Institute for Sociological Investigations of Youth, Institute for Research and Training at the Central Council of the Trade Unions, sociological section at the Television and Radio Research Institute, sociological chair at the Academy of Social Sciences and Social Management, section of Sociology of Labor at the Institute of Labor (Ministry of Labor and Wages), Sociological Research Center at the *Bulgarska Kniga* (Bulgarian Book), Sport Sociology Research Center at the Higher Institute of Physical Culture, and Council of Criminological Research at the Office of the Attorney General of the People's Republic of Bulgaria.

The affirmation of sociology as an independent scientific discipline, its institutionalization, and the growing need for empirical sociological investigations brought to the fore the problem of the training of sociological cadres and the improvement in the professional culture of the existing cadres. Courses of lectures in sociology have been given in Bulgaria ever since 1880 in the law faculty of the University of Sofia, and this tradition is still followed. Nowadays, however, lectures in sociology are also given for the students of philosophy and journalism in the University of Sofia, the students of the Academy of Social Sciences and Social Management, the higher institute of National Economy (Varna), the highest finance and accountancy institute (Svishtov), and elsewhere.

The main pattern of training of professional sociological cadres is within the framework of university education. Since the 1968–1969 school year, specialized training in sociology was started at the University of Sofia, as well as in the higher economical institute in Sofia. The study plans and curricula comprise courses of lectures on general sociology, statistics, social psychology, sociology of social groups, and other more particular sector sociological disciplines. These universities prepare professional sociologists. Lectures in sociology are read at all higher schools.

An important pattern of formation of sociological cadres is also the postgraduate studies. Through the system of postgraduate studies, higher qualified cadres are prepared for research activities and for the management of various units of applied social research. Through this system, higher qualification is given not only to those who have obtained a university education in sociology but also to specialists with the university education in philosophy, economics, law, psychology, pedagogy, mathematics, literature, architecture, engineering, and other areas. Postgraduate students specialize at the Institute of Sociology at the Bulgarian Academy of Sciences, at the Sofia University, and abroad.

Moreover, in collective works and monographs, and in several periodical publications, Bulgarian sociologists report their sociological investigations. The main role in this respect belongs to *Sotsiologicheski Problemi* (Sociological Problems), the bimonthly organ of the Institute of Sociology and the Bulgarian Sociological Association (publication was started in 1969). Major articles and abstracts are published annually in one volume in Russian and English. Besides this a thick bulletin, *Sotsiologicheski Pregled* (Sociological Review), plays in fact a role of a magazine, publishing many articles and much information about empirical researches. These periodicals publish articles on all basic and topical questions of sociology; on the methodology, technique, and organization of empirical sociological investigations; and information about scientific sociological life at home and abroad. Other periodical organs in which sociological materials are published are the proceedings of the various research institutes of the Bulgarian Academy of Sciences, of different universities.

The International Varna Sociological School in Bulgaria plays the role of an important center of international collaborations of sociologists. It was founded in 1980 in Varna by the Bulgarian Academy of Sciences, respectively by the Institute of Sociology and by the Bulgarian Sociological Association. Its aim is to promote international cooperation of sociologists for the development of sociological theory as well as the methodology and practice of sociological researchers.

CURRENT TRENDS IN THEORETICAL AND METHODOLOGICAL STUDIES

Among the great number of theoretical questions discussed in contemporary sociological literature in Bulgaria, pride of place is given to the problems of the sociological model of society, and the system and structure of sociology as a science. Sociologists of all generations accept that sociology as a science is something different from historical materialism as a philosophy. But what is it?

The first attempt to answer this question was a construction of a theoretical model of society well known as Sociological Structure of Society.[12] The idea of the sociological structure of society is an attempt to reveal the main components of the macrostructure of society in order to substantiate sociology's specific peculiarities compared not only with philosophy but also with the other social sciences.

There are various approaches to the solution of this complex task. A number of authors adopt as their starting point the fundamental Marxist idea of the role of *human activity* and especially the role of labor in the formation and development of human society. The model of sociological structure is described as an interaction of main spheres or components of society's system, namely, material production, spiritual production, sociobiological reproduction of people, governments, and communications.[13]

Efforts to reveal society's sociological structure more thoroughly are accompanied by corresponding definitions of the subject of sociology. According to Z. Oshavkov, sociology studies "the general structure and the specific peculiarities of society to the difference of nature, and the specific general laws of its integral development."[14] According to K. Vassilev, sociology studies "the structure and structural formations of human society, the specific laws of the latter's development."[15]

Despite some merits, the idea of sociological structure of society is strongly criticized by many authors because of its macro- but not microorientation and because of its static but not dynamic character. It also fails to take account of the relations between objective social conditions of human activity and its subjective meaning.[16] The efforts are directed at an improvement of the Marxist sociological paradigm in order to make it reproduce more adequately interactions in social reality: the interaction of subjective and objective, of material and ideal, of stability and change, of functioning and development, of individual and collective.[17]

A model of sociology as a scientific system of theories on various levels, incorporating in its structure the sociological content of society, has been developing in Bulgaria over the past twenty years. General sociology has the widest range of explanation since its subject covers the most general, the most profound social regularities for functioning and development of society. Next come the middle-range sociological theories or particular sociologies, which have for their subject social interactions of different subsystems of the society. The degree of abstraction in our knowledge of society gives an opportunity for sociological knowledge to exist in two basic forms and levels: abstract-theoretical and concrete-empirical.

The considerable development of sociology in Bulgaria brought to the fore *the problems of the methodology of sociology in general, and the methodology of empirical sociological research in particular.* It may be said that sociology's methodological problems are elaborated on three levels: a philosophical, a nonphilosophical (theoretical), and an empirical level. The first level concerns epistemological questions, that is, questions of the role of philosophy in sociological knowledge. The second level relates to the system of theoretical methods that service both sociology and some other sciences in a specific way. Such are the systemic method, the structural method, and also the theoretical, historical, and comparative methods. The proper sociological method plays a particular role here since it involves the study of all social phenomena and processes from the angle of social interactions on their various levels.

Finally, the level method concerns the methods and techniques of what we call empirical sociological investigation. One of the important questions of these investigations relates to the representativeness of the empirical information gathered. The approach to this problem, which has been substantiated and is being applied by Bulgarian sociologists, is characterized by some peculiarities. There is a striving to calculate the size of the sampling on the basis of the probability theory under a random selection of the investigated persons. During the 1960s there was a striving to conduct investigations on the scale of the country as a whole, but now the great majority of all empirical researches are on the scale of different districts, communities, enterprises, and many particular organizations. The ensuring of the reliability of the data is another essential methodological problem of sociological investigations to the elaboration of which Bulgarian sociologists have devoted their attention.[18]

The studies in history of sociology are an integral part of the development of sociological theory. The historical sociological studies include the history of sociological thought in Bulgaria as well as the history of different sociological thought in the world.[19]

CURRENT TRENDS IN EMPIRICAL SOCIOLOGICAL RESEARCH

Sociological investigations in Bulgaria are characterized by successful attempts to apply the entire methodological tooling for *the study of various problems of society, both on a macrolevel and a microlevel.*

On the basis of the achievements of the social sciences and of a huge amount of historical facts and statistical data, sociological thought in Bulgaria endeavors to provide a creative solution to a number of urgent sociological problems of the country's integral social development. Such problems are, for instance, the problems of the framework, criterion, content, and place of the new stage in the development of Bulgaria after

World War II. But most of these studies are predominantly ideological, not strictly sociological.

A great many investigations are devoted to various sociological problems of the Bulgarian society at the present stage of its development. Of all investigations conducted so far in Bulgaria, the 1968 *Town and Countryside* "superinvestigation" (it comprised 18,996 persons), prepared and carried out by an organization headed by Z. Oshavkov, possessed the most extensive program and proved to be the most important. The program of this sociological investigation comprised interactions of all main fields of social life, such as material and intellectual production, social classes and groups, politics, education, public health, physical culture, communications, time budget, and everyday life. The data gathered in this investigation facilitate the analyses of various aspects of the sociological structure of the society in Bulgaria.[20] The institute of sociology at the Bulgarian Academy of Sciences repeated the investigation in 1985 with the respective improvements in the program and the methodology, with a view to establishing and measuring the dynamics of social processes and to creating reliable bases for their prognostication.

Continuing the traditions of progressive sociological thought, contemporary Bulgarian sociologists are conducting empirical sociological investigations with a growing scope. An impressive network of research units of sociology and sociological investigations, on the scale of the country's present stage of development, has been created; and in it many qualified sociologists are developing their activity. The ongoing sociological investigations vary in range and content. Besides the ones directed at individual enterprises, settlements, districts, or areas, there are also investigations on a national scale. The sociological investigations are also different by their content. Some aim at studying a definite mark or group of marks of concrete social phenomena, whereas others attempt the thorough examination of a given social class, group, or profession.

The sociological analyses of *the socio-class structure of society,* of the changes of the working class, the cooperative peasants, and the intellectuals in Bulgaria, are traditionally priority tasks in Bulgaria. The radical restructuring of the system of social relations has found a particularly vivid expression in the dynamic processes of change in the social-class relationships in the country. Particular attention is given to the elucidation of the conceptual apparatus, in terms of which socio-class relationships are studied. It is accepted by many sociologists that the socio-differentiating and stratifying criteria are the nature and the content of labor, the education and the qualification; sources and size of incomes. Empirical findings show high rates of numerical growth of the working class, civil servants, and intelligentsia and a rapid decrease of the share of cooperated peasants within the socio-class structure of the country. Quite complex and considerable in its swing is the social stratification of the separate social groups according to the material conditions of life and living standard, particularly according to the income, house-and-living, and property stratification. The picture of the internal class social distinctions is complemented with that of the interclass (macro-social) distinctions. In the course of development, education attains even greater and more decisive significance as a socially integrating and socially differentiating factor.[21]

A considerable number of monographs, studies, and articles develop some of the most important sectors of sociology. The problems of the *sociology of economics* and of the *sociology of labor,* in particular, are elaborated. The research work on sociology of work covers the problems of labor groups, the participation of working people in the management of production, the working and the leisure time, the influence of various factors on the work activity of the people, and so on. The studies of population and work force, the organization of remuneration, professional orientation, and the affectivity of work have a sociological aspect. Still along these lines a number of authors address their efforts to the study of the division of labor and professions, the raising of the standard of education and qualification of the working people, labor discipline, emulation, and so forth. In the late 1970s, extensive research was devoted to the problems of possibilities for work of the Bulgarian population and their practical realization. The findings address the significance of social organization of labor.[22]

Traditionally, *the problems of the family* are studied mostly from their demographic aspect, that is, from the point of view of the function of the family in the reproduction of the population. In recent years, however, a definite tendency to study it as a complete social system is making its way, integrating in the analysis another social problem—women. The sociological study of the family carried out in 1978–1979 is of particular importance in this respect. It was focused on the problem of the basic social functions of the family and the relationship between family and society.[23]

When science has a growing and effective impact on all spheres of social life, the efforts of accelerated development of the *sociology of science and technology* are quite natural. This branch of sociology in Bulgaria is characterized by an elaboration of theoretical and methodological problems combined with empirical studies. The studies in this field cover a broad range of problems: the interaction between society and science, social relations in the sphere of science, scientific groups as social systems, and so on. The main purpose of all studies is to reveal the most significant factors which stimulate or lay obstacles to the technological improvement of the country.[24]

The *sociology of culture and mass communications* is developed with intensity. Theoretical and empirical studies are focused on processes such as creation as well as dissemination and consumption of culture. The writings of the researchers throw light on the problem of the genesis, the essence and development of culture, its social function, and the social dynamics of culture in Bulgaria. Sociological researchers put in the forefront a number of fundamental problems of the communication process, including its social structure, its social function, the mass audience, and the specifics of various communicative forms. The considerable number of empirical studies characterize efforts of Bulgarian sociologists in this field.[25]

Important contributions are made by Bulgarian sociologists who study sociological problems of youth, urbanization, migration, and others.[26] Practically all sociological researches cover all subfields of sociology. The number of empirical observations, more than two hundred in a year, is quite enough for a small country but the main problem remains their quality and social effectiveness.

OUTSTANDING PROBLEMS

Like any other precipitous forward movement, the rapid advance of sociology raises a number of important problems. The growing interest in this scientific discipline has brought it many recruits with very dissimilar scientific qualifications, such as philosophers, economists, lawyers, engineers, and medical men; whereas the relatively rapid expansion of the empirical sector of sociology, that is, the concrete sociological investigations, makes more and more strongly felt the need for more development in the field of sociological theory. Without the harmonious and timely development of sociological theory on all levels and in all aspects, and without the continuous and close integration of empirical sociological research, the most general sociological theory, and the various particular sociological theories, sociology as a scientific discipline will not be able to develop successfully; it will sink into empiricism and will fail to live up to expectations.

That is why one of the major problems now is to overcome the relative lag of theoretical sociology, especially in the field of the particular sociological disciplines such as the sociology of management, the sociology of education, the sociology of law, the sociology of art, and the sociology of social groups.

Another problem that is closely related to the further advance of sociology is the development in the professional sociologists (the sociological teaching and research staffs) of a high sociological culture, required by the very subject matter and content of sociology, and by its enormous methodological and practical importance.

The rapid expansion of sociological institutions and the growing number of those who devote their energies to various kinds of sociological activities increase the need for and the importance of the coordination of these activities in order to impart more unity and purposefulness to the development of sociological thought.

And last, as a result of the radical political and economic changes which we call *Perestroika,* there is a new situation for the development of sociological studies in the country. I expect a most intensive development of different sociological perspectives, an increase of social effectiveness of empirical studies in the process of democratization of society. An example of this is the publication now of the results of public opinion observations, which was not possible earlier. The process of democratization of all spheres of society will have great significance for further promotion of sociological thought in Bulgaria.

These, as well as many other significant problems, reveal the need for more discussion of the most urgent questions of sociological theory, the theoretical generalization of the results of the extensive sociological investigations, the methodology, and pragmaticism of sociology.

NOTES

1. Lyubcn Karavelov (1834–1879), eminent Bulgarian Revolutionary democrat, writer, and publicist. *Collected Works,* 9 vols. (Sofia, 1965–1968).

2. Vassil Levski (1837–1873), ideologist and great organizer, strategist, and tactician of the revolutionary movement in Bulgaria in the struggle for national and social liberation. See *Vassil Levski, The Apostle of Freedom* (London: Allen and Unwin, 1967).

3. Hristo Botev (1849–1876), great Bulgarian revolutionary, utopian socialist, scientist, poet, publicist, and head of an insurgent detachment, killed in a fierce fight with the Ottoman armies. *Collected Works,* 2 vols. (Sofia, 1971).

4. Dimitur Blagoev (1856–1924), remarkable Bulgarian politician, founder and ideologist of the Bulgarian Social-Democratic party, literary critic, and philosopher. He laid the foundations of Marxist sociology in Bulgaria. He had enormous impact on the country's spiritual life at the end of the nineteenth century and the beginning of the twentieth century. *Collected Works* (Sofia, 1957–1964).

5. Georgi Bakalov (1873–1939), Bulgarian publicist, literary historian and critic, and sociologist. He elaborated mainly the sociological problems of art.

6. Iliya Yanoulov (1880–1962), jurist and sociologist, one of the founders of empirical sociological research in Bulgaria at the beginning of the twentieth century. Main works: *Sotsialna Politika V Chouzhbina I V Bulgaria, Prichina, Razvitie I Sistema* (Social Policy Abroad and in Bulgaria: Causes, Development and System) (Sofia, 1924); *Izouchavane Prestupnostta V. Bulgaria. Kakvi Tryabva I Kakvi Netryabva da Budat Metodite Na Tova Izouchavane* (Study of Crime in Bulgaria: What Should and Should Not Be the Methods of This Study) (Sofia, 1925); *Moralna Statistica. Chast I. Samooubiystva. Razmeri, Prichini, Borba—Ou Nas I V Chuzhbina* (Moral Statistics: Part I. Suicides: Rate, Causes, and Fight against Them—At Home and Abroad) (Sofia, 1927).

7. Ivan Hadzhiyski (1907–1944), Bulgarian publicist and sociologist, killed in

the patriotic war against German fascism. Main works: *Bit I Doushevnost Na Nashiya Narod* (Mode of Life and Mentality of the Bulgarian People) (Sofia, 1966), p. 463; *Optimistichna Teoriya Za Nashiya Narod* (An Optimistic Theory of the Bulgarian People) (Sofia, 1966), p. 432.

8. See G. Bakalov, *Questionnaire for Gathering Data on the Situation of the Working Class* (Bulg.) (Sofia, 1903).

9. Todor Pavlov (1890–1977), prominent Bulgarian philosopher, sociologist, aesthetician, and literary critic. *Selected Works,* 10 vols. (Sofia, 1957–1970). His major works are: *Osnovni Vuprosi Na Teoriya Na Poznanieto* (Basic Questions of the Theory of Knowledge: Theory of Reflection) (Sofia: Nov Svyat, 1938), p. 402; *Shto E Obshtestvo. Filosofsko-Sotsiologicheski Ocherk* (What Is Society: A Philosophic-Sociological Essay) (Sofia: Pechatnitsa V. Ivanov, 1939), p. 31; *Sotsiologiya I Biologiya* (Sociology and Biology) (Sofia: Bulgarska Knizhnina, 1940), p. 31; "Sociology and Philosophy" (Bulg.), *Sotsiologicheski Problemi,* Vol. 6, 1969.

10. Zhivko Oshavkov (1913–1982), professor, Ph.D., vice-president of the International Sociological Association (1970–1974), president of the Bulgarian Sociological Association (1968–1982), the first director of the Institute of Sociology at the Bulgarian Academy of Sciences (1968–1974). Main works: *Istoricheskiyat Materializm I Sotsiologiyata* (Historical Materialism and Sociology) (Sofia: Naouka I Izkoustvo, 1970), p. 379; *Sotsiologiyata Kato Nauka* (Sociology as a Scientific Discipline) (Sofia: Naouka I Izkoustvo, 1970), p. 336; K. Vassilev, *Uvod Kum Filosofia Na Istoriyata* (Introduction to Philosophy of History) (Sofia: Naouka I Izkoustvo, 1961).

11. Michail Buchvarov, Ed., *Anthology of Bulgarian Sociological Thought* (Bulg.) (Sofia, Vol. I, 1978; Vol. II, 1979); Velichko Dobrianov, Ed., *Anthology of Sociological Thought* (Bulg.) (Sofia, 1985), p. 750.

12. Zhivko Oshavkov, *Sotsiologiyata Kato Naouka* (Sociology as a Science) (Sofia, 1970).

13. Stoyan Mihailov, *Sotsiologicheski Studi* (Sociological Articles) (Sofia: Naouka I Izkoustvo, 1982).

14. Z. Oshavkov, *Sociology as a Scientific Discipline* (Bulg.) (Sofia, 1970), pp. 32–33.

15. K. Vassilev, *Introduction to the Philosophy of History* (Sofia, 1961), p. 69.

16. V. Dobriyanov, *Society from Sociological Point of View* (Bulg.), Sotsiologichesko Poznanie (Sofia: Ban, 1976); Stefan Donchev, *Social System and Industrial Situation* (Bulg.) (Sofia, N.I., 1982); Lyuben Nikolov, *Structure of Human Activity* (Bulg.) (Sofia, N.I., 1982); Dobrianov, *Critical View on Activity Model of Sociological System of Society* (Bulg.), *Sotsiologicheski Problemi* 6 (Sofia, 1987); Zhelyo Vladimirov, *Concept of "Sociological Structure of Society"—Methodological Dignity and Shortcomings* (Bulg.), *Sotsiologicheski Problemi* 6 (Sofia, 1987).

17. Nikolai Genov, *Talcott Parsons and the Theoretical Sociology* (Bulg.) (Sofia: Ban, 1982); V. Dobrianov, *The Marxist Sociological Paradigm,* in: A. G. Zdravomyslov, Ed., *Developments in Marxist Sociological Theory* (London, Sage Publications, 1986).

18. Z. Oshavkov, *Historical Materialism and Sociology* (Bulg.) (Sofia, 1970); *Sociology as a Scientific Discipline* (Bulg.) (Sofia, 1970), pp. 139–164; "On the Selection Method in Sociological Investigations" (Russ.), *Voprosi Filosofii* 5 (1967): 50–60; Venets Tsonev, *On the Logical Basis of the Statistical Method*

(Bulg.) (Sofia: Naouka I Izkoustvo, 1951), p. 31; *Dialectics and Statistics* (Bulg.) (Sofia: Naouka I Izkoustvo, 1959), p. 36; *The Bases of Representative Investigation* (Bulg.) (Sofia: Naouka I Izkoustvo, 1958), p. 284; Stoyan Mihailov, *Empirical Sociological Research* (Bulg.) (Sofia: Partizdat, 1973).

19. V. Dobrianov, *The Poverty of Anti-Historicism: Criticism of Philosophical and Sociological Views of Karl Popper* (Bulg.) (Sofia, 1969); N. Iribadzhakov, *Sociological Thought of Ancient World* (Bulg.) (Sofia, Vol. I, 1978; Vol. II, 1981; Vol. III, 1982); V. Dobrianov, B. Stavrov, N. Genov, *Contemporary Sociology in Bulgaria: A Historical Outline* (Bulg.) (Sofia, 1978); G. Fotev, *Sociological Theories of E. Durkheim, M. Weber and V. Pareto: A Comparative Critical Analysis* (Bulg.) (Sofia, 1982); N. Genov, *Talcott Parsons and the Theoretical Sociology* (Bulg.) (Sofia, 1982); G. Fotev, *Principles of the Positivistic Sociology* (Bulg.) (Sofia, 1982).

20. Z. Oshavkov, Ed., *Sociological Structure of Contemporary Bulgarian Society* (Bulg.) (Sofia, 1976).

21. Vassil Ivanov, *Class Structure and Social Unity* (Bulg.) (Sofia, 1971); Krustyo Dimitrov, *Bulgarian Intelligentsia under Capitalism* (Bulg.) (Sofia, 1974); Chavdar Kiuranov, *Social Classes and Social Stratification* (Bulg.) (Sofia, 1977); V. Ivanov, *The Social Structure* (Bulg.), Book 1: *Theoretical and Methodological Problems* (Sofia, 1977), Book 2: *The Working Class* (Sofia, 1979), Book 3: *The Class of Cooperative Farmers* (Sofia, 1979), Book 4: *The Intelligentsia* (Sofia, 1981); K. Dimitrov, Ed., *Social Class Structure of the Contemporary Bulgarian Society: Problems and Trends* (Bulg.) (Sofia, 1986); K. Dimitrov, *Sociology of Social Class Structure* (Bulg.) (Sofia, 1988).

22. M. Minkov, T. Avrakov, *Labor Resources in the People's Republic of Bulgaria* (Bulg.) (Sofia, 1968); M. Minkov, D. Ivanov, G. Stoev, *The Intersectoral Balance of Labor* (Bulg.) (Varna, 1969); I. Kapitanski, *Changes in the Structure and Qualification of the Labor Force in Bulgarian Agriculture* (Bulg.) (Sofia, 1971); S. Vlaikov, *Planning the Social Development of Work Teams* (Bulg.) (Sofia, 1973); St. Donchev, *Social System and Industrial Situation* (Bulg.) (Sofia, 1979); G. Kostov, *Sociological Aspects of the Sociologist Organization of Labor* (Bulg.) (Sofia, 1979); D. Dimitrov, *Labor Turnover—Labor Force—Industry: Sociological Aspects* (Bulg.) (Sofia, 1980); G. Kostov, *Sociology of Labor* (Bulg.) (Sofia, 1986); P. Bliznakov, *Sociological Problems of Economy* (Bulg.) (Sofia, 1987); V. Topalova, *The Meaning of Work: Value Orientations, Motivation, Satisfaction* (Bulg.) (Sofia, 1988).

23. M. Dinkova, *Contemporary Bulgarian Family* (Bulg.) (Sofia, 1976); L. Spasovska, *The Family: A Sociological Essay* (Bulg.) (Sofia, 1980); M. Dinkov, *The Social Picture of Bulgarian Woman* (Bulg.) (Sofia, 1980); Ch. Kiuranov, *Bulgarian Family* (Bulg.) (Sofia, 1987).

24. Y. Minkov, *Science and Man* (Bulg.) (Sofia, 1973); K. Gospodinov, *Scientific Teams as a Social System* (Bulg.) (Sofia, 1973); Y. Minkov, *Weal or Malediction: Scientific Achievements and Their Impact on Man* (Bulg.) (Sofia, 1980); V. Samoilov, *Conformity in Scientific Activity* (Bulg.) (Sofia, 1980); H. Domozetov, *Innovation and Implementation* (Bulg.) (Sofia, 1980); A. Yossifov, *Professionalization of Scientists* (Bulg.) (Sofia, 1983); N. Yahiel, *Sociology of Science* (Bulg.) (Sofia, 1987).

25. Elit Nikolov, *Phenomenology and Aesthetics* (Bulg.) (Sofia, 1965); Kruystyu Goranov, *Art and Social Life: Essay on the Aesthetics and Sociology of Artistic*

Culture (Bulg.) (Sofia, 1973); V. Kunchev, *Mass Media and Personality* (Bulg.) (Sofia, 1974); I. Stefanov, *Art and Communication in the Cinema* (Bulg.) (Sofia, 1976); T. Petev, *Upon the Sociology of Mass Communications* (Bulg.) (Sofia, 1969).

26. P. Mitev, *Social Progress and the Youth* (Bulg.) (Sofia, 1969); P. Mitev, Ed., *Youth Studies: Theory, Methods, Practice* (Bulg.) (Sofia, 1978); M. Zhelyazkova, *Social Creativity of Youth* (Bulg.) (Sofia, 1987); K. Kertikov, *Society and Urbanization* (Bulg.) (Sofia, 1987); K. Kertikov, *Society and Urbanization* (Bulg.) (Sofia, 1979); V. Todorov, *Migration Processes and Some Sociopolitical and Cultural Problems of the Village* (Bulg.) (Sofia, 1968); M. Minkovk, *Population and Basic Social Structures* (Bulg.) (Sofia, 1976).

18

The History of Modern Sociology in Hungary

Tibor Huszár

While assessing Comte's work in the 1870s, the eminent Hungarian historian Gyula Pauler once wrote: "By the time Western ideas and institutions reach us, they usually become obsolete at home and are about to be replaced by other ideas in their own country."[1] A few years later Károly Tagányi repudiated that view in the same journal: "it's nonsense to say that thoughts are delayed by a century before they reach us, or that all the ideas we have, have been brought here from abroad."[2] In a strange way, there was some truth in what both men said as far as Hungarian social science in general, particularly sociology, was concerned.

HUNGARY'S INTRODUCTION TO SOCIAL SCIENCES

In the 1840s, a time when desire for social and political reform reached a high pitch, political writers and young scholars tried to "subject elements of social structure to analysis" and reregulate the "fundamental institutions of society," for example, family, marriage, and wealth.

"Collecting information about the fatherland" was the slogan of the day. *Athenaeum,* an outstanding journal of the time, carried numerous articles in this vein. Despite the seductiveness of the slogan, many scholars at universities remained indifferent to this initiative because they were conservative and were committed to the self-contradictory tenet of reform-minded nationalism.[3]

The demand for social sciences reemerged following the Compromise of 1867. The exponents of this movement were statesmen who were familiar with international social science literature. They wanted to modernize and liberalize Hungary. They were influenced by the works of Auguste

Comte, Herbert Spencer, John Stuart Mill, and Adolphe Quetelet. They aspired to what they described as "authentic knowledge" and reliance on what they called "scientific experience."[4]

Some of them had set out to explore the country during the heady years of the reform-minded 1840s. After the disastrous social effects of a crushed revolution and the ensuing stifling of political thought and culture, these statesmen supported efforts to examine social conditions in their reality.

Those in the vanguard of this movement were aware of related achievements in more advanced parts of Europe. Károly Keleti and his associates laid the foundations of statistics in Hungary by introducing advanced techniques of collecting data about society and applying the comparative method.[5] Leó Beöthy and Gyula Pauler tried to modernize attitudes and techniques in historiography and the study of society. They took it for granted that these disciplines employed the methodology of the natural sciences.[6]

Unfortunately, the steam of the movement was spent on causes lying outside science. The intellectual elite opted for caution in the face of crises which accompanied the political scuffles over suffrage.

At that time attempts were made to reinterpret and reconcile the contradictions of reform-minded nationalism, but all these efforts led to the conclusion that liberalism could not be reconciled with democracy, provided the latter was consistently asserted. It was feared that if nationalities were granted the status of nationhood, Greater Hungary would disintegrate.

Social sciences were not the only disciplines to be affected by these changes in approach. During this era the entire language of research and politics was restructured. Social scientists, who (among other things) studied the process in which the institutions of science were created, were more aware of the changes than others.

The most popular argument of the time went as follows: in the course of history Hungarians became the dominant nation of the Carpathian Basin through natural selection, and therefore they did not have the right to voluntarily give up this "evolutionary achievement." Consequently, they have to subordinate the struggle among classes to that among nationalities.[7]

This tenet emerged in various forms in the works of several noted thinkers of the era.[8] To use the terminology of Thomas Kuhn, marked differences in views apart, there was consensus over a paradigm which, perhaps with an updated set of arguments, consolidated the positions of historicism and the conservative and hierarchical approach to social issues.

On one hand, more and more essays were devoted to the works of Comte, Quatelet, and Spencer.[9] On the other, members of the academic establishment dismissed positivism as a theory dangerous to the Hungarian nation's supremacy, the family, property, and the state.[10]

The exponents of this paradigm were hostile to scholarly efforts which attempted to expose social conflicts and reveal other aspects of reality.[11] Moreover, the advocates of this school of thought rejected the theory and method of positivism. They were convinced that scholars preoccupied with the facts of life could not grapple with notions like national spirit (*Volksgeist*), national character, national soul, national temperament, and national genius.

This attitude was eloquently set forth in a paper written by Ferenc Toldy on the causes of Hungary's backwardness in science.[12] He presented the paper in 1868, yet his arguments were embraced well into the middle of the 1870s—even by thinkers who had urged a fresh start on collecting first-hand information about Hungary in the years following the Compromise.

Modernization picked up speed in Hungary during the 1880s and 1890s. All branches of the economy were affected by the rise of capitalism. The massive response to this development was socially heterogeneous. The attitude of the landed aristocracy differed from that of some advocates of reform-minded conservatism[13] who belonged to the new middle class, which rose from the landless gentry and the bureaucracy.

Although this newly formed elite had some affinity to sociology, they aspired to adopt only those non-Hungarian research findings that could be connected with what they termed as organic processes rooted in the past of the Hungarians. Once again, the criterion for determining what was good or bad was whether a tenet served to maintain the integrity of Greater Hungary.

There was a new element in their approach, though: in addition to considering capitalism as a force that disintegrates traditional patterns, they exaggerated the importance of the role of purportedly rootless, but in effect assimilated, German and Jewish intellectuals. Consequently, they used whatever doctrines they could find to counterbalance the sway of liberalism and to promote organization, equilibrium, cohesion, solidarity, and the perpetuation of traditions. Creating a theory of their own was beyond them. They concentrated on evolving the institutions for social policy, primarily agricultural policy.[14]

THE "FIRST WORKSHOP OF SOCIOLOGY IN HUNGARY," 1900–1918

Initial Steps/Failures

Having established its economic position, the bourgeoisie sought influence on the country's intellectual life. Also, the progress of research and arts abroad had an impact on research and arts in Hungary. At the turn of the century, in response to this neoconservatism the Hungarian Society for Social Sciences (MTT) and the journal *Huszadik Század* (Twentieth Century) were formed.

Their appearance marked a new chapter in the history of social sciences in Hungary. The first issue of *Twentieth Century* carried a letter by Herbert Spencer.[15] He expressed his pleasure over the decision to launch a journal that was committed to the propagation of scientifically sound ideas on social issues. The publication of this letter marked a milestone in the history of the Hungarian reception of this eminent British sociologist.

The journal and the Society became the first Hungarian workshops for sociology. They rallied gifted, erudite thinkers and journalists, old and young. Their patrons were Ágost Pulszky and Gyula Pikler, renowned professors at the Budapest Faculty of Legal and Administrative Sciences, and Bódog Somló, lecturer at the Oradea (then called Nagyvárad) law school. Their early works can be indirectly associated with Leó Beöthy's writings on primitive society.[16]

The young social scientists, law school graduates, and political writers rallying behind *Twentieth Century* sought positive solutions for the challenges posed by modernization. These responses included the growing role of people with college or university diplomas in industry and trade in Budapest and certain other regions. Simultaneous to the evolution of a modern public administration and the development of transport and communication infrastructure, the size of certain groups of professional men rapidly increased. Social mobility and migration accelerated. New interpretations were given to the history of the Hungarian intelligentsia when these developments were discussed by members of the Society.[17]

The professionalization and institutionalization of a discipline do not necessarily take place simultaneously, and their criteria are not identical. For a discipline to reach maturity it must reach a certain level in terms of content, theory, terminology, and method.[18]

Two crucial questions emerge when the actions of the Society are examined: Why were these intellectuals unable to formally institutionalize sociology in Hungary? Why was this workshop not integrated into Hungary's network of academic (and collegiate) institutions, when such integration would have created the basis for the professionalization of sociology?

All went well in the beginning. The patrons were respected professors of the Budapest Law School. The leaders and members of the Society were popular and influential. Some members of the Society and of the editorial staff of *Twentieth Century* were in contact with noted sociological workshops abroad. They published numerous sociological and other social science works in the series "Társadalomtudományi Könyvtár" (Social Science Library). Surveys were made about nearly all social strata. A section of sociology was set up under the auspices of the Society and it took part in an international comparative project.

The Society failed to institutionalize sociology for a number of reasons, not the least of which was the asymmetrical modernization of Hungarian society. Although modernization in general accelerated, Hungarian agriculture continued to be dominated by large estates. The aristocracy and the major churches wielded a strong influence, whereas the bourgeoisie had only a limited influence.

In such a situation the alliance of the liberal-conservative national[19] intellectuals, and of the radical bourgeois intellectuals, could not last for long. The members of the liberal-conservative national wing left the Society in 1906 to form their own association (MTE) and journal (MTSz).

The increasingly marked division showed—among other things—that the intellectual elite of the first workshop of sociology in Hungary could not find a common platform for evaluating Hungarian historical conditions, patterns of thought, and values.

There were additional barriers to the institutionalization and professionalization of sociology in Hungary. The radical camp failed, even within its own ranks, to firmly establish the intellectual, structural, and methodological aspects of a cognitive identity. At that time sociology was treated as a natural science. The (so-called) organic theory was initially more widely embraced than any other theory. The theoretical debates concentrated on the reception and critical analysis of Spencerism, later of Marxism. By contrast, seminal works by French and German thinkers were examined either belatedly or not at all.[20]

Oszkár Jászi visited É. Durkheim as early as 1905. After their discussion Jászi realized how backward Hungarian sociology was in terms of theory. However, having reservations about the theories of this French sociologist, Jászi did not adopt such Durkheimian terms as "social fact," "division of labor," "solidarity," and "anomie."[21]

Conflicts rent the Society for Social Sciences in 1905 through 1906 and obliged the members of the association, and particularly Jászi, to give unequivocal wording to their political conclusions.[22] In response to passionate contributions during the general meeting at which the split of the Society was decided, Jászi declared that differentiation between theory and practice would become increasingly marked. He added that theory and praxis, science and politics, would benefit from this differentiation.[23] He argued that this process was in line with the universal law under which progress necessitates functional differentiation. This tendency, he went on, may only unfold entirely in advanced societies where a nation is developed enough to facilitate an articulated social division of labor.[24] Jászi conceded that the lines of division were not rigid, yet phenomena that qualify as exceptions in functionally differentiated societies can become the rule in backward and hardly differentiated societies.[25] He concluded that the Society for Social Sciences, the scientific body of an extremely undifferentiated society, may not confine itself to pursuing pure science. Instead it should lay down in its bylaws the commitment to tackle, among other things, issues of social policy. Furthermore, it should organize public readings and debates. He said that with these activities the Society could launch practical movements.[26]

These statements were motivated by real social needs, as there was a genuine thirst for new ideas. Jászi wished to steer the Society toward using observations of the facts of life for "writing out appropriate recipes for curing social ills."[27] It is clear from Jászi's words that he was committed to progress. Unfortunately, the program he outlined was suitable neither for turning sociology into a modern specialized discipline nor for adequately institutionalizing it.

It seems from the nature of the debates going on at the time that the members of the Society were not aware of the theoretical debates which took place during an early phase of the development of sociology in Germany on delimiting sociology, social policy, and politics, nor were they aware of the works of Max Weber.[28] Although cognitive identity was not reached in German sociology prior to World War I, the debates and empirical experiments carried out there enabled German sociologists to elaborate the essential questions of theory and method. It was on this basis that later, during the Weimar Republic, sociology became a mature discipline and was accepted as such.[29]

In Hungary no member of the movement, not even the best informed, noticed that the intellectual map of Europe had been redrawn. They failed to realize that the crisis of naturalist positivism resulted in (1) the renaissance of neo-Kantian tendencies, and (2) the conclusion that science may aspire to more than mere observation of empirical reality. The question of how to use outward traits of human behavior to trace inner motivations (i.e., how to subject to analysis the meaning of human behavior) was not raised in Hungary either.

The Society for Social Sciences retained its appeal well into the first decade of this century: numerous young and able scholars joined the program of surveying traditional Hungarian social values.[30]

While the *Twentieth Century* carried profound essays on timely social issues, the changes in the social and political climate gradually turned the attention of the brightest minds of the Society to politics. Thus they became divorced from the academic establishment. Professors embracing national conservatism and/or status quo liberalism came to dominate the universities. With time the theoretical questions of social science decreased in importance in articles published by the *Twentieth Century*.

Another noteworthy development occurred when a group of talented and progressive young men realized that the tenets of positivist sociology had become obsolete. They turned to the method of *Geisteswissenschaften* (sciences of the mind, or human sciences). At first they published articles in the *Twentieth Century* and participated in its discussion evenings. Then they opted for a path of their own by launching the journal *Szellem* (Mind) and the Free School of Geisteswissenschaften.[31] György (Georg) Lukács, Lajos Fülep, Károly (Karl) Mannheim, Arnold Hauser, and Frigyes Antal were some of the notable names among these editors and lecturers.

They concentrated on the theory of knowledge, on logic and psychology. Lukács—who, with Lajos Fülep, was the spiritual leader of this group— came into contact with intellectuals in Heidelberg. He attended seminars by Max Weber. Simmel read some of his essays.

It was probably due to the influence of these thinkers that the group did not reject sociology as such. On the contrary, Lukács's writings on the history of drama are believed to have helped found the sociology of literature.[32] Oszkár Jászi and Ervin Szabó also attended some of the meetings organized by this group, and they were prepared to accept critical remarks about their views. Conditions were favorable for a constructive dialogue between 1916 and 1918, as the various camps were undergoing realignment and many participants in the debates had modified their position.

In the meantime, the advocates of the conservative-liberal tendency continued their efforts to evolve a Hungarian institution for sociology.[33] They were preoccupied with protecting and improving indigenous institutions and opposing what they described as a "forcible adoption of alien models." On these grounds they became hostile to theory. More precisely, they attempted to replace theoretically founded analyses of society in Hungary, and elsewhere in Europe, with writings that were confined to abstract generalities and speculation. They tried to make the empirical research of society a function of the social welfare system.[34]

It was a logical consequence of their interpretation of sociology that no committee of sociology was set up under the auspices of the Hungarian Association for Social Sciences, nor was any section of the *Hungarian Social Science Review* devoted exclusively to sociology.[35]

The Association and the *Review* came to take positions close to reform-minded agrarian tendencies,[36] and there was interpenetration between these organizations.[37]

There was a bourgeois democratic revolution in Hungary in October 1918. It was as short-lived as the communist dictatorship that followed it in 1919. This episode of a few months had positive and negative consequences for the institutionalization of sociology in Hungary.

Only two aspects of the developments need to be described. In November 1918, acting on the initiative of the Ministry of Culture, the Faculty of Legal and Administrative Sciences of Budapest University admitted to its staff Bódog Somló "without observing the relevant stipulations of the university bylaws." The minister granted him full professorship (ignoring the schedule of appointments) on December 3, 1918.[38] A week later the minister, in a letter to the university, recommended the appointment of additional professors and the creation of departments of economic policy and of political sociology.[39]

The ministry intended to reform the faculty by transforming it into one of legal, administrative, and social sciences. However, the leadership of the faculty considered the proposals to be a violation of the university's autonomy and rejected all of them.[40]

In January 1918 Zsigmond Kunfi, a leading personality in the Association, became minister of culture. On January 22, realizing that the leaders of the faculty were not prepared to transform the faculty at their own initiative, the new minister proposed the creation of new departments and appointed the head of the newly established department of sociology. But the faculty's resistance increased. On February 4, 1918, the minister appointed Oszkár Jászi government commissioner of the university. He did not serve on the post for long. After March 21, 1919, during the communist dictatorship, university faculties lost their independent status, several faculty members were banned from teaching, and Oszkár Jászi resigned.[41]

Following the fall of the communist dictatorship, in autumn 1919, the seven professorial appointments made during the bourgeois democratic revolution were declared illegal. They were found to be "unsuitable" for teaching at the university.[42] (The authorities wished to treat the case of Bódog Somló as an exception, but he refused to accept his renewed appointment. In 1920 he committed suicide in Cluj, then called Kolozsvár.) The newly established departments were also dissolved. It signaled the end of the first attempt to win university recognition for sociology.

The other blow that scholarship in Hungary suffered from this turn of events was the emigration of numerous scholars who had started their careers in the first workshop of sociology in Hungary and/or in the Sunday Circle. Many became noted sociologists abroad.[43]

SOCIOLOGY IN THE INTERWAR PERIOD (1919–1945)

There was no real progress in institutionalizing sociology between the two world wars for several reasons. Conservatives and reform-minded intellectuals formed a social science section within the Ethnographical Society as early as 1920. Later the section continued under the name Social Science Society (TT) and launched a journal called *Social Science.*

These names were selected in order to neutralize the influence of radicals. As there was no other journal devoted exclusively to sociology at that time, the Social Science Society and its journal became the principal institutions for sociological issues. They regularly organized discussion meetings and sent representatives to international sociological conferences. The journal, just like the *Social Science Booklets* which were

launched in 1925, regularly carried (among other things) statistical analyses and essays on social history which helped popularize sociology.

In the absence of any domestic institutions devoted to the training of
sociologists, the Social Science Society could not recruit more students to
study sociology. The periodical did not foster a workshop to encourage
sociological research in Hungary. The writings it carried, especially the
sociological ones, were abstract and lacked originality. The sociological
contributors lacked a clear-cut theoretical position. Their writings eclectically mixed aspects of pure science and/or an endeavor to establish Hungarian national sociology, as well as syntheses of remedial programs to
heal the ills of society.[44]

In 1921 the essentials of sociology and economics became a school subject in colleges and in the eighth class of the grammar schools. It also
became an optional subject at the Faculty of Economics of Budapest University, at the Academy of Law of Kecskemét, and at some church schools.
But these attempts at institutionalizing sociology remained isolated due to
certain tendencies in the official scientific life and ideology of the time. In
the late 1920s and early 1930s the *Geisteswissenschaften* method gained
broader currency. This development was encouraged by the framers of the
official scientific policy, even though there were differences in the evaluation of this method by the scientific policy makers and the framers of the
policy of higher education. The makers of scientific policy ensured preference for so-called national sciences when deciding which new institutions
to create. Theoretically speaking, they supported historicism and an approach that centered on the concept of nationhood.

They were not consistent in asserting these considerations, though. One
reason for this inconsistency was the natural alternation between reform-
minded conservatism and national radicalism, which happened in connection with changes in the international political environment of the country.

That decision making was often improvised in moments of crisis (even
though certain attitudes and conditions were there to stay for a long period) was proven by the wrangling over the establishment of certain departments at the Budapest University, little veiled resistance to their
establishment, the isolation of the advocates of their establishment, and
the virtual failure of attempts to institutionalize sociology.[45]

Hans Freyer served as a visiting professor at the Faculty of Arts of the
Péter Pázmány University between 1939 and 1944.[46] He did not teach
sociology but held lectures on German cultural history under the auspices
of the Institute of German Studies.

Although the opening sociology courses by professors of some prestigious university departments of social sciences did not directly mean the
adoption of sociology as an independent university discipline, it signaled
an important stage on the road of professionalization.

Hungarian works on the history of domestic sociology mix facts with myths. It is an often-quoted fact that in the course of his research into the theory of law Barna Horváth, professor of the Faculty of Legal and Administrative Sciences of the Szeged University, became attracted to sociology. In 1934 he published a monograph in Germany entitled *Rechtssoziologie.*[47] He called attention to numerous debated issues of Ferenc Erdei and István Bibó, two scholars who were to play a major role in the history of Hungarian sociology later, and his theoretical teaching activity had a positive influence on their thinking.[48] However, Barna Horváth was not among the founders of sociology (of law) as a full-fledged discipline in Hungary, nor did he play a pioneering role in elaborating cognitive aspects, which are so vital to the institutionalization of each discipline.[49]

By contrast, István Hajnal's research output was of seminal importance in the field of social history, the comparative method, and the sociology of history. Furthermore, his sociological analysis of the history of written records was already up to international standards in the 1920s. In his essay "Történelem és szociológia" (History and Sociology) he surveyed the sociological literature of his time and made an ambitious theoretical attempt to contrast historical and sociological methods and to reinterpret some categories of social theory (socialization, the rise of forms, intellectualization, and regional development).[50]

It is little wonder that his disciples wrote outstanding works in the field of sociology, sociography, the sociology of history, and the sociology of law.[51]

Immediately prior to World War II critical tendencies could not gain ground. Bourgeois radicalism could not recover from the loss caused by the emigration of its brightest minds. The journal of this camp (*Századunk*) continued, but its editors (Sándor Braun, Rusztem Vámbéri, and István Varró) could not create a new intellectual workshop. The Marxists were doctrinaire and were hostile to sociology. It was exclusively for political considerations that they supported critical sociography. Conditions were not suitable for field work. In this respect an essay by Ferenc Földes was exceptional.[52]

Rural sociography was a noteworthy tendency among the critical schools. Describing this movement would go beyond the scope of this chapter.[53] We only address one question. Why did Ferenc Erdei, Gyula Ortutay, and Béla Reitzer, all with scholarly ambitions, abandon their plan to pursue the theoretical and methodological questions they defined during the formative 1930s, when these questions would have been essential for the cognitive institutionalization of sociology and for their own professionalism?[54]

Paradoxical as it may sound, these thinkers could not promote the institutionalization of sociology because at that time conditions necessary for the efficient operation of sociology did not exist. In fact, the institutions under whose auspices they could have operated had not even come into existence. What is more, they could not establish lasting relations with international workshops of sociology for various reasons. Furthermore, they could not entirely distance themselves from the influence of *Geisteswissenschaften*-related Hungarian studies which treated social conflicts as "fateful questions" (*Schicksalsfrage*).[55] They would not entirely adopt the value considerations of "official" Hungarian studies: the critical attitude is "the art of seeing the essential things," the capability for empathy, which "obliges one to announce the prophecy of possibility."[56]

The advocates of Hungarian studies did not question the importance of field work, yet they gave preference to a writer's method of collecting material over the systematic scholarly method of collecting data. This was true even for the two most important projects of the time: *Magyarország felfedezése* (Discovering Hungary) and the activities of *Szolgálat és írás Munkaközösség* (Team for Service and Writing).

It is possible to classify the works published between 1936 and 1938 according to types. Taking as criteria patterns of description and interpretation, it is possible to differentiate between works belonging to scholarly sociography, journalism with sociographical ambition, and literary sociography. The works created in these years shared the trait of utilizing a literary approach.[57]

Involvement in politics diverted the attention of representatives of rural sociology from some of the professional issues of sociology, but their literary instinct showed even in their politically motivated writings.

That their writing is called "literary" should not be counted as a denigration of the output of these "founding fathers" of sociography. Their writings were informative and had a powerful appeal to readers. Rural sociologists outdid all others in portraying the peasantry vividly and with artistic authenticity. However, sociologically speaking, their achievement was deficient. Ferenc Erdei stated in 1941: "Had any of us been able to synthesize our findings, a brilliant social theory, say, a sociological tendency, would have been born. . . . But we were not able to."[58]

In the early 1940s there was a shift toward scientifically sound sociology. The most noteworthy works in this respect belonged to Ferenc Erdei: *A magyar paraszttársadalom* (The Society of Hungarian Peasants) and an unfinished work on the structure of Hungarian society.[59] His cooperation with István Hajnal was a key factor in his shift toward sociology proper. Hajnal's original thoughts on the evolution of social forms, and on the characteristics of the development of European regions, inspired both Erdei and István Bibó. They benefited from Hajnal's methodology of examining the emergence of the middle class. Erdei later discussed this phenomenon in the context of Hungary's complex social structure, in which traits of vassalage, feudal estates, and capitalism coexisted.[60]

In the early 1940s Ferenc Erdei was also engaged in field work sponsored by the Research Center for Country and People. He made a sociological study of the history of the village of Nagykôrös in cooperation with István Márkus and Jolán Majlát.

István Hajnal regarded this project as noteworthy and pointed out its merits and shortcomings. If the achievements of the Erdei team had attracted greater professional attention and served as a general topic of discussion, they could have created a research workshop wherein a leap could have been made toward professionalization and genuine theoretical analysis.[61] World War II, the events after, and changes in the careers of the people concerned postponed this opportunity. In 1945 István Hajnal made an attempt to institutionalize this workshop, but the conditions necessary for success did not then exist. Now that nearly fifty years have passed, it is clear that the influence of the work of István Hajnal, Ferenc Erdei, István Bibó, and later of István Márkus, István Kemény, and their students, was there to stay, even if (at times) in disguise. When sociology became institutionalized in the second half of the 1960s, their thoughts forcefully resurfaced.

The demand for modernization, and the increasing reliance on the central state redistribution of goods (the war economy), created a need for empirical surveys in areas where no such surveys had been made before. Two examples include (1) the empirical research related to the modernization of public administration (carried out in part by the Research Center for Country and People and in part by the University Department of Hungarian Public Administration and Financial Law under Professor Zoltán Magyary); and (2) the empirical surveys covering the condition of factory workers, carried out by the Hungarian Research Institute for Economy.[62] It was probably the team of these researchers who, with the mediation of Gyula Rézler, initiated the trail-blazing empirical survey of a machine-building factory in the Kispest district of Budapest.[63] This survey was conducted by Rezsô Hilscher.[64]

The end of World War II in 1945 marked the beginning of a new chapter in the history of sociology in Hungary. The Society for Social Sciences was relaunched, and the editors of the journal *Valóság* (Reality) started rallying a new generation of sociographers. There were signs that sociology might be recognized as an academic discipline. István Hajnal, the dean of the Faculty of Arts of Budapest's ELTE University, proposed the creation of a department of sociology as early as April 1945.[65] In September 1945 the chance arose to put this idea into practice. After István Dékány resigned, the post of head of the department of social theory became vacant. Hajnal set up a committee under László Mátrai to seek a successor, and he recommended the invitation of Károly Mannheim from London to fill the post.[66]

Hajnal also proposed the creation of a department of sociography with Ferenc Erdei as head. The minutes of the meeting at which he spoke do not reflect how heated the debate over his proposal was, yet a letter Hajnal sent to Jolán Majlát does.[67] The opponents to this proposal argued that Ferenc Erdei was working as a government minister at the time.

No rapid decision was made. The letter in which Mannheim politely dismissed the proposal was read aloud at a meeting on December 13, 1945.[68] Mannheim cited his engagement in London but remained silent about his chief motivation—his relationships with György Lukács, Béla Fogarasi, and József Révai (who had assumed control over the official intellectual life of Hungary) had turned sour in the early years of his emigration.[69] Mannheim knew that if a political turn for the worse took place in Hungary, he would be trapped. In a related development, in 1947 Fogarasi published a pamphlet (written in 1930) attacking Mannheim.[70]

The Council of the Faculty of Arts set up another committee. Following a proposal submitted during a council meeting on July 11, 1946, the application of Sándor Szalai was accepted. He was appointed full professor of the department of social theory on August 18, 1946.[71]

The plan to set up a department of sociography did not come to fruition.[72] Although groups of students submitted a petition proposing Ferenc Erdei for the professorship,[73] the university's leadership was divided on the issue and he himself rejected the offer. The issue was finally taken from the agenda in 1946.

By contrast, the department of social theory appeared to have gotten into the best of hands. Sándor Szalai (age 34 at the time) did not have Erdei's prestige by virtue of his sociological works, but thanks to his excellent skill as a lecturer, it took little time for him to make sociology a popular subject. The lectures he held, and the seminars he conducted, made the Szalai name and sociology synonymous in students' minds.

To lay the theoretical foundations of teaching this discipline—to achieve cognitive identity—he wrote *Társadalmi valóság és társadalomtudomány*.[74]

In 1948 he published *Bevezetés a társadalomtudományba* with the sole purpose of helping teach sociology at the university. In the second book he adhered to the theoretical position of the first but presented a more comprehensive overview of the sociological tendencies of the time. He devoted an entire chapter to teaching sociology and its importance in teacher training.[75] Apart from the concessions he had to make to the Marxist ideology of the time, it is a merit of his works that they established sociology as a full-fledged discipline, made an attempt at finding its place in the system of social sciences, and defined its relationship to social practice, especially politics and social policy.[76]

In the early postwar years universities worked under adverse conditions. The department of social theory had an especially difficult time, as it lacked the traditions which helped maintain more established departments.[77]

At that time István Bibó started a course in sociology at the Faculty of Legal and Administrative Sciences at the University of Szeged. His lecture notes have come down to us, but he did not have the time to write a textbook. However, the essays he published in *Valóság* and *Válasz* (Response) opened new vistas for the sociological analysis of sociopsychological phenomena.[78]

These promising beginnings could not reach fruition owing to changes in ideological and political conditions, and to a radical alteration of the sociocultural environment. Hostile journal articles heralded the start of an offensive against the department of sociology. Concrete measures followed.[79] Even though Sándor Szalai agreed to make several concessions, the Institute of Social Sciences first lost its independence, then was closed. Szalai was fired and became a defendant in a show trial. The professorship of István Bibó was suspended, and both were expelled from the Academy of Sciences. Sociology and sociography were branded as bourgeois science and silenced. Once again the institutionalization and professionalization of sociology was stopped in Hungary.

THE PROBLEMATIC PROCESS OF PROFESSIONALIZATION AND INSTITUTIONALIZATION DURING THE YEARS OF STATE SOCIALISM

Sociology was to be revived in Hungary after the suppression of the 1956 revolution under conditions of crisis. Open physical and intellectual repression was the order of the day until about 1960. The crisis, which affected all strata of society, called for a novel, critical attitude to social phenomena.

The first initiatives to revive sociology were rejected with rigorous ideological arguments.[80] The pioneering "free groups" were rather heterogeneous in background.[81] The political leaders of the country were ambiguous in their attitude to sociology. They agreed with the intention to maintain the primacy of ideology, but unlike in 1948, they neither obstructed nor encouraged the slow and controlled process of the institutionalization of sociology.

The process of sociology's institutionalization and becoming a full-fledged discipline was full of setbacks well into the 1970s and 1980s. No monograph has yet been written about this era, and the scope of this chapter allows little room for more than an outline of major events.

The post-Stalinist regimes adhered to the party-state pattern, continued to rely on the central redistribution of goods, and adhered to one-party rule and rubber-stamp parliamentarism. The autonomy of sciences was restricted.

Yet for several reasons (which cannot be described in this chapter) and despite cruel repression after 1956, Hungary had a relatively flexible version of the Stalinist model. Pre-1956 institutions were maintained, but the room to maneuver was greater in the economy and intellectual life, and there was greater freedom of speech than in the other countries of Eastern Europe. In other words, at stake in the behind-the-scene infighting was— depending on the ebb and flow of developments in the Soviet Union— the narrowing or broadening of elbow room.[82]

The development of the intellectual sphere in general, and that of the individual disciplines in particular, could not be strictly associated with the dates just given, especially in the case of autonomous disciplines. However, these historical junctures were of importance in the history of attempts to secure the emancipation of sociology in Hungary. During this period sociology lacked strong institutions and consolidated international relations, and initially it had limited room to maneuver.

The process of the institutionalization of sociology started in the early 1960s. The most important event in this context was the foundation of the sociological group of the Hungarian Academy of Sciences.[83] Sociology began to be taught at several universities,[84] and empirical surveys were launched.[85] Sociography, which had a long-standing tradition in Hungary, was also revived.

As the number of strictly scientific surveys increased, sociographers were keen to emphasize their independence from academic sociology. However, the influence of sociology remained limited at that time. This was due to several factors: the network of institutions was underdeveloped, the cognitive aspects of sociology were not elaborated, and professionalism was at a low level.

As far as cognitive aspects were concerned, the debates in the early years of the 1960s made it clear that however cautiously the object and method of sociology were defined by the thinkers who had the courage to "reopen this case," concessions to the Marxist system were inevitable. There was no other option in the sociocultural environment of the time but to present sociology as a Marxist discipline.

For some sociologists this was no concession at all. This group intended to treat sociology as part of a Marxist social theory, free of dogma. During the 1960s this meant advocacy of the line represented by György Lukács. Ágnes Heller, a member of the staff of the research group for sociology, was an outstanding representative of this school.

Marxism was the dominant ideology of the time and as such served mainly functional aims. After the publication of the first few major sociological works, some of which synthesized the findings of empirical surveys,[86] it became evident, both in content and method, that there was no way to avoid drawing a demarcation line between the findings of the surveys on society and what the political regime considered as a legitimate image of society. The preparations that were made in the middle of the 1960s to introduce a reform of central economic management allowed an increasing role for the articulation of conflicting views. It can now be seen that the opening at that time was temporary. Of importance were András Hegedûs's essay on the structure of society, which appeared in 1964,[87] and the survey on social stratification carried out under the auspices of the Central Statistical Office with the participation of Zsuzsa Ferge and István Kemény. Ferge published an article and a book on this topic.[88] These works challenged both the then prevalent dichotomous structural pattern of society and the theoretical foundations of class structure in general.

The works written by György Konrád and Iván Szelényi, together or separately, defined a new paradigm: they systematically described the latent and manifest dysfunctions of the socialist economic system of central redistribution.[89]

The publication of classic works of sociology, which had been banned for many years, resumed.[90] This helped popularize sociology. The series *Társadalomtudományi Könyvtár*[91] was relaunched, and several aptly edited omnibus volumes were published on sociology. These books helped a specific section of intellectuals to acquire a new language for argumentation. New sociological institutions were created, research was carried out in more and more places, and training was also done in more and more institutions.[92]

Sociology in Hungary in the late 1960s was beset by contradictions when, in the wake of student movements in the United States and Western Europe and of the events of 1968 in Paris, the New Left tendency reached Hungary. So-called critical sociology gained ground here.

In the early 1960s positivism, due to its genuine or ostensible objectivity, was a widely accepted form of tacit opposition to official ideology, but critical sociology proved to be a much more effective tool to use in opposition to Marxist ideology. Consequently, the views of C. Wright Mills, Alvin Gouldner, and Alain Touraine had an appeal, not only to radical groups of young sociologists but also to several former followers of the structuralist-functional school. These researchers decided to give preference to the critical function of sociology over its objective merits.[93] This resulted in peculiar instances of consensus between representatives of the markedly nonconformist neo-Marxist tendency and that of critical sociology. At the time important sociological works highly critical of alienated labor and lifestyles carried references to Max Horkheimer, Theodor Adorno, Herbert Marcuse, Jürgen Habermas, and the young Georg Lukács side by side.

Furthermore, in this period a counteroffensive by conservative forces took place. This was another consequence of 1968, especially of the intervention in Czechoslovakia. Hungary's political leaders strove to create the impression that a reform would be introduced in science policy.[94]

However, it took but a short time for fundamentalists, who enjoyed international support, to gain the upper hand. Thinkers like András Hegedûs, Ågnes Heller, and Mária Márkus, who used to be neo-Marxists, were publicly criticized.[95] Iván Szelényi and the internationally renowned writer György Konrád were harassed by the police.[96] Surveys, led by István Kemény, which focused on poverty and the conditions of gypsies, received no further funds and were later banned.[97] With the exception of András Hegedûs, they were all forced to emigrate between 1973 and 1976.[98]

These thinkers addressed themes the political leadership considered taboo, but average academic sociology in Hungary either fully ignored or only tacitly touched upon—themes such as the mode of production under state socialism, the one-party system, the social hierarchy that was partly bureaucratic and partly feudalistic, and the interplay between the prerogatives of certain hereditary elite groups and poverty.

In Hungary victories and defeats were always temporary in the tug-of-war between fundamentalists and reformers. The "left-wing" turn that occurred between 1973 and 1975 showed that the reforms could hardly be fully implemented within the framework of the given social system. There was another conclusion: due to the widening economic recession, the scope for further reforms was continuously recreated—within certain limits.

Although Hungarian sociology was suffering from a serious blow, it could survive if it made certain concessions. During the mid-1970s one form of survival was putting strong emphasis on the requirements of professionalization.[99]

This incentive to professionalize sociology and bring it up to international standards was powerful enough to finally, at least in part, achieve these long-desired goals. Hungarian sociology was integrated into international sociological life better than ever before.[100] Surveys were of higher standards theoretically and methodologically. In some areas (social stratification and social mobility) research was absolutely at a par with international standards.

Progress was most dynamic in institutionalization. New research centers were created and existing ones increasingly turned toward sociology.[101] Sociology was introduced as a subject to more university and college departments.[102] The Hungarian Sociological Association was established.[103]

From the second half of the 1970s an increasing number of surveys were commissioned, often with the cooperation of several institutions. Some of the surveys covered sizable samples.[104]

The sophistication of methods promoted both institutionalization and professionalization. However, the Weberian creed of objectivity could not be consistently implemented. Members of the various sociological schools of thought shared the view that the differentiation of society could only be portrayed in multidimensional fields, and that the features of this differentiation were related to the reproduction of social inequalities. This reasoning led to the conclusion that there were conflict-ridden, definable, and quantifiable differences in interests and values in Marxist societies as well as in capitalist societies.

At this juncture sociology, willy-nilly, entered the realm of politics. It became clear that the opportunity—or lack of it—to articulate interests, the size of the income, the quality of education, and social policy in its broadest sense are all structure-forming factors. In other words, the social structure is not a mere derivative of objective processes that are independent of people's actions.

Sociological findings, synthesized in part with the tenets of critical sociology, were used to further explore reality and discard myths about it. Some taboo subjects were also challenged.

However, the most fundamental issues raised between 1968 and 1974 were only addressed on the level of abstract generalities, or were relegated to questions of method. This was the price paid to the existing polity for institutionalization. The sociologists on the staff of government-subsidized institutes made indirect criticism of the model of existing socialism, but they either accepted its existence as historically given or carefully avoided an open challenge to its legitimacy.[105]

Professionalization was therefore problematic, and cognitive consensus was based either on hushing up questions or on using an esoteric code for questions left unanswered by Marxist theology. This lack of professionalization was the consequence of the following facts: the precondition and a key component of the professionalization of all disciplines, including sociology, is autonomy—autonomy in the sense that scholars are given free reign to evaluate, reject, or reward rival views among themselves independently of government politics.

The ever more manifest legitimation crises of the socialist societies in the 1980s gave rise to new processes in sociology. They led toward the definition of a new paradigm.

Sociological works were published in Hungary that discussed the following themes: how the Communist party and government officials are recruited, and what privileges they have; what dysfunctions are caused by the over-politicization of all spheres of life; what are the problems in national identity; which irregularities in the assessment of student and scholarly performance are due to restrictions in the autonomy of universities and research institutes; what does the so-called second society (the tolerated, at times encouraged, private market) really consist of, and so forth. These issues were raised in the broad context of the rise of the middle class and of modernization.[106] Some researchers openly called for the re-definition of the premises of the theory of sociology.

The history of the institutionalization and professionalization of sociology in Hungary offers an important message for those who fought for the new paradigm: the expansion and smooth operation of the network of sociological institutions are indispensable preconditions to professionalization, but they are not sufficient in themselves. Full professionalization, the perfection of the cognitive dimensions of institutionalization, may only take place provided the functions of a scholar (lecturer and researcher) are clearly separated from those of a politician and a social policy official—in short, under conditions of autonomy.

Hungary's newly won freedom, the institutions of parliamentarism, offer its scholars new opportunities in this respect, yet it will take some time before Hungary's East European backwardness can be overcome.

NOTES

1. Gyula Pauler, "Auguste Comte és a történelem" (Auguste Comte and History), *Századunk,* 1876, pp. 70–71.

2. Károly Tagányi, "Styl és történelem" (Style and History), *Századunk,* 1884, p. 503.

3. As early as the reform era of the 1840s, the thinkers realized that there could be no modernization without the rise of a middle class, an officially approved and used mother tongue, and national consciousness. They also saw that the evolution of these might be a challenge to the territorial integrity of the multinational Kingdom of Hungary.

4. Tibor Huszár, "Az értelmiségszociológia és szociográfia hazai történetéhez" (On the History of the Sociological and Sociographical Study of the Intelligentsia in Hungary), in *Nemzetlét—nemzettudat—értelmiség* (National Existence—National Consciousness—Intelligentsia), Budapest, pp. 115–22.

5. For a vivid description of the process, see *Statisztikai Nemzetgazdasági Közlemények* (Statistical Bulletin on the Economy), I–VII, Pest, the volumes of 1865–1871.

6. Gyula Pauler, "A pozitvizmus hatása a történetírásra" (The Influence of Positivism on Historiography), *Századok,* 1873; Leó Beöthy, "Auguste Comte társadalomtani nézetei" (Auguste Comte's View of Society), Budapest, 1879; cf. *A társadalomfejlôdés kezdetei* (The Early Stage in the Evolution of Society), I–II, Budapest, 1882.

7. See János Asbóth, *Három nemzedék* (Three Generations), Budapest, 1873; cf. *Irodalmi arcképek* (Portraits of Writers), Budapest, 1976.

8. See Gábor Zsigmond, *A magyar társadalomnépraiz kezdetei* (The Birth of Ethnography in Hungary), Budapest, 1974; Béla G. Németh, "Létharc és nemzetiség. Az irodalmi értelmiség felsô rétegeinek ideológiájához 1876. után" (Struggle for Life and the Nationalities. On the Ideology of the Upper Strata of Literary Intelligentsia after 1876), in *Létharc és nemzetiséq,* Budapest, 1976, pp. 6–42.

9. József Buday, "Comte Ágost: a positivismus jövôje. Comte Ágost szociológiája nyomán" (Auguste Comte: The Future of Positivism. In the Footsteps of Auguste Comte's Sociology), *Magyar Philosophiai Szemle* (Hungarian Philosophical Review), I–IV, 1887; I–IV, 1888; I–V, 1889; IV, 1890. Leó Beöthy, "Auguste Comte társadalomtani nézetei" (Auguste Comte's View of Society), *Budapesti Szemle* (Budapest Review), 1879, pp. 19–20. László Pápay, "Quatelet és a társadalmi természettan" (Quatelet and the Science of Society), *Természettudományi Közlöny* (Natural Science Gazette), 1872, pp. 167–71.

10. Gyula Pauler, "Konzervatív liberalizmus" (Conservative Liberalism), *Athenaeum,* V, 1879. Referring to Cimet (as so many thinkers did), Pauler attacked liberalism, which he described as the policy of material prosperity. He contrasted liberalism with the duty to foster time-honored morals and ideals.

11. Dominant as this tendency was, it was not the only one in existence. Other tendencies are represented by articles printed in the journal *Figyelö* (Observer), 1871–1875, or are expressed in the words of István Hegedüs.

12. It is both a rewarding challenge and a dangerous dream for us, Hungarians, to aspire to contribute to universal scientific progress. The price to be paid for that may be the loss of national integrity. Universal science is cosmopolitan. It may undermine a nation's healthy sense of danger. As the territory of our country is vast and there are a lot of nationalities, dangers from the outside may combine with those from the inside. Our task therefore is to create a national science, one that can supply intellectual and emotional ammunition for the nation's struggle for life.

Ferenc Toldy, "Tudománybéli hátramaradásunk okai s ezek tekintetében Akadémiánk feladása" (On the Causes of Our Backwardness in Science and the Related Tasks of Our Academy), 1868, pp. 144–49.

13. On how the neoconservative ideology and movement feature in the social sciences, see Miklós Szabó, "A kontinentális Európa konzervatív ideológiájának új vonásai a századfordulón" (New Features of Conservative Ideology in Continental Europe on the Turn of the Century), pp. 7–47; Miklós Szabó, "Középosztály és újkonzervatizmus" (Middle Class and Neoconservatism), pp. 176–90.

14. It is worth examining the history of the National Széchenyi Federation [OSzSz]. See Mihály Kerék, *Az Országos Széchenyi Szövetség története, mûködése és hivatása* (The History, Operation and Calling of the NSzF), Budapest, 1932. See also Jenô Czettler, *Magyar mezôgazdasági szociálpolitika* (Social Policy in Hungarian Agricultural Policy), Budapest, 1914.

15. *Huszadik Század,* vol. 1, no. 1, in *A magyar szociológia elsô mûhelye* (The First Workshop of Sociology in Hungary), ed. György Litván and László Szûcs, 1979, p. 64.

16. See Leó Beöthy, *A magyar társadalmi fejlôdés kezdetei, I–II* (The Earliest Phase of Social Development in Hungary), Budapest, 1882; B. Somló, *Der Güterkehr in der Urgesellschaft.* The first related publication in German: "Entwicklung und Literature der Soziologie in Ungarn," *Monatschrift für Soziologie,* vol. 10, 1909, pp. 325–35.

17. For the programs of and the names of participants in the approximately fifty evenings devoted to debates, see The First Workshop of Sociology, op. cit., vol. 2, pp. 537–48.

18. When talking about a full-fledged discipline, we mean (at least in this century) a complexly articulated social subsystem, not (as was the case earlier) a loose integration of researchers busy pursuing similar projects. Major scientific organizations have the trappings of a bureaucracy, but unlike the situation in agencies of public administration, scholarly achievements are evaluated by international scientific discussions instead of administrative or legal institutions. Ideally, therefore, the vehicles of scientific tradition are teams of researchers who enjoy varying degrees of autonomy. Scientific tradition imparts a social form to scientific content and innovative effort. From the beginning of this century the institutionalization of a discipline has ensured it the conditions for efficient and well-coordinated operation. Lepienes, *Geschichte der Soziologie. Studien zur kognitiven, sozialen und historischen Identitaet einer Disziplin,* p. 1. Robert L. Geiger, "Die Institutionalieserung soziologischer Paradigmen: Drei Beispiel der Frühzeit der französchien Soziologie." In: W. Lepienes, vol. 2, pp. 140–45. Victor Karády, "Strategien und vorgehenweisen der Durkheim Schule im Bemühen und die Anerkennung der Soziologie." In Lepienes, vol. 2, pp. 231–32.

19. The first president of the Society was the Count Gyula Andrássy, a widely respected personality of his age. The liberal-conservative wing within the Society included Gusztáv Gratz, Loránt Hegedüs, and Pál Wolfner. In 1905 there was a political crisis in Hungary, the details of which would go beyond the scope of this chapter. It sparked a series of events, one of which was this wing's departure from the Society in the summer of 1906. Andrássy resigned from the post of president. There was an unsuccessful attempt to seize power within the Society, and then the 37-member conservative-liberal wing of the Society also left the Society. (For the history of the crucial general meeting, see *Huszadik Század,* 1906, II, pp. 147–75.) The organization that was subsequently formed received the name Hungarian Association for Social Sciences (MTE). Its president was István Apáthy. The editor-in-chief of its journal, the *Magyar Társadalomtudományi Szemle* (Hungarian Social Science Review, or MTSz), was Menyhért Palágyi.

20. See Bódog Somló, "A társadalmi fejlôdés elméletérôl és néhány gyakorlati alkalmazásáról" (On the Theory of Social Progress and Some of Its Practical Applications), *Huszadik Század,* vol. 1, 1903, pp. 397–409. Ervin Szabó, "Természet és társadalom" (Nature and Society), *Huszadik Század,* vol. 2, 1903, pp. 747–72. Gyula Pikler, "A materialista történelmi felfogás legnagyobb hiánya" (The Most Important Deficiency of the Materialistic Interpretation of History), *Huszadik Század,* vol. 1, pp. 138–40. Oszkár Jászi, *A történelmi materializmus állambölcselete* (The Theory of State as Interpreted by Historical Materialism), Budapest, 1908.

21. Oszkár Jászi's letter to Ervin Szabó, March 12, 1905, in *Szabó Ervin levelezése* (E. Sz.'s Correspondence), Budapest, 1978, pp. 75–76.

22. Oszkár Jászi, "Tudomány és politika" (Science and Politics), in "A szociológia elsô magyarországi mûhelye" (The First Workshop of Sociology in Hungary), in *Magyarországi mûhelyek,* Budapest, vol. 1, 1973, pp. 60–80.

23. Oszkár Jászi, op. cit., p. 70.

24. "Why should a Durkheim or a Ribot interfere in politics when that job is done properly by a Jaures, a Guesde or a Clemenceau" Oszkár Jászi: op. cit., pp. 70–71.

25. Oszkár Jászi, op. cit., p. 72.

26. Ibid.

27. Ibid.

28. Even Bódog Somlò, who was better informed in theoretical questions than any of his contemporaries, embraced the ideas of Spencer. On occasions when he went beyond positivism, he addressed questions other than sociological. Works by Bódog Somlò, *Az objektiv szociológia* (Objective Sociology), Budapest, 1903; *A helyes jog elmélete* (The Theory of Proper Law), Budapest, 1904; cf. *Gedanken zu einer ersten Philosophie*, Berlin-Leipzig, 1925; cf. *Juristische Grundlehre*, Leipzig, 1927.

29. R. Maria Lespius, "Die Soziologie der Zwissenkriegzeit. Entwicklungtendzen und Beurteilungskriterien," in *Soziologie in Deutschland und österreich, 1918–1945*, p. 23. On how the theory of evolution and positivism lost ground in the beginning of this century, see I. W. Burow, *Evolution and Society*, London, 1966.

30. Oszkár Jászi, "Tiz év" (Ten Years), *Huszadik Század*, vol. 1, pp. 1–10.

31. For further details, see *A vasárnapi kör* (The Sunday Circle), Documents. Compiled and introduced by Éva Karádi and Erzsébet Vezér, Budapest, 1980.

32. Georg Lukács, *A modern dráma fejlôdésének története* (A History of the Development of Modern Drama), Budapest, 1911. Georg Lukács, "Zum Wesen und zur Methodike der Kultursoziologie," in *Schriften zur Soziologie der Kultur*, Ed. A. Weber, vol. 1, Jena, 1913. Karl Mannheim, *Seele und Kultur*, Budapest, 1918.

33. See Jenô Gaál, "A Magyar Társadalomtudományi Szemle rendeltetése" (The Mission of the Hungarian Social Science Review, MTSz), vol. 1, 1908, pp. 1–8. Dr. István Apáthy, "A Magyar Társadalomtudományi Egyesület legelsô teendôi" (The First Priorities of the Hungarian Association for Social Sciences), *MTSz*, 1908, pp. 8–13.

34. See the Programme of the Hungarian Association for Social Sciences, *MTSz*, vol. 3, 1910, pp. 555–58.

35. The following committees operated in 1905: legal, economic, social science, social policy, labor, and finally, one devoted to private and liberal education. Op. cit. Supplement to *MTSz*, 1909, pp. 32–33.

36. Miklós Szabó, "Magyar konzervatizmus" (Conservatism in Hungary), in *Politikai kultúra Magyarországon, 1898–1986* (Political Culture in Hungary, 1898–1986), 1989, p. 15.

37. István Bernát, József Hajós, Endre György, Károly Schandl, and later, Jenô Czettler, who was promoted to a senior post in a university in the 1920s, advocated the institutionalizing of interest associations and social policy organizations, first in the domain of social policy for agriculture. For an encyclopedic summary of these experiments, see Jenô Czettler, *Magyar mezôgazdasági szociálpolitika* (Social Policy in Hungarian Agriculture), 1914.

38. Ferenc Eckhardt, *A Jog- ás Államtudományi Kar története, 1867–1935* (A History of the Faculty of Legal and Administrative Sciences, 1867–1935), Budapest, 1936, p. 647.

39. Ibid, p. 648.

40. The minutes of the meeting of the leadership of the Faculty of Legal and Administrative Sciences, January 17, 1919.

41. *A Jog- ás Államtudományi Kar története*, op. cit., pp. 647–49.

42. The government, called Council of People's Commissioners, made Hungary a Soviet-type republic in 1919. Ibid., pp. 651–52.

43. Karl Mannheim resettled in Vienna, then in Heidelberg. In 1930 he became a university professor in Frankfurt. He played an important role in institutionalizing sociology in Germany. Between 1933 and his death in 1947 he taught at the London School of Economics. His principal works are *Ideology and Utopia,* English trans. 1936, *Man and Society in an Age of Reconstruction,* trans. 1940. (Neither have been translated into Hungarian.) Pál Szende did not become a university lecturer. However, two of his works, *Verhüllung und Enthüllung,* Leipzig, 1922, and *Eine soziologische Theorie der Abstraktion,* 1923, are still noted in German-speaking countries. (They have not been translated into Hungarian either.) Arnold Hauser settled in Vienna. From 1933 he lived in London. From 1951 he was a professor at Leeds University. He wrote the following sociological works: *Sozialgeschichte der Kunst und Literatur,* Munich, 1953, and *Soziologie der Kunst,* Munich, 1974. Antal Frigyes first lived in Italy, then, from 1933, in Britain. His principal works are: *Florentine Painting and Its Social Background,* London, 1947, and *Hoggarth and His Place in European Art,* 1962. There was also a delay in the scholarly university career of Karl Polányi in Vienna, his first base. Then he moved to Oxford. Between 1947 and 1953 he was a professor at Columbia University, New York. His principal works are: *The Great Transformation,* New York–Toronto, 1957, and *Trade and Market in the Early Empires,* London, 1957. Oszkár Jászi worked as a professor at Oberlin University from 1925. His *Dissolution of the Habsburg Monarchy,* Chicago, 1929, has become an often-quoted reference.

44. The most eloquent example from this point of view is "Nemzeti és nemzetietlen szociológia" (National and Un-National Sociology), *Társadalomtudomány* (Social Science), 1927, pp. 337–47. An example for the opposite point of view is "A szociológia feladata" (The Task of Sociology), an article by the eminent economist Farkas Heller (*Társadalomtudomány,* vol. 1, pp. 6–12. However, his initiative had no response and he did not raise this subject in further writings either.

45. BTK KKr. 1930–131. ELTE Archives. June 20, 1931. 1080 DSZ. BTK jkr ih, June 1, 1932. IX. 3. ü. BTK. IV. VII. r. meeting. 41366 DSZ BTK Jkr. March 7, 1939. IV. r. meeting. ih. 1089 DSZ BTK KKr. 22 May, 1939. II. r. meeting, 1316 DSZ. Finally, in 1942 a Department of Social Theory was set up with István Dékány as head. Dékány was a philosopher of society rather than a sociologist. His works on the social phenomena are of a deductive, speculative character. See *Társadalomfilozófia alapfogalmai,* Budapest, 1939.

46. Hans Freyer was a professor of sociology at Leipzig University. His works in social philosophy, history, and ethnography were often referred to by Hungarian scholars. From 1934 he acted as president and the most influential member of the German Sociological Society.

47. Barna Horváth, *Rechtssoziologie,* Berlin, 1934.

48. Tibor Huszár, *Bibó István. Beszélgetések, politikai életrajzok, dokumentumok* (István Bibó. Conversations, Political Biographies, and Documents), Budapest, 1989, pp. 24–25.

49. This what he had to say of the relationship of sociology and the philosophy of society in 1943:

Research on social reality and values is philosophical provided it aspires to encompass the whole, and it falls under the category of a specialized science provided it focuses on certain partial aspects. It follows from the tenet of "entia praeter necessitatem non sunt multiciplanda" that we may only speak of specialized social sciences and the theory of society, and the latter may be called sociology or philosophy of society.

"A mai filozófia," in op. cit., pp. 115–16. Oral contribution by Barna Horváth.

50. István Hajnal, "Történelem és szociológia," *Századunk* (Our Century), 1939, pp. 1–32, 137–66; *Írásbeliség, írástörténet a felújulás korából* (The Evolution of Written Records in the Age of Revival), Budapest, 1921; "A kis nemzetek történetírásának munkaközössége" (Joining the Efforts of Historiographers of Small Nations), *Századunk,* 1942, pp. 1–42, 133–65.

51. See György Bónis, *Hűbériség és rendiség a középkori jogban* (Vassaldom and Estates in Medieval Law), Cluj, 1943; Ferenc Erdei, *A magyar paraszttársadalom* (The Society of Hungarian Peasants), Budapest, 1942; István Bibó, *A keleteurópai kis államok nyomorúsága* (The Misery of the Small States of Eastern Europe), Budapest, 1946; Jolán Majlát-István Márkus, *Nagykőrös beilleszkedése a magyar rendi társadalomba a XVIII. században* (The Integration of Nagykőrös into Hungary's Society of Estates in the 18th Century), Budapest, 1943.

52. Ferenc Földes, "A munkásság és a parasztság kulturális helyzete" (The Cultural Situation of the Workers and Peasants), in *Válogatott írások* (Selected Writings), Budapest, 1967.

53. For a detailed analysis, see Dénes Némedi, *Népi szociográfia. 1932–33* (Rural Sociography), Budapest, 1985; Tibor Huszár, "A tudós és politikus Erdei Ferenc műhelyében" (In the Workshop of Ferenc Erdei, the Scholar and Politician), in *Történelem és szociológia,* Budapest, 1979, pp. 249–553.

54. Gyula Ortutay, "A magyar falukutatás új útjai," *Vigília,* February 1935, p. 116; Béla Reitzer, "A szociográfia módszertani problémái," *Fiatal Magyarság* (Young Hungarians), November 1, 1934.

55. The concept was borrowed by Hungarian essayists and social scientists from German ethnographical and culture historical works, namely, from Leo Frobenius, *Schicksalskunde im Sinne des Kulturwendens,* Leipzig, 1932.

56. "The real qualification for anyone to practise the scholarship of fate is mankind as it is tried by fate. That has to reach out for the things known." László Németh, "A magyarságtudomány feladatai" (The Tasks of Hungarian Studies), in *Kiadatlan tanulmányok* (Unpublished Essays), vol. 1, Budapest, 1968, p. 383.

57. Ferenc Erdei, the archetype of authors of scholarly sociography, wrote in 1941:

The movement attained an additional marked trait, it became literary. At that time we described it as intellectual. With hindsight now it can be unequivocally classified as one belonging to writers. The social analysis was typical of writers, it was writers who kept the movement going, and the response was also reminiscent of literature: the public reacted as a reading audience.

Ferenc Erdei, "A reformkorszak epilógusa" (Epilogue to the Reform Era), *Kelet Népe* (People of the East), vol. 6, 1941, pp. 3–4.

58. Ferenc Erdei, "A reformkorszak epilógusa" (Epilogue to the Reform Era), *Kelet Népe* (People of the East), vol. 6, 1941, p. 3. Inconsistencies in their method were also criticized by the conservative Gyula Rézler. Gyula Rézler, *Falukutatók és szociográfusok. A magyar társadalom önvizsgálata az elmúlt évtizedben* (Rural Sociologists and Sociographers. The Self-Examination of Hungarian Society in the Past Decade), Budapest, 1943.

59. Ferenc Erdei, *A magyar paraszttársadalom,* Budapest, 1942. Now available in *A magyar társadalomról* (On Hungarian Society), Budapest, 1983, pp. 33–217. In English: "The Society of Hungarian Peasants," in Ferenc Erdei: *Selected Writings,* Ed. Tibor Huszár, Budapest, 1988, pp. 156–204. See also "Hungarian Society between the Two World Wars," in *Selected Writings,* pp. 7–95. In Hungarian: Ferenc Erdei, "A magyar társadalom a két világháború között," in *A magyar társadalomról,* pp. 291–347.

60. Ferenc Erdei, *Selected Writings,* p. 12.

61. István Hajnal's letter to Ferenc Erdei, November 10, 1943. Archive of the Sociological Institute of ELTE University, Budapest.

62. Zoltán Magyary–István Kis, *A közigazgatás és az emberek* (Public Administration and People), Pécs, 1933. *Magyar gyári munkások. Szociális helyzetkép* (Factory Workers in Hungary. Their Living Conditions), Ed. Gyula Rézler, Budapest, 1946. Gyula Rézler made a pioneering contribution to surveying the lives of factory workers in Hungary well before this book. His major sociographical-historical piece, *A magyar nagyipari munkásság kialakulása (1867–1914)* (The Rise of Factory Labor in Hungary, 1867–1914), could only be published in 1948.

63. The survey of 1,200 workers covered essential sociological data. The questionnaires remained unprocessed but were preserved in the archive of a grammar school of Sárospatak. Miklós Lackó processed them fifty years later. See "Gépgyári munkások az 1930-as években" (Machine Factory Workers in the 1930s), *Századunk,* vol. 1–2, 1989, pp. 2–43.

64. Rezsô Hilscher, a lecturer at the Budapest University of Economics, headed the social welfare department of the Institute of Social Policy.

65. Péter Pázmány University, minutes of the council of the Faculty of Arts, April 17, 1945.

66. Ibid., September 21, 1945.

67. See István Hajnal's letter to Ferenc Erdei, Budapest, September 29, 1945. Copy held in the sociological archive of ELTE University. Ferenc Erdei published writings even during his spell as a minister. In May 1945 he presented a paper at a session of the reorganized Society for Social Sciences.

68. Minutes of the Pázmány University's Arts Faculty Council, December 13, 1945.

69. In a letter to Béla Balázs, Mannheim gave a terse explanation for this. Heidelberg, February 15, 1930. In *Vasárnapi Kör* (Sunday Circle), Eds. Éva Karádi and Erzsébet Vezér, Budapest, 1980, p. 145.

70. Published first as Adalbert Fogarasi: "Die Soziologie der Intelligenz and die Intelligenz der Soziologie," *Unter dem Banner des Marxismus,* 1930.

71. Dezso Keresztúry's letter to the rector of the university, August 23, 1946. Archive of ELTE University, correspondence of rectors.

72. Minutes of the Pázmány University's Arts Faculty Council, September 9, 1946.

73. Dezso Keresztúry's letter to the rector of the university, August 23, 1946, ELTE correspondence.

74. Sándor Szalai, *Társadalmi valóság és társadalomtudomány* (Social Reality and Social Science).

75. Sándor Szalai, *Bevezetés a társadalomtudományba* (Introduction to Social

Science), in the series Nevelôk Könyvtára, No. 4, Budapest, 1948, pp. 149–58, 175–79.

76. Sociology goes beyond examining certain phenomena for a practical purpose. It applies scientific methods and seeks general principles. Ibid., p. 171.

77. Elek Karsai joined the department in 1946 as junior lecturer presenting the recommendation of Emma Léderer. His doctoral dissertation was in the field of history. Evidently, he had no sociological qualifications. The department, which was later to become an institute, had two other full-time staff members: historian Géza Perjés, who worked as librarian, and Iván Sugár, who handled the institute's administrative affairs. In 1947, János Harsányi joined the institute as an unpaid trainee.

78. István Bibó, *A kelet-európai kis államok nyomorúsága* (see note 51); *Eltorzult magyar alkat, zsákutcás magyar történelem* (Distorted Hungarian Character, Dead Alley in Hungarian History), *Zsidókérdés Magyarországon* (Jewish Question in Hungary), in *Válogatott Tanulmányok* (Selected Essays), Ed. Tibor Huszár, Budapest, 1986.

79. The tone of the polemic writings was becoming increasingly sharper. Articles by László Rudas anticipated the subsequent repressive measures. See "Mi változott tavaly ôsz óta? Válasz Szalai Sándornak" (What Has Changed since Last Fall? An Answer to Sándor Szalai), in László Rudas, *Elmélet és gyakorlat* (Theory and Practice), Budapest, 1950, pp. 217–250.

80. For the debate, see "A hazánkban folyó szociológiai kutatások helyzete és idôszerû problémái" (The Situation and Timely Issues of Sociological Research in Our Homeland), *Magyar Filozófiai Szemle* (Hungarian Philosophical Review), 1960, no. 2, pp. 615–631.

81. Sándor Szalai, who had been politically rehabilitated, represented the older generation. The majority of the representatives of the middle generation came from disciplines like law, economics, or ethnography. Others came from politics, like András Hegedûs, who had been prime minister of Hungary between 1954 and 1956. Others, for instance István Kemény, got involved in politics in 1956. There were, furthermore, younger people who expected sociology to free social science from ideological content.

82. From the political and economic point of view the periods of 1963–1968, 1968–1973, 1973–1978, 1978–1985 saw alternating waves of partial reform and hard-liners counteroffensive. From 1985 the communist system began to come unstuck. The process led into a negotiated revolution, to free parliamentary elections and take aim at establishing a market economy.

83. Characteristically, the research group for sociology initially operated under the auspices of the Institute of Philosophy. Its independent operation in 1965 was the first step toward sociology becoming a discipline on its own. The founder and head of the group was András Hegedûs.

84. At the department of philosophy of the Faculty of Arts of ELTE University; at departments of law, economics, and legal theory in Budapest, Pécs, and Szeged; at the department of philosophy of the Budapest University of Economics.

85. The most important empirical project was conducted by the economics department of the Central Statistical Office in early 1963. The survey, which covered 15,000 households, focused on the dynamics of social stratification. See "Tár-

sadalmi rétegzôdés Magyarországon" (Social Stratification in Hungary). KSH (Central Statistical Office), *Idôszaki Közlemények,* 1964.

86. See Sándor Csoóri, *Tudósítás a toronyból* (Report from the Tower), Budapest, 1963; Gyula Csák, *Mélytenger áramlás* (Deep-Sea Currents), Budapest, 1963. The series "The Discovery of Hungary" was relaunched at the end of the 1960s. It generally contains works falling under the category of literary sociography. For the so-called scholarly sociography, see *Város és vidéke* (Town and Its Surroundings), Budapest, 1971; István Márkus, *Az ismeretlen fôszereplô* (The Unknown Protagonist), Budapest, 1991.

87. András Hegedûs, "A szocialista társadalom struktúrális modellie és a társadalmi rétegzôdés" (Structural Model of Socialist Society and Social Stratification), *Valóság* (Reality), vol. 5, 1964, pp. 1–15.

88. Zsuzsa Ferge, "Társadalmi rétegzôdés Magyarországon" (Social Stratification in Hungary), *Valóság,* 1966, no. 10. Cf. *Társadalmunk rétegzôdése* (The Stratification of Our Society), Budapest, 1969.

89. See György Konrád–Iván Szelényi, *úi lakótelepek szociológiai vizsgálatának problémái* (Problems of the Sociological Examination of New Housing Estates), Budapest, 1969. Konrád-Szelényi, "ùj lakótelepek szociológiai vizsgálata," *Valóság,* 1969, no. 8, p. 28. György Konrád, "A késleltetett városfejlesztés társadalmi konfliktusai" (Social Conflicts of Retarded Urban Development), *Valóság,* 1971, no. 12.

90. Durkheim, *Suicide,* 1967. Max Weber, *Economy and Society* (excerpts), Comp. Iván Varga, 1967. Max Weber, *Állam, politika, tudomány* (State, Politics, Science), Comps. István Kemény and Iván Varga, 1970.

91. This series was started in the early years of this century. It includes nearly seventy authors, early and modern. Eminent thinkers from universities and the Academy have been on its editorial board.

92. The research group was transformed into an institute. In 1969 the department for public opinion research of the Hungarian Radio and Television continued as the Institute for Media Research and became a center for domestic sociological surveys. It was headed by Tamás Szecskô. In 1970 a department of social statistics was set up within the Central Statistical Office. Social phenomena that used to be taboo were examined by its three sections with sophisticated methodology. The sections were as follows: social mobility (headed by Rudolf Andorka), social stratification (headed by László Cseh-Szombathy), poverty (headed by István Kemény). Two postgraduate courses, organized by the Institute for Social Sciences, played an important role in the training of sociologists. The courses were led by Tibor Huszár, Iván Szelényi, Zsuzsa Ferge, and Kálmán Kulcsár. A sociology group was set up at ELTE University's Arts Faculty in 1969 and became an independent department one year later. An independent sociology group started at the Budapest University of Economics in 1967 under Tibor Huszár.

93. See András Hegedûs–Mária Márkus, *Ember, munka, közösség* (Man, Labor, Community), Budapest, 1966. Zoltán Zsille, "Fiatal diplomások esélyei" (Young Graduates' Chances of Success in Career), *Valóság,* 1971, no. 7. Lajos Héthy–Csaba Makó, *Munkásmagatartások és gazdasági szervezet* (Patterns of Worker Behavior and Economic Organization), Budapest, 1972.

94. A document entitled "Guidelines for Science Policy" was issued in 1969. It paid lip service to the freedom of research but in effect restricted the scholars'

ability to publish their writings. "MSzMP KB Tudománypolitikai Irányelvei, June 27, 1969," in *Határozatok és dokumentumok 1967–1970* (Resolutions and Documents 1967–1970), Budapest, 1974, pp. 335–67. As initiated by the Secretariat of the Communist party, two men were simultaneously removed from senior posts: the director of the Institute of Philosophy, who was well known for his sectarian and dogmatic views, and András Hegedûs, the director of the Institute of Sociology of the Academy, who played a pioneering role in reviving sociology. "MSzMP Titkárságának határozata" (Resolution of the Communist Party Secretariat), *Pártélet* (Party Life), December 1969.

95. "A Magyar Szocialista Munkáspárt KB. Kulturpolitikai Munkaközösségének állásfoglalása néhány társadalomkutató antimarxista nézeteirôl" (Statement of the Culture Policy Panel Set Up by the Central Committee of the Hungarian Socialist Workers' Party on the Anti-Marxist Views of Certain Social Scientists), *Határozatok és dokumentumok 1971–1975* (Resolutions and Documents 1971–1975), Budapest, 1978, pp. 456–69.

96. *The Road of the Intellectuals to Class Power: Sociological Study of the Intelligentsia in Socialism,* New York, 1979, written by György Konrád and Iván Szelényi, was confiscated by police in typescript form. It was published abroad.

97. The Central Statistical Office dismissed István Kemény; a new head was appointed to the department of social statistics and the department itself was reorganized.

98. In his preface to the Hungarian edition of their book, Iván Szelényi gives a vivid description of this process. Konrád–Szelényi, *Az értelmiség útja az osztályhatalomhoz* (The Road of the Intellectuals), Budapest, 1989, pp. 5–6:

From the moment we started working on the book we were clearly aware that the task we had set ourselves was an impossible one: we have to write a book that is unacceptable for the Hungarian political authorities and police and is bound to remain such in the foreseeable future. After all, by the end of 1973 we had become outcasts from the official intellectual life and were jobless. As a result of the reactionary turnabout that took place in Hungary after 1968 and especially in the early 1970s, which we describe in this book as the counteroffensive of the ruling class, the conservative party and secret-police bureaucracy pushed us to the margin of intellectual livelihood. The same happened to many of our friends and like-minded acquaintants. True, it was partly our fault to become outcasts: the more conservative the political regime became, the more radical we grew intellectually. We refused to use the ideological muzzle that was required. On the contrary, we aimed at drawing ever more consistent conclusions from our research. We could not retreat and behave. Our aim was to formulate our ideas as precisely and sharply as possible. We wished to write a book free of taboos and sacred cows. We consciously prepared ourselves for committing "scholarly suicide." We were aware that, once we publish this essay, we cannot work as sociologists in Eastern Europe any more.

99. Kálmán Kulcsár, *Társadalom, politika, jog* (Society, Politics, Law), Budapest, 1974. See also Lajos Héthy–Csaba Makó, "Antimarxista szociológia és a valóságfeltárás" (Anti-Marxist Sociology and Exploring Reality), *Társadalmi Szemle* (Social Review), 1973, no. 11, pp. 19–30. Cf. "A marxista szociológia önismeretének kérdéséhez" (On the Question of the Self-Knowledge of Marxist Sociology), *Társadalmi Szemle,* 1974, no. 1.

100. More and more Hungarian researchers attend the congresses of the International Sociological Association. The papers they present are published in Eng-

lish before the congresses; they are active in the working groups and in projects organized by the Vienna-based UNESCO center.

101. The Institute for Social Sciences, which was founded in 1967, became the hub of research on social stratification by the middle of the 1970s. The periodical it published, *Társadalomtudományi Közlemények* (Issues in Social Science), became an important forum. Other noteworthy workshops of sociology were the Research Center for Higher Education, the Institute for Culture Research (founded in 1980), and the Institute for Educational Research (founded in 1981). They too had a periodical of their own: *Kultúra és közösség* (Culture and Community), launched in 1979, which grew to be the most important journal for Hungarian sociology of culture. From 1980 the Research Institute for Mass Media published a periodical entitled *Jel-Kép* (Symbol and Image). The Research Center of Cooperatives (founded in 1967) fostered rural sociology.

102. After becoming an independent institute, the department of sociology of the Faculty of Arts at ELTE University launched a sociology course in 1971. Initially it was an evening course, but in 1972 it became a day course. The postgraduate training of lecturers of sociology started in 1980. Sociology has been taught at the Budapest University of Economics since 1972; the research group for economic sociology started operation in 1980, and training started at the Institute of Sociology in 1980. A department of sociology was set up at the Szeged University in 1979, and at the Pécs University in 1981. At the Debrecen University a sociology group was set up in 1978 and a department of sociology in 1985.

103. The Hungarian Sociological Association was formed in 1978. Its first president was Sándor Szalai.

104. The projects were coordinated by the Institute for Social Sciences. The surveys focused on the following issues: how to measure and classify social differences, how to describe the social strata and evolve a comprehensive model of strata. See: "Stratification Model Investigation. I," Budapest, Institute for Social Sciences, 1982. Rudolf Andorka and István Harcsa, *The Short-Range and Long-Range Modernization of Hungarian Society, Measured by Social Indicators 1870–1984,* 2 vols., Budapest, 1986. University of Economics, Department of Sociology, Research Reports; István R. Gábor and Péter Galasi, *A "második gazdaság": Tények és hipotézisek* (The "Second Economy": Facts and Hypotheses), Budapest, 1981; Elemér Hankiss, *Érték és társadalom* (Values and Society), Budapest, 1977; Hankiss, *Diagnózisok* (Diagnoses), I and II, Budapest, 1982 and 1986.

105. Those were authors who considered the regime as state socialist, a party-state, or a "soft dictatorship," and referred to the "state of workers" as a state that represses its workers. They either retreated into literary sociography or found it impossible to publish in Hungary at all. Some of them published their works abroad or in samizdat form at home in the genre of political essays. István Kemény, "The Unregistered Economy in Hungary," *Soviet Studies,* vol. 3, no. 34, 1982, pp. 349–66; Kemény, "A második gazdaság Magyarországon" (The Second Economy in Hungary), *Magyar Füzetek,* Paris, 1984, no. 13; Kemény, "Hongrie économie et société civile," *L'Autre Europe,* 1987, no. 13, pp. 38–59, Péter Kende, Ed., *A létező kecske. Dialógusok a mozgástérről* (The Existing Goat: Dialogues about the Room of Maneuver), *Magyar Füzetek,* Paris; Iván Szelényi, "The Prospects and Limits of the East European New Class Project. An Auto-Critical Reflection on 'The Intellectuals on the Road to Class Power,' " *Politics and Society,*

vol. 2, no. 15, 1986–1987, pp. 103–44; Szelényi, *Socialist Entrepreneurs: Embour-geoisement in Rural Hungary,* Cambridge, 1988.

106. István R. Gábor, "Reformok, második gazdaság, államszocializmus," *Va-lóság,* 1981, no. 7–8; László Bruszt, "Jogformálás, társadalom és legitimitás" (Law-making, Society and Legitimacy), Institute for Social Sciences, research report, Budapest, 1984; Iván Szelényi and Róbert Manchin, "Piac, redisztribúció és tár-sadalmi egyenlôtlenségek a kelet-európai szocialista társadalmakban" (Market, Redistribution and Social Inequalities in the East European Socialist Societies), *Medvetánc* (Bear Dance), 1988, no. 2–3. See also *Magyar gazdaság és szociológia a nyolcvanas években* (Hungarian Economy and Sociology in the 1980s), Comp. Tamás Miklós, Budapest, 1988; Attila Bicskeházi, "A világképpé kövült ráció mi-tosza" (The Myth of Reason That Turned into a World View), *Valóság,* 1989, no. 8, pp. 52–61.

19

Polish Sociology, 1975–1990: Between Involvement and Detachment

Anna Giza-Poleszczuk

The fifteen years between 1975 and 1990 were by no means the most important ones for Polish sociology. Its empirical as well as theoretical interests and orientations were intimately connected with the course of social and political events. The Sixth Congress of the Polish Sociological Association held in September 1981 was dominated by the problem of the Solidarity movement, and some of its participants came there directly from "Oliwia" hall, where the first Solidarity convention took place. Opening the Eighth Congress of the Polish Sociological Association in September 1990, Antonina Kłoskowska said:

> The Congress we are just opening will have its place in the history of Polish sociology because for the first time in postwar Poland we can say everything we believe to be true, everything we want to, without any external limits. But I would like to stress that this very opportunity entails great and difficult challenges for sociology at the same time. We do not have any historical alibi any more, and no censorship, no external constraint can justify our mistakes, our silence, distortions and limits on what we say. Now the time has come to take responsibility for ourselves, and as citizens we should take responsibility for something more than our discipline, more than our profession.

Periodization of the history of Polish sociology is marked by the events that shaped the postwar history of Poland. The influence of the general situation was both direct and indirect. The direct influence consisted of the political decisions closing and opening sociological faculties, putting limits on sociological research, influencing the possibility of establishing links with the new trends in world sociology, censorship, and establishing the status of intellectuals in the social system. Indirectly it influenced sociological interests, research problems, and the choice of the theoretical frameworks. Sociology—the institutionalized body of practice and thought—as part of the social system, has always been sensitive to its problems.

In Poland both the direct and indirect influences of the social system on sociology were particularly strong: sociologists, in both their professional and civil roles, were much more involved in the course of events than elsewhere.

One should not be surprised by this. Polish sociologists were educated, especially beginning with the 1970s, in the Western sociological tradition. Their view on social reality was shaped by the notions of rationality and modernization forming the mainstream of sociological tradition, and Western societies—their structure and functioning—served as the comparative background for their theorizing and empirical research. They were by necessity the carriers of a specific rationality, which was in sharp conflict with the reality that was the object of their studies and determined their own professional standing. For them the malfunctioning of the recent social system was not only a "scientific" but also a personal problem. They suffered all the disadvantages of belonging to the intellectual class more acutely, precisely because they could see more clearly the reasons and consequences of this flawed system. As a result, their attention focused on two main problems. The first concerned the macrostructural features of socialist society. In a sense, arguments were gathered to prove the necessity of social change. The second concerned the state of social consciousness. In a sense, to paraphrase the well-known notion, the process of changing "society in itself" into "society for itself" was monitored. The most influential sociological works were those examining the "ontology" and/or performance of socialism and those examining the legitimation of socialism.

1975–1980: WAITING FOR THE "INEVITABLE"

In the second half of the 1970s the decline of the Gierek period of prosperity began, together with the decline of its social legitimation. In 1975 Poland was on the eve of the workers' revolt in Radom and at the beginning of the long queues before ever more empty shops. If the Stalin era was marked by omnipresent fear, the Gierek era was marked by an overall feeling of absurdity. As for sociologists, they were faced with three main problems.

Gierek "imported modernization" and the relative opening to the West affected sociology in many ways. Sociologists were much more free to conduct research, to become familiar with the developments of Western sociology and recent sociological literature. Many classics and recent works were translated into Polish (e.g., works of Dahrendorf, Lipset, Bendix, Crozier). Marxism, although still officially present and obligatory, in fact disappeared from the sociological faculties. Sociologists thus got both new theoretical and empirical insight into reality. Gierek, promoting the modernization of Polish industry, created a new labor market for sociologists. Huge industrial enterprises were obliged to employ sociologists and psychologists in order to improve the functioning of work teams and production. Sociologists thus got the opportunity to observe the planned economy "from the inside," and at the same time they experienced their professional uselessness. Nobody needed their expertise and nobody from the industrial management knew what to do with them. Where the organization of work is completely irrational and an enterprise acts under the pressure of the economy of shortage, the "human relations" dimension cannot be improved. Sociologists, who were unable to defend their professional standards of action, in most cases busied themselves with purely administrative work. To see what is going wrong and to be helpless is an unbearable experience. In the circles of "practicing" sociologists, one could observe growing frustration.

The same was true in academic circles. In the late 1970s the academic sociology experienced the "elusiveness" of the society it was trying to describe. Two sets of questions were of special importance: (1) What is the validity of the data gathered by means of surveys? and (2) What are the mechanisms of social stratification in the socialist society?

To understand those questions, one should remember that Polish sociology of that time was dominated by surveys in its empirical dimension and by Western theories of social structure. That society "escaped" measurement and theorizing of that kind was visible in two main classes of facts.

As for measurement by means of the survey, Jacek Kurczewski put the problem clearly by asking: "Does it make any sense to examine public opinion in a society where such a thing does not exist?" It became clear, especially due to the works of the Lodz school (under Jan Lutyński), that Polish respondents reacted strangely toward sociological studies, perceiving them as a way of checking citizens' loyalty or, in a more optimistic version, as a way of gathering material for completely unpractical sociological dissertations. If the respondents' role is defined in such a way, what is the validity of their answers to survey questions?

Polish sociology began to search for new instruments. It is not by accident that in the late 1970s "interpretative" sociology—together with qualitative methods of research—began to gain popularity, especially among the younger generation.

However, the same set of sociodemographic and economic variables which in Western research formed the stable basis of statistical analysis began to lose its explanatory potential in Poland. Not only were the cor-

relations among the variables composing that set more and more insignificant, but in addition they did not explain (in the statistical sense) the
differentiation of beliefs and opinions. As Bogdan Cichomski has put it,
social consciousness together with such "hard" variables as income or
prestige began to "levitate." Neither social structure nor the structure of
opinion and beliefs could be linked to the "classic" demographics. It was
clear to everybody, not only sociologists, that there were social groups in
Poland, mechanisms of social differentiation, systematic inequality—but
they could not be grasped in the stratification categories elaborated in the
West. Later on Włodzimierz Wesołowski offered an answer to that apparent paradox: "Does socialist stratification exist?"

It is not surprising that Polish sociology began to search not only for
new research instruments but for a new theoretical framework as well.
Together with qualitative methodology, the "interpretative paradigm" began to gain more and more adherents. This was possible mainly because
of the relative liberty of communication with Western science: the intellectual crisis of Western sociology in the late 1960s and early 1970s was
"imported" to Poland. The affinity became much more visible in 1980:
like the youth revolt in the West, the Solidarity movement was not predicted by Polish sociology.

The period 1975–1980 was thus marked by the search for a new paradigm, by the growing frustration of sociologists as professionals (and intellectuals generally), and by the growing awareness that the socialist
system needed a new theoretical framework and empirical tools to be
understood and described.

In the period mentioned many important works were written—but not
always published. Some focused on the macrostructural level of the socialist system (Jadwiga Staniszkis, Winicjusz Narojek, Antoni Z. Kamiń-
ski), showing its limits and contradictions. Some focused on the
microstructural level of individual consciousness (Stefan Nowak and his
collaborators), showing its fuzziness and limitation to the level of primary
bonds and loyalties. Both were deeply involved in the recent course of
events in Poland.

One could also observe a generational change. The great generation of
"humanists and sages" like Stanisław Ossowski, Maria Ossowska, Kazimierz Dobrowolski, and Józef Chałasiński was gone. Together with the
strong involvement in social reality and the shortage of recent sociological
literature, the new generation might be responsible for a slight decline in
purely theoretical (academic) sociology. Nonetheless, in the period mentioned many important books were translated and also written in the domain of theory and/or foundations of sociological theory (Antonina
Kłoskowska on the theory of culture, Jerzy Szacki on the history of sociological thought).

At the end of 1970s the atmosphere was clearly one of expectation: as

it was put later, almost everybody felt that "it could not last any longer"—
something was going to happen.

1980–1981: THE RISE AND DECLINE OF A COLLECTIVE DREAM

The input of Polish sociologists to the ideas of the Solidarity movement
was invaluable. It seems that Polish sociologists, as advisers, experts, and
teachers, fulfilled the role Comte had dreamed about: they actively influenced decisions and the course of affairs. They were joined by Western
colleagues conducting research on the Solidarity phenomenon. Solidarity
became the main object of sociological studies, both those adopting macrostructural (as "Self-Limiting Revolution" by Jadwiga Staniszkis) and
microstructural categories (Mira Marody and her team, Ireneusz Krzem-
iński and his collaborators). Thus sociologists offered Solidarity their
knowledge and expertise; Solidarity offered them the unique opportunity
to study social change and a social movement.

Nevertheless, I would risk the thesis that fascination with Solidarity and
the great hopes it brought caused some distortions in the sociological perception of it. Solidarity was conceptualized mainly in value-categories: the
stress was put on its moral dimension (Solidarity ethos), and its ethical
roots. The structural dimension of political conflict, the divisions emerging
inside Solidarity, were largely neglected. The unrealistic view of a mono-
lithic society joined together against the communist regime resulted in
what Jadwiga Staniszkis called the "Titanic complex": the "Titanic is so
beautiful and great that it cannot go to the bottom." The real society—
with its divisions, habits of action, people trying to secure "normal standards of life"—was forgotten. Solidarity, if I may recall the metaphor used
by Bogdan Cichomski, "levitated" over the structure of everyday life. The
situation described was to a certain extent a result of the unpredictability
of what had happened. The Solidarity movement had not been predicted
by any sociological research or theory. As mentioned, socialist society escaped sociological description; on the other side, in the atmosphere of a
collective feast it would be tactless to explain people's behavior in mun-
dane categories of interests. Spiritual motivation—such as searching for
human dignity—fitted much better. Indeed, the experience of social solidarity of that period was absolutely unique.

The main works written in that period—although in some cases they
had to wait to be published—concerned Solidarity.

1981–1989: THE WITHERING AWAY OF COMMUNISM

December 13, 1981, put an end to the dreams of reforming the social
system. It should be stressed here that nobody, sociologists included, ex-

pected the imposition of martial law. I think the lack of "objectivity" in the perception of the Solidarity period was largely responsible for that collective shortsightedness.

The sociological community suffered in martial law like all intellectuals involved in the Solidarity movement: some were interned, later on some were imprisoned because of their activity in the underground Solidarity. Universities and institutes of the Polish Academy of Sciences were closed for some time and then forced to "verify" their scientific staff.

It is not surprising that sociological attention focused on the problems of legitimization and, more generally, on people's reactions to the imposed rule. "Social reality and ways of dealing with it" became the subject of interdisciplinary work. Once more, two main views were adopted to theoretical and empirical studies. On the one hand, social consciousness and values inherent in it—especially religious values—were explored. On the other hand, the structural barriers to solving systemic problems were reconstructed.

It can be said without exaggeration that December 13 was the beginning of the withering away of the socialist system in Poland. For sociologists it was clear that martial law had been the last possible way of securing its position in Poland and that the system could not be reformed, not only because of its internal contradictions but also because of its lack of legitimacy. After the imposition of martial law—identified as an act against the nation—the Party could not mobilize social support any more. Many important works were written in that period displaying the limits of reproducing the socialist system—in the sphere of economy, politics, and legitimacy. The situation was widely recognized as "a stalemate."

The results of sociological research revealed changes in social consciousness. For the first time in postwar history people began to realize that it was the system of collective life—in its economic, political, and social dimensions—and not "the bad will" of the ruling class that was responsible for the state of affairs. The system itself became visible. Along with the feeling of helplessness, Polish society experienced the deterioration of living conditions. The decline of life expectancy—especially for men aged 45 to 54—was the most dramatic manifestation of it. During the same period a lot of young people left Poland, mainly the best educated ones.

The period 1981–1989 brought extensive theoretical and empirical reflection on the socialist society.

First, sociologists began to demystify many facts that previously had been interpreted as indices of acceptation of socialist reality. When interpreted carefully, beliefs about equality revealed the rejection of socialist principles of distribution rather than "egalitarianism." The normative views on social organization turned out to be very similar to those accepted in other societies. Moreover, the patterns of social mobility or marriages were not so different from those prevailing in Western countries. Polish society turned out to be much more "normal" and oriented toward securing "normality" than it had seemed before.

Second, sociological attention began to focus on the people's real behavior, trying to re-create the prevailing patterns of adaptation to socialist reality. Socialism was more and more often perceived as a peculiar set of pressures and fringe opportunities shaping individual decisions. People had to live there, bear and rear their children, work, fall in love, invest in their future and the future of their children. By finding the nexus of pressures and circumstances, individual decisions, habits of action, and beliefs could be understood. "Socialism" began to be perceived as a set of problems people had to cope with, using those opportunities, institutions, and people that were at hand.

From that point of view society was much more real than when purely "ethos" categories were adopted. On the other hand, the image of society emerging from the reconstruction of those everyday solutions and adaptations was not so optimistic. In a sense, the thesis put forward in the 1970s by Stefan Nowak revived. Studying the social affiliations of individuals, he observed a "social vacuum" spreading out between the level of primary groups and the level of nation. There were no social bonds linking individuals to institutions, local communities, or associations. Polish society, Nowak concluded, was "a federation of primary groups." The works written in the 1980s strongly supported that diagnosis. In a society where the initiative of action was state-controlled, spontaneous individualism— or rather particularism—reigned. In a society where the public sphere was inefficient, "amoral familism" served as a means to individual expansion.

The habits of action and thought elaborated under socialism were recognized more and more often as creating a barrier to social transformation. That diagnosis would become important later on, after 1989, when the "legacy of communism" became the subject of research.

The period 1981–1989 brought a lot of important works concerning both the institutional system of socialism and the patterns of everyday behavior.

It could be observed, however, that the memory about the Solidarity period has distorted to a certain extent the view on Polish society: the past experience of being together made it difficult to realize the structures and habits of everyday actions. Viewed from the perspective of the past solidarity, society provided a kind of disappointment: it was not fighting hard enough against the imposed rule.

FROM 1989: SOCIOLOGY IN SEARCH OF SOCIETY

The June 1989 election, which brought the spectacular defeat of Party candidates in the first round, drew away a lot of sociologists from the universities and academies. They entered political and governmental institutions. Together with market reforms, a demand for market research emerged: public opinion and market research companies mushroomed all over the country. Sociological expertise was strongly needed in the various domains of social life. The boundaries have been opened for international cooperation. A lot of Western sociologists have come to Poland to study social transformation. In general, sociology is "in transition" together with changing society. But, as Antonina Kłoskowska observed when opening the last sociological congress in Poland, the new situation creates a great challenge for both sociology and sociologists. We ought to remember that "socialism" as a project for collective life is deeply rooted in the tradition of social thought. Does the implosion of "real socialism" prove anything or solve any of the eternal problems of sociological theorizing? Could it provide us with any new insights, any new understanding of the imperatives of social life? The experience of East and Central European countries has not been thought through sufficiently.

On the other side, recent events in the post-socialist part of Europe create enormous practical problems which have to be solved. One can recall here the original dreams of the sociological vocation embodied in the works of Saint-Simon or Comte: they both believed sociological theory could improve social life, put an end to wars and social injustice, and serve as a basis for an efficient social policy.

Nobody believes it today. Nevertheless, sociologists in Poland have to define anew their place in the social system. The task they have to face is particularly difficult. The economic crisis has its effects on the situation of science and education systems: the universities and academies become empty (e.g., Law Faculty of University of Warsaw has lost 40 percent of its teachers) not only because of the political involvement of scientists but also because of the relative worsening of material conditions and salaries. On the other side, both the isolation from the development of world sociologies and the concentration on the "socialist reality" and strong value-orientation has its results in the theoretical backwardness of Polish sociology, especially in the domain of formal theories. And as we know, the problem of "objectivity" of social science and social scientists is one of the greatest theoretical problems. I do not know whether sociologists in Poland should "as citizens take responsibility for something *more* than their discipline." But I am sure they have to take responsibility for the construction of reality free from ideology and wishful thinking image of what is going on.

BIBLIOGRAPHY

These are some of the main sociological works published in Poland 1975–1990. These are included here for those interested in the contemporary sociology in Poland.

Adamski, W., Jasiewicz, K., Rychard, A. (red.). (1986). Polacy '84. Dynamika konfliktu i konsensusu. IFiS, Warszawa.

———. (1989). Polacy '88. Dynamika konfliktu a szanse reform. IFiS, Warszawa.

Kłoskowska, Antonina. (1980). Kultura masowa. PWN, Warszawa.

———. (1981). Socjologia kultury. PWN, Warszawa.

———. (1991). Przemówienie na otwarcie VIII Zjazdu, w: Przełom i wyzwanie. Pamiętnik VIII Ogólnopolskiego Zjazdu Socjologicznego. Sułek A., Wincławski W., (red.), PTS, Warszawa–Toruń.

Koralewicz, Jadwiga. (1982). Wartości rodzicielskie a stratyfikacja społeczna. Ossolineum.

Mach, Bogdan. Wesołowski Włodzimierz. (1982). Ruchliwość społeczna a teoria struktury społecznej. PWN, Warszawa.

———. (1986). Systemowe funcke ruchliwości społecznej w Polsce. IFiS Publishers.

Marody, Mirosława. (1987). Technologie intelektu. PWN, Warszawa.

———. (ed.). (1991). Co nam zostało z tych lat . . . Polskie społeczeństwo u progu lat 90-tych. Aneks Londyn.

Marody, M., Sułek, A., (red.). (1987). Rzeczywistość polska i sposoby radzenia sobie z nią. IS UW, Warszawa.

Marody, Mirosława, et al. (1981). Polacy '80. IS UW, Warszawa.

Morawski, W., Kozek W. (red.). (1988). Załamanie porządku etatystycznego. IS UW, Warszawa.

Morawski, Witold (red.). (1983). Demokracja i gospodarka. IS UW, Warszawa.

Narojek, Winicjusz. (1976). Społeczeństwo planujące. PWN, Warszawa.

———. (1980). Społeczeństwo otwartej rekrutacji. PWN, Warszawa.

———. (1983). Struktura społeczna w doświadczeniu jednostki. PIW, Warszawa.

———. (1986). Perspektywy pluralizmu w upaństwowionym społeczeństwie. Aneks, Londyn.

———. (1990). Socjalistyczne welfare state. Studium z psychologii społecznej Polski Ludowej. Aneks, Londyn.

Nowak, Stefan. (1979). System wartości społeczeństwa polskiego. Studia Socjologiczne, nr 4, s. 155–173.

———. (red.). (1989). Ciągłość i zmiana tradycji kulturowej. PWN, Warszawa.

Rychard, A., Sułek A., (red.). Legitymizacja. Klasyczne teorie i polskie doświadczenia. PTS, UW, Warszawa.

Siemieńska, Renata. (1984). Polskie systemy wartości i modele konsumpcji. Warsaw University.

Słomczyński, Kazimierz M. (1985). Pozycja zawodowa i jej związki z wykształceniem. IFiS Publishers.

Staniszkis, Jadwiga. (1989). Ontol Staniszkis Jadwiga. (1989). Ontologia socjalizmu, Kryty.

Szacki, Jerzy. (1981). Historia myśli socjologicznej, v. 1–2. PWN, Warszawa.

———. (red.). (1981). Czy kryzys socjologii. Czytelnik, Warszawa.

20

Russian Sociology: Its Origins and Current Trends

Gennady S. Batygin and Inna F. Deviatko

THE SOCIOLOGISM AS ETHOS AND *WELTANSCHAUUNG:* PRELIMINARY NOTES TO CONCEPTUAL FRAMEWORK OF SOVIET SOCIOLOGY

The most striking feature of Soviet sociology appears to be its exceptional influence on public and political life. The history of human community has never known a similar submission to theoretical scheme. The most simple explanation of "the Marxist effect" was proposed by Boris N. Tchicherin, who qualified it as the most colossal example of human stupidity to be found in the history of thought.[1] Even if one doubts Tchicherin's diagnosis, one can hardly deny the fact that a Soviet man's being reminds one of a sociological concept in its development. Therefore, in order to learn the intention of Soviet sociology as an intellectual discipline, we need a sociologism contour, the ethos and outlook of a certain species of human being. Let it be *"homo sociologicus."*

Nikolaj A. Berdyaev, compiling a review of Soviet philosophy, was struck by its social giantism. "Only two lines are available for a man, two completely different standpoints," he wrote.

A man may face God and the Mystery of being and existence.... Then his mind and conscience are pure, then he is favored with revelation and intuition is being granted to him; then he is capable of true first-born creation, then he does find his way to primary source. But man may turn his face to others, to society. Then his mind and conscience can never be pure, then the truth of revelation is being distorted, then religion itself turns into a mere social fact and the sparkling light of intuition dies out, then lie comes to its rights, being considered socially useful and even necessary. Then man is determined by social routine, whether he is a conservator or a revolutionary. . . . So it has to be said that a Marxist-Leninist never does face God and the Mystery of being, he always faces others, the society, the Communist Party Central Committee. . . . This exclusive stand in face of others, the society, this rejection of primary source gives rise to charlatanism, sometimes to a subjectively frank and honest one, which is more or less characteristic of all parties, trends, schools and sects. . . . In Marxist-Leninist outlook this frank and self-sacrificial charlatanism is brought to the point of utter perfection and takes the place of a sacred duty.[2]

Soviet sociology is unique because it brings into life the imperative of Enlightenment millenarianism and—as far as its ample possibilities afford—accomplishes the procedure of "God's Funeral," thus inheriting the Western tradition of critics.[3] It comes into realization through the transposition of the intellectual prejudices of sociology into ethos and a matter of vital interests. This metamorphosis in its madness could be analogous to one of ornithologists learning to fly,[4] and we may state that every ordinary Soviet man-on-the-street would be a sociologist. Of all the dimensions of sociological mentality, our first attention should be given to that of constant readiness *to explain* anything that happens—nothing in the world can escape this immediate and ruthless explanation. Gustav G. Schpet, as he became sure of the fact, remarked that he would have liked to be a Marxist[5]—but naturally he failed.

Standards of sociological ethos are represented in spiritual physiognomies of K. Marx and V. I. Lenin, for whom personality was nothing more than a derivative of the regular development of classes and social groups.[6] The social theory of Marxism discovers here a surprising *Wahlverwandschaft* with "mass revolt" ethos and the practice of life, when ideas, free will, and individual responsibility are said to be a mere reflection of the interests of certain social groups. People were turned into sociological categories. The transformation of life into "social matter," akin to forced reconstruction, makes it possible to operate on human material as analytically as on sociological categories. Thus, the sociological idea of total explanation and mastering of social development laws has been brought by Soviet sociology to epistemic and praxeological limits. Perhaps it is the last, but not the final, contribution to world science made by Soviet sociologists.

Following historiographical canons, we are bound to offer a chronological framework of the birth of Soviet sociology. Its major postulates and thematic programs had been formed long before the October revolution of 1917 when Marxism became the official ideology of the communist regime.

By then Russia had acquired more than a hundred-year tradition of sociological thought. It is represented by the names of Katherine II, N. Ya. Danilevski, K. N. Leontiev, V. S. Solovyov, P. Ya. Chaadayev, N. G.

Chernyshevski, M. A. Bakunin, P. L. Lavrov, N. K. Mikhailovski, S. N. Yuzhakov, N. I. Kareev, G. V. Plekhanov, P. B. Struve, M. I. Tugan-Baranovski, E. V. De Roberti, P. A. Kropotkin, M. M. Kovalevski, N. M. Korkunov, and others.[7]

Although Marx's and Engels's vocabulary was missing the word "sociology," the reception of Marxist ideas was going on within the context of sociological problems. The first attempts to make a sociological synthesis of A. Comte's, H. Spencer's, and K. Marx's concepts belong to N. K. Mikhailovski, founder of the "subjective school" in Russian sociology. In Russian sociological thought, polemics between the representatives of organic, psychological, and materialistic-economic trends were combined with the dominating struggle for learning the universal laws of social evolution, with progressist eschatologism and critical activism of wide scope—from liberal reformism to political terrorism. At any rate, the Russian intelligentsia with its belief in the scientific reconstruction of society became one of the essential premises of the victory of Marxist social outlook.[8] In 1915 J. Hecker made a shrewd remark that Russian sociology represented a theoretical aspect of the Russian people's dynamic progressive forces[9]—the question is, who were these "progressive forces"?

After the revolution of 1917, the sociological thought of Russian liberals was rapidly developing. The books of K. M. Takhtaryov, V. M. Khvostov, V. M. Bekhterev, P. A. Sorokin, S. L. Frank, and L. P. Karsavin were published. M. M. Kovalevski's "Russian Sociological Society," founded in 1916, had irregular sessions, as did the "Sociological Institute" where K. M. Takhtaryov, N. A. Gredeskul, N. I. Kareev, P. A. Sorokin, and others gave lectures.[10] The "Marxist's Scientific Society" (M. V. Serebryakov and N. A. Gredeskul), for the time being, was also peacefully working.[11] In 1922 the "bourgeois professionate" was attacked by the Bolshevist power and the "Rotshtein commission"; since then, non-Marxist sociology ceased to exist in Russia. Many of the intellectuals were deported from the country;[12] the rest were either killed or became adopted to the regime.

LENINIST TRADITION IN SOCIOLOGY AND THE POSTERIOR TERMINOLOGICAL ABERRATIONS

We may take the summer of 1894 for a starting point of Soviet sociology, though neither Lenin nor his opponents could imagine then that sociology might become "Soviet." That very year in polemics with Mikhailovski and other authors of the magazine "Russkoye bogatstvo," Lenin gave a canonic definition of "a scientific method in sociology." The history of Soviet sociology has been developing for almost a century under the sign of this definition:

Just as Darwin put an end to the view of animal and plant species being unconnected, fortuitous, "created by God" and immutable, and was the first to put biology on an absolutely scientific basis by establishing the mutability and the succession of species, so Marx put an end to the view of society being a mechanical aggregation of individuals which allows all sorts of modification at the will of the authorities (or, if you like, at the will of society and the government) and which emerges and changes casually, [Marx] was the first to put sociology on a scientific basis by establishing the concept of the economic formation of society as the sum-total of given production relations, by establishing the fact that the development of such formation is a process of natural history.[13]

Attention should be given to the way in which Lenin's dialectical method is combined with a scientific-organic view of society (such inter-pretation of dialectics occurs only in his early works; after his discovery of Hegel's "Logic," it is never reproduced any more):

What Marx and Engels called the dialectical method—as against the metaphysi-cal—is nothing else than the scientific method in sociology, which consists of re-garding society as a living organism in a state of constant development, . . . an organism the study of which requires an objective analysis of the production re-lations that constitute the given social formation and an investigation of its laws of functioning and development.[14]

Lenin's formulas require further comment. Despite some later collisions inside the Marxist theory, the term "sociology" could not be removed from the conceptual vocabulary. Therefore, information concerning a "ban on sociology" during the Stalin period and in the 1950s has no sufficient foundation.[15] One could only speak of aberrations of sense, connected with the struggle on the "philosophical front." Lenin's interpretation of soci-ology in 1894 was a bit naive, and he could not imagine that "scientific character" would unavoidably come into conflict with the exaltation of class struggle. It is a rational, that is, sociological, argument that dominates in Marxism—but a pure interest; "revolutions do not happen, they are being made," noted Berdyaev.[16] As for sociology in its conceptualized form, it turned out to be incapable of fitting that romantic revolutionary gust because of its inclination toward reasoning and rationalizing. Lenin must have felt this unreliability of "sociology," its hidden opposition to the Party principle, its air of "bourgeois objectivism"—that's why he avoided the word. If he still preserved any illusions about "the scientific approach," they were all finally dispersed in 1909, when A. A. Bogdanov,[17] an influential theorist of Marxism, gave a sociological explanation of ma-terialistic *Dingen an Sich* and suggested an empiriomonistical version of Marxist science, which later developed into "tectology"—the general or-ganizational science.

The Russian intelligentsia in general were obsessed with the idea of the scientific approach. This euphoria reached its peak in the first post–revo-lutionary years. The whole world was regarded as an object for transformation, and sociological ignorance was considered one of the main reasons for its imperfection. P. A. Sorokin used this very argument in emphasizing the necessity of teaching sociological subjects. In 1919 the future president of the American Sociological Association wrote:

It is for our ignorance in the field of social phenomena that up to this time we do not know how to fight the disasters which start in people's social life. We can't make a clever man out of a fool, we can't make a criminal honest, we can't make a loafer industrious. . . . People go on bickering with one another. When we study people's social life properly, when we learn the laws of its functioning, only then may we expect success in our struggle with social disasters.[18]

Within the same course of total sociologism, the sociology of plants' and animals' populations was developing; and Bogdanov, who disassociated himself from the Bolsheviks, was nursing the idea of "physiological collectivism" on the grounds of all-embracing interchangeable blood transfusions. The Psycho-neurological Institute was working out methods of reflexological upbringing,[19] and all that was crowned with faith that the "complete triumph of the proletariat" would establish the "complete triumph of the proletariat" would establish the "complete triumph of pure science."[20]

The sociological version of Marxist theory was advanced in the early 1920s by Bukharin and became an object of hard criticism from Lenin, who left his marginalia in Bukharin's "Economics of Transitional Period." These notes, written in May 1929, remained unknown except to the narrow circle in the Socialist Academy, until Stalin's triumph over Bukharin in 1929.[21] They are of primary importance for understanding the views of the "late" Lenin on sociology; besides, they clarify some theoretical and political reasons for his attempts to stamp the word "sociology" as one already "vulgarized by bourgeois scientists." Lenin felt open antipathy toward all of Bogdanov's "gibberish." He first read Bogdanov's book at the beginning of May; three weeks later he came across another Bukharin work, wherein without effort he discovered traces of organizational-sociological "ideas." We are interested in Lenin's reactions to the words "sociology," "sociological," and so forth. These words were underlined and commented on in Lenin's typical marginalia: "uph!," "ha-ha!," "eclectism!," "help," and so on. A detailed argument in one place leaves no doubt about Lenin's attitude toward the term discussed: "What is good here [on page 84] is that at last Bukharin 'the sociologist' has ironically put the word 'sociologist' into inverted commas! Bravo!"[22]

Afterwards "the red professors" worked a lot in order to oppose Bukharin to Lenin, and it would have been a sin not to use the controversy between Lenin's "Party principle" and Bukharin's "sociology" (and "scientific approach" in general). "Oh, academism! Oh, pseudo-classicism!

Oh, Tretyakovsk!" Lenin used to exclaim ironically while reading Buk-harin's scientific arguments.[23] By then he had already stopped looking back to his own "scientific-sociological" definitions of 1894. Bukharin did not take Lenin's criticism into account, and he made another attempt to work out "the sociology of Marxism" in his book *The Theory of Historical Materialism.* Bukharin's sociological concept emanated from the assump-tion that the "practical task of social reconstruction may be carried out successfully only with the help of a proletarian *scientific* policy, i.e., the policy based on a *scientific* theory of the kind the proletariat has got al-ready—the theory substantiated by Marx."[24] The defeat of Bukharin's "heresy" prompted an active struggle against "abstract sociologism" and "mechanicism" during the 1930s.

"Proletarian sociology" was, truly enough, a chimerical idea. Historical materialism was obliged to hate its own "scientific approach" personified by "sociologist law." The wishes of the proletariat and the Party, its avant-garde, act like laws. Therefore, the sociological theory of "balance be-tween things, people, and ideas" was doomed to become heretical from the very beginning. Sociology in its relation to historical materialism looked like neurotic rationalization as intolerable as the last witness to the design and circumstances of the crime. That is what the Soviet sociological version of *Ressentiment* looks like.

There is one more point of seizure (or of love-enmity, to be precise) of philosophical and sociological impulses in Soviet Marxism.[25] Imagine, on one side, the "dialectics" of which Lenin was such a brilliant master. Flex-ibility, relativity, and imperceptibility of dialectical thought turned histor-ical materialism (in spite of the clarity of its formulas) into something mysteriously unpredictable and esoteric. Here lies the origin of its vocab-ulary, truly analogous to Orwell's "newlang" with its upside-down words claiming for initiation into invisible spheres of party and class struggle. Besides all that, historical materialism appears to be a poetic theory of revolutionary hermitage, with a suffering inability to articulate itself.

But sociology in its striving for the "laws of functioning and develop-ment" makes the very mystery obvious with an air of idiotic sincerity and profanes revolutionary romanticism with rationalized schemes. At the same time, a sociologist may successfully play the role of "Furious Ro-land." Bukharin was just like that. He suggested (logically enough, but with a catastrophic naivete) that if under the conditions of capitalism the proletariat's chief goal was to blow up "the social entity," then the dic-tatorship of the proletariat was aimed at its consolidation. Bukharin was as great a sociologist as Stalin—a dialectitian.

Having exterminated Bukharin's sociological heresy, the A. M. Deborin group soon became an object of political persecution itself. The Debori-ners were called "idealists of Mensheviks style," and "sociology" regained its position in the theoretical vocabulary. In 1936 in the magazine *Pod znamenyem marxisma* it was explained that sociology was nothing but that very Marxist social science and that there were no grounds to consider it vulgarized by bourgeois scientists.[26] Most important of all, it was established that J. V. Stalin happened to use the word "sociology" "in positive meaning."[27] At least, Soviet history knows no repressions against sociologists.

SOCIOLOGY BY THE END OF THE 1940s AND IN THE 1950s

By the autumn of 1946, while plans for new political persecutions were being discussed in the offices of the Kremlin, a new sociological subdivision appeared within the USSR Academy of Sciences Institute of Philosophy, and that was the department headed by Professor M. P. Baskin. According to its reports the program of the department was the following: "At the present moment, when the word 'sociology' is introduced into practice, it is important to throw away the archives' categories of sociology. We must borrow from sociological studies only the flesh and blood of the matter."[28] M. P. Baskin dealt with the study and criticism of foreign sociological concepts and received tremendous support from G. F. Aleksandrov, head of the CC ACP(b) Department of Propaganda, and Yu. P. Frantsev, a high-ranking official in the USSR Ministry of Foreign Affairs at that time. Aleksandrov, Frantsev, and Baskin were actively publishing articles on the analysis and criticism of Western sociological concepts in scientific and political periodicals. P. N. Fedoseyev, chief editor of the Party's theoretical journal *Bolshevik,* was another participant in the group. Baskin's task was to provide "the sociological triumvirate" with review material and to ensure the scientific respectability of publications.

"Criticism of bourgeois sociology" requires some commentary as a genre. It was linked with ideological struggle on the one hand and was strongly influenced by the West on the other. Not taking into account some insulting attacks on the bourgeoisie, we might say that within the limits of the genre, thanks to thorough reviews of foreign literature an intensive reception of Western social thought by the terrified Soviet audience was going on. During not less than four postwar decades, many "critics" were deservedly considered intellectual elites among Soviet social scientists, who were usually rather ignorant. There is no need to explain why the contingent of professional sociologists that was formed in the second half of the 1950s mostly comprised people who knew English.

In 1950 Soviet Marxism adopted a new combination of words—"concrete research." The task was to study "people's real life,"[29] to overcome "dogmatism and talmudism." F. V. Konstantinov in his article formulated the principal question: Is there the danger of slipping into "creeping empiricism"? On the contrary, the author answers (from 1951 he was director of the USSR Academy of Sciences Institute of Philosophy), "theoretical research and concrete research are going to feed one another. It will be sort of a division of labor."[30] Despite the leading directive, "concrete research" never went farther than the organization of philosophical-propagandistic conferences in the leading enterprises; however, some factual information on labor heroism more and more often appeared in scientific articles. It was already empirical sociology. Foreign contacts of philosophy leadership and those who accompanied them played a role of great significance in the formation of Soviet sociology in the 1950s.

In 1956 energetic steps toward establishing cooperation with the Academy of Sciences were undertaken by UNESCO. For the first time, a Soviet delegation (led by P. N. Fedoseyev) took part in the World Congress of Sociology (Amsterdam, August 1956). Sociological problems became points of frequent discussions at "scientific councils," and in the autumn of 1956 a yet unrealistic claim for a sociological journal rang out for the first time. The initiative belonged to M. D. Kammary.[31] In 1957 a discussion on the relations between sociology and historical materialism was started and since then has been going on without visible results. At the International Conference of Sociologists (Moscow, January 1958) the term "sociological research" was sanctified by academic power.[32] To a certain extent it was a propagandistic declaration, designed for Western guests T. Marshall, J. Friedman, P. Hollander, R. Aron, H. Schelski, and others. However, there are sufficient grounds to think that the influence of Khruschev's liberal reforms on the development of Soviet sociology was many times reinforced by Western phraseology. During the period 1957–1961, 217 foreign philosophers and sociologists visited the Institute of Philosophy in Moscow alone.[33] To a certain degree Soviet sociology was produced "for export." Deliberately for export the Soviet Sociological Association was created in June 1958. Speaking of foreign influence, we must emphasize R. Angell's, R. Merton's, T. Parsons's, A. Gouldner's, and recently (June 1991) J. Alexander's contributions to the development of Soviet sociology.

By the beginning of the 1960s, "concrete research" was advanced in the country. A Department of New Forms of Labor and Daily Life Research in the Institute of Philosophy, led by G. V. Osipov, was making a study of Moscow enterprises and labor collectives. A study of Leningrad workers in their attitude to labor was started (V. P. Rozhin). The Urals sociological school (M. N. Rutkievic) must have been of utmost success, for it carried out a large study of industrial enterprises of the Sverdlovsk Council of National Economy (*sovnarkhoz*) and published a book on the cultural and technical development of the working class. This book gained approval and support in high political quarters. The question of the creation of a sociological institution was discussed in academic quarters. The initiative belonged to M. T. Yovtchuk, an experienced and careful ideological functionary who took the Urals school under his special patronage.

KHRUSCHEV'S THAW AND SOCIOLOGICAL CHALLENGE

We are hardly mistaken if we say that sociological reformation was the essence of Khruschev's thaw. In order to speed up the building of communism he needed "new men," and sociologists ought to have created a methodology of their upbringing. It was a convenient moment to capture both ideological and institutional springboards or even to occupy a position in the avant-garde of communist reorganizations. In the 1960s a relatively autonomic development of at least three trends could be observed in sociological thought. The first—the export-imported one—was already mentioned. The second is represented by academician V. S. Nemtchinov and his group of "mathematical economists." Nemtchinov openly declared the ideas of social engineering on the grounds of planned calculations.[34] Thus started mathematical sociology (Yu. N. Gavriletz, A. G. Aganbegian, F. M. Borodkin). The third trend was connected with the theory of "scientific communism" (this specialization was introduced into practice in 1963–1964) and was terrorizing politically unsteady sociologists and working out its own, rather specific sociological programs. "Scientific communism" had no institutional base in the Academy of Sciences (attempts on the part of a "scientific communist," Tz. A. Stepanyan, to prove the necessity of a scientific communism department in the Academy were met with fierce counteraction from president M. V. Keldysh), and "scientific communist" sociology was affiliated by Party structures and departments of social sciences in higher educational institutions. They needed a sociology of their own as a means of total "control and registration." In 1966 at the All-Union Conference on Concrete Sociological Researches in the CC CPSU Academy of Social Sciences, E. M. Tiazhelnikov, future chief of the CC CPSU Department of Propaganda, demanded creating a Party-state structure of sociological centers throughout the Soviet Union[35] and Party quarters regarded sociology as a new, effective way of ideological work. According to the published archives documents, sociology had additional support from the academic leadership; the plan of creating a sociological institution on the basis of Osipov's department in the Institute of Philosophy was being worked out, and Osipov himself was appointed president of the Soviet Sociological Association.[36]

According to official estimation, in 1966 about 2,000 specialists in the Soviet Union were preoccupied with sociological research.[37] By then a certain amount of experience in sociological work had already been obtained. Studies of public opinion and of central newspapers' readers were made (B. A. Grushin, V. E. Shlapentokh); the Leningrad project "Man and His Work" (V. P. Rozhin, A. G. Zdravomyslov, V. A. Yadov) served as a perfect example of methodological work for decades; an active study of professional orientations of schoolchildren was made in Novosibirsk (V. N. Shubkin); an edition of the annual *Social Research* was started, and the sociological library comprised more than several dozen names. Sociology was on the rise.[38]

The beginning of a new period in the development of Soviet sociology dates back to 1968, when the USSR Academy of Sciences Institute of Concrete Social Research (AS ICSR) was founded. Academician A. M. Rumiantsev, the Academy of Sciences vice-president, became its director. During the period 1968–1971, the Institute was working on serious sociological projects which were published in "The USSR AS ICSR Information Bulletins." With a certain amount of relativity this period may be said to be a golden age of Soviet sociology, though the first ideological attack came already in autumn of 1969 when Yu. A. Levada's "Lectures on Sociology" were fiercely criticized.[39] The second show was dedicated to the book *The Modeling of Social Processes.*[40] For one version, partocracy simply could not tolerate the sociologists' liberalism and free thinking. However, the circumstances of the matter were far more complicated than the scheme. With an air of sociological euphoria and enthusiasm many intellectuals were unambiguously declaring the priority of "scientific sociology" over philosophical demagogy. As an alternative to "philosophy," structural-functional analysis and mathematics were put foward. Even the bravest of sociologists never belonged to the dissidents; nevertheless, some were unable to hide an air of scornful superiority over the ideologists. Thus, the attack was not incidental (confrontation occurred not for the reason of Levada's "Lectures"), but it was prompted by a long-accumulated tension between the "intellectuals" and "the Party supporters" and no doubt was organized by high Party elements. Anyway, S. P. Trapeznikov, chief of the CC CPSU Department of Science; N. F. Pilipenko, head of a subdepartment; G. G. Kvasav, a consultant; and particularly V. N. Yagodkin, the secretary of the Moscow City Committee, took part in it.

In 1971 the head of the Institute became M. N. Rutkevich, whom many of the liberals considered an agent of the Party ideological apparatus.[41] Being a man of iron will and stubborn as a bulldozer (as he was called in the lobby), Rutkevich dismissed from the Institute dozens of scientists.[42] We must say that he was not only a convinced and consistent Marxist but also a professional of high qualification and broad knowledge. This fact cannot be denied. Shortly afterwards, Rutkevich with all his natural resoluteness entered into direct conflict with P. N. Fedoseyev, an ideological mentor of the Academy (taking into account that the motive of the conflict could not be compared to the things staked), and was removed from his leading post in 1976. In general, the period of the 1970s and 1980s could be qualified as a time of "sociological diaspora": "the Temple" had been ruined, the Institute of Sociological Research had lost its authority, and separate groups of specialists went on working as far as their mights and possibilities could afford. However, in spite of the defeat and with the exception of Levada, who became a symbol of sociological dissent, the majority of the intellectuals had sufficient status within the academic structure and could publish their works. By the beginning of the 1980s a considerable drop in the number of reports on empirical sociological research was registered—it was nearly halved—and in 1983 only ninety-nine accomplished studies were registered throughout the country.[43]

In 1974 the only Soviet sociological professional journal, *Sociological Studies,* was started. Its editorial board managed to maintain neutrality and to publish essays of sufficient skill at the same time. Its editor-in-chief, A. G. Kharchev, managed to lead the journal through the narrow passage between ideological Scilla and sociological Haribda in the worst of the times, though not without excesses.[44]

From 1976 to 1988 the AS USSR Institute of Sociological Research was working in an atmosphere of fright and professional demoralization. Actually, V. E. Shlapentokh has reasons to call this period "the age of greyness,"[45] but rapid accumulation of methodological experience and formation of a professional community were still going on. V. A. Yadov's group published in Leningrad an excellent monograph on the measurement of value orientations;[46] the school of T. I. Zaslavskaya in Novosibirsk achieved interesting results in the field of system analysis of a Siberian village;[47] the collection of essays "Mathematics in Sociology," issued in Novosibirsk, became widely recognized;[48] genuine sociological works were published in Kiev;[49] and even many of the Moscovites made successful attempts. There is no good without evil, and vice versa. Another characteristic feature of the gloomy Brezhnev times was a deliberate separation of professionals from political activity and assumption of self-contained scientific values (not without a degree of cynicism). That is the difference between the generation of the 1970s and the politically active and ideologically literate sociologists of the 1960s. Political ataraxic played a dominating role in the scientific ethos of a new generation. At that, sociology became associated not so much with bookish knowledge but with distributing questionnaires and counting up the respondents "by noses," in the words of Paul Lazarsfeld. The subsequent events ended in the renovation of both ideological and scientific values of the discipline—in particular, it has been discovered that sociology has no place in theoretical doctrine.

INSTITUTIONAL REFORMS AND "GROUPS OF INTERESTS"

Before 1988, the political reforms of Gorbachev had had little influence on Soviet sociology. It was revealed mostly by means of pseudo-democratic phraseology. Social scientists were searching for ways of accommodation to the new political vocabulary, not doubting the strength of the partocracy, which was going through another painful rotation. Notes of criticism in sociological publications sounded more and more loud, and censorship step by step was exceeding the limits of what was permitted. But questions of research themes and the status of scientific researchers remained under the supervision of the CC CPSU Department of Sciences and of the Department of Philosophy and Law Study directly in the Academy of Sciences. In June 1988 the CC CPSU resolution "About the Increasing of the Marxist-Leninist Sociology's Role in the Solution of the Main Questions of Soviet Society" was passed[50]—the first and probably the last precedent in our history when the communist regime appealed to sociology. As a result of this resolution, "sociology" was separated from "philosophy" within the nomenclature of scientific specialities and the institute acquired the name of the AS USSR Institute of Sociology. For some reason, the public welcomed this change of name as the sign of a disciplinary autonomy, though the situation depended on the change of sociological leadership. V. A. Yadov's appointment to the post of director-organizer may be regarded as a "usurpation of power." Being a man of high professional and moral authority and a liberal by convictions, Yadov had never before entered the scientific-political hierarchy (i.e., nomenclature) and in the recent period had been a leading scientific researcher in the AS USSR Institute of Natural Sciences, History, and Technology in Leningrad. His appointment was an act of major importance in the reorganization of Soviet sociology, and it was prepared by academician T. I. Zaslavskaya, president of the Soviet Sociological Association. Her personal acquaintance with M. S. Gorbachev and her high authority allowed the problem to be solved at the highest level of power. Yadov was appointed "from above" beside the will of social sciences hierarchies in the Academy.

Polarization of interests immediately followed. Rejecting the traditional system of administrating and planning, the director-organizer allowed his employees (by 1989 there were more than 400 persons on the staff of the Institute) to make a free choice of research themes ("projects"). This action substantially weakened the administrative structure of the Institute. The majority of the sociologists prefered Yadov's program. The contingent of those who took the side of Osipov was clearly determined: as a rule, they were interested in renovating socialism and leaving traditional institutional structures untouched. Nevertheless, this sign seems to be of dubious validity. Apparently, the polarization of sociological personnel during the period of "glasnost" should be explained with the help of latent ethico-intellectual dimensions. "The Strange War" broke out. A letter to the CC CPSU may be regarded as its first "shot"—there Yadov was accused of authoritarianism and restriction of creative freedom. The letter was signed by a Dorogovtsev, a man without principles who specialized in ideological activity under the leadership of the Party bureau of the Institute. The letter "accidentally" emerged at the end of 1988 at the bureau session of the Department of Philosophy and Law Study, where Yadov's candidacy to the post of director of the Institute was being discussed. A similar motive appeared in an interview with Osipov, published in January 1990, wherein he remarked (though not mentioning the name of Yadov): "Many of the scientists including sociologists are falling into authoritarianism and they are establishing their authority by whip and cake."[51]

In spring 1989, democratic elections for director of the Institute of Sociology were announced. Yadov's candidacy was the first. Osipov was not put to the vote, but his "camp" put forward four candidates, neither of whom had a real chance to win. Their task must have been to prevent Yadov from polling the majority of votes. But 64 percent of the scientists voted for Yadov, and he became full-right director of the Institute of Sociology for five years.

The "diarchy" situation in the central sociological institution of the country lasted for about two years, until the beginning of 1991. Osipov insisted on the division of the Institute and then a new one was created—the AS USSR Institute of Social and Political Problems. This event institutionalized the distribution by "groups of interest."

These changes had as background a noticeable growth of sociological prestige as well as the struggle for leadership in scientific and political communities. Academician T. I. Zaslavskaya became a recognized leader. She was elected People's Deputy of the USSR and put at the head of the All-Union Public Opinion Research Center, a new kind of institution for the Soviet System. A similar Public Opinion Research Center has been created in the CC CPSU Academy of Social Sciences. It is directed by J. T. Toshchenko. Sociological surveys have become common practice. Substantial changes have occurred in the regional structure of Soviet sociology as well. Baltic sociologists have left the Soviet Sociological Association and have created a self-dependent society. Sharpening of national and political problems has influenced the work of sociological schools not only in Baltic countries but also in Armenia, Azerbaidzan, and Ukraine. Sociologists have been taking an active part in political movements.

Moscow sociologists have got a demand on dominating positions in social sciences. This was evidenced, for instance, by the nomination of candidates for the elections to the USSR Academy of Sciences in the autumn of 1990. Out of 41 applicants to member-correspondents and 8 applicants to members of the Academy, standing for the Department of Philosophy and Law Study, at least 12 were closely connected with sociological science.[52] None of the sociologists, however, has achieved success.

"The Strange War" at the Institute of Sociology was a reflection of a general process of polarization of the scientific community. "Yadov's line" focusing on democratic reforms and the de-ideologization of science received active support from Moscow sociologists of authority who achieved relative independence from power structures. At the same time, the Congress of the Soviet Sociological Association in January 1991 demonstrated that the liberal-democratic wing of Soviet sociologists had not yet consolidated organizationally.

One more trend in the sociological movement at the end of the 1980s and the beginning of the 1990s, which holds the line of Party and academic establishment, should not be qualified as "conservative," for from that time we can also hear constant demands for revolutionary renovation of the society. A more precise definition of this trend would be "ideological sociology." Its stronghold in the Academy of Sciences is guarded by the Department of Philosophy and Law Study and by the Institute of Social and Political Problems. An important role in "ideological sociology" is played by the CC CPSU Academy of Social Sciences, which has mighty resources and carries out mass sociological surveys. In the institutional disposition observed, the sociological faculty of the Moscow University, formed on the basis of a scientific communism department, occupies a peculiar position. In any case, its professoriate in the majority wears a strong mark of its scientific communist past.

Another curious feature of institutional reforms in the field of Soviet social sciences is the tendency to change the names of scientific communism departments in higher educational institutions. Glasnost has caused students' refusal to study the theory of scientific communism, the history of the CPSU, and political economy as obligatory disciplines. Institutes and universities, having acquired a bit of freedom in the compilation of educational programs, lightheartedly agree to social sciences departments' dissolution. About a thousand scientific communism departments under the threat of disappearance and job loss have started a hasty reorganization of curricula and have changed their names to politology and sociology departments. Never in the history of the Soviet Union has there been such a number of politologists and sociologists as there are in 1991—and they are still to multiply.

Rarely will any historian of science take a risk to apply Kuhn's concept of "scientific revolution" to the Soviet sociology. But we may state that in 1989–1990 a "normal" paradigm of Soviet sociology was ruined by one mighty blow. That traditional paradigm was based on intellectual values and self-sufficient sociological erudition, even if a specialist was talking of "practical recommendations." Along with the intellectual dignity, a sociologist's "Olympian" position was supported by his status as a state employee with firm wages. At that, academic employees were not allowed to undertake commercial research. In 1989–1990 academic science rapidly assumed the priorities of the market—it has become obvious that there's nothing to earn at the library. A market for sociological service has formed, dozens of small sociological enterprises have been created, and to sell information for hard currency has become the highest criterion of success. The field of sociological work wherein nonscientific norms and priorities rule may be defined as "gescheft-sociology."

DIVERSIFICATION OF THEMATICAL PROGRAM

Changes in the thematic of sociological research at the end of the 1980s and the beginning of the 1990s were due primarily to ideological circumstances. Soviet sociology after the decades of ideological suppression turned out a scientific paraphrasis of "ideological mind" itself. Like all the maid-servants, *ancilla ideologiae* is very much like its mistress. The conceptual apparatus of the discipline, its scientific inference schemes, its rhetoric—all that duplicated the Party's political stereotypes and depended on officially declared ideologems. Perestroika's phraseology was immediately caught up by sociology's conceptual vocabulary. Questions taken from a questionnaire such as: "Did you manage to rebuild yourself in time?" represent the idiotic side of this metamorphosis, but reproduction of ideologically spoilt schemes of sociological thought is still going on. A classic example of such a scheme is represented in a questionnaire worked out in the Institute of Sociological Research in 1987:

What of the country's current issues are of your greatest concern?

• Speeding up the social and economic development
• Growth of people's wealth level
• Reorientation of social consciousness of the people
• Further development of democracy, of civil and political liberties
• Education of people in the spirit of communist consciousness
• Improvement of mutual national relations
• Struggle against bourgeois ideology
• Molding of people's political culture
• Rooting out the survivals of past from people's life and behavior
• Other (write yourself)[53]

This "write yourself" shows the inmost pursuit of the Party's inquest, and clinical symptoms of sociology on the whole are to be found in its vocabulary. Among other scientific problems, the 1991 research plan of the Institute of Sociology includes the following: "New way of thought—social and ideological problems of its assertion," "Glasnost under the conditions of perestroika: Premises for development and hampering factors," "Man in the labor collective under the conditions of perestroika," and so on.[54] Even when explorers are ready to keep to the criteria of scientific respectability, thematic programs are applied to social and political conjuncture.

The policy of glasnost has freed the press from censorial restrictions, thus providing every possibility to sociological publicism. Traditional statements of the Soviet Marxism about the class structure of society, the "planned" character of its social and economic development, the leading role of the Communist party, "cooperation and flourishing of Soviet nations," and the like have become objects of critical attack. In 1988 "Progress Publishers" started publication of the series "Perestroika, glastnos't', demokratiya, sotsialism," wherein new sociological ideas found their reflection. The first book of the series, "No Other Way," appeared against the will of ideological quarters and had great influence on the intelligentsia. For Soviet sociology its value is defined, in the first place, by its resolute attack against the traditional concept of the social structure of society (working class, collective farms' peasantry, plus intelligentsia). T. I. Zaslavskaya rejected the "motion toward social uniformity" postulate and advanced a multifactorial stratificational model. A typology of social groups in their connection with perestroika, described by Zaslavskaya, has gained wide recognition: according to her survey, advanced workers, collective farmers, political and economic bosses, and humanitarian intelligentsia are initiators, supporters, and allies of perestroika; and those responsible for directing, unreasonably privileged workers, and representatives of organized criminality are conservators and reactioners.[55]

New sociological ideas on the ways of development of Soviet society are represented in the following books of the "Progress Publishers" series: *Comprehension: Sociology, Social Politics, Economic Reform,*[56] *Economic Sociology and Perestroika,*[57] and in a monograph wherein an attempt is made to translate the ideas of the ruling democracy of industry into the language of sociological variables.[58] By the end of the 1980s, "economic sociology" came to be a leading trend in Soviet sociology. Its range of problems is not limited by the fields of labor and production control, of social structure and economic behavior. It would be better to define it as a concept of Soviet society in its development, connected with the intellectual style of the Novosibirsk school. Anyway, "economic sociology" acts like the center of gravity of an "invisible college," which determines nowadays the Soviet sociological community's dynamics and thematic priorities of prestige.

Diagnosis of the modern social and political situation—that's what is in the focus of the sociologists' attention. An example of such diagnosis is a collection of articles, "The Society under Different Dimensions," wherein various screen scripts of perestroika are represented.[59]

A separate position in the disciplinary structure of Soviet sociology is occupied by the area of *public opinion studies.* Its thematic scope usually encompasses learning the political sympathies of the population, conducting the leaders' popularity rating research, investigating the people's attitude toward various programs on how to find a way out of the crisis, and exploring the problems of international relations. In this field research standards are worked out by the All-Union Center of Public Opinion Studies, where methodologists and theorists of high skill do their work and their analytical reviews are regularly published. The distinguishing feature of the Center's intellectual style is its combination of permanent polls technology of the all-Union sample network (a sample's average size is about 2,000–5,000 respondents) with theoretical work on the nature and functioning of public opinion in Soviet society.[60]

At the same time, mass surveys are actively organized by the Public Opinion Research Center at the Institute of Sociology[61] (judging by publications, in February 1989 a record amount of responses was collected here—1.2 million from people in Moscow and Kuibyshev); by the CC CPSU Public Opinion Center at the Academy of Social Sciences; by sociological services of newspapers and magazines; and by independent firms which do it on commercial terms. In 1990 a firm of this kind named "Vox Populi" was founded by B. A. Grushin.[62]

Since the 1960s the field of utmost prestige in sociology was considered the *methodology of research.* The methodologists' professional level was much higher than that of "average" Soviet sociologists, and ideological dictates in this field acted irregularly. During the period 1974–1988, the methodological department of the journal *Sociological Studies* held priority by its number of publications.[63] That was the only possibility left to follow professional priorities. In 1988–1989 the journal leadership was passed to "ideologists," and soon it acquired a distinct "conjunctural" line. By the end of the 1980s "methodological sociology" lost its superior position. Under the circumstances of perestroika and commercialization of science this specialty has become economically ineffective, and nowadays serious publications on the methodology of sociological research appear only occasionally. A compendium of data collection methods,[64] published in 1990, looks like a mausoleum of systematic methodological work. An essay on the interpreting of data,[65] written by one of the best Soviet methodologists, Victor Moin, was published at the very moment when the author received an immigration visa to Israel. In 1991 at the Institute of Sociology an attempt was made to reanimate methodological specialization in sociology and to create a new journal on mathematical methods and modeling. But it is still just a project.

History of sociology is sufficiently separated from the other social sciences trends. The History of Western Sociology Department at the Institute of Sociology (led by Ju. N. Davydov) is specialized on the preparation of monographs on the history of social thought; during the 1980s the main tendencies in Western sociology were regarded here from the point of view of "Weber's Renaissance,"[66] not without the influence of T. Mommsen, W. Schlüchter, and other German Weberists. In 1989 work on an academic edition of classical sociological studies of Western and Russian scientists was started. In 1990 selected works of M. Weber and S. N. Bulgakov were published; in 1991 E. Durkheim's and P. Sorokin's writings are coming; and H. Spencer's, W. Sombart's, and G. Simmel's editions are in project. It will take many years to overcome theoretical literature's isolation of Soviet sociology and to build up the Russian sociological library.

Theoretical and methodological research is now in a dubious position. Since the end of the 1980s, leaden conceptual schemes of Soviet Marxism have not only lost their cognitive interest but look rather unbecoming on the background of the generally critical state of mind. An attempt to surround the "materialistic view of history," "objective laws," and a lot of empirical data with a pseudo-human ornament is represented in a fundamental monograph under the simple name of *Sociology*.[67] Marxism as the only scientific sociology and its adjoining standpoint, mentioned by Berdyaev in 1932, should be at the end of its adaptational resources.

Much imagination is needed to discern within the conglomerate of Soviet sociology the symptoms of theoretical-methodological trends: positivism, structural functionalism, phenomenology. The theoretical affiliation of professionals depends to a great extent on their capacity to analyze data (one who knows how to count percentages is nearly a positivist) or their taste for rhetoric (a sign of phenomenological preferences). One who has neither analytic, nor artistic talents finds himself in system construction. Evidently, theoretical pluralism of such a kind is already developing in Soviet sociology.

In order to complete our panorama of sociological trends in the former Soviet Union, we must mention numerous local studies in the industrial enterprises and in the regions. They are carried out mostly by amateurs, and this "parasociological" line together with the "gescheft sociology" becomes more and more noticeable.

CONCLUSION: ON THE PHILOSOPHY OF SOVIET SOCIOLOGICAL RESEARCH

We believe that during the last decade of the twentieth century Soviet sociology will be developing under the sign of growing diversification. Diversification will show itself, first, in the appearance of numerous sociological institutions, which will be busy collecting and organizing current political information. The market is going to form new demands for sociological personnel, and thousands of scientists will leave libraries for the sake of "field research." However, we are interested in the fate of the academic sociology that creates epistemic standards for the discipline. Analyzing the content of sociological publications during the period of glasnost, D. Shalin has discovered a curious taste on the part of Soviet sociologists for disclosure of totalitarianism's horrors. Taking a famous admission that sociological research may develop only under the conditions of a certain political system (i.e, a democracy) for a starting point, he makes a conclusion about the sociological Renaissance of the Gorbachev reformation period.[68] A certain analytical skepticism should not prevent us from understanding the origin of supercriticism as a metamorphosis of power—or, to be precise, a claim to power. At any rate, the hypothesis of the alliance of sociology and power is too smart to be true. It could be more useful to recall the alliance of German empirical sociology of the 1930s and the "third reich." S. L. Frank wrote "The Essay of Methodology of Social Sciences" during the period of dictatorship of the proletariat. Hence, substantially different imperatives do act within the depth of sociology itself, waiting for their time to come. No doubt Soviet sociologists will soon master both LISREL and TETRAD. It is a question of technique. It is not so easy to master the art of respectful treatment of truth, which is not indifferent to the fact of who approaches it. The ethos of a scholar demands not only pure conscience, pure mind, and schoolish diligence but also a transcendental urge toward things as they are. J. Mathisen expressed this demand by a simple question: "Could I be a Christian and at the same time a sociologist?"[69]

In order to find the way to itself, sociology should overcome itself. On the other hand, the creation of an ethical-intellectual tradition in science is very much like that of lawn-raising in England: once the grass is sown, it has to be cultivated for a hundred years.

NOTES

We express gratitude to Marina A. Georgadze for the translation of this chapter. Since this chapter was written, there have been changes in the former Soviet Union. Among these are the renaming of educational institutions. For example, the USSR Academy of Sciences is now called the Russian Academy of Sciences, among others.

1. Boris N. Tchicherin, *Istoriya politicheskikh uchenij* (The History of Political Thought), Part 5 (Moscow: I. N. Kushnerev and Co., Publishing House, 1902), 228.

2. Nikolaj A. Berdyaev, *Generalnaya liniya sovetskoy philosophii i voinstvujustchij ateism* (The General Line of Soviet Philosophy and Militant Atheism) (Paris: YMCA Press, 1932), 7–8.

3. Michael Harrington, *The Politics at God's Funeral: The Spiritual Crisis of Western Civilization* (New York: Holt, Rinehart and Winston, 1983), 174–196.

4. The authors owe this extraordinary metaphor to Professor Vladimir Yadov.

5. Gustav G. Schpet, *Otcherk rasvitija russkoj philosophii* (An Essay on Russian Philosophy Development) (Petrograd: Kolos, 1922), ix.

6. Sergey Bulgakov wrote: "Elimination of personality problem is the main trait of marxism." Sergey N. Bulgakov, *Karl Marx kak religiosniy tip* (Karl Marx as a Religious Type) (Paris: YMCA Press, 1929), 9.

7. A brief but informative review of Russian sociology of the nineteenth and the beginning of the twentieth century is represented in Julius Hecker, *Russian Sociology* (New York: Augustus M. Kelley Publishers, 1969). The earlier period is represented in Alexander S. Lappo-Danilevsky, *Istoriya russkoy obshchestvennoj mysli i kuitury* (The History of Russian Social Thought and Culture, XVII–XVIII Centuries). (Moscow: Nauka, 1990).

8. Hecker, op. cit., 286.

9. An account of spiritual and moral seekings of the Russian intelligentsia in a pre-revolutionary period can be found in the following collections of essays: *Problemy idealisma* (The Problems of Idealism) (S. Petersburg: Moscow Psychological Society, 1902); *Vekhi* (Landmarks: The Essays of Russian Intelligentsia) (Moscow: Sablin's Publishing House, 1909).

10. Pitirim A. Sorokin, "Sostoyaniye russkoy sotsiologii za 1918–1922" (The State of Russian Sociology in 1918–1922), *Novaya russkaya kniga* (New Russian Book. Monthly journal of critics and bibliography) (Ladyzhnikov's Publishing House, 10, 1922), 7–10.

11. I.V. Znamenskaya and M. A. Kudryavtsev, "Nautchnoye obshchestvo marxistov Petrograda-Leningrada" (The Scientific Society of Marxists in Petrograd-Leningrad), *Istoki. Voprosy istorii narodnogo hoziaystva i ekonomicheskoy mysly* (The Sources: Problems of History of Economics and Economic Thought), vol. 1. (Moscow: Economics, 1989), 331–35.

12. Vadim V. Sapov, "Vysylka 1922 goda: popytki osmysleniya" (Deportation of 1922: Attempts to Investigation), *Socio-gicheskiye Issledovaniya* (Sociological Studies) 3, 1990, 112–14.

13. Vladimir I. Lenin, *Collected Works* (Moscow: Foreign Languages Publishing House, 1963), 142.

14. Ibid., 165.

15. Nikolay V. Novikov, "The Sociological Movement in the USSR (1960–1970) and the Institutionalization of Soviet Sociology," *Studies in Soviet Thought* (Dordrecht–Boston: Reidel Publishing Co.), vol. 23, no. 2, February 1982, 142.

16. Berdyaev, op. cit., 11.

17. Alexander A. Bogdanov, "Strana idolov i philosophia marxisma" (The Land of Idols and the Marxist Philosophy), *Otcherki po philosophii marxisma* (The Essays on Philosophy of Marxism) (S. Petersburg: V. Bezobrazov and Co., 1908), 215–42. Alexander A. Bogdanov, *Tektologia. Vseobshchaya organizatsionnaya nauka* (Tectology: The General Organizational Science) (Berlin–Petersburg–Moscow: Z. Grzhebin's Publication, 1922).

18. Pitirim A. Sorokin, *Obshchedostupnyi utchebnik sociologii* (The Handbook on Sociology for Common Uses) (Yaroslavl: The Yaroslavl' Union of Cooperatives for Mutual Credit, 1920), 19.

19. Vladimir M. Bekhterev, ed., *Voprosy izutcheniya i vospitaniya lichnosti* (The Questions of Exploration and Upbringing of Personality), vol. 4–5 (Petersburg: Gosizdat, 1922). Bekhterev, *Kollektivnaya reflexologiya* (The Collective Reflexology) (Petrograd: "Kolos" Pub., 1922).

20. Eugeny A. Engel, *Otcherki materialisticheskoy sotsiologii* (The Essays on Materialistic Sociology) (Moscow: A. D. Frenkel Publishers, 1923), 4.

21. *Leninskij sbornik, XI* (Lenin's Collections) (Moscow–Leningrad: The Lenin's Institute of All-Union Communist Party–Bolshevics, 1929), 348–402.

22. Ibid., 369.

23. Ibid., 385.

24. Nikolaj I. Bukharin, *Teoriya istoricheskogo materialisma. Popularnyi utchebnik po istorii sotsiologii* (The Theory of Historical Materialism: Popular Manual on History of Sociology) (Moscow: Gosizdat, 1921), 8.

25. Nikolaj Karev, "Itogi raboty i zadatchi v oblasti teorii istoritcheskogo materialisma" (The Total of Work and Current Tasks in the Field of Historical Materialism), *Pod Znamenyem marxisma* (Under the Banner of Marxism) 5, 1930, 25–35.

26. Fyodor V. Konstantinov, "Sotsialisticheskoye obshchestvo i istoritcheskij materialism" (The Socialist Society and Historical Materialism), *Pod Znamenyem Marxisma* 2, 1936, 47–48.

27. Josef V. Stalin, *Ob oppozitsii* (On opposition) (Moscow: Gosizdat, 1928), 532.

28. The USSR Academy of Sciences Archives. Fund 1922, inventory 1, file 214, 14.

29. "Life" and "practice" are the metaphors of major significance for Marxists. Sergei Bulgakov wrote: "The last saying of street philosophy and the last recipe of solution of all the philosophical questions has been an invitation to cover oneself with mud of life." Bulgakov, op. cit., 12.

30. Fyodor V. Konstantinov, "Protiv dogmatizma i natchetnitchestva" (Against Dogmatism and Talmudism), *Voprosy philosophii* (The Questions of Philosophy) 3, 1950, 110.

31. *Voprosy philosophii* 4, 1957, 223.

32. Piotr N. Fedoseyev, "Problema mirnogo sosushchestvovaniya v sotsiologicheskikh issledovaniyakh i prepodavanii sotsiologii" (The Problem of Peaceful Coexistence in Sociological Research and Teaching of Sociology), *Voprosy philosophii* 4, 1958, 3–14.

33. The USSR Academy of Sciences Archives, 499, 1, 669, 77.

34. Vasily S. Nemtchinov, "Sotsiologitcheskij aspect planirovaniya" (The Sociological Aspect of Plan-making), *Voprosy philosophii* 10, 1959. The idea of social engineering for the first time was proclaimed in Nemtchinov's report "Sociology and Statistics," *Voprosy philosophii* 6, 1955, 19–30.

35. *Problemy nautchnogo kommunisma* (The Problems of Scientific Communism), vol. 2 (Moscow: Mysl Publishers, 1968), 8.

36. There are essential doubts about evidences published by G. V. Osipov under the title "Sociological Drama in Two Actions," *Vestnik Akademii nauk SSSR* (The Messenger of USSR Academy of Sciences) 1, 1990, 119–28.

37. "Razvitiye issledovanij v oblasti obshchestvennykh nauk" (The Develop-

ment of Studies in the Field of Social Sciences), *Vestnik Akademii nauk SSSR* 5, 1956, 15.

38. The state of Soviet sociological studies of the 1960s is represented in: E. Weinberg, *The Development of Sociology in the Soviet Union* (London: Routledge and Kegan Paul, 1974); Joseph S. Roucek and Raj P. Mohan, "Contemporary Sociology in the Soviet Union," Raj P. Mohan and Don Martindale, eds., *Handbook of Contemporary Developments in World Sociology* (Westport, Conn.: Greenwood Press, 1975), 287–301; Vladimir E. Shlapentokh, *The Politics of Sociology in the Soviet Union* (Boulder: Westview Press, 1987).

39. Yury A. Levada, *Lektsii po sotsiologii* (Lectures on Sociology) (Moscow: The Institute of Concrete Social Research, 1969).

40. Edvard P. Andreyev and Yuri N. Gavriletz, eds., *Modelirovaniye sotsialnykh processov* (The Modeling of Social Processes) (Moscow: Nauka, 1970).

41. This point of view is represented, for example, in: Novikov, op. cit., 46. Dmitry Shalin considers M. Rutkevich to be a "veteran of many ideological pogroms." Dmitry N. Shalin, "Sociology for the Glasnost Era: Institutional and Substantive Changes in Recent Soviet Sociology," *Social Forces* 68, no. 4, 1990, 1019–39.

42. In a personal interview in March 1991, Michail N. Rutkevich said that "the situation was predetermined." Nevertheless, several well-skilled professionals preserved their positions in the Institute (I. Bestuzhev-Lada, Yu. Davydov, V. Shlapentokh).

43. *Empiritcheskiye sotsiologicheskiye issledovaniya v SSSR. 1981–1982* (The Empiric Sociological Surveys in the USSR, 1981–1982) (Moscow: Institute of Sociological Research, 1985), 2.

44. G. Batygin (one of the editors in the 1980s) has evidence of the censorship meddling in practically every issue of the *Sotsiologicheskiye issledovaniya* journal.

45. Shlapentokh, op. cit., 57.

46. Vladimir A. Yadov, ed., *Samoregulatsiya i prognozirovaniye sotsialnogo povedeniya lichnosti* (The Self-Regulation and Anticipation of Social Behavior of Personality) (Leningrad: Nauka, 1979).

47. Tatiana I. Zaslavskaya, "K metodologii sistemnogo izutcheniya derevni" (Toward the Methodology of System Research of Village), *Sotsiologicheskiye issledovaniya* 3, 1975.

48. Abel Aganbegian, Hubert Blalock, et al., eds., *Matematika v sotsiologii* (Mathematics in Sociology. Model-Constructing and Data-Processing) (Moscow: Mir Publishers, 1977).

49. V. Chernovolenko, V. Ossovsky, and V. Paniotto, *Prestizh professiy i problemy sotsialno-professionalnoy orientatsii molodyozii* (The Prestige of Occupations and the Problems of Youth's Social and Professional Orientation) (Kiev: Naukova dumka, 1979).

50. "O povyshenii roli marksistsko-leninskoy sotsiologii v reshenii uzlovykh problem sovetskogo obshchestva" (About the Increasing of the Marxist-Leninist Sociology's Role in the Solution of the Main Questions of Soviet Society: Resolution of the Central Committee of CPSU), *Sotsiologicheskiye issledovaniya* 5, 1988, 3–5.

51. "Moltchali ne vse" (Not Everyone Was Silent), *Vestnik Akademii nauk SSSR* 1, 1990, 120.

52. The list of applicants for the Academy of Sciences election can be found in: *Vestnik Akademii nauk SSSR* 11, 1990, 129 and 153–54.

53. *Kompleksnaya programma sotsiologicheskogo issledovaniya "Problemy sotsialnogo razvitiya sovetskoy intelligentsii. . . "* (The Complex Program for the Sociological Research "The Problems of Social Developments of Soviet Intelligentsia. . . " Questionaire) (Moscow: Institute of Sociological Research, 1987), 42–43.

54. *Institut sotsiologii* (The Institute of Sociology) (Moscow: Institute of Sociology, 1990), 14–24.

55. Tatiana I. Zaslavskaya, "O strategii socialnogo upravleniya perestroikoy" (Toward the Strategy of the Social Control over the Perestroika), *Inogo ne dano* (No Other Way) (Moscow: Progress, 1988), 39.

56. Fridrich M. Borodkin, Leonid Ya. Kosals, et al., eds., *Postizheniye. Sotsiologiya, sotsialnaya politika, ekonomicheskaya reforma* (Comprehension: Sociology, Social Politics, Economic Reform) (Moscow: Progress, 1989).

57. Tatiana I. Zaslavskaya, ed., *Ekonomicheskaya sotsiologiya i perestroika* (The Economic Sociology and Perestroika) (Moscow: Progress, 1989).

58. Inna V. Ryvkina and Vladimir A. Yadov, eds., *Sotsialno-upravlencheskiy mekhanism razvitiya proizvodstva* (Social and Managerial Mechanism of Production's Developments) (Novosibirsk: Nauka, 1989).

59. Leonid A. Gordon and Edward V. Klopov, eds., *Obshchestvo v raznykh izmereniyakh. Sotsiology otvechayut na voprosy* (The Society under the Different Dimensions: Sociologists Answer Questions) (Moscow: Moskovsky rabochiy, 1990).

60. Yury A. Levada, ed., *Yest' mnenie. Itogi sotsiologicheskogo oprosa* (There Is Opinion: The Results of Sociological Survey) (Moscow: Progress, 1990).

61. Vilen N. Ivanov, "Utverzhdeniye novogo politicheskogo myshleniya" (The Establishing of the New Sociological Mind), *Sotsiologicheskiye issledovaniya* 2, 1991, 7.

62. See, for example, Vladimir Boykov and Jan Toshchenko, "Mneniya delegatov 28 s'ezda KPSS" (The Opinions of Delegates at the 28th Congress of the Communist Party), *Sotsiologicheskiye issledovaniya* 11, 1990, 99–104.

63. Dina D. Raikova, "Sotsiobybliometricheskiy analis zhurnala 'Sotsiologicheskiye Studies" Journal), *Sotsiologiche issledovaniya'* " (Sociobibliometrical Analysis of the "Sociological Studies" Journal, *Sotsiologicheskiye issledovaniya* 1, 1991, 77.

64. Vladimir G. Andreyenkov and Olga M. Maslova, eds., *Metody sbora sotsiologicheskoy informatzii* (The Methods of Sociological Data Collection), 2 vols (Moscow: Nauka, 1990).

65. Victor B. Moin, "Alternativnaya interpretatziya dannykh: atributivnyi podkhod" (The Alternative Data Interpretation: Attributive Approach), *Sotsiologicheskiye issledovaniya* 11, 1990, 62–71.

66. Vilen N. Ivanov and Yury N. Davydov, eds., *Burzhuaznaya sotsiologiya na iskhode XX veka* (The Bourgeois Sociology in the End of the Twentieth Century) (Moscow: Nauka, 1986).

67. Gennady V. Osipov, et al., *Sotsiologiya* (Sociology) (Moscow: Mysl, 1990).

68. Shalin, op. cit., 1034.

69. James Mathisen, "The Origin of Sociology: Why No Christian Influence," *Christian Scholar Review* 19, no. 1, 1989, 49.

Part IV

Sociology in Southern Europe

As attention turns to Southern Europe, the Northern European–North American axis in the formation and institutionalization of sociology is seen even more critically. This region, abutting the Mediterranean Sea, has been a caldron of changing programs of domination. Ancient Greek and Roman influences once swept the region. In the wake of Rome's domination, the Holy Roman Empire and its successor system, the Roman Catholic Church, emerged, as did the oppositional Greek Orthodox Church in the East. Islamic influences also swept the region. Even today, uneasy relationships exist between nations hosting predominantly Christian populations, such as Greece, and neighboring countries which are the home of large numbers of followers of Islam, such as Turkey. And some of the adjacent countries such as Bulgaria and the former Yugoslavia were, until recently, in the orbit of influence of the former Soviet Union. Three European countries manifest the development of sociology: Greece, Italy, and Spain.

In the twentieth century, Greece has been involved in conflicts involving in various ways Russia and Turkey. In the post–World War II era the conflict in Cyprus over Orthodox versus Islamic influence was intense. So too were political intrigues which projected Greece into conflicts related to the cold war between the United States and the former Soviet Union. Without any substantial foundation prior to World War II, George Kourvetaris reports, sociology did not find a receptive home in Greece. Even today its institutional identity is frequently indistinct from social work and other social activist concerns. It does not enjoy an independent identity in most of Greek public higher education.

Sociology in Greece is an emergent subject due in part to the growth of other institutional opportunities, such as with the Center for Social Research and the Center of Planning and Economic Research. In a recent study it was found that Greek sociologists were exploring a standard range of specialty topics. Still, sociology in Greece confronts a number of obstacles, some institutional and others geopolitical.

Italian sociology is discussed by Franco Ferrarotti in terms of the activities in prefascist and postfascist Italy. Ferrarotti sees the debate between Croce and Pareto at the turn of the century as the watershed event. Though apparently more bitter, the debate was similar to the *Methodenstreit* controversy raging in Germany during the same epoch. But whereas in Germany the nature of social science as a natural or cultural science was the dividing issue, Ferrarotti reports that Croce's criticisms were more venomous, questioning the very possibility of social science. This is seen as compatible with the fascist criticisms of social science in later generations. Although the postfascist age has been more receptive to sociology, Italy, Ferrarotti reports, remains inhospitable to the discipline. Sociology is confused with socialism, whereas intellectual life is dominated by what is described as "artistico-prophetic intuition," a style which shuns this-worldly interests.

Because Croce looms so large over the intellectual landscape, efforts to establish an intellectual wedge came through efforts such as those of Antonio Gramsci. One senses in Ferrarotti's review that the nature of Italian life contributes significantly to some lack of disciplinary focus. A diverse nation, characterized by a cosmopolitan, industrial north and a less developed south, means that the way in which various facets of Italian life relate to local, regional, and global concerns is quite varied. As a result, sociological attention does not reveal consistency in reporting and analyzing various micro- and macro-links. Meanwhile, various migration waves and communities have, until late, eluded attention, labor has received some attention, though in a way more in harmony with Fordism than other traditions.

In his discussion of systems theory, Ferrarotti shows that Italian sociology through figures such as Achille Ardigo is resonating with international works, such as those of Germany's Niklas Luhmann and the neofunctionalist project of North America's Jeffrey Alexander. In another vein, works such as those of Luciano Gallino reveal some reception to sociobiology. Ferrarotti himself has entered into the discussion about criteria for sociological theory and practice with his historically sensitive program for a revised positivism.

Traversing from the northeastern shores of the Mediterranean to the northwestern ones, one comes upon Spain. In Spain, Carlota Solé reports, the institutionalization of sociology has been growing since the 1960s. A number of texts appeared during the 1970s. Sociology's intrusion into academic affairs became more pronounced in the 1980s. An area attracting attention, Solé reports, is the sociology of knowledge along with general interest in subfields such as theory, methodology, political sociology, social stratification, social change, and medicine.

21

Social Science with the Emphasis on the Present Status of Sociology in Greece

George A. Kourvetaris

INTRODUCTION

The purpose of this chapter is to give a brief account of the development and present status of sociology in Greece, and to some extent that of the other social sciences there.[1] The overriding feature of sociology and its subsequent inception both as an academic discipline and as a research enterprise is one of interrupted and fragmented development. Although sociology emerged early, at the turn of the twentieth century, in Greece, only recently can one find a genuine effort to institutionalize sociology in Greece. In the past, sociology was not able to establish legitimacy, let alone a broader sociological base that could be used as a "frame of reference" by future Greek sociologists, similar to the ones in place in other European countries and the United States. The academic community in modern Greece has been and still is, above all, national. It has not succeeded in developing a broader intellectual base.

The development of sociology and its present status in Greece must be seen in the context of the processes of legitimation of social science in general and the increasing rationality of the Greek social structure in the last thirty or so years. It is within this time span that Greek society has undergone (and still is undergoing) rapid changes, moving from a society basically bounded by tradition until the 1950s, to one developing more along the West European and American models.

In 1981, Greece became a full member of the European Economic Community (EEC). The twelve member nation-states of the EEC are working to implement a free common market. Sociology and other social sciences will play an important role in the processes of European economic and political integration. Greece no longer can afford to ignore the contributions of sociology and other social sciences in these processes. My argument throughout this analysis will be the growing need for Greece to develop along the European and American models of rationality and organization. To be able to compete with its European partners it needs the empirical and theoretical contributions and insights of sociology and other social sciences in general. Greece needs sociology more than sociology needs Greece.

EMERGENCE OF SOCIOLOGY

In the past, sociology in Greece commenced both as a social reform movement (as in the United States) and somewhat as an outgrowth of the German tradition of philosophy and folklore studies. While both folklore and sociology were introduced during the same period (1908–1909) in Greece, one can discern different developments. The study of Greek folklore, founded and introduced by the German-educated Greek scholar Nicholas Politis, was more readily accepted in Greece because it was patriotically inspired. The first chair in folklore was established in 1926 at the University of Salonica. More recently, chairs have been established at the University of Athens and at the newly founded University of Ioannina in Epirus (northwest Greece). At the same time that the folklore society was founded, sociology was introduced in Greece by Alexandros Papanastasiou,[2] a liberal political activist and supporter of the liberal politician Eleftherios Venizelos. Papanastasiou founded the first Sociological Society in 1908. While the stated objectives of the society were to "conduct and popularize philosophical, sociological, and economic studies," its main latent functions were political and social reform. Indeed, it was used as a base for organizing the working class into economic interest groups and a self-contained political party.[3]

Thus, sociology started in Greece more as a social reform movement than as a social science. Because of its close affinity with social reform and being, by its very nature preoccupied with social conditions, it was hardly distinguished from the ideology of socialism, especially by the more conservative elements of Greek society.[4] The first sociological society and its publication, *Journal of the Social and Legal Sciences,* were short-lived, and by 1915 both ceased to exist. A year later, the same founder of the first Sociological Society and his associates established the "Society of Social and Political Science" along with a second publication, the *Review of Social and Political Sciences.* Despite the reorientation of its journal and its new members, who included the late professor and former prime minister Panagiotis Kanellopoulos, both the journal and the society were again short-lived. Later, a few similar efforts were made to establish sociological societies, centers, and journals, but they also met only limited success.

These pioneering efforts to introduce sociology as a reform movement failed primarily because of (1) the populist/socialist ideas of their founders, which were ahead of their times; (2) the lack of interest on the part of the educated public; (3) the reluctance on the part of established disciplines (philosophy, history, philology, theology) to accord legitimacy to sociology at the university level; and (4) the speculative and armchair orientation of sociology and lack of professionalism at the time.

In 1926, Demetrios Kalitsounakis, a Greek economist educated in Germany, founded the *Archive of Economic and Social Science,* a social science publication with both theoretical and empirical emphases in sociology and other social sciences. This journal and its founder had a lasting impact on promoting and disseminating social science research and knowledge in Greece for the next half-century. The *Archive* ceased to be published in the 1970s, but its late founder, Professor Kalitsounakis, received the National Academy award for his journal.

Like the societies, sociology as an academic subject underwent a somewhat sporadic historical development. It took almost twenty years from the time of the founding of the first sociological society for sociology to be taught in the two major universities. Avrotelis Eleftheropoulos[5] and Panagiotis Kanellopoulos[6] were credited with the introduction of sociology into academia at the universities of Salonica (1926–1936) and Athens (1929–1935), respectively. The two protosociologists in Greece, influenced by the European tenor and their German education, followed a historical approach and stressed the study of sociological theories—especially those of the German idealist and philosophical schools of thought—over British or empirical sociology. Indeed, Eleftheropoulos was a professor of philosophy at Zurich when he received this appointment to teach sociology in Salonica; he then divided his teaching time between the two universities. Among his special areas of interest were the role of the individual in society, symbiotic characteristics of human societies, and the origin of social institutions. Owing to religious and political pressures, Eleftheropoulos resigned his position. Instead of declaring the chair vacant, the university faculties abolished it. Following the Metaxas dictatorship in 1936, sociology no longer was taught as an academic subject. It was perceived as subversive because of its close affiliation with social reform and socialist ideas. During the Metaxas regime all the leftists and communists were persecuted.

A somewhat similar fate for sociology awaited at the University of Athens. Kanellopoulos, who was better known in Greece as a politician than as a sociologist, occupied the chair of sociology at the School of Law, University of Athens, from 1929 until 1935. He resigned to enter national politics during the Venizelist movement in Northern Greece, and his position was declared vacant. It took almost another forty years before sociology was reintroduced at the University of Athens; from 1935 to 1973 it was not offered. It should be noted that the emergence of sociology in Greece and its subsequent growth were associated both with the prestige of the person occupying the chair and with the amount of approval given to it by the Faculty of Law. Although sociology has been taught as an academic and research subject in Greece for some time, it still is not distinguishable from social work, social reform, and social activist roles. In many instances a lawyer in Greece calls himself a sociologist as well. Thus, sociology has often been described and taught as an auxiliary discipline under the rubrics of philosophy and jurisprudence. This was also true in Germany and other European universities at the turn of the century. Even during Weber's time sociology was taught in the departments of law and jurisprudence.

Although Eleftheropoulos and Kanellapoulos helped to introduce sociology in Greece and had some impact on disseminating sociological knowledge in the academic community, they failed to establish a broader sociological base that the future generations of Greek scholars could use as a frame of reference to further the institutionalization and legitimation of sociology in Greece. In many ways their failure was not of their own making. The political and structural constraints of Greek society did not favor the uninterrupted growth and development of sociology. Efforts by a few more individuals later, including professors Sakellariou, Karavidas, Danielides, Skleros, Lembesis, and Kalitsounakis, failed to establish the foundation and legitimacy of sociology as both an academic and a research enterprise in Greece (Lambiri-Demaki, 1987: 31). It is overstating matters to even speak of sociology as a distinct discipline with its own identity, subject matter, methods, and theories during the first half of the twentieth century. There were no groups or departments of sociology, only individuals who taught sociology as part of other cognate fields or interests.

While sociology in the United States in the 1920s and 1930s was well established and moving toward an empirical and positivist orientation, sociology in Greece was scarcely known. In Europe at that time, sociology was more theoretical than empirical, as witnessed in the works of Durkheim, Weber, Simmel, Tönnies, and others. By the 1950s, when Greece launched a vigorous program of reconstruction from the ravages of war and needed the insights and empirical findings of sociology and other social sciences to plan a future course of modernization and reconstruction, the nation was faced with the gloomy situation of finding that sociology and the other social sciences were undeveloped and undernourished disciplines in Greece. Therefore, in any effort to give a brief account of the present status and development of sociology in modern Greece, it is only proper to start with the decade of the 1960s. By the 1960s sociology emerged as an applied research enterprise first, and in the 1970s as an academic subject. More specifically it is only within the last fifteen years or so, following the demise of military dictatorship in 1974, that sociology has received legitimacy as an academic discipline. However, despite its institutionalization, one must keep in mind that sociology in Greece still can be described as deficient by West European and North American standards, and in many instances it compares unfavorably with the development of sociology in a number of the developing independent states of the Third World.

THE PRESENT ACADEMIC STATUS OF SOCIOLOGY

Regarding the overall system of higher education in Greece, there has been a concentration of university and college level institutions as well as research centers in the Athens and Salonica areas (especially the former). However, more recently an effort has been made to decentralize higher education by establishing five additional state-supported universities: one in Patra (northwest Peloponnese); one in Ioannina (Epirus–northwest Greece), which is an affiliate of the University of Salonica; one in Evros (northeast Greece); one on the island of Crete; more recently the Aegean University on the Greek islands of Lesbos, Chios, and Rhodes of the Aegean archipelago; the Ionian at Corfu (Kerkyra); and Volos (in central Greece).

While sociology is taught as an academic subject in most institutions of higher learning, including in the third year of high school (Lyceum), it has not generally been accorded recognition and legitimacy as a distinct subject in which academic degrees (both undergraduate and graduate) could be awarded at the university level. For example, at the universities of Athens and Salonica, by far the two largest, oldest, and most prestigious state-supported institutions in Greece, there are no departments of sociology. While sociology at the universities has not established itself as a legitimate academic subject in its own right (owing perhaps to the reaction of the more traditional and established disciplines or to the lack of qualified persons to assume such positions), one finds that sociology has gained recognition and legitimacy at smaller and more modest state colleges (and one private), which operate independently of the larger state universities. In 1983–1984, for example, sociology was established at the Panteios School of Political Sciences. Likewise, in 1984 a Department of Sociology was established at the University of Crete at Rethymnon, and the Aegean University has introduced social anthropology and postgraduate work in sociology. Since 1982, sociology has been taught regularly in the school of law at the University of Athens. The school of law is divided into three specializations: law, politics, and economics. In all three, sociology is taught but not as an independent specialty, rather as a prerequisite course.

Beyond academics, sociologists are employed in public organizations and civil services and some technical and trade schools.

It must be noted that while sociology in Greece has only been recently legitimized and institutionalized in state-supported Greek universities and colleges, it has been taught outside the state-supported system of higher education much longer in private colleges and universities organized by foreign institutions of higher learning, especially the United States. Sociology is taught at Deree-Pierce College, an American college that was founded in Turkey in 1875 by the American Board of Commissioners for Foreign Missions, transferred to Greece in 1923 (following the Asia Minor disaster), and reopened later as a nonsectarian institution. In 1961 the school was incorporated under a separate board of trustees in the state of Colorado. Originally established as an all-women's school, Deree-Pierce College, located in Agia Paraskevi, a suburb north of Athens, is now a co-educational four-year liberal arts college. The sociology offerings at Deree-Pierce College are substantial and are equivalent to what one would find in a good liberal arts college in the United States. All courses are taught in English. While the college has become co-educational, it continues to train primarily women from upper-middle and upper-class Athenian families. Other foreign universities have, or used to have, extension programs in Greece which included courses in sociology. The University of Maryland offered extension courses until the recent closing of the Hellenikon military base. The University of Laverne no longer serves the United States Navy, since the N. Makri naval base was closed, but continues to operate as a private institution. A number of Greek sociologists and social scientists teach courses in sociology which earn credit from the home-type universities, a sort of multinational university.

Although the private and foreign colleges have complete programs and courses in sociology, their courses and degrees are not accepted by state universities. In Athens, sociology is taught by two trained sociologists as a subject, but the university does not offer a complete program in sociology. This is also true in most other business and technical schools, where sociology is taught as a subject by sociologists or individuals who express an interest in sociology as a minor. The following schools also have listed sociology in their curricula but have no chairs: the Supreme School of Economics and Commercial Sciences in Athens, School of Social Workers, the Center of Retraining of Public (Civil) Employees in Athens, the Higher School of Agricultural Cooperatives, and the military service academies.

The late and partial institutionalization and legitimation of sociology in Greece is due to many factors, including the failure of early sociologists to establish a strong foundation and legitimacy for sociology. The political situation and frequent military interventions into politics contributed to the underdevelopment of sociology in Greece. From the beginning, the emphasis in sociology has been general and limited to the more applied aspects of the discipline. There is less interest in conducting vigorous empirical research within a theoretical and methodological framework at the university level. This should be understood in terms of the bifurcation of teaching and research phases, which are not the same in Greece as in the United States. In Greece, most research is conducted outside the university or college settings by sociologists and other social scientists. Sociology at various schools of state universities is taught by professors, who, as a rule, are not engaged in sociological research as part of the academic profession.

THE PRESENT RESEARCH STATUS OF SOCIOLOGY

Despite the partial institutionalization and acceptance of sociology in the Greek academic world, it has come to play an increasingly greater role in the various research institutes and organizations not directly associated with the institutions of higher learning. It must be noted, however, that in most of these research institutes, sociology is normally incorporated only as a part of the overall interest in other areas of social and behavioral sciences, and thus it (as in academia) has not been able to develop its own differentiated and distinct research identity.

Furthermore, although one can distinguish a number of independent research organizations[7] (private, quasi-public, or public) that currently conduct social and political research in Greece (most of which are located in the Athens area), the National Center of Social Research is the only organization with primary emphasis on sociological research. The other research groups rely in varying degrees on sociologists. The National Center of Social Research (previously known as the Social Science Center) was established in 1959 through a collaborative effort of the Greek government and UNESCO experts that began in 1956. Dr. John Peristiany, once a UNESCO advisor and professor of social anthropology at Oxford, England, was the scientific director of the center's research projects from 1962 to 1968. Professor Peristiany was also associated with the newly established Center of Social Research in Nicosia, Cyprus. During this period the research activities of the Social Science Center were rather limited and had a more social anthropological and applied orientation.

In 1968 the National Center of Social Research, known by its Greek acronym EKKE, thoroughly reorganized by establishing a new administrative council and by expanding its research personnel and research output. At present it is under the general directorship of Professor Constantine Tsoukalas, who has been trained as a sociologist in France. Sociologists are prominent on the center's research staff, and research projects are planned and carried out mostly by Greek social scientists. The objectives of the center reflect both the need for vigorous research and objective analyses in sociology and the demand for applied knowledge that may facilitate social development in Greece.

The center is financed through a yearly government grant, special research grants, revenue from its publications, and gifts, bequests, or special grants from its property. Certain of the studies carried out by EKKE are partially supported by foreign universities, both European and American. The center also issues a quarterly journal, *The Greek Review of Social Research,* now published in Greek. In the past it was published in English and French. The center acts as a clearinghouse for social science information and to encourage interest in the social sciences through (1) its publications (over 100 books, monographs, and research reports since its inception); (2) its participation in seminars, lectures, and international meetings; and (3) its invitation to Greek and non-Greek sociologists from overseas to undertake research projects and participate in seminars.[8]

Although the National Center of Social Research is the only organization in Greece with a major focus on sociological research, other research groups and institutes exist that participate in sociological research and rely in varying degrees on sociologists. The Athens Center of Ekistics (ACE), founded in 1963 by Dr. Constantinos Doxiadis, an internationally renowned city planner and architect, emphasizes interdisciplinary instruction.[9] Ekistics (roughly translated, the science of human settlements) draws its instructors and students from specialities in administration, architecture, engineering, city planning, and the social sciences. Its main aim is to foster a concerted program of research, education, documentation, and international cooperation in all major fields related to the development of human settlements. ACE examines human settlements (from the smallest dwelling unit to the *ecumenopolis,* or universal city) by considering five basic ekistic elements—nature, people, society, shells (housing, community services, industrial and transportation facilities), and networks (public utility systems, transportation, communications systems, and the like). It also seeks as a new discipline to integrate skills and perspectives from a heterogeneous group of scholars, including sociologists, especially urbanologists and futurologists from Greece and foreign countries, in order to solve various urban and population problems and to forecast the future urban development of human populations.

The Ekistics Center includes a graduate program that provides a wide selection of courses ranging from neighborhood redevelopment to the creation of entirely new urban areas and offers a certificate of higher studies in ekistics. Candidates for the degree must have an M.A. or M.S. in any of the disciplines related to ekistics (including sociology) or have obtained a B.S. or B.A. plus three years of practical or research experience. Through its manifold activities and publication of a monograph series, a monthly journal *Ekistics,* an *Ekistic Index,* and an ATO-ACE newsletter, the center has exerted a worldwide influence on community/city planning and urban development and renewal. It also conducts international symposia to mobilize international resources to meet the crisis of human settlements.

Paralleling the objectives of the ACE but existing at an international level is the World Society of Ekistics, which has a substantial number of members. This group has received acceptance as an International Non-Governmental Organization in Consultative Status with the United Nations. Its secretariat is located at the ACE headquarters in Athens, Greece.

Also of interest to sociologists are the activities of the Center of Planning and Economic Research.[10] This research organization (by far the largest in Greece) was established in 1961 under the name Center of Economic Research. Its functions included basic research in the structure, behavior, and problems of development of the Greek economy, as well as the advanced training of young Greek economists. In its initial stages, the Ford and Rockefeller foundations and the U.S. Mission to Greece provided the center substantial financial assistance.

In 1964 the center was reorganized and given its present title. In addition to serving as a research and training institute, it took on certain responsibilities allocated by the state, including the preparation of draft plans for economic development, the study of short-term developments in the Greek economy, and the making of recommendations on current economic problems. An effort is being made by the center to coordinate Greece's economic integration with the European Common Market. Although the center's research monograph series obviously is concerned with economic matters, it seems that many of its studies are carried out in conjunction with the National Center of Social Research or have direct sociological relevance.

Finally, there are a number of research organizations that have some bearing on sociological interests, including the Athenian Institute of Anthropos, the Athens Center for Mental Health and Research, the Hellenic Society for Humanistic Studies, the Institute for Balkan Studies, the Athens Plan Section of the Ministry of Public Works, the Greek Center of Production, the National Statistical Service of Greece, and more recently Eurodim, the Center for Political Research, and the Mediterranean Institute for Women's Studies. The Athenian Institute of Anthropos (AIA), directed by Drs. George and Vasso Vassiliou (M.D. in psychiatry and Ph.D. in psychology, respectively), is an independent social science organization focusing on research, training, and the development of applications in the behavioral-social sciences, the sciences of Anthropos.

Since its incorporation in 1963, the AIA has organized many international meetings, has contributed to many symposia formed within the framework of international congresses, and has offered many seminars and workshops given at the invitation of academic centers and scientific societies in Europe and the United States. The major portion of its publications is concerned with subjective culture (the perception of social environment), family relations, group relations, and group techniques for which AIA has developed its own approach, the Transactional Group Image Technique. The AIA publishes a newsletter that gives information on the institute's ongoing research projects, staff activities, seminars, and international involvements and conferences.

Somewhat similar to the AIA is the Athens Center for Mental Health, a nonprofit private agency (established in 1956). Its research areas include sociology of the family, social psychology, and medical sociology. The Institute for Balkan Studies (in Thessaloniki, Northern Greece) fosters research and conducts seminars on the Balkan societies with special emphases on Greece and Greek Macedonia. Its journal *Balkan Studies* is a trilingual publication (English, French, and German) focusing primarily on historical, political, religious, philological, and linguistic studies.

The Athens Plan Section of the Ministry of Public Works is concerned with transportation and urban planning studies conducted by a staff consisting of urban planners, while the Greek Center of Production (EL-KEPA) conducts research and seminars on the sociology of industry and industrialization. The National Statistical Service of Greece, the census bureau of Greece, conducts various surveys on social, economic, demographic, occupational, and population aspects of Greece.

Eurodim is a well-known Greek public opinion organization owned and operated by Harvard-trained political economist Dr. Panayote E. Dimitras. Eurodim conducts public opinion surveys on a variety of political, economic, and sociological issues. It publishes *Greek Opinion: A Bimonthly Survey of Greek Public Opinion Trends.* In addition, it carries out public polls on voting and electoral behavior. A number of these surveys have a sociological significance and indicate social trends and social attitudes on a variety of current issues, both domestic and foreign. Eurodim provides useful current information for decision makers, politicians, and the mass media, both within and outside Greece.

In short, sociological research and social science in Greece have been advancing and clearly surpass the development of sociology in the academic world. However, with the exception of the work of the National Center of Social Research, sociological aspects of studies are often only auxiliary to the research of the major institutions of Greece. While sociology has made progress in the more applied aspects of social research, it has a long way to go before it catches up with the more advanced countries of Europe and the United States.

SURVEY ANALYSES

So far we have discussed the development and present status of sociology in Greece as both an academic and a research enterprise by looking at what is published or written about sociology and other social sciences by various individuals, research organizations, colleges, and universities. The next part of the analysis is based on two types of survey data: the Lambiri-Demaki survey of twenty-three Greek sociologists, and the author's questionnaire to thirty-four Greek professionals who took a class in sociology in the spring of 1984. The questionnaire was administered by Professor Dimitri Carmocolias, who taught a sociology research methods class at the Center of Mental Health. Sociology as a regular subject is not taught there.

The results of the Lambiri-Demaki survey were published in the book *Sociology in Greece Today* (1987). On the basis of three criteria, the possession of a Ph.D. in sociology, the teaching of sociology at the university level or work at a research center, and the publication of articles or studies in the field of sociology, the author selected thirty-one Greek sociologists. Then she administered a half-dozen questions concerning professional characteristics, the nature of their work, their views about sociology in general, and the way sociology is practiced in Greece in particular. Out of the thirty-one sociologists, fifteen women and sixteen men, twenty-three completed the questionnaire. Most of them studied in England and France, (ten in each country, five in the United States, three in Germany, and three in Greece). Most of them received their Ph.D.s in the 1970s and 1980s. Those who studied in the United States and England tended to be empirically oriented, while those who received their training in France and Germany had a more theoretical orientation (Lambiri-Demaki, 1987: 44). According to Lambiri-Demaki, most of the studies conducted by Greek sociologists tend to be empirical and applied. They deal primarily with Greek social structure. Furthermore, most of the studies deal with special areas of sociology such as education, political sociology, social development, stratification, family, work, mobility, social change, immigration, youth, and the like; or general sociology, history of sociology, and social institutions. Almost all the specialized studies were based on data derived from questionnaires. Overall the author concluded that sociology in Greece deals primarily with Greek social structure, with emphasis on the specialized areas of sociology, and with particular emphasis on education and political sociology. However, most specialized studies were independent and isolated without a systematic comparative analysis of one study with another between urban and rural areas of Greece (Lambiri-Demaki, 1987: 4).

In addition, Lambiri-Demaki reported the attitudes of the twenty-three Greek sociologists who answered the questionnaire. The majority, or seventeen of the twenty-three, believed that sociology is undergoing some worldwide crisis. The respondents saw this crisis generated by the inadequacy of the theoretical models and methodology, the weak scientific legitimacy and influence of sociology, and the lack of a distinct identity of sociology as a scientific discipline. There was the feeling, which is shared by many sociologists throughout the world, that sociology is not doing very well. The responses to her question "What are the main causes of under-development of sociology in Greece?" were, in order of frequency, as follows: (1) the general academic climate in Greece, which is non-conducive to the growth of sociology; (2) the slow introduction of sociological research in Greece; (3) the introduction of scientific thought from the capitalist countries; (4) the underdeveloped character of Greek society; (5) the political crises and instability of the country; and finally (6) a host of other reasons including lack of funding and planning, and the emphasis on economic rather than social aspects of Greek society.

On another question about the "role of the sociologist in Greece," the majority of the respondents believed that there is a need for the upgrading of social science in general and sociology in particular. Most Greek sociologists wished the role of the sociologist in Greece to be more interpretative, critical, social, and problem-solving, rather than political and ideological. The respondents believed that there should be a separation of the ideological role of the sociologist from the scientific role. In a somewhat similar question, "What do Greek sociologists try to do with their work?" Lambiri-Demaki found that the majority of the respondents thought that Greek sociologists should contribute to the development of a Greek sociology and promote the sociological thinking and research of Greek society. In general, the author of the article concluded that despite the difficulties the Greek sociologists are facing, the majority of them still believe in the role of sociology as a genuinely objective and value-free social science.

My own survey asked somewhat similar questions. It was circulated to a seminar sociology class taught by Dr. Carmocolias during my sabbatical in Athens, Greece, in the spring of 1984. The questionnaire contained three types of questions: (1) questions concerning the meaning and role of sociology and sociologists in Greece; (2) questions dealing with the present and future status of sociology; and (3) questions concerning the sociodemographic background of the respondent. The questions asked were both open-ended and structured.

Sociodemographic Characteristics

There were thirty-four students who completed the questionnaire; eighteen of the students were college graduates, ten had done postgraduate work, and the rest had some college education or were high school graduates. Most students were employed or self-employed professionals (twenty-four), seven had white-collar jobs, three were students or were unemployed. There were seven psychologists, seven educators, three social workers, two doctors, two sociologists, a historian, a political scientist, and an architect. One could not ascertain the respondents' occupation. Almost

Table 21.1
Perceptions by Students of Occupational Roles of Sociologists in
Greece

Occupational Role	Number of Times Mentioned
Social scientist	34
Social reformer	13
Social worker	11
Ideologist/activist/socialist	11
Journalist	2

half were married and two were divorced. In terms of age distribution, they were almost equally distributed between the ages of twenty to twenty-nine and thirty to thirty-nine (twelve and eleven respectively); five respondents were between forty and forty-nine years of age; the rest did not mention their age.

Meaning and Role of Sociologists

One of the first questions that the students were asked was to check three terms out of nine listed in the questionnaire which in their judgment closely described what the students perceived as the role of sociologists in Greece. Students were asked to list any additional terms or give any description of their perceptions of sociologists in Greece. Table 21.1 shows the distributions of their perceptions concerning the role of sociologists in Greece.

Almost all the respondents perceived the role of the sociologist to be that of a social scientist and to a lesser extent a social reformer, social worker, and/or ideologist/activist/socialist. These responses, however, must be interpreted with caution. We do not know, for example, how representative these views are of the entire Greek population. This group was an educated professional group; the majority of Greeks may not necessarily share similar views. Related to the role of sociologist in Greece, the question was asked, "Where do sociologists usually find employment or work?" The respondents were asked to check the following alternatives provided for them (education, research, syndicalism, administration, industry, civil service, etc.), or respondents were requested to list other options of their own. Table 21.2 shows the distributions of the work options for sociologists in Greece.

The majority of the respondents marked the options of research, public service, and education as the possible areas of work for sociologists. A

Table 21.2
Work Options for Sociologists in Greece

Types of Work or Employment	Number of Times Mentioned
Research	25
Public service	17
Education	17
Administration	7
Public opinion, unions, industry	6

number of the respondents felt that the work options for sociologists must increase, or did not feel there were many options for sociologists; still others felt that sociologists have not managed to carve a niche and utilize their expertise properly.

Meaning and Status of Sociology

Five questions were asked concerning the meaning of sociology in Greece, reasons for its underdevelopment, the present status of sociology, and the future possibilities of sociology. Most respondents perceived sociology as the study of the social structure (mentioned twenty-nine times), the study of social institutions (twenty times), the study of social relationships (fifteen times), the study of social groups (eighteen times), and the study of social behavior (fifteen times).

In the query "What in your opinion are the reasons of slow development of sociology and other social sciences in Greece?" students were asked to check the options listed in the questionnaire (humanities, Greek establishment, the socialist/reform beginnings, inability of sociology to develop its own autonomy). Other reasons that students mentioned as important were also considered in the analysis. In order of frequency, the students' responses were as follows: inability of sociology to develop its own autonomy (mentioned twenty-seven times), Greek establishment (mentioned twenty-six times), humanities (mentioned seventeen times), and socialist/reform beginnings (nine times). For the question "How do you perceive the nature of sociology in Greece today?" the options listed were empirical, applied, theoretical, ideological, Marxist, other—please describe. The distribution of the responses was as follows: most students perceived sociology as developing along a theoretical path (mentioned nineteen times), empirical (mentioned nine times), applied (mentioned nine times), and ideological/Marxist (mentioned nine times). "Don't know" was mentioned three times.

A somewhat related question, "How would you like to see sociology develop in Greece in the future?" was also asked. Most students felt that they would prefer to see sociology develop along applied and social engineering lines (mentioned twenty-two times). A number of students felt sociology should develop at the theoretical, scientific, and empirical levels (mentioned thirteen times). Two of the students believed that sociology should develop along an empirical Marxist model, and one mentioned the Western model.

The last question was "How do you envision the development of sociology and that of the role of sociologists in the next five years?" The answers to this question were rather a mixed bag. There were those who saw good prospects or favorable development for sociology (mentioned ten times). On the opposite side, there were those who saw limited opportunity and development of sociology in Greece (mentioned nine times). Many saw it as developing along an applied orientation (mentioned seven times), four saw it as theoretical, and a smattering of others saw it as Marxist (one time), lacking in objectivity (one time), or uncertainty (two times).

The extent to which the responses of the sociology class represent the trends and perceptions of most educated Greeks cannot be known. However, the responses of the thirty-four professionals who took a sociology class were not significantly different from the findings of the twenty-three professional sociologists reported by Lambiri-Demaki. In general, one can tentatively conclude that there is the perception that although sociology in Greece made certain strides and became more legitimate during the last fifteen years as both a teaching and a research enterprise, sociology is not doing very well in Greece. I share this overall assessment. In my judgment, sociology still lags far behind; we cannot speak of a well-developed discipline of sociology in Greece with its own professional identity, autonomy, legitimacy, and equal footing as an academic subject with the more established disciplines of the humanities and the natural sciences in Greece.

SOCIOLOGICAL INTEREST IN GREECE

One possibly significant factor contributing to the future growth and development of sociology in Greece is the interest of both Greek and non-Greek social scientists working inside or outside Greece proper and interested in conducting sociological research in Greece. The areas for sociological research seem to be quite varied. In a recent survey of articles, papers, and books on Greece indexed over a twelve-year period in *Sociological Abstracts,* there were 140 listings on Greece. There were abstracts in the following areas of Sociology: History and Theory; Culture and Social Structure; Demography and Human Biology; and Social Differentiation. Numerous other topics had five or more publications: Group Interaction; Social Change and Economic Development; Mass Phenomena; Sociology of Religion, the Family, and Socialization; Sociology of Knowledge; Rural Sociology and Agricultural Economics; Urban Structures and Ecology; Political Interaction; Complex Organizations (including military sociology); Social Psychology; Sociology of Arts; and Sociology of Health and Medicine. In addition, a number of Greek and non-Greek students write their Ph.D. dissertations on some aspect of Greek social and political structures. A number of Greek or non-Greek students working in foreign universities collaborate with professors who teach in these institutions and collect sociological data on modern Greece.

Social science publications in the Greek language are quite minor. Although not an exhaustive record, the *World List of Social Science Periodicals,* which was compiled and revised by the International Committee for Social Sciences Documentation[11] reported that less than 1 percent of the world's total of social science journals were in Greek. Kourvetaris and Dobratz[12] mentioned nineteen journals and periodicals published in the English language. With exception of the *Greek Review of Social Research* (Greek), most of these are published outside Greece. Many of these periodicals publish articles and studies of sociological and social science relevance.

Enthusiasm for Greek studies can be illustrated by the following organizations or groups, which have varying degrees of emphases on social science research. All are located in the United States unless noted otherwise. The Modern Greek Studies Association (MGSA) was founded by a group of Greek and non-Greek social scientists and humanities professors in 1968 in order to promote Greek studies through teaching, research, publication, and cooperative exchanges among university-level scholars in the United States and elsewhere in various fields of study (literature, language, history, fine arts, and the social sciences). Every two years the association conducts a symposium on a particular theme in which a number of members present papers, panel discussions, debates, and the like. Most of the themes deal with modern Greece and include a range of topics and themes including modernization, urbanization, social stratification, political sociology, mobility, migration, work, sociology of music, and other similar subjects. The association also has a biannual publication.

In the past the MGSA used to circulate to its members a *Bulletin,* which provided information on its programs and activities. For example, one issue (Vol. 5, No. 1, June 1973) contained a useful bibliography of more than 200 doctoral dissertations and 130 master's theses on modern Greece, most of which had been written in the previous ten years or so, compiled by Professor George Giannaris, then at Queens College, CUNY, and now at the University of Patras. To mention only a few, one has to include Betty Dobratz's dissertation, "Politics, Class, and Mobility" (1980—University of Wisconsin: the data was collected by Kourvetaris and Dobratz in 1976–1977); Yota Papageorge dissertation, "Political Involvement of Greek Women" (1985), and Joannis M. Katsillis, "Education and Social Selection: A Model of High School Achievement in Greece" (1987). Most of these dissertations are written by Greek students studying abroad. However, overall the MGSA tends to have a humanistic rather than a social science orientation with emphases on modern Greek literature, modern Greek history, and language studies. At present the MGSA is sponsoring a biannual publication, *Modern Greek Society: A Social Science Newsletter,* which serves as a source of recent publications and bibliographies on modern Greece including sociological studies, recent conferences, and events of interest to scholars who conduct research and teach in Greece. In addition, MGSA published a bi-annual journal. Another journal of some interest to sociology and social sciences is the *Journal of Hellenic Diaspora,* founded by Dr. Nikos Petropoulos before he moved to Greece; he along with a score of other Greek sociologists was instrumental in establishing the association of Greek sociologists in Greece in 1983.

FUTURE STATUS OF SOCIOLOGY

In conjunction with the delineation of the present state of sociology in Greece, four tentative propositions concerning the future development of this field were suggested by Charles Moskos and myself in 1968.[13] Over twenty years later, I believe these propositions still hold true.

1. Sociology will continue to encounter resistance from the traditionally established disciplines (e.g., philosophy, history, philology, and jurisprudence) before it is accepted as a genuine intellectual and scientific subject.

2. Whenever sociology is hindered in its growth and development by its traditional predecessors and is now allowed a formal place in the university program, it will be taught more diffusely under the rubric of history, social philosophy, and jurisprudence.

3. Although not a viable part of the university curriculum, sociological research—and to a lesser degree sociological training—will be carried on under the direction of nonacademic research centers and institutions.

4. In Greece, as in certain other semi-developed countries, the major portion of sociological research will be conducted under governmental auspices and control. When this occurs, the major thrust of sociological research will be toward applied social science research.

SUGGESTIONS FOR FURTHER GROWTH

In view of the present status of sociology in Greece, some general recommendations may be offered that could help sociology attain greater
recognition and legitimacy as a distinct discipline with its own social science identity in both the academic and research phases. It must be
stressed, however, that economic, political, structural, and cultural difficulties, and the lack of trained sociologists and experts in other social
science disciplines, admittedly handicap and limit the rapid adoption of
the following recommendations.

1. Reorganize the major universities along the American model of departments
   and university research institutes. This has been partially initiated in the last
   fifteen years following the restoration of democracy.

2. Extend the programs in sociology by (1) offering more substantive courses in
   sociology at the major universities, and (2) eventually developing programs
   that lead to both undergraduate and graduate degrees in sociology (besides
   the B.A. degree at Deree-Pierce College and Panteios School).

3. Encourage and promote empirical research concurrently with teaching at the
   university level in addition to that carried out by the research centers. Avoid
   the parochialism and ethnocentrism of Greek sociological research. Diversify
   sociological research from applied models to theoretical as well as methodological studies.

4. Expand the sociological research activities of the present centers (for only
   EKKE presently has such a major orientation) and/or develop new institutes
   that are primarily concerned with sociological research in other urban centers
   besides Athens, in order to establish a better geographical balance instead of
   the present extreme concentration of research centers in the capital of Greece.

5. Maintain academic freedom and a posture of value-free intellectual honesty
   and objectivity in both the teaching and research aspects of sociology. Sociologists and sociological research must be judged by universal criteria of mer-
   itocracy and not Greek political criteria. Political orientations and party
   affiliations should not be criteria of one's employment and work.

6. Encourage Greek sociologists trained abroad to initiate a series of publications
   including textbooks, anthologies, and monographs but use Greece as the social
   setting and incorporate all the empirical findings by Greek and non-Greek
   social scientists concerning modern culture and social structure in Greece.

7. Invite Greek and non-Greek social scientists, particularly sociologists who
   have had to go abroad in order to obtain their education and training and
   practice their profession, to return to Greece to teach and conduct sociological
   research especially during their sabbaticals. At the same time, however, encourage non-Greek sociologists to carry out sociological research in Greece,
   independently or jointly with their Greek colleagues, and thus counter the
   possible parochialism of Greek sociologists. It would be possible to develop a

genuine sociology in modern Greece rather than one advanced by only a few Greek sociologists. Develop a link or exchange program between Greek sociologists and Greek and non-Greek sociologists teaching and doing research abroad.

8. Increase interest and seek greater professional and financial support from the broader sociological academic and research communities. For example, sociology departments in major universities, grant-giving institutions in other countries, and international agencies could sponsor sociological training and research and also help disseminate sociological findings in Greece.

9. Expand the sociological base in Greece through memberships in national, regional, and international sociological associations and related fields. Encourage Greek sociologists to attend these professional groups and international conferences and encourage them to present papers and their research findings.

10. Increase the number of social science journals and expand the readership by using English and other languages as media of communication, in addition to Greek. Develop a critical posture for Greek sociology by encouraging inter-professional conferences and seminars. Referee professional journals by cadres of Greek and non-Greek professional sociologists, both in Greece proper and abroad, or the Greek professional sociologists in the diaspora. Increase the number of professional and trained sociologists in Greece. The number of sociologists reported by Lambiri-Demaki of thirty-one is very small indeed. In the United States a medium-size department of sociology in a state university has that number.

11. Encourage the establishment of private colleges with full programs in the social sciences and recognize the existing ones. The promise of the new government to change the constitution to allow for the establishment of private colleges is, I believe, a move in the right direction.

12. Generate funds and economic support for higher education including the social sciences, from private sources and international organizations. State funding of higher education and research institutes should not be the only source of support.

SUMMARY AND CONCLUSION

Although one can speak of only partial development and growth of sociology in modern Greece, one finds encouraging signs, particularly in the last fifteen or so years, of a genuine effort on the part of a number of Greek and non-Greek sociologists and educational institutions to promote sociology in Greece. The introduction of sociology as subject matter at various state colleges and universities, the research centers, the establishment of a Greek sociological association, and the teaching of sociology at high schools (Lycea) are positive steps. All these initiatives have helped to establish sociology as a respectable academic and research enterprise. This is not to suggest, however, that sociology in Greece has reached the level of legitimacy and institutionalization that it enjoys in some of the more advanced nations and even in developing nations of the Third World. In the last analysis, the full institutionalization of sociology in Greece has not yet taken place.

In this chapter an effort was made to briefly trace the historical development of sociology and analyze its present status in Greece. Initially an effort was made to show the emergence of sociology as an outgrowth of folklore studies and as a social reform movement that had strong German influences, because the first Greek sociologists were educated in Germany during the first quarter of this century. Second, prior to the 1950s a somewhat sporadic and interrupted development of sociology in both its academic and research phases was noted. Third, the present status of sociology as both an academic and a research enterprise was analyzed as a concomitant development of the broader processes of modernization and social change in postwar Greece. It was pointed out that the academic status of sociology still lags. In contrast, sociology as an ongoing process of social research outside academia was found to be more successful, but with an emphasis on an applied social science orientation. Finally, the growing sociological interest on the part of scholars and educational institutions outside Greece proper along with a number of suggestions for its future status and growth were suggested. In a final analysis it seems to me that Greece, especially now, needs the insights and empirical findings of sociology and other social sciences. In order for Greece to continue and plan its processes of social modernization and development on a more realistic and rational basis, it must encourage and support the development and growth of sociology and other social sciences as both an academic and a research enterprise at the university and college levels.

NOTES

1. This is an updated and thoroughly revised chapter on the "present status of sociology of Greece" published in 1975. Both Greek and English sources were used. The revision was also based not only on recent publications but on survey material conducted by Ionna Lambiri-Demaki in *Koinoniologia Stin Ellada Simera* (*Sociology in Greece Today*) (Athens: Papazisis Publishers, 1957), and material collected from and an analysis of a questionnaire administered to a class of students and professionals taking a sociology class in Athens, Greece, taught by Dr. Dimitri Carmocolias in the Mental Health Institute of Athens, Greece.

I would like to express my gratitude for their prompt and kind responses to my inquiries to the director of the National Center of Social Research, Dr. Constantine Tsoukalas; and Dr. Nikos Fakiolas, past president and editor of the equivalent of the American Sociological Association's *Footnotes* in Greece, and social scientist of EKKE. Last but not least, my thanks are extended to my old friend and colleague Dimitri Carmocolias, who is my professional link with the development of sociology and social science in general in Greece. It must be stressed, however, that the usual caveat that the author alone accepts responsibility for interpretations is particularly relevant here.

2. Papanastasiou studied law, political economy, and philosophy in Athens and Berlin. He was in favor of radical reforms and the breakup of large land holdings to be distributed to small farmers. He became prime minister but was also imprisoned for his political views in 1922 (Lambiri-Demaki, 1987: 17). Members of the first sociological society were mainly lawyers and educators. For further studies about the development of sociology in Greece, see Artemis Emmanouel, "Sociology in Greece: One Science in Search of Its Scientific and Academic Identity" (Greek), *Review of Social Science Research* 4–5 (1981): 36–42; Litsa N. Nicolaou-Smokovitis, *"The Growth and Development of Sociology in Greece,"* Boston: 1974 (pre-publication form).

3. J. G. Peristiany, "Sociology in Greece," in *Contemporary Sociology in Western Europe and in America,* Rome, Italy, 1968: First International Congress of Social Sciences of the Luigi Sturzo Institute, pp. 272–73.

4. Lambiri-Demaki, *Sociology in Greece Today,* p. 19.

5. Avrotelis Eleftheropoulos (1873–1955) was born in Constantinople. He studied theology in the school of Chalkis and philosophy in Germany. In 1914 he was appointed professor of philosophy at the University of Zurich, and in 1929 he taught historical sociology at the University of Thessaloniki (Northern Greece).

6. Panagiotis Kanellopoulos (1902–1989) was educated in both Greece and Heidelberg, Germany. He studied law, philosophy, and sociology. He taught sociology at the law school, University of Athens, from 1929 until 1935. He became involved in national politics, founded a political party, became prime minister, served as minister more than fifteen times, and was active in the political life of Greece until his death in 1989. He wrote many other works (see Lambiri-Demaki, 1987: 25). In the first quarter of the twentieth century, Greece sent some of its brightest students to study overseas, especially in Germany. Some of the most prominent professors were Tsatsos (professor of philosophy who became president of Greece), Zolotas (professor of economics, and former prime minister of Greece), and Theodorakopoulos (professor of philosophy).

7. In addition, "Research Sources" of the *Modern Greek Society: A Newsletter* 1 (October 1973): 11–12, noted a proliferation of other resources and institutions that are tangentially related to the development of sociology. Included among them are (1) Neo-Hellenic Research Center of the National Research Foundation, Athens; (2) Institute for Research in Communications, Athens; (3) University Center of Demographic Studies, Medical School, University of Athens; (4) Psychology and Education Laboratory, School of Philosophy, University of Ioannina; (5) Social Research Center of Cyprus, Nicosia; (6) Academy of Athens, Research Center for the Study of Modern Greek History; (7) National Library, Athens; (8) Parliament Library, Athens; (9) Gennadeios Library, Athens; (10) General State Archives, Athens; and (11) various other provincial archives, most recently research institutes of Mediterranean Studies, Women's Studies, Political Research Studies, and so on.

8. In its efforts to provide sociological research in Greece and disseminate its ongoing research activities, EKKE has participated or helped to organize numerous professional activities. EKKE was instrumental in helping to establish and

revive the Greek Sociological Society, "Alexandros Papanastasiou," named after its founder in 1908. The society includes over thirty Greek social scientists from academic and research organizations. In 1983 the Greek Sociological Association was established, which publishes a bimonthly bulletin. Also of sociological interest is the establishment by Drs. Lambiri-Demaki and Nikos Mouzelis of the London School of Politics and Economics of an informal sociological group, the purpose of which is to present ongoing research reports and keep in touch with sociological developments among sociologists. In the past, efforts were made by EKKE to establish a Greek-American Center of Social Research in the United States. A number of conferences and/or symposia on Mediterranean and Balkan societies have been convened since the inception of the center.

In a 1989 publication by EKKE one notices an ambitious and extensive agenda of applied sociological research on a number of areas and topics of empirical investigation of the Greek social structure. These include work and occupations (empirical and diachronic development) encompassing tourism and farming occupations, social mobility, poverty, class and social stratification, immigration and repatriation, economic and social transformation of agrarian communities, political culture and political sociology, social geography, demography, family, education, social psychology, sociology of youth, the agrarian community, health, prisons, aging, singlehood, drugs, housing, consumption patterns, and mass media. EKKE has in its research agenda the formation of a dictionary of social science terminology. Each topic of investigation is a team enterprise, with one person being in charge of research coordination and guidance. It is difficult to know how many of these researchers are professionally trained sociologists. Lambiri-Demaki (1987: 41–42) mentions that EKKE has 120 employees, of whom 65 are research personnel. Most of the studies are applied oriented and deal with Greek society.

9. Peter Lengyel, "Athens Centre of Ekistics and Graduate School of Ekistics," *International Social Science Journal* 18 (1966): 98–101. See also Athens Center of Ekistics, "Fifth Annual Report: Reviews on the Problems and Science of Human Settlements," *Ekistics,* June 1969, pp. 357–444, and the September 1973 (Vol. 36, No. 214) issue of *Ekistics.*

10. A leading figure in the founding of the Center of Planning and Economic Research was the former prime minister Andreas Papandreou, professor of economics at a number of American universities and son of the late Greek prime minister George Papandreou.

11. International Committee for Social Sciences Documentation, *World List of Social Science Periodicals,* New York: UNESCO, 1966.

12. For more information, see George Kourvetaris and Betty A. Dobratz, *A Profile of Modern Greece in Search of Identity,* Oxford: Clarendon Press, 1987. The book is a concise analysis of social institutions in modern Greece based on research conducted in the last twenty years. It includes topics on the economy, education, politics, military, culture, history, and geography.

13. George Kourvetaris and Charles C. Moskos, Jr., "A Report on Sociology in Greece," *The American Sociologist* 3 (1968): 243–245.

22

Sociology in Italy: Problems and Perspectives

Franco Ferrarotti

THE BREAKDOWN OF GLOBAL IDEOLOGIES AND ITS IMPACT

The breakdown of global ideologies by the end of the 1980s has given rise in Europe, both East and West, and in the Soviet Union, to informal, fluid social movements. At present these seem to be confused and at the same time flourishing; they are likely to act on the basis of a piecemeal approach, focusing quite casually on different issues, supposedly following the American model of policy making. In this way, the present-day social movements have apparently taken advantage of the misfortunes of ideology, as it were, and have acquired a certain significance as signals of societal requests as well as anomalous representative bodies of the so-called invisible society, that is to say of those marginal groups and "underclasses" which are not easily accommodated within the formally codified institution of society. An interesting phenomenon is taking place. While global society seems to be filled with ferments and expectations advocating profound structural changes, formal institutions, instead of opening up to these social demands, clam up and—perhaps because of a defensive conditioned reflex—become more and more self-enclosed, sternly opposing the palingenetic dreams of those extremist groups which claim to obtain everything at once, here and now. Between the global ideology in crisis and the malaise of everyday life, it seems there is a vacuum which should be filled by the sociological culture, or by the "third culture," to use the formula invented by Wolf Lepenies to indicate a way out of the contradiction between the scientific and the humanistic cultures (see C. P. Snow, *The Two Cultures and The Scientific Revolution,* London, 1962).

This is nothing new to the Italian intellectual landscape. The ambiguity of the sociological enterprise in Italy has been a constant feature of the general culture of the country. In fact, as I have elsewhere pointed out, the fate of sociology in Italy displays the aspects of paradox. At the end of the last century there were few countries which could boast even remotely of such a variety and richness of sociological research comparable to that which flourished in Italy.[1] Nor was this just a matter of philosophical or pseudo-literary speculation. Positions and assumptions adopted by Enrico Ferri and the positive juridical school influenced the conceptual development and drawing up of the constitutions of European countries of some importance. Cesare Lombroso's theories of criminality, not to mention Alfredo Niceforo's, had considerable weight in administering criminal justice.[2] At that period, Saverio Merlino worked out the basic outlines of a libertarian socialism which may have had its precursor, however artisan or even parochial, in Pierre Joseph Proudhon. Georges Sorel often published his brilliant historical and sociological articles in Italian before they appeared in French. At that time, Herbert Spencer's evolutionist approach held sway over the entire extent of social thought. With some reason, he was seen as the great systematizer of the social sciences and also the natural, and the more specifically philosophical and moral, sciences. This was done in the name of the "unknowable," and thereby precisely because of its unknowability (about which Spencer, however, knew all too many contradictory things), it was destined to ensure the encounter between religion and science, and their synthesis in the ultimate mystery of the universe.[3]

It is not hard to understand the reasons which effectively blocked a settling of accents, and thereby a reunion, however critical, with prefascist sociology when Italian sociology resumed its path after World War II. This prefascist sociology had been taught for years as course material but not officially by university chairs in faculties of jurisprudence and medicine, in the guise, somewhat reductively, of criminology. That sociology had been literally swept away by Croce's criticism from the beginning of the century (*La critica* had been published by Giuseppe Laterza since 1902–1903). Moreover, that criticism had also availed itself of the antisociological support of the only authority the self-taught Croce ever recognized and from whom he had ever accepted specific research assignments, for example, the attack of Achille Loria and the study of the evidently unfindable historical basis of "natural law." In fact, Antonio Labriola had for some time polemically laid bare from a Marxist viewpoint the misunderstanding into which many Italian scholars in the social sciences had fallen toward the end of the last century, especially the great majority inspired by positivism. They had unconsciously confused Spencerian and

Darwinian evolutionism with Marx and Engels's dialectical historicism, to the extent of validating Labriola's assertion that a new trinity had been created in the place of the old theological one, but resting on the same irrational, credulous principles: that of Spencer, Darwin, and Marx. Labriola's *Lettere a Engels* are still stimulating in this context.

It is too easy to attribute the weakening and the subsequent fall and disappearance of the social sciences, especially sociology, to the "fascist dictatorship." In prefascist sociology there were weaknesses of method and substance. These prevented effective resistance to Croce's "clarification," which was in many ways ignorant and unaware of modern scientific procedure. Certainly fascism, with its autarky in the cultural sphere as well, favored that critique.[4] However, sociology seemed uncertain and unable to confront it, with perhaps the sole exception being the polemical exchange between Pareto and Croce.[5]

I have remarked elsewhere that neo-idealism's criticism of sociology also had a positive side. It prevented reductive understanding. In the "plan of research" with which I founded the *Quaderni di sociologia* in 1951, I observed that sociology in the full sense did not exist in the United States or in Italy: in the United States because of the fragmentation of research thoroughly worthy of the paleo-positivism which quite naturally allied itself with the dominant pragmatist-scientistic cultural background, and in Italy because of the "dictatorship of idealism" (the phrase is Remo Cantoni's). This led to a lack of research in the field, to which no real value as knowledge was recognized. Such research was considered as having mere pseudo-concepts, and so to be debased as "inferior means of intellectual life."[6]

Forty years after the end of the war it is quite incredible to still stress that the dominant culture in Italy is profoundly a-sociological, if not antisociological. This culture is still, rhetoric aside, in some basic aspects profoundly antisocial. On examination, this surprise is suspect. There is no sociology without society—society of a certain kind, that is, functional enough and able, or at least not averse, to listen to itself, using the methods of social analysis instead of surrendering to improvisation. This last may be brilliant or lucky, but it is erratic and breathless, the fruit of a passionate and equally untrustworthy "life-force," instead of reason and rational planning. The proofs of resistance of Italian culture to the criteria and bases of sociological reasoning, which exhibits both individual problematic awareness and standardized, intersubjective scientific judgment, are many. They are to be found at the roots of a veterohumanist tradition which is at once the betrayal of humanism's values and recalcitrance toward scientific culture.

In Italy, the "two cultures" continue to turn their backs on each other, despite the theoretical proposal of the "two tensions" suggested by a famous man of letters. And they end up mutually impoverishing each other.

It is no wonder that, just to take one example, in the monumental Einaudi *Storia d'Italia,* the volume edited by the Italianist Alberto Asor Rosa on the *Cultura del Novecento* rapidly liquidates the whole theoretical argument and field research of the "human sciences." He manages this by turning to semiology, which, however, understands society as a group of signs or at most as a more or less elegant linguistic metaphor derived from the humors of traditional philosophers and writers on politics to whom rigorously applied social analysis is, by their own admission, quite alien.[7] This lack of attachment, of the absence of a logically grounded link between purely doctrinal statements and empirical data collected in a methodologically controlled manner, weighs negatively on Italian cultural dialogue—also as regards subjects of current interest such as the relation and impact of the mass media on society as a totality and on individual strata, groups, and social classes. The paraliterary nature and reasoning to the point of unreasoning on pure topicality appear in all their capricious ideological character in this context. False dilemmas, like that borrowed from Marshall MacLuhan's famous heading "apocalyptics or integrated," take the place of ordered, logical research. They produce discussion wherein the polemicist's skill and dexterous wordsmithing win out over modest field research. It has been justly remarked that "evidently, in the current Gutenberg-electronic reality, relations between the different media and means of information, co-present, are not reducible to simple or radical *alternatives,* but require a much more flexible view of their respective, often complementary, function."[8]

However, it is just this sober capacity for research that Italian culture evidently lacks, to the point that even today in otherwise well-informed circles sociology is understood as "allology," to use Indro Montanelli's quip. There are even lapses into confusing sociology and socialism, as in late nineteenth-century propagandists, or sociology and contestation as (especially after May 1968) regularly happens. The fact is that sociology returned to Italy in this postwar period and has again earned the right to academic citizenship. (The first chair in the full sense in the history of the university in Italy dates from 1960, and it is symptomatic that it was requested by a "minor" faculty, Pedagogy at Rome: minor, that is, and thereby open to novelty according to the sociological "law" which sees a close connection between marginality and creativity, as is duly witnessed in such teachers as Antonio Labriola, Luigi Pirandello, and Guido De Ruggiero.) Yet sociology was not accepted with all its consequences, and above all without social research being recognized as a permanent, crucial function of a modern society which had rejected the great traditions of the past as legitimating sources for its important decisions and orientations.[9]

The average Italian intellectual, if I may use this shorthand expression, is still somewhat of a certain brilliance, at times with artistico-prophetic intuition; he wavers, however, between two opposite and symmetrical poles which emphasize his extraneousness regarding the practical needs of the society in which he lives. This holds whether, as a good revolutionary, he dons the cap of liberty and mounts the barricades, or whether, sated with immediate cares, he retires to the walled garden of his prized intimacy. In both cases, he confirms his—probably congenital—difficulty in connecting positively and responsibly with the problems of his community, leaving behind the aristocratic distance from which he surveys the everyday needs of the great masses of citizens to whose service he likes proclaiming himself dedicated.[10]

The return of sociology to Italy in the postwar period was brought about by many factors, some of which, it must not be forgotten nor omitted, are of an intellectual nature. However, there is no doubt that the decisive impetus came from the real structural and sociopsychological conditions Italy found itself in after the process of industrialization, which affected it from the 1950s. It was impossible to go on taking important social decisions, or simply to understand the processes of change simultaneously occurring in multiple spheres of social life (from politics and generally cultural ones to the family, economic-industrial and microsocial ones at the community level), without leaving behind traditional cognitive and value perspectives. These were constitutionally incapable of providing a global, articulated vision of the change under way. Neither the diachronic perspective of the old historicism, the juridical one, nor the philosophical perspective appeared able to describe, interpret, and predict what was happening. The first perspective was obsessed by what is really history and what is mere chronicle. The second was jealous to a fault of its perfect but enclosed, internal logic. And the philosophical perspective was linked to a highly individualized, intimate climate which on the practical level was inclined to provide ideological arguments rather than empirically demonstrated findings. Sociological research, though surrounded by understandable suspicions, took its first steps in a country which had decided to start along the road of modernization, and which was literally pushed forward by the process of industrialization with all the disturbances this process implied—the concentration and massive internal migrations of the population which for centuries had been distributed in villages and towns; the nuclearization of the family and its urbanization; the rationalization of productive process in the factories and new forms of class struggle with the advent of mass parties and unions; a different conception of power; a crisis of religious practices and innovative ways of perceiving and living the experience of the sacred.

THE RESURRECTION OF ITALIAN SOCIOLOGY AFTER WORLD WAR II

In the first phase of the resumption of Italian sociology where instruments for wide-ranging surveys were not yet available, community studies expressed rather well the broadly felt need to resume, or plunge into, contact with local reality, restricted and limited, in all its historical specificity. The latter was very pronounced in a situation characterized by the recent political unification—fragile at the national level, but, on the other hand, strong as regards a subnational community, a sociocultural identity. This occurred after—and counter to—the spurious globalities of fascism's rhetorical centralization, beyond the purely speculative, all-embracing "systems" of metaphysical-dialectical rationalism in neo-idealism. It also occurred after that typically Italian Marxism which one of its exponents was to define as "saturated with idealism" and which Antonio Gramsci himself, in his long, taut polemical dialogue with Croce from his fascist jail, never managed to free himself as he too succumbed to a heavy subjectivist, voluntaristic content. The historical terms which community studies so usefully identified on the micro-sociological scale were also valid as a warning against the "dialectical impatience" of global ideological systems and their doctrinaire nature, one intolerant of empirical checking. They were formally opposite systems, but in reality they converged in their tendency toward dogmatic closure as regards the effectiveness of dated, experienced historical events. Despite their undeniable limits, community studies in this perspective presented themselves as valuable criteria for calculating political-economic and sociocultural change, which at that time was involving the whole national system.

The limitations of these early sociological studies in the postwar period are obvious and do not merit more than a glance here:

1. The link between macro and micro social system is usually weak; and functional interdependence, which is expressed in this link, is almost never made explicit in dynamic terms. The problem is a hard one and even today cannot be regarded as solved. Even in the most recent research, the problem is often not even posed at a critical level. However, it is the case that in contemporary conditions of a society even starting to be developed, the community is part of the system and seems conditioned by it, even though it can never be considered as wholly determined by it in every aspect, from popular, customary culture to ways of working and producing, and family and religious behavior. Indeed, in specific historical circumstances the community seems able to react decisively on the global system, on the general conditions of its stability, and "civil society" presses against—to the point of rupture—the rigid facade of formally codified institutions.

2. Even today some studies of the massive process of internal migration which took place in Italy in the 1960s in a climate of fierce social Darwinism are worthy of note. While politicians were passionately discussing in Parliament the conditions for just cause for dismissal of agricultural workers, these workers simply left the farms in a rural exodus of biblical proportions in order to become workers in industry. Directors such as Luchino Visconti, with *Rocco and His Brothers,* and, in addition, the whole

of Italian comedy with its formulas somewhere between farce and the picturesque, were to comment on the phenomenon even earlier than the social analysts. However, there is no shortage of studies on migration, rushed but deserving; however, the problem of assimilating, homogenizing, and integrating the immigrant in the hosting culture is stressed, whereas interest in the point of departure is slight or absent. Today one understands that this perspective, wholly intended to assist the solution of the problem of those who receive the immigrant, must be inverted or at least balanced; whereas the immigration of foreign (especially nonwhite) workers presents sociological analysts and also the Italian authorities with a historically unheard-of problem, whose sociological and anthropologico-cultural dimensions are of equal importance as the economico-structural ones.

3. The world of labor, that of the unions and the employers, has been in many ways a privileged area of study: from the first research on "human relations" (too readily used by some unscrupulous managers of firms as techniques for conformism, if not as crude instruments for industrial espionage, instead of seeing in them the opportunity for realistic description and well-founded interpretation of social relations in the workplace, in place of the doctrinaire "ideological spectacles"); to analyses of the labor market with its bottlenecks and rigidity; of the peripheral economy and the wrongly named "invisible" or submerged one, called upon to provide that degree of flexibility which the system needed and still needs acutely.

4. Italian sociologists study the community, emphasizing neighborhood groups, changes in family structure, the young, the processes of primary and secondary socialization, and environmental and feminist social movements among others. Attention to "social" facts is a staple although these have always eluded or were neglected by official culture. Within the panorama of Italian sociology, one school has made universally recognized contributions—ones still widely used by scholars (on an international level too): the "elitist school." Its representatives include Gaetano Mosca, Vilfredo Pareto, and Roberto Michels, no strangers to considering themselves distant disciplines of Machiavelli. Thus, there opens up the rich and, as expected, variously oriented picture of the sociological analysis of politics in the broad sense, that of political structures, behaviors, and attitudes; but also of cultural processes and phenomena of the "average social awareness" which define the citizen's awareness and political values—even if it is still true that we are now, in Italy perhaps more than in other countries, faced with a blocked democracy and an incomplete citizenship.

A New Socially Oriented Culture Is Emerging

This new way of "looking" at human and social situations was a provocation and challenge to postwar Italian culture. After the appearance of the second issue of the *Quaderni di sociologia,* founded in 1951, in which contributions of a theoretical nature the "second" part of the Castellamonte research was published (now in my *Lineamenti di sociologia,* Naples: Liguori, 1973), Carlo Antoni's critique appeared.[11] While recognizing so-called sociology's merit of having investigated "primitive mentality" (and here the reference was to the Marxist-Crocean Ernesto De Martino), Antoni brought out how this science tended to reduce humans to nature. To Antoni sociology had tried to "freeze" a sentiment or idea appearing in the same instant in all individuals in a group, and which produced the same behavior. Sociology, Antoni then concluded, is nothing other than the "science of the puppets." Nicola Abbagnano's response, published in the third issue of the *Quaderni,*[12] was swift and caustic. In that issue there also appeared the third part of the Castellamonte study, with a comment by Luigi Eindudi, sent directly to the editor in charge.

We can thus relate to the "community studies" the first empirical verification of the concept of "group,"[13] realized in a wide area of functional interdependencies such as appear, precisely, in community life. A series of studies began to flourish in Italy, directed toward the study of the community. These,[14] even though not carried out with strictly sociological conceptualizations but rather—usefully, I think—mediated through concepts of an anthropological kind (e.g., the concept of "culture"), nonetheless provided a basic contribution to the diffusion and understanding of the concept of the "social group" as an indispensable structural foundation, of empirical research.

In this period, the "theoretical" contributions[15] were added to the empirical studies. Among the latter was Guido Vincelli's study of the community of Montorio, in the Frentani, known for its internal coherence and the abundance of qualitative data—which are not, however, separate from the originality exhibited in organizing the statistical data. Appearing in installments in the *Quaderni di sociologia* between 1955 and 1957, it essentially proposed to measure Weber's *Kulturbedeutung* regarding the "cultural themes" suggested by the concrete behavior of the community's members. Vincelli's research, published in book form by the Taylor Publishing House[16] in 1968, prompted other studies, which at times were inferior in tone, even if methodologically exact and more "centered" on a specific problem of the community being investigated.

The importance of community studies had by now been established. In this kind of study one glimpsed a possibility for researchers to propound social modifications of an economic, political, and cultural order in the regional contexts of which the communities were part. If this program was never realized, it was certainly not the fault of sociology, whose task was that of "identifying" the most important phenomena of Italian society in transformation, to study them and possibly propose general courses of renewal. By way of community studies, therefore, the concept of the group came to take on a certain vitality, especially as an instrument of empirical investigation. In this spirit I returned "to the field" to investigate a "community" once again. Involved in the summer of 1956 in a study which proposed to identify the basic variables of the "company atmosphere" of a factory in the South, I let the experience of Elton Mayo, Fritz Roethlisberger, Charles Whitehead, George Homans, and William Whyte come to fruition. The factory was not seen as a simple place of production, but rather as a "type" of social organization dedicated to productive ends, as the seat of collective behavior, manifest or latent motivations—in a word, as a "group" place. From these premises there arose the desire, in a confined space, to coordinate a research project which would look at the "small town," the center of complex social situations, including the following:

1. the pre-worker, post-peasant laborer, silent witness of the breakup of the traditional social order

2. the worker in a pre-industrial situation (personalism, irrationality of productive organization, absence of entrepreneurship, etc.)

3. the "weight" of the family, still of the peasant kind

4. the disturbance of the cultural themes of the peasant world (sense of time, quality, myth)

5. the rise of new demands for progress

The study of Castellammare[17] suggested, for further research, the collection of personal histories which would constitute an indispensable legacy of information for composing the headings for the inquiry. This study in a sense "finishes up" community studies in the 1950s.[18] Indeed, in the following decade this kind of study was to dwindle; whereas research on factories, on the political system, and so forth increased. The subject of the social group also began to undergo theoretical examination, while studies and research on a basic aspect of the group relation started to spread: that of the *voluntary association.*

The decade of the 1960s began, in a way, with Allessandro Pizzorno's study, in which Bianca Beccalli, Giovanni Pellicciari, Francesco Alberoni, Guido Carboni, Umberto Dragone, and many others materially collaborated.[19] The work's main aim was to study urbanization in a community just 22 kms. from Milan and its "mediated" consequences by way of the media and social relations as the latter developed in an area particularly rich in urban centers. Pizzorno's study, cumbersome in its overall structure, also proposed an analysis of the "associative groups" as basic subgroups of the community. It seemed in some way to "liquidate" the preceding decade, which was so rich in empirical studies on the specific theme of community reality. The study of the community, using social group as

unit of analysis, inspired researchers to observe the community increasingly in its wider context (the region). Communities in agricultural regions
even exhibited strong correlates with "rurality."

For the period after 1964, it has been correctly noted[20] that sociological
studies of community tended to analyze from "below" the disequilibria of
social, economic, and cultural factors, the awareness of which were needed
for correct regional planning. However, I am driven to stress that in many
investigations, the conceptual frameworks of reference were "blurred" if
not wholly forgotten.

One study that deserves singling out for its organic character and internal logic of inquiry is the one by Pietro Crespi on Sardinian society.[21] The
basic themes of culture, values, and social change are joined together in
a problematic framework brought to light by the gathering of "oral tes-
timonies," which for him were to mark for the future the method of investigating social phenomena. This theoretical incisiveness revived by
empirical research does not seem present (save in a few flashes) in the
work on the community of Cerveteri, republished by Achille Ardigò in
Innovazione e comunita'. Rather, it seems in that volume that the theoretical section on the subject of innovation is redolent of a kind of "jux-
taposition" as regards the empirical inquiry; it is essentially a descriptive
effort on the community of "oxherds" scarcely touched by the agrarian
reform. The very theme of innovation seems to encounter a certain forcing
of its cohesion where there is an attempt to reconcile American with European problematics.

The concept of social group, especially the specific sociological form of
the basic essentially extrafamilial "primary group," began to take on importance in sociological investigations. The first social ferments which affected the world of the young—and which, at the end of the 1960s, came
together in the great general protest of the young—gave rise to these
studies. The research by A. Carbonaro and F. Luachi on youth attitudes,
and the contribution by V. Cesareo on voluntary associationism,[22] are illustrative. The theme of associations, which was to characterize sociological studies on the concept of group in the following decade, was addressed
in broad, coordinated empirical research concentrating on issues such as
the "role" and "function" of cultural clubs in a big city such as Milan.[23]
Changes of *associationism* and *social participation,* were detected particularly in the aspirations and needs of the young facing breakup, whether
they are in a "rural" setting (narrow, without services, with little information, worn away by emigration, etc.) or in a larger setting (inorganic
wide-open spaces, unserviced rudimentary peripheries, encouragement to
consumerism, etc.).

Already visible are the first distinguishable signs, of the rejection of the
political "party" as an organic structure that suppresses "creativity" and
"fantasy" in relation to "needs" (massification). The first resisting groups

are thus born, and these new formations have an essential characteristic: they are largely the new "primary groups" coalescing against the parties and the traditional "family." These groups, to a large extent, gave young people, for nearly a decade, new desires and new certainties. In empirical studies, public debates, and contributions to influential journals, this theme was widely represented, thus becoming, up to the first half of the 1970s, a focus of significant sociological research interest.[24]

The problematic of voluntary associations as basic prepolitical groupings is one that belongs to the sociological concept of "group." In the period from about 1971 to 1976, some empirical studies stand out for having dealt with this specific topic. Franco De Marchi's research on the phenomenon of association in the province of Gorizia and Renato Cavallaro's in the Molise are several. De Marchi's study[25] ties in with investigations carried out on this subject in the United States, and it reveals how the "aims" of associations may be defined in relation to (1) achieving "ideal" values (cultural, religious associationism, etc.), (2) acquiring practical advantages and consistency in achieving "power," prestige, or pay (political, economic associationism, etc.), or (3) achieving a "physical" balance (sporting and recreational associations).

A more coherent treatment in my view, since it is preceded by a wide-ranging theoretical analysis of the concept of the group, is provided by Renato Cavallaro's study.[26] Cavallaro analyzed all the associational forms present in about forty communes selected in two "integrated areas" of Molise. Classified as "traditional" and "intermediate," associationism in Molise is marked by the following: class identification; social, political, and cultural crystallization; conflicts of age and culture. Cavallaro's research is connected to the great sociological theme of participation as subjective incitement to action (motivation); it constituted for the writer the basic theme of many of his studies, which are still today focused on the concept of the group.[27] As I recalled a few years ago, the sociological prospects in the study of groups have been, unfortunately, neglected of late, as a result of the spread of petty psychologism (and sometimes sociologism) as a technique for studying the phenomena of social cohesion. The making of "group" a myth of the sole expression of subjectivity—and I want to stress this forcefully—leads to reductions in the interpretative sphere of social phenomena, since the group is identified only as a placid, soft, slow instrument of manipulation.

From a sociological point of view, it still remains to explore the (formal and informal) associative forms, the spontaneous groups in their territorial dynamic (rural community, urban district, etc.), "cooperative" and economic associationism—in other words, the individual's interaction within the group, whether "primary" or "secondary," which deserves special attention. Today, empirical research is moving in this direction by way of the application of instruments of a "biographical" type. *Humans* and their *group* context seem to me today the fertile meeting-ground between sociology and the dynamics of culture,[28] which I have tried to emphasize in recent publications: from the phase of *Vite di baraccati,*[29] where I analyzed critically (especially in relation to Lewis's concept of "poverty") a group of marginal persons in the Roman context of the *borgate,* to my research in a "community" type of settlement grown up around a brickworks. I refer especially to the Valle Aurelia study wherein biographies were collected which tended to demonstrate not only situations of family dynamics but more complex interactions between individuals and the community settlement.[30] In this sense I believe the study of "contextualized" biographical data is fundamental, in the sphere of the *primary group* and *basic* associations. This kind of analysis should be especially focused on fundamental variables such as experience of work, class structure, overall structural position, and specific existential content—and, in addition, the given, experienced "context" in the framework of a defined "historical horizon."[31]

SYSTEMS THEORY AND "CONSCIENCE" AS AN INDIVIDUAL SOURCE OF MORAL OBLIGATION

I should like to restrict myself here to making a few remarks about some recent studies I believe are worthy of note. Achille Ardigò critically rehearses the unfolding and development of Niklas Luhmann's sociological thought. Ardigò has devoted much attention to this thinker which is as passionate as it is critically alert.[32] His book is not an easy one, packed as it is with formulations which the purists' demanding palates may find at times esoteric or barbarous, or redundantly jargon-filled, but which should not be allowed to discourage the reader. The Bologna sociologist declares his ambitious purpose at the outset, that of advancing both a post-postmodern theory and an epistemology. To this end, he does not hesitate to tackle supremely philosophical questions, while cautioning the reader that "sociology cannot be returned—reduced or exalted, according to one's viewpoint—to social philosophy" (p. 2).

In a period of sociological study which even an indulgent critic would not hesitate to describe as wishy-washy (to the extent that Jeffrey C. Alexander and his collaborators' effort to refurbish the Parsonian system has to be recognized as a theoretical interlude of exceptional vigor), I find Ardigò's attempt timely and important. As regards Alexander, it is well known that vigor is not always accompanied by philological precision and conceptual acumen. Ardigò's work is important both as a symptom of dissatisfaction with the prevailing paradigms and as a demand for new areas for study, and from the point of view of findings already made and established. In particular, his understanding of the moral weakness of "weak thought" (if you will pardon the involuntary play on words), is striking for its accuracy. This comes into play where the Heideggerian "identity between being and language" is remarked upon, and thus the insurmountable limitation involved in this identity when dealing with historically determinate, dated, and circumscribed social phenomena. Ardigò's critical reservations seem to me wholly acceptable in this regard, except for one's surprise at seeing him so positively "impressed" with the notion of "empathy," elaborated by Edmund Husserl's disciple, Edith Stein. This notion seems to me not so distant from Heidegger's idea of *Gelassenheit,* or "abandon," which has an echo in Kurt H. Wolff's "surrender" or my own "sociology of participation" (1961).

It is true that Edith Stein had long taken her distance from her master, Husserl. Whereas the latter seemed essentially concerned to establish the "objective world" (especially in *Ideen* I and II) by means of a basically idealistic orientation, for Stein the "constitution" of an "objective world" was not to be understood in idealistic terms, since this required "on the one hand a really existing physical nature, and on the other, a subjectivity endowed with a determinate structure; at all events, without these two preconditions, it is impossible to constitute an intuitive nature."[33]

In this way Stein deals with "empathy" trying to avoid the idealistic orientation typical of Husserl from the first volume of his *Ideen* onwards. It is furthermore well known that Husserl never concerned himself with "empathy" in the specific sense. Edith Stein, on the other hand, dealt with "empathy" by comparing exactly and systematically the positions of Theodor Lipps and Max Scheler. She remarked that "what misled Theodor Lipps in his description (of empathy and unipathy) was that he confused self-forgetfulness, in which we identify ourselves with some object or other, with the act of opening ourselves up to the object. For this reason, empathy is not unipathy, if it is rigorously conceived."[34]

As regards Max Scheler, and especially his study *Sympathiegefühle,* Stein finds his notion of the "extraneous subject" problematic and ultimately unacceptable. This subject was equated with the internal experience of one's own subjectivity, in terms of lived experience. Scheler's theory, insofar as it was distinguished from traditional theories, was, according to Stein, "very seductive." Unfortunately, in her view, "whilst it is true that a glance of a smile is sufficient to obtain a fragment of the inner core of a person," Scheler's theory ends up reducing empathy and identifying it with a generic "co-feeling," or *mitfühlen.* For Stein, on the contrary, empathy remained an instrument (or, if you will, a basic procedure) for understanding "spiritual persons." As such it involves an attitude of acceptance in the face of the fragmentary and disjointed nature of empathic experience. Here lies its obvious importance for the biographical approach and especially for the collection of life histories; bear in mind that the latter implies a personal interaction, since nobody seems prepared, still less desirous, to tell their *Erlebnisse* to a tape-recorder.[35] In my humble opinion, the empathic attitude chimes meaningfully with Heidegger's concept of *Gelassenheit,* and especially with what Heidegger calls *die Gelassenheit zu den Dingen* (abandonment to things themselves). In fact, this is an attitude which consists of abandoning oneself to the logically unprotected experience of things, and of opening oneself to the mystery of otherness—in such a way as to appear the antithesis of Nietzsche's "will to power," which reveals the essence of the *homo religious.*

One can see in the concept of *Gelassenheit* the notion of allowing oneself to open up and to accept others, and things. This denies and removes itself from the traditional tendency in our technically advanced Western civilization of conquering, dominating, and transforming people and things by means of the technical industrial system and of psychological manipulation. Despite this, *Gelassenheit* does not necessarily mean a passive waiting. There is certainly an idea of waiting in it; but it is active, watchful waiting. It is waiting which is also an act of listening: listening to the other and accepting the otherness of the other.

In this regard, it is perhaps opportune to recall the concept of "surrender" as it was set out by Kurt H. Wolff. In developing this concept, Wolff proceeds with great precision, distinguishing it from other similar conceptual instruments currently in use in sociological research and in cultural anthropology as well as in everyday language. In particular he distinguishes his usage from the military connotation and other meanings current, but basically misleading.[36] However, it seems clear that despite both the linguistic and essential differences between the various terms (empathy, co-feeling, *Gelassenheit,* surrender), we more or less consciously leave behind, using these conceptual apparatuses, the Cartesian standpoint of thinking which has characterized the Western world for centuries. Now, instead of turning to a thinking subjectivity—an *Ego* or *Ichheit* (only French permitting the distinction between *je* and *moi*)—ever seemingly imperious and dominant, we now turn to a subject that accepts and recognizes that in some way it is thought by thought. It is thus far from being able to choose freely the object of its thought. The insight is owed to—among others—Michel Foucault in *L'ordre du discours.* One can say in the same way that one does not speak but is spoken by language, as though immersed in a cosmic flux where thought stops being a purely individual initiative or "project" and recovers its nature as purely human experience. The attitude of domination in the predatory culture thus gives way to an idea and practice of social research radically different from paleo-positivistic, systemic, or quantitativistic sociology, which today is in the majority. The researcher cannot consider himself or herself extraneous to the process of research, cannot enjoy a kind of extraterritorial immunity, insofar as every researcher is also "researched." Thus, the researcher cannot treat the "objects" of research like the subordinate population of a colony without risking the possibility of carrying out research into their problems without having the faintest idea of what they are. Common language, like the everyday knowledge of everyday life, takes on in this perspective a much greater and more decisive importance than the pompous technical jargon where in science is often confused with scientism.[37]

That Ardigò, borrowing Edith Stein's concepts, seems to entertain no fear of slipping into the bog of psychologism seems to be more a proof of intellectual courage—I won't say, of Don Juanesque unconstraint—than of conceptual rigor. In reality, the reduction of the Durkheimian "social fact" to a plastic, if noble, state of mind is a serious risk for sociological analysis. I think Ardigò is aware of this when he recalls the "difficult" transition from the subjectivity of consciousness to intersubjective "objectivity" (p. 8) and stresses that "the life of relationship between human beings, especially in the present condition of humanity, increasingly needs—in the daily relation between individuals as in between the representatives of the powerful—empathy, intuition, and of the difficult, laborious, and yet possible, search even for transcategorial communication ... between persons belonging even to distant, different, ideologically opposed cultural outlooks" (p. 11). All right: empathy, intuition, even a-rational feeling. But not irrationality. Transcategorial communication, certainly, but with the warning that no possibility for struggle is conceded to the traditionally established categories except by new categorizations. The alternative is the refusal to leave the ego, letting oneself sink in the dim quicksand of a cloudy, ungraspable, and incommunicable interiority.

It does not surprise me that at this point Ardigò mounts a precise, compact critique against Jürgen Habermas as theorist of a "verbal competence" which serves as presupposition for discursive dialogue. This latter-day (though unusually logical and greatly cultured) enlightenment thinker meticulously seeks the foundation of the legitimacy of power and politico-state law. However, it does not seem to me that the accounts with Habermas have been perfectly calculated and settled. Rather, in Ardigò's project, his criticism of the Frankfurt philosopher-sociologist seems to have the function of smoothing the way for the return and accurate exposition of the complex views of the Bielefeld sociologist. Indeed, here in Ardigò's redefinition of the purpose of his study: "it involves the following, with some innovations, a path and an example already opened up by others, especially Luhmann, even though the important 'discoveries' made have then been virtually cemented up by Luhmann himself, in a kind of fortress, very well endowed within, but not without some affinities with Kafka's castle" (pp. 26–27).

The reference to Kafka and his labyrinthine constructs is certainly evocative, yet it does not seem from this initial statement of intent that the Bologna sociologist is fully aware of the basic problem: how to widen the historical perspective against the attempts made in the name of sociobiology or systemic-abstraction or scientism to "block" history by "scientificizing" it. It is hard to overemphasize the impact of Luhmann's systemic construct on Ardigò's standpoint. One could almost say that he has to some extent been "gorgonized"—not only as regards the substance but even in his language and style of thought, to the extent of remaining captured by it even when he does not spare it his critical reservations:

"The conclusion Luhmann shares with authoritative political scientists, especially at the end of the '70s, is clear: if it is desired to obtain governability in democracies with greater degrees of social differentiation, the decision-makers must be able to dominate, manipulate, and postpone the excessive claims for inclusion (participation) for the non-experts" (p. 210); "the political decision-centers of a complex social system . . . cannot . . . then appeal, even in difficult situations, to the unpaid commitment and co-responsibility of the citizens and their families" (p. 213); "neo-enlightenment responses to the growth of human environmental complexity are thus limited for Luhmann to the following: (a) functional-structural differentiation, with more abstraction and more specialization of systemic intervention, along with more skilful manipulations of the response time (postponements, evasion, subdivision of subjects, etc.); (b) stimulation as regards the human environment, excluded or self-excluded from systemic self-referentiality, so that in turn it may increase its own autonomous differentiation; (c) a 'semantic' support of neo-enlightenment counsellors in favor of the leaders (so that they should be able to discount the motivations and legitimations of personal moralities of solidarity and pity in the face of the human environment)" (p. 214).

The scandal for a socially aware Catholic scholar such as Ardigò can be imagined, however nobly contained and efficiently entrusted to understatement. Faced with the drastic character of Luhmann's assertions, which call to mind the schematic systematics, quite unadorned, of some of Schmitt's theorizations on the essence of politics as the supreme technique of elimination of the deadly enemy—the *hostis,* not to be confused with the *inimicus*—it is no wonder that a "supplement of soul" should be invoked. There springs to mind, from quite a different context, the case of those willing neoscholastic philosophers (F. Olgiati, G. Bontadini) striving in the 1930s to endow Giovanni Gentile's actualism with a Christian chrism. The commitment is a respectable one. The citing of Paul VI's Encyclical (p. 222) is pertinent. All this may be ethically desirable, highly to be wished, but it does not dent Luhmann's iron logic. I now understand Ardigò's underlying purpose, and I sympathize with it: to complete—so to speak—Niklas Luhmann's system by giving it a meaning, importing into it conscience. But meaning and conscience are historical products, and Luhmann's system is rigorously impersonal and ahistorical. Luhmann's mocking remarks at the expense of the "classics" of sociology and history are innumerable. Moreover, conscience, as Ardigò shows perfectly well in these pages, is an attribute of the individual; but for Luhmann the individual is none other than the "system environment."

Finally, Ardigò observes, "Luhmann too . . . wanted to break the strange links which join macro- and micro-wholes (mutually referential) by introducing a hierarchy of types whereby wholes of a higher type, communicating with formal languages, should not be accessible, still less compatible, with wholes of a lower type speaking non-formalized everyday language. But when it is a question of language," to conclude with Hofstadter's words, "which is an omnipresent aspect of our life, a stratification of that kind seems absurd." Here, however, it is not just a question of language. Luhmann is right for once. Moreover, was it not Ardigò who criticized a few chapters earlier the importance given to language in Heidegger, and later on in Habermas? I feel I can conclude, upset by my natural disagreement with Ardigò, that Luhmann simply "extremizes" Parsons, whose "individual agents" were certainly not "free agents." His "social system" too was certainly not capable of taking note of social change, though it is true that in the late Parsons there survived at least the ghost of history as "developmental process" (cf. especially *Structure and Process in Modern Societies*). It is simply impossible to harmonize Luhmann's "self-referential system" and the oral conscience of the individual conceived of as a person.

One can undoubtedly share Ardigò's suggestion of an "open system, beyond Luhmann's theory," but the essentially exhortatory tone, the imperatives and shrillness, betray all too clearly its character as mere assertion of praiseworthy points of view, which nonetheless lie beyond any demonstrable scientific status—that is, the intersubjective condition. "(T)he social system and its selective 'meaning' . . . *have to find channels* that are not wholly self-referential. . . . I *believe* that the 'actual' relation . . . sociological research today . . . *should be directed towards*. . . " (p. 223, my emphasis). It is hard to deny that there is a good ration of normative optimism here. Orders are given, instructions, views. Are we into fieldwork, or in the field? More modestly, are we in camp? Or in the barracks? Or in a convent? These doubts seem legitimate to me.

The Limits of Sociobiology and Paleopositivism

Sharp, rather than probing, perhaps, are the critical demands Ardigò levels at Luciano Gallino and his well-informed sociobiological suggestions. I restrict myself to noting that their two positions are paradoxically convergent in their ultimate negation of history. However, anyone who assesses the latest development of this hardworking Turin sociologist and reflects on how one fits the "preface" to the imminent publication *La sociologia,* for the Utet Press, will not be slow to grasp that Gallino is returning with rare consistency to the old ambition of forever petrifying a dynamic, "taut" science such as sociology. Certainly this guarantees its scientificity, but meanwhile extracts it from the flow of changing historical events and their fickle climate. It is no wonder that Gallino proposes reducing sociology to a "method": "a method—like grammar—to generate infinite descriptions of any society whatsoever," so long as, naturally, they scrupulously follow the directions for use. Gallino thus wants to reinvent the alphabet, the sociological alphabet. Sociology would thus be freed from the tiresome concern to take social questions and phenomena for its own object. It will suffice to busy oneself with the general rules in order to study these problems—rules understood to be changeless, timeless, and eternal. These will constitute the sociological grammar from which the specific fields of analysis may be "generated." But, as Gallino too once taught us, are sociological concepts not themselves, perhaps, historical? And is it not true that Noam Chomsky himself, as inventor of "generative grammar" in linguistics, now recognizes the importance of the historical context as more "potent" than any linguistic text? Must we resign ourselves to viewing Gallino as the Derrida of sociology? Are we sure that the "control over a limited number of rules" enriches, rather than stifles, sociological analysis? Behind such attempts one can glimpse the terror of historical indeterminacy and thence the necessity of turning to iron laws which never cease, are few but good, and transcend the capriciousness of the historical horizon. I see similar motives at work in quantitativism and systems theory. In both cases, it is to be feared that the dehistoricization of sociological analysis, even when dictated by the desire to ensure it a granitic methodological base, leads it permanently into a blind alley.

Franco Crespi's proposals seem more productive[38] (though the argument is complex and should be expounded more extensively elsewhere) but are perhaps too dependent on philosophical hermeneutics not to make one fear for the theoretical autonomy of social research. However, in this context one cannot pass silently over Filippo Barbano's remarks on the new way of "doing theory" and regarding the concept of "reciprocal exposition" wherein he sees sociology, hermeneutics, and history as inextricably linked.[39] According to Barbano,

since the constructive and reflexive modes of "doing theory" tend to optimize multiple theoretical and empirical borrowings, one must question oneself regarding the criteria of selection and choice of these contributions and their sources of legitimation. Then, one perceives that these criteria and sources . . . are thoroughly involved in the *interactive* and *inter-theoretical* character which scientific interests have historically come to assume . . . both as regards the diffused conventionalism as regards the choice of means and theoretical units (concepts, methods), and for the awareness of their *historicity,* or historical structure of the sciences or science in general. (pp. 15–16, emphasis in original)

I believe it would be wrong to mistake the interactive and intertheoretical nature of contemporary sciences for a superficial invitation to gratuitousness or intellectual free-for-all. Once the historicity of scientific knowledge and the multidisciplinary, "cross-breed" nature of the sciences is acknowledged, problems of a considerable weight remain open. It has recently been remarked that "it is possible that two relativisms are combined, that of facts and that of values, where the latter is understood as the view that values are wholly subjective and incommensurable. Scientific relativism would thus be closely linked to a form of ethical noncognitivism."[40] However, no form of relativism can appear as an absolute one, given the communitarian nature of the social base which upholds and makes truth plausible—thereby giving it the moral quality of obligation at the very moment when it is verified, for all those who feel themselves participants in a common "historical horizon." In this context, I feel justified in referring the reader to my *La sociologia alla riscoperta della qualià* and Chapter 3, "I limiti della scienza e il suo illusorio trionfo," in the already-cited *Una fede senza dogmi.* I can briefly summarize the basic arguments in these works as follows:

1. Positivism is not "factualism," and one should not confuse paleopositivism and neopositivism. Whereas one should undoubtedly reject "Comtean infallibilism," it seems one should on the contrary retain Comte's basic contribution, showing the nexus between science and industrial society, scientific judgment as the basis of social consensus, and thence the *new social nature of science.*

2. The historical context is a determining factor in scientific knowledge, which thus cannot be conceived of as atemporal and universally binding. The historicity of science and its full acceptance help make explicit an awareness of the problem which directs research and justifies it. The problematization of scientific discourse is essential, so as to avoid falling into scientism.

3. The cult of numerical precision and quantitativism adopted as sole criterion of scientific truth is an impoverishment of the concept of science—the fallacy of the "two cultures." The absence of history suppresses the dimension of individual, social, and collective memory. It opens up the risk of fragmentary arbitrariness. It sees in the market of commissioning bodies the decision-making source of subjects for study, outside the requirements of a logical theoretical development.

4. The bursting in of the category "time" to scientific reasoning acts as a typical "transmigratory concept," allowing one to reestablish a unitary perspective between sciences of nature and those of culture, with the subsequent resolution of the related dichotomies. The critical questioning of *Edmund Husserl contro Galileo* and overall mathematization of the human experience should be retained. But Husserl himself falls victim to the problematic demand when, in *The Crisis of European Sciences and Transcendental Phenomenology,* he asserts that "positivism decapitates philosophy." Is it possible to decapitate philosophy without doing philosophy? The question returns when, in the same book, he criticizes the exemplary nature of the natural sciences' method but then does not go on, in agreement with his critical presuppositions, to explicit reevaluation

of experience as actual everydayness. He is thus unable to overcome the ambiguity between an essentially idealist position (the need for an infinite rationality) and the aspiration toward rigorously delimited research, directed by verifiable hypotheses—even though with the awareness (see the *Cartesian Meditations*) that there is never a definitive verification, and that every test can only lead back to other, infinite tests. This *"regressus in indefinitum"* already appeared absurd to Kant (in the *Critique of Pure Reason*).

THE PROBLEM OF QUALITATIVE ANALYSIS

Examining the theme of quality as a problem in the social sciences means being aware that even today the real problem for scholars in the field (at least for the majority of them) is another symmetrical but opposing one. The real problem has always been—and still is—that of quantity, or precise measurement, expressed in mathematical formulas with nothing left over. Thus, human knowledge can be reduced to rigorous measuring, which reflects quite adequately the inferiority complex of sociology with regard to old-time physics. For a start, one must establish for which social sciences quality is a problem. It is proposed to examine the social sciences as divided between the ancient, tested ones, as it were—law, economics, and history—and the recent, or "new" ones—sociology, cultural anthropology, social psychology. This is clearly a division for the sake of convenience which for the time being takes no account of the process of erosion of the disciplines and their academic-bureaucratic organization. This last lets us glimpse not only a general inter- or multidisciplinary outlook, but indeed a *postdisciplinary* one.

1. For the older social sciences quality has never really been a problem, whereas for the new ones it is (however, one should not neglect, for example, the tendency toward a quantified, not narrative, history; computerization in some sectors of legal studies; and so on).

2. It is worth emphasizing the misunderstanding of Comte's position, wherein "the luminous guidance of theory" appears basic. A purely descriptive paleopositivism would at most be acceptable as sociography, not sociology.

3. The discussion on quality in the social sciences has as a necessary presupposition the critique of ahistorical formalism (for the new social sciences, see Morton White, *The Revolt against Formalism*). In the wider view, the antiformalist critique was undertaken by Bertrand Russell and Gödel, who established it in the field of mathematical analysis against every type or model of formalism. In this regard, one must maintain the distinction between context of discovery and context of validation: in other words, the critique of formalism should not be confused with a slackening of rigor (it is not only mathematics that rests on the dialectic between rigorous analyses of concepts, and an appeal to unfettered intuition—a dialectic present in all the sciences).

4. More specifically, a wholly formalized system (where the context of discovery

fails or falters)—Niklas Luhmann's, for example—is by definition an incomplete system and thus has limited significance.

5. If this limited significance is not explicitly set out, there appears a risk of general implication—the formal and necessarily omni-comprehensive system is really based on the hypostasis of a specific meaning. Thus, if a system is *formal,* it is incomplete; and if it is presented as complete, it is *informal,* it is incomplete, in the sense that it is arbitrarily presented as formally closed.

6. A formal-logical system is a closed one, and if it appears "open" it is not without incoherent meanings.

7. In this case, what is proposed as formal is formal only in appearance, since its formal character is simply "decided" as such.

8. This decision may have subjective psychological or extrasubjective historical justifications, but *in any event it cannot be rigorously defended.*

9. A deductive theory has to be coherent and complete. If, however, formal systems manifest the previously mentioned incoherences, it is doubtful whether a theory of knowledge can be purely deductive and formal.

10. The categories of this theory (as a totality of terms and propositions) must rest on a basis that is not formal-deductive but historico-inductive (leaving aside the deductive-formal apparatus theory many employ in analyzing specific situations).

11. Formal coherence in treating human meanings thus includes the explicit assumption of meaning as frame of reference or coherence.

12. The opening up of the formal system demands the *reincorporation of the formal system into a system that transcends it, since it produces the former system historically, as a specific case.* Hence, a complete system includes coherence and rigor but is not limited to this, in that it considers these functions as part of a more general coherence as regards the modes of placing oneself within the thought act.

These propositions can also serve as a premise to the demonstration of the historicity of science and thence of the impossibility of scientific "laws" that are absolutely timeless, necessary and compelling, and universally valid for every time and place irrespective of the sociocultural and economico-historical context. Science as the overall activity of sciences of both nature and culture is nothing other than a human enterprise trying to give answers to society's questions in a determinate time and space. It cannot dispense a "divine wisdom." It must be content with a tendential, probabilistic knowledge, intrinsically vulnerable to skeptical demands. Failing this, it congeals into dogmatic propositions which contradict its basically problematic character.

To conclude, attention has been directed at the historical horizon and point of view of the observer. All history is contemporary history in the sense that the field of experience of contemporaries is the center of all histories. The temporal interconnection of history depends on the position the observer occupies in it, be that as eyewitness or as professional historian. Every contemporary individual is a historical witness in the exact sense that every contemporary is the depository of an experience made up of everything that the past has sedimented in him or her. This can be activated in the present by memory. At the same time, together with memory of the past which brings it to the present, expectation reflects but at the same time anticipates in the present the whole-prevision-imagination of the future.[41]

NOTES

1. See the remarks by R. H. Inglis Palgrave, *Dictionary of Political Economy,* London, MacMillan, 1899.

2. See my Preface to C. Lombroso, *Gli anarchici,* Rome, Napoleone, 1972. For an overview, see my "Sociology in Italy: Problems and Perspectives," in H. Becker and A. Boskoff, eds., *Modern Sociological Theory in Continuity and Change,* New York, Dryden 1957; even before this, "La situazione degli studi sociologici in Italia," in *Quaderni di Sociologia* 16, Spring 1955, p. 55ff.; "Orientrenti e caratteristiche della sociologia in Italia," now in *Societa' e filosofia di oggi in Italia,* Pubblicazioni Intituto di Filosofia dell "Universita" di Roma, 1958, p. 367. For the earliest introduction, see my "Nuovi orizzonti della sociologia," in *Aut Aut* 1950.

3. See the Introduction to H. Spencer, *Principi di sociologia,* 2 vols. Turin, Utet, 1958.

4. The totalitarian regimes, especially the fascist and later the nazi, could not tolerate sociology, supposedly a "corrosive science," save by reducing it to a technical service for information especially in the demographic sector, for the use of the dictatorship. On sociological activity, which despite everything remained alive under fascism, see O. Lentini, *L'analisi sociale durante il fascismo,* Naples, Liguori, 1974.

5. See the *Giornale degli economisti, 1900–1901.* The polemic rested on the possibility of pure concepts in economics and naturally also concerned sociology, whose lack of theoretical autonomy was to be linked as well to the incomplete institutionalization of the discipline, as the recent research by Joseph Ben-David has conclusively documented. On the other hand, the less-than-full recognition of autonomous scientific dignity confirmed sociology in its hybrid state as "infirm science," devoted to occasional and fragmentary research, with which Croce fed his destructive critique in, among others, the *Storia d'Italia dal 1871 al 1914.* It is interesting to note how Croce was to repeat the same arguments four decades later, when cutting down (in the *Corriere della Sera,* 15.1.1949) Thorstein Veblen's *The Theory of the Leisure Class,* which I translated for Einaudi—and also how the Marxists of *Critica Marxista* moved in aid of Croce; especially the editor-in-chief of the review (managed by Antonio Pesenti), Vittorio Angiolini, who was surprised by the intellectual ardor of an obscure translator.

6. I have noted elsewhere that Max Weber did not spare his criticisms of Croce in the context of his general critique of the methodology of intuitionism or, more exactly, of "the unwary and uncontrolled adoption of the intuitive method as re-

gards the empirical approach to the social sciences or sciences of civilization" (*Gesammelte Aufsätze zur Wissenshaftslehre,* Tübingen, Mohr, 1951; 2nd. edn., ed. J. Winckelmann, p. 105ff.). See my "Sociologia e societa' nell' Italia moderna," now in *Idee per la nuova societa',* Florence, Vallecchi, 1974, p. 212–39.

7. See my "La Sociologie en Italie," *Cahiers Internationaux de Sociologie,* PUF, Paris, 38, 1985.

8. See G. Corsini, "Umanesimo e mass media: un contributo di ricerca," in *La Critica Sociologica* 80, Winter 1986–87, p. 85. The two cultures referred to were long debated, also in Italy, in the wake of the little book by C. P. Snow, *The Two Cultures and the Scientific Revolution,* London, 1960, which was later echoed in Italy by the tireless Elio Vittorini (in his *Le due tensioni,* Milan, II Saggiatore 1962). Together with Italo Calvino and others, Vittorini launched the literary review *II Menabo',* which had ambitions toward scientific discussion; this was not so distant from the earlier efforts in that direction by Leonardo Sinisgalli, engineer-poet-mathematician, whose support for reviews like *La civilta' delle machine* is well known.

9. It should come as no surprise that much of the first phase of Italian sociological research centered on the problem of the "transition" from the peasant world to industrial society, stressing somewhat ingenuously the old-new dichotomy without giving a sign of ascertaining how much of the old was still present in the new, nor realistically evaluating the typical "stickiness" of social change, save for what could be glimpsed in pure legal formulas.

10. Whereas ideological research on the intellectual abounds, sociologically grounded studies seem relatively rare. Aside from Antonio Gramsci, *Gli Intellettuali e l'organizzazione della cultura,* Turin, Einaudi, 1960—to which A. Asor Rosa responds critically in *Scrittori e popolo,* Rome, Savelli, 1965—S. Piccone Stella attempts an analysis of the intellectuals' means of subsistence in *Intellettuali e capitale nel dopoguerra,* Bari, De Donato, 1972, still on a level of pure politico-cultural discussion. F. Ferrarotti, M. Michetti, J. Fraser, and M. I. Macioti (*II libro come bene di consumo,* Rome, Ianua, 1984) study the intellectual as provider of labor in the passage from artisan-publishers to publisher-entrepreneurs on an industrial scale. As against Alberto Moravia, who sees in Pier Paolo Pasolini a "civil poet" (though of the Left), I have often (*Corriere della Sera, La Critica Sociologica*) tried to show that in reality Pasolini was a "representative Italian intellectual," especially as regards the use in an aesthetic manner of social problems and their instrumentalizing as material for essentially solipsistic experience, and moreover socially irresponsible ones. Apart from the well-known contributions of Luigi Barzini and the moody pages of Curzio Malaparte (not to speak of Giuseppe Prezzolini's) on the "national character" of the Italians, see the recent contribution by Giulio Bollati, *L'Italiano,* Turin, Einaudi, 1983.

11. See *II Mondo,* 17.11.1951, p. 6.

12. N. Abbagnano, "Risposta a Carlo Antoni," in *Quaderni di Sociologia* 3, 1952, pp. 137–40.

13. I suggested, among other things, in my contribution aimed mainly at "social service": "The study of primary groups, or of groups whose members are not yet divided by defined hierarchical barriers, so that they know each other and deal directly, face to face, without recourse to bureaucratic mediation, can provide the

social worker with valuable indications regarding the probable behavior of the individual in the group." See F. Ferrarotti, "Sociologia e servizio sociale," in *Quaderni di sociologia* 12, 1954, p. 64.

14. I draw attention to G. Ambrico, "Un'indagine sperimentale sulla civilta' contadina nel sud," in *Realta' sociale d'oggi* 11–12, 1954, pp. 563–76; L. De Rita, *Il vicinato a Grassano (aspetti di psicologia communitaria),* Bari, Laterza, 1954; G. Di Stefano, "Una comunita' calabrese: Mileto," in *Nord e Sud* 4, 1957, pp. 104–18; U. Serbi and R. Volpi, *Borgo a Mozzano: Vicende e prospettive dell'economia contadina di un comune rappresentativa in provincia di Lucca,* Genoa: Esso, 1955; L. De Rita, "I sassi sotto inchiesta," in *Civilta' delle macchine* 2, 1956, pp. 106–19; A. Ardigo', "Il villaggio come forma sociale," in *Rivista di politica agraria* 3, 1955; A. Ciabattoni, *Problemi umani e sociali del mondo rurale,* Rome, Studium, 1957; T. Tentori, *Il sistema di vita della comunita' materana,* Relazione della Commissione per lo studio della citta' e dell'agro di Matera, Ensiss, Rome, 1955; L. Cavalli, "Inchiesta sugli abituri," in *Notizie sociologiche,* Genoa, 1957.

15. Among the many articles of a "theoretical" cast, at times shot through with residual psychologism or idealism, I should point out: G. Nirchio, "La sociologia come scienza autonoma. Tecniche sociografiche e sociometriche," in *Il Politico* 18, 1953, pp. 366–72; G. Nirchio, "Microsociologia e sociometria. Interpersonalismo del Moreno," in *Il Politico* 19, 1954, pp. 74–88; G. Sarfatti, "Dissidi e conflitti fra varie specie di gruppo," in *Rivista del lavoro,* July–August 1952; G. Sarfatti, *Conflitti di gruppo,* Rome, 1952; A. Fabris, "Introduzione allo studio della dinamica di gruppo," in *Produttivita'* 9, 1956, pp. 803–7; G. Goretti, "Sociologia e gruppi sociali," in *Scritti di sociologia e politica in onore di Luigi Sturzo,* vol. 1, Bologna, 1953; F. Leonardi, "Teoria dei gruppi sociali," in *Atti del xiv° congresso internazionale di sociologia,* vol. 3, Rome, 1950–53, pp. 117–38; G. Frisella Vella, *Classi e gruppi sociali nella vita moderna,* Palermo, Patron, 1949; F. Leonardi, "Psicologia di gruppo. Contributo alle tecniche nella valutazione dei gruppi sociali," in *Contributi dell'Istituto nazionale di psicologia del Cnr,* Rome, 1950; V. De Capraris, "Gruppi di pressione," in *Nord e Sud* 25, 1956, pp. 66–69.

16. G. Vincelli, *Una comunita' meridionale: Montorio dei Frentani. Preliminari ad un'indagine sociologico-culturale,* Turin, 1958. To better understand certain problematics related to the concept of "community" and "group," I refer the reader to my introduction in that volume, pp. v–x.

17. See F. Ferrarotti, E. Uccelli, and G. Giorgi Rossi, *La piccola citta' Dati per l'analisi sociologica di una comunita' meridionale,* Milan, Comunita', 1959.

18. I note in addition at the conclusion to this intense decade: L. Lopreato and D. Lococo, "Stefanoconi; un villaggio agricolo meridionale in relazione al suo mondo," in *Quaderni di sociologia* 34, 1959, pp. 239–60; A. Ardigo', *Un'inchiesta sociologica in una comunita' arretrata confinante con Roma, Atti del 1° congresso nazionale di scienze sociali,* vol. 2, Bologna, 1959, pp. 365–69; M. Marotta, "Societa' e uomo in Sardegna, ricerca di sociologia positiva," in *Annali economico-sociali della Sardegna,* Cagliari, 1958, vol. 1; A. Anfossi, M. Talamo, and F. Indovina, *Ragusa comunita' in transizione—Saggio sociologico,* Turin, Taylor, 1959; A. Signorelli, *Alcuni aspetti del rapporto citta'—campagna in un villaggio della Lucania, Atti del 1° congresso dazionale di scienze sociali,* Bologna, vol. 2, 1959, pp. 379–85.

19. A. Pizzorno, *Communita' e razionalizzazione,* Turin, Einaudi, 1960; in this

period, L. Potesta', "Nuovi orientamenti nella teoria sociologica, la studio del 'gruppo umano,' " in *Quaderni di sociologia* 35, 1960, pp. 29–64, is a treatment of some interest.

20. See G. Catelli, "Gli studi di comunita' tra storia ed esplorazione sociale," in *Sociologia urbana e rurale* 4, 1980, pp. 11–52.

21. *Una societa' tra costume e storia—Introduzione a uno studio d'ambiente in Sardegna*, Milan, 1966. I draw attention also to an example of a late historical study, generally acritical, by A. Palazo, *Nomia e autonomia in societa' particolari*, Milan, 1963, in which the problems of marble workers were studied in the area of the Alpi Apuane, including Carrara.

22. See "Aspetti e tendenze dell'associazionismo volontario," in *Studi di Sociolgia* 3, 1966, pp. 299–316.

23. U. Melotti, *Cultura e partecipazione sociale nella cittal in trasformazione*, Milan, Ed. Terzo Mondo, 1966.

24. Among the studies which grasp these new ferments, see: F. Mnoukian Olivetti, "Il gruppo come esperienza critica," in *Il Mulino* 4, 1966, pp. 28–46; E. Spaltro, R. Ronza, and P. De Carli, *Le associazioni studentesche cosa sono?*, Milan, 1967; M. Spinella, "I circoli culturali—strumento di contestazione," in *Rinascita* 33, 1965; R. Agostini, "L'associazionismo giovanile oggi: inchiesta sociologica," in *Incontri cultruali* 1, 1968, pp. 189–92. G. Gozzer, "La partecipazione e la responsabilita' giovanile," in *Formazione e lavoro*, ed. Enaip, 37, 1969, pp. 32–37; P. P. Benedetti, "I circoli culturali in Italia," in *Quaderni di azione sociale*, February 1968, pp. 3–15; P. Bellasi and G. Pellicciari, "Partecipazione e gruppi di contestazione," in *Quaderni di azione sociale*, 6, 1970, p. 774–82; P. P. Benedetti, "Dove sono finiti i gruppi spontarei?" in *Quaderni di azione sociale* 1, 1971, pp. 79–92.

25. See *L'associazionismo in provincia di Gorizia*, ed. F. De Marchi, Bologna, 1971. I should like to recall here the study by P. P. Benedetti, *I giovani e la politica*, Rome, Isvet 45, 1972. In this study he examined the voting, political attitudes, and membership in party organizations of the young; as well as the experience of the university student movement and the formation of spontaneous groups, including the extraparliamentary kind. Aside from remarks on the methodological structure of the research, I should like to draw attention to the degree of differentiation achieved.

26. *La sociologia dei gruppi primari—Formazione e dinamica dei ragruppamenti sociali di base*, Naples, 1975.

27. See by R. Cavallaro on the concept of the group, "Aspetti e problemi dell'aggregazione sociale in ambiente urbano," in *International Review of Community Development* 35–36, 1976, pp. 217–52; "Mezzogiorno, periferia urbana e gruppi sociali," in *La critica sociologica* 45–46, 1978, pp. 47–59; "Roma, io decentro, tu partecipi?" in *La critica sociologica* 41, 1977, pp 64–67; "La serie, il gruppo e il flusso armonioso del 'désir,' " in *La critica sociologica* 50, 1979, pp. 108–38; "Sul concetto di gruppo, dalla teoria della Gemeinschaft alla Beziehungsoziologie," in *Sociologia* 2–3, 1981, pp. 41–81; "Individuo, gruppo e societa': un confronto tra quattro classici," in *Sociologia* 1, 1983, pp. 31–65; "Analisi sociologica e teoria dei gruppi sociali. Alcune proposte della sociologia contemporanea," in *Sociologia* 1, 1983, pp. 89–113. Overall, the 1970s was quite a rich decade for studies on the group concept viewed in its "associatve" dimension. See also P. P. Benedetti, "Associazionismo familiare o lotte operaie?" in *Quaderni di azione sociale* 6, 1970,

23

The Current Status of Sociology in Spain

Carlota Solé

It was not until the 1970s that sociology in Spain finally gained academic and professional recognition and associations of Spanish sociologists were formed. The first Faculty of Political Sciences and Economics, later known as the Faculty of Political Sciences and Sociology, was founded in Madrid in 1973 and opened the way to full acceptance of the discipline. During the 1980s many young graduates of the Faculty (which is part of Madrid's Universidad Complutense) went to work in local, provincial, and regional governments, political parties, labor unions, official agencies, business firms, schools, research centers, consultants' offices, and so forth. The appearance of sociologists in the communications media also helped make the profession known and generally accepted by the Spanish public, as did the opening of new Faculties of Political Science and Sociology at the Universidad Autónoma de Barcelona (1986), UNED/University of Distance Learning (1987), and the Universities of Granada (1988), the Basque Country (1988), and Alicante (1990). Moreover, new faculties are scheduled to open soon in Orense, Palencia, Valladolid, and Valencia.

The boom in Spanish sociology in the past twenty years responds to the need to face up to and analyze the complex and dynamic economic and social scene in contemporary Spain, following the decade of economic growth and political restriction in the 1960s. Among the major sociological works published is Volume I (*La Sociedad*) of the Sociological Report on *La España de los 70,* compiled by Salustiano del Campo and containing work by such prominent sociologists as Juan Diez Nicolás, Luis González Seara, Carlos Moya, Manuel Navarro, José Antonio Garmendia, Carmelo Lisón, Juan del Pino, Juan Ramón Torregrosa, José Caballero, and others. In 1966 and 1970 the FOESSA Foundation published important quantitative studies of the social situation in Spain, written by Amando de Miguel, Juan Linz, Juan Salcedo, and others. These studies examined subjects which were relevant to Spain in the Franco years, such as the new breed of Spanish businessmen, the economic elite, the value system, and so forth. The work of these sociologists was hindered by the censorship of those years, during which time Carlos Moya spoke out in recognition of the difficult but necessary role of sociologists working under the tight social and political restrictions imposed by the dictatorship.

In the 1970s there was a proliferation of introductory books on sociology, making this brand-new social science familiar to a country that was open to any general explanation for the radical changes then taking place. This explains the impact of work of a general and critical nature that examined these social changes and the role of sociology and sociologists. Among the authors whose work attracted most attention were Salvador Giner (*Sociologia,* 1968), Carlos Moya (*Sociologia y sociólogos,* 1970), Luis González Seara (*La Sociologia, aventura dialéctica,* 1970), Salustiano del Campo (*Cambios sociales y formas de vida,* 1973), Juan Díez Nicolás (*Especialización funcional y dominación en la España urbana,* 1972), and Amando de Miguel (*Sociologia o subversión,* 1972). Other young thinkers of the time successfully examined particular features of Spanish life. Among them was Victor Pérez Diaz, who wrote about rural Spain (*Estructura social del campo y éxodo rural,* 1966; *Emigración y cambio social,* 1971; *Pueblos y clases sociales en el campo español,* 1974). José Maria Maravall analyzed the emergence of a working class as the result of an industrialization process that began in the traditionally more developed regions of Catalonia and the Basque Country, and later spread to the rest of Spain (*El desarrollo económico y la clase obrera,* 1970).

Although they continued to be concerned with what were the most burning issues in Spain in the 1970s (the exodus from the countryside to the industrial cities, the emergence of a new working class), Spanish sociologists became increasingly specialized as the discipline became ever more developed. Soon there were two generations or cohorts of sociology teachers and practitioners who had been trained either in Spain or abroad. By the end of the 1970s there were groups of sociologists whose field of expertise was the population and the family; others who specialized in social structure and nationalisms; theory of sociology and the sociology of knowledge; research methodology and techniques; urban sociology, sociology of education, labor, religion, communications, organizations, daily life, health, sport, the armed forces, women, young people, senior citizens, poverty, delinquency, and drug addiction.

Still the tradition of more general works endured, with the material collected by Luis González Seara was published in 1975 under the title *Estudios sociológicos sobre la situación social en España;* and later, in 1981, the *Informe sociológico sobre el cambio político en Españoa, 1975–1981,* directed by Juan Linz; *La transición democrática española,* edited by José Félix Texanos, Ramón Cotarelo, and Andrés de Blas and published in 1989; and *España, Sociedad y Politica,* compiled by Salvador Giner and published in 1990. These research studies are required reading for anyone wishing to become acquainted with the period of history immediately before and after the death of Franco as well as the transition from dictatorship to democracy. At this time a good deal of work was also published on the culture, politics, economy, and society of Spain's different regions. These studies combined quantitative analyses with qualitative observations on population, social structure, social movements, the largely domestic nature of the economy, economic sectors, the ideological evolution of political parties, the status of the language of the particular region under study, the creation of regional culture, and so forth. A good example of this kind of work is *Catalunya: 77–88,* published in 1990 by the Jaume Bofill Foundation of Barcelona.

The two decades from 1970 to 1990 also saw the consolidation of professional associations for sociologists and the institutionalization of public and private research centers. Although various associations of sociologists had previously existed, their size and importance varied greatly depending upon the extent to which sociology was recognized by the academic world and the labor market in the different areas of the country; and it was not until 1979 that these associations united to form FASEE (The Federation of Spanish Sociological Associations). FASEE includes the Sociological Associations of Asturias, the Canary Islands, Catalonia, Galicia, Madrid, Murcia, Valencia, and the Basque Country. It reflects the desire of Spain's sociologists to work together to define a joint plan of action that would guarantee the professional quality of sociologists while maintaining the progressive and critical spirit which marked the early years of sociology in Spain. The fact that the association is a federation and the members of its governing bodies (President, Standing Committee, General Council) have no links to the Spanish university structure of the Franco years demonstrates FASEE's professional, democratic, and decentralized nature, as does the variety of events the Federation organizes (national congresses, symposia, international conferences, and seminars).

In 1981, the Sociology Association of Aragon organized the first national congress with the theme "Our Sociology Today"; in 1984 the Sociology Association of Asturias hosted the second congress, dedicated to "Conflict and Social Structure"; in 1989 the Sociology Association of the Basque Country organized the third national congress in San Sebastian to examine "Sociology and the Challenges of the 21st Century." In addition, the Catalan Sociology Association organized the "1st Workshop on Sociology" in 1981; and the Valencia Sociology Association coordinated an international seminar on "Modernization and Social Change" in 1986. In 1987, FASEE, a Category A member of the International Sociology Association, created a Spanish Committee to organize the Twelfth World Sociology Congress, which was held in Madrid in 1990.

Parallel to these activities, the Colegio Nacional de Doctores y Licenciados en Ciencias Politicas y Sociologia (National Association of University Graduates and Ph.D.s in Political Science and Sociology) has worked tirelessly during the past two decades to defend the professional interests and working conditions of Spanish sociologists. Because membership in professional associations is subject to a number of legal restrictions, this association does not represent all the sociologists working in Spain (many of the sociologists ineligible for membership hold postgraduate degrees— Ph.D., *doctorat d'etat*—conferred by universities abroad), but it has nonetheless made every effort to guarantee the normalization of the practice of sociology during the vital years in which the discipline and the profession had not yet become fully accepted and institutionalized. Although the Association dates back to the Franco years (it was founded around 1953), its most recent governing bodies (President, Executive Committee, General Assembly) have worked hard to promote institutional support for the post-Franco generations of sociologists and political scientists entering the labor market.

The Sociedad Española de Profesores de Sociologia (SEPS), founded in 1987, is a strictly corporatist association, representing the interests of university faculty members (particularly former associate professors) in terms of job opportunities and chances for promotion through the system of state examinations.

In addition to defending the corporate interests of the profession, FASEE, the regional sociology associations, and the Colegio Nacional de Doctores y Licenciados en Ciencias Politicas y Sociologia organize training courses and keep practitioners up-to-date through journals such as the Catalan Sociology Association's *Revista de Ciéncies Socials* or the *Cuadernos de Ciencias Politicas y Sociologia* published by the Colegio Nacional de Doctores y Licenciados. The Colegio also gives two annual awards to sociologists: one for research and the other for the best published work.

The best example of how research centers have become institutionalized is the Centro de Investigaciones Sociológicas (CIS) in Madrid, which promotes basic research, builds up data banks for use by Spanish sociologists, and publishes their work in the form of books, monographs, surveys, and so on. The Centro's *Revista Española de Investigaciones Sociológicas* is one of the most prestigious journals in Spain. The predecessor of CIS, the Public Opinion Institute, founded in 1963, was a true trailblazer at a time when the political situation of the country made it difficult for such an organization to survive. In 1977, the Centro de Investigaciones Sociológicas took over, and many of the sociologists who formerly worked for the Institute continued working for the CIS. Among them are the former directors of the Institute, Salustiano del Campo and Rafael López Pintor, as well as numerous other professional sociologists and academics such as Juan Díez Nicolás, Francisco Alvira, José Caballero, and many others. All now work together with a new generation of sociologists such as Luis Rodríguez Zúñiga, Juan Salcedo, Ubaldo Martínez, Jacinto Rodríguez Osuna, and others. During this period, the Universidad Complutense's ICE (Institute of Educational Sciences) in Madrid also engaged in painstaking research, largely under the direction of Julio Carabaña.

These years (1970–1990) also saw the rational and inevitable division of labor among sociologists in Spain. Groups of social thinkers emerged and were classified more by their common interest in a particular area of specialization than by virtue of belonging to a particular school. During recent years the traditional scheme of distinguished masters and their followers or disciples has to some extent given way to a new order in which people with shared viewpoints or interests group together. Naturally, theoretical, methodological, and ideological affinities still exist, but they overlap and become interdisciplinary to such an extent that one can actually speak of new channels of social thought and new experiences in sociological praxis.

Thus, in the field of sociology of knowledge (as distinguished from epistemology as such) we have E. Lamo de Espinosa, E. Medina, and J. Trías, who are experts on the social production of knowledge, the distribution of knowledge in society, and the symbolic reproduction of this knowledge in close relationship to the structure of society and the cognoscent subject's knowledge. Their attempts to define this area of knowledge involve an approach that combines the object of their study with the "progressive revelation of the concrete and empirical nature of the cognoscent subject" (1987). Thus, the material object of knowledge ends up becoming the subject of all other knowledge or science. This field of knowledge involves analyzing the context of the knowledge or research and discovery, the relation between thought and society, object and subject, no matter what the conditioning or determining factors of this interaction may be. In contrast, José Trías (1971) represents the Marxist approach to sociology of knowledge in Spain. In his studies on ideology and false conscience, determinism is questioned in terms of the shape society takes in the social or symbolic representation of social phenomena. The belief that these forms give power structures their legitimacy has been examined from a more or less confirmed Marxist viewpoint, the more critical approach of the Frankfurt school (José Vericat, 1974), and in relation to present-day mass culture (Ludolfo Paramio, 1971).

The differentiation between sociology of knowledge and epistemology immediately presents problems. Esteban Medina (1982) attempted to resolve the dilemma by placing the problem in the context of the discussion on what criteria should be used to determine what is science and what is not science, the usefulness of research programs, and the border line between discovery and justification. Controversies over the philosophy of science have had a definite impact in this field of sociological knowledge. Despite writings on the crisis of American sociology by academics such as Juan F. Marsal (1979), one of the most influential schools of thought was neopositivism, with its long tradition in the United States. Recent discussions on the philosophy of science (U. C. Moulines; F. Suppe; W. Stegmüller; M. Bunge et al.) have triggered major social and philosophical studies of science by such sociologists as Carlos Moya, Pedro González Blasco, José Enrique Rodríguez Ibáñez, José Vericat, and Ramón Ramos.

The works of Francisco Parra Luna (closely linked to the theory of systems); Manuel García Ferrando (statistics); and Francisco Alvira, Jesús Ibáñez, Alfonso Ortí, Rafael López Pintor, and García Ferrando (on research methods and techniques) deal more with the field of methodology. Sociologists such as Miguel Beltrán, Pedro González Blasco, Carlota Solé, and Teresa González have repeatedly explored the science of social reality, the conceptualization of subjects for sociological study, the influence of different philosophical schools of thought on sociology, and the scientific approaches to social phenomena designed by various classic and contemporary authors. A number of contemporary Spanish sociologists, among them Victor Pérez Díaz, José Ma. Maravall, and Carlota Solé, have attempted to unite theoretical/scientific reflections on the subject studied with the application of the methods and techniques used in empirical studies. Although the sociology of science has not yet been formally institutionalized in Spain, certain sociologists have done considerable work in this area. Among them are José Jiménez Blanco, Pedro González Blasco, José Ma. López Piñeiro, and a large number of internationally recognized sociologists such as Manuel Castells, Ricardo Montoro, Juan José Castillo, and Diego López Garrido, who have researched the new technologies in Spain's society and economy.

Sociological theory, particularly epistemology and the sociology of knowledge, made notable progress at the same time that abundant studies were made of social inequalities and the existence of social classes in contemporary Spain. Theoretical and empirical studies of the country's social situation carried out in the 1960s and 1970s (the FOESSA reports published in 1967 and 1970) were the first in a long line of works dealing with the social structure of Spain. Among the pioneers in this field were Ignacio Fernández de Castro and Antonio Goytre, José Cazorla, Salvador Giner, and José Félix Tezanos. All adopted a critical approach, sometimes rooted in theory and doctrine, which grew out of the conditions prevalent at the time (as the Franco regime was coming to an end) when many of their works were published. Others openly disagreed with this approach and perhaps went to opposite extremes, designing strata studies of the Spanish social structure which were more descriptive than analytical. Thus, some sociologists viewed Spain as a class society typical of a capitalist production system, while others emphasized the inherent conflict in relations between

different social groups and classes, and still others advocated that economic or professional categories be used to analyze the country's social
structure.

These contrasting approaches were also mirrored in two distinct visions
of Spain. Some authors (Amando de Miguel, José Cazorla) considered the
country as a whole, and their studies employed such pragmatic indicators
as professional and occupational categories or earnings. Others (José Félix
Tezanos, Salvador Giner) had a more pluralistic vision and took the different histories of the different Spanish regions into consideration when
examining the subsystems of social inequality in Spain. The former described social strata, which can be measured or quantified on the basis of
the indicators used, and which at most makes it possible to speak about
the distance between them. Phenomena such as social conscience, conflict,
class struggle, and so forth were not taken into consideration. Holders of
the latter point of view expressly attempted to examine social classes as
defined in terms of their class conscience and classify them in relation to
other social classes. Rather than regarding facts as data, these authors
attempted to delve deeper and find an explanation for the causes of social
inequality (capitalist production, industrialization and urbanization processes, etc.) and the class struggle.

These two viewpoints have converged in work published during the past
fifteen years. The reasons are partly political (the transition to democracy,
the disappearance of the tendency to assign sociology the role of a pseudo-
agitator dedicated to explaining the true picture of the country) but also
partly due to the development of Spanish sociology itself. Thus, the late
1970s saw the appearance of the first studies reflecting the radical economic changes that had taken place in Spain since the 1960s and their
impact on the social structure of a country in the throes of accelerated
modernization (Victor Pérez Díaz, José Félix Texanos, Luis Garcia San
Miguel, Miguel Beltrán). This approach involved the use of statistical and
empirical data and explorations together with theoretical reflections on
the agents of social change, their strategies for deflecting social conflict,
the coexistence of various analytical categories, and so forth. Meanwhile,
studies that were empirical in nature continued to appear, exploring the
population and its unequal distribution in statistical categories (Juan Díez
Nicolás, Juan Salcedo). These studies were by no means incompatible with
the proliferation of research on specific sectors or subclasses (farm workers, the middle class, the working class, the upper class; employers, employees, etc.) at both a national and regional level.

There was also an abundance of studies on the class system in the various regions of Spain, which are historically, economically, and culturally
different from one another. This was when scholars began to openly deal
with the subject of nationalism as related to social structure. The 1980s
saw the appearance of a number of books and articles on social structure

and nationalism in Andalusia (José Cazorla), Catalonia (Carlota Solé, Faustino Miguélez, Francesc Mercadé, Francesc Hernández), and Galicia (José Pérez Vilariño).

Social classes and groups were studied in detail, and special attention was paid to the region in which these groups currently predominate or predominated in the past. Andalusian farm workers and their corporative associations were studied by Eduardo Sevilla, Manuel Pérez Yruela, and Eduardo Moyano; the population, its class structure and interest groups, representative associations and social organizations, the party system, and the modernization process in Catalonia were analyzed by Carlota Solé and Faustino Miguélez; the national issue and intellectuals were examined by Francesc Mercadé and Francesc Hernández. The following decade saw the publication of works that analyzed Spain's society and politics as a whole. Among these were the study directed by Salvador Giner and the report published by the Fundación Jaume Bofill on Catalan society, economy, politics, and culture from 1977 to 1988.

Around 1980 studies began appearing on the social changes taking place in post-Franco democratic Spain—a country open to Europe and the world and frankly anxious to make a mark on the international scene (José Félix Texanos, Ramón Cotarelo, Andrés de Blas). New social movements such as ecology and pacifism were studied by Louis Lemkow and Juan José García de la Cruz. Movements that are less new and have more of a tradition in Spain were also studied during this time. Inés Alberdi, Teresa Torns, and Judith Astellara worked with the Center for Feminist Studies at the Universidad Autónoma de Barcelona to analyze the feminist movement; Manuel Castells, Alice Gail Bier, and Anna Alabart studied urban movements and civic associations. Enrique Laraña, Andrés Guruchaga, and Antonio Arganzo studied the student movement; and José Sanromá analyzed the consumer movement.

One of the most interesting features of the transition period in Spain is the consolidation of negotiation as the way to settle labor and other conflicts. Employers' associations and labor unions turned corporatism and social pacts into standard practices in employer/employee relations. Just as in Austria, Germany, and other West European societies where social conflicts have been negotiated and employees have participated in company management as a matter of course since immediately after World War II, the years in Spain just after Franco's death saw a plethora of meetings, agreements, and corporatist pacts between the social forces, which made Spain one of the least conflictive countries in Europe—at least until the general strike protesting socialist government measures in December 1988.

These subjects have been explored by numerous authors. The February 1984 issue of *Revista Española de Investigaciones Sociológicas* carried an article by Carlota Solé describing the theoretical framework of the debate on corporatism/neocorporatism. Shortly thereafter, other work appeared on the corporatist society (Salvador Giner), corporatism in agriculture (Eduardo Moyano), and a number of other variations on the theme.

The latter half of the 1980s saw the publication of work analyzing the situation in Spain. Some of this work was reflective (Victor Pérez Díaz, Salvador Giner), and some consisted of empirical research on specific sections of the economy (Carlota Solé, Harry Rijnen, J. Pedro López Novo, Juan Jesús González, Pilar Rivilla) carried out by the Spanish team that worked under the direction of Victor Pérez Díaz on Philippe Schmitter and Wolfgang Streeck's international research project. At the same time a few voices were raised in criticism of the threats or dangers of neocorporatism. The most eloquent protests came first from Juan Martínez Alier, followed by Jordi Roca.

The work of Faustino Miguélez, Santos Juliá, and Angel Zaragoza was dedicated more specifically to labor relations and the impact of corporatist pacts in negotiating conflict in business firms. Their work could be classified as the sociology of labor—or, in broader terms, as part of the sociology of the economy. Business-labor-government pacts were the subject of detailed study, taking the shape of both empirical analysis and journalistic reporting. Sectorial and regional analyses were combined in order to illustrate the regional differences in solving labor and industrial problems. Employers and politicians (Victor Pérez Díaz), employers' associations (Carlota Solé), and labor unions (Faustino Miguélez) were among the specific subjects studied in the 1980s.

Specialization has been a striking characteristic of Spanish sociology during the past two decades. Some fields of specialization are survivors of previous years, but others first appeared around the latter half of the 1970s. There is a sizable group of experts in the sociology of labor (Juan José Castillo, Carlos Prieto, Andrés Bilbao, Faustino Miguélez) and education (Julio Carabaña, Juan Fernández Anguita, Marina Subirats, Josep María Masjoan), whose members have been studying old and new issues in these fields for over twenty years. The most significant contributions to urban sociology have been made by Mario Gavira, Manuel Castells, Jordi Borja, Jesús Leal, Josep Olives, Rosa Junyent, and Victor Urrutia, who have been involved in this field since its very beginnings. The sociology of religion has its specialists, among them Rogeli Duocastella, Joan Estruch, Juan González Anleo, Pedro González Blasco, José Pérez Vilariño, and José Alberto Prades.

In the 1980s a good deal of attention started being paid to the sociology of medicine and health. The Catalan Sociology Association's First Workshop in Barcelona and the First National Sociology Congress in Zaragoza, both held in 1981, revealed the existence of a considerable group of sociologists who work with members of the medical profession examining, writing, and publishing on this subject; organizing interdisciplinary retraining courses; and continually making themselves known abroad. Among the best-known members of this group are Jesús de Miguel, Vicente Navarro, Benjamín González, Carmen Domínguez-Alcón, Josep Rodríguez, Mauro Guillén, and Isidoro Alonso Hinojal. Prominent sociologists such as Salustiano del Campo and Maria Angeles Durán, who are not directly involved in this group, have nonetheless published important work on the subject of health.

Ever since the birth of modern sociology in Spain at the beginning of the 1960s, the family as an institution has been one of the major concerns of Spanish sociologists. The family has been continually analyzed not only in connection with the changes taking place in Spanish society, but also with other subjects such as women, youth, fertility and birth rates, industrialization, the labor market, mating habits, and so forth. The family has also been the subject of interdisciplinary analyses, especially by anthropologists and psychologists. During the 1970s the sociology of the family became a recognized field of specialization, and ten years later major works on the subject were published by such sociologists as Julio Iglesias de Ussel, Inés Alberdi, Salustiano del Campo, Rosa Conde, Juan Díez Nicolás, Lluís Flaquer, Joan Soler, Salvador Pérez Peñasco, Anna Alabart, Anna Cabré, and others.

At first, women's studies were included in the category of sociology of the family, but they soon became an independent field of knowledge and analysis. Twenty years later, by the 1980s, the field was flourishing. By the end of the 1970s, the first seminars on women had been held in the sociology departments of the Universities of Madrid, Barcelona, and Granada. Some of the most significant work on the subject was published by Maria Angeles Durán, Inés Alberdi, Julio Iglesias de Ussel, Jesús de Miguel, Marina Subirats, Maria Jesús Miranda, Enrique Gil Calvo, and Amando de Miguel. As time went on, traditional studies of women as related to the family or to work were enriched by studies which examined women's problems in terms of education, health, and participation in politics. Obviously, the evolution of Spain as a democratic society in which steps have been taken to eliminate discrimination against women in the educational system, legalize abortion, and admit women to the highest jobs and political offices in all types of organizations has contributed to the popularity of this field of study. The extensive literature that is now available includes work by Maria Jesús Izquierdo, Judith Astelarra, Teresa Torns, Rosa Ma. Capel, Pilar Folguera, Maria Teresa Gallego, Lois Méndez, and Pilar Escario. Their work has had enough impact that the current socialist government has created institutions to protect Spanish women from the discrimination they are likely to encounter in their daily existence.

Daily existence and, more specifically, such issues as privacy, intimacy, and individualism have become popular fields of study in the past ten years, thanks to the valuable contributions of specialists like Lluis Flaquer, who analyzes the private lives of families in rural and urban areas. Helena Bejar studies privacy in relation to the increase in individualism registered in the past ten to fifteen years; she bases her analysis on the historic origin of the distinction between what is public and what is private, explaining how this distinction relates to the construction of civil society and the liberal tradition with its exaltation of privacy.

In recent years, youth has been the subject of systematic study. In 1982, 1984, and 1989 surveys were made of the values and attitudes of young Spaniards. These studies were sponsored by the Fundación Santa Maria and directed by Miguel Beltrán, Francisco Andrés Orizo, and Pedro González Blasco. Among the sociologists collaborating on the studies were Juan Linz, José Juan Toharia, Rafael López Pintor, Manuel García Ferrando, Juan Gonzlez Anleo, and Manuel Gómez Reyno. Particularly noteworthy is the work done by Juan González, Antonio de Lucas, and Angel Ortí on young people's working and living conditions in rural areas; Luis Zárraga's two reports on young people in Spain (1985 and 1989); the 1989 report on the problems of entering the labor market and becoming integrated in society by Joaquím Casals, Josep Maria Masjoan, and Jordi Planas; Domingo Comas's 1985 work on the use of drugs; Francisco Alvira and Antonio Canteras Murillo's 1985 study of delinquency and social dropouts; and Enrique Gil Calvo's 1985 work on cultural activities and use of leisure time.

Electoral sociology is another area of specialization that has developed within the last fifteen years. This is a field midway between sociology and political science. The demise of the Franco regime and the ensuing switch to democracy doubtless inspired the formation of the Barcelona group (Josep Maria Vallés, Francesc Pallarés, Rosa Virós, Montserrat Tresseres, and others), the Madrid group (Rafael López Pintor, José Juan Toharia, Manuel Santillán, Miguel Martínez Cuadrado, Jorge de Esteban, Luis López Guerra, José Ramón Montero, Alejandro Muñoz Alonso), and the Basque Country specialists (the team led by Francisco Liera), as well as other, more recent groups working in the Canary Islands and Andalusia. Since 1978 these teams have published studies, maps, reports, and analyses of the various national, regional, and local elections held in Spain since the beginning of democracy. The party system and political change have been much studied. One of the most prolific writers on this subject is Juan Linz.

Other, more recent but equally important issues being studied by Spanish sociologists include the sociology of public administration, the legal system, ecology, leisure time and sports, new technologies, mass communications, religion, migrations, the armed forces, poverty and welfare, delinquents, and drug addiction. Some of the best-known sociologists working with these subjects are Miguel Beltrán, Mariano Baena, José Maria García Madaria, Alberto Gutiérrez Reñón, Rafael Bañón; Louis Lemkow, Mario Gavira, Josep Vicens Marqués; Manuel Garcia Ferrando, Nuria Puig, Luis González Seara; Manuel Martín Serrano, José Luis Piñuel, Manuel Parés, Miguel Moragas; Joan Estruch, Juan González Anleo, José Pérez Vilariño, Pedro González Blasco; Carlota Solé, José Cazorla, Angeles Pascual, Lluís Recolons, José Antonio Garmendia; Juli Busquets, Jesús Maria Paricio, José Antonio Olmeda, Carlos Santamaría, Carlos Seco Serrano; Tomás Calvo, Josep Picó, Gregorio Rodríguez Cabrero; Domingo Comas, Juli Gabaté, José Navarro, Javier Elzo, and Javier Blanco.

The list of these authors' works is a long one; it demonstrates how prolific Spanish sociologists have been during the past two decades. They gradually refined their methodology until they reached the level of scientific rigor which has earned them acceptance on an international level. Their theoretical and conceptual approaches and tendencies have also been refined. Thus, a great deal of the critical sociology of the 1960s, which was customarily influenced by Marxist thought and cohabited uneasily with the empirical sociology of the United States (which had such a great influence in Spain during the 1970s), has now given way to a more analytical, comparative, and pluralist production in which the influences of Weber, Dahrendorf, and Parsons not only coexist but are combined with the most empirical descriptive approaches in order to illustrate theoretical affirmations with hard facts. Spanish sociology is still young, but perhaps the 1990s will mark its coming of age.

BIBLIOGRAPHY

It is impossible to list all the books written by the authors mentioned in the text. The following bibliography contains only the most important collections of sociological writings published in Spain during the past twenty years and is by no means a complete list of the material available.

del Campo, Salustiano (ed). 1984. *Tratado de Sociología.* Ed. Taurus, Madrid.
Fundación, Jaume Bofill (ed). 1989. *Catalunya, 77–88.* Ed. La Magrana, Barcelona.
Giner, Salvador (ed). 1990. *España. Sociedad y Política.* Ed. Espasa Calpe, Madrid.
Iglesias, Carmen; R. Aramberri, Julio; R. Zúñiga, Luis. 1980. *Los orígenes de la teoría sociológica.* Akal, Madrid.
Jiménez Blanco, José; Moya Valgañón, Carlots (eds.). 1978. *Teoría Sociológica Contemporánea.* Ed. Tecnos, Madrid.
Texanos, José Félix; Cotarelo, Ramón; de Blas, Andrés. 1989. *La transición democrática española.* Ed. Sistema, Madrid.

REFERENCES

Aguilar, F.; et al. 1990. "Intereses individuales y acción colectiva." *Zona Abierta* 54–55, Madrid.

Aguilar Piñar, F. 1967. *Los comienzos de la crisis universitaria en España.* Madrid: El Magisterio Español.

Alabart, A.; A. Cabré; et al. 1988. *La cohabitaciòn en España.* Madrid: CIS.

Alberdi, I. 1978. *El fin de la Família.* Barcelona: Bruguera.

Alberdi, I. 1979. *Historia y Sociología del divorcio en España.* Madrid: Centro de Investigaciones Sociológicas.

Alberdi I.; and P. Escario. 1986. *El impacto de las nuevas tecnologías en la formación y el trabajo de las mujeres.* Madrid: Instituto de la Mujer.

Alberdi I.; and P. Escario. 1988. *La situación social de las viudas en España.* Madrid: Ministerio de Trabajo. Alberoni, F. (1977) 1984. "La formación del grupo" in *Movimiento e Institución.* Madrid: Editorial Nacional, 185–235.

Alvira, F.; et al. 1983. *El papel de politólogos y sociólogos en la sociedad española.* Datos CIS, estudio no. 1.369. Madrid: Colegio de Doctores y Licenciados en CCPP y sociología, CIS.

Alvira, F.; M. García Fernando; and J. Ibañez. 1986. *Análisis de la realidad social.* Madrid: Alianza.

Beltran, M. 1987. "Perceptores de ingresos y familias" in *Política y Sociedad,* vol. 2. Madrid: CIS.

Beltran, M. 1989. *Los funcionarios ante la reforma de la Administraciòn.* Madrid: CIS.

Carabaña, J. 1983. *Educación, ocupación e ingresos en la España del siglo XX.* Madrid: Ministerio de Educación.

Carabaña, J. 1983. "¿Racionalidad o discriminación?. Sobre los estudios acerca del sexismo ocupacional y la família" in J. Jiménez Blanco, and C. Moya (eds.), *Teoría sociológica contemporánea.* Madrid: Tecnos.

Carabaña J.; and E. Lamo. 1978. "Resumen y valoración crítica del interaccionismo simbólico" in J. Jiménez Blanco and C. Moya (eds.), *Teoría sociológica contemporánea.* Madrid: Tecnos.

Castells, M. 1983. *El desafio tecnológico. España y las nuevas tecnologías.* Madrid: Alianza.

Castells, M. 1986. *La ciudad y las masas. Sociología de los movimientos sociales urbanos.* Madrid: Alianza.

Castells, M.; et al. 1986. *Nuevas Tecnologías, Economía y Sociedad en España.* Madrid: Alianza Ediotorial.

Castillo Castillo, J. 1983. "Los hijos de la sociedad de consumo" in J. L. López Aranguren et al., *Infancia y sociedad en España.* Madrid: Hesperia, 65–80.

Castillo Castillo, J. "Consumo y bienestar" in J. Vidal Beneyto (ed.), *España a debate vol. II La sociedad.* Madrid: Tecnos.

Castillo, J. 1968. *Introducción a la sociología.* Madrid: Guadarrama.

Castillo, J. 1987. *Sociedad de consumo a la española.* Madrid: Eudema.

Cazorla, J. 1989. "Estudios empíricos de la sociología española." *Anales de Sociología* 3, Madrid.

Conde, R.; et al. 1982. *Familia y cambio social en España.* Madrid: CIS.

De Miguel, A. 1965. "Cambio, movilidad y promoción social." *Revista de trabajo* 11–12, 93–127.

De Miguel, A. 1966. "Análisis general de la movilidad social en España" in Varios, *La promoción social en España.* Madrid: Valle de los Caídos.

De Miguel, A. 1969. *Introducción a la sociología de la vida cotidiana*. Madrid: Cuadernos para el diálogo.

De Miguel, A. 1970. "Evolución y perspectivas de la población escolar en España, 1960–1980." *Arbor* 220, 33–51.

De Miguel, A. 1972. *España, marca registrada*. Barcelona: Kairós.

De Miguel, A. 1974. *Manual de estructura social de España*. Madrid: Tecnos.

De Miguel, A. 1984. *La bola de cristal. Los intelectuales norteamericanos y el futuro del capitalismo*. Barcelona: Argos Vergara.

De Miguel, A.; et al. 1970. *Síntesis del informe sociológico sobre la situación social de España 1970*. Madrid: Euramérica.

De Miguel A.; J. M. De Miguel; et al. 1972. *Informe sociológico sobre la situación social de España*. Madrid: FOESSA Euramérica.

De Miguel, J. M. 1973. *El ritmo de la vida social*. Madrid: Tecnos.

De Miguel, J. M. 1978. *Anatomía de una Universidad*. Barcelona: Dopesa.

De Miguel, J. M. 1984. *La amorosa dictadura*. Barcelona: Anagrama.

De Miguel, J. M. 1985. *La salud pública del futuro*. Madrid: Ariel.

De Miguel, J. M. 1990. *El mito de la sociedad organizada*. Barcelona: Península.

De Miguel, J. M.; et al. 1988. *El futuro de la salud*. Madrid: Centro de Estudios Constitucionales.

De Miguel, J. M.; and J. Díez Nicolás. 1985. *Politicas de población*. Madrid: Espasa Calpe.

De Miguel, J. M.; and M. G. Moyer. 1979. "Sociology in Spain." *Current Sociology* 27, no. 1.

Del Campo, S. 1969. *La Sociología científica moderna*. Madrid: Centro de Estudios Constitucionales.

Del Campo, S. 1973. *Cambios Sociales y Formas de Vida*. Barcelona: Ariel.

Del Campo, S. (Ed.). 1984. *Tratado de Sociología*. Madrid: Taurus.

Del Pino Artacho, J. 1986. *Perspectivas teóricas de la Sociología*. Málaga: Universidad de Málaga.

Del Pino Artacho, J. (Ed.). 1987. *El Conflicto Social*. Málaga: UNED.

Del Pino Artacho, J. 1987. "Paradigmas y teorías como marcos de referencia en la enseñanza expositiva de la sociología" in *Política y Sociedad. Estudios en homenaje a Francisco Murillo Ferrol*. Madrid: CIS and CESCO, 159–70.

Del Pino Artacho, J. 1990. *Teoría Sociológica*. Madrid: Tecnos.

Díez Nicolás, J. 1966. "Motivación, aspiraciones e información en la promoción social" in Varios, *La promoción social en España*. Madrid: Valle de los Caídos.

Díez Nicolás, J. 1971. *La sociología: entre el funcionalismo y la dialéctica*. Madrid: Guadiana.

Díez Nicolás, J. 1972. "La urbanización y el urbanismo en la década de los 70" in M. Fraga Iribarne et al., *La España de los 70. Vol. 1 La Sociedad*. Madrid: Moneda y Crédito.

Díez Nicolás, J. 1990. "La población española" in S. Giner (dir.), *España, Sociedad y Política*. Madrid: Espasa-Calpe.

Díez Nicolás, J.; et al. 1984. *50 años de sociología en España*. Málaga: Universidad de Málaga:

Díez Nicolás, J.; and J. del Pino. 1973. "Estratificación y movilidad social en España en la década de los años setenta" in S. del Campo (ed.), *La sociedad española en la década de los setenta.* Madrid: CECA.

Díez Nicolás, J.; and J. M. De Miguel. 1981. *Control de la natalidad en España.* Barcelona: Fontanella.

Durán, M. A. 1972. *El trabajo de la mujer en España.* Madrid: Tecnos.

Durán, M. A. 1977. *Dominación, sexo y cambio social.* Madrid: Edicusa.

Durán, M. A. 1982. *Liberación y utopía.* Madrid: Akal.

Durán, M. A. 1983. "Socialización diferencias de clase y sexo" in Aranguren et al., *Infancia y sociedad en España.* Madrid: Hesperia, 81–97.

Durán, M. A. 1988. *De puertas adentro.* Madrid: Ministerio de Cultura.

Flaquer, L. L.; and J. Soler. 1990. *Permanencia y cambio en la familia española.* Madrid: CIS.

García Ferrando, M. 1976. "La investigación sociológica y los datos estadísticos: una crítica al positivismo y el sujetivismo" in *Papers: Revista Sociológica* 6, Barcelona: Univ. Autónoma.

García Ferrando, M. 1978. "La sociología, ¿una ciencia multiparadigmática?." in J. Jiménez Blanco and C. Moya (eds.), *Teoría sociológica contemporánea.* Madrid: Tecnos, 445–64.

García Ferrando, M. 1979. *Sobre el método.* Madrid: CIS.

García Ferrando, M. 1984. *Socioestadística. Introducción a la Estadística en Sociología.* Madrid: CIS.

García Ferrando, (Comp.). 1988. *Pensar nuestra sociedad.* Valencia: Mestral.

García Ferrando, M.; J. Ibáñez; and F. Alvira. 1986. *El análisis de la realidad social.* Madrid: Alianza Textos.

Garmendia, J. A. 1979. *Sociología.* Madrid: CIS.

Garmendia, J. A. (Comp.). 1981. "El análisis de entre-vistas libres a emigrantes y expertos españoles" in *La emigración española en la encrucijada.* Madrid: CIS, 389–422.

Garmendia, J. A. 1985. "Comportamientos variantes y desorganización social" in S. del Campo, *Tratado de sociología.* Madrid: Taurus.

Garmendia, J. A. 1990. *Desarrollo de la organización y cultura de la empresa.* Madrid: ESIC.

Garmendia, J. A.; M. Navarro; and F. Parra Luna. 1987. *Sociología Industrial y de la empresa.* Madrid: Aguilar.

Giner, S. 1968. *Sociología.* Barcelona: Península.

Giner, S. 1974. *El progreso de la conciencia sociológica.* Barcelona: Península.

Giner, S. 1975. *História del pensamiento social.* Barcelona: Ariel.

Giner, S. 1976. *Introducción a la sociología.* Barcelona: Península.

Giner, S. 1979. *Sociedad masa.* Barcelona: Península.

Giner, S. 1987. *Ensayos civiles.* Barcelona: Península.

Giner, S. 1991. "Una incierta victoria: la inteligencia sociológica" in T. González de la Fe (ed.), *Sociología: unidad y diversidad.* Madrid: CESIC.

Giner, S.; et al. 1990. *España. Sociedad y Política.* Madrid: Espasa Calpe.

Giner, S.; and M. Pérez Iruela. 1979. *La sociedad corporativa.* Madrid: Centro de Investigaciones Sociológicas.

Gómez Arboleya, E. 1976. *História de la estructura y del pensamiento social.* Madrid: Instituto de Estudios Políticos.

Gómez Arboleya, E. 1982. *Estudios de teoría de la sociedad y del Estado.* Madrid: Centro de Estudios Constitucionales.

Gómez de Liaño, I. 1989. *La mentira social. Imágenes, mitos y conducta.* Madrid: Tecnos.

Gómez Pérez, R. 1972. "La demanda de Universidades en España." *Nuestro Tiempo* 212, 41–45.

González, J. J. 1985. "Las asociaciones profesionales agrarias." *Papeles de Economía Española* 22, Madrid.

González Anleo, J. 1976. *Catolicismo Nacional: nostalgia y crisis.* Madrid: Paulinas.

González Blasco, P. 1980. *El investigador científico en España.* Madrid: Centro de Investigaciones Sociológicas.

González Seara, L. 1970. *La sociología, aventura dialéctica.* Madrid: Tecnos.

Ibañez, J. 1979. *Mas allá de la sociología. El grupo de discusión: técnica y crítica.* Madrid: Siglo XXI.

Ibañez, J. 1985. *Del algoritmo al sujeto. Perspectivas de la investigación social.* Madrid: Siglo XXI.

Iglesias, M. C. 1983. *Paradigma de la naturaleza. Montesquieu. Rousseau. Compte.* Madrid: Fundación Juan March.

Iglesias, M. C. 1984. *El pensamiento de Montesquieu.* Madrid: Alianza.

Iglesias, M. C.; J. Rodriguez Aramberri; and L. Rodriguez Zúñiga. 1980. *Los Origenes de la Teoría Sociológica.* Madrid: Akal.

Iglesias de Ussel, J. 1983. "Infancia y família en España" in J. L. López Aranguren et al., *Infancia y sociedad en España.* Madrid: Hesperia, 229–60.

Iglesias de Ussel, J. 1987. "El tiempo en la sociedad contemporánea" in *Política y Sociedad.* Madrid: Centro de Investigaciones Sociológicas, 113–33.

Jiménez Blanco, J. (Ed.). 1968. "Personalización y socialización en las ciencias sociales modernas" in *La persona humana en la sociedad contemporánea. Personalización y socialización.* Madrid: Anales de Moral Social y Económica.

Jiménez Blanco, J. 1973. "Sociedad, individuo, homosociologicus." Presentación de la versión española de R. Dahrendorf en *Homo sociologicus.* Madrid: IEP.

Jiménez Blanco, J. 1974. "Sobre la disputa del positivismo en la sociología alemana." *REIS* 36, 37.

Jiménez Blanco, J.; et al. 1986. *Sociología general.* Madrid: UNED.

Jiménez Landi, A. 1973. *La Institución Libre de Enseñanza.* Madrid: Taurus.

Lamo de Espinosa, E. 1975. *Juicios de valor y ciencia social.* Valencia: Fernando Torres.

Lamo de Espinosa, E. 1981. *La teoría de la cosificación. De Marx a la escuela de Frankfurt.* Madrid: Alianza.

Lamo de Espinosa, E. 1990. *La sociedad reflexiva.* Madrid: Centro de Investigaciones Sociológicas.

Laraña, E. 1986. "Cambio social" in S. del Campo (ed.), *Tratado de sociología.* Madrid: Taurus, vol. 2, 243–77.

Lerena, C. 1976. *Escuela, ideología y clases sociales en España.* Barcelona: Ariel.

Lerena, C. 1983. *Reprimir y liberar. Crítica sociológica de la educación y la cultura contemporánea.* Madrid: Akal.

Lerena, C. 1985. *Materiales de sociología de la educación.* Madrid: Grupo Zero.

Lerena, C. (Comp.). 1987. *Educación y Sociología en España* (Selección de textos). Madrid: Akal.

Linz, J. J. (Ed.). 1984. *España, un pasado para un futuro*. La sociedad, vol. 1. Madrid: Instituto de Estudios Económicos.

Linz, J. J. 1988. "Política e intereses a lo largo de un siglo en España: 1880–1980" in M. Pérez Yruela and S. Giner (eds.), *El corporativismo en España*. Barcelona: Península.

Linz, J. J.; and A. De Miguel. 1966. *Los empresarios ante el poder público*. Madrid: IEP.

López Aranguren, J. L. 1962. *La juventud europea et al. ensayos*. Barcelona: Seix-Barral.

López Aranguren, J. L. 1967. "Introducción" to P. Bourdieu and J. C. Passeron, *Los estudiantes y la cultural*. Barcelona: Labor.

López Aranguren, J. L. 1973. *Moralidades de hoy y de mañana*. Madrid: Taurus.

López Aranguren, J. L. 1981. "La vida moral" in *Etica*. Madrid: Alianza, 279–97.

López Aranguren, J. L. 1986. *La comunicación humana*. Madrid: Tecnos.

López Pintor, R. 1991. "Opinión pública, valor y ura política en España" in J. Vidal Beneyto (ed.), *España a debate vol. II La sociedad*. Madrid: Tecnos.

Maravall, J. M. 1970. *El desarrollo económico y la clase obrera*. Barcelona: Ariel.

Maravall, J. M. 1972. *Sociología de lo posible*. Madrid: Siglo XXI.

Maravall, J. M. 1978. *Dictadura y disentimiento político*. Madrid: Alfaguara.

Maravall, J. M. 1978. "Sociología y explicación funcional" in J. Jiménez Blanco and C. Moya, *Teoría Sociológica Contemporánea*. 148–57.

Marsal, J. F. 1977. *La crisis de la sociología norte-americana*. Barcelona: Península.

Marsal, J. F. 1978. *Conocer Max Weber y su obra*. Barcelona: Dopesa.

Marsal, J. F. 1979. *Dependencia e independencia*. Madrid: CIS.

Marsal, J. F.; and B. Oltra. 1977. *Nuestra sociedad: Introducción a la sociología*. Barcelona: Ed. Vicens Universidad.

Martín López, E. 1966. *Guiones de sociología general*. Madrid: Ed. Zagos.

Martín López, E. 1982. "Datos globales Tercera edad" and "Trabajos actuales hacia el trabajo en la Tercera Edad" in Lucenesa Nacional a la *Revista de Seguridad social* 16, Oct.–Dec. 1982.

Martín López, E. 1986. *Fundamentos sociales de la felicidad individual*. Piura, Perú: Universidad de Piura.

Martín López, E. 1990. "Los intelectuales y su papel en la formación de la opinión pública" in *Sociología de la opinión pública,* Vol. 1. Madrid: Facultad Ciencias Políticas y Sociología, Univ. Complutense.

Martín López, E. 1990. *Sociología de la opinión pública*. Madrid: Facultad Cienias Políticas y Sociología, Univ. Complutense.

Martín Moreno, J.; and A. de Miguel. 1979. *Universidad, fábrica de parados*. Barcelona: Vicens Vives.

Martín Santos, L. 1990. "Teoría de las catástrofes" in *Política y Sociedad*. Invierno 90.

Martín Serrano, M. 1973. "Libertad y predicción en las ciencias sociales." *Revista de ciencias sociales* 7, Madrid.

Martín Serrano, M. 1977. *La mediación Social*. Madrid: Akal.

Martín Serrano, M. 1978. *Métodos actuales de investigación social*. Madrid: Akal.

Martín Serrano, M. 1981. *Teoría de la comunicación*. Madrid: UIMP.

Martín Serrano, M. 1986. *La producción social de la comunicación.* Madrid: Alianza.

Martínez, R.; and R. Pardo. 1985. "El asociacionismo español en la transiciòn." *Papeles de Economía Española* 22, Madrid.

Medina, E. 1989. *Conocimiento y sociología de la ciencia.* Madrid: CIS.

Mercadé, F.; F. Hernandez; and B. Oltra. 1988. *Once tesis sobre la cuestión nacional en España.* Barcelona: Ed. Anthropos.

Miguélez, F. 1985. "Corporatismo y relaciones laborales en Europa en tiempos de crisis." *Revista Española de Investigaciones Sociológicas* 30, Madrid.

Moya, C. 1967. "Emile Durkheim: la autonomía metodológica de la sociología y los orígenes del análisis estructural funcional." *Revista Española de la Opinión Pública* 8, Madrid.

Moya, C. 1970. *Sociología y sociológos.* Madrid: Siglo XXI.

Moya, C. 1971. *Burocracia y sociedad industrial.* Madrid: Edicusa.

Moya, C. 1971. *Teoría Sociológica. Una introducción crítica.* Madrid: Taurus.

Moyano, E. 1984. *Corporatismo y Agricultura,* Madrid: Mº de Agricultura.

Muñoz-Alonso, A. 1990. "Génesis y aparación del concepto de opinión pública" in A. Muñoz Alonso et al., *Opinión pública y comunicación política.* Madrid: Eudema Universidad.

Navarro, M. (Dir.). 1978. *La sociedad de consumo y su futuro.* Madrid: Instituto Nacional del Consumo.

Navarro, M. 1985. "Economía" in *Tratado de Sociología.* Madrid: Taurus, 61–96.

Navarro, M. 1987. "Producción y consumo" in J.A. Garmendia et al. (eds.), *Sociología industrial y de la empresa.* Madrid: Aguilar.

Oltra, B. 1978. *Una sociología de los intelectuales.* Barcelona: Ed. Vicencs.

Ortí, A. 1984. "Crisis del modelo neogritalista y reproducciòn del proletariado rural" in E. Sevilla Guzman (ed.), *Sobre agricultura y campesinos.* Madrid: Mo Agricultura.

Paramio, L. 1984. "Marxismo y explicación funcional: una reivindicación de la filosofía de la historia de Marx" in L. Rodríguez and F. Bouza, *Sociología contemporánea. Ocho temas a debate.* Madrid: CIS Siglo XXI.

Pareto, W. 1967. *Forma y equilibrio sociales.* Madrid: Revista de Occidente.

Parra Luna, F. "Balance social de la empresa" in J. A. Garmendia et al., *Sociología industrial de la empresa.* Madrid: Aguilar, 299–329.

Pérez Agote, A. (Ed.). 1989. *Sociologia del Nacionalismo.* Bilbao: Universidad del País Vasco.

Pérez Díaz, V. 1972. *Cambio tecnológico y procesos educativos en España.* Madrid: Seminarios y Ediciones.

Pérez Díaz, V. M. 1978. *Estado, Burocracia y Sociedad Civil.* Madrid: Alfaguara.

Pérez Díaz, V. 1979. *Clases obrera, partidos y sindicatos.* Madrid: Instituto Nacional de la Industria.

Pérez Díaz, V. 1980. *Clase obrera, orden social y conciencia de clase.* Madrid: Fundación del INI.

Pérez Díaz, V. M. 1980. *Introducción a la Sociolog,aaia.* Madrid: Alianza.

Pérez Díaz, V. 1987. "La calidad de la educación superior en España y la resignación al status de país periférico" in *El retorno de la sociedad civil.* Madrid: Instituto de Estudios Económicos, 261–97.

Pérez Díaz, V. 1987. "La doble cara del neocorporativismo. Políticas económicas y pactos sociales" in *La España de la transición.* 95–125.

Pérez Díaz, V. 1987. *El retorno de la sociedad civil.* Madrid: Instituto de Estudios Económicos.

Pérez Yruela, M.; and S. Giner. 1988. *El corporativismo en España.* Barcelona: Ariel.

Perpiña Grau, R. 1954. *Corología. Teoría estructural y estructurante de la población española (1900–1950).* Madrid: Inst. Sancho de Moncada.

Picó, J. 1987. *Teorías sobre el estado del Bienestar.* Madrid: Siglo XXI.

Ramos, R. 1989. "El calendario sagrado: el problema del tiempo en la sociología durkheimiana." *Revista Española de Sociología* 46, 48.

Rodriguez Cabrero, G. 1985. "Tendencias actuales del intervencionismo estatal y su influencia en los modos de estructuración social." *Revista Española de Investigaciones Sociológicas* 31, Madrid.

Rodriguez Cabrero, G. 1988. *La integración social de la drogodependencia.* Madrid: Plan Nacional de la Droga.

Rodríguez Ibañez, J. E. 1989. *La perspectiva sociológica.* Madrid: Taurus.

Rodríguez Ibañez, J. E. 1990. "De la crisis de legitimación al corporatismo: las paradojas políticas de las sociedades contemporáneas" in *Centro de Estudios Constitucionales.* Madrid, 219–52.

Rodríguez Ibáñez, J. E. 1991. "Decisión racional versus holismo." *Revista Española de Investigaciones Sociológicas* 54, Madrid.

Rodríguez Zúñiga, L. 1973. *Raymond Aron y la Sociedad Industrial.* Madrid: Centro de Investigaciones Sociológicas.

Rodríguez Zúñiga, L. 1976. *Elites y democrácia.* Valencia: F. Torres.

Rodríguez Zúñiga, L. 1978. *Para una lectura crítica de Durkheim.* Madrid: Akal.

Rodriguez Zúñiga, L. 1984. "El desarrollo de la teoría sociológica" in S. del Campo (ed.), *Tratado de sociología,* Vol. 1. Madrid: Taurus.

Rodríguez Zúñiga, L. 1988. "Sobre el problema de los orígenes de la Sociología" in *Homenaje a José Antonio Maravall.* Madrid: Centro de Investigaciones Sociológicas.

Rodríguez Zúñiga, L.; and F. Bouza. 1984. *Sociología contemporánea.* Madrid: Centro de Investigaciones Sociológicas.

Roemer, J. C. 1982. *A General Theory of Exploitation and Class.* Cambridge, Mass.: Harvard University Press.

Rojo, L. A.; and V. Pérez Díaz. 1984. *Marx, economía y moral.* Madrid: Alianza.

Salcedo, S. 1989. "La tercera revolución industrial (De la revolución científico-técnica a la sociedad post-industrial)" in *Cambio Social y Modernización.* Valencia: Publicaciones de la Generalitat Valenciana.

Salcedo, S. 1990. "Entre la era industrial y la era tecnológica." *Business* 2. Valencia: Escuela Universitatria de Empresariales de Valencia (AIESEC).

Solé, C. 1976. *Modernización. Un análisis sociológico.* Barcelona: Península.

Solé, C. 1981. *La integración sociocultural de los inmigrantes en Cataluña.* Madrid: Centro de Investigaciones Sociológicas.

Solé, C. 1982. *Los inmigrantes en la sociedad y en la cultura catalanas.* Barcelona: Península.

Solé, C. 1984. "Tendencias actuales en la explicación de la sociedad." *Perspectiva Social* 19, Barcelona.

Solé, C. 1986. *Sociología. Fundamentos filosóficos y cuestiones metodológicas.* Barcelona: Ed. Hispano Europea.

Solé, C. (Comp.). 1987. *Corporatismo y diferenciación regional.* Madrid: Ministerio de Trabajo y Seguridad Social.

Solé, C. 1987. *Ensayos de teoría sociológica. Modernización y postmodernidad.* Madrid: Paraninfo.

Solé, C. 1990. "Las clases medias: criterios de definición." *Revista Española de Investigaciónes Sociológicas* 49, Madrid, 7–25.

Texanos, J. F. 1975. *Estructura de clases en la España actual.* Madrid: Edicusa.

Texanos, J. F. 1977. *Alienación, dialéctica y libertad.* Valencia: Fdo. Torres Editor.

Texanos, J. F. 1982. *¿Crisis de la conciencia obrera?.* Madrid: Mezquita.

Texanos, J. F. 1984. "Análisis de la estratificación social" in S. del Campo (ed.), *Tratado de Sociología.* Madrid: Taurus, 235–66.

Texanos, J. F. 1990. *La explicación sociológica: una introducción a la sociología.* Madrid: UNED.

Toharia, J. J. 1989. *Cambios recientes en la sociedad española.* Madrid: IEE.

Toharia, L. (Comp.). 1983. *El mercado de trabajo: teorías y aplicaciones.* Madrid: Alianza.

Torregrosa, J. R.; and B. Saravia (Eds.). 1983. *Perspectivas y Contexto de la Psicología Social.* Barcelona: Ed. Hispano Europea.

Uña, O.; et al. 1989. *Conocimiento y comunicación.* Madrid: Montesinos.

Vallés, J. M. 1989. "Political Science in Contemporany Spain: An overview." Barcelona: ICPS (Working Paper).

Varela, Julia (Ed.). 1983. *Perspectivas actuales en sociología de la educación.* Madrid: ICE de la UAM.

Veira, J. L. 1983. *Análisis sociológico del profesorado universitario.* Santiago: Universidad de Santiago de Compostela.

Vericat, J. 1974. "El sentido de la sociología." *Revista de la Opinión Pública* 37, Madrid.

Zaragoza, A. 1988. "El ocio en las sociedades avanzadas." *Sistema* 76, Madrid.

Part V

Sociology in Africa and the Middle East

Long dominated by colonial powers, much of Africa and the Middle East obtained national independence after World War II. These newly independent states have confronted numerous problems. In many instances the colonial traditions either did not provide a sufficient foundation for building institutions and intellectual traditions or were openly rejected. Others used some of the residues of colonial scholarship to extend earlier traditions or to resist and fashion oppositional styles. Others found themselves wedged in by contesting religious traditions and pan-national sentiments. Many found that the cold war between the United States and the former Soviet Union constituted a contingency of a major dimension, in some ways not unlike that of the earlier colonial period. Overall, the conditions for effective nation-building have not been uniformly present. Sociology has not significantly penetrated the institutional and intellectual landscape. The shadow of the colonial past still looms large in many settings; and in the scheme of world affairs, much attention is directed toward examining prenational formations and conditions which are of interest to developmentalists.

M'hammed Sabour sketches the history of sociology in Morocco, noting how work in the colonial period is now being eclipsed in this post-independence epoch. The earlier epoch focused on politics, the tribal system, Islam, and rural and urban life. In the postcolonial period, Moroccan sociology retains ties with French sociology, continuing a long-forged relationship, although there are English-speaking enclaves and an emergent nationalistic sociology. Sabour, citing A. Dialmy, classifies sociological interest into three broad types: " 'happy' (technocratic) sociology, 'worried' (epistemological) sociology, and 'merry' (metaphysical) sociology." Though sociology as a recognized activity continues to struggle, the effort to make sociology primarily a Moroccan activity continues even though its institutional autonomy is not yet ensured.

Detailing the colonial influences on Zimbabwe, formerly Northern Rhodesia, A. P. Cheater highlights the locations and personalities which dominated sociology. The contemporary period is characterized by certain theoretical and methodological problems, reflecting a reliance on earlier colonial-inspired formulations. The research agenda of contemporary Zimbabwean sociologists centers on social issues of central concern to the state: medicine, rural development, labor-industrial studies, urbanization, and religion. Reflective of the colonial epoch, the distinction between sociology and social anthropology is often unclear.

Eva Etzioni-Halevy and Rina Shapira trace the growth of sociology in Israel with the growth of the Israeli state. Unlike many former colonies, Israel had the advantage of building a national-political order immediately. Many of those who attained leadership positions in the formative years of Israel were well versed in the ways and operations of Western political-military regimes.

After surveying the early history, the authors note that the pluralism of the inhabitants of Israel, most of whom are immigrants, commands sociological attention on highlighting and exploring divisions and consensus. Theoretically, attention follows Western lines—structural functionalism, symbolic interactionism, phenomenology. The role of S. N. Eisenstadt as a purveyor of the functionalist tradition is noted. The substantive areas of primary interest include examinations of the kibbutz (communal settlement), immigration and accommodation, ethnic and nationality studies, social stratification, education, politics, and religion. Meanwhile, Israel's sociology is sufficiently institutionalized that numerous other topical areas are also explored. A nation which remakes itself in the wake of changing political and economic conditions, and whose population dynamics strain competing national and religious interests, establishes, the authors suggest, conditions for sociology to be a voice of pluralism.

24

Contemporary Sociology in Israel

Eva Etzioni-Halevy and Rina Shapira

Sociology in Israel developed with the development of Israeli society: as society grew and expanded, so did sociology. As society became more differentiated and heterogeneous, so did sociology. From modest beginnings in one center, the Hebrew University in Jerusalem, it has now proliferated and taken root in seven institutions of higher learning, as well as in various colleges and (as a topic of study) in a large number of high schools. Israeli sociology has also branched out into various applied areas; and from being an elite discipline, dominated first by one and then by a small group of leaders, it has become almost a "mass" discipline, including several hundreds of professional sociologists and thousands of students. Whether this quantitative growth also spells a qualitative growth is still an open question, to which we cannot purport to supply an answer. One point is clear, at any rate: Israeli sociology has very much held its hand on the pulse of Israeli society. Generally speaking, and with some exceptions, the major problems of Israeli society have also become the major problems of Israeli sociology.

THE ORIGINS AND PROLIFERATION OF ISRAELI SOCIOLOGY

In the beginning there was Martin Buber. Buber was, of course, world-renowned. However, he was not strictly speaking a sociologist, but rather a social philosopher and a Judaic scholar. He became the pioneer of sociology in Israel for reasons that had little to do with sociology itself. When he emigrated from Germany to what was then Palestine in 1938, the only existing university was the Hebrew University in Jerusalem. As the chairs

in Philosophy and in Biblical Studies were occupied already, a special chair
was created for him and, perhaps for lack of a better name, was named
Sociology of Culture. Thereby he was made head of a program, not of a
department. But the program, once created, assumed a dynamic of its own:
it gradually developed into one of sociology in general. In 1948–1949, the
first year of Israel's independence, a full-fledged curriculum in sociology
was offered. The first Department of Sociology in Israel had been born.

Thus, sociology in Israel was born almost by chance. But it established
itself rapidly. In 1950 Buber retired and was replaced by Shmuel Noah
Eisenstadt as head of the department. Eisenstadt quickly established an
international reputation both as a theorist and as a student of various
societies and civilizations, including Israeli society. Another member of
the department was Yonina Garber-Talmon, who became well known on
the basis of her studies of the Israeli kibbutz. More junior in the department was Joseph Ben-David, who subsequently established an international reputation in the sociology of science and the professions. Another
member of the staff was Yaakov Katz, who established a reputation in
historical sociology on the basis of his studies of Jewish society in the
diaspora at the end of the Middle Ages and in modern times.

Both on the basis of their positions at the only (then) existing department of sociology, and on the basis of their stature, these scholars became
the founding fathers of sociology in Israel. They were then responsible for
the education of following generations of Israeli sociologists, and also for
the shape that sociology subsequently assumed in Israel. Eisenstadt, Garber-Talmon, and Ben-David received their training in England, and a certain European influence on Israeli sociology thus became visible. At the
same time, at least Eisenstadt and Ben-David were also influenced by
American, most prominently structural-functional, Parsonian sociology.
Concomitantly, a tradition of empirical research was established, and the
department's staff and students set out to study various aspects of Israeli
social life.

The department at the Hebrew University remained the sole department of sociology in Israel until the beginning of the 1960s. By that time,
the Israeli population had grown substantially, as had the numbers of potential students. Young sociologists, many of whom had graduated from
the Hebrew University and had taken graduate studies abroad, were hoping to establish themselves in Israel. Thus, relevant departments at Israel's
other universities—Tel-Aviv University, Bar-Ilan University (a religiously
oriented university) in Ramat Gan, the University of Haifa, and Ben-
Gurion University in Beer Sheba—were gradually established. These became combined departments of sociology and anthropology—or (in the
case of Ben-Gurion University) a department of behavioral studies in
which sociology was a major component. Also, the Technion, Israel's technological university in Haifa, established a program in sociology; and the

Open University, in Tel-Aviv, has been offering studies in sociology as well.

Each of these units has acquired some distinctive characteristics. The department at the Hebrew University was and has remained particularly strong in theory. On the empirical front it began with a particular emphasis on the study of the kibbutz and of immigrant absorption, but today it is particularly strong in the analysis of politics. The Tel-Aviv University department was the first to introduce sophisticated quantitative research methods, and it is still strong in this area. It also focuses on the study of organizations, ethnicity, stratification, politics, and education. The department at Bar-Ilan University has made its most distinctive contribution in the study of religion, Jewishness, and Jewish communities. Over the years it has also developed a particular strength in social psychology, the sociology of organizations, of women, and of health. The department at Haifa University has made a special contribution to the study of the kibbutz and also to that of disadvantaged groups, ethnicities, and nationalities, particularly Israeli Arabs. The distinctiveness of the department at Ben-Gurion University lies in its interdisciplinary structure (in Israel rather unique); its studies of the population of the Negev, the southern part of Israel; and its focus on the sociology of health. The program at the Technion has focused on work and industrial relations, and the Open University has, of course, offered distance learning to a wide array of students who otherwise might have been deprived of higher education altogether. On top of this, the regional and other colleges have made their contribution by offering some basic sociological studies, inter alia to future university students, thereby easing their transition into higher education.

The increasing variety of sociology has also been evident in the establishment of research institutes. Some have been academic in orientation and/or attached to universities; others have been more applied and outside the confines of academic institutions. Most prominent among these have been the Institute of Applied Social Research, established in 1948 under the leadership of the world-renowned methodologist Louis Guttman, and now under the directorship of the no less renowned Elihu Katz; and the Henrietta Szold Institute, now under the leadership of Dr. Yitzchak Friedman. Both institutes are located in Jerusalem. But other research institutes, in Jerusalem and in other cities, have mushroomed as well.

Israeli sociologists have branched out into applied areas as well. They have been employed or engaged as consultants by policy makers (including politicians), top governmental bureaucrats, and town planners. They have also been employed or used as consultants by the military and its affiliated institutions, as well as by various organizations in the private sector.

The department at the Hebrew University, which at first held a monopoly over the field, has thus had to face increasing competition from other departments and centers of study; and sociology has generally become a more open, competitive, and diversified discipline. Thereby, sociology has also gained a degree of legitimacy and recognition in Israeli society at large. This is evidenced, for instance, by the fact that results of sociological research and interviews with sociologists are frequently reported in the press, and quite a few sociological terms have penetrated (some would say; have enriched) the everyday Hebrew language.

By now Garber-Talmon, Guttman, and Ben-David have passed away, to the greater loss of Israeli sociology. But over the years, as new generations of sociologists have entered the field, they have made their own contributions to sociology through a variety of research methods, including historical, other qualitative, and (from the simplest to the most sophisticated) quantitative methods. The harvest of their research and analyses has been published in a considerable number of books, in two sociological journals in Israel, and in a great number of journals abroad. Also, various social issues and trends—mainly those of Israeli society—have been tackled, various theoretical paradigms have developed, and areas of study have proliferated. The most distinctive of these are briefly reviewed in this chapter.[1]

ANALYSIS OF ISRAELI SOCIETY: MAIN ISSUES AND TRENDS

If the whole variety of social issues and problems that have been analyzed by Israeli sociologists with respect to Israeli society can be put under one general heading, and at the risk of oversimplification, it would be this: the various social processes based on solidarity, identification with common values, and consensus which unify Israeli society, counterbalanced by the various cleavages and divisions which rend it apart. The commonality which unifies most (though not necessarily all) of Israeli society has to do with commitment to the existence of Israel as such, identification with its Jewish and Zionist values, solidarity with Jews abroad, and adherence to patterns of modernity and to the principles of democracy.

Conversely, the schisms that divide Israeli society have to do with differentiation between the center and the periphery, or between elites and the rank and file; the gap between old-timers and newcomers; the divisions between ethnicities (Westerners and Oriental Jews), nationalities (Jews and Arabs), and socioeconomic strata or classes (expressed inter alia in gaps in educational achievements); ideological divisions between Left and Right; and controversies between religious and nonreligious Jews. Each of these divisions has created a multitude of social problems, which have been the main topics of analysis for Israeli sociologists.

Superimposed on all these, however, has been one central issue of concern to Israeli sociologists, namely, the degree to which these various cleavages are not only counterbalanced by consensus and solidarity but also crosscut each other to create a pluralist yet well-integrated society—or, conversely, the extent to which solidarity and consensus have weakened, and/or the cleavages have coincided, to create one or two fundamental and possibly insuperable chasms within Israeli society. Many sociologists have also devoted major attention to trends of change in both the processes that unify Israeli society and the cleavages that divide it. Several sociologists have been concerned with attempts to help solve the problems which emanate from these divisions. In all this, sociologists have been guided by several theoretical paradigms.

SOCIOLOGICAL THEORY: THE MAIN PARADIGMS

Although theory has played an important role in the work of Israeli sociologists, it is difficult to compartmentalize this work into theoretical pigeonholes. Some sociologists have worked without any explicit theories in mind; others have worked with a combination of two or more theoretical approaches, which themselves have also been partly overlapping. Nonetheless, and (once again) at the peril of oversimplification, some theoretical paradigms may be identified.

At first, the theoretical orientation adhered to by most Israeli sociologists was the structural-functional consensus model, the proponents of which have put special emphasis on the consensus, cohesion, and solidarity that has been one of the most prominent characteristics of Israeli society. Gradually other paradigms have developed, including a power and conflict perspective, whose adherents have highlighted the divisions, inequalities, and struggles that have been equally prominent in Israeli society. Within this broad perspective, some have been working with a neo-Marxist framework, and they have conceptualized many of the gaps and conflicts in terms of classes and the social reproduction of inequality. Partly overlapping with these has been the phenomenological and symbolic interaction perspective, highlighting the role of symbols and meanings in Israeli social interaction.

The structural-functional, consensus model has been employed in quite a few areas of study, including the study of the kibbutz, the absorption of immigrants, and ethnic relations. The power and conflict paradigm has been employed in several areas as well, including ethnic relations, classes, and politics. Within the broader power and conflict perspective, neo-Marxism has been used in the study of ethnic relations and classes, and in the sociology of education. But although the power and conflict paradigm in the broader sense has been prevalent in the analysis of politics as well, Marxism has not emerged as a prominent paradigm in this particular field.

In a way this is surprising, since socialism has long been an important ideology in Israel, and since many, if not most, Israeli sociologists have been leftist in their ideological stance. In another sense, the weakness of Marxist political sociology in Israel is quite self-evident: because of the long-time socialist tendencies of Israeli society, economic power has been concentrated largely in public, and most prominently labor federation–controlled, enterprises. The capitalist class has thus remained weak and partly subdued by the bureaucratic and political establishment. This does not mean that there have not been class-related political inequalities in Israel. But the weakness of the capitalist class has made it difficult to argue the case for seeing it as Israel's ruling class, an argument without which Marxist theory of politics has little to build on.

The most prominent general theorist in Israel has been Eisenstadt. At the beginning it seemed that the paramount influence on his work was that of Talcott Parsons and to a lesser degree that of Robert Merton. It was mainly their theories that students were obliged to study, and Eisenstadt's early students could be excused for believing that those were the only theories then prevalent in sociology. But it soon became apparent that Eisenstadt's own theoretical orientation could not be classified strictly as Parsonian.

Like Parsons, Eisenstadt has focused on general theory. But much more than Parsons, Eisenstadt has been interested not merely in theory but in society, engaging in comparative studies of various empires and civilizations, as well as in studies of Israeli society. Like Parsons, Eisenstadt has been interested in modernization. But much more than Parsons, Eisenstadt has been interested in issues of power—hence in elites, whether in the process of modernization or in society in general. From Edward Shils, Eisenstadt has adopted the terms *center* and *periphery.* But his concern with power, authority, and charisma, no less than his comparative studies of cultures and civilizations, has also placed him within the Weberian tradition. Thus, Eisenstadt's contribution lies in the fact that he has managed to reconcile various, seemingly incompatible, theoretical paradigms and forge them into a new, distinctly Eisenstadtian entity, which he has employed in his comparative studies as well as in his studies of various facets of Israeli society.[2]

Apart from Eisenstadt, there have been few if any grand theorists as such. Mostly, the theoretical concerns of Israeli sociologists have come through in their studies of various social issues and trends of Israeli society. This has been evident, first, in the study of the Israeli kibbutz.

THE SOCIOLOGY OF THE KIBBUTZ

The kibbutz (communal settlement) movement in Israel has attracted unusual sociological attention—an attention that is blatantly disproportional to the size of its population (a mere 4 percent of the Jewish population in Israel). Consequently, research and publications on the kibbutz have been legion. This attention may be attributed to the fact that the kibbutz has fulfilled a pivotal, pioneering role in Israeli society, and consequently has been central in its collective, national consciousness. It may also be due to the fact that the kibbutz has been considered not only as a unique venture into utopia but also, and perhaps because of this very fact, as a substitute social laboratory, in which sociological theories such as those on the inevitability of inequality and of the family could be tested.

The first comprehensive attempt by Israeli sociologists to study the kibbutz took place in the early 1950s under the tutelage of Yonina Garber-Talmon. According to Menachem Rosner,[3] himself a prominent student of the kibbutz, this study came at a time in kibbutz history characterized by self-doubt and crisis. The kibbutz, which had fulfilled a pioneering role in the pre-state era, now had to face the problem of whether it could still fulfill such a role in a normalizing Israeli state.

In this context, one major question, which was also highly relevant for sociological theory, was whether the kibbutz would be able to realize its ideal of building an egalitarian community, even within a broader, semi-capitalist Israeli society, or whether it, too, like society at large, would be divided into an elite and a rank and file. Eva Rosenfeld had previously argued, on the basis of a functionalist theory, that despite the kibbutz's egalitarian ideology there was a process of internal stratification in which at least two strata, an elite and a rank and file, could be distinguished. Contrary to this view, Garber-Talmon's study led to the conclusion that no such division could be identified.

This conclusion was in turn contradicted by other students of the kibbutz, such as E. Cohen and Yuchtman, who argued that the emergence of inequalities and elites in the kibbutz could be explained on the basis of kibbutz economic development, specialization, and the quest for rationality and efficiency. On the other side of the fence, Rosner, in his earlier analyses, found that contrary to what one would expect if there were a well-differentiated elite, there was in fact a continuous rotation of central positions among various kibbutz members. Subsequently, however, Rosner himself in his later studies (as well as Ben-Rafael, among others) once again contradicted this conclusion by showing that rotation was basically horizontal, rather than vertical. In this manner, position-holders did indeed move out of central positions, but they tended to move into other central positions—rather than return to the rank and file—thus forming a long-term elite after all.

Another core question for both the kibbutz movement and sociological theory has been the position of the family in the kibbutz. The kibbutz had originally aimed at reducing the functions of the family to a minimum and at transferring some of its functions to the collective. In her studies, however, Garber-Talmon detected a growing familistic trend and the growing pervasiveness of the kibbutz family; and Bar-Yosef showed how the kibbutz family had come to be integrated with the collective. Later on, in the 1970s, Tiger and Shepher proposed a sociobiological explanation for this trend. Arguing that women were its chief instigators, they explained women's tendencies in this respect on the basis of a female "biogrammar" and mammarian physiology, prescribing for them a higher parental drive than that of men. This theory has subsequently met with fierce criticism, although as such the growing familistic tendencies in the kibbutz—and the growing tendencies of kibbutz women to revert to more traditional feminine roles—have also been identified by other researchers (e.g., M. Palgi, Rosner) and generally have not been disputed.

Recently the kibbutz has become more individualized in its patterns and, perhaps partly in relation to this, has been facing a new socioeconomic crisis. This has been manifested among other things in a high rate of attrition, particularly among its second generation. The problem of attrition has attracted some new research, such as that by Leviatan, Orchan, and Avnat. In general, however, it is too early to tell how this crisis will be reflected in sociological research.

THE STUDY OF THE ABSORPTION OF IMMIGRANTS

Apart from the study of the kibbutz, another area in which theoretical concerns have been integrated with empirical research, as well as with attempts to help solve the problems of Israeli society, has been the study of the absorption of immigrants. The Jewish society in Israel has obviously been an immigration-society from its inception. But in the absence of an empirically oriented sociology in the pre-state era, the problems involved in immigration were not being studied until the early 1950s. At that time—as an unprecedented mass immigration more than doubled Israel's population within a few years—the study of the absorption of immigrants became a central, concerted effort of Israeli sociologists.

As A. Weingrod[4] and D. Bernstein[5] note, the paradigm in which these studies have worked has been a functional consensus model, with special stress on modernization theory. The central figure during the early period of these studies was Eisenstadt, who set the conceptual framework. In this framework, Israel has been viewed as faced by various divisions yet marked by widespread consensus regarding its core values. These are seen as a combination of modern, Western values, with values of Zionism and Jewish solidarity. Accordingly, immigrants from Western countries, whose cultural background was more similar to that of Israeli society, have been seen to be quite easily absorbed into the mainstream of Israeli society.

Since, however, a majority of the newcomers in the 1950s were from Middle Eastern, Muslim countries, the encounter between them and the old-timers has been conceptualized as marked by a cultural gap. This was seen as created by the virtual absence of a modern, Western culture among the immigrants. The essence of the absorption process has thus been conceived (by Eisenstadt, Ben-David, and Bar-Yosef, among others) as the modernization and resocialization of traditional newcomers by the more modern veterans. Accordingly, factors seen as aiding in the absorption process were an immigrant group's willingness to change, coupled with the emergence of ethnic leaders with positive attitudes toward the absorbing society. By contrast, resistance to change, particularly occupational inflexibility, coupled with alienated ethnic leaders who ignite frustrations, was apt to lead to breakdowns of the absorption process and created foci of political tension.

A modified version of this theory has stressed that the retention of some of their previous traditions provided immigrants with supportive values and social networks which aided their integration into the new society. But here, too, the process of immigrant absorption has basically been visualized (e.g., by F. Bernstein and Weintraub) as one of modernization. Although both versions of this approach have been criticized for diverting attention from conflicts of interest inherent in the class and power structure, they have remained dominant until recent years.

In later years, as the mass immigration of the 1950s gave way to a mere trickle of immigrants, the previous major collective endeavor of the study of immigrant absorption turned into a trickle as well. Still, in the 1970s individual sociologists continued to work in the area. Some of these, such as Deshen and Shokeid, focused on the problems of immigrant adaptation in rural settlements; others, such as Ginzberg, analyzed similar problems in small towns known as "development towns." Still others, such as Lazerwitz or Shuval, have done the same in urban neighborhoods, or else (like E. Cohen) have compared the latter two.

In the 1980s, immigration fizzled out and so did immigration research. At some stage, emigration from Israel practically counterbalanced immigration. At that point some Israeli sociologists (e.g., Shokeid or Sobel) did research on emigration and emigrants from Israel. The numbers of sociologists studying emigration might well have come to outnumber those studying immigration, were it not for the fact that toward the end of the 1980s and the beginning of the 1990s, large-scale immigration resumed. The absorption of these immigrants—mainly from the former Soviet Union and Ethiopia—has raised new problems, and these have been analyzed for example by Adler and his group, by Goldberg, by Hasson, and by T. Horowitz.

Some initial research with respect to immigrants from Ethiopia, for instance, has found that they evince cultural codes that are totally different from those of Israelis—and incomprehensible to them. Yet they also display a strong identification with Israel and a strong (one would almost say, modern) ambition to succeed within it. This situation has been found to put major obstacles in the way of their absorption, but also to open prospects for more successful absorption if and when the communication gaps between the Israelis and the Ethiopians may be bridged.

So far, the resurgence in immigration has not led to a refocusing of major, collective attention on this topic.[6] But as of this writing (1991), it is too early to tell whether this will be the case in the near future, and what direction research in the area may now take.

THE STUDY OF ETHNICITIES: WESTERNERS AND ORIENTALS

Since the majority of immigrants who arrived with the mass immigration of the 1950s were from Middle Eastern, Muslim countries, and since those who arrived from other countries soon lost their identity as new immigrants, the division between old-timers and newcomers has become partly overlapping, with a major ethnic division within the Jewish community in Israel. This is the division between people originating in European and Western countries, also known as Westerners or Ashkenazi, and those originating in Middle Eastern, Muslim countries, also known as Orientals or Sephardi. For that reason, the study of the absorption of immigrants has inevitably shaded over into the study of these two ethnicities and the relations between them.

The Oriental or Sephardi ethnicity now makes up somewhat more than 50 percent of the Jewish population in Israel. However, the numerical superiority of Orientals has not been translated into social dominance: Westerners or Ashkenazi have emerged as dominant, while Orientals or Sephardi have been relatively disadvantaged. Gaps in income, education, and standard of living between the two ethnicities have become evident, and it did not take long for sociologists to discover these gaps and focus their attention on them.

According to S. Smooha,[7] the dominant approach in this area has been the structural-functional consensus approach, largely overlapping with the same approach to the absorption of immigrants. According to this approach, (espoused for instance by Eisenstadt, Bar-Yosef, Ben-David, Ben-Rafael, Krausz in some of his writings, and Peres in his earlier writings, the Orientals' relatively weaker position derives from their different—and less modern—cultural background. But ethnic divisions, though exploited by political interests, have been diminishing. For instance, interethnic marriages have reached a rate of about two-fifths of the maximum possible. And the large numbers of youngsters issuing from these marriages lack ethnic identity as either Westerners or Orientals. All in all, the Israelization of Orientals has advanced considerably over the years.

Criticizing this approach as overly optimistic, some recent students have been drawing on Marxist and neo-Marxist class theory. Their basic assumption has been that ethnic relations are essentially similar to class relations in their asymmetry and potential for conflict. According to their view, the Oriental immigrants deliberately had been made to enter the labor market at the bottom, as unskilled laborers, and from then onward they have been exploited as a cheap labor force. This has created extreme dependency on their part on the state and on Ashkenazi employers, and it has turned them into a permanent working class.

That state of affairs has worked in the interests of the Ashkenazi, by allowing most of them to advance into the middle class. The Ahskenazi establishment then created an ideology to justify it. According to this ideology, Orientals are backward and incompetent, hence have no one to blame for their problems but themselves. Despite this ideology, the Orientals' sense of ethnic deprivation is becoming more acute, and friction is mounting (e.g., D. Bernstein, Elbaz, Hasson, Swirski).

This approach has been criticized as overly pessimistic, and others have worked with a composite approach which Smooha[8] (who is also one of its chief proponents) terms the "pluralist approach." Lacking a linkage to grand theory, this approach depicts a more complex picture of ethnic relations. Its proponents—who include Lissak, Lotan, Peres in his later work, Weingrod, and others—view Israel as possessing a plural ethnic structure marked by several interlocking processes: continuity and change; integration but also separation; conflict but also compromise, solidarity, and common nation building; Ashkenazi dominance but also its gradual erosion; ethnic stratification but also mobility within the Oriental ethnicity, whereby about two-fifths of Orientals have now moved into the middle class and above. A good example of this approach may be found in a recently published book by Bensky, Krausz, and some (interdisciplinary) colleagues, who identify many of these complex and contradictory trends among Iraqi Jews. Overall, though eclectic, this seems to be the most realistic approach to ethnicity.

Several studies have linked ethnicity to politics. Of these, some (e.g., D. Bernstein, E. Cohen, E. Etzioni-Halevy) have analyzed ethnic protest which emerged (and soon subsided) in the 1970s. Others have studied the ethnic factor in politics, reaching divergent conclusions. Deshen has concluded that the business of ethnicity, far from being finished in Israeli politics, was being utilized particularly in election campaigns. By contrast, Herzog has endeavored to show that ethnicity has served as a tool for political bargaining and thus has assisted in integrating the various ethnic groups into the political system.

THE STUDY OF NATIONALITIES: JEWS AND ARABS

In the Israeli context, ethnicity refers to a division within Jewish Israeli society. There is, however, another and more fundamental division that has overshadowed it: that between Jews and Arabs, usually subsumed under the label of nationality. Contrary to the topic of ethnicities, which has been pivotal in Israeli sociology, the topic of nationalities and their relations, and the analysis of the Arab nationality in Israel (some 18 percent of the population), has been relegated to the margins.

Among the few who have dealt with this topic are Peres, H. Rosenfeld, Shalev, Smooha, and Swirski. What emerges from the work of such scholars is that Arabs in Israel are separate and unequal. While they enjoy full civil liberties, they are disadvantaged by institutional arrangements. These include their position as a minority in a largely Jewish institutional structure, their being considered a security risk, their consequent exclusion from several occupational fields, endogamy, separate residence and school systems, and labor market segmentation encouraged by Israel's federation of labor, the Histadrut. As a consequence of these arrangements, the Arab minority is lower in all aspects of socioeconomic status than the Jewish population. Despite all this, the Arabs' standard of living has risen; they have taken part in a shift in the Israeli occupational structure toward higher-ranking occupations, thereby enjoying upward (structural) mobility; and a sizable middle class, as well as elites, has emerged.

This overall characterization of the situation has been supplemented by more specific studies, such as those of Arabs in the labor market (e.g., by Y. Cohen, Lewin-Epstein, Semyonov, Tyree, and Yaar. In this context it has been found, for instance, that Arabs employed in the protective environment of a segregated labor market enclave in their own communities have enjoyed better job and income opportunities than Arabs who had to find employment outside this enclave and have thus been exposed to discriminatory competition with Jews.

To this has been added the analysis of the labor market participation of Arabs from the territories occupied by Israel in 1967. While they are not Israeli citizens, many of them commute daily to work in Israel. In their study, Semyonov and Lewin-Epstein have found that although some of these Arabs have advanced on the occupational ladder, and although their wages and social benefits have improved, they have generally been relegated to nonskilled menial jobs in building, industry, and the services. Though lower than Israelis in their average level of schooling, they have not obtained rewards commensurate with the human capital that they do have. They have thus become the hewers of wood and drawers of water of Israeli society. Interestingly, their situation has been found to be surprisingly similar to that of migrant and guest workers in Europe in the 1950s and 1960s, and to that of seasonal Mexican workers in the United States.

A window with a view into Arab society itself has been opened by Al-Haj, in his description of changes in the Arab family, as it has been coping with the challenge of adaptation to the modern world. A similar window, with a view into the world of Arab Bedouins, has been opened by Kressel and by Marx, who have explored the Bedouins' ability to adapt to modernity by weaving elements of modern economic activity into their traditional culture and social networks. All in all, then, separation, inequality, but also mobility and tradition-linked overtures toward modernity have been found to characterize the situation of Israeli Arabs.

THE STUDY OF STRATIFICATION AND CLASSES

As noted before, the division between old-timers and newcomers has shaded over into a division between ethnicities, which has been overshadowed by the division between nationalities. The division between both ethnicities and nationalities, in turn, has been partly overlapping with that between socioeconomic strata or classes. The majority of sociologists, however, have preferred to focus their attention on the study of ethnicities, relegating the study of strata and classes as such (like the study of nationalities) to a less central place. Moreover, most sociologists who have dealt with socioeconomic inequalities have preferred to conceptualize them in terms of the distribution of income (e.g., Zandberg), in terms of occupations and professions (e.g., Ben-David, Kahane, Matras), in terms of social mobility (e.g., Ben-Rafael, Lissak, Semyonov, Yaar), or in terms of a status-attainment model (e.g., Hodge, Kraus, Samuel, S. Smooha, Yaar) rather than in terms of classes.

In the framework of the status-attainment model, for instance, it has been found that in Israel (as elsewhere) family background, as measured by father's education and occupation, affects educational attainment, which affects occupational status, which affects income. The effect of such background on individual achievements is greatly reduced after controlling for level of education. Yet gender and ethnicity retain significant effects on socioeconomic attainment even after other variables are controlled for. In the framework of mobility studies, a prominent finding has been that because of an upgrading of the occupational structure, structural mobility has been considerable. Moreover, the established channel of social mobility via education is often bypassed by some of the educationally disadvantaged, particularly by Orientals, who use (for instance) small-scale economic entrepreneurship as a significant alternative path of advancement into the middle class.

The fact that most sociologists have worked with the individual achievement rather than the class model should not be taken to indicate that class divisions proper are nonexistent in Israel. From a neo-Marxist class perspective, Bernstein has argued that even the pre-state era—which is usually considered as the epitome of solidarity, disturbed only by ideological controversies—was actually marked by contradictory interests and fierce struggles between wage earners and employers; and this has been the case after the establishment of the state as well. By the same token, the fact that classes with opposing interests do exist does not, of course, invalidate the findings of other sociologists concerning trends of significant social mobility from one class to another.

THE SOCIOLOGY OF EDUCATION

One area in which divisions in Israeli society have been especially visible is education. Much of the sociology of education has thus focused on some of these gaps, namely, those between ethnicities. Other educational gaps, particularly those between nationalities, on the other hand, have not been adequately analyzed.

With the influx of mass immigration from Middle Eastern countries, it soon became clear that youngsters of Oriental origin did not equal their Western counterparts in educational achievements. During the first decade of the state's existence, policy makers dealt with this situation by endeavoring to provide all children with equal educational programs and facilities. It soon transpired that this policy of formal equality was not effective, and the educational gaps between the ethnicities persisted. Accordingly, in the 1950s, research was concerned to identify the explanatory factors for these gaps. These were pinpointed (e.g., by Adar, Ortar, or Smilansky) as lying in a combination of Oriental children's cultural "disadvantage" with school factors (e.g., the inability of schools to adapt to the requirements of Oriental children).

In the second decade, policy makers attempted to rectify this situation by setting up various projects of compensatory education for disadvantaged (i.e., Oriental) children. At that time, research (e.g., by Adler, Chen, Dar, Ichilov, Kahane, Peleg, Resh, or Starr) focused on evaluating the outcomes of this new policy. Its general conclusion was that the new policy was not effective either, and that the second generation of Israeli-born or Israeli-raised Orientals was now joining the ranks of the disadvantaged.

In view of this failure, the next step, taken in Israel's third decade, was an overall reform of the educational system. Its essence was the introduction of a comprehensive secondary school in which children of different social backgrounds were to meet and be socially integrated, and in which all children were to be given educational opportunities appropriate for their abilities. However, subsequent research (e.g., by Amir, Chen, Guttmann, Schmida, Sharan) has shown that the reform has not worked out as planned. The retention rate of disadvantaged youngsters increased, and an elite of achievers was emerging among them. But their general achievements did not improve as much as had been expected, the gaps in achievements between them and the more advantaged youngsters were not significantly narrowed, and social integration did not come about either.

As time went by, and as it has become clear that the educational disadvantage of Oriental children has eroded, but at only a snail's pace, the theoretical approaches of researchers have shifted. While earlier research emphasized the alleged cultural disadvantages of Oriental children, in later research the neo-Marxist perspective has become prominent as well. Scholars such as Ayalon, Swirski, and Yogev have conceptualized persistent disadvantages as resulting from a social reproduction of inequalities, and from an increasingly pervasive credentialism. These scholars have shown how despite all good intentions manifested in educational reforms, the system is geared to perpetuate inequalities. It does so by channeling advantaged youngsters into academically oriented schools and streams while leaving the disadvantaged little choice but to turn to lower streams and vocational schools. Credentialism then does the rest, by transplanting educational disadvantages into occupational and socioeconomic ones.

On the micro-level, researchers have concentrated on the study of educational institutions as organizations in relation to the surrounding community and society. Some of these have focused attention on boarding schools, which fulfill an unusually prominent role in Israeli education: some 20 percent of adolescents are educated in them. Two major types of boarding schools exist: religious boarding schools, or Yeshivot, whose role has been analyzed by Bar-Lev; and boarding schools for youngsters of disadvantaged background. Arieli and Kashti (working with a phenomenological paradigm) and other researchers, including Izikovich or R. Shapira, have all reached the conclusion that despite their efforts and minor successes in promoting the achievements of disadvantaged youngsters, in the end they, too, like the educational system in general, serve as agents of social reproduction.

Studying regular schools as organizations, several researchers (e.g., Adler, Y. Friedman, Goldring, and R. Shapira) have recently brought out their expanding ties with the surrounding community, and particularly with parents. Given the fact that the Ministry of Education has long held centralized control of the educational system, research has traced growing pluralism, brought about by (1) parents' increasingly prevalent struggles with the ministry, and (2) their successively more vocal demands to have a say in determining educational policy for their offspring and in shaping schools in line with their particular views and needs.

Another topic that has attracted the attention of sociologists is that of Israel's distinctive youth movements, which were found to have generated a paradox. Exploring their structure, Kahane found them to be unique among educational institutions in having symmetrical (i.e., egalitarian) as well as informal relations between educators and the youngsters being educated in them. Other researchers (e.g., Adler, Ben-David, Chen, Peres, and R. Shapira) have found members of youth movements to be more imbued with collectivist, egalitarian, and service-oriented values than other youngsters. But despite their egalitarian setting and values, they were also found to have more elitist self-images, stronger ambitions, and higher aspirations than other youngsters.

One other salient topic has been the study of higher education and university students, (e.g., by Ayalon or Bar-Lev). A major study in this area has been conducted at Tel-Aviv University by R. Shapira and E. Etzioni-Halevy. Designed as a follow-up study and also as a study of consecutive generations of students at ten-year intervals, it has highlighted the students' distinctive subculture. In contrast to many students in other Western democracies, Israeli students (who reach university after a lengthy term in the army) were found to show little interest in the "moratorium" aspect of their studies: prolonging adolescence and having a "good time" in the process. Despite a tendency to be moderately anti-establishment in their political views, they had not created a nonconformist subculture. Rather, they were found to be mainly vocationally oriented, viewing their studies as preparation for their roles as adults and as a channel of mobility into elite positions in Israeli society.

POLITICAL SOCIOLOGY

Apart from the divisions already mentioned, another pivotal division in Israeli (as in all other) society is that between the center of political power holders—the elites—on the one hand, and the public at large on the other hand. Israeli political sociology has been concerned with both levels: the study of elites and of the public.

As is almost inevitable in the study of elites, Israeli sociologists have—in general terms, and loosely—worked within a power and conflict perspective. In this framework, the view has been that at the beginning the political center has been a relatively more concerted and cohesive one, and that over the years it has changed into a somewhat more dispersed and variegated or complex one. However, in some cases the interpretation of this trend has been more in line with elite theory, while in other cases it has had some elements of pluralism and functionalism mixed into it. Also evident have been a corporatist perspective (a prominent proponent of which has been Shalev) and a democratic elite perspective, both of which have occupied their own ground among the other points of view.

Here, Eisenstadt has argued that during the first years of Israel's independence, increasing differentiation and autonomy of elites was counterbalanced by basic elite solidarity and consensus. Subsequently, and especially since the right-wing Likud came to power in 1977, this balance has broken down. While elite differentiation has continued to grow, elite solidarity and consensus have been eroding. The balance between elite consensus and solidarity on the one hand and elite autonomy on the other hand—which Eisenstadt sees as a crucial condition for the success of democracy—thus seemingly no longer prevails. Yet, as Eisenstadt admits, vigorous democratic processes continue to inform Israeli politics.

Working within an elite framework, Y. Shapiro has demonstrated how pre-state and Israeli society have been ruled by a concerted elite of the labor movement, which was marked by ideological consensus yet was also pragmatic and perpetuated its rule through an elaborate system of machine politics. This ruling elite, however, has not been able to reproduce itself: the next generation of labor leaders has no longer formed a cohesive elite. Thus, a contradiction has emerged between the system, which has remained centralized, and the elite, which has become internally divided and therefore has no longer been able to control the system.

Adopting a more pluralist frame of reference, Lissak and D. Horowitz maintain that during the labor era Israeli politics was characterized by rule of a centralized elite—whose power was counterbalanced, however, by its need to compromise with various lesser parties and pressure groups. The change of government in 1977 led to greater decentralization. Like its predecessor, the new, right-wing ruling elite ensures its hegemony by monopolizing the state's major resources. But there has recently been a polarization of attitudes among the various government and opposition parties, as well as a dispersion of power centers. The resulting multiple controversies and pressures have led to an overload, a weakening, and even a paralysis of the political system.

Lissak and Horowitz, as well as several other sociologists, have seen the general trends toward greater pluralism as reflected, inter alia, in the role of the military elite, which for obvious reasons is of strategic importance in Israel. They have pointed to the fact that contrary to what might have been expected in a society under constant siege, militarization, or a "garrison state," never developed in Israel. But there has been a conglomeration of elites based on intimately close connections between the political and the military elites under Labor rule, expressed in political appointments in the army, in informal social ties between members of the two elites, and in the tendency of high-ranking officers to join the political elite after retirement from the army. Recently, however, the relations between the military and the political elite have not been as close as they were before, and a greater bifurcation of the two power centers has thus occurred.

In line with the tradition of democratic elite theory, Etzioni-Halevy has accepted the tenet, also presented by Eisenstadt, that Western democracy depends on a balance of elite cooperation and elite autonomy. Her main emphasis, however, has been on the relative autonomy of elites from the state and the government. She has seen this relative autonomy (rather than more diffuse "pluralism") as forming a basic requirement for, as well as one of the most distinctive features of, Western democracy. Conversely, she has seen erosion of such autonomy as presenting one of the most visible threats to democracy. In Israel, despite a greater diversification of power, she has identified some continuously close ties among elites, expressed in weaknesses in elite autonomy—as exemplified, for instance, in the politicization and partial subjugation of the elite of the state bureaucracy by the political elite. This in turn has led to political corruption, which at times has come close to invalidating the electoral processes of Israeli democracy.

Analyzing Israel's political center within a power and conflict, yet rather original, perspective, Kimmerling argues that since 1967 a new periphery, the occupied territories, has been added to the system, and that this fact has wrought a fundamental change in the center itself. Whereas previously the boundaries of the sociopolitical system controlled by this center were clear and simple, a duality has now emerged. The center incorporates the new periphery in some respects—as part of the economy, and as an object of political and military control—yet keeps it beyond the pale in other respects—particularly in respect to collective identification and citizens' rights. It is from this duality that some of Israel's most severe problems arise.

As for the public, one distinctive trend has been a gradual shift from the left to the right, which was pinpointed by social scientists even before it became evident at the ballot box, in 1977. Another distinctive trend has been the fact that the relatively disadvantaged (i.e., the Oriental Jews) have come to be the major supporters of the right-wing party, the Likud. Under Labor rule, a majority of Orientals have moved toward the Likud because, feeling disadvantaged, they wished to express their protest against the establishment. But Israeli sociologists are still puzzling over the fact that the majority of Orientals have remained loyal to the right-wing Likud even after this party itself came into office and thus became the dominant establishment.

Another intriguing fact has been revealed by Danet, on the basis of her research on the interface between the public and the bureaucracy. Working within the tradition of symbolic interactionism, she has reported that although the majority of the Israeli public is staunchly opposed to the use of personal connections (*protekzia* in the Israeli slang) when dealing with the bureaucracy, the majority of those who have had the opportunity to do so, have actually used such connections. The interface between elites and the public has also been analyzed by Ichilov in her extensive studies of political socialization and, in particular, education toward democracy, and by Herzog who has presented a phenomenological interpretation of parties' election propaganda.

THE SOCIOLOGY OF RELIGION AND JEWISHNESS

Israeli sociologists of religion have had to face a paradox: the fact that in one sense the Jewish religion is coextensive with the Jewish people, as no one can belong to that people and adhere to another religion, and any one joining the Jewish people must (formally at least) join the Jewish religion as well. Yet, while many Jews are religious, many more are non- or even antireligious. Thus, another division in the Jewish part of Israeli society has been that between religious and nonreligious Jews. Each of these larger categories has been divided into several subcategories, distinguished from each other on one side of the fence by the degree of their religious orthodoxy, and on the other side of the fence by the degree of their secularism. Despite the internal divisions in both camps, the overall relations between them have been wrought by friction.

In view of this, several sociologists of religion have focused on the ramification of religion for the relations between religious and nonreligious Jews. Prominent among these has been M. Friedman, who has provided a historical analysis of the development of what has been known as the status quo, the fragile yet persistent modus vivendi between the two groups. Friedman has also traced the development of the society of the ultra-orthodox, the religious zealots, its internal divisions and controversies, its violent confrontations with secular society—but also its geographical and social separatism, or ghettoization, which has helped moderate friction, thus making it possible for the modus vivendi between the ultra-orthodox and the rest of society to be perpetuated.

A unique type of modus vivendi has been described by L. and S. Weller in their study of the domestic relations of "mixed" religious and nonreligious couples. A different attempt to work out a coexistence has been depicted by Liebman and Don-Yehiya. These scholars have shown that part of the Jewish religious inheritance has been reinterpreted by the government and the media so as to form a new "civil religion" in which the contrast between religious and secular Judaism has been reduced, with the aim of increasing solidarity between religious and secular Jews.

A further peculiarity in this area is the fact that the state of Israel has been established explicitly as a Jewish state, yet the majority of Jews reside outside its boundaries. This has provided scope for analysis of Jewish communities in the diaspora and their relations with Israel. Thus, for instance, Krausz has studied the Jewish community in Britain, and Lazerwitz and Harrison, among others, have analyzed various aspects of the Jewish community in the United States.

Concentrating on the study of Jewish religion itself, and its ramifications on various facets of social life, Fishman has pointed to its role in stimulating economic achievement (as evidenced by the high economic performance of the religious kibbutzim); and L. Weller has reviewed the impact of religious adherence on a variety of social attitudes. Working within the phenomenological tradition, Rubin has interpreted the significance of rituals of passage and of mourning, as well as that of time, in the Jewish religious teachings. Rubin has shown how, in the scriptures, time was used not in a historical but in a didactic manner, to drive home a certain religious message concerning in particular the importance of rituals such as circumcision. Cooper has analyzed the symbolic significance of Jewish holidays, and Sered has depicted the manner in which some rituals and symbols of the Jewish religion have been personalized and utilized to help elderly women in particular cope with their alien modern environment.

The complex interrelationship between Jewish religion, Jewish identity, Israeli nationalism, and the state has been explored by Tabory. Tabory has shown how Israeli nationalism and religious Zionism coincide with the interest of increasing Israel's Jewish population, in shaping Israel's policy toward immigration from the former Soviet Union. This policy has made it difficult for Soviet Jews to use Israeli help in order to migrate to other countries. This, however, stands in contradiction to a more general Jewish identity which places priority on Israeli responsibility for Jews everywhere, whether they settle in Israel or not. The complex relationship between religion and the state has also been expressed in the fact that the Orthodox establishment is the only one that has gained full legitimacy and has become intertwined with the state. Yet non-orthodox denominations, the Reform and Conservative movements, have been established in Israel as well. Their development in Israel, and the challenge thus posed to the Orthodox establishment, have also been analyzed by Tabory.

THIS, AND MUCH MORE

The tyranny of space makes it impossible to cover all areas of Israeli sociology. One area, for instance, that deserves extensive elaboration is the sociology of science, in which lies the particular contribution of the renowned Ben-David. Science has long been of special concern to Israel, inter alia because of its dire need to maintain a gap in sophistication of weapon-related technology between itself and the hostile Arab neighbors that surround it. In this, Israel has been disadvantaged by its small size; Ben-David's concern was to understand the conditions which could aid Israel in overcoming this disadvantage.

Another area that deserves more attention than we can give it is the sociology of health and illness. As Shuval and Antonovsky pointed out in 1990, a large part of Israeli sociology in this area has focused on the health-related features of Israel's distinctive social structure and problems. For instance, some sociologists (e.g., E. Cohen, Shuval) have analyzed Israel's politically linked health system. Others (e.g., Krausz, Ronen, Shuval, Bareli) have compared patterns of health, illness, and their related behavior among various waves of immigrants, ethnicities, and strata. Still others, particularly Antonovsky and Rosen (in separate studies), have analyzed the impact on health of the unique stress characterizing life in Israel. Their conclusion has been that because this stress was countervailed by Israel's especially tight solidary networks, its population is not higher than average on most parameters of chronic and infectious diseases.

One distinctive feature of Israeli society that cannot be reviewed here either is the plethora of social movements with which it has been blessed. These have been analyzed by Bareli, Bensky, and Kalekin-Fischman, among others. However, one movement that has not been very prominent is the women's movement; for many years, this has been reflected in the fact that the analysis of women and gender in Israeli sociology has not been prominent either. But recently this trend has changed, and most stimulating work has been done by D. Amir, Atzmon, Bar-Yosef, Bernstein, Herzog, Izraeli, Kraus, Padan-Eisenstark, R. Shapira, Shenhav, Toren, and others.

This work—which can only be hinted at here—has focused on how features common to Western societies combine with factors peculiar to Israel to shape the disadvantages of Israeli women. One of the features, highlighted for instance by Izraeli, has been the burden of defense and security carried disproportionally by men, which has made women reluctant to stand up for their rights in rectifying occupational and other disadvantages. Another factor identified by Izraeli is Israel's social policy, which encourages a high birth rate and also encourages women to work outside their homes, yet discourages them from embarking on occupational careers. Women's disadvantages in the political arena have been analyzed by Atzmon and by Herzog, among others. The position of women in higher education has been studied by Toren and by Shenhav; their position on the other pole of the social spectrum, namely, as cleaning women, has been studied by D. Bernstein; and the analysis of women's health and illness has been the particular contribution of D. Amir.

One area that is especially popular among Israeli students, but which shortage of space makes it impossible to discuss in depth here, is the sociology of organizations, occupations, and professions. This area in Israeli sociology developed in particular from the late 1960s and the beginning of the 1970s. Although the leaders in this field (including Bachrach, Bamberger, Goldberg, Harrison, Chermesh, Izraeli, Kirschenbaum, Lachman Mannheim, Phillips, Samuel, Shenhav, and Yaar) have contributed to organizational theory, most of their work has been empirical-quantitative and/or diagnostic and applied. In the wake of recent shifts in American organizational studies, in Israel too the emphasis has shifted from sociodemographical and economic variables to political and cultural (including symbolic) ones. Consequently, qualitative research methods have come to be emphasized as well, though quantitative ones still predominate. Thereby, too, interest has almost inadvertently shifted toward greater emphasis on factors that are special to the Israeli organizational scene.

Whereas the study of organizations has attracted the attention of quite a few sociologists, this has not been the case with the study of cities. Despite the fact that some 90 percent of the Israeli population is urban, urban sociology has not caught the imagination of many sociologists. Much work has been done on problems of the absorption of immigrants and other social problems, as they have found expression inter alia in urban neighborhoods. But urban life as a phenomenon in its own right has not been at the center of attention, though interesting work in the area (which cannot be covered here either) has been done, for instance, by Ginzberg, Karmon, and Menachem. A similar point may be made about the sociology of the media: although the media fulfill a prominent role in Israeli society (media-channeled interest in politics is higher in Israel than it is in most other Western countries), analysis of the media has not been central to Israeli sociology. This, however, has made the few sociologists working in the area (e.g., Katz or Weiman) all the more prominent. Other areas which had to be left out include the study of the family (e.g., by Peres or Schrift), community studies (e.g., by Hazan, E. Cohen, and O. Shapiro), the study of deviance (by M. Amir, Shoham, and Shelef), and the study of old age, most prominently by Hazan.

Finally, certain intriguing studies, though outside the mainstream of Israeli sociology, should at least be mentioned. These include phenomenological and historical studies of changes from collectivism to greater individualism in Israeli society, documented through changing choices of names by Weitman, and through changes in texts in children's memory books, by R. Shapira and Herzog. They also include a phenomenological study in sociolinguistics by Katriel, documenting the outspoken character of Israelis through their speech patterns; the studies of tourism by E. Cohen; the study of trust and mistrust by Roniger; and the study of death-related symbols by P. Palgi.

CONCLUSION

A brief overview such as this cannot possibly do justice to the great variety and richness of Israeli sociology. All that we could hope to accomplish is to bring out some of its special flavor, and some of its central themes and trends, in relation to those of Israeli society.

In this respect we have identified some major foci of solidarity and consensus, as well as some divisions and foci of conflict, two facets of Israeli society that have also become foci of analysis for Israeli sociology. If there is a common denominator to the conclusions reached by a large number (though not by all) sociologists on these issues, it is that contrary to initial misgivings, the various divisions and arenas of conflict have not hardened and become increasingly overlapping, but rather, and with some exceptions, increasingly distinct and crosscutting.

Thus, although there are classes in Israel, processes of social mobility have prevented the ossification of their boundaries. In this respect, it is of special importance that Orientals, though they have not achieved equal status with Westerners, have not become a homogeneous lower class; and trends of internal differentiation and mobility within this group, as well as interethnic marriages, have become increasingly evident. The division between religious and nonreligious Jews, wrought with friction, has not been consistently coextensive with any other division. In some respects political power centers have become more diversified and decentralized. Thus, the periphery has gained increasing power to counterbalance that of the center, a process that has been evident, for instance, in increasing parental involvement in determining educational policy.

In this kaleidoscope of crisscrossing categories, loyalties, divisions, and conflicts, the ultra-orthodox community and the Arab minority have remained largely separate. Yet the Israeli component of the Arab community (as distinct from Arabs of the territories) is not totally disconnected from wider trends in Israeli society: here, too, processes of mobility have been discerned. And the ultra-orthodox community is indirectly tied to the rest of the religious community, and to Israeli society at large, through the vulnerable yet still surviving arrangements known as the status quo. To the extent that beyond all divisions and conflicts there is still a certain integration within the Jewish part of Israeli society, it thus seems to rest on such mechanisms for working out compromises (analyzed by sociologists of religion) and on the increasingly crosscutting divisions and struggles (identified by the power and conflict school) no less than on consensus on fundamental values (identified by the structural-functional school of Israeli sociologists).

Israeli sociologists have long been involved in the formation of social policy. Whether, and to what extent, they have had a share in bringing about the current patterns of Israeli society is a moot question. At the moment, sociologists face the task of trying to help this society solve the problems it currently faces. It seems to us that most sociologists involved in social policy issues are intent on doing so not by turning Israeli society into a more homogeneous and consensual one, a project that would be futile to begin with. Rather, they seem intent on making policy makers more aware of Israeli society's pluralist dimensions, thus encouraging society's advancement along the path toward greater pluralism—on which it seems set to move in any case. Given the obvious limits of sociology in the policy area, its influence in these respects should not be overestimated. Neither should it be dismissed as irrelevant; and only in our next analysis (which we intend to present in thirty years' time) will we be able to tell what degree of success sociology will have had in this respect.

NOTES

The authors' names are listed in alphabetical order.

We wish to thank Professor Akiva Deutsch, Professor Helmut Mjusam, Dr. Ephraim Tabory, and Dr. Peter Bamberger for their most helpful comments and suggestions. We are also grateful to Ms. Anat Kalka and Mr. Siomi Brill for their excellent assistance in researching this chapter.

1. Space constraints, the fact that there has been a veritable explosion of sociological work in Israel, and the fact that the studies of sociologists have been reported in several publications preclude the listing of references to their work. Instead, names only have been mentioned, and references are cited only in those cases in which a point in this chapter is based on an argument made by another sociologist.

2. Eisenstadt's ideas have found expression in eighteen books, in sixteen collections of readings of which he has been editor or co-editor, and in articles too numerous to mention.

3. Menachem Rosner, "Social Research, Change and the Kibbutz," in Ernest Krausz, ed., *The Sociology of the Kibbutz*. New Brunswick, N.J.: Transaction Books, 1983, 7–22.

4. Alex Weingrod, "The State of the Art," in Ernest Krausz, ed., *Migration, Ethnicity and Community*. New Brunswick, N.J.: Transaction Books, 1980, 5–17.

5. Deborah Bernstein, "Immigrants and Society," *British Journal of Sociology* 31 (2), June 1980, 246–64.

6. This point has been made by Professor Moshe Lissak at a recent conference of the Israel Sociological Society.

7. Sammy Smooha, *Jewish Ethnicity in Israel 1948–1986*. Haifa: Haifa University Press, 1987.

8. Ibid.

25

Contemporary Sociology in Morocco

M'hammed Sabour

The work of Abderahman Ibn Khaldun (1332–1406),[1] which appears in his seminal book *The Muqaddimah: An Introduction to History,*[2] represents a scientific and historical masterpiece of undeniable sociological value.[3] The book places greatest emphasis on North Africa and especially Morocco, with Ibn Khaldun analyzing such subjects as the social hierarchy, the division and strategies of power, group solidarity, the rise and fall of political power and Arab-Islamic civilization, the impact of rural and urban ways of life on the flourishing and decay of culture. For these many reasons he has been designated by many as one of the most prominent forerunners of sociology.[4] His work, however, appeared at a time when Arab-Islamic civilization was going through a period of decline, with the result that he remained relatively unknown until the middle of the nineteenth century, when he was rediscovered by European scholars. His work had no followers, nor did it form the basis for any school of thought.

The genesis of contemporary sociology in Morocco came only at the beginning of this century. Hence the development of sociology in the country can be divided into two stages: the colonial and the postcolonial periods.

THE COMMITTED SOCIOLOGY OF THE COLONIAL PERIOD

By the turn of the twentieth century Morocco had become a coveted object among the European nations. After various treaties and negotiations, France (and to some extent Spain) reserved the right to take over Morocco. But gaining control of Morocco and subjugating its population demanded a knowledge of its fundamental realities (customs, traditions, structures, beliefs, etc.). With this in mind, the sciences, or "scientific research," were called upon to prepare the ground by supplying the information required by the business groups interested in investing in and monopolizing the Moroccan market. In addition, the political-military elite needed information essential for the successful completion of its colonial project.[5] Although some individual scholars and scientific groups who worked independently were interested in Morocco for its own sake, the majority of the studies were organized and sponsored by the French authorities and accordingly had aims which were more political than scientific. Therefore, sociology as a discipline and a means of social investigation emerged in Morocco under the impulse of French colonial policy. This first materialized in the constitution of the so-called Mission Scientifique and the foundation of the Institut des Hautes Etudes Marocaines, which facilitated the emergence—or, more exactly, the creation—of a politically committed sociology which had an avowed vocation to serve particular interests and which, as a consequence, served as a dependent and partial instrument.[6] As we will see later, until the 1950s the foundation and evolution of sociology in Morocco followed the political trajectory of the colonial process.

In spite of the conflicting intellectual and political forces behind its foundation, The Mission Scientifique (1904), became very active during the early part of this century (1900–1930). This is reflected in the appearance of many reviews and journals: *Les Archives Marocaines, La Revue du Monde Musulman, Villes et Tribus du Maroc, Les Archives Berbères.* Under the guidance of Edouard Michaux-Bellaire,[7] the goals of the Mission Scientifique were defined in the study of Moroccan social organization by means of oral and written sources, popular traditions, and religious practices through an "empirical sociology." This sociology consisted of the drawing up of an inventory and description of tribes, rituals, and ethnic groups in Morocco.

After the official imposition of protectorate status on Morocco (1912), France set up the administration and general control of Moroccan society. Some colonial administrators, such as Jacques Berque,[8] became influential scholars and sociologists who specialized in the Moroccan society. Their scientific contribution was relatively impartial and perceptive. Moreover, their contribution to some extent helped in establishing a Moroccan tradition of social sciences. But it was not until the 1920s, when the headquarters of the Mission Scientifique was transferred from Tangier to Rabat (the capital), that sociology as such actually obtained an independent and distinguished status through the foundation of a Sociological Department. Like the other French scientific institutions, this department was closely tied to the colonial administration, since it relied totally on its moral and financial sponsorship.

With the establishment of French colonization and the pacification of the main regions of the country, French sociologists and anthropologists had the opportunity to penetrate into zones which had thus far remained inaccessible. This factor helped increase significantly the number of studies written on Morocco, which in turn probably stimulated the need for a center to coordinate and publish the works of an ever-increasing number of scholars studying Moroccan society. In 1920, therefore, the Institut des Hautes Etudes Marocaines was founded, with finance from the colonial administration and under the supervision of the academic institutions of the Metropolis (France). The Institut provided education and training for French civil servants and army assistants, but research remained its main function. Apart from a few isolated and independent scholars Edward Westermarck[9] (a Finn), Moroccan society was a monopoly of the French. Orientations and activities were directed and motivated by the interests of colonial policy, receiving no significant theoretical or empirical influence from the Durkheimian sociological current prevailing in the Metropolis in the 1920s. The review *Hesperis,* which replaced the *Archives Berbères,* became the forum wherein the Institut published its works.

Faithful to its vocation, conditioned by colonial policy, and reacting to the evolution of Moroccan society, sociology during the colonial period (1900–1956) took an interest in many themes and issues. Following M. Bentahar and E.-T. Bouasla,[10] these can be divided into six domains: political system, tribal system, maraboutism, rural sociology, urban sociology, and education and acculturation.

Political system (the Makhzen)[11]: In studies concerned with the political system, the military and bureaucratic structures of the Makhzen were analyzed, as well as their relation to the tribal system. If the sultan was presented as a prominent element in the Moroccan political system, for ideological reasons no attempt was made to examine either the origin or the legitimacy of his power. In addition to the characteristics, function, and authority of the Makhzen and the social origin of its members, detailed descriptions were provided of the social space within which the sultan and the Makhzen exercised authority.[12]

Tribal system: The tribal system was a favorite domain for French researchers because it represented a key element in the colonial policy. In this respect, we find the tribal organization and hierarchy amply described in various publications, as well as customs, rituals, traditions, and lifestyles. In an attempt to justify colonial intentions, the sociocultural and political specificities of the Berbers[13] were often presented in a positive light in comparison with those of the Arabs.[14]

Maraboutism: Moroccan Islam consists of three main components: the religious brotherhoods, sharifism, and maraboutism,[15] the last component constituting what is called popular Islam. The maraboutic phenomena (practices, symbolic power, social signification, cultural influence, and eth-

nographic dimensions) provide the main foci of these studies, in relation
to the religious brotherhoods and their social role.[16]

Rural sociology: Morocco as a society, culture, and landscape is a whole
formed of many diversities. This diversity is visible in the variety of its
ethnic groups, its numerous languages and dialects, and its lifestyles. The
sociologists and anthropologists of the colonial period were fascinated by
this diversity, which was rooted in the rural reality and its socioeconomic
structures.[17] In this respect, some studies provide interesting analyses of
the rural way of life and economic activity based on traditional agriculture
and living conditions, as well as discussions of the problems which faced
the countryside as a result of emigration. However, with the exception of
a few works like those of Jacques Berque,[18] which provide "interesting
sociological reflexions on the use of soil, the social relations and the production, the relation of the sacred to the agrarian practice,"[19] most studies
represent an anthropological and ethnographic literature which is broadly
descriptive and simplifying. Berque's theoretical contributions to the Moroccan rural sociology are, therefore, of undeniable value.

Urban sociology: Owing to their Arab-Islamic architectural aspect, Moroccan towns—especially the imperial cities Fès, Rabat, Meknès, and Mar-
rakech—attracted an undue amount of the attention of the French
sociologists. While the majority were interested in describing their culture,
religion, and history, others, in a sociohistorical vein, emphasized the hierarchy of the city dwellers, their professional activity, and their crafts.
Here, the works of Louis Massignon[20] on the corporation of craftsmen and
merchants are especially well known. His theory and methodology were
distinguished by their scientific rigor. Elsewhere, the increase in the European population emigrating to Morocco and the establishment of many
new urban centers have incited sociologists to draw attention to subjects
such as the "exodus to the cities," the "formation of the proletariat,"
"spare-time activities," and the "socioeconomic evolution of the urban
sector."[21]

Acculturation and education: Traditional values, education, and the
Moroccan personality have been at the center of interest for European
scholars ever since the Middle Ages; and contact with the Moroccan population has increased this tendency. The result has been descriptions of
the mentality, intellectual aptitudes, and social psychology of Moroccans.
The literature associates the image of the Moroccans, compared to Europeans (especially the French), with such aspects as fatalism, lack of fore-
sight, and laziness—stereotypes which existed before the colonial
sociology and which continue to exist today.[22] Other studies address Islamic education (mosque, medersa), the impact of modern education on
Moroccan society, and the universe of the Moroccan schoolboy and the
education of young people.[23]

THE PERIOD OF INDEPENDENCE: THE SEARCH FOR STATUS AND IDENTITY

After independence in 1956 the sociological field became de facto inheritor of a large number of works accumulated over half a century. Although some scholars, like A. Adam,[24] contend that the colonial sociology is "of inestimable importance from the point of view of knowledge and civilisation in general because it has planified all possible sociological thought on Morocco,"[25] these works must be viewed with caution. In fact, the genesis, theoretical and methodological content, and motifs of this sociology require meticulous reassessment in the light of the political-ideological context which produced it and which has tainted most of it.[26]

The transition from colonial sociology to a postcolonial, culturally authentic Moroccan sociology has not been without problems. The imprint of the past (structures, archives, logistics, etc.), the linguistic dependence[27] of young Moroccan sociologists (frame of conception and analysis, references), and the effort demanded by the construction of the new nation-state has placed the social sciences among the last priorities. In this context, sociology began to develop various activities: (1) the continuation of a French-influenced sociology emphasizing fields such as "proletarianization-urbanization," the "decolonization" (sociological, intellectual), and the "position of women and gender"; (2) the emergence of an English-speaking school[28] which applies segmentist theory in the study of different Moroccan tribes (religion, authority, social solidarity, etc.); (3) the emergence of sociological activities (theorization, empirical studies) led by Moroccans whose goal has been to promote a national sociology distanced from any theoretical and methodological dependence.[29]

For his part, A. Dialmy[30] has typified three forms of practice in the sociological field in Morocco over the last thirty years: "happy" (technocratic) sociology, "worried" (epistemological) sociology, and "merry" (metaphysical) sociology. The first includes the kind of studies which apply Western theories and methods to Moroccan society without taking sufficiently into consideration the nature of this society. This orientation follows a conciliatory pragmatism which is satisfied or "happy" with using a simplifying empiricism with no consistent theory. In this synthetic orientation the theorization is often a mix and patching-up wherein speculative argumentation has taken over concrete empirical reference. The "happiness" of this sociology is to be found in the use of ideas and concepts without concern for their contextual and cultural fitness.

"Worried" (epistemological) sociology represents studies characterized by a certain skepticism toward the adaptation of Western sociological apparatus. This orientation does not ask for a total break with the Western theories but argues for distancing from them and refusing to accept them as the only valid means of reference. This orientation therefore works toward developing an alternative which draws on roots in the reality of Moroccan society. Attachment to the roots is performed without regret, with neither an inferiority nor a superiority complex. The main goal is the search for authenticity (in relation to the past and/or the future) in sociological action.

The third orientation has been termed "merry" sociology. This is strongly linked with the Western model, from which it borrows its inspiration and for which it mainly directs its production (which in most cases is in French). The Western frame of thinking is so omnipresent in the activity of sociologists belonging to this orientation that we may speak of an acculturation and assimilation. In fact, the studies of these sociologists are marked by a conflicting rejection-adoption[31] of the Western knowledge (language, ideas, symbols, ideals, etc.). This can be seen in their writing about identity, the sacred, interaction, gender, phenomenology, and so forth.

Accordingly, we can outline two characteristics in the sociological activity in Morocco: (1) the techno-empiric branch situated in departments which form part of the state apparatus and which practice a *sur commande* sociology according to the requirements of these departments[32] (this situation has placed sociology in a position of subjugation to the directives and will of the political status quo), and (2) academic sociology, which is more theoretically oriented. This is explained by the fact that after independence a process of decolonization took place in the field of sociology which crystallized in numerous critical theoretical writings for the revival of cultural identity. In addition, the weakness of empirical sociology[33] is due to the lack of an institutional and organizational basis. In 1960, with the assistance of UNESCO, an Institut de Sociologie was created; but it was closed ten years later as a result of conflict with the political and academic authorities. This was followed by the integration of sociology into the departments of philosophy at the Universities of Rabat and Fès.[34] The nonexistence of independent material support for significant empirical studies has pushed academic sociology toward speculative and interpretative criticism and theorization. The philosophically rooted French sociology, from which the Moroccan tradition has received a relative influence, has also had an impact on this orientation.

Furthermore, there is a declared will to underrate and marginalize the social sciences in general and sociology in particular. As in many Third World countries sociology[35] is seen as associated with critical if not subversive forces which challenge the political paradigm. In addition, sociology, as a discipline oriented toward and inspired by cultural, social, and political phenomena and issues, is by nature sensitive to the ongoing discourse. This sensitivity, whether in written or spoken form, makes sociology a troublemaker in the eyes of the political leadership, which is—at least in some Arab countries—characterized by a visceral anti-intellectualism.[36]

However, the difficult status of sociology does not mean that the sociological field is totally inactive or sterile. Despite the lack of support and the limited means, many Moroccan researchers and scholars have been able to produce studies of high scientific quality. Nevertheless, during the last two decades these studies have been cut back, especially with regard to social stratification, urban-rural change, popular culture, and the family (gender, sex, division of labor, etc.).[37]

CONCLUSION

Because of contemporary socioeconomic and political conditions, sociology in Morocco is undergoing a threefold crisis: the first is linked to its raison d'être, the second to its vocation, and the third to its autonomy.

1. Underestimated to a considerable extent as a science by the powers-that-be, sociology is struggling to survive. The situation is highly visible: a shortage of financial support, weakness in the library services, an uncertainty about vocational opportunities, limited freedom to carry out studies in certain social fields, and flagrant intervention and control on the part of administrative authorities.[38]

2. The genesis and history of Moroccan sociology cause it problems of identity and vocation. However, contrary to those who contend that the present Moroccan sociology is more or less a continuation of the colonial sociology,[39] it can be argued that even though there remain links between culture and language and schools of thought with France, there is no direct dependence. There exists, in my view, rather a metamorphosed and conscious relationship on the part of Moroccan sociologists. But this is not the main problem. In fact, the crucial matter for sociology in a developing Moroccan society is its scientific quality, its analytical objectivity, and its position vis-à-vis the social reality with all the dialectics and components it embodies.

3. The autonomy of science is a vital prerequisite for the establishment of its credibility. Sociology in Morocco was created under political and administrative supervision during the colonial period, and in a way, it still exists under another supervision, that of independent Morocco. Except for a few cases, sociology and sociologists remain to a large extent dependent on the state and are therefore subject to its mercy and humor for their survival and support. If sociology in Morocco has passed through many stages on its path toward maturity, it is nevertheless still searching for recognition of its status, scientific legitimacy, and social indispensability.

NOTES

1. Ibn Khaldun was active in various fields (1370–1404). He was scholar (*'alim*), professor (e.g., University Al-Qarawiyyin, Morocco), judge (*qadi*), and diplomat.

2. Ibn Khaldun Abdelrahman, *The Muqaddimah: An Introduction to History.* English translation by F. Rosenthal (New York: Bollingen Foundation, 3 vols., 1958).

3. M. Mahdi, *Ibn Khaldun's Philosophy of History: A Study in the Philosophical Foundations of the Science of Culture* (London: Chicago University Press, 1957); M. Sabour, *The Sociology of Ibn Khaldun* (Helsinki: Marhaba [Finnish], 1981); A. Al-Azmeh, *Ibn Khaldun: An Essay in Reinterpretation* (London: Frank Cass, 1982).

4. G. Bouthoul, *Ibn Khaldoun, sa philosophie sociale* (Paris: 1930); N. Schmidt, *Ibn Kaldun: Historian, Sociologist and Philosopher* (New York: 1967).

5. A. Khatibi, *Bilan de la sociologie au Maroc* (Rabat: Publication de l'association pour les sciences humaines, 1967).

6. F. M. Houroro, *Sociologie coloniale au Maroc: Cas de Michaux-Bellaire* (Paris: Editions Afrique-Orient, 1988).

7. Edouard Michaux-Bellaire is considered to be one of the main initiators of Moroccan colonial sociology. This French civil servant was an Arabist, a historian by training who converted himself to sociology. He directed the Mission Scientifique from 1906 until 1920. When the Mission was transferred to Rabat and incorporated in the Institut des Hautes Etudes Marocaines, he was nominated "counsellor of native affairs." He carried out and directed a large number of studies of Moroccan society. While some of these studies constitute valuable historical documents on Moroccan society at the beginning of this century, the majority of his works were ideologically and politically committed to the service of French colonial policy. See E. Michaux-Bellaire (ed.), *La Mission scientifique au Maroc* (Rabat: Série renseignement, 1925), p. 22; E. Michaux-Bellaire, "La sociologie marocaine," *Archives marocaines* 27 (1927).

8. J. Berque, *Structures sociales du Haut Atlas* (Paris: PUF, 1955).

9. E. Westermarck's socio-anthropological works on Morocco are important, which cover almost three decades of study (1904–1930). Three of his main works can be mentioned here: E. Westermarck, *Les cérémonies du mariage au Maroc,* Ecole supérieure de Langue Arabe et de Dialectes Berbères de Rabat, Vol. 7 (Paris: Editions E. Leroux, 1921); *Ritual and Belief in Morocco,* 2 vols. (London: Macmillan, 1926); *Wit and Wisdom in Morocco: A Study of Native Proverbs,* With the Assistance of Sharif Abdelsalam El-Baqqali (London: 1930).

10. M. Bentahar and E.-T. Bouasla, *La Sociologie coloniale et la société marocaine de 1830 à 1960. La Sociologie Marocaine Contemporaine: Bilan et Perspectives* (Rabat: Publications de la Faculté de Lettres et des Sciences Humaines, 1988), pp. 27–43.

11. Literally, a storehouse; by extension, the central government in Morocco.

12. F. de La Chapelle, "La formation du pouvoir monarchique dans les tribus du haut Atlas occidental," *Hespéris* (1928): 263–83; R. Montagne, *Les berbères et le Makhzen dans le sud du Maroc: essai sur les transformation politique des berbères sédentaires, groupe chleuh* (Paris: Librairie Félix Alcan, 1930).

13. The Berbers constitute the second largest ethnic group after the Arabs in Morocco (between 30% and 40%).

14. H. Bruno and G. H. Bousquet, "Les pactes d'alliance chez les berbères du Maroc central," *Hespéris* (1946): 353–72.

15. M. Gilsenan, *Recognizing Islam: Religion and Society in the Modern Arab World* (New York: Pantheon Books, 1982); M. Sabour, *The Cultural Identification and Alienation of the Arab Intelligentsia: An Empirical Study of the Moroccan Educated* (Joensuu: University of Joensuu, 1985).

16. G. Spillmann, *Les confréries religieuses au Maroc* (Paris: Centre des hautes études sur l'Afrique et l'Asie modernes, 1938).

17. M. Faust, *La colonisation rurale au Maroc, 1919–1929* (Alger: 1931).

18. J. Berque, *Les pactes pastoraux Beni Meskine* (Alger: 1936); J. Berque, *Etudes d'histoire rurale maghrébine* (Tanger: 1938); J. Berque, *Structures sociales du Haut Atlas* (Paris: PUF, 1955); J. Berque, "Cent vingt-cinq ans de sociologie maghrébine," *Annales Economies Sociétés, Civilisations* 11, no. 3, Juillet-Septembre, 1956.

19. M. Bentahar and E.-T. Bouasla, *La Sociologie coloniale et la société marocaine de 1830 à 1960. La Sociologie Marocaine Contemporaine: Bilan et Perspectives* (Rabat: Publications de la Faculté de Lettres et des Sciences Humaines, 1988), p. 39.

20. L. Massignon, "Le corps de métier et la cité islamique," *Revue Internationale de Sociologie* (1920): 473–89; L. Massignon, "Enquête sur les corporations d'artisans et de commerçants au Maroc (1923–1924)," *Revue du Monde Musulman* (1924); J. Tharaud, *Fés ou les bourgeois de l'Islam* (Paris: Plon, 1951); L. Villeme, "L'évolution de la vie citadine," L'évolution sociale du Maroc, *Les Cahiers de l'Afrique et de l'Asie* (1951).

21. M. Zimmermann, *Paysages et villes du Maroc* (Lyon: 1923); Ch. Lecoeur, "Métiers et classes sociales d'azemmour," *Revue Africaine* (1936): 933–56; R. LeTourneau, *Fés avant le protectorat: une étude économique et sociale d'une ville de l'Occident musulman* (Casablanca: Publications de l'Institut des hautes études marocaines, 1949); A. Adam, "La prolétarisation de l'habitat dans l'anciènne Médina de Casablanca," *BESM* 12, no. 45; 13, no. 46, 1950; A. Adam, "Le 'bidonville' de Ben Msik à Casablanca: Contribution à l'étude de prolétariat musulman au Maroc," *Annales de l'Institut d'études orientales,* 1949–1950; R. Montagne, *Naissance du prolétariat marocain: enquête collective, 1948–1950* (Paris: Peyronnet, 1951).

22. L. Brunot, "L'espirit marocain: les caractères essentiels de la personalité Marocaine," *Bulletin d'Enseignement Public* (1923): 35–59; G. Surdon, "Psychologies marocaines vues à travers le droit," *Afrique Française* (1930): 373–80; A. Koller, *Essai sur l'esprit des Berbères marocains* (Fribourg: Editions Franciscaines, 1949); P. Brachet, *Descartes n'est pas marocain* (Paris: La Pensée Universelle, 1982); M. van der Yeught, *Le Maroc à nu* (Paris: L'Harmattan, 1989).

23. R. LeTourneau, *Les collèges musulmans et leur fonctionnement* (Paris: Centre des Hautes Etudes sur L'Afrique et l'Asie Modernes, 1938); L. Paye, *L'éducation de la jeunesse marocaine, réflexions et principe d'action* (Rabat: 1940); P. Bourgeois, *L'univers de l'écolier marocain* (Rabat: Faculté des lettres et des sciences sociales, fascule 1–2, 1959); P. Bourgeois, *L'univers de l'écolier marocain* (Rabat: Faculté des lettres et des sciences sociales, fascule 3–5, 1960).

24. A. Adam, *Bibliographie critique de sociologie, d'éthnologie et de géographie humaine du Maroc* (Alger: CRAPE, 1972).

25. Ibid., p. 53.

26. T. Benjelloun, "Décolonisation de la sociologie au Maghreb," *Le Monde diplomatique* (Août, 1974): 18; A. Khatibi, "Double Criticism: The Decolonization of Arab Sociology," in H. Barakat, *Contemporary North Africa* (Washington, D.C.: Center for Contemporary Arab Studies, Georgetown University, 1985).

27. Teaching, research, and publication are still conducted mainly in French.

28. E. Gellner, *Tribalism and Social Change in North Africa: French-Speaking North Africa, a Search of Identity* (New York: 1965); E. Gellner, *Saints of the Atlas* (London: Chicago University Press, 1969).

29. M. Chekroun, "Crisis of Sociology or Crisis of Society," *Towards an Arab Sociology,* Centre for Arab Unity Studies (1986): 68–82 (Arabic).

30. A. Dialmy, *The Sociological Affair* (Casablanca: Publications Afrique-Orient, 1989, Arabic): 66–75.

31. A. Khatibi, *La blessure du nom propre* (Paris: DuNoël, 1974).

32. Sociology in its techno-empiric orientation has an important status in the Institut Agronomique et Vétérinaire Hassan II as part of the Départment Humain Sciences. In spite of its pragmatic situation it is the most empirically fertile and active. So far, as a result of official financial support and the consequent logistical possibilities, this area of sociology has produced important rural studies.

33. M. Chekroun, "Crisis of Sociology or Crisis of Society," *Towards an Arab Sociology,* Centre for Arab Unity Studies (1986): 68–82 (Arabic); A. Dialmy, *The Sociological Affair* (Casablanca: Publications Afrique-Orient, 1989, Arabic).

34. A. Dialmy, "Aspects in the Development of Sociology in Morocco," *Towards an Arab Sociology,* Centre for Arab Unity Studies (1986): 287–308 (Arabic).

35. L. A. Jinadu, "The Social Sciences and Development in Africa," *Sarec Report,* R. 1, Stockholm, 1985; M. E. Hijazi, "The Present Crisis of Sociology in the Arab World," *Towards an Arab Sociology,* Centre for Arab Unity Studies (1986): 13–44 (Arabic); A. Akiwowo, "Building National Sociological Tradition in an African Subregion," in N. Genov, *National Traditions in Sociology* (London: SAGE Publications, 1989), pp. 151–67.

36. M. Sabour, *Homo Academicus Arabicus* (Joensuu: University of Joensuu Publications in Social Sciences, 1988).

37. F. Mernissi, *Beyond the Veil: Male-Female Dynamics in a Modern Muslim Society* (Cambridge, Mass.: Schenkman, 1975); F. Mernissi, *Le Maroc raconté par ses femmes* (Casablanca: Editions Le Fennec, 1983); F. Mernissi, *Chahrazad n'est pas marocaine* (Casablanca: Editions Le Fennec, 1988); M. Salahdine, *Les petits métiers clandestins* (Casablanca: Eddif Maroc, 1987); M. Bentahar, *Villes et campagnes au Maroc, les problèmes sociaux de l'urbanisation* (Rabat: Editell, 1988).

38. M. Sabour, "The Status and Ontology of Arab Intellectuals: The Academic Group," *International Journal of Contemporary Sociology* 28 (July–October 1991): 221–32.

39. A. Adam, *Bibliographie critique de sociologie, d'éthnologie et de géographie humaine du Maroc* (Alger: CRAPE, 1972).

26

Contemporary Sociology in Zimbabwe

Angela Penelope Cheater

A SHORT HISTORY OF SOCIOLOGY IN ZIMBABWE

Zimbabwe was colonized, toward the end of the "scramble for Africa," in 1890, by the British South Africa Company (BSAC) rather than by any colonial power proper. The BSAC was formed by Cecil John Rhodes for the purpose of colonizing territory then unclaimed by any European power on the Cape-to-Cairo route on behalf of Great Britain. The company took over what were then called Southern and Northern Rhodesia (excluding the Protectorate over Barotseland). Northern Rhodesia, which in 1964 became the independent Republic of Zambia, is not part of the purvue of this chapter, although there were important academic links between Northern and Southern Rhodesia and Nyasaland (now Malawi) during the period of political federation from 1953 to 1963. The University College of Rhodesia and Nyasaland, which opened for teaching at the beginning of 1957, served all three countries; and its social scientists had research experience in all three. After the breakup of the Central African Federation, the college successively became the University College of Rhodesia, the University of Rhodesia, and finally the University of Zimbabwe.

Southern Rhodesia was administered under the BSAC Charter until 1923, when its white settlers voted (by a narrow margin) to become a self-governing territory under the British Crown, rather than to become a (fifth) province of their southern neighbor, the Union of South Africa. However, both its policy of racial segregation and its system of law (Roman-Dutch principles leavened by English common law) reflected the geopolitical impact of South Africa on this new country, rather than the influence of its nominal metropolitan parent. Indeed, almost exactly seventy-five years after the foundation of this new state, on 11 November 1965, its white settlers, having recurrently been in conflict with metropolitan thinking (especially but not exclusively on racial issues), unilaterally declared their independence (UDI) from Britain. UDI led directly to the formation of guerrilla armies fighting against the illegality of the white settlers' declaration, and for their own democratic rights in their own country. On 18 April 1980, after thirteen years of war and two general elections based on universal suffrage (in April 1979 and February 1980), the Republic of Zimbabwe was born. As a modern state, Zimbabwe celebrated its centenary in 1990. Its academic history is correspondingly even shorter.

Its political history and the South African influence on its social policy have influenced the development of sociology in Zimbabwe. A large minority of the white settlers came from South Africa. Racial attitudes and social policy alike penetrated north of the Limpopo not only through the social networks of these settlers but also through trade links and capital investment. Until the 1950s, the nearest institutions of tertiary education lay in South Africa; even today, "family traditions" require that thousands of young Zimbabweans, almost exclusively white, attend the South African alma maters of their parent(s)—a pattern which, because it relieves pressure on the limited places available at Zimbabwean institutions, has the acquiescence of the new state. Within the sphere of university education, of course, the South African influence has been liberal—even radical—as well as conservative; it has affected blacks, who attended Fort Hare, Cape Town, and Witwatersrand universities, as well as whites. Joshua Nkomo, for example, in 1947 obtained his diploma from the Jan Hofmeyr School of Social Work associated with Witwatersrand University.[1]

One can trace an early, humanitarian concern with studies of urban poverty to Percy Ibbotson, a Wesleyan Methodist priest who arrived from Britain in 1922 and was based in Bulawayo. From 1942 to 1946 Ibbotson was the organizing secretary of the Association of Native Welfare Societies. During this time he undertook national surveys of urban employment, wages, rents, food rations, educational and health facilities, and juvenile delinquency, among blacks. He later became a "native representative" in the federal legislature. Such concern with poverty developed in parallel with the philanthropy of black Christians such as Matthew Rusike, who established rural orphanages in the 1930s; and Jairos Jiri, whose battle after World War II to establish urban rehabilitation centers for the disabled was ultimately very successful.[2] But social work as an *academic* discipline responding to black urban poverty developed only a generation ago as an adjunct of sociology; sociology itself had earlier grown out of social anthropology, the discipline of major importance to a settler administration grappling with the problems arising from a racially segregated society subject to rapid economic development.

Early "native administrators" dabbled in anthropology,[3] seeking to understand, for example, the adjustment of indigenous cultures to the newly imposed systems of "native administration" involving new roles for chiefs and headmen, and new rules regarding land tenure. Later, such efforts to understand rural societies and the ways in which they were changing, not least under the impact of labor migration to the towns and cities, would be assisted by professional anthropologists.[4] In the cities themselves, although some anthropologists retained both research[5] and administrative interests,[6] they tended over time to give way to sociologists.[7]

So there arose something of the traditional division of labor separating urban-based sociologists from anthropologists willing to get their boots dirty in the countryside. In Zimbabwe, this separation arose not because the theoretical ancestors of social anthropology and sociology were different—on the contrary, they are shared—but rather for reasons of practical, administrative convenience in the context of colonization. Where parallel systems of statutory and customary law operated, "native administrators" and appeal-hearing magistrates had to know what the customs were with which they had to deal.[8] Where local authorities, especially chiefs, faced extreme difficulties in reconciling the demands of the state with those of their people, the state had to resolve such problems if it wished its own apparatus to continue to function.[9] When people refused to bury deceased bodies until their property demands were met, "good government" required a response.[10] With respect to these examples of continuing problems of administration, the major difference between the colonial and independent states is that the independent state either rejects, or has not thought of using, the anthropological expertise on which the colonial state relied.

Most social anthropologists were recurrently professionally embarrassed by the willingness of the colonial settler regime to take their discipline seriously. When, in 1964, the then prime minister, Ian Smith (later the architect of UDI), noted publicly that he wanted anthropological advice on how to consult blacks on the desirability of full independence from Britain, the reaction of those at the local university was to publish a letter in the United Kingdom–based *Manchester Guardian,* stating that a secret ballot was "the only way . . . to give at least every man the opportunity to express his own view" and rejecting the government's proposal to take the opinion of its own salaried chiefs as representative of the people's views.[11]

In contrast to the administrative problems of the central state, which arose from cultural differences in a polyethnic system, the problems of urban poverty and municipal administration were less diffuse, more localized, and more amenable to what R. Chambers[12] has called "quick and dirty" (or, sometimes, "pathological long and dirty") survey investigations by people who do not themselves experience such problems directly. Many problems arose from the policy of discouraging permanent urbanization in favor of circulatory migration among black workers, and its corollaries of "single-person wages" and the extremely limited provision of family housing, which caused poverty among blacks in Zimbabwe's small but growing towns. Yet for decades such practical problems were regarded if not as an adjunct of anthropology, then certainly as unworthy of disciplinary specialization.

Anthropology in colonial Rhodesia was, as suggested in its orientation to solving practical problems, theoretically somewhat eclectic. Radcliffe-Brownian structural-functionalism, the dominant paradigm of South African English-language universities in which A. R. Radcliffe-Brown himself established social anthropology as a teaching subject, undoubtedly predominated (e.g., in the works of J. F. Holleman, later a professor at the University of Leiden in Holland). Leavened by the theoretical premises pertaining to situational analysis (which were influenced by Max Gluckman's variety of Marxism) of the so-called Manchester School,[13] important representatives of which were teaching at the local university in the 1960s, structural-functionalism sometimes became very critical of the colonial regime[14] without undergoing any major theoretical transformation. Even neo-Marxist approaches, which finally arrived in the late 1970s, responded to the requirements of practical utility.[15]

Nonetheless, important theoretical advances were made by the local representatives of the Manchester School working in both Zimbabwe and Zambia. The most significant of these concerning Zimbabwe involved micro-sociological network analysis among urban populations, and all were firmly grounded in the people's reaction to colonization.[16]

THE ACADEMIC INSTITUTIONALIZATION OF SOCIOLOGY

After the cessation of World War II hostilities in 1945, the question of establishing a local university was raised in Southern Rhodesia and funds were donated specifically to that end.[17] In 1952 the settler government passed the Southern Rhodesia University Act to legitimize fund-raising activities for its future establishment. In 1953 the Carr-Saunders Commission recommended the initial establishment of Science and Arts faculties to award General degrees, and Queen Elizabeth the Queen Mother laid the foundation stone on the Harare campus. In 1955 a Royal Charter was granted to the University College of Rhodesia and Nyasaland, as an external college of the University of London, to replace the Southern Rhodesia University Act. (Its many advantages, not least in placing the control of university affairs above direction by the state, were abrogated after Independence by the 1982 University of Zimbabwe Act, which reestablished the state domination considered undesirable during the colonial period and strengthened the indirect political influence on university affairs which had, in 1965, caused the first professor of sociology to resign.)

Among other appointments in 1955, Clyde Mitchell, formerly director of the Rhodes-Livingstone Institute in Lusaka (Zambia), became the first professor of one of the founding departments, that of African Studies. In 1964, at the instigation of Professor Mitchell, it was renamed Sociology.

I was very unhappy with the appellation. To me it seemed to imply that Africans were an object of study *sui generis.* I had to decide what London university subject should be taught . . . [and] naturally chose social anthropology. I hoped to demonstrate to the students both Black and White that social anthropology was a general theoretical subject and could be applied to any society. But of course the only real solution was [to] change the name of the department. So eventually after talking things over with the staff we decided not to call it social anthropology but the more general sociology.[18]

Clyde Mitchell had taken his first degree, in sociology, psychology, and social work, in his native South Africa. He responded successfully to an advertisement for a "sociologist" at the Rhodes-Livingstone Institute and was appointed in 1945, taking up the post after his demobilization. At the Institute, he undertook rural research in both Zambia and Malawi and spent some time at the University of Cape Town, with his research colleagues, studying anthropological theory under Isaac Schapera, before proceeding to an Oxford doctorate in social anthropology supervised by Max Gluckman. Mitchell's teaching in Zimbabwe, like his research, married the two disciplines of sociology and social anthropology; he emphasized the importance of working toward generalizing propositions on the basis of specific case studies[19] in the inductive approach typical of social anthropology.

Sociology was one of the "good departments" of the new university,[20] which itself achieved an international reputation within its first ten years of operation. Although the university initially offered only courses within the BA General degree, by 1963, in the new Faculty of Social Studies, African Studies was offering in addition a single Honours degree in social anthropology. Its staff went on to much grander appointments: Clyde Mitchell to a chair at Manchester; Ioan Lewis to become professor of social anthropology at the London School of Economics; Axel Sommerfelt (after being arrested and declared a prohibited immigrant, along with Jaap van Velsen and others protesting racial politics in 1966), to take the Chair of Social Anthropology at the University of Oslo in his native Norway.

By 1967, as a consequence of its staff's opposition to the racial politics

of UDI Rhodesia, which had penetrated the university college via conditions attached to student grants, the Department of Sociology was in crisis.
It had no professor and had lost two of its four lecturing staff. Another
left at the end of that year. One lecturer and a temporary teaching assistant held the department together in 1967, when no second-year teaching
in either the General or the Honours programs was available. Students
had to be sent to London to complete their degrees.[21] As an emergency
measure, Hansi Pollak, recently retired from the Chair of Sociology at the
University of Natal, Durban, South Africa, was persuaded to accept an
interim contract while the chair was advertised. The first black lecturing
appointment was made: Gordon Chavunduka (later, in 1979, to become
the department's first black professor) had been sent abroad by Clyde
Mitchell to the Universities of California at Los Angeles and Manchester,
in the United Kingdom, where his training straddled both anthropology
and sociology; he had completed his Master's degree at just the right academic time—even though it was also, for him, something of a political
embarrassment.

In 1968 Desmond Reader was appointed permanently to the Chair of
Sociology, where he stayed until moving in 1978 to a chair at Chelsea
College in the University of London. Reader was, in the pattern of past
appointments, a Cambridge-trained social anthropologist turned industrial
sociologist-cum-psychologist. Under his chairmanship the first lecturers
were appointed who had trained only in sociology, in the United States,
South Africa, and the United Kingdom. In the late 1960s, then, the Department of Sociology started teaching American-style sociology, while A.
K. H. Weinrich and Chavunduka continued the older anthropological tradition. The past practice of amalgamating the two disciplines thus became
difficult to maintain. Similarly, on the research side, the Institute of Social
Research was founded within the department. It conducted predominantly
urban, survey-type projects[22] before being dissolved (for lack of funds) in
the late 1970s.

For the past two decades, in teaching if not also in research, sociology
has predominated over social anthropology; and the content of specific
courses has emphasized one or the other of the two disciplines depending
on who has taught them. At present, in addition to separate introductory
courses in social anthropology and sociology, one-year courses are offered
in the second and third years of the B.Sc. (Sociology) Honours degree, in
Social Research Methods, Social Theory, Industrial Sociology, Rural Development, Ideas and Society, Urban Sociology, Sociology of Medicine,
Women in Development, Economy and Society, Social Policy and Social
Administration, Social Change and Demography. A Special Area Study
and Political Sociology are also taught from time to time, but not regularly.
It is important to note that certain specialties have never been taught

within the department: the sociology of education, for example, has always been located within teacher training in the Faculty of Education, since Dr. D. R. Manley (from Jamaica) was appointed to the first lectureship in 1964. But at the same time, psychology was for some years taught within the Department of Sociology as one of four options within a very complex Honours degree structure, before becoming an independent department.

Sociology is therefore not the only department at the University of Zimbabwe which teaches sociology. Although it is primarily concerned with research, since the mid-1980s the Centre for Applied Social Sciences (CASS) has been teaching methodology at the Master's level. The origins of this center lie in the privately funded Chair of Race Relations, endowed in the early 1960s, to which Kenneth Kirkwood (later Rhodes Professor of Race Relations at the University of Oxford) was appointed in 1964. For the past two decades the CASS chair has been occupied by a Zimbabwean social anthropologist, Marshall Murphree, who has also taught an undergraduate course on race and ethnic relations. By the late 1980s, the new Department of Rural and Urban Planning was servicing its own undergraduate students in all social science inputs, including sociology. The Department of Community Medicine also had its own sociologist. However, students in medical rehabilitation attended the introductory course in sociology. And although Department of Agricultural Economics students had previously read introductory social anthropology, by the 1990s their department hired a rural sociologist for its specialist requirements. Clearly, as sociology became fully institutionalized at the University of Zimbabwe, it also became more fragmented in specialist services.

Despite its problems of the mid- to late 1960s, teaching in the Department of Sociology recovered quite rapidly following the new appointments. By 1971 a coursework M.Sc. (Sociology) was on offer, in addition to research degrees at the Master's and Doctoral levels. The postgraduate coursework degree has never proved fully satisfactory, however, and teaching has recurrently been suspended for restructuring. Even after a decision has been taken to confirm that this degree is *not* a "conversion" but a "build-on" degree, there have been problems in operationalizing that decision.

As far as I am aware, and in marked contrast to the more recently established discipline of psychology, there has never been any attempt to reinforce the institutionalization of sociology in Zimbabwe by forming a national professional association. The Students' Sociological Association has waxed and waned, occasionally going completely defunct, although in the early 1970s it produced a student journal for a couple of years. It has always been more concerned with gaining access to financial resources within the university bureaucracy than with professional disciplinary issues. Nor have the social anthropologists, most of them individual members of the Association of Social Anthropologists of the Commonwealth and numbering the minimum required to establish a local chapter of this association, chosen to start such a chapter.

Concerning the institutionalization of sociology and social anthropology through professional publication, again there is little differentiation of these disciplines from the social sciences more generally. *Zambezia,* the journal of the University of Zimbabwe (UZ), publishes across disciplines, though the social sciences and humanities provide most of its articles. In addition to the university itself, which is currently assessing the viability of establishing a university press, half a dozen local publishing houses provide outlets for books across the social sciences spectrum. Some firms co-publish both local and international work with overseas publishing houses. Nonetheless, there remains an acute shortage of imported books; and over the past five years the University of Zimbabwe Library has had to restrict its journal subscriptions to the most basic, as the Zimbabwean dollar has declined in value against harder currencies. Although designated a regional "center of excellence" on the basis of its past holdings, the UZ Library can no longer serve as an adequate reference source for contemporary publications, in sociology or any other discipline. This very sad state of affairs has implications not only for local research but also for the quality and content of teaching in the future.

In contrast to the amorphous nature of sociology, its offshoot, social work, has professionalized, perhaps because it has never been regarded with much favor by the local academy. The first suggestion, which came from Kitwe (a copper-mining town in Zambia) in the early 1960s, to establish "a university certificate of proficiency in social studies and practices," was rejected. A nongraduate diploma was regarded as diverting teaching resources from their proper target, and "the College preferred not to train social workers."[23] By 1964, however, the Jesuits founded, in Harare, a School of Social Services offering a one-year training in group-work. In 1966 it expanded to offer a three-year diploma in social work. Following Professor Reader's appointment (from South Africa) to the Chair of Sociology at the university, in 1969, the renamed School of Social Work became the university's first "associate college" under the administrative aegis of the Department of Sociology. In 1975 the School added a one-year, post-diploma Bachelor of Social Work to its repertoire; in 1982 an Honours option in Clinical Social Work; and in 1983 the first course-work Master's degree in Social Work at any sub-Saharan university outside South Africa. More recently it has rationalized its degree structure into standard General and Honours streams.[24] All these degrees are awarded by the University of Zimbabwe and are overseen by the Department of Sociology, whose Board is responsible for the quality of the programs. The social work profession further consolidated its position in

1986, when the school began to publish the *Journal of Social Development in Africa.*

Another development occurred in the social sciences, not just sociology, in 1980, with the establishment of a new parastatal "think-tank" by the newly independent government, called the Zimbabwe Institute of Development Studies (ZIDS).[25] Although it never achieved the size originally envisaged, by 1987 ZIDS employed some thirty social scientists as researchers, primarily to produce policy position papers and recommendations to government. The staff complement by 1990 had fallen to twenty, employed in six multidisciplinary departments (agriculture and rural development; labor studies; education and social development; industry, science, and technology; history and politics; and Southern Africa and international relations). Three sociologists were among the research staff at the time of the unilateral cabinet decision, in mid-1989, that ZIDS would become part of the University of Zimbabwe. This decision was not without its difficulties; and at the time of this writing, the modalities of this incorporation are still under discussion by the university.

CURRENT TRENDS IN THEORETICAL AND METHODOLOGICAL STUDIES

The advent of Zimbabwe's independence under a nominally socialist government made it necessary for everyone, not merely sociologists and anthropologists, to take Marxist paradigms more seriously than they had in the past, and to examine in detail the experiences of socialist countries. However, in the opinion of self-confessed Marxist-Leninists, the result was yet more eclecticism and a distressing lack of dialectical rigor.

In self-defense, as one who strives for ongoing synthesis in the dialectic, and on behalf of those who believe that theory is only as good as its practical applicability, I would say that there have been genuine attempts to fashion Marxist ideas into a shape usable by independent Zimbabwe in its further development. Few of us in small university departments with very heavy teaching loads are theorists in our own right; the best we can hope for is small, incremental changes to established positions, perhaps a sharpened critique. For my own part, I have tried to "domesticate" Marxism, not least for teaching purposes.[26] In the same way that social scientists in our position need introductory texts that speak to our own condition using the insights of relevant theory, so (in my view) we desperately need to re-think the cultural provenance of existing theories. The issues of rationality and relativism should be alive and well in Third World social science, but often they yield to the repetitive domination of established theoretical ideas. Theories of bureaucracy are a classic example in which Western views do not begin to address the modes of socio-politico-economic strangulation practiced by socialist and Third World bureaucracies.

Neo-Marxist concepts are by no means the only ones used in Zimbabwean sociology. Interactional and transactional perspectives are at least as popular—sometimes independently, sometimes in combination with Marxist insights. C. Pearce is right to note that my own work is—very deliberately—such an amalgam.[27] Such combinations are arguably more useful (e.g., in gender studies in a country such as Zimbabwe) than "purer" theoretical imports from advanced, postindustrial economies.

It is important to note what theoretical approaches are *not* found as well as those that *are* found in contemporary theorizing in Zimbabwe. Perhaps the most notable theoretical omission—again, one reflecting our specific social conditions—is that of postmodernism, which seems almost totally irrelevant to our realities.

If theory is so often accepted uncritically in Third World sociology and social anthropology, the position concerning methodology is even more distressing. Often driven by external research funding to establish "a standard methodology" (meaning a structured, precoded questionnaire), we run the risk of eliminating the record of our own uniqueness, expunging it from future theoretical examination, by insensitive techniques of data collection. This is, of course, an unashamedly anthropological perspective; but I am happy to report that direct and participant observation, although they have taken a battering in the last two decades, are still alive and well among Zimbabwean postgraduate research students in the two disciplines. This is largely because there is some local, untied funding available from the Research Board of the university.

There has also been some methodological innovation, somewhat ironically among those working against time on consultancy projects rather than among those who teach research methods. As Chambers[28] has so sensitively detailed, traditional survey techniques, as well as those of participation, have had to yield to "rapid appraisal" methods among consultants on rural development and project evaluation. Such new techniques rely heavily on direct observation and the refocusing of limited research attention. "Interviewing wheeled carts," for example, may be a quicker way of assessing their impact on rural women and their work than interviewing sampled women themselves.

Nonetheless, there also exists an extremely disturbing trend whereby competent graduates are reluctant to undertake research, as opposed to coursework, degrees. There are a number of reasons for this situation—including the time and difficulty factors, and levels of available funding. As long as this reluctance continues, however, it is highly unlikely that independent Zimbabwe will be able to define its own problems and priorities and conduct its own research into these problems—including the development of appropriate new investigative techniques—without external assistance. In this respect we have definitively regressed, I believe, from local capacities in the 1950s and early 1960s, when it was believed that the university had "special obligations to the world of scholarship in matters of research . . . unique opportunities of exploring certain fields, such as in the biological and social sciences," and that "every lecturer should have 'a considerable amount of time to devote to research.' "[29] In the past decade, this earlier emphasis on research has been replaced by an emphasis on undergraduate teaching, especially in the social sciences. Over the last twenty-five years, staff-student ratios have risen from 1:7 to 1:30 in the Department of Sociology, thus impairing not only staff research but also the capacity of staff to supervise research students. In such contexts, methodological issues do tend to die!

CURRENT TRENDS IN RESEARCH

For the students who have graduated in our jointly taught disciplines, the old distinctions between social anthropology and sociology are irrelevant. Indeed, I have had assessments, couched in complaint form, from social theory students to the effect that they have been "totally confused" as to the distinction between the two disciplines! In my view, this is as it should be, at least in the Third World as it comes to reflect upon itself using concepts borrowed from outside. Much of the current research being undertaken is equally blind, not only to the distinctions between sociology and social anthropology but also between these two and sister social sciences. Many of the "traditional" specializations and classifications of the sociological world are, therefore, difficult to uphold when discussing "sociological" research in contemporary Zimbabwe. However, in order to communicate with colleagues elsewhere, I shall try!

For example, in the sociology of medicine, recent, broadly sociological research has covered the following: professionalization of traditional practitioners, detailed investigations into the transmission of knowledge by these practitioners to younger acolytes and "apprentices," domestic hygiene, rural sanitation and water supplies, the problems of recruiting and retaining highly qualified "modern" health personnel in rural hospitals and clinics, and the operations of a clinic employing both traditional and modern practitioners in a major city.[30] It should be noted here that *all* health-related research must now be formally approved by the Medical Research Council, irrespective of its disciplinary nature and whether or not on-site investigations of government infrastructure are involved. That the sociology of medicine is one of the most important areas of contemporary research reflects not merely individual interests but the practical problems involved in developing health services in a Third World economy and society. In this respect, research into the impact of AIDS by staff of the School of Social Work merits special note.[31]

Likewise, research in the field of gender studies has major practical implications for socialist policy. Ironically, however, most gender-related research has been and is being done not by the ZIDS policy think-tank, but by female Zimbabweans (and some foreigners) actively concerned with gender-differentiated access to land, income, and employment,[32] and legal issues affecting women.[33] As such, their perspectives stray well beyond classical sociology or anthropology into economics, politics, and law.

Again, rural development is an area in which disciplinary specialties and subspecializations are difficult—and inappropriate—to maintain, as both Marxism and social anthropology have maintained for many decades. In particular, it is often difficult to distinguish economic anthropology from agricultural economics (as some have remarked of my own work, and as is certainly true of the work of some of my postgraduate students, whether or not they have been trained in economics as well as sociology). The special developmental relationship between rural people and wildlife is currently the focus of a large-scale, long-term research project linking socioanthropologists in the Centre for Applied Social Sciences with colleagues in the biosciences and tropical ecology.

Although few results are as yet in the public domain,[34] labor studies and industrial sociology/anthropology have flourished since Independence, partly as a result of academic interest in policy attempts to restructure the social relations of production through altered legislation (the Labour Relations Act of 1985), and partly through the demand for consultancy in this area from firms experiencing difficulty in making the legal provisions work in practice. It is in this context that existing theories of bureaucratic organization have, in my view, proved totally inadequate for contemporary Zimbabwe.

An area of developing interest which was almost totally ignored in the past is "crime and deviance." Again, its growing importance is a reflection of a growing social problem consequent upon rising unemployment, especially among young school-leavers. Both sociologists and social workers are currently actively engaged in studies of "street kids," with a view to influencing social policy in this and other related areas. Juvenile delinquency more generally, as well as adult "street-sleepers," are also of current research interest.

Housing, as one of the classic interests of urban sociology, has long been on the research agenda,[35] as has urban class differentiation.[36] Today, however, the housing squeeze has worsened and is the subject of specific aid programs; it has therefore become an interest as much of planners as sociologists. But family structure in the cities, and correlated issues such as mate selection, have very recently re-interested sociologists/anthropologists, not least because of their relationship to the developing problem of juvenile behavior which departs from past norms. Of considerable interest to ordinary people (but not, as yet, the subject of specific sociological research) is the related issue of urban youth subcultures differentiated by class (the "nose brigades"—who speak English through their noses—and the *rasta* or *jah* groups of working-class origin).

There has been substantial past investigation into matters falling under the sociology of religion.[37] However, notwithstanding ongoing teaching in this area and the recent growth of Christian fundamentalism among Zimbabweans both black and white, at present almost no sociological or anthropological research is being conducted in this field. A new textbook, however, is in press.[38] The sociology of religion is regarded as a low priority area even by its specialists, in comparison with issues of rural and urban development. Perhaps it is also a reflection of contemporary Zimbabwean society, in the context of debates concerning the desirability of a one-party state, that there is little research—though much personal—interest in political sociology per se, as opposed to the micropolitics of development.

Practically all the contemporary sociological research agendas reflect the urgency of specific social problems and the importance of different areas of social policy in the newly independent state of Zimbabwe. In this respect, our research priorities lag behind those of societies which have been independent for a longer time. After a decade of emphasizing the utility of potential findings as a necessary adjunct of obtaining funds for research, we are only just beginning to appreciate anew the longer-term importance of "basic research" that is not tied to immediate ends but is instead defined theoretically. This realization comes as the availability of both time and money is in decline.

NOTES

At the outset, I should make clear that I write with the biases of a social anthropologist working in a joint department that has more recently been extended to include demography as well. I am grateful to all who have assisted me in various ways in the production of this chapter, most particularly to Clyde Mitchell for his detailed historical reminiscences, to Rudo Gaidzanwa for critical comment on an early draft, to Eileen Haddon and Ray Roberts for additional sources of data, and to colleagues in the Department of Sociology for details of their current research.

1. J. Nkomo, *The Story of My Life,* London: Methuen, 1984, Ch. 4.

2. P. Ibbotson, "Survey of Urban African Conditions in Southern Rhodesia," in D. Forde, ed., *Social Implications of Industrialization and Urbanization in Africa South of the Sahara,* Paris: UNESCO, 1956, 166–69; J. Farquhar, *Jairos Jiri: The Man and His Work, 1921–1982,* Gweru: Mambo Press, 1987, 31–32.

3. For example, Charles Bullock, later Chief Native Commissioner, authored *Mashona Laws and Customs,* 1913 (no publication details given), and *The Mashona,* Cape Town (South Africa): Juta, 1928.

4. For example, J. F. Holleman, *Shona Customary Law,* Cape Town: Oxford University Press, 1952; *Chief, Council and Commissioner,* Assen: Royal van-

Gorcum, 1969; G. K. Garbett, *Growth and Change in a Shona Ward* (Occasional Paper 1), Salisbury: UCRN Department of African Studies, 1960; G. K. Garbett, "Circulatory Migration in Rhodesia: Towards a Decision Model," and J. C. Mitchell, "Factors in Male Absenteeism in Rhodesia," both in D. Parkin, ed., *Town and Country in Eastern and Central Africa,* London: Oxford University Press for International African Institute, 1972; J. C. Mitchell, "Structural Plurality, Urbanization and Labour Circulation in Rhodesia," in J. A. Jackson, ed., *Migration,* Cambridge: Cambridge University Press, 1969; M. F. C. Bourdillon, *The Shona Peoples,* Gweru (Zimbabwe): Mambo Press, 1976 (2nd. ed. 1982; 3rd ed. 1988).

5. Clyde Mitchell did extensive work in urban Zambia, as well as occupational rating studies in Harare, reported in his *Cities, Society, and Social Perception: A Central African Perspective,* Oxford: Clarendon Press, 1987; as well as "Aspects of Occupational Prestige in a Plural Society," in P. C. Lloyd, ed., *The New Elites of Tropical Africa,* London: Oxford University Press for International African Institute, 1966. See also J. F. Holleman, "Town and Tribe," in P. Smith, ed., *Africa in Transition,* London: Max Reinhardt, 1958; C. Kileff, *Black Suburbanites: Adaptation to Western Culture in Salisbury, Rhodesia* (Ph.D. thesis, Rice University), Houston, Texas, 1970; C. Kileff and W. C. Pendleton, eds., *Urban Man in Southern Africa,* Gwelo: Mambo Press, 1975.

6. Dr. Hugh Ashton, an anthropologist, was for many years director of African housing for the City of Bulawayo.

7. Notably to Peter Stopforth, a research fellow at the Institute of Social Research in the early 1970s, who produced: *Survey of Highfield African Township* (Occasional Paper 6), 1971, and *Two Aspects of Social Change, Highfield African Township, Salisbury* (Occasional Paper 7), 1972, Salisbury: University of Rhodesia, Department of Sociology; *Comparative Data for the Assessment of Problems of Social Change among Urban Africans, Salisbury* (Research Report 4) and *Comparative Differential Social Change: Highfield African Township and Chitepo Road, Salisbury* (Research Report 5), Salisbury: UR Institute of Social Research, 1973. Stopforth was later joined by Valerie Moller, and they both moved to the Centre for Applied Social Sciences, University of Natal, Durban, South Africa, in the late 1970s.

8. Holleman, *Shona Customary Law.*

9. G. K. Garbett, "The Rhodesian Chief's Dilemma: Government Officer or Tribal Leader?" *Race* 8, 2, 1966, 113–28; Holleman, *Chief, Council and Commissioner.*

10. Hans (J. F.) Holleman, Address delivered to the Annual General Meeting of the [Tribal Areas of Rhodesia Research] Foundation, Salisbury, 24 February 1975. (Typescript held by the Zimbabwe National Archives.)

11. M. Gelfand, *A Non-Racial Island of Learning: A History of the University College of Rhodesia and Nyasaland from Its Inception to 1966,* Gwelo: Mambo Press, 1978, 247–48.

12. R. Chambers, *Rural Development: Putting the Last First,* London: Longman, 1983, 199.

13. Clyde Mitchell regards the Manchester School as "a construction of reality from the outside" (personal communication, July 1990). He allows, however, that those who worked at the Rhodes-Livingstone Institute in Lusaka, Zambia, and later at the University of Manchester under Max Gluckman's academic and ad-

ministrative leadership did share the "crucially important" approach of situational analysis based on "detailed and systematic fieldwork" and in-service "group learning." See R. P. Werbner, "The Manchester School in South-Central Africa," *Annual Review of Anthropology* 13, 1984, 157–85.

14. For example, A. K. H. Weinrich, *Chiefs and Councils in Rhodesia,* London: Heinemann, 1971; *African Farmers in Rhodesia,* London: Oxford University Press for International African Institute, 1975.

15. A. P. Cheater, *Idioms of Accumulation,* Gweru: Mambo Press, 1984; *Social Anthropology: An Alternative Introduction,* Gweru: Mambo Press, 1986 (overseas edition published by Unwin Hyman, London, 1989).

16. See J. C. Mitchell, "Theoretical Orientations in African Urban Studies," in M. Banton, ed., *The Social Anthropology of Complex Societies* (ASA 4), London: Tavistock, 1966; and Banton, ed., *Social Networks in Urban Situations,* Manchester: Manchester University Press, 1969.

17. Details in this section concerning the local university come from Gelfand, *A Non-Racial Island of Learning.*

18. Clyde Mitchell, personal communication, July 1990. Much of what follows is also based on this communication.

19. Personal communication, 1987.

20. Gelfand, *A Non-Racial Island of Learning,* 195.

21. Ibid., 298, 297.

22. See note 7; also V. Moller, *Urban Commitment and Involvement among Black Rhodesians,* Durban (South Africa): University of Natal, Centre for Applied Social Sciences, 1978; and J. May, *Drinking in a Rhodesian African Township* (Occasional Paper 8), Salisbury: University of Rhodesia, Department of Sociology, 1973.

23. Gelfand, *A Non-Racial Island of Learning,* 149.

24. Historical details on the School of Social Work are taken from its undated Newsletter, produced to celebrate its silver anniversary in 1989.

25. For the information on ZIDS, I am indebted to its director, Dr. A. M. Rukobo, for an interview on 14 May 1990. University papers concerning the proposed incorporation of ZIDS have also been useful.

26. Cheater, *Social Anthropology;* C. Pearce, "A Dialogue with Marxism," *Zambezia* 15, 2, 1989, 181–97.

27. Pearce, "A Dialogue," 196.

28. Chambers, *Rural Development,* Ch. 3.

29. Gelfand, *A Non-Racial Island of Learning,* 115, 171.

30. G. L. Chavunduka, *Interaction of Folk and Scientific Beliefs in Shona Medical Practice* (Ph.D. thesis), London: University of London, 1972; M. Last and G. L. Chavunduka, eds., *The Professionalisation of African Medicine,* Manchester: Manchester University Press for International African Institute, 1986.

31. H. Jackson, *AIDS: Action Now: Information, Prevention and Support in Zimbabwe,* Harare: AIDS Counselling Trust, 1988.

32. R. B. Gaidzanwa, *Promised Land: Towards a Land Policy in Zimbabwe* (M.Dev. Studs. thesis), The Hague: Institute of Social Studies, 1981; *Women's Land Rights in Zimbabwe: An Overview* (Occasional Paper 13), Harare: University of Zimbabwe, Department of Rural and Urban Planning, 1988; S. Jacobs, *The Effect of Agricultural Policies on Women in Zimbabwe* (D.Phil. thesis), Brighton,

UK: University of Sussex, 1981: "Women and Land Resettlement in Zimbabwe," *Review of African Political Economy* 27–28, 1983, 35–50; A. P. Cheater, "Women and Their Participation in Commercial Agricultural Production: The Case of Medium-Scale Freehold in Zimbabwe," *Development and Change* 12, 3, 1981, 349–77.

33. G. L. Chavunduka, *A Shona Urban Court,* Gwelo: Mambo Press, 1978; J. May, *Social Aspects of the Legal Position of Women in Rhodesia* (M.Phil. thesis), Salisbury: University of Rhodesia, Department of Sociology, 1979; *The Women's Guide to Law through Life,* Salisbury: University of Zimbabwe, CASS, 1980; *Zimbabwean Women in Customary and Colonial Law,* Gweru: Mambo Press, 1983; *Changing People, Changing Laws,* Gweru: Mambo Press, 1987; A. Armstrong, ed., *Women and Law in Southern Africa,* Harare: Zimbabwe Publishing House, 1987; A. P. Cheater, "Fighting over Property. . . ," *Africa* 57, 2, 1987, 173–95.

34. G. J. Maphosa, *Workers' Participation in Industry: A Case Study* (M.Phil. thesis), Harare: UZ Department of Sociology, 1985; A. P. Cheater, *The Politics of Factory Organisation,* Gweru: Mambo Press, 1986; D. Mutizwa-Mangiza, *An Evaluation of the Effectiveness of Workers' Participation in a Zimbabwean Parastatal Enterprise* (M.Sc. dissertation), Harare: UZ Department of Sociology, 1988. Mark Shadur's research for a doctorate at the Australian National University, Canberra, was also in this area.

35. R. J. Adams and D. H. Patel, *Chirambahuyo: A Case Study of Low-Income Housing,* Gwelo: Mambo Press, 1981.

36. M. B. Lukhero, "The Social Characteristics of an Emergent Elite in Harare," in P. C. Lloyd, ed., *The New Elites of Tropical Africa,* London: Oxford University Press for International African Institute, 1966; Kileff, *Black Suburbanites.*

37. Ignoring theological writings, the more important of these studies include: J. F. Holleman, *Accommodating the Spirit amongst Some North-Eastern Shona Tribes* (Rhodes-Livingstone Paper 22), Cape Town: Oxford University Press, 1953; G. K. Garbett, *The Political System of a Central African Tribe with Particular Reference to the Role of Spirit Mediums* (Ph.D. thesis), Manchester: University of Manchester, 1963; M. W. Murphree, *Christianity and the Shona,* London: Athlone Press, 1969; P. Fry, *Spirits of Protest,* Cambridge: Cambridge University Press, 1976; M. L. Daneel, *The God of the Matopo Hills,* The Hague: Mouton, 1970; *Old and New in Southern Shona Independent Churches,* vols. 1 and 2, The Hague: Mouton, 1971, 1974, and vol. 3, Gweru: Mambo Press, 1988; plus many dozens of journal articles.

38. M. F. C. Bourdillon, title forthcoming, Gweru: Mambo Press.

Part VI

Sociology in the East

Ideas do not have a permanent home. By their very nature they drift and diffuse. When the colonization of the Eastern nations occurred by the Western nations, it was inevitable that social sciences would eventually find their way here. There are major differences culturally and physically between the Eastern and the Western worlds. Older generations of scholars and anthropologists thought that basic cultural styles, to use their language, were different between the East and the West. These cultural styles or mentalities are related to habits of thought. It was hypothesized that whereas Western ways of thinking were "analytical," in the Eastern nations these were "synthetic." They argued further that whereas the West preferred "individualistic" types of societies, Eastern preferences were for "collectivistic" types of societies. In other words, they were arguing that the worldview, or *Weltanschauung,* of East and West were different. It is an old debate, and this is no place to indulge in reactivating it. These are probably stereotypical oversimplifications.

When sociology emerged in Western Europe in the nineteenth century, it was dominated by positivism of methodological preference and an organismic theory of society. Objective idealism, which was a German counterpart to sociology, counterposed a form of holism to the elementariness of the seventeenth and eighteenth centuries. At about the same time, many scholars were trying to grapple with Eastern philosophies, translating many of the writings and exploring many forms of holistic and collectivistic ideas unheard of in the West. Sociology was the closest approach the West had to the holistic philosophies of the East. When sociological ideas drifted from Europe to North America, the result was an individualistic and elementaristic type of interpretation and social theory; and when these ideas diffused toward the East, holistic forms of social theory and preference became evident in the explanation of social change in terms of dialectical play of counterposed forces within the whole. These and other changes in the emphasis resulted from the type of societies to which sociology migrated. This may reflect, in part, the ancient cultural differences in styles of thought, cultural assumptions, and preferences between East and West. The fate of sociology, and its development and forms of thought, are tied to the nation-state.

In China as early as 1905 a Chair of Sociology was founded, but its incumbents were British Baptists who were interested in social reform rather than theory. After 1920, following Sun Yat-sen's national revolution, sociology was established as an academic discipline. Research institutions were established, journals were founded, and a Chinese Sociological Society was established. The works of foreign sociologists were translated and community studies were carried out. However, even at this time Chinese sociologists showed a preference for dialectical modes of reasoning and theories of historical materialism. The development of sociology was cut short with the victory of Mao Tse-tung.

Sociology in Australia and New Zealand, as reviewed by Cora Baldock, was a relatively late arrival; however, toward the end of the 1950s it began to develop rapidly on all fronts with the expansion of tertiary education, which created several new universities. Whereas Australian and New Zealand sociology belongs more to the West than to Asia, Baldock traces a growing restiveness with the uncritical transplantation of American empirical methods to the local scene. Once again a system of sociology seems to be moving in the direction of establishing a distinctive identity of its own. Culturally, Australia and New Zealand are not part of the Pacific Rim countries; they are dominantly Western in orientation, thinking, and traditions. But the classification of Australian and New Zealand sociologies under Pacific Rim or under Oceania, according to Baldock, are obstacles to the development of authentic sociology in these countries. The point is well taken.

The influence of U.S. sociology is dominant in both Australia and New Zealand, but this is not to say that sociology in these countries is dependent upon U.S. sociology. Actually, the current scene attests to the contrary. The current state of scholarship in sociologies in Australia and New Zealand is breaking away from American and British models of society and in specific subfields like class, gender, and race. Australian and New Zealand sociologies are building their own authentic traditions.

The development of sociology in Bangladesh is intimately tied with political development by the British rule in pre-independence unified India. However, as compared to India, the development of sociology in Bangladesh is late. Even today it is not a fledgling field of study. According to A. H. G. Quddus there is a paucity of theoretical works and research, and sociological methodology is relatively underdeveloped. However, demography and social development areas receive preference from the sociological community in Bangladesh. Sociology is intimately tied with the development of nation-states. Bangladesh is a relatively new nation-state with a checkered history of military coups and political upheavals. It is still going through birth pangs. Despite the foreign assistance, Bangladesh has to come to grips with its own reality. So does sociology.

Ming Yan examines the development of sociology in China. She identifies three distinct historical phases in the development and institutionalization of sociology as a discipline in terms of training, publications, research funding, and activities of professional associations. According to her, the early influence of U.S. sociology was not direct—it occurred through the Japanese translations of the writings of Franklin Henry Giddings, among others. However, contemporary sociology is under the direct influence of U.S. sociology.

Sociology in Hong Kong is a product of liberal society, the Chinese heritage, and Western intellectual influences. Sociology's development in Hong Kong is also intimately tied with the growth of its industrial sector, economy, population, and international trade; the influence of visiting American sociologists; and the trained sociologists who have earned postgraduate degrees in the United States, Britain, Canada, and Australia.

Sociology was introduced early into India by British administrators and missionaries; and Indian social theorists quickly became familiar with the theories of Spencer, Comte, Darwin, LePlay, and others and with the development of Western positivism. In a review of sociology in India by Raj Mohan and Vijayan K. Pillai, the content of Western positivism and specifically Indian traditional humanism is seen as moving toward a new type of sociological synthesis that is providing Indian sociology with a distinct identity. New support for social research during the 1980s and at present has helped the institutional status and stature of sociology as a field of study. The influence of U.S. sociology has been increasing since the early 1970s, and it is fairly dominant today due to the travel and research opportunities afforded to both American sociologists and their Indian counterparts.

Soon after Japan was opened to Western influence in 1865, the works of Western social scientists were introduced: Spencer, Mill, Bentham, and exponents of Social Darwinism from England; Montesquieu, Comte, Tarde, and Durkheim from France; Small, Giddings, Ross, and Ellwood from America; Toennies, Von Wiese, Simmel, and Weber from Germany. Among early Japanese social scientists, Masamicki Shimmei and Yunichiro Matsumoto undertook to establish sociology as a comprehensive system of explanations of social reality. Under the nationalist government in World War II, sociology was discouraged; but after the war, the Japanese universities were reorganized and, as traced by Tsuyoshi Ishida, Japanese sociology underwent a virtual knowledge explosion. Ishida thinks that Japanese sociology is a combination of Western ideas and the indigenous thought of Japanese society. In addition, he shows that changing social conditions bring changes to the research interests and areas of inquiry. At present, sociology in Japan does not have a strong foothold in higher education.

Sociology in Nepal is the most recent phenomenon. The first university in Nepal was established during the early 1960s, and the first department of sociology was established at Tribhuvan University in 1981. Since the 1980s, sociology in Nepal has grown considerably on the one hand by trained Nepalese students and on the other hand by visiting sociologists and anthropologists from the United States, England, and other countries. Current research areas in sociology in Nepal are population and demography, and social change and development. Sociology in Nepal is yet to come of age. It is only beginning at present.

In contemporary Pakistan, according to Hassan Gardezi, sociology is primarily an American-dominated import that at present is rapidly seeking an identity of its own. However, the influence of North American sociological thought is very much in place in the mainstream teaching, research, and writings of Pakistani sociologists. With increasing frequency contemporary sociologists in Pakistan are restive with American theories and methods and are tending to experiment with dialectical modes of reasoning. Primary areas of research in sociology in Pakistan are rural life, inequality, communalism, gender and ethnic studies, and other problem areas of society.

27

Sociology in Australia and New Zealand

Cora Vellekoop Baldock

Any return to the past tends to reflect the preoccupations of the present, and issues which concern us today were not necessarily of concern or visible around twenty years ago.[1] This chapter takes a fresh look at the pre-1975 development of sociology in Australia and New Zealand as described by J. Lally and C. V. Baldock in the first edition of this Handbook.[2] At the same time, the chapter does not dwell on that early history. The main concern of its author is to document the changes in Australian and New Zealand sociology since 1975, and in particular to highlight the exciting new directions in theory and research which have taken place in both countries during the last twenty years.

HISTORY OF SOCIOLOGY IN AUSTRALIA AND NEW ZEALAND

Prehistory

There is possibly a subtle irony in the fact that the indigenous people of Australia and New Zealand played such a significant part (albeit not with their consent) in the early history of European social sciences, especially of sociology and anthropology. Would Friedrich Engels have written *The Origins of the Family, Private Property and the State* if Karl Marx had not read, with approval, Lewis Henry Morgan's *Ancient Society*—a study which contained data on Aboriginal culture collected by Australian missionaries? And would Durkheim have written his influential *Les Formes elementaire de la vie religieuse,* were it not for the same amateur anthropological research by Australian missionaries? In New Zealand the earliest research was also on indigenous people.[3]

Research on the European population during the early period of white colonization of Australia and New Zealand was sporadic, and mostly "conducted" by visitors wishing to comment on work conditions in the new colonies. There are famous examples: Albert Metin, who came and declared Australia to be a country typified by *"socialisme sans doctrine"*;[4] and the Webbs, Sidney and Beatrice, who summed up their impressions of Australia by saying that "muddling on with a high standard of honour and a low standard of efficiency is the dominant note of Australian Public Life."[5] None of these observations could be defined as genuinely sociological,[6] and they were comments made by outsiders. Local sociological research could hardly be expected. In these "young" countries,[7] universities were not established until the 1850s: Sydney University, the first university in Australia, dates from 1852; the first New Zealand university, Otago University, was founded in 1869; and sociology as an independent discipline did not appear until one hundred years later.

There were a few early attempts to introduce sociology courses in some of the new universities, for example, at Sydney University in 1909, and at the University of New Zealand in 1921.[8] In Australia, Francis Anderson, philosophy professor in the 1920s at Sydney University, introduced a sociology course and encouraged his students to take up sociology and anthropology. His course disappeared three years after his retirement in 1925, but his influence lived on through his students.[9] At Melbourne University in the 1920s there was a professorship in economics and sociology sponsored by the Workers' Educational Association.[10] Personal animosity between the incumbent of the post and the professor of economics led to the demise of sociology at Melbourne and may have contributed to the ascendency of economics as a major social science in Australia.[11] In New Zealand, one of the "founding" fathers of sociology was Crawford Somerset, an educationalist by training who campaigned from the 1930s for the introduction of sociology as an academic discipline and initiated important "socioeducational" research in his social survey *Littledene*.[12]

The Late Development of Sociology

Until World War II, Australia and New Zealand remained culturally and geographically isolated. Their main preoccupations were with practical matters (e.g., agriculture and engineering) directly related to "pioneering needs," and the course of development was deemed to be generally peaceful.[13] This was nothwithstanding the fact that both countries experienced severe social problems. Both countries faced serious depressions, first in the late nineteenth century and again in the 1930s. Racial inequality, as shown in the atrocious treatment of the indigenous Maori and Aboriginal people, and the systematic discrimination against any non Anglo-Saxon immigrants, was rampant during most of colonial history.[14] There was also considerable evidence of discrimination against women in both countries.[15] Many of these problems of racial, social, and sex inequality were of the same magnitude as those found in other Western nations.

Due to pressure from the trade union movement, governments took some ameliorative action to overcome the effects of poverty and unemployment;[16] but with patriarchal and racist attitudes dominant in the community, it was easy for policy makers, unionists, and academics to ignore the problems of racial and gender discrimination. In countries where the motto of "she'll be right mate" was invoked for most occasions, there was limited interest in sociological analysis to assess the effects of such social problems.[17] Within the university system there was also little interest in sociology.[18] Given the long-standing tradition, right up to the postwar years, of hiring senior academics trained in the United Kingdom, where sociology had not been received well,[19] knowledge and appreciation of sociology among university administrators and senior professors in Australia and New Zealand were inevitably colored by the attitudes of the British university system.

After World War II, Australia experienced accelerated industrialization and extensive immigration. New Zealand also had a large influx of migrants, although not on the same scale as Australia. The immigration movement in both countries broke their cultural isolation and created greater cultural heterogeneity. In the hitherto homogeneous white Anglo-Saxon environment created by colonial settlement, these changes were seen as disruptive, with the overwhelming sentiment favoring a policy of assimilation—that is, migrants adjusting to the cultural and political climate of their host countries.[20] It was at this time that sociology first emerged as an independent discipline and its research efforts taken seriously. In fact, a number of staff members in the newly established Australian sociology departments were themselves migrants or refugees, and several among them took up the study of immigration as one of their first and major research foci.[21] While these sociologists were not yet ready to deal with issues of racial or gender inequality, immigration and population studies were certainly within their ambit.[22]

Sociology emerged at a time when both Australia and New Zealand experienced a vast expansion of tertiary education, with the establishment of several new universities and large increases in the number of students. When sociology became established in Australia, it was instituted mainly within these newer universities (e.g., the University of New South Wales established the first department and the first professorship in sociology in 1959) and gained little foothold in the long-established tertiary institutions (with the exception of the University of Tasmania). A special stumbling block was the attitude of anthropologists toward the establishment of separate sociology departments, a problem that also occurred in New Zealand. Anthropology had incorporated sociology for so long, especially in the Australian context, that the development of separate departments was seen by some as unnecessary.[23] In New Zealand, the first sociology course was introduced within the social work program at Victoria University, in 1957; Canterbury University followed in 1958 with a sociology major within the psychology department. However, Auckland University was late in developing sociology, and Otago does not have a sociology department to this day; in both cases, it has been argued that the competing interests of anthropology held sociology back in these two institutions.[24]

Another possible factor in Australia was that because of sociology's failure in the years immediately preceding World War II "to speak to the realities of Australian political and social life in the way that, for example, economics was able to," economics, rather than sociology, had gained the right to speak on behalf of the social sciences.[25] It was to economists and not to sociologists that the federal government turned for the task of postwar social and economic reconstruction.

INSTITUTIONALIZATION OF SOCIOLOGY AS AN ACADEMIC DISCIPLINE

The Teaching of Sociology

There are currently seven universities within New Zealand. Of these, five have departments of sociology: Victoria University in Wellington, Canterbury University in Christchurch, Auckland University, Waikato University, and Massey University. The five departments vary in size from 6 to 14 tenured staff, and they employ in all approximately 60 full-time staff and about the same number of part-time and "junior" staff, teaching undergraduate, honors, and postgraduate courses.[26] There is one professor in each department. These departments have been in operation as separate entities for at least 30 years.[27] Other departments—for example, education at Massey University and medicine at Auckland—also employ sociologists.

At Otago University, which has no separate sociology department, there are around 9 people in areas such as anthropology, community studies, education, and medicine who are strongly interested in sociology. At Lincoln, the newest New Zealand university, 4 staff members apply sociological perspectives to their work in the teaching of leisure and tourism studies. There are courses in sociology in teachers' colleges, and even some in secondary schools.[28]

In Australia, the situation is more complex because of a major restructuring in the tertiary education system (dating from the late 1980s), which led to the creation of a number of new universities and to the amalgamation of others.[29] Of the 19 universities established before this major restructuring, 13 offer a sociology degree (8 in separate sociology departments offering undergraduate, honors, and postgraduate degrees; 3 in joint anthropology and sociology departments offering the full range of sociology degrees; and 2 within an interdisciplinary structure, rather than an autonomous department). They are, in order of establishment, the University of New South Wales; Australian National University; New England; Monash; Queensland; La Trobe; Flinders; Newcastle; Tasmania; Macquarie; Wollongong; Murdoch; and Deakin universities. The departments vary in size from 8 to 36 full-time staff, to an overall total of about 180 tenured staff members across the 13 institutions.[30] Seven of these 13 institutions have had sociology departments for 30 years or more. As in New Zealand, each department has only one sociology professor (except for Monash, which appointed a second sociology professor in 1992). In all these universities sociological perspectives are also incorporated in other departments, specifically in education, social work, and where applicable, legal studies, medicine, and nursing.

Of the nineteen universities established prior to the recent restructuring, six do not have separate sociology departments nor do they offer a sociology degree (yet). These include Sydney, Melbourne, and Adelaide universities and the University of Western Australia—old, well-established universities in which sociological perspectives have remained embedded in departments of anthropology, education, and social work; and James Cook and Griffith universities, which were established in the 1970s as innovative interdisciplinary ventures where sociology is part of broad interdisciplinary programs.[31]

Since 1987, nine new universities have been created from former Colleges of Advanced Education and Institutes of Technology; while four Institutes of Technology and four University Colleges have remained.[32] Some of these have had flourishing undergraduate programs in sociology dating from the 1970s, but generally no honors and postgraduate studies.[33] It appears sociology has in all cases been part of interdisciplinary programs in the social sciences in these institutions. New universities which have substantial sociology offerings include Charles Sturt University; Curtin University of Technology; the University of Technology, Sydney; and the University of Western Sydney; among the Institutes, the Royal Melbourne Institute of Technology has offered sociology for many years. Most of the new universities are likely to establish honors and postgraduate studies within sociology as soon as resources allow.

Research Facilities

Both in Australia and New Zealand, sociologists' opportunities to gain access to research funding have been limited because research priorities have tended to favor the sciences, to the detriment of the social sciences.

In both countries, most of the funding for academic research comes from government.[34] In Australia, the main granting body for academic research (except in the area of medicine) is the Australian Research Council (ARC), a Commonwealth organization with five subcommittees, including one for the humanities and social sciences. In 1991 the ARC allocated 8 percent of its budget to social sciences and 7 percent to humanities.[35]

The costs involved in doing sociological research often appear to be underestimated by the ARC, and the common assumption is that research assistance can be provided by part-time, casual workers rather than by full-time senior research personnel, as is common in the sciences.[36] This results in a paucity of people who are researchers *only* within academic sociology. Overall, few sociologists receive ARC funding, although it is also clear that the number of sociologists applying to the scheme has so far been limited.[37] There are, of course, other government sources of funding, but these are frequently "mission-oriented"—that is, academics tend to engage in specific government-commissioned applied research, usually projects of short duration with no guarantee of continuation.[38] In recent years the federal government has instituted major reviews in areas such as social security and housing, providing an opportunity for sociological research.[39] In all instances important sociological work is done, but there is limited public recognition of its significance qua sociology.

In 1990, New Zealand established a new research funding organization, the Foundation for Research, Science and Technology. A subcommittee of this foundation (the Social Science Committee) deals with the social sciences, which until 1990 had been served by a separate body, the Social Science Research Fund Committee (SSRFC). In its infancy in 1990, only $500,000 of the Foundation's grant money was allocated to social science research within the university.[40] A positive feature is that there are sociologists represented on the Social Science Committee (as had been on the SSRFC), whereas in Australia sociologists are not represented on the ARC as a matter of course.[41]

In both countries there are research institutes, either government-based or attached to universities, with a strong sociological emphasis. In New Zealand the Centre of Labour and Trade Union Studies, the Centre for Population Studies, and the Women's Studies Centre at Waikato employ sociologists; there is also an independent Society for Research on Women which has produced valuable sociological research. In Australia, the Institute of Family Studies in Melbourne, the Social Policy Research Centre at the University of New South Wales, the Centre of Multicultural Studies at Wollongong University, and the Government Bureaus of Criminology and of Migration Research all have sociologists at work in senior positions. There are also several major nongovernment welfare bodies (e.g., the Brotherhood of St. Laurence and the Australian Council of Social Service) which have from time to time commissioned sociological research.[42]

Other Indices of Institutionalization

Professional Associations

An important step in achieving professional recognition for sociology in New Zealand and Australia was the establishment of a professional sociological association. In the first instance, this was a joint organization—the Sociological Association of Australia and New Zealand (SAANZ), formed in 1963. This body has been responsible for the organization of annual conferences and the publication of a journal (since 1965), the *Australian and New Zealand Journal of Sociology (ANZJS)*. In 1980 SAANZ instituted a biannual award, the so-called Jean Martin Award, for the best Ph.D. thesis in sociology produced in Australia or New Zealand. In addition, the Association has subsidized several other journals and has produced guides to postgraduate studies and other informational material about sociology. Issues of special concern for the Association have been the establishment of a code of ethics; questions regarding the definition of membership; and whether locally trained rather than foreign-trained sociologists should be given preference in academic appointments.

The Secession of New Zealand Sociology

Throughout the history of SAANZ, New Zealand had maintained a New Zealand Sociological Association as a branch of the umbrella organization. Within this body, debates became increasingly frequent during the 1980s regarding the possibility of establishing a separate association. Those arguing in favor emphasized the differences between Australian and New Zealand sociology. They expressed an overall concern for the dominance of Australian interests in SAANZ and in the journal, but also argued that there were substantial differences in the membership: more than half of the New Zealand members of the association were employed in nonacademic jobs, whereas in Australia the overwhelming majority of members were academics. Another argument was the unique emphasis on biculturalism in New Zealand sociology.[43]

The secessionists won the debate, and the formal connection between New Zealand and Australian sociology came to an end in 1988 when separate organizations were formed—the Sociological Association of Aotearoa[44] (New Zealand), or SAA (NZ), and The Australian Sociological Association (TASA). Membership of SAA (NZ) stands at 170; TASA membership is about 450 (1991 figures). Both organizations are members in their own right of the International Sociological Association. New Zealand sociologists continue to have access to the prestigious Jean Martin Award, although SAA (NZ) has now also established its own award, the Oxford University Press Sociology Prize.

Since the establishment of the SAA (NZ), this organization appears to

have made enormous strides. A code of ethics was established within a
year of formation; a sociologist became president of a newly established
organization of social scientists, the Foundation of New Zealand Social
Science Organizations (FoNZSSO); and sociologists have engaged in vigorous interaction with high school teachers interested in the teaching of
sociology. Also, as mentioned, SAA (NZ) negotiated with Oxford University Press for the establishment of a prize for the best Ph.D. or M.A.
thesis in sociology. The "house" journal of the association, *New Zealand
Sociology,* is also gaining in prominence. Much of the high level of activity
must be attributed to the work of Paul Spoonley from Massey University,
founding president of SAA(NZ), and of FoNZSSO. TASA, which went
through a downturn in the late 1980s, has regained its strength, due mainly
to its energetic 1991–1992 president, Katy Richmond. A code of ethics has
been drafted, and recent conferences have been well attended. Several
individual sociologists have gained prestigious positions on national bodies, although the sociological association as such does not appear to have
reached the same national standing as the SAA (NZ) in its brief period
of existence.

Textbooks

In 1975, when the first edition of this handbook appeared, there were
only two introductory sociology texts written for an Australian or New
Zealand student readership—although there were more introductory texts
in subfields such as educational sociology and political sociology.[45] Textbooks were mainly American: for example, Berger, *Introduction to Sociology;* Homans, *The Human Group;* and Smelser, *Sociology.*

Now, close to twenty years later, there are at least a dozen Australian
introductory texts including several readers, and about half a dozen published for a New Zealand audience. A shortcoming of most texts is that
they do not provide an overview of the general body of internationally
recognized sociological theory and concepts. They can thus be used only
as supplementary texts, or alternatively—if used as main texts—students
need to be provided with a great deal of additional reading matter to
acquaint them with broader sociological perspectives.[46] Of recent Australian texts, only Waters and Crook's *Sociology One* and Austin's *Australian
Sociologies* skillfully integrate general theory with local examples.[47] In
New Zealand, one of the most successful examples of such an interweaving
is the text *New Zealand: Sociological Perspectives.*[48]

Several international publishers established local branches within New
Zealand and Australia in the 1970s. Of these, Allen and Unwin Australia
forged the closest links with sociology in both countries, inter alia through
its participation in the Jean Martin Award, and through the establishment
of a *Studies in Sociology Series,* which has more than forty titles so far.[49]
Other important publishers of Australian sociology texts have been (Long-

man) Cheshire and MacMillan Australia, while Longman has been active in New Zealand. In recent years, both Dunmore Press, a New Zealand-owned publisher, and Oxford University Press have shown an interest in New Zealand sociological publications. In the case of Oxford University Press, this has led to the establishment of a *Critical Issues in New Zealand Society Series,* and the establishment of the Oxford University Press Sociology Prize.

Institutionalization and Interdisciplinarity

In summary, it may be said that according to conventional indices, New Zealand sociology has indeed become institutionalized as a separate discipline. There are five well-established, autonomous sociology departments situated in the major universities, and these departments train a considerable number of students at undergraduate and postgraduate levels; there is an active professional association with national standing; and there is a lively production of local texts. Where sociologists engage in interdisciplinary research and teaching (e.g., in women's studies) or in joint lobbies on policy issues with other social scientists, they come to these projects with a well-established identity. That sociology is accepted as a profession, not only within the academy but also within the community at large, is shown in the large number of sociologists employed outside tertiary institutions.

The situation in Australia does not appear to be quite as favorable. As in New Zealand, sociologists have been prolific in the production of good sociological texts. As in New Zealand, there are a number of tertiary institutions, eleven in all, where sociology is well established in separate departments or as a strong partner in joint ventures with anthropology. However, four of the most prestigious universities have never recognized sociology in its own right. This may have repercussions not only within those institutions but also in major national forums such as the Academy of Social Sciences, the Australian Research Council, and other policy bodies on which senior professors and administrators of these four highly prestigious universities are represented. There are 21 tertiary institutions (4 universities established in the 1970s as interdisciplinary ventures; 9 new universities established since 1987; and 8 institutes or colleges) where sociology also lacks a separate identity, because it has been incorporated within interdisciplinary programs without a separate department.[50]

At its best, such interdisciplinarity broadens the boundaries of sociology and leads to exciting new possibilities in research and teaching. However, in institutions where sociologists are employed in interdisciplinary teaching programs without the benefit of a strong and acknowledged discipline core and without the support of senior academics trained in sociology, such interdisciplinarity can be detrimental. This is especially the case in some

of the new universities where efforts to cut costs and to avoid retrenchment of academic staff have led to the appointment of on-the-cheap casual
workers, and to the teaching of sociology by people unqualified in the
subject.

CURRENT TRENDS IN THEORY AND METHODOLOGY

Prominent Contributors and Their Perspectives

Centers of Intellectual Leadership: Australia

M. Waters and R. Crook argue that there are three centers of intellectual leadership in Australian sociology, each representing a different theoretical perspective: positivist research at the Australian National
University; Weberian sociology at Flinders University; and Marxism at the
Macquarie University.[51] This chapter uses Waters and Crook's classification with some modifications, while adding a fourth "network" (rather
than a center), that of feminist scholarship.

Research in the tradition of positivism. Sociology at the Australian National University has been characterized by large-scale studies of stratification and social mobility, based on the consensual assumption that
Australia is an open society without rigid class differences. This idea of a
democratic and egalitarian ethos started early within Australian social sciences, in fact well before the establishment of sociology, and was perhaps
inaugurated by W. K. Hancock, an influential Australian historian writing
in the 1930s.[52] Bob Connell, a severe critic of positivist consensus-based
sociology, showed in an amusing article that Hancock's ideas have been
repeated (but not referenced) in innumerable articles on Australian society by authors trying to demonstrate how egalitarian Australians are.[53]

It is this tradition which was perpetuated in the 1960s and 1970s at the
Research School of the Australian National University, albeit not in an-
ecdote but in large-scale, survey-based research on social stratification,
social mobility, and social elites by sociologists Frank Lancaster Jones,
Leonard Broom, Jerzy Zubrzycki, and John Higley. The tradition is maintained today in the work of Jonathan Kelley and Ian McAllister.[54]
Whereas early studies of this kind focused nearly exclusively on male,
"white" Australian samples, more recent versions have attempted to incorporate data on women and on ethnic minorities.[55] An example of such
a study is M. D. R. Evans and J. Kelley on the work experiences of migrants: their conclusion is that migrants' occupational attainments are to
be explained by their training and skills levels (especially language skills)
gained in their country of origin, and not by discrimination in the labor
market.[56] B. Graetz and I. McAllister, in an introductory text in which
they make extensive use of multivariate statistical procedures, sum up the

main conclusions of sociologists following this consensual viewpoint: they see Australia as an open society with considerable social mobility, in which privileges transmitted from one generation to the next seldom persist beyond two generations. They acknowledge that there are considerable differences in wages, work conditions, and job autonomy—they note, for example, that clerical jobs require limited training and draw low incomes, but they do not see these differences as being indicative of rigid class divisions.[57] If there is any social theory which informs these positivist scholars, it would be Weberianism in the stratificationist sense—in other words, a belief in multidimensional systems of inequality, which can be measured through quantitative analysis.

The sociology department at Queensland University, headed by John Western, should rank as a second center of large-scale survey research in the positivist tradition.[58] The interesting aspect of Queensland sociology is the attempt to merge conflict perspectives and quantitative analysis, Erik Olin Wright's neo-Marxist analysis of class and socialist feminist theories of patriarchal relations being the main recent sources of inspiration.[59] As with all research based on Wright's class analysis, the Queensland studies deal only with paid workers and do not provide an assessment of the placement of unemployed and welfare recipients within the class structure of Australia.[60] Janeen Baxter and Diane Gibson have rectified one shortcoming of this research by their focus on the class placement of women; in addition they have undertaken research on the relation between women's participation in paid employment and the extent of their involvement in domestic labor.[61]

Marxist perspectives on research and theory. As Waters and Crook note, Macquarie University is the center of Marxist sociological analysis. The research methodology employed in the work of the Macquarie school of sociology is generally historical and qualitative, with an emphasis on in-depth interviews and critical analysis of policy documents. The most prominent representative of this tradition is Bob Connell, until recently professor of sociology at that institution. Connell is arguably the only Australian-born sociologist who could be defined as a theorist of international standing in the sense of having developed a comprehensive theory of his own society.

Most elements of class analysis are found in Connell's work. He has conducted historical studies of the development of capitalism in Australia, analyzed the ingredients of Australian bourgeois ideology, and studied the role of the school in the socialization of children within this bourgeois culture. He is possibly the only Australian male sociologist who has engaged seriously with feminist theory: his most recent contributions concern the construction of masculinity, and the relationship between gender and power.[62]

The most profound influence on Connell's work, apart from Marx, is

Antonio Gramsci; and the study of cultural hegemony in Australian society has been a central focus in Connell's work. Similar to British historians such as E. P. Thompson and J. Foster, Connell sees the class structure as a set of relations rather than as abstract categories, and the working class not as a victim of the class system but as an active agent of history. A controversial aspect of his account is his emphasis on childhood socialization, rather than upon union solidarity as a determinant of class consciousness; and the role assigned to intellectuals, rather than the working class, as a revolutionary force. He argues that the Australian union movement has always been controlled by the state, and that Australian workers have incorporated the bourgeois suburban culture of consumerism and welfare.[63] Notwithstanding his belief in the working class as an agent of history, Connell at the same time assumes the persistence of ruling-class hegemony.

Also of significance has been the work of socialist feminists working at Macquarie—feminists such as Rosemary Pringle, who, with Ann Game from the University of New South Wales, conducted research in the tradition of labor process theory.[64] Game and Pringle affirm what has been argued by all Australian feminists—that sex segregation is deeply embedded in Australian society. This, in their view, is because the sexual division of labor is *intrinsic* to capitalism, in fact is a "defining feature of it, as central as wage labour or surplus value."[65] This means that even when changes in technology (e.g., technological advances leading to de-skilling) could bring an erosion of distinctions between men's and women's jobs, sex segregation in the paid labor force will not disappear. Other feminists at Macquarie have given special attention to the relation between class, gender, and ethnicity, and have analyzed the inequalities among women within the sex-segregated labor force when race and ethnicity are taken into account.[66]

Sociology in the Marxist tradition is not restricted to Macquarie University. Other sociologists who have conducted research on issues of class and class consciousness are Chris Chamberlain at Monash and Andrew Metcalfe at the University of New South Wales.[67] Both have tackled Connell's notion of ruling class hegemony and have argued for the existence of a clearly identifiable working-class consciousness. Metcalfe's work is particularly interesting. Using historical and anthropological methods, Metcalfe undertook to study the lives of the coalminers in the Hunter Valley, New South Wales, under the assumption that people make their own history, albeit "under social circumstances and social structures beyond their control."[68] His study emphasized workers' ability to shape (although not control) their own destiny. In this, Metcalfe took issue with both deterministic theories such as Althusser's and voluntaristic ones such as E. P. Thompson's.

Several socialist feminist researchers are at work in various institutions—for example, Judy Wacjman and Claire Williams, both in the tradition of labor process theory, at the University of New South Wales and Flinders University, respectively.[69] Williams's study forms an interesting contrast with that of Game and Pringle: whereas Game and Pringle assume that male employers and male workers share a common interest in maintaining patriarchal relations to the detriment of women, Williams argues, in a study of a Queensland coal mining town, that workers' acceptance of patriarchal values is a consequence of hegemonic control by the ruling classes.[70]

There are also a number of Marxist sociologists across Australia who have written general theoretical treatises for international audiences which make no reference to the specific Australian context.[71]

Weberian traditions in research. Several members of the sociology department at Flinders University concentrate on long-term historical studies in the Weberian tradition. This work was started by one-time professor Ivan Szelenyi, continued by Bryan Turner, and is now maintained by Bob Holton.[72] Holton has also conducted studies of class analysis using the Eric Olin Wright framework.[73] Another Weberian is Anna Yeatman, now at Monash University, who for many years worked at Flinders. Yeatman's main concern has been the study of bureaucratic structures in government administration and the influence of neorationalist and technocratic models of decision making in government.[74]

A reference to Flinders University alone obscures the important Weberian tradition initiated by Sol Encel at the University of New South Wales.[75] In his best-known work, *Equality and Authority,* Encel combined Weberian analytical categories of class, status, and power with a multidimensional approach to stratification. Sol Encel's tradition has been maintained at the University of New South Wales by Ann Daniel in her work on occupational prestige, and, more recently, by the widely acclaimed work of Michael Pusey on the social and political background and ideologies of bureaucrats responsible for the 1980s shift to economic rationalism in Australian federal government policies.[76] A Weberian perspective is also clearly discernible in the work done by Malcolm Waters and by Jan Pakulski at the University of Tasmania, and in the research by political sociologist Eva Etzioni-Halevy at the Australian National University.[77] Few of these scholars follow the positivist application of Weberian sociology; they favor historical and conceptual analyses, or qualitative studies in the social-anthropological tradition.

Feminist theoretical perspectives on sociology. In the case of feminist sociology, it is appropriate to speak of a closely interlinked network of scholars who focus on common concerns. These concerns are fivefold:

1. a theoretical understanding of, and attempts to overcome, the dichotomy between public and private spheres, with its concomitant divisions between work and welfare, formal and domestic economy;

2. the study of women's paid and unpaid work;

3. the development of a theory of the state, with special attention to agency and social control;

4. sociology of the family;

5. general feminist theories as critique and construct.[78]

There are feminist scholars at work in all the mainstream centers of sociological research identified by Waters and Crook. These feminists usually follow theoretical perspectives which deviate from the theories *en vogue* in their institution: Dorothy Broom, for example, follows a decidedly feminist train of thought in the midst of Australian National University positivism; Rosemary Pringle at Macquarie has moved away from socialist feminism into postmodern feminist theory; and Claire Williams applies a socialist feminist framework at Weberian Flinders University.[79]

In some tertiary institutions, there are significant clusters of feminist sociologists. This is the case, for example, at Murdoch University,[80] where feminists have gained inspiration from the theoretical insights of three overseas feminist sociologists—Mary O'Brien, Hilary Rose, and Dorothy E. Smith.[81] The work of political scientist Carole Pateman, who is now in the United States but who still maintains close contact with Australian feminists, has also had a considerable influence.[82]

Feminist sociologists generally have developed sophisticated critical assessments of mainstream research methodology. The emphasis in their work has been upon action research and qualitative methods, including the use of in-depth interviews. They generally work within an interdisciplinary framework and maintain close contact with feminists in anthropology, economics, cultural studies, history, philosophy, and political science. Several work within, or in conjunction with, women's studies programs. Feminist sociological research has led to a number of significant publications, and texts written by feminists have been the major academic output of the publisher Allen and Unwin Australia.[83]

Centers of Intellectual Leadership: New Zealand

When in 1987 N. Perry assessed the viability of a separate New Zealand Sociological Association, he argued that it was not possible to speak of New Zealand sociology but only of Massey sociology, Canterbury sociology, or Auckland sociology. In listing these three centers, Perry signified at the same time that these were the only ones with any strength in terms of their research productivity.[84] Although arguing that there was no unified national sociology, Perry did not specify how each of the centers differed, other than through what he described as "rudimentary modes of specialisation."[85] Massey, he noted, had capitalized on its large number of external students and its political base on campus; Canterbury had gained considerable strength in the area of social policy, with close links to government; and Auckland had maintained and developed strong links with the Pacific and Australia.

In evaluating Perry's comments, it is important to keep in mind that he was an opponent of "secession" and therefore was possibly inclined to underestimate the value of New Zealand sociology. There is no doubt that sociology in New Zealand is small in scale. However, to an outsider what is apparent is an increasingly strong and coherent sociological paradigm across New Zealand universities. This is shown, in particular, in two major publications, both edited works, with contributors from across the country including several from outside academia. One is an introductory text edited by P. Spoonley, D. Pearson, and I. Shirley, the other a book on social problems, edited by P. F. Green.[86] Both books are written from a conflict perspective and problematize issues of class, gender, and race. Most authors in both books reject what the editors of one of the texts see as the "traditional emphasis on social pathology which has characterised sociological research in New Zealand."[87]

Of course, this is not to say that other perspectives do not occur. There is a fair amount of large-scale demographic research in the tradition of positivism at Waikato;[88] and there are Weberian sociologists at Victoria University—for example, David Pearson, whose community studies and research on social inequality (with David Thorns from Canterbury) have a clear Weberian emphasis.[89] As Pearson and Thorns conclude in their *Eclipse of Equality,* patterns of inequality in New Zealand emerge from the "combined effects of the operation of the labour and property markets, and state allocative practices."[90] This conclusion is in sharp contrast to the views of David Bedggood, a sociologist at Auckland, who over the years has maintained an orthodox Marxist perspective and for whom the production of value by labor power remains the "essential premise of all social life."[91]

As in Australia, feminist theoretical insights inform the work of many sociologists, with especially strong centers of feminist work at Canterbury and Waikato. Feminists include Rosemary Du Plessis Novitz at Canterbury, who has theoretical interests in women and the state and in theories of paid and unpaid work; and Bev James, a graduate from Waikato, who has written on the family and on feminist research methodology.[92] An active researcher outside the university system is Roberta Hill, the head of the Social Science Unit at the government Department of Scientific and Industrial Research (DSIR). Hill works in the tradition of labor process theory and has researched technological changes in the print media.[93] The theoretical and methodological preoccupations of feminists in New Zealand are similar to those of Australian feminist sociologists: the artificial dichotomy between public and private spheres; feminist theories of women and the state; family policies; the relationship between women's unpaid and paid work; and the development of a feminist research methodology.

The one noticeable difference lies in the greater attention given to issues of race by New Zealand feminists.[94]

New Zealand society has experienced profound changes in the period following the writing of the first edition of this handbook, and these changes have led to deep social and political divisions. On the one hand there remains entrenched conservatism, but on the other there is outspoken radicalism. Under successive Labour governments, New Zealanders have taken a strong stand on issues of apartheid, demonstrating en masse against South African rugby teams playing in New Zealand; they have argued for a nuclear-free Pacific Ocean region; and they have reaffirmed the original Treaty of Waitangi, drawn over 150 years ago between Maori chieftains and the British colonial government.

What appears a unique feature of New Zealand, and of central importance to sociology, is the notion of a genuinely bicultural society which is signified by the recognition of the Treaty of Waitangi. This implies that the Maori population, as the original owners of the country, are granted sovereignty—or at least equal partnership—with non-Maori. The Sociological Association of Aotearoa has taken this concept seriously, and the constitution of the Association contains the clause: "The aims and objectives of the Association shall be pursued in a manner consistent with Te Tiriti o Waitangi." The implications of this for sociological research and theory are at least as profound as those provided by feminism.[95] As Miriama Scott, a Maori sociologist, has commented,

From the Maori point of view, then, the subjective/objective distinction is a Pakeha myth. Its incorporation into research may lead to an intensification of unequal power relations between researcher and researched, and is likely to produce a predictably biased end result. Ways of categorising methodology often reinforce this bias because they stem from European methodology, also based on the objectivity myth. Sociology as a critique of society becomes oppressive when it is taken into minority ethnic groups without proper awareness of essential and often intrinsic differences.[96]

There are several sociologists in New Zealand who conduct research on racism and ethnic relations, and the issue of race is of central concern to feminist sociologists. The political challenge of the Treaty of Waitangi, however, if taken seriously, will no doubt have a profound effect on New Zealand sociology as a whole.

From Positivist to Anti-Positivist Perspectives

Contrasting theoretical perspectives have been at times a source of division within the sociological community. They were at the basis of a crisis in the Sociological Association of Australia and New Zealand (SAANZ)

in 1972, when young conflict theorists attacked the predominant positivistic emphasis in the *Australian and New Zealand Journal of Sociology,* the house journal of the association, and staged a coup ousting the editors.[97] Conflicting theoretical viewpoints were the source of an intense debate ten years later in the journal *Search;* on the one hand were Kelley and McAllister, and on the other Connell—representatives respectively of positivist and Marxist theories.[98] Such conflicts also flared up at conferences.[99] What is interesting to note is that notwithstanding the ideological differences between these camps, positivists have, in their analyses of social inequality, generally come to the same conclusions as Marxists.[100]

These divisions have become much less pronounced in recent years. There are few writers left within the Australian and New Zealand context who acknowledge that they are positivists, and there has been a clear trend toward an anti-positivist and a conflict perspective. Whatever divisions still exist are muted and largely unacknowledged. For some, no debate is necessary, because they do not take a theoretical stance themselves, arguing instead for the value of a range of discourses. They are sociologists who have embraced postmodernist and/or poststructuralist theoretical perspectives. For them, feminism, as well as the traditional sociological paradigms of positivism and Marxism, are metatheoretical orthodoxies to be avoided. What this signifies is that the debates which do occur are now more likely to be between modernists (working within the tradition of positivism, Marxism, and feminism) and postmodernists, rather than between positivists and Marxists.[101]

Overseas Influences

In the early stages of its postwar development, sociology in Australia and New Zealand was heavily influenced by American sociology. This situation has changed markedly. With very few exceptions, textbooks are produced locally or come from Britain, and staff members are no longer recruited from the United States. It may be argued that the only American social theorists still used with approval are Harry Braverman, who has inspired local research in the tradition of labor process theory;[102] Erik Olin Wright, who has had an impact on class analysis at Massey, Flinders, and Queensland universities; and writers in the tradition of ethnomethodology such as Harold Garfinkel, who are continuing to influence sociologists working in communication studies.[103] Even within specialist areas, American texts are only used to a limited extent, and then mainly by positivist researchers publishing comparative material in international journals.[104]

On the other hand, British and European texts are read widely. Of the British authors, Anthony Giddens remains an important gatekeeper due to the influence of his textbooks, and Raymond Williams has had considerable influence in the area of cultural theory.[105] A number of Australian sociologists are followers of the Frankfurt School, and Jurgen Habermas is widely read.[106] Foucault is another major influence, especially in inter-disciplinary centers and within the context of cultural studies.[107] British feminist sociologists, such as Michelle Barrett, Hilary Rose, and Mary MacIntosh, are also held in high regard.[108] The Canadian feminist sociol-ogist Dorothy E. Smith has gained a considerable following, especially at Canterbury and Murdoch universities, for her complex interweaving of Marxist and ethnomethodological principles into a sociology for women. It should be noted also that New Zealand sociologists are on the whole well aware of Australian sociological literature, but the reverse is not al-ways the case.

A recurrent problem in the 1950s and 1960s was the lack of qualified staff,[109] and full-time faculty were actively recruited from overseas. Many of these overseas recruits have settled in Australia and New Zealand and have made these countries their home, conducting research on local issues, with a commitment to developing a local sociology.[110] In recent years there has been a new wave of such immigration. A number of influential British social theorists, already well known internationally, have moved to Aus-tralia or New Zealand. All are British men in their early forties who have been appointed to professorships. One of the first in this category was Bryan Turner, who took up a chair at Flinders in the early 1980s (and after an interlude in Europe returned to a chair at Deakin); more recent examples are Barry Hindess at the Australian National University, Ste-phen Mennell at Monash, and Barry Smart at Auckland. It is rather early to see to what extent the more recently arrived international scholars will become involved in the development of theoretical work which adds to authentic Australian and New Zealand sociology.[111] The strength of their contribution may well be considerable—Hindess, for example, has already been a co-editor of the *ANZJS,* but the fact that these appointments were made remains problematic. This is especially so because there are many very able Australian and New Zealand sociologists, including several well-published and highly qualified women, who should have the opportunity to compete for these top positions. The paucity of female professors has been particularly noteworthy. In Australia, there are now eight female sociologists who are professors, but only three of these currently work in a sociology department, and all but one were appointed within the last three to five years. In New Zealand, all professors within sociology de-partments are male.[112]

CURRENT RESEARCH IN PROMINENT SUBFIELDS

Overview

Lally and Baldock's review of Australian and New Zealand sociology in the first edition of this handbook included six major subfields of study:

demographic and family-related studies; ethnic minorities; community studies; social stratification; political sociology; and sociology of education. Lally and Baldock judged most of the studies at that time to be functionalist and modeled on American examples. Just over twenty-five years later, the picture has altered radically. Sociologists have moved away from positivist to antipositivist perspectives, and from naive functionalism to a much more sophisticated and eclectic approach to theory and methodology. This shows even in the terminology of subfields used: no longer do sociologists speak of the study of stratification, or of ethnic minorities; rather, they define their work as being in class and inequality, or in race and ethnic relations.

There has also been a vast increase in the number of subfields, several new areas of specialization having appeared since the 1970s. The new areas include deviance and social control; sociology of sport and leisure; rural sociology; work and industry; social policy and interdisciplinary work in cultural studies; health studies; socio-legal studies; youth studies; and women's studies.

Of current subfields, possibly the most important remains the field of class and inequality, which replaced the earlier study of social stratification. This subfield was dealt with at length in the discussion of current trends in theory and methodology. Women's studies, another subject dealt with in connection with feminist sociology, has also produced a great deal of valuable work. That these two subfields figured so strongly in the overview of theoretical perspectives in this chapter is, of course, an indication that they have had a profound influence on sociology as a whole. Lack of space precludes discussion of each of the subfields mentioned. Having already covered class and inequality and feminist studies, this chapter will now focus on five subfields: demographic/family studies; race and ethnic relations; community studies; work and industry; and social policy.[113]

Demographic and Family Studies

Demographic studies, still conducted at the Australian National University and also at Waikato University, inform sociological analysis but are much less central to sociology proper than in the past, except possibly in terms of their political implications—demographic data have been used in the Australian political arena to argue for or against restrictions on immigration.[114]

On the other hand, family studies have gained importance in their own right and have lost their functionalist flavor. As may be expected from the strength of feminist sociology, studies of the family have increasingly scrutinized the concept of the "nuclear family" and highlighted the conflicts inherent in modern family life.[115] An important aspect of family studies is their focus on government policies. This includes study of the effect of government policy on the incidence of poverty among women and children in single-parent families, and on the incidence of homelessness among adolescent children.[116] A broad conclusion drawn in this research is that government policies reinforce the ideology of the nuclear family, thereby rendering other family types (e.g., the sole parent family, or Aboriginal and Maori extended families) "deviant."[117] Some feminist sociologists have extended this analysis of the state to include health and welfare professionals as agents of social control over family life and women.[118] There are also a number of studies of the relationship between home and paid work, which highlight the double or triple burden taken on by women engaged in paid work as well as domestic labor, child care, and volunteer community service, and the as yet very limited contribution made by men to child care and other household duties.[119] Particularly detailed and vivid accounts of family life and domesticity are contained in Jan Harper's and Lyn Richards's qualitative studies based on in-depth interviews with Australian women and men, and also in Betsy Wearing's work on the ideology of motherhood.[120]

Race and Ethnic Relations

Studies of ethnic minorities have continued, but the issue of race, virtually absent from study in the 1970s, is now an integral part of a new field of race and ethnic relations. Again, a critique of government policies on race relations and immigration forms an important ingredient of this research. An example is M. de Lepervanche's critical analysis of the shifting use of concepts in Australian social theory—a move, in fact, from the use of "race" to "ethnicity"—and its ideological connotations.[121] Paul Spoonley, writing about the New Zealand situation, has developed a political economy perspective on labor relations as an alternative to the sociology of race and ethnic relations.[122] Both de Lepervanche and Spoonley give considerable attention to the role of government in shaping policies which have led to the subordination of indigenous people and non-English-speaking immigrants.

Most of the current research conducted on issues of race and ethnicity rejects the assimilationist stance taken by the sociologists of the 1960s and 1970s, and argues for political autonomy of racial and ethnic groups.[123] The commitment of sociologists in New Zealand to the notion of biculturalism has been discussed already. Paradigm shifts in the study of race and ethnic relations unfortunately have not led to a greater representation of Maori and Aboriginal people among academic sociologists. There are a few Maori working within sociology departments now, but there are no Aboriginal academic sociologists. In other words, the indigenous people of Australia and New Zealand have very limited opportunity to articulate their own sociology—in sharp contrast to female sociologists, who have been able to do so within feminist sociology.[124] And there are still some sociologists who can engage in theoretical debate regarding the concept of race without once referring to the specific plight of Aboriginal people or Maori.[125]

Community Studies

One of the notable aspects of research in New Zealand and Australia is the continued interest in community studies. Among the more recent studies of this kind are Bev James's *Report to the Kawerau Community,* David Pearson's *Johnsonville,* Claire Williams's *Open Cut,* and Ken Dempsey's *Smalltown.*[126] Compared with earlier community studies, which were mostly consensual in orientation, the community studies of the 1980s have been increasingly conflict-oriented in their approach and incorporate careful analyses of class and gender relations.[127] Dempsey, for example, paints what appears to be a chilling portrait of small-town conservatism. In the town he studied, egalitarianism and community solidarity are maintained by *men* through the rigid rejection of outsiders (especially those who belong to ethnic minorities) *and* through the subordination of the women in the community. Most members of the working class, "no-hopers," elderly people, women—particularly those who breach the community code of respectability—are marginalized from mateship, from the sporting and work activities of the men, and from the prestigious and major decision-making processes of the town.[128] The community solidarity that exists is reinforced through the persistent reiteration of an ideology of community. Dempsey's study is not dealing with a community which is radically different from those studied in the 1970s;[129] it is his interpretation, and especially his greater concern for issues of marginality and gender relations, which is different.

Solidly in the Marxist tradition are small-town studies by Williams and by Metcalfe.[130] Their preoccupation is with the study of what are effectively company towns, that is, towns built and run by a single company employing all or most of the people living in the community. It is not surprising that in their studies industrial relations between bosses and workers are given prime attention. But, following the trends of the 1980s, they also put gender issues in focus. Some of their conclusions have already been recounted in our discussion of the Marxist tradition in sociology.

Work and Industry

As mentioned in the description of feminist and Marxist perspectives, there are a number of sociologists in Australia and New Zealand who work in the tradition of labor process theory. One strand of this research deals with the broad social and economic conditions of international cap-

italism which have led to changes in the labor process. A prime example
of this kind of work is Paul Boreham and Geoff Dow's *Work and Inequality,* which they describe as dealing with the dialectic between state
power, capitalist production, and economic crisis. Although deeply embedded within the neo-Marxist paradigm, their work has a distinct functionalist flavor.[131] The other strand of research in labor process studies has
in the main been concerned with the detailed analysis of the labor process
through participant observation and in-depth interviews.[132] This approach
allows greater opportunity for the study of working-class agency. Although
not strictly dealing with labor process, an emphasis on agency is also found
in recent studies on working-class youth and the school culture.[133]

There has also been research on the participation of women in paid and
unpaid work, with a particular emphasis on the marginalization of women
from paid work.[134] An example is Cora Baldock's research on volunteers,
in which she applies feminist theories of women's work to unpaid workers
in nongovernment welfare organizations.[135] Recent changes in the Australian system of industrial relations, which have led to a restructuring of all
industrial contracts for the sake of productivity and "structural efficiency,"
have also inspired sociological research and policy analysis. The focus of
these studies has again been primarily on women's work, with particular
attention to the definition of skill and productivity in so-called caring labor, and the increasing casualization in areas of work in which women
predominate.[136]

Social Policy

Sociologists within Australia have made major contributions to public
policy in the areas of social welfare, social security, poverty, housing, and
Equal Employment Opportunity (EEO) issues; and they have also contributed in the areas of population policy, immigration, and ethnic policies.[137] The most prominent sociologist in public policy is Bettina Cass, a
sociology graduate from the University of New South Wales who is now
a professor in the Department of Social Work and Social Administration
at Sydney University. In the late 1980s she was the director of the Commonwealth Social Security Review; currently she is a major contributor to
the National Housing Strategy, a policy review of federal government
housing priorities, and to the Population Issues Committee of the National
Population Council.[138] As a feminist sociologist, she has focused on women
in poverty; the relationship between family allowance and wage fixation;
female unemployment; and women's participation in paid work.[139]

Others who have made important contributions to policy studies in the
areas of social welfare, social inequality, and social security are Lois Bryson (now professor of sociology at Newcastle University), who for a num-

ber of years worked as senior policy advisor within the Victorian State Government; Sheila Shaver from Macquarie University, now on secondment to the Social Policy Research Centre at the University of New South Wales; and Patricia Harris, a Murdoch sociologist who acted as a consultant on a major review of child poverty conducted by the Brotherhood of St. Laurence.[140] Policy-related work in the area of social welfare has also been done by Adam Graycar, one-time director of the Social Policy Research Centre.[141]

Feminist sociologists (together with feminist political scientists) have also made major contributions to policies in the field of Equal Employment Opportunity. Most prominent in this area have been Hester Eisenstein, who for many years acted as the director of Equal Opportunity in Public Employment for the New South Wales (State) Government, and a more recent incumbent of that position, Clare Burton. The latter has become an authority on issues of job restructuring, equity, and skills assessment for women throughout Australia.[142]

In the area of migration policy, extensive research has been done by Lois Foster, currently acting director of the Government Bureau of Migration Research.[143] Robert Birrell, a Monash sociologist, who also works in this area, is a current member of the Population Issues Committee.[144] One of the most prominent social policy analysts in Australia in the field of criminology is Paul Wilson, one-time director of research at the federal government Bureau of Criminology.[145] Of the various research centers which have produced sociological research, the Australian Institute for Family Studies has possibly been most influential in the area of policy studies. Its findings on the costs of supporting children, for example, were of crucial importance to government policies on the amount of child maintenance to be paid by noncustodial parents after separation or divorce; and the specific studies on homeless and unemployed youth have also had considerable impact on policy.[146]

In New Zealand, sociologists have been acknowledged qua sociologists in policy making for a long time, and they have occupied prominent positions on major government committees and written extensively on policy issues. Peggy Koopman-Boyden has possibly made the most significant contribution as an expert on the family and the aged; she was for some time a member of the New Zealand Planning Council, the highest planning and advisory body in the country. Her research focuses on family policy and policies in the area of aged care.[147] Ivanica Vodanovich, from Auckland University, is on the New Zealand National Commission of UNESCO; Penny Fenwick, a sociologist with the New Zealand government, and Ted Douglas, from Waikato University, were manager and senior researcher with the Royal Commission on Social Policy (the discussion of the Treaty of Waitangi being one of major issues of concern).

As mentioned earlier, several sociologists are members of the Social Science Committee of the Foundation for Research, Science and Technology, the main research grant–issuing body in New Zealand.

All sociologists in Australia and New Zealand who write in the area of social policy, or more generally on issues in political sociology, recognize the central role of the state in Australian and New Zealand colonial histories. Feminist sociologists' involvement in policy making has led them to reflect on the role of the state for women in Australia and New Zealand. Generally, they have concluded that there is a basic contradiction between the patriarchal nature of the state and the reliance of women on the state to ameliorate their condition.[148] In this context feminists have also critically examined their own position as policy makers in the service of the state.[149]

TOWARD AN INDIGENOUS SOCIOLOGY? AN EVALUATION

In her conclusion to *Australian Sociologies,* Diane Austin puts a case for the development of a truly Australian sociology. More recently, Paul Spoonley has described the specific research agenda required for a genuine New Zealand sociology.[150] Both argue that such sociologies must take their starting point from Australia and New Zealand's colonial histories, histories in which the state has played a crucial role in the development and maintenance of class and race relations.[151] This review of Australian and New Zealand sociological literature makes it clear that issues of class, gender, and race would indeed be the central ingredients in the construction of such local sociologies.

My own evaluation of the current state of scholarship in Australian and New Zealand sociology is that sociologists in both countries have come a long way toward the development of such local knowledges. Many have broken away from the slavish application of British and American models of society and have began to construct explanations—within their area of specialization—which are pertinent to the local context. Perhaps the only author who has brought specific insights together in one overarching theoretical perspective is Bob Connell, but others have provided insightful, partial theoretical analyses of their own society.[152]

There are obstacles to the creation of a genuinely Australian or New Zealand sociology. In both countries tensions remain between the cultural cringe mentality of university administrators who award academic recognition only to those who write for international audiences, and the genuine desire of academics to write specifically about local issues. This is aggravated by the inclination of international publishers to see as internationally marketable those books that are situated in Britain and the United States, but not in Australia and New Zealand. A further manifestation is in the tendency to appoint overseas scholars to senior academic appointments—indicative of a lesser acknowledgment of local products.

New trends in sociological theory may also create obstacles to the development of authentic Australian and New Zealand sociologies. On the face of it, the poststructuralist and postmodernist rejection of "big stories," and the new interest in the "local," "particular," and "specific" ought to be helpful in the application of specific knowledges to local contexts.[153] However, the interest of postmodernists and poststructuralists in the local and specific has not necessarily led to a commitment to the development of an authentic *local* sociology. What is needed for the development of a local sociology is a close connection between theory and praxis, and the grounding of theory within lived experience. It may well be that an authentic Australian and New Zealand sociology will develop only in particular subfields of Australian and New Zealand sociology—namely, feminist sociology, community studies, or work and industry in the labor process tradition—where this close connection between experience, theory, and praxis is maintained.

There is a further obstacle to the development of an authentic Australian and New Zealand sociology. This is the lack of acknowledgment by the international sociological community of Australian and New Zealand sociologies as significant in their own right. When contributing to international publications, I myself have variously been classified under Pacific Rim countries, under Oceania, and—in the first edition of this handbook—Sociology of the East. Such terminological and geographical confusion does not augur well for the recognition of Australian and New Zealand sociologies as separate entities. My suggestion to the editor of this handbook that I write again—as for the first edition—on Australia *and* New Zealand, was my own—misguided—contribution to the persistence of this obstacle.

NOTES

1. The author is indebted to Victoria Rogers, Patricia Harris, and Beth Leslie for critical comments and editorial corrections to this chapter; to Gary Wickham for bibliographical references; and to Lynne Alice and Paul Spoonley for providing materials on recent developments in New Zealand sociology.

2. J. Lally and C. V. Baldock, "Contemporary Sociology in Australia and New Zealand," in R. P. Mohan and Don Martindale, eds., *Handbook of Contemporary Developments in World Sociology,* Westport, Conn.: Greenwood Press, 1975, 453–69. See also C. V. Baldock and J. Lally, *Sociology in Australia and New Zealand,* Westport, Conn.: Greenwood Press, 1974.

3. E.g., R. Firth, *Primitive Economics of the New Zealand Maori,* London: Routledge, 1929. Other eminent social anthropologists who conducted fieldwork in Australasia were Malinowksi, Lloyd Warner, and Radcliffe-Brown.

4. Albert Metin defined Australia as the workers' paradise in his book *La Socialisme sans doctrines,* Paris: no publisher, 1901.

5. A. G. Austin, ed., *The Webbs' Australian Diary 1898,* Melbourne: Pitman and Sons, 1965, 109.

6. Beatrice Webb defined herself as a social investigator and a first-rate interviewer; but as noted by Austin, "one feels that both she and Sidney were so forbidding that they must have inhibited and infuriated many of the Australians they met." See Austin, ibid., 13.

7. Australia and New Zealand are often misleadingly described as young countries because white settlement did not occur until the eighteenth century.

8. D. W. G. Timms and J. Zubrzycki, "A Rationale for Sociology Teaching in Australasia," *Australian and New Zealand Journal of Sociology* 7, April 1971, 4.

9. See Lally and Baldock, op. cit., 5–6. The most influential of Anderson's students was anthropologist A. P. Elkin, whose anthropology students Morven Brown and Jean Martin became foundation professors of sociology departments at the University of New South Wales and La Trobe, respectively.

10. H. Bourke, "Sociology and the Social Sciences in Australia, 1912–1928," *Australian and New Zealand Journal of Sociology* 17, 1, 1981, 26–35.

11. Ibid., 32.

12. H. C. D. Somerset, *Littledene: A New Zealand Rural Community,* Wellington: NZ Council of Educational Research, 1938.

13. R. H. T. Thompson, "Sociology in New Zealand," *Sociology and Social Research* 51, July 1967, 503; also J. Zubrzycki, professor of sociology at the Australian National University, who argued in 1971 that there is "much less need in Australia for social amelioration than in Britain at the turn of the century" (J. Zubrzycki, ed., *The Teaching of Sociology in Australia and New Zealand,* Melbourne: Cheshire, 1971, 4).

14. E.g., P. Spoonley, "The Political Economy of Racism," in P. F. Green, ed., *Studies in New Zealand Social Problems,* Dunmore Press: Palmerston North, 1990, 128–44; M. de Lepervanche, "Immigrants and Ethnic Groups," in S. Encel and L. Bryson, eds., *Australian Society,* 4th ed., Melbourne: Longman Cheshire, 1984, 170–228.

15. E.g., B. James and K. Saville-Smith, *Gender, Culture and Power,* Auckland: Oxford University Press, 1989; A. Summers, *Damned Whores and God's Police,* Melbourne: Penguin, 1975.

16. Francis G. Castles, *The Working Class and Welfare: Reflections on the Political Development of the Welfare State in Australia and New Zealand 1890–1980,* Wellington: Allen and Unwin, 1985.

17. In New Zealand, a sociological study of the living conditions of farmers in the late 1930s was rejected by the government of the day, and the research bureau which had conducted the study was abolished as a consequence. See R. H. T. Thompson, op. cit., 503.

18. In 1955, P. H. Partridge, an influential Australian social scientist, argued that "many Australian social scientists judge sociology by the very inferior work that has been produced by some sociologists in other countries, and they regard sociology as a synonym for woolliness and pretentiousness" (as quoted by J. Zubrzycki, op. cit., 7). As late as 1966, a New Zealand psychology professor thought

that he would have no difficulty teaching sociology, because he had read his daughter's sociology textbooks (personal communication to the author).

19. P. Abrams, *The Origins of British Sociology: 1834–1914,* Chicago: University of Chicago Press, 1968, 152–53.

20. E.g., Spoonley, op. cit.; de Lepervanche, op. cit.

21. E.g., J. Zubrzycki, *Immigrants in Australia,* Melbourne University Press, 1960; Zubrzycki, *Settlers of the Latrobe Valley,* Canberra: ANU Press, 1964; E. Kunz, "Refugees and Eastern Europeans in Australia," in Ch. A. Price, ed., *Australian Immigration,* Canberra: ANU Press, 1966; J. Krupinski and A. Stoller, "Family Life and Mental Ill-Health in Migrants," in A. Stoller, ed., *New Faces,* Melbourne: Cheshire, 1966.

22. Sociologists' policy recommendations, however, were not always heeded. See, for example, de Lepervanche, op. cit., 173–74.

23. See C. V. Baldock, "Academic Recruitment and Dependency: An Australian Case Study," paper presented at the SAANZ Conference, Brisbane, May 1978, for an account of the resistance in the 1970s to the development of sociology at the University of Western Australia.

24. D. W. G. Timms, "Sociology in Auckland," *University of Auckland Gazette* 12, April 1970, 2–4; D. A. Hansen and R. J. R. King, "Sociology and Social Research in New Zealand," *Sociology and Social Research* 50, October 1965, 36–46; see, however, for a dissenting voice on this issue, R. H. T. Thompson, op. cit., 503.

25. Bourke, op. cit., 34.

26. P. Spoonley, "The Development of Sociology in New Zealand," *Footnotes,* January 1990, 7.

27. In an interesting reversal of historical trends, in 1989 the Waikato department became the Department of Sociology and Anthropology.

28. Information derived from various newsletters of SAA (NZ).

29. The process of restructuring meant the eradication of the distinction between universities and colleges or institutes. The process began in 1987 with the upgrading of the Western Australian Institute of Technology to Curtin University of Technology; all other changes took place in 1989 or after.

30. The Australian Sociological Association, *Postgraduate Study in Sociology,* 1991.

31. Murdoch and Deakin universities were also established in the 1970s with an interdisciplinary structure; Murdoch developed a separate sociology major in 1990, Deakin in 1991.

32. D. Ashenden and S. Milligan, *The Independent Good Universities Guide to Australian Universities,* Melbourne: Mandarin, 1991.

33. Colleges of advanced education and institutes of technology have traditionally been defined as teaching-only institutions. Thus, very high teaching loads and lack of time and resources for research have been symptomatic of these institutions.

34. I. Lowe, "University Research Funding: The Wheel Still Is Spinnin'," *Australian Universities' Review* 1, 1987, 2–12, estimates that 95 percent of academic research funding in Australia comes from this source.

35. Public address by Professor P. Sheehan, Chairman, Social Sciences Panel, ARC, at Murdoch University, 15 July 1991.

36. A disturbing aspect of this is that women applicants in the social sciences

appear to be less successful than men in gaining funds and are awarded more often than men at a lower level than requested. See G. Poiner and D. Temple, *The Participation of Women in Academic Research. Research Report No 1*, Sydney: Women's Studies Centre, University of Sydney, 1990, 31.

37. G. Poiner and D. Temple, ibid., 17, found that over a four-year period (1986–1989) sociologists from three universities in Sydney made only 23 grant applications to the ARC; this compares with, for example, 196 applications from chemistry.

38. For example, one medium-sized sociology department with a good track record in gaining grants, that of the University of Queensland, received a total of $323,404 in external grants in 1991; 18 percent of these came from nongovernment sources, 49 percent from "mission-oriented" research, and the remaining 33 percent from ARC (Dept. of Anthropology and Sociology, Queensland University, *Annual Review,* 1991).

39. E.g., B. Cass, *Income Support for Families with Children,* Social Security Review, Issues Paper No. 1., Canberra: Australian Government Publishing Service (AGPS), 1986; ibid., *Income Support for the Unemployed in Australia: Towards a More Active System,* Social Security Review, Issues Paper No. 4., Canberra: AGPS, 1988; see also Human Rights and Equal Opportunity Commission, *Our Homeless Children. Report on the National Inquiry into Homeless Children,* Canberra: AGPS, 1989; National Housing Strategy, *Australian Housing: The Demographic, Economic and Social Environment,* Canberra: AGPS, 1991.

40. Sociological Association of Aotearoa (NZ) *Newsletter* 2, August 1990, 1.

41. There have been no sociologists on the Australian Research Council since 1986.

42. E.g., P. Harris, *Child Poverty, Inequality and Social Justice,* Child Poverty Policy Review 1, Melbourne: Brotherhood of St. Laurence, 1989; ibid., *All Our Children,* Child Poverty Policy Review 4, Melbourne: Brotherhood of St. Laurence, 1990.

43. Spoonley, "The Development of Sociology," op. cit., 7. See, for opposing arguments, N. Perry, "Absent Centre: New Zealand Sociology and the Conditions of Cultural Production," *NZSA Newsletter* 2, 1987, 17; C. Crothers and C. Gribben, "The State of New Zealand Sociology," *New Zealand Sociology* 1, 1, May 1986, 1–17.

44. In bicultural New Zealand, the Maori name for the country is now used with pride in many public documents, and New Zealand sociologists have chosen the Maori name for their professional association.

45. In New Zealand, J. Forster, ed., *Social Process in New Zealand,* Auckland: Longman Paul, 1969; in Australia, A. F. Davies and S. Encel, eds., *Australian Society, a Sociological Introduction.* New York: Atherton Press, 1965.

46. Australian or New Zealand writers are usually asked by publishers to specify in the titles of their books that they refer to Australian or New Zealand conditions. The consequence of this is that very few books written by Australian and New Zealand scholars, however excellent, reach an international readership. British or American textbook writers seldom follow such a practice, under the assumption that their analysis has general application. An example is Giddens's *Sociology,* a British text with predominantly European and American illustrations, which is widely used as an introductory text in Australia.

47. M. Waters and R. Crook, *Sociology One, Principles of Sociological Analysis for Australians,* Melbourne: Longman Cheshire, 2nd ed., 1990; D. J. Austin, *Australian Sociologies,* Sydney: Allen and Unwin, 1984.

48. P. Spoonley, D. Pearson, and I. Shirley, eds., *New Zealand: Sociological Perspectives,* Palmerston North: Dunmore Press, 1982 (reprinted 1986).

49. The Series started in 1978; by 1991, in addition to books in the Series, Allen and Unwin had published 12 other sociology titles, and about 10 books by sociologists in its Women's Studies list (personal communication, Robert Gorman, Allen and Unwin, 1991).

50. It appears there are as yet only three full professors in any of these 21 tertiary institutions who are sociologists—at the University of Western Sydney, Nepean, at the Queensland University of Technology, and at Deakin University.

51. Waters and Crook, op. cit., 19.

52. W. K. Hancock, *Australia,* London: Benn, 1930. While presenting "popsociology" in this book, Hancock described sociology as "mumbo-jumbo." See Bourke, op. cit., 30.

53. R. W. Connell, "Images of Australia," in D. F. Edgar, ed., *Social Change in Australia: Readings in Sociology,* Melbourne: Cheshire, 1974, 27–41.

54. E.g., L. Broom, F. L. Jones, and J. Zubrzycki, "Social Stratification in Australia," in J. A. Jackson, ed., *Social Stratification,* Cambridge: Cambridge University Press, 1968; L. Broom and F. L. Jones, *Opportunity and Attainment in Australia,* Canberra: Australian National University Press, 1976; J. Higley, D. Deacon, and D. Smart, *Elites in Australia,* London: Routledge and Kegan Paul, 1979; B. Graetz and I. McAllister, *Dimensions of Australian Society,* Melbourne: MacMillan Australia, 1988.

55. E.g., F. L. Jones, "Sources of Gender Inequality in Income: What the Australian Census Says," *Social Forces* 62, 1983, 134–52; F. L. Jones and P. Davis, *Models of Society: Class, Stratification and Gender in Australia and New Zealand,* Sydney: Croom Helm, 1986; Graetz and McAllister, op cit., 46–116.

56. M. D. R. Evans and J. Kelley, "Immigrants' Work: Equality and Discrimination in the Australian Labour Market," *Australian and New Zealand Journal of Sociology* 22, 2, July 1986, 187–207.

57. Graetz and McAllister, op. cit., 176–232.

58. John Western himself has expressed a disdain for social theory; see his *Social Inequality in Australian Society,* Melbourne: MacMillan, 1983, 10.

59. J. H. Baxter, P. R. Boreham, S. R. Clegg, M. Emmison, D. M. Gibson, G. N. Marks, J. S. Western, and M. C. Western, "The Australian Class Structure: Some Preliminary Results from the Australian Class Project," *Australian and New Zealand Journal of Sociology* 25, 1, May 1989, 100–20; J. H. Baxter, "Gender and Class Analysis: The Position of Women in the Class Structure," *Australian and New Zealand Journal of Sociology* 24, 1, 1988, 106–23; J. H. Baxter, D. Gibson, with M. Lynne-Blosse, *Double Take: The Links between Paid and Unpaid Work,* Canberra: Australian Government Publishing Service, 1990.

60. E.g., G. N. Marks, J. S. Western, and M. C. Western, "Class and Income in Australia," *ANZJS* 25, 3, November 1989, 410–27, does not make any reference to income levels of the unemployed.

61. Baxter, "Gender and Class," op. cit.; Baxter and Gibson, op. cit.

62. R. W. Connell, *The Child's Construction of Politics,* Melbourne: Melbourne

University Press, 1971; Connell, *Ruling Class, Ruling Culture,* Cambridge: Cambridge University Press, 1977; R. W. Connell and T. Irving, *Class Structure in Australian History,* Melbourne: Longman Cheshire, 1980; R. W. Connell, D. J. Ashenden, S. Kessler, and G. W. Dowsett, *Making the Difference: Schools, Family and Social Division,* Sydney: Allen and Unwin, 1982; Connell, *Which Way Is Up?* Sydney: Allen and Unwin, 1983; Connell, *Teachers' Work,* Sydney: Allen and Unwin, 1985; Connell, *Gender and Power,* Oxford: Polity Press, 1987.

63. E.g., Connell and Irving, op. cit., 298. See, for a critical review of Connell's ideas, D. Austin, op. cit., especially 33–36.

64. A. Game and R. Pringle, *Gender at Work,* Sydney: Allen and Unwin, 1983.

65. Ibid., 14.

66. E.g., G. Bottomley and M. de Lepervanche, eds., *Ethnicity, Class and Gender in Australia,* Sydney: Allen and Unwin, 1984. See on this issue also M. Kalantzis, "Ethnicity Meets Gender Meets Class in Australia," in S. Watson, ed., *Playing the State,* Sydney: Allen and Unwin, 1990, 21–38.

67. C. Chamberlain, *Class Consciousness in Australia,* Sydney: Allen and Unwin, 1983; A. Metcalfe, *For Freedom and Dignity, Historical Agency and Class Structures in the Coalfields of NSW,* Sydney: Allen and Unwin, 1988.

68. Metcalfe, op. cit., 210.

69. J. Wacjman, *Women in Control,* Milton Keynes: Open University Press, 1983; C. Williams, *Open Cut,* Sydney: Allen and Unwin, 1981; Williams, *Blue, White and Pink Collar Workers in Australia,* Sydney: Allen and Unwin, 1988.

70. Williams, *Open Cut,* op. cit. See Metcalfe, op. cit., 187, for a critique of Williams's somewhat deterministic account of patriarchal relations.

71. E.g., J. M. Barbalet, *Marx's Construction of Social Theory,* London and Melbourne: Routledge, 1983; S. Clegg, P. Boreham, and G. Dow, *Class, Politics and the Economy,* London: Routledge, 1986.

72. E.g., G. Konrad and I. Szelenyi, *Intellectuals on the Road to Class Power,* London: Harvester, 1979; B. Turner, *For Weber, Essays on the Sociology of Fate,* London: Routledge, 1981; R. J. Holton, *The Transition from Feudalism to Capitalism,* London: Macmillan, 1985; Holton, *Crisis, Capitalism and Civilisation,* London: Allen and Unwin, 1986.

73. R. J. Holton and W. Martin, "The Class Structure of Metropolitan Adelaide," *Australian and New Zealand Journal of Sociology* 23, 1, 1987, 5–22.

74. A. Yeatman, *Bureaucrats, Technocrats, Femocrats: Essays on the Contemporary State,* Sydney: Allen and Unwin, 1990.

75. S. Encel, *Equality and Authority: A Study of Class, Status and Power,* Melbourne: Cheshire, 1970. See, for a critical assessment of Encel's work, D. Austin, op. cit.

76. A. Daniel, *Power, Privilege and Prestige: Occupations in Australia,* Melbourne: Longman Cheshire, 1983; M. Pusey, *Economic Rationalism in Canberra,* Cambridge/New York/Melbourne: Cambridge University Press, 1991.

77. J. Pakulski, *Social Movements. The Politics of Moral Protest,* Melbourne: Longman Cheshire, 1991; M. Waters, *Class and Stratification,* Melbourne: Longman Cheshire, 1990; Waters and Crook, *Sociology One,* op. cit.; Eva Etzioni-Halevy, *Bureaucracy and Democracy,* London and Melbourne: Routledge, rev. ed. 1985; Etzioni-Halevy, *The Knowledge Elite and the Failure of Prophesy,* London and Sydney: Allen and Unwin, 1985.

78. E.g., C. V. Baldock, *Volunteers in Welfare,* Sydney: Allen and Unwin, 1990; C. V. Baldock and B. Cass, eds., *Women, Social Welfare and the State,* 2nd ed. Sydney: Allen and Unwin, 1988; L. Bryson, "The Australian Patriarchal Family," in S. Encel and L. Bryson, op. cit., 113–69; Bryson, "Women as Welfare Recipients: Women, Poverty and the State," in Baldock and Cass, op. cit., 134–49; Bryson, *Welfare and the State,* London: MacMillan, 1992; C. Burton, *Subordination: Feminism and Social Theory,* Sydney: Allen and Unwin, 1985; A. Edwards, *Regulation and Repression: The Study of Social Control,* Sydney: Allen and Unwin, 1988; H. Eisenstein, *Contemporary Feminist Thought,* Sydney: Allen and Unwin, 1984; S. Franzway, D. Court, and R.W. Connell, *Staking a Claim. Feminism, Bureaucracy and the State,* Sydney: Allen and Unwin, 1989; E. Pengelly, "A Feminist Critique of Max Weber's Economy and Society," unpublished honors thesis, Perth: Murdoch University, 1983; S. Shaver, "Sex and Money in the Welfare State," in C. V. Baldock and B. Cass, op. cit., 150–67; B. Thiele, "Vanishing Acts in Social and Political Thought: Tricks of the Trade," in C. Pateman and E. Gross, eds., *Feminist Challenges,* Sydney: Allen and Unwin, 1986, 30–43; S. Watson, ed., *Playing the State,* Sydney: Allen and Unwin, 1990; B. Wearing, *The Ideology of Motherhood,* Sydney: Allen and Unwin, 1984.

79. D. Broom, ed., *Unfinished Business,* Sydney: Allen and Unwin, 1984; R. Pringle, *Secretaries Talk; Sexuality, Power and Work,* Sydney: Allen and Unwin, 1988; Williams, op. cit.

80. These include Lynne Alice, Cora V. Baldock, Patricia Harris, Beth Pengelly, Lynne Star, and Bev Thiele.

81. M. O'Brien, *The Politics of Reproduction,* London: Routledge, 1981; H. Rose, "Hand, Brain, and Heart: A Feminist Epistemology for the Natural Sciences," *Signs* 9, 1, 1983, 73–90; D. E. Smith, *The Everyday World as Problematic. A Feminist Sociology,* Milton Keynes: Open University Press, 1988.

82. E.g., C. Pateman, *The Sexual Contract,* Oxford: Polity Press, 1988. A highlight for feminist sociology in Australia was the ANZAAS conference 1983, held in Perth, when Hilary Rose and Carole Pateman presented papers, and Murdoch and Monash feminist coordinated a workshop on Mary O'Brien's work.

83. Since 1978, Allen and Unwin Australia has published approximately 10 texts by feminists in its series *Studies in Society* and at least 45—10 of which were by sociologists—in its *Women's Studies Series.*

84. N. Perry, op. cit. See also Crothers and Gribben, op. cit.

85. Perry, op. cit., 23.

86. Spoonley, Pearson, and Shirley, op. cit; P. F. Green, ed., *Studies in New Zealand Social Problems,* Palmerston North: Dunmore Press, 1990.

87. I. Shirley, P. Spoonley, and D. Pearson, "Conclusion," in Spoonley, Pearson, and Shirley, op. cit., 382.

88. E.g., I. Pool and J. Sceats, "Population: Human Resource and Social Determinant," in Green, op. cit., Ch. 1.

89. D. G. Pearson, *Johnsonville,* Auckland: Allen and Unwin, 1980; D. G. Pearson and D. C. Thorns, *Eclipse of Equality,* Sydney: Allen and Unwin, 1983.

90. Pearson and Thorns, op. cit., 249.

91. D. Bedggood, "The Welfare State," in Spoonley, Pearson, and Shirley, op. cit., 197; see also Bedggood, *Rich and Poor in New Zealand,* Sydney: Allen and Unwin, 1980.

92. E.g., R. Novitz, "Bridging the Gap: Paid and Unpaid Work," in S. Cox, ed., *Public and Private Worlds,* Sydney and Wellington: Allen and Unwin and Port Nicholson Press, 1987, 23–52; B. James, "Taking Gender into Account: Feminist and Sociological Issues in Social Research," *New Zealand Sociology* 1, 1, May 1986, 18–33; B. James and K. Saville-Smith, op. cit.

93. R. Hill, "From Hot Metal to Cold Type: New Technology in the Newspaper Industry," *New Zealand Journal of Industrial Relations* 9, 3, 1984, 161–75.

94. E.g., James and Saville-Smith, op. cit.; see also the journal *Race, Gender, Class.*

95. See, for extensive discussions on the implications of this clause, B. Willmott, "Contribution to the Symposium on the SAA(NZ) and Te Tiriti o Waitangi," *SAA(NZ) Newsletter* 1, April 1990, 23–27.

96. M. Scott, "'Sociology and the Treaty of Waitangi" (interview with M. Roth), *SAA(NZ) Newsletter* 1, March 1989, 2–3.

97. Lally and Baldock, op cit., 453–54.

98. R. W. Connell, "Social Class in Australia," *Search* 14, 9–10, 247–48; J. Kelley and I. McAllister, "Modern Sociology and the Analysis of Class," *Search* 14, 9–10, 249–52; Connell et al., "The Colonial Mentality in Social Science," *Search* 15, 3–4, 110–11.

99. E.g., F. L. Jones, W. E. Willmott, R. Wild, "Dialogue: Crisis in Sociology," *Australian and New Zealand Journal of Sociology* 19, 2, July 1983, 195–215, for a heated debate between positivist, Marxist, and Weberian sociologists. The papers had their origin in a panel discussion at a SAANZ conference.

100. See Austin, op. cit., 84.

101. E.g., Pringle, *Secretaries Talk,* op. cit.; G. Wickham, "The Political Possibilities of Postmodernism," *Economy and Society* 19, 1, 1990; A. Milner and C. Worth, eds., *Discourse and Difference: Post-Structuralism, Feminism and the Moment of History,* Clayton: Monash University, 1990.

102. Braverman's work has inspired studies by Game and Pringle, op. cit.; Williams, op. cit.; Hill, op. cit; and R. Kriegler, *Working for the Company,* Melbourne: Oxford University Press, 1980; see also E. Willis, ed., *Technology and the Labour Process,* Sydney: Allen and Unwin, 1988.

103. Sociologists in Australia influenced by ethnomethodology include A. MacHoul, *Telling How Texts Talk: Essays on Reading and Ethnomethodology,* London: Routledge, 1982; K. Liberman, *Understanding Interaction in Central Australia: An Ethnomethodological Study of Australian Aboriginal People,* Boston: Routledge, 1985; M. Campion, *Worry: A Maieutic Analysis,* Hampshire, England: Gower Press, 1986.

104. A major model for Australian positivist stratification research has been P. M. Blau and O. D. Duncan, *The American Occupational Structure,* New York: Wiley, 1967. See, for example, Kelley and McAllister, "Modern Sociology and the Analysis of Class," op. cit.

105. Giddens's textbook *Sociology* is very widely used, but his other theoretical texts are also prominent. It does not appear, though, that Giddens's own theoretical perspectives are given serious consideration. Williams and other authors in the tradition of the Birmingham Centre for Cultural Studies have inspired some Australian research (e.g., Connell, Ashenden, Kessler, and Dowset, op. cit.; L. Johnson, *The Unseen Voice. A Cultural Study of Early Australian Radio,* London:

Routledge, 1988). The recently established Cultural Studies Association follows a "soft" Marxist approach in the Williams tradition.

106. Work inspired by Habermas has appeared in the journal *Thesis Eleven,* e.g., M. Pusey, "Rationality, Organisations and Language: Towards a Critical Theory of Bureaucracy," *Thesis Eleven* 10/11, November 1984–March 1985, 89–109; G. Munster, R. Poole, T. Rowse, A. K. Salleh, and T. Smith, "Special Symposium: Australian Intellectuals and the Left," *Thesis Eleven* 10/11, November 1984/March 1985, 145–65. See also Pusey, *Economic Rationalism in Canberra,* op. cit.

107. Foucault is a major influence on the work of the Centre for Cultural Policy Studies at Griffith University. See, e.g., I. Hunter, *Culture and Government,* Basingstoke: MacMillan, 1988. Feminist sociologists who have made imaginative use of discourse analysis are Edwards, op. cit; and K. Reiger, *The Disenchantment of the Home. Modernizing the Australian Family 1880–1940,* Oxford: Oxford University Press, 1985. See also B. Wearing, "Beyond the Ideology of Motherhood: Leisure as Resistance," *ANZJS* 26, 1, March 1990, 36–58.

108. M. Barrett, *Women's Oppression Today,* London: Verso, 1988, is used as a text in feminist sociology courses; see also M. Barrett and M. MacIntosh, *The Anti-Social Family,* London: Verso, 1982; Rose, op. cit.

109. A continuing problem has been the brain drain of sociologists going overseas for further studies or jobs, never to return. This includes a brain drain from New Zealand to Australia.

110. Even today there are sociology departments in Australia and New Zealand in which the majority of staff come from abroad. For example, in 1990 the eight staff members of one New Zealand sociology department welcomed a new colleague as the "only New Zealand born and bred sociologist amongst us." SAA(NZ) *Newsletter* 1, April 1990, 6.

111. Turner's description of Australian sociology as at the periphery of the global marketplace of sociology did not sit well with Australian sociologists. See B. S. Turner, "Sociology as an Academic Trade," *Australian and New Zealand Journal of Sociology* 22, 2, July 1986, 272–82; and L. Bryson, M. Emmison, and B. S. Turner, "Responses and a Reply," 283–90, in the same journal issue.

112. In 1991 there were five female sociologists in full professorial positions in Australia: Lois Bryson, professor of sociology at the University of New England; Jane Marceau, professor of social policy at the Australian National University; Bettina Cass, at Sydney University, who holds a personal chair in the Department of Social Work; Lesley Johnson, professor of communications at the University of Western Sydney, Nepean; and Sophie Watson, chair in planning at Sydney University. Two new appointments were made in 1992—Anne Edwards, to a chair in sociology at Monash's Department of Sociology and Anthropology; and Gisela Kaplan, head of social sciences at Queensland University of Technology. In New Zealand, sociologist Anna Yeatman held the chair in women's studies at Waikato for two years, before returning to Australia to take up the second sociology chair in the Monash department.

113. For reviews and examples of the subfields which are not discussed, see the following: A. Edwards, op. cit.; P. O'Malley and K. Carson, "The Institutional Foundations of Contemporary Australian Criminology," *ANZJS* 25, 3, November 1989, 333–55; B. Gidlow, "Deviance," in Spoonley, Pearson, and Shirley, op. cit., 325–52; K. Pearson, *Surfing Subculture of Australia and New Zealand,* Brisbane:

University of Queensland Press, 1979; L. Bryson, "Sport and the Oppression of Women," *ANZJS* 19, 1983, 413–26; J McKay, "Leisure and Social Inequality in Australia," *ANZJS* 22, 3, November 1986, 343–67; G. Kaplan, "Welfare Issues and Rural Economy," paper presented at TASA Conference, Perth, December 1991; A. Milner, *Contemporary Cultural Theory,* Sydney: Allen and Unwin, 1991; L. Johnson, op. cit.; T. Bennett, C. Mercer, and J. Woollacott, eds., *Popular Culture and Social Relations,* Milton Keynes: Open University Press, 1986; P. Davis, *Health and Health Care in New Zealand,* Auckland: Longman, 1981; E. Willis, *Medical Dominance,* Sydney: Allen and Unwin, 1983; C. Russell and T. Schofield, *Where It Hurts,* Sydney: Allen and Unwin, 1986; Pat O'Malley, *Law, Capitalism and Democracy: A Sociology of the Australian Legal Order,* Sydney: Allen and Unwin, 1983; B. Wilson and J. Wyn, *Shaping Futures. Youth Action for Livelihood,* Sydney: Allen and Unwin, 1987; P. Dwyer, B. Wilson, and R. Woock, *Confronting School and Work,* Sydney: Allen and Unwin, 1984.

114. A valuable critique of the descriptive nature of demographic studies for New Zealand was given by J. Johnston, "Population," in Spoonley, Pearson, and Shirley, op. cit., 13–38. See, for the immigration debate, F. Lewins, "The Blainey Debate in Hindsight," *ANZJS* 23, 2, July 1987, 261–73.

115. The best review of the literature for Australia is in Bryson, "The Patriarchal Family," in Encel and Bryson, op cit.; for New Zealand in Novitz, op. cit; or James and Saville-Smith, op. cit. See also Baldock and Cass, op. cit.; A. Burns, G. Bottomley, P. Jools, eds., *The Family in the Modern World,* Sydney: Allen and Unwin, 1983; C. O'Donnell and J. Craney, *Family Violence in Australia,* Melbourne: Longman, 1982; P. Bunkle and B. Hughes, *Women in New Zealand Society,* Auckland: Allen and Unwin, 1980; P. G. Koopman-Boyden and C. Scott, *The Family and Government Policy in New Zealand,* Sydney: Allen and Unwin, 1984.

116. E.g., Harris, op. cit; Bryson, "Women as Welfare Recipients," op. cit.; Human Rights and Equal Opportunity Commission, op. cit.

117. E.g., Edwards, op. cit.; James and Saville-Smith, op. cit..

118. Reiger, op. cit.; Edwards, op. cit.; K. Reiger, "The Coming of the Counsellors: The Development of Marriage Guidance in Australia," *ANZJS* 23, 3, November 1987, 375–87.

119. Bryson, "The Patriarchal Family," op. cit.; Baldock, *Volunteers in Welfare,* op. cit.; Baxter and Gibson, op. cit.; M. Bittman, *Juggling Time: How Australian Women Use Time,* Canberra: Office of the Status of Women, Department of the Prime Minister and Cabinet, 1991.

120. J. Harper and L. Richards, *Mothers and Working Mothers,* Melbourne: Penguin, rev. ed. 1986; J. Harper, *Fathers at Home,* Penguin: Melbourne, 1980; L. Richards, *Nobody's Home. Dreams and Realities in a New Suburb,* Melbourne: Oxford University Press, 1989; Wearing, *The Ideology of Motherhood,* op. cit.

121. M. de Lepervanche, "From Race to Ethnicity," *ANZJS* 16, 1, 1980, 24–37.

122. R. Miles and P. Spoonley, "The Political Economy of Labour Migration: An Alternative to the Sociology of 'race' and 'ethnic relations'," *ANZJS* 21, 1, March 1985, 3–26. See also Spoonley, "The Political Economy of Racism," in P. F. Green, op. cit., 128–44.

123. In some instances the paradigm shifts led to lively debates. See for example, responses by C. Macpherson and D. Pearson to the article by Miles and

Spoonley: C. Macpherson, "On the Silences in Emerging Pluralism: A Reply to Miles and Spoonley," *ANZJS* 21, 2, July 1985, 267–68; D. Pearson, "The Political Economy of Labour Migration in New Zealand: A Reply to Miles and Spoonley," *ANZJS* 21, 2, July 1985, 269–74.

124. The author is indebted to Patricia Harris for bringing this point to her attention.

125. E.g., K. M. Brown, "Keeping Their Distance. The Cultural Production and Reproduction of 'Racist Non-Racism'," *ANZJS* 22, 3, November 1986, 387–98.

126. B. James, *A Report to the Kawerau Community,* Hamilton: University of Waikato, 1979; D. Pearson, *Johnsonville,* Auckland: Allen and Unwin, 1980; Williams, *Open Cut,* op. cit.; K. Dempsey, *Smalltown: A Study of Social Inequality, Cohesion and Belonging,* Melbourne: Oxford University Press, 1990.

127. See L. Bryson and B. Wearing, "Australian Community Studies—A Feminist Critique," *ANZJS* 21, 3, November 1985, 349–66, for a critique of earlier studies.

128. Dempsey, op. cit., 306.

129. E.g., R. Wild, *Bradstow, a Study of Status, Class and Power in a Small Australian Town,* Sydney: Angus and Robertson, 1974; Wild, *Heathcote,* Sydney: Allen and Unwin, 1983; H. G. Oxley, *Mateship in Local Organisation,* Brisbane: Queensland University Press, 1974.

130. Williams, op. cit.; Metcalfe, op. cit.

131. P. Boreham and G. Dow, eds., *Work and Inequality,* vols. I and II. Melbourne: MacMillan, 1980.

132. E.g., Williams, op. cit.; Game and Pringle, op. cit.; Willis, *Technology and the Labour Process,* op. cit.; Kriegler, op. cit.; R. Hill, op. cit. See, for a review of the New Zealand literature, R. Hill, P. Couchman, and B. Gidlow, "Work and Technology," in Green, op. cit., 213–33.

133. E.g., P. Dwyer, B. Wilson, R. Woock, op. cit.

134. R. Novitz, op. cit.

135. Baldock, *Volunteers in Welfare,* op. cit; Baldock, Chapter 2 in Baldock and Cass, op. cit.

136. E.g., C. Burton, *The Promise and the Price,* Sydney: Allen and Unwin, 1990; C. V. Baldock, "Award Restructuring for Women. Tools of Change or Stagnation," *Australian Feminist Studies* 12, 1990, 43–49; C. O'Donnell and P. Hall, *Getting Equal,* Sydney: Allen and Unwin, 1988.

137. The distinction between public and social policy made among Australian academics and policy makers often signifies an artificial division (and rank ordering) between "hard" and "soft" social sciences, as well as between male and female policy makers. See S. Dowse, "The Women's Movement's Fandango with the State: The Movement's Role in Public Policy since 1972," in C. V. Baldock and B. Cass, eds., *Women, Social Welfare and the State,* Sydney: Allen and Unwin, 2nd ed. 1988, 204.

138. See notes 39 and 78 for references to her work.

139. E.g., B. Cass, "Redistribution to Children and Mothers, a History of Child Endowment and Family Allowances," in Baldock and Cass, op. cit., 54–88.

140. For work by L. Bryson and S. Shaver, see, for example, Baldock and Cass, op. cit., Chs. 6 and 7; for Harris, see Harris, op. cit., 1989, 1990.

141. E.g., A. Graycar, ed., *Retreat from the Welfare State,* Sydney: Allen and

Unwin, 1983; A. Graycar and J. Jamrozik, *How Australians Live,* Melbourne: Mac-Millan, 1989.

142. See, e.g., C. Burton, *The Promise and the Price,* op. cit.

143. E.g., L. Foster and A. Seitz, "Legality and Illegality: The Issue of Non-Citizens in Australia," *ANZJS* 22, 3, November 1986, 446–61; L. Foster and D. Stockley, *Multiculturalism: The Changing Australian Paradigm,* Avon: Multilingual Matters, 1985.

144. R. Birrell, D. Hill, and J. Nevill, eds., *Populate and Perish? The Stresses of Population Growth in Australia,* Melbourne: Fontana, 1984; Population Issues Committee, National Population Council, *Population Issues and Australia's Future. A Discussion Paper,* Canberra: AGPS, 1991.

145. E.g., D. Chappell and P. Wilson, eds., *The Australian Criminal Justice System: The Mid-1980s,* Sydney: Butterworth, 1986.; P. R. Wilson, *Murder of the Innocents: Child-Killers and Their Victims,* Adelaide: Rigby, 1985.

146. E.g., T. Burke, *A Roof over Their Heads. Housing Issues and Families in Australia,* Melbourne: Australian Institute of Family Studies (AIFS), 1984; K. Lovering, *Cost of Children in Australia. Working Paper 8,* Melbourne: AIFS, 1984; P. McDonald, *The Economic Consequences of Marriage Breakdown in Australia,* Melbourne: AIFS, 1985; M. Harrison, "Child Support Assessment," *Family Matters* 21, 1988, 36–40; F. Maas, "Homeless Youth in Australia," *Family Matters* 21, 1988, 43–47.

147. P. Koopman-Boyden and C. Scott, op. cit.

148. E.g., K. Saville-Smith, "Women and the State," in Cox, op. cit., 193–210; Dowse, op. cit. See also Novitz, op. cit.; James and Saville-Smith, op. cit; Yeatman, op. cit.; Watson, op. cit.

149. In the Australian context the term "femocrat" has been used to describe a feminist working in the government bureaucracy. See L. Ryan, "Feminism and the Federal Bureaucracy 1972–1983," in Watson, op. cit., 71–84.

150. Austin, op. cit., 185; Spoonley, "The Development of Sociology in New Zealand," op. cit., 7.

151. Austin, op. cit., 184; Miles and Spoonley, op. cit.

152. Particularly noteworthy in this respect are the contributions by Diane Austin, Anne Edwards, Andrew Metcalfe, Rosemary Du Plessis Novitz, and David Pearson. See also, for an early attempt, C. V. Baldock, *Australia and Social Change Theory,* Sydney: Novak, 1978.

153. The author thanks Patricia Harris for her thoughts on this issue.

28

Contemporary Sociology in Bangladesh

Abul Hasnat Golam Quddus

INTRODUCTION

Soon after the occupation of India, the British colonial administrators re-alized that perpetuation of the rule would be difficult without knowing the people, the land, and the culture of the country. Although India was rich in philosophy, mythology, and literature, there was no systematic in-formation available about the social complexities of the country[1] for the newly arrived bureaucrats to set their administrative strategies. To solve this problem, the colonial authority decided to collect information of their own on the social, economic, and religious life of the people. This infor-mation was mostly collected by the administrators as part of their profes-sional duties; much of the data were finally organized and published in books and journal articles.[2] These books and articles are still considered valuable resources on the social history of India and Bengal.

Despite the importance of these books and articles in laying the foun-dation of sociology in the subcontinent, formal sociology did not come into existence until three universities were established—in Calcutta, Bom-bay, and Madras—immediately after the war of independence against the British in 1857. The importance of sociology as a supportive tool for the smooth functioning of the colonial administration was reflected in 1924 in a letter written by the education commissioner to the vice-chancellor of Dhaka University, in which he asked for the inclusion of sociology as an elective subject in the Indian civil service examination.[3] That was the time when political unrest heightened for the independence of India. Therefore, all evidence tends to support the claim that sociology arrived in the sub-continent as a nonacademic reactionary science. Despite its controversial role during the colonial period, sociology gradually and steadily made its way into the academic world of this subcontinent during the later part of the British rule.

INSTITUTIONALIZATION OF SOCIOLOGY IN BANGLADESH

The formal study of social science began in this subcontinent with the establishment of three universities in India.[4] Sociology was first introduced in the Economics Department of Calcutta University and then in the Philosophy Department of Dhaka University as a full course and a half course, respectively. It became a full course in the Political Science Department of Dhaka University in the early 1940s. It was one of fifteen courses for the honors degree in political science.[5]

Sociology as a recognized discipline was not formally instituted until 1957 at Dhaka University. Prior to that during the period 1940–1957, many articles and research papers of sociological importance were presented in conferences and professional seminars by well-known scholars of the subcontinent.[6] Their efforts contributed significantly to the awareness of the policy makers and thus the establishment of a separate Department of Sociology at Dhaka University.

The actual creation of the department began with the visit of the noted French anthropologist Claude Lévi-Strauss. Professor Lévi-Strauss came to Dhaka as a UNESCO consultant in 1950 to assess the position of social science studies in the country. He visited Chittagong Hill Tracts and was very impressed with this living human laboratory. He termed it a "vertible paradise" for social anthropologists.[7] He asked the government and intellectuals to give adequate attention to the promotion of social science in the country. His assessment showed that the possibilities for development of social science were good at Dhaka University.

On his return to Paris, he made arrangements to send three scholars in 1955 to Dhaka University for promoting teaching and research in social science. They were Den Hollander from the Netherlands, John Humlum from Denmark, and John S. Arid from the United States.[8] These UNESCO consultants were attached to the Department of Political Science at Dhaka University to teach sociology and other related courses and to conduct anthropological studies. Besides these teaching consultants, two other anthropologists were directly engaged in tribal studies in Chittagong Hill Tracts; they would occasionally return to Dhaka to present their findings to the students of social science.[9] On completion of the UNESCO assignment, Professor Hollander recommended the establishment of a separate Department of Sociology, but it was not accepted on the grounds that there would not be enough jobs for the sociology graduates. This attitude, however, quickly changed when sociology was included as an optional subject in the Central Superior Service Examination of Pakistan, the most prestigious administrative examination in the country.[10] The entry of sociology into the group of elite subjects raised its public and academic image in the country.

During the same time Professor Pierre Bessaignet of France became the new consultant with the specific assignment to help in the organization of a Department of Sociology, in the regrouping of social science departments in a separate Faculty, and in the promotion of whatever research seemed indispensable for their organization.[11] He was unsuccessful in regrouping the social science departments into a separate Faculty, but his efforts did give concrete shape to the Sociology Department. In the spring of 1957, the creation of the Sociology Department was formally approved; on the first of July 1957, the Department of Sociology was launched. Professor Pierre Bessaignet became the first head of the department. The department began with two full-time and two part-time teachers. The two full-time teachers were Professor Bessaignet and Dr. Margaret Elizabeth Shaw.[12] The two part-time teachers were Mr. Nazmul Karim and Dr. H. Zaidi. UNESCO continued its support to the department until 1967 by providing consultants from different parts of the world. All Bangladeshi teachers initially appointed in this department were from the discipline of political science. Most, however, later earned sociology degrees from different foreign universities.[13] In the early years, the department was staffed by people of different disciplines and national origins, such as anthropology (mostly European), sociology (all except Mr. Karim were foreigners), political science (mostly Bangladeshi), and social psychology (Dr. Zaidi). The impact of blending people from different disciplines and different national origins was reflected in the syllabus of the department. It was biased toward philosophy, history, and anthropology. In recent years these orientations have started to change with the recruitment of indigeneous and North American–trained graduates. However, the Dhaka University courses still reflect greater European more than North American influences.

Dhaka University's Sociology Department began with two courses: B.A. first-year honors and B.A. subsidiary.[14] Forty students were in the former and thirty in the latter. The first part of an M.A. was opened in the 1964–1965 academic year. Student enrollments grew significantly over the years. In the academic year 1982–1983, exactly twenty-five years after the establishment of the department, the total number of students in sociology was over 2,000. Today Dhaka University offers B.S.S. (Honours), M.S.S., M. Phil., and Ph.D. degrees in Sociology.

The birth process of sociology at Rajshahi University was different than at Dhaka University. It made its appearance in August 1964 as a full-fledged curriculum in a joint department with political science. Administratively, both disciplines were under one head; but academically they were independent of each other. Mr. Badruddin Omar was the head of the joint department. The first head of the independent Sociology Department of Rajshahi was Dr. Fazlur Rashid Khan, who assumed leadership on October 7, 1969. It started with an M.A. program; but later in 1970, B.A. honors along with subsidiary courses were included in the program. There are some differences in the contents of courses at Dhaka and Rajshahi universities, but very little difference regarding patterns and orientation of courses. The reason could be that the most of the early faculty members of Rajshahi University were graduates of Dhaka University. At present B.S.S., M.S.S., M. Phil., and Ph.D. degrees are offered in sociology at Rajshahi University. Besides the Sociology Department, there is an institute at Rajshahi University known as the Institute of Bangladesh Studies. It also offers M. Phil. and Ph.D. degrees in sociology in collaboration with the department. The institute, by now, has already awarded a few M. Phil. and Ph.D. degrees to Bangladeshis.[15]

At Chittagong University, sociology was first taught in 1968 as subsidiary papers by two full-time teachers attached to the Political Science Department. An independent Sociology Department came into existence in 1969. Initially an M.A. program was introduced, followed two years later by B.A. honors degree. Professor R. I. Chowdhury, then head of the Department of Political Science, remained the interim head of the department until Dr. Badrud Duza took over as department head in 1970. The orientation of Chittagong University in terms of selection of courses was different from that of the other two universities. It emphasized more contemporary courses than other universities, such as quantitative research, development (including courses on communication, social change, population, and rural development), and applied sociology. The total number of undergraduate and graduate students now majoring in sociology at Chittagong University is more than four hundred. The department offers B.S.S. (Honours), M.S.S., M. Phil., and Ph.D. degrees.[16]

Besides these general universities, Agricultural University at Mymensingh, Bangladesh University of Engineering and Technology in Dhaka, and Jagannath University College have full-fledged departments of sociology. Sociology in agricultural and engineering universities is taught as a partial fulfillment of the requirements of professional degrees. The Jagannath University College, however, offers honors and master's degrees in sociology. At present, many colleges under general universities and secondary education boards[17] offer two to three sociology courses. Specialized sociology courses are also offered at certain specialized institutes in Bangladesh, such as social forestry at the Institute of Forestry, sociology of public administration at the Civil Service Training Academy, sociology of management at the Bangladesh Management Development Centre, and so forth. In short, during the last thirty-three years sociology has grown much faster as an academic as well as applied discipline than many traditional subjects.

KEY CONTRIBUTORS TO THE FIELD

Professor A. K. Nazmul Karim is the founding father of sociology in Bangladesh. From a well-educated family, Professor Karim's untiring efforts not only helped to institutionalize sociology in the universities of the country but also made it a prestigious academic discipline in the Faculty of Social Science in all three general universities. He began his career as a sociologist before sociology was institutionalized in the country. As an undergraduate student he wrote articles of sociological importance such as "Muslim Aristocracy and Middle Class," "Religious Transformation and Marxism," and "Transformation of Culture."[18] In 1951 he became a lecturer at Dhaka University and taught a sociology course in the Political Science Department. In addition to his M.A. in political science from Dhaka University, Professor Karim earned a master's degree in sociology from Columbia University, New York, and a Ph.D. from London University. He has four books to his credit, two in Bengali and two in English.[19] He has also published as many as thirty Bengali and twenty-two English articles in local and international journals.[20] Notable works of Professor Karim are his two English books[21] and articles on Muslim beliefs, crime, family, and methodology.[22] One of his books addresses the impact of British rule on social change and social stratification in India, Pakistan, and Bangladesh. His most recent book addresses the social structure of Bangladesh. Although Professor Karim showed interest in many areas, his chosen area was social structure. He liberally used Marxist models in his analysis but remained conscious of not being a Marxist.

Professor Karim was the first Bengali full-time teacher in the department, the first head of the Department of Sociology, the first professor of sociology, and the first president of the Sociological Association of Bangladesh. He was directly involved in opening up sociology departments at Rajshahi and Chittagong universities. Despite his frail physical condition he provided continuous guidance to all three universities in developing courses, recruiting teachers, and promoting research activities until his death on November 18, 1982.

After Professor Karim, only a few names can be mentioned as second generation contributors to the field in Bangladesh. Professor Mohammad Afsaruddin, a student of Professor Karim, came to the field from political science. He showed interest in many areas of sociology, including social structure, juvenile delinquency, and social research. He published three books in these areas.[23] His most significant contribution was the publication of the first sociology journal in the country in 1983, the *Bangladesh*

Journal of Sociology. It has opened up a new opportunities for the sociologists who were unable to publish their works due to the absence of such a professional outlet in the country.

Professor M. Badrud Duza, a student of Professor Karim, is one of the pioneers in the field of social demography. He received his Ph.D. from Cornell University in the United States. He began his career as a teacher at Dhaka University and later became the first chairman of the Sociology Department at Chittagong University after it was separated from political science. Under his guidance, the Sociology Department at Chittagong University achieved a sound academic footing. Professor Duza deviated from the tradition of his predecessors. He introduced more development- and empirical research–oriented courses at Chittagong University than other universities in the country offered. He left Chittagong University in 1973 to accept an international assignment in New York. Since then he continued, until very recently, to work in many population program–related international agencies. Professor Duza has published a considerable number of research and theoretical articles in national and international journals. Professor Duza differs from most of the demographers of the country in that he combines both theoretical as well as practical experiences in analyzing the country's population problems. His book entitled *Cultural Consequences of Population Change in Bangladesh*[24] deals specifically with cultural factors affecting the fertility behaviors of couples in Bangladesh. His contributions in the field have made him known at home and abroad in the field of demography.

A relatively young but well-known sociologist in the country is Professor Anupam Sen of Chittagong University. Educated in Dhaka and Canada, he embraces a neo-Marxist analytical perspective. Professor Sen is the only sociologist of the country who has published a book through the prestigious publishing company, in this case Routledge and Kegan Paul of Great Britain.[25] The book, entitled *The State, Industrialization and Class Formations in India: A Neo-Marxist Perspective on Colonialism, Underdevelopment and Development,* provides a theoretical and empirical analysis of the modes of production, social classes, and the state of India. In addition to this major work, Professor Sen has contributed scores of articles to both English and Bengali journals. Recently he has published a book in the vernacular which contains some of his previously published articles.[26] Professor Sen is the present president of the Bangladesh Sociological Association.

Besides these four major sociologists, a number of others have contributed significantly to the field. Since it is not possible in this short chapter to include all who have contributed or who are contributing in different areas, I will refer to a few of the other relatively well known sociologists. Professor F. R. Khan, one of the early sociology graduates of Dhaka University, has written on social control, the family, social structure, and social stratification. Professor Anwarullah Chowdhury has done some work on social stratification and village communities. Professor Qadir, who died prematurely, did one of the most pioneering village studies in the country.[27] Professor Rangalal Sen of Dhaka University has done some work on social stratification and elites in Bangladesh.

Besides sociologists, a number of scholars from other disciplines have contributed to the enrichment of sociology in the country. These include Abdus Satter on the tribal cultures of Bangladesh, Ameerul Huq on the rural power structure, Aminul Islam on rural factionalism, Hafeez Zaidi on cultural change in rural Bangladesh, and A. F. A. Hossain on the impact of technological change.[28] These names, however, do not exhaust the list of contributors to the field. In fact, a significant number of foreigners as well have worked in this country, producing insightful books and articles.

CURRENT TRENDS IN THEORETICAL AND METHODOLOGICAL STUDIES

Current trends in theoretical and methodological studies are very difficult to assess since it would require complete enumeration of all works done in all areas of sociology. This is not possible because of limited time and resources and the poor preservation system of our libraries. Instead, we have examined all issues of sociology journals (which number only two), seminar and workshop proceedings in the field of sociology, and other social science journals of the last five years.[29] Therefore this assessment should be taken with some caution, although we expect it to show the general pattern of development of sociology in the country.

Theoretical studies are very few in Bangladesh. Only about 3 percent of the articles can be classified as theoretical (Table 28.1). These articles are mostly on the appropriateness or inappropriateness of Marxist or neo-Marxist paradigms for analyzing Bangladesh society. It may be mentioned that this is the only theoretical paradigm discussed in the journals of Bangladesh. However, the number of direct articles on the theory being too few, it is difficult to draw any conclusion about the theoretical preference of the majority of sociologists in the country. Despite the limited number of theoretical studies, the majority of research articles have used various theoretical paradigms. A little over one-third of the articles have used Marxist and neo-Marxist paradigms particularly in studying rural power structures. These are the only paradigms which have been explicitly mentioned by authors (Table 28.2). This is not the case for those who have used non-Marxist paradigms. They usually implicitly use the theoretical paradigm for their explanation. Since the use of non-Marxist paradigms is implicit, we have tried to identify the theoretical orientation from the analytical models and conceptual frameworks[30] used by the authors. It has been found that about one-fourth of the research articles belong to the

Table 28.1
Percentage Distribution of Subfields of Sociology as Reflected in Journals and Seminar/Workship Proceedings

	BJS* N=45	SR** N=30	OJ*** N=90	WSP**** N=41	Total N=206
Fields	26.7	20.0	36.7	19.5	28.6
Development/Social Change	20.0	16.7	27.8	9.8	20.9
Methodology	6.7	6.7	11.1	58.5	18.9
Demography	6.7	13.3	10.1	-	7.8
Marriage and the Family	13.3	-	2.2	2.4	4.4
Women*****	6.7	6.7	3.3	2.4	4.4
Social Stratification	2.2	20.0	2.2	-	4.4
General Theory	-	10.0	3.3	-	2.9
Social Thought	13.3	-	1.1	-	3.4
Others	4.4	6.7	2.2	7.3	4.4
Total	100.0	100.0	99.9	99.9	100.0

Source: *BJS = Bangladesh Journal of Sociology.*
**SR = *Sociological Review.*
***OJ = Other journals.
****WSP = Workshop and seminar proceedings.
*****A large number of studies are conducted in the country but are published elsewhere. Here we have mentioned only those which are published in sociological and social science journals to indicate the trend of sociological research.

structural-functional school (Table 28.2). The authors may not have consciously used this paradigm; rather, it may have been used simply because the paradigm appears most suitable to explain the phenomena under study. Other paradigms used by a few authors are symbolic interactionism and exchange theory. It is interesting to observe that over 30 percent of the articles cannot be classified under any theoretical paradigm. Most of these articles are descriptive in nature. Tables 28.1 and 28.2 indicate that as of today, the conscious use of theoretical paradigms in sociological studies is limited in Bangladesh.

Table 28.2
Percentage Distribution of Theoretical Paradigms Used in the Articles
of Different Journals and Seminar/Workshop Proceedings

Theoretical Framework	BJS N=45	SR N=30	OJ N=90	WSP N=41	Total N=206
Conflict: Marxist/ Neo-Marxist	11.1	33.3	35.6	9.8	24.8
Conflict: Non- Marxist	11.1	20.0	5.6	-	7.8
Structural-Functional School	26.7	30.0	21.1	19.5	23.3
Descriptive	8.9	3.3	6.7	14.6	8.3
Others	4.4	3.3	1.1	-	1.9
No Theoretical Paradigm	37.8	10.0	30.0	56.1	34.0
Total	100.0	99.9	100.0	100.0	100.0

Compared to theory, the advancement of methodological studies is more extensive in Bangladesh. Professor Bessaignet, the first chairman of the Sociology Department at Dhaka University, strongly felt the need for research in the field.[31] He took the initiative to edit the first book of research articles in 1960.[32] A landmark article by Professor Karim, which has had a profound effect upon the sociologists of the country regarding the appropriateness of method for studying Bangladesh society, was published in the same book.[33] Karim strongly advocated use of the anthropological method at the initial stage of the discipline and a gradual movement to other methods with the advancement of society.

The debate about appropriate methods actually began with this article, and it is still continuing. Although the debate is as old as the birth of sociology in this country, the studies on methodology are few. In fact, except for workshop and seminar proceedings, methodological studies are minimal in journals and books. However, including all sources the number of total articles focusing on methodological issues stands at the third position, about 19 percent. Of these articles, a significant number debate the appropriate methods for studying Bangladesh society. A few articles, however, have discussed the pains and pleasures of anthropological fieldwork, modification of techniques of survey methods to suit local needs, and criticisms of blindly following Western techniques of research.[34]

In Bangladesh, historical method dominates sociological studies (about 47 percent, Table 28.3). This could be because many of the early sociologists were not trained in survey and anthropological methods. Professor

their own works in book or report form rather than in journals. Therefore, the actual number of women's studies is much higher than the journal publications indicate. The vast majority of the women's studies describe the present subordinate status of women in the country. The latent objectives of these studies are to make people aware of the status of women and to influence public policies to improve their social standing. Both quantitative as well as qualitative methodologies are used in these studies. Theoretically, the conflict perspective predominates. Other areas which are gradually receiving attention of the sociologists of Bangladesh are marriage and the family, social stratification, and social thought.

All these discussions reveal some important facts about the state of sociology in Bangladesh. Theoretical studies not only are very underdeveloped but also receive low priority from the researchers. The most high priority research topic is social structure. This could be because it was the preferred area of most of the founding fathers of the discipline. The most debated area of sociology is methodology, but very little is actually done to improve or modify the existing methods to address the cultural environment of the country. Because of the availability of funds and the high priority placed by the government on demography, development, and social change, these areas receive preferential treatment from the sociologists. Quality of research, except in the areas of demography and social structure, is still at a very low level. However, in recent years it has been rapidly improving.

A new trend is observed in the field. More and more textbooks are written in the vernacular and published by the government and private publishing houses. The government is also encouraging individual sociologists to write books in the vernacular by providing financial support. Another positive aspect of sociology in the country is its growing importance in national planning. Sociologists are being consulted in planning and implementing development programs; this has generated employment opportunities for sociologists at higher-level positions in both private and governmental organizations.

NOTES

1. M. N. Srinivas and M. N. Panini, "The Development of Sociology and Social Anthropology in India," *Sociological Bulletin* 22(2), 1973: 215.

2. Francis Buchanan Hamilton, *A Geographical, Statistical and Historical Description of the District or Zilla of Dinajpur in the Province or Sobah of Bengal,* Calcutta Baptist Mission Press, 1833; W. W. Hunter, *A Statistical Account of Bengal,* Vol. II, District of Nadiya and Jassore, 1875; W. W. Hunter, *A Statistical Account of Bengal,* Vol. V, District of Dacca, Bakerganj, Faridpur, and Mymensingh, 1975; B. H. Baden-Powell, *The Land Systems of British India,* 3 Vols., Oxford, 1892; B. H. Baden-Powell, *The Indian Village Community,* London, 1896; W.

W. Hunter, *The Indian Mussalmans,* 3rd ed., London, 1876; W. W. Hunter, *Annals of Rural Bengal,* London: Smith, Elder, and Company, 1897; H. H. Risely, *The Tribes and Castes of Bengal,* 2 vols., Calcutta, 1891.

3. Minutes of the Academic Council of Dhaka University, 1924: 1–2.

4. Rangalal Sen, "Development of Sociology in Bangladesh," Mohammad Afsaruddin (ed.), in *A. K. Nazmul Karim Commemorative Volume,* Department of Sociology, Dhaka University, 1985: 127–63. (The book is written in Bengali. The title of the book is translated in English.)

5. Mohammad Afsaruddin, "Bangladesh," Yogesh Atal (ed.), in *Sociology and Social Anthropology in Asia and the Pacific,* Wiley Eastern Limited, Paris: UNESCO, 1985: 388–409.

6. Rangalal Sen, op: cit., 1984: 130–37.

7. Mohammad Afsaruddin, op. cit., 1985: 390.

8. Pierre Bessaignet, "Introduction," Pierre Bessaignet (ed.), in *Social Research in East Pakistan,* Asiatic Society of Pakistan, 1960: viii.

9. Rangalal Sen, op. cit., 1984: 136.

10. Mohammad Afsaruddin, op. cit., 1985: 391.

11. Pierre Bessaignet, op. cit., 1960: ii.

12. Rangalal Sen, op. cit., 1984: 137.

13. Dr. H. Zaidi was a non-Bengali who migrated from India.

14. All honors students must study two subjects other than their major area. These are called subsidiary subjects.

15. Rangalal Sen, op. cit., 1985: 143.

16. This information has been collected from different office documents and personal interviews with relevant persons by the author.

17. Secondary and higher secondary education in the country are controlled by boards. These boards are responsible for developing syllabi, sanctioning permission to open different courses, and conducting secondary and higher secondary examinations.

18. Mohammad Afsaruddin, op. cit., 1984: 11–14, 15–21, 39–44. These articles were in Bengali.

19. Professor Karim's Bengali books are: *Falgunkara,* Dhaka, Sesecur Book Corner, 1958; and *Samaj Bijnan Somikkhan,* Dhaka, Newroze Kitabistan, 1973. Professor Karim's English books are: *Changing Society in India, Pakistan and Bangladesh,* Dhaka, Newroze Kitabistan, 1976; and *The Dynamics of Bangladesh Society,* New Delhi, Vikas Publishing House Private Ltd., 1980.

20. Mohammad Afsaruddin, op. cit., 1984: 4–7.

21. Nazmul Karim, op. cit., 1976, 1980.

22. "Some Aspects of Popular Beliefs among Muslims of Bengal," *Eastern Anthropologists* 9(1), Lucknow, September–November 1955: 29–51. "Crime in East Pakistan since 1947," *International Review of Crime Policy,* No. 16, October 1960, New York. "The Methodology for a Sociology of East Pakistan," in *Social Research in East Pakistan,* ed. Pierre Bassaignet, The Asiatic Society of Pakistan, Dacca, 1960; "Changing Patterns of an East Pakistan Family," in *Women in New Asia,* ed. Barbara Ward, UNESCO, 1965.

23. Mohammad Afsaruddin: *The Rural Life in Bangladesh,* Nawroze Kitabistan, Dacca, 1979; *Juvenile Delinquency in East Pakistan,* Samakal Mudrayan, Dacca, 1965; *Sociology and Social Research in Pakistan,* Dhaka, The Pakistan Sociological

Association, 1967. Besides these, he has a few articles in different areas of sociology.

24. Badrud Duza, *Cultural Consequences of Population Change in Bangladesh,* Dhaka, Ali Publications, 77 Patuatuly, 1, 1977.

25. Anupam Sem, *The State, Industrialization and Class Formations in India: A Neo-Marxist Perspective on Colonialism, Underdevelopment and Development,* London: Routledge and Kegan Paul, 1982.

26. Anupam Sen, *Bangladesh: The State and Society: A Socio-Economic Study,* Dhaka: Sahitya Samabaya, 102/A Dinanath Sen Rd.,–1204, 1988. (The book is in Bengali.)

27. S. A. Qadir, *Village Dhaneswar: Three Generations of Man-Land Adjustment in an East Pakistan Village,* BARD, Comilla, 1960.

28. Abdus Sattar, *Tribal Culture in Bangladesh,* Dacca, Muktadhara, 1975; Ameerul Huq (ed.), *Exploitation of Rural Poor,* Comilla: BARD, 1976; Aminul Islam, *A Bangladesh Village, and Conflict and Cohesion,* Anthropological Study of Politics, Cambridge: Schenkman Publishing Company, 1974; S. M. Hafeez Zaidi, *The Village Culture in Transition,* Honolulu; East-West Center Press, 1970; A. F. A. Hossain, *Human Impact of Technological Change in Pakistan,* 2 vols., Oxford University Press, Pakistan, 1956.

29. The number of articles used in our analysis is not exhaustive. However, we believe these articles are enough to demonstrate the trend of theoretical and methodological studies in the country. Articles from the following journals, books, and proceedings of seminars and workshops have been reviewed for table presentation: *Bangladesh Journal of Sociology; Sociological Review; Asian Affairs; Chittagong University Studies; Dhaka University Studies; Rajshahi University Studies; Journal of Social Studies; Bangladesh Development Studies; Journal of the Institute of Bangladesh Studies; Village in Bangladesh,* ed. Hasnat Abdul Hye, 1985; *Sociology of Bangladesh: Problems and Prospects,* Proceedings of the workshop jointly organized by Bangladesh Sociology Association and Bangladesh Academy for Rural Development, May 1986; *Bangladesh: Society and Development,* Seminar proceedings of the Second National Conference of the Bangladesh Sociology Association, 8 and 9 November, Chittagong, 1985.

30. "Conceptual frameworks" refers to clusters of concepts but not theory or theories. This term is used by R. Hill and D. A. Hansan in "The Identification of Conceptual Frameworks Utilized in Family Study," *Marriage and Family Living* 22 (November) 1960: 299–311.

31. Pierre Bessaignet (ed.), *Tribesmen of the Chittagong Hill Tracts,* Asiatic Society of Pakistan, Publication No. 1, 1958.

32. Pierre Bessaignet (ed.), *Social Research in Bangladesh,* Asiatic Society of Pakistan, Publication No. 5, 1960.

33. A. K. M. Nazmul Karim, "The Methodology for a Sociology of East Pakistan," in *Social Research in East Pakistan,* ed. Pierre Bessaignet, Asiatic Society of Pakistan, Publication No. 5, 1960: 1–6.

34. Anwarullah Chowdhury (ed.), *Pains and Pleasures of Field Work,* Dhaka: National Institute of Local Government, 1985; Kamal Siddique, "The Pains and Pleasure of Field Research: A Personal Account," in Hasnat Abdul Hye (ed.), *Village Studies in Bangladesh,* Bangladesh Academy for Rural Development, 1985: 66–88; B. K. Jahangi, "An Evaluation of Rural Study Methodologies in Bangla-

desh," in Hasnat Abdul Hye (ed.), *Village Studies in Bangladesh,* Bangladesh Academy for Rural Development, 1985: 89–105; Abul Hasnat Golam Quddus, "Some Experience of Scale Construction for Illiterate or Near Illiterate Spouses Who Live Apart," *Chittagong University Studies,* Social Science Vol. 10, No. 1, June 1987: 149–53.

35. Professor Karim in his formal and informal discussions considered social structure as the core of all areas of sociology. Most of his students who contributed most to the field continued his tradition.

36. During the last two decades a group of professional women has taken the initiative to promote the cause of women. One of their approaches was to conduct and publish research on women to make people aware of their actual condition. Women for Women Research and Study Group took the lead in this regard, publishing a number of books and papers. One of those books is *Situation of Women in Bangladesh,* edited by Women for Women Research and Study Group, Dhaka, UNICEF.

29

The Development of Sociology in China

Ming Yan

The intent of this chapter is to delineate the development of sociology in China. Chinese sociology can be roughly divided into three parts, representing the three broad historical periods: sociology's introduction and institutionalization from the late nineteenth century to 1979, its suspension period between 1950 and 1978, and the reestablishment since 1979. Within each part, three dimensions of the subject are identified: the sociohistorical contexts in which sociology evolves; the institutional structure of sociology, including training, publications, research funding, activities of professional associations, and so forth; and the intellectual content, that is, sociological theories, research methods, and substantive areas. We will examine characteristics of each dimension in every phase of Chinese sociology.

SOCIOLOGY IN CHINA FROM THE LATE NINETEENTH CENTURY TO 1949

Introduction of Sociology from the West

The late nineteenth century and the beginning of the twentieth century witnessed the rise of sociology in China. This was closely related to the national crisis China faced then. For some two thousand years Chinese society was characterized by a dynastic political system, self-sufficient economy, and kin- and clan-oriented social relations. As one of the oldest civilizations with a rich cultural and historical tradition, China had developed sophisticated philosophy and literature, but not science in the modern sense. Due to the high achievements of Chinese civilization, this "middle kingdom" manifested a strong sense of cultural superiority and regarded foreign countries as barbarian tribes.

By the mid-nineteenth century when the West imposed full-fledged intrusion, China began to face unprecedented change and unparalleled crisis. To the Western world, this was the age of imperialism and colonialism; experiencing industrialization, the Western countries were eager to seek overseas markets and resources. The refusal of China to deal with non-Chinese on a basis of equality brought China into constant conflict with the West. From the Opium War with Britain in 1840 to the Sino-Japanese War of 1894, China was defeated many times in military conflict; so was its pride. As responses to the Western influence, a series of painstaking reforms were implemented to learn from the West—first Western weapons and technology, languages, and geography; then Western philosophy and social thought. At the end of the nineteenth century, China was ready to accept any prescription that might cure its disease of weakness, bringing wealth and power and promoting modernization.

It was under such an atmosphere of self-doubt and self-criticism that sociology was introduced into China. The dominant theme of national survival at that time may well explain why Herbert Spencer and his Social Darwinism prevailed in the country. In 1895, Herbert Spencer and his sociology were introduced by Yan Fu (1854–1921) in a political essay, "Yuan Qiang" (On Strength).[1] *Qunxue Yiyan,* a translation of Spencer's *Study of Sociology* by Yan Fu, came out in 1903. At that time, the ideas of other Western Social Darwinists, such as Thomas H. Huxley and Benjamin Kidd, and other Western social thinkers, such as Adam Smith, Montesquieu, and Mill, were all introduced into China. The message was clear: in order to achieve national strength and social progress, China ought to know the laws governing society discovered by Western social sciences. Group strength and survival of the race were emphasized by Chinese intellectuals, and the methodological individualism embedded in Social Darwinism was simply ignored then.

It is noted that at the turn of the twentieth century, besides Yan Fu's translation of Spencer, almost all the sociological texts that appeared were translations from Japanese by those who had studied in Japan. Some were direct Japanese translations of American sociological works, such as Franklin H. Giddings's *Theory of Socialization;* others were Japanese compilations of Western sociology. The Chinese term for sociology, *shehuixue,* came from the Japanese word, *shakaigaku.* This was due to the wave of Chinese studying in Japan around the turn of the twentieth century.

The forerunners of sociology in China, mainly the scholar-reformers, held strong political positions. They regarded sociology as one of the possible solutions to the national crisis, rather than as a specialized academic field. Therefore, thorough study of society as well as systematic social research would not emerge until the new generation of professional sociologists arrived.

Institutionalization of Sociology in China

Sporadic teaching of sociology in Chinese higher education appeared in the first two decades of this century. But not until a cohort of professional sociologists emerged and chairs or departments of sociology were created could we say that the subject was institutionalized. The first generation of Chinese sociologists were all Western-trained; the majority of them received their Ph.D.s or M.A.s from American universities (this was common to other fields as well); they returned to China by the 1920s and held chairs of sociology in the newly established institutions of Chinese higher education. They included Zhu Yuyu, Tao Menghe, Yu Tianxiu, Sun Benwen, Chen Da, Xu Shilian, Li Jinghan, Yang Kaidao, Wu Wenzao, and Wu Jingchao.

While Chinese sociologists were trained in the West, chairs and even full-fledged departments of sociology were established in missionary colleges and universities in China. As early as 1914, the founding of a sociology department at the Shanghai Baptist College was claimed by Daniel Kulp II, an American missionary who taught there.[2] Just as in the Western countries at that time, the terms "social science" and "sociology" were used interchangeably. In some cases, sociology departments could be as small as just one faculty member offering a couple of general courses in sociology. The level of academic standards was gradually enhanced. By 1947, sociology departments had been established in twenty-one universities out of forty-nine. All these departments offered undergraduate courses in sociology. After the 1930s, graduate programs in sociology were established in several universities such as Yanjing, National Zhongshan, and National Qinghua. Since none of them offered Ph.D. degrees, Chinese students went abroad for advanced study.

At first, sociological instruction was given by American missionaries. They were then joined by Chinese who had done graduate work or traveled abroad; foreign scholars presented on a short-term basis, such as the eminent Robert E. Park and Alfred R. Radcliffe-Brown. After retiring from the University of Chicago, Park went to teach at Yanjing University in Beijing, China, in the fall of 1932 for one semester. The anthropologist Radcliffe-Brown also went to China and taught one semester in 1935. In the teaching of sociological courses, textbooks by British authors and translations of Japanese texts were sometimes used. Yet American textbooks predominated. Authors such as F. W. Blackmar, E. S. Bogardus, C. M. Case, F. S. Chapin, J. Q. Dealey, C. A. Ellwood, F. H. Giddings, E. C. Hayes, and W. I. Thomas were very popular. Heavy reliance on imported texts seemed unavoidable when the teaching subject itself was imported, but this did bring problems of unfamiliar concepts, language, and values.

In China prior to 1949, universities served as both training and research centers in which scholars were mainly employed to teach and to do research. The few research institutes took the form of (1) university-affiliated research institutes, such as the Institute of Census Research of National Qinghua University, which existed between 1939 and 1946; or (2) institutes sponsored by American religious organizations, such as the Institute of Social Research in Peking, in the late 1920s; or (3) government-sponsored bodies, such as the section of sociology in the Institute of Social Science of the Academia Sinica, which concentrated on studying rural economy.

As early as 1921, the Chinese Sociological Society was founded by Yu Tianxiu (Ph.D., Clark, 1920); and the Society's quarterly *Journal of Sociology* was published in the following year. As the first professional organization of sociology in China, this society seemed to be ahead of the times because few scholars in China had an interest in the subject and few sociologists existed to serve as a support group for it. The second attempt at establishing the Chinese Sociological Society in 1930 by Sun Benwen, Chen Da, and others turned out to be much more successful. From 1930 to 1948, the Society held nine annual meetings. Themes of these meetings included Chinese population problems (1930), the family (1932), and social reconstruction after the war (1943). The membership of the Society grew from 66 in the first year to 132 in 1943, and it increased to 160 by 1947.

The Nature of Sociological Inquiry

Sociological training in China was closely related to foreign sources. Therefore, it seems unavoidable that sociological inquiry in the country took the form of a "shadow science," merely reflecting the tides of the Western mainstream.

Ways to keep up with Western scholarship are many. The most common one was through the reading and translation of Western works. Among all the translated foreign works, a significant portion represents the works of well-known Western scholars such as H. Spencer, F. Giddings, E. Durkheim, C. Ellwood, W. F. Ogburn, B. Malinowski, M. Weber, L. T. Hobhouse, P. A. Sorokin, G. LeBon, W. McDougall, R. H. Lowie, K. Mannheim, and T. Abel. Even in their own writings, Chinese sociologists could not escape the "magic" of foreign influence. A close examination of the sociological publications before 1949 shows that many books written by Chinese scholars were simply compilations of foreign texts. This is especially evident in the works of those who were identified as theorists. Sun Benwen (1894–1979) is illustrative. Sun received his Ph.D. in the United States in 1925, and he was several times the chairman of the Chinese Sociological Society and editor of the *Journal of Sociology.* He had also been the director of the Higher Education Department of the Ministry of Education in China. As the most prolific writer, Sun published fifteen monographs and four translated books. His solid and well-knit writings won him tremendous respect among colleagues, and he was regarded as one of the foremost social theorists in China. However, in almost all his works he analyzed and tried to synthesize various schools of Western sociology; he stressed W. F. Ogburn and W. I. Thomas, who profoundly influenced him. Apart from his well-versed discussion of Western social theories, he formulated no original conception or appreciable independent theory.

The influence of Western sociology on the Chinese sociological community was nothing unusual. Chinese sociologists, trained by teachers from a variety of cultural backgrounds and ideological stances, inevitably introduced into their classrooms the vocabulary of their mentors and colleagues. It seemed that from the earlier evolutionism to the British functionalism, every Western school could find its representatives in China. This strong Western influence, however, faced challenge by some scholars:

The various schools of Western sociology were each introduced into China by its followers. That which made Chinese sociology less than identical with Western sociology lay in its relationship to the real society. Whatever the particular one, the various schools of Western sociology each reflected a portion of social phenomenon, but when they were brought into China, they became empty theories divorced from social reality.[3]

Fei Xiaotong's viewpoints reflected two underlying antagonisms within the sociological enterprise in China: one was the confrontation of Western sociology with the national and intellectual identity of the country; the other was the conflict between theoretical conceptualization and empirical research there. Thus, there did exist a force within Chinese sociology prior to 1949, yearning for the building of a "sinicized" sociology; this tendency was mainly embedded in the empirical studies of Chinese society based on firsthand collection of data.

Earlier empirical researches were mostly conducted by missionary teachers and their students for the purpose of social melioration, for example, *Peking: A Social Survey* by Sidney Gambles and John Burgess (1921). In the late 1920s and early 1930s, many social surveys came out as byproducts of the Rural Reconstruction Movement, a large-scale reform by intellectuals to solve the crisis of the rural areas caused by industrialization and urbanization. General social surveys were conducted, such as *Ching-ho: A Sociological Analysis* (1930), written by sociology professors and students at Yanjing University, and Li Jinghan's *Survey of Ding County* (1933). The Sino-Japanese War (1937–1945) served as a turning point for the country as well as for sociological inquiry. As Japan occupied the coastal cities, government agencies and schools moved to the hinterland. Scholars who had previously spent their lives with no contact with the common people were sent to dilapidated temples and peasant huts. The loss of books and the unavailability of foreign periodicals made it difficult to keep up with Western ideas. Above all, with the national crisis and the seriousness of real problems, they had no choice but to confront reality and try to resolve the problems of actual people's lives. Among all the works published during this period, at least two scholars won international recognition. One was Chen Da, whose *Population in Modern China* (Chicago, 1946) was based on regional censuses. The other was Fei Xiaotong, who undertook community studies from a functionalist perspective, which was the prevailing method applied in Chinese sociology in those days.

Fei Xiaotong (1910–) studied with Malinowski and received his Ph.D. in social anthropology at the London School of Economics in Britain in 1938. He seemed satisfied with neither pure scholarship nor the strong foreign influence on Chinese sociology.[4] He complained that sociology students in China were more familiar with crime and Russian immigration in Chicago than with the daily life of ordinary people in Peking. Devoting himself to field research, he studied the peasant life in south China and published *Peasant Life in China: A Field Study of Country Life in the Yangtze Valley* (London: Routledge & Kegan Paul, 1939). Malinowski praised this work as "a landmark in the development of anthropological field-work theory" because Fei had applied the functionalist approach to the study of contemporary Chinese society.[5] Continuing with more extensive studies, Fei moved on to the second stage of a more ambitious work, *Xiangtu Zhongguo* (Earthbound China, 1947), in which he applied the method of ideal type to the conceptualization of unique Chinese culture as well as social structure.

Compared with the Western orientation, the sinicization process within Chinese sociology seemed a more promising one. It might have become the dominant force had there been no Communist Revolution, or had there been no Marxism. Marxism, along with other Western social thoughts, was introduced into China at the beginning of the twentieth century as a possible solution to China's problems. Marxism became popular in China after the 1917 revolution in Russia; it became the ideology of the Chinese Communist Party (CCP) for political struggle after the founding of the CCP in July 1921.

Most sociologists in China, like their counterparts in many other countries, believed in reformism and scientism rather than radical revolution, and were politically inert. Sociologists in general did not accept Marxism as "orthodox" sociology. At that time Chinese sociologists were afraid of being identified with Marxism or socialism, because the latter was officially forbidden. The fact that the two terms "sociology" (*shehuixue*) and "socialism" (*shehui zhuyi*) are similar in the Chinese language made the situation more complicated. To clarify the "misunderstanding" of sociology and socialism, sociologists claimed that the former was a science but the latter an ideology. The line between the two, however, was not that clear. On one hand, a few Western-trained sociologists became Marxists, for example, Xu Deheng. Xu Deheng studied sociology at the University of Paris in the 1920s. He published the translation of Durkheim's *Rules of Sociological Method* in 1925 but later regretted it after he became a Communist.[6]

On the other hand, a sociology department was established at Shanghai University, which was strongly influenced by the Chinese Communist Party, in 1923. Compared with departments of sociology at other universities, this one had a distinctive historical-philosophical orientation. Courses such as Social Philosophy, History of Social Evolution, History of Social Thought, and History of Social Movement were emphasized. Qu Qiubai, one of the earlier leaders of the CCP, was chairman of the department. Li Da, a Marxist social scientist, taught there. Li later published *New Sociology* (1926) and *An Outline of Sociology* (1935). An examination of their works shows that both acknowledged Western sociology in their earlier works and later solely discussed historical materialism. Neither academic sociologists nor Marxists expected that Marxism would decisively change the fate of sociology some years later.

SOCIOLOGY IN CHINA UNDER THE COMMUNIST REGIME

The Chinese Communist Party took power in China in 1949. This opened an entirely new chapter for Chinese society as well as for the discipline of sociology there. Fundamental social transition took place which included the leadership of the CCP, central-planned economy, and Marxism as the official ideology. Meanwhile, through a series of reforms China's system of higher education underwent some basic changes. Institutions of higher education supported by foreign missionaries had to be eliminated. The Chinese attempted to duplicate the Soviet system by eliminating most of the comprehensive universities; schools were reorganized, and the training of high-level technical personnel became the priority. It was in such a context that the status of sociology was seriously questioned.

Chinese sociologists anxiously defended the discipline by stressing its usefulness to socialist construction. They stressed that Chinese sociologists in the past had always emphasized field research and had accumulated rich materials, systematic methods, and experience, which could be critically inherited. Furthermore, Chinese sociologists acknowledged Marxism and Leninism as the foundation of and guideline for social sciences through rigorous "thought reform" and reading of Marxist works. All these efforts worked to no effect. After the Higher Education Reform in 1952, disciplines of long tradition such as philosophy, history, and literature were retained; departments of economics concentrated on political economy and national economic planning; departments of Marxism-Leninism studies were established. The nightmare of sociologists finally came true: all sociology departments were closed. Former sociologists were transferred to other jobs, academic as well as nonacademic. Some taught or did research on labor economy, national minorities, or statistics; others took unrelated jobs as librarians and the like.

Now we can summarize the reasons for the abolishment of sociology. On one hand, this was brought about by a combination of domestic and international factors. In the international realm, China's break with the Western world caused the Chinese government to adopt a hostile attitude toward Western culture, including its social sciences. Also, China desired to follow the Soviet model, especially in the area of higher education. Since Soviet universities had halted sociological studies, China decided it did not need them either. This seems simplistic at first glance. The spread of the Soviet model, nevertheless, stemmed from (1) the influence achieved by the Soviet Union as a result of the Sino-Soviet Treaty of February 1950 and the accompanying series of agreements providing for Soviet economic aid; as well as (2) its historical role as the pioneer of socialist planned development. Thus, under the supervision of Soviet experts, China followed the Soviet model in every aspect of social construction as well as daily life. By the time the Soviet sociology was restored in the late 1950s, China had broken its relationship with the Soviet Union— which was, in some sense, a tragedy for Chinese sociology.

In the domestic realm, China stressed the development of heavy industry and basic sciences, generally ignoring the humanities and social sciences. Development of the humanities and social sciences was further hindered when strong ideological and political control by the state was imposed upon academia. Since Marxism had achieved the status of official ideology, historical materialism, the "true" science of the proletariat, should replace sociology, the bourgeois "pseudoscience." In fact, Marxist studies, comprised of historical and dialectical materialism, political economy, and scientific socialism, were substituted for studies of all social sciences and philosophy in China at that time. Finally, the new leadership regarded Chinese socialist society as something of a flawless white jade, untouched by the sorts of social problems sociology purported to address.

While some of these sociohistorical factors have been identified and discussed in previous studies, no one has yet mentioned internal factors that contributed to the abolition of Chinese sociology. By this we mean the characteristics of the intellectual content of sociology that distinguish it from all other fields, that is, natural sciences, other social sciences, or humanities. Three such factors seem to be highly relevant. First, sociology is frequently criticized by nonprofessionals for its almost limitless subject matter and vague boundaries. In some outsiders' eyes, sociology does not deserve to be treated as a specialized subject. Second, the nature of sociological inquiry—its value orientation—makes it much more vulnerable than other fields to political and ideological control. Compared to professionals in other fields, sociologists in most societies, regardless of the political systems, tend to include more political deviants and adversaries who are critical of the status quo.[7] Third, prior to 1949, Chinese sociology had experienced systematic institutionalization in academic settings but had not achieved intellectual maturity or autonomy, that is, independent theorizing and methods. Sociology's lack of rootedness in Chinese intellectual soil provided flank support for its abolition under the communist regime.

From 1952 to 1979, criticisms of the "bourgeois" sociology appeared here and there in journal articles and books. Some social investigations continued to be made, for example, in the area of national minority studies. By and large, however, true sociological inquiry had ceased to exist, sociologists were summarily reviled, and sociology as a discipline was abolished.

Only for a few months in 1957 was there a somewhat relaxed atmosphere, ushered in by the policy of "Let A Hundred Flowers Blossom and A Hundred Schools of Thought Contend," set forth by Mao for promoting the progress of the arts and the sciences and the development of a flourishing socialist culture. Free expressions were encouraged, and criticisms of the Party were welcomed. At first intellectuals hesitated, but soon they freed their minds of apprehensions. Some former sociologists felt that the opportunity had finally arrived for them to express their viewpoints on the status of sociology. They were further encouraged by the news that the Soviet Union and several East European countries had sent delegates to the 3rd World Congress of Sociology of the International Sociological Association held in Amsterdam. From January to June 1957, a series of discussion meetings was held by some former leading sociologists, and proposals were made to restore sociology. They discussed theoretical schools of sociology and their recent development in the capitalist states; they also claimed that social problems under socialism constituted a subject for sociological research. Their institutional plans included the founding of a research institute of sociology at the Chinese Academy of Sciences, establishing sociology departments at certain universities, and organizing the Chinese Sociological Association.[8]

Meanwhile, social research was partially resumed. Chen Da came forward with a comprehensive plan for research on population problems; he started to prepare a paper, "New China's Population Census of 1953 and Its Relations to National Reconstruction and Demographic Research," for the Thirtieth Session of the International Statistical Institute to be held in

July 1957. Li Jinghan did a re-study of current conditions in the suburbs of Beijing, which he had first investigated and written on twenty years before, attempting to assess social changes in the Chinese villages brought about by the Revolution.

But in July 1957, the wind direction all of a sudden changed and a large-scale "Anti-Rightist Movement" was launched by the Communist Party. Almost all the former sociologists who were involved in restoring the discipline were branded antiparty "rightists." These "rightists" were attacked not only for trying to restore bourgeois sociology but also for having a grand political design of overthrowing the Communist Party, Marxism, and socialism. From then on, sociology teaching and research remained a "forbidden area" until some twenty-seven years later.

REESTABLISHMENT OF SOCIOLOGY IN CHINA

The new era in contemporary China began in the late 1970s after Mao's death and the end of the Cultural Revolution. The Third Plenum of the Eleventh Central Committee of the CCP was held in December 1978 when Deng Xiaoping took power and implemented economic reform and open-door policies. The CCP has now made the transition from a revolutionary party to a ruling party. The new leadership has shifted emphasis from political struggle to economic modernization, from Marxist orthodoxy to a pragmatic way of thinking; an open-door policy has been implemented to introduce Western advanced technology. As general political and economic changes take place, policies regarding intellectuals change as well. It is now admitted that in 1957, although a few rightists took advantage of the "Hundred Flowers" policy, attacked the Party and socialism, and had to be opposed, most were branded rightists erroneously; this had an unfortunate inhibiting effect on the careers and lives of intellectuals, as well as on the development of the country. Academic activities, standards, and reward systems in universities and research institutes have been resumed. As part of the open-door policy and new educational system, thousands of students or scholars have been sent to study abroad. This historical moment also marked the reestablishment of Chinese sociology.

Instead of fighting for it this time, the handful of surviving sociologists were called up to revive the discipline. Fei Xiaotong was invited by the Planning and Liaison Bureau of the newly established Chinese Academy of Social Sciences to convene meetings of the former sociologists. Four such discussion meetings were held before the formal gathering in March 1979.[9] When they were called to discuss the possibility of re-studying the subject, these scholars, who had experienced tremendous vicissitudes of life, still had their hearts fluttering with fear. Yuan Fang, a student of Chen Da in the 1940s and chairman of the Department of Sociology at Beijing University in the 1980s, had been rehabilitated from the label "rightist" not long before. Despite the invitation he received, Yuan could not show up because none of his family members liked the idea of his going back to study sociology. "Don't get into trouble again," they told him. Another scholar did attend the meetings but claimed that he would not participate in the discussions; if he had to, he would speak after everyone else did.[10]

As we examine the discussions of these sociologists on the status of sociology, it is striking how similar the arguments are to those of the 1950–1952 efforts and the 1957 campaign:

1. Sociology in China should be transformed and not abolished, since there were progressive as well as useful elements.

2. Marxism is the guideline and basis of sociological inquiry.

3. Social problems arise in socialist construction (e.g., population, family, crime, labor, national minorities, and urban and rural development) and are the subject matter of sociological research.

4. The findings of sociological research can be used in the decision-making process of the government.

5. Attitudes toward Western sociology should reflect "critical absorption"; not all of Western sociology is ideologically problematic and its research methods useful.

Therefore, it is the change of the larger sociohistorical environment that has made the restoration of sociology possible. In March 1979, the formal discussion meeting on sociology was held. Hu Qiaomu, then president of the Chinese Academy of Social Sciences and a member of the Secretariat of the Central Committee of the CCP, was invited to deliver a speech, which symbolized the support of the CCP. At the meeting, the Chinese Sociological Research Association (subsequently renamed the Chinese Sociological Association) was founded, and Fei Xiaotong was appointed the president.

Re-institutionalization

After its revival, the first step for Chinese sociology was to train professional sociologists to teach and conduct research. Among the first-generation sociologists, some had passed away (e.g., Chen Da and Sun Benwen); others were too aged to take active roles in the reestablishment of sociology. They simply served as advisers (e.g., Wu Wenzao, Li Jinghan, and Wu Zelin).

With the joint efforts of Chinese sociologists of the older generation, sociology professors from foreign countries (mostly the United States), and overseas sociologists of Chinese descent, short-term programs and regular departments of sociology have been set up. Short-term programs ran in the early 1980s to rapidly train teachers and researchers to fill the urgent demand. In April 1980, the first sociology department was established in the Branch School of Fudan University (later known as Shanghai University). Since then some twelve universities have successively established sociology departments that have undergraduate programs in sociology. Among them nine offer master's degrees, and there is one doctoral program at Beijing University. There are two universities offering non-degree graduate training in sociology.[11] In addition, the first sociology textbook since 1979, *Shehuixue gailun* (Introduction to Sociology), was published in 1984.

The Chinese academic community after 1949, taking the Soviet model, has two separate systems: higher education and research institutions. Higher education is mainly responsible for training, but there are two university-affiliated research institutes of sociology: the Institute of Sociology at the People's University, and the Research Center of Chinese Society and Development at Beijing University. Research institutions concentrate on developing research, although some offer graduate training as well.

Among the academic research institutions, the leader is the Institute of Sociology at the Chinese Academy of Social Sciences. Founded in January 1980, the institute now has over seventy researchers who work in six sections: (1) sociological theory, (2) sociology of science and development, (3) rural sociology, (4) social psychology, (5) lifestyles, and marriage and the family, and (6) youth and adolescence. The researchers at the institute can work on topics that they are personally interested in; they are also involved in national planning projects, from which the main fundings come. In regional academies of social sciences, by 1989 twenty-seven out of thirty provinces (or municipalities, or autonomous regions) have either sociology institutes (nineteen) or sociology sections (eight) within other institutes. Altogether, some four hundred scholars conduct sociological research in these institutes.[12] It is noted that the research projects proposed are based on individual scholars' specialties and interests; they are also determined by the geographic features of the institutions. For instance, Yunnan Institute and the Inner Mongolia Institute orient themselves in studies of national minorities and frontier issues. The Institute of Sociology at Sichuan, a major agricultural province, concentrates on rural sociology. Outside academia, sociologists are employed in government agencies. Research projects are usually funded by all levels of government agencies.

The Chinese Sociological Association (CSA), founded in March 1979, is the foremost professional organization of sociology in the country. The official aims of the association are to unite sociologists, to follow the instruction of Marxism and Maoist thought, to hold to the principle of integrating theory with practice, to work hard to establish Marxist sociology, and to serve socialist construction. In spite of its ambitious goals, this organization does not seem to have much of a practical function. It is the provincial sociological associations (twenty-one out of thirty provinces have them) that organize the majority of academic activities. There are also branch organizations specializing in subfields of sociology, such as marriage and the family, sociology of lifestyle, and juvenile delinquency.

At present there are over ten professional journals of sociology that publish empirical studies and theoretical articles. *Shehui* (Society), published by the Sociology Department of Shanghai University in 1981, was the first sociological journal to appear in China after 1979. Today it has a more popular appeal than scholarly. *Shehuixue Yanjiu* (Sociological Studies), a bimonthly published by the Institute of Sociology at the Chinese Academy of Social Sciences, is currently the foremost academic journal of sociology in China. Other journals, such as *Shehuixue yu Shehui Diaocha* (Sociology and Social Research), *Shehuixue Tansuo* (Sociological Exploration), and *Shehuixue yu Xiandaihua* (Sociology and Modernization), tend to focus on applied studies. *Guowai Shehuixue* (Sociology in Foreign Countries) features translations and evaluations of sociological inquiry in the West, the former Soviet Union, and Eastern Europe, as well as in Third World countries.

At least two points can be made when we compare the institutional aspect of the reborn Chinese sociology since 1979 and that of the "old" sociology prior to 1949. First, the new Chinese sociology has rapidly advanced and operates on a much larger scale than the old one, as is shown in its vast number of scientists, numerous research areas, and large body of publications. Second, the organization of the reborn sociology is under government control. Since all the universities and colleges are government-sponsored, academic institutions are manipulated by the government through the control of their personnel and funding.

The Chinese Dilemmas

In examining the intellectual content of sociology in China since 1979, we are most interested in questions such as the following: What are the characteristics of Chinese sociology in terms of theories, methods, and substantive areas? Has Chinese sociology evolved into an enterprise with a high degree of autonomy? It seems that the new sociology could be generally characterized as a "Marxist sociology serving the socialist construction in China," as stated in many Chinese sociological publications. But we may examine its relationships with its own sociological tradition, with Western sociology, with Marxism, as well as with contemporary Chinese politics.

After 1979, most sociologists of the older generation either were deceased or were too old to play active roles in research, yet their early works were published or reprinted: for example, Chen Da's *Population*

Problems in Modern China ([1946], 1981), Li Jinghan's *Survey of Ding County* ([1933], 1986), Pan Guangdan's *The Principle of Eugenics* (1981), and Fei Xiaotong's *Reproductive Institution* (1981). What has been inherited from the old sociology is the applied tradition—specifically, the method of community studies that prevailed before 1949. This has been mainly applied by Fei Xiaotong in his small-town studies, which were listed as one of the three "key research projects" during the Sixth Five-Year National Plan Period (1981–1985) (the other two were studies on marriage and the family, and urban population problems). Fei has advocated the development of small towns rather than big cities, which have already encountered the problem of overpopulation, as the unique pattern of urbanization in China. His viewpoint has been the overwhelmingly dominant one, partly because of his prestige as the leading scholar in the discipline and partly because his keen insights have netted him substantial government support.

However, the new generation of Chinese sociologists do not necessarily resort to studies conducted several decades ago as the models or basis for their own research. In fact, most sociologists prefer to call the new sociology a *chongjian* (reestablished) sociology rather than a *huifu* (revived) one, which indicates their intention of breaking away from the "old sociology." They are especially resistant to the strong Western or American orientation of the old Chinese sociology. Instead, they carry forward the tendency toward sinicization and have as a major concern the study of Chinese society. This, on one hand, reflects forty years of largely independent development of China; on the other hand, it is related to the composition of the new generation of Chinese sociologists. Today's sociologists who form the backbone of teaching and research in China are almost all Chinese and were trained in China after 1979. Although foreign sociology professors have been invited to teach in China, they are usually present on a short-term basis. Those who have gone abroad to receive sociological training in the 1980s will not be able to make their mark upon Chinese sociology in the very near future.

Though breaking away from the shadow of Western sociology, sociologists in China since 1979 have had extensive academic exchange with sociologists in other countries. Hundreds of Chinese have gone abroad—for example, to the United States, Japan, the former Soviet Union, Eastern and Western Europe—to study sociology; a Chinese delegation attended the 80th annual meeting of the American Sociological Association in Chicago in 1985; a group of Chinese sociologists went to Rome, Italy, to attend the Conference of the International Institute of Sociology in 1989;[13] collaborative studies have been carried out in the areas of population studies, marriage and the family, and so forth; and foreign works, that is, articles and books, have been translated into Chinese.

Between 1979 and 1989, translated articles accounted for 34 percent of the total number of articles published.[14] From 1979 to 1990, there were 133 translations out of a total of 415 published sociological books (i.e., 32 percent), among which translations of American works account for 41 percent (54 books), the highest.[15] Translated Soviet works comprise 27 percent (36 books) of the total translation, the second highest. One reason for this is that in the 1950s, a great number of Chinese scholars studied Russian or went to the Soviet Union to study. Now they take advantage of their knowledge of the language to do translations. Western classical as well as popular works of sociology that have been translated into Chinese include Emile Durkheim's *On Suicide* (1988), Robert K. Merton's *Science, Technology and Society in Seventeenth-Century England* (1986), Max Weber's *Protestant Ethics and the Spirit of Capitalism* (1986), Talcott Parsons's *The Structure of Social Action,* C. Wright Mills's *White Collar: American Middle Class* (1987), Alex Inkeles's *What Is Sociology? An Introduction to the Discipline and Profession* (1981), and Earl Babbie's *The Practice of Social Research* (1988).

Compared with their counterparts before 1949, however, Chinese sociologists do not thoroughly and intensively study foreign texts. None of the Chinese sociologists claim that they belong to any of the Western schools of sociology. Instead, the introduction of methods and techniques, especially survey research, arouses more enthusiasm than the absorption of foreign theory. Survey research and computer programs are widely applied to empirical studies, although the statistical techniques utilized are rather preliminary. Other methods (e.g., experimentation, participant observation) have so far not been explicitly applied in research. In addition, the long-standing methodological debate between positivism and humanism in Western sociology does not seem to have caught the attention of Chinese sociologists. Sociologists in China either ignore the issue or claim to follow Marxist dialectical materialism.

Since 1979, the relationship between Marxism and sociology has been a major topic of discussion, and it still perplexes Chinese sociologists. After years of "education," most sociologists do not see the building of a Marxist sociology in China as a perfunctory genuflection in the direction of the CCP. They genuinely accept Marxism as a part of the sociological framework. Marxism, or historical materialism and sociology, for the first time in China are not regarded as diametrically opposing each other. Rather, it is now generally held that Marxist historical materialism and sociology, both taking society as the subject of study, cannot substitute for one another. Historical materialism, dealing with the fundamental law and general pattern of society, serves as the basis of, and the guideline for, sociology; sociology, as an academic discipline, offers supporting evidence to replenish or expand Marxism through empirical research on concrete social phenomena. Yet the problem remains unsolved as to how to establish this "Marxist sociology" in China. Furthermore, some deviation from the doctrine of Marxism finds its expression in the popularity of Max Weber in the circle of the Chinese sociological community. Weber's theory of stratification, combined with Marx's notion of class, is applied in the study of Chinese social structure;[16] Weber's emphasis on cultural factors in social change, in addition to Marxist economic determinism, is also recognized.[17]

This has a lot to do with the general view of Marxism in China. The typical viewpoint is that Marxism itself is not wrong; it was we who had misunderstandings about Marxism. Marxism demands always to develop with the times, that is, with the new experiences of man's practice. Socialism is bound to have various models in the course of its development in different countries with different historical, economic, political, and cultural backgrounds. We should build a "socialism with Chinese characteristics," which allows playing to market forces but retains predominantly public ownership. The Chinese have to make a new assessment of capitalism because capitalism today is not the same as it was during the days of Marx, Engels, or even Lenin.

Studying social problems and not catering purely to academic purposes have been a tradition of Chinese sociology. In the 1950s, sociologists in China defended the discipline by stressing its utility. Since 1979, Chinese sociologists have been doing research in such areas as population, housing, marriage and the family, and delinquency. For the past ten years, articles published on social problems account for 44 percent of all sociological publications, the highest of all categories. In doing so, Chinese sociologists are not only addressing key issues with the hope of resolving them; they are, in essence, legitimizing the very discipline they had struggled with for so long.

The studies of sociologists on social problems also arouse the interests of government. The government increasingly relies on academic diagnoses and practical recommendations made by sociologists to policy making, implementation, and feedback. One such instance is the "Survey of One Thousand Households" in Tianjin, the second-largest city in China. This has been conducted once a year since 1983 jointly by the Sociology Institute of the Tianjin Academy of Social Sciences and the Tianjin Municipal Government. Survey reports are distributed by the municipal government to its subordinate departments, so that officials of these departments may gain insights into public opinion on policy matters. Surveys have also been conducted on the relationship between economic reform (e.g., reforms on price, labor, and wages) and public opinion on the effect of these structural changes. In addition, sociological studies on social developments and significant social problems are being brought into line with state planning. Population problems, small towns, marriage and the family, social development, social structure, class and strata, lifestyle, the elderly, and social indicators have all been listed under national "key projects" in the Seventh Five-Year Plan (1986–1990). By conducting policy-oriented research, sociologists receive from the government human resources as well as material, financial, and moral support. We may proclaim that this problem-cum-policy orientation, a hybrid of sociology and Chinese politics, is the most distinctive feature of contemporary Chinese sociology.

We have so far discussed the dilemmas of the reborn Chinese sociology. They reflect the difficulties China itself has been facing: (1) in the economic realm, accelerating inflation, corruption resulting from the mix of free and controlled prices, urban discontent at the increasing prosperity of rural areas and Special Economic Zones while urban areas have been left behind; (2) politically, the loss of interest in Marxist-Leninist ideology, a power struggle to determine whether conservatives or reformers will take the helm of China's economy, and the difficulty of trying to introduce markets and rational prices without establishing private property rights and a constitution of liberty providing for the depoliticization of economic life. The focus is on how the transition to a market system can be made without creating chaos and inflation. China's leaders still face the problem of resolving the contradictions while at the same time providing the institutional framework for markets to effectively function—namely, private property, freedom of contract, constitutional safeguards for the rights of persons and property, and most crucially a multiparty government.

SUMMARY

We have so far examined the development of sociology in China and have focused on the unique Chinese sociohistorical conditions that shaped the discipline. Sociology was introduced into China from the West at the end of the nineteenth century as a response to the national crisis. It then evolved under a strong Western—especially American—influence, although it later underwent a sinicization process. After the Communist Revolution took place in China in 1949, Chinese sociology was officially abolished as a bourgeois pseudoscience for twenty-seven years. After rebirth in the late 1970s, the new Chinese sociology, which is still in growth, has been constrained by Marxism and Chinese politics.

Therefore, we can say that sociology has evolved as an inseparable part of social change in China. The tortuous course of Chinese sociology reflects the ups and downs of larger social factors. The sociological enterprise tries to grow out of the crevices of conflicting nationalism and Western intrusion, a traditional framework and modernization, an ideological stance and liberalism, reformism and scientism. Western scholars often ask whether sociological inquiry can be freely pursued in China; specifically, what repercussions the June 4 incident of 1989 have had on the development of Chinese sociology. It seems that the institutional effects were local and short-term: in the fall semester of 1989, the Sociology Department at Beijing University did not enroll new students in the sociology major (there is also a social work major in the department); a couple of universities (e.g., the Chinese People's University) reduced the planned enrollment of sociology students; the China Research Institute of Economic Reform, which has been founded by leading reformists, shut down, and a few sociologists there were imprisoned. More profound impact, however, is subtly psychological. Chinese sociologists now have to readjust to the severe political atmosphere and not do research on more "sensitive" topics. Following the rule of "self-censorship," they themselves, rather than government officials, have been acting as gatekeepers of the discipline.

NOTES

1. Yan Fu, "Yuan Qiang" (On Strength), *Zhi bao,* Tianjin, March 4, 1895.

2. Reported by Kulp in the *Bulletin of the Shanghai Baptist College and Seminary* 2, no. 1, June 1915, p. 5; and the Catalogue, 1914, p. 13.

3. Fei Xiaotong, "The Growth of Chinese Sociology," in James P. McGough, *Fei Hsiao-t'ung, The Dilemma of a Chinese Intellectual,* White Plains, NY: M. E. Sharpe, 1979, p. 25.

4. For more on Fei, see R. David Arkush, *Fei Xiaotong and Sociology in Revolutionary China,* Cambridge, Mass.: Harvard University Press, 1981.

5. Fei Xiaotong, *Peasant Life in China,* London: Routledge & Kegan Paul, 1939, p. xiii. Some forty years later, Fei received the Malinowski Award of the Society for Applied Anthropology in Denver in 1980, and the Huxley Award of the Royal Anthropological Institute in London in 1981.

6. Xu Deheng, *Weile Minzhu yu Kexue—Xu Deheng Huiyilu* (For Democracy and Science—Reminiscences of Xu Deheng), Beijing, 1987.

7. Wong Siu-lun, *Sociology and Socialism in Contemporary China,* London: Routledge & Kegan Paul, 1979, p. 108.

8. Yuan Fang, "Yaogao Makesi zhuyi shehuixue, bugao zichanjeji shehuixue" (Do Marxist Sociology, Not Bourgeois Sociology), mimeographed, March 15, 1979; "Guanyu kaizhan shehuixue yanjou de jidian yijian" (Some Suggestions on the Study of Sociology), mimeographed, April 8, 1957.

9. See "Guanyu kaizhan shehuixue yanjou de jidian yijian," in *Zhexue shehui kexue guiha tongxun* (Newsletter of Philosophy and Social Sciences Planning), February 27, 1979, Beijing.

10. Yuan Fang, op. cit.

11. This is intended to rapidly train sociology instructors. Those enrolled in such programs take regular graduate courses and graduate without writing a thesis. They could write the thesis to obtain M.A. degrees later on while working at their jobs.

12. It is extremely difficult to obtain precise information due to the lack of official statistics. The author of this chapter made reference to the following publications (some of them conflict each other): *Difang shehui kexueyuan jianjie* (A Brief Introduction to the Regional Academies of Social Sciences), Beijing,

1988; *Zhongguo shehuikexueyuan shehuixue yanjiusuo jianjie* (A Brief Introduction to the Institute of Sociology at the Chinese Academy of Social Sciences), ms., Beijing, 1989; *Zhongguo shehuixue shouce* (Handbook of Chinese Sociology), Shenyang, 1988; *Zhongguo putong gaodeng xuexiao jiaoshou minglu* (A List of Professors in Universities in China), Beijing, 1988; and *Zhongguo shehuixue nianjian, 1979–1989* (Yearbook of Sociology in China, 1979–1989), Beijing, 1989.

13. The Chinese sociologists, arriving in Rome right after the June 4 incident, were not permitted to attend the meeting as official representatives.

14. Over two thousand sociology articles were published between 1979 and 1989, according to Zhou Guihua, "Chongjianhou de Zhongguo shehuixue de yanjiu xuanti qingxiang fenxi," (An Analysis of the Subject Matters of the Chinese Sociology after Its Reestablishment), *Shehuixue yanjiu* 2, 1989.

15. This is based on *Chuanguo xinshumu* (National New Books List), January 1979–July 1991.

16. Pang Shuqi and Qiu Liping, "Wuoguo shehui xian-jieduan jieji jieceng jiegou yanjiu chutan" (Preliminary Study of the Current Structure of Social Classes and Strata in China," *Shehuixue Yanjiu* (Sociological Studies) 3, 1989, 63–75.

17. These become significant if one considers how great the impact of Marxism has been in China. Among outstanding Western sociologists, Max Weber seems to be the only one on whom a critical biography has been written in the Chinese language. See Su Guoxun, *An Introduction to Weberian Thoughts: Rationalization and Its Limitations,* Beijing, 1989.

30

Development of Sociology in Hong Kong

Rance P. L. Lee and Lau Siu-kai

There have been ample opportunities for the development of sociology in Hong Kong. These opportunities have been created by a liberal society which permits freedom of academic pursuits and a rapidly industrializing society which experiences intensive interplay between Chinese heritage and Western influence. Indeed, sociology as an academic field has grown robustly in the past two to three decades. Sociologists have also emerged as respectable intellectuals in society.

HISTORY AND SOCIAL CONTEXT

Sociology is undoubtedly a product of Western civilization. It was transplanted to China at the beginning of the twentieth century and was received by Chinese intellectuals with great enthusiasm.[1] Numerous empirical studies were conducted, resulting in a large number of sociological publications. Most of the writings were in Chinese and were preoccupied with social issues and problems. Ta Chen, Hsiao-tung Fe, Kuang-tan Pan, Penwen Sun, Wen-tsao Wu, and C. K. Yang were some of the prominent sociologists. Their works are still respected by academic sociologists and their students in Hong Kong today.

When the Communist regime was instituted in China in 1949, some sociologists migrated to Hong Kong and introduced sociology to college students on a small scale. The initial development of sociology in Hong Kong was slow, but in the last two decades it has become a rapidly growing field in both teaching and research. The rapid growth, however, cannot be properly appreciated without understanding its social context.

Hong Kong has been a British colony for about one and a half centuries, but political control of social research and intellectual activities is limited. Moreover, despite the political upheaval in neighboring countries in the postwar period, Hong Kong's own political system has been remarkably stable over many decades.[2] Academic freedom, coupled with political stability, creates a favorable breeding ground for the development of social science in general and sociology in particular.

The growth of sociology in Hong Kong has also been facilitated by social and economic development. Hong Kong is a city with limited space (about one thousand square kilometers). Its total population has grown from about two million to nearly six million over the last forty years. Meanwhile, Hong Kong's economy has progressed tremendously, making the city one of the greatest commercial-industrial centers in Asia.[3] Rapid population growth, coupled with miraculous economic advancement, has created a great demand for social scientific information for comprehending the emerging social problems and for making future plans and actions. No less important, the society is capable of allocating more resources to the promotion of social research and the expansion of educational opportunities at all levels.

The expansion of education at the tertiary level deserves special attention. Recent decades and particularly recent years have seen rapid growth in both the number of academic institutions and the size of student enrollment at each institution. This contributes to the growth of a variety of academic disciplines, including sociology.

DEVELOPMENT OF TEACHING PROGRAMS

Sociology courses are currently offered in all the major universities and colleges in Hong Kong. The two publicly supported universities, the University of Hong Kong and the Chinese University of Hong Kong, have been playing the leading role in the development of sociology as an academic discipline.

Some historical facts should be mentioned. The immigrant scholars from China to Hong Kong around the year 1949 helped establish several liberal arts colleges, of which the prominent ones were New Asia College, Chung Chi College, United College, and Baptist College. The first teaching program in sociology was introduced by Chung Chi College in 1951, followed by both United College and Baptist College in 1956, and by New Asia College in 1959. Some of the pioneer sociologists from China included C. C. Hu, Tsun Leng, and Shau-lam Wong. A significant development was the combining of Chung Chi College, New Asia College, and United College to form the Chinese University of Hong Kong in 1963. As a result, the sociology staff and students in these three colleges were integrated into a single Department of Sociology.

Another significant event was the involvement of C. K. Yang, then pro-

fessor of sociology at the University of Pittsburgh, in the curriculum reform and manpower development of the Chinese University's Department
of Sociology. Through Yang's match-making arrangements, several sociologists (Morris Berkowitz, Jiri Nehnevajsa, Burkart Holzner, and Hiroshi
Wagatsuma) from the University of Pittsburgh and a social psychologist
(Robert Chin) from Boston University came to teach at the Chinese University, while several Chinese University graduates were sent to Pittsburgh
for postgraduate studies in sociology. This helped to build up and to lo-
calize the Department of Sociology at the Chinese University, making it
a leading center of sociology teaching and research in Hong Kong. Ambrose King and Rance Lee are two local sociologists who have been leading the development of the department since the mid-1970s. Recently, the
department had a total of fifteen sociologists, all of them Chinese in origin.
They offer about forty courses in sociology, some of which have become
popular subjects in the university's general education program.

The University of Hong Kong (founded in 1911) has also been active
in the development of sociology. Its Department of Sociology was established in 1967, but some sociology courses were offered as early as 1952.
Henry Lethbridge was a founding member. For many years the department was chaired by overseas scholars: Keith Hopkins and Murray
Groves. Siu-lun Wong, a local Chinese sociologist, took over the chairmanship recently. At present the department has a total of eleven sociologists, of whom five are Chinese.

On top of the full-fledged undergraduate programs of studies in sociology, the two universities provide opportunities for studies in sociology
at both the master's and the doctoral level. While the Chinese University
has more postgraduate students in sociology than the University of Hong
Kong, the latter has set up a special program of criminology at the master's
level.

The third major Department of Sociology is located at Baptist College.
The department offers undergraduate studies and is planning to enroll
students at the master's level. A special feature of the department is its
participation, through offering several courses, in the college's interdisciplinary teaching program on China Studies. Presently the department has
a total of eleven sociologists, of whom eight are Chinese. William Liu, an
American sociologist of Chinese descent, is now playing a key role in the
development of the department.

It should be pointed out that in the three academic institutions just
mentioned, there are sociologists serving in the other departments or faculties, such as business administration, medicine, and social work. Moreover, there are sociologists teaching in the other institutions of higher
learning in Hong Kong. For instance, sociology courses have been offered
at the Lingnan College since 1976. The college established an independent
Department of Sociology in 1981 but dismissed it in 1984. Most of the

sociology courses are now integrated into a multidisciplinary teaching program on Social Issues and Policy. The Hong Kong Polytechnic and the
City Polytechnic of Hong Kong offer sociology as part of their interdisciplinary Department of Applied Social Studies. The Shue Yan College
has maintained a small Department of Sociology for nearly twenty years.
In 1988, the Hong Kong University of Science and Technology was
founded as the third university in Hong Kong. It also has plans to offer
some service courses in sociology under its School of Humanities and Social Science.

It is estimated that at present there are about seventy sociologists teaching at tertiary academic institutions in Hong Kong. Most have received
postgraduate training in the United States, followed by Britain, Canada,
and Australia.

RESEARCH DEVELOPMENT FROM 1950 TO 1980

There was no sociological research in Hong Kong before 1950. Social
research was given birth by overseas scholars in the 1950s and has been
undertaken largely by local Chinese scholars since the beginning of the
1970s.

Hong Kong is located along the southeast coast of the Chinese main-
land. It was part of China before it became a British colony in 1842. It is
essentially a Chinese society, as over 98 percent of the population is Chinese in origin. With its intellectual freedom, political stability, and economic prosperity, Hong Kong represents an ideal place for the study of
Chinese social structure and culture in the context of modernization. In
comparison with Communist China and even Taiwan and Singapore, the
abundance of research opportunities in Hong Kong is unique. As a result,
it attracted a number of overseas scholars to conduct research in Hong
Kong in the 1950s and the 1960s. Most were social anthropologists from
Britain or America, such as E. N. Anderson, Hugh Baker, James Hayes,
Graham Johnson, Jack Potter, Marjorie Topley, Barbara E. Ward, and
James Watson. They were mainly interested in the study of rural Hong
Kong as a traditional Chinese society, focusing on such topics as clan and
lineage organization, ancestor worship and religious rituals, family and
economic life, and diet and health behavior.[4] It is here that some concrete
and well-circulated results have been obtained. Their spillover effect upon
the development of modern sociology in Hong Kong should not be overestimated. Still, as forerunners in social scientific studies in Hong Kong,
their collective impact cannot be discounted.[5]

Special mention should be made of the contributions of Barbara E.
Ward and Marjorie Topley, social anthropologists from Britain. While Topley contributed numerous insights about traditional religious practices,
economic organization, and illness behavior in Hong Kong, Ward was well

known for her application of the "conscious models" to the understanding of the social and economic life of Chinese fishermen and factory workers in Hong Kong. Both of them conducted fieldwork in Hong Kong for many years and taught courses for sociology students in local academic institutions. They are highly regarded by both foreign and local scholars.

Until the mid-1960s there were very few local sociologists in Hong Kong, and they were mostly engaged in teaching rather than research. It was in the mid-1960s that sociologists at the three constituent colleges of the Chinese University decided to promote research by setting up their own research centers. The Rural Research Centre at Chung Chi College organized intensive fieldwork in a Chinese village to study how its cultural values and social life were affected by the growth of industrial urbanism in Hong Kong. The Urban Research Centre at the United College promoted survey research on family life and neighborhood associations in urban Hong Kong. The Sociology Laboratory at New Asia College concentrated on running experimental studies of small-group behavior. All the studies complemented each other by addressing different sociological problems (rural community studies, urban life and problems, and small group dynamics) and by adopting different research strategies (case study, sample survey, and laboratory experiment). Moreover, they shared one common objective: to provide sociology students with empirical research training under the supervision of teachers. The educational function of these research centers was as significant as, if not more significant than, the research function. However, they were dismantled in the late 1960s. Their resources were pooled to form the Social Research Centre.

It was toward the end of the 1960s that sociological research in Hong Kong approached the "take-off" stage. Since then, it has been growing at a faster pace and the bulk of studies have been undertaken by local sociologists. A major reason is the expansion of university education. This permitted the recruitment of a large number of relatively young Chinese sociologists who had just completed postgraduate studies abroad and were eager to launch empirical studies. Meanwhile, the universities began to recognize the importance of research as well as teaching, and the government also began to see a need for supporting research activities in addition to educational programs.

As Hong Kong was undergoing rapid social and economic transformation in the 1960s, a number of social issues and problems began to emerge. In 1965 the government invited Lady Gertrude Williams from Britain to examine the social welfare conditions in Hong Kong. Her report urged the government to start compiling systematic and comprehensive information on which to devise plans for social services.[6] Subsequently, the government allocated a sizable grant for a large-scale sample survey of urban family life in Hong Kong during the period 1966–1969. This was a milestone in the history of sociological research in Hong Kong, as a social survey of such magnitude had never been undertaken before. The Chinese University set up the Social Survey Research Centre specifically for undertaking this task. Local sociologists, however, were not involved. Robert E. Mitchell, an American sociologist, was contracted to direct the Centre and to carry out the survey. A large volume of information about family life was collected through personal interviews with structured questionnaires from a random sample of nearly four thousand households in the urban sector of Hong Kong.

During the late 1960s, academic sociologists were mostly interested in urban family life or rural community studies. Since the beginning of the 1970s, the increase in the number of sociologists made it more and more feasible for sociological research to diversify. A significant event was the formation of the Social Research Centre at the Chinese University at the end of 1969. It was established under the advice of C. K. Yang from the University of Pittsburgh. It replaced the Social Survey Research Centre and collectivized the manpower resources of the aforementioned college-based research units at the Chinese University. The teaching staff in sociology served as the core members of the Centre, but there were also participants from other teaching departments, such as social work, psychology, geography, and economics. The policy was to ensure the integration of teaching and research and to encourage cooperation of sociologists with other social scientists.

The Social Research Centre promoted a wide range of studies on Hong Kong society. The most notable ones were studies of fertility attitudes and practices, social life and new town development, patterns of hawking activities and their social-economic functions, bureaucratic corruption and its control, high-density living and its effect on health, juvenile crime and its social causes, and Chinese familism and its economic and political implications.[7] There were also some studies on China. The most notable was a study of the organization of the people's commune and its implication for rural development in contemporary China. A total of nine sociologists, together with one anthropologist and one psychologist, participated in the study, collecting data from both documentary sources and field trips to China during the late 1970s.

The Social Research Centre was the dominant institution of social research in Hong Kong during the 1970s. In 1982 the Centre was closed down and was integrated with the research units of other social science disciplines to form a larger and more interdisciplinary research organization at the Chinese University, namely, the Institute of Social Studies. This consisted of two research centers: the Centre for Hong Kong Studies and the Centre for Contemporary Asian Studies. Sociologists played a key role in the development of the Institute, especially in studies of Hong Kong society.

Apart from the Chinese University, sociologists at the other academic institutions, especially the University of Hong Kong, were increasingly active in research during the 1970s. They took up issues such as the social needs and housing conditions of the poor, the social attitudes and life quality of industrial workers, the growth and characteristics of the population, the evolution of traditional Chinese voluntary associations, and the role of Europeans in the early history of Hong Kong.[8] The Centre of Asian Studies (founded in 1967) at the University of Hong Kong helped promote some of these sociological studies.

Roughly speaking, sociological research in Hong Kong was in a nascent stage during the 1950s and early 1960s. Social anthropologists from the West played an important part. From the middle of the 1960s to the end of the 1970s, sociological research was at an infancy stage. Local sociologists began to take over the enterprise. It should be recognized that despite the government's generous support of the aforementioned urban family life survey, most sociological studies were supported by international foundations, such as the Asia Foundation, Ford Foundation, Harvard-Yenching Institute, International Development Research Centre, Lingnan University Board of Trustees, Nuffield Foundation, and Rockefeller Foundation. Since 1980, however, the tendency of these funding bodies to classify Hong Kong as a developed area has made it increasingly difficult for local sociologists to obtain funds from them.

RESEARCH TRENDS SINCE 1980

Sociological research in Hong Kong entered its adolescence in the 1980s. It began to flourish. The increase in the number of academic sociologists was one reason. No less important, as the economy continued to grow at a rapid pace, the society became increasingly complex. There were increasing demands for research and also increasing resources for the support of research. The government began to play a more active role in promoting and funding research, including social research. A Research Grants Council was set up under the government's University and Polytechnic Grants Committee for allocating research funds to the academic institutions. This helped to push forward sociological studies in Hong Kong. Recent years have seen an increase in both the number and the scale of social research projects.

Since the beginning of the 1980s, an area of research that has attracted the interest of many sociologists and their students is political culture and political development in Hong Kong. As the sovereignty of Hong Kong will be resumed by China in 1997, there is considerable interest both inside and outside the academic circle about the changes in the political system of Hong Kong. Academic sociologists have initiated studies on such issues as the legal and political attitudes of the Hong Kong Chinese and their participation in political activities, the transfer of power in the decolonization process, the formation and consolidation of political leadership, the emergence and strategies of political groups and parties, and the changing role of civil servants. Political sociology has emerged as a dominant field in Hong Kong.

The study of industrial relations and economic behavior is another popular research area. It is generally recognized that the future of Hong Kong greatly depends upon its economic vitality. Sociologists can hardly avoid addressing such issues in Hong Kong as the motivation for economic pursuit, the social attitudes and job satisfaction of industrial workers, the distribution of the labor force and the problem of labor shortage, the adjustment and life quality of alien workers, the strategies of employers in coping with economic restructuring, and the social and political factors in national strategies for economic development. There are also studies to identify the salient characteristics of industrial culture in China.

The family as a basic unit of society was and still is an area of concern to academic sociologists in Hong Kong. The theoretical interest and research focus, however, have changed.[9] The pioneering work of F. M. Wong in the early 1970s led many sociologists to accept that as a result of industrialization there had arisen a predominant trend toward the small nuclear family pattern in Hong Kong. Subsequently, there were some major studies on the internal structure and processes of the family, such as family values, power differentiation and division of labor, parent-child conflict, and child care and control. In recent years, however, some sociologists have raised doubts about the role of industrialization in the increase of nuclear families in the context of Hong Kong society.[10] Meanwhile, there has emerged an increasing emphasis on the study of the extended network of the family, especially its contribution to political participation, economic pursuit, and social support of the family members. It is increasingly recognized that the Chinese families in Hong Kong are predominantly of the nuclear family type in form but of the modified extended family type in actual practice. Increasing attention has also been paid to the changing role of women and the family life cycle.

Another area of growing interest is the study of social class structure and social mobility patterns in Hong Kong. Efforts are being made to construct a socioeconomic status index, to identify the rates and channels of both intra- and intergenerational mobility of different socioeconomic groups, to assess the extent to which opportunities for mobility are based on achievement rather than ascription, and to investigate individual experiences of mobility in terms of normative and relational discontinuities. A major focus is on the role of the expanding middle class, especially their values and aspirations, and their social and political participation.

Recent years have also seen a rising interest in youth behavior and popular culture in Hong Kong. Both the government and the public are increasingly aware of youths' discontent with various domains of life. This has led to a series of sociological studies on youth behavior, especially regarding their mentalities, school adjustment, leisure patterns, and life satisfaction. There are also studies to identify and conceptualize the central characteristics of popular culture in Hong Kong, and to study its impact on the social and political orientations of youth as well as people in other age categories.

Like many other rapidly industrializing societies, Hong Kong is facing increasing incidence of crime and delinquency. In response to growing concern in the community, academic sociologists in Hong Kong have been compiling data about crime trends and have initiated studies on organized crime, drug abuse, and the organization of the police force.

Hong Kong has enjoyed a relatively high degree of political stability over many decades. Nevertheless, there were massive riots in 1966–1967 and a number of industrial actions and social protests, particularly in the last decade or so. Academic sociologists have started compiling a database on collective behavior in Hong Kong since the middle of the present century. The data can be used for identifying the trends of collective actions and for identifying their causes, patterns, and consequences.

With regard to population studies, fertility behavior was a major focus of research during the 1970s. Since the mid-1980s, public apprehension about China's resumption of sovereignty over Hong Kong in 1997 has led to increasing emigration, particularly among the middle and lower classes. Meanwhile, immigration from China continues and the influx of Vietnamese boat people rises. Both immigration and emigration have become issues of overwhelming concern in Hong Kong today. As a result, academic sociologists have shifted their interest from the study of fertility behavior to the study of migration. They have initiated studies on the patterns of emigration and their social and economic consequences. There are also studies on the social adjustment and economic implication of immigrants to Hong Kong.

Health and medical care constitute another major area of research by academic sociologists and their students in Hong Kong. There have been studies on occupational accidents and injury, health problems and social support of the elderly, social correlates of psychiatric illness, social and cultural factors in stress management, and the development of primary health care. There has also been a series of studies on the perceptions and utilization of traditional Chinese and modern Western medical care among different socioeconomic groups. Recently some sociologists have participated in studies of AIDS, especially about the related beliefs, attitudes, and practices of the Hong Kong Chinese.

Last, it should be mentioned that a group of sociologists from several academic institutions have jointly formed a Social Indicators Research Program. The aim is to accumulate longitudinal data that will allow for the analysis of social change and the exploration of social issues and problems. Beginning in 1988, there would be a series of biennial sample surveys focusing on a wide range of subjective social indicators, that is, the perceptions, aspirations, and life satisfaction of Hong Kong residents.[11]

Over the last decade, social research in Hong Kong has been making continuous progress. A large number of subject matters have been covered and the quantity of research findings is impressive. However, there is much room for improvement. Empirical research with borrowed concepts and theories from the West represents the substance of sociology in Hong Kong. Moreover, most sociologists are relatively young and are thus short of maturity in theoretical innovations. Partly because of the dominance of young scholars, the community of sociologists in Hong Kong also suffers from a lack of strong intellectual leadership. As a result, individual sociologists are pretty much on their own in their quest for theoretical guideposts. Scattered and fragmented studies abound, providing occasional inspirations. Synthetic work of theoretical significance is sorely needed, and coordination of individual research efforts still awaits the emergence of intellectual "masters."

Sociology in Hong Kong further suffers from the absence of a professional forum or a professional association which can chart intellectual fields and promote intellectual exchanges among sociologists. Hong Kong does not have a professional journal specifically for sociology. The Hong Kong Sociological Society was established in 1966 and registered as a member of the International Sociological Association in 1967. However, as the membership at that time was too small to function effectively, the Society became inactive after 1970. In recent years, the number of sociologists has greatly increased. There are voices for revitalizing the Society, but concrete action has yet to be taken.

Nevertheless, over the last decade some new organizations for promoting collaborative research have been established by academic institutions. In view of the momentous changes and the growing importance of the Asia-Pacific region, the Chinese University restructured its Institute of Social Studies to form the Hong Kong Institute of Asia-Pacific Studies in 1990. Special research emphasis is laid on the role of Hong Kong in the development of the Asia-Pacific region. The University of Hong Kong established the Social Science Research Centre in 1990, promoting not only academic studies but also public opinion surveys and other applied studies. The Baptist College set up the Centre for East-West Studies in 1992, planning to encourage intellectual dialogues and empirical studies on Hong Kong in relation to other parts of the world. Moreover, the Chinese University recently succeeded in taking over the Universities Service Centre (established in 1963), which would help accumulate research materials for both local and foreign scholars to study changes in contemporary China. These various research organizations promise to facilitate social research, but the results have yet to be seen.

Outside the academic community, there are research sociologists working for the government or the nongovernmental organizations. Attention should be paid to the government's Census and Statistics Department, which employs some sociologists and plays a key role in providing research support to other departments—particularly in the areas of questionnaire design, sampling, data processing, and interpretation. Among the nongovernmental organizations, the Hong Kong Council of Social Service is most active in applied social research. Staffed with some sociologists, it compiles welfare statistics, surveys social service needs, and evaluates social service programs. Furthermore, numerous marketing research firms in Hong Kong have sociologists on their staff lists.

PROBLEMS AND PROSPECTS

As mentioned earlier, an overwhelming majority of Hong Kong sociologists received their postgraduate education in American or British universities. In spite of the increasing use of local materials for classroom instruction in recent years, the bulk of textbooks are still imported from America or Britain. Furthermore, Hong Kong sociologists generally publish their research findings in American or British journals. All these facts suggest that Hong Kong sociology has been developing under the shadow of American and British sociology.

Nevertheless, contacts with other Asian sociologists have expanded over the last two decades. Most of the contacts during the 1970s were developed through participation in regional seminars and workshops. Since the mid-1980s, an increasing number of Hong Kong sociologists have participated in collaborative research projects with their counterparts in China and in the Asia-Pacific region. Collaboration with sociologists and other social scientists in China has produced studies on topics such as the interaction between demographic changes and economic development in China, the dynamic aspects of the work ethic and human relations in an industrial setting, and social stratification patterns in urban areas. It is noteworthy that the Hong Kong Institute of Asia-Pacific Studies at the Chinese University has recently collaborated with Yale University to establish a special research program on South China. It intends to build up research materials and to support research by faculty members and postgraduate students on recent developments in the South China region. Attempts will be made to study the economic collaboration and cultural interaction of South China with Hong Kong and Taiwan.

Hong Kong sociologists also collaborate with other Asian sociologists, especially those in South Korea, Japan, Taiwan, and Singapore. There are, for instance, comparative studies of bureaucratic corruption in Asia, the making of the middle classes in East Asia, the problem of industrial restructuring and labor market adjustment in East and Southeast Asia, and the national strategies for economic development among the four "little dragons" in Asia. Most recently, urban sociologists in Hong Kong and Japan have been planning to organize joint studies on problems related to the social integration of heterogeneous populations in Hong Kong and Tokyo.

It is expected that the intellectual contact and research collaboration with sociologists in China and other Asia-Pacific countries will continue to grow. As Hong Kong is an industrial-commercial center in Asia, Hong Kong sociologists generally consider it not only desirable but also necessary to strengthen intellectual ties with their counterparts in other Asian countries, particularly those in the nearby Asia-Pacific region. It is noteworthy that in recent years there have been active moves among Asian sociologists to establish an association of Asian sociologists. This would help to strengthen the ties between Hong Kong and other Asian sociologists.

It should be admitted that despite the increasing contact and collaboration with other Asian sociologists, dependency on American and British sociology remains a central feature of Hong Kong sociology. Another important feature is the strong emphasis on the study of Chinese culture and social structure. This generally shared research emphasis, coupled with the sociologists' American or British training, constitutes the integrative elements that make the community of sociologists in Hong Kong a rather homogeneous one. Regardless of the results so far achieved, the common goal of Hong Kong sociologists is to discover and verify general sociological propositions through systematic studies of social life and social development in the context of Hong Kong and China.

The application and verification of sociological ideas from the West in a Chinese setting has its own merits; but what is equally, if not more, important is the development of new concepts and new paradigms consequent upon empirical research on local development. It is gratifying to see that Hong Kong sociologists have recently expressed growing interest in this direction. Discussion groups have been formed, and systematic observations have attempted to identify the distinctive characteristics of Chinese social behavior. Some results have been achieved. For instance, Ambrose King developed the concept of "administrative absorption of politics," while Siu-kai Lau developed the concept of "utilitarianistic familism" for explaining why political stability can be achieved in Hong Kong, a Chinese society under British rule.[12] Although Lau's concept also touches on Chinese economic behavior, Siu-lan Wong modified it and formulated his own concept of "entrepreneurial familism" to explain how the Shanghai industrialists actively organize and mobilize their family resources for economic advancement in the competitive and changing environment of Hong Kong.[13] As a challenge to Weber's thesis on the Protestant ethic and the rise of capitalism, both Ambrose King and Tak-sing Cheung have reexamined the Confucian ethic and explained how it could contribute to the economic modernization of China.[14] In a comparative analysis of the medical care systems in China, Hong Kong, and Taiwan, Rance Lee has proposed the concept of "hierarchial medical pluralism," suggesting that the dynamic relationships among different medical traditions within a national society in the course of modernization could be studied in terms of their structural superiority (power, prestige, and wealth) and functional strength (distribution and utilization).[15] As a result of these various efforts, Hong Kong sociologists have begun to plant their own tradition of sociology, making their research relevant to both the local Chinese society and the development of sociology as a worldwide academic discipline. Gradually, there has emerged a sense of self-confidence among academic sociologists in Hong Kong.

Hong Kong sociologists are not alone in making sociology relevant to Chinese society. Similar movements have occurred in China, Singapore, and Taiwan. It is noteworthy that in recent years attempts have been made to bring together Chinese sociologists from different national societies for the purpose of comparing their insights about Chinese social behavior in different sociopolitical contexts and at different stages of economic development.[16] For instance, Hong Kong sociologists have recently organized two academic conferences for this purpose, one on "Modernization and Chinese Culture" and another on "Chinese Family and Its Changes."[17] The exchange and collaboration among Chinese sociologists from different parts of the world will continue to grow. This will help develop a distinctive identity for Chinese sociology.

It should be noted that the dominance of Comtean positivism is another important feature of the Hong Kong sociology. It is generally believed that social phenomena are patterned and that the goal of sociology is to construct a set of law-like propositions amenable to empirical verification. This orientation has been largely due to the influence of sociology in China and America. Comtean positivism was a central theme of sociology in China in the first half of the present century, resulting in a massive number of social surveys and community studies.[18] The Chinese sociologists immigrating to Hong Kong in the middle of the century brought with them the empirical tradition and passed it on to the younger generation. Moreover, as mentioned before, most sociologists in Hong Kong were trained in American universities which had a long tradition of emphasis on empirical studies.

The scientific conception of sociology has been clearly expressed in both teaching and research programs in Hong Kong. In the instructional programs, strong emphasis has been placed on the training in scientific methods and the conduct of field studies by students. Over the years, sociologists and their students have undertaken numerous studies, of which most are cross-sectional sample surveys. The variable analysis approach, advocated by Paul F. Lazarsfeld and his associates, is the dominant methodological orientation in Hong Kong. Data are collected mainly through questionnaires and interviews, although there have been some significant studies using case study designs and relying on observational methods and historical documents. The availability of computer facilities has led to an increasing use of multivariate statistical techniques. Quantification is a major trend in Hong Kong's sociological research.

Elements of positivism can also be found in the theoretical orientations of Hong Kong sociology. For many years, structural-functionalism in a broad sense has reigned as the dominant paradigm in the sociological community of Hong Kong. The works by such contemporary sociologists as Talcott Parsons, Robert Merton, Edward Shils, Lewis Coser, S. N. Eisenstadt, Marion Levey, Neil Smelser, and Alvin Gouldner have been widely read. Among the other perspectives, symbolic interactionism and critical theory are well covered in the teaching programs and are of great interest to students. However, their bearing on empirical research in Hong Kong is still marginal.

Academic sociologists in Hong Kong are overwhelmingly concerned with objective empirical studies of Chinese social behavior. It should be pointed out that the concern is motivated more by the production of scientific knowledge than by the making of a direct contribution to practical problem solving. To most academic sociologists in Hong Kong, the reference group is the worldwide professional community rather than the immediate society in which they live and work. Of course, this does not mean that their research is of no practical value. On the contrary, their conceptual insights and research findings have attracted the attention of decision makers as well as the general public in Hong Kong. Nevertheless, it is the academic publication rather than the practical contribution that is of major concern to the academic sociologists.

The situation is gradually changing. Even though applied research is presently overshadowed by basic research, there is increasing pressure to undertake studies with practical implications. A major source of the pressure comes from the rise of social issues and problems in society.

There have emerged numerous social issues and problems in Hong Kong in recent years. Many of them are probably legacies of a disintegrating social fabric, as Hong Kong has been undergoing rapid social and economic changes. There are, however, other factors, such as the expansion of educational opportunities, the growing awareness of the concept of human rights, and the increasing number of active political and pressure groups in the community. These factors elevate public awareness of social issues and problems. The salient ones include violent crime, juvenile delinquency, housing shortage, rising cost of living, traffic congestion, environmental pollution, chronic illnesses, labor shortage, emigration of skilled workers, and aging.

For many centuries, the Chinese treasured the value of tolerance of existing conditions. This traditional value is now being replaced by rising social expectations. Recent years have seen various forms of civic actions putting pressure on the government to initiate social reforms and to provide better services. Meanwhile, sociologists are being invited to present their views on social issues, to conduct systematic investigations related to social problems, and to give advice on policies and action programs. Willingly or not, academic sociologists can hardly resist the pressure or the temptation to apply their sociological knowledge and skills to the complex issues and problems in society. It is noteworthy that the universities—particularly the polytechnics—have come to place emphasis on social impact as a criterion for funding research.

To conclude, sociology as an academic field was given birth by scholars from China and the West in the 1950s. Since then, it has kept growing and localizing. It has now come to the stage of adolescence. It has acquired a sense of self-confidence and is actively searching for its own identity. Despite the influence of American and British sociology, Hong Kong sociologists generally share the ambition to plant sociology on the Chinese soil, making it both theoretically and practically relevant to Chinese social life and development in Hong Kong and other societies. It is their conviction that such efforts would also contribute to the development of sociology as a worldwide academic discipline.

NOTES

The following persons should be acknowledged for their assistance in collecting some of the information for this chapter: Ki-yung Au, Frances Lai, Wing-kin Law, Ming-kwan Lee, William T. Liu, Alex Kwan, and Siu-lun Wong.

1. Ambrose Y. C. King, "The Development and Death of Chinese Academic Sociology: A Chapter in the Sociology of Sociology," *Modern Asian Studies* 12, 1978, 37–58.

2. T. B. Lin, Rance P. L. Lee, and U. E. Simonis, eds., *Hong Kong: Economic, Social and Political Studies in Development,* New York: M. E. Sharpe, 1979, 145–66.

3. Ibid., 9–30 and 225–331.

4. For an overview, see *Anthropology and Sociology in Hong Kong: Field Projects and Problems of Overseas Scholars* (Proceedings of a Symposium, February 8–9, 1969), compiled by Marjorie Topley, Hong Kong: Centre of Asian Studies, University of Hong Kong, 1969.

5. For some of the major essays that have been widely read by local scholars and students, see J. C. Jarvie, ed., *Hong Kong: A Society in Transition,* London: Routledge & Kegan Paul, 1969; and Barbara E. Ward, *Through Other Eyes: Essays in Understanding "Conscious Models" in Hong Kong,* Hong Kong: The Chinese University Press, 1985.

6. G. Williams, *Report on the Feasibility Survey into Social Welfare Provision and Allied Topics in Hong Kong,* Hong Kong: Government Printer, 1966.

7. For some of the major publications, see Lin, Lee, and Simonis, op. cit.; Ambrose Y. C. King and Rance P. L. Lee, eds., *Social Life and Development in Hong Kong,* Hong Kong: The Chinese University Press, 1981; and Rance P. L. Lee, ed., *Corruption and Its Control in Hong Kong,* Hong Kong: The Chinese University Press, 1981.

8. See Keith Hopkin, ed., *Hong Kong: The Industrial Colony,* Hong Kong: Oxford University Press, 1971; H. J. Lethbridge, *Hong Kong: Stability and Change* (a collection of essays), Hong Kong: Oxford University Press, 1978.

9. For a review of major issues and related studies, see Rance P. L. Lee, "Change in the Family and Kinship Structure in Hong Kong," in K. Aoi, K. Morioka, and J. Suginohara, eds., *Family and Community Changes in East Asia,* Japan: Japan Sociological Society, 1985, pp. 133–57.

10. For some of the arguments, see Chapters 11 and 12 in Ming-kwan Lee, *Hong Kong Politics and Society in Transition,* Hong Kong: Commercial Press, 1987 (in Chinese).

11. Siu-kai Lau et al., eds., *Indicators of Social Development: Hong Kong 1988,* Hong Kong Institute of Asia-Pacific Studies, The Chinese University of Hong Kong, 1991.

12. See King and Lee, op. cit., 127–46; Siu-kai Lau, *Society and Politics in Hong Kong,* Hong Kong: The Chinese University Press, 1982; and Siu-kai Lau and Hsin-chi Kuan, *The Ethos of the Hong Kong Chinese,* Hong Kong: The Chinese University Press, 1988.

13. Siu-lan Wong, *Emigrant Entrepreneurs: Shanghai Industrialists in Hong Kong,* Hong Kong: Oxford University Press, 1988.

14. Ambrose Y. C. King, "Confucian Ethics and Economic Development: A Re-examination of Max Weber's Thesis," in Chien Chiao, ed., *Proceedings of the Conference on Modernization and Chinese Culture,* Faculty of Social Science and Institute of Social Studies, The Chinese University of Hong Kong, 1985, pp. 133–46; and Tak-sing Cheung, *The Order Complex and Confucian Ethic,* Taiwan: Chu Liu Press, 1989 (in Chinese).

15. Rance P. L. Lee, "Comparative Studies of Health Care Systems," *Social Science and Medicine* 16, 1982, 629–42.

16. For a pioneering work, see K. S. Yang and C. I. Wen, eds., *The Sinicization of Social and Behavioral Science Research,* Taiwan: Institute of Ethnology, Academia Sinica, 1982 (in Chinese).

17. See Chien Chiao, op. cit.; and Chien Chiao, ed., *Chinese Family and Its Changes,* Hong Kong: The Chinese University Press, 1991 (in Chinese).

18. King, op. cit., 1978.

31

Contemporary Sociology in India

Raj P. Mohan and Vijayan K. Pillai

INTELLECTUAL HERITAGE

Contemporary Indian sociology is a product of two cultural streams: (1) India's traditional culture, with ideas deriving from its ancient scriptures and philosophy; and (2) recent Western culture, with ideas deriving from the works of European and North American scholars. The intellectual traditions from those two sources have yet to be synthesized. In the seesaw interplay of the Indological and Western traditions, now one, now the other has dominated. The Indological tradition has been dominant at times, particularly during the 1950s, but its impact is currently lessening![1] Understandably, then, among the much debated issues of Indian sociology,[2] the most fundamental issue concerns "the spirit of Indian sociology" as contrasted with "the spirit of the West." Account must be taken of this debate in sketching the nature of and trends in contemporary sociology in India. In order to put the nature of Indian sociology in proper perspective, it is essential that we understand the intellectual heritage of Indian society. Understanding of the philosophical underpinnings which have motivated or facilitated the development of Indian sociology is also essential for seeing the sociopolitical forces at work in shaping the culture and institutions of a society. To this we now turn.

This chapter is not concerned with constructing any new concepts in sociology as a result of the analysis of Indian society, nor is any attempt being made to develop a unique Indian sociology as distinct from that of the West. Rather, the aim is simply to put forward ideas which might explain the continuation of one of the oldest social systems in the world, that is, Indian society. This approach might give us an understanding of the dynamics of Indian culture and civilization and provide clues to the unity and functioning of its social system. Because India is a land of diverse religious beliefs and practices, different languages and dialects, different cultural and ethnic groups, there is some truth in the observation by R. N. Saksena that "till the establishment of the Republic of India there was not much in common in the Indian society, which according to the Western thinking, could be either observed or experienced in a concrete shape so as to form a homogeneous social organization."[3] However, according to Saksena, "Indian people have always been conscious of the fact that they have a common social heritage, both in their thinking and living."[4] He further claims:

As it has been repeatedly observed by the historians and other thinkers, there has always existed a fundamental unity amidst the diversities in our culture, if we look at the Indian society as a whole. This unity has always existed in ideas and values. It gives us the proper material for observing Indian society in its correct sociological perspective, as a whole, by laying greater stress of unity more in relations than in isolated elements. This approach has also a unique advantage of not only explaining the continuity of Indian society but also its vitality. Thus India's past is to be regarded as a key to India's present.[5]

Various scholars and their studies reveal that even the pre-Aryans of India had a highly developed religious faith, now called Hinduism. Accordingly, through India's history, Hinduism—as the common denomination of Buddhism, Brahmanism, and Jainism—has significantly influenced the social thought and the lifestyle of the people.

Relatively sophisticated and self-conscious social thought in India is at least as old as Gautama and Kautilya, in fact, older still because Gautama and Kautilya drew on the works of predecessors who postulated a geometry of social relations.[6] In India the oldest sources of social thought are the religious texts, the Vedas, the Upanishads, the Sutras, and the Puranas, which deal with—among many other subjects—customary law, history, and morality. Other sources of the Hindu social thought include epics like the *Mahabharata,* the *Ramayana,* and the *Bhagavad Gita. The Laws of Manu* is a classic work on Hindu social organization in which rites, social laws, customs, and social ideas are described and theorized. In variety, richness, and empirical accuracy, this treasure of comparative social observation and thought equals or surpasses anything available to Western intellectuals at the time sociology was making its debut.

Among the famous authors in ancient India, mention should be made of Usanas or Sukracharya, one of the early *Rishis* (saints) who, in a classic work, the *Nitishastra,* deals with the science of morals and discusses at length questions of social, economic, and political character. The famous *Arthasastra* of Kautilya, the minister of King Chandragupta Maurya (317–

321 B.C.), is a treatise on practical and theoretical economics, politics, sociology, and the law of the whole period, done with the empirical objectivity of a Machiavelli. It was once the recognized authority for the rules and legal codes of acquiring wealth, by either an individual or the government. It provides a working manual to guide the ruler in the conduct of his daily affairs. It should be stressed here that as a result of being lost and only recently discovered, Kautilya's *Arthasastra* is both ancient and amazingly modern. According to D. M. Brown, "the dramatic nature of this discovery, together with the utilitarian character of the material, caused something like an upheaval in Indian political studies. It was hailed as welcome proof of the practical turn of the Indian mind, which has been subject of the Western criticism because of its alleged preoccupation with mysticism and idealism. A flood of Indian books and articles on Kautilya followed Shamasastry's publication of the text in 1909."[7]

The *Manusamhita,* or *The Laws of Manu,* contains the fourfold classification of Indian society. Kewal Motwani believes that Manu's system provides the moral foundation of human society in general, though it has specific relevancy to the Indian social system.[8]

INTELLECTUAL LEGITIMATION

Intellectual legitimation of sociology in India is basically a post-independence phenomenon; however, it is not to say that there was no sociology in India before this time. The major expansion of sociology in India occurred during the five-year plans for social and educational reconstruction. During this period many new universities came into existence and departments of sociology followed.

The origins of the teaching of sociology as a subject of study can be traced back to around the year 1915; however, origins of sociology in India go back to the day when British officials discovered that knowledge of Indian culture and social life was indispensable to the smooth functioning of the government. According to M. N. Srinivas and M. N. Panini,[9] the first sociological study can be traced back to 1769 when Henry Verelest, then governor of Bihar and Bengal, understood the need and importance of gathering information regarding the leading Indian families and their customs in his directives to revenue supervisors. Since then many British civil servants and missionaries have made efforts to record the life and culture of the Indian people. "For instance, Francis Buchanan undertook an ethnographic survey of Bengal in 1807 at the insistence of the Governor-General-in-Council. Abbe Dubois, a French Missionary in Mysore, wrote in 1816, a book entitled *Hindu Manners, Customs and Ceremonies,* which is even now valuable."[10] His book is concerned with the life, customs, and rituals of people he lived among. After this study by Dubois, Walter Hamilton produced *A Geographical, Statistical and Historical De-*

scription of Hindostan and Adjacent Countries, which was published in 1820. He attempted to locate many towns and places in India in terms of their longitude and latitude in relation to other places and the history of various towns. He estimated the population of India at that time to be 123 million. In 1871, British officials undertook the first census of India. In 1901, Herbert Risley attempted the first ethnographic survey of India which would develop as a part of the census.

According to Bernard Cohn, they justified the huge expense by saying that this type of survey, with superior data, would help solve some of the problems in Europe and that they needed to collect the data before it disappeared with social and cultural changes. They also argued that such data would be indispensable for the purposes of legislation, famine relief, control of epidemics, sanitation and judicial procedures, and so forth.[11] Many scholars such as A. Baines, J. Wilson, H. H. Risley, D. O'Malley, J. H. Hutton, B. S. Guha, and others made use of the census as an important tool not only for demographic studies but also for social and cultural analyses of Indian society. It also helped the British officialdom in making social policies for India. Many types of legislation during this period would bear out the use of census and demographic data in making policy decisions.

During this period, the procedures for gathering information outlined by Henry Verelest were extended by the East India Company and afterwards the British Imperial Government to all castes and class of people. This resulted in a wealth of data as contained in the British parliamentary reports and papers.[12]

Warren Hastings, when he became the governor of Bengal (1772–1774) and later the governor general of India (1774–1786), asked the jurists to prepare a compendium of Hindu law. It contains a wealth of sociological data of significant value. Another effort of Hastings was to prepare a compendium of Muslim law. During this period there were many other similar and sporadic efforts toward collection of data on life and lifestyles of Indian people. This was the period when the British government was trying to consolidate its power in India in the second half of the eighteenth century.

Preparation of the imperial and district *Gazetteers* became the routine task of the British administration—as it was with a socioeconomic account of the people in the reports of the population census from 1880, which contained a wealth of sociological information. Other agencies such as the All-India Ethnographical Surveys of Castes and Tribes were also formed; these gathered information on Indian castes and tribes from the last decade of the nineteenth century. During this period, J. C. Nesfield produced *A Brief View of the Caste System of the North-Western Provinces and Oudh*[13] in 1885; and H. H. Risley did a fascinating study, *The Tribes and Castes of Bengal,*[14] published in 1891 in two volumes. Even today these works are of importance and merit. The role of the Christian missionaries in the study of society and culture, people and community life, of India cannot be neglected. Important works during this period were two books by Henry S. Maine entitled *The Ancient Law*[15] and *Village Communities in the East and West.*[16] B. H. Baden-Powell also wrote two books during this period, *The Indian Village Community*[17] and *The Origin and Growth of Village Communities in India.*[18] Both are significant in understanding the village and communal life in India of the time.

It is to the Asiatic Society of Bengal that Indian sociologists and social anthropologists owe immense debt. The society was organized in 1774 by Sir William Jones, who was also its first president. He defined the scope of this organization to encourage the study of "nature and man." A number of researchers and publications were initiated by this group. Since then large amounts of data on tribal and rural groups have been collected by British administrators, travelers, missionaries, and trained anthropologists. Because of these research-oriented activities of the Asiatic Society of Bengal, a number of research reports and research papers were developed. Because of the need to disseminate knowledge, a number of journals came into existence: *Journal of the Asiatic Society of Bengal* (1784), *Indian Antiquary* (1872), *Journal of Bihar and Orissa Research Society* (1915), and *Man in India* (1921).

At this time a number of research-oriented British administrators were locating themselves in different parts of India. For example, Dalton O'Malley and H. H. Risley were in East India, R. V. Russell in Middle India, E. Thurston in South India, and T. Creek in North India. They all wrote encyclopedic inventories about the castes and tribes of India. Their works, even today, provide basic information about the life and culture of people of different parts of India. Some of their works either have been or are in the process of being reprinted by the Anthropological Survey of India.

These works were followed by detailed accounts about specific castes and tribes. For example, George Briggs published his study, *The Charmars,*[19] in 1920; P.R.T Gurdon published his major work, *The Khasi,* in 1912.[20] J. P. Mills[21] and N. E. Parry[22] wrote scholarly monographs on specific tribes.

These publications and others inspired many Indian scholars, and S. V. Ketkar published his *History of Caste in India*[23] in 1909. In 1921 G. S. Ghurye was doing his research work on caste at Cambridge University in England. He emphasized race as the basis for the emergence of caste. His monograph, *Caste and Race in India,*[24] appeared in 1932. The report of the Indian census in 1931 contained J. H. Hutton's contribution to the theory of caste.

During the last part of the nineteenth century—and even before that— knowledge of these studies by Western intellectuals began to disseminate in India through journals, newspapers, and others sources. Because of these and other studies by Western scholars, Indians found a new interest to look at themselves and learn about themselves. According to Howard Becker and Harry Barnes,

Confronted by the disquieting spectacle of what seemed superior social organization as well as superior material culture, Indian thinkers began to look at the family, law, education, and religion in ways different from those honored by century-old traditions.[25]

The major precursors of this trend were people like Raja Rammohun Roy (1772–1833), Swami Dayanand Saraswati (1824–1883), Mahadev Govinda Ranade (1842–1901), and Swami Vivekananda (1863–1902). With these persons came a reinterpretation of old values and traditions of Indian society as contained in the old texts and scriptures. They all can be called the harbingers of modern India. This period also marks a break with the past, and Ramkrishana Mukherjee has called it the Indian renaissance.[26]

The new movement brought modern rationalism to the forefront and led to the collection and codification of empirical data as well as documentary evidence to reinterpret India's past. For example, it is believed that Raja Rammohun Roy had collected data on widows who were burned on their husbands' funeral pyres. He also reinterpreted Hinduism in the light of universal values and wrote on the utility of English education as a gateway to Western knowledge and science. In Rammohun Roy, India had a true cosmopolitan and modernizer. The Arya Samaj and Brahmo Samaj movements were two facets of the nineteenth century: the Hindu revivalism against Christianity and the influence of Christian social ethics. The social reforms of these movements ran parallel, but their language of communication was different. In Brahmo Samaj the primary language seems to have been English, and with Keshab Chander Sen the vocabulary became entirely Christian in a reaffirmation of Bhaktiism. As the leader of Arya Samaj, Dayanand Saraswati stressed the use of Indian languages and reinterpreted the four Vedas. This reinterpretation created a much-needed change in the attitude of the Indian people toward their religious beliefs and practices and paved the way for the acceptance of rationalism and modernism. The movement he initiated has stood for equality among people and the consequent abolition of caste and sex discrimination, as well as the cessation of "idol worship." This is, in short, the early background and the process of legitimation for sociology in India. Now let us turn to its professionalization as an academic discipline.

PROFESSIONALIZATION

With the beginning of the twentieth century, sociology entered the early phase of professionalization. Even though the Indological tradition, which relied heavily on the early literary works (particularly scriptures, epics, and law books), continued, studies based on direct empirical observation and on available census and other reports began to be popular. Even though most of the ethnographic work was carried out by British officials connected with the census operations, professional sociologists and social anthropologists continued to be attracted to India. For example, W.H.R. Rivers (with his 1906 book *The Todas*—in the modern social-anthropological tradition—and his papers on kinship and marriage, and *Social Organization*) and A. R. Radcliffe-Brown (with his study of An-daman Islanders) significantly influenced Indian sociology and social anthropology, as did C. Bougle, M. Mauss, and Max Weber with their use of secondary sources to formulate ideas and theories. During the first two decades of the twentieth century, two Indian scholars (L. K. Ananthak-rishna Iyer, with his accounts of castes and tribes of Cochin and Mysore; and S. C. Roy, with his monographic accounts of the tribes of Bihar) made their mark on sociology and social anthropology in India. Roy also founded the journal *Man in India* and wrote a book entitled *Caste, Race and Religion in India* in 1934.[27]

Indian sociology reflects the wider historical and intellectual milieu. As a "legitimate" academic discipline it is a recent phenomenon. In the early part of the twentieth century, Sir Brajendra Nath Seal, of the Department of Philosophy at Calcutta University, used to deliver occasional lectures in "comparative sociology." But as a special course sociology was first introduced in the Department of Economics at Calcutta University in 1917.[28] In 1919 an independent Department of Sociology was established at the University of Bombay, by Patric Geddes. In 1924 C. S. Ghurye, a famous Indologist, succeeded Geddes as head of the department. At the University of Lucknow some courses in sociology were introduced in the economics department in 1921 when Radhakamal Mukerjee became the head of the department. During the 1930s sociology was systematically taught only in the universities of Bombay, Calcutta, and Mysore.[29] The discipline grew very slowly thereafter. At Lucknow University sociology had only a minor place in the curriculum, and until the 1940s there was no separate paper required for the B.A. degree. From the beginning at the University of Bombay, sociology held an important place in the cur-riculum. In fact, there were four sociology papers required for the M.A. degree, and after 1924 it was possible by completing a thesis to take the degree entirely in sociology. A few years later, sociology was established as an independent subject for both the M.A. and the Ph.D. degrees.

Until 1947, sociology was taught only in four universities; moreover, only one of these universities had a separate department. Between 1940 and 1947 significant efforts were made by the Indian Science Congress and the Inter-University Board of India to encourage the major universities to introduce the subject.[30]

The University of Poona established a department of sociology in the

Deccan College in 1949 under the supervision of Dr. (Mrs.) Iravati Karve. Karnatak University introduced the subject in 1950 as one of the papers whereby it could be combined with four papers in economics, history, and political science. In 1959, a separate department of sociology came into being at Karnatak. The M.S. University in Broada introduced the subject in 1950, and a separate department of sociology was established in 1954. The Agra University initiated studies in sociology during 1950 at the postgraduate level; however, it had initiated sociology courses at the undergraduate level in 1948. The Institute of Social Sciences at Agra under the direction of Professor R. N. Saksena was set up in 1956. The Andhra University started a sociology department in 1959. In the Gujrat University, sociology was taught for many years before a department of sociology was set up in 1954 in the School of Social Sciences. The S.N.D.T. University in Bombay was teaching sociology as far back as 1916 for the B.A. (Pass) examination. Sociology was introduced for M.A. course in 1957 and B.A. (Honors) in 1961. The Jabalpur University established a department of sociology in 1960. At the Benaras Hindu University, the subject has been taught in the departments of philosophy and psychology since 1950; however, a department of sociology was started only in 1966 under the direction of Professor S. K. Srivastva. At the Utkal University there is no separate department of sociology; however, sociology can be taken as one of the optional papers at the B.A. examination. The University of Saugar has recently established separate master's level courses, one in general sociology and the other in the sociology of development.[31]

According to G. C. Hallen, sociology departments have also been established at the universities of Patna (1951), Annamalai (1954), Bhagalpur (1956), Gorakhpur (1958), Delhi (1959), Punjab (1960), Nagpur (1960), Rajasthan (1961), Kashi Vidyapeeth (1962), Jodhpur (1962), Udaipur (1966), Ravi Shankar (1967), and South Gujrat Gandi (1968).[32] Although no separate departments of sociology exist, the subject is taught in various colleges affiliated with such universities as Vikram (1957), S. V. Vidyapeeth (1959), Kalyani (1961), Kerala (1963), Jiwaji (1964), Indore (1964), Shivaji (1964), Meerut (1967), Kanpur (1967), and Marathawada and Bihar universities and institutes. Only 51 universities had departments of sociology in 1973. Since 1973 two additional universities, namely, Jawaharlal Nehru University and National Indira Gandhi Open University, have established sociology departments.[33]

The period between 1940 and 1947 was dominated by the struggle for freedom and the milieu was characterized by constant tension on the intellectual as well as the lay mind in India. There was little room at this time for significant changes in the development of sociology as an intellectual enterprise in India. However, while sociology was in eclipse as a discipline during this period, other intellectuals visualized its importance. T. B. Bottomore has speculated on the forces that ran counter to the development of sociology:

The failure to develop is seen, however, not only in the fact that sociology did not establish itself as an independent discipline outside Bombay, but also in the character of sociological thought and research. Much of the theoretical writing has developed to presenting speculative schemes of social evolution, and was remote from the major intellectual controversies of the times. Empirical research which was on a small scale, was almost entirely descriptive and largely confined to the sphere of social work (or "social problems") in the narrow sense. Several reasons might be adduced to account for this lack of progress; but there are two which seem particularly important. In the first place, Indian sociology, like other disciplines, was intellectually dependent upon British universities, and since academic sociology in Britain itself developed slowly in this period, it was hardly to be expected that it should burst into vigorous life in India. Secondly, while sociology is not necessarily subversive it is always likely to engender social criticism; in order to flourish it needs, in greater measure than many other disciplines, a general freedom of thought, and it does not flourish under authoritarianism, or colonial governments.[34]

With independence Indian sociology was free to develop.

The history of the development of sociology in India during the post-independence years may be divided into five periods. In the first period, from 1947 to 1949, Indian sociology remained by and large in the same general state as in the prewar period, both with regard to the departments at the universities and the courses given. The same is true with respect to publications and research.[35]

The second period, between 1950 and 1956, brought important changes as sociology began to emerge as a distinct discipline within the departments of philosophy, economics, and anthropology. The Indian Sociological Society was formed, and the first issue of the *Sociological Bulletin* appeared in 1952. At this time only four universities possessed independent departments of sociology, as is evident from D. P. Mukerji's statement in 1952:

Seats of higher learning do not yet recognize the fundamental nature of sociology, seats of political power do not seem to appreciate its importance for legislation and administration ... and big economic interests, with a few honorable exceptions, are still not cognizant of the elementary fact that even production for profit is a socioeconomic problem. At the present, the course in civics at the pre-university stage is a hodge-podge of politics, economics and administration with little or no emphasis on sociology. Only four universities in India teach sociology with any seriousness in the under- and postgraduate classes. In two, it is an independent subject with full course of eight papers at the postgraduate level alone; in one, it is for all practical purposes, separate, making sociology compulsory for economics and optional for politics students; and a fourth has just introduced it. ... Only three universities have a respectable number of students in the sociology class.[36]

The third period began in 1956 with the activation of various institutions, government and private, for study and research in sociology.[37] Creative research work was initiated during this period; independent departments of sociology emerged at various universities and colleges teaching sociology at the graduate and postgraduate levels. Universities which received smaller funds for research began to concentrate on teaching. This period also marked a rapid evolution of the social sciences and a noticeable development of the history of social thought, chiefly of the ancient period and middle ages.[38]

During the fourth period, from 1960 to 1975, which accompanied a basic reorganization of Indian society through five-year plans, sociology experienced accelerated growth as both an academic and research enterprise throughout the entire country. At many universities the social sciences, among them sociology, gained supremacy. Rapid growth also occurred in sociological research under the guidance of noted scholars. Several specialized research departments began to function during this period in India. These were devoted to the promotion of mathematical and statistical procedures, inductive logic, and the exploration of the interrelation between theory and practices. Much stress was also placed on methodological problems.

Transformation of historical sociology into a logico-historical tradition also occurred. Four basic trends may be distinguished in sociological research during this period. The first was the description, recording, and monographic interpretation of the manuscripts of ancient Indian thought.[39] The second involved research on the development and changes in traditions of religious and philosophical thought in India.[40] The third, based on ancient chronicles of philosophy and social thought,[41] consisted of research on changes in sociological doctrines over time and among social groups. The last consisted of an attempt to modify Western research techniques and methods for their utilization in the study of Indian social phenomena.[42] Research in the sciences of ontology and epistemology was conducted on a smaller scale on the ideas of regularity, causality, and determinism.

Sociological research during this period concentrated on the complex problem of changes in the class and caste structures and social consciousness in post-independence India. Work was also being carried out in fields closely related to major trends abroad, including sociology of literature,[43] sociology of religion,[44] urban sociology,[45] community structure and change,[46] sociology of economic phenomena,[47] medical sociology,[48] and social change.[49] Specialists were also conducting studies on the scope, function, and significance of mass media,[50] social relations in work establishments, chiefly in industrial enterprises,[51] rural social change,[52] the process of urbanization in India and sociological characterization of Indian cities,[53] the impact of urbanization on rural families,[54] crime and delinquency,[55] social relations in family and small professional groups,[56] and fertility behavior.[57] Family planning provided a field of research in both sociology and demography. The values of interdisciplinary approaches in research were recognized. Research in the sociology of the family was also gaining momentum.

India's dual social-intellectual heritage, those of India and of the West, is unique. Through the interplay of forces, indigenous and external, sociology in India has been advancing toward a fuller development. In no sense is it a replica of the sociology of any other country, nor could it be.[58]

Some studies during this period had claimed that the dominant trend in sociology in India was empirical.[59] In our opinion, caution must be exercised in making such interpretations. While empiricism, as contrasted with rationalism and historicism, had made some headway in sociological circles in India, it could hardly be called a dominant tendency. While positivism and empiricism were being more widely accepted during this period than previously, such acceptance did not result in the abandonment of traditional modes of inquiry. In accord with an ancient tendency to believe that all things have a proper place, scientism and positivism have been welcome in Indian sociology, and efforts have been made to harmonize them with other perspectives like traditionalism, humanism, and rationalism. This tendency harmonizes with the traditional values of the Indian mind as well as the Indian social system.

A review of some of the studies during this period reveals the degree to which sociology in India showed a synthesis of traditionalism and modernism and acceptance of the conceptual schemes as well as methods and techniques in research from the West, particularly the United States and England. But it would be an overstatement to say that the dominant tendency in sociology in India at the time was empirical.[60]

The emergence of sociological positivism in India during this period may not be Benoy Kumar Sarkar's "transcendental posivitism," but it can well be labeled logico-historical positivism. It also appears that this logico-historical positivism would eventually emerge as an integral theory of cognition and creativity, which, according to Pitirim Sorokin,[61] is becoming increasingly accepted by sociologists in the West. In the contemporary Indian sociology, there is an attempt to balance quantitative and qualitative research as well as theory and methods.

T.K.N. Unnithan is of the opinion that if sociology is to develop in India, it must follow an integrative "middle path" between "sociological universalism" and "sociological regionalism," adapting sociological concepts to the peculiarities of Indian social phenomena. He posits that "only this way can I conceive of an Indian sociology, i.e., a body of related concepts enabling us to comprehend peculiarities of social phenomena, characteristics of Indian society."[62]

R.N. Saksena has put forward his conviction that "even the current sociological view cannot be said to be divorced from metaphysical thinking." He stresses the sociological significance of spiritual values (of the

Hindu social system) as manifested in the social unity and conformity in Indian society, the origin and validity of ritual affirmation of these ends, and a scheme of reward and punishment. He further asserts that the aim of sociological study of Indian social phenomena should be to interpret the synthesis in culture and thought, and to find continua of stability and change in Indian society. He also posits that sociology in India cannot be entirely objective in its contents:

Even now in our society an individual's behavior and values are interrelated as part and whole. Hence sociology in India cannot be entirely "objective" in its contents and approach. It has to contain a little bit of abstract philosophy, which provided a continuum between the past and the present, which constitutes the dynamics of Indian society.[63]

Y. B. Damle[64] sees adoption of features, of the Parsonian model as a primary hope for Indian sociology. These features include: culture as a system; personality as a system; society as a system; the functional prerequisites; hierarchy of control; anomic breakdown; and pattern variables. He further urges the reinterpretation of these conceptual notions with reference to the Indian social system.

Unnithan et al.,[65] while editing a study on the sociology of culture in India, commented on the difficulties facing the development of a "conceptual content of a comprehensive model for the study of Indian culture and its dynamics." Unnithan's concerns are well taken, though, since in most of the recorded history of Indian traditions and customs, the material transmitted has been processed through mythological and metaphysical frames of reference.

We partly share the views expressed by Unnithan et al.; because of forces indigenous and external, Indian sociology has already advanced somewhat toward a fuller development in its own right. We share the views expressed by S.K. Nandy in the following lines:

Indian sociology has advanced towards a fuller development. It has not all together been a replica of the sociology of any other country, from the perspective of the "sociology of sociology," what can be called a "duplicate sociology" appears to be an academic impossibility. Much critical discussion of Indian sociology is available in monographs, journal articles, speeches, and conference proceedings in India and abroad. And among the issues handled by these discussions, one of the most fundamental is that of what can be called "the spirit of Indian sociology."[66]

In view of these comments, the notion of regionalism in sociology seems to us to be of no special significance as applied to Indian sociology. Sociology is a universal science and the concepts developed have a universal appeal and application. As the research becomes more and more sophisticated, the development of principles universal in space and time is to be expected. The differences in sociology developed in different countries may in time be matters of *spirit* but not of *content,* that is, rules, rationales, methods, and the logic behind sociological formulations. Meanwhile, sociology speaks the language of the locality.

The major drawback to the present development of Indian sociology has been the lack of conceptual tools and concepts applicable to Indian social phenomena. It would not be out of place to say that the entire field of Indian sociology as such, despite its relatively broad development, is nebulous and unexplored in the modern scientific sense. Most of the works available on Indian sociology are confined to analytical discussions of theoretical problems substantiating arguments here and there with facts drawn from ancient Indian scriptures and religious texts. Some studies have been conducted, although not with the deliberate intention of systematically contributing to Indian sociology. D. P. Mukerji's work on the relationship between social structure and intellectual professional culture is unusual in this respect. In many of his essays, he has offered both analytical concepts and historical perspectives for the study of the relationship between class structure and changes in social structure. However, the logico-historical-positivistic tradition of analysis of change in Indian social structure and systems has been a recent one.

From a theoretical standpoint, Radhakamal Mukerjee has made a series of attempts to bring about a synthesis in the relativistic concept of values within the scope of the traditional Indian theory of values.

Since the logico-historical-positivistic tradition in Indian sociology is a recent one, most of the studies in this tradition are confined to very small areas. Moreover, in all these studies there is a lack of uniformly defined concepts and categories; limited results are generalized for the nation as a whole. In the present stage of development, Indian sociology does not need "grand" generalizations applicable to the whole nation, but "middle range" studies appropriate to the empirical reality of Indian social phenomena.

In "Sociology in India: Some Considerations," R. M. Srivastva[67] has formulated the view that sociology in India has developed under the foster care of economics and, to a lesser degree, political science. Only in post-independence India has sociology received the status and recognition it deserves. Srivastva further develops five guidelines for Indian sociologists, for the development of sociology in India. Sociology should (1) focus attention upon problems of basic conceptualization and terminology, within the frame of Indian social data; (2) develop analyses and explanations of Indian social structure which will meet the critical demand of professional colleagues and sociologists all over the world as well as the students at Indian universities; (3) enable expert sociologists to fit the available funds of Indian social data into a reasonable framework of theory construction; (4) present its postulates so lucidly that it would not only stimulate continuous research and investigation in the field but encourage scholars to challenge it from time to time, so as to pave the way for a sound general theory; and (5) provide analytical tools and categories to permit significantly systematic, logical, coherent, and consistent interpretations of research-based material concerning social problems. Srivastva also found trends toward scientism in Indian sociology but believes it inadequate in its present form. He argues that mathematical complexity should not be identified with completeness, nor sophistication with wisdom. As long as Indian sociologists remain concerned with only specialized aspects or segments of a problem rather than with the organic whole, there is little hope for sound and healthy development in the time to come. India is confronted by many urgent problems which demand the aid of sociology along with the other social sciences, but the historical perspective and theoretical considerations must not be neglected. Indian and non-Indian social phenomena must be seen as opposite ends of the same continuum, not as a dichotomy. Also, it is essential to disregard the tendency among some sociologists to view Indian society as in every respect different from non-Indian or Western societies.

An impartial student of the history of sociology in India would agree that the discipline of sociology in India has immensely benefited from the theoretical developments and research of other countries, particularly Britain and the U.S. Saksena posits this point:

But the contact of Indian society with the West, unlike that of modern with medieval society in Europe, introduced a foreign element into Indian culture. It is in this context that the modern sociological thought of India has to be understood. This impact led some thinkers who wanted to return to traditional principles, to reject Western civilization altogether.[68]

The most important modern thinkers who subscribe to such a view are Bhagwandas and Coomaraswamy. Coomaraswamy presents a strong, uncompromising critique of Western civilization; Bhagwandas, though adhering to traditional Indian sociological thought, tries to bring about a synthesis (based, however, upon religion). There are others who have attempted to interpret traditional concepts and values from a modern rationalistic-positivistic standpoint.[69]

In the view of Saksena, sociology in India poses this problem; and if no solution is found, it constitutes a serious dilemma for the Indian sociologists. This predicament is the key to understanding the fundamental trends in contemporary sociological thought in India.[70]

Radhakamal Mukerjee has observed that social interests and experiences must express Indian conceptions of the nature and functions of divinity. From the beginning of his intellectual career, Mukerjee's main concern has been the reorganization of the social sciences as expounded by Western thinkers. Mukerjee's thought is clearly indicative of the rise of sociology in India. His interests range widely from ecological studies to religion and mysticism. He has even endeavored to integrate such diverse material as ecology and mysticism in one whole. In A. K. Saran's opinion, the bases of Mukerjee's synthesis of traditional and modern thought are found in the concepts of level, hierarchy, and themes of symbolism and in the method of reinterpretation and adaptation. The concepts and methods are all traditional.[71]

D. P. Mukerji, another exponent of the synthesis theory of Indian culture and nonpositivistic Indian sociology, analyzes the impact of the West on Indian society as a phase in cultural assimilation. In his view, Indian culture has grown by a series of responses to successive challenges of many races and cultures, which have resulted in a synthesis. He finds the tradition of Indian society as a symbolic system to be the most significant core of human action.[72]

The common practice is to play down empirical positivism and to treat the traditional knowledge and tradition as the superstructural property of the group (D. P. Mukerji) or to view philosophy (Saksena) or dharma (Motwani) as the key sociological phenomena to be understood and analyzed by sociologists. Hence, despite the increase in the number of colleges and universities offering instruction in the field, sociology in India still has far to go. A major factor in the slow progress of sociology as an academic discipline in India has been confusion over the proper scope of course offerings and over the areas of sociological inquiry to be included. There has also been a lack of consensus on the professional role of sociologists. Those wishing to pursue graduate-level studies in sociology have been unsure about the opportunities and fields in which they may be required to invest their talent.

In the mid-1960s a volume entitled *Sociology in India,*[73] based upon a seminar on the subject organized by R. N. Saksena under the auspices of the Institute of Social Science (of which he was the director), assembled valuable contributions on the topic of the development of sociology in India. The papers included in this volume discuss and analyze the growth of sociology and its teaching in Indian universities, the major institutional areas of Indian society and social changes, the nature and content of courses to be adopted for students of sociology in India, the inventory of topics in the areas of methodology and statistical techniques, and the responsibility of sociologists for molding social policy in India. It is suggested in the volume that there is no need to develop an "Indian sociology" as contrasted with a "Western sociology," in the general sense of a conceptual and theoretical framework. What is needed to develop general sociological theories, concepts, and methods in such a way that they become more fully applicable to the study of Indian or non-Western civilizations. However, from the present perspective this is probably premature.

It appears that sociology in India is moving toward synthesis of traditional Indian and modern Western cultural materials as well as an awareness of sociologies developed elsewhere in various models and schools of thought. Indian sociology is a complex of traditional and modern values and systems of thought, a reflection of past and present, a synthesis of East and West.[74]

Initially, the impact of foreign scholars (especially those from England and the United States) on the development of the discipline was very prominent.[75] Many studies were conducted by these foreign scholars and Indian sociologists on several different aspects of Indian life and social structure. As a result, numerous subdisciplines within Indian sociology emerged: for example, industrial sociology, urban sociology, political sociology, sociology of education, social demography, and women's studies.

TRENDS IN THE 1970s AND 1980s

There have been three approaches in studying the structure of sociology in India. The first is structuralism, which is based on locating social structure in the symbols and representations of the Indian tradition but does not rule out universal generalizations based on comparison. The second approach is ethnosociology, or the cultural analysis approach, which postulates the notion of social structure from the source material drawn largely from textual traditions relying on myths and legends. The third is the structural-historical approach, which is based on examining the process of change and transformation in a historical setting.

The Marxist approach is extensively used to study the Indian social structure. Sociologists and social anthropologists use the notions of mode of production in their analysis of social structure to introduce new perspectives on class and caste differentiation and emerging forces of change.[76] Village studies have been a predominant focus of research, even before independence. These studies often were very large and comprehensive. Interest in village studies was to a large extent the result of community development programs that needed evaluation, and many sociologists made use of these opportunities to study the village setting.[77]

The caste system has been an important focus of research.[78] One influential study was conducted by Louis Dumont (1970). Dumont's study encouraged other studies on Indian social structure to be undertaken, some using varying approaches of Dumont's methodology. Dumont's study provoked some debate. His study of the caste system is a study in tradition, and he borrowed parts of his methodology from the structuralists.

Another area of sociological research in India is modernization. Modernization is a transformation of the social, political, cultural, and economic processes which by nature are accumulative and adaptive, and which selectively encourage structural replacements and differentiation in society.[79] Scholars were interested in studying the effect of modernization on a society that has a strong history of tradition. Questions were raised as to whether traditional India could evolve into a modern society.

One way in which sociologists study modernization is by studying institutions. The legal system has played a key role in the modernization of India. The modernization began with the introduction of British common law, which is dissimilar to the traditional Indian legal system. British law introduced universal principles and individual-oriented principles, and it implied a separation between the judicial and executive functions. The traditional legal system is based on principles of holism or communitarian responsibilities, and a hierarchy wherein the judicial and executive functions overlap.

Professions, another area of sociological interest, have existed for centuries in India but have changed as governments and authorities have changed. The Indian studies on professions are mainly concentrated on Western medicine, law, teaching, civil service, and nursing,[80] although India still hosts many traditional practitioners in areas such as medicine. The modern professions require formal education, credentials, and regular training for a prescribed period. Their orientation is secular and scientific, whereas the legitimacy of the traditional professions generally depends upon religious support and theology.[81]

The studies done on traditional professions focus on the priestly functions of the Brahmins. Topics include the following: the high priestly caste of Kerala; occupational patterns, education, and income of priests, the relationships between senior and junior priests, their kinship-professional relationship, and teacher-trainee relationship; and the social organization of different groups of priests. Studies on modern professions have examined such things as relations between lawyers and their clients, the professional middle class, physicians, and nurses. The professions are often analyzed in terms of dimensions such as stratification, mobility, training, social background, relationships, and role structure. Stratification and hierarchy within a profession provides insights into the role of professions in the general system of social stratification and class organization.[82]

The study of urban sociology gained momentum in the 1970s and 1980s. Though this particular subdiscipline has been around for a while, it was essentially neglected until the 1970s. The importance of urban studies was overlooked, as it was felt that India was mostly made up of villages. The emergence of serious urban problems saw the reintroduction of this subdiscipline. The problems of rural-urban migration, urban development, and slums attracted the attention of sociologists and social anthropologists. Within the broad field of urban sociology, urban phenomena such as slums, ethnic conflicts, urban kinship patterns, and the impact of urbanization on rural areas have been extensively investigated. The growth of urbanization and its impact on villages seems to be of special interest for many sociologists.

The study of rural sociology developed in the 1970s and continues in the 1980s. There have been studies on peasantry, land reforms, agricultural laborers, and agrarian relations. These studies dealt with problems of the rural masses and the nature and degrees of exploitation of the lower classes by the upper classes.[83] The impact of land reforms on rural society with an emphasis on the dynamics of social and economic life was thoroughly researched. Agrarian social structure was the focus of studies on agrarian relations.

The study of social movements became very popular in the 1980s. This subject had rarely been explored before the 1970s. Examples include studies of the Indian national movement, peasant movements, messianic tribal movements, agrarian movements, revolutionary and religious movements, tribal movements, and cultural movements. Every sociologist who has studied a particular movement has looked at different parts of that movement using different methodologies to analyze the movement. In 1974–1975 there were a series of seminars, and in 1976 several papers were published on social movements in India. The seminars were established to work out the theoretical and methodological perspectives of studying social movements, and they resulted in empirical studies of agrarian, revolutionary, and religious movements.

A large proportion of social movement studies are related to peasant movements. There were many peasant uprisings after independence. Studies of peasant movements follow two types of methodological orientation, including the Marxist orientation and the historical structure orientation. Thus, many studies on peasant movements involved a class analysis of the movements. The social structure and class formation of the peasantry were also analyzed. It has been found that a common characteristic of all the movements is their rootedness in class structure and class alliances.[84] Studies have shown that in general the peasant movements have not been successful, probably because they were often led by leaders from non-peasant classes and their struggle lacked a wider range of alliances with other classes. The outcomes of the movements in most cases were legislative and ameliorative reforms in favor of the peasantry within the overall social system.

Cultural and religious movements have been studied not only by sociologists but also by political scientists, social thinkers, and historians who made use of empirical and observational methods.[85] These studies mainly address aspects of collective mobilization on religious grounds relating to protests. These studies have focused upon the impact of changes in the economic, political, and social aspects of the various segments of castes, communities, and social categories which engender a feeling of collective identity.[86]

Sociology in India, through the 1970s and 1980s, witnessed several developments. In the 1970s programs of study began to emerge in the fields of agrarian relations, peasants, land reforms, agricultural laborers, scheduled castes, and tribes. The focus was on the problems of the rural masses and the degree of exploitation among lower classes.[87] Agrarian relations and peasant studies have continued into the 1980s. There are conventions, journal articles, and workshops which emphasize an increasing interest in this area.[88] Social movements, as mentioned earlier, gained attention in the 1980s.[89] There have been studies on "backward classes" movements, religious movements, tribal movements, and women's movements.

The 1970s also saw the emergence of subdisciplines such as sociology of development, medical sociology, and social demography.[90] In the initial stages there was some confusion with regard to the boundaries of these subdisciplines. Studies which analytically belonged to the area of profession and organization were passed off as studies in medical sociology[91] merely because terms like *doctors, nurses,* or *hospitals* appeared in the title. Social demography in the 1970s remained descriptive. There were two reasons for this. First, hypotheses related to population control, fertility behavior, and family planning were not formulated on the basis of intensive microstudies. Second, sociologists and social anthropologists did not develop a body of interrelated concepts to analyze fertility. A number of studies were published in the area of sociology of development. Entrepreneurship, management of change, and rural development were among the topics that received greater attention during that period.

Two other significant areas of interest in the 1970s were industrial sociology, and social stratification. Industrial sociology gained interest throughout the 1970s. Several doctoral dissertations were written in this area, covering industrial relations, industrial entrepreneurs, workers, and trade unions.[92] Several courses on social stratification are currently being taught in almost all universities.[93] One trend that was present during the 1970s and continued to grow into the 1980s is the sociology of education. There seems to be a shift from the problems of higher education to the problems of lower education. These include primary and nonformal education.[94] Other new fields of study in the 1980s were sociology of law, deviance, knowledge, science, and historical sociology. Two other areas of expansion are child development, and food and nutrition. These two areas were stimulated by conferences and seminars in connection with the 1979 International Year of the Child.

The number of research studies using the Marxist analytical framework increased through the 1970s and gained strength in the 1980s. Alongside the Marxian approach, historical analysis also became popular in the

1980s. Another theoretical development that has gained strength because of the need to process and analyze dynamic situations is processual analysis. This is based on networks, roles, and interactions.[95]

Methods of sociology in the 1970s saw a debate between surveyors and observers. Eventually, they both came to realize that they could complement each other. The social survey method became popular in the 1970s and 1980s. The 1970s saw an increased appreciation of mathematical approaches to the study of social phenomena; for example, game theory and structural equation models have been introduced into the field of sociology in India.

In the 1980s, peasant studies and agrarian relations studies continued to enjoy popularity. Social demography and medical sociology crystallized during this time. Two surveys conducted by the Indian Council of Social Science Research in 1974 and 1985 provide insights into the new Indian sociology of the 1980s.[96] The 1974 survey identified areas such as social demography, tribal studies, rural studies, urban studies, industrial sociology, social stratification, sociology of religion, education, law, and political sociology as growth areas with an expected high level of research activity in the 1970s and 1980s. The 1985 survey identified a few new areas of growth, including the sociology of science, communications, and deviant behavior.

Demographic studies in general may be classified into two groups. Some studies focus on demographic variables, such as age at marriage, population composition, mortality, and migration. Sociocultural studies have dealt with institutional, normative, and cultural aspects of Indian fertility.

The dominant areas of inquiry in the field of mortality are infant, childhood, and maternal mortality.[97] The Khanna study[98] and the WHO (World Health Organization) Asian study[99] are among the pioneering studies which carried out investigations of fetal wastage and health and socioeconomic determinants of mortality in India.

Very few migration studies were conducted before independence. These studies dealt with the patterns, streams, and causes of long-distance as well as short-distance (internal) migration, especially rural to urban migration. There is very little literature on rural to rural, urban to rural, and urban to urban migration. Sociocultural studies of migration have examined the effects of determinants such as occupation, caste, and kinship ties on patterns of migration.[100]

Fertility research plays a crucial role in the development and growth of population research in India. The Indian family planning program was considerably strengthened in its outreach by the National Family Planning Program, which started in 1952. The 1980s emerged as a decade of fertility research in India. In spite of an extensive national family planning program, India has become the most important contributor to the world population growth rate. The total fertility rate remains high, about 4.4 children per woman.

Demographic studies on fertility have focused on three important variables: age at marriage, place of residence, and contraceptive use. In India, age at marriage has been found to be an important predictor of fertility.[101] India's birth rate could be reduced by almost a third (30 percent) by 1992 if Indians delayed marriage beyond the age of nineteen.[102]

Research on contraceptive use was accelerated by the National Family Planning Program. Several population research centers have been established to conduct studies on the social and economic determinants of contraceptive use. A number of family planning communication action research centers were established during the 1960s. A number of studies have examined the role of community leaders and family planning adopters in increasing the use of contraceptives.[103]

A rural/urban fertility differential has contributed to a growing interest in identifying the impact of urban living on fertility in India. The crude urban and rural birth rates in 1979 were 32.8 and 38.9, respectively. Several studies have pointed out that in India the differential is very small, with urban fertility sometimes exceeding rural fertility.[104]

In addition, several studies on sociocultural factors such as family structure,[105] kinship,[106] religion,[107] socioeconomic status,[108] caste,[109] and modernization[110] have been carried out. A large portion of the population studies continued in the 1980s emphasized the importance of sociocultural factors.[111]

Women's studies became a very popular and an important focus of study in the 1980s. While most of the studies concerning Indian society have been conducted by male sociologists, women's studies have been mostly conducted by female sociologists, social activists, and research workers. Several areas of investigation within the field of women's studies became important in the 1980s. These areas include women's position in the context of culture in India, women in the police force and their public image, women's political participation, specific categories of Muslim and tribal women in the process of change, women in the work force, and women's movements.[112] The role conflict of working women has also been a subject of inquiry in women's studies. These studies on women will continue to be important as further understanding of their position in society is attained.

The profession of sociology became a topic of study in India through the 1970s and 1980s. Sociology as a profession in India has grown in terms of quality and size. Annual conferences are held to discuss problems and concerns about the teaching of sociology.[113] Unfortunately, those who graduate with sociology degrees have not been involved in the sociology profession. In 1971, 60 percent of the graduates were unemployed; a majority of these graduates were women who were not seeking employment. Students who did take on careers seemed to go into fields other than sociology; some went into business and others into governmental positions. In sum, many students of sociology in India have emerged over the years. Fields which were popular in the 1960s and 1970s have changed somewhat and created new ones in the 1980s. Indian sociologists in India and abroad continue to play an important role in the development of Indian sociology. Although there is a lack of sociology professionals, the sociologists in the field seem to have more confidence than in the past. Through the 1970s and 1980s several support organizations were established. These organizations are making funds and facilities available, and therefore sociological research is growing. Further growth of the study of sociology lies in the changing social conditions of the profession and in the commitment to sociology.

NOTES

1. This is an expanded and revised version of a previous chapter: Raj P. Mohan, "Contemporary Sociology in India," in Raj P. Mohan and Don Martindale (eds.), *Handbook of Contemporary Developments in World Sociology,* Westport, Conn.: Greenwood Press, 1975, pp. 423–37.

2. For example, see the controversial article in Indological tradition by Louis Dumont and D. F. Pocock, "For a Sociology of India," *Contributions to Indian Sociology* 1, 1957. For a commentary on this article, see F. G. Bailey, "For a Sociology of India?" *Contributions to Indian Sociology* 3, 1959, and a rejoinder to Bailey by Dumont and Pocock, "For a Sociology of India: A Rejoinder to Dr. Bailey," *Contributions to Indian Sociology* 4, 1960. See also Dan A. Chekki, "Toward Reconstructing National Traditions in Sociology," *Journal of Sociological Studies* 7, 1988. See also R. K. Pachauri, *Contemporary India,* New Delhi: Vikas, 1991.

3. R. N. Saksena, "Sociology in India," in *Sociology in India,* Agra: Institute of Social Sciences, 1965, p. 1.

4. Ibid., p. 1.

5. Ibid., pp. 1–2.

6. For a comprehensive discussion of such ideas, see Benoy Kumar Sarkar, *Positive Background of Hindu Sociology,* Allahabad: Panini Office, 1937, p. 657. See also Brajendranath Seal, *Positive Sciences of Ancient Hindus,* Delhi: Motilal, 1985.

7. D. Mackenzie Brown, *The White Umbrella,* Berkeley: University of California Press, 1968, p. 49.

8. Kewal Motwani, *Manu Dharma Sastra,* Madras: Ganesh and Co., 1958, p. 35.

9. M. N. Srinivas and M. N. Panini, "The Development of Sociology and Social Anthropology in India," *Sociological Bulletin* 22, no. 2, September 1973, pp. 181–83. This is an excellent essay on the development of both sociology and social anthropology in India.

10. Ibid., p. 182.

11. Bernard S. Cohn, "The Study of Indian Society and Culture," in Milton Singer and Bernard S. Cohn (eds.), *Structure and Change in Indian Society,* New York: Wennder-Gren Foundation for Anthropological Research, 1968.

12. See Ramkrishna Mukherjee, "Trends in Indian Sociology," *Current Sociology* 25, no. 3, 1977.

13. Allahabad: Government Press, 1885.

14. Calcutta: Bengal Secretariat Press, 1891.

15. London: John Murray, 1861.

16. London: John Murray, 1871.

17. London: John Murray, 1872.

18. London: Swan Sonnesnsheir, 1899.

19. George W. Briggs, *The Chamars,* Calcutta: Calcutta Association Press, 1920.

20. P.R.T. Gurdon, *The Khasi,* London: Macmillan, 1914.

21. J. P. Mills, *The Lhota Naga,* London: Macmillan, 1922.

22. N. E. Parry, *The Lakhers,* London: Macmillan, 1932.

23. S. V. Ketkar, *History of Caste in India,* Ithaca, N.Y.: Cornell University Press, 1909.

24. The monograph entitled *Caste and Race in India* was reissued as *Caste and Class in India,* Bombay: Popular Book Depot, 1950.

25. Howard Becker and Harry Elmer Barnes, *Social Thought from Lore to Science,* Vols. 1 and 2, 3rd ed., New York: Dover Publications, 1961, pp. 1135–36.

26. Ramkrishana Mukherjee, *What Will It Be? Explorations in Inductive Sociology,* Bombay: Allied Publishers, 1979.

27. Srinivas and Panini, op. cit., p. 185.

28. Howard Becker and Harry Elmer Barnes, *Social Thought from Lore to Science,* rev. ed., Washington, D.C.: Harren Press, 1952, especially Chapter 21.

29. Benoy Kumar Sarkar, *Creative India, from Mohanjo Daro to the Age of Ramkrishana-Vivekananda,* Lahore: Motilal Banarsi Das, 1937, p. 653.

30. Kewal Motwani, "The Next Step," in Kewal Motwani (ed.), *A Critique of Empiricism in Sociology,* Bombay: Allied Publishers, 1966, pp. 299–302.

31. For further details, see G. C. Hallen, "Progress of Sociology as an Academic Discipline in India," *Indian Journal of Social Research* 10, no. 1, April 1969, pp. 48–54.

32. Ibid., p. 53.

33. T.K.N. Unnithan, "Sociology in India since Independence," *International Journal of Contemporary Sociology* 18, no. 3–4, 1981, pp. 81–134.

34. T. B. Bottomore, "Sociology in India," *British Journal of Sociology,* June 1962, pp. 98–105.

35. Raj P. Mohan, "Contemporary Sociology in India: Historical Aspects, Comments, and Some Trends," pp. 341–54, and "Contemporary Sociology in India: Synthesis of Traditional and Modern Values," pp. 184–92, in G. C. Hallen (ed.), *Indian Sociology,* Meerut, India: Rohini Publications, 1986.

36. D. P. Mukerji, "Sociology in Independent India," *Sociological Bulletin* 1, no. 1, 1952. Also see R. N. Saksena, "Sociology in India," *Transactions of the Fourth World Congress of Sociology* 1, 1959, pp. 57–71.

37. Reference can be made to numerous organizations like the Indian Council

of Agricultural Research; Council of Scientific and Industrial Research; Institute of Social Sciences, Agra; A. N. Sinha Institute of Social Sciences; Tata Institute of Social Sciences, Tatanagar and Bombay; Institute of Economic Growth; Indian Statistical Institute; India Institute of Management; Indian Institute of Technology; Gokhle Institute of Politics and Economics; and Central Institute of Community Development, to mention a few. Also, several universities and numerous colleges have independent departments of sociology.

38. See, for instance, Iravati Karve, *Hindu Society: An Interpretation,* Poona: Deccan College, 1961; A. R. Pillai, *Origin and Development of Caste,* Bombay: Kitab Mahal, 1959. For more recent explorations in the concepts of caste and class and their implications in industrial organizations, see G. Karunanithi, *Caste and Class in Industrial Organization,* New Delhi: Commonwealth, 1991. See also Bam Dev Sharda, *Tribes, Castes, and Harijans,* New Delhi: Ajanta, 1991; and V. T. Rajshekar, *The Dilemma of the Caste and Class in India,* Banglore: Dalit Sahitya Akademy, 1984.

39. Bhagwan Das, *The Science of Social Organization,* Banaras: Anand Publishing House, 1948; Jadunath Sarkar, *Military History of India,* Calcutta: M. C. Sarkar & Sons, 1960; E. Shils, *The Intellectual between Tradition and Modernity,* The Hague: Mouton & Co., 1961; D. P. Mukherji, *Diversities,* New Delhi: People's Publishing House, 1958; and Raj P. Mohan and Arthur S. Wilke, "Intellectuals in India: Between Tradition and Modernity," *Journal of National Development* 3, no. 1, 1990.

40. K. M. Kapadia, *Marriage and Family in India,* Bombay: Oxford University Press, 1958; R. C. Majumdar and A. D. Pusalkar, *The History and Culture of Indian People,* 4 vols., Bombay: Bharitya Vidya Bhawan, 1960; P. H. Prabhu, *Hindu Social Organization,* Bombay: Popular Book Depot, 1959; and Dan A. Chekki, "Recent Directions in Family Research: India and North America," *Journal of Comparative Family Studies* 19, no. 2, 1988.

41. B. B. Misra, *The Indian Middle Classes: Their Growth in Modern Times,* Bombay: Oxford University Press, 1961; Ramkrishana Mukherjee, *Sociologists and Social Change in India Today,* New Delhi: Prentice-Hall, 1965; and T. K. Oommen and P. N. Mukherji (eds.), *Indian Society: Reflections and Introspections,* Bombay: Popular Parkashan, 1986.

42. Y. B. Damle, "Reference Group Theory with Regard to Mobility in Caste," *Social Action,* April 1963; P. N. Rastogi, "Functional Analysis of Sanskritisation," *Eastern Anthropologist,* January–April 1963.

43. G. C. Hallen, "Sociology of Literature," *Social Science* 14, no. 1, 1965.

44. S. L. Sharma and R. N. Sirivasta, "Institutional Resistance to Induced Islamization in a Convert Community: An Empiric Study in Sociology of Religion," *Sociological Bulletin* 16, no. 1, March 1967.

45. D. N. Majumdar, *Social Contours of an Industrial City in India,* Bombay: Asia Publishing House, 1960; Radhakamal Mukerjee and Baljit Singh, *Social Profiles of a Metropolis,* New York: Asia Publishing House, 1961.

46. See, for instance, studies by McKim Marriott, *Caste Ranking and Community Structure in Five Regions of India and Pakistan,* Poona: Deccan College, 1960, and the various references in this volume. See also Arthur S. Wilke and Raj P. Mohan, "An Approach to Community Study: An Examination of Merchant Castes in Two Indian Cities," *Sociological Bulletin* 25, no. 2, 1976, and "Caste,

Caste Association, Caste Federation and Inequality as Vocabularies," *Contributions to Indian Sociology* 12, no. 2, 1978.

47. B. Prasad, "Foreign Technology and India's Economic Development," *International Development Review* 10, no. 2, January 1968; and R. T. Tewari, *Development and Change in India,* Delhi: Ashish, 1988.

48. Parmatma Saran, "Medical Care and Its Determining Factors at an Indian Hospital," *Indian Sociological Bulletin* 5, no. 4, July 1968. For recent studies, see the special issue on "Social Science and Health," *Journal of Social and Economic Studies* 3, no. 4, 1986; and R. Venkataratnam, *Medical Sociology in an Indian Setting,* Delhi: The MacMillan Co. of India, 1979.

49. See, for instance, Ramkrishana Mukherji, op. cit., and especially the extensive bibliography on pp. 219–29.

50. Raj P. Mohan, "Local Newspapers: Case Study of Newspapers of an Industrial City in India," in *La Prensa,* Barcelona: Instituto De Ciencias Sociales, 1964.

51. S. D. Kapoor, "Employee Job Satisfaction: Basic Imperatives and Measurement," *Indian Sociological Bulletin* 4, no. 4, July 1967; and especially the work done by the Siriram Institute of Industrial Management in New Delhi. See also A. D. Moddie (ed.), *Concept of Work in Indian Society,* Delhi: Manohar, 1990; Biswajit Ghosh, "Organizing Unorganized Workers: The Case of Bindery Workers in Calcutta," *Sociological Bulletin* 37, nos. 1–2, 1988, pp. 97–112; and Baldev Sharma, *Not by Bread Alone: A Study of Organizational Climate and Employer-Employee Relations in India,* New Delhi: Shri Ram Centre for Industrial Relations and Human Resources, 1987.

52. See M. S. Gore (ed.), *Problems of Rural Change: Some Case Studies,* Delhi: Delhi School of Social Work, 1963.

53. A. Bopegamage, *Delhi: A Study in Urban Sociology,* Bombay: University of Bombay Press, 1957, especially the bibliography on this subject.

54. See note 31.

55. G. Bose, "Delinquency in India," in K. R. Eissier (ed.), *Searchlight on Delinquency,* London: Imago, 1949; S. D. Gokhle, "Juvenile Delinquency in Relation to Social Influence," *Indian Journal of Social Research,* June 1954.

56. I. P. Desail, "Effects of Changes in Occupations on Social Relationship with Reference to Family," *Journal of M. S. University of Baroda* 10, no. 2, July 1961; Chanderkala A. Hate, *Hindu Woman and Her Future,* Bombay: New Book Company, 1948.

57. Ajit Das Gupta, "Determination of Fertility Level and Trend in Defective Registration Areas," *Bulletin de l'Institut International Statistique* 38, 1958; S. Chandersekhar, *Asia's Population Problem,* London: Allen and Unwin, 1967.

58. Santosh Kumar Nandy, op. cit.

59. Imtiaz Ahmad, op. cit.

60. Santosh Kumar Nandy, op. cit.

61. Pitirim A. Sorokin, *Sociological Theories of Today,* New York: Harper and Row, 1968.

62. T.K.N. Unnithan et al. (eds.), op. cit.

63. R. N. Saksena, "Sociology in India," *Transactions of the Fourth World Congress of Sociology* 1, 1959, pp. 57–71.

64. Y. B. Damle, "For a Theory of Indian Sociology" (unpublished paper).

65. T.K.N. Unnithan et al. (eds.), op. cit.

66. Santosh Kumar Nandy, op. cit.

67. R. M. Srivastva, "Sociology for India: Some Considerations," *Indian Journal of Social Research* 7, no. 3, 1966, pp. 198–205.

68. R. N. Saksena, op. cit., p. 59.

69. Ibid.

70. Ibid.

71. Ibid., pp. 59–60; see also A. K. Saran, "India," in Joseph S. Roucek (ed.), *Contemporary Sociology,* New York: Philosophical Library, 1958, reprinted by Greenwood Press, Westport, Conn., 1969, pp. 1013–34.

72. Saran, "India," p. 60.

73. Institute of Social Sciences, *Sociology in India,* Agra: Agra University, 1965, p. 173.

74. See the article by Y. B. Damle, "Theoretical Orientations and Methodological Perspectives for Sociology in India in the 1980s," in P.K.B. Nayar (ed.), *Sociology in the 1980s: Retrospect and Prospect,* New Delhi: D. K. Publishers and Distributors, B. R. Publishing Corp., 1982, pp. 45–59.

75. See Anant Ram Sharay, *Development of Sociology in India,* Bombay: Allied Publishers, 1988.

76. See A. R. Desai, "Relevance of the Marxist Approach to the Study of Indian Society," in P.K.B. Nayar (ed.), *Sociology in the 1980s: Retrospect and Prospect,* New Delhi: D. K. Publishers and Distributors, B. R. Publishing Corp., 1982, pp. 93–114; and the writings of Yogendra Singh, *Indian Sociology: Social Conditioning and Emerging Concerns,* New Delhi: Vistaar Publications, 1986.

77. Anant Ram Sharay, op. cit.

78. See the writings of G. Omvedt, "Toward a Marxist Analysis of Caste," *Social Scientist* 6, no. 11, 1978, pp. 70–76.

79. Yogendra Singh, op. cit.

80. See S. M. Dubey, "Sociology of the Professions in India: Emerging and Needed Studies," in P.K.B. Nayar (ed.), *Sociology in the 1980s: Retrospect and Prospect,* New Delhi: D. K. Publishers and Distributors, B. R. Publishing Corp., 1982, pp. 245–72.

81. Ibid.

82. Ibid.

83. See M.S.A. Rao, "Sociology in the 1980s: Retrospect and Prospect," in P.K.B. Nayar (ed.), *Sociology in the 1980s: Retrospect and Prospect,* New Delhi: D. K. Publishers and Distributors, B. R. Publishing Corp., 1982, pp. 15–43.

84. Yogendra Singh, op. cit.

85. See R. S. Khare, *The Hindu Hearth and Home,* New Delhi: Vikas, 1976.

86. Yogendra Singh, op. cit.

87. M.S.A. Rao, op. cit.

88. For more information, see T. K. Oommen, "Sociological Issues in the Analysis of Special Movements in Independent India," *Sociological Bulletin* 26, no. 1, 1977, pp. 14–37.

89. See P. N. Mukherjee, "Social Movement and Social Change: Towards a Conceptual Clarification and Theoretical Framework," *Sociological Bulletin* 26, no. 1, 1977, pp. 38–59.

90. M.S.A. Rao, "Sociology in India in the Seventies and Eighties," *Economic and Political Weekly* 14, 1979, pp. 678–90.

91. See T. N. Madan, "Who Chooses Modern Medicine and Why," *Economic and Political Weekly* 4, no. 37, 1969, pp. 1475–84; and D. Banerji, "Social and Cultural Foundations of Health Services System," *Economic and Political Weekly* (Special Number), no. 9, 1974, pp. 123–26.

92. M.S.A. Rao, 1982, op. cit.

93. Ibid.

94. See J. P. Naik, *Some Perspectives on Non-Formal Education*, New Delhi: Allied, 1977.

95. M.S.A. Rao, op. cit.

96. Indian Council of Social Science Research (ICSSR), *Surveys of Research in Sociology and Social Anthropology*, vols. 1 and 2, Bombay: Popular Prakashan, 1985.

97. See S. P. Jain, *A Status Study of Population Research in India*, New Delhi: McGraw Hill, 1975; K. E. Vaidyanathan, *Studies on Morality in India*, Gandhigram: GIRH & FF, 1972; Sarah Abraham and K. B. Gotpagar, *An Annotated Bibliography of Mortality Studies in India*, Bombay: Himalaya Publishing House, 1985; Anurudh Jain and Pravin Visaria (eds.), *Infant Mortality in India: Differentials and Determinants*, Newbury Park, CA: Sage Publications, 1988; Barbara J. Isely, *Modernization and Sex Differences in Mortality in India: A New Perspective*, East Lansing: International Center, Michigan State University, 1988.

98. J. B. Wyon and J. E. Gordon, *The Khanna Study: Population in Rural Punjab*, Cambridge, Mass.: Harvard University Press, 1971.

99. A. R. Omran and C. C. Standley, *Family Formation and Health: An International Collaborative Study in India, Philippines, and Turkey*, New York: WHO Publications Center, 1976.

100. Susan Lewandowski, *Migration and Ethnicity in Urban India: Kerala Migrants in the City of Madras, 1870–1970*, New Delhi: Manohar, 1980; Biplab Dasgupta, *Migration and Development: Major Features of Migratory Movements in India*, New York: UNESCO, 1982; J. P. Singh, *Patterns of Rururban Migration in India*, New Delhi: Inter-India Publications, 1986; Haraprasad Chattopadyaya, *Internal Migration in India: A Case Study of Bengal*, Calcutta: K. P. Bagchi, 1987; A. S. Oberai, P. H. Pradhan, and M. G. Sardana, *Determinants and Consequences of Internal Migration in India: Studies in Bihar, Kerala and Uttar Pradesh*, New York: Oxford University Press, 1989.

101. S. N. Agarwal, *Age at Marriage in India*, Bombay: Kitab Mahal, 1962; G. Arora, "Changing Dimensions of Social Stratification and Fertility Behavior in India," *Eastern Anthropologist* 39, no. 4, 1986, pp. 123–34.

102. N. V. Sovani, *Internal Migration and the Future Trend of Population in India*, Belgrade: World Population Conference.

103. K. A. Pisharoti, *The Alhoor Experience*, Gandhigram: GIRH & PE, 1971; K. Mahadevan, *Differentials in South India*, New Delhi: Sterling Publishers, 1979.

104. K. Anand, "An Analysis of Differential Fertility in Chandigarh," *Journal on Family Welfare* 12, no. 3, 1966; Edwin D. Driver, *Differential Fertility in Central India*, Princeton: Princeton University Press, 1963.

105. Prafulla Bebarta, *Family Type and Fertility in India*, Hanover, Mass.: Christopher Pub. House, 1977.

106. T. Poffenberger, "Motivational Aspects of Resistance to Family Planning in an Indian Village," *Demography* 5, no. 2, 1968, pp. 757–66; D. A. May and David Heer, "Son Survivorship and Motivation and Family Size in India," *Population Studies* 22, no. 2, 1961, pp. 256–85; Mahmood Mamdani, *The Myth of Population Control: Family, Caste and Class in Indian Village,* New York: Monthly, 1972.

107. Edwin D. Driver, op. cit.; and Leela Visaria, "Demographic Transition among the Parsis: 1881–1971," *Economic and Political Weekly* 9, no. 43, 1974, pp. 1828–36.

108. K. A. Srinivasan, "Perspective Study of the Fertility Behavior of a Group of Married Women in Rural India: Design and Findings of the First Round of Inquiry," *Population Review* 11, no. 2, 1967, pp. 46–60; G. Arora, "Caste, Socioeconomic Status and Fertility: A Study of the Proximate Determinants of Fertility in Village Riwasa," *Guru Nanak Journal of Sociology* 6, no. 2, 1985, pp. 145–60.

109. V. M. Dandekar and Kumudini Dandekar, *Survey of Fertility and Mortality in Poona,* Poona: Gokhale Institute of Politics and Economics, 1953.

110. Udai Pareek and V. Kothandapani, "Modernization and Attitudes toward Family Size and Family Planning," *Social Biology* 16, no. 1, 1969, p. 999; G. Arora, "Changing Dimensions of Social Stratification and Fertility Behavior in India," *Eastern Anthropologist* 39, no. 4, 1986, pp. 123–34.

111. S. C. Gulati, *Fertility in India: An Econometric Analysis of a Metropolis,* New Delhi: Sage Publications, 1988; Prafulla Bebarta, op. cit.; and Marilyn Fernandez, *Fertility Patterns in Kerala, India: An Assessment of the Role of Modernization and Family Planning in Determining Fertility Norms and Behavior,* doctoral dissertation, Loyola University of Chicago, 1982; Abusaleh Shariff, *Fertility Transition in Rural South India,* New Delhi: Gain Publishing House, 1989.

112. For more information, see Doranne Jacobson and Susan Wadley, *Women in India: Two Perspectives,* Columbia, SC: South Asia Books, 1977; and K. N. Jha, *Women toward Modernization,* Patna: Janaki Prakashan, 1985.

113. M.S.A. Rao, op. cit.

32

Sociology and Sociological Works in Japan

Tsuyoshi Ishida

Ever since Howard Becker[1] and Jesse Frederick Steiner[2] introduced Japanese sociology to American sociologists, some Japanese sociologists have endeavored to inform Western specialists about Japanese society and about the contribution they have made toward understanding their society. Until a decade or so ago, resources relating to Japanese society and sociology written in English by Japanese sociologists included books prepared by Chie Nakane,[3] Takeshi Ishida,[4] George K. Yamamoto and Tsuyoshi Ishida,[5] and Tsuyoshi Ishida.[6] The quarterly journal *Japanese Sociological Review* has a brief introduction to the contents in English, which also helps Western sociologists understand Japanese society and sociology. Adding to these resources, works published between 1975 and 1990, the author of this chapter intends to introduce Japanese sociology to the Western world.

What a coincidence to learn that the foundation of leading sociological thought in the world and the newly established Japanese central government were both in the forefront of news around the 1860s! Leading world sociologists and social thinkers whose theories strongly affected Japan during the Meiji period (1868–1912) were Herbert Spencer (1820–1903), Auguste Comte (1798–1857), Lorenz von Stein (1815–1890), Albert E. F. Schäffle (1831–1903), Lester F. Ward (1841–1913), Jean Gabriel Tarde (1843–1904), Leonard T. Hobhouse (1864–1929), Franklin H. Giddings (1855–1931), Albion W. Small (1854–1926), Ferdinand Tönnies (1855–1936), and Charles H. Cooley (1864–1929).

As in most developing countries, Japan gradually introduced and started to discuss Western thought and practice of law, institution, custom, and industrialization when the new Meiji government started in 1868. Also,

higher educational institutions were established around the middle of the
Meiji period. Sociology as a core subject was part of the curriculum of the
newly established Tokyo University. An American social scientist, Ernest
Francisco Fenollosa (1853–1908), came to Japan in 1878 and taught political science, economics, and philosophy as a visiting professor. One of his
main objectives in teaching political science was to lecture on a sociology
developed by Herbert Spencer. This course was essential for those who
were going to go into government or politics. For Fenollosa, teaching sociology was a byproduct of teaching economics based on John Stuart Mill's
works; teaching political science based on Francis Lieber's and Theodore
D. Woolsey's works; and teaching philosophy based on Immanuel Kant's
and G.W.F. Hegel's works.[7] Tokyo University admitted sociology under
the name *Setai-gaku* (a study of world conditions) as an independent subject in 1881; it was taught by Shoichi Toyama (1848–1900), who was a
historian and, at the time, dean of letters. In 1885 the contemporary Japanese name of the subject, *Shakai-gaku* (a study of society or sociology),
was adopted formally by the university. Fenollosa's lectures were based
on social evolutionism; with his interpretation of Hegel's works, he wanted
to develop his own evolutional thought. He used textbooks written by
Herbert Spencer, Walter Bagehot, and Lewis Henry Morgan.[8]

Shoichi Toyama first went to England in 1866 and learned about Spencerian social evolutionism, which dominated all his later works. He went
to the United States in 1872 and studied philosophy and physics at the
University of Michigan. He became the first occupant of the chair of sociology when it was established at Tokyo University in 1893.[9] His research
interests, however, were Japanese mythology, mythological society, and
the moral history of traditional Japan. Nevertheless, his works were
counted as the first positive sociological ones.

Nagao Ariga (1860–1920) learned sociology under Fenollosa at Tokyo
University and taught sociology there until his interest moved to law. Nevertheless, he is a pioneer of sociology in Japan because the main focus in
his lectures was the social organismic theory of Spencer. He published two
volumes, *Shakai-Shinka Ron* (Social Evolution) and *Shukyo-Shinka Ron*
(Evolution in Religion), both in 1883. Ariga collected materials from Ezo
(Hokkaido), China, and Korea, and he interpreted how the traditional
Japanese large family system evolved. He firmly believed that loyalty to
the emperor, ancestor worship, and respect for the head of the household
were the three major factors which upheld the Meiji regime.[10] Both Toyama and Ariga considered sociology a fundamental subject for those who
were going to enter politics. However, they did not accept or support a
major sociopolitical movement called Jiyu-Minken Undo, the Liberty and
People's Rights Movement, which was active in Japan around the 1880s
and which was responsible for establishing the election system and install-
ing the national Diet. They were indifferent because they thought that

those who participated in the movement were acting too hastily. In other words, Toyama and Ariga were conservative in regard to sociopolitical mass movements.

Japanese sociology, in essence, is a combination of imported Western thought on society and indigenous interpretations or approaches to Japanese society. At the outset of Japanese sociology about 100 years ago, the power of imported thoughts and practices from the Western world was strong. This trend, however, gradually diminished. Then, the interpretation of these thoughts and the application of Western thought to Japanese society were eagerly pursued. Following a period of strong impact of ultra-nationalism upon sociology and social sciences in Japan during World War II, Japanese sociologists gradually gained freedom of action and thought. Today, most of them teach at colleges and/or pursue theoretical discussions or fieldwork. I believe that the number of sociologists teaching at colleges in Japan and the number of books published by them in Japan are the largest in the world besides that of the United States. Although their research funds and materials are limited, they are active in introducing new theories, new ideas, and new methods in sociology using their own Japanese society as a sample. The remainder of this chapter focuses on five aspects of Japanese sociology: a short history of the discipline; the institutionalization of sociology as an academic discipline; current trends in theoretical and methodological studies; current trends in research in the prominent subfields of sociology; and recent works on contemporary Japanese society which are mainly conducted by American researchers.

SHORT HISTORY OF JAPANESE SOCIOLOGY

Japanese sociology has a history of approximately 100 years beginning with the first two Japanese books on sociology, *Shakai-Shinka Ron* (Social Evolution) and *Shukyo-Shinka Ron* (Evolution in Religion), both by Nagao Ariga, which appeared in 1883. This was about 30 years after the publication of Herbert Spencer's *Social Statics,* 1850; 40 years after John Stuart Mill's *A System of Logic, Ratiocinative and Inductive,* 1843; and about 50 years after Auguste Comte's *Cours de philosophie positive,* 1830–1842. Although Japanese society dissolved its feudal organization in 1868, it could not establish a constitutional monarchy until there was an Imperial Constitution, which was not complete until 1889. Japan experienced the Liberty and People's Rights Movement in the Meiji era (1868–1912), the Democracy Movement in the Taisho era (1912–1926), and the Militarism and Democratic Change Movement in the Showa era (1926–1989). Because of these unstable political systems and radical changes in political regime, Japanese sociologists were expected to work closely with the central government during most of these eras.

One of the early debates among sociologists was what they should study and on what they should lecture. Sociology was considered a fundamental scholarship of political science, and therefore those planning to enter government and politics had to study sociology. The original name of sociology, *Setai-gaku* (a study of world conditions), indicated this trend.

English words such as "society," "sociology," "nation," and "people" prompted much discussion among early sociologists and social scientists in Japan. As primary discussions centered on what these words meant and what Chinese characters were to be assigned to these words, sociological discussions could not get to the heart of social organismic theory. Today, for example, "nation" is translated into Japanese as *kokka* or *kokumin,* depending on its context. Assigned Chinese characters for *kokka* mean "houses belonging to a country," whereas the ones for *kokumin* mean "people belonging to a country." What about "people"? Government officials do not use the word, because it refers either to the solidarity of the human being beyond the boundary of a country or to those who are not identified by their nationalities. Naturally, words convey ideologies, so the government and social scientists were sensitive in choosing words.

Early sociological works were produced by those who either had taught or had been interested in studying sociology. Shoichi Toyama published three articles, "Kamiyo no Josei" (Women in Mythology), "Kamiyo no Kon' in oyobi Kazoku Seido" (Marriage and Family System in Mythology), and "Kamiyo niokeru Seiji Shiso oyobi Seido" (Political Thought and System in Mythology), in 1909. Besides teaching psychology and English in his early career, and history and logic later, he gave lectures on sociology based on the thought of Herbert Spencer.

An advocate of the natural rights of man, Hiroyuki Kato wrote *Jinken Shinsetsu* (A New Theory of Human Rights, 1882) and became an example of how difficult it is to maintain one's original thought on politics and society throughout one's academic life. He originally maintained that Japan needed to introduce a European type of Diet system and that man had indigenous human rights given by nature. He later denied his original idea of human rights and gradually shifted his thinking to Social Darwinism, wherein human rights evolved within society. Influenced by Ernst Heinrich Häckel and Albert Eberhard Friedrich Schäffle, he published *Shinsei Taii* (An Introduction to True Politics, 1870), *Kokutai Shinron* (True Theory of the National Body, 1875), *Shakaigaku Ippan* (General Sociology, 1891), and other books.

As a law professor, Nobushige Hozumi wrote *Ancestor Worship and Japanese Law* (1901), the first English publication in the field of sociology of law. He employed sociological methods in researching ancestor worship and other social customs in order to clarify social relationships in specific social settings. Tongo Takebe tried to establish his own system of sociology after the one developed by Auguste Comte. Takebe wanted to combine the social perspectives of Confucianism with Comte's positivism. He published four volumes of *Riron Futsu Shakaigaku* (Theoretical General Sociology, 1905–1918) and in these writings asserted that society is an unknown organism. By studying sociology, he concluded that the ideal government embodying peace could be realized only through the cooperation of people and that no one would accept extreme socialism or egalitarianism.

After learning sociology from Spencer and Comte, Japanese sociologists moved their emphasis from organismic sociology to psychological sociology, which originated in the United States. Ryukichi Endo's book, *Genkon no Shakaigaku* (Sociology Today, 1901), was heavily influenced by Franklin H. Giddings. Endo emphasized that society was based on collective consciousness; that is, social phenomena could be explained by the combination of the will of human beings. Besides Giddings, American sociologists Lester F. Ward, Charles H. Cooley, and Charles A. Ellwood strongly influenced Japanese sociologists around the turn of the century. Shotaro Yoneda, Iku Kobayashi, and Hideo Higuchi were proponents of psychological sociology. In his book *Gendai Jin no Shinri to Gendai Bunmei* (Contemporary Psychology and Modern Civilization, 1919) and others, Yoneda introduced various theories of sociology which he had learned while he was in Europe and the United States. He was especially influenced by Jean Gabriel Tarde and Georg Simmel. Kobayashi published *Shakai Shinrigaku* (Social Psychology, 1909) as the first Japanese book under this title; Higuchi published *Shakaigaku Shoshi* (A Short History of Sociology, 1911).

Until then, many sociologists discussed how sociology should be systematized, and snythetic sociology was popular. Synthetic sociology tried to interpret all kinds of social issues, and its supporters wanted to include all social sciences under one umbrella called sociology. Therefore, whoever wanted to enter the field of government and/or politics was required to study sociology before deciding to pursue careers in these areas.

Yasuma Takata studied sociology under Yoneda, but he is probably the first Japanese sociologist who established his own theory of society and sociology. In one of his major books, *Shakaigaku Gairon* (Introductory Sociology, 1922), Takata departed from Yoneda's psychological sociology and switched his viewpoint of sociology to a framework of a branch of social sciences. He also was against synthetic sociology. He insisted that sociology should be one of the scholastic fields under social sciences, such as economics, political science, administration, and so forth. Following his interpretation of sociology, Japanese sociologists became sufficiently confident to assert that sociology is a branch of social sciences in Japan.

Takata's theoretical sociology was attacked by both militarists and Marxists. Although the militarists came from the central government, the Marxists were sociologists and philosophers teaching Marxism at colleges in Japan. Thus, Takata moved from sociology to theoretical economics, based on his interests and institutional affiliations. Many sociologists thought his move was a great loss to Japanese sociology.[11]

Around 1920, Japanese sociologists started to establish individual fields of study and research, such as family, rural communities, cities, industries, ideologies, and social welfare. Sociologists shifted their concern from building an independent science of sociology to having specific fields of study in society. This move was made so as to understand how critical thinking applies to a real social world. There were only a handful of sociologists at that time, and they often interacted with scholars in philosophy, economics, political science, finance, administration, and law.

The founders of specialized fields in sociology included Teizo Toda in the field of family, Eitaro Suzuki and Kizaemon Aruga in the field of rural society, Fukutaro Okui in urban society, and Kunio Odaka in occupation. Other fields such as social behavior or consciousness, social problems, social pathology, social policy, and sociology of knowledge drew the attention of Japanese sociologists in the 1920s and 1930s. Although there were only around 100 Japanese sociologists and social practitioners at that time, and only 30 who taught sociology at colleges before 1945,[12] they were eager to produce research results. According to Takashi Koyama,[13] sociological works from 1932 to 1936 numbered 238 books and 1,424 articles. This was a clear indication that Japanese sociologists wanted to discuss and publish the results of their studies related to sociological theories and/or practices.

Sociological discussions were conducted either through publications or in personal communications. Even before World War II more than twenty publishers were interested in publishing sociological works in Japan. As most Japanese sociologists teaching at small colleges worked by themselves, those who wanted to promote their sociological works had to continue personal relationships with their former teachers at their alma maters or had to be active in informal sociology study groups. Few schools nurtured sociologists before World War II. Tokyo, Kyoto, and Waseda universities, together with Hitotsubashi College and a few other minor institutions, were dominant in developing younger sociologists. If younger sociologists wanted to work in the profession of sociology, they had to establish informal personal contacts with their former teachers. Japanese sociologists also came from the fields of philosophy, social policy, history, and law. If those who came from other fields hadn't established relationships with their alma maters but wanted to promote their scholarship, they had to establish or belong to informal research communities.

The journal *Shakaigaku Hyoron* (Sociological Review), edited by Toshio Hayase and published through October 1935, was one of the sources to which sociologists could contribute to enhance their scholarship.[14] The journals *Nempo Shakaigaku* (Annual Sociology),[15] *Shakaigaku Kenkyu* (Sociological Studies), *Minzokugaku Kenkyu* (Folklore Studies),[16] *Shak-*

aigaku Zasshi (Journal of Sociology),[17] *Kikan Shakaigaku* (Sociology Quarterly),[18] and *Shakai Jigyo Kenkyu* (Study of Social Welfare)[19] invited sociologists to publish their sociological works during the 1920s and 1930s. The variety of sociological journals published during that period exceeds those we find in Japan today.

In countries which have lost wars, the loss changes almost every social structure which existed previously in that country, including family, marriage, rural community, employment, social welfare, tax, franchise, communication, education including higher learning, and so on. After 1945, a major change occurred in Japanese sociology. As the number of colleges and universities increased, the number of sociologists in colleges increased accordingly. Before World War II sociology was seldom installed in the college curriculum, but this trend changed after the war. Thus, the number of Japanese sociologists increased over twofold during the decade after 1945. This increase will continue. As of today, the number of Japanese sociologists is around 1,200.

SOCIOLOGY AS AN INSTITUTION

Most academic associations have their own informal preludes. So does the Japan Sociological Association, which has about 1,200 members today. Shakai Seisaku Gakkai (the Academic Association of Social Policy), organized in 1897, intended to support social goals of the government which were pursued under privately owned economic systems. Shakai Mondai Kenkyukai (the Study Group for Social Problems), also organized in 1897, intended to pursue socialistic solutions concerning government goals. These organizations continued for only two to three years after being founded.

During the time when social policies and social problems were being debated by various specialists through their publications, *Shakai Zasshi* (Journal of Society) was published in 1897. The name of this journal used the word "society," not "sociology." It carefully avoided academic discussions and instead dealt with solutions to real and social problems in order to improve the social conditions of Japan at the time.

Shakaigaku Kenkyu-kai (the Study Group for Sociology), organized in 1898, was active for five years. Its journal, *Shakai* (Society), first published in 1899, was renamed *Shakaigaku Zasshi* (Journal of Sociology) in 1902.

These groups and activities symbolized the bewilderment of academicians in sociology and social sciences at the time. Although the new nation had started only a few decades earlier, the government could not decide what policies should be adopted and what assistance it could ask from colleges. Sociologists themselves were questioning what issues they should discuss—socialistic society, social policy, relief, policies for the poor community, as well as the ideal society proposed by Marxian ideology. Many

Western sociological ideas were being interpreted, published, and introduced in Japan by Japanese social scientists by the end of the nineteenth century.

Nihon Shakaigakkai (the Japan Sociological Association) was formed in 1924, and its first journal, *Shakaigaku Zasshi* (Journal of Sociology), was published in the same year. The journal's name was changed to *Kikan Shakaigaku* (Sociology Quarterly) in 1931, and then to *Nempo Shakaigaku* (Annual Sociology) in 1933. In 1935 a new journal, *Shakaigaku Hyoron* (Sociological Review), was published.[20] Also, a less formal sociological organization, Nihon Shakaigaku-in (Japan Academy of Sociology) was formed in 1913; it started to publish *Nihon Shakaigakuin Nempo* (Annual Sociology of Japan Academy) in the same year.

Sociologists and sociological activities in Japan proliferated after 1950. Where new universities, colleges, and junior colleges were established, sociology was legitimately recognized as a teaching subject. Empirical research on social conditions was encouraged, and almost every college and university began employing sociologists as full-time or part-time instructors. Within twenty years after 1945, the number of sociologists teaching sociology at higher institutions of learning in Japan exceeded 400, almost ten times the number from the 1930s.[21] Membership in the Japan Sociological Association around 1965 was more than 1,100, and this number is still increasing due to the proliferation of schools and departments in colleges.

Today most graduate students who have finished coursework for a Ph.D. teach at colleges or junior colleges. At times it is easy for them to find teaching jobs, but at other times they face difficulties. Since employment is a matter of balance between supply and demand, it is difficult to predict if new candidates will find employment after successfully completing their degree.

Furthermore, Japanese graduate schools seldom confer Ph.D. degrees to their graduates even if they finish required coursework. This is especially true for doctoral students majoring in humanities and social sciences. The schools themselves are not the only problem. Professors at graduate schools rarely advise students regarding the themes for Ph.D. theses and the know-how of successfully completing them. Furthermore, both professors and students at graduate schools lack confidence in their respective teaching and learning roles. In fact, a large number of professors do not have Ph.D. degrees.

Graduate students with M.A. degrees may choose to get a job either in private enterprise or in public service. Others may choose to advance their scholarship by staying in graduate school for an additional three years, hoping they may have opportunities to teach in some college in the future. How soon? Nobody knows. The future is uncertain for those who are unemployed despite having completed their coursework. Many unconferred Ph.D. graduates do research without much compensation. In 1986, there were 145 graduates who had finished their coursework but were unemployed. There were 31 graduate schools with Ph.D. programs in sociology in 1992. There were 251 professors, including assistant professors and instructors, in graduate schools which confer Ph.D.s in sociology in 1986.[22] In essence, Japanese sociology in higher education is still not fully established.

Japanese Sociologists in Colleges

In order to understand the characteristics of Japanese sociology professors, factors such as institutional affiliation, age structure, affiliated departments, educational background, and others will be presented, because they are quite different from what American sociologists assume. The ecological differences of Japanese sociologists are clear in education, training, employment, mobility, promotion, and retirement. The observations are based on information gathered through two publications of *Zenkoku Daigaku Shokuin-roku* (College Professors in Japan) published in 1989.[23] There were 499 colleges and universities in Japan in 1989, with the following breakdown: 364 private, 96 national, and 39 public institutions. Listed in these publications are 121,140 professors, assistant professors, and instructors. Some qualified assistants are also included. Those teaching at private institutions represent 50.8 percent, those at national institutions 43.9 percent, and those in public institutions 5.3 percent.

Of the 121,140 professors, those who teach sociology or a subfield of sociology number 1,149. With this sample number, an analysis was done of who they are and what they teach. Some are not necessarily sociology specialists, although they may be assigned to teach sociology or a related subject. Also, their interest may be in pursuing research in other fields. Their rank at colleges, in most cases, is either professor (*kyoju*) or assistant professor (*jo-kyoju*). There are a few Ph.D.s, whose doctoral degrees include not only literature or sociology but also education, economics, medicine, and agriculture. It should be noted that the Ph.D. in literature (*Bungaku Hakushi*) in a Japanese university was and even today is the only Ph.D. conferred to sociology majors. Recently, however, some universities have started to grant Ph.D.s in sociology (*Shakaigaku Hakushi*).

Institutional Affiliation

The majority (65.8%) of Japanese sociologists teach in the Kanto (Tokyo) area (41.9%) or Kinki (Kyoto-Osaka) area (23.9%). Those who teach in the Chubu (Nagoya), Kyushu (Fukuoka), and Tohoku (Sendai) areas represent 11.2 percent, 7.2 percent, and 6.0 percent, respectively. Those who teach in the Chugoku (4.2%), Hokkaido (2.9%), and Shikoku (2.7%)

areas represent the smallest proportion of Japanese sociologists. The allocation of teaching staff is based on the allocation of Japanese colleges and universities. In other words, many colleges are located in the Tokyo and Kyoto-Osaka areas. This indicates that major educational institutions not only of sociology but also of other academic fields are located in either the Tokyo or Kyoto-Osaka areas. There are no special geographical allocations of sociology professors among institutions, that is, among private, national, or public colleges. If a region happens to have more sociology professors, it is because that region has more colleges than other regions.

Age Structure

The age structure of Japanese sociology professors by rank is shown in Table 32.1 According to my survey, the age span of full professors of sociology ranges from 41 to 74, with private institutions having the widest range. National institutions have an age range of 44 to 65, whereas public institutions range from 46 to 64. Although private institutions tend to employ professors who are advanced in age, the table indicates that the mean difference in age of professors between private and national is 4, and between private and public, only 2.

The age span of assistant professors is equally wide. At private institutions it is between 33 and 63. Respective age figures for national and public institutions are 33 and 50, and 32 and 48. The mean age difference of assistant professors at different institutions, however, is not as large as is shown in the table. The table shows that the mean age of assistant professors among the three different categories of institutions is 43 (private) and 41 (national and public). Therefore, difference in age is negligible.

There are different kinds of sociology lecturers in Japanese colleges and universities. Most are young and prospective students of sociology who recently completed their graduate requirements. Some lecturers were previously in business or public service but had recently moved to colleges to teach, using their work background and experience.

Some lecturers were not promoted to assistant professors for various reasons such as seniority, available vacancy, or productivity. Even if lecturers were not productive in research, they were not terminated or forced to move to other institutions. Once a person is appointed a lecturer, he/she enjoys tenure until the age of retirement, which is usually between 63 and 70.

The age span of lecturers is 32 to 64 at private institutions, which is similar to that of national institutions (29 to 62). In public institutions, it is 28 to 42. These differences are not reflected in the mean ages of lecturers as shown in Table 32.1. The mean age of lecturers in private institutions is 38.3, which is three years more than the mean age of those teaching at national institutions (35.2). There are some institutions which have assis-

Table 32.1
Age Structure of Japanese Sociology Professors by Rank and Character of Institutions, 1989

	Private Institutions		National Institutions		Public Institutions		Percent by Positions
	Number of Incumbents	Mean of Age	Number of Incumbents	Mean of Age	Number of Incumbents	Mean of Age	
Professors	400	58.1	189	54.1	22	56.2	53.2
Assistant professors	187	43.2	162	41.2	23	40.7	32.4
Lecturers, and foreign instructors	84	38.3	33	35.2	7	37.0	10.8
Assistants	7	35.0	33	33.4	1	38.0	3.6
Total	678	51.3	417	46.0	53	46.6	100.0

tant positions in sociology, but the number of assistants is decreasing because of institutional preferences for more instructors rather than more researchers and/or assistant professors. The average age across the institutions is between 33 (national) and 38 (public). Assistants at private institutions were not considered in the sources with which the survey was conducted.

As shown in the last column of Table 32.1, more than half (53.2%) the instructors of sociology are professors. Assistant professors number only one-third (32.4%), and those who are lecturers, foreign instructors, and assistants are a much smaller percentage (14.4%).

In What Department Do They Teach?

Sociologists teach everywhere. It is true that most sociologists prefer to teach at schools of sociology, literature, humanities, or economics. However, these schools do not necessarily accept those sociologists who apply. To better understand where sociologists teach, we have classified schools into four groups. The first is a combination of schools of literature, humanities, education, foreign languages, and others. This is where sociology originally developed. The second group is composed of organizations which emphasize liberal arts, arts and sciences, or general education. Organizations in this group do not necessarily form schools. Sociologists in this group primarily teach introductory sociology or related subjects. Official names of schools and organizations included in this group are as follows: School of Arts and Sciences (Kyoyo Gakubu), Curricula for Arts and Sciences (Kyoyo Katei), General Education (Ippan Kyoiku), School of Whole Sciences (Sogo-Kagaku-bu), and School of Liberal Arts (Gakugei Gakubu). The third group combines schools of sociology, economics, law, and commerce. This is where a large number of sociologists want to be tenured; but this is not always the case, because once a sociologist starts to teach in a school, he or she tends to stay there. The fourth group is composed of schools of engineering, medicine, agriculture, physical training, home economics, music, and others. Some sociologists prefer this group because of its relative independence, the availability of financial aid, and the accessibility to interdisciplinary professionals.

Table 32.2 shows the following results. The first group—that is, the schools of literature, humanities, education, and foreign languages—employs the largest number of sociologists. There are 288 sociologists in private, 233 in national, and 26 in public institutions. This total of 547 is about 60 percent larger than the number of those who teach in schools of social sciences. The figures reflect the fact that sociology originated in the School of Literature in Japan. After 1950, a new organization called the School of Sociology was established as a larger entity than the Department of Sociology. Although Japanese institutions had schools of economics and

Table 32.2
Schools Where Sociologists Teach

Institution	Literature, Humanities, and Others	Arts and Sciences	Sociology, Economics, and Others	Engineering, Medicine, and Others	Total
Private	288	70	254	66	678
National	233	81	75	28	417
Public	26	6	17	5	54
Total	547	157	346	99	1,149

schools of law before 1945, sociology professors in these schools were few. Once the schools started to expand to accommodate more students, they separated that portion of curriculum which included sociology; this change eventually led to an independent school, the School of Sociology (Shakai Gakubu). The trend was stronger in private institutions than in national or public institutions. Whereas about 37 percent of sociologists in private institutions belong to schools of social sciences, only 18 percent belong to such schools in national institutions.

Compared to sociologists teaching in literature or social sciences, those teaching in arts and sciences or engineering, medicine, and others are relatively few. Their representation in private institutions is 20 percent; in national, 26 percent; and in public, 20 percent.

Education, Degrees, Gender, and Ethnicity

Most college professors were educated in major national universities, and this trend is still evident today. However, the tendency is decreasing. About a quarter-century ago, one-third of all college professors in Japan were graduates of Tokyo University; Kyoto University graduated one-third of the rest. According to our statistics, 18 percent of all sociologists who teach in Japanese colleges and universities today graduated from Tokyo University. Kyoto University graduates represent 11 percent. Therefore, about one-third of the sociologists teaching in Japan today are graduates of either Tokyo or Kyoto. The second largest group of graduates are from Tohoku (6.4%), Keio (4.8%), Waseda (4.4%), and Kyushu (4.0%). Other universities such as Tokyo Educational, Osaka, Hokkaido, and Hitotsubashi graduated 3 percent or less. It is interesting to note that 13 percent of the sociologists who were educated at less prestigious colleges or universities teach at their alma maters. Those who were educated at minor colleges and teach at other minor colleges represent 21 percent.

Their number is the largest in proportion to the other groups. Those who received advanced degrees overseas compose 3 percent, a very small number. Although Tokyo and Kyoto tend to allocate their graduates to national institutions (30.7%) rather than private institutions (26.1%), the two institutions continue to be interested in distributing their graduates evenly to private as well as public institutions.

As mentioned earlier, few professors have attained their Ph.D. The number with doctoral degrees in private institutions is 85 out of 678, or 12.5 percent. This trend also applies to national institutions, where 51 out of 417, or 12.2 percent, have Ph.D. degrees. Among public institutions only 5.6 percent belong in this category. The statistics by status show that the ratio of Ph.D. degree holders among full professors is 17.8 percent. Only 5.9 percent of assistant professors fall into this group. Among lecturers and foreign instructors there are only 2.4 percent. These figures indicate that the higher the status, the more Ph.D. degree holders there are. The figures do not apply to assistants, the lowest in academic rank. The ratio of degree holders in this group is the second highest, next to full professors: 12.2 percent hold Ph.D. degrees. It indicates that graduate schools have recently started to confer Ph.D.s to those satisfactorily completing their theses. This was not the case a decade ago.

The percentage of women professors in public institutions (11.1%) is higher than in private (6.5%) or national (4.8%) institutions. But public institutions still have not employed women as full professors, whereas in private institutions female full professors make up 40.9 percent of all female instructors. In national institutions they represent 15 percent. It is obvious that most colleges and universities prefer employing male faculties. Equal employment in this respect is far behind that of the United States.

Ethnic distribution among students as well as faculties is a vital national concern today. Japanese higher educational institutions rarely accept applications from students for enrollment and faculty for employment from ethnic groups other than Japanese. However, some colleges have recently started to employ *Gaikokujin Kyoshi* (foreign instructors). It can be said that many Protestant- and Catholic-supported colleges and universities in Japan have traditionally employed foreign professors. The tradition is still maintained among these schools. Apart from this custom, many Japanese colleges and universities today realize how important it is to employ foreign instructors because many faculty members, students, and businesspeople are increasingly traveling to all parts of the world. These travelers feel they should be exposed to different people and cultures before going abroad.

Some private institutions have begun to employ foreign instructors for the first time, whereas others have increased their numbers gradually. Most private institutions, however, do not realize that they segregate foreign instructors. For example, they set up different employment systems for foreign faculty, such as limited terms of employment, limited chances of promotion, different salary scales, and closed membership to certain levels of meetings. Segregation practices are more widespread among national institutions than among private institutions. Foreign faculties in national institutions are employed only as *Gaikokujin Kyoshi.* They are separate in status and role. There are twenty-three sociologists as *Gaikokujin Kyoshi* in national institutions today.

Japanese sociologists teach various subjects related to sociology. The main subjects they teach are classified into four groups. The first is introductory sociology; lectures center on the subject of sociology together with the principles of sociology, social structure, sociocultural change, human behavior, and modern society. The second group comes under applied sociology and includes industrial sociology, medical sociology, legal sociology, educational sociology, urban sociology, rural sociology, management sociology, and social planning. The third group consists of community-related subjects such as community sociology, community studies, social survey and community culture. The fourth group covers such subjects as social information, measurement sociology, and social system.

But do Japanese sociologists teach only these subjects? No, they teach more. For example, they also teach subjects such as social thought, social policy, social welfare, social security, social education, social anthropology, social psychology, social sciences, American studies, and Japanese studies. Thus, Japanese sociologists not only lecture in their fields of expertise and interest but also are committed to teach subjects that are related to sociology and social concerns.

CURRENT TRENDS IN THEORETICAL AND METHODOLOGICAL STUDIES

Japanese sociologists, like American sociologists, are sensitive to sociological works in the world. Both Japanese and American sociologists are interested in acquiring knowledge of contemporary sociology and actively publish their works. However, there are a few differences. There are only thirty-one graduate schools which produce sociologists in Japan, and most of these started to grant Ph.D.s only in the last decade or two; in the United States there are many more schools which bestow Ph.D.s in sociology, and most have been granting Ph.D. degrees for at least thirty years. Japanese sociologists are in fact novices in teaching and researching when compared to American sociologists. Japanese sociologists are still learning from their American counterparts how to organize departments of sociology at both the undergraduate and graduate levels.

The primary difference comes from the development of higher educational institutions. When the first Japanese colleges were established in the late nineteenth century, Japan was already late in promoting scholarship in comparison to the United States. While the quality and quantity of colleges and universities in Japan were and still are under the control of the central government, in the United States these factors depend on regional or national accreditation standards. Higher education is still a great concern of national policy in Japan.

The rebirth of Japanese sociology after World War II was welcomed by both Japanese and American sociologists. For the Japanese this marked a foundation for scholastic proliferation, and for the Americans it provided momentum for interaction with Japan and the Japanese. Talcott Parsons, Pitirim A. Sorokin, David Riesman, William Lloyd Warner, C. Wright Mills, and others have influenced Japanese sociologists in one way or another. Their works have been widely read by many Japanese sociologists; works such as *Toward a General Theory of Action* by Parsons, *Reconstruction of Humanity* by Sorokin, *Lonely Crowd* by Riesman, *Who Shall be Educated?* by Warner, and *White Collar* by Mills have been translated into Japanese and published.

The writings of Yasujiro Daido (*America Shakaigaku no Choryu,* or Trends of American Sociology, 1948), Toshio Hayase and Akio Baba (*Gendai America Shakaigaku,* or Modern American Sociology, 1954), and Takashi Muraki and Ayako Kikuchi (*Nijisseiki America Shakaigaku no Tembo,* or Prospect of Twentieth-Century American Sociology, 1955) indicate how Japanese sociologists reacted to the introduction of American sociology right after World War II.

During the period 1945–1985 most Japanese sociologists concentrated their research interests in one of these fields: sociological theory, family, rural society, urban society, industries, education, social psychology, social welfare, and social problems. Marxian sociology, French sociology, studies of Asian family and society, mathematical sociology, medical sociology, and social planning are the fields of research either carried out by some prewar specialists or established recently to promote the mutual interests of professionals. These fields such as Marxian sociology and mathematical sociology, however, have been and are likely to continue to be organized and maintained by informal and personal relationships rather than formal and associational exchanges. Saburo Yasuda[24] referred to this type of organization as oligarchic, but he thinks Japanese sociologists need to have these types of professional activities in order to promote their scholarship.

Current theoretical studies by Japanese sociologists can be classified into three groups. The first are studies by those who are interested in theories of sociology; the second, by those who are interested in introducing and discussing the accomplishments of great Western sociologists; and the third, by those who are interested in devoting themselves to their own fieldwork and want to introduce and expand their theories through their work. The three groups are characterized as general theorists, discussants, and field-workers, respectively.

General Theorists

Although some Japanese sociologists question whether sociology should be synthetic or formal, others discuss what society is and what sociology should be like. Ken'ichi Tominaga[25] is very interested in how theories of sociology are understood and systematized. Starting his discussions from Adam Smith, he examines why and how John Locke, Karl Marx, Ferdinand Tönnies, Max Weber, and Talcott Parsons could not develop a suitable concept of sociology (which many sociologists are still researching today). He introduces two concepts of society—wider and limited. He examines how the concept of wider society applies to (1) the whole society in which all social scientists scrutinize the utilization of their concepts, and (2) the concept of limited society, in which only sociologists examine the application of their concepts. He tries to reorganize the following: individualistic social theory, a dialectical social theory, a positivistic social theory, a social evolutionistic theory, a social change theory, and a structural-functional theory—while using his concepts of wider versus limited society and micro versus macro theories. In his theoretical scheme, action theory, role formation theory, and interaction theory are reclassified and defined as micro theory. The social system theory, the structural-functional theory, the social structural theory, and social change theory are likewise reclassified and defined as macro theory.[26] Tominaga is keenly aware of the strong and weak points of these theories. He also has a thorough knowledge of historical developments.

While Tominaga's classification of sociology theories can be considered an analysis of theories, Takeshi Yamagishi[27] explores how Western sociologists developed their ideas of examining and interpreting society in a limited sociohistorical setting. Yamagishi discusses how human beings behave in a social setting as members of a larger society. World, science, culture, role, and self meld together to determine why and how a person decides what to do. Yamagishi interprets the social reality of a human being. Although an understanding of human action requires a lot of sociological imagination, he concludes that personal behavior is based on "absurdity" and is "often alienated."

Although his classification of theories in sociology is simple and limited, Atsuhiro Terada[28] interpreted how these theories contribute in understanding social behavior and social structure. Other than these theorists, recent works by Kanji Naito,[29] Takashi Noguchi,[30] Yusuke Maki,[31] and Mamoru Funatsu[32] are well known in general theories, social typology, Marxian sociology, and symbolic interactionism, respectively.

Discussions on Western Thought

Japanese sociologists believe they cannot develop their own idea of sociology without consulting Western thinkers. Currently, the history of Western sociological thought in Europe and the United States is the basis of discussions on sociological thought in Japan. Some sociologists[33] think that Japanese society should be understood by its own theoretical framework, which earlier Japanese sociologists tried to develop, but these scholars are few.

It is clear that Japanese sociologists have introduced a large number of Western theories and works into their own theoretical discussions. Western sociologists whose works have been translated into Japanese or have been discussed extensively among Japanese sociologists are as follows: Peter Blau, Isidore Auguste M. F. X. Comte, Emile Durkheim, Erik H. Erikson, Sigmund Freud, Jürgen Habermas, George C. Homns, Claude Lévi-Strauss, John Locke, Niklas Luhmann, Robert M. MacIver, Thomas Robert Malthus, Karl Marx, George H. Mead, Robert K. Merton, Robert Michels, John Stuart Mill, Wilbert E. Moore, George P. Murdock, Talcott Parsons, Alfred R. Radcliffe-Brown, Edward A. Ross, Jean Jacques Rousseau, Alfred Schütz, Georg Simmel, Albion W. Small, Pitirim A. Sorokin, Herbert Spencer, Ferdinand Tönnies, Lester F. Ward, and Max Weber.

Among these influential Western sociologists, Max Weber and Emile Durkheim were extensively discussed by Japanese sociologists during the past decade. Yoshio Atoji[34] emphasizes that understanding is the most important concept in clarifying why and how a study of history is different from natural sciences. Starting from this concept, he discusses political thought, economic values, dimensions in law, and the rationalization of religion. Atoji not only employs Weber's works. He simultaneously describes the sociohistorical background of Weber's theories and refers to the influence of other works on Weber's theories published both in Germany and the rest of the world. As most Japanese sociologists acknowledge the importance of Weber's concepts (e.g., ideal types, two types of authority, the Protestant ethic, and capitalism), they may well want to examine further the sociohistorical background of Weber's theories. Yoshiyuki Sato[35] discusses the social action theory and value theory of Max Weber and tries to apply them to social change and professionalism in modern society. Yosuke Koto[36] uses Weber's work to reinterpret how conflict by the gods (the role of religion) applies to a modern society, which has two characteristics—surplus of conflict and surplus of order. Toshio Nakano's contribution[37] was the personifying of Weber's theory of understanding and typology of actions.

There is no doubt that Max Weber presented Japanese sociologists with many effective ideas to understand modern society. His theories continue to attract Japanese sociologists today. From a comparative point of view, the theory of Max Weber has been contrasted with that of Emile Durkheim by Hiroshi Orihara.[38] His main focus centered on methods of social sciences. Two volumes of his work are discussions of *The Protestant Ethic and the Spirit of Capitalism,* by Weber, and *Suicide,* by Durkheim. Kosei Sakuma compared Weber's methods of social understanding with those of Marx[39] and other European social scientists.[40] Comparative discussions on Max Weber and Ernst Troeltsch,[41] and on Max Weber and Jürgen Habermas,[42] have also contributed to enrich Western sociological thought in Japan.

Besides Max Weber, Emile Durkheim has figured in many sociological discussions in Japan. Collective conscience, collective representations, social recognition, functional analysis, action theory, and the four types of suicide have been discussed by Hisao Naka,[43] Koken Sasaki,[44] Takashi Miyajima,[45] and Toichiro Koseki.[46] Their main focus was the precise interpretation of interrelations of Durkheim's basic concepts and their sociohistorical backgrounds.

Other Western sociologists whose works have been recently discussed in Japan include Georg Simmel, Karl Marx, Talcott Parsons, Alfred Schütz, Claude Lévi-Strauss, and Jean Jacques Rousseau. Yoshio Atoji[47] discusses the critiques and anti-critiques of Simmel sociology done by Wilhelm Dilthey, Alfred Jules Emile Fouillée, Th. Kistiakowski, Hans Freyer, Siegfried Kracauer, Rudolf Heberle, Othmar Spann, Hans Kelsen, Maria Steinhoff, Albert Salomon, George Lukác, Emile Durkheim, and Max Weber. As most Japanese sociologists place a person's surname in front of "sociology" to denote that person's specific theory of sociology, so Atoji puts Simmel's name in front of "sociology" and calls it "Simmel sociology." Atoji interpreted the concepts of small group, authority, and conflict after scrutinizing Simmel's work and a large number of related works. In his second book on Simmel, Atoji[48] focused on the concepts of exchange, education, and religion.

Karl Marx is another social thinker whose works were well read among Japanese social scientists. Takashi Hosoya's recent work[49] focused on Marx's materialistic social thought and showed how thought was historically as well as socially built into his ideology. Akio Tanosaki[50] tried to summarize Parsons's entire works, from *The Structure of Social Action* through *The American University,* in one volume with the help of eight sociologists. He included in this book Parsons's original paper, which was prepared for a lecture at Harvard University in 1971. If one wants to understand why Parsons was so popular among Japanese sociologists, this book gives some clues. Alfred Schütz introduced the concept of life world and emphasized the importance of meaning and understanding between two actors. Masataka Katagiri[51] interpreted Schütz's idea of human relations by pointing out that personal relevance, which often is based on a stock of knowledge, gives an active world to an actor. Claude Lévi-Strauss's work was interpreted by Takashi Noguchi.[52] Keiichi Sakuda[53] discussed Jean Jacques Rousseau's attitude of ambivalence and utopia.

A different approach to American society and sociology has been taken by Akira Takahashi,[54] Tsuyoshi Ishida,[55] and Mamoru Funatsu.[56] Takahashi accumulated his findings to understand how American intellectuals, radicals, and the New Left were organized and have contributed to American society since the 1960s. Ishida, after observing American higher education, authored two volumes on Yale University. Funatsu completed sociohistorical studies of symbolism in American society.

Other studies by Japanese sociologists to introduce Western sociological thought to Japan were conducted by Shizuo Yamamoto,[57] Ritsuo Akimoto,[58] Takashi Miyajima,[59] and Shigeru Susato.[60] Starting with descriptions of sociological studies in Germany during the Weimar Republic, Yamamoto follows the retention and development of German sociology from 1930 to 1980. His research reveals that the argument between René König and Helmut Schelsky was crucial to German sociology, for it showed historically how German sociology contributed to the world. Akimoto focuses on German society from 1830 through 1930, which he considers to be a late and incomplete civilization. This was when German sociology flourished. The sociologists Akimoto examined were Lorenz von Stein, Robert von Mohl, and Ferdinand Tönnies. Miyajima, on the other hand, points out how traditional French sociology—led by Emile Durkheim, Claude-Henri de Saint-Simon, Pierre Joseph Proudhon, Armand Cuvillier, Georges Gurvitch, Raymond Aron, and Alain Touraine—was formed and how it affected the May Revolution of 1968. Susato has studied the social structure of contemporary France. His work focuses on the occupational structure, the old middle class, the white-collar class, the elites, and the working class. Putting these areas of thinking in perspective, he interprets how the structures and classes were supported by education and what the May Revolution attempted to change.

These works by contemporary Japanese sociologists during the past decade or so show several characteristics of Japanese sociology. First, Japanese sociologists are interested in Western sociology, namely, that of Germany, France, and the United States. Second, employing their original and related works, they are interested in understanding the effects of great thinkers upon contemporary theories of sociology. Third, based on their understanding of revolutionary changes in Western societies over the past 150 years through their studies of sociological works done by Western sociologists, Japanese sociologists and social scientists want to learn what are the lessons for Japan and Japanese society.

Fieldwork and Research in Understanding Contemporary Japanese Society

Japanese society is advanced in its economy and engineering, unique in its history and culture, but it has closed its eyes and systems to foreign people. There are lots of social themes and problems in Japanese society that have been studied by sociologists. As a matter of fact, there are so many publications dealing with these issues that specialists are kept busy trying to follow what research has recently been published. The publications related to contemporary Japanese society can be classified according to the following fields: population and family, village, religion, community, urbanization, stratification, politics, industries, pathology, and others. Only several fields out of those listed will be discussed here.

It is obvious that Japanese society is different from American and European societies as well as other Asian societies. The process of modernization, the experiences of world wars, the curiosity about and longing for democracy, and the attitudes toward catching up with Western standards of living are so different from the rest of the world that many sociologists worldwide think that understanding Japanese society is difficult and impossible. Even Japanese sociologists find the characteristics typifying Japanese society hard to grasp. Some people think the Japanese enjoy a high quality of life, whereas others point out that they spend too much money for fundamental items, namely, clothes, food, and shelter.

Hiromichi Nakamoto[61] edited a book on population. Chapters contributed to this book explore population in relation to urbanization, family problems, regional distribution, employment, education, the aged, poverty, and Asian problems. One of the contributors, Tsuneo Yamane,[62] develops a theoretical framework for the analysis of the modern family, such as the meaning of raising children. Having children and the role of parents in nurturing children in a Japanese family may be quite different from that of a Western family. Another contributor, Takeji Kamiko,[63] in studying contemporary Japanese families tries to understand how a traditional family and a dual-income family are different in terms of their roles within the family. Role taking in a three-generation family, which used to be a traditional family pattern in Japan, was studied by Takeji Kamiko and Kokichi Masuda.[64] Although most of the extended Japanese family system has diminished during the past three decades, some of this pattern still exists today.

One might question where the model of the traditional Japanese family came from and how it was formed. Michio Aoyama[65] tried to answer these questions by analyzing research on Japanese families by Kizaemon Aruga and Seiichi Kitano. His discussion centers on the meaning and implication of "house." A Japanese house, called "*ie*," is a shelter where a family lives. It also functions as a place where the altar is kept and the spirits of deceased family members are worshipped. Its structure and function are much more complex than in the Western world. Kiyomi Morioka,[66] whose interests are Japanese religious organizations and the family system, had his students discuss the maintenance and change of religious functions in a Japanese family. Japanese families have changed tremendously during the past four decades, and they are still changing. As examples, nuclear families are widely accepted, women are now working outside the home, children's education and school careers regardless of gender are important for family members, men's lifetime commitment to occupation is changing, and traditional gender roles are being questioned. Yoriko Meguro[67] has extensively studied these trends. So has Shuhei Yamamuro,[68] who reports that family theories in Japan were developed long before George P. Murdock and Margaret Meade wrote on how the family was organized. Yamamuro says that John Locke and Mary Wollstonecraft wrote on the structure of family before Johann Jakob Bachofen of *Das Mutterrecht,* although the latter was referred to as the first researcher on family by Friedrich Engels.

There are some Japanese sociologists who have devoted themselves to studying Japanese villages. Although Eiichi Yamaoka's work is a collection of papers written over twenty years, his comprehensive summary[69] helps us understand how Japanese villages have changed during the past four decades. Land reforms (1947–1950), introduction of machines into farming, and migration of villagers to cities characterize significant changes of village life during this period. The residue of the traditional village life system, however, can still be observed. Itsuo Emori[70] discusses how the fictive parents-children relationship, which is widely observed in Japan, was historically developed. Japanese villages experienced a tremendous change after World War II. Villagers started to allow people who had lost their homes as well as jobs to live in their villages. Likewise, ravaged cities gradually recovered their energy and accepted those who had left their villages. Gradually a dynamic change occurred in the socioeconomic structure of Japan, and as a result the traditional roles of villages were affected. Mitsuru Shimpo and Sonoko Kumagai Matsuda[71] surveyed a village in northern Japan and analyzed how Japanese villages lost their population due to the mechanization of agriculture and urbanization. The applicability of social systems theory to Japanese villages was tested by Hisayoshi Mitsuda.[72] He tried to systematize why and how Japanese rural societies disappeared. He prepared a structural model, a change model, and an evaluation model in an attempt to understand the contemporary change of rural societies in Japan.

Current Trends in Research

It seems that Japanese sociologists disagree with each other in their theoretical outlooks and research. As mentioned previously, about 1,200

Japanese sociologists teach at Japanese colleges and universities and perform various kinds of research. Their research results have been published in professional journals and college bulletins or as books. College bulletins in Japanese colleges and universities are periodical publications featuring faculties' research and/or findings. Japanese sociologists also are interested in knowing and introducing results of Western scholarship into Japanese academic circles. Translations of Western sociological works into Japanese and their subsequent publications are prevalent. These trends indicate that at least a certain group of Japanese sociologists is active in research and publication. One may ask, however, to what extent new research and publication is read and/or understood among researchers and specialists, and whether the studies have contributed to a new orientation of research. It is difficult to answer these questions. It is obvious that limitations in the circulation of research results bring inactivity in academic discussions. It is an established fact that most Japanese sociologists are not supported financially either by their colleges or by academic foundations. Consequently, a large-scale survey has to be postponed until a researcher can secure financial aid. Even if some financial aid is available, the researcher may come across other problems, such as difficulties in obtaining coworkers or interviewers and suitable sites for fieldwork. Also, not many organizations are concerned or agree with a researcher's survey. They are too busy maintaining their own organizations and population, and are not willing to help others.

This situation may be explained from a different perspective. A few decades ago sociologists could perform fieldwork with the cooperation of city governments, town organizations, corporations, or schools. Today a large-scale field survey is almost impossible because a researcher lacks funds, field assistants, or both. Consequently, Japanese sociologists tend to limit themselves to descriptive, analytical, or historical research. Government organizations, central or local, occasionally want to conduct surveys to determine the sort of policies inhabitants want to have introduced. An organization in this kind of situation often comes to a college professor for advice on conducting a survey. The professor is hired temporarily by the organization and is requested to provide the needed expertise and advice.

Another reason why field surveys are unsuccessful stems from the general attitude of Japanese people. They are reluctant to express themselves without some benefit or compensation. This attitude may be applicable all over the world. Further, some people today feel there is already too much information and no need to acquire any more.

Kazuko Tsurumi[73] is one of the early Japanese sociologists whose English-translated study of Japanese thinking was published through an American publisher. Hiroshi Mannari[74] contributed his results of research on Japanese business leaders in English. Recently, Kunio Odaka[75] and Kyoichi Sonoda[76] also published their works—on the Japanese employment system and health care system—in English.

RECENT WORKS IN ENGLISH

During the period 1988–1991, more than 200 books on Japan and Japanese society, excluding literature, history, art, and religion, appeared for review in the *Journal of Asian Studies* or *American Journal of Sociology*. Who would believe that so much is being published so fast? American sociologists may find it hard to believe that many Westerners are interested in Japanese society, especially in such topics as employment, management, technology, productivity, economics, politics, law, war, international relations, cities, agriculture, education, and belief systems. Many Japanese sociologists may also wonder why so many Japan studies have appeared during the past few years. Sociocultural curiosity about Japan by Westerners may have been enhanced by their interest in Japan's economic success. Government officials and college professors have introduced Western thought to modernize law, administration, taxation, and education.

From the 1940s through the 1960s, anthropological works by American researchers were well known and discussed by many Japanese sociologists. Probably American anthropologists and some field research specialists of Japanese studies programs in major American universities during the 1960s and 1970s contributed to the training of younger researchers in such fields as biotechnology,[77] government policy,[78] industry,[79] and education.[80]

Westerners' greatest interest in Japanese society is in understanding why and how Japanese products acquired a large worldwide market share during the past few decades. Obviously, cheap labor costs were one contributing factor. In addition, the quality of education, diligence, ability to understand the international market, and individual discretion as well as group-mindedness worked to produce many market-oriented items. In the past thirty years the toy and camera industries have been supplemented by car, ship, boat, computer, and robot industries.

Even Japanese researchers often face difficulties in understanding how Japanese low-tech industries have become high-tech. Many Japan specialists admit that college-level education in Japan seems not to contribute to the production of new technology and management, and Japanese companies do not invest in basic research. Instead, the Ministry of International Trade and Industry, a branch of the Japanese government, may work to organize and help promote private industries in order to produce competitive products in international markets. All this is true, but there remains much more to be discovered and understood in Japanese society.

Works by Gene Gregory,[81] Richard Samuels,[82] K. Odaka, K. Ono, and F. Adachi,[83] Daniel Okimoto,[84] Sheridan Tatsuno,[85] Thomas Pugel,[86] K.

Yamamura and Y. Yasuba,[87] Jon Woronoff,[88] and F.M. Rosenbluth[89] on Japanese productivity in industry and its sociopolitical environments are particularly specialized.

As sociology is expected to contribute to "an understanding of the 'value systems' that are at the heart of the world's societies, . . . [it is our hope that we can] work with the other social sciences and with the physical sciences and engineers to tackle the major problems of our times."[90]

CONCLUSION

This chapter has attempted to show how Japanese sociology has developed and where it is presently. Historically, Japanese sociology started with an influx of Western social and evolutional thought. Thereafter, it took a couple of decades to nurture Japanese sociologists. At the outset, influenced strongly by Western sociological works, Japanese sociologists tried to find a theme for their own research and field. Although the impact of sociopolitical and socioeconomic influences upon fundamental discussions of sociology in Japan was evident during the past hundred years, quite a number of Japanese sociologists are still debating which Western theory of sociology is most appropriate for the analysis of Japanese society. Sociologists may add a few concepts to the existing theories, but they are afraid to revise the total structure of theories or to develop a new frame of reference.

It seems to me that most Japanese sociologists need an extensive retraining in sociology and social sciences in order to understand what is occurring within the profession throughout the world. The breakdown of traditional family and village practices, excessive proliferation of business, the traditional and indecisive character of politics, emphasis on competition and allocation of human resources through formal education, and rapid changes in values and attitudes and their implications for the future are important areas for sociological studies in Japan.

In preparing this chapter, more than 160 books published in Japan during the past fifteen years and reviewed in *Shakaigaku Hyoron* (Japanese Sociological Review), and more than 200 books on Japanese society published mainly English worldwide, were collected, classified, and reviewed by the author.

Japanese sociologists have different ideas regarding their publications. Some prefer publishing in Japanese, while others prefer English. Inasmuch as English-language publications are more useful when writers want to circulate their findings in the professional world, this matter warrants discussion. Although many Japanese sociologists may want a portion of their works translated and published in English, others are much more concerned with having a Japanese version of their works.

It is a fact that academic publications are not a profitable business in

Japan. Therefore, many Japanese publishers are reluctant to publish academic works. Although departments of sociology or related departments may be very popular, many students are interested only in their future occupations, such as in mass media, advertising, publications, international business, and tourism. Most students are not interested in what they are learning; they are much more concerned with the knowledge they need for future occupations. As a result, faculties presenting lectures based on their research and work do not interest or excite students.

There are several reasons why Japanese professional studies have not been published in English thus far. Most Japanese scholars work more comfortably with their native language. Also, even if their command of English is reasonable, there are problems because the development of logic in discussions tends to be tautological. This is partly because Japanese society lacks constructive expressions for developing ideas logically. Also, seniority, tradition, training, and availability of fundamental materials for discussions make Japanese sociologists feel that the given position and work are satisfactory. Some Japanese people know there is a thick wall of Japanese traditional structure of institutions and human relations.

My hope is that a new world for Japanese sociologists will surface within a decade or two, utilizing as themes of study the rapidly changing world societies with Japan at the forefront. To meet this challenge, we will need a new breed of Japanese sociologists who can perform in an international academic world.

NOTES

1. Howard Becker, "Sociology in Japan," *American Sociological Review* 1, no. 3 (June 1936), 455–71.

2. Jesse Frederick Steiner, "The Development and Present Status of Sociology in Japanese Universities," *American Journal of Sociology* 41, no. 6 (May 1936), 707–22.

3. Chie Nakane, *Japanese Society*. Berkeley and Los Angeles: University of California Press, 1970.

4. Takeshi Ishida, *Japanese Society*. New York: Random House, 1971.

5. George K. Yamamoto and Tsuyoshi Ishida, eds. *Selected Readings on Modern Japanese Society*. Berkeley, Calif.: McCutchan, 1971.

6. Tsuyoshi Ishida, "Contemporary Sociology in Japan," in Raj P. Mohan and Don Martindale, eds., *Handbook of Contemporary Developments in World Sociology*. Westport, Conn.: Greenwood Press, 1975, 439–52.

7. Takeshi Ishida, *Nihon no Shakai Kagaku* (Social Sciences in Japan). Tokyo: Tokyo University Press, 1984, 23–34.

8. Tadashi Fukutake, *Shakaigaku no Hoho to Kadai* (Methods and Problems in Sociology). Tokyo: Tokyo University Press, 1969, 309–14.

9. Howard Becker, op. cit., 455–71.

10. Shoji Yonemura, "Kazoku Kenkyu no Doko" (Trends in the Sociology of Family), *Japanese Sociological Review* 28, no. 2 (October 1977), 30.

11. Tadashi Fukutake, op. cit., 318.

12. Ibid., 332.

13. Takashi Koyama, "Senzen no Jisshoteki Kazokukenkyu no Kaiko" (Reminiscence of Positive Family Studies in Prewar Japan), *Japanese Sociological Review* 28, no. 2 (October 1977), 145–48.

14. Toshio Hayase, "Senzen no Nihon Shakaigaku" (Prewar Japanese Sociology), *Japanese Sociological Review* 28, no. 2 (October 1977), 21.

15. Shoji Yonemura, op. cit., 50.

16. Kazuo Goto, "Senzen niokeru Nihon Noson Shakaigaku" (Japanese Rural Sociology before World War II), *Japanese Sociological Review* 28, no. 2 (October 1977), 56.

17. Takeshi Yamagishi, "Senzen no Toshi Kenkyu" (Urban Studies in Prewar Japan), *Japanese Sociological Review* 28, no. 2 (October 1977), 68.

18. Kazuo Goto, op. cit., 54.

19. Takeshi Yamagishi, op. cit., 77.

20. Ritsuo Akimoto, *Nihon Shakaigaku Shi* (A History of Japanese Sociology). Tokyo: Waseda University Press, 1979, 265–74.

21. Tadashi Fukutake, op. cit., 349–55.

22. Nihon Shakaigakkai and Shakaigaku Kyoiku Iinkai, "Daigakuin Mondai Chosa ni tsuiteno Chosa Hokoku" (Survey Report on Graduate Schools), *Japanese Sociological Review* 39, no. 3 (December 1988), 314–34.

23. Kojunsha, ed., *Zenkoku Daigaku Shokuinroku* (College Professors in Japan). Tokyo: Kojunsha, 1989. vols. 1 and 2.

24. Saburo Yasuda, "Gendai Shakaigaku Kaigi nitsuite" (On Modern Sociology Conference), *Japanese Sociological Review* 29, no. 1 (July 1978), 91–92.

25. Ken'ichi Tominaga, *Shakaigaku Genri* (Principles of Sociology). Tokyo: Iwanami, 1986, 7–12.

26. Ibid.

27. Takeshi Yamagishi, *Shakaiteki Sekai no Tankyu* (A Search for a Social World). Tokyo: Keio Tsushin, 1985.

28. Atsuhiro Terada, *Shakaigaku no Hoho to Riron* (Methods and Theories of Sociology). Tokyo: Shinsen-sha, 1989.

29. Kanji Naito, *Shakaigaku Ronko* (Discussions on Sociology). Tokyo: Ochanomizu Shobo, 1980.

30. Takashi Noguchi, *Shakaigaku no Shiza* (Perspectives in Sociology). Kyoto: Koyo Shobo, 1981.

31. Yusuke Maki, *Gendai Shakai no Sonritsu Kozo* (Existing Structure of Modern Society). Tokyo: Chikuma Shobo, 1977.

32. Mamoru Funatsu, *Symbolic Sogosayo Ron* (Symbolic Interactionism). Tokyo: Koseisha-Koseikaku, 1976.

33. Akiko Fuse, "Kazoku Kenkyu no Kiseki to Kadai" (A History of Japanese Family Research and Today's Problems), *Japanese Sociological Review* 38, no. 2 (September 1987), 150–66; and Takeshi Ishida, *Nihon no Shakai Kagaku* (Social Sciences in Japan). Tokyo: Tokyo University Press, 1984, 225–41.

34. Yoshio Atoji, *Weber Shakaigaku no Shiten* (The Perspective of Weber Sociology). Tokyo: Keiso Shobo, 1976.

35. Yoshiyuki Sato, *Koi no Shakaigaku* (Sociology of Actions). Tokyo: Shinsen-sha, 1976.

36. Yosuke Koto, *Weber Shakai Riron no Kenkyu* (A Study of Social Theory of Weber). Tokyo: Tokyo University Press, 1977.

37. Toshio Nakano, *Max Weber to Gendai* (Max Weber and Today). Tokyo: San'ichi Shobo, 1983.

38. Hiroshi Orihara, *Durkheim to Weber* (Durkheim and Weber). Tokyo: San-'ichi Shobo, 1981, vols. 1 and 2.

39. Kosei Sakuma, *Weber to Marx* (Weber and Marx). Tokyo: Sekai Shoin, 1984.

40. Kosei Sakuma, *Weber to Hikaku Shakaigaku* (Weber and Comparative Sociology). Tokyo: Safu-sha, 1986.

41. Kunichika Yagyu, *Weber to Troeltsch* (Weber and Troeltsch). Tokyo: Misuzu Shobo, 1983.

42. Yoshiyuki Sato, *Weber kara Habermas e* (From Weber to Habermas). Tokyo: Sekai Shoin, 1986.

43. Hisao Naka, *Durkheim no Shakai Riron* (The Social Theory of Durkheim). Tokyo: Sobunsha, 1979.

44. Koken Sasaki, *Durkheim Shakaigaku Kenkyu* (A Study of Sociology of Durkheim). Tokyo: Koseisha-Koseikaku, 1978.

45. Takashi Miyajima, *Durkheim Sahkairiron no Kenkyu* (A Study of Social Theory of Durkheim). Tokyo: Tokyo University Press, 1977.

46. Toichiro Koseki, *Durkheim to Kindai Shakai* (Durkheim and Modern Society). Tokyo: Hosei University Press, 1978.

47. Yoshio Atoji, *Simmel Shakaigaku no Hoho* (Methods of Simmel Sociology). Tokyo: Ochano-mizu Shobo, 1979.

48. Yoshio Atoji, *Simmel no Shiten* (Perspectives of Simmel). Tokyo: Keiso Shobo, 1985.

49. Takashi Hosoya, *Marx Shakai Riron no Kenkyu* (A Study of Social Theory of Marx). Tokyo: Tokyo University Press, 1979.

50. Akio Tanosaki, ed., *Parsons no Shakai Riron* (The Social Theory of Parsons). Tokyo: Seishin Shobo, 1975.

51. Masataka Katagiri, *Nichijo Sekai no Kosei to Schutz Shakaigaku* (The Structure of the Life World and Schutz Sociology). Tokyo: Jicho-sha, 1982.

52. Takashi Noguchi, *Lévi-Strauss to sono Shuhen* (Lévi-Strauss and His Environment). Kyoto: Koyo Shobo, 1986.

53. Keiichi Sakuda, *Jean Jacques Rousseau* (in Japanese). Kyoto: Jinbun Shoin, 1980.

54. Akira Takahashi, *Gendai America Chishiki-Jin Ron* (Contemporary American Intellectuals). Tokyo: Shinsen-sha, 1987.

55. Tsuyoshi Ishida, *Yale Daigaku no Kyoiku System* (The Educational System of Yale University). Hiroshima: Keisui-sha, 1986; and Tsuyoshi Ishida, *Yale Daigaku niokeru Gakumon Kaihatsu System* (The Academic Development System of Yale University). Hiroshima: Keisui-sha, 1987.

56. Mamoru Funatsu, op. cit.

57. Shizuo Yamamoto, *Nishi-Doitsu Shakaigaku no Kenkyu* (A Study of West German Sociology). Tokyo: Koseisha-Koseikaku, 1986.

58. Ritsuo Akimoto, *Doitsu Shakaigaku Shiso no Keisei to Tenkai* (The Formation and Development of Thought in German Sociology). Tokyo: Waseda University Press, 1976.

59. Takashi Miyajima, *Gendai France to Shakaigaku* (Contemporary France and Sociology). Tokyo: Bokutaku-sha, 1979.

60. Shigeru Susato, *Gendai France no Shakai Kozo* (The Social Structure of Contemporary France). Tokyo: Tokyo University Press, 1984.

61. Hiromichi Nakamoto, ed., *Jinko to Shakai Mondai* (Population and Social Problems). Tokyo: Nanso-sha, 1982.

62. Tsuneo Yamane, *Kazoku to Jinkaku* (Family and Personality). Tokyo: Kasei Kyoiku-sha, 1986.

63. Takeji Kamiko, *Kazoku Yakuwari no Kenkyu* (A Study of Roles in Family). Kyoto: Minerva, 1979.

64. Takeji Kamiko and Kokichi Masuda, eds., *San-sedai Kazoku* (Three Generations Family). Tokyo: Kakiuchi Shuppan, 1976.

65. Michio Aoyama, *Nihon Kazoku Seidoron* (The Japanese Family System). Fukuoka: Kyushu University Press, 1978.

66. Kiyomi Morioka, ed., *Kin-Gendai niokeru Ie no Henshitsu to Shukyo* (Change of House and Religion in Modern Japan). Tokyo: Shinchi Shobo, 1986.

67. Yoriko Meguro, *Kojinka suru Kazoku* (Individualized Family Members). Tokyo: Keiso Shobo, 1987.

68. Shuhei Yamamuro, *Kazoku Gakusetsushi no Kenkyu* (A Study of Theoretical History of Family). Tokyo: Kakiuchi Shuppan, 1987.

69. Eiichi Yamaoka, *Noson Kenkyu no Kiseki* (A Locus of Village Studies). Tokyo: Daimeido, 1976.

70. Itsuo Emori, *Nihon Sonraku Shakai no Kozo* (The Structure of Japanese Village Communities). Tokyo: Kobundo, 1976.

71. Mitsuru Shimpo and Sonoko Kumagai Matsuda, *Gendai Nihon Nosonshakai no Hendo* (Social Change of a Contemporary Japanese Village). Tokyo: Ochanomizu Shobo, 1986.

72. Hisayoshi Mitsuda, *Sonraku Shakai Taikei Ron* (The Social Systems Theory of a Village). Kyoto: Minerva, 1987.

73. Kazuko Tsurumi, *Social Change and the Individual*. Princeton, N.J.: Princeton University Press, 1970.

74. Hiroshi Mannari, *The Japanese Business Leaders*. Tokyo: University of Tokyo Press, 1974.

75. Kunio Odaka, *Toward Industrial Democracy*. Cambridge, Mass.: Harvard University Press, 1975.

76. Kyoichi Sonoda, *Health and Illness in Changing Japanese Society*. Tokyo: University of Tokyo Press, 1988.

77. Malcolm V. Brock, *Biotechnology in Japan*. London and New York: Routledge, 1989.

78. John C. Campbell, *How Policies Change*. Princeton: Princeton University Press, 1992.

79. Hugh Patrick, ed., *Japan's High Technology Industries*. Seattle: University of Washington Press, 1987.

80. Lois Peak, *Learning to Go to School in Japan*. Berkeley and Los Angeles: University of California Press, 1991.

81. Gene Gregory, *Japanese Electronics Technology*. New York: John Wiley and Sons, 1986.

82. Richard J. Samuels, *The Business of the Japanese State.* Ithaca, N.Y.: Cornell University Press, 1987.

83. Konosuke Odaka, Keinosuke Ono, and Fumihiko Adachi, *The Automobile Industry in Japan.* New York: Oxford University Press, 1988.

84. Daniel I. Okimoto, *Between MITI and the Market.* Stanford: Stanford University Press, 1989.

85. Sheridan M. Tatsuno, *Created in Japan.* New York: Harper and Row, 1990.

86. Thomas A. Pugel, ed., *Fragile Interdependence.* Lexington, Mass.: Lexington Books, 1986.

87. Kozo Yamamura and Yasukichi Yasuba, *The Political Economy of Japan.* Stanford: Stanford University Press, 1987.

88. Jon Woronoff, *Politics the Japanese Way.* New York: St. Martin's Press, 1988.

89. Frances McCall Rosenbluth, *Financial Politics in Contemporary Japan.* Ithaca, N.Y.: Cornell University Press, 1989.

90. William V. D'Antonio, "Bidding a Fond Farewell to ASA and Its Staff," *Footnotes* 19, no. 6 (August 1991), 2–12.

33

Contemporary Sociology in Nepal

Krishna B. Bhattachan and James F. Fisher

HISTORY

Our title is something of a misnomer. The development of sociology in Nepal is so recent that all the sociology that now exists or ever did exist is contemporary—there is no "traditional" or "formative" sociology to which it can be contrasted. The history of sociology in Nepal is indeed very brief compared with its development in other parts of the world, including even the neighboring countries of China, where sociology was taught as early as 1898, and India, where the first department of sociology was established (at Bombay University) in 1919. Until the early 1960s there was not even a university in Nepal, and until 1981 there was no department of sociology in Tribhuvan University, as the institution that had emerged in the meantime—the nation's only university—had been christened.

This does not mean that Nepal was utterly devoid of sociology before a department devoted to it was established at Tribhuvan University. The bare-bones beginnings of sociology can be traced back as far as the 1950s, not in an academic institution but in a government agency. Rural sociology has been one of the major courses offered since 1953 in the Village Development Program (known as the Panchayat Training Centre from 1968 until April 1990) of His Majesty's Government of Nepal. The Centre was designed to familiarize village development workers with rural society.[1] As an impetus for the growth of academic sociology, this development was a dead end; but today sociologists continue to work in applied programs under the aegis of foreign development agencies and offices of His Majesty's Government.

Sociological research accordingly suffered exactly the fate one would expect of a discipline with no institutional base to support it. Whatever sociological research was done prior to the 1980s was accomplished in a stumbling, ad hoc fashion, either by the occasional Nepalese sociologist trained in India or elsewhere, or by the scattering of Western sociologists who came to Nepal to do research for their Ph.D. dissertations or similar projects.

Western and Nepalese anthropologists and other social scientists also made significant contributions to the sociological literature on Nepal.[2] Once Nepal was opened up to the outside world after the revolution of 1950, pioneering research in anthropology slowly but steadily began to be carried out in the 1950s by Christoph von Furer-Haimendorf, Jiro Kawakita, Shigeru Iijima, Collin Rosser, and Dor Bahadur Bista, and in sociology by G. S. Nepali. Their efforts dominated the anthropological and sociological research arena during the 1950s and, along with John T. Hitchcock, the early 1960s.[3]

Professor Ernest Gellner's visit to Nepal in September 1970 was a preliminary step toward the institutionalization of sociology and anthropology in Nepal. On his recommendation, Tribhuvan University initiated a program of M.A. and Ph.D. degrees in sociology and anthropology by dissertation. The program, conducted under the auspices of the university's Institute of Nepal and Asian Studies, was launched on July 15, 1973, under the leadership of A. W. MacDonald. This short-lived initiative was terminated after producing disappointing results—only two M.A. degrees.[4]

After a few subsequent moribund years, Chaitanya Mishra, having recently obtained his Ph.D. in sociology from the University of Florida (1978), assumed an instrumental role in reviving the academic study of sociology and anthropology. Although there was some initial skepticism about starting a new university department, Mishra was convinced that the time was ripe to do so.

The development of a department of sociology and anthropology began with a meeting convened in March 1978, at which various existing departments within the Institute of Humanities and Social Sciences were represented. Mishra represented sociology at that meeting, and at a series of subsequent meetings in which more and more sociologists and anthropologists were included.

The primary initial problem blocking the creation of the incipient department was the extreme shortage of teaching staff. Tribhuvan University assisted by providing faculty development scholarships to pursue master's degree programs in India to two students in sociology and three in anthropology. When all these graduate students returned to Nepal in early 1981 with their newly minted M.A. degrees, a critical mass of personnel was finally in place to begin a program of instruction. Thus it was that the department of sociology and anthropology, located at the central campus of Tribhuvan University in Kirtipur, just south of Kathmandu, was opened in July 1981. The department, with Mishra serving as its first chair,[5] offered courses (called "papers," following Anglo-Indian terminology) leading to the master's degree. A student request for separate degrees in each discipline was approved by the Faculty Board, although the curriculum for both degrees was largely identical.

The anthropologist Dor Bahadur Bista succeeded Mishra as chair in 1982. In 1984, just as the first students from the first "batch" were beginning to finish their degrees,[6] the Fulbright program sent James F. Fisher as a visiting professor on a two-year assignment to the department to help build up and strengthen its various programs. In 1985 Krishna B. Bhattachan was appointed chair of what had in the meantime come to be called the Sociology and Anthropology Instruction Committee. (This change in nomenclature was meant to suggest that the main job of the faculty was classroom teaching, as opposed to such tangential activities as hiring and firing, curriculum development, making up and grading examinations, etc.) In 1986 the department was expanded to include B.A.-level programs on four campuses elsewhere in Nepal: Biratnagar in the east, Kathmandu and Patan in the center, and Pokhara in the west. Subsequently the university agreed, in principle, to expand the B.A. program to twelve additional campuses throughout the country. In 1987 the department (by now called the Central Department of Sociology and Anthropology) published Volume 1 of *Occasional Papers in Sociology and Anthropology.*[7]

It will probably take another decade or more before Tribhuvan University will be able to institute its own Ph.D. degree program in sociology. Although the department has recently made available Ph.D. degrees by dissertation, lack of coursework in advanced theory and research methodology will force many students wanting to pursue doctoral degrees in sociology to continue to go to foreign countries, especially the United States, for further education.

As the number of Nepalese and Western sociologists and anthropologists continued to grow, a professional society called the Sociological and Anthropological Society of Nepal (SASON) was formed in 1986, with Dor Bahadur Bista as president and Krishna B. Bhattachan as general secretary. Following an inactive period, SASON's current president (as of 1993), Kailash N. Pyakuryal, initiated new activities, such as an interparty seminar on the election platforms of various political parties for the general election of 1991, and SASON's first national convention in 1992.

A small but growing number of trained Nepalese and Western sociologists have contributed to the development of sociology in Nepal through research and publications.[8] In addition, a number of anthropologists have published works of considerable sociological significance.[9]

INSTITUTIONALIZATION OF SOCIOLOGY AS AN ACADEMIC DISCIPLINE

As mentioned earlier, although some efforts were made to institutionalize sociology as an academic discipline in Tribhuvan University during the 1970s, it was not embodied in a full-fledged academic department until July 1981, with the opening of the graduate department of sociology and anthropology under the Institute of Humanities and Social Science, Tribhuvan University. A master's level curriculum of sociology and anthropology was prepared by the curriculum development committee, whose members represented various social science departments within the Institute of Humanities and Social Science.[10] According to its brochure, the department's goal is as follows:

To provide a broad, interdisciplinary introduction to the two fields of sociology and anthropology, emphasizing the common theoretical roots that unite and the disparate methodologies that separate the two fields. In this respect the Department is like its counterparts elsewhere, but with one crucial difference: unlike its sister departments in other countries, the Department makes every effort to relate its curriculum and field research to the ongoing development needs of Nepal.[11]

The Faculty Development Program of Tribhuvan University, the Research Centre for Nepal and Asian Studies, the Fulbright Program, Carleton College, the University of Wisconsin, and the Winrock International Foundation (formerly the Agricultural Development Council) have played crucial roles in building up the infrastructure of the faculty by assisting in training, study abroad, research grants, library acquisitions, and publications. In addition, the department's graduate students benefit from ample opportunities to share experiences and ideas with foreign graduate students affiliated with the department.

Faculty represent considerable diversity—of ethnic and educational background, theoretical interests, and research experiences. They have earned master's and Ph.D. degrees from a variety of institutions of higher education in the United States, Great Britain, the Philippines, Italy, and India. Similarly, students enter the department with different backgrounds. Their B.A. degrees include majors in economics, political science, history, psychology, home science, culture, geography, sociology, anthropology, and, since 1989, physics, chemistry, biology, engineering, agriculture, forestry, and management.

Close interaction in formal and informal settings between faculty and students, added to the factors already mentioned, have contributed to the department's considerable popularity among prospective students, despite the short span of its existence. Every year the sociology and anthropology department receives about 700 student applications for admission, out of which about 500 are admitted. Foreign students from Japan, Thailand, Germany, the United States, Sri Lanka, Bangladesh, and India have also been admitted to the master's program. The department has tried, with a limited degree of success, to resist the pressures of "source and force" in its admission policy. The Student Union also exerts considerable pressure on the department to admit a larger number of students.

Although the department has made a promising beginning, many problems continue to plague it. Principal among them are the following:

1. Lack of sufficient classrooms, conference rooms, office space for faculty, teaching materials such as overhead and slide projectors (classrooms are unheated and lack electricity), and equipment such as photocopying machines and computers. Many of the required texts, as well as reference books, are published in Western countries and are unavailable in Kathmandu bookstores; those that are available are often too expensive for students to buy. There is no university bookstore.

2. Lack of sufficient books, journals, and other literature in the central university library. Until 1987 the library subscribed to no anthropological or sociological journals, and its holdings in sociology and anthropology were extremely limited.

3. Lack of funding and personnel to publish the research of department faculty on a regular basis.

4. Bureaucratic difficulties in expediting changes in the curriculum to respond to the constantly evolving needs of students, faculty, and the disciplines.

5. An excessive number of local and official holidays and student strikes, which disrupt teaching and result in unconscionable delays in the academic calendar.

6. Continuing centralization of power within the university bureaucracy, which affords little scope for the department to design and run programs of its own choosing even though it has more authority now than formerly.

7. Limited input for graduate students in the design of specialized fields and choice of courses. Also, graduate students cannot enroll in courses offered in other departments.

CURRENT THEORETICAL AND METHODOLOGICAL TRENDS

Theoretical underpinnings of sociological as well as general social scientific research in Nepal continue to involve, in Thomas Kuhn's[12] terms, "puzzle solving" rather than "problem solving." That is, both Nepalese and Western sociologists, anthropologists, and other social scientists conduct research following theoretical paradigms generated in the West, namely, structural-functional, conflict-critical, symbolic, historical, ecological, psychological, and public philosophy. Nepalese and Western sociologists and anthropologists working in Nepal are thus engaged in filling up "empty boxes" generated by one or the other world-renowned social scientist.

Several factors account for this lack of original theorizing. First, the existence of so many unsolved puzzles in Nepal tends to divert the attention of sociologists and anthropologists working there from novel problems. Second, many researchers believe that puzzle solving is more feasible, important, and relevant to national needs than problem solving. Third, more fundamental theoretical problem-solving efforts can only be attempted after an adequate puzzle-solving base has been erected.

Finally, there is a serious lack of what Imre Lakatos[13] calls a "hard core" indigenous research program, with ancillary theories to protect it and rival research programs with which it can compete. Chaitanya Mishra[14] has proposed some tentative features of a Nepalese sociological research program. First, he holds that sociology should substantively locate itself within the central life experiences of the masses of the Nepalese people. Second, it should incorporate a critical-dialectical reconstitutive bias in its theorizing. Third, it should be epistemologically rooted in history. Finally, institutionally it should strengthen teaching and research. This will constitute the theoretical and methodological agenda for some Nepalese sociologists in the 1990s. The ever-increasing number of trained sociologists in Nepal will probably make some joint effort to delineate their research program along these or alternative lines, but rival research strategies to challenge it have not yet appeared. The future is likely to see the proliferation of a few rival research programs as well as the strengthening of existing ones.

Nepalese and Western sociologists have utilized a variety of methods, including comparative and historical, survey, case study, and participant observation. A few of these are quantitative, but most are qualitative.

CURRENT TRENDS IN RESEARCH

Although our sketch makes clear that sociology in Nepal has grown by leaps and bounds in the 1980s, there are still only a few trained Nepalese sociologists engaged in teaching, research, and publication of their findings. This partially accounts for the limited number of subfields within the discipline. Another reason is that most Nepalese social scientists work on interdisciplinary or multidisciplinary joint research projects funded by foreign or national agencies. Dependence on such agencies for support has forced individuals to jump from one field to another, as they follow funding sources flowing from this or that project. Thus, rather than building up expertise in a limited number of topical or theoretical areas, Nepalese sociologists tend to stretch themselves all over the disciplinary map.

Many research projects funded by donor/funding agencies and carried out by social scientists, including sociologists, involve feasibility, monitoring, and evaluation assessments of various development projects and programs. In other words, most of this research is applied research, or studies that arise out of action programs. Because sociology is such a latecomer to Nepal, many publications by Nepalese sociologists and other social scientists have been byproducts of Ph.D. dissertation research. Even today, much of the research done in Nepal, whether by foreigners or Nepalis, is being conducted in pursuit of an advanced degree.

Finally, at the institutional level, Tribhuvan University faculty do not face the "publish or perish" pressure which their counterparts in Western universities face. Thus far, Nepalese sociologists have published only articles at most. Books and monographs have yet to appear. However, many other social scientists, especially anthropologists, have done sociologically significant research and produced publications in a wide range of areas relevant to sociology. A thorough description of research relevant to sociology would have to refer to these publications (see note 9 at the end of this chapter).

Current trends in research in some of the prominent subfields of sociology are described in the following sections.

Population/Demography

The population problem in Nepal is regarded as one of the most intractable difficulties facing the nation. The present annual population growth rate of 2.6 percent has drawn the attention of politicians, development experts, international donor agencies, and social scientists, including sociologists. Considerable research has been done in areas of fertility, mortality, and migration. In most of the studies on internal and international migration in Nepal, a gravity model (measuring the strength of push and pull factors) is used. Anthropologists like Alan Macfarlane (1976)[15] have also done significant work on the relationship between resources and population.

One of the most influential studies in the demographic/population area was research on migration conducted by a task force, headed by the geographer Harka Gurung, which the National Commission on Population established in 1983. It made its controversial findings and recommendations available to the public in a national daily newspaper on September 8, 1983. One of its major recommendations was that the perennially open border between Nepal and India should be regulated by the use of passports. This created—perhaps for the first time in the history of social scientific work in Nepal—a national, public debate at various levels.

In doctoral dissertations, Shyam Thapa (1985) has done a sociodemographic analysis of fertility in Nepal, and Chaitanya Misra (1986) has analyzed the determinants of family size norms in the Terai.

Social Change and Development

All sociological and many other social scientific studies done in Nepal pertain, in one way or another, to the field of social change and development. Most such research done by sociologists focuses on the macro level, while that done by anthropologists focuses on the micro level. Chaitanya Mishra (1984)[16] has criticized the anthropological emphasis on micro studies, which are undertaken with insufficient attention to contextualizing them in a broader macro, theoretical-substantive frame of reference. In turn, anthropologists criticize sociologists for ignoring the realities of everyday life and the theoretical issues that their symbolic and historical analysis entails.

A number of studies have already been published in this fertile field: Lionel Caplan's (1970)[17] study on the Hindu-tribal conflict on the land issue in eastern Nepal; Patricia Caplan's (1972)[18] work on the conflict between higher and lower castes at the village level; Judith Justice's (1986)[19] study of culture and health development; and James Fisher's (1986)[20] work on the process of integration of trans-Himalayan traders from a remote village community into the global market economy through cycles of exchange interaction. These are a few of the theoretical works with implications for issues of development and/or underdevelopment at the micro level. At the macro level, studies done by Frederick Gaige (1975)[21] on regional conflict in linguistic and citizenship issues; P. Blaikie, J. Cameron, and D. Seddon (1980)[22] on the center/metropolis and periphery/satellite relationship; Prakash Lohani (1980)[23] on people's participation in development through single-polar or multi-polar institutions; L. Stiller and R. P. Yadav (1979)[24] on planning for people; Chaitanya Mishra (1987)[25] on development and underdevelopment; and Mahesh Regmi in a series of publications (1971, 1976)[26] on economic history—all these are noteworthy additions to our knowledge of change and development in Nepalese society.

Bista's recent *Fatalism and Development* (1990) has stirred a debate among Nepalese social scientists over development issues in Nepal. Bista blames Brahmanic values for the continuing underdevelopment of the country. Bhattachan (1993) has analyzed the public debate on development after the people's movement of 1990, arguing that the Nepalese public's strong belief that "politics precedes development" has been more myth than reality. These recent studies represent a clear shift in focus from rural development (as in Shrestha's [1980] and Pyakuryal's [1982] dissertations) to large-scale issues of economic development.

Caste and Ethnicity

Most anthropological literature on Nepal is concerned with caste and ethnic groups, often considered in isolation. Comparative studies are relatively underrepresented. Comparative caste and ethnic studies focusing on social, economic, political, and regional inequalities were regarded as "communal" (or "fascist") during the Panchayat era. More research in this field is likely to follow the advent of the multiparty political system after April 1990. Ethnic issues will remain a dominant political theme in Nepal and will provide a fertile research field for sociologists and anthropologists.

Public Philosophy

Bhattachan (1993) has used the public philosophy approach developed by Robert N. Bellah and his colleagues to study the public debate on Nepalese development during the people's movement of 1990, the framing of the 1990 Constitution, and the general election of May 12, 1991. Bhattachan argues that the peoples' voice should have priority over theory, data, and observer, and that public debate is a missing link between modernization and dependency theories of development.

Marxism

Most of the few books and articles about Nepal written by sociologists take a Marxist perspective (see Seddon [1987] and Mishra [1987]). Mikesell's anthropology dissertation (1988) uses historical materialism to describe community relations and ritual in terms of global processes. A. Kondos, V. Kondos, and I. Ban[27] analyze the origin and behavior of Nepal's industrial capitalist class and its relation to caste.

In summary, the discipline of sociology is, like many other Western novelties, a latecomer to Nepal. It has established a beachhead in the national university, but much remains to be done to establish it as a pervasive presence in the educational system and in the myriad agencies and offices, both domestic and foreign, which are attempting to develop the country. The possibilities for establishment of private universities may contribute to the further expansion of sociology in Nepal. The people's movement of 1990 and the subsequent reestablishment of a multiparty political system have altered the academic climate substantially. The teaching and research agenda of Nepalese sociologists is likely to be heavily influenced by whatever political ideologies prevail. The route and direction of the future development of sociology in Nepal are now charted, if not the precise timetables for its arrival at various stations along the way.

NOTES

1. T. S. Thapa, "The Development of Sociology in Nepal," in P. R. Sharma (ed.), *Social Science in Nepal,* a report on a seminar on social science in Nepal held at the Institute of Nepal and Asian Studies in October 1973. Kathmandu: INAS, Tribhuvan University, pp 21–38, 1974.

2. Since the development of sociology in Nepal has proceeded in a somewhat parallel and coordinated fashion with that of anthropology, our account will frequently refer to both disciplines. Also, we refer to works by other social scientists because of the paucity of books and articles by Nepalese or Western sociologists.

3. For details on the history of anthropology in Nepal, see James F. Fisher, "The Historical Development of Himalayan Anthropology," *Mountain Research and Development* 5, no. 1, February 1985.

4. For details on the development of social science in Nepal, see Prayag Raj Sharma (ed.), *Social Science in Nepal,* Kathmandu: Institute of Nepal and Asian Studies, Tribhuvan University, 1974; and Mohan P. Lohani (ed.), *Social Science in Nepal: Infrastructure and Development,* Kathmandu: Institute of Humanities and Social Science, Tribhuvan University, 1985.

5. Departmental chairs are as follows:

1. Chaitanya Mishra (sociologist): 1981–1982
2. Dor Bahadur Bista (anthropologist): 1982–1984
   Padam Lal Devkota (Acting chair, anthropologist): 1983–1984
3. Kailash Nath Pyakurel (sociologist): 1984–1985
4. Krishna B. Bhattachan (sociologist): 1985–1987
5. Dor Bahadur Bista (anthropologist): 1987–1988
6. Om Prasad Gurung (anthropologist): 1988–1990
7. Rishikeshab Raj Regmi (anthropologist): 1990–

6. The M.A. program was designed to be completed in two years, but a combination of strikes, holidays, and other institutional delays roughly doubled the amount of time needed to complete the degree.

7. James F. Fisher (ed.), *Occasional Papers in Sociology and Anthropology,* vol. 1. Kathmandu, Nepal: Tribhuvan University Press, 1987. Volume 2, edited by Stephen L. Mikesell, followed in 1990.

8. Nepalese sociologists include G. S. Nepali, Mohammad Mohasin, Mohammad Sharif, T. S. Thapa, Keshav Prasad Sharma, Kailash Nath Pyakurel, Santa Bahadur Gurung, Chaitanya Mishra, Bijaya Shrestha, Bishnu Bhandari, Bina Pandey, Ganesh Man Gurung, Sudha Paneru, Padma Dikshit, Jitpal Kirant, Zahid Muhammad Parwez, Krishna Bahadur Bhattachan, Kiran Dutta Upadhyaya, Phanindreswor Paudel, Minu Amatya, Raman Raj Mishra, Khagendra Sangam, Dhuti Baral, and Tulsi Ram Pandey. Of these, G. S. Nepali and Chaitanya Mishra are the best known.

The following list includes most Nepalese sociologists with doctoral degrees, in chronological order of the degree granting date:

Nepali, Gopal Singh. 1960. *The Newars of Nepal.* Bombay University.

Mohasin, Mohammad. 1962. *Sociological Study of a Workshop Town (with Particular Reference to Chittaranjam).* Bombay University.

Sharif, Mohammad. 1969. *Perception of Village Needs by Four Categories of Need Definers in Nepal.* Iowa State University.

Mishra, Chaitanya Sharma. 1978. *Sex, Race, and Occupational Inequalities in the United States.* University of Florida.

Shrestha, Vijaya. 1980. *Community Leadership in Rural Nepal.* Mississippi State University.

Pyakuryal, Kailash. 1982. *Ethnicity and Rural Development: A Sociological Study of Four Villages in Chitwan, Nepal.* Michigan State University.

Bhandari, Bishnu. 1985. *Landownership and Social Inequality in the Rural Terai Area of Nepal.* University of Wisconsin.

Gurung, Ganesh Man. 1985. *The Chepangs: A Sociological Study.* Banaras Hindu University.

Thapa, Shyam Pratap. 1985. *Fertility in Nepal: A Sociodemographic Analysis.* Brown University.

Misra, Ramana Raj. 1986. *Determinants of Family Size Norm in Terai of Nepal.* University of Kentucky.

Singh, Jay Puram. 1986. *Legislative Elites of Nepal (Sociological Study).* Bombay University.

Chalise, Suresh. 1990. *The Rastriya Panchayat Elite of Nepal: A Sociological Study of Their Social Origin and Value Orientation.* Banaras Hindu University.

Bhattachan, Krishna Bahadur. 1993. *Public Debate on Development: Sociological Perspectives on the Public Philosophy of the Development of Nepal.* University of California, Berkeley.

Similarly, Western sociologists such as the following have made contributions to the development of sociology in Nepal: George H. Axinn, Joseph W. Elder, David Seddon, John Elder, Brian Douglas Smith, Alex Kondos, Vivienne Kondos, Indra Sohan, Sonam Ram Yadav, and Mary Dagmar Bar. David Seddon achieved prominence through a series of books (coauthored with Piers Blaikie and John Cameron) on Nepalese political economy as seen from a dependency perspective.

9. A partial but representative listing would include the following: Lionel Caplan, Patricia Caplan, Christoph von Furer-Haimendorf, John Hitchcock, Alan Macfarlane, Nick Allen, Sherry Ortner, Don Messerschmidt, James F. Fisher, Rex L. Jones, A. W. MacDonald, Joe Reinhard, Nancy Levine, Dilli Ram Dahal, Navin Rai, David Holmberg, Kathryn March, Judith Justice, Dor Bahadur Bista, Hiroshi Iishi, Shigeru Iijima, William Fisher, Vincanne Adams, Linda Stone, Gerard Toffin, Stacey Pigg, Ernestine McHugh, Stephen Mikesell, and Melvyn Goldstein. For references, see the bibliographies by Boulnois (*Bibliographie du Nepal,* vol 1. Paris: Centre National de la Recherche Scientifique, 1975) and the Royal Nepal Academy (*Bibliography of Nepal.* Kathmandu: Royal Nepal Academy, 1975).

10. For a detailed discussion of curricular issues, see Krishna B. Bhattachan, "Sociology and Anthropology Curricululm and the Needs of Nepal," in James F. Fisher, *Occasional Papers in Sociology and Anthropology,* vol 1. Kathmandu: Tribhuvan University Press, 1987, 11–28.

11. For a fuller statement of this ideology, see Dor Bahadur Bista, "Nepal School of Sociology/Anthropology," in Fisher, op. cit., 6–10.

12. Thomas S. Kuhn, *The Structure of Scientific Revolutions.* Princeton: Princeton University Press, 1962.

13. Imre Lakatos, *The Methodology of Scientific Research Programmes,* Philosophical Papers, vol. 1. Cambridge: Cambridge University Press, 1978.

14. Chaitanya Mishra, "Sociology in Nepal: Challenges for the 1980s." Unpublished paper read at the Social Science seminar, Tribhuvan University, 1981.

15. Alan Macfarlane, *Resources and Population: A Study of the Gurungs of Nepal.* Cambridge: Cambridge University Press, 1976.

16. Chaitanya Mishra, "Social Research in Nepal: A Critique and a Proposal," *Contributions to Nepalese Studies* 11, no. 2, 1984, pp. 1–10. Kathmandu: Centre for Nepal and Asian Studies, Tribhuvan University.

17. Lionel Caplan, *Land and Social Change in East Nepal.* Berkeley: University of California Press, 1970.

18. Patricia Caplan, *Priests and Cobblers.* San Francisco: Chandler Publishing, 1972.

19. Judith Justice, *Policies, Plans, and People.* Berkeley: University of California Press, 1986.

20. James F. Fisher, *Trans-Himalayan Traders: Economy, Society, and Culture in Northwest Nepal.* Berkeley: University of California Press, 1986.

21. Frederick H. Gaige, *Regionalism and National Unity in Nepal.* Berkeley: University of California Press, 1975.

22. Piers Blaikie, John Cameron, and David Seddon, *Nepal in Crisis: Growth and Stagnation at the Periphery.* Oxford: Oxford University Press, 1980.

23. Prakash C. Lohani, *People's Participation in Development.* Kathmandu: Centre for Economic Development and Administration, Tribhuvan University, 1980.

24. Ludwig F. Stiller and Ram Prakash Yadav, *Planning for the People.* Kathmandu: Sahayogi Prakashan, 1979.

25. Chaitanya Mishra, "Development and Underdevelopment: A Preliminary Sociological Perspective," in Fisher, *Occasional Papers in Sociology,* 109–37.

26. Mahesh C. Regmi, *Economic History, 1768–1846.* New Delhi: Manjusri Publishing House, 1971. *Land Ownership in Nepal.* Berkeley: University of California Press, 1976.

27. Alex Kondos, Vivienne Kondos, and Indra Ban, "Nepal's Industrial Capitalist Class: 'Origin' and 'Behaviour,'" *South Asia* 15, no. 1 1992, pp. 81–103.

34

Contemporary Sociology in Pakistan

Hassan N. Gardezi

The growth of sociology in Pakistan covers a brief historical span. Full academic recognition of the subject came in 1955, seven years after the inception of the new state, when Punjab University inaugurated the first department of sociology in the country. From this perspective, one could regard all academic sociology in Pakistan as contemporary. However, the student of contemporary sociology must attempt to cover at least three basic steps while investigating the current state of the discipline. In our view these steps include (1) search for dominant trends and orientations in the literature with respect to methodology, philosophical assumptions, and ideological bias; (2) explanation of these trends with respect to some criteria of validity and relevance; and (3) forecasting the course of future developments.

THE BEGINNINGS OF ACADEMIC SOCIOLOGY

In Pakistan, as elsewhere, the production of sociological thought and analysis did not await the introduction of sociology as an academic discipline in the universities of the country. However, once the first university department of sociology was opened in 1955, sociological teaching, writing, and professional application became quickly dominated by university-trained sociologists. It is with the work of these scholars, formally labeled as sociologists, that this chapter will be concerned.

EARLY INFLUENCE OF AMERICAN SOCIOLOGY

With a few exceptions, all these sociologists received postgraduate training after 1955. A strong influence of American (U.S.) sociology became

remarkable in their work and orientations at the outset. American scholars, training facilities, and textbooks exercised a powerful impact on the
initial planning of sociological teaching and research projects in Pakistan.
Professors and experts assigned by the U.S. Agency for International Development (AID) played major roles in founding the sociology departments and socioeconomic research projects of the Punjab University and
the West Pakistan Agricultural University. In addition, some Americans
became involved with the newly created departments of sociology at the
Karachi and Dhaka universities through the Fulbright and UNESCO projects. Almost all Pakistani foreign-trained professors and research administrators received their education in American universities during the
period 1955–1970.

As an outcome of this extensive influence, Pakistani sociology in teaching, research, and professional application adopted a course which has
been predominantly ahistorical, eclectic, and narrowly empirical. This was
particularly the case in the Punjab University, which was a major producer
of trained sociologists and sociological research during the period 1955–
1968. The syllabi and courses of reading at this institution reveal attempts
to copy closely the graduate and undergraduate programs of American
universities current at the time.[1] Similarly, dissertations written as part of
the requirements of the M.A. degree in sociology, with very few exceptions, indicate an exclusive preoccupation with testing of propositions derived haphazardly from American sociological literature.[2] For example,
one student thesis tests correlations between "broken homes," "permis-
siveness," "overprotection at home," "lack of parental affection," "working mothers," and so forth via frustration and aggression to the crime of
homicide among a sample of Pakistani women convicts taken from a local
jail.[3] The frustration-aggression hypothesis is, of course, credited to the
works of American authors J. Dollard and others.[4] No cognizance is taken
of the fact that in Pakistan an overwhelmingly large proportion of female
homicide convicts continue to be those who have murdered their husbands.

Generally, the extensive infusion of concepts and propositions with primary validation in American sociology and sociocultural realities had an
overpowering effect on the thought and work of Pakistani sociologists
right from the inception of the discipline as a formal enterprise. "Sir, all
my hypotheses have been disproved," was a common protestation of the
bewildered sociology students at the Punjab University, who had been
carefully instructed in operationalizing borrowed concepts by their mentors and testing statistical relationships between variables. The instructors
were often themselves puzzled at these results because of insufficient
awareness that such middle-range theory as they were using, along with
survey and research techniques, had received its primary validation in the
middle-class, Western, urban, industrial societies.

A review of the master's theses written in the sociology departments of the Punjab and Karachi universities, two of the largest in the country, since the 1970s suggests that there is a continued reliance on survey analysis of attitudes toward different issues and social events within the previously mentioned frameworks. One exception to this observation is a new trend to undertake descriptive studies of the social organization of tribal groupings and case studies of deviant behavior.[5]

Since the 1970s there have also appeared a number of textbooks catering to the needs of undergraduate students, as more and more colleges have introduced sociology at the B.A. level. These books, both in Urdu and English, have also borrowed conceptual frameworks, terminology, and methodological approaches from the American/European textbooks. Their only redeeming feature lies in attempts to introduce illustrative material from local sources, such as the national census and socioeconomic studies conducted by governmental and nongovernmental agencies. Textbooks literally translated from English into Urdu are also commonly used in teaching sociology at the undergraduate level.

THE PROFESSIONAL ORGANIZATION OF SOCIOLOGISTS

As the decade 1960–1970 began, almost all major universities and colleges in the country were offering formal programs in sociology, and the number of Pakistani sociologists increased considerably.[6] Some of them began to see the need to form a professional body that could sponsor periodic conferences of the country's sociologists. A wider exchange of ideas, and discussion of the unique problems of Pakistani sociology, was seen as one way of resolving some of the critical issues that the practitioners of the new discipline were facing. The Pakistan Sociological Association was formed in April 1963 and was followed by a National Seminar held in June of the same year at the Dhaka University in East Pakistan (now Bangladesh). In this seminar, for the first time several participants expressed concern regarding a number of issues affecting their sociological practice.[7] These issues revolved around the consequences of a heavy and uncritical reliance on Western substantive sociology, its philosophical and methodological premises, and its techniques and models of research. Not all the delegates were equally critical of the "imported sociology." Some felt that the fundamental principle of sociology and corresponding methodological premises are universal and flow from a common and continuous tradition which was simply carried forward from its Mediterranean origins to Europe and North America. According to this view, contemporary American sociology was as good a grounds for initiation into the discipline as any.

Nevertheless, others persisted in noting that the unique elements of the culture and social organization of Pakistani society called for the development of concepts and theoretical models bearing greater relevance to the indigenous social experience. Although no concrete course of action emerged from this seminar, it did arouse a lasting interest in examining the fundamental problems of practicing sociology in Pakistan. Thus, in the following year when the Pakistan Sociological Association held its first annual meeting, the issue was given poignant expression by one of the participants:

There is the impossible alternative of inventing an *ad hoc* sociology, custom tailored to local conditions, from a nationalistic point of view, an attractive prospect. This will lead to as many so-called sociologies as there are cultures and subcultures in the world but this would be the death of sociology in any objective *scientific*, universalistic sense of the word and sociology will become vulnerable to increasing diversion for political ends. The other alternative is to continue the application of concepts and techniques rooted in a western industrial society to the rural social system of the East. In this direction lies barren scolasticism, where our students continue to memorize definitions that baffle understanding in any empirical context known to them.[8]

Such reminders continued to be registered at the annual meetings of the Pakistan Sociological Association. As late as 1966, the president of the Association reminded his colleagues:

We will be closing our eyes to reality if we deny that in a hurry to establish separate departments of sociology in various Pakistani universities, we have almost blindly depended on such type of textbooks which have little or no relevance to our society.... It is time that we take the warning against the pitfalls that lie hidden in the unexamined application of theory and methodology of certain Western writers for the study of our society. Sociology like any other science is, doubtless, universal in its approach, but society being the outcome of many particularistic and parochial forces has to be understood in the context of those forces.[9]

These reminders did not produce any significant immediate shifts in the orientations of the country's sociologists. Unfortunately, the Pakistan Sociological Association itself was allowed to die after the movement of some of its active members out of the country and the later secession of East Pakistan.

FOCUS ON RURAL LIFE

Pakistan being a predominantly rural society, studies of social organization and change in the rural setting became popular at an early stage of formal sociological work. A number of such studies were produced from

1959 onward by the Social Sciences Research Centre of the Punjab University, the Department of Rural Sociology of the West Pakistan Agricultural University, and the Pakistan Academy for Rural Development. These studies reflect two major foci of investigation.

The first has to do with interest in investigating villagers' responses to programs of induced change and agricultural innovations. This interest was strongly promoted and sustained by the U.S.-AID funds and personnel. All the previously named institutions, along with several rural development centers, were in fact established in Pakistan at the initiative of the U.S.-AID advisors. Most of these advisors came from land grant colleges and universities, which had laid the foundations of research and extension work credited with the transformation of agricultural production and rural life in America. Thus, a number of village studies using statistical survey methods replicated research already conducted in the United States to identify the social and behavioral characteristics of farmers most likely to use new agricultural practices recommended by experts. The respondents were divided into categories such as "non-adopters," "low adopters," "medium adopters," and "high adopters." These categories were correlated with independent variables such as age, literacy, social class, attitudes, and values with statistical limits of confidence.[10]

An interesting extension of this type of research involved constructing "modernity scales," based on the theoretical frameworks developed by American sociologists David McClelland, Daniel Lerner, and Alex Inkles, with all their veiled racist assumptions.[11] A Pakistani researcher, for example, asks a sample of Punjab peasants if they believe in *bhootnas* (hobgoblins) to determine how free from superstition, and therefore modern, they are.[12] Whether this has anything to do with modernity or not, the existence of *bhootna,* a cultural construct, will be hard to deny if one has had the experience of venturing out on the unlit, dark, and spooky nights of rural Punjab.

A second and more fruitful trend in the study of rural life focused on the social organization of village communities in Pakistan. Initially, studies in this perspective were descriptive. They seemed to assume an audience of nonvillagers, Pakistani upper-class urbanites, curious foreign tourists, and development experts. Village life was described for this audience with some demonstration of scientific objectivity and statistical expertise, for example, an analysis of sampling errors.[13] Apart from the atomistic description of villagers' material possessions, institutional performance, and management of life crises, a few references are made to certain authentic elements of the social organization of Punjab villages, such as factionalism, *biradri, zat* and *quom* distinctions, *syep* contracts, and so forth. However, these elements of the social organization are rarely used as a meaningful conceptual basis for analysis, and a predominant tendency is to subsume all particularistic patterns of differentiation of social structures under the generic and hackneyed concept of *caste*. An improvement over these works is an independent village study by Zekiye Eglar, which investigates kinship networks in depth as a basis for mutual duties and obligations and patterns of interaction within the village community.[14]

However, the earlier studies by and large present a static and closed view of rural life in which the villager seems to be caught as a passive object of manipulation by internal and external forces. The basic elements of the village social organization are not treated as a set of possibilities and constraints through which the villagers actively realize their survival goals in an environment of economic hardship and political pressures. Significant departures from this orientation began to appear in the late 1960s with another independent village study by Hamza Alavi.[15] Here the author develops a dynamic framework as he carefully observes how the villagers pragmatically and innovatively solve their day-to-day dilemmas and problems; how they translate their positions in various networks of kinship, tenancy, government, and market systems into concrete strategies of action. Thus, the social organization of the village is given a refreshingly original and vivid portrayal as a working and ongoing dynamics.

This outstanding departure from the past orientation was soon followed by two other major studies undertaken in 1964–1965 and 1978–1980.[16] By now the countryside in Pakistan had several years of experience with adult franchise, land reforms, and projects of modernizing agriculture through innovations associated with the "green revolution." Focusing on the impact of changes, both of these latter studies demonstrate that class and power relations are more fundamental for the villagers' life experiences than their membership in kinship circles and castelike status groups. While sociocultural phenomena do play a role, the system of property relations sets the boundaries within which classes relate to each other and the struggle for survival takes place for an overwhelming segment of small landowners and landless cultivators. The researchers conclude that the introduction of agrarian reforms and innovations have had the cumulative effect of increasing the political and economic power of big landowners, while at the same time creating a small class of middle farmers and reducing a majority of the village population to an impoverished rural proletariat.

It is significant that few noteworthy studies of rural life in Pakistan today ignore the realities of class and distribution of power while investigating the issues of social organization and change.[17]

APPLIED SOCIOLOGY

Sociology in Pakistan adopted an applied orientation from the beginning. In a society with a low level of development of productive forces and a history of colonial exploitation, a strong concern with problems of a practical and developmental nature was almost a prerequisite for the acceptance of the discipline. Heavy emphasis on the study of social problems was also a reflection of the American sociological tradition. P. A. Wakil estimates that between 1957 and 1967, 327 master's theses were submitted to the Punjab University, out of which over 95 percent addressed social problems.[18] Topical areas included crime, poverty, overpopulation, deterioration of educational standards, status of women, low agricultural production, and various urban "vices." The definitions of social problems were generally derived from American sociological literature; Richard Fuller and Richard Myers's framework was the one most popularly used.[19]

However, since 1965 the trend of conducting social problem surveys within arbitrary and negative definitions of social situations has been balanced to a degree by applied research in the framework of change theory. Reviewing a volume of collected papers, presented at the meetings of the Pakistan Sociological Association, Raymond Ries remarks: "The empirical studies represented in these collections represent the practical sociological concerns of a developing society, and it is in this area that more innovation and originality appear."[20] Such concerns have continued to dominate more recent social research, with or without elaborate theoretical frameworks, as humanistic awareness of the problems of the underprivileged sections of society has intensified. To the list of subjects for sociological inquiry popular in the earlier decades (e.g., fertility control, modernization of agriculture, community development, and crime) have been added new areas of investigation having to do with the growth of rural and urban poverty, health and sanitation, the plight of children, the status of women, and the rise of religious fundamentalism. The salient features of the latter type of studies are noted in our subsequent discussion.

A few studies focusing on rural and urban poverty that have appeared more recently have been conducted in the context of changes introduced through the adoption of official plans and strategies of change in the economic and technological spheres. A statistical survey of poverty in Pakistan covering the period 1950–1980 revealed that while the growth-oriented industrialization policies adopted in Pakistan produced remarkable increases in the country's gross national product (GNP), they had little impact on the reduction of poverty.[21] The statistical findings of this survey were corroborated by another study which provides a theoretical connection between poverty and high growth rates. The author argues that the regime of accumulation developed in Pakistan's peripheral capitalist mode of production makes a highly exploitative use of human labor, which explains the coincidence of poverty and economic growth measured in terms of increases in the country's GNP.[22] Similarly, another study indicates that the aggravation of rural poverty and economic disparities was to a large extent the result of the "elite farmer strategy" followed in conjunction with the measures introduced to promote the so-called green revolution.[23]

FOCUS ON AGE AND GENDER

Since the 1970s Pakistani sociologists have also turned their attention to age- and gender-specific issues. This has partly been a result of global interest in the welfare of children and women. A number of studies sponsored by UNESCO are exploratory fact-finding projects with the aim of effecting improvements in the life situation of children in Pakistan. Two recent studies have collected extensive information on the educational, health, nutritional, and environmental conditions and needs of children in the sociocultural milieu of the rural society.[24]

Greater social concern and maturity of sociological formulations begin to appear from 1970 onward in studies pertaining to the position of women in Pakistani society. These studies can be divided into two categories. First, there are studies that go beyond the earlier preoccupation with more or less descriptive expositions of the female role and status in the traditional, patrimonial household economy, marriage, and family along with discussions of customs such as dowry and *purdah* (seclusion of women). These studies, while still basically descriptive, examine the impact of wider societal changes on the socioeconomic status of women. One of the studies based on a series of surveys, for example, focuses on the impact of urbanization on the position of women. These surveys show that working women lag far behind men in terms of salaries, promotions, and working conditions; and that they suffer from the negative attitudes of bureaucrats, who are invariably men.[25] Other studies aimed at compiling socioeconomic and demographic data are often sponsored by governmental and nongovernmental agencies interested in improving the life and work of the female population.[26] The sociological importance of these studies can hardly be overemphasized in a society in which much of women's life and work remains invisible.

Although progress had been made, however modest, in creating awareness of the socioeconomic conditions of Pakistani women and protecting their fundamental rights through legislation since independence, a setback occurred with the imposition of a new military regime in 1977. This regime, under the presidency of General Ziaul Haq, produced several ordinances throughout the 1980s curtailing the rights of women—ostensibly to "Islamize" the society of Pakistan. The challenge of these attempts to reverse the gains made by women in their struggle for equality was picked up not only by female activists but also by female social scientists, who refused to put up with the age-old patriarchal system that was not necessarily of Islamic origin. It was in this context that the second category of sociological literature, on women by women, began to appear in Pakistan. This

literature is not only politically better informed and critical but more sophisticated in making use of empirical information to theorize on the life
and work of Pakistani women. Khawar Mumtaz and Farida Shaheed, for
example, produced an important study of the structural and political basis
of oppression of Pakistani women in the context of culturally evolving
asymmetrical gender relations.[27] Needless to say, a sociological understanding of the roots of gender inequalities in Pakistan, as elsewhere, is
accompanied by an earnest debate over the course of action to be followed
to mobilize resistance against male domination and abuse. Some women
argue that the issue of women's rights is a secular one of human rights
and therefore should be treated as such, while others feel that in order
not to be perceived as alien there is a need to mobilize the women of
Pakistan for the recovery of their rights around a cultural, and therefore
an Islamic, discourse.[28] The debate highlights the power of the Islamic
fundamentalists in Pakistan, who have used religion as a weapon to per-
petrate patriarchal gender relations in society.

FOCUS ON POLITICAL ECONOMY

Although Pakistani sociologists showed an early interest in developing
an indigenous disciplinary perspective, for a considerable time their research work represented little more than replications of Western empirical
methodology and theoretical orientations. The vogue of structural-
functionalism of the North American variety was in particular responsible
for giving Pakistani sociology a nonhistorical character whereby the existing institutional arrangements, systems of social stratification, and mechanisms of social control were taken for granted. Social change was viewed
as a product of discrete, unrelated events caused by internal strains, accidents, or reformist (modernizing) interventions.

However, the situation began to change as a succession of political and
economic crises began to transform the Pakistani society in ways not con-
ductive to general well-being. The rise to power in the 1950s of a bureaucratic military oligarchy, and its collaborators among the landed gentry
and an emergent class of industrial capitalists, led to the dismantling of
the country's federal structure through a highly unpopular amalgamation
of ethnically distinct provinces. The 1958 martial law produced conspicuous class and regional inequalities, tied Pakistan to Western powers
through neocolonial alliances, and eventually led to the dismemberment
of the nation in 1971. After an interlude of civilian government from 1972
to 1977, Pakistan once again came under military dictatorship, this time
initiating a rapid process of decline in the autonomy and integrity of civilian institutions. Furthermore, in its pursuit of total power, the state
under this long military regime resorted to unprecedented physical and

ideological coercion, which brought to the surface serious gender, communal, and ethnic conflicts.

It was in the context of these sociopolitical realities that some Pakistani sociologists turned to investigate the dynamics of their society using the multidisciplinary approach of political economy. Hamza Alavi was one of the first to develop a theoretical framework to analyze the social significance of class and state in societies situated in the periphery of world capitalism.[29] He applied this framework to a detailed analysis of the social base of authoritarian rule in Pakistan and substantiated the now-famous thesis of the relative autonomy and overdevelopment of the state in postcolonial societies relative to other civil institutions. The relationship between state, society, and ideology has emerged as a central focus of a number of studies that deal with some of the pervasive conflicts that have characterized the recent history of Pakistani society. These conflicts crosscut the spheres of class, gender relations, religion, and ethnicity. It is therefore not surprising that sociologists using the holistic approach of political economy have succeeded in dealing with them most effectively and have in the process produced a coherent body of research and theoretical formulations distinctively based on Pakistani experience, without being parochial. It is not possible to discuss the content of all the relevant individual contributions in the short scope of this chapter, but a few significant ones are listed in the notes.[30]

CONCLUSION

The formal discipline of sociology has a short history in Pakistan. Its methodological and theoretical orientations have been strongly influenced by North American sociology. The restrictive nature of this influence is still evident in the mainstream teaching, research, and writings of Pakistani sociologists. However, over time there has also emerged a noticeable trend toward the use of more flexible research strategies, such as participant observation and historical analysis, as well as application of concepts better suited to study the social realities of Pakistani society. Soon after independence from colonial rule, this society has faced growing social and political conflicts giving rise to new issues and problems. New dimensions have been added to the study of rural life, inequality, communalism, gender, and ethnic relations. In order to study these issues a number of Pakistani sociologists have turned to the interdisciplinary perspective of political economy. Their work shows the promise of developing into a more relevant and distinctively Pakistani tradition of sociological discourse.

NOTES

The author acknowledges the help of Dr. Abdur Rauf in preparing the revised version of this chapter.

1. Punjab University, Department of Sociology, *Prospectus, 1965–1967,* Lahore: Punjab University Press, 1965.

2. Muhammad Fayyaz and Qaiyum Lodhi, *Thesis Index, 1957–1967,* Lahore: Department of Sociology, Punjab University, 1968.

3. Irshad Malik, "Crime of Murder among Women Convicts of the Womens' Jail" (M.A. thesis, Department of Sociology, Punjab University, 1958.)

4. J. Dollard et al., *Frustration and Aggression,* New Haven: Yale University Press, 1939.

5. To cite two random examples: Manzoor Hussain, "A Study of Social Organization of Thori Tribe" (M.A. thesis, Department of Sociology, Punjab University, 1976); and Muhammad Razzak, "A Case Study of Swindlers" (M.A. thesis, Department of Sociology, Punjab University, 1978).

6. Hassan N. Gardezi, ed., *Sociology in Pakistan,* Lahore: Punjab University Press, 1966.

7. M. Afsaruddin, ed., *Sociology and Social Research in Pakistan,* Dhaka: Pakistan Sociological Association, East Pakistan Unit, 1963.

8. M. Barash, "Prospects for Sociology in Pakistan: A Comparative Analysis," *Pakistan Sociological Studies,* Lahore: Pakistan Sociological Association, 1965, pp. 8–9.

9. A. K. Nazmul Karim, "Presidential Address to the Third Annual Conference," in Haider Ali Chaudhari et al., eds., *Pakistan Sociological Perspectives,* Lahore: Ferozesons Ltd., 1968, p. 78.

10. For a typical example, see Haider Ali Chaudhari, Eugene C. Erickson, and Ijaz Ahmad Bajwa, "Some Social Characteristics of Agricultural Innovators in Pakistan," in Chaudhari et al., eds., *Pakistan Sociological Perspectives,* 1968, pp. 95–102.

11. Daniel Lerner, *The Passing of Traditional Society: Modernizing the Middle East,* New York: The Free Press, 1958; David C. McClelland, *The Achieving Society,* Toronto: Collier MacMillan, 1961; Alex Inkles, *Making Men Modern,* in Amitai Atzioni, ed., *Social Change,* New York: Basic Books, 1973.

12. Muhammad Rafiq Raza, *Two Pakistani Villages,* Lahore: Department of Sociology, Punjab University, 1969. (A publication based on the author's doctoral thesis submitted to the Department of Sociology, Cornell University, Ithaca, New York, 1966.)

13. W. L. Slocum, Jamila Akhter, and A. F. Sahi, *Village Life in Lahore District,* Lahore: Punjab University Press, 1959.

14. Zekiye Eglar, *A Punjabi Village in Pakistan,* New York: Columbia University Press, 1960.

15. Hamza Alavi, "The Politics of Dependence: A Village in West Punjab," *South Asian Review,* January 1971, pp. 111–28.

16. Saghir Ahmad, *Class and Power in a Punjabi Village,* Lahore: Punjabi Adbi Markaz, 1977; and Shahnaz Rouse, "Systemic Injustices and Inequalities: Maliki and Rayia in a Punjab Village," in Hassan N. Gardezi and Jamil Rashid, eds., *Pakistan, the Roots of Dictatorship: The Political Economy of a Praetorian State,* London: Zed press, 1983. (The latter publication is a preliminary report. For the completed work, see the author's Ph.D. dissertation, "Agrarian Transformation in a Punjabi Village: Structural Change and Its Consequences," submitted to the Department of Sociology, University of Wisconsin, Madison, Wisconsin.) It should be noted that the recurrence of Punjab as the regional focus of village studies is

not a coincidence. This province, having the largest number of villages and the bulk of the country's oldest irrigated lands, has attracted the greatest resources for agricultural research and development.

17. See, for example, David M. Freeman, Hosein Azadi, and Max K. Lowdermilk, "Power Distribution and Adoption of Agricultural Innovations: A Structural Analysis of Villages in Pakistan," *Rural Sociology* 47, no. 1, 1982; David M. Freeman and Hosein Azadi, "Education, Power Distribution, and Adoption of Improved Farm Practices in Pakistan," *Community Development Journal* 18, no. 1, 1983; Mahmood Hassan Khan, "Classes and Agrarian Transformation in Pakistan," *Pakistan Development Review* 22, no. 3, 1983.

18. P. A. Wakil, "Sociology in Developing Nations: The Case of Pakistan," paper presented to the Seventh World Congress of Sociology, Varna, Bulgaria, 1970.

19. Richard C. Fuller and Richard R. Myers, "Some Aspects of a Theory of Social Problems," *American Sociological Review,* February 1941.

20. Raymond Ries, "Pakistan Sociological Perspectives: Book Review," *American Sociological Review,* February 1970, p. 181.

21. S. M. Naseem, *Underdevelopment, Poverty and Inequality in Pakistan,* Lahore: Vanguard Publications, 1981.

22. Hassan N. Gardezi, "Labour, Poverty, and Growth in Pakistan's Peripheral Accumulation," *South Asia Bulletin* 8, nos. 1 and 2, 1988, pp. 12–19.

23. Hamza Alavi, "Elite Farmer Strategy and Regional Disparities in Agricultural Development," in Hassan N. Gardezi and Jamil Rashid, eds., *Pakistan: The Roots of Dictatorship,* pp. 290–307.

24. Muhammad Anwar and Muhammad Naeem, *Situation of Children in Rural Punjab,* Lahore: Department of Sociology, Punjab University, 1980; Muhammad Anwar, *Maternity and Child Care in Rural Mianwali,* Lahore: UNICEF, 1982.

25. Sabiha Hafeez, *Metropolitan Women in Pakistan,* Karachi: Asia Printers and Publishers, 1981.

26. M. B. Abbas, *Socio-Economic Characteristics of Women in Sind,* Karachi: Sind Regional Plan Organization Economic Studies Centre, 1980; Nasra M. Shah, ed., *Pakistani Women: A Socioeconomic and Demographic Profile,* Islamabad: Pakistan Institute of Development Economics, 1986; Muhammad Anwar, *Female Work Load/Time Use Patterns,* Lahore: Department of Sociology, Punjab University, 1991; Abdur Rauf, "Rural Women and the Family: A Study of a Punjabi Village in Pakistan," *Journal of Contemporary Studies* 18, no. 3, 1987, pp. 403–15; Farida Shaheed and Mumtaz Khawar, *Invisible Workers,* Islamabad: Womens' Division, Government of Pakistan, 1986.

27. Khawar Mumtaz and Farida Shaheed, eds., *Women of Pakistan: Two Steps Forward, One Step Back?,* London: Zed Books, 1987.

28. Fauzia Gardezi, "Islam, Feminism and Womens' Movement in Pakistan," *South Asia Bulletin* 10, no. 2, 1990, pp. 18–24.

29. Hamza Alavi, "The State of Postcolonial Societies: Pakistan and Bangladesh," in Kathleen Gough and Hari P. Sharma, eds., *Imperialism and Revolution in South Asia,* New York: Monthly Review Press, 1973; Hamza Alavi, "Class and State," in Hassan N. Gardezi and Jamil Rashid, eds., *Pakistan: The Roots of Dictatorship, the Political Economy of a Praetorian State,* London: Zed Books, 1983.

30. For one of the first major works in this perspective, see Hassan N. Gardezi

and Jamil Rashid, eds., *Pakistan: The Roots of Dictatorship,* 1983. See also Feroz Ahmed, "Ethnicity and Politics: The Rise of Muhajir Nationalism," *South Asia Bulletin* 8, nos. 1 and 2, 1988; Muhammad Asghar Khan, ed., *Islam, Politics and State: The Pakistan Experience,* London: Zed Books, 1985; Hamza Alavi, "Pakistan and Islam: Ethnicity and Ideology," in Fred Halliday and Hamza Alavi, eds., *State and Ideology in the Middle East and Pakistan,* New York: Monthly Review and Press, 1988; Hassan N. Gardezi, *Understanding Pakistan: Colonial Factor in Societal Development,* Lahore: Maktaba, 1990.

Selected Bibliography

AUSTRALIA AND NEW ZEALAND

Austin, D.J. *Australian Sociologies*. Sydney: Allen & Unwin, 1984.

Baldock, C.V., and J. Lally. *Sociology in Australia and New Zealand: Theory and Methods*. Westport, CT: Greenwood Press, 1974.

Balmen, C.J. "Cities Unlimited—The Sociology of Urban Development in Australia and New Zealand." *Australian Journal of Politics and History* 25 (3): 423–24. 1980.

Bottomley, W.J. "The Climate of Opinion in Australian Sociology." *Australian and New Zealand Journal of Sociology* 10 (1): 64–69. 1974.

———. "Professional Social Science: Responsible as Well as Respectable." *Australian Journal of Social Issues* 9 (2): 100–107. 1974.

Bourke, H. "Sociology and the Social Sciences in Australia, 1912–1928." *Australian and New Zealand Journal of Sociology* 17 (1): 26–35. 1981.

Dunphy, D. "Putting Sociology to Work. The Social Relevance of Sociology—An Immediate Issue." *Australian and New Zealand Journal of Sociology* 10 (1): 3–7. 1974.

Hansen, D.A., and R.J.R. King. "Sociology and Social Research in New Zealand." *Sociology and Social Research* 50 (October): 36–46. 1965.

Lally, J., and C.V. Baldock. "Contemporary Sociology in Australia and New Zealand." In R.P. Mohan and D. Martindale (eds.), *Handbook of Contemporary Developments in World Sociology*, pp. 453–69. Westport, CT: Greenwood Press, 1975.

Spoonley, P. "The Development of Sociology in New Zealand." *Footnotes* 7, January 1990.

Spoonley, P., and I. Shirley (eds.). *New Zealand: Sociological Perspectives*. Palmerston North: Dunmore Press, 1982 (reprinted 1986).

Thompson, R.H.T. "Sociology in New Zealand." *Sociology and Social Research* 51 (July): 503. 1967.

Timms, D.W.G. "Sociology in Auckland." *University of Auckland Gazette* 12 (April): 2–4. 1970.

Timms, D.W.G., and J. Zubryzcki. "A Rationale for Sociology Teaching in Australia." *Australian and New Zealand Journal of Sociology* 7 (April): 4. 1971.

Turner, B.S. "Sociology as an Academic Trade." *Australian and New Zealand Journal of Sociology* 22 (2): 272–82. July 1986.

Zubrzycki, J. "The Relevance of Sociology." *Australian and New Zealand Journal of Sociology* 9 (1). February 1973.

———— (ed.). *The Teaching of Sociology in Australia and New Zealand.* Melbourne: Cheshire, 1974.

AUSTRIA

Bunzel, J.S. "Contemporary Sociology in Austria." In R.P. Mohan and D. Martindale (eds.), *Handbook of Contemporary Developments in World Sociology.* Westport, CT: Greenwood Press, 1975.

Torrance, J. "The Emergence of Sociology in Austria 1885–1935." *Archives Européennes de Sociologie* 17 (2): 185–219. 1976.

Wieser, G. "Sociology in Austria." *International Review of Modern Sociology* 13 (1–2): 1–33. 1974.

BANGLADESH

Chowdhury, A. "Sociology in Bangladesh: The Need for Empirical Research." *Sociological Bulletin* 22 (1): 112–19. 1973.

BELGIUM

DeBie, P. "The Beginnings of Sociology in Belgium: Part II, The Preparation: Pioneers and Topics of the Nineteenth Century." *Recherches Sociologigues* 16 (1): 3–37. 1985.

————. "Contemporary Sociology in Belgium." *International Journal of Contemporary Sociology* 8 (3–4). 1971. Reprinted in R.P. Mohan and D. Martindale (eds.), *Handbook of Contemporary Developments in World Sociology.* Westport, CT: Greenwood Press, 1975.

BRITAIN

Abrams, P. *The Origins of British Sociology: 1834–1914.* Chicago: University of Chicago Press, pp. 152–53. 1968.

Abrams, P., R. Deem, J. Finch, and P. Rock (eds.). *Practice and Progress: British Sociology, 1950–1980.* London: George Allen and Unwin, 1981.

Bryant, G.A. "Development and Direction in Sociology." *British Journal of Sociology* 35 (4): 608–18. 1984.

————. *Positivism in Social Theory and Research.* New York: St. Martin's Press, 1985.

Collini, S. "Sociology and Idealism in Britain 1880–1920." *Archives Européennes de Sociologie* 19 (1): 3–50. 1978.

Eldridge, J.E.T. *Recent British Sociology.* London: MacMillan, 1980.

———. "Space for Sociology." *Sociology* 15 (1): 94–103. 1981.

Goldman, L. "A Peculiarity of the English—The Social Science Association and the Absence of Sociology in 19th Century Britain." *Past and Present* 114: 133–71. 1987.

Goldthorpe, J.H. "Review Article: A Revolution in Sociology?" *Sociology* 7 (3): 449–62. 1973.

Jackson, J.A. "Sociology in Contemporary Britain." In R.P. Mohan and D. Martindale (eds.), *Handbook of Contemporary Developments in World Sociology.* Westport, CT: Greenwood Press, 1975.

Kent, R. *A History of British Empirical Sociology.* Aldershot: Gower, 1981.

Morris, P. "Utilization of the Social Sciences in Britain and the U.S.A." *Current Sociology/La Sociologie Contemporaine* 23 (1): 129–41. 1975.

Mulkay, M.J. *Science and Sociology of Knowledge.* Winchester, MA: Allen and Unwin, 1979.

Outhwaite, W. "The Sociology of Knowledge in the United Kingdom since the 60s." *Cahiers Internationaux de Sociologie* 78 (January): 103–8. 1985.

Owen, J.E. "Sociology in Britain: Some Recent Developments." *Social Science* 54 (2): 93–100. 1979.

Rex, J. (ed.). *Approaches to Sociology: An Introduction to Major Trends in British Sociology.* London: Routledge and Kegan Paul, 1974.

———. "British Sociology 1960–1980: An Essay." *Social Forces* 61 (4): 999–1009. 1983.

Smith, C.S. "The Employment of Sociologists in Research Occupations in Britain in 1973." *Sociology* 9 (2): 309–16. 1975.

Smith, D.N. "The State of British Sociology." *Insurgent Sociologist* 9 (2): 309–16. 1975.

Urry, J. "Sociology: A Brief Survey of Recent Developments." In B. Dufour (ed.), *New Perspectives in the Humanities and Social Sciences.* London: Temple Smith, 1980.

BULGARIA

Dobrianov, V., and B. Stavrov. "Contemporary Sociology in Bulgaria." In R.P. Mohan and D. Martindale (eds.), *Handbook of Contemporary Developments in World Sociology.* Westport, CT: Greenwood Press, 1975.

Dobrianov, V., B. Stavrov, and N. Genov. *Contemporary Sociology in Bulgaria: A Historical Outline.* Sofia: Izn na Ban, 1978.

Kohout, J. "Contemporary Bulgarian Sociology." *Sociologicky Casopis* 23 (4): 358–68. 1987.

Michajlov, S. "Founder of the Bulgarian School in Marxist-Leninist Sociology— Scientific Methodological Work of Osavkov Zivko." *Sociologicky Casopis* 20 (3): 249–57. 1984.

Oshavkor, J. "Topical Problems of Bulgarian Sociology." *Sociologicky Casopis* 14 (6): 577–81. 1979.

Vasilev, R., M. Dragnov, S. Mikhailov, and B. Stavrov. "Sociology in Bulgaria." *International Review of Modern Sociology* 13 (1–2): 35–77. 1983.

CANADA

Anand, A. *A Sociological History of French-Canadian Sociology: 1900–1920.* MA thesis, Carleton University, 1973.

Anderson, A.B., P.A. Sinclair, B.S. Bolaria, and S.P. Wakil. "Sociology in Canada: A Developmental Overview." In R.P. Mohan and D. Martindale (eds.), *Handbook of Contemporary Developments in World Sociology.* Westport, CT: Greenwood Press, 1975.

Breton, R. "Quebec Sociology: Agendas from Society or from Sociologists." *Canadian Review of Sociology and Anthropology* 26 (3): 557–70. 1989.

Brym, R., with B. Fox. *From Culture to Power: The Sociology of English Canada.* Toronto: Oxford University Press, 1989.

Card, B.Y. *The Expanding Relation: Sociology in Prairie Universities.* Regina: Canadian Plains Research Center, 1975.

Clark, S.D. "The Changing Image of Sociology in English-Speaking Canada." *Canadian Journal of Sociology* 4 (4). 1979.

———. "Sociology in Canada: An Historical Overview." *Canadian Journal of Sociology/Cahiers Canadiens de Sociologie* 1 (2): 225–34. 1975.

Clement, W. "Approaches toward a Canadian Sociology." In L. Pepperman and J. Curtis (eds), *Readings in Sociology: An Introduction.* Toronto: McGraw-Hill Ryeson, 1989.

———. "Macro-Sociological Approaches toward a Canadian Sociology." *Alternate Routes* 1: 5–7. 1977.

Davis, A.K. "The Failure of American Import Sociology in Anglophone Canada." In R.W. Nelsen and D. Nock (eds.), *Reading, Writing and Riches: Education and the Socio-Economic Order in North America,* pp. 212–30. Kitchener, Ontario: Between the Lines Publishers, 1978.

Dumas, B. "Philosophy and Sociology in Quebec—A Socioepistemic Inversion." *Canadian Journal of Sociology* 12 (1–2): 111–33. 1987.

Felt, L.F. "Nationalism and the Possibility of Relevant Anglo-Canadian-Sociology." *Canadian Journal of Sociology/Cahiers Canadiens de Sociologie* 7 (3): 377–85. 1975.

Forcese, D., and S. Richer. "Social Issues Sociology in Canada." In *Issues in Canadian Society: An Introduction to Sociology,* pp. 449–66. Scarborough, Ontario: Prentice-Hall, 1975.

Gurstein, M. "Towards the Nationalization of Canadian Sociology." *Journal of Canadian Studies* 7 (3): 50–58. 1972.

Harrison, D. *The Limits of Liberalism: The Making of Canadian Sociology.* Montreal: Black Rose Books, 1981.

———. "The Limits of Liberalism in Canadian Sociology: Some Notes on S.D. Clark." *Canadian Review of Sociology and Anthropology* 2 (2): 150–66. 1983.

Hiller, H.H. "The Canadian Sociology Movement: Analysis and Assessment." *Canadian Journal of Sociology* 4 (2): 125–50. 1979.

————. "Paradigmatic Shifts, Indigenization, and the Development of Sociology in Canada." *Journal of the History of Behavioral Sciences* 16: 263–74. 1980.

————. *Society and Change: S. D. Clark and the Development of Canadian Sociology.* Toronto: University of Toronto Press, 1982.

————. "Universality of Science and the Question of National Sociologies." *American Sociologist* 14 (3): 125–35. 1979.

Hofley, J.R. "J. Porter—His Analysis of Class and His Contribution to Canadian Sociology." *Canadian Review of Sociology and Anthropology* 18 (5): 595–606. 1982.

Jones, F.E. "Current Sociological Research in Canada: Views of a Journal Editor." *Journal of the History of the Behavioral Sciences* 13 (2): 160–72. 1977.

Kuhn, M.A. "Characteristics of Canadian Sociology Theses: A Note on Some Differences." *Society-Société* 2 (7): 11–13. 1978.

Nock, D. "History and Evolution of French Canadian Sociology." *Insurgent Sociologist* 4 (4): 15–29. 1974.

Nock, D.A. "S.D. Clark in the Context of Canadian Sociology." *Canadian Journal of Sociology* 8 (1): 79–97. 1983.

Ramu, G.N., and S.D. Johnson (eds.). "Toward a Canadian Sociology." In *Introduction to Canadian Society: Sociological Analysis.* Toronto: MacMillan Company of Canada. 1976.

Rush, G.B., E. Christensen, and J. Malcolmson. "Lament for a Notion: The Development of Social Science in Canada." *Canadian Review of Sociology and Anthropology* 18 (4): 519–44. 1981.

Spray, L.S. "Some Observations on the Social Organization of Canadian Sociology." *Sociological Focus* 9 (2): 209–13. 1976.

Stolzman, J., and H. Gamber. "The National Question and Canadian Sociology." *Canadian Journal of Sociology/Cahiers Canadiens de Sociologie* 1 (1): 91–106. 1975.

Tepperman, L. "Sociology in English-Speaking Canada: The Last Five Years." *Canadian Historical Review* 59 (4): 435–46. 1978.

Timlin, M.F., and A. Faucher. *The Social Sciences in Canada: Two Studies.* Ottawa: Social Science Research Council of Canada, 1968.

Tomovic, V.A. "Sociology in Canada: An Analysis of Sociology in Canada: An Analysis of Its Growth in English Language Universities." Ph.D. thesis, University of Waterloo, 1975.

Watson, L. "The Poverty of Sociology in a Changing Canadian Society." *Canadian Journal of Sociology/Cahiers Canadiens de Sociologie* 1 (3): 345–62. 1975.

Whyte, O. "Sociology and the Nationalist Challenge in Canada." *Journal of Canadian Studies* 19 (4): 106–29. 1985.

CHINA

Arkush, R.D. *Fei Xiaotong and Sociology in Revolutionary China.* Cambridge, MA: Harvard University Press, 1981.

Benwen, S. "The Content of Bourgeoisie Sociology in Imperialist Times and Its Impact on the Old China." *Xin jianshe* (New Construction) 11. 1956.

King, Y., and W. Tse-sang. "The Development and Death of Chinese Academic

Sociology: A Chapter in the Sociology of Sociology." *Modern Asian Studies* 12 (1): 44. 1978.

Ming-mo, H. *Zhongguuo shehuixue shi* (History of Chinese Sociology), Tianjin, 172. 1987.

Ross, A.S. (ed.). *Sociology and Anthropology in People's Republic of China.* Washington, DC: National Academy Press, 1984.

Wang, Y. C. *Chinese Intellectuals and the West, 1872–1949,* pp. 34–35. Chapel Hill: University of North Carolina Press, 1966.

DENMARK

Blegvad, B.-M. "The Consumer and the Scandinavian Sociology of Law," and "Sociology of Law in Denmark, Its Origin, Development and Present Perspective." *Archiv für Rechts- und Sozialphilospohie* 57 (1). 1971.

Blegvad, B.-M. (ed.). "Contributions of Sociology of Law," *Acta Sociologica* 10, Fasc. 1–2, Copenhagen. 1966.

———. "The System Position of Sociology of Law in Current Scandinavian Research." *Acta Sociologica* 10, Fasc. 1–2, Copenhagen. 1966.

Eckhoff, T. "Sociology of Law in Scandinavia." *Scandinavian Studies in Law 1960,* pp. 31–58.

Jesper D., and J.S. Madsen. *Slip sociologien los,* pp. 113–35. Kobenhavn: Hans Reitzel, 1983.

Mogens, B. " 'Sociology and Philosophy'—Some Reflections." Paper presented by H. Hoffding at the First Meeting of the Society for Philosophy and Psychology. *Danish Yearbook of Philosophy* 13: 221–41. 1976.

EGYPT

El-Saaty, H. "Sociology and Development in Contemporary Egypt." *Die Dritte Welt* 5 (2–3): 242–55. 1977.

Hegazy, E. (ed.). *Bibliography of the Works of Egyptian Sociologists.* Cairo: National Center for Social and Criminological Research, 1973.

Murphy, L. "Social Science Research in the Middle East: The American University in Cairo, Egypt." *Journal of the History of the Behavioral Sciences* 15 (2): 115–27. 1979.

FINLAND

Allardt, E. "Contemporary Sociology in Finland." In R.P. Mohan and D. Martindale (eds.), *Handbook of Contemporary Developments in World Sociology,* pp. 107–25. Westport, CT: Greenwood Press, 1975.

———. "Sociology in Finland." *Current Sociology* 25 (1): 29–56. 1977.

Kaukonen, E. "Finnish Sociology in a Sociology of Science Perspective." *Sociologia* 21 (2): 128–38. 1984.

Lamminen, H.S. "Bibliography of Finnish Sociology 1960–1969." *Transactions of the Westmarck Society* 19. 1973.

Leimu, H. "Sociology in Finland—Notes on Main Traditions in Sociology and on

Some of Their Exponents with an Emphasis on Period since 1945." *Zeitschrift Fur Soziologie* 6 (2): 222–49. 1977.

Rabier, J.C. "Sociology in Finland." *Revue Française de Sociologie* 18 (1): 109–31. 1977.

FRANCE

Amiot, M. "Urban Sociology in France." *International Social Science Journal* 38 (2): 311–22. 1986.

Kaufmann, J.C. "French Urban Sociology—Problems and Prospects." *Urban Affairs Quarterly* 19 (3): 287–302. 1984.

Leenhardt, J. "Ideologies and Trends in Contemporary French Sociology." In R.P. Mohan and D. Martindale (eds.), *Handbook of Contemporary Developments in World Sociology,* pp. 9–18. Westport, CT: Greenwood Press, 1975.

Peloille, B. "Return to a Sociology of a French Nation." *Cahiers Internationaux de Sociologie* 75 (July): 239–61. 1983.

GERMANY

Hertz, T.A., and H. Stegemann. "Empirical Social Science Research in the Federal Republic of Germany." *Social Science Information/Informahou derles Sociales* 15 (1): 143–76. 1976.

Matthes, J. "Sociology without Sociologists—Academic Situation of Sociology in Federal Republic of Germany." *Zeitschrift fur Soziologie* 2 (1): 47. 1973.

Ranier, L. "The Development of Sociology after WWII: 1945 to 1967." *Kolner Zeitschrift fur Soziologie und Sozialpsychologie* 21: 25–30. 1979.

Schafers, B. "Sociology and Social-Development Report from the 22nd German Sociology Meeting in Dortmund, October 9–12, 1984." *Kolner Zeitschrift fur Soziologie und Sozialpsychologie* 37 (1): 184–87. 1985.

Schissler, H. "Report on the 19th German Sociology Conference, Berlin 1979." *Geschichte Und Gesellschaft* 6 (1): 157–61. 1980.

Silbermann, A. "How Sick Is the Sociology in the Federal Republic of Germany?" *International Social Science Journal* 27 (4): 787–89. 1975.

Urs, J. "Developmental Interaction between American and German Sociology." *Social Research* 43 (1): 62–76. 1976.

Viehoff, L. "The Development of Sociology in West German Universities between 1960 and 1981." *Zeitschrift fur Soziologie* 13 (3): 264–72. 1984.

Wurzlacher, G., D. Blaschlee, G. Cyprian, H.P. Frey, J. Hamers, F. Heckmann, F. Kroll, I. Lukatis, W. Lukatis, U. Schlottmann, E. Schmickl, and D. Walz. "Sociology in East and West Germany." *International Review of Modern Sociology* 13 (1–2): 139–230. 1983.

GREECE

Kourvetaris, G., and B.A. Dobratz. "Present Status of Sociology in Greece." In R.P. Mohan and D. Martindale (eds.), *Handbook of Contemporary Developments in World Sociology.* Westport, CT: Greenwood Press, 1975.

Peristiany, J.G. "Sociology in Greece." In *Contemporary Sociology in Western Europe and in America,* pp. 272–73. Rome, Italy: First International Congress of Social Sciences of the Luigi Sturzo Institute.

HUNGARY

Keresz, G. "Sociologists in Hungary: Their Professional Orientation and Requirements." *Sociologia,* 1973.

Kulcsar, K. "Marxian Sociology in Hungarian Society of Year 1970." *Sociologicky Casopis* 13 (4): 372–82. 1977.

Rezler, J. "Rebirth of Sociology in Hungary." *Eastern European Quarterly* 8 (2): 223. 1974.

Roucek, J.S., and R.P. Mohan. "Contemporary Sociology in Hungary." In R.P. Mohan and D. Martindale (eds.), *Handbook of Contemporary Developments in World Sociology.* Westport, CT: Greenwood Press, 1975.

Unnithan, T.K.N. "Recent Trends and Issues in Hungarian Sociology." *Sociological Bulletin* 25 (1): 95–100. 1977.

Varga, K. "Sociology in Hungary." *International Review of Modern Sociology* 13 (1–2): 231–66.

INDIA

Ahmad, A. "For a Sociology of India." *Contributions to Indian Sociology* (New Series) 6: 172–78. 1972.

Bailey, F.G. "For a Sociology of India?" *Contributions to Indian Sociology* 3. 1959. (A commentary on Dumont and Pocock's article.)

Barnett, S. "Comparative Sociology of India—Reply." *Journal of Asian Studies* 36 (3): 599–601. 1987.

Bottomore, T.B. "Sociology in India." *British Journal of Sociology* (June): 98–105. 1962.

Chekki, D.A. "Toward Reconstructing National Traditions in Sociology." *Journal of Sociological Studies* 7. 1988.

Damle, Y.B. "Sociology in India." *New Quest* 24 (November–December): 355–59. 1980.

———. "Sociology in India: Its Teaching and Status." *International Social Science Journal* 26 (2): 343–48. 1974.

———. "Theoretical Orientations and Methodological Perspectives for Sociology in India in the 1980s." In P.K.B. Nayar (ed.), *Sociology in India: Retrospect and Prospect,* pp. 45–59. Delhi: B.R. Publishing Corporation, 1982.

Desai, I.P. "Craft of Sociology in India: An Autobiographical Perspective." *Economic and Political Weekly* 16 (6): 197–204, February 7, 1981; 11 (5–6): 246–51, February 14, 1981.

Dube, S.C. "Indian Sociology at the Turning Point." *Sociological Bulletin* 26 (1): 1–13. 1977.

Dumont, L., and D.F. Pocock. "For a Sociology of India." *Contributions to Indian Sociology* 1. 1957.

———. "For a Sociology of India." *Contributions to Indian Sociology* 4. 1960.

Dutta, G.B. *Sociology in India.* Center for Sociological Research, 1972.

Gupta, R. "Bibliographical Tools in Sociology: An Evaluation—Part 1: Growth of Sociology in India." *Library Herald* 16 (1–2): 83–172. 1974.

Hallen, G.C. "Progress of Sociology as an Academic Discipline in India." *Indian Journal of Social Research* 10 (1): 48–54. April 1969.

ICSSR. *Training in Research Methodology in the Social Sciences in India, No. 1.* Occasional Monograph on Research Methodology in the Social Sciences. New Delhi: Indian Council of Social Science Research, 1974.

———. *A Survey of Sociology and Anthropology,* vols. 1 and 2. Bombay: Popular Prakashan, 1974.

———. *A Survey of Sociology and Social Anthropology,* vol. 3. Bombay: Popular Prakashan, 1972.

Indian Institute of Advanced Study. *Social Sciences and Social Realities—Role of the Social Sciences in Contemporary India.* Simla: Indian Institute of Advanced Studies, 1976.

Joshi, P.C. "Reflections on Social Science Research in India." *Sociological Bulletin* 24 (2): 139–62. 1975.

Lakshmannya, C. "Teaching and Research in Sociology in India." *Sociological Bulletin* 23 (1): 1–13. 1974.

Madan, T.N. "For a Sociology of India." *Contributions to Indian Sociology* (New Series) 15 (1–2): 403–19. 1981.

———. "The Teaching of Sociology in India: Some Comments." *Sociological Bulletin* 23 (1): 113–18. 1974.

Mohan, R.P. "Contemporary Sociology in India." In R.P. Mohan and D. Martindale (eds.), *Handbook of Contemporary Developments in World Sociology,* pp. 423–37. Westport, CT: Greenwood Press, 1975.

———. "Contemporary Sociology in India: Historical Aspects, Comments, and Some Trends." In G.C. Hallen (ed.), *Indian Sociology,* pp. 341–54. Meerut, India: Rohini Publications, 1986.

———. "Contemporary Sociology in India: Synthesis of Traditional and Modern Values." In G.C. Hallen (ed.), *Indian Sociology,* pp. 184–92. Meerut, India: Rohini Publications, 1986.

Momin, A.R. "Indian Sociology: Search for Authentic Identity." *Sociological Bulletin* 27 (2): 154–72. 1979.

Mukherjee, R. "Indian Sociology: Historical Development and Present Problems." *Sociological Bulletin* 22 (1): 29–58. 1973.

———. "I.P. Desai and Sociology of India." *Economic and Political Weekly* 21 (4): 164–68. 1986.

———. "The Sociologist of the Social Reality." *Sociological Bulletin* 25 (2): 169–92. 1974.

———. "Trends in Indian Sociology." *Contributions to Indian Sociology* (New Series) 13 (2): 319–32. 1979.

Nayar, P.K.B. (ed.). *Sociology in India: Retrospect and Prospect.* Delhi: B.E. Publishing Corporation, 1980.

Oommen, T.K. "Sociological Issues in the Analysis of Special Movements in Independent India." *Sociological Bulletin* 26 (1): 14–37. 1977.

Rao, M.S.A. "Sociology in the 1980s." *Economic and Political Weekly* 14 (44): 1810–15. 3 November 1979.

————. *Urban Sociology in India.* New Delhi: Orient Longmans, 1974.

Rao, S.V.V., and C.R.P. Rao. "Reflections on the Crisis of Indian Sociology." *Sociological Bulletin* 26 (2): 259–63. 1977.

Saxena, B.C. "Teaching of Sociology in India—Some Comments." *Sociological Bulletin* 23 (2): 246–47. 1975.

Sharma, C.L. "Recognition of Hindi in the Profession of Sociology in India." *Sociological Bulletin* 27 (2): 258–59. 1979.

Singh, Y. *Indian Sociology: Social Conditioning and Emerging Concerns.* New Delhi: Vistaar Publications, 1986.

Srinivas, M.N. "Development of Sociology in India—An Overview." *Economic and Political Weekly* 22 (4): 135–38. 1987.

Srinivas, M.N., and M.N. Panini. "The Development of Sociology and Social Anthropology in India." *Sociological Bulletin* 22 (2): 179–215. 1973.

Srivastara, R.N. "The New Role of Sociologist in India Today." *Bharati Utkal University Journal* 8 (14): 85–92. 1974.

Unnithan, T.K.N. "Sociology in India since Independence." *International Journal of Contemporary Sociology* 18 (3–4): 81–134. 1981.

Yogendra, S. "Some Reflections on Indian Sociology Today." *Indian Journal of Political Studies* 2 (1): 10–18. 1978.

Yogesh, A. "Professionalization of Sociologist." *Indian Journal of Social Research* 12 (2): 137–42. 1971.

IRAQ

Algazzaz, A. "Impressions of Sociology in Iraq." *International Social Science Journal* 27 (4): 781–86. 1976.

ITALY

Direnzo, G.J. "Contemporary Sociology in Italy." *International Journal of Contemporary Sociology* 8 (3–4): 410–26. 1971.

Ferrarotti, F. *Societa'.* Milan: Mondadori, 1980, especially the chapter "La Sociologia dei gruppi," pp. 169–89.

————. "Sociologia e servizio sociale." *Quaderni di Sociologia* 12: 64. 1954.

————. "La Sociologie en Italie." *Cahiers Internationaux de Sociologie* (PUF, Paris) 38. 1985.

Fiamingo, G. "Sociology in Italy: The Sociological Tendency of Today." *Quaderni di Sociologia* 29 (2): 267–79. 1980–1981.

Fraser, J. "Italian Sociology Facing the Eighties: Points for Discussion." *La Critica Sociologica* 73: 22–32. 1985.

Kurzweil, E. "Reflections on Contemporary Italian Sociology." *Contemporary Sociology* 2: 247–54. 1973.

Pinto, D. (ed.). *Contemporary Italian Sociology.* New York and Cambridge: Cambridge University Press, 1981.

Piperno, A. "Contemporary Italian Sociology." *International Journal of Contemporary Sociology* 12 (1–2): 113–23. 1975.

Renato, T. "Thirty Years of Sociology in Italy and the Association Problem." *Quaderni di Sociologia* 29 (4): 727–31. 1980–1981.

JAPAN

Ishida, T. "Contemporary Sociology in Japan." In R.P. Mohan and D. Martindale (eds.), *Handbook of Contemporary Developments in World Sociology.* Westport, CT: Greenwood Press, 1975.

Isomura, E. "New Selection of Sociology in Japan." *Japanese Sociological Review* 35, 4 (140): 64–71. 1985.

Koyano, S. "Sociological Studies in Japan: Prewar, Postwar and Contemporary Stages." *Current Sociology* 24 (1): 7–196. 1976.

Kuravti, K. "Advancement of Modern Sociology in Japan." *Cahiers Internationaux de Sociologie* 57 (July): 197. 1974.

LATIN AMERICA

Deev, V.A. "Mexican Sociology: Historical Development and Contemporary Theoretical Approaches." *Sotaiologicheskie Issledovaniya* 9 (3): 49–54.

Ferrari, T.A. "The Expansion of Sociology in Brazil." *Revista Brasileira de Sociologia* 6 (1–2): 3–22. 1974.

Ianni, O. *Sociology and Dependence in Latin America.* Asuncion, Paraguay: Centro Paraguayo De Estudios Sociologicos, 1972.

Marinho, M.J.M. "The Professionalization of Sociology in Brazil." *Dados Revista De Ciencias Sociais* 30 (2): 223–33. 1988.

Motta, R. "Sociology in Brazil." *Cahiers Internationaux de Sociologie* 78 (January): 109–14. 1985.

Smith, T.L. "Social Change in Latin America." *International Journal of Contemporary Sociology* 12 (1–2): 49–62. 1975.

Valladares, L. "Urban Sociology in Brazil—A Research Report." *International Journal of Urban and Regional Research* 12 (2): 285–302. 1988.

MOROCCO

Bentahar, M., and E.T. Bouasla. *La Sociologie coloniale et la société marocaine de 1830 à 1960. La Sociologie Marocaine Contemporaine: Bilan et Perspectives,* pp. 27–43. Rabat: Publications de la Faculté de Lettres et des Sciences Humaines, 1988.

Dialmy, A. *The Sociological Affair,* pp. 66–75. Casablanca: Publications Afrique-Orient, 1989 (Arabic).

Khatibi, A. *Bilan de la sociologie au Maroc.* Rabat: Publication de l'association pour les sciences humaines, 1967.

———. "Double Criticism: The Decolonization of Arab Sociology." In H. Barakat, *Contemporary North Africa.* Washington, DC: Center for Contemporary Arab Studies, Georgetown University, 1985.

Sabour, M. *Homo Academicus Arabicus.* Joensuu: University of Joensuu Publications in Social Sciences, 1988.

———. "The Status and Ontology of Arab Intellectuals: The Academic Group." *International Journal of Contemporary Sociology* 28 (July–October): 221–32. 1991.

NETHERLANDS

Bovenkerk, F., and L. Brunt. "Where Sociology Falls Short: How Dutch Sociologists Observe Social Reality." *Netherlands Journal of Sociology* 19 (1): 65–78. 1983.

Devalk, J.M.M. "Contemporary Sociology in the Netherlands." *International Journal of Contemporary Sociology* 8 (3–4): 396–404. 1971.

Mok, A.L. "Professing Sociology in the Netherlands." *Sociologia Neerlandica* 10 (1): 92–98. 1974.

Rademaker, L. *Sociologie in Nederland.* Deventer: Von Loghum Slaterus, 1977.

Ultee, W.C. "Progress in Sociology: Nooji Interpretation." *Sociologische Gids* 29 (20): 159–70. 1982.

Van de Vall, M., and F.L. Leeuw. "Unity and Diversity: Sociology in the Netherlands." *Sociological Inquiry* 57 (2): 183–203. 1987.

Van Rossum, W. "The Problem of Cognitive Institutionalization in the Social Sciences: The Case of Dutch Sociology." *Social Science Information/Information sur les Sciences Sociales* 14 (2): 155–77. 1975.

Zijderveld, A.C. "On Rigidity in Dutch Sociology." *Sociale Wetenschappen* 24 (1): 44–50. 1981.

NIGERIA

Akiwowo, A. *Sociology in Africa Today.* Beverly Hills: Sage Publications, 1983.

Akiwowo, A.A. "Contemporary Sociology in Nigeria." In R.P. Mohan and D. Martindale (eds.), *Handbook of Contemporary Developments in World Sociology,* pp. 391–407. Westport, CT: Greenwood Press, 1975.

———. "Sociology in Africa Today." *Current Sociology/La Sociologie Contemporaine* 28 (2): 1–126. 1980.

Temu, P.E. "Reflections on the Role of Social Scientists in Africa." *International Social Science Journal* 27 (1): 190–94. 1975.

Waterman, P. "Whither Nigerian Sociology?" *West Africa* 2853: 189. 1972.

NORWAY

Lochen, Y. "Norwegian Sociology—Social Rebellion and/or Professional Participation." *Acta Sociologica* 25 (4): 359–65. 1983.

PAKISTAN

Gardezi, H.N. "Contemporary Sociology in Pakistan and Bangladesh." In R.P. Mohan and D. Martindale (eds.), *Handbook of Contemporary Developments in World Sociology.* Westport, CT: Greenwood Press, 1975.

Wakil, S.P. "Sociology in Pakistan: Some Lessons and Prospects." *International Journal of Contemporary Sociology* 12 (3–4): 244–54. 1975.

POLAND

Borowski, K. "Sociology in Poland." *International Review of Modern Sociology* 13 (1–2): 267–312. 1983.

Gella, A. "Contemporary Sociology in Poland." In R.P. Mohan and D. Martindale (eds.), *Handbook of Contemporary Developments in World Sociology.* Westport, CT: Greenwood Press, 1975.

———. "Contemporary Sociology in Poland." *International Journal of Contemporary Sociology* 8 (3–4): 224–40. 1971.

Kloskowska, A. "Empiricism and Theory in Polish Sociology." *Prezeglad Socjologiczny* 31 (1): 17–32. 1979.

Mink, G. "Polish Sociology: History and Trends." *Sociologie du Travail* 24 (3): 249–61. 1982.

Podgorecki, A. "Comment on Review of Masters of Polish Sociology, A Reply." *Contemporary Sociology* 16 (1): 3–4. 1986.

Smolicz, J.J. "Some Impressions of Polish Sociology." *Australian and New Zealand Journal of Sociology* 10 (1): 17–23. 1974.

Suxek, A., and R. Suxek. "1980 Bibliography of Sociological Works by Polish Authors and Published in a Language Other Than Polish, Part III." *Polish Sociological Bulletin* 1 (49): 49–78. 1980.

Sztompka, P. "Comment on Review of Masters of Polish Sociology." *Contemporary Sociology* 16 (1): 3. 1987.

Walaszek, Z. "Recent Developments in Polish Sociology." *Annual Review of Sociology* 3: 331–62. 1977.

ROMANIA

Badina, O. "Sociology in Romania." *International Review of Modern Sociology* 13 (102): 313–74. 1983.

Costea, S. *A Concise History of Romanian Sociology.* Bucharest: Editura Stintific a si Encicopedic a 1983–1985 Fishe. 1981.

Roucek, J., and R.P. Mohan. "Contemporary Sociology in Romania." In R.P. Mohan and D. Martindale (eds.), *Handbook of Contemporary Developments in World Sociology.* Westport, CT: Greenwood Press, 1975.

SOUTH AFRICA

Lever, H. "Sociology of South Africa—Supplementary Comments." *Annual Review of Sociology* 7: 249–62. 1981.

SOVIET UNION

Crique, E. "Sociology of the Ruling Class in the USSR." *Revue Française de Sociologie* 30 (6): 1272–1300. 1981.

Frolic, M. "Soviet Urban Sociology." *International Journal of Comparative Sociology* 12 (4): 234–51. 1971.

Gapachka, M.F. "Aspects of the Social Sciences in the Union of Soviet Socialist Republics." *International Social Science Journal* 26 (2): 349–52. 1974.

Jonson, L. "Coordinating and Planning Sociological Research in the Soviet Union." *Acta Sociologica* 21 (2): 181–91. 1978.

Lipset, S.M., and R.B. Dobson. "Social Stratification and Sociology in the Soviet Union." *Survey* 3: 114–85. 1973.

Matthews, M., and A. Jones. *Soviet Sociology 1964–75: A Bibliography.* New York: Praeger Publishers, 1978.

Merton, R.K., and H.W. Riecken. "Notes on Sociology in the USSR." In *Current Problems in Social-Behavioral Research,* Symposia Studies No. 10. Washington, DC: National Institute of Social and Behavioral Science, 1962.

Nystrom, K. "Soviet Sociology and the Scientific Technological Revolution." *Acta Sociologica* 17 (7): 55–77. 1973.

Osipov, G.V., and M.N. Rutkevick. "Sociology in the USSR, 1965–1975." *Current Sociology* 26 (2): 1–154. 1978.

Roucek, J.S., and R.P. Mohan. "Contemporary Sociology in the Soviet Union." In R.P. Mohan and D. Martindale (eds.), *Handbook of Contemporary Developments in World Sociology.* Westport, CT: Greenwood Press, 1975.

Rutkevick, M.N., et al. *Sociology and the Present Age.* Moscow: Soviet Sociological Association, 1974.

Rutkowski, E.H. "Soviet Sociology—An Exchange of Letters." *Studies in Soviet Thought* 26 (2): 151–53. 1983.

Shalin, D.N. "On Current Trends in Soviet Sociology." *La Critica Sociologica* 38: 173–84. 1976.

Shaw, K. "The Dilemma of the Soviet Sociologist." *New Society* 40 (764): 392–93. 1977.

Weinberg, E.A. *The Development of Sociology in the Soviet Union.* London: Routledge and Kegan Paul, 1974.

Zaslavsky, V. "Sociology in the Contemporary Soviet Union." *Social Research* 44 (2): 330–53. 1977.

SPAIN

Eljabeitia, C. de, and I.C.F. de Castro. "Sociology in Spain Today." *International Social Science Journal* 31 (2): 355–59. 1979.

Miguel, A. de. "Sociology in an Authoritarian Society: A Pessimistic Reflection on the Case of Spain." In Tom Bottomore (ed.), *Crisis and Contention in Sociology,* pp. 25–53. London: Sage, 1975.

Miguel, J.M. de, and M.G. Mayor. "Trend Report: Sociology in Spain." *Current Sociology* 27 (1): 5–140. 1979.

SWEDEN

Allardtl, E. "Swedish Sociology." *International Journal of Sociology* 3: 50–71.

Boalt, G. "Swedish Sociology—Trends and Prospects." *Contemporary Sociology* 25 (1): 101. 1987.

Boalt, G., and B. Abrahamsson. "Swedish Sociology—Trends and Prospects." *Current Sociology/La Sociologie Contemporaine* 25 (1): 101–26. 1977.

Janson, C.-G. "The Case for a Scandinavian Sociology." *Sociology and Social Research* 57 (2): 153–55. 1973.

———. "The Case for a Scandinavian Sociology." *Sociology and Social Research* 58 (3): 278–85. 1974.

———. "The Current State of Swedish Sociology: A Review Essay." *Social Forces* 53 (1): 124–26. 1974.

SWITZERLAND

Heintz, P. "Problems of Developing Sociology in Switzerland." *International Social Science Journal* 27 (4): 777–80. 1975.

UNITED STATES

Angell, R.C. "Reflections on the Project, Sociological Resources for the Social Sciences." *American Sociologist* 16 (1): 41–43. 1981.

Armer, J.M. "Provincialism and Internationalism in Contemporary American Sociology." *International Sociology* 2 (3): 315–24. 1987.

Becker, H.S. "What's Happening to Sociology?" *Society* 16 (5): 19–24. 1979.

Bernert, C. "The Career of Causal Analysis in American Sociology." *British Journal of Sociology* 34 (2): 230–54. 1983.

Birnbaum, N. "An End to Sociology?" *Social Research* 42 (3): 433–66. 1975.

Blackwell, J.E., and M. Janowitz. *Black Sociologists: Historical and Contemporary Perspectives.* Chicago: University of Chicago Press, 1972.

Block, F. "Alternative Sociological Perspectives." *Catalyst* 7: 29–41. 1973.

Blomdahl, U. "American Sociology at the Beginning of the 1980s: Some Publications." *Sociologisk Forskning* 20 (1): 82–89. 1983.

Bode, J.G. "The Silent Science." *American Sociologist* 7 (5): 5–6. 1972.

Bogardus, E.S. "Twenty-Five Years of American Sociology: 1947–1972." *National Taiwan University Journal of Sociology* 77: 21–24. 1975.

———. "Twenty-Five Years of American Sociology: 1947–1972." *Sociology and Social Research* 57 (2): 145–52. 1973.

Carneiro, R.L. "Herbert Spencer's *The Study of Sociology* and the Rise of Social Science in America." *Proceedings of the American Philosophical Society* 118 (6): 540–54. 1974.

Coleman, J.S. "Recent Developments in American Sociological Methods." *Polish Sociological Bulletin* 2 (30): 11–23. 1974.

Curtis, J.E., and J.W. Petras. "The Sociology of Sociology: Some Lines of Inquiry in the Study of the Discipline." *Sociological Quarterly* 13 (2): 197–209. 1972.

Denzin, N.K. "American Sociology—Plight and Promise—Comment." *American Sociologist* 14 (1): 42–44. 1979.

Dynes, R.R. "On the Institutionalization of Sociology in the United States." *Sociological Focus* 6 (3): 1–34. 1973.

Erikson, K.T. "Sociology: That Awkward Age." *Social Problems* 19 (4): 431–36. 1972.

Ferrarotti, F. "Preliminary Remarks on the Interaction between American and European Social Science." *Social Research* 43 (1): 25–45. 1976.

Flacks, R. "Radical Sociology—Emergence of Neo-Marxian Perspectives in United States Sociology." *Annual Review of Sociology* 4: 193–238. 1978.

Foote, N.N. "Putting Sociologists to Work." *American Sociologist* 9 (3): 123–34. 1974.

Frisbie, W.P. "Urban Sociology in the United States—The Past 20 Years." *American Behavioral Scientist* 24 (2): 177–214. 1980.

Frumkin, R.M. "Contemporary Sociology in the United States." In R.P. Mohan and D. Martindale (eds.), *Handbook of Contemporary Developments in World Sociology.* Westport, CT: Greenwood Press, 1975.

Fuhrman, E.R., and W.E. Snizek. "Finnish and American Sociology: A Cross-Cultural Comparison." *Sociological Inquiry* 57 (2): 204–19. 1987.

Gelfand, D.E. "The Challenge of Applied Sociology." *American Sociologist* 10 (1): 13–18. 1975.

Gibbs, J.P. "Causation and Theory Construction." *Social Science Quarterly* 52 (4): 815–26. 1972.

Giddens, A. "American Sociology Today." *New Society* 33 (676): 633–34. 1975.

Glass, J.F. "Toward a Sociology of Being: The Humanistic Potential." *Sociological Analysis* 32 (4): 191–98. 1971.

Glenn, N. "Standards of Quality in American Sociology." *Contemporary Sociology* 8 (3): 335–36. 1979.

Goodwin, G.A. "The Emergence of Various Theoretical Trends and Their Prospects in Sociology." *Sociological Focus* 6 (2): 1–9. 1973.

Gordon, M. "The Social Survey Movement and Sociology in the United States." *Social Problems* 21 (2): 284–98. 1973.

Gray, D.J. "American Sociology—Plight and Promise." *American Sociologist* 14 (1): 35–42. 1979.

Hauser, P.M. "Sociology's Progress toward Science." *American Sociologist* 16 (1): 62–64. 1981.

Hayes, J.R. "Images of Persons in Early American Sociology—Three Social Groups." *Journal of the History of the Behavioral Sciences* 10 (4): 391. 1974.

Heferkamp, H. "Theory of Social Problems: Critique of the North American Problem Sociology." *Kolner Zeitschrift fur Soziologie und Sozial Psychologie* 39 (1): 121–31. 1987.

Heise, D.R. "American Sociology—Plight and Promise." *American Sociologist* 14 (1): 44–45. 1979.

Julesrosette, B. "Comprehensive Sociology in the United States—Paradigms and Perspectives." *Cahiers Internationaux de Sociologie* 78 (January): 91–101. 1985.

Kinloch, G. "The Development of American Sociology as Reflected in Journal Debates." *International Journal of Contemporary Sociology* 21 (1–2): 65–81. 1984.

Kivisto, P. "Sociology as a Vocation—A Weberian Analysis of the Origins and Subsequent Development of American Sociology." *British Journal of Sociology* 38 (1): 112–20.

Kuklick, H.A. "Scientific Revolution: Sociological Theory in the United States, 1930–1945." *Sociological Inquiry* 43 (1): 3–22. 1973.

Lantz, H.R. "Urban-Rural Differences in American Sociology." *International Review of Modern Sociology* 8 (2): 179–91. 1979.

Lee, R., J.C. Runda, and A.B. Lee. "The Intradiscipline Status Hierarchy: Prestige Ranking of Sociology's Specialty Areas." *Sociological Focus* 7 (2): 7–19. 1973.

Lindsey, D. "American Sociology—Plight and Promise—Comment." *American Sociologist* 14 (1): 45–46. 1979.

Lundberg, C.C. "Sociology and Science: Notes toward an Alternative Strategy of Inquiry." *Humanity and Society* 1 (1): 12–17. 1977.

Luschen, G. "Two Sociologies—German and American Sociology in Representative Compendia." *Kolner Zeitschrift fur Soziologie und Sozialpsychologie* 35 (1): 133–41. 1983.

MacClung, A.L. "A Different Kind of Sociological Society." *Humanity and Society* 17 (1): 1–11. 1977.

Manning, P.K. "Existential Sociology." *Sociological Quarterly* 14 (2): 200–225. 1973.

Patel, N. "Collaboration in the Professional Growth of American Sociology." *Social Sciences Information/Information sur les Sciences Sociales* 12 (6): 77–92. 1973.

Peillon, M. "American Sociology in France." *Cahiers Internationaux de Sociologie* 72 (January): 159–72. 1982.

Perruci, R. "On the Liberation of a Liberating Discipline." *Sociological Focus* 7 (3): 1–12. 1974.

Ritzer, G. "A Multiple Paradigm Science." *American Sociologist* 10 (3): 156–67. 1975.

Rubin, L.B. "Sociological Research: The Subjective Dimension." *Symbolic Interaction* 4 (1): 97–112. 1981.

Schvessler, K. "Sociology toward the Year 2000." *Society* 16 (5): 31–35. 1979.

Short, J.F. "American Sociology—Plight and Promise—Comment." *American Sociologist* 14 (1): 47–49. 1979.

Street, D., and E.A. Weinstein. "Problems and Prospects of Applied Sociology." *American Sociologist* 10 (2): 65–72. 1975.

Taylor, L. "A Brief History of Sociology." *International Review of Modern Sociology* 11 (1–2): 1–23. 1981.

Turner, J.H. "Sociology as a Theory Building Enterprise: Detours from the Early Masters." *Pacific Sociological Review* 22 (4): 427–56, 1979.

Turner, R.E. "Sociological Theory Today: A Symposium." *Rocky Mountain Social Science Journal* 12 (2): 1–27. 1975.

Wei, Z.L. "The Development of Sociology in the United States." *Chinese Sociology and Anthropology* 13 (3): 75–90. 1981.

Wells, R.H., and J.S. Picou. *American Sociology: Theoretical and Methodological Structure.* Washington, DC: University Press of America, 1981.

Wiley, N. "The Current Interregnum in American Sociology." *Social Research* 52 (1): 179–207.

Wilke, A.S., and R.P. Mohan. "Units of Analysis and Paradigms in Contemporary Sociological Theory." *Social Science* 54 (1): 28–34. 1979.

Williams, R.M., Jr. "Sociology in America: The Experience of Two Centuries." *Social Science Quarterly* 57 (1): 77–111. 1976.

Yinger, J.M. "American Sociology—Plight and Promise—Comment." *American Sociologist* 14 (1): 49–50. 1979.

Yoels, W.C. "On the Social Organization of American Sociology." *British Journal of Sociology* 25 (2): 150–61. 1974.

Young, T.R. "Research in the Land of Oz: The Yellow Brick Road to Success in American Sociology." *Sociological Inquiry* 47 (1): 65–71. 1977.

Zelditch, M. "American Sociology—Plight and Promise—Comment." *American Sociologist* 14 (1): 52–55. 1979.

YUGOSLAVIA

Cuetko, K. "Sociology in Yugoslavia: 1960–1978." *International Review of Modern Sociology* 13 (1–2): 375–95. 1983.

Deutsch, S. "Sociological Currents in Contemporary Yugoslavia." *American Sociologist* 12 (3): 141–47. 1977.

Gobetz, G., J. Goricar, and P. Jambrek. "Yugoslav Sociology." In R.P. Mohan and D. Martindale (eds.), *Handbook of Contemporary Developments in World Sociology*. Westport, CT: Greenwood Press, 1975.

Kostic, C. "Sociology in Yugoslavia 1960–1970." *International Review of Modern Sociology* 13 (1–2): 375–95. 1985.

Mirkovic, D. "Sociology in Yugoslavia Today." *International Review of Modern Sociology* 6 (2): 227–52. 1976.

Name Index

Abbagnano, Nicola, 490, 505 n.12
Abbas, M. B., 754 n.26
Abbott, Pamela, 50, 61 n.23
Abel, Richard L., 38 n.39, 39 n.47
Abel, T., 641
Åberg, Rune, 191, 200
Abraham, R. H., 149 n.96
Abraham, Sarah, 699 n.97
Abrahamson, Peter, 82 n.6
Abrahamsson, Bengt, 201, 204 n.35
Abrams, P., 613 n.19
Adachi, F., 724
Adam, A., 561, 565 n.21, 566 nn.24, 25, 39
Adams, R. J., 582 n.35
Adams, Vincanne, 741 n.9
Adamski, W., 435
Adar, Prof., 546
Adler, Frank, 145 n.31
Adler, Max, 9, 10, 15 n.7
Adler, Prof., 541, 546, 547
Adorno, Theodor W., 16 n.25, 123, 124, 128, 130, 145 n.36, 179 n.17, 412
Afsaruddin, Mohammad, 626, 635 nn.5, 7, 10, 18, 20, 23, 753 n.7
Aganbegian, Abel G., 444, 457 n.48
Agarwal, S. N., 699 n.101
Agersnap, Torben, 65, 66, 67, 79, 81
Agger, Ben, 315, 325, 336 n.18, 338 nn.43, 45
Agostini, R., 507 n.24
Aguilar, F., 521
Aguilar Pinar, F., 522
Ahmad, Imtiaz, 697 n.60
Ahmad, Saghir, 753 n.16

Ahmavaara, Yrjö, 93, 103 n.52
Ahmed, Feroz, 755 n.30
Ahrne, Göran, 191, 200
Ahtola, Olli T., 303 n.11
Aikio, Marjut, 98, 105 n.93
Akhter, Jamila, 753 n.13
Akimoto, Ritsuo, 720, 727 n.20, 728 n.58
Alabart Anna, 517, 519, 522
Alapuro, Risto, 98, 101, 105 n.10, 84, 85
Alasuutari, Pertti, 105 n.80
Alavi, Hamza, 748, 752, 753 n.15, 754 nn.23, 29
Al-Azmeh, A., 564 n.3
Alberdi, Inés, 517, 519, 522
Alberoni, Fracesco, 491
Albrecht, G., 145 n.28
Aldous, Joan, 41 n.59
Aldrich, John H., 304 n.23
Aleksandrov, G. F., 442
Alemann, Heine von, 144 n.6
Alestalo, Marja, 107 n.121
Alestalo, Matti, 96, 98, 101 nn.14, 71, 104 nn.71, 73, 105 nn.85, 90
Alexander, Jeffrey C., 131, 146 n.46, 149 n.86, 226 n.14, 306, 313, 314, 335 nn.2, 3, 443, 460, 494
Alice, Lynne, 611 n.1, 617 n.80
Allardt, Erik, xvii, 92, 98, 102, 104, nn. 29, 30, 32, 40, 41, 44, 45, 53, 69, 70, 105 n.92, 193, 197, 199, 200, 201, 204 nn.27, 31, 34
Allen, Nick, 741 n.9
Allen, Woody, xv
Allison, Paul D., 304 nn.20, 21

About the Editors and Contributors

RAJ P. MOHAN is Professor of Sociology at Auburn University and Adjunct Professor of Sociology at the University of Joensuu in Finland. His previous publications include *Handbook of Contemporary Developments in World Sociology* (with Don Martindale, 1975), *Management and Complex Organizations in Comparative Perspective* (1979), and *The Mythmakers: Intellectuals and the Intelligentsia in Comparative Perspective* (1987), all published by Greenwood Press. He is Editor of *International Journal of Contemporary Sociology.*

ARTHUR S. WILKE is Professor of Sociology at Auburn University. He is Associate Editor of the *International Journal of Contemporary Sociology* and Co-Editor of *Sociological Spectrum.* His current research interests include the sociology of science, knowledge, and technology, and the political implications of social problems. He has published a variety of articles and chapters, edited: *The Hidden Professoriate* (Greenwood, 1979), and co-edited (with R. Mohan) *Swedish Sociology* (1980) and *Critical Realism and Sociological Theory* (1980).

ERIK ALLARDT is Chancellor of Åbo Akademi University. He was Professor of Sociology at the University of Helsinki from 1958 to 1991, and he has been Visiting Professor at the University of California–Berkeley, University of Illinois–Urbana, University of Wisconsin–Madison, Lund University, and Universität Mannheim. He was President of the Academy of Finland from 1986 to 1991. He was Chair of the ISA and IPSA Committee on Political Sociology (1979–85), and he was 1990 Vice-President of the European Science Foundation. He was Editor of *Acta*

Sociologica (1968–71) and of *Scandinavian Political Studies* (1975–76). His publications include *Mass Politics* (with Stein Rokkan, 1970), *About Dimensions of Welfare* (1973), and *Finland and Poland, Comparative Perspective* (with Wlodimierz Wesolowski, 1978).

HEINE ANDERSEN is Professor at the Copenhagen Business School. He has published works on philosophy of social sciences, sociological theory, moral philosophy, and national choice theory, including the recent article, "Morality in Three Social Theories: Parsons, Analytical Marxism and Habermas." He is Editor of the Danish sociological journal *Dansk Sociologi.*

PIERRE ANSART is Professor Emerite at the University Paris VII–Jussieu. He has published works on the history of sociology (*Sociologie de Proudhon* [1968], *Marx et l'anarchisme* [1969], and *Sociologie de Saint-Simon* [1970]; on the problems of ideology ("Les idéologies politiques" [1974], *Idéologies, conflicts et pouvoir* [1977], and *La Gestion des passions politiques* [1983]; and on sociological theory (*Les Sociologies contemporaines* [1990]).

CORA VELLEKOOP BALDOCK is Associate Professor of Sociology at Murdoch University in Perth, Western Australia. Her previous academic appointments were in sociology departments at the Australian National University, City University of New York, San Diego State University, Canterbury University (New Zealand) and Leiden University. Her publications include *Volunteers in Welfare* (1990), *Women, Social Welfare and the State* (1988), *Australia and Social Change Theory* (1978), and *Sociology in Australia and New Zealand* (1974). Dr. Baldock is a former President of the Sociological Association of Australia and New Zealand, and a former member of the Australian Research Grants Committee.

GENNADY S. BATYGIN is a leading Research Associate at the Institute of Sociology, USSR Academy of Sciences. He is the author of "Substantiations of Scientific Inference in Applied Sociology" (1986) and numerous articles in sociological symposia and journals. He is a councillor of the journal *Messenger of the USSR Academy of Sciences.* His current interests are history and methodology of social research.

HENK A. BECKER is Professor of Sociology and Policy Sciences in the Department of Sociology, Utrecht University, the Netherlands. His research interest is the pattern of generations that has emerged in Western societies. His recent publications explore impact assessment (technology assessment and demographic impact assessment) and the state of the art in sociology.

KRISHNA B. BHATTACHAN is completing his Ph.D dissertation in Sociology at the University of California, Berkeley. Prior to being awarded a Fulbright scholarship, he was Chair of the Department of Sociology and Anthropology at Tribhuvan University in Kathmandu, Nepal.

BRITT-MARI BLEGVAD teaches at the Faculty of Economics at the Copenhagen Business School, where she now holds the position of Docent (Reader). In 1970 she was Guest Professor with the Department of Sociology, University of California, Santa Barbara. She is a Research Fellow at the Law School of the University of Wisconsin–Madison as well as at the Onati International Institute for the Sociology of Law. She was President of the Danish Society for Sociology of Law and for the Institute of Sociology of Law for Europe. She is Co-Editor of *European Yearbook in the Sociology of Law.* She edited *Contributions to the Sociology of Law* (1966) and has since written surveys of Scandinavian sociology of law and reports on her own research, including criminology, organizational theory, and legal sociology.

MOGENS BLEGVAD has worked as a Psychologist and a Research Librarian. He was Mary Taylor Williams Fellow at the University of North Carolina at Chapel Hill; Professor of Philosophy at the University of Copenhagen, where he taught ethics and the history of philosophy of social science; Guest Professor at the Department of Sociology, University of California, Santa Barbara; and Fellow of the Royal Danish Academy of Sciences and Letters, where he served twelve years on the Governing Board. He is a Member of the ISA-Research Council for History of Sociology and for eight years served on its Executive Board. In *Danish Yearbook of Philosophy,* which he founded in 1964, he published papers in English.

LOUIS H. BLUHM is Professor of Sociology at Mississippi State University. He received a predoctoral internship for research in Brazil from the Midwest Universities Consortium for International Activities, Inc. In 1987, he was a Senior Fulbright Scholar in Campina Grande, Paraiba, Brazil. He is included in *The International Directory of Distinguished Leadership* and in *Personalities of the South* and was nominated to *Men of Achievement.* During his professional career, he has conducted research in Latin America and Africa and is the author of numerous articles and professional papers treating such topics as social change, development, terrorism, and trust. In conjunction with Latin American colleagues, his current research includes a three-year, joint project focusing on the reestablishment of trust in previously defunct Brazilian cooperatives.

B. SINGH BOLARIA is Professor of Sociology at the University of Saskatchewan. He has published widely in the areas of health care, racial inequality, and labor migrations. His most recent publications include *Racial Oppression in Canada* (1985), *Sociology of Health-Care in Canada* (1988), and *Social Issues and Contradictions in Canadian Society* (1991).

WALTER L. BÜHL has been Professor of Sociology at the University of Munich since 1974. He is author of many German publications about social change and sociological theory, including *Evolution und Revolution* (1970); *Transnationale Politik* (1978); *Struktur und Dynamik des menschlichen Sozialverhaltens* (1982); *Die Ordnung des Wissens* (1984); *Eine Zukunft für Deutschland* (1985); and *Sozialer Wandel im Ungleichgewicht* (1990).

ANGELA PENELOPE CHEATER is with the Department of Sociology and Anthropology at the University of Waikato, Hamilton, New Zealand, and author of an introductory textbook, three research monographs (co-author of a fourth), and over three dozen journal articles. She was also Research Fellow, Lecturer, Senior Lecturer, and associate Professor (Social Anthropology), at the University of Zimbabwe.

JACQUES COENEN-HUTHER is Associate Professor in the Department of Sociology at the University of Geneva. He was Associate Editor of *International Sociology* (1986–90) and is now Editor of a Swiss journal of sociology (*Schweizerische Zeitschrift für Soziologie/Revue suisse de sociologie*). He is a member of the Executive Committees of the Swiss Sociological Association and the International Association of French-speaking Sociologists (AISLF). He published *Le fonctionnalisme en sociologie: et après?* (1984) and numerous articles.

INNA F. DEVIATKO is Research Associate at the Institute of Sociology in Moscow. Among her recent publications are "Auxiliary Theories of Measurement in American Empirical Sociology" (in Russian, 1990) and "TETRAD-Methodology: Is It the End of Procedural Epistheme?" (1991).

HARLEY D. DICKINSON is Associate Professor, Department of Sociology, University of Saskatchewan. His research interests are in the areas of medicine and health care, mental health services and policy, and work organization. He has written numerous articles, chapters, and books, including: *The Two Psychiatries: The Transformation of Psychiatric Work in Saskatchewan* (1989). He co-edited, with B. Singh Bolaria, *Sociology of Health Care in Canada* (1988).

KAREL DOBBELAERE is Professor in Sociology and Sociology of Religion and Culture at the Catholic University of Leuven, Belgium. He is also Dean of the Faculty of Social and Political Sciences. His current publications are on changes in the Catholic world and on secularization.

VELICHKO DOBRIANOV is Professor at the Institute of Sociology, Bulgarian Academy of Sciences, and Head of the Department of the History of Sociology. He is Editor-in-Chief of *Sociological Problems* and has been Member of the Executive Committee of the Bulgarian Sociological Association. His major scientific works include *Theory and History* (1965); *Methodological Problems of Theoretical and Historical Cognition* (1968); *Poverty of the Antihistorical Method: Criticism of Karl Popper's Philosophy and Sociology* (1969); *The Elections-Electors and Elected: A Sociological Essay on the Presidential Elections in the USA* (1969); and *The Building of the Developed Socialist Society* (1973).

EVA ETZIONI-HALEVY is Professor of Sociology at Bar-Ilan University, Israel. She is the author of numerous articles and several books, including *The Knowledge Elite and the Failure of Prophecy* (1985), *Fragile Democracy* (1989), and *The Elite Connection* (1992). She is a Fellow of the Academy of the Social Sciences in Australia.

FRANCO FERRAROTTI has been Full Professor of Sociology and President of the Ph.D. Program in Social Science at the University of Rome; Director of Social Research Projects at the OEEC (now OECD in Paris); Independent Member of the Italian Parliament; and Founder of the *Quaderni di Sociologia*. At present, he is Editor of the journal *La Critica sociologica*. His numerous publications include *Toward the Social Production of the Sacred* (1975); *Max Weber and the Destiny of Reason* (1976); *An Alternative Sociology* (1978); *The Paradox of the Sacred* (1980); *Time, Memory, and Society* (Greenwood, 1984); *The End of Conversation* (Greenwood, 1989).

JAMES F. FISHER is Professor of Anthropology at Carleton College. His books include *Trans-Himalayan Traders* (1986) and *Sherpas: Reflections on Change in Himalayan Nepal* (1990). As a Fulbright Professor, he helped found the Department of Sociology and Anthropology at Tribhuvan University in Kathmandu, Nepal.

CHRISTIAN FLECK is Associate Professor at the Institute for Sociology, Graz University. He is also Co-Founder and Partner of the Bureau of Social Research, Graz, and Director of the Archive for the History of Sociology in Austria (AGSO) since its start in 1987. His publications include *Korruption. Zur Soziologie nicht immer abweichenden Verhaltens*

(1985), *Koralmpartisanen. Uber abweichende Karrieren politisch moti-
vierter Widerstanskämpfer* (1986), and *Der Fall Brandweiner Universität im
Kalten Krieg* (1987). He is also co-author of a sociological field research
about the unemployed and author of several professional articles.

HASSAN N. GARDEZI is Associate Professor of Sociology at Algoma
University in Canada. He is the author of numerous articles and book
chapters. Among his four books are *A Reexamination of the Socio-Political
History of Pakistan: Reproduction of Class Relations and Ideology* (1991)
and *Chairs to Lose: Life and Struggle of a Revolutionary* (1989).

ANNA GIZA-POLESZCZUK is Deputy Director of the Institute of Sociology, Warsaw University, where she teaches Methodology of Social Sciences and Theoretical Sociology. She is the winner the Helmuth Plessner
Award (in the domain of the philosophy of social sciences), Ministry of
Education Award (for the best sociological book), and S. Ossowski Award
(for the best sociological work). Currently, she is working on the problem
of the relations between social system and individual life-strategies, and
especially the strategies of family formation.

TIBOR HUSZÁR is Professor at Eötvös Loránd University, Budapest
(since 1961) and Organizer and Chair (since 1966) of the sociological department (Institute of Sociology and Social Policy). His main areas of
research are history of Hungarian social thought, sociology of intellectuals,
and Hungarian social structure.

TSUYOSHI ISHIDA is Professor of Sociology and Education at the Hiroshima Institute of Technology. Besides serving as a Postdoctoral Fellow
at the Department of Sociology, Cornell University, he taught as a Visiting
Associate Professor of Sociology at the University of Hawaii, Manoa; Fulbright Visiting Lecturer of Sociology at Yale University; and Visiting Professor of Sociology and Asian Studies at Bowdoin College. His recent
books are *Educational System of Yale University* (1986) and *Academic
Development System of Yale University* (1987). Presently, he is conducting
a research on knowledge, exploration, and development of intellectual
youths.

GRAHAM C. KINLOCH is presently Associate Dean of Academic Affairs in the College of Social Sciences at Florida State University. He completed his doctorate at Purdue University and has spent most of his career
in Florida, focusing on minority group relations and sociological theory.
He is presently interested in the comparative analysis of intergroup relations on a worldwide basis.

GEORGE A. KOURVETARIS is Professor of Sociology at Northern Illinois University. His major academic and research interests include political and military sociology, social stratification, intergroup relations, and comparative sociology. He is the author of *On Military Intervention* (1971) and *First and Second Generation Greeks in Chicago: An Inquiry into Their Stratification and Mobility Patterns* (1971). *Social Thought* (1993) Also, he has published articles in the *American Sociologist, International Journal of Contemporary Sociology, International Review of Modern Sociology, Pacific Sociological Review,* and others. He is Founder and Editor of the *Journal of Political and Military Sociology* and serves as an Associate Editor of six social science journals.

RANCE P. L. LEE is Professor of Sociology and Chairman of the Department of Sociology at the Chinese University of Hong Kong. He has served, concurrently, as Director of the Social Research Centre (1973–82), Director of the Institute of Social Studies (1982–90), and Chair of the Management Committee of the Hong Kong Institute of Asia-Pacific Studies (1990–present). He was Secretary-Treasurer of the Research Committee on the Sociology of Health, International Sociological Association (1982–90), and has been serving on the editorial boards of several international journals, such as *Southeast Asian Journal of Social Science, Chinese Sociology and Anthropology, International Review of Modern Sociology, Social Science and Medicine,* and *Health Transition Review.*

FRANS L. LEEUW is Director of the Netherlands' Court of Audit Department of Policy Evaluation. He also holds the Chair of Professor of Policy Effectiveness Research at Utrecht University. His recent publications are on policy theories, similarities and dissimilarities of auditing and evaluation research, and the utilization of policy research by government officials.

THOMAS A. PETEE is Associate Professor of Sociology at Auburn University. He has published articles in *Criminal Justice and Behavior, Journal of Social Psychology, Sociology and Social Research,* and *Journal for the Scientific Study of Religion.*

VIJAYAN K. PILLAI is Assistant Professor of Sociology at the University of North Texas. He was Research Associate at the Iowa Urban Community Research Center, at the University of Iowa, from 1987 to 1989. He is author and co-author of several articles, monographs, and book chapters.

ABUL HASNAT GOLAM QUDDUS is Professor in and Chair of the Department of Sociology at University of Chittagong, Bangladesh. For-

merly, he was Lecturer at Southern Illinois University at Carbondale. He
has written numerous journal articles; conducted several research projects;
and taught courses on methodology, social statistics, applied sociology, and
marriage and the family. From 1965 to 1974 he worked in the population
control program of Bangladesh.

M'HAMMED SABOUR is Associate Professor of Sociology of Culture
and Comparative Development in the Department of Sociology at the
University of Joensuu. He is author of several books and papers on development, cultural identification, and intellectuals. His most recent book
is *Homo Academicus Arabicus,* (1988) and he is presently working on
Femina Academica Arabica.

RINA SHAPIRA is Professor of Sociology of Education at the Tel-Aviv
University. She is the author of three books and many articles. Her current
research interests include sociology of education, educational organizations, education and community, and stratification and politics.

LAU SIU-KAI is Professor of Sociology at the Chinese University of
Hong Kong and Associate Director of its Hong Kong Institute of Asia-
Pacific Studies. He is the author of *Society and Politics in Hong Kong*
(1982) and the co-author of *The Ethos of the Hong Kong Chinese* (1988),
as well as many monographs and journal articles.

CARLOTA SOLÉ is Professor of Sociology in the College of Political
Sciences and Sociology at the Universidad Autonoma de Barcelona, Spain,
where he holds the Chair of Sociology. He is a keen observer of the Spanish sociological scene and has published his writings in journals and monographs.

RICHARD SWEDBERG is Associate Professor of Sociology at the University of Stockholm, Sweden, and was Visiting Scholar at Harvard University. He was Secretary of the section on Economy and Society of the
International Sociological Association. He is the author of numerous articles and book chapters. His most recent books are *Economics and Sociology: Redrawing Their Boundaries, Conversations on Redrawing Their
Borders* (1990) and *The Sociology of Economic Life: A Book of Readings*
(co-edited with Mark Granovetter, 1990).

LILIANE VOYÉ is Professor and President of the Department of Sociology at the Catholic University of Louvain (Belgium). Her current
publications are on urban and rural society and on religion and culture in
Belgium and Europe.

MING YAN completed her Ph.D. and is currently associated with St. Johns University.

STEVEN YEARLEY worked for several years at the Queen's University of Belfast before becoming the University of Ulster's first Professor of Sociology. His research has chiefly concentrated on the sociology of science and of environmentalism, although he has also published on sociological theory and sociolinguistics. His most recent book is *The Green Case* (1992), a study of the rise of environmentalism.

ISBN 0-313-26719-7

90000>

EAN

9 780313 267192

HARDCOVER BAR CODE

FORREST GENERAL MEDICAL CENTER

ADVANCED MEDICAL TERMINOLOGY AND TRANSCRIPTION COURSE

DONNA L. CONERLY, Ed.D.
Chair and Associate Professor
Department of Business Education
University of Southern Mississippi
Hattiesburg, MS

WANDA L. LOTT, A.R.T.
Director
Medical Records Department
Forrest General Hospital
Hattiesburg, MS

Published by

K31 **SOUTH-WESTERN PUBLISHING CO.**

CINCINNATI   WEST CHICAGO, IL   DALLAS   PELHAM MANOR, NY   LIVERMORE, CA

ISBN: 0-538-11310-3

Library of Congress Catalog Card Number: 85-61353

4 5 6 7 8 9 H 5 4 3 2

Printed in the United States of America

PREFACE

Beginning a career as a medical transcriber can be either extremely exciting or totally frightening. FORREST GENERAL MEDICAL CENTER has been written to prepare one to enter this profession with excitement rather than with fright or frustration.

In writing this text, the authors were guided by their belief that for an educational experience to be of maximum benefit to the student involved in a medical terminology/transcription course, there must be exposure to the most realistic kinds of dictation during the learning period—the type one will encounter on the job.

A unique feature of this text/workbook is the atmosphere of realism that has been created by having actual doctors dictate the medical reports that make up each chapter. Since a medical transcriber is confronted with realistic dictation from the first day on the job—dictation that can be indistinct, very rapid, and sometimes unintelligible—his or her training time could be shortened and productivity could be increased by having worked through the learning activities provided in this text.

At the beginning of each chapter, a brief description of the medical specialty is provided to serve as a foundation for the terminology and transcription one will encounter relative to that specialty. An additional feature of this text is the inclusion of material to be transcribed as letters, as a speech, and as a white paper (journal article). Advanced terminology most frequently heard in dictation of reports in the specialty, illustrations relative to anatomical location (in most chapters), common abbreviations, and forms upon which medical reports are to be typed are provided.

At the completion of each chapter, the material was submitted to either a physician or an oral surgeon for confirmation of facts.

While transcribing the tape for each specialty, the student will hear approximately one to nine doctors. An attempt has been made to provide the best quality dictation at the beginning of each tape with more difficult, but very realistic, dictation occurring at the end of the tape.

Because of the design of this book, the materials would be applicable for use in any post-secondary educational setting, in a course offered to practitioners who desire to upgrade current skills or to acquire new ones, in an open-ended program to be used on an individualized basis, or in any medical setting to provide practice in realistic learning experiences.

The appendix includes such helpful items as confusing medical terms; types of incisions, sutures, suture materials, dressings, anesthesia, instruments, operative positions; common lab tests; common drugs; prefixes; combining forms; suffixes; model report forms; and sample footnote entries.

In addition to the physicians, oral surgeons, and dentist listed on the following pages, many other people assisted in the production of this text. The authors are particularly indebted to the following people: Lowery A. Woodall, Executive Director, Forrest General Hospital; Freeman Parker, Assistant Executive Director, Forrest General Hospital; Dr. Annelle Bonner, retired Chair, Department of Business Education, University of Southern Mississippi; Dr. Bobby D. Anderson, Professor, Department of Educational Leadership and Research, University of Southern Mississippi; Ladoris Nicholoson, Supervisor of Medical Transcriptionists, Forrest General Hospital.

To Gene Owens, President of Allen-Owens Business Machines, Inc., for his office systems assistance, and to Tom Smith, Coordinator, Teaching-Learning

Resources Center, University of Southern Mississippi, for his technical assistance, we are particularly grateful.

And, most of all, to our families, Perry, Keith, Michelle, and Brett, Hayward, Larry, and Kim, we are thankful for their encouragement and patience.

Wanda Lott   Donna Conerly

SPECIAL ACKNOWLEDGMENTS

Without the support of the following physicians, oral surgeons, and dentist, this text would have not been a reality:

Ralph Abraham, M.D.
   Fellow, American College of Surgeons
   Diplomate, American Board of Surgery
   Diplomate, American Board of Thoracic Surgery

David Bomboy, M.D.
   Diplomate, American Board of Orthopedic Surgeons

Paul C. Charbonneau, D.D.S.
   Fellow, American College of Oral and Maxillo-Facial Surgery
   Diplomate, American Board of Oral and Maxillo-Facial Surgery

Dawson B. Conerly, M.D.
   Fellow, American College of Surgeons
   Diplomate, American Board of Surgery

Kenneth C. Crawley, D.D.S.
   Member, Mississippi State Board of Dental Examiners

William Gullung, M.D.
   Fellow, American Academy of Dermatology
   Diplomate, American Board of Dermatology

Larry Hammett, M.D.
   Fellow, American Academy of Otolaryngology, Head, and Neck
   Diplomate, American Board of Otolaryngology, Head, and Neck

Marcus L. Hogan, M.D.
   Fellow, American College of Obstetricians and Gynecologists
   Diplomate, American Board of Obstetricians and Gynecologists

G. Eli Howell II, M.D.
   Diplomate, American Society of Plastic and Reconstructive Surgeons

A. Jerald Jackson, M.D.
   Fellow, American College of Physicians

Ronald Lubritz, M.D.
   Fellow, American College of Physicians
   Clinical Professor of Dermatology, Tulane University School of Medicine, New Orleans, LA

Richard F. McCarthy, M.D.
   Diplomate, American Board of Radiology, American College of Radiology

Robert H. McCrary, M.D.
   Fellow, American Academy of Otolaryngic Allergy
   Diplomate, American Board of Otolaryngology, Head, and Neck

Lynn B. McMahan, M.D.
   Fellow, American Academy of Opthalmology

Toxey M. Morris, M.D.
Fellow, American College of Surgeons
Diplomate, American Board of Urology

Gerald Robertson, M.D.
Diplomate of the American Board of Psychiatry and Neurology

Ralph T. Wicker, M.D.
Fellow, American College of Surgeons
Diplomate, American Board of Neurological Surgery

James E. Williams III, M.D.
Diplomate, American Board of Pathology

Bennett V. York, D.D.S.
Fellow, American College of Oral and Maxillo-Facial Surgery
Diplomate, American Board of Oral and Maxillo-Facial Surgery

CONTENTS

INTRODUCTION

You are about to enter the exciting world of "realistic" medical transcription. The task will be much easier if you have had exposure to medical terminology and basic transcription; if you have not, these materials will really offer a challenge to you. With a lot of hard work, however, you can be successful in your study of these advanced transcription activities.

FORREST GENERAL MEDICAL CENTER has been designed to provide learning activities that will equip you with very competitive skills. Since the transcription exercises you will be listening to were dictated by physicians in realistic settings, you will become accustomed to transcribing dictation that is very similar to that encountered on the job. This exposure should enable you to be productive from your first day as a medical transcriber. If you presently work in a medical setting in which you transcribe, your skills should be sharpened and your production rate increased.

If you will follow suggestions made in the sections below and any specific directions given by your instructor, you will find the challenge much easier.

STRUCTURE OF THE LEARNING ACTIVITIES

The learning materials have been arranged in chapters alphabetically by name of the medical specialty; no effort was made to arrange the material according to level of difficulty. Therefore, you may find Chapter 12 to be "easier" than Chapter 1, etc. If you are in a class situation, your instructor will choose the specific order in which he/she would like you to proceed.

At the beginning of each chapter, you will read about the specialty, note a list of some of the more difficult common terms used in that specialty, see visuals to help you more readily assimilate the anatomical parts associated with the particular specialty, learn common abbreviations used in transcribing dictation in the specialized area, and hear medical reports commonly encountered in the specialty. Once you have become familiar with the terms from having listened to the terminology tape, you should transcribe the medical reports given on the accompanying set of tapes.

In most chapters you will be transcribing the types of medical reports one deals with in a hospital or clinic setting, such as operative reports, discharge summaries, x-ray reports, etc. In one chapter, though, you will be asked to type material for a speech; in another, a white paper (or journal article); and in another, some letters.

Be sure to become completely familiar with the lists provided in the appendix. There you will find such items as confusing medical terms; types of incisions, sutures, suture materials, dressings, instruments, anesthesia; operative positions; common lab tests; common drugs; prefixes; combining forms; suffixes; model report forms; and sample footnote entries. As you transcribe, you will find these reference materials invaluable.

An index of all the medical terms listed at the beginning of each chapter is also provided in the back of the text. This list will serve as a quick reference when you are unsure as to the spelling of words you will hear when transcribing the tapes.

In order to work most efficiently and with the most accuracy, we encourage you to have at your disposal the list of references suggested in the appendix. Of course, other materials can be used which may be just as useful. The sources recommended in the appendix were consulted in doing research for this text.

Although forms have been provided onto which you will transcribe the exercises from the tapes, many hospitals and/or medical facilities do not use forms. The medical reports are either transcribed onto plain white sheets or onto colored sheets with the different colors being used for different reports; for example, an x-ray report would be typed on green paper, a discharge summary on yellow paper, and a consultation on pink paper. When this is the case, no headings are provided and the transcriptionist must also type these.

As you type the information onto the forms provided in your text, from time to time you may hear more "headings" than are printed on the form. In this case, simply type the additional heading(s) in all caps in an appropriate place on the form and proceed with the dictation. If more headings appear than you need, simply leave blank those for which you do not have information.

In your examination of Model Report Forms in the appendix, you will notice at the end of each report the name of the doctor has been typed together with a "/" and the initials of the transcriber. Sometimes the name and initials are typed in all caps and sometimes not. In actuality the doctor may not dictate his/her name at the end of the report; it is your responsibility as transcriber to type it followed by your initials. Since medical records are subpoenaed in court cases from time to time, it is vital that the transcriber of the materials be identifiable; therefore, always type your initials. In addition, because medical records are subject to subpoena, they must be prepared in a way that qualifies them as "legal" documents. This means that any errors made must be corrected by some means other than use of either correction tape or liquid paper.

You will also notice that at the bottom of each model form "dd" and "dt" appear together with dates. "Dd" indicates the day the material was dictated by the doctor, and "dt" indicates the day it was transcribed. Since these dates can be very critical at times, be sure you type in the correct date. And although you will not hear these on the tapes, you should supply the information.

Even though we have made an attempt to be consistent in all the reports, there is more than one correct way to transcribe many things you will hear in medical transcription. For example, if the doctor dictates "four 0 chromic catgut," you may type it either "4-0" or "0000." You should be guided by the preference of the doctor or medical facility for which you are working. So you see, you must learn to be flexible.

Although in medical transcription one should be more concerned that the correct words have been transcribed than that each punctuation mark is placed in the proper place, strive to apply the various grammar, punctuation, etc., rules correctly as you would in any other setting.

Good luck as you begin an interesting and challenging training program!

CHAPTER 1
CARDIOLOGY

The cardiovascular system has numerous functions, two of which are carrying oxygen from the lungs to individual cells and transporting carbon dioxide from the cells back to the lungs. This system is composed of the heart, blood vessels, and blood, which consists of cells and plasma.

The primary duty of the heart, which serves as the functional center of the system, is to serve as a muscular pump propelling blood into and through vessels to and from all parts of the body. After the heart performs the function of pumping the blood, the network of blood vessels (vascular system) carries it to all parts of the body.

The blood travels in a circular route beginning and ending at the same place. This course starts at the heart and is composed of the arteries, arterioles, capillaries, vessels, and veins. An artery is a blood vessel that carries blood away from the heart; a vein is a blood vessel that carries blood back to the heart.

The heart is the source of the power that maintains the circulation of the blood. It beats 100,000 times a day and moves more than 2,000 gallons of blood through the body via the arteries and veins.

The specialty of vascular surgery concerns itself with the diagnosis, repair, and reconstruction of heart and blood vessel defects.

ABBREVIATIONS

A2	aortic second sound		LA	left atrium
AP	anteroposterior		LAD	left anterior descending coronary artery
ASHD	arteriosclerotic heart disease			
AV	atrioventricular node		LBBB	left bundle branch block
			LV	left ventricle
BP	blood pressure			
			M2	mitral second sound
CHF	congestive heart failure		MI	mitral insufficiency or myocardial infarction
CT	cardiothoracic ratio			
CV	cardiovascular		MS	mitral stenosis
CVA	cerebrovascular accident or costovertebral angle			
			NSR	normal sinus rhythm
ECG	electrocardiogram		OPG	occular plethysmography
EKG	elektrokardiogram (German)			
			P2	pulmonic second sound
HCVD	hypertensive cardiovascular disease		PAC	premature atrial contraction
HVD	hypertensive vascular disease		PAT	paroxysmal atrial tachycardia
			PMI	point of maximum impulse
IASD	interatrial septal defect		PND	paroxysmal nocturnal dyspnea
IVC	inferior vena cava		PTT	partial thromboplastin time
IVSD	interventricular septal defect		PVC	premature ventricular contraction

RBBB	right bundle branch block	SVPT	supraventricular premature contraction
RHD	rheumatic heart disease		
RSR	regular sinus rhythm		
		TIA	transient ischemic attack
SA	sinoatrial node		
SGOT	serum glutamic oxylacetic transaminase	VDH	valvular disease of heart
		VHD	valvular heart disease
SGPT	serum glutamic pyruvic transaminase	VPC	ventricular premature contraction
SVC	superior vena cava	VSD	ventricular septal defect

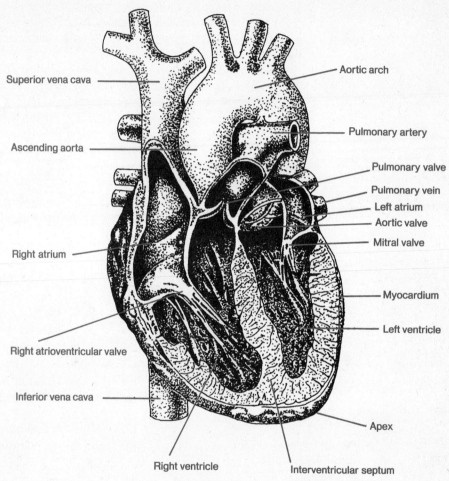

1-1   Structures of the Heart

DEFINITIONS OF TERMINOLOGY

adenocarcinoma – carcinoma derived from the glandular tissue or in which the tumor cells form recognizable glandular structures

akinesis (akinesia) – absence or poverty of movements or the temporary paralysis of a muscle by the injection of procaine

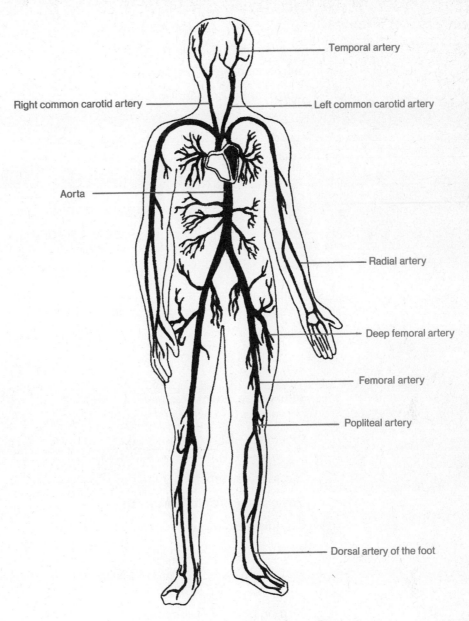

Temporal artery

Right common carotid artery

Left common carotid artery

Aorta

Radial artery

Deep femoral artery

Femoral artery

Popliteal artery

Dorsal artery of the foot

1-2   Arteriole System of the Body

aneurysmectomy – the surgical removal of an aneurysm by removing the sac

angina pectoris – a paroxysmal thoracic pain, with a feeling of suffocation and impending death due, most often, to anoxia of the myocardium and precipitated by effort or excitement

*angiocath

antegrade (anterograde) – moving or extending forward

*These terms were used in dictation but were not located in any of the references consulted. You will encounter this situation throughout this text. For a list of the reference books consulted, see page 502.

anteromedial (anteromedian) – in front and toward the middle line

anulus – a term used to designate a ringlike anatomical structure (has replaced the spelling "annulus")

aorticocoronary bypass (no definition given)

*aorto ramus coronary bypass

*aortobifemoral

aortotomy incision – incision of the aorta

arcus senilis – a gray opaque ring surrounding the margin of the cornea but separated from the margin by an area of clear cornea

arrhythmia – any variation from the normal rhythm of the heartbeat

arteriosclerosis – a group of diseases characterized by thickening and loss of elasticity of arterial walls

arteriotomy – division or opening of an artery by surgery

atheromatous – affected with a mass or plaque of degenerated, thickened arterial intima occurring in atherosclerosis

atriotomy – surgical incision of an atrium of the heart

backflow – the flowing of a current in a direction the reverse of that normally taken

bifurcation – division into two branches; the site where a single structure divides into two

bigeminy – the condition of occurring in pairs; especially the occurrence of two beats of the pulse in rapid succession

Bjork-Shiley prosthesis (no definition given)

Bovie unit (no definition given)

cannula – a tube for insertion into a duct or cavity

cannulating – the insertion of a cannula

cardiomyopathy – a general diagnostic term designating primary myocardial disease, often of obscure or unknown etiology

cardioplegia – interruption of contraction of the myocardium as may be induced by the use of chemical compounds or of cold (cryocardioplegia) in the performance of surgery upon the heart

*Carpentier-Edwards valve

cavae, superior and inferior – plural of cava, which is plural of cavum, which is a general term used to designate a cavity or space

caval – pertaining to a vena cava

celiac axis – the arterial trunk that arises from the abdominal aorta, gives off the left gastric, common hepatic, and splenic arteries, and supplies the esophagus, stomach, duodenum, spleen, pancreas, liver, and gallbladder

cephalically – of or relating to the head; directed toward or situated on or in or near the head

cineangiocardiography – study of the chambers of the heart and pulmonary

circulation by the use of motion picture techniques (while the structures
motion) following injection of radiopaque material

circumferentially – encircling

contractility – capacity for becoming short in response to a suitable stimulus

cor pulmonale – heart disease due to pulmonary hypertension secondary to
diseases of the blood vessels of the lungs

Cournand cardiac catheter – named for American physiologist; co-winner of
Nobel prize in medicine and physiology in 1956 for the development of new
techniques to measure more precisely lung and heart function

Crafoord clamps, scissors, forceps – instruments used in heart and lung
operations

Crawford aorta retractor – instrument used in heart surgery

cristy region (crista) – a projection or projecting structure, or ridge, especially
one surmounting a bone or its border

cusp – a tapering projection; especially one of the triangular segments of a
cardiac valve

decannulated – without a cannula

decrescendo murmur (no definition given)

dextrocardia – location of the heart on the right side of the midline of the chest

Dopamine – a compound, hydroxytyramine, produced by the decarboxylation
of dopa, an intermediate product in the synthesis of norepinephrine

Doppler pulses (no definition given)

dyspneic – characterized by difficult or labored breathing

ectasia – dilatation, expansion, or distention

ectatic – distended or stretched

embolectomy – surgical removal of an embolus or clot from a blood vessel

endarterectomy – removal of the interior portion of an artery

Epinephrine – a potent stimulator of the sympathetic nervous system, being a
powerful vasopressor, increasing blood pressure, stimulating the heart muscle,
accelerating the heart rate, and increasing cardiac output

Ethibond suture – a type of suture material

*femoroanterior bypass

femoropopliteal bypass (no definition given)

Fogarty catheter (no definition given)

foramen ovale – in the fetal heart, the oval opening in septum secundum; the
persistent part of septum primum acts as a valve for this interatrial
communication during fetal life and postnatally becomes fused to septum
secundum to close it

gastrocnemius muscle – popliteal surface of femur, upper part of medial
condyle, and capsule of knee

geniculate – bent, like a knee

GORE-TEX – material used for graft

Grade I, II, III, etc., murmur – refers to the varying degrees of intensity of the murmur

heparinization – the treatment with heparin in order to increase the clotting time of the blood

hyperemic – condition present when there is an excess of blood in a part

hypokalemic – condition present when there is an abnormally low potassium concentration in the blood

hyponatremia – deficiency of sodium in the blood; salt depletion

idioventricular rhythm – relating to or affecting the cardiac ventricle alone

intima – a general term denoting an innermost structure

*intra-aortic balloon pump

intra-arterially – occurring within an artery or arteries

intramyocardial – within the myocardium, the heart muscle

*Ioprep

Javid shunt (no definition given)

Lidocaine – a white or yellow powder used as a topical anesthetic and in the treatment of ventricular arrhythmias

LOA Cines – left occipitoanterior position

*MA-1

Mannitol – an IV solution used in varying concentrations (5, 10, 15, 20%) as an osmotic diuretic; it is used to prevent oliguria during surgical procedures

*Medrad pressure

Medtronic external pacemaker (no definition given)

midportion – a middle part

modalities – a condition under which symptoms develop, becoming better or worse

Mycitracin Ointment – a drug

obliquity – the state of being oblique or slanting

ohm resistance – the unit of electrical resistance in the M.K.S. system of measurement, being equivalent to that of a column of mercury one square millimeter in cross-section and 106 centimeters long

ostium primum – an opening in the lowest aspect of the septum primum of the embryonic heart, posteriorly, in the neighborhood of the atrioventricular valve

ostium secundum – an opening high in the septum primum of the embryonic heart, approximately where the foramen ovale will be later

parenchymal – pertaining to or of the nature of parenchyma, which refers to the

---

**The correct spelling of this term was obtained from the manufacturer.

essential elements of an organ; a general term to designate the functional elements of an organ

perforator – an instrument for piercing the bones and especially for perforating the fetal head

pericarditis – inflammation of the pericardium

peroneal artery – artery located on the outer side of the leg; fibular artery

platysma muscle – a platelike muscle that originates from the fascia of the cervical region and inserts in the mandible and the skin around the mouth

pledget – a small compress or tuft, as of wool or lint

Potts scissors (no definition given)

profunda femoris artery – deep femoral artery

***profundoplasty**

quadrigeminy – quadrigeminal or four-fold rhythm

rami communicans – a communicating branch between two nerves; a branch connecting two arteries

ramus branch of the circumflex – ramus is a general term for a smaller structure given off by a larger one, or into which the larger structure, such as a blood vessel, divides

reanastomosis – a reattachment between two vessels by collateral channels

Renografin-76 – a drug

retrograde – going backward; retracing a former course

retroperitoneal – behind the peritoneum

Rumel tourniquets (no definition given)

run off (verb form)

run-off (noun form)

saphenous vein – pertaining to or associated with a saphena, which is either of two larger superficial veins of the leg

sartorius muscle – muscle that flexes the thigh and leg

Satinsky clamp (no definition given)

Seldinger technique – a technique for percutaneous puncture of arteries or veins, used in angiography

Sones' catheter (no definition given)

sternotomy – the operation of cutting through the sternum

***Stress Thallium test**

***subadventitial**

***subcutaneum**

subsartorial tunnel – beneath the sartorius muscle; denoting a nerve plexus

suprapatellar – situated above the patella

supraventricular – above the ventricles; especially applied to rhythms originating from centers proximal to the ventricles, namely in the atrium or A-V node, in contrast to rhythms arising in the ventricles themselves

Surgicel – trademark for an absorbable cellulose gauze used as a hemostatic vehicle

Swan-Ganz catheter – a thin, very flexible, flow-directed catheter using a balloon to carry it through the heart to a pulmonary artery; when it is positioned in a small arterial branch, pulmonary wedge pressure is measured in front of the temporarily inflated and wedged balloon

sympathectomy – the transection, resection, or other interruption of some portion of the sympathetic nervous pathways

tangential – of the nature of a tangent

Tevdek – a type of suture material

thermistor – a thermometer whose impedance varies with the ambient temperature and so is able to measure extremely small changes in temperature

thoracentesis (thoracocentesis) – surgical puncture of the chest wall for drainage of fluid

thoracotomy – surgical incision of the wall of the chest

thrombectomy – removal of a thrombus from a blood vessel

tracheobronchial – pertaining to the trachea and bronchi

transducer – a device that translates one form of energy to another; e.g., the pressure, temperature, or pulse to an electrical signal

*trifascicular block

trifurcation – division into three branches

trigeminy – the condition of occurring in threes, especially in the occurrence of three pulse beats in rapid succession

Tycron sutures – a type of suture material

valvuloplasty – plastic operation on a valve

vasopressor – stimulating contraction of the muscular tissue of the capillaries and arteries; an agent that stimulates contractions of the muscular tissue of the capillaries and arteries

vena cava, inferior and superior – inferior refers to the venous trunk for the lower extremities and for the pelvic and abdominal viscera; superior refers to the venous trunk draining blood from the head, neck, upper extremities, and chest

*venocath

venotomy (phlebotomy) – incision of a vein, as for the letting of blood

ventriculogram – an x-ray of the cerebral ventricles

ventriculography catheter (no definition given)

*ventriculoseptal

*vessel loop

visceromegaly – enlargement of viscera

HISTORY

Patient Name: **Date:**

Doctor:

PHYSICAL

Patient Name: **Date:**

Doctor:

Patient Name: Date:

PREOP DIAGNOSIS:

POSTOP DIAGNOSIS:

OPERATION:

SURGEON:

PROCEDURE:

Patient Name: Date:

PREOP DIAGNOSIS:

POSTOP DIAGNOSIS:

OPERATION:

SURGEON:

PROCEDURE:

Patient Name: Date:

SURGEON:

DESCRIPTION OF CATHETERIZATION PROCEDURE AND SUMMARY OF FINDINGS:

Patient Name: Date:

SURGEON:

ANESTHETIC:

OPERATION:

PREOP DIAGNOSIS:

POSTOP DIAGNOSIS:

FINDINGS:

Patient Name: Date:

SURGEON:

FIRST ASSISTANT: SECOND ASSISTANT:

ANESTHETIST: ANESTHETIC:

OPERATION:

PROCEDURE:

Patient Name: **Date:**

SURGEON:

ASSISTANT:

PREOP DIAG:

POSTOP DIAG:

OPERATION:

ANES:

INDICATIONS:

PROCEDURE:

Patient Name: Date:

PREOP DIAG:

POSTOP DIAG:

OPERATION:

SURGEON:

ASSISTANT:

PROCEDURE:

CHAPTER 2
DENTISTRY/ORAL SURGERY

Physicians in the practice of dentistry are concerned with the teeth, oral cavity, and associated structures, including the diagnosis and treatment of their diseases and the restoration of defective and missing tissue.

A dentist may become an oral surgeon by taking two or more years of graduate study in oral surgery at a recognized graduate school or hospital.

Surgical diseases, injuries, and developmental abnormalities of the oral cavity, teeth, jaws, and adjacent structures are the concerns of oral surgeons.

ABBREVIATIONS

AFH	anterior facial height	MOD	mesio-occlusodistal
BWX	bite-wing x-rays	OC	occlusocervical
CRN	crown		
		P/	partial upper denture
DL	distolingual	/P	partial lower denture
DMF	decayed, missing, and filled	PFH	posterior facial height
DO	disto-occlusal	PNS	posterior nasal spine
D5RL	Dextrose 5% with Lactated Ringers	PRP	posterior ramal plane
		PTM	pterygomaxillary fissure
F/	full upper denture		
/F	full lower denture	RC	root canal
FCC	fracture-compound comminuted	REC CRN	recement crown
F/M	full mouth		
FMX	full mouth x-rays	SSC	stainless steel crown
FSC	fracture-simple comminuted		
IP	incisoproximal	TMJ	temporomandibular joint

DEFINITIONS OF TERMINOLOGY

actinomycosis – fungal infection, characterized by chronic suppurative inflammatory lesions

adenoameloblastoma – neoplasm of odontogenic epithelium, producing ductlike structures and frequently calcification

agnathia – congenital absence of the maxilla or mandible, or of a portion thereof

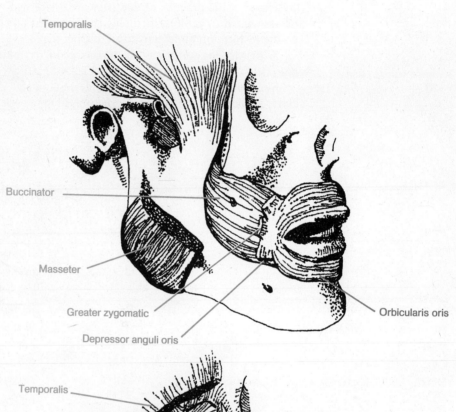

Temporalis

Buccinator

Masseter

Greater zygomatic

Depressor anguli oris

Orbicularis oris

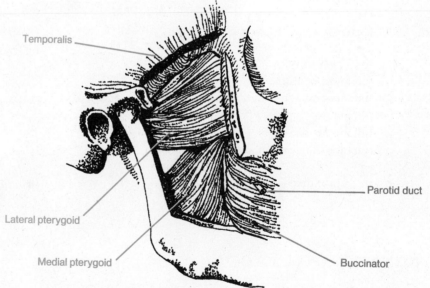

Temporalis

Lateral pterygoid

Medial pterygoid

Parotid duct

Buccinator

2-1   Muscles of the Face

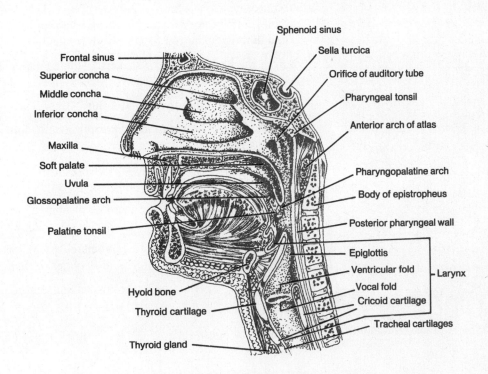

Frontal sinus
Superior concha
Middle concha
Inferior concha
Maxilla
Soft palate
Uvula
Glossopalatine arch
Palatine tonsil

Sphenoid sinus
Sella turcica
Orifice of auditory tube
Pharyngeal tonsil
Anterior arch of atlas
Pharyngopalatine arch
Body of epistropheus
Posterior pharyngeal wall
Epiglottis
Ventricular fold
Vocal fold
Cricoid cartilage
Tracheal cartilages
Larynx

Hyoid bone
Thyroid cartilage
Thyroid gland

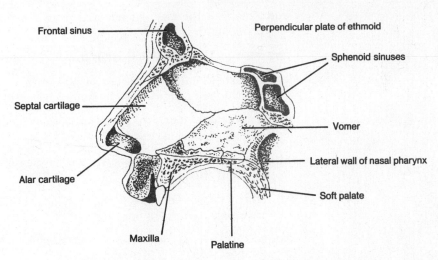

Frontal sinus
Septal cartilage
Alar cartilage
Maxilla
Palatine

Perpendicular plate of ethmoid
Sphenoid sinuses
Vomer
Lateral wall of nasal pharynx
Soft palate

2-2   Structures of the Oral and Nasal Cavities

ala – a general term for a winglike structure or process

alveolalgia – pain occurring in a dental alveolus

alveolar – pertaining to that portion of the upper or lower jaw that contains the teeth and forms the dental arch

alveolectomy – excision of a portion of alveolar bone to aid in the removal of teeth, in the restoration of the normal contour following the removal of teeth, and in the preparation of the mouth for dentures

alveoli – the bony cavities or sockets in the mandible and maxilla in which the roots of the teeth are attached

alveolitis – inflammation of an alveolus

alveoloclasia – disintegration or resorption of the inner wall of a tooth alveolus, causing looseness of the teeth

alveoloplasty – the surgical alteration of the shape and order of the alveolar process in preparation for immediate or future denture construction

alveolus – a general term used in anatomical nomenclature to designate a small saclike dilatation

amalgam – an alloy of silver, tin, and mercury with low concentration of copper and sometimes zinc; used for filling cavities in teeth

amelodentinal – pertaining to the enamel and dentin of a tooth

ankyloglossia – tongue-tie

anodontia – congenital absence of the teeth; it may involve all or only some of the teeth

apertognathia – open-bite deformity

apoxemena – the material removed from a periodontal pocket; treatment of periodontitis

apoxesis – the removal of detritus from a periodontal pocket

apththous stomatitis – disease of unknown etiology, characterized by the formation of painful single or multiple ulcers of the oral cavity

arcus dentalis – the curving structure formed by the crowns of the teeth in their normal position in the jaw

atraumatically – in a way that is specially designed or planned to minimize injurious effects

attrition – the physiologic wearing away of a substance or structure (such as the teeth) in the course of normal use

avulsed teeth – traumatic loss of teeth from their bony alveoli or sockets

bone bur – a form of drill used for creating openings in bone or similar hard substances

bone rongeur – an instrument for cutting tissue, particularly bone

brachygnathia – "bird face"; retrognathic or small mandible, either congenital or associated with the interference of condylar growth because of trauma or infection

Brophy bistoury – a long, narrow surgical knife, straight or curved, used for incising abscesses and enlarging sinuses, fistulas, etc.

buccinator muscle – muscle of chin that compresses the cheek and retracts the angle of the mouth

buccogingival – pertaining to the cheek and gum

buccolingual – pertaining to the cheek and tongue; pertaining to the buccal and lingual surfaces of a posterior tooth

caries – gradual decay and disintegration of a tooth

carious – affected with or of the nature of caries

cephalometrics – method of measuring distances between bony landmarks of the cranium and face, from a reproducible cephalogram, for the purpose of evaluating facial growth and development, including soft tissue profiles

cheilorraphy – surgical repair of a deformed lip

circummandibular – pertaining to fixation in stabilization by wire passed around the mandible

coapt – to approximate, as the edges of a wound or the ends of a fractured bone

collodion – a clear or slightly opalescent, highly flammable, syrupy liquid compounded of pyroxylin, ether, and alcohol, which dries to a transparent, tenacious film; used as a topical protectant

concrescence – union of two completely formed teeth by fusion of the roots

condylectomy – surgical removal of a condyle or a portion thereof

cricothyrotomy – emergency incision between the cricoid and thyroid cartilages for the purpose of maintaining a patent airway

crossbite – a tooth (or teeth) that is either buccal to its supposedly normal position with the tooth (or teeth) in the opposing arch

decidious teeth – the teeth of the first dentition, which are shed and followed, in the dental arch, by the permanent teeth

Deknatel sutures (no definition given)

Denhardt mouth gag (no definition given)

dens-in-dente – developmental anomaly of a tooth that gives the impression of a "tooth within a tooth"

dental alveoli – the bony cavities or sockets in the mandible or maxilla in which the roots of the teeth are attached

dentibuccal – pertaining to the teeth and cheek

dentigerous cyst – containing or bearing a tooth or teeth

dentinogenesis – the formation of dentin

dentition – the teeth in the dental arch; ordinarily used to designate the natural teeth in position in their alveoli

dentoalveolar – pertaining to a tooth and its alveolus

dentritus – particulate matter produced by or remaining after the wearing away or disintegration of a substance or tissue diastema – a space between two adjacent teeth in the same dental arch

edentulous – without teeth; having lost the natural teeth

eminectomy – removal of the eminence of the temporomandibular joint

endodontia – endodontics

endodontics – that branch of dentistry which is concerned with the etiology, prevention, diagnosis, and treatment of diseases and injuries that affect the tooth pulp, root, and periapical tissue

*Endosseous implant

endosteal – occurring or located within a bone

epulis – benign giant-cell tumor arising in the gums

exodontia – exodontics

exodontics – that branch of dentistry dealing with extraction of the teeth

*exognathism

fluorosis – a mottled discoloration of the enamel of the teeth resulting from ingestion of excessive amounts of fluorine during tooth development

frenectomy – excision of a frenum

friable – easily pulverized or crumbled

gingivae – the gums

gingivectomy – surgical excision of all loose, infected, and diseased gum tissue from necks of teeth

gingivitis – inflammation involving the gingival tissue only

gingivolabial – pertaining to the gums and lips

gingivosis – chronic ulcerative, inflammatory disease of the gingivae

glossopalatinius muscle – muscle originating in the undersurface of the soft palate that elevates the tongue and constricts the throat

gnathion – most anterior/inferior point of the mandible

gomphosis – a type of fibrous joint in which a conical process is inserted into a socket-like portion, such as the styloid process

gutta-percha – rubber-based compound used as a temporary filling material in dentistry or used as a permanent root canal filling in endodontics

Hajek mallet (no definition given)

harelip – a congenital cleft or defect in the upper lip, usually due to failure of the median nasal and maxillary processes to unite

hydroxyapatite – an inorganic compound found in the matrix of bone and the teeth, which gives rigidity to these structures

---

*These terms were used in dictation but were not located in any of the references consulted. You will encounter this situation throughout this text. For a list of the reference books consulted, see page 502.

hypercementosis – excessive development of secondary cementum on the surfaces of tooth roots

incisolabial – denoting the incisal and labial surfaces of an anterior tooth

intermaxillary – situated between the two maxillae

intraoral – being or occurring within the mouth

Kirschner wire – heavy, rigid wire, threaded at one end, used with a hand drill to pass through a fractured bone or a segment of a bone to which traction can be applied

laterognathia – horizontal deformity to one or the other side of the maxilla or mandible in relation to the rest of the face

Le Fort's fracture – bilateral horizontal fracture of the maxilla

lingual – pertaining to or toward the tongue

macrodontia – abnormal increase in the size of the teeth

malocclusion – such abnormal position and contact of the upper and lower teeth as to interfere with the highest efficiency during the process of chewing

malposed – not in the normal position

mandible – the bone of the lower jaw

mandibular – pertaining to the lower jaw bone, or mandible

masseteric – pertaining to the masseter muscle

masticating – chewing

maxilla – upper jaw

maxillary – pertaining to the maxilla

maxillomandibular – pertaining to the maxilla and the mandible

mesial – nearer the center line of the dental arch

meso – a prefix signifying "middle," either situated in the middle or intermediate

micrognathia – unusual or undue smallness of the jaws

*mucobuccal

mucocele – dilatation of a cavity with accumulated mucous secretion

mucoperiosteum – periosteum having a mucous surface, as in parts of the auditory apparatus

mylohyoid – relating to molar teeth or posterior portion of lower jaw

mylohyoid muscle – the muscle that elevates the hyoid bone and supports the floor of the mouth

*Obwegaser AWL technique

occlusal – pertaining to the masticating surface of a tooth

odontalgia (dentalgia) – pain in a tooth

odontectomy – excision of an erupted tooth, or of an unerupted or impacted tooth

odontogenic – forming teeth; arising in tissues which give rise to the teeth

odontolithiasis – a condition marked by the presence of deposits of calcium on the teeth

odontome – a tumor found only in the jaws, consisting of the constituent parts of teeth in aberrant forms

oligodontia – presence of less than the normal number of teeth, some of them being congenitally absent

operculectomy – surgical removal of the mucosal flap partially or completely covering an unerupted tooth

overbite – extension of the maxillary teeth over the mandibular teeth in a vertical direction when the opposing posterior teeth are in contact

overjet – projection of the maxillary anterior and/or posterior teeth beyond their contagonists in a horizontal direction

periapical – relating to tissues encompassing the apex of a tooth, including periodontal membrane and alveolar bone

pericementitis – inflammation of the tissues adjacent to the tooth root

pericementoclasia – disintegration of the periodontal ligament and alveolar bone without loss of overlying gingival tissue

peridontoclasia – periodontoclasia; a term used for degeneration and destructive diseases of the periodontium

periocoronitis – inflammation of the gingiva surrounding the crown of a partially erupted tooth

periodontitis – inflammatory reaction of the tissues surrounding a tooth

periodontoclasia – a general term sometimes used for any degenerative and destructive disease of the periodontium

periodontosis – a degenerative, noninflammatory condition of the periodontium, originating in one or more of the periodontal structures and characterized by destruction of the tissues

pogonion – most anterior, prominent point on the mandible

prognathism – marked forward projection of the mandible or the maxilla beyond a normal distance from the cranial base

prosthodontics – that branch of dentistry concerned with the construction of artificial appliances designed to restore and maintain oral function by replacing missing teeth and sometimes other oral structures or parts of the face

pterygoid muscle – one of four muscles, in two sets (internal and external), running from the mandible to the pterygoid plate of the sphenoid bone

pterygomandibular – pertaining to the pterygoid process and the mandible

pulp extirpation – complete removal of the dental pulp from the pulp chamber and root canal of a tooth

pulpitis – inflammation of the dental pulp

pyorrhea – disease of the supporting tissues of the teeth

retrognathic – pertaining to or characterized by retrognathia, underdevelopment of the maxilla and/or mandible

rhizodontropy – the fixation of an artificial crown upon the natural root of a tooth

rhizodontrypy – perforation of the root of a tooth for the escape of morbid material

rhizoid – rootlike

sagittal – shaped like or resembling an arrow; straight

sialodochoplasty – surgical procedure for the repair of a defect and/or restoration of a portion of a salivary gland duct

staphylorrhaphy – surgical procedure performed on the soft palate

submandibular – below the mandible

temporomandibular joint – the fibrous or true bony union between the condyles of the mandible and the base of the skull

thermocautery – cauterization by means of a hot wire or point

torus – a bulging projection; a swelling

torus mandibularis – bone projections on the inside of the mandible

vermilion border – the exposed red portion of the upper or lower lip

vestibuloplasty – the surgical modification of the gingival-mucous membrane relationships in the vestibule of the mouth, including deepening of the vestibular trough, repositioning of the frenum or muscle attachments, and broadening of the zone of attached gingiva after periodontal treatment

Z-plasty – a plastic operation for the relaxation of contractures in which a Z-shaped incision is made, the middle bar of the Z being over the contracted scar, and the triangular flaps rotated so that their apices cross the line of contracture

OP NOTE

Patient Name: Date:

    Doctor:

PREOP DIAG:

POSTOP DIAG:

PROCEDURE:

OPERATION

Patient Name: Date:

     Doctor:

PREOP DIAG:

POSTOP DIAG:

PROCEDURE:

SURGEON:

PROCEDURE:

OPERATION

Patient Name: Date:

    Doctor:

PREOP DIAG:

POSTOP DIAG:

SURGEON:

PROCEDURE:

SURGERY

Patient Name: Date:

Doctor:

PREOPERATIVE DIAGNOSIS:

POSTOPERATIVE DIAGNOSIS:

OPERATION:

PROCEDURE:

OP NOTE

Patient Name: Date:

    Doctor:

PREOP DIAGNOSIS:

POSTOP DIAGNOSIS:

OPERATION:

PROCEDURE:

OPERATION

Patient Name: Date:

    Doctor:

PREOP DIAG:

POSTOP DIAG:

PROCEDURE:

SURGERY

Patient Name: Date:

    Doctor:

PREOP DIAGNOSIS:

POSTOP DIAGNOSIS:

OPERATION:

SURGEON:

PROCEDURE:

SURGERY

Patient Name: Date:

  Doctor:

PREOP DIAG:

POSTOP DIAG:

OPERATION:

PROCEDURE:

SURGICAL

Patient Name: Date:

Doctor:

PREOP DIAG:

POSTOP DIAG:

OPERATION:

SURGERY

Patient Name: Date:

   Doctor:

PREOP DIAG:

OPERATION:

PROCEDURE:

OPERATION

Patient Name: Date:

    Doctor:

PREOP DIAG:

POSTOP DIAG:

PROCEDURE:

PROCEDURE IN DETAIL:

SURGERY

Patient Name: Date:

    Doctor:

PREOP DIAG:

POSTOP DIAG:

OPERATION:

PROCEDURE:

OPERATION

Patient Name: Date:

    Doctor:

PREOP DIAG:

POSTOP DIAG:

OPERATIVE PROCEDURES:

PROCEDURE IN DETAIL:

CHAPTER 3
DERMATOLOGY

That branch of medical practice concerned with the diagnosis and treatment of diseases of the skin and accessible linings of body openings is known as dermatology. A physician specializing in this field is known as a dermatologist.

A dermatologist must have knowledge of internal medicine as well as a comprehensive knowledge of skin diseases so that any relationships between an external manifestation of a disease and the body as a whole can be evaluated. In addition, a knowledge of allergies is required as many common skin lesions are of an allergic nature.

In recent years, much progress has been made in dermatology. For example, knowledge of many of the causative factors and anatomic sequences of acne has led to logical, effective treatments for this common disfiguring disorder. Determination of the factors causing or worsening eczema has made preventive medicine an important part of its treatment. Determination of the early signs of malignant melanoma provides for early recognition of these tumors and allows many more lives to be saved than was possible in the past.

To manage skin diseases, dermatologists utilize many methods; for example, internal and external medications; electrosurgical procedures; cold, in the form of solidified carbon dioxide gas or liquid nitrogen; heat; ultraviolet light; x-rays; various scalpel surgical procedures; and more recently, lasers.

ABBREVIATIONS

BCE	basal cell epithelioma	HLA	human leukocyte antigens
BCH	bullous disease of childhood	HTT	halo thaw time
BP	bullous pemphigoid		
		LSF	lateral spread of freeze
CTT	complete thaw time		
		SCE	squamous cell epithelioma
DF	depth of freeze		
DH	dermatitis herpetiformis		
		TC	thermocouple
FT	freezing time	TMT	thermocouple minimum temperature

Permission was granted by the Yorke Medical Group to reproduce the white paper[1] included in this chapter:

[1]Lubritz, Ronald, R., M.D. "Cryosurgery of Benign Lesions." *Cutis*, Vol. 16 (September, 1975), pp. 426-432. (portions of article)

acantholysis – dissolution of the intercellular bridges in the prickle-cell layer of the epidermis

acanthoma – a tumor composed of epidermal or squamous cells

acariasis – an infestation with mites

acarodermatitis – any skin inflammation caused by mites

acne rosacea (rosacea) – a chronic disease affecting the skin of the nose, forehead, and cheeks, marked by flushing, followed by red coloration due to dilatation of the capillaries, with the appearance of papules and acne-like pustules

actinic keratosis – a sharply outlined, red or skin-colored, flat or elevated, verrucous or keratotic growth, which may develop into a cutaneous horn and may give rise to a squamous-cell carcinoma

acuminata verruca (condyloma acuminatum) – a papilloma with a central core of connective tissue in a treelike structure covered with epithelium

adenoma sebaceum (sebaceous hyperplasia) – nevoid hyperplasia with sebaceous glands, forming multiple yellow papules or nodules of the face

anaphylaxis – an unusual or exaggerated allergic reaction of an organism to foreign protein or other substances

argyria – poisoning by silver or a silver salt

atrophodermatosis – any skin disease having cutaneous atrophy as a prominent symptom

aurantiasis (carotenemia) – presence of excessive carotene in the blood; it sometimes occurs in sufficient quantities to produce yellowing of the skin resembling jaundice

bullous pemphigoid – a chronic, generalized, bullous eruption, occurring in elderly adults predominantly, and usually not fatal

cafe au lait spots – pigmented macules of a distinctive light brown color, like coffee and milk

callositas – a callus

carbunculosis – a condition marked by the development of carbuncles

cheilitis – inflammation affecting the lips

chloasma (melasma) – a condition in which blotchy, brown macules from one to several centimeters in diameter occur typically on the cheeks, temples, and forehead

chondrodermatitis – an inflammatory process involving cartilage and skin

chrysiasis – the deposition of gold in the tissues

collagenosis – collagen disease

comedo – a blackhead

congelation – frostbite or freezing

corium – the dermis; the layer of the skin deep to the epidermis

cryobiology – the science dealing with the effect of low temperatures on biological systems

cryogen – a substance used for lowering temperatures

cryoprobe – an instrument for applying extreme cold to tissue

denudation – removal of the epithelial covering from any surface, by surgery, trauma, or pathologic change

Dermacentor andersoni – wood tick

Dermacentor variabilis – dog tick

dermatitis herpetiformis – chronic dermatitis

dermatitis venenata – a form of contact dermatitis in which an acute allergic inflammation of the skin occurs as a result of contact with various substances of a chemical, animal, or vegetable nature to which delayed hypersensitivity has been acquired

*dermatocryosurgery

dermatophytosis – a fungous infection of the skin, or infection caused by a dermatophyte, which is a fungus parasitic upon the skin; athlete's foot

desiccation – the act of drying up

dyshidrosis – any disorder of the eccrine sweat glands

dyskeratosis – abnormal, premature, or imperfect keratinization of the keratinocytes

dyskeratotic – of, relating to, or affected by dyskeratosis

ectodermosis – a disorder based on congenital maldevelopment of the organs of ectodermal derivation

eczema – a superficial inflammatory process involving primarily the epidermis

eczematoid – resembling eczema

eczematous – affected with or of the nature of eczema

electrodesiccation – dehydration of tissue by the use of a high-frequency electric current

epidermodysplasia verruciformis – a condition caused by a virus identical with or closely related to the virus of common warts

epidermophytosis (athlete's foot) – infection by fungi; dermatophytosis

erythropoietic – pertaining to, characterized by, or promoting erythropoiesis

exanthematous – pertaining to, characterized by, or of the nature of an exanthem, which is any eruptive disease or eruptive fever

excoriation – any superficial loss of substance, such as that produced on the skin by scratching

---

*These terms were used in dictation but were not located in any of the references consulted. You will encounter this situation throughout this text. For a list of the reference books consulted, see page 502.

exfoliation – a falling off in scales or layers

fasciitis – inflammation of fascia

folliculitis – inflammation of a follicle

fragilitas – fragility

furunculosis – the persistent sequential occurrence of furuncles over a period of weeks or months

gangrenous – pertaining to, characterized by, or of the nature of gangrene

gargoylism – Hurler's syndrome

granuloma pyogenicum – a fungating pedunculated growth in which the granulations consist of masses of pyogenic organisms

guttate – characterized by lesions that are drop-shaped

hemangioma – a benign tumor made up of new-formed blood vessels

hemangiomatosis – a condition in which multiple hemangiomas are developed

hidradenitis – inflammation of a sweat gland

hidradenoma – a general term for tumors of the skin the components of which resemble epithelial elements of sweat glands

hydroquinone – a compound occurring as fine white needles and used as a depigmenting agent

*hyperadrenocorticoidism

hypertrichosis – excessive growth of hair

hypocomplementemia – diminution of complement levels in the blood

ichthyosis – any of several generalized skin disorders characterized by dryness, roughness, and scaliness

ichthyosis hystrix – a rare form of epidermolytic hyperkeratosis, characterized by generalized, dark brown, linear verrucoid ridges somewhat like porcupine skin

ichthyosis vulgaris – a hereditary form of ichthyosis transmitted as an autosomal dominant or sex-linked recessive trait

impedance – the opposition to the flow of an alternating current

impetigo contagiosa – impetigo

incontinentia pigmenti – a hereditary disorder almost exclusively in females, in which early vesicular and later verrucous and bizarrely pigmented skin lesions are associated with developmental defects of the eyes, bones, and central nervous system

intertriginous – affected with or of the nature of intertrigo—superficial dermatitis occurring on apposed surfaces of the skin, about the creases of the neck, folds of the groin and armpit, and beneath pendulous breasts

keratinocytes – the epidermal cell which synthesizes keratin

keratohyaline – both horny and hyaline, like the material of the stratum granulosum of the epidermis keratosis – any horny growth, such as a wart or callosity

lentigines – round or oval, flat, brown, pigmented spots on the skin due to increased deposition of melanin and associated with an increased number of melanocytes at the epidermodermal junction

lentigo maligna – a noninvasive malignant melanoma occurring most frequently on the face of women during the fourth decade, but also in both sexes at any age, and of any part of the body

leukoderma – an acquired type of localized loss of melanin pigmentation of the skin

lichen planus – an inflammatory skin disease with wide, flat, violaceous, itchy, polygonal papules having a characteristic sheen, occurring in circumscribed patches, and often very persistent

lichenification – thickening of the epidermis

lipoidosis – a disturbance of lipid metabolism with abnormal deposits of lipids in the cells

livedo – a discolored spot or patch on the skin

macule – a macula—a stain, spot, or thickening

melanocyte – the cell responsible for the synthesis of melanin

milium – a whitish nodule in the skin, especially of the face, usually 1 to 4 mm in diameter

molluscum – the name given to various skin diseases characterized by the formation of soft rounded cutaneous tumors

moniliform – shaped like a necklace or string of beads

mycotic tumors – tumors caused by fungi

Neisseria meningitidis – a prominent cause of meningitis and the specific etiologic agent of epidemic cerebrospinal meningitis

nevus – mole

onychia – inflammation of the matrix of the nail resulting in shedding of the nail

papilloma – a branching or lobulated benign tumor derived from epithelium

parapsoriasis – a name applied to a group of maculopapular scaly erythrodermas of slow development

*parokeratosis

paronychia – inflammation involving the folds of tissue surrounding the fingernail

pemphigus vulgaris – a rare relapsing disease manifested by suprabasal, intraepidermal bullae of the skin and mucous membranes; invariably fatal if untreated

petechia – a pinpoint, nonraised, perfectly round, purplish red spot caused by intradermal or submucous hemorrhage

phthiriasis – infestation with crab or pubic lice

podophyllum – a caustic for topical application to certain papillomas porphyria – any of a group of disturbances of porphyrin metabolism, characterized by marked increase in formation and excretion of porphyrins or their precursors

*pseudoepitheliomatous

pseudoepitheliomatous hyperplasia – an irregular, penetrating acanthosis accompanied by chronic inflammation in the dermis, found in chronic ulcers of the skin and chronic granulomatous infections

*pseudosarcomatous

Pseudoxanthoma elasticum – a rare skin disease marked by small yellowish macules and papules

psoriasis – a chronic, hereditary, recurrent, papulosquamous dermatosis, the distinctive lesion of which is a vivid red macule, papule, or plaque covered almost to its edge by silvery lamellated scales

purpura – a group of disorders characterized by purplish or brownish red discoloration, easily visible through the epidermis, caused by hemorrhage into the tissues

purpura fulminans – a form of nonthrombocytopenic purpura, observed mainly in children, usually following an infectious disease such as scarlet fever

pyemia – a general septicemia in which secondary foci of suppuration occur and multiple abscesses are formed

pyoderma faciale – a condition characterized by formation of a few or many abscesses and cysts on the face, with intense erythema, and sinus tracts linking the deep-seated lesions

pyodermatisis – pyoderma, which is any purulent skin disease

Quincke's edema (angioneurotic edema) – a condition characterized by the sudden appearance of temporary edematous areas of the skin or mucous membranes and occasionally of the viscera

Rendu-Osler-Weber disease – hereditary hemorrhagic telangiectasia

rhinophyma – a form of rosacea characterized by redness, sebaceous hyperplasia, and nodular swelling and congestion of the skin of the nose

Rickettsia – a genus of bacteria which cause epidemic typhus, murine or endemic typhus, Rocky Mountain spotted fever, tsutsugamushi disease, rickettsialpox, and other diseases

rosacea – a chronic disease affecting the skin of the nose, forehead, and cheeks, marked by flushing, followed by red coloration due to dilatation of the capillaries, with the appearance of papules and acne-like pustules

saccharomycosis – a pathologic condition due to yeasts or Saccharomyces

Salmonella typhi – the etiologic agent of typhoid fever, occurring mainly in man

seborrheic keratosis – a benign, noninvasive tumor of epidermal origin, characterized by hyperplasia of the keratinocytes, ordinarily developing in middle life in the form of numerous yellow or brown, sharply marginated, oval, raised lesions

sebum – the secretion of the sebaceous glands

serpiginous – having a wavy or much indented margin, as a lesion in noduloulcerative cutaneous syphilis

spiradenoma – adenoma sudoriparum

steatoma – a sebaceous cyst

stratum – a general term for a sheetlike mass of substance of nearly uniform thickness, particularly when the layer is one of several associated layers

stratum malpighii (stratum germinativum epidermis) – the innermost layer of the epidermis

sycosis – a disease marked by inflammation of the hair follicles, especially of the beard

syringoma – a benign tumor of sweat glands, occurring most often in females and developing after puberty

telangiectodes – marked by telangiectasia

therapeutic armamentarium – equipment of a practitioner or institution, including books, instruments, medicines, and surgical appliances

thermocouple – a pair of dissimilar electrical conductors so joined that an electromotive force is developed between thermoelectric effects when the junctions are at different temperatures

tinea – a name applied to many different kinds of superficial fungal infections of the skin

torulosis – cryptococcosis

Treponema – a genus of microorganisms

trichoepithelioma – a benign skin tumor whose cell growth starts in the follicles of the lanugo

trichomycosis – any disease of the hair due to infection by a fungus

truncated – having had the end cut squarely off

urtication – the development or formation of urticaria; a burning sensation as of stinging with nettles

variola – smallpox

vesication – the process of blistering

vesiculobullous – characterized by both vesicles and bullae at the same time

vitiligo – acquired leukoderma or leukopathia; the appearance on the otherwise normal skin of loss of melanin pigment with white patches of varied sizes, often symmetrically distributed

Weil's disease – infectious icterus; infectious jaundice

xeroderma – a mild form of ichthyosis characterized by excessive dryness of the skin due to a slight increase of the horny layer and diminished cutaneous secretion

Since this chapter contains no forms for you to use, type the article on plain paper. Use the following information when typing footnotes (in an accepted form) to be used with the article entitled "Cryosurgery of Benign Lesions":

1. "Liquid Nitrogen Neuropathy," ARCH DERM, Vol. 92, p. 185, 1965, by TW Nix Jr.

2. SKIN SURGERY by AA Gage, E Epstein, Editor. Published in Springfield, IL, by Charles C. Thomas, 1970.

3. "Cryosurgery in Dermatology," by D. Torre. Appeared in CRYOGENICS IN SURGERY, von Leyden H, Cahan W, Editors. Published in New York by Medical Examination Pub, 1971.

4. "Dermatological Cryosurgery: A Progress Report," by D. Torre. CUTIS, Vol. 11, page 782, 1973.

5. CUTIS, "Swimming Pool Granuloma: Treatment with Cryosurgery," by SC Atkinson and F Daniels, Jr. Vol. 11, p. 818, 1973.

6. Data in current preparation for publication by RR Lubritz.

7. CRYOSURGERY OF TUMORS OF THE SKIN AND ORAL CAVITY by S Zacarian. Published by Charles C Thomas, Springfield, IL, 1973.

8. Personal communication from D. Torre.

9. "Liquid Nitrogen Therapy, Histological Observation," ARCH DERM, 1961, Vol. 83, p. 563, by RH Grimmett.

10. Personal communication from D. Torre.

11. Same reference as footnote #4.

CHAPTER 4
GENERAL SURGERY

Surgery is a specialized field of medicine which requires further educational training—usually four years beyond internship—of one who wishes to become a surgeon. After training in general surgery, one may further specialize into areas such as orthopedics, urology, thoracic, or plastic surgery.

Surgeons receive referrals from other physicians when it is felt that a diseased organ needs to be removed or when surgical reconstruction is required to make a patient well.

ABBREVIATIONS

Abdom	abdomen/abdominal	CEA	carcino-embryonic antigen
ABG	arterial blood gas	CNS	central nervous system
a.c.	before meals	C/O	complaining of
a.d.	alternating days	coag	coagulation
adm	admission	Con, CON, Cons	consultation
AFB	Acid Fast Bacilli	COPD	chronic obstructive pulmonary disease
AJ	ankle jerk	CPAP	continuous positive airway pressure
AK	above knee	CPK	creatine phosphokinase
ANA	antinuclear antibodies	CR	cardiorespiratory
anes	anesthesia	CRNA	Certified Registered Nurse Anesthetist
ant	anterior	CXR	chest x-ray
A & P	auscultation and percussion		
AS	left ear	dc	discontinue
ASA	acetylsalicylic acid (aspirin)	diag	diagnosis
ASAP	as soon as possible	diff	differential
ASD	atrial septal defect	dil	dilute
ax	axillary	Disch	discharge
		D.M.	diabetes mellitus
BE	barium enema	DOA	dead on arrival
BCC	basal cell carcinoma	DOE	dyspnea on exertion
BI, Bx	biopsy	DTR	deep tendon reflexes
bilat	bilateral	Dx	diagnosis
BK	below the knee		
BPH	benign prostatic hypertrophy		
BUN	blood urea nitrogen	EBL	estimated blood loss
		E. coli	Escherichia coli
c	with	EDC	estimated day of confinement
CA	carcinoma	EGD	esophagogastroduodenoscopy
cath	catheter	EOM	extraocular movement
CBC	complete blood count	EXP LAP	exploratory laparotomy
CBD	common bile duct	ext	extremity

F.B.	foreign body	OR	operating room
FBS	fasting blood sugar		
FS	frozen section	PA	posteroanterior
FUO	fever of unknown origin	path	pathology
Fx	fracture	PERLA	pupils equal and react to light and accommodation
gb, GB	gallbladder	PO	by mouth
GI	gastrointestinal	pos	positive
glob	globulin	postop	postoperative
Glu	glucose	prn	as often as needed
GSW	gunshot wound	PTA	prior to admission
GTT	glucose tolerance test		
		RAD	radium
HEENT	head, ears, eyes, nose, throat	RBC	red blood cell
HNP	herniated nucleus pulposus	RLE	right lower extremity
Hx	history	RLL	right lower lobe
		RLQ	right lower quadrant
ICU	Intensive Care Unit	RML	right middle lobe
I & D	incision and drainage	RO, R/O	rule out
IM	intramuscular	ROM	range of motion
I & O	intake and output	ROS:	review of systems
IPPB	intermittent positive pressure breathing	RR	recovery room
		RUL	right upper lobe
IV	intravenous	RUQ	right upper quadrant
IVP	intravenous pyelogram	Rx	prescription/take
jt	joint	SOB	short of breath
		spec	specimen
KJ	knee joint	Sp. Gr.	specific gravity
KUB	kidneys, ureters, bladder	Spon	spontaneous
		S & S	signs and symptoms
L	left	staph	staphylococcus
L&A, l/a	light and accommodation	stat	at once
lac	laceration	strep	streptococcus
lat	lateral	STSG	split thickness skin graft
LKS	liver, kidneys, and spleen	sub ling	sublingual
LLL	left lower lobe	subcu, subq	subcutaneous
LLQ	left lower quadrant	surg	surgery
LP	lumbar puncture	sut	sutures
LUL	left upper lobe	sym	symmetrical
LUQ	left upper quadrant	symp	symptom
lymphs	lymphocytes		
		TBA	to be admitted
mEq	milliequivalent	T&C	type and crossmatch
		temp	temperature
neg	negative	TNTC	too numerous to count
NG	nasogastric	tol	tolerate
NKA	no known allergies	tr,tinct	tincture
noct	night		
NPO	nothing by mouth	UA	urinalysis
NSR	nasal septal reconstruction		

UGI	upper gastrointestinal	VS	vital signs
unk,UNKN	unknown		
		WBC	white blood count
VO	verbal order	W/C	wheelchair
VP	venous pressure		

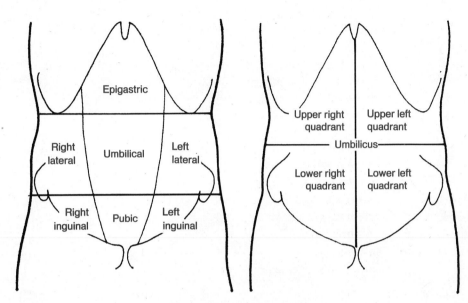

4-1   Abdominal Regions

DEFINITIONS OF TERMINOLOGY

abdominoperineal (no definition given)

adenoma – a benign epithelial tumor in which the cells form recognizable glandular structures or in which the cells are clearly derived from glandular epithelium

adjuvant – assisting or aiding; a substance which aids another, such as an auxiliary remedy

adventitia – outermost; denoting the layer of loose connective tissue forming the outermost coating of an organ

anastomosis – a communication between two vessels by collateral channels; an opening created by surgical, traumatic, or pathological means between two normally distinct spaces or organs

anesthesia, types – brachial plexus block, endobronchial, endotracheal, epidural, pudendal block

anthrocotic lymph nodes (no definition given)

aperture – an opening or orifice

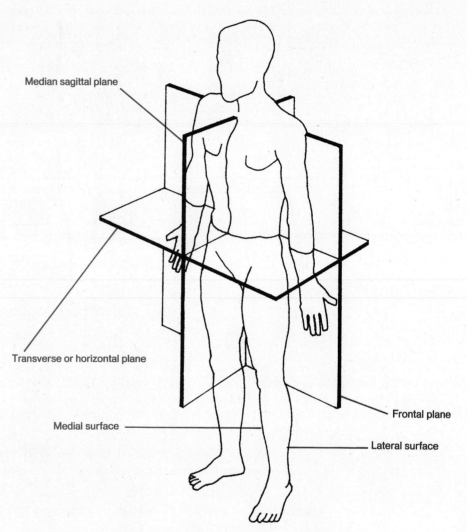

Median sagittal plane

Transverse or horizontal plane

Frontal plane

Medial surface

Lateral surface

4-2   Body Planes and Surfaces

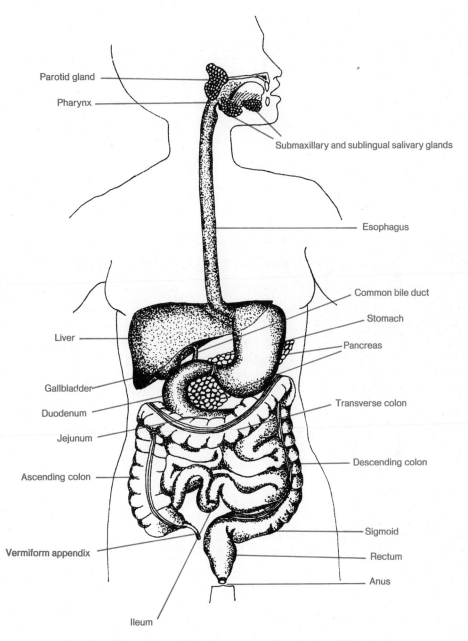

Parotid gland

Pharynx

Submaxillary and sublingual salivary glands

Esophagus

Common bile duct

Stomach

Liver

Pancreas

Gallbladder

Duodenum

Transverse colon

Jejunum

Ascending colon

Descending colon

Sigmoid

Vermiform appendix

Rectum

Anus

Ileum

4-3   The Digestive System and Associated Structures

areola – a circular area in tissue, usually of a color differing from that around it; it may be primary, occurring naturally, such as the areola of the breast, or it may be secondary, caused by some pathological state, such as the red area around a boil or the white area around an allergic reaction

areolar – pertaining to or containing areola; containing minute interspaces

arteriovenous – both arterial and venous; pertaining to or affecting an artery and a vein

ascites – effusion and accumulation of serous fluid in the abdominal cavity

asthenic – pertaining to or characterized by asthenia, which is the lack or loss of strength and energy; weakness

atelectasis – incomplete expansion of the lungs at birth; collapse of the adult lung

azygos – unpaired; any unpaired part, such as the azygos vein

Betadine scrub – trademark for preparations of povidone-iodine

biliary – of or relating to bile, the bile ducts, or the gallbladder

bilirubin – a bile pigment

Billroth's procedure (no definition given)

borborygmus (mi) – a rumbling noise caused by the propulsion of gas through the intestines

bougie – a slender, flexible, hollow or solid, cylindrical instrument for introduction into the urethra or other tubular organ, usually for the purpose of calibrating or dilating constricted areas

buccal – pertaining to or directed toward the cheek

canalization – the formation of canals, natural or morbid

carbuncle – a necrotizing infection of skin and subcutaneous tissue composed of a cluster of boils, usually due to Staphylococcus aureus, with multiple formed or incipient drainage sinuses

carcinomatosis – the condition of widespread dissemination of cancer through the body; also called carcinosis

carina – a ridgelike structure

cavagram (no definition given)

cavitary area – characterized by the presence of a cavity or cavities

cephalad margin – toward the head

cholangiogram – an x-ray of the gallbladder and bile ducts

cholangitis – inflammation of a bile duct

cholecystectomy – surgical removal of the gallbladder

cholecystitis – inflammation of the gallbladder

cholecystogram – an x-ray of the gallbladder

choledocholithiasis – the occurrence of calculi in the common bile duct

choledochoscope – an instrument for direct inspection of the interior of the common bile duct by artificial light

choledochotomy – incision into the common bile duct for exploration or removal of a calculus

cholelithiasis – the presence or formation of gallstones

chondritis – inflammation of cartilage

cicatrix – a scar; the new tissue formed in the healing of a wound

circumareolar incision (no definition given)

colorectal – pertaining to or affecting the colon and rectum

colostomy – the surgical creation of an opening between the colon and the surface of the body; also used to refer to the opening, or stoma, so created

condyloma – condyloma acuminatum; a papilloma with a central core of connective tissue in a treelike structure covered with epithelium; caused by a filterable virus

cortical – pertaining to or of the nature of a cortex or bark

costophrenic – pertaining to the ribs and diaphragm

crescentic margin – resembling a crescent

cryosurgery – destruction of tissue by the application of extreme cold; utilized in some forms of intracranial and cutaneous surgery

cul-de-sac – a blind pouch or cecum

cystostomy – the formation of an opening into the bladder

decortication – removal of portions of the cortical substance of a structure or organ, as of the brain, kidney, lung, etc.

decubitus – the act of lying down; also the position assumed in lying down

dehiscence – a splitting open

denude – make bare; strip something of its covering

dermatome – an instrument for cutting thin skin slices for skin grafts

descensus – the process of descending or falling

desquamation – the shedding of epithelial elements, chiefly of the skin, in scales or small sheets

devascularize – to interrupt the circulation of blood to a part causing obstruction or destruction of the blood vessels supplying it

diastalsis – a downward moving wave of contraction with a preceding wave of inhibition occurring in the digestive tube

diverticulitis – inflammation of a diverticulum

diverticulosis – the presence of diverticula, particularly of intestinal diverticula

diverticulum (la) – a circumscribed pouch or sac of variable size occurring normally or created by herniation of the lining mucous membrane through a defect in the muscular coat of a tubular organ

donor site (no definition given)

dorsalis pedis pulse (no definition given)

dressings, types – aeroplast, collodion, iodoform, stent, Velpeau

ductus – a duct; a general term for a passage with well-defined walls, especially such a channel for the passage of excretions or secretions

duodenum – the first or proximal portion of the small intestine, extending from the pylorus to the jejunum

dysphagia – difficulty in swallowing

dysplasia – abnormality of development

ecchymosis – a small hemorrhagic spot in the skin or mucous membrane forming a nonelevated, rounded or irregular, blue or purplish patch

efflux – the action or process of flowing or seeming to flow out

emesis – vomiting; an act of vomiting

empyema – accumulation of pus in a cavity of the body

endoscopy – visual inspection of any cavity of the body by means of an endoscope

endothelium (la) – the layer of epithelial cells that lines the cavities of the heart and of the blood and lymph vessels, and the serous cavities of the body, originating from the mesoderm

enteric – pertaining to the small intestine

enterocolectomy – resection of the intestines, including the ileum, cecum, and ascending colon

enucleation – the removal of an organ, of a tumor, or of another body in such a way that it comes out clean and whole, like a nut from its shell

epididymis – the elongated cordlike structure along the posterior border of the testis, in the ducts of which the spermatozoa are stored

epiplocele – a hernia that contains omentum

epithelialization – healing by the growth of epithelium over a denuded surface

epitrochlea – the inner condyle of the humerus

eructation – the act of belching, or of casting up wind from the stomach through the mouth

erythematous – characterized by erythemia

eschar – a slough produced by a thermal burn, by a corrosive application, or by gangrene

esophagogastrectomy – excision of the esophagus and stomach, usually the distal portion of the esophagus and the entire stomach

esophagogram – an x-ray of the esophagus

esophagojejunostomy – surgical anastomosis between the esophagus and the jejunum

esophagopharynx – the distal portion of the pharynx where the fibers of the inferior constrictor are arranged in a circular form

Ethicon clips, suture (no definition given)

excavation – the act of hollowing out; a hollowed-out space or pouchlike cavity

exteriorization (no definition given)

extirpation – complete removal or eradication of an organ or a tissue

extraluminal (no definition given)

extraperitoneal – situated or occurring outside the peritoneal cavity

extravasation – a discharge or escape, as of blood, from a vessel into the tissues

extubation – the removal of a previously inserted tube

fiberoptic – pertaining to fiberoptics; coated with glass or plastic fibers with special optical properties

fimbriated – fringed

fingerbreadth – a unit of length based on the breadth of one finger

Finochietto rib spreader (no definition given)

fistulectomy – excision of a fistulous tract

forceps, types – Allis, Halstead mosquito, Heaney, Kocher, Lahey

Freer nasal elevator (no definition given)

frenulum (la) – a general term for a small fold of integument or mucous membrane that checks, curbs, or limits the movements of an organ or a part

gastroduodenostomy – surgical creation of an anastomosis between the stomach and the duodenum

gastroenteroanastomosis – anastomosis between the stomach and small intestine in gastroenterostomy

gastroenterostomy – surgical creation of an artificial passage between the stomach and intestines

gastroesophagostomy – surgical creation of an anastomosis between the stomach and the esophagus

gastrojejunocolic – pertaining to or communicating with the stomach, jejunum, and colon

gastroscope – an endoscope for inspecting the interior of the stomach

gastrostomy – surgical creation of an artificial opening into the stomach; also, the opening so established

Gomco suction (no definition given)

granulomatous – composed of granulomas

Hartmann's pouch of the colon – an abnormal sacculation of the neck of the gallbladder

Hashimoto's disease (struma lymphomatosa) – chronic inflammatory disease of the thyroid gland characterized by infiltration of lymphocytes

hematochezia – the passage of bloody stools

hemoperitoneum – an effusion of blood in the peritoneal cavity

hepatic flexure (flexura coli dextra) – right flexure of colon; the bend in the large intestine at which the ascending colon becomes the transverse colon

herniae (more than one hernia) – the protrusion of a loop or knuckle of an organ or a tissue through an abnormal opening

hernioplasty – operation for the repair of a hernia

Hesselbach's hernia – hernia with a diverticulum through the cribriform fascia

hilum (us) – a general term for a depression or pit at that part of an organ where the vessels and nerves enter

histiocytosis – a condition marked by the abnormal appearance of histiocytes in the blood

Hofmeister type gastrectomy (no definition given)

Holinger bronchoscope (no definition given)

Homan's sign – discomfort behind the knee on forced dorsiflexion of the foot; a sign of thrombosis in the veins of the calf

hydrocele – a circumscribed collection of fluid, especially a collection of fluid in the tunica vaginalis of the testicle or along the spermatic cord

hydrops – the abnormal accumulation of serous fluid in the tissues or in a body cavity; called also dropsy

hyperbilirubinemia – an excess of bilirubin in the blood

hyperplasia – the abnormal multiplication or increase in the number of normal cells in normal arrangement in a tissue

hypoglycemia – an abnormally diminished content of glucose in the blood

ileocecal – pertaining to the ileum and cecum

ileostomy – surgical creation of an opening into the ileum, usually by establishing an ileal stoma on the abdominal wall

imbrication – the overlapping of opposing surfaces, like shingles on a roof

in toto – totally, entirely

incarcerated – imprisoned; constricted; subjected to incarceration

incisions, types – Kocher, McBurney, Pfannenstiel, Rocky-Davis, semilunar

infraorbital – lying under or on the floor of the orbit

infundibulopelvic – pertaining to an infundibulum and a pelvis, as of the kidney

insufflation – the act of blowing a powder, vapor, gas, or air into a body cavity

intraluminal – within the lumen of a tube, as of a blood vessel

intussusception – a receiving within; specifically, the prolapse of one part of the intestine into the lumen of an immediately adjoining part

isoperistaltic (no definition given)

isthmus (mi) – a narrow connection between two major bodies or parts

jejunectomy – excision of the jejunum

jejunojejunostomy – the operative formation of an anastomosis between two portions of the jejunum; also the union so established

jejunum – that portion of the small intestine which extends from the duodenum to the ileum

Jesberg esophagoscope (no definition given)

keratotic – pertaining to, characterized by, or permitting keratosis, which is any horny growth, such as a wart or callosity

Kerrison's ronguer (no definition given)

laryngectomy – extirpation of the larynx

leukoplakia – a disease marked by the development upon the mucous membrane of the cheeks, gums, or tongue of white, thickened patches which cannot be rubbed off and which sometimes show a tendency to fissure

Levin tube – a gastroduodenal catheter of sufficiently small caliber to permit transnasal passage

ligament of Treitz – a small ligamentous extension of the posterior peritoneum reflected up onto the duodenum as it emerges from the retroperitoneal area

linea alba – the tendinous median line on the anterior abdominal wall between the two rectus muscles, formed by the decussating fibers of the aponeuroses of the three flat abdominal muscles

lingular – pertaining to a lingula, which is a general term for a small tongue-like structure

liposarcoma – a malignant tumor derived from primitive or embryonal lipoblastic cells which exhibit varying degrees of lipoblastic and/or lipomatous differentiation

lymphadenectomy – surgical excision of one or more lymph nodes

lysis – destruction, as of cells by a specific lysin or antibody

macro follicular (no definition given)

Mallory-Weiss (no definition given)

marsupialization – the creation of a pouch

Meckel's diverticulectomy – a congenital outpouching of the wall of the ileum 12 to 18 inches from the ileocecal junction

meconium – a dark green mucilaginous material in the intestine of the full-term fetus, being a mixture of the secretions of the intestinal glands and some amniotic fluid

mediastinoscopy – examination of the mediastinum by means of a tubular instrument permitting direct inspection of the tissues in the area

mediastinum – a median septum or partition; the mass of tissues and organs separating the two lungs, between the sternum in front and the vertebral column behind, and from the thoracic inlet above to the diaphragm below

mesentery – a membranous fold attaching various organs to the body wall

mesocolon – the process of the peritoneum by which the colon is attached to the posterior abdominal wall

Metzenbaum scissors (no definition given)

Meyer retractor (no definition given)

mucocutaneous – pertaining to or affecting the mucous membrane and the skin

nasolabial – pertaining to the nose and lip

Nissen fundoplication – mobilization of the lower end of the esophagus and plication of the fundus of the stomach up around it, in treatment of reflux esophagitis

normocephalic – refers to a normal-shaped head

omentum – a fold of peritoneum extending from the stomach to adjacent organs in the abdominal cavity

orchiectomy – removal of one or both testes

osteoarthritic – of, relating to, or affected with degenerative arthritis

pancreas – a large, elongated, racemose gland situated transversely behind the stomach, between the spleen and the duodenum

paracentesis – surgical puncture of a cavity for the aspiration of fluid

paramedian – situated near the midline or midplane

peau d'orange – a dimpled condition of the skin, resembling that of an orange

pedunculated – provided with a stemlike connecting part

perinephric – around the kidney

peripancreatic – surrounding the pancreas

phlegmon – inflammation of the connective tissue, often leading to ulceration or abscess; cellulitis

pneumatocele – hernial protrusion of lung tissue, as through a congenital fissure of the chest

porta hepatis (hepatic portal) – the transverse fissure on the visceral surface of the liver where the portal vein and hepatic artery enter the liver and the hepatic ducts leave

postauricular (no definition given)

Poupart's ligament – the inguinal ligament; a fibrous band running from the anterior superior spine of the ilium to the spine of the pubis

presacral – situated in front of the sacrum

proctalgia – neuralgia of the lower rectum

pyloric area – pertaining to the pylorus or to the pyloric part of the stomach

pyloromyotomy – incision of the longitudinal and circular muscles of the pylorus; Fredet-Ramstedt's operation

rectosigmoid – the lower portion of the sigmoid and upper portion of the rectum

resonance – the prolongation and intensification of sound produced by the transmission of its vibrations to a cavity, especially a sound elicited by percussion

retrocolic – behind the colon

rubin – fuchsin

sanguineous – abounding in blood; pertaining to blood

sarcoma – a tumor made up of a substance like the embryonic connective tissue; tissue composed of closely packed cells embedded in a fibrillar or homogeneous substance

Scarpa's fascia – a sheet of thin, ligament-like tissue passing from the mid-abdominal line to the dorsal root of the penis and to the symphysis pubis; very low in the pelvis of the male

sequelae – plural of sequela, which is any lesion or affection following or caused by an attack of disease

serosa – any serous membrane

serosanguineous – pertaining to or containing both serum and blood

silhouette – a dark image outlined against a lighter background

sphincteroplasty – surgical repair of a defective sphincter

splenectomy – excision or complete removal of the spleen

Staphylococcus aureus – a species of microorganisms comprising the pigmented, coagulase-positive, mannitol-fermenting pathogenic form

stent sutures – stent graft or surgical dressings

stylet/stilet/stilette – a wire run through a catheter or cannula to render it stiff or to remove debris from its lumen

symptomatology – that branch of medicine which treats of symptoms; the combined symptoms of a disease

tenesmus – straining; especially ineffectual and painful straining at stool or in urination

tetany – a syndrome manifested by sharp flexion of the wrist and ankle joints, muscle twitchings, cramps, and convulsions, sometimes with attacks of stridor

thenar eminence – the mound on the palm at the base of the thumb

thoracodorsal nerve – a nerve running from the brachial plexus to the latissimus dorsi muscle that helps provide nerve supply for the upper extremities

tomography – a special technique to show in detail images of structures lying in a predetermined plane of tissue, while blurring or eliminating detail in images of structures in the other planes

tracheostomy – the surgical creation of an opening into the trachea through the neck; also, the opening so created

transversalis fascia – part of the inner investing layer of the abdominal wall, continuous with the fascia of the other side behind the rectus abdominis and the rectus sheath

Trendelenburg – surgeon in Leipzig; a position

trocar – a cannula with a sharp-pointed obturator for piercing the wall of a cavity

ultrasonography – the visualization of deep structures of the body by recording the reflection of ultrasonic waves directed into the tissues

Unna's paste boot – a dressing for varicose ulcers

vas – a vessel; any canal for carrying a fluid; a general term for such channels especially those carrying blood, lymph, or spermatozoa

vermilion – the exposed red portion of the upper and lower lip

vermilionectomy – excision of the vermilion border of the lip, the surgically created defect being resurfaced by advancement of the undermined labial mucosa

verruca (ae) – an epidermal tumor caused by a papillomavirus

Vi Drape film and adhesive (no definition given)

villous (villose) – shaggy with soft hairs; covered with villi

Vim-Silverman needle (no definition given)

Xeroform – a gauze dressing

xiphoid – shaped like a sword; the xiphoid process

SURGICAL

Patient Name: **Date:**

PREOP DIAGNOSIS:

POSTOP DIAGNOSIS:

OPERATION:

SURGEON:

PROCEDURE:

SURGERY

Patient Name: **Date:**

PREOP DIAGNOSIS:

POSTOP DIAGNOSIS:

SURGEON:

ANESTHETIC:

OPERATION:

PROCEDURE:

X-RAY REPORT

Patient Name: **Date:**

Doctor:

OPERATION

Patient Name: Date:

PREOPERATIVE DIAGNOSIS:

POSTOPERATIVE DIAGNOSIS:

TITLE OF OPERATION:

SURGEON:

ANESTHESIA:

INDICATIONS:

DISCHARGE SUMMARY

Patient Name: **Date:**

    Doctor:

X-RAY REPORT

Patient Name: **Date:**

Doctor:

OPERATION

Patient Name: Date:

PREOP DIAG:

POSTOP DIAG:

SURGEON:

OPERATION:

PROCEDURE:

OP NOTE

Patient Name: **Date:**

   Doctor:

OPERATION:

PREOP DIAG:

POSTOP DIAG:

OPERATION

Patient Name: **Date:**

Doctor:

PREOP DIAG:

POSTOP DIAG:

OPERATION:

PROCEDURE:

SURGERY

Patient Name: Date:

PREOP DIAGNOSIS:

POSTOP DIAGNOSIS:

OPERATION:

SURGEON:

ASSISTANT:

PROCEDURE:

SURGERY

Patient Name: Date:

PREOP DIAG:

POSTOP DIAG:

OPERATION:

SURGEON:

INDICATIONS:

CHAPTER 5
INTERNAL MEDICINE

Internal medicine is that branch of medicine concerned with the diagnosis and treatment of internal organs and functions of the body. The disciplines included in the practice of this specialty are cardiology, gastroenterology, nephrology, oncology, chest diseases, and rheumatology. Since examples of cardiology and nephrology terminology and dictation are presented in other sections of the text, this particular unit will sample dictation from the remaining specialties. A short discussion of each follows.

Gastroenterology is the branch of medicine concerned with the esophagus, stomach, small and large intestines (colon), liver, and pancreas, or to define it broadly, with digestive diseases.

Chest disease, or pulmonary disease, is the branch of medicine concerned with diseases of the lungs, bronchial tubes, and upper respiratory tract which consists of the nose, pharynx, larynx, and heart.

The branch of medicine concerned with the diagnosis and treatment of cancer and the overall management and care of the patient who has cancer is known as medical oncology.

Rheumatology, the science of rheumatism, is concerned with a variety of disorders marked by inflammation, degeneration, or metabolic derangement of the connective tissue structures of the body, especially the joints and related structures, including muscles, bursae, tendons, and fibrous tissue.

ABBREVIATIONS

ANA	antinuclear antibodies	Hb F	fetal hemoglobin
ASHD	arteriosclerotic heart disease	Hb S	sickle cell hemoglobin
		HH	hiatal hernia
BMR	basic metabolic rate		
BX	biopsy	IPPB	intermittent positive pressure breathing
CEA	carcinoembryonic antigen		
COPD	chronic obstructive pulmonary disease	LH	luteinizing hormone
CPK	creatine phosphokinase		
		MCV	mean clinical value or mean corpuscular volume
DPT	diphtheria-pertussis-tetanus		
EGD	esophagogastroduodenoscopy	N&V	nausea and vomiting
ERCP	endoscopic retrograde cholangiopancreatography	OCP	ova, culture, parasites
ESR	erythrocytic sedimentation rate	PKU	phenylketonuria
FBS	fasting blood sugar	PND	paroxysmal nocturnal dyspnea
		PT	prothrombin time
GFR	glomerular filtration rate		
GGTP	gamma-glutamyl transpeptidase	RPR	rapid plasma reagin
Hb A	adult hemoglobin	URI	upper respiratory infection

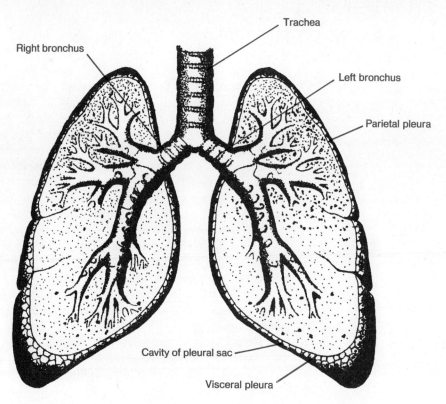

Right bronchus

Trachea

Left bronchus

Parietal pleura

Cavity of pleural sac

Visceral pleura

5-1 Trachea, Bronchi, Lungs, and Pleural Sacs

DEFINITIONS OF TERMINOLOGY

achalasia – a failure to relax of the smooth muscle fibers of the gastrointestinal tract at any point of junction of one part with another

achlorhydria – absence of hydrochloric acid in the gastric juice

achylia – absence of gastric juice

acrocyanosis – a condition marked by symmetrical cyanosis of the extremities, with persistent, uneven, mottled blue or red discoloration of the skin of the digits, wrists, and ankles and with profuse sweating and coldness of the digits

acromegaly – a condition caused by hypersecretion of the pituitary growth hormone after maturity and characterized by enlargement of the extremities of the skeleton

adiposis – obesity; an excessive accumulation of fat in the body

adrenalectomy – excision of one or both adrenal glands

aerophagia – spasmodic swallowing of air followed by eructations

agranulocytosis – a symptom complex characterized by marked decrease in the number of granulocytes and by lesions of the throat and other mucous membranes, of the gastrointestinal tract, and of the skin

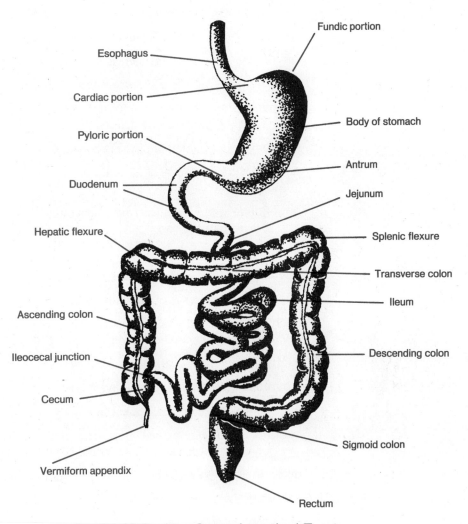

Fundic portion

Esophagus

Cardiac portion

Pyloric portion

Duodenum

Body of stomach

Antrum

Jejunum

Hepatic flexure

Splenic flexure

Transverse colon

Ileum

Ascending colon

Ileocecal junction

Descending colon

Cecum

Sigmoid colon

Vermiform appendix

Rectum

5-2   The Gastrointestinal Tract

allantiasis – sausage poisoning

amebiasis – the state of being infected with amebae

amelioration – improvement, as of the condition of a patient

amylase – one of the three digestive enzymes produced by the pancreas

amylasuria – an excess of amylase in the urine; a sign of pancreatitis

anaphylactic – decreasing immunity instead of increasing it

anasarca – generalized massive edema

ancylostomiasis – hookworm disease

anemia, myelophthisic – leukoerythroblastosis

anemia, pernicious – a megaloblastic anemia occurring in children but more commonly in later life

angiomatosis – a diseased state of the vessels with the formation of multiple angiomas

angioneurotic – denoting a neuropathy affecting the vascular system

angiosarcoma – a hemangiosarcoma

anhidrosis – an abnormal deficiency of sweat

anhydremia – deficiency of water in the blood

anomaly – marked deviation from the normal standard, especially as a result of congenital or hereditary defects

anoxemia – reduction of oxygen content of the blood below physiologic levels

anthracosis – a disease of the lungs caused by inhalation of fine particles of coal dust

anticholinergic – an agent that blocks the passage of impulses through the parasympathetic nerves

antidiuresis – suppression of urinary secretion

apepsinia – total absence or lack of secretion of pepsinogen by the stomach

aperistalsis – absence of peristaltic action

asphyxia – a condition due to lack of oxygen in respired air, resulting in impending or actual cessation of apparent life

asphyxiation – suffocation

athyreosis (athyrosis) – hypothyroidism

bacteremia – the presence of bacteria in the blood

beriberi – a disease caused by a deficiency of thiamine and characterized by polyneuritis, cardiac pathology, and edema

bilirubinemia – the presence of bilirubin in the blood

bronchiectasis – a chronic distention of the bronchi or bronchioles

bronchiolitis – bronchopneumonia

bronchopneumonia – a name given to an inflammation of the lungs which usually begins in the terminal bronchioles

bronchospirometry – determination of the vital capacity, oxygen intake, and carbon dioxide excretion of a single lung, or simultaneous measurement of the function of each lung separately

bruxism – rhythmic or spasmodic grinding of teeth in other than chewing movements

Buerger's disease – thromboangiitis obliterans

cachexia – a profound and marked state of constitutional disorder; general ill health and malnutrition

cancericidal (cancerocidal) – destructive to cancer or malignant cells

carcinoid – a yellow circumscribed tumor occurring in the small intestine, appendix, stomach, or colon

carotenemia (carotinemia) – presence of excessive carotene in the blood

catamnesis – the history of a patient from the time of discharge from treatment or from a hospital to the time of death

catecholamines – the chemical substances secreted by the adrenal gland, which are excreted in relatively constant amounts in the urine in conditions of good health

chancre – the primary sore of syphilis, a painless, indurated, eroded papule occurring at the site of entry of the infection

Cheyne-Stokes respiration – one type of breathing seen in deeply comatose patients in which there is deep regular breathing for a time alternating with quite long periods of no breathing

chloremia – iron deficiency anemia

chlorosis – iron deficiency anemia

cholangiolitis – inflammation of the cholangioles, the fine terminal elements of the bile duct system

cholecystogastric – referring to the gallbladder and stomach

choledocholithotomy – removal of stone from the bile duct

choledochoplasty – plastic repair or reconstruction of the bile duct

cholemia – the occurrence of bile or bile pigment in the blood

cholestasis – stoppage or suppression of the flow of bile

cholesterinemia (cholesterolemia) – hypercholesterolemia

cholesterosis (cholesterolosis) – a condition in which cholesterol is deposited in tissues in abnormal quantities

choriomeningitis – cerebral meningitis with lymphocytic infiltration of the choroid plexuses

chyme – the mixture of gastric juices with food

coxsackievirus – one of a heterogeneous group of enteroviruses producing, in man, a disease resembling poliomyelitis, but without paralysis

Cruveilhier's disease – spinal muscular atrophy

Cruveilhier-Baumgarten syndrome – cirrhosis of the liver with portal hypertension, associated with congenital patency of the umbilical or paraumbilical veins

cystadenocarcinoma – carcinoma and cystadenoma

de Toni-Fanconi syndrome (Fanconi's syndrome) – a congenital hereditary disease

defervescence – the period of abatement of fever

dehydrogenase – an enzyme

deleterious – hurtful; injurious

duodenitis – inflammation of the duodenum

duodenoduodenostomy – operative formation of an artificial opening between two segments of the duodenum

duodenoileostomy – operative formation of an artificial opening between the duodenum and ileum

duodenojejunostomy – operative formation of an artificial opening between the duodenum and jejunum

dysarthria – imperfect articulation of speech due to disturbances of muscular control which result from damage to the central or peripheral nervous system

dyssymmetry – a condition characterized by absence of symmetry

dyssynergia – disturbance of muscular coordination

Ebstein's disease – hyaline degeneration and necrosis of the epithelial cells of the renal tubules; seen in diabetes

echinococcosis – hydatid disease

electrophoresis – the movement of charged particles suspended in a liquid under the influence of an applied electric field

enterolith – a stone in the bowel

eosinophilia – the formation and accumulation of an abnormally large number of eosinophils in the blood

erysipelas – a contagious disease of skin and subcutaneous tissue due to infection with Streptococcus pyogenes and marked by redness and swelling of affected areas, with constitutional symptoms

erythroblastosis – the presence of erythroblasts in the circulating blood

erythromelalgia (erythermalgia) – a disease affecting chiefly the extremities of the body, the feet more often than the hands, and marked by paroxysmal, bilateral vasodilatation, particularly of the extremities, with burning pain, and increased skin temperature and redness

esophagoscope – an endoscope for examination of the esophagus

eucrasia – a state of health; proper balance of different factors constituting a healthy state

eurhythmia – harmonious relationships in body or organ development; regularity of the pulse

euthyroid – having a normally functioning thyroid gland

evanescent – vanishing; passing away quickly; unstable, unfixed

exanthema subitum – a condition frequently seen in children, marked by remittent fever lasting three days, followed by crisis, and followed a few hours later by a rash on the trunk

excrescence – any abnormal outgrowth; a projection of morbid origin

fecalith – a fecal concretion

fibrinogenopenia – deficiency of fibrinogen in the blood

fibrinolysis – the dissolution of fibrin by enzymatic action

fibromyoma – leiomyoma

filariasis – a diseased state due to the presence of filariae within the body

fremitus – a vibration perceptible on palpation

fundoplication – operative procedure to relieve gastroesophageal reflux of large amounts of acid-peptic juice and to restore gastroesophageal competence

galactosemia – a hereditary disorder of galactose metabolism

gastrectomy – excision of the whole or part of the stomach

gastrojejunostomy – surgical creation of an anastomosis between the stomach and jejunum

gastrorrhea – excessive secretion of mucus or gastric juice in the stomach

gastrosuccorrhea – excessive and continuous secretion of gastric juice

gelatinase – an enzyme that liquifies gelatin but does not affect fibrin and egg albumin

gingivostomatitis – inflammation involving both the gingivae and the oral mucosa

Graefe's sign – failure of the upper lid to move downward promptly and evenly with the eyeball in looking downward; instead it moves tardily and jerkingly

granulocytopenia – agranulocytosis

habitus – physique

Hanot-Chauffard syndrome – hypertrophic cirrhosis with pigmentation and diabetes mellitus

hemachromatosis – an excess of iron absorption and the presence of iron-containing deposits in the liver, pancreas, kidneys, adrenals, and heart

hematoporphyria – porphyria

hepatomalacia – softening of the liver

hepatomegaly – enlargement of the liver

hepatorrhea – a morbidly excessive secretion of bile; any morbid flow from the liver

hepatotoxic – toxic to liver cells

herpangina – a specific infectious disease characterized by sudden onset of fever of short duration and appearance of typical vesicular or ulcerated lesions in the faucial area or on the soft palate

hidrorrhea – hyperhidrosis

Hirschowitz gastroduodenal fibroscope (no definition given)

Hirschsprung's disease – excessive enlargement of the colon associated with an absence of ganglion cells in the narrowed bowel wall distally

hyperalimentation – the ingestion or administration of a greater than optimal amount of nutrients

hyperchlorhydria – excessive amount of hydrochloric acid in the gastric juice

hyperhidrosis – excessive perspiration

hyperinsulinism – excessive secretion of insulin by the pancreas, resulting in hypoglycemia; insulin shock

hyperparathyroidism – abnormally increased activity of the parathyroid glands

hyperpituitarism – a condition due to pathologically increased activity of the pituitary gland

hypervitaminosis – a condition due to ingestion of an excess of one or more vitamins

hypervolemia – abnormal increase in the volume of circulating fluid in the body

hypochlorhydria – deficiency of hydrochloric acid in the gastric juice

hypoestrogenemia – an abnormally diminished amount of estrogen in the blood, as in the menopause

hypopotassemia (hypokalemia) – abnormally low potassium concentration in the blood

hypoprothrombinemia – deficiency of prothrombin in the blood

hyposthenuria – a condition characterized by inability to form urine of high specific gravity

hypothermia – low temperature, especially a state of low temperature of the body induced as a means of decreasing metabolism of tissues and thereby the need for oxygen, as used in various surgical procedures

icterus – jaundice

icterus neonatorum – jaundice in the newborn

ileitis – inflammation of the ileum

ileocolitis – inflammation of the ileum and colon

inspissated – being thickened, dried, or rendered less fluid

kalemia (kaliemia) – the presence of potassium in the blood

kinetosis (kinesia) – any disorder caused by unaccustomed motion; motion sickness

Laennec's cirrhosis – cirrhosis of the liver closely associated with chronic excessive alcohol ingestion

leukocytosis – a transient increase in the number of leukocytes in the blood, resulting from various causes

leukopenia – reduction in the number of leukocytes in the blood

lipase – one of the three digestive enzymes produced by the pancreas

lipomatosis – a condition characterized by abnormal localized, or tumor-like, accumulations of fat in the tissues

Loffler's syndrome – a condition characterized by transient infiltrations of the lungs associated with an increase of the eosinophilic leukocytes in the blood

lues – syphilis

lymphadenoleukopoiesis – the production of leukocytes by the lymphadenoid tissue

lymphangioma – a tumor composed of new-formed lymph spaces and channels

lymphedema praecox – primarily of young females, characterized by puffiness and swelling of the lower limbs, and occurring at or near puberty

lymphocytoma – well-differentiated lymphocytic malignant lymphoma

maculopapular – both macular and papular

maduromycosis – a chronic disease caused by a variety of fungi or actinomycetes, affecting the foot, hand, legs, or other parts, including the internal organs

marasmus – a form of protein-caloric malnutrition chiefly occurring during the first year of life

megacolon – abnormally large or dilated colon

meningococcemia – invasion of the blood stream by meningococci

meningoencephalomyelitis – inflammation of the meninges, brain, and spinal cord

meniscocytosis – sickle cell anemia

microcythemia (microcytosis) – a condition in which the erythrocytes are smaller than normal

mononucleosis – the presence of an abnormally large number of mononuclear leukocytes in the blood

moribund – in a dying state

myeloproliferative – pertaining to or characterized by medullary and extramedullary proliferation of bone marrow constituents

neutropenia – a decrease in the number of neutrophilic leukocytes in the blood

ochronosis (ochronosus) – a peculiar discoloration of certain tissues of the body, caused by the deposit of alkapton bodies as the result of a metabolic disorder

oncology – the sum of knowledge concerning tumors; the study of tumors

oxyuriasis – pinworm

pancytopenia – deficiency of all cell elements of the blood; aplastic anemia

panniculitis – inflammation of the fatty tissue that is deposited as broad sheets in any part of the body

panniculus – a layer of membrane

parascarlatina – a febrile disease of childhood characterized by an exanthematous eruption, probably a mild form of scarlet fever

pediculosis – infestation with lice

pellagra – a clinical deficiency syndrome due to deficiency of niacin

pemphigus – a name applied to a distinctive group of diseases characterized by successive crops of bullae

periarteritis nodosa – an inflammatory disease of the coats of the smaller and medium-sized arteries of the body, associated with a variety of systemic symptoms

peritonitis – inflammation of the peritoneum

phenylketonuria – an inborn error of metabolism attributable to a deficiency of or a defect in phenylalanine hydroxylase, the enzyme that catalyzes the conversion of phenylalanine to tyrosine

phenylpyruvic oligophrenia – mental deficiency associated with phenylketonuria

phrenicotomy – surgical division of the phrenic nerve in order to cause one-sided paralysis of the diaphragm, which then becomes pushed up by viscera so as to compress a diseased lung

phrenicotripsy – crushing of a phrenic nerve

pneumoconiosis – a chronic fibrous reaction in the lungs due to the inhalation of irritating dust of varying types

poikilocytosis – presence of red blood corpuscles of a variety of shapes—some elongated, some round, and some oval

polyserositis – general inflammation of serous membranes with serous effusion

postprandial – occurring after dinner, or after a meal

pseudohemophilia – angiohemophilia

psychogenic – having an emotional or psychologic origin

ptyalocele – cystic tumor of a salivary gland

pylorectomy – excision of the pylorus

pyloroplasty – a plastic operation to relieve pyloric obstruction or to accelerate gastric emptying

pyrosis – heartburn

quiescent – marked by a state of inactivity or repose; causing no symptoms

quinsy – peritonsillar abscess

recalcitrant – stubbornly resistant to authority, domination, or guidance

reticulocytosis – an increase in the number of reticulocytes in the peripheral blood

rhabdomyosarcoma – a highly malignant tumor of striated muscle derived from primitive mesenchymal cells and exhibiting differentiation along rhabdomyoblastic lines, including but not limited to the presence of cells with recognizable cross striations

rugae – irregular folds of the mucous membrane of the stomach in which gastric glands are embedded

scarlatina – scarlet fever

Schlesinger's sign – in tetany, if a patient's leg is held at the knee joint and flexed strongly at the hip joint, there will follow within a short time an extensor spasm at the knee joint, with extreme supination of the foot

sessile – attached by a base

sialaden – a salivary gland

sialoadenectomy – excision of a salivary gland

sialozemia – involuntary flow of saliva

sideropenia – iron deficiency

silicatosis – pneumoconiosis caused by the inhalation of the dust of silicates

silicosis – pneumoconiosis due to the inhalation of the dust of stone, sand, or flint containing silicon dioxide, with formation of generalized nodular fibrotic changes in both lungs

singultus – hiccup due to a nervous state of the stomach

spherocytosis – the presence of spherocytes in the blood

stomatitis – inflammation of the oral mucosa, due to local or systemic factors, which may involve the buccal and labial mucosa, palate, tongue, floor of the mouth, and the gingivae

telangiectasis – the spot formed, most commonly on the skin, by a dilated capillary or terminal artery

thalassemia – a heterogeneous group of hereditary hemolytic anemias which have in common a decreased rate of synthesis of one or more hemoglobin polypeptide chains and are classified according to the chain involved

thromboangiitis obliterans – an inflammation and obliterative disease of the blood vessels of the extremities, primarily the lower extremities, occurring chiefly in young men and leading to ischemia of the tissues and gangrene

thrombocytopenia – decrease in the number of blood platelets

thyrotoxicosis – a morbid condition resulting from overactivity of the thyroid gland

Tietze's syndrome – an acute rheumatoid inflammation of the costochrondral junction

toxicosis – any disease condition due to poisoning

trichobezoar – a ball composed of hair and mucoid material; usually found as a foreign body in the stomach

trypsin – one of the three digestive enzymes produced by the pancreas

tsutsugamushi disease, fever (scrub typhus) – a self-limited, febrile disease of two weeks' duration

uricosuric – pertaining to, characterized by, or promoting uricosuria, which is the excretion of uric acid in the urine

urobilinogenuria – the presence of urobilinogen in the urine

uropepsinogen – pepsinogen occurring in the urine

urticaria – a vascular reaction of the skin marked by the transient appearance of smooth, slightly elevated patches which are redder or paler than the surrounding skin and often attended by severe itching

valvulitis – inflammation of a valve or valvula, especially a valve of the heart

vermiform – shaped like a worm

volvulus – intestinal obstruction due to a knotting and twisting of the bowel

Wharton's duct – the principal duct of the submaxillary salivary gland

xanthomatosis – an accumulation of an excess of lipids in the body due to disturbance of lipid metabolism and marked by the formation of foam cells in skin lesions

ESOPHAGOGASTRODUODENOSCOPY REPORT WITH GASTRIC BIOPSY AND CYTOLOGY

Patient Name: Date:

    Doctor:

PROCEDURE:

CONSULTATION

Patient Name: Date:

    Doctor:

CONSULTANT:

CONSULTATION

Patient Name: **Date:**

Doctor:

CONSULTANT:

DISCHARGE SUMMARY

Patient Name: **Date:**

   Doctor:

Admitted:
Discharged:

CONSULTATION

Patient Name: Date:

Doctor:

DISCHARGE SUMMARY

Patient Name: Date:

    Doctor:

DISCHARGE DIAGNOSIS:

DISCHARGE SUMMARY

Patient Name: **Date:**

    Doctor:

Admitted:
Discharged:

DISCHARGE SUMMARY

Patient Name: Date:

      Doctor:

Admitted:
Discharged:

HISTORY

Patient Name: Date:

Doctor:

PHYSICAL

Patient Name: Date:

    Doctor:

DISCHARGE SUMMARY

Patient Name: Date:

Doctor:

OPERATION

Patient Name: Date:

Doctor:

SURGEON:

ASSISTANT:

ANESTHESIA:

OPERATION PERFORMED:

PREOP DIAG:

POSTOP DIAG:

PROCEDURE:

CONSULTATION

Patient Name: Date:

Doctor:

DEATH SUMMARY

Patient Name: Date:

  Doctor:

CHAPTER 6
NEUROLOGY/NEUROSURGERY

Neurology is the medical specialty concerned with the diagnosis and treatment of disorders of the brain, spinal cord, and peripheral nerves.

Serving as the complicated communication network of the body, the neurological system provides the mechanism for the sending and receiving of messages between the brain and the nerves, which in turn makes man an intelligent, functioning individual.

Anatomically and functionally, the nervous system is divided into the brain, spinal cord, and nerves. The brain (encephalon) and the spinal cord (medulla spinalis) make up the central nervous system. The peripheral nervous system is composed of a series of nerves that extend from the central nervous system to all portions of the body enabling all other body systems to be coordinated and work together as a unit.

Strokes, epilepsy, Parkinson's disease, and brain tumors are common disorders treated by the neurologist. These disorders may be caused by organic injury, congenital defects, or diseases such as infections.

The related specialty of neurosurgery treats the surgical aspects of neurological disease. A neurologist who wishes to become a neurosurgeon must take three additional years of specialized training.

ABBREVIATIONS

AJ	ankle jerk		LOA	left occiput anterior
			LOP	left occiput posterior
CAT	computerized axial tomography		LP	lumbar puncture
CNS	central nervous system			
CP	cerebral palsy		MD	muscular dystrophy
CSF	cerebrospinal fluid		MS	multiple sclerosis
CVA	cerebrovascular accident		MVA	motor vehicle accident
CVP	central venous pressure		MVV	maximal voluntary ventilation
DTP	distal tingling on percussion		Neuro	neurology
DTR	deep tendon reflexes		N.S.	neurosurgery
ECF	extended care facility		OBS	organic brain syndrome
EEG	electroencephalogram		OKN	opticokinetic nystagmus
EMG	electromyogram			
ENG	electronystagmograph		PEG	pneumoencephalography
FS	frozen section		RA	rheumatoid arthritis
			RNA	ribose nucleic acid
GSW	gunshot wound		ROA	right occiput anterior
			ROM	range of motion
HNP	herniated nucleus pulposus		ROP	right occiput posterior
IMV	intermittent mandatory ventilation		SLR	straight leg raising
KJ	knee jerk		TIA	transient ischemic attack

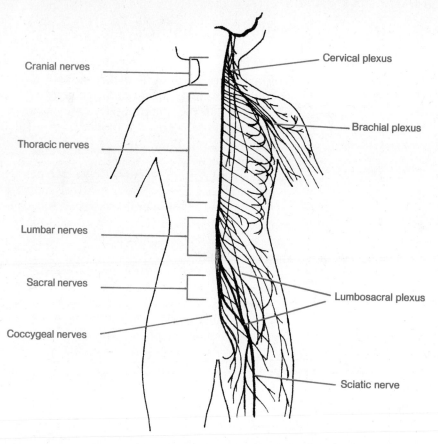

6-1 Spinal Nerve System of the Body

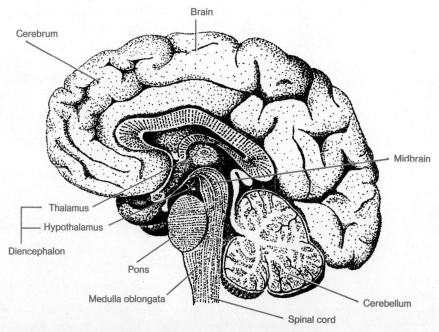

6-2 Central Nervous System

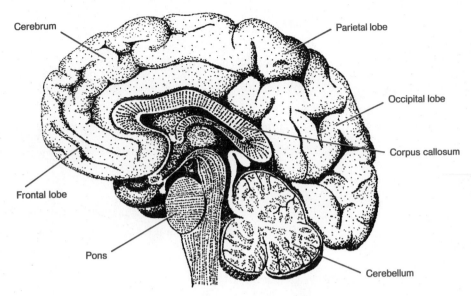

Cerebrum

Parietal lobe

Occipital lobe

Corpus callosum

Frontal lobe

Pons

Cerebellum

6-3   Interbrain Structures

DEFINITIONS OF TERMINOLOGY

acrocephalosyndactyly – a congenital malformation consisting of a pointed shape of the top of the head and syndactyly of the four extremities

adiadochokinesia – inability to perform rapid alternating movements

agrammatism – inability to speak grammatically because of brain injury or disease

akinesia – absence or poverty of movements; the temporary paralysis of a muscle by the injection of procaine

allochiria – a condition in which, if one extremity is stimulated, the sensation is referred to the opposite side

Alzheimer's disease (presenile dementia) – mental deterioration of unknown etiology beginning at middle age and characterized by a cortical atrophy and secondary ventricular dilatation

amyelia – congenital absence of spinal cord

amyotrophic lateral sclerosis – a combined motor system degeneration involving the principal pyramidal tracts and the anterior horn cells of the brain; usually death occurs due to pharyngeal muscle failure

anencephalia (anencephaly) – congenital absence of the cranial vault, with cerebral hemispheres completely missing or reduced to small masses attached to the base of the skull

aphemia – loss of the power of speech, due to a central lesion

apraxia – inability to carry out purposeful movements in the absence of paralysis or other motor or sensory impairment, especially inability to make proper use of an object

aqueduct – a passage or channel in a body structure or an organ

arachnoid – the almost invisible membrane that covers the brain and spinal cord; resembles a cobweb

arachnoidea – a delicate membrane interposed between the dura mater and the pia mater, being separated from the pia mater by the subarachnoid space

arachnoiditis – inflammation of the arachnoidea

astereognosis – loss of power to recognize objects or to appreciate their form by touching or feeling them

aura – a subjective sensation or motor phenomenon that precedes and marks the onset of a paroxysmal attack, such as an epileptic attack

axon – the appendage of a nerve cell that conducts impulses away from the cell body

basioccipital – pertaining to the basilar process of the occipital bone

Biernacki's sign – analgesia of the ulnar nerve in paralytic dementia and tabes dorsalis

brachycephaly – the fact or quality of having a short head

bregma – the point on the surface of the skull at the junction of the coronal and sagittal sutures

Brown-Sequard's disease – a syndrome due to damage of one-half of the spinal cord

Brudzinski's sign – a physical sign that suggests the presence of meningitis

cauda equina – the terminal portion of the spinal cord

cella – an enclosure or a compartment

cephalhematocele – a bloody tumor under the pericranium, communicating with one or more sinuses of the dura through the cranial bones

cephalhematoma – a tumor or swelling filled with blood beneath the pericranium

cephalodynia (cephalalgia) – pain in the head; headache

cephalogyric – pertaining to turning motions of the head

cerebellopontine (cerebellopontile) – conducting or proceeding from the cerebellum to the pons varolii

cerebellum – the second largest portion of the brain; it is concerned with the coordination of movements

cerebral dysrhythmia – irregularity in the electrical impulses given off by the brain

cerebromalacia – abnormal softening of the substance of the cerebrum

cerebromeningitis – meningoencephalitis

cerebrosclerosis – morbid hardening of the substance of the cerebrum

cerebrum – the largest and uppermost portion of the brain; the mass of nervous matter within the cranium

Charcot-Marie-Tooth disease – progressive neuropathic (peroneal) muscular atrophy

chorea – the ceaseless occurrence of a wide variety of rapid, highly complex, jerky movements that appear to be well coordinated but are performed involuntarily

choreiform – resembling chorea

choreoathetosis – a condition marked by choreic and athetoid movements

cinerea – the gray matter of the nervous system

cingulum – an encircling structure or part

cisterna – a closed space serving as a reservoir for lymph or other body fluid, especially one of the enlarged subarachnoid spaces containing cerebrospinal fluid

conus medullaris – medullary cone; the cone-shaped lower end of the spinal cord, at the level of the upper lumbar vertebrae

cordectomy – removal of a portion of the spinal cord

corticodiencephalic – pertaining to or connecting the cerebral cortex and the diencephalon

craniectomy – excision of a part of the skull

craniobuccal – pertaining to the head and mouth

craniocele – a protrusion of any part of the cranial contents through a defect in the skull

cranioclast – an instrument for performing craniotomy

craniolacunia – defective development of the bones of the vault of the fetal skull marked by depressed areas on the inner surfaces of the bones

craniopharyngioma – a tumor arising from cell rests derived from the hypophyseal stalk or Rathke's pouch, frequently associated with increased intracranial pressure, and showing calcium deposits in the capsule or in the tumor proper

craniorachischisis – congenital fissure of the skull and spinal column

craniotomy – any operation on the cranium; an operation to decrease the size of the head of a dead fetus and facilitate delivery by puncturing the skull and removing its contents

cribriform – perforated with small apertures like a sieve

cryptococcosis – an infection which may involve the skin, lungs, or other parts, but has a predilection to the brain and meninges

decerebrate – to eliminate cerebral function by transecting the brain stem between the anterior colliculi and the vestibular nuclei or by ligating the common carotid arteries and the basilar artery at the center of the pons

dementia – a general designation for mental deterioration

demyelinate – to destroy or remove the myelin sheath of a nerve or nerves

diadochokinesia – the function of arresting one motor impulse and substituting for it one that is diametrically opposite

diastematomyelia – a congenital defect, often associated with spina bifida, in which the spinal cord is split into halves by a bony spicule or fibrous band, each half being surrounded by a dural sac

diencephalon – the innerbrain

diplegia – paralysis affecting like parts on both sides of the body; bilateral paralysis

dolichocephalism (dolichocephaly) – the quality of being long headed

Duchenne's disease – spinal muscular atrophy; bulbar paralysis

dura mater – the outermost, toughest, and most fibrous of the three membranes (meninges) covering the brain and spinal cord

dysesthesia – impairment of any sense, especially of that of touch

dyskinesia – impairment of the power of voluntary movement, resulting in fragmentary or incomplete movements

encephalitis – inflammation of the brain

encephalocele – a herniation of a part of the brain through any opening in the skull

encephalomalacia – softening of the brain

encephalomyeloradiculitis – inflammation of the brain, spinal cord, and spinal nerve roots

encephalopathy – any degenerative disease of the brain

encephalosis – any organic brain disease

enervation – removal of a nerve or a section of a nerve

epencephalon – cerebellum; metencephalon

ependymitis – inflammation of the ependyma, which is the lining membrane of the ventricles of the brain and of the central canal of the spinal cord

glabella – the smooth areas on the frontal bone between the superciliary arches

glioblastoma multiforme – a rapidly growing malignant tumor, usually of the cerebral hemispheres, arising from cells called astrocytes; now called astrocytoma, Grade IV

glioma – a tumor arising from specialized connective tissue found in the brain and spinal cord

gliosarcoma – a spindle cell glioma

grand mal – a severe or major attack of epilepsy, marked by convulsions, oscillating pupils, feeble pulse, stupor, and unconsciousness

Gullian-Barré syndrome – a rare disease of the nervous system involving peripheral nerves, nerve roots, and spinal cord

hemangioendothelioma – a hemangioma in which the endothelial cells are the most prominent component

hemilaminectomy – removal of the vertebral laminae on one side only

hemiparesis – muscular weakness affecting one side of the body

heterotopia – displacement or misplacement of parts or organs; the presence of a tissue in an abnormal location

hydrocephalus – a condition characterized by abnormal accumulation of fluid within the ventricles of the brain

hygroma – a sac, cyst, or bursa distended by a fluid

hyperostosis frontalis – a new formation of bone tissue protruding in patches on the internal surface of the cranial bones in the frontal region

hypothalamus – the portion of the diencephalon which forms the floor and part of the lateral wall of the third ventricle

idiocy – severe mental retardation; a former category of mental retardation which comprised individuals with an IQ of less than 25

inion – the most prominent point of the external occipital protuberance

innervation – the distribution or supply of nerves to a part

ischogyria – a condition in which the cerebral convolutions have a jagged appearance, as in bulbar sclerosis

kernicterus – a condition with severe neural symptoms, associated with high levels of bilirubin in the blood

kinesioneurosis – a functional nervous disorder characterized by motor disturbances, such as spasms or tics

kinesthesia – the sense by which movement, weight, position, etc., are perceived

L-dopa (levodopa) – a drug used as an anticholinergic in the treatment of Parkinson's disease

lateropulsion – an involuntary tendency to go to one side while walking

lemniscus – a general term for a band or bundle of fibers in the central nervous system

leptomeninges – the pia-arachnoid, a combined delicate weblike membrane that ultimately covers the brain; also called the pia mater

leptomeningitis – inflammation of the pia and arachnoid of the brain or spinal cord

leukodystrophy – disturbance of the white substance of the brain

lobulus – a general term for a small lobe or one of the primary divisions of a lobe

macrocrania – abnormal increase in the size of the skull, the facial area being disproportionately small in comparison

macrogyria – moderate reduction in the number of sulci of the cerebrum, sometimes with increase in the brain substance, resulting in excessive size of the gyri

Magendie's foramen – a deficiency in the lower portion of the roof of the fourth ventricle through which the ventricle cavity communicates with the subarachnoid space

medulla oblongata – the brainstem

megalencephaly (macrencephaly) – overgrowth of the brain

meninges – the covering membranes of the brain and spinal cord

meningioma – a hard, slow-growing, usually vascular tumor which occurs mainly along the meningeal vessels and superior longitudinal sinus, invading the dura and skull and leading to erosion and thinning of the skull

meningoencephalitis – inflammation of the brain and meninges

meningomyelocele – hernial protrusion of a part of the meninges and substance of the spinal cord through a defect in the vertebral column

metencephalon – the anterior portion of the rhombencephalon comprising the cerebellum and the pons

microgyria (polymicrogyria) – a malformation of the brain characterized by development of numerous small convolutions

myelencephalon – the posterior portion of the rhombencephalon, including the medulla oblongata and the lower part of the fourth ventricle

myelinoclasis – destruction of myelin

myelomalacia – morbid softening of the spinal cord

myokymia – persistent quivering of the muscles

narcolepsy – a condition marked by an uncontrollable desire for sleep or by sudden attacks of sleep occurring at intervals

neopallium – that portion of the pallium (cerebral cortex) showing stratification and organization characteristic of the most highly evolved type of cerebral tissue

neurectomy – excision of a nerve

neurilemma – the delicate membranous sheath, or covering, of a nerve fiber

neurilemoma – usually a benign, encapsulated, solitary tumor, produced by the proliferation of Schwann cells

neurofibromatosis – a familial condition characterized by developmental changes in the nervous system, muscles, bones, and skin and marked superficially by the formation of multiple pedunculated soft tumors (neurofibromas) distributed over the entire body associated with areas of pigmentation

neurolysis – the process of freeing a nerve from adhesions

neuromatous – affected with or of the nature of a tumor or new growth largely made up of nerve cells and nerve fibers

neuropathy – a general term denoting functional disturbances and/or pathological changes in the peripheral nervous system

oligodendroglia – the non-neural cells of ectodermal origin forming part of the adventitial structure of the central nervous system

oligodendroglioma – a neoplasm derived from and composed of oligodendrogliocytes in varying stages of differentiation

opisthotonos – a form of spasm in which the head and the heels are bent backward and the body bowed forward

oxycephaly – a condition in which the top of the head is pointed

pacchionian – smooth granular structures found in the meninges of the brain

pachycephalia (pachycephaly) – abnormal thickness of the bones of the skull

pachyleptomeningitis – inflammation of the dura and pia together

paramyotonia – a disease marked by tonic spasms due to disorder of muscular tonicity, especially a hereditary and congenital affection

paresthesia – morbid or perverted sensation

parieto-occipital – pertaining to the parietal and occipital bones or lobes

petit mal – small seizures

pheochromocytoma – a well-encapsulated, lobular, vascular tumor of chromaffin tissue of the adrenal medulla or sympathetic paraganglia

pia mater – the innermost of the three membranes (meninges) covering the brain and spinal cord, investing them closely and extending into the depths of the fissures and sulci

platybasia – basilar impression

pleocytosis – presence of a greater than normal number of cells in the cerebrospinal fluid

pneumoencephalogram – radiographic visualization of the fluid-containing structures of the brain after cerebrospinal fluid is intermittently withdrawn by lumbar puncture and replaced by air, oxygen, or helium

porencephalia – the presence of cysts or cavities in the brain cortex communicating by a "pore" with the arachnoid space

precuneus – a small, square-shaped convolution on the medial surface of the parietal lobe of the cerebrum

pseudoathetosis – movements of the fingers elicited when the patient closes his/her eyes and extends the arms, associated with impairment of joint position sense

rachialgia – pain in the vertebral column

rachicentesis – lumbar puncture

rachidian – pertaining to the spine

rachilysis – mechanical treatment of a curved vertebral column by combining traction and pressure

radiculitis – inflammation of the root of a spinal nerve, especially of that portion of the root that lies between the spinal cord and the intervertebral canal

radiculopathy – disease of the nerve roots

rhinencephalon – a term generally applied to certain parts of the brain previously thought to be concerned entirely with olfactory mechanisms

rhombencephalon – the part of the brain developed from the posterior of the three primary brain vesicles of the embryonic neural tube

satellitosis – accumulation of neuroglial cells about neurons; seen whenever neurons are damaged

scaphocephalia (scaphocephaly) – a condition in which the skull is abnormally long and narrow

schwannoma – a neoplasm of the white substance of Schwann; i.e., of a nerve sheath

sella turcica – a bony shelf in approximately the central portion of the base of the skull that houses the pituitary gland

splanchnicotomy – division of a splanchnic nerve

stereognosis – the faculty of perceiving and understanding the form and nature of objects by the sense of touch

subarachnoid – situated or occurring between the arachnoid and the pia mater

subgaleal – situated beneath the galea aponeurotica

suprasellar – above the sella turcica

synkinesia (synkinesis) – an associated movement; an unintentional movement accompanying a volitional movement

syringobulbia – the presence of cavities in the medulla oblongata

tapetum – a covering structure or layer of cells

tegmentum – a covering

teratomas – a true neoplasm made up of a number of different types of tissue, none of which is native to the area in which it occurs

thalamus – a structure within the diencephalon which serves as the main relay center for sensory impulses

tic douloureux (trigeminal neuralgia) – disorder of cranial nerves

topagnosis – loss of touch localization

trismus – motor disturbance of the trigeminal nerve, especially spasm of the masticatory muscles, with difficulty in opening the mouth (lockjaw); a characteristic early symptom of tetanus

vagotomy – interruption of impulses carried by the vagus nerve or nerves

vagotonia – hyperexcitability of the vagus nerve; a condition in which the vagus nerve dominates in the general functioning of the body organs

*ventriculocaval

ventriculocisternostomy (ventriculostomy) – surgical establishment of a communication between the third ventricle of the brain and the cisterna magna for flow of cerebrospinal fluid in hydrocephalus

wallerian degeneration – fatty degeneration of a nerve fiber which has been severed from its nutritive centers

---

*These terms were used in dictation but were not located in any of the references consulted. You will encounter this situation throughout this text. For a list of the reference books consulted, see page 502.

SURGERY

Patient Name: Date:

   Doctor:

PREOP DIAGNOSIS:

POSTOP DIAGNOSIS:

OPERATION:

SURGEON:

PROCEDURE:

OPERATION

Patient Name: Date:

     Doctor:

PREOP DIAG:

POSTOP DIAG:

OPERATION:

PROCEDURE:

OPERATION

Patient Name: Date:

   Doctor:

DATE OF OPERATION:

SURGEON:

ASSISTANT:

PREOPERATIVE DIAGNOSIS:

POSTOPERATIVE DIAGNOSIS:

TITLE OF OPERATION:

ANESTHESIA:

PROCEDURE:

HISTORY

Patient Name: **Date:**

Doctor:

PHYSICAL

Patient Name: Date:

    Doctor:

SURGERY

Patient Name: Date:

    Doctor:

PREOP DIAG:

POSTOP DIAG:

OPERATION AND SPECIAL PROCEDURES:

PROCEDURE:

DISCHARGE SUMMARY

Patient Name: Date:

Doctor:

DISCHARGE DIAG:

OPERATIONS AND SPECIAL PROCEDURES:

HISTORY:

SURGERY

Patient Name: Date:

     Doctor:

SURGEON:
OPERATION:
ANES:

PROCEDURE:

SURGERY

Patient Name:

Doctor:

DATE:

PREOP DIAGNOSIS:

POSTOP DIAGNOSIS:

OPERATION:

SURGEON:

PROCEDURE:

OPERATION

Patient Name:

Doctor:

DATE OF OPERATION:

SURGEON:

PREOPERATIVE DIAGNOSIS:

POSTOPERATIVE DIAGNOSIS:

TITLE OF OPERATION:

PROCEDURE:

CHAPTER 7
OBSTETRICS/GYNECOLOGY

Obstetrics and gynecology (OB/GYN) is the medical specialty that attends to the care of women during pregnancy, childbirth, contraception, and periods of disease. More specifically, a gynecologist is a doctor who diagnoses and treats medical problems of the reproductive organs of women and, when necessary, also performs surgery. An obstetrician is the doctor who cares for pregnant women before, during, and after delivery.

All gynecologists are also obstetricians, but not all obstetricians are gynecologists. Some general practitioners also perform obstetrical services and call in an obstetrician only when difficulties arise in the delivery process.

Anyone working as an assistant for a gynecologist or obstetrician should have a basic understanding of the processes of pregnancy, childbirth, and its aftermath.

ABBREVIATIONS

AP	anteroposterior (AP vaginal vault repair)	GPA	gravida, para, abortio
		gyn	gynecology
BOW	bag of waters (BOW rupture)	HCG	human chorionic gonadotropin
B&S	Bartholin's and Skene's glands		
BUS	Bartholin's, urethral, and Skene's glands	LMP	last menstrual period
		LNMP	last normal menstrual period
CPD	cephalopelvic disproportion	NB	newborn
C.S.	cesarean section		
D & C	dilatation and curettage	OB	obstetrics
EBL	estimated blood loss	PID	pelvic inflammatory disease
EDC	expected date of confinement	POC	products of conception
EUA	examination under anesthesia	PUD	pregnancy undelivered
FHT	fetal heart tone	Rh neg.	Rhesus factor negative
FT	full term	Rh pos.	Rhesus factor positive

DEFINITIONS OF TERMINOLOGY

abortion – the premature expulsion from the uterus of the products of conception

abruptio placentae – premature detachment of the placenta

adnexa – adjoining parts; the uterine adnexa are the fallopian tubes and ovaries

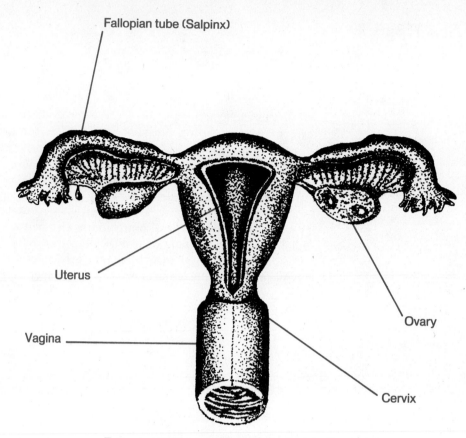

Fallopian tube (Salpinx)

Uterus

Vagina

Ovary

Cervix

7-1 Internal Genital Organs of Female

amenorrhea – the complete or abnormal cessation of menstruation

amniocentesis – the process whereby the uterus is entered through the abdomen to extract amniotic fluid

amnionitis – inflammation of the amnion

amniorrhea – the escape of the amniotic fluid

ante partum – the period before the onset of labor

anteflexion of uterus – condition present when the uterus is abnormally bent forward

Apgar score – a numerical expression of the condition of a newborn infant, usually determined at 60 seconds after birth, being the sum of points gained on assessment of the heart rate, respiratory effort, muscle tone, reflex irritability, and color

ballottement – the use of a finger to push sharply against the uterus and detect the presence or position of a fetus

bimanual examination – examination with both hands

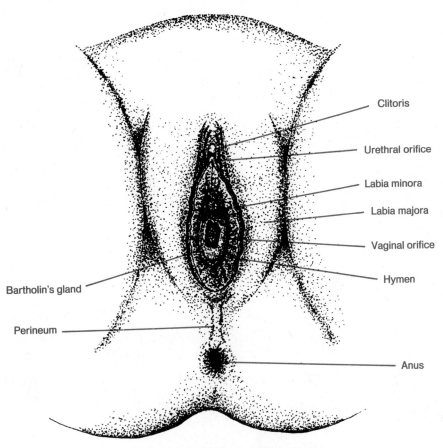

7-2 External Female Genitalia

Clitoris

Urethral orifice

Labia minora

Labia majora

Vaginal orifice

Hymen

Anus

Bartholin's gland

Perineum

Candida vaginitis – an infection of the vagina caused by a yeastlike fungus of the genus Candida

candidiasis – fungal infection of the vagina

caudal – referring to a position toward the tail

cauterize – to destroy tissue with a hot iron, electric current, or a caustic substance

cephalopelvic disproportion – condition where the head of the fetus is too large for the mother's pelvis

cerclage – encircling of a part with a ring or loop, such as encirclement of the incompetent cervix uteri, or the binding together of the ends of a fractured bone with a metal ring or wire loop

cervicectomy – excision of the cervix uteri

cervicitis – inflammation of the cervix uteri

cervix – the narrow passage at the lower end of the uterus which connects with the vagina

cesarean section – incision through the abdominal and uterine walls for delivery of a fetus

chorion – the outer membrane enclosing the embryo

chorionic villi – one of the threadlike projections growing in tufts on the external surface of the chorion

clitoris – a small, pea-shaped organ composed of erectile tissue similar in sensitivity to the penis in the male

clonus – alternate muscular contraction and relaxation in rapid succession

coitus – the act of intercourse

colostrum – the thin, yellow, milky fluid secreted by the mammary gland a few days before or after childbirth

colpectomy – excision of the vagina

colpoperineorrhaphy – suture of the ruptured vagina and perineum

colporrhaphy – the operation of suturing the vagina; the operation of denuding and suturing the vaginal wall for the purpose of narrowing the vagina

conjugate measurements – the distance between two specified opposite points on the periphery of the pelvic inlet, usually used in reference to the true conjugate diameter

copulation – sexual union between male and female; usually used in reference to animals lower than man

cornu – a hornlike projection

culdocentesis – aspiration of fluid from the rectouterine excavation by puncture of the vaginal wall

curettage – the removal of growths or other material from the wall of a cavity or other surface by scraping

cystocele – hernial protrusion of the urinary bladder through the vaginal wall

decidua – refers to the mucous lining of the uterus which comes off after childbirth

defervesced – fever decreased

descensus uteri – prolapse of the uterus

diaphragm – any separating membrane or structure

dilatation – the condition, as of an orifice or a tubular structure, of being dilated or stretched beyond the normal dimensions

dysmenorrhea – painful menstruation

dyspareunia – painful or difficult intercourse

dystocia – abnormal labor or childbirth

eclampsia – convulsions and coma, rarely coma alone, occurring in a pregnant or puerperal woman, associated with hypertension, edema, and/or proteinuria eclamptic toxemia – toxemia during pregnancy

ectopic pregnancy – development of the fertilized ovum outside of the uterine cavity; tubal pregnancy

ectropion – the turning outward (eversion) of an edge or margin

effacement – the obliteration of the cervix in labor when it is so changed that only the thin external os remains

endocervical – pertaining to the interior of the cervix uteri

endocervicitis – inflammation of the mucous membrane of the cervix uteri

endometrial – pertaining to the endometrium

endometrium – the mucous membrane of the uterus, the thickness and structure of which vary with the phase of the menstrual cycle

episiotomy – surgical incision of the vulvar orifice for obstetrical purposes

epithelium – the covering of internal and external surfaces of the body, including the lining of vessels and other small cavities

fallopian tube – the tube leading from the ovary to the uterus carrying the egg to the womb where it will develop

fibroid – having a fibrous structure; resembling a fibroma

fibroma – a tumor composed mainly of fibrous or fully developed connective tissue

fimbria – a fringe, border, or edge

fontanelle – soft spot in the skull of an infant

fornix – a vaulted space

fundus – the small rounded part of the uterus above where the fallopian tubes enter

Gelfoam pack – an absorbable gelatin sponge

genital – pertaining to the reproductive organs

genitalia – the reproductive organs of the male and female

gestation – the period of development of the young in viviparous animals, from the time of fertilization of the ovum

gravid – pregnant

gravida – a pregnant woman

Gravida III, Para II, Aborta I – pregnant three times, gave birth two times, and aborted once

Hegar's dilator – a slender, flexible instrument used for dilating the cervix

hirsutism – abnormal hairiness, especially in women

hydatid – any cystlike structure

hydatid of Morgagni – a cystlike remnant of the mullerian duct attached to a testis or to the oviduct

hydatidiform mole – an abnormal pregnancy characterized by a shapeless mass resembling a bunch of grapes

hymen – the membranous fold which partially or wholly occludes the external orifice of the vagina

hyperemesis gravidarum – excessive vomiting during pregnancy

hysterectomy – the operation to remove the uterus, performed either through the abdominal wall or the vagina

intrapartum – occurring during childbirth or during delivery

introitus – a general term for the entrance to a cavity or space

ischiorectal – pertaining to the ischium and rectum

labia majora – two folds of skin which extend backward and downward to the perineum; the outer surfaces are covered with hair

labia minora – two folds of skinlike lips located within the labia majora

lactation – the period of the secretion of milk

laparoscopy – examination of the interior of the abdomen by means of an instrument, the laparoscope, which is introduced through the abdominal wall

laparotomy – surgical incision through the abdomen to explore the abdominal contents

leiomyoma – a benign tumor of smooth muscle and fibrous connective tissue

Lembert's suture – a type of suture used in a cesarean section

leukorrhea – a whitish, viscid discharge from the vagina and uterine cavity

lithotomy position – a position assumed where the patient is on the back with legs raised and apart with feet or ankles in stirrups

lochia – the vaginal discharge that occurs during the first week or two after childbirth

macerated – softened by wetting or soaking

mammary – pertaining to the breast

mastitis – inflammation of the breast

meatus – an opening or passage

menarche – the beginning of the menstrual function

menometrorrhagia – excessive uterine bleeding occurring both during the menses and at irregular intervals

menopause – cessation of menstruation in the human female

menorrhagia – excessive uterine bleeding during the menstrual period

metritis – inflammation of the uterus

metrorrhagia – uterine bleeding, usually of normal amount, occurring at completely irregular intervals, the period of flow sometimes being prolonged

mittelschmerz – intermenstrual pain

Monilia vaginitis – an inflammation of the vagina caused by a fungus of the genus Moniliaceae

mucopurulent discharge – an excretion containing mucus and pus

mucous membranes – the membranes lining all bodily channels that communicate with the air

multigravida – a woman who has been pregnant several times

multiparity – the condition of having two or more pregnancies which resulted in viable fetuses

myoma – a common tumor of the uterus made up of muscular elements

myomectomy – surgical removal of a myoma

myometritis – inflammation of the muscular substance, or myometrium, of the uterus

myometrium – the smooth muscle coat of the uterus which forms the main mass of the organ

nabothian cyst – cystlike formation caused by occlusion of the lumina of glands in the mucosa of the uterine cervix, causing them to be distended with retained secretion

Nuck (canal of Nuck or Nuck's canal) – processus vaginitis peritonei

nulliparous – having never given birth to a viable infant

oligomenorrhea – markedly diminished menstrual flow; relative amenorrhea

omphalus – the umbilicus

oophorectomy – the removal of an ovary or ovaries

oophoropexy – ovariopexy; the operation of elevating or fixing an ovary to the abdominal wall

oophoroplasty – the plastic repair of an ovary

oophritis – inflammation of an ovary

os – a general term which is qualified by the appropriate adjective to designate a specific type of bony structure or a specific segment of the skeleton

ova – plural of ovum

ovarian – pertaining to an ovary or ovaries

ovarian follicle – refers to the egg and its encasing cells at any stage of its development

ovary – the female reproductive gland

ovum – the female reproductive cell

panhysterectomy – complete removal of the uterus and cervix; total hysterectomy

Papanicolaou's stain (PAP smear) – routine cancer detection test

parenchymatous – pertaining to or of the nature of parenchyma, the essential elements of an organ

parietal – of or pertaining to the walls of a cavity

parous – having borne one or more viable offspring

patulous – spreading widely apart; open; distended

pedicle – the area of an organ where the major nutrient blood vessels enter

pelvimetry – the measurement of the dimensions and capacity of the pelvis

perimetritis – inflammation of the perimetrium

perimetrium – the serous coat of the uterus

perineum – the pelvic floor and the associated structures occupying the pelvic outlet

peritonealize – to cover with peritoneum

peritoneum – the serous membrane lining the abdominopelvic walls

pessary – an instrument placed in the vagina to support the uterus or rectum or as a contraceptive device

Pfannenstiel incision – a curved abdominal incision named for Hermann Johann Pfannenstiel, a gynecologist in Breslaw

placenta praevia – a placenta which develops in the lower uterine segment, so that it obstructs the internal opening of the cervix

polyhydramnios – too much amniotic fluid

polymenorrhea – abnormally frequent menstruation

postpartum – after childbirth, or after delivery

preeclampsia – a toxemia of late pregnancy, characterized by hypertension, albuminuria, and edema

prenatal – existing or occurring before birth, with reference to the fetus

primigravida – a woman who is pregnant for the first time

procidentia – condition present when the uterus falls to the degree that the cervix protrudes from the vagina

progesterone – a female hormone whose function it is to prepare the uterus for the reception and development of the fertilized ovum by inducing secretion in the proliferated glands

prolapse uteri – protrusion of the uterus through the vaginal orifice

pruritus vulvae – intense itching of the external genitals of the female

pudendal block – a type of anesthesia used in childbirth

pyosalpinx – a collection of pus in an oviduct

raphe – a seam

retrocession – a going backward; backward displacement; specifically a dropping backward of the entire uterus

retroflexion – the bending backward of the body of the uterus toward the cervix

retroversion – the tipping of an entire organ backward

Rubella titer (no definition given)

salpingectomy – surgical removal of the uterine tube

salpingitis – inflammation of the uterine tube

salpingo – a combining form denoting relationship to a tube, specifically to the uterine or to the auditory tube

salpingo-oophorectomy – surgical removal of a uterine tube and ovary

secundines – the afterbirth

sonolucent – without echoes

speculum – an instrument for exposing the interior of a passage or cavity of the body

sphincter – a ringlike band of muscle fibers that constricts a passage or closes a natural orifice

Stein-Leventhal syndrome – a clinical symptom complex characterized by secondary amenorrhea and anovulation (hence sterility), and regularly associated with bilateral polycystic ovaries

stress incontinence – involuntary discharge of urine due to anatomic displacement which exerts an opening pull on the bladder orifice, as in straining or coughing

stria – a streak or line; a narrow bandlike structure

striated – striped; marked by striae

Sturmdorf sutures – No. 1 chromic catgut mattress sutures

subinvolution – failure of a part to return to its normal size and condition after enlargement due to functional activity

suprapubic – situated or performed above the pubic arch

symphysis pubis – the joint formed by union of the bodies of the pubic bones in the median plane by a thick mass of fibrocartilage

tampon – a plug made of cotton or sponge

tenaculum – a hooklike instrument for seizing and holding tissues

thrombocytopenic purpura – a disease of undefined cause, characterized by thrombocytopenia, hemolytic anemia, bizarre neurological manifestations, azotemia, fever, and thromboses in terminal arterioles and capillaries

toxemia – a general intoxication sometimes due to the absorption of bacterial products (toxins) formed in a local source of infection

Trichomonas – parasitic protozoa that cause urogenital infection

tubal ligation – the process of tying off the fallopian tubes to prevent conception

ultrasound – mechanical radiant energy, with a frequency greater than 20,000 cycles per second

umbilicus – the navel

utero-ovarian – pertaining to the uterus and ovary

uterosacral ligament – a part of the thickening of the visceral pelvic fascia beside the cervix and vagina, passing posteriorly in the rectouterine fold to attach to the front of the sacrum

uterovesical – pertaining to the uterus and bladder

uterus – the womb

vagina – the birth canal

vaginitis – inflammation of the vagina

varicosities – refers to the condition of varicose veins

vesicouterine – pertaining to or communicating with the urinary bladder and the uterus

vesicovaginal – pertaining to the urinary bladder and vagina

vulva – the external aspect of the female genitalia

vulvectomy – excision of the vulva

HISTORY

Patient Name: **Date:**

Doctor:

PHYSICAL

Patient Name: Date:

   Doctor:

OPERATION

Patient Name: Date:

    Doctor:

PREOP DIAG:

POSTOP DIAG:

OPERATION:

SURGEON:

ANES:

FINDINGS:

PROCEDURE:

OPERATION

Patient Name: Date:

    Doctor:

PREOPERATIVE DIAGNOSIS:

POSTOPERATIVE DIAGNOSIS:

OPERATION:

SURGEON:

PROCEDURE:

OP NOTE

Patient Name: Date:

    Doctor:

PREOP DIAGNOSIS:

POSTOP DIAGNOSIS:

SURGEON:

ANESTHESIA:

OPERATION:

OPERATIVE FINDINGS:

OP NOTE

Patient Name: Date:

     Doctor:

PREOP DIAG:

POSTOP DIAG:

PROCEDURE:

ANESTHESIA:

OPERATION

Patient Name: Date:

    Doctor:

OPERATIVE PROCEDURE:

PREOP DIAG:

POSTOP DIAG:

SURGEON:

ANESTHESIA:

COMPLICATIONS:

DRAINS:

ESTIMATED BLOOD LOSS:

DESCRIPTION OF PROCEDURE:

OP NOTE

Patient Name: Date:

    Doctor:

DATE OF SURGERY:

SURGEON:

ASSISTANT:

PREOPERATIVE DIAG:

POSTOPERATIVE DIAG:

OPERATION:

PROCEDURE:

SURGERY

Patient Name: Date:

     Doctor:

PREOP DIAG:

POSTOP DIAG:

OPERATION:

SURGEON:

ANES:

PEDIATRICIAN:

SURGERY

Patient Name: Date:

   Doctor:

PREOP DIAG:

POSTOP DIAG:

OPERATION:

SURGEON:

PROCEDURE:

CONSULTATION

Patient Name: Date:

   Doctor:

CONSULTANT:

PATIENT PROFILE:

DISCHARGE SUMMARY

Patient Name: Date:

    Doctor:

ADMITTED:
DISCHARGED:

DISCHARGE DIAGNOSIS:

OP NOTE

Patient Name: Date:

     Doctor:

PREOP DIAG:

POSTOP DIAG:

SURGEON:

ANESTHESIA:

OPERATION:

OPERATION

Patient Name: Date:

Doctor:

DATE OF SURGERY:

SURGEON:

PREOP DIAG:

POSTOP DIAG:

PROCEDURE:

ANESTHESIA:

CHAPTER 8
OPHTHALMOLOGY

The specialized field of medicine which deals with the medical and surgical disorders of the eyes, as well as the treatment thereof, is known as ophthalmology. Physicians specializing in this field are called ophthalmologists and must have an M.D. degree, of course, plus three to five years of specialized training in a hospital.

Ophthalmologists treat eye diseases, such as glaucoma, tumors, and infections. In addition, they prescribe glasses to correct visual problems such as nearsightedness, farsightedness, and other visual defects.

A distinction needs to be made between the ophthalmologist, the optometrist, and the optician. Whereas the ophthalmologist, or oculist as one is sometimes called, prescribes glasses and treats diseases of the eyes, the optometrist is skilled in measuring a patient's vision and prescribing glasses. This physician may also prescribe eye exercises to improve vision or correct visual defects.

When given the prescription by an optometrist or oculist, the optician makes and sells the proper glasses. An optometrist is usually also an optician, whereas the ophthalmologist is not.

ABBREVIATIONS

ARC	anomalous retinal correspondence
AV	arteriovenous
Em	emmetropia
EOM	extraocular movement
EPF	exophthalmos-producing factor
EPS	exophthalmos-producing substance
IOL	intraocular lens
IOP	intraocular pressure
LASER	light amplification by stimulated emission of radiation
L & A, l/a	light and accommodation
NPC	near point of convergence
NRC	normal retinal correspondence
OD, RE	right eye (oculus dexter)
OS, LE	left eye (oculus sinister)
OU	each eye (oculus uterque)
PD	prism diopter
PERLA	pupils equal and react to light and accommodation
PERRLA	pupils equal, round, and react to light and accommodation
ST	esotropia
TOD	tension of right eye
TOS	tension of left eye
TU, T	intraocular tension
VA	visual acuity
VC	acuity of color vision
VF	visual field
VOU	vision of each eye
XT	exotropia

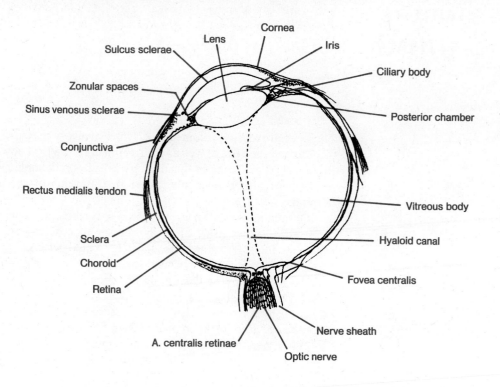

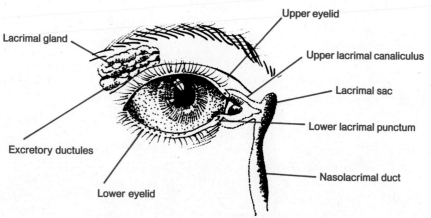

8-1   Structures of the Eye

DEFINITIONS OF TERMINOLOGY

agnosia – loss of the power to recognize the import of sensory stimuli

amaurosis – blindness, especially blindness occurring without apparent lesion of the eye, as from disease of the optic nerve, spine, or brain

amaurosis centralis – blindness due to disease of the central nervous system

amblyopia – dimness of vision without detectable organic lesion of the eye ametropia – discrepancy between the size and refractive powers of the eye, such that images are not brought to a proper focus on the retina

aniridia – absence of the iris

aniseikonia – a condition in which the ocular image of an object as seen by one eye differs in size and shape from that seen by the other

anisocoria – inequality of the pupils in diameter

anisometropia – a difference in the refractive power of the two eyes

ankyloblepharon – the adhesion of the ciliary edges of the eyelid to each other

anophthalmia – a developmental defect characterized by complete absence of the eyes (rare) or by the presence of vestigial eyes

aphakia – absence of the lens of the eye; it may occur congenitally or from trauma but is most commonly caused by extraction of a cataract

aphakic – pertaining to aphakia; having no lens in the eye

arcus lipiodes corneae – a crescentic deposit of fat and cholesterol crystals in the cornea

Argyll-Robertson pupil – a pupil that is miotic and which responds to accommodation effort, but not to light

asthenopia – weakness or easy fatigue of the visual organs, attended by pain in the eyes, headache, dimness of vision, etc.

Barraquer's operation (phacoerysis) – removal of the lens in cataract by means of suction with an instrument known as an erysiphake

binocular – pertaining to both eyes

Bitot's spots – superficial, foamy gray, triangular spots on the conjunctiva, consisting of keratinized epithelium

blepharitis – inflammation of the eyelids

blepharophimosis – abnormal narrowness of the palpebral fissures in the horizontal direction, caused by lateral displacement of the inner canthi

blepharoplegia – paralysis of an eyelid

blepharorrhaphy – the operation of suturing the eyelids together

buphthalmos – enlargement and distention of the fibrous coats of the eye

canthectomy – surgical removal of a canthus

cantholysis – surgical division of the canthus of an eye or of a canthal ligament

canthorrhaphy – the suturing of the palpebral fissure at either canthus

canthotomy – surgical division of the outer canthus

cataract, cerulean – blue cataract

cataract, intumescent – a cataract in which the lens is swollen and opaque

chalazion – an eyelid mass that results from chronic inflammation of a meibomian gland

chloropsia – a visual defect in which all objects seen appear to have a greenish tinge chorioretinal – pertaining to the choroid and retina

choroid – the middle coat of the eyeball (like a membrane)

choroidea – the choroid

choroideremia – hereditary primary choroidal degeneration

choroiditis – inflammation of the choroid

choroidocyclitis – inflammation of the choroid and ciliary processes

chromatopsia – a visual defect in which colorless objects appear to be tinged with color

ciliectomy – excision of a portion of the ciliary margin of the eyelid and the roots of the lashes

Cloquet's canal – a passage running from in front of the optic disk to the lens of the eye

coloboma – an apparent absence or defect of some ocular tissue, usually resulting from a failure of a part of the fetal fissure to close

conjunctivitis – inflammation of the conjunctiva

conjunctivoplasty – repair of a defect of the conjunctiva by plastic operation

corectopia – abnormal situation of the pupil

corneal abscission – excision of the prominence of the cornea in staphyloma

corneoiritis – inflammation of the cornea and iris

corneosclera – the cornea and sclera regarded as forming one organ

cryophake (no definition given)

cryptophthalmos – a developmental anomaly in which the skin is continuous over the eyeballs without any indication of the formation of eyelids

cyclectomy – excision of a portion of the ciliary border of the eyelid

cyclochoroiditis – inflammation of the choroid and ciliary body

cyclodiathermy – destruction of a portion of the ciliary body by diathermy; employed as therapy in cases of glaucoma

dacryoadenectomy – excision of a lacrimal gland

dacryoadenitis – inflammation of a lacrimal gland

dacryocystectomy – excision of the wall of the lacrimal sac

dacryocystoptosis – prolapse or downward displacement of the lacrimal sac

dacryocystorhinostomy – surgical creation of a communication between the lacrimal sac and the nasal cavity

dacryops – a watery state of the eye

Dalrymple's disease (cyclokeratitis) – inflammation of the cornea and ciliary body

diopsimeter – a device for measuring the field of vision

diplopia – the perception of two images of a single object

discission – the surgical rupturing of the capsule so that the aqueous humor may gain access to the lens of the eye

distichia – the presence of a double row of eyelashes on an eyelid, one or both of which are turned in against the eyeball

dysmegalopsia – a disturbance of the visual appreciation of the size of objects, in which they appear larger than they are

dysopia – defective vision

eikonometer – an instrument used in making examination for aniseikonia

Elschnig's bodies – clear grapelike clusters formed by proliferation of epithelial cells after extracapsular extraction of a cataractous lens

embryotoxon – a ringlike opacity of the margin of the cornea

emmetropia – the normal condition of the eye as far as refraction is concerned

endophthalmitis – inflammation involving the ocular cavities and their adjacent structures

enophthalmos – a backward displacement of the eyeball into the orbit

entropion – the turning inward of an edge or margin, as of the margin of the eyelid, with the tarsal cartilage turned inward toward the eyeball

epiphora – an abnormal overflow of tears down the cheek, mainly due to stricture of the lacrimal passages

epischleritis – inflammation of the tissues overlying the sclera

erysiphake – an instrument for removing the lens in cataract by suction

erythropsia – a visual defect in which all objects appear to have a red tinge

esotropia – strabismus in which there is manifest deviation of the visual axis of an eye toward that of the other eye, resulting in diplopia

euchromatopsy – normal color vision

euryopia – abnormally wide opening of the eyes

evisceration – removal of the contents of the eyeball, with the sclera being left intact

excyclophoria – cyclophoria in which the upper pole of the vertical axis of the eye deviates away from the midline of the face and toward the temple

exophthalmometer – an instrument for measuring the amount of exophthalmos

exophthalmos – abnormal protrusion of the eyeball

fluorescein dye – the simplest of the fluorane dyes and the parent compound of eosin; used intravenously in tests to assess by its fluorescence the adequacy of the circulation

glaucoma – a group of eye diseases characterized by an increase in intraocular pressure which causes pathological changes in the optic disk and typical defects in the field of vision

goniotomy – Barkan's operation for that type of glaucoma which is characterized by an open angle and normal depth of the anterior chamber

hemeralopia – day blindness; defective vision in a bright light hemianopia – defective vision or blindness in half of the visual field

hemoglobinopathy – a hematologic disorder caused by alteration in the genetically determined molecular structure of hemoglobin

heterochromia – diversity of color in a part or parts that should normally be of one color

heterochromia iridis – difference in color in the two irides, or in different areas of the same iris

Hippel's disease – angiomatosis confined principally to the retina

*histoplasmosis

Holth's operation – excision of the sclera by punch operation

homokeratoplasty – corneal grafting with tissue derived from another individual of the same species

hordeolum – a stye

hydrophthalmos – a form of glaucoma characterized by marked enlargement and distention of the fibrous coats of the eye

hyperopia – farsightedness

hyphema – hemorrhage within the anterior chamber of the eye

hypopyon – an accumulation of pus in the anterior chamber of the eye

hypoxic – pertaining to or characterized by hypoxia, low oxygen content or tension

ianthinopsia – violet vision; a condition in which objects seem to be violet colored

iridectomize – to remove part of the iris by excision

iridectomy – surgical excision of part of the iris

iridencleisis – the surgical creation of a permanent drain by incarceration of a slip of the iris within a corneal or limbal incision to act as a wick through which the aqueous is filtered from the anterior chamber to the subconjunctival tissues; done to reduce intraocular pressure

iridesis – the operation of repositioning the pupil by bringing a sector of the iris through a corneal or limbal incision and fixing the sector with a suture

iridocorneosclerectomy – surgical incision of a portion of the iris, cornea, and sclera for glaucoma

iridocyclectomy – surgical removal of a portion of the iris and of the ciliary body

iridocyclitis – inflammation of the iris and of the ciliary body

iridodonesis – abnormal tremulousness of the iris on movements of the eye, occurring in subluxation of the lens, depriving the iris of this support

*These terms were used in dictation but were not located in any of the references consulted. You will encounter this situation throughout this text. For a list of the reference books consulted, see page 502.

iridokeratitis – inflammation of the iris and cornea

iridoleptynsis – thinning or atrophy of the iris

iridomesodialysis – surgical loosening of adhesions around the inner edge of the iris

iridotomy – incision of the iris, as in creating an artificial pupil

Ishihara's test – a test for color vision made by the use of a series of plates composed of round dots of various sizes and colors

isopia – equality of vision in the two eyes

keratectasia – protrusion of a thinned, scarred cornea

keratoconjunctivitis – inflammation of the cornea and conjunctiva

keratoiritis – inflammation of the cornea and iris

keratoleptynsis – removal of the anterior portion of the cornea and covering of the denuded area with bulbar conjunctiva

keratometry – the measurement of the cornea, made by an instrument called a keratometer, which measures the curve of the cornea

keratopathy – a noninflammatory disease of the cornea

kerectomy – surgical removal of a part of the cornea

lagophthalmos – inability to close the eyelids

lenticulo-optic – pertaining to the lenticular nucleus and the optic thalamus

lenticulothalamic – relating to the lenticular nucleus and the thalamus

leukokoria – a condition characterized by appearance of a whitish reflex or mass in the pupillary area back of the lens

levator palpebrae muscle – a muscle that raises the upper eyelid

lipemia retinalis – a high level of lipids in the blood, manifested by a milky appearance of the veins and arteries of the retina

megalophthalmos – abnormally large size of the eyes

meibomianitis – inflammation of the meibomian glands

metamorphopsia – a disturbance of vision in which objects are seen as distorted in shape

microphthalmia – abnormal smallness of the eyes

miosis – abnormal contraction of the pupil

myope – a nearsighted person; one affected with myopia

myopia – nearsightedness

neovascularization (no definition given)

nyctalopia – night blindness

oculopathy – any morbid condition of the eyes

*ocutome

ophthalmodynamometer – an instrument for measuring the retinal arterial pressure ophthalmodynamometry – determination of the retinal arterial pressure

ophthalmodynia – pain in the eye

ophthalmoplegia – inability to move the eye

ophthalmosteresis – loss of an eye

ophthalmotropometer – an instrument for measuring eye movements

pachyblepharon – a thickening of the eyelid, chiefly near the border

panophthalmitis – inflammation of all the structures or tissues of the eyes

perimetry – determination of the extent of the peripheral visual field by use of a perimeter

periotomy (no definition given)

phacoemulsification (no definition given)

phlyctena – a small vesicle containing lymph seen on the conjunctiva in certain conditions

phlyctenule – a small vesicle, or an ulcerated nodule of the cornea or of the conjunctiva

photo-ophthalmia – ophthalmia caused by intense light, such as electric light, rays of welding arc, or reflection from snow

photocoagulation (laser treatment) – condensation of protein material by the controlled use of light rays

phthisis bulbi – shrinkage and wasting of the eyeball

phthisis corneae – the shriveling and disappearance of the cornea after suppurative keratitis

pinguecula – a yellowish spot of proliferation on the bulbar conjunctiva near the sclerocorneal junction, usually on the nasal side

plica semilunaris conjunctivae – a fold of mucous membrane at the medial angle of the eye

proptosis – a forward displacement or bulging, especially of the eye

Purkinje-Sanson images – reflected images formed on the anterior surface of the cornea and the anterior and posterior surfaces of the crystalline lens

retinochoroiditis – inflammation of the retina and choroid

retinopathy – any noninflammatory disease of the retina

retrobulbar – behind the eyeball

rhinommectomy – excision of the inner canthus of the eye

Schiotz's tonometer – an instrument that registers intraocular pressure by direct application to the cornea

sclerectoiridectomy – the operation of excision of a portion of the sclera and of the iris for glaucoma

scleriasis – a hardened state of an eyelid

scleriritomy – incision of the sclera and iris in anterior staphyloma

scleritis – inflammation of the sclera

scleronyxis (scleroticopuncture) – surgical puncture of the sclera

scleroticectomy (sclerectomy) – excision of the sclera by scissors, by punch, or by trephining

scotoma – an area of depressed vision within the visual field, surrounded by an area of less depressed or of normal vision

sphincterectomy – excision of any sphincter, such as the sphincter iridis

Stellwag's sign – retraction of the upper eyelids producing apparent widening of the palpebral opening with which is associated infrequent and incomplete blinking

stigmatism – the condition due to or marked by stigmas

strabismus – deviation of the eye which the patient cannot overcome

stye – hordeolum; a localized, purulent, inflammatory staphylococcal infection of one or more sebaceous glands of the eyelids

symblepharon – an adhesion between the tarsal conjunctiva and the bulbar conjunctiva

synchysis – a softening or fluid condition of the vitreous body of the eye

synechia – adhesion of parts, especially adhesion of the iris to the cornea or to the lens

teichopsia – the sensation of a luminous appearance before the eyes, with a zigzag, wall-like outline

torulus – a small elevation; a papilla

trichiasis – the condition of ingrowing eyelashes

ulectomy – excision of scar tissue; i.e., in secondary iridectomy

uvea – the iris, ciliary body, and choroid considered together

Van Lint akinesia – a type of seventh nerve block, by local anesthetic, to stop the patient from closing the lids during an operation

vitrectomy – excision of the vitreous body

vitreous – glasslike or hyaline; often used alone to designate the vitreous body of the eye

Weiss procedure – blepharoplasty

xanthelasma – the commonest form of xanthoma affecting the eyelids and characterized by soft yellowish spots or plaques

xanthoma – a papule, nodule, or plaque of yellow color in the skin, due to deposits of lipids

xerophthalmia – dryness of the conjunctiva and cornea due to vitamin A deficiency

OUTPATIENT SURGERY

Patient Name: Date:

   Doctor:

PREOP DIAG:

POSTOP DIAG:

OPERATION:

ANES:

PROCEDURE:

OPERATION

Patient Name: Date:

  Doctor:

PREOP DIAG:

POSTOP DIAG:

OPERATION:

SURGEON: ASSISTANT:

PROCEDURE:

Transcription Exercise #3 is material for a speech and is to be typed on plain paper.

CHAPTER 9
ORTHOPEDICS

Orthopedics is that branch of medicine which is concerned with the preservation and restoration of the function of the skeletal system and the treatment of muscular and skeletal diseases, such as poliomyelitis and muscular dystrophy. Disorders of vertebral discs, fractures, and the correction of deformities are also concerns of orthopedics.

The human body is made up of about 40 to 50 percent muscle and 206 bones. The spinal column consists of seven cervical, twelve thoracic, and five lumbar vertebrae. The sacrum is one fused vertebra, and the coccyx is the last bone in the vertebral column.

The muscles are connected to the bones, ligaments, cartilage, and skin either directly or through the intervention of fibrous structures called tendons or fasciae, sometimes called aponeuroses.

An orthopedic surgeon is a physician who treats surgical disorders of the musculoskeletal system, which includes the joints, tendons, ligaments, tissues, muscles, and bones that support and form the human skeleton.

ABBREVIATIONS

AE	above elbow	IPJ	interphalangeal joint
AK	above knee		
AP	anteroposterior	KB	knee bearing
Arth.	arthrotomy	KD	knee disarticulation
		LOM	limitation of motion
BE	below elbow		
BK	below knee	MPJ	metacarpophalangeal joint
DIP	distal interphalangeal joint	ORIF	open reduction and internal fixation
DP	dorsalis pedis	orth	orthopedics
Fx	fracture	PIPJ	proximal interphalangeal joint
HD	hip disarticulation	ROM	range of motion
HNP	herniated nucleus pulposus		
HP	hemipelvectomy	SD	shoulder disarticulation
		SLR	straight leg raising
IDK	internal derangement of the knee		
IM	intramuscular	THR	total hip replacement

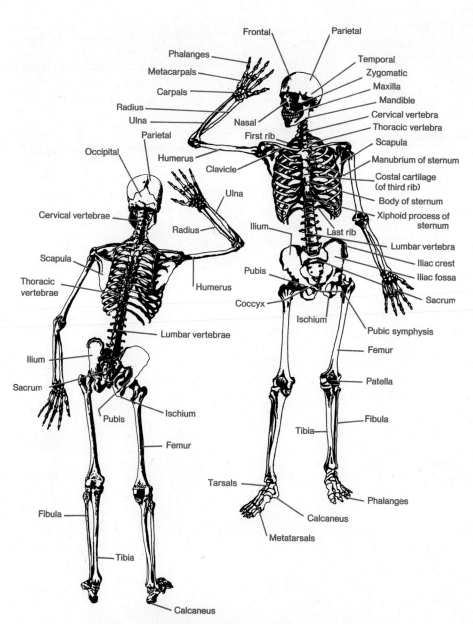

9-1 Skeletons, Front and Back Views

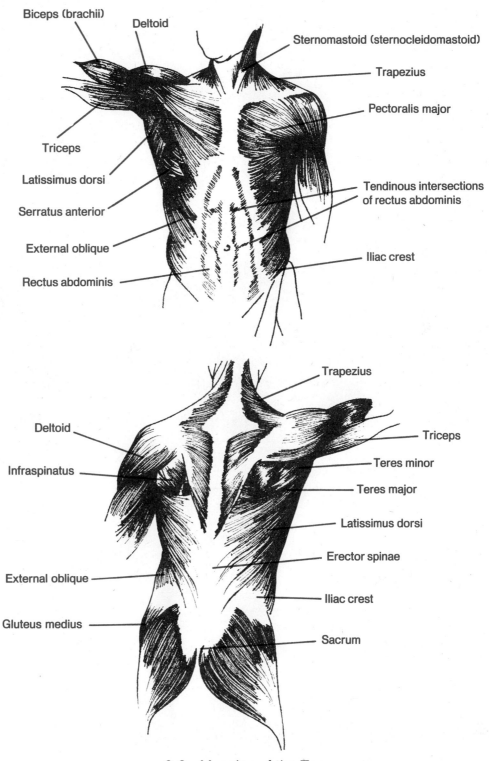

Biceps (brachii)

Deltoid

Sternomastoid (sternocleidomastoid)

Trapezius

Pectoralis major

Triceps

Latissimus dorsi

Serratus anterior

External oblique

Rectus abdominis

Tendinous intersections
of rectus abdominis

Iliac crest

Trapezius

Deltoid

Triceps

Infraspinatus

Teres minor

Teres major

Latissimus dorsi

Erector spinae

External oblique

Iliac crest

Gluteus medius

Sacrum

9-2 Muscles of the Torso

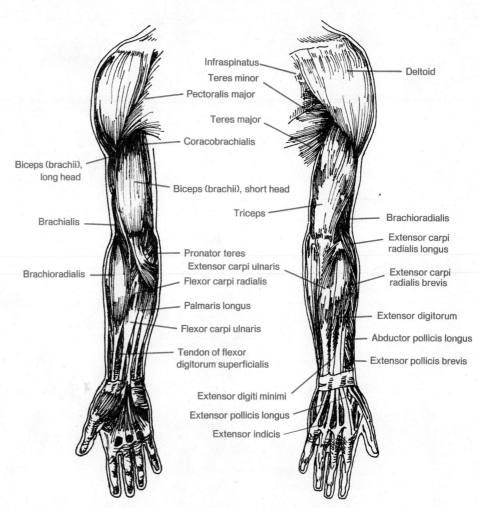

Infraspinatus

Teres minor

Pectoralis major

Teres major

Coracobrachialis

Biceps (brachii),
long head

Biceps (brachii), short head

Brachialis

Triceps

Pronator teres

Brachioradialis

Extensor carpi ulnaris

Flexor carpi radialis

Palmaris longus

Flexor carpi ulnaris

Tendon of flexor
digitorum superficialis

Extensor digiti minimi

Extensor pollicis longus

Extensor indicis

Deltoid

Brachioradialis

Extensor carpi
radialis longus

Extensor carpi
radialis brevis

Extensor digitorum

Abductor pollicis longus

Extensor pollicis brevis

9-3   Muscles of the Arm

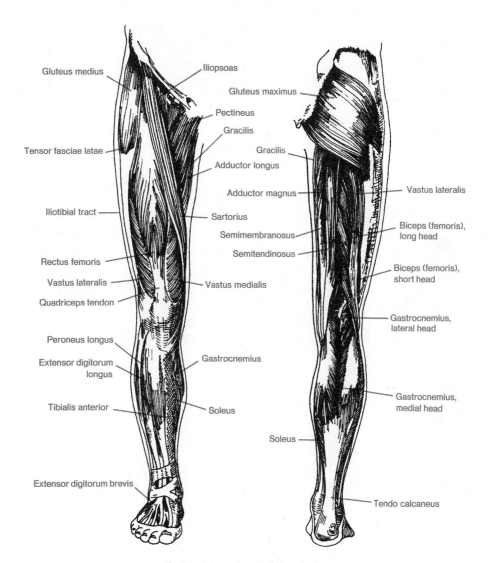

Gluteus medius

Iliopsoas

Gluteus maximus

Pectineus

Gracilis

Tensor fasciae latae

Gracilis

Adductor longus

Adductor magnus

Vastus lateralis

Iliotibial tract

Sartorius

Semimembranosus

Biceps (femoris), long head

Semitendinosus

Rectus femoris

Biceps (femoris), short head

Vastus lateralis

Vastus medialis

Quadriceps tendon

Gastrocnemius, lateral head

Peroneus longus

Extensor digitorum longus

Gastrocnemius

Gastrocnemius, medial head

Tibialis anterior

Soleus

Soleus

Extensor digitorum brevis

Tendo calcaneus

9-4 Muscles of the Leg

acetabulum – a cup-shaped bony recess in the ilium that holds the head of the femur

achondroplasia – a hereditary, congenital disturbance of epiphyseal chondro-blastic growth and maturation, causing inadequate enchondral bone forma-tion and resulting in a peculiar form of dwarfism with short limbs, normal trunk, small face, normal vault, lordosis, and trident hand

acromial – pertaining to the lateral extension of the spine of the scapula, projecting over the shoulder joint and forming the highest point of the shoulder

acromioclavicular – pertaining to the acromion and clavicle, especially to the articulation between the acromion and clavicle

ankylosing spondylitis – the form of rheumatoid arthritis that affects the spine

ankylosis – the fusion of two or more bones at a joint

aponeurosis – the end of a muscle where it becomes a tendon

arthroclasia – the surgical breaking down of an ankylosis in order to secure free movement in a joint

arthrodesis – the surgical fixation of a joint by a procedure designed to accomplish fusion of the joint surfaces by promoting the proliferation of bone cells

arthrogryposis – persistent flexure or contracture of a joint

arthroscopy – examination of the interior of a joint with an arthroscope

arytenoidectomy – surgical removal of an arytenoid cartilage

astragalus – the ankle bone (talus)

brachiocrural – pertaining to the arm and leg

brachium – the arm; specifically the arm from the shoulder to elbow

bunionectomy – excision of an abnormal prominence on the mesial aspect of the great toe

bursa – a sac or saclike cavity filled with a viscid fluid and situated at places in the tissues at which friction would otherwise develop

bursae – small, fluid-filled sacs which are located between the bone and moving tissue

bursitis – inflammation of a bursa wall or its contents

calcaneoapophysitis – an affection of the posterior part of the calcaneus marked by pain at the point of insertion of the Achilles tendon, with swelling of the soft parts

calcaneocavus – clubfoot in which talipes calcaneus is combined with talipes cavus

calcification – the process by which organic tissue becomes hardened by a deposit of calcium salts within its substance

callosity – a callus

callus – an unorganized meshwork of woven bone developed on the pattern of the original fibrin clot, which is formed following fracture of a bone and is normally ultimately replaced by hard adult bone

calvaria – the domelike superior portion of the cranium

cancellus – any structure arranged like a lattice

capitellum – an eminence on the distal end of the lateral epicondyle of the humerus for articulation with the head of the radius

capsuloplasty – a plastic operation on a joint capsule

carpometacarpal – pertaining to the carpus and metacarpus

carponavicular (no definition given)

chemonucleolysis – the enzymatic dissolution of the nucleus pulposus by injection of chymopapain; this procedure is used in the treatment of intervertebral disc lesions

chondrochondral (no definition given)

chondrolysis – the degeneration of cartilage cells that occurs in the process of intracartilaginous ossification

chondromalacia – softening of the articular cartilage, most frequently in the patella

Chvostek's symptom – the test for lack of calcium in children

chymopapain – an enzyme from the latex of a chiefly tropical tree

clavicle – the collarbone

clinoid – resembling a bed; bed-shaped, as the clinoid process

coccydynia (coccygodynia) – pain in the coccyx and neighboring region

coccyx – the terminal bony complex of the caudal end of the vertebral column composed of three to five fused bones

condyle – a rounded projection on a bone

coracoacromial – pertaining to the coracoid and acromion processes

coracoclavicular – pertaining to the coracoid process and the clavicle

coracoid – the coracoid process; a strong curved process that arises from the upper part of the neck of the scapula and overhangs the shoulder joint

costovertebral – pertaining to a rib and a vertebra

coxalgia – hip-joint disease; pain in the hip

crepitation – the noise made by rubbing together the ends of a fractured bone

deossification – loss of or removal of the mineral elements of bone

diaphyseal – pertaining to or affecting the shaft of a long bone

diaphysis – the long, narrow shaft of the bone

diastasis – a form of dislocation in which there is separation of two bones normally attached to each other without the existence of a true joint; as in separation of the pubic symphysis discogram (diskogram) – an x-ray of the intervertebral disc

dorsolumbar – pertaining to the back and the loins

dorsoradial – pertaining to the radial or outer side of the back of the forearm or hand

Dupuytren's contracture – shortening, thickening, and fibrosis of the palmar fascia, producing a flexion deformity of a finger

dysostosis – defective ossification; defect in the normal ossification of fetal cartilages

enarthrosis – a joint in which the globular head of one bone is received into a socket in another, as in the hip joint

enchondromatosis – a condition characterized by hamartomatous proliferation of cartilage cells within the metaphysis of several bones, causing thinning of the overlying cortex and distortion of the growth in length

endosteum – the tissue lining the inner surfaces of bone

epicondyle – an eminence upon a bone, above its condyle

epiphyseal – pertaining to or of the nature of an epiphysis

epiphysiodesis – the operation of fixing a separated epiphysis to its diaphysis to produce healing and fusion of the epiphyseal plate

epiphysis (es) – the knoblike end of a long bone

epiphysitis – inflammation of an epiphysis or of the cartilage that separates it from the main bone

epitroclea – the inner condyle of the humerus

exarticulation – amputation at a joint; removal of a portion of a joint

exostosis – a benign bony growth projecting outward from the surface of a bone, characteristically capped by cartilage

facetectomy – excision of the articular facet of a vertebra

fasciculation – the formation of a small bundle of nerve, muscle, or tendon fibers

fasciodesis – the operation of suturing a fascia to skeletal attachment

fasciotomy – a surgical incision or transection of fascia

fenestra – a general term for an opening or open area

foramen – a natural opening or passage, especially one into or through a bone

genu valgum – a deformity in which the knees are abnormally close together and the space between the ankles is increased; known also as knock knee

glenohumeral – pertaining to the glenoid cavity and to the humerus

glenoid – resembling a pit or socket

hallux – the great toe, or first digit of the foot

hallux valgus – everted foot; displacement of the great toe toward the other toes

hemarthrosis – extravasation of blood into a joint or its synovial cavity

humeroradial – pertaining to the humerus and the radius

humeroscapular – pertaining to the humerus and the scapula

humerus – the bone that reaches from the shoulder to elbow

hydrarthrosis – an accumulation of watery fluid in the cavity of a joint

iliotibial – pertaining to or extending between the ilium and tibia

ilium – the expansive superior portion of the hip bone

infraspinous – beneath the spine of the scapula

innominate – nameless

interosseous – between bones

intertrochanteric – situated in or pertaining to the space between the greater and the lesser trochanter

intervertebral disc – the fibrocartilaginous disc between each vertebra

intramedullary – within the spinal cord

ischiopubic – pertaining to the ischium and pubis

ischium – the inferior dorsal part of the hip bone

kyphoscoliosis – backward and lateral curvature of the spinal column, as in vertebral osteochondrosis

kyphosis – hunchback

lamella(ae) – a thin leaf or plate, as of bone

laminectomy – excision of the posterior arch of a vertebra

latissimus – a general term denoting a broad structure, as a muscle

lordosis – a condition in which the lower portion of the spinal column is bowed forward

*Magnuson-Stack procedure

malleolus(li) – a rounded process, such as the protuberance on each side of the ankle joint

Marie-Strumpell disease – rheumatoid spondylitis

McMurray's test – test for cartilage injury

meniscectomy – removal of the meniscus

meniscus(ci) – a disc of fibrocartilage found in certain joints

metaphysis – the wider part at the extremity of the shaft of a long bone, adjacent to the epiphyseal disc

myalgia – pain in a muscle

myasthenia – muscular debility

myelomeningocele – hernial protrusion of the cord and its meninges through a defect in the vertebral canal

---

*These terms were used in dictation but were not located in any of the references consulted. You will encounter this situation throughout this text. For a list of the reference books consulted, see page 502.

myesthesia – muscle sensibility

myositis ossificans – a condition in which the healing lesion creates new bone formed in the muscle; this may occur as the result of repeated injury or severe injury to a muscle

navicular – boat-shaped, as the navicular bone (one of the wrist bones)

olecranon – the proximal bony projection of the ulna at the elbow

os calcis – alternative of calcaneus (the irregular quadrangular bone at the back of the tarsus)

osseous – of the nature or quality of bone; bony

ossific – forming or becoming bone

ossification – the conversion of muscle into a bony substance

osteitis – inflammation of bone

osteoarthritis – a degenerative, inflammatory disease of joint; involving the cartilage, membranes, and bones

osteoarthrosis – chronic arthritis of noninflammatory character

osteoarthrotomy (ostearthrotomy) – excision of an articular end of a bone

osteochondritis – inflammation of both bone and cartilage

osteoclasia – the absorption and destruction of bony tissue

osteodystrophy – defective bone formation

osteomyelitis – inflammation of bone and bone marrow usually caused by a pus-forming bacteria

osteophyte – a bony outgrowth

osteoplasty – plastic surgery on bones

osteoporosis – a disease characterized by an abnormal absorption of bone

osteotomy – cutting or transecting bone

Paget's disease (osteitis deformans) – a degenerative disease of bone, cause unknown, with associated inflammation and resultant deformity

patella – the knee cap

perichondrium – the layer of dense fibrous connective tissue which invests all cartilage except the articular cartilage of synovial joints

periosteum – a tough fibrous membrane that covers the outside of the diaphysis

Perthes' disease – osteochondrosis of the capital femoral epiphysis

phalanx(ges) – a general term for any bone of the finger or toe

plantar – pertaining to the sole of the foot

polydactylism (polydactyly) – a developmental anomaly characterized by the presence of supernumerary fingers or toes on the hands or feet

polymyositis – inflammation of several or many muscles at once

porosis – the formation of the callus in the repair of a fractured bone porotic – pertaining to or characterized by porosis favoring the growth of connective tissue

pseudoarthrosis (pseudarthrosis) – a false joint

psoas – a muscle in the back wall of the abdomen

rachitis – inflammatory disease of the vertebral column

rhabdomyoma – a benign tumor of striated muscle

*Richard's Lag Screw

sarcolemma – the delicate plasma membrane which invests every striated muscle fiber

scaphoid – shaped like a boat; used especially in reference to the most lateral bone in the proximal row of carpal bones

Scheuermann's disease (kyphosis) – osteochondrosis of vertebral epiphyses in juveniles

sciatic notch – pertaining to or located near the ischium

sciatica – a syndrome characterized by pain radiating from the back into the buttock and into the lower extremity along its posterior or lateral aspect; the term is also used to refer to pain anywhere along the course of the sciatic nerve

sclerosing – causing or undergoing sclerosis

sclerotic – hard, or hardening; affected with sclerosis

scoliosis – a lateral or sideways curvature of the spinal column

sequestrectomy – surgical removal of dead bone

sequestrum – a piece of dead bone that has become separated during the process of necrosis from the sound bone

sesamoid – denoting a small nodular bone embedded in a tendon or joint capsule

sphenoid – designating a very irregular wedge-shaped bone at the base of the skull

spina bifida – a developmental anomaly characterized by defective closure of the bony encasement of the spinal cord through which the cord and meninges may or may not protrude

spondylitis – inflammation of the vertebrae

spondylitis rhizomelica (rheumatoid spondylitis) – the form of rheumatoid arthritis that affects the spine

spondylodesis – the operation of fusing vertebrae

spondylolisthesis – forward subluxation of the body of one of the lower lumbar vertebrae on the vertebra below it or on the sacrum

subluxation – an incomplete luxation or dislocation

subtrochanteric – situated below a trochanter

supracondylar – situated above a condyle or condyles

supraspinous – situated above a spine or a spinous process

symphysis joint – permits slight movement

synchondrosis – a type of cartilaginous joint that is usually temporary, the intervening hyaline cartilage ordinarily being converted into bone before adult life

syndactylia (syndactyly) – the most common congenital anomaly of the hand, marked by persistence of the webbing between adjacent digits so they are more or less completely attached

syndesmosis – a type of fibrous joint in which the intervening fibrous connective tissue forms an interosseous membrane or ligament

synovectomy – excision of a synovial membrane, as of that lining the capsule of the knee joint, performed in treatment of rheumatoid arthritis of the knee

synovial joints – move freely like in the jaw, elbows, fingers, etc.

synovitis – inflammation of a synovial membrane

synovium – a synovial membrane; a membrane that secretes a transparent alkaline viscid fluid, resembling the white of an egg

talipes – a congenital deformity of the foot, which is twisted out of shape or position

talocalcaneal – pertaining to the talus and calcaneus

tendinitis – inflammation of tendons and of tendon-muscle attachments

tendolysis – the operation of freeing a tendon from its adhesions

tenodesis – tendon fixation; suturing the end of a tendon to a bone

tenosynovitis – inflammation of a tendon sheath

tibiofibular – pertaining to the tibia and the fibula

torticollis – wryneck; a contracted state of the cervical muscles, producing twisting of the neck and an unnatural position of the head

trochanter – either of the two processes below the neck of the femur

trochlea(ae) – a pulley-shaped part or structure

tuberosity – an elevation or a protuberance

valgus – bent outward, twisted; the term is an adjective and should be used only with the noun it describes, as talipes valgus, genu valgum, etc.

varus – bent inward; the term is an adjective and should be used only with the noun it describes, as talipes varus, genu varum, etc.

vertebra(ae) – any of the 33 bones of the spinal column

xiphoid process – the pointed bottom part of the sternum or breastbone

OPERATION

Patient Name: Date:

    Doctor:

PREOP DIAGNOSIS:

POSTOP DIAGNOSIS:

PROCEDURE:

OPERATION

Patient Name:

Doctor:

DATE:

PREOP DIAG:

POSTOP DIAG:

SURGEON:

ASSISTANT:

OPERATION PERFORMED:

PROCEDURE:

SURGERY

Patient Name: Date:

    Doctor:

SURGEON:

ANESTHESIA:

PREOP DIAGNOSIS:

POSTOP DIAGNOSIS:

OPERATION:

PROCEDURE:

SURGERY

Patient Name: Date:

    Doctor:

PREOP DIAG:

POSTOP DIAG:

OPERATION:

SURGEON:

ASST:

ANES:

DRAINS:

BLOOD LOSS:

PROCEDURE:

SURGERY

Patient Name: Date:

Doctor:

PREOP DIAG:

POSTOP DIAG:

OPERATION:

PROCEDURE:

DISCHARGE SUMMARY

Patient Name: Date:

    Doctor:

Admitted:
Discharged:

DISCHARGE DIAG:

OPERATION:

SURGERY

Patient Name: Date:

    Doctor:

OPERATION:

PREOP DIAGNOSIS:

POSTOP DIAGNOSIS:

SURGEON:

ANESTHESIA:

PROCEDURE:

OPERATION

Patient Name:

Doctor:

DATE:

PREOP DIAG:

POSTOP DIAG:

OPERATIVE PROCEDURES:

SURGEON:

ASSISTANT:

ANESTHESIA:

DRAINS: BLOOD LOSS:

PROCEDURE:

OPERATION

Patient Name: Date:

    Doctor:

PREOP DIAG:

POSTOP DIAG:

OPERATIVE PROCEDURE:

SURGEON: ASSISTANT:

DRAINS: BLOOD LOSS:

ANESTHESIA:

PROCEDURE:

OPERATION

Patient Name:

Doctor:

DATE:

PREOP DIAG:

POSTOP DIAG:

OPERATIVE PROCEDURE:

SURGEON:

ASSISTANT:

ANESTHESIA:

DRAINS: BLOOD LOSS:

PROCEDURE:

DISCHARGE SUMMARY

Patient Name: Date:

    Doctor:

ADMITTED:
DISCHARGED:

DIAGNOSIS:

OPERATION:

COMPLICATIONS:

SPECIAL PROC:

OPERATION

Patient Name:

    Doctor:

DATE:

PREOP DIAG:

POSTOP DIAG:

OPERATION PERFORMED:

SURGEON:

ASSISTANT:

PROCEDURE:

OPERATION

Patient Name:

Doctor:

DATE:

PREOP DIAG:

POSTOP DIAG:

OPERATIVE PROCEDURE:

SURGEON:

ASSISTANT:

ANESTHESIA:

DRAINS: BLOOD LOSS:

PROCEDURE:

CHAPTER 10
OTORHINOLARYNGOLOGY

The three medical specialties of otology, rhinology, and laryngology refer to the structure, function, and diseases of the ears, nose, and throat respectively and are usually practiced together.

An otologist is a physician who is concerned with the medical and surgical diagnoses of the diseases of the ear, which is composed of three basic parts—the external ear or the pinna, the middle ear or tympanic cavity, and the internal ear or the labyrinth.

A rhinologist is a doctor who treats the nose and its diseases. The three basic parts of the nose are the external nose, the internal nose, and the sinuses, which are the openings that appear in the interior of the nose and occur in pairs, one for each side of the face. They are known as the maxillary, frontal, ethmoid, and sphenoid sinuses.

A physician who studies the throat and the tracheobronchial tree is called a laryngologist. What lay people call the throat is referred to by medical people as the pharynx and is composed of three natural divisions—the nasopharynx, the oropharynx, and the laryngopharynx (hypopharynx).

Physicians who are concerned with the medical and surgical diagnoses of diseases of all three divisions—ears, nose, and throat—are known as otorhinolaryngologists.

ABBREVIATIONS

AC	air conduction		PND	postnasal drip
AD	right ear		PORP	partial ossicular replacement prosthesis
AS	left ear			
BC	bone conduction		SAL	sensory acuity level
BOM	bilateral otitis media		SD	septal defect/speech discrimination
			SISI	short increment sensitivity index
ENG	electronystagmograph		SMR	submucous resection
ENT	ears, nose, throat		SOM	serous otitis media
ETF	eustachian tubal function		Staph	Staphylococcus
			Strep	Streptococcus
HD	hearing distance			
			T & A	tonsillectomy and adenoidectomy
IAC	internal auditory canal		TM	tympanic membrane
			TMJ	temporomandibular joint
mp	mouthpiece		TORP	total ossicular replacement prosthesis
NSR	nasal septal reconstruction		URIs	upper respiratory infections

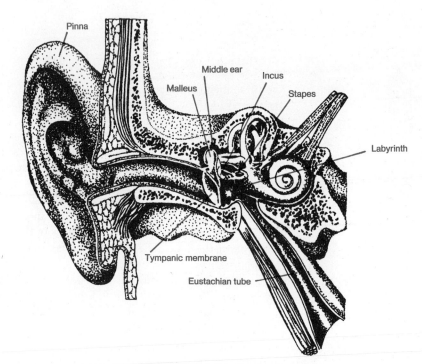

10-1   External Auditory Canal

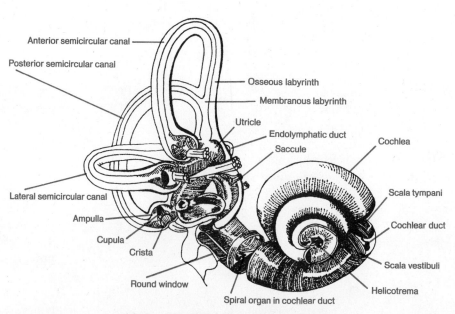

10-2   Middle and Internal Ear

adenoidectomy – removal of adenoids

aditus – a general term for the entrance or approach to an organ or a part

antrostomy – the operation of making an opening into an antrum for purposes of drainage

attic – a cavity situated on the tegmental wall of the tympanic cavity, just above the facial canal

audiogram – a test to measure hearing ability

Bellucci scissors (no definition given)

bevel incision (no definition given)

Boies elevator (no definition given)

Caldwell-Luc procedure – sinus operation

canaliculus(li) – an extremely narrow tubular passage or channel

cartilaginous – consisting of or of the nature of cartilage

cauda helicis – the termination of the posterior margin of the cartilage of the helix

cerumen – earwax

cheilectropion – eversion of the lip

cheiloschisis – hairlip

cheilosis – a condition marked by fissuring and dry scaling of the vermilion surface of the lips and angles of the mouth

cholesteatoma – a cystlike mass filled with desquamating debris frequently including cholesterol

chorda tympani nerve – a nerve originating from the facial nerve and distributed to the submandibular, sublingual, and lingual glands and the anterior two-thirds of the tongue

Chvostek's sign – a spasm of the facial muscles resulting from tapping the muscles or the branches of the facial nerve

Coakley's operation – an operation for disease of the frontal sinus by incising through the cheek, removing the anterior wall, and curetting away the mucous membrane

cochlea – the essential organ of hearing

cochleariform – shaped like a spoon

columella – a little column

commissure – a site of union of corresponding parts

concha – a structure or part that resembles a shell in shape; also called the turbinate

corniculum laryngis – a conical nodule of elastic cartilage surmounting the apex of each arytenoid cartilage coryza – head cold

Cottle tunnel (no definition given)

cricoid – the cricoid cartilage; a ringlike cartilage forming the lower and back part of the larynx

cricoidectomy – complete removal of the cricoid cartilage

cricothyroidotomy (cricothyreotomy) – incision through the cricoid and thyroid cartilages

Crow-Davis mouth gag (no definition given)

crura (pl. of crus) – general term used to designate a leglike part

decibel – a unit used to express the ratio of two powers; one decibel is equal to approximately the smallest difference in acoustic power that the human ear can detect

desensitization – a condition in which the organism does not react immunologically to a specific antigen

eardrum – the middle ear

endolymphatic – pertaining to the endolymph, the fluid contained in the membranous labyrinth of the ear

epiglottectomy (epiglottidectomy) – excision of the epiglottis

epiglottis – the lidlike cartilaginous structure overhanging the entrance to the larynx and serving to prevent food from entering the larynx and trachea while swallowing

epistaxis – nosebleed

epitympanum – the upper portion of the tympanic cavity above the tympanic membrane; it contains the head of the malleus and the body of the incus

ethmoid – cribriform; sievelike

eustachian tube (auditory tube) – a canal connecting the nasopharynx and the middle ear cavity

exanthem (exanthema) – any eruptive disease or eruptive fever

extirpated – completely removed an organ or a tissue

fenestration – the surgical creation of a new opening in the labyrinth of the ear for the restoration of hearing in cases of otosclerosis

follicular tonsillitis – an acute inflammation of the tonsils and their crypts

fronto-occipital – pertaining to the forehead and the occiput

frontoparietal – pertaining to the frontal and parietal bones

frontotemporal – pertaining to the frontal and temporal bones

furuncular otitis – pertaining to or of the nature of a furuncle or boil

geniohyoid – pertaining to the chin and hyoid bone

genyantralgia – pain in the maxillary sinus

glossoepiglottic – pertaining to the tongue and epiglottis

glossopharyngeal – pertaining to the tongue and the pharynx

glossotomy – incision of the tongue

Grommett tube (no definition given)

guillotine – an instrument for excising a tonsil or the uvula

Hartmann forceps (no definition given)

hemilaryngectomy – excision of one-half of the larynx

Hurd dissector (no definition given)

hyoid bone – a horseshoe-shaped bone situated at the base of the tongue, just above the thyroid cartilage

hyperkeratosis lacunaris – a condition in which the tonsillar crypts contain hard, firmly attached masses

hypopharynx – that division of the pharynx which lies below the upper edge of the epiglottis and opens into the larynx and esophagus

in situ – in the natural or normal place

incisura – a general term for an indention or depression, chiefly on the edge of a bone or other structure

incudostapedial – pertaining to the incus and stapes

incus – the middle of the three bones of the ear, which, with the stapes and malleus, serves to conduct vibrations from the tympanic membrane to the inner ear; also called the anvil

Jako laryngoscope (no definition given)

Kesselbach's area – the nose

La Force adenotome (no definition given)

labyrinth – a system of intercommunicating cavities or canals, especially that constituting the internal ear

labyrinthitis – inflammation of the labyrinth

landmark – a readily recognizable anatomical structure used as a point of reference in establishing the location of another structure or in determining certain measurements

laryngitis – an inflammation of the mucous membrane lining the larynx accompanied by edema of the vocal cords

laryngocentesis – surgical puncture of the larynx

laryngoparalysis – paralysis of the larynx

laryngopharyngectomy – excision of the larynx and pharynx

laryngoscopy – examination of the interior of the larynx, especially that performed with the laryngoscope

lenticular – pertaining to or shaped like a lens

lymphoepithelioma – a poorly differentiated radiosensitive squamous cell carcinoma involving lymphoid tissue of the region of the tonsils and nasopharynx

malleus – the largest of the auditory bones and the one attached to the membrana tympani; also called the hammer because of its shape

mastoiditis – infection of the middle ear which extends to the antrum and mastoid cells

membrana tympani – eardrum

Ménière's disease – deafness, tinnitus, and vertigo resulting from nonsuppurative disease of the labyrinth

mucoperichondrium (no definition given)

myasthenia gravis – a syndrome of fatigue and exhaustion of the muscular system marked by progressive paralysis of muscles without sensory disturbance or atrophy; it may affect any muscle of the body, but especially those of the face, lips, tongue, throat, and neck

myringitis – inflammation of the eardrum

myringitis bullosa – a form of viral otitis media in which serous or hemmorrhagic blebs appear on the eardrum and often on the adjacent wall of the auditory meatus

myringotomy – surgical incision of the eardrum in an area which tends to heal readily, to avoid spontaneous rupture at a site which rarely closes

naris – one of the openings of the nose

nasolacrimal – pertaining to the nose and lacrimal apparatus

nuchal – pertaining to the back of the neck

nystagmus – constant moving of the eyeballs

occipitomastoid – pertaining to the occipital bone and the mastoid process

omohyoid – pertaining to the shoulder and the hyoid bone

opisthognathism – the condition of having receding jaws

oropharynx – that division of the pharynx which lies between the soft palate and the upper edge of the epiglottis

ossicle – a small bone

otalgia – earache; pain in the ear

otitis media – inflammation of the middle ear

otorhinolaryngology – summary of knowledge regarding the ear, nose, and larynx and their diseases

otorrhagia – bleeding from the ear

otorrhea – purulent drainage from the ear

otosclerosis – a progressive condition in which the normal bone of the inner ear is replaced by abnormal osseous tissue

otospongiosis – otosclerosis

outfracture (no definition given)

palatoglossal – pertaining to the palate and tongue

palatopharyngeal – pertaining to the palate and pharynx

pansinusitis – inflammation of all the sinuses

paracentesis tympani – incision of the tympanic membrane for drainage or irrigation

parotid – situated or occurring near the ear, as the parotid gland

parotidectomy – removal of the parotid gland

parotitis – inflammation of the parotid gland

PE tube – polyethylene tube; type of tympanotomy tube

perilymphatic – pertaining to the perilymph, or around a lymphatic vessel

peritonsillar abscess – abscess near or around a tonsil; infection extends from the tonsil to form an abscess in surrounding tissue

pharyngitis – inflammation of the throat and pharynx

pharyngoplegia – paralysis of the muscles of the pharynx

phlegm – mucus secreted in abnormally large amounts, usually discharged through the mouth

pinna – the flap of the ear; also called the auricle

piriform sinus – pear-shaped sinus

polymyxin – a generic term used to designate a number of antibiotic substances derived from strains of a soil bacterium

preauricular – situated in front of the auricle of the ear

presbycusis – a progressive, bilateral hearing loss occurring with age

pseudocholesteatoma – a mass of cornified epithelial cells resembling cholesteatoma in the tympanic cavity in chronic middle ear inflammation

pterygopalatine – pertaining to a pterygoid process and to the palate bone

purulent – containing pus

pyramidal – shaped like a pyramid

rhinitis – an inflammatory condition of the mucous membranes of the nose and accessory sinuses

rhinoantritis – inflammation of the nasal cavity and the antrum of Highmore

rhinorrhea – "runny nose"

rhinoscleroma – a granulomatous disease involving the nose and nasopharynx

Rivinus, notch of – tympanic notch; a defect in the upper portion of the tympanic part of the temporal bone, between the greater and lesser tympanic spines, which is filled in by the pars flaccida of the tympanic membrane

Rosenmuller's fossa (no definition given)

Scarpa's membrane – secondary tympanic membrane

secretory otitis media – thick, cloudy, viscous exudate in the middle ear containing cells and mucous strands

sepsis – the presence in the blood or other tissues of pathogenic microorganisms or their toxins

septoplasty – plastic surgery on the nasal septum

septorhinoplasty – a combined operation to repair defects or deformities of the nasal septum and of the external nasal pyramid

serous otitis media – thin, clear, amber fluid in the middle ear

Shea holder (no definition given)

sialadenitis – inflammation of a salivary gland

Silastic tube – trademark for polymeric silicone substance having the properties of rubber; it is used in surgical prostheses

sinus tympani – a deep fossa on the medial wall of the tympanic cavity

sinusitis – inflammation of one or more of the sinuses

Sjogren's syndrome – a symptom complex of unknown etiology, usually occurring in middle-aged women, in which keratoconjunctivitis is associated with pharyngitis sicca, enlargement of the parotid glands, chronic polyarthritis, and xerostomia

sphenopalatine – pertaining to or in relation with the sphenoid and palatine bones

stapedectomy – complete removal of the stapes

stapediotenotomy – the cutting of the tendon of the stapedius muscle

stapes – the innermost of the auditory ossicles, shaped somewhat like a stirrup; also called the stirrup

staphyledema – an enlargement or swollen part of the uvula

Stensen's duct, foramen – the duct that drains the parotid gland and empties into the oral cavity opposite the second superior molar

sternohyoid muscle – depresses the hyoid bone and larynx

sternothyroid muscle – depresses thyroid cartilage

stomatomycosis – any oral disease due to a fungus

sulcus – a groove or furrow

suppurative – producing pus

temporomandibular – pertaining to the temporal bone and the mandible

tests for hearing – Bekesy, Doerfler-Stewart, Lombard, Rinne, Weber

thyromegaly – enlargement of the thyroid gland; goiter

tinnitus – a noise in the ears, as ringing, buzzing, roaring, clicking, etc.

tonsillitis – inflammation of the tonsils

tragus – the cartilaginous projection anterior to the external opening of the ear

turbinate – bone shaped like a top

tympanic membrane – eardrum; the membrane separating the external from the middle ear

tympanitis – inflammation of the eardrum

tympanoeustachian – pertaining to the tympanic cavity and auditory tube

tympanomandibular – pertaining to the middle ear and the mandible

tympanomastoiditis – inflammation of the middle ear and the pneumatic cells of the mastoid process

tympanomeatal (no definition given)

tympanoplasty – surgical reconstruction of the hearing mechanism of the middle ear

tympanotomy tube – tube inserted in the membrane tympani

tympanum – middle ear

umbo – a round projection

uvula – the soft, fleshy mass hanging from the soft palate

vallecula – the depression between the epiglottis and the root of the tongue on either side

Van Alyea irrigator (no definition given)

verrucous – rough; warty

vestibule – a space or cavity at the entrance to a canal

vomer – the unpaired flat bone that forms the inferior and posterior part of the nasal septum

zygomaticomaxillary – pertaining to the zygoma and maxilla

OP NOTE

Patient Name:

Doctor:

Date:

PREOP DIAG:

POSTOP DIAG:

SURGERY

Patient Name: Date:

    Doctor:

PREOP DIAG:

ANESTHESIA:

SURGEON:

OPERATION:

PROCEDURE:

OPERATION

Patient Name: Date:

    Doctor:

PREOP DIAG:

POSTOP DIAG:

OPERATION:

SURGEON: ANESTHESIA:

PROCEDURE:

SURGERY

Patient Name: Date:

    Doctor:

PREOP DIAG:

POSTOP DIAG:

OPERATION:

PROCEDURE:

OP NOTE

Patient Name: Date:

    Doctor:

PREOP DIAG:

POSTOP DIAG:

OPERATION:

PROCEDURE:

FORREST GENERAL MEDICAL CENTER

2201 PERSHING ROAD   HOLLYWOOD, FL 33020-7116   (305) 231-3400

SURGERY

Patient Name:

Doctor:

Date:

PREOP DIAGNOSIS:

POSTOP DIAGNOSIS:

ANESTHESIOLOGIST:

SURGEONS:

OPERATION:

PROCEDURE:

SURGERY

Patient Name: Date:

    Doctor:

PREOP DIAG:

POSTOP DIAG:

ANESTHESIA:

SURGEON:

OPERATION:

PROCEDURE:

FORREST GENERAL MEDICAL CENTER

2201 PERSHING ROAD   HOLLYWOOD, FL 33020-7116   (305) 231-3400

SURGERY

Patient Name: Date:

    Doctor:

PREOP DIAGNOSIS:

POSTOP DIAGNOSIS:

SURGEONS:

OPERATION:

PROCEDURE:

CHAPTER 11
PATHOLOGY

Pathology is a specialized branch of medicine concerned with the detailed study of any deviation from normal in anatomy or physiology.

The pathologist seeks to determine the cause of disease as well as the changes it causes in cells, tissues, organs, and the body as a whole. Additionally, the pathologist studies the form the disease may take, together with the complications which may follow. If the disease leads to the individual's death, the autopsy can then be performed by the pathologist, providing additional clues to the process and termination of the disease.

One of the methods by which a pathologist obtains tissue for examination is through the removal of specimens during surgery. Such tissue specimens are examined grossly (for structure) and, if warranted, microscopically (for tissue analysis).

A biopsy, a small piece of tissue removed for pathological examination, is widely used for detection of malignant cells.

Another aspect of the work of the pathologist is obtaining, through various means, body fluids, blood, and other materials that are either brought or sent to the lab for analysis and study.

Pathologic examinations, both gross and microscopic, at the time of autopsy are the ultimate answer in assessing tissue and organ damage to the body in establishing the cause or contributing cause of death.

ABBREVIATIONS

ABG	arterial blood gas		GGTP	gamma-glutamyl transpeptidase
ACTH	adrenocorticotropic hormone		GTM	glucose tolerance meal
AFB	acid-fast bacilli		GTT	glucose tolerance test
A/G	albumin-globulin ratio			
AHT	antihyalurindase titer		HAA	hepatitis associated antigen
ANF	antinuclear fluorescent antibodies		HBD	hydroxybutyrate dehydrogenase
ASLO	antistreptolysin-O		HCG	human chorionic gonadotropin
			Hct	hematocrit
BX	biopsy		Hgb,Hb	hemoglobin
			HIAA	hydroxyindoleacetic acid
CPK	creatine phosphokinase		HNP	herniated nucleus pulposus
			hpf	high power field
E. coli	Escherichia coli			
			IgG	gamma G immunoglobulin
FAN	fluorescent antinuclear antibodies			
FBS	fasting blood sugar		LDH	lactic dehydrogenase
FS	frozen section		LFT	liver function test
FSH	follicle-stimulating hormone			
FTA	fluorescent treponemal antibody		MCH	mean corpuscular hemoglobin

MCHC	mean corpuscular hemoglobin concentration	SMAC	sequential multiple analysis computerized
MCV	mean corpuscular volume	SP GR	specific gravity
		SSKI	saturated solution of potassium iodide
OCP	ova, cysts, parasites		
		STS	serologic test for syphilis
PKU	phenylketonuria		
PPD	paraphenylenediamine purified protein derivative	TSH	thyroid-stimulating hormone
PPLO	pleuropneumonia-like organism	UCG	urinary chorionic gonadotropin
QNS	quantity not sufficient	VDRL	Venereal Disease Research Laboratories
RIA	radioimmunoassay	VMA	vanillylmandelic acid

DEFINITIONS OF TERMINOLOGY

achromia – absence of normal color; specifically, a condition of the red cells of the blood in which the centers of the cells are paler than normal

acinus – a general term used to designate a small saclike dilatation, particularly one found in various glands

adamantinoma – a benign tumor arising from cells that resemble the enamel cells of the teeth; it occurs most frequently in the jaws and tibia

adenoacanthoma – an adenocarcinoma in which some or the majority of the cells exhibit squamous differentiation

aleukemic – marked by aleukemia, the absence or deficiency of leukocytes in the blood

aleukocytic – showing no leukocytes

amelanotic – containing no melanin; unpigmented

amitotic – of the nature of amitosis; not occurring by mitosis

anisocytosis – presence in the blood of erythrocytes showing excessive variation in size

anisotropic – having unlike properties in different directions, as in any unit lacking spherical symmetry

anoxic – characterized by absence or lack of oxygen

apocrine – denoting that type of glandular secretion in which the free end or apical portion of the secreting cell is cast off along with the secretory products that have accumulated therein

argentaffinoma – carcinoid; a tumor of the gastroenteric tract formed from the argentaffin cells found in the enteric canal

Armanni-Ebstein changes – intercellular glycogen vacuolization of the distal loops of Henle; occurs in diabetes mellitus

arrector pili muscle – a muscle located in the dermis next to the pilosebaceous apparatus

arrhenoblastoma – a neoplasm of the ovary, arising from the ovarian stroma

arteriolonephrosclerosis – arteriolar nephrosclerosis

artifact – any change in tissue structure made accidentally while preparing a specimen

Askanazy cells – follicular cells of the thyroid that show increased eosinophilia and nuclear enlargement

astrup – an instrument designed to determine the pH of the blood and with it partial carbon dioxide and bicarbonates of the blood

atypia – deviation from normal in morphology

Auer's bodies – elongated bacteria-like inclusions found in the cytoplasm of myeloblasts, myelocytes, monoblasts, and granular histiocytes; they are thought to be nucleoprotein material

autolysis – the spontaneous disintegration of tissues or of cells by the action of their own autogenous enzymes, such as occurs after death and in some pathological conditions

autolyze – to undergo or to cause to undergo autolysis

Autotechnicon – an instrument in which selected tissue sections are successively passed through different solutions by a timed mechanism in preparation for sectioning, staining, and mounting in microscopic slides

azure eosin – a stain for chromaffin

azurophilic – staining well with blue aniline dyes

Bacteroides – a genus of nonsporulating obligate anaerobic filamentous bacteria occurring as normal flora in the mouth and large bowel; often found in necrotic tissue, probably as secondary invaders

basophilic – staining readily with basic dyes

Bielschowsky's stain – a silver stain for demonstrating axons and neurofibrils

Boeck's sarcoid – a nonmalignant, granulomatous disease with an unknown cause that affects mainly the lungs, skin, and bone

bosselation – a small eminence

Bouin's solution – a fixative solution for tissue which is especially good for skin and other tissue in which cellular detail is important

Breus' mole – a malformation of the ovum consisting of tuberous subchorional hematoma of the decidua

Brill-Symmers disease – a form of malignant lymphosarcoma occurring in lymph nodes and giving rise to large germinal centers

bulla – a large vesicle, usually 2 cm or more in diameter

calcospherite – one of the small globular bodies formed during the process of calcification

Call-Exner bodies – the accumulations of densely staining material that appear among granulosa cells in maturing ovarian follicles and that may be intracellular precursors of follicular fluid

*calor mortis

calvarium – the calvaria, the domelike superior portion of the cranium

carbolfuchsin stain – a stain for acid-fast bacteria

carcinoma en cuirasse – term used when the skin is thickened and immovable because of cancer of the breast

carneous – fleshy or meatlike

caseation – becoming like cheese; a coagulation necrosis of tissue

celloidin – a material used for embedding specimens

centrilobular – pertaining to the central portion of a lobule

cholesterolosis (cholesterosis) – a condition in which cholesterol is deposited in tissues in abnormal quantities

chondromyxofibroma – a benign connective tissue tumor in which there are cartilage cells, fibrocytes, and a degenerated granular material spoken of as myxoid tissue

chordae tendineae – cordlike structures extending from the margins of the leaflets of the mitral and tricuspid valves to the papillary muscles in the walls of the ventricles

chordoma – a malignant tumor arising from the embryonic remains of the notochord

chromaffin – taking up and staining strongly with chromium salts

chromaffinoma – a tumor of one of several glandular structures characterized by the presence of pigmented material, found notably in the adrenal gland, the carotid body, and some other locations

coccidioidal – pertaining to a genus of pathogenic fungi of the family Endomycetales

coccidiosis – infection by coccidia

comedocarcinoma – an intraductal carcinoma of the breast

condyloma acuminatum – a papilloma with a central core of connective tissue in a treelike structure covered with epithelium; caused by a virus, it is infectious and autoinoculable

contiguous – in contact or nearly so

conus arteriosus – the portion of the right ventricle of the heart that lets blood into the pulmonary arterial orifice

Coomb's test – a test using various antisera, usually employed to detect the presence of proteins on the surface of red cells

*These terms were used in dictation but were not located in any of the references consulted. You will encounter this situation throughout this text. For a list of the reference books consulted, see page 502.

corpora amylacea – small hyaline masses of degenerate cells found in the prostate, neuroglia, etc.

corpora arantii – nodules of the aortic valve

*corticomedullary

cotyledon – any one of the subdivisions of the uterine surface of a discoidal placenta

Crohn's disease – regional ileitis

cystosarcoma pyhlloides – a low-grade malignant tumor of the human breast resembling a giant fibroadenoma and often containing cleftlike cystic spaces

cytotrophoblast – the cellular (inner) layer of the trophoblast

deciduoma – an intrauterine mass containing decidual cells

Demodex folliculorum – a species of mite found in hair follicles and in secretions of the sebaceous glands, especially of the face and nose

diapedesis – the outward passage through intact vessel walls of corpuscular elements of the blood

Diplococcus pneumoniae – the type species, a facultative anaerobe which is the commonest cause of lobar pneumonia

Dohle's inclusion bodies – small coccus-shaped bodies occurring in the polynuclear leukocytes of the blood in several diseases, especially scarlet fever

dysontogenesis – defective embryonic development

eccrine gland – one of the ordinary, or simple, sweat glands of the body

Ehrlich's test – a test for urobilinogen in the urine

enchondroma – a benign growth of cartilage arising in the metaphysis of a bone

endophytic – growing inward; proliferating on the interior or inside of an organ or other structure, as a tumor

enteropathy – any disease of the intestine

eosinophil – a structure, cell, or histologic element readily stained by eosin

ependymoma – a neoplasm composed of differentiated ependymal cells

epicrisis – a critical analysis or discussion of a case of disease after its termination

epithelioma of Malherbe – a benign tumor of squamous epithelial cells in which there is some calcification

erythropoiesis – the production of erythrocytes

Escherichia coli (E. coli) – a species of organisms constituting the greater part of the intestinal flora of man and other animals

exophytic – growing outward; in oncology, proliferating on the exterior or surface epithelium of an organ or other structure in which the growth originated

faucial – pertaining to the throat

ferrugination – mineralization (with iron) of the blood vessels of the brain fetus papyraceus – extreme compression of a dead fetus by its living twin

Fibrindex test – a test to determine the adequacy of fibrinogen of the blood

fibrofatty – both fibrous and fatty

fossa navicularis – a shallow depression between the hymen and the frenulum of the vaginal labia

fovea – a general term for a small pit in the surface of a structure or an organ

fusiform – spindle shaped

gemistocytic – composed of large round cells (gemistocytes)

Ghon's complex, lungs – the sign of healed primary tuberculosis

Giemsa stain – a solution used for staining protozoan parasites such as trypanosomes

gitter cells – ovoid phagocytic cells found in areas of softening of the brain that contain devoured fragments of broken-down brain tissue

glomangioma – a benign, often painful tumor derived from a neuromyoarterial glomus, usually occurring on the distal portions of the fingers and toes, in the skin, or in deeper structures

Gomori's methenamine silver stain – stain used specifically for fungus

*granulomata

grumous – clotted or lumpy

gynandroblastoma – a rare ovarian tumor containing histological features of both arrhenoblastoma and granulosa cell tumor

gyri – the tortuous elevations on the surface of the brain caused by infolding of the cortex

hamartoma – a benign tumor-like nodule composed of an overgrowth of mature cells and tissues that normally occur in the affected part, but often with one element predominating

Hamman-Rich syndrome – a disease characterized by widespread fibrosis of the lung parenchyma

Hassall's corpuscles – small concentrically striated bodies in the thymus

haustral folds – the folds of the mucosa of the large bowel caused by the underlying arrangement of its musculature

hemangiopericytoma – a tumor composed of spindle cells with a rich vascular network, which apparently arises from pericytes

hematoxylin stain – an intense blue stain used in the preparation of microscopic tissue specimens; it stains the nucleus of the cell

hemofuscin – a brownish-yellow pigment that results from the decomposition of hemoglobin; it gives the urine a deep ruddy color

hemosiderin – an insoluble form of storage iron in which the micelles of ferric hydroxide are so arranged as to be visible microscopically both with and without the use of specific staining methods

hemosiderosis – a focal or general increase in tissue iron stores without associated tissue damage

heterotopic – occurring at an abnormal place or upon the wrong part of the body

histolytic – pertaining to, characterized by, or causing histolysis

Hurthle cells – large eosinophilic cells sometimes found in the thyroid gland

hypereosinophilia – excessive eosinophilia, the formation and accumulation of an abnormally large number of eosinophils in the blood

hypogammaglobulinemia – an immunological deficiency state characterized by an abnormally low level of generally all classes of gamma globulin in the blood

iatrogenic – resulting from the activity of physicians

islets – clusters of cells or isolated pieces of tissue

Jakob-Creutzfeldt disease – a progressive dementia involving gray matter and basal ganglia

Kaposi's sarcoma – a multifocal, metastasizing, malignant reticulosis with features resembling those of angiosarcoma, principally involving the skin

karyolysis – destruction or breakdown of the cell's nucleus, at least the loss of affinity of its chromatin for basic dyes

karyorrhexis – the process of breaking up of the cell's nucleus

keratoacanthoma – a rapidly growing papular lesion, with a crater filled with a keratin plug, which reaches maximum size and then resolves spontaneously within four to six months from onset

Kerchring's, folds of – circular folds of mucous membranes that form elevations in the inner wall of the small intestine

Kienbock's disease – a slowly progressive degenerative disorder of the semilunar bone of the wrist

Krukenberg's tumor – a special type of carcinoma of the ovary, usually metastatic from cancer of the gastrointestinal tract, especially of the stomach

Kupffer's cells – large star-shaped or pyramidal cells with a large oval nucleus and a small prominent nucleolus

Lambl's excrescence – small papillary projections on the cardiac valves seen post mortem on many adult hearts

Langhans' cells – polyhedral epithelial cells constituting cytotrophoblast

Leriche's disease – a trophic injury or disorder that causes thickening of an artery wall and diminished blood supply to the dependent tissue

Letterer-Siwe disease – a serious disease characterized by a proliferation of reticuloendothelial cells in many organs, especially lymph nodes, spleen, and bone

leucine – acid essential for optimal growth in infants and for nitrogen equilibrium in human adults

leucine aminopeptidase – an enzyme found in the pancreas

Leydig's cells – the interstitial cells of the testes that furnish the internal secretion of the testicle

lines of Zahn – the white lines that are present in thrombosed blood clots and consist of coagulated blood serum that has separated from cellular components

lipofuscin – any one of a class of fatty pigments formed by the solution of a pigment in fat

littoral cells – flattened cells that line the walls of lymph or blood sinuses

lividity – the quality of being discolored, as of dependent parts, by the gravitation of the blood

lutein – a yellow pigment, or lipochrome, from the corpus luteum, from fat cells, and from the yolk of eggs

Lutembacher's syndrome – atrial septal defect with mitral stenosis

macrogametocyte – the infected red blood cell containing the female form of the malarial parasite which, transferred from man to the mosquito, becomes a macrogamete

macrophage – any of the large, mononuclear highly phagocytic cells with a small, oval, sometimes indented nucleus and inconspicuous nucleoli, occurring in the walls of blood vessels and in loose connective tissue

Malherbe's epithelioma – a tumor made up of squamous epithelial cells in which heterotopic calcification is present

malpighian corpuscles – ovoid collections of lymphocytes that are present around the small penicilliary blood vessels in the spleen

May-Grunwald stain – an alcoholic neutral mixture of methylene blue and eosin

Mayer's mucicarmine stain – a tissue stain for the substance mucin

megakaryocyte – the giant cell of bone marrow

Meissner's corpuscles – encapsulated nerve endings found mainly in the skin of the soles and palms that receive sensitive touch stimuli

mesenchyma – the meshwork of embryonic connective tissue in the mesoderm from which are formed the connective tissues of the body and also the blood vessels and lymphatic vessels

mesenchymoma – a mixed mesenchymal tumor composed of two or more cellular elements not commonly associated, not counting fibrous tissue as one of the elements

molluscum contagiosum – a mildly contagious viral disease characterized by lesions in the skin or trunk, face, and genital areas

mosaicism – the presence of cells that have different chromosomal constitution

mucicarmine stain – a reddish stain designed to show selectively the presence of mucinous material

myelocyte – any cell of the gray matter of the nervous system

myelophthisis – reduction of the cell-forming functions of the bone marrow

myxoid – resembling mucus

myxomatous – of the nature of a myxoma

necropsy – examination of a body after death; autopsy

neutrophil – any cell, structure, or histologic element readily stainable by neutral dyes

nidus – the point of origin or focus of a morbid process

osseocartilaginous – pertaining to or composed of bone and cartilage

pacchionian bodies – smooth, granular structures found in the meninges of the brain

pacinian corpuscles – small, but enlarged, nerve endings concerned with the perception of pressure

Paneth's cells – narrow, pyramidal, or columnar epithelial cells with a round or an oval nucleus close to the base of the cell

papillomatosis – the development of multiple papillomas

parenchyma – the essential elements of an organ

Pel-Ebstein fever – a fever in which the temperature rises by steps over several days and then goes down in steps the same way; common in Hodgkin's disease

phagocyte – any cell that ingests microorganisms or other cells and foreign particles

phagocytized – said of particles engulfed by an active cell (a phagocyte), especially a histiocyte

phthisis – a wasting away of the body or a part of the body; tuberculosis especially of the lungs

plicae palmatae – the grooves in the cervical canal

poikilocyte – a red blood cell showing abnormal variation in shape

polycythemia ruba, vera – a disease characterized by an absolute increase in red cell mass and total blood volume, associated frequently with splenomegaly, leukocytosis, and thrombocythemia

polysaccharides – compounds made up of multiple sugar linkages

*propria

proteinaceous – pertaining to or of the nature of a protein

Proteus vulgaris – the type species of Proteus, occurring, often as a secondary invader, in a variety of localized suppurative pathologic processes, and being a common cause of cystitis

psammoma body – a spherical, smooth, homogeneous, laminated mass, sometimes containing calcium, arising in cells; such bodies occur in both benign and malignant epithelial and connective-tissue tumors, and are sometimes associated with chronic inflammation

pseudohypha – a chain of easily disrupted fungal cells that is intermediate between a chain of budding cells and a true hypha, marked by constrictions rather than septa at the junctions

Pseudomonas aeruginosa – the causative agent of a variety of human diseases, including common cases of endocarditis, pneumonia, and meningitis

pultaceous – like a pulp or poultice; soft and pulplike

Purkinje's cells – large branching neurons in the middle layer of the cortex cerebelli

putamen – one of the paired large nuclei in the midbrain

pyknosis – condensation and increased basophilic staining of a cell's nucleus

pyknotic – serving to close the pores; pertaining to pyknosis

Queyrat's erythroplasia – squamous cell carcinoma in situ that manifests as a circumscribed, velvety, erythematous papular lesion on the glans penis, coronal sulcus, or prepuce, leading to scaling and superficial ulceration

Recklinghausen's disease – a disease characterized by multiple neurocutaneous fibromas; sometimes similar tumors of the central nervous system occur

rete pegs – the downward sawtooth-like projections of the epidermis into the dermis

Rokitansky-Aschoff, crypts of – small folds of the gallbladder mucosa that extend into the muscular wall

Rokitansky's disease, tumor – acute yellow tumor atrophy of the liver

rouleaux formation – a closely packed arrangement of red blood corpuscles in rows that resemble a collapsed column of coins

saprophytic actinomycosis – nonpathogenic form of actinomycosis

Schimmelbusch's disease – a form of productive mastitis marked by the production of many small cysts

scirrhous – pertaining to or of the nature of a hard cancer

scrofuloderma – suppurating abscesses and fistulous passages opening on the skin, secondary to tuberculosis of lymph nodes, most commonly those of the neck, and sometimes of bones and joint

siderogenous – producing or forming iron

sinusoid – a form of terminal blood channel consisting of a large, irregular anastomosing vessel, having a lining of reticuloendothelium but little or no adventitia

squamocolumnar – pertaining to the junction between a stratified squamous epithelial surface and one lined by columnar epithelium

struma – goiter

sudoriferous glands – the sweat glands

sympathicoblastoma – a malignant tumor containing sympathicoblasts

sympathicogonioma – sympathicoblastoma

syncytium – a multinucleate mass of protoplasm produced by the merging of cells

syringocystadenoma – adenoma of the sweat glands

telangiectatic – pertaining to or characterized by telangiectasia, which is a vascular lesion formed by dilatation of a group of small blood vessels and is the basis for a variety of angiomas

thalamic – pertaining to the thalamus

thrombocythemia – a fixed increase in the number of circulating blood platelets

trabeculae carneae – rounded, ridgelike elevations on the interior walls of the ventricles of the heart

unci – plural of uncus, which is any hook-shaped process or structure

van Gieson's stain – a stain for connective tissue, consisting of acid fuchsin and aqueous solution of trinitrophenol

variegated – marked by patches of differing color

Vater-Pacini corpuscles – sensory nerve structures deep in the hands and feet and around joints serving proprioceptive function

Verhoeff's elastic stain – a stain for demonstrating elastic tissue

vernix caseosa – the white, clinging, greasy material found on the skin of newborn infants

Verocay bodies – small groups of fibrils surrounded by rows of palisaded nuclei; seen in nerve tumors

Virchow-Robin spaces – the spaces around the blood vessels where they enter the brain

von Willebrand's disease – angiohemophilia

Zenker's fixation – a method of hardening tissue in preparation for section (microscopic slide preparation)

Ziehl-Neelsen's method, stain – a staining procedure for demonstrating acid-fast microorganisms

Case Number:

SPECIMEN:

GROSS:

MICROSCOPIC DIAGNOSIS:

SPECIMEN:

CLINICAL:

GROSS EXAMINATION:

SPECIMEN:

CLINICAL:

GROSS EXAMINATION:

COMMENT:

MICROSCOPIC DIAGNOSIS:

AUTOPSY REPORT

Number:

GROSS DESCRIPTION:

SPECIMEN:

CLINICAL:

GROSS EXAMINATION:

Case Number:

SPECIMEN:

HISTORY:

GROSS EXAMINATION:

SPECIMENS:

CLINICAL HISTORY:

GROSS EXAMINATION:

SPECIMEN:

GROSS EXAMINATION:

SPECIMEN:

CLINICAL:

GROSS:

AUTOPSY REPORT

Number:

GROSS DESCRIPTION:

DATE OF AUTOPSY:

DATE AND HOUR OF DEATH:

CHAPTER 12
PLASTIC SURGERY

Simply stated, plastic surgery is the surgical method of repairing and/or reconstructing body structures that are defective or damaged by injury or disease. Some of these deformities may be present at birth or may have been caused by burns, wounds, injury, disease, or the aging process. This method of surgery is employed to restore both function and appearance.

The word *plastic* is defined simply as "giving form or shape to a substance." As might be thought by many, neither the word *plastic* nor the substance which also bears this name has any relationship to commercially prepared synthetic plastic materials and products. It is true, however, that in some cases medical-grade plastic materials may be required in some areas of reconstructive and cosmetic surgery.

The essence of plastic surgery is tissue transplantation and repositioning. Tissues, which include nerves, skin, bone, cartilage, tendon, mucous membrane, and fat, can be moved from sites near the damaged area or from remote parts of the body. In the new location, such tissue can substitute for damaged, deformed, or lost tissue and can protect exposed and functioning areas.

For optimum and lasting results, grafts are transferred from one part of the body to another part of the same individual. It is possible, though, for bone, cartilage, and cornea to be transplanted from one person to another.

In recent years advances in plastic surgery have been many. Improved techniques have enabled surgeons to repair cleft lips so that the remaining scars are almost imperceptible. It is now common practice to transfer ultrathin sheets of good skin from one area to another by use of an instrument called the dermatome. New materials such as the rubber-silicone compound, Silastic, and medical mesh grafts are being used safely and successfully to round out facial contours and fill in depressions.

The practice of plastic surgery is not confined to the head and neck but is performed on all parts of the body by general and specialty plastic surgeons with successful results. The general plastic surgeon performs surgery on virtually any area of the body.

ABBREVIATIONS

Abd. DM	abductor digiti minimi	DIP	distal interphalangeal joint
Abd. PB	abductor pollicis brevis		
Abd. PL	abductor pollicis longus	ECRB	extensor carpi radialis brevis
Add. P	adductor pollicis	ECRL	extensor carpi radialis longus
AROM	active range of motion	ECU	extensor carpi ulnaris
		EDC	extensor digitorum communis
BC Ca	basal cell carcinoma	EDM	extensor digiti minimi
		EHB	extensor hallucis brevis
CL	cleft lip	EHL	extensor hallucis longus
CP	cleft palate	EI	extensor indicis
CRFZ	closed reduction of fractured zygoma	EIP	extensor indicis proprius
CRIF	closed reduction & internal fixation	EPB	extensor pollicis brevis

EPL	extensor pollicis longus	MS	morphine sulfate
EUA	examination under anesthesia		
		ODM	opponens digiti minimi
FCR	flexor carpi radialis	OP	opponens pollicis
FCU	flexor carpi ulnaris	ORIF	open reduction & internal fixation
FDM	flexor digiti minimi		
FDP	flexor digitorum profundus		
FPB	flexor pollicis brevis	PIP	proximal interphalangeal joint
FPL	flexor pollicis longus	PL	palmaris longus
FTSG	full-thickness skin grafting	PROM	passive range of motion
FX	frozen section		
		SC Ca	squamous cell carcinoma
GSW	gunshot wound	SLE	systemic lupus erythematosus
		SMR	submucous resection
I & D	incision and drainage	STSG	split-thickness skin grafting
IMF	intermaxillary fixation	subcu,subq	subcutaneous
IP	interphalangeal		
		WP	whirlpool
MCP	metacarpophalangeal joint		

DEFINITIONS OF TERMINOLOGY

abdominoplasty – the surgery to remove excess skin and tighten the protuberant abdomen that results from multiple pregnancies

allograft (homograft) – graft from one individual to another in the same species

asymmetry – dissimilarity in corresponding parts or organs on opposite sides of the body which are normally alike

augmentation – the act or process of enlarging or increasing

autograft – graft from one place to another on the same individual

avulsion – the tearing away of a part of structure

benzoin – a balsamic resin with an aromatic odor and taste, which is used as a topical protectant

blepharochalasis – relaxation of the skin of the eyelid due to atrophy of the intercellular tissue

blepharoplasty – plastic surgery of the eyelids

blepharoptosis – drooping of an upper eyelid due to paralysis

callosum – corpus callosum

canthoplasty – plastic surgery of the medial and/or lateral canthus, especially section of the lateral canthus to lengthen the palpebral fissure

canthus – the angle at either end of the fissure between the eyelids

cheilectomy – excision of a lip

cheiloplasty – surgical repair of a defect of the lip

cheilotomy – incision into the lip

cicatrectomy – excision of a cicatrix

dermabrasion – surgical removal of the frozen epidermis and as much of the dermis as necessary, by mechanical means

*dermolipectomy

DIP joint – distal interphalangeal joint

electrodermatome – an electrical dermatome for cutting off even layers of large areas of skin in a short time; used in skin grafting, shaving scars, etc.

electromyography – a method of recording the electrical currents generated in an active muscle

escharotomy – a surgical incision in a burn eschar to lessen constriction

exenteration – surgical removal of the inner organs

exsanguinate – to deprive of blood; bloodless

facioplasty – plastic surgery of the face

genioplasty – plastic surgery of the chin

gentian violet – a faintly odorous compound occurring as a dark green powder, or as glistening pieces with a metallic luster; it is used as a dye and in medicine as a topical anti-infective

gingivoplasty – surgical modeling of the gingival margin and papillae to obtain a normal gingival contour

hamulus – a general term denoting a hook-shaped process

Heyer-Schulte implant (no definition given)

hypermastia – hypertrophy of the mammary gland

hypomastia – abnormal smallness of the mammary glands

inframammary incisions – incisions made below the mammary gland

keloid – a mass of hyperplastic, fibrous connective tissue, usually at the site of a scar

keloplasty – operative removal of a scar or keloid

labiomental – pertaining to the lip and chin

leMesurier technique for cleft lip repair (no definition given)

lipectomy – the excision of a mass of subcutaneous adipose tissue, as from the abdominal wall

mamilla (papilla) – a nipple

mammoplasty/mammiplasty/mammaplasty – plastic reconstruction of the breast as may be done to augment or reduce its size

mastectomy – removal of a breast

*These terms were used in dictation but were not located in any of the references consulted. You will encounter this situation throughout this text. For a list of the reference books consulted, see page 502.

mastopexy – mammoplasty performed to correct a pendulous breast

mastoplasty – mammoplasty

mucinous – resembling or marked by the formation of mucin

*myocutaneous

nevus/nevi – a circumscribed stable malformation of the skin and occasionally of the oral mucosa, which is not due to external causes and therefore presumed to be of hereditary origin

otoplasty – plastic surgery of the ear; the surgical correction of ear deformities and defects

palatine – pertaining to the palate

palatoplasty – plastic reconstruction of the palate, including cleft palate operations

palatorrhaphy – surgical correction of a cleft palate

palpebra – eyelid

palpebral – pertaining to an eyelid

Panas' operation – the attachment of the upper eyelid to the occipitofrontalis muscle for ptosis

pharyngoplasty – plastic operation on the pharynx

PIP joint – proximal interphalangeal joint

plication – the taking of tucks in any structure to shorten it, or in the walls of a hollow viscus; a folding

ptosis – prolapse of an organ or a part

retrenchment – the cutting away of superfluous tissue

retroposed – displaced backward or posteriorly

rhinocheiloplasty – plastic surgery of the nose and lip

rhinokyphectomy – a plastic operation for rhinokyphosis, a humpback deformity of the nose

rhinoplasty – plastic surgical operation on the nose, either reconstructive, restorative, or cosmetic

rhinorrhaphy – an operation for epicanthus performed by excising a fold of skin from the nose and closing the opening with sutures

rhinotomy – incision into the nose

rhytidectomy – excision of skin for the elimination of wrinkles; facelift

rhytidoplasty – plastic surgery for the elimination of wrinkles from the skin

rhytidosis – a wrinkling of the cornea

semilunar – resembling a crescent or half-moon

Steristrip (no definition given)

stomatoplasty – plastic surgery of, or operative repair of, defects of the mouth or of the ostium uteri

synchronous – occurring at the same time

tantalum – a noncorrosive and malleable metal which has been used for plates or disks to replace cranial defects, for wire sutures, and for making prosthetic appliances

tarsorrhaphy – the operation of suturing together a portion of or the entire upper and lower eyelids for the purpose of shortening or closing entirely the palpebral fissure

thelitis – chronic or acute inflammation of the nipple

*thoracodorsal

turgor – the condition of being turgid; normal or other fullness

uranoplasty – palatoplasty

xenograft (heterograft) – graft from one individual to another of a different species

SURGERY

Patient Name: Date:

    Doctor:

ANESTHETIC:

OPERATION:

PREOP DIAG:

POSTOP DIAG:

FINDINGS:

OPERATIVE PROCEDURE:

OPERATION

Patient Name: Date:

    Doctor:

OPERATION:

PREOP DIAG:

POSTOP DIAG:

INDICATIONS:

OPERATION

Patient Name: Date:

    Doctor:

SURGEON:

OPERATION:

PREOP DIAG:

POSTOP DIAG:

INDICATIONS FOR PROCEDURE:

SURGERY

Patient Name: Date:

    Doctor:

ANESTHETIC:

OPERATION:

PREOP DIAG:

POSTOP DIAG:

FINDINGS:

SURGERY

Patient Name: Date:

    Doctor:

OPERATION:

PREOP DIAG:

POSTOP DIAG:

FINDINGS:

OP NOTE

Patient Name: Date:

    Doctor:

OPERATION:

PREOP DIAG:

POSTOP DIAG:

FINDINGS:

OUTPATIENT SURGERY

Patient Name: Date:

    Doctor:

SURGEON:

OPERATION:

PREOP DIAG:

POSTOP DIAG:

INDICATIONS FOR PROCEDURE:

SURGERY

Patient Name: Date:

     Doctor:

SURGEON:

OPERATION:

PREOP DIAG:

POSTOP DIAG:

INDICATIONS FOR PROCEDURE:

SURGERY

Patient Name: Date:

Doctor:

ANESTHETIC:

OPERATION:

PREOP DIAG:

POSTOP DIAG:

FINDINGS:

SURGERY

Patient Name: Date:

    Doctor:

OPERATION:

PREOP DIAG:

POSTOP DIAG:

FINDINGS:

SURGERY

Patient Name: Date:

   Doctor:

OPERATION:

PREOP DIAG:

POSTOP DIAG:

FINDINGS:

CHAPTER 13
PSYCHIATRY

That branch of medicine which deals with functional nervous disorders or mental disease is known as psychiatry. Both conscious and unconscious processes of the psyche—the human faculty for thought, judgment, and emotion—are treated by the psychiatrist.

The study, treatment, and prevention of mental illness is performed by psychiatrists who analyze the thinking and actions of patients suffering from psychiatric illnesses.

Patients with psychiatric problems are treated by physical means, drugs, or psychotherapy which makes use of reassurance, suggestions, hypnosis, or discussion of the patient's condition in an effort to help the patient understand the nature of the problem and meaning of the symptoms.

Naturally, different psychiatrists use different therapeutic methods.

ABBREVIATIONS

CA	chronological age		MSRPP	Multidimensional Scale for Rating Psychiatric Patients
CBS	chronic brain syndrome			
CR	conditioned reflex			
CS	conditioned stimulus		OBS	organic brain syndrome
			OT	occupational therapy
DSM	Diagnostic and Statistical Manual of Mental Disorders			
			PEG	pneumoencephalogram
DT	delirium tremens		PMA	Primary Mental Abilities Tests
ECT	electroconvulsive therapy		SB	Stanford-Binet Test
EEG	electroencephalogram			
ESP	extrasensory perception		TAT	Thematic Apperception Test
EST	electric shock therapy			
IMP	Inpatient Multidimensional Psychiatric (Scale)		UCR	unconditioned reflex
			WAIS	Wechsler Adult Intelligence Scale
MMPI	Minnesota Multiphasic Personality Inventory		WISC	Wechsler Intelligence Scale for Children

DEFINITIONS OF TERMINOLOGY

abreaction – a form of psychotherapy that encourages a reliving of repressed emotional stress situations in a therapeutic setting

acarophobia – morbid dread of mites or of small objects

acrophobia – morbid dread of high places

agoraphobia – fear of being in a large open space

akathisia – a syndrome characterized by an inability to remain in a sitting posture, with motor restlessness and a feeling of muscular quivering

ambivalence – the simultaneous existence of conflicting attitudes, as of love and hate toward the same object

amentia – feeblemindedness; a mental disorder characterized by marked mental confusion, sometimes so severe as to approach stupor

amok – a psychic disturbance marked by a period of depression, followed by violent attempts to kill people

amusia – inability to produce or to comprehend musical sounds

anaclitic – leaning against or depending on something

analysand – one who is being psychoanalyzed

anamnesis – the collected data concerning a patient, his/her previous environment and experiences, including any abnormal sensations, moods, or acts observed by the patient or by others, and the dates of their appearance and duration, as well as any results of treatment

anorexia nervosa – a serious nervous condition in which the patient loses his/her appetite and systematically takes but little food, so that he/she becomes greatly emaciated

antianxiety agents – drugs which have a central calming effect

antipsychotic – denoting a neuropharmacolic agent that has antipsychotic action affecting principally psychomotor activity and is generally without hypnotic effects, as a tranquilizer

aphonia paranoica – stubborn willful silence

apperception – conscious perception and appreciation; the power of receiving, appreciating, and interpreting sensory impressions

ataractics – tranquilizing agents widely used in psychiatric disorders such as agitation, aggressive outbursts, psychomotor overactivity, and the like; they are the same as antianxiety agents

autism – the condition of being dominated by subjective, self-centered trends of thought or behavior which are not subject to correction by external information

autognosis – self-diagnosis

barbiturate – a salt or derivative of barbituric acid

Bender Gestalt test – a psychological test used for evaluating perceptual-motor coordination, for assessing personality dynamics, as a test of organic brain impairment, and for measuring neurological maturation

bradyphrasia – slowness of speech due to mental disorder

bradypsychia – slowness of mental reactions

bulimia – abnormal increase in the sensation of hunger

cacesthesia – any morbid sensation or any disorder of sensibility

cachinnation – laughter without apparent cause often found in schizophrenia

camptocormia – a static deformity consisting of forward flexion of the trunk

carphology – the involuntary picking at the bedclothes seen in grave fevers and in conditions of great exhaustion

catalepsy – a morbid state in which there is a waxy rigidity of the limbs that may be placed in various positions which will be maintained for a time

catatonia – stupor

catharsis – Freud's treatment of psychoneuroses to bring about abreaction, by encouraging the patient to tell everything that happens to be associated with a given train of thought, thus "purging" the mind of the repressed material that is the cause of the symptoms

cathexis – the charge or attachment of mental or emotional energy upon an idea or object

chorea insaniens – chorea with symptoms of insanity, chiefly seen in pregnant women

conation – in psychology, the power that impels to effort of any kind; the conscious tendency to act

coprophilia – a psychopathologic interested in filth, especially in feces and in defecation

cryptomnesia – the recall of events not recognized as part of one's conscious experience

cybernetics – the science of the processes of communication and control in the animal and in the machine

cyclothymia – a temperament characterized by cyclic alternations of mood between elation and depression

cyclothymic personality – an individual manifesting mood swings from elation to depression

déjà vu – an illusion in which a new situation is incorrectly viewed as a repetition of a previous situation

dereism – mental activity in which fantasy runs on unhampered by logic and experience

disdiadochokinesia (dysdiadochokinesia) – derangement of the function of diadochokinesia

dysbulia – abnormal weakness or disturbance of the will

dyslexia – an inability to read understandingly, due to a central lesion

echolalia – the repetition by a patient of words addressed to him/her

echopraxis (echopraxia) – the spasmodic and involuntary imitation of the movements of another

ectomorphic – pertaining to or characteristic of an ectomorph

ego-dystonic – denoting any impulse, idea, or the like, that is repugnant to and inconsistent with an individual's conception of himself/herself

eidetic – pertaining to or characterized by exact visualization of events or of objects previously seen

electronarcosis – anesthesia produced by passing an electric current through the brain by electrodes placed on the temples

empathy – the recognition of and entering into the feelings of another person

encopresis – incontinence of feces not due to organic defect or illness

enosimania – obsessive belief of having committed an unpardonable offense

euphoria – in psychiatry, an abnormal or exaggerated sense of well-being, particularly common in the manic state

fetishism – the worship or adoration of an inanimate object as a symbol of a loved person

flagellation – whipping or being whipped to achieve erotic pleasure

flexibilitas cerea – a cataleptic state in which the limbs retain any position in which they may be placed

gestaltism – that theory in psychology which claims that the objects of mind, as immediately presented to direct experience, come as complete unanalyzable wholes or forms which cannot be split up into parts

grandiosity – a condition characterized by delusions of grandeur

hallucination – a sense perception without a source in the external world

hallucinogen – an agent which induces hallucinations

hebephrenia – hebephrenic schizophrenia

hebephrenic schizophrenia – shallow inappropriate emotions, disorganized thinking, unpredictable childish behavior and mannerisms, indicative of gross personality disorganization

hypnopompic – persisting after sleep; applied to visions or dreams that persist prior to complete awakening

ideation – the distinct mental presentation of objects

Karsokov's psychosis – a chronic brain syndrome associated with a prolonged use of alcohol

kleptomania – an uncontrollable impulse to steal

lability – in psychiatry, emotional instability; a tendency to show alternating states of gaiety and somberness

lethargy – a condition of drowsiness or indifference

libido – in psychoanalysis the term applied to the motive power of the sex life

malingering – the willful, deliberate, and fraudulent feigning or exaggeration of the symptoms of illness or injury, done for the purpose of a consciously desired end

manic-depressive – alternating between attacks of mania and depression

masochism – a form of sexual perversion in which cruel or humiliating treatment gives sexual gratification to the recipient

mesmerism – hypnotism

metaphrenia – the mental condition in which the interests are withdrawn from the family or group and directed to personal gain or aggrandizement

milieu therapy – the utilization of a modified and controlled environment in the treatment of mental disease

misanthropia (misanthropy) – hatred of mankind

mydriasis – extreme or morbid dilatation of the pupil; dilatation of the pupil as the effect of a drug

mysophobia – morbid dread of filth or contamination

narcissism – self-love

neurasthenic neurosis (neurasthenia) – a neurosis characterized by chronic weakness, easy fatigability, and sometimes exhaustion

neurosis – disorder in which the dominant trait is anxiety

neurotic – a nervous person in whom emotions predominate over reason; pertaining to or affected with a neurosis

nihilism – a form of delusion in which, to the patient, everything no longer exists

nympholepsy – ecstasy; transport, especially one of an erotic nature

obnubilation – a clouded state of the mind

oligophrenia – defective mental development

oneirodynia – nightmare

pantophobia (panphobia) – fear of everything; a vague morbid dread of some unknown evil

paresthetic – relating to or marked by paresthesia

petit mal epilepsy – epilepsy in which there is sudden momentary loss of consciousness with only minor myoclonic jerks, seen especially in children

phagomania – an insatiable craving for food, or an obsessive preoccupation with the subject of eating

postictal – following a stroke or seizure, such as an acute epileptic attack

psychedelic – pertaining to or characterized by visual hallucinations, intensified perception, and, sometimes, behavior similar to that seen in psychosis

psychodynamics – the science of mental processes

psychometry – the measurement of intelligence; psychological testing

psychoneurosis – an emotional disorder due to unresolved conflicts, anxiety being its chief characteristic

psychosis – a general term for any major mental disorder of organic and/or emotional origin characterized by derangement of the personality and loss of contact with reality

psychosomatic – pertaining to the mind-body relationship; having bodily symptoms of psychic, emotional, or mental origin

psychotogen – a drug that produces psychotic manifestations

recidivism – the relapse or recurrence of a disease

CHAPTER 14
RADIOLOGY/NUCLEAR MEDICINE

The specialty of radiology is concerned with the diagnostic and therapeutic application of radiant energy, including roentgen rays (x-rays) and radium.

Nuclear Medicine is that branch of radiology which employs the use of radioactive material in diagnosis and/or treatment of human disease. The amount of radiation used is quite small, and there is no hazard to the patient or to any medical employee.

Various body systems are tested through the administration of usually intravenous medications found in the Nuclear Medicine Department. Cameras that are attuned to or focused to these drugs take serial pictures of the systems that are being studied. The studies can be either dynamic, in which the series are read almost as motion pictures, or static, in which after a certain period of time, the images are evaluated either for progress or change in the anatomy of the organ system studied.

Almost all the body systems can be evaluated by this intravenous method through the use of one or more different drugs tagged with Technetium, a radionuclide. Because radionuclides emit gamma rays which can be detected and recorded in many ways, thus providing statistical information or images, they are used commonly in all phases of medicine.

After the studies are made, the reports are interpreted by a radiologist and should be signed by the radiologist, since the definitive report is his/her responsibility.

ABBREVIATIONS

ACTH	adrenocorticotropic hormone	HEG	high energy gamma
ASD	atrial septal defect	HVL	half value layer
AV	arteriovenous		
		ICS	intercostal space
Ba	barium	IHSA	iodinated human serum albumin
Ci	curie	LAO	left anterior oblique
CPB	competitive protein binding	LD	lethal dose
CPM	count per minute		
		MAA	macroaggregated albumin
EGD	esophagogastroduodenoscopy	mCi	millicurie
EOB	end of bombardment	MFB	metallic foreign body
ERCP	endoscopic retrograde cholangiopancreatogram	MLD	median lethal dose
		MPC	maximum permissible concentration
ESD	esophagus, stomach, and duodenum	MPL	maximum permissible level or limit
FTI	free thyroxine index	N	neutron
FUT	fibrinogen uptake test		
		PBI-131	protein bound radioiodine
GM	Geiger-Muller (counter)	PIT	plasma iron turnover rate

PTC	percutaneous transhepatic cholangiogram	TBG	thyroxine binding globulin
		TBI	thyroxine binding index
		TBP	thyroxine binding protein
r	roentgen	TBPA	thyroxine binding prealbumin
RAD,rad	radiation absorbed dose	TD	tumor dose
RAIU	radioactive iodine uptake	TRF	thyrotropin-releasing factor
RAO	right anterior oblique	TRH	thyrotropin-releasing hormone
RBE	relative biological effectiveness	TSD	tumor skin distance
REG	radiation exposure guide	TSH	thyroid-stimulating hormone
RISA	radioiodinated serum albumin		

DEFINITIONS OF TERMINOLOGY

aerated – charged with air or with carbon dioxide; oxygenated

angiocardiography – examination of the chambers of the heart and pulmonary circulation after injection of radiopaque material

angiogram – an x-ray of blood vessels filled with a contrast medium

angiography (no definition given)

anomalous – irregular; applied particularly to congenital and hereditary defects

aortogram (no definition given)

apices – points of greatest activity, or points of greatest response to any type of stimulation, such as electrical stimulation of muscles

arteriogram – an x-ray of an artery

attenuation – the process by which a beam of radiation is reduced in energy when passed through tissue or other material

bleb – a large flaccid vesicle, usually at least 1 cm in diameter

bolus – a rounded mass of food, or a pharmaceutical preparation ready to swallow, or such a mass passing through the gastrointestinal tract

cardiothoracic (no definition given)

Cesium 137 – radionuclide used for external radiation therapy of cancer

choledochogram – an x-ray of the common bile duct

cineangiography – the photographic recording of fluoroscopic images of the blood vessels by motion picture techniques

cinefluorography – cineradiography

cineradiography – x-ray motion pictures

cisternography – the roentgenographic study of the basal cisterns of the brain after the subarachnoid introduction of an opaque or other contrast medium, or a radiopharmaceutical

collimator – a diaphragm or system of diaphragms made of an absorbing material, designed to define the dimensions and direction of a beam of radiation

colpostat – an appliance for retaining something, such as radium, in the vagina

coxa – the part of the body lateral to and including the hip joint; also loosely used to denote the hip joint

curie – the unit for measuring the activity for all radioactive substances

cyclotron – a particle accelerator in which charged particles receive repeated synchronized accelerations or "kicks" by electrical fields as the particles spiral outward from their source; they are a valuable source of radionuclides for medical diagnosis and research

cystogram – an x-ray of the bladder

cystourethrogram – an x-ray of the urinary bladder and ureters

deglutition – the act of swallowing

desiccate – to render thoroughly dry

dextroposition – displacement to the right

diathermy – heating of the body tissues due to their resistance to the passage of high-frequency electromagnetic radiation

dosimeter – an instrument for measuring the dose of radiation

eburnation – the conversion of a bone into an ivory-like mass

echoencephalography – a diagnostic technique in which pulses of ultrasonic waves are beamed through the head from both sides, and echoes from the midline structures of the brain are recorded as graphic tracings

encephalogram – an x-ray made after the injection of a contrast material, usually air, into the cerebrospinal fluid in order to outline the spinal cord and brain

fasciogram (no definition given)

fibrocaseous – both fibrous and caseous

fluoroscopy (no definition given)

hematogenous – produced by or derived from the blood; disseminated by the circulation or through the blood stream

hemodynamic – pertaining to the movements involved in circulation of the blood

hemopneumothorax – pneumopericardium with hemorrhagic effusion

hyalinization – conversion into a substance resembling glass

Hypaque – in combination with sodium hydroxide or meglumine, used as a radiopaque medium in angiocardiography and excretory urography

hyperaerated (no definition given)

hyperlucent (no definition given)

hypermotility – excessive or abnormally increased motility, as of the gastrointestinal tract

hysterogram – an x-ray of the uterus

hysterosalpingography – an x-ray of the uterus and uterine tubes after injection of a contrast medium, under pressure

idiopathic – self-originated; of unknown causation

intermural – situated between the walls of an organ or organs

Iridium-192 – a radioisotope used for selected cases of cancer

laminagram (laminogram) – an x-ray of a selected layer of the body made by body-section roentgenography

laminagraphy – the taking of x-rays at varying levels of tissue

lobulated – made up of or divided into lobules

loculate – divided into small spaces or cavities

lymphangiography – x-ray study of the lymphatic system after the injection of a contrast medium

mammography – x-ray of the mammary gland

meglumine – a chemical used in the preparation of certain radiopaque media

metastasis – the transfer of disease from one organ or part to another not directly connected with it

microcurie – unit for measuring the energy of a radionuclide in a tracer dose

miliary – characterized by the formation of lesions resembling millet seeds, as in miliary tuberculosis

millicurie – unit for measuring the energy of a radionuclide in a therapeutic dose

mucoviscidosis – cystic fibrosis of the pancreas

myelogram – an x-ray of the spinal cord

myelography – x-ray of the spinal cord after injection of a radiopaque substance into the subarachnoid space

necrosis – death of tissue

nephrogram – an x-ray of the kidney

nephrotomography – body-section roentgenography as applied to the kidney

nonopaque – not opaque to the roentgen ray

nuclide – a general term denoting all nuclear species of chemical elements, both stable and unstable; it is used synonymously with isotope

obliteration – complete removal, whether by disease, degeneration, surgical procedure, irradiation, etc.

opaque – neither transparent nor translucent

orifice – the entrance or outlet of any cavity in the body

osteopenia – reduced bone mass due to a decrease in the rate of osteoid synthesis to a level insufficient to compensate normal bone lysis

oxycephalic – pertaining to or characterized by a condition in which the top of the head is pointed

palliative – affording relief, but not cure; an alleviating medicine

Pantopaque – a contrast medium or radiopaque dye used in x-ray studies

peristalsis – the wormlike movement by which the alimentary canal or other tubular organs provided with both longitudinal and circular muscle fibers propel their contents

picogram – a unit of weight of the metric system; also called a micromicrogram or one-trillionth of a gram

pneumothorax – an accumulation of air or gas in the pleural space, which may occur spontaneously or as a result of trauma or a pathological process, or be introduced deliberately

portogram – an x-ray of the portal vein

presbyesophagus – a condition characterized by alteration in motor function of the esophagus as a result of degenerative changes occurring with advancing age

prominence – a protrusion or projection

pyelogram – x-ray in which the pelvis of the kidney is shown filled with contrast material, which may be injected directly into the urinary system through a catheter or into a vein to reach the kidneys through the blood

pyeloureterography (pyelography) – radiologic study of the kidney and renal collecting system, usually performed with the aid of a contrast agent

Pyrophosphate – any salt of pyrophosphoric acid

radiodensity (no definition given)

radioisotope – an isotope of a chemical element made radioactive by bombardment with neutrons; term has become obsolete—radionuclide is the accepted term

radionuclide – a nuclide that displays the property of radioactivity

radiopaque – not permitting radiant energy, such as x-rays, to pass

Reno M-DIP – Diatrizoate Meglumine Injection U.S.P., a radiopaque contrast agent

roentgen – the international unit of x- or y-radiation

roentgenography – picture of an organ or a region by means of roentgen rays

sarcoidosis – a chronic, progressive, generalized granulomatous reticulosis of unknown etiology, involving almost any organ or tissue, including the skin, lungs, lymph nodes, liver, spleen, eyes, or small bones of the hands and feet

scintigram (scintiscan) – a two-dimensional representation (map) of the gamma rays emitted by a radioisotope, revealing its varying concentration in a specific tissue of the body, such as the brain, kidney, or thyroid gland

scintillation scan – image made by a scintillation counter to determine the size of a tumor, goiter, or other involvement and to locate aberrant, metastatic lesions

scybalum – a dry, hard mass of fecal matter in the intestine

selenium – a metallic element chemically similar to sulfur

senescent – exhibiting senescence or the process or condition of growing old, especially the condition resulting from the transitions and accumulations of the deleterious aging processes

sialogram – radiographic visualization of the salivary glands and ducts after injection of radiopaque material

siphon – a bent tube with two arms of unequal length, used to transfer liquids from a higher to a lower level by the force of atmospheric pressure

stereoroentgenography – the making of an x-ray giving an impression of depth as well as width and height

Strontium-90 – radionuclide used for lesions of the eye and removal of benign small tumors

submental – situated below the chin

suppuration – the formation of pus; the act of becoming converted into and discharging pus

Technetium 99m – a radionuclide used in brain, thyroid, parotid, and heart blood pool scans

Technetium Sulfur Colloid – radionuclide used in liver, spleen, and bone marrow scans

Telepaque – a contrast media, or radiopaque dye, used in x-ray studies

teleroentgenogram – the picture or film obtained by teleroentgenography

tertiary – third in order

Thallium 201 – radionuclide used in myocardial scans

tortuous – twisted

turricephalic (no definition given)

ureteropyelogram – an x-ray of the ureter and pelvis of the kidney

vasodilation – dilation of a vessel, especially dilation of arterioles leading to increased blood flow to a part

ventriculography – an x-ray of the head following removal of cerebrospinal fluid from the cerebral ventricles and its replacement by air or other contrast medium

Xenon 133 – a radionuclide used in studies of lung and blood flow

Yttrium-90 – radionuclide used for ascites and effusions associated with malignant metastatic involvement; i.e., hepatomegaly, splenomegaly, chronic leukemia, and polycythemia

X-RAY REPORT

Patient Name:

Doctor:

X-RAY REPORT

Patient Name:

Doctor:

X-RAY REPORT

Patient Name:

Doctor:

X-RAY REPORT

Patient Name:

    Doctor:

X-RAY REPORT

Patient Name:

Doctor:

X-RAY REPORT

Patient Name:

Doctor:

X-RAY REPORT

Patient Name:

Doctor:

X-RAY REPORT

Patient Name:

Doctor:

Patient Name:

Doctor:

X-RAY REPORT

Patient Name:

Doctor:

X-RAY REPORT

Patient Name:

Doctor:

X-RAY REPORT

Patient Name:

Doctor:

X-RAY REPORT

Patient Name:

Doctor:

Patient Name:

    Doctor:

X-RAY REPORT

Patient Name:

Doctor:

X-RAY REPORT

Patient Name:

Doctor:

X-RAY REPORT

Patient Name:

Doctor:

X-RAY REPORT

Patient Name:

    Doctor:

HISTORY:

X-RAY REPORT

Patient Name:

Doctor:

CHAPTER 15
UROLOGY/NEPHROLOGY

Urology is a study of the urinary tract in the male and female as well as the reproductive system in the male; nephrology is a study of the kidney and its disorders. A urologist is the name given to a surgeon who treats surgical disorders of the kidney, ureter, bladder, and male reproductive system. A physician who treats only kidney disorders is called a nephrologist.

Disorders that would be treated by a urologist include kidney stones, blood in the urine, inflammation of the bladder, and prostate problems in men.

The urinary system is made up of two kidneys, which form and excrete urine, removing various poisons from the body; two ureters, which carry urine from the kidneys down to the bladder; the urinary bladder, which serves as a collecting reservoir for urine; and the urethra, which transports the urine to the outside of the body.

ABBREVIATIONS

BNO	bladder neck obstruction	TPN	triphosphopyridine nucleotide
BPH	benign prostatic hypertrophy	TUE	transurethral extraction
BUN	blood urea nitrogen	TUR	transurethral resection
		TURB	transurethral resection, bladder
CAPD	continuous ambulatory peritoneal dialysis	TURP	transurethral resection, prostate
CT scan	computerized tomography		
		UA	urinalysis
ESRD	end stage renal disease	UPJ	ureteropelvic junction
		UTI	urinary tract infection
GU	genitourinary	UVJ	ureterovesical junction
KUB	kidneys, ureters, bladder	VCUG	voiding cystourethrogram
LDH	lactic dehydrogenase (enzyme in blood and tissues)	XC	excretory cystogram
		XU	excretory urogram
PVC	postvoiding cystogram		

DEFINITIONS OF TERMINOLOGY

acidosis – a pathologic condition resulting from accumulation of acid in, or loss of base from, the body

aciduria – the presence of acid in the urine

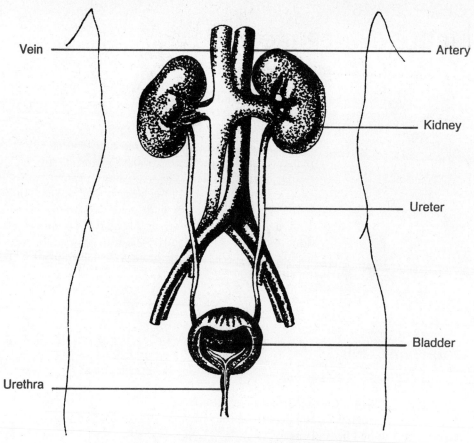

Vein — — Artery

— Kidney

— Ureter

— Bladder

Urethra —

15-1   The Genitourinary System

Albarran's disease – presence of E. coli in the urine

albuminuria – presence in the urine of serum albumin

alkalosis – a pathologic condition resulting from accumulation of base in, or loss of acid from, the body

aminoaciduria – an excess of amino acids in the urine

amyloidosis – the accumulation of amyloid in various body tissues

amyotrophia (amyotrophy) – atrophy of muscle tissue

anorchism – congenital absence of the testis, which may occur unilaterally or bilaterally

anorexia – lack or loss of the appetite for food

antidiuretic – agent used to suppress the rate of urine formation

antigen – any substance which is capable, under appropriate conditions, of inducing the formation of antibodies and of reacting specifically in some detectable manner with the antibodies so induced

antipyrine – chemical compound used as an analgesic

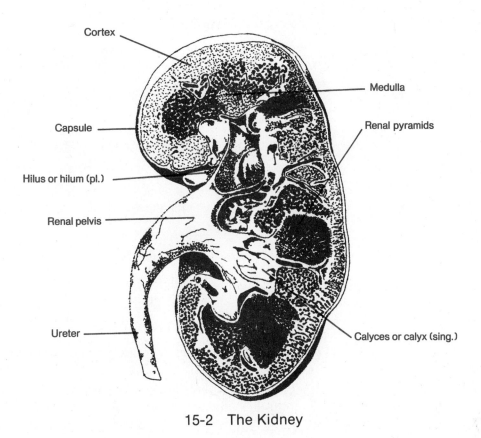

Cortex

Medulla

Capsule

Renal pyramids

Hilus or hilum (pl.)

Renal pelvis

Ureter

Calyces or calyx (sing.)

15-2   The Kidney

antistreptolysin – an antibody that inhibits streptolysin

anuria – absence of excretion of urine from the body

aplasia – lack of development of an organ or tissue, or of the cellular products from an organ or tissue

aspermia – failure of formation or emission of semen

asthenia – lack or loss of strength and energy; weakness

atheroma – a mass of plaque of degenerated, thickened arterial intima occurring in atherosclerosis

athrocytosis – absorption of macromolecules from the lumen of the renal tubular cells by means of a process similar to phagocytosis

atrophic – pertaining to or characterized by a wasting away

autoimmune – directed against the body's own tissue

autoimmunization – the induction in an individual of an immune response to its own tissue constituents, which may lead to pathological sequelae

azoospermia – the absence of living sperm

azotemia – an excess of urea or other nitrogenous bodies in the blood

bacteriuria – the presence of bacteria in the urine

balanitis – inflammation of the glans penis

Bence Jones protein – an abnormal urinary protein, which is found almost exclusively in multiple myeloma and constitutes the light-chain component of myeloma globulin

brucellosis – a generalized infection of humans involving primarily the reticuloendothelial system

bulbourethral – pertaining to the bulb of the urethra

calcareous – pertaining to or containing lime or calcium; chalky

calculus – an abnormal concretion occurring within the animal body and usually composed of mineral salts

caliectasis (calicectasis) – dilatation of a calix of a kidney

calyceal (caliceal) – pertaining to or affecting a calix

calyx (calix) – a cup-shaped organ or cavity

capsulectomy – excision of a capsule

capsulotomy – the incision of a capsule

caruncle – a small fleshy eminence, whether normal or abnormal

choriocarcinoma – any epithelial malignancy of trophoblastic cells, formed by the abnormal proliferation of cuboidal and syncytial cells of the placental epithelium, without the production of chorionic villi

chylocele – elephantiasis scroti

chyluria – the presence of chyle in the urine, giving it a milky appearance

cirrhosis – liver disease characterized pathologically by loss of the normal microscopic lobular architecture, with fibrosis and nodular regeneration

cloaca(ae) – the terminal end of the hindgut before division into the rectum, bladder, and genital primordia

colliculitis – inflammation about the colliculus seminalis

colloid – glutinous or resembling glue

corona – a crownlike eminence or an encircling structure

corticosteroid – any of the steroids produced by the adrenal cortex

creatinine – a basic substance, creatine anhydride, procurable from creatine and from urine

cremasteric – pertaining to the cremaster

cretinism – a chronic condition due to congenital lack of thyroid secretion, marked by arrested physical and mental development, dystrophy of the bone and soft parts, and lowered basal metabolism

cryesthesia – abnormal sensitiveness to cold

cryptorchism (cryptorchidism) – a developmental defect characterized by failure of the testes to descend into the scrotum

crystalluria – the excretion of crystals in the urine, producing renal irritation

cystine – an amino acid produced by the digestion or acid hydrolysis of proteins cystinosis (Fanconi's syndrome) – a congenital hereditary disease

cystinuria – the occurrence of cystine in the urine

cystolithectomy – the removal of a calculus by cutting into the urinary bladder

cystoureteritis – inflammation involving the urinary bladder and ureters

cystoureterolithotomy (no definition given)

cytotoxicity – the quality of being capable of producing a specific toxic action upon cells of special organs

dartos (tunica dartos) – a layer of smooth muscle fibers situated in the superficial fascia of the scrotum

dehydration – the condition that results from excessive loss of body water

descensus testis – the descent of the testis from its fetal position in the abdominal cavity to the scrotum

detrusor – a general term for any body part that pushes down

dialysis – the process of separating crystalloids and colloids in solution by the difference in their rates of diffusion through a semipermeable membrane

diuresis – increased secretion of urine

diuretic – increasing the secretion of urine; an agent that promotes the secretion of urine

dysgerminoma – a solid, often radiosensitive, neoplasm derived from undifferentiated germinal cells; it is found most often in the ovary or testis

dysproteinemia – derangement of the protein content of the blood

dysuria – painful or difficult urination

elephantiasis – a chronic filarial disease due to infection of the lymphatic channels, and characterized by inflammation and obstruction of the lymphatics and hypertrophy of the skin and subcutaneous tissues

endogenous – growing from within

enuresis – involuntary discharge of the urine

epispadia (epispadias) – a congenital defect in which the urethra opens on the dorsum of the penis

filiform – thread shaped; an extremely slender bougie

Foroblique – trademark for an obliquely forward visual telescopic system used in certain cystoscopes

frenum – a restraining structure or part

fulguration – destruction of living tissue by electric sparks generated by a high frequency current

funiculitis – inflammation of the spermatic cord

galactosuria – presence of galactose in the urine

gamma globulin – a group of plasma globulins which, in neutral or alkaline solutions, have the slowest electrophoretic mobility and which have sites of antibody activity

genitourinary – pertaining to the genital and urinary organs

Gerota's fascia or capsule – the fascia surrounding the kidney

glomerular – pertaining to or of the nature of a glomerulus, especially a renal glomerulus

glomerulitis – inflammation of the glomeruli of the kidney, with proliferative or necrotizing changes of the endothelial or epithelial cells or thickening of the basement membrane

glomerulonephritis – a variety of nephritis characterized by inflammation of the capillary loops in the glomeruli of the kidney

glomerulosclerosis – fibrosis and scarring which result in senescence of the renal glomeruli

glomerulus – a tuft or cluster; often used alone to designate one of the glomeruli of the kidney

glycosuria – the presence of glucose in the urine; especially the excretion of an abnormally large amount of sugar (glucose) in the urine

gonadectomy – removal of an ovary or a testis

gonadotropin – a substance having affinity for, or a stimulating effect on, the gonads

gonococcal – pertaining to gonococci

gonorrhea – infection due to Neisseria gonorrhoeae transmitted venerally in most cases

gubernaculum – something which guides

hematuria – blood in the urine

hemoconcentration – decrease of the fluid content of the blood, with resulting increase in its concentration

hemodialysis – the removal of certain elements from the blood by virtue of the difference in the rates of their diffusion through a semipermeable membrane

hemoglobinuria – the presence of free hemoglobin in the urine

hemolytic – pertaining to, characterized by, or producing hemolysis

hemorrhagic – pertaining to or characterized by hemorrhage; descriptive of any tissue into which bleeding has occurred

hermaphroditism – a condition characterized by the presence of both male and female sex organs

Hesselbach's triangle (trigonum inguinale) – the area on the inferoanterior abdominal wall bounded by the rectus abdominis muscle, the inguinal ligament, and the inferior epigastric vessels

hiatus – general term for a gap, a cleft, or an opening

hilus – a general term for a depression or pit at that part of an organ where the vessels and nerves enter

Hippuran – trademark for preparations of iodohippurate sodium

Hodgkin's disease – a malignant condition characterized by painless, progressive enlargement of the lymph nodes, spleen, and general lymphoid tissue

hyaline – glassy and transparent or nearly so

hydronephrosis – distention of the pelvis and calices of the kidney with urine, as a result of obstruction of the ureter, with accompanying atrophy of the parenchyma of the organ

hypercalcemia – an excess of calcium in the blood

hypercalciuria – excess of calcium in the urine

hypercapnia – excess of carbon dioxide in the blood

hyperchloremia – an excess of chloride in the blood

hypercholesterolemia – excess of cholesterol in the blood

hyperglycemia – abnormally increased content of sugar in the blood

hyperkalemia – abnormally high potassium concentration in the blood, most often due to defective renal excretion

hyperlipemia – an excess of lipids in the blood

hypernatremia – excessive amount of sodium in the blood

hypernephroma – renal cell carcinoma whose structure resembles that of the cortical tissue of the adrenal gland

hyperosmolarity – abnormally increased osmular concentration

hyperoxaluria – the excretion of an excessive amount of oxalate in the urine

hyperphosphatemia – an excessive amount of phosphates in the blood

hyperuricuria – excess of uric acid in the urine

hypoalbuminemia – an abnormally low albumin content of the blood

hypocalcemia – reduction of the blood calcium below normal

hypogonadism – a condition resulting from or characterized by abnormally decreased functional activity of the gonads, with retardation of growth and sexual development

hypoproteinemia – abnormal decrease in the amount of protein in the blood, sometimes resulting in edema and fluid accumulation in serous cavities

hypospadias – a developmental anomaly in the male in which the urethra opens on the underside of the penis or on the perineum

immunoelectrophoresis – a method combining electrophoresis and double diffusion for distinguishing between proteins and other materials by means of differences in their electrophoretic mobility and antigenic specificities

infundibulum – a funnel-shaped passage

interstitial – pertaining to or situated between parts or in the interspaces of a tissue

intrarenal – within the kidney

isoimmunization – development of antibodies against an antigen derived from a genetically dissimilar individual of the same species

kraurosis – a dry, shriveled condition of a part, especially of the vulva

kwashiorkor – a syndrome produced by severe protein deficiency characterized by retarded growth, changes in skin and hair pigment, edema, and pathological changes in the liver including fatty infiltration, necrosis, and fibrosis

leukocyturia – the discharge of leukocytes in the urine

lipoiduria (lipiduria) – the presence of lipids in the urine

lithiasis – a condition characterized by the formation of calculi and concretions

litholapaxy – the crushing of a calculus in the bladder, followed at once by the washing out of the fragments

macroglobulinemia – a condition characterized by increase in macroglobulins in the blood

malacoplakia – the formation of soft patches on the mucous membrane of a hollow organ

Marshall-Marchetti technique (no definition given)

meatotomy – incision of the urinary meatus in order to enlarge it

medulla – a general term for the inmost portion of an organ or a structure

micturition – the passage of urine; urination

myoglobinuria – the presence of myoglobin in the urine

myxedema – a condition characterized by a dry, waxy type of swelling with abnormal deposits of mucin in the skin and other tissues and associated with hypothyroidism

necrotizing – causing necrosis

neocystostomy (no definition given)

nephrectomy – excision of a kidney

nephritis – inflammation of the kidney

nephroblastoma – Wilm's tumor

nephrocalcinosis – a condition characterized by precipitation of calcium phosphate in the tubules of the kidney, with resultant renal insufficiency

nephrocystitis – inflammation of the kidney and bladder

nephrolithiasis – a condition marked by the presence of renal calculi

nephrolithotomy – the removal of renal calculi by cutting through the body of the kidney

nephrology – scientific study of the kidney, its anatomy, physiology, and pathology

nephropathy – disease of the kidneys

nephropexy – the fixation or suspension of a floating kidney

nephrosclerosis – hardening of the kidney; the condition of the kidney due to renovascular disease

nephrosis – any disease of the kidney

nephroureterectomy – excision of a kidney and a whole or part of the ureter

obturator – a disk, or plate, natural or artificial, which closes an opening, such as a prosthetic appliance used to close a congenital or acquired opening in the palate

oligospermia – deficiency in the number of spermatozoa in the semen

oliguria – secretion of a diminished amount of urine in relation to the fluid intake

orchiocele – hernial protrusion of a testis

orchiodynia (orchialgia) – pain in a testis

orchiopexy – surgical fixation in the scrotum of an undescended testis

orchitis – inflammation of a testis

os pubis – the pubic bone

oxalate – a salt of oxalic acid

oxalosis – primary hyperoxaluria

paraphimosis – retraction of phimotic foreskin, causing a painful swelling of the glans that, if severe, may cause dry gangrene unless corrected

pelviolithotomy (pyelolithotomy) – the operation of excising a renal calculus from the pelvis of the kidney

perineostomy (no definition given)

perinephritis – inflammation of the perinephrium

periurethral – occurring around the urethra

Peyronie's disease – induration of the corpora cavernosa of the penis, producing a fribrous chordee

phalloplasty – plastic surgery of the penis

phallus – the penis

phimosis – tightness of the foreskin, so that it cannot be drawn back from over the glans

phlebolith – a calculus or concretion in a vein; a vein stone

photon – a particle (quantum) of radiant energy

plasmapheresis – the removal of blood, separation of plasma by centrifugation, and reinjection of the packed cells suspended in citrate-saline or other suitable medium

polycystic – containing or made up of many cysts

polydipsia – excessive thirst persisting for long periods of time, as in diabetes mellitus

polyuria – the passage of a large volume of urine in a given period, a characteristic of diabetes

porphyruria (porphyrinuria) – the presence in the urine of porphyrin in excess of the normal amount

posthitis – inflammation of the prepuce

preputial – pertaining to the prepuce (a covering fold of skin; often used alone to designate the preputium penis)

prevesical – situated in front of the bladder

priapism – persistent abnormal erection of the penis, usually without sexual desire, and accompanied by pain and tenderness

prostatectomy – surgical removal of the prostate or of a part of it

proteinuria – the presence of an excess of serum proteins in the urine

pseudomembranous – marked by or pertaining to a pseudomembrane (false membrane)

pyelectasis – dilatation of the renal pelvis

pyelitis – inflammation of the pelvis of the kidney

pyelocaliectasis – dilatation of the kidney pelvis and calices

pyelonephritis – inflammation of the kidney and its pelvis

pyonephrosis – suppurative destruction of the parenchyma of the kidney, with total or almost complete loss of renal function

pyuria – the presence of pus in the urine

resectoscope – an instrument for transurethral prostatic resection

retropubic (no definition given)

Retzius' foramen, space, etc. (no definition given)

scintiscan (scan) – a two-dimensional representation (map) of the gamma rays emitted by a radioisotope, revealing its varying concentration in a specific tissue of the body, such as the brain, kidney, or thyroid gland

seminoma – a malignant tumor of the testis thought to arise from primitive gonadal cells

septicemia – systemic disease associated with the presence and persistence of pathogenic microorganisms or their toxins in the blood

spermatogenesis – the process of formation of spermatozoa

spermatogonium – an undifferentiated germ cell of a male, originating in a seminal tubule and dividing into two primary spermatocytes

spermaturia (seminuria) – the presence of semen in the urine

symphysis – a site or line or union; used to designate a type of cartilaginous joint in which the opposed bony surfaces are firmly united by a plate of fibrocartilage

synorchism – fusion of the two testes into one mass, which may be located in the scrotum or in the abdomen

trabeculation – the formation of trabeculae in a part

transilluminates (no definition given)

transvesical – through the bladder

trigone – a triangular area

trigonitis – inflammation or localized hyperemia of the trigone of the bladder

tunica – a general term for a membrane or other structure covering or lining a body part or an organ

tunica albuginea – a dense, white, fibrous sheath enclosing a part or an organ

urea – a white, crystalline substance found in the urine, blood, and lymph

ureterectasis – distention of the ureter

ureteritis – inflammation of a ureter

ureteroenteric – pertaining to or connecting the ureter and the intestine

ureterolithiasis – the formation of a calculus in the ureter

ureterolithotomy – the removal of a calculus from the ureter by incision

ureteropelvic – pertaining to or affecting the ureter and the renal pelvis

ureteroureterostomy – end-to-end anastomosis of the two portions of a transected ureter

urethrovesical – pertaining to or communicating with the urethra and the bladder

uriniferous – transporting or conveying the urine

urotoxia – the toxicity of the urine; the toxic substance of the urine

utriculus – a small sac

varicocele – a varicose condition of the veins of the scrotum

vasectomy – surgical removal of the ductus (vas) deferens, or of a portion of it; done in association with prostatectomy, or to induce infertility

verumontanum (colliculus seminalis) – a prominent portion of the urethral crest on which are the opening of the prostatic utricle and, on either side of it, the orifices of the ejaculatory ducts

*vesicourethropexy

---

*These terms were used in dictation but were not located in any of the references consulted. You will encounter this situation throughout this text. For a list of the reference books consulted, see page 502.

SURGICAL

Patient Name: Date:

    Doctor:

PREOP DIAGNOSIS:

POSTOP DIAGNOSIS:

PROCEDURE:

OPERATION

Patient Name: Date:

    Doctor:

PREOP DIAG:

POSTOP DIAG:

SURGEON:

PROCEDURE:

   PROCEDURE:

SURGERY

Patient Name: Date:

    Doctor:

PREOP DIAGNOSIS:

POSTOP DIAGNOSIS:

OPERATION:

SURGEON:

PROCEDURE:

SURGERY

Patient Name: Date:

    Doctor:

SURGEON:

ASST:

PREOP DIAG:

POSTOP DIAG:

OPERATION:

PROCEDURE:

OPERATION

Patient Name: Date:

    Doctor:

OPERATION:

SURGEON:

ANESTHESIA:

ASSISTANT:

PROCEDURE:

OPERATION

Patient Name:

Doctor:

DATE OF OPERATION:

SURGEON:

ASSISTANT:

ANESTHESIA:

PREOPERATIVE DIAGNOSIS:

POSTOPERATIVE DIAGNOSIS:

TITLE OF OPERATION:

PROCEDURE:

HISTORY

Patient Name: Date:

Doctor:

PHYSICAL

Patient Name: Date:

Doctor:

SURGERY

Patient Name: Date:

    Doctor:

PREOP DIAG:

POSTOP DIAG:

SURGEON:

OPERATION:

PROCEDURE:

SURGERY

Patient Name:

Doctor:

DATE OF SURGERY:

PREOP DIAGNOSIS:

POSTOP DIAGNOSIS:

SURGEON:

OPERATION:

ANESTHESIA:

PROCEDURE:

OPERATION

Patient Name:

Doctor:

DATE:

SURGEON:

ASSISTANT:

OPERATION PERFORMED:

PROCEDURE:

DISCHARGE SUMMARY

Patient Name: Date:

Doctor:

Admitted:
Discharged:

PROBLEM #1:

SUBJECTIVE:

OBJECTIVE:

ASSESSMENT:

PROBLEM #2:

SUBJECTIVE:

OBJECTIVE:

APPENDIX

MODEL REPORT FORMS

HISTORY

Aultman, Johnny   March 14, 19--

Sachi Dazai, M.D.

PI: This is a 76-year-old white male who presented to the ER because of black tarry stools. He had been having these for just a short period of time and only has had two stools. He has not been having any indigestion or heartburn. He has a past history of peptic ulcer disease twice in the past with bleeding. Each of those two times he had no pain or indigestion. He has not had any nausea or vomiting.

PH: He has been in relatively good health. He has had hypertension for about 6 years. No history of thyroid disease or history of asthma, TB, or pneumonia. He has been a borderline diabetic about 6 years.

He has no known allergies.

He has had no previous surgery.

ROS:

HEENT: Has a cataract on the right eye. He has decreased vision in that eye.

PUL: He has some chronic productive cough and does have some shortness of breath with exertion. There is no hemoptysis. He has no PND or orthopnea.

CV: No chest pains, palpitations, or fluttering.

GI: See PI.

GU: No dysuria, hematuria, frequency, or urgency. He does have some decrease in size and force of his stream at times. He also has some terminal dribbling. He has nocturia 1 to 2 times per night.

NM: He has stiffness in his left shoulder. He has some pain at times in the right shoulder.

SH: He smoked about two packs a day for about 25 yrs. but stopped about 16 yrs. ago. He does not drink.

CURRENT MEDS: Dyazide one daily; a 1,500 calorie ADA diet.

FH: Father had a CVA. He has a brother with prostate CA and a sister with CA of the spleen.

PHYSICAL

Aultman, Johnny   March 15, 19--

Sachi Dazai, M.D.

GENERAL: Well-developed white male in no acute distress

VITAL SIGNS: BP - 142/70. Resp - 18. Pulse - 100. Temp - 97.5.

HEENT: Pupils are equal, round, and reactive to light and
                  accommodation. He has a right cataract. Fundi are
                  normal. He has dentures.

NECK: There are no carotid bruits. There is some fullness over
                  the thyroid but no palpable gland.

HEART: Regular without a murmur, rub, or gallop.

LUNGS: Clear to auscultation and percussion.

ABDOMEN: Soft and nontender. No masses are palpable. He has no
                  bruits. There is no palpable organomegaly. No masses
                  palpable.

RECTAL: He has some black tarry stool in the rectal vault that is
                  hemocult positive. His prostate is 1 to 2+ enlarged but
                  there are no hard nodules.

NEUROLOGICAL: He moves all extremities well. Sensory and motor
                  function is normal. DTRs are symmetrical.

EXTREMITIES: No clubbing, cyanosis, or edema.

IMPRESSION: Melena; rule out bleeding peptic ulcer disease.

Sachi Dazai, M.D./eod

dd: 3/14/--
dt: 3/14/--

OPERATION

Benson, Craig T.

Sandra Loftin, M.D.

DATE OF OPERATION:	March 13, 19--
SURGEON:	Sandra Loftin, M.D.
ASSISTANT:	Ed Torres, M.D.
PREOPERATIVE DIAGNOSIS:	Pituitary adenoma
POSTOPERATIVE DIAGNOSIS:	Same
TITLE OF OPERATION:	Sublabial transphenoidal-transseptal approach for excision of pituitary adenoma
ANESTHESIA:	CRNA

PROCEDURE: The patient had been previously anesthetized and placed in neurosurgical head holder. The anterior nares were inspected and two neurosurgical Cottonoids impregnated with 4% Cocaine solution were placed into the anterior nasal chambers bilaterally. The anterior nasal septum, floor of the nose, and premaxillary area were infiltrated with approximately 8 cc of 2% Xylocaine with Epinephrine 1:100,000. The face and abdomen were then prepped and draped in the usual manner. A left anterior hemitransfixion incision was performed and an anteroposterior mucoperichondrial/mucoperiosteal tunnel was created on the left. There was marked dislocation of the quadrilateral cartilage with fragmentation and multiple dense adhesions along the floor of the nose and anteriorly along the previous septal fracture line. Using blunt and sharp dissection, the adhesions were lysed. Several small fenestra were created along the inferior ridge and anteriorly. A right posterior mucoperiosteal tunnel was created after disarticulating the quadrilateral cartilage. An inferior floor of the nose tunnel on the left was created using Freer elevator. Due to the extreme deformity of the nasal cartilage, essentially submucous resection of quadrilateral cartilage and radical bony septectomy was performed. Thereafter, the remaining quadrilateral cartilage could be displaced from the maxillary crest into the right nasal chamber. A retrograde dissection was performed and an inferior tunnel on the right created. There was a large maxillary crest spur which was removed with a chisel. The face of the maxilla was then dissected beneath the piriform aperture. The anterior nasal spine was identified and removed with Jansen-Middleton. Attention was turned to the anterior gingival labial sulcus. Incision was performed from the left canine fossa to the contralateral canine fossa.   Mucoperiosteum overlying the premaxilla was incised and the previously encountered dissection plane was found.   Therefore, the Hardy was placed sublabially and used to visualize the face of the sphenoid. The mucoperiosteum was cleaned off of the face of the sphenoid.   The sphenoid sinus ostea was identified and small anterior fenestrae were created in the face of the sphenoid.   Thereafter, Dr. Torres enlarged the sphenotomy and completed his portion of the procedure which will be dictated.   Following removal of the adenoma and packing of the sphenoid sinus, we were again called to close the wound.   Severe fenestra of the mucoperichondrial were closed with interrupted sutures of #4-0 chromic. The septum was quilted with interrupted sutures of #3-0 chromic.   The left hemitransfixion incision was closed with interrupted sutures of #4-0 chromic.   Two interrupted sutures of Vicryl were placed in the columella and lateral alar areas to prevent collapse of the nose on the face of the premaxilla.   The sublabial incision was then closed with interrupted sutures of #3-0 chromic and bilateral intranasal trumpets were placed along with Telfa packing.   The patient was uneventfully awakened from general anesthesia and removed to the Recovery Room in stable condition.

Sandra Loftin, M.D./rt

dd: 3/13/--
dt: 3/13/--

SURGERY

Toups, Wallis

March 15, 19--

SURGEON: Susan Woods, M.D.

ANESTHETIC: Local, 1% Xylocaine

OPERATION: Implantation of permanent transvenous cardiac
                    pacemaker (Medtronic model 5985)

PREOP DIAGNOSIS: Intermittent atrial flutter/fibrillation with severe
                    ventricular bradycardia

POSTOP DIAGNOSIS: Same

FINDINGS: (including the condition of all organs examined)

Patient was admitted with episodes of atrial flutter/fibrillation with
very slow ventricular response in low 40's. Patient was entirely
uncooperative and combative during the course of operation. It took
five people to hold him on the cath table. Also, his heart rate was
between 140 and 180. He had very small veins in the region of the
deltopectoral groove. All these problems led to great difficulty
putting this pacemaker in. However, the electrode was finally
positioned in the apex of the right ventricle; and I assumed that his
threshold was satisfactory; but we could not be entirely sure of this
because of his very fast ventricular rate of 140 to 160. It appeared
that the threshold was an MA of 0.8, voltage 0.5 with resistance of 610
ohms. R-wave sensitivity was 7.3.

PROCEDURE: With the patient in the supine position, right pectoral
region was prepped and draped in the usual fashion. As mentioned above,
patient was entirely combative and uncooperative so that five people had
to hold him down. After satisfactory local anesthesia and regional
anesthesia were induced, transverse incision was made and the
deltopectoral groove was dissected. One vein appeared to be slightly
larger than the rest of the very small venules in this area; and it was
cannulated with a cardiac electrode, which with some difficulty was
gotten into the apex of the right ventricle under fluoroscopic control.
As mentioned above, patient's threshold appeared to be satisfactory,
though this was not entirely certain. Electrode was ligated in place
with heavy silk, after which it was attached to the Medtronic pacemaker
model 5985. The unit was implanted into the subcutaneous pocket. It
should be noted that the patient had practically no subcutaneous fat, so
that only a very, very thin layer of subcutaneous tissue and skin

overlies the pacemaker. The wound was closed in two layers. Dressings
were applied, and the patient was taken back to his room.

SUSAN WOODS, M.D./wst

dd: 3/15/--
dt: 3/15/--

PATHOLOGY REPORT

SPECIMENS: A. Right spermatic cord lipoma
              B. Right inguinal node

CLINICAL: Not given.

GROSS EXAMINATION: A. Received is a fragment of fibromembranous and fatty tissue which measures 4.4 x 3.0 x 2.0 cm. On cut section most of the tissue appears to be fat which is circumscribed and appears to be partially encapsulated. One representative section is submitted.

B. Received is a fragment of yellow fatty tissue measuring 1.5 x 1.4 x 0.8 cm. On cut section all of the tissue appears to be fat, and it appears to be partially encapsulated. No evident lymph node structure is identified grossly. Representative section is submitted.

MICROSCOPIC DIAGNOSES: A.   Hernia sac and lipoma
                          B.   Lymph node showing extensive fatty
                                replacement

                                        Joel Sundeen, M.D./br
                                        Pathologist

dd: 4/8/--
dt: 4/9/--

PATHOLOGY REPORT

SPECIMEN: Gallbladder

GROSS: There is a single calculus that is yellow to brown 0.7 cm
mulberry in type. The previously opened gallbladder consists of two
portions, one showing abundant fat and multiple staples. The other
portion is the portion of the fundus that is previously opened presently
measuring 6.0 x 3.5 x 1.2 cm, the remaining portion measuring 6.0 x 3.0
x 1.5 cm. Representative portion of soft tissue embedded.

MICROSCOPIC DIAGNOSES:
   1. Chronic cholecystitis--no evidence of malignancy these
sections.
   2. Cholelithiasis.

Michi Iwasaki, M.D./ba
Pathologist

dd: 5/18/--
dt: 5/18--

X-RAY REPORT

Welch, Leona   March 14, 19--

Dr. Ghetti

HISTORY: LEFT URETERAL STONE

IVP:

The scout film shows a large calcification measuring about 4 x 6 mm in the left pelvis. There is also a calcification overlying the right kidney region. There is good excretion of contrast material bilaterally. The size and shape of both kidneys are normal. There is a dromedary hump on the left side. There is minimal dilatation of the collecting system on the left, and there is moderate dilatation of the left ureter. The calyceal system on the right shows partial duplication but is otherwise normal. The right ureter is normal.

The bladder is also within normal limits. The distal left ureter does point right towards the stone seen on the scout film.

IMPRESSION:

Large left ureteral stone in the distal left ureter which is causing only minimal obstructive symptoms.

THOMAS P. GHETTI, M.D./jok

dd: 3/14/--
dt: 3/14/--

COLONOSCOPY

Carpenter, Rosa

Vincent Prell, M.D.

INSTRUMENT: Olympus CF1TL flexible colonoscope.

PROCEDURE: The patient was premedicated with Demerol 50 mg and Valium 20 mg and an additional 10 mg of Valium IV was given during the procedure. The colonoscope was passed to the cecum with mild difficulty.

FINDINGS: The patient was poorly prepped and there was some spasm in the sigmoid colon; but, otherwise, there were no mucosal lesions, mass lesions, friability, or ulceration seen throughout the colon.

IMPRESSION: Normal examination except for some spasm in the sigmoid colon.

RECOMMENDATIONS: Antispasmodics.
High-fiber diet.

Vincent Prell, M.D./rt

dd: 11/21/—
dt: 11/22/—

cc: Milton Toups, M.D.

CONSULTATION

Levi, Moses T.   March 11, 19--

Dr. Presley

CONSULTANT: Dr. Terry

The patient is a 25-year-old right-handed black male who around 6 a.m.
on 3/10 was coming to work. He states he lost control of his car and
was involved in motor vehicle accident. He was brought to Wallis
Emergency Room where he was seen and evaluated by Dr. Presley. He had
fracture involving his mandible and also fracture involving his left
clavicle. He complained of pain in the same region plus pain in his
thoracic region of his back.

Examination of this left shoulder reveals he has large area of
ecchymosis over the clavicle. The area is tender. The skin is intact.
He has full passive range of motion involving the left shoulder. All
muscle tendon units in the left upper extremity were tested and found to
be intact.

Examination of his neck revealed that he had some tenderness in the
region of the left sternocleidomastoid muscle and left pericervical
muscles. He could put his chin on his chest without any difficulty. He
had full rotation of his cervical spine.

Examination of his back revealed tenderness over the region of the
dorsal spinous process to T6. No swelling and increased heat and no
tenderness elsewhere.

X-rays taken of the thoracic spine revealed no fractures or
dislocations.

X-ray performed of the left clavicle reveals undisplaced fracture
involving the left clavicle.

IMP: 1.   Undisplaced fracture involving the left clavicle.
      2.   Multiple abrasions and contusions.
      3.   Fracture involving the mandible.

I discussed the care of the fractured clavicle with the patient and his
wife in detail. He is currently in figure-of-eight clavicular strap.
This may be removed for hygiene following his discharge. We need to
follow him back up in the office regarding this particular fracture.
Potential complications of this fracture were discussed with the patient
and his family in detail.

Thank you for this consultation.

MICHAEL S. TERRY, M.D./crd

dd: 3/11/--
dt: 3/11/--

ESOPHAGEAL MOTILITY STUDY AND BERNSTEIN TEST

Salters, Vivian

Dr. Dews

The esophageal motility study was done in the usual manner using the Beckman manometer. Using the slow pull-through technique, the lower esophageal sphincter pressure was measured. The mean was 15 mm of mercury, location at 40 cm and there was normal relaxation. Using both wet and dry swallows, the peristaltic waves were measured. In the mid esophagus, the mean pressure was 41 mm of mercury, duration five seconds and in the distal esophagus, 38 mm of mercury, duration of six seconds. The upper esophageal sphincter pressure was measured and was 55 mm of mercury in the anterior and posterior lead and 34 mm of mercury in the lateral lead. These were all within normal limits. The motility appeared normal even during the episode of chest pain that the patient experienced in the Bernstein test. There was one episode noted on the tracing of some simultaneous waves. However, there were no repetitive waves noted.

IMPRESSION: Positive Bernstein test with a normal esophageal motility study except for a few simultaneous waves.

Jim Dews, M.D./prt

dd: 3/7/--
dt: 3/7/--

cc: Endoscopy Lab

X-RAY REPORT

Presley, Andrea

Dr. Salem Poole   March 15, 19--

RENAL DYNAMIC AND STATIC SCINTIGRAPHY:

HISTORY: LONG HISTORY OF RECURRENT URINARY TRACT INFECTIONS, SMALL
ATROPHIC RIGHT KIDNEY

Nuclide:

Technetium Glucoheptonate Complex 10 mCi - IV

Serial Posterior Photoscintiscans:

There is prompt progression of photon activity down the abdominal
aorta with good visualization of the bifurcation and prompt appearance
of activity in both renal vascular beds simultaneously.

Blood Pool and Delayed Posterior and Oblique Photoscintiscans:

The renal functioning parenchyma vary in size. Diameters are on the
right 7 1/2 x 5 1/2 cm. and on the left 11 x 6 1/2 cm. Distribution of
photon activity is homogeneous and there is collecting system activity
in both collecting systems on delayed scan.

Scan:

Hippuran tagged Iodine 131-200 uCi - IV

Serial Posterior Two-Minute Photoscintiscans:

There is activity in both parenchyma at two minutes and collecting
system activity bilaterally at four minutes and bladder activity at six
minutes. Parenchymal washout is identified bilaterally at eight
minutes. No obstruction is present.

Histograms:

Activity curves are generated over both kidneys and on the right,
Phase I curve is initially sharp with a decreasing rate in the last part
of the curve peaking at 250 seconds at a 500-count intensity followed by
an efficient-appearing washout curve.

On the left, Phase I curve is sharp and peaking occurs at about 270 or 280 seconds at 600-count intensity followed by a sharp washout curve.

Michi Iwasaki, M.D./ba
Pathologist

dd: 3/15/--
dt: 3/15/--

DISCHARGE SUMMARY

Donaldson, Gayle

Dr. T. McGuffey

ADMITTED: 6/10/--
DISCHARGED: 6/14/--

DIAGNOSIS: 1. Atrophic gastritis.
              2. Irritable bowel syndrome.

OPERATIONS & PROCEDURES: Esophagogastroduodenoscopy 6/11/--

This 78-year-old white female was admitted for evaluation of abdominal
pain, nausea, and vomiting and reports of coffee-ground emesis. Several
weeks ago she was evaluated at the Danielson Hospital for similar
symptoms and was told she had several ulcers in her distal esophagus and
that she would require surgery. She was subsequently started on
medications; however, she was told that she might have to have surgery.
She did fairly well after the initiation of medication; but over the
three days prior to admission she had increasing left upper quadrant
discomfort along with nausea, vomiting, hematemesis. She also gives
history of 35-pound weight loss over the last 18 months. In October
1983 she underwent evaluation at Speed Hospital and was found to have
erosive gastritis with duodenitis as well as reflux esophagitis. She
also had some left upper quadrant pain at that time which was attributed
to some post herpes zoster neuritis. The patient has previously had
cholecystectomy and appendectomy.

Physical exam on admission showed multiple well-healed abdominal scars.
No masses were palpable. There was some mild discomfort in the left
upper quadrant on palpation and bowel sounds were normal.

Laboratory data on admission: hemoglobin 13.8, WBC 8,000. Urinalysis
showed 3+ protein with 1 to 3 RBCs/HPF. SMAC was normal except for
slight elevation of BUN at 38.

HOSPITAL COURSE: The patient underwent EGD by Dr. Andrew Friend on
6/11/-- with findings of some mild erythema in the prepyloric area but,
otherwise, was unremarkable. CT scan of the abdomen was normal. Serum
Gastrin was slightly elevated at 256 and gastric analysis was done which
showed basal of 0.3mEq/hr which was quite low, maximal acid output 7.1
which is also low and peak acid output of 10mEq/hr. The Zantac had been
discontinued about 24 hours prior to gastric analysis. Lactose
tolerance test was done and this showed normal curve. Barium enema was
done which was normal grossly.

My impression is that the patient has element of atrophic gastritis.
She was started on Reglan while in the hospital and has shown marked
improvement with regard to her nausea and abdominal discomfort. I

suspect that she has some element of irritable bowel syndrome and we are
instituting high-fiber diet and continuing Reglan and Zantac. She has
been instructed to continue bland diet and to add additional foods one
at a time. She is to return to my office in three weeks for follow up.
MEDS at time of discharge: Zantac 150 mg p.o. b.i.d., Reglan 10 mg p.o.
a.c. and h.s., Restoril 30 mg h.s. p.r.n. sleep, Darvocet-N 100 1 q. 4
hours p.r.n. pain.

DAVID HAMMETT, M.D./rt

dd: 6/14/--
dt: 6/14/--

REPORT OF TISSUE EXAMINATION

Patient: Dagget, Danny

Doctor: James Z. Sherman, M.D.

Specimen Number: 93804-76

Date Removed: 3/11/--

Date Received: 3/11--

Waters General Hospital
476 Danielson Avenue
Superior, AL   57890-3302

Specimen: B-3894-76

Date Reported: 3/13/--

GROSS AUTOPSY DESCRIPTION:

Autopsy was performed on Wednesday, March 11, 19--, at Waller Funeral Home beginning at 11:30 a.m. Funeral home attendants were present during the proceedings.

External Description--The body is that of a well-developed, well-nourished elderly caucasian male, identified as Danny Dagget by funeral home employees. The head is normal in size and shape, scalp partially covered with long white hair. Facial features are not remarkable. The right cornea has a cloudy, glazed appearance. The mouth is largely edentulous, the mucosal surfaces having a pasty grayish-green appearance. There is a slight degree of beard growth. The neck is symmetrical. The chest is slightly increased in AP diameter, and the abdomen is protuberant. External genitalia are normal adult male except for reddish-purple discoloration of the scrotum. Extremities are bilaterally symmetrical. There is no rigor or livor mortis.

Body Cavities--The body is opened by the usual Y-shaped incision and the sternum removed. There is no abnormal accumulation of blood or fluid in any of the body cavities. There are a few fibrous adhesions in the apical portions of the upper lobes of both lungs.

Cardiovascular System--The heart is of normal size and shape. Coronary arteries are in their usual distribution and show a moderate degree of atherosclerosis with areas of up to 50 percent narrowing of the lumen. No thrombi or other occlusions are identified. The myocardium is firm reddish-brown and of normal thickness. The valves of the heart are normally disposed and appear grossly normal except for slight fusion of the aortic cusps. The aorta and great vessels show a mild to moderate degree of atherosclerosis.

Respiratory System--The larynx and trachea are patent and contain a small amount of brownish-green mucoid material. The mucosal surfaces have a grayish-green to reddish-purple discolored appearance, a similar appearance extending into the major bronchi of both lungs. The lungs are of normal size and shape with increased weight. There is nodular consolidation in the posterior and lateral aspects of the lower lobes of both lungs, more marked on the right where there is a fairly solid nodular friable area approximately 5.0 cm diameter. Overlying pleural surface has a slightly granular reddish-gray appearance. Similar nodular consolidation is present in the posterior aspect of the upper lobe of the right lung and to a lesser degree in the upper lobe of the left lung. There is marked emphysematous change of the apical portions of both upper lungs, more marked on the right. In the area of the apical fibrous adhesions on the right, there is a focal grayish-tan nodular lesion 1.5 cm diameter, grossly resembling an old granuloma. Hilar lymph nodes are slightly enlarged and anthracotic.

Gastrointestinal System--The esophagus is intact. The stomach is dilated and contains semiliquid reddish-gray material. The marked gaseous distention of the entire intestinal tract, particularly the colon. Lumen contains the usual fecal material. The liver is of normal size and shape, capsules smooth reddish-tan, parenchyma reddish-brown with normal architectural markings. The gallbladder is large, measuring 10.5 cm greatest dimension and contains thick, dark green bile, no stones present. Extra-hepatic ducts are normal. The pancreas has a normal lobulated grayish-tan appearance and is of normal size.

Spleen--The spleen is submitted twice normal size and has a smooth reddish-purple capsule, parenchyma firm, dark reddish-purple with no gross lesions.

Endocrine System--The adrenal glands are of normal size and appearance with yellow cortex and gray-white medulla. The thyroid gland is of normal size and grossly normal. Parathyroid glands are not identified.

Genitourinary System--The kidneys are of normal size and shape, cortical surfaces smooth, cut surfaces showing normal architectural markings. The calices and pelvis are of normal size, both ureters patent and normal in size. The urinary bladder is grossly not remarkable. The prostate gland is slightly enlarged.

Central Nervous System--The scalp is reflected in the usual manner and the calvarium removed. There is no abnormal accumulation of blood or fluid in the cranial cavity. The dura and leptomeninges are smooth and glistening with no exudate or other lesions identified. The brain is removed and is found to be externally symmetrical with the usual architectural markings. Vessels at the base of the brain show scattered moderate atheromatous plaques. On the anterior medial aspect of the tip of the right temporal lobe, there is a 1.0 cm granular reddish—gray area which appears to represent superficial necrosis. Multiple coronal sections through the cerebrum, cerebellum, and brain stem reveal normal architectural markings. Ventricles are of normal size and shape with smooth, glistening linings.

Skull——Examination of the internal bones of the cranial vault reveal an eroding lesion extending through the sphenoid bone on the right, immediately adjacent and partially involving the sella turcica. The tumor has a grayish—tan appearance. Cut surface through the area reveals an infiltrating mass approximately 2.5 cm greatest dimension which appears to involve the bony walls of the sphenoid sinus and the wall of the orbit. Cranial nerves 3, 4, 5, and 6 appear to be encroached upon by tumor. The pituitary gland is removed and is grossly normal in size and shape with a slight granular appearance on the right aspect of the anterior lobe. The internal carotid artery appears to be partially surrounded by neoplasm but is not grossly penetrated.

MICROSCOPIC DESCRIPTION:

Heart——Sections of heart show irregular areas of atrophy of myocardial fibers associated with a slight degree of fatty infiltration from the epicardium. In one section, there is an irregular area of considerably increased fibrous interstitial tissue forming a small scar near the center. Coronary arteries have moderately sclerotic walls.

Lungs——Sections from various areas of lungs show extensive intra—alveolar organizing pneumonitis with patchy areas showing almost complete filling of the alveolar spaces by fibroblastic plugs containing inflammatory cells and hemosiderin—laden macrophages. Clumps of fibrin and erythrocytes are prominent in some areas. Vessels are dilated and engorged. Focal accumulations of neutrophils are present in some of the alveolar spaces and in some bronchial lumens. There is a thick layer of fibrin on the pleural surface, and in one section, numerous neutrophils are also present. Bronchial walls are thickened and show a chronic inflammatory infiltrate with extraordinary numbers of plasma cells in some instances. Bronchial mucosa appears somewhat hyperplastic. In a section from the right apex, there is a dense fibrotic scar with calcification consistent with old granuloma. Throughout the lung there are varying degrees of emphysema associated with interstitial fibrosis. Peribronchial hilar lymph nodes show reactive hyperplasia.

Spleen——The spleen is markedly congested with dilatation and engorgement of sinusoids. Plasma cells are greatly increased in the red pulp and there are scattered accumulations of hemosiderin—laden macrophages. Malpighian corpuscles are not remarkable.

Liver——Architecture of the liver is preserved. Central veins and sinusoids are moderately dilated. There is a minimal degree of fatty change of hepatocytes with no particular zonal distribution. Portal areas are not remarkable.

Pancreas—There is a moderate interlobular fatty infiltration. Islets appear more numerous than usual. Acini are well preserved.

Adrenal Gland—There are no significant histologic abnormalities.

Kidneys—The kidneys are congested. Glomeruli are generally well preserved and are congested. Tubules show slight dilatation of the lumens, and some in the medullary areas have hyaline casts in their lumens. There is mild to moderate hyalinized thickening of the walls of arterioles as well as small muscular arteries.

Primary Neoplasm—Sections from the right sphenoid sinus area reveal areas of extensive tumor necrosis with scattered foci of residual viable cells, generally surrounding intact blood vessels. The cells are poorly differentiated, variable in size, but generally small with hyperchromatic nuclei and no visible cytoplasm. There is extension into intratrabecular spaces in the bone associated with fibrosis. A section of the internal carotid artery on the right shows infiltrating neoplasm invading the adventitia and minimally into the media of the artery. No neoplasm is present in the lumen. The arterial wall also shows severe atherosclerosis with calcification.

Pituitary Gland—There is superficial invasion of the capsule of the anterior lobe of the pituitary gland with minimal involvement of the parenchyma.

Brain—Sections of the right temporal lobe in the area adjacent to the penetrating neoplasm reveal infiltration of carcinoma into the subarachnoid space and underlying cerebral tissue. There is associated tissue necrosis adjacent to the tumor. Other areas of the brain show essentially normal histologic features with exception of engorgement of vessels and slight increase in perivascular space. Though there is some necrosis associated with the infiltrating neoplasm, there are no histologic findings in the adjacent brain tissue to suggest any degree of radiation effect.

COMMENT:

The patient died primarily as a result of extensive bilateral bronchopneumonia resulting from repeated aspiration, occurring as complication of longstanding carcinoma of the right nasal area and sphenoid sinus. The bulk of the tumor mass at autopsy was found in the area of the sphenoid sinus with erosion into the adjacent bony structures involving the wall of the sella turcica. The pituitary gland was superficially invaded, and the internal carotid artery was nearly surrounded by tumor which partially invaded its wall. The adjacent temporal lobe of the brain was also invaded, though there was relatively superficial destruction in this area. There were extensive areas of tumor necrosis suggesting radiation effect, though radiation damage was not appreciable in the adjacent brain tissue. Cranial nerves 3 through

6 were encroached upon by tumor, resulting in loss of function of these nerves as detected clinically.

DIAGNOSIS:

Bilateral bronchopneumonia, secondary to aspiration, staphylococcus aureus, Klebsiella pneumoniae, and Proteus mirabilis grown from sputum culture prior to death.
Fibrinopurulent pleuritis, associated with bronchopneumonia.
Poorly differentiated squamous cell carcinoma of right sphenoid sinus with invasion into cranial cavity, right temporal lobe of pituitary gland.
Partial radiation necrosis of neoplasm.
Moderate inanition, secondary to neoplasm and infection.
Marked passive congestion of liver and spleen.
Marked gaseous distention of small and large intestine, consistent with adynamic ileus.
Pulmonary emphysema and interstitial fibrosis.
Fibrotic calcified nodule, apex of right lung, consistent with old granuloma.
Fibrous pleural adhesions, bilateral.
Minimal fatty change of liver.

JZS/DLC

_____, M.D.
Pathologist

James Z. Sherman

dd: 3/11/--
dt: 3/11/--

CONFUSING MEDICAL TERMS

abduction – the act of drawing away from the axis of the body
adduction – the act of drawing toward a center

aberration – deviation from the usual course or condition
abrasion – the wearing away of a substance or structure through some unusual or abnormal mechanical process

absorption – the soaking up of a substance by skin or other surface
adsorption – the adherence of a substance to a surface

afferent – designates nerves or neurons that convey impulses from sense organs and other receptors to the brain or spinal cord
efferent – designates nerves or neurons that convey impulses from the brain or spinal cord to muscles, glands, and other effectors

aphagia – abstention from eating
aphasia – a disorder of language affecting the generation of speech and its understanding and not simply a disorder of articulation

areola – a circular area of a different color surrounding a central point
areolae – plural of areola
areolar – pertaining to or containing areolae

arteriosclerosis – a group of diseases characterized by thickening and the loss of elasticity of arterial walls.
arteriostenosis – ossification of an artery
atherosclerosis – hardening of the arteries caused by the deposition of calcium and cholesterol in the arterial walls

aural – pertaining to the ear
oral – pertaining to the mouth

calculous – pertaining to, of the nature of, or affected with calculus
calculus – a hard, pebble-like mass formed within the body, particularly in the gallbladder

callous (adj) – unfeeling; the adjective form of callus
callus (n) – a callosity

cancellous – of a reticular, spongy, or lattice-like structure; said mainly of bony tissue
cancellus – any structure arranged like a lattice

canker – an ulceration, primarily of the mouth and lips
chancre – the primary lesion of syphilis

cerebellum – that part of the brain behind the cerebrum
cerebrum – the main portion of the brain

cystoscopy – direct visual examination of the urinary tract with a cystoscope
cystostomy – the formation of an opening into the bladder
cystotomy – surgical incision of the urinary bladder

dysphagia – difficulty in swallowing
dysphasia – impairment of speech
dysplasia – abnormality of development
dyspragia – painful performance of any function

enervation – lack of nervous energy
innervation – the supply of nervous energy or of nerve stimulus sent to a part

enterocleisis – closure of a wound in the intestine
enteroclysis – the injection of a nutrient or medicinal liquid into the bowel

facial – pertaining to the face
fascial – pertaining to the fascia

fossa – a trench or channel; a general term for a hollow or depressed area
fossae – plural of fossa

ileum – part of the small intestine
ilium – part of the pelvis

malleolus – a bone of the ankle
malleus – a bone of the ear

mucosa – a mucous membrane
mucosal – pertaining to the mucous membrane

mucous (adj) – pertaining to or resembling mucus
mucus (n) – secretion of the mucous membrane

myelitis – inflammation of the spinal cord
myositis – inflammation of a voluntary muscle

palpation – the act of feeling with the hand
palpitation – unduly rapid action of the heart

pericardium – the membrane surrounding the heart
precordium – the region of the thorax immediately over the heart

perineal – pertaining to the perineum, or genital region
peritoneal – pertaining to the peritoneum, or membrane lining the abdominal
    wall
peroneal – pertaining to the fibula

psychosis – a general term for any major mental disorder of organic and/or
    emotional origin
sycosis – a disease marked by inflammation of the hair follicles

radical – directed to the cause; directed to the root or source of a morbid process
radicle – any one of the smallest branches of a vessel or nerve

scirrhous – pertaining to a cancer that is stony hard to the touch
scirrhus – scirrhous carcinoma

ureter – the tube through which urine travels to the bladder
urethra – a membranous canal through which urine travels from the bladder to
    the surface

ureteral – pertaining to the ureters
urethral – pertaining to the urethra

vesical – pertaining to the bladder
vesicle – a small bladder or sac containing liquid

villous – shaggy with soft hairs; covered with villi
villus – a small vascular process or protrusion

FREQUENTLY USED DRUGS

Actifed
Adriamycin
Afrin Nasal Spray
Aldoril
Amoxicillin
Ampicillin
Apresoline
Ativan
Azo Gantrisin
Azulfidine

Bactrim
Benadryl
Betadine
Butabell
Butisol Sodium Elixir

CaldeCORT Hydrocortisone
    Cream
Cardizem
Ceclor
Celestone
Chloromycetin
Choledyl
Cleocin
Coly-Mycin
Cortef Acetate
Cytoxan

Darvocet-N
Darvon
Dasikon
Decadron
Diabinese
Dialose
Dicumarol
Diethylstilbestrol
Digoxin
Dilantin
Dimetane
Dimetapp
Dimethyl Sulfoxide Cream
Dolobid
Dolonil
Dopamine
Dramamine
Dulcolax
Dyazide

Emetrol
Equagesic

Erythromycin
Evac-Q-Kit

Flagyl
Fluorouracil
Furadantin

Gantanol
Gantrisin
Garamycin
Gentamicin Cream

Haldol
Heparin Lock
Hepatitis B Immune Globulin
Herplex Liquifilm ophthalmic
    solution
Histalog, Ampoules
Histamine Phosphate
Hydrocortisone
HydroDIURIL

Ilosonc
Inderal
Indocin
Insulin
Ipecac
Isordil
Isosorbide Dinitrate Oral Tablets
Isuprel Hydrochloride Glossets

K-Lyte
Keflex
Keflin
Kenalog
Kenpectin
Kolantyl Gel
Kondremul with Cascara
Konsyl

Lactinex Granules
Lanoxin
Lasix
Leukeran
Librax
Lidocaine
Lincocin
Lithium Carbonate
Lopressor
Luminal

Maalox

Magnesium Sulfate
Mandol
Marcaine Hydrochloride
Mefoxin
Mellaril
Mercresin Tincture
Metamucil
Methadone Hydrochloride
Mi-Cebrin
Minipress
Minocin
Monistat
Motrin
Mycostatin
Mycostatin Oral Tablets
Mylicon

Naldecon
Narcan
Nembutal
Neodecadron
Neomycin
Neosporin Ointment
Neo-Synalar Cream
Neo-Synephrine
Nitroglycerin
Norgesic
Norpace
Novahistine
Nupercainal Cream

Ophthocort
Orinase
Ornade Spansule
Ortho-Novum
Oxytocin

Panheprin
Parafon Forte
Parepectolin
Pathibamate
Pathilon
Penicillin
Pentothal
Phenergan
Phenobarbital
Polycillin
Prednisone
Premarin
Pro-Banthine

Procaine
Provera
Pyridium

Quāālude
Quinidex
Quinidine

Rauserpin
Reglan
Reserpine
RhoGAM
Rifamate
Riopan
Ritalin
Robaxin
Robitussin
Roniacol
Ru-Tuss

Scopolamine

Seconal
Serpasil
Serpate
Similac
Sinequan
Slow-K
Sodium Bicarbonate
Solu-Medrol
Sorbide
Sorbitrate
Surfacaine

TACE
Tagamet
Talwin
Tegopen
Terramycin
Thyrolar
Tigan
Tofranil

Tolbutamide
Triavil
Tuss-Ornade

Urised
Urispas

Valisone
Valisone Cream
Valium
Vibramycin
Vitron-C

Wyanoid Ointment
Wydase

Xanax
Xylocaine

Yutopar

MEDICAL INSTRUMENTS

(Partial List)

A

Abadie clamp
ACMI gastroscope
Adair–Allis tissue forceps
Adson forceps
Adson–Brown forceps
Allport–Babcock mastoid retractor
argon laser

B

Babcock forceps
Backhaus dilator
Backhaus towel clamps
Bacon rongeur
Bailey-Gibbon rib contractor
Bainbridge goiter clamp
Bakes common duct dilator
Balfour retractor
Ballenger-Lillie mastoid bur
Ballenger tonsil forceps
Bard-Parker blade
Barraquer iris forceps
Beck-Schenck tonsil snare

Beckman goiter retractor
Bellucci scissors
Benedict gastroscope
Bennett retractor
Berens lens expressor
Berens mastectomy retractor
Bernstein gastroscope
Bethune rib shears
Beyer rongeur forceps
Blanchard hemorrhoid forceps
Blohmka tonsil hemostat
Boettcher antrum trocar
Bonney dissecting forceps
Boucheron ear speculum
Bovie unit
Bozeman forceps
Braasch bulb ureteral catheter
Bronson-Turtz iris retractor
Brown-Buerger cystoscope
Burford rib spreader

C

Cameron flexible gastroscope

Caparosa burs
Carmel clamps
Castroviejo-Arruga forceps
Cavanaugh-Wells tonsil suturing forceps
Chevalier Jackson gastroscope
Church scissors
Cicherelli rongeur forceps
Clark common duct dilator
Collin forceps
Cottle-Neivert retractor
C-P suction (Chaffin-Pratt)
Crile hemostatic forceps
Crutchfield tongs
Cushing retractor
Cushing vein retractor

D

Dandy forceps
Davidson electric bur
Davis-Crowe mouth gag
Deaver retractor
DeBakey-Cooley retractor
deCourcy goiter clamp
DeMartel-Wolfson forceps
Depuy-Weiss tonsil needle
Deschamps' ligature needles
Desjardin gallstone forceps
Desmarres lid elevator
Deutschman cataract knife
DeVilbiss cranial rongeur
DeWecker eye scissors
Dormia bracket
Doubilet sphincterotome
Doyen intestinal occlusion clamp
Doyen raspatory
Doyen retractor
Duckbill rongeur
Duffield scissors
Dunning periosteal elevator
Duval-Allis forceps

E

Eder gastroscope
Elliott forceps
Ellsner gastroscope
Elschnig cataract knife
Emerson suction

F

Farabeuf periosteal elevator
Faulkner antrum gouge
Fehland clamps

Fein antrum trocar
Fenger forceps
Ferguson needle
Ferris-Robb tonsil knife
Finochietto rib spreader
Foley catheter
Frankfeldt grasping forceps
Frazier retractor
Freer elevator
French catheter
Fritsch's retractor
Furniss-Clute clamp

G

Gavin-Miller forceps
Gelpi retractor
Gerzog mallet
Gifford curette
Gigli saw
Gill scissors
Gomco clamp
Gomco suction
Goodhill tonsil forceps
Graham scalene elevator
Grover meniscotome
Gruenwald rongeur
Guyton-Park lid speculum

H

Hajek mallet
Harrison-Shea knife
Hartmann forceps
Heaney forceps
Heermann chisel
Hegar dilator
Herrick clamp
Heymann-Paparella angular scissors
Hibbs retractor
Hibbs-Spratt curette
Hirschowitz gastroduodenal fiberscope
Hotz ear probe
House-Dieter malleus nipper
House myringotomy knife
Housset-Debray gastroscope

J

Jaboulay button
Jackson laryngoscope
Janeway gastroscope
Jansen forceps
Jesberg scope
Jewett osteotomy plate

Johns Hopkins forceps
Joker dissector
Judd-DeMartel forceps

K

Kahler forceps
Keeler pantoscope
Kehr's T tube
Kelly forceps
Kelly-Murphy forceps
Kelman forceps
Kerrison rongeur forceps
Key periosteal elevator
Kifa skin clip
Kirschner wire
Klebanoff gallstone scoop
Knapp cataract knife
Kocher clamp
Krukenberg pigment spindle
Krwawicz cataract extractor

L

Lahey forceps
Lambotte osteotome
Lane forceps
Langenbeck retractor
LeFort catheter
Lempert knife
Luer bone rongeur
Luer-Korte scoop
Luer-Whiting rongeur forceps

M

MacDonald dissector
Mackenrodt ligament
Mahoney speculum
Malecot catheter
Mathieu's retractor
Mayo scissors
McCaskey curette
McGuire scissors
McIndoe scissors
McIvor gag
Mentor wet field coagulator
Metzenbaum scissors
Meyerding finger retractor
Michel clips
Moersch esophagoscope
Mollison mastoid retractor
Molt mouth gag
Morris retractor
mosquito forceps

Moynihan artery forceps
Mueller mastoid curette

N

Nesbit resectoscope

O

O'Brien forceps
Ochsner forceps
Olivercrona rongeur forceps
Ollier rake retractor
O'Sullivan-O'Connor retractor

P

Parker-Heath cautery
Parker ribbon retractor
Payr clamps
Pean forceps
Penrose drain
Pezzer catheter
Potts-Smith forceps

R

Rampley sponge holding forceps
Rapaport common duct dilators
Reich-Nechtow forceps
Reiner rongeur
Rigby self-retaining retractor
Rizzuti iris retractor
Roux retractor
Rubinstein cryoprobe
Ruskin mastoid rongeur

S

Sam Roberts head rest
Sarot needle holder
Satinsky clamp
Sauerbruch box rib rongeur
scalpel
Schiotz tenonometer
Schnidt forceps
Schoemaker thyroid scissors
Schroeder forceps
Schuknecht knife
Sengstaken balloon
Senn retractor
Shallcross forceps
Shambaugh irrigator
Shea curette
Siker laryngoscope
Sims probe

Storz-Beck tonsil snare
Sump drain

T

Thorek scissors
Timberlake obturator

V

Van Buren urethral sounds
Varco forceps
Volkmann rake retractor
von Graefe cataract knife
von Petz clamp

Y

Yankauer antrum punch
Yankauer suction tube

W

Wagner antrum punch
Wangensteen clamp
Weiner-Pierce antrum trocar
Weitlaner retractor
Weitlaner self-retaining retractor
Wellaminski antrum perforator
Westcott scissors
Winsbury-White deep retractor

Z

Zeiss operating microscope
Ziegler knife
Zipser clamp

LABORATORY TESTS

A-1 Antitrypsin
A-1 Fetoprotein (fetoglobulin), quantitative
    (tumor marker)
A-E-DHA (androsterone, etiocholanoione,
    dehydroepiandrosterone)
Acetaminophen
Acetazolamide
Acetone plus acetoacetic acid
Acetone, GLC
Acid phosphatase colorimetric
Acid phosphatase, prostatic by RIA
ACTH
AHT (antistreptococcal hyaluronidase)
ALT—alanine aminotransferase (SGPT)
Albumin, serum
Alcohol, blood or urine, GLC
Aldolase
Aldosterone, serum
Alkaline Phosphatase
Alkaline phosphatase, heat fractionation
Alkaline phosphatase isoenzymes
Aluminum, serum
Aluminum, urine
Amenorrhea profile
Amikacin (Amikin®)
Amino acid screen, urine and blood
Aminolevulinic acid (D-ALA)

Aminophylline (theophylline)
Amitriptyline (Elavil®)
Ammonia
Amniotic fluid scan, (bilirubin) Delta OD scan
Amniotic fluid, creatinine
Amylase, serum or urine
Androstenedione
Androsterone, etiocholanolone,
    dehydroepiandrosterone
Angiotensin converting enzyme
Anti-DNA
Antibody identification panel
Antihyaluronidase (antistreptococcal
    hyaluronidase—AHT)
Antimitochondral antibodies
Antinuclear antibodies
Antiparietal cell antibodies
Antismooth muscle antibodies
Antistreptolysin-O (ASO)
Arsenic in miscellaneous substances
Arsenic, whole blood
ASO (antistreptolysin-O)
AST—aspartate aminotransferase (SGOT)

Bacteria identification
Bacterial meningitis antigens
Barbiturates

Beta lactamase activity, bacterial isolate
Bile acid/cholylglycine
Bilirubin, total
Bilirubin, total and direct
Bleeding time, modified Mielke
Blood group and type
Blood group—ABO
Blood smears, interpretation
Blood, Rh factor
Bromides, serum
Brucella abortus agglutination
BUN/Creatinine ratio

C-Reactive protein, CSF
C-Peptide
C-Reactive protein
Cadmium, urine
Caffeine, serum
Calcium, serum, atomic absorption
Calcium-dialysate
Calcium/Phosphorus, serum
Calcium/Phosphorus, urine
Calcium, serum, by atomic absorption
Calcium, urine
Calculus, infrared spectroscopy
Campylobacter, stool
Cannabinoids, urine
Carbamazepine (Tegretol®)
Carbon monoxide, blood
Carcinoembryonic antigen
Carotene
Catecholamines, free, urinary
Catecholamines, fractionated, plasma
Catecholamines, total, urine
CBC (Hemoglobin, hematocrit, RBC, WBC,
     MCH, MCV, MCHC, platelet count)
CBC with differential
Cell count
Celontin® (methsuximide)
Ceruloplasmin
Chloral hydrate/Trichloroethanol
Chloramphenicol
Chlordiazepoxide
Chloride, serum
Chloride, urine
Chlorides, iontophoresis
Chlorinated pesticides
Chlorpromazine
Cholesterol, total
Cholinesterase (pseudo), serum
Cholinesterase, dibucaine number
Clonazepam (Clonopin®)
Clorazepate (Tranxene®)
Cold agglutinins

Complement, C-4
Complement, C-3 and C-4
Complement, (beta 1A) C-3
Compound 5 (deoxycortisol)
Coombs test, direct
Coombs test, indirect
Copper, serum
Copper, urine
Copro/Protoporphyrins, feces
Cortisol, plasma
Cortisol, urinary free
Cosyntropin test (cortisol X3)
Co2/Carbon dioxide, content
CPK isoenzymes
CPK isoenzymes and LDH isoenzymes (D-9)
Creatine phosphokinase (CPK)
Creatine, serum
Creatine, urine
Creatinine clearance
Creatinine, serum
Creatinine, urine
Cryofibrinogen
Cryoglobulins
Cryptococcus antigen
Crystals, fluid
Culture for Neisseria
Culture, acid fast bacilli
Culture, blood
Culture, spinal fluid
Culture, sputum
Culture, stool
Culture, throat
Culture, urine
Cyclic AMP, plasma
Cyclic AMP, urine
Cystine
Cytochemistries for leukemia classification,
     with interpretation
Cytologic exam for presence of sperm
Cytology breast, fluid aspirate
Cytology, bronchial washings or brushings
Cytology, cerebrospinal fluid
Cytology, cervical
Cytology, esophageal brushings
Cytology, fluid, not specified
Cytology, gastric
Cytology, sputum
Cytology, urine
Cytomegalovirus, CMV-G
Cytomegalovirus, CMV-M

D-Xylose, blood
D-Xylose, urine
Dalmane® (flurazepam)

Darvon® (propoxyphene)
Dehydroepiandrosterone
Deoxycorticosterone
Deoxycortisol (compound S)
Depakene® (valproic acid)
Desipramine
Desyrel® (trazedone)
DHEA
DHEA, sulfate
Dilantin® (phenytoin)
Diazepam (Valium®)
Digitoxin
Digoxin
Diphenylhydantoin (phenytoin)
Diphenylhydantoin, free
Disopyramide (Norpace®)
Doriden® (glutethimide)
Doxepin
Drug screen, miscellaneous, TLC
Drug screen, blood, GLC
Drug screen, gastric, TLC
Drug screen, miscellaneous, GLC
Drug screen, serum, TLC
Drug screen, urine, GLC
Drug screen, gastric, GLC
Dyphylline

Elavil® (amitriptyline)
Electrolytes, urine
Electrophoresis, CSF (oligoclonal bands)
Electrophoresis, serum
Electrophoresis, urine
Eosinophils, total
Estradiol (E2)
Estriol, serum
Estriol, urine
Estrogens, total urine
Estrone, (E1)
Estrone and Estradiol
Ethclorvynol (Placidyl®)
Ethosuximide (Zarontin®)
Ethotoin (Peganone®)
Etiocholanolene

Factor V assay
Factor VII assay
Factor VIII assay
Factor IX assay
Factor X
Factor XIII
Fat globules, serum
Fat globules, urine
Fat stain, stool
Febrile agglutination, tube titer

Febrile agglutination series
Ferritin
Febrin Degradation products
Fibrinogen
Fluoride, serum
Flurazepam (Dalmane®)
Folates (folic acid)
Folates, red cell
Follicle stimulating hormone
Free phenytoin (Dilantin®)
Free T4 (thyroxine), includes total T4
Fructose, semen
FSH/LH
FSH/LH/Prolactin
Fungal antibodies, R.I.D
Fungus identification

Galactose
Gammaglutamyl Transpeptidase
Garamycin® (gentamicin)
Gastrin
Gemonil® (metharbital)
Glucagon
Glucose
Glucose tolerance
Glucose, 6-phosphate dehydrogenase
Glucose, fractionated, 24 hour urine
Glucose, post prandial
Glucose, spinal fluid
Glucose, 24 hour urine
Glucose, fasting and 2 hour post prandial
Glutamic oxalacetic transaminase-GOT
Glutamic pyruvic transaminase—GPT
Glutethimide (Doriden®), GLC
Gold, serum
Gold, urine
Gram stain
Growth Hormone (HGH)

H-1 profile
H-2 profile
H-3 profile
H-4 profile
H-5 profile
H-6 profile
H-7 profile
H-8 profile
Haloperidol, haldol
Ham's acid serum test
Haptoglobin
HCG-beta subunit
HDL-cholesterol
HDL/LDL-cholesterol
Heavy metal screen, urine

Hemoglobin
Hemoglobin A-2
Hemoglobin A-2 and F
Hemoglobin and hematocrit
Hemoglobin electrophoresis
Hemoglobin F
Hemoglobin, glycosylated
Hemoglobin, plasma or serum
Hemophilus influenzae antigen
Hemosiderin
Hepatitis B surface antibody
Hepatitis B "e" antigen and B "e" antibody
Hepatitis A antibody
Hepatitis B core antibody
Hepatitis B surface antigen
Herpes simplex virus culture
Herpes smear
Heterophile antibodies, absorption
Histochemistry enzyme battery, muscle biopsy
Histochemistry stains, Class I, miscellaneous
Histochemistry stains, Class II, miscellaneous
Histoplasmosis, titer
HLA phenotype
HLA-B27
Homocystine, urine
Homogentisic acid, urine
Homovanillic acid, urine
Human placental lactogen, serum
17 Hydroxycorticosterone, urine
17 Hydroxyprogesterone, serum
5 Hydroxyindoleacetic acid, urine
Hydroxyproline, free and total, urine
Hydroxyproline, total, urine

Immunoelectrophoresis, serum, K&L chains
Immunoelectrophoresis, urine, K&L chains
Immunoglobulin A (IgA)
Immunoglobulin E
Immunoglobulin G (IgG)
Immunoglobulin G in CSF
Immunoglobulins (IgA, IgG, IgM)
Immunoperoxidase, special stains
India Ink preparation
Indican, as potassium indoxyl sulfate
Insulin by RIA
Iron and iron binding capacity
Iron binding capacity
Iron in miscellaneous solutions
Iron stain
Iron, serum
Iron, urinary, excretion
Isohemagglutinin titer

17 Ketosteroids, 17 hydroxycorticoids

17 Ketogenic steroids
17 Ketosteroids, full fractionation
17 Ketosteroids, total neutral
17 Ketosteroids, 17 ketogenic
Kleihauer-Betke, stain

LE latex
Lactic acid (lactate)
Lactic dehydrogenase isoenzymes
Lactose in urine
LDH isoenzymes CSF
Lead, blood
Lead, urine
Lecithin-sphingomyelin ratio, includes
       phosphatidylglycerol
Leucine aminopeptidase
Leukemia, cytochemistry classification, with
       interpretation
Leukocyte alkaline phosphatase
Lipase
Lipids, total, serum
Lipids, total, feces
Lipoproteins
Lithium, serum
Lithium in erythrocytes
Luteinizing hormone

Magnesium, urine
Magnesium (water soluble) feces
Magnesium, serum
Malaria, blood smears
Manganese, serum
Melanin, random urine
Mercury, urine
Mesantoin® (mephenytoin)
Metanephrines, 12 hours
Metanephrines, fractionated
Metanephrines, total
Methemalbumin
Methemoglobin
MHPG
       (methoxyhydroxyphenylethyleneglycol)
Micro assay, water/dialysate
Minimal inhibitory concentration (MIC)
Mono test
Mucopolysaccharide screen, urine
Muscle fibers, stool
Mycobacterium identification
Myoglobin, serum
Myoglobin, urine

NA+, K+, water soluble, stool
Nortriptyline
5 Nucleotidase

Oligoclonal bands, CSF (electrophoresis)
Osmolality, serum or urine
Osmolality, stool
Ova, parasites, occult blood
Oxalate as oxalic acid

Paramethadione®
Parathyroid hormone mid-molecule
Parathyroid hormone C-terminal
Partial thromboplastin
PAS for fungus
Peganone® (ethotoin)
Pesticides screening, miscellaneous
PH, NA+, K+, osmolality, stool
PH, stool, meter
PH, urine, meter
Phenol, total, urine
Phenophthalein, stool
Phenothiazines, serum
Phenylalanine, quantitative
Phosphorus, inorganic, serum
Phosphorus, inorganic, urine
Pinworm preparation
PKU—Guthrie
Platelet count
PN-1 profile
PN-2 profile
PN-3 profile
PN-4 profile
PN-5 profile
PN-6 profile
Pneumococcal bacterial antigen
Porphobilinogen
Porphyrins, fecal
Potassium in water
Potassium, urine
Potassium (water soluble) stool
Potassium, serum
Pregnancy screen, serum
Pregnancy test, urine
Pregnanediol, urine
Pregnanetriol, urine
Progesterone
Prolactin
Prostatic acid phosphatase RIA
Protein, total urine
Protein, CSF
Protein, miscellaneous substances
Protein, serum
Proteus agglutinins
Prothrombin time
Protoporphyrin, zinc
Protoporphyrins, fecal
Protriptyline

Renin activity
Reticulocytes
RH titre/Antibody identification
Rheumatoid factor
Rotavirus antigen
RPR (serological test syphilis)
Rubella antibodies

S. pneumoniae bacterial antigen
Salicylates, serum
Sedimentation rate modified, Westergren
Sensitivity
Serum inhibitory level
Sex chromatin (Barr bodies)
Sialic acid, serum
Sickle cell preparation
SGOT—serum glutamate oxalacetate
        transaminase
SGPT—serum glutamate pyruvate
        transaminase
Smear, acid fast bacilli
Sodium and potassium, serum
Sodium and potassium, urine
Sodium, serum
Sodium, urine
Stains, Histochemistry
Stains, Cytochemistries
Stercobilinogen-urobilinogen, stool
Streptococcus group B latex
Streptonase-B
Streptozyme
Strychnine, qual, identification
Sugars, fractionated in urine
Sulfa
Sulfhemoglobin

T-3 total circulating
T-3 uptake
T3 uptake and T4 (D-18)
T4, free
T4, neonatal
T4 (thyroxine) by RIA
Testosterone/Luteinizing hormone
Testosterone
Thallium
Thrombin time
Thyroglobulin antibody
Thyroid antibody group (D-20)
Thyroid microsomal antibodies
Thyroid stimulating hormone
Thyroxine (T4) by RIA
Thyroxine, free
Thyroxine binding globulin
Tissue exam, gross

Tissue exam, gross and micro
Tissue, stains
Total protein and A/G ratio, serum
Total protein, fluid
Toxicology study, miscellaneous
Toxoplasma antibodies, IgM specific
Toxoplasma antibodies, IgG specific
Transferrin
Treponemal antibodies-FTA/ABS
TRH stimulation (cortisol X3)
Triglycerides
Trimethadione
Trypsin, stool
TSH, neonatal
Tubular reabsorption phosphorus
Tularemia agglutination
Tyrosine

Urea nitrogen, serum
Urea nitrogen, urine
Uric acid, serum
Uric acid, urine
Urinalysis
Urine isolate
Urobilinogen, fecal

Urobilinogen, urine
Uroporphyrinogen-1 Synthetase
Uroporphyrins, fecal
Uroporphyrins, urine

Valproic acid (Depakene®)
Vanillylmandelic acid
Vanillylmandelic acid, 12 hours
VDRL, CSF
VDRL, quantitative
VDRL, serum
Vibrio, stool
Viscosity
Vitamin B-12
Volatiles

Water quality analysis, aluminum
Water quality analysis, calcium
Water quality analysis, iron
Water quality analysis, sodium
White blood cells and differential

Yersinia, stool

Zinc, serum or urine

ANESTHETIC AGENTS

(Partial List)

Anestacon
Brevital
Carbocaine
Cocaine
Demerol
Ethrane
Fentanyl
Fluothane
Forane
Halothane

Ketamine hydrochloride
Lidocaine
Marcaine hydrochloride
Morphine
Nembutal
Nesacaine
Nisentil
Nitrous Oxide
Novocain
Nupercaine hydrochloride

Pontocaine
Procaine hydrochloride
Sodium Pentothal
Sufentanyl
Tetracaine hydrochloride
Thiopental Sodium
Topical Cocaine
Valium
Xylocaine

TYPES OF DRESSINGS

(Partial List)

ABD pad
Adaptic
Aeroplast
Desault's bandage, ligature
Esmarch bandage, tourniquet
Kerlix gauze
Kling bandage, dressing
Kos-House
Owen's cloth

Robert-Jones compression
   bandage
Sayre bandage
scultetus binder
Semken dressing
spica cast
stent surgical dressing
Steri-drape (3-M drape)

Steri-strip skin closure
Steri-tape
Telfa
Unna's paste boot
Vaseline wick dressing
Velpeau bandage
Xeroform gauze dressing

TYPES OF INCISIONS

(Partial List)

ab-externo
Auvray
buttonhole
Cherney
circumferential
collar
coronal
crosshatch
cruciate
curvilinear
Deaver
Dührssen
elliptical
endaural

Fowler
gridiron
hockey stick
infraumbilical
intracapsular
Kehr
Kocher
Küstner
Langenbeck
lateral flank
lateral rectus
Mackenrodt
McBurney
median

midline
muscle splitting
paramedian
Parker
Pfannenstiel
racquet
rectus muscle splitting
Rockey-Davis
Schuchardt
suprapubic
transverse
Vischer lumboiliac
Z-flap
Z-shaped

OPERATIVE POSITIONS

(Partial List)

decubitus
dorsal recumbent
jackknife
knee-chest

Kraske's
lateral
lithotomy
Proetz

prone
Sims
supine
Trendelenburg

TYPES OF SUTURES AND SUTURE MATERIALS

(Partial List)

Atralease
atraumatic
bridle
buried
button
chromic catgut
coaptation
Connell
continuous
Cushing
cutaneous
Dacron
Deknatel
Dermalene
Dermalon
Dexon
D-Tach
Ethibond
Ethicon
Ethiflex
Ethilon

Ethistrip skin closures
everting
figure-of-eight
Flexon
Halsted
hemostatic
Lembert
Limbal
Littre
lock-stitch vertical mattress
mattress
Maunsell
Mersilene
monofilament
multifilament
Nurolon
Palfyn
Petit
Polydek
polyethylene

prolene
purse-string
Ramdohr
retention
right-angle
Ritisch
silk braided
stainless steel
steel mesh
stick tie
subcuticular
Surgilon
Tevdek
through-and-through
tongue-and-groove
traction
Tycron or Ti-Cron
Vicryl
visceroparietal
Y-suture

MEDICAL PREFIXES AND MEANINGS

(Partial List)

Prefixes are always located at the beginning of a word and are generally one or two syllables. A prefix can never stand alone; it is always used in conjunction with a medical combining form or with a combining form and suffix.

a-	without
ab-	from, away
ad-	to, toward
ambi-	both
ante-	forward, before
antero-	in front of
apo-	away, from
arter-, arteri-	artery
arthr-	joint
auto-	self
bi-, bis-	twice, double
bio-	pertaining to life
carcin-	cancer
cardi-	heart
cata-	down, lower
cervic-	neck

circum-	around, about
contra-	against, counter
crani-	skull
cyst-	bladder
de-	down from
derm-	skin
di-	double
dia-	through
dis-	apart from
dys-	bad, painful
e-, ec,- ex-	out of
ecto-	outside
endo-	within
entero-	intestine
epi-	upon
gastr-	stomach
gyn-	woman
hemi-	half
hemo-, hema-	blood
hyper-	increased, over, excessive
hypo-	decreased, below
hyster-	womb, uterus
infra-	below, beneath
inter-	between, among
intra-	within, into
intro-	into
iso-	equal
laryng-	windpipe
leuk-	white
lig-	tie
macro-, mega-, megalo-	large, great
mast-	breast
meso-, media-	in middle of, center
meta-	from one place to another
micro-	small
myo-	muscle
neur-	pertaining to nerves
ortho-	normal, straight
oss-, oste-, osteo-	bone
ot-, oto-	ear
ov-	egg
patho-	disease
peri-	around
phleb-	vein
pneumo-	lung
postero-	in back, behind
psyche-	the mind
pulmo-	lung
retro-	backward
supra-, super-	upon, above
thorac-	chest
thromb-	lump, clot
tox-	poison
ultra-	excess

MEDICAL SUFFIXES AND MEANINGS
(Partial List)

A suffix is always located at the end of a word. It may be found in combination
with a prefix and combining form(s) or with only a combining form. A suffix
should never be used alone.

-able, -ible	denoting an ability or tendency toward
-ac	pertaining to
-aemia	condition of blood
-algia, -dynia	painful
-asis, -iasis	state resulting from
-cele	pouching, hernia
-centesis	puncture for aspiration
-cle	expresses diminution
-cyte	cell
-ectomy	excision; surgical removal of
-edema	swelling
-emia	blood
-genic	producing
-ia	denoting state or condition
-ic	pertaining to, resembling
-id	state or condition
-ist	one who practices a skill
-itis	inflammation
-logy, -ology	science of
-mania	madness or insane desire
-megaly	enlargement
-ness	state of being
-oma	a swelling, usually a tumor, either benign or malignant
-opia	sight
-oscopy	observation by means of an instrument
-osis	condition, state, process
-otomy, -ostomy	opening, incision
-pexy	fixation
-phagia, -phagy	eating, swallowing
-phasia	speaking
-phobia	fear, dread of
-plasty	plastic surgery
-plegia	paralysis
-ptosis	falling, downward displacement
-rhagia	hemorrhage
-rhea	discharge, flow
-rrhaphy	suture
-scope	instrument for inspection or examination
-scopy	examination
-sis	denoting condition; act of
-trophy	nutrition or growth

MEDICAL COMBINING FORMS AND MEANINGS
(Partial List)

The combining form is the main stem of each medical term. Combining forms are always found in conjunction with a prefix, suffix, another combining form, or any combination of these.

abdomino	abdomen
acro	extremity
adeno, aden	gland
adreno	adrenal gland
aero, aer	air, gas
angio, angi	vessel
arterio	artery
arthro, arthr	joint
atrio	atrium of the heart
brady	slow
broncho	bronchus, bronchi
carcino	carcinoma
cardio, card	heart
celio,	abdomen
cephalo, cephal	head
cheilo, cheil	lip
chole, chol, cholo	bile
chondro, chondr	cartilage
chordo	cord
colpo, colp	vagina
costo	rib
cranio	cranium, skull
cyano, cyan	blue
cysto, cyst, cysti, cystido	sac, bladder
cyto, cyt	cell
dermato, dermat, derma, dermo	skin
duodeno	duodenum
encephalo	brain
entero, enter	intestines
episio	vulva
erythro	red
eu	normal
fibro	fibers
ganglio, gangli	ganglion
gastro, gastr	stomach
glosso, gloss	tongue
gluco	glucose
glyco	sugar
gyneco, gyn, gyne, gyno	woman
hem, hema, hemo, hemat, hemato	blood
hepato, hepat	liver
hydro, hydr	water
hystero	uterus, hysteria
ileo	ileum

ilio	ilium, flank
jejuno	jejunum
kerato	cornea, horny tissue
laparo	flank, abdomen
laryngo	larynx
leuco, leuko	white
lipo	fat
litho, lith	stone, calculus
lyso	breaking down, dissolution
macro	large, long
malaco	softening
mammo	breast
masto, mast	breast
melano	black
meningo	meninges
meno	menses
micro, micr	small
myelo, myel	bone marrow, spinal cord
myo, my	muscle
myringo	eardrum
naso	nose
necro	death
neo	new
nephro, nephr	kidney
neuro, neur	nerve
oculo	eye
oligo	few, deficient
oophoro, oophor	ovary
ophthalmo, ophthalm	eye
orchio, orchi, orchido	testis, testes
oro	mouth
ortho	straight, normal, correct
osteo, oste	bone
oto, ot	ear
patho	disease
pedo	child, foot
phago	eating, engulfing
pharyngo	pharynx
phlebo, phleb	vein
phono, phon	sound
pleuro, pleur	pleura
pneo	breathing
pneumo	lung
poly	many, excessive
procto, proct	rectum
psycho	mind
pulmo, pulmono	lung
py, pyo	pus
pyelo, pyel	pelvis of the kidney
recto	rectum
rhino, rhin	nose
salpingo, salping	tube, uterine or eustachian

sclero, scler	hard, sclera
splanchno	viscera
spleno, splen	spleen
steno	narrowed
sterno	sternum
tachy	fast
thoraco	chest
thrombo	clot
thyro	thyroid
toxico, toxo	poison
tracheo	trachea
tropho	nourishment
uretero	ureter
urethro	urethra
uro, ur	urine
utero	uterus
vaso	vessel
veno	vein
ventriculo	ventricle of the heart or brain

SUGGESTED REFERENCE MATERIALS

Any good English dictionary, preferably unabridged.

Coleman, Frances. Guide to Surgical Terminology. Oradell, NJ: Medical Economics Company, 1978.

Dorland's Illustrated Medical Dictionary (Philadelphia: W. B. Saunders, 1974).

Doyle, Jean Monty and Robert Lee Dennis. The Complete Handbook for Medical Secretaries and Assistants. Boston: Little, Brown and Company, 1978.

Humphrey, Doris D., and Kathie Sigler. The Modern Medical Office: A Reference Manual. Cincinnati: South-Western Publishing Company, 1986.

Physicians' Desk Reference (Oradell, NJ: Medical Economics Company, 1983).

Rimer, Evelyn Harbeck. Harbeck's Glossary of Medical Terms. Menlo Park, CA: Pacific Coast Publishers, 1967.

SAMPLE FOOTNOTE REFERENCES

JOURNAL ARTICLES

Jones TW: New Frontiers in Psychiatry. JAMA 1981;182:150.

Hogue C, and Parvin D: Cancerous Agents. JAMA 1979;17:204.

BOOKS

Davis SE: Reyes syndrome, in Savoy T and Taylor CW (eds): <u>Pediatrics</u>. New York, John Wiley & Sons, 1975, pp 235–237.

Loftin CE: Cancer of the lungs, in Powell CB (ed): <u>Emphysema</u>. Boston, Little, Brown & Co, 1980, pp 5–8.

Warren TM: <u>Pediatric Cardiology</u>. Los Angeles: Harper & Bros, 1976, pp 59–62.

MISCELLANEOUS

Goss W: Personal communication.

INDEX

A

abdominoperineal, 75
abdominoplasty, 334
abortion, 179
abreaction, 361
abruptio placentae, 179
acantholysis, 66
acanthoma, 66
acariasis, 66
acarodermatitis, 66
acarophobia, 362
acetabulum, 238
achalasia, 110
achlorhydria, 110
achondroplasia, 238
achromia, 302
achylia, 110
acidosis, 423
aciduria, 423
acinus, 302
acne rosacea, 66
acrocephalosyndactyly, 151
acrocyanosis, 110
acromegaly, 110
acromial, 238
acromioclavicular, 238
acrophobia, 362
actinic keratosis, 66
actinomycosis, 29
acuminata verruca, 66
adamantinoma, 302
adenoacanthoma, 302
adenoameloblastoma, 29
adenocarcinoma, 4
adenoidectomy, 273
adenoma, 75
adenoma sebaceum, 66
adiadochokinesia, 151
adiposis, 110
aditus, 273
adjuvant, 75
adnexa, 179
adrenalectomy, 110
adventitia, 75
aerated, 380
aerophagia, 110
aeroplast dressing, 80
agnathia, 29
agnosia, 218
agoraphobia, 362
agrammatism, 151
agranulocytosis, 110

akathisia, 362
akinesia, 4, 151
akinesis, 4
ala, 32
Albarran's disease, 424
albuminuria, 424
aleukemic, 302
aleukocytic, 302
alkalosis, 424
allantiasis, 111
Allis forceps, 81
allochiria, 151
allograft, 334
alveolalgia, 32
alveolar, 32
alveolectomy, 32
alveoli, 32
alveolitis, 32
alveoloclasia, 32
alveoloplasty, 32
alveolus, 32
Alzheimer's disease, 151
amalgam, 32
amaurosis, 218
amaurosis centralis, 218
ambivalence, 362
amblyopia, 218
amebiasis, 111
amelanotic, 302
amelioration, 111
amelodentinal, 32
amenorrhea, 180
amentia, 362
ametropia, 219
aminoaciduria, 424
amitotic, 302
amniocentesis, 180
amnionitis, 180
amniorrhea, 180
amok, 362
amusia, 362
amyelia, 151
amylase, 111
amylasuria, 111
amyloidosis, 424
amyotrophia, 424
amyotrophic lateral sclerosis, 151
anaclitic, 362
analysand, 362
anamnesis, 362
anaphylactic, 111

anaphylaxis, 66
anasarca, 111
anastomosis, 75
ancylostomiasis, 111
anemia, 111
anencephalia, 151
aneurysmectomy, 5
angina pectoris, 5
angiocardiography, 380
angiocath, 5
angiogram, 380
angiography, 380
angiomatosis, 111
angioneurotic, 112
angiosarcoma, 112
anhidrosis, 112
anhydremia, 112
aniridia, 219
aniseikonia, 219
anisocoria, 219
anisocytosis, 302
anisometropia, 219
anisotropic, 302
ankyloblepharon, 219
ankyloglossia, 32
ankylosing spondylitis, 238
ankylosis, 238
anodontia, 32
anomalous, 380
anomaly, 112
anophthalmia, 219
anorchism, 424
anorexia, 424
anorexia nervosa, 362
anoxemia, 112
anoxic, 302
ante partum, 180
anteflexion of uterus, 180
antegrade, 5
anteromedial, 6
anthracosis, 112
anthrocotic lymph nodes, 75
antianxiety agents, 362
anticholinergic, 112
antidiuresis, 112
antidiuretic, 424
antigen, 424
antipsychotic, 362
antipyrine, 424
antistreptolysin, 425
antrostomy, 273

cystoureteritis, 427
cystoureterolithotomy, 427
cystourethrogram, 381
cytotoxicity, 427
cytotrophoblast, 305

D

dacryoadenectomy, 220
dacryoadenitis, 220
dacryocystectomy, 220
dacryocystoptosis, 220
dacryocystorhinostomy, 220
dacryops, 220
Dalrymple's disease, 220
dartos, 427
de Toni-Fanconi syndrome, 113
decannulated, 7
decerebrate, 153
decibel, 274
decidious teeth, 33
decidua, 182
deciduoma, 305
decortication, 79
decrescendo murmur, 7
decubitus, 79
defervesced, 182
defervescence, 113
deglutition, 381
dehiscence, 79
dehydration, 427
dehydrogenase, 113
déjà vu, 363
Deknatel sutures, 33
deleterious, 113
dementia, 153
Demodex folliculorum, 305
demyelinate, 153
Denhardt mouth gag, 33
dens-in-dente, 33
dental alveoli, 33
dentibuccal, 33
dentigerous cyst, 33
dentinogenesis, 33
dentition, 33
dentoalveolar, 33
dentritus, 33
denudation, 67
denude, 79
deossification, 239
dereism, 363
dermabrasion, 335
Dermacentor andersoni, 67
Dermacentor variabilis, 67
dermatitis herpetiformis, 67
dermatitis venenata, 67
dermatocryosurgery, 67

dermatome, 79
dermatophytosis, 67
dermolipectomy, 335
descensus, 79
descensus testis, 427
descensus uteri, 182
desensitization, 274
desiccate, 381
desiccation, 67
desquamation, 79
detrusor, 427
devascularize, 79
dextrocardia, 7
dextroposition, 381
diadochokinesia, 153
dialysis, 427
diapedesis, 305
diaphragm, 182
diaphyseal, 239
diaphysis, 239
diastalsis, 79
diastasis, 239
diastema, 34
diastematomyelia, 154
diathermy, 381
diencephalon, 154
dilatation, 182
diopsimeter, 220
DIP joint, 335
diplegia, 154
Diplococcus pneumoniae, 305
diplopia, 220
discission, 221
discogram, 240
disdiadochokinesia, 363
distichia, 221
diuresis, 427
diuretic, 427
diverticulitis, 79
diverticulosis, 79
diverticulum, 79
Doerfler-Stewart test, 278
Dohle's inclusion bodies, 305
dolichocephalism, 154
donor site, 80
Dopamine, 7
Doppler pulses, 7
dorsalis pedis pulse, 80
dorsolumbar, 240
dorsoradial, 240
dosimeter, 381
Duchenne's disease, 154
ductus, 80
duodenitis, 113
duodenoduodenostomy, 113
duodenoileostomy, 113
duodenojejunostomy, 114

duodenum, 80
Dupuytren's contracture, 240
dura mater, 154
dysarthria, 114
dysbulia, 363
dysesthesia, 154
dysgerminoma, 427
dyshidrosis, 67
dyskeratosis, 67
dyskeratotic, 67
dyskinesia, 154
dyslexia, 363
dysmegalopsia, 221
dysmenorrhea, 182
dysontogenesis, 305
dysopia, 221
dysostosis, 240
dyspareunia, 182
dysphagia, 80
dysplasia, 80
dyspneic, 7
dysproteinemia, 427
dyssymmetry, 114
dyssynergia, 114
dystocia, 182
dysuria, 427

E

eardrum, 274
Ebstein's disease, 114
eburnation, 381
ecchymosis, 80
eccrine gland, 305
echinococcosis, 114
echoencephalography, 381
echolalia, 363
echopraxis, 363
eclampsia, 182
eclamptic toxemia, 183
ectasia, 7
ectatic, 7
ectodermosis, 67
ectomorphic, 363
ectopic pregnancy, 183
ectropion, 183
eczema, 67
eczematoid, 67
eczematous, 67
edentulous, 34
effacement, 183
efflux, 80
ego-dystonic, 363
Ehrlich's test, 305
eidetic, 364
eikonometer, 221
electrodermatome, 335

inion, 155
innervation, 155
innominate, 241
inspissated, 116
insufflation, 82
intermaxillary, 35
intermural, 382
interosseous, 241
interstitial, 429
intertriginous, 68
intertrochanteric, 241
intervertebral disc, 241
intima, 8
intra-aortic balloon pump, 8
intra-arterially, 8
intraluminal, 82
intramedullary, 241
intramyocardial, 8
intraoral, 35
intrapartum, 184
intrarenal, 429
introitus, 184
intumescent cataract, 219
intussusception, 88
iodoform dressing, 80
Ioprep, 8
iridectomize, 222
iridectomy, 222
iridencleisis, 222
iridesis, 222
Iridium-192, 382
iridocorneosclerectomy, 222
iridocyclectomy, 222
iridocyclitis, 222
iridodonesis, 222
iridokeratitis, 223
iridoleptynsis, 223
iridomesodialysis, 223
iridotomy, 223
ischiopubic, 241
ischiorectal, 184
ischium, 241
ischogyria, 155
Ishihara's test, 223
islets, 307
isoimmunization, 429
isoperistaltic, 82
isopia, 223
isthmus, 82

J

Jako laryngoscope, 275
Jakob-Creutzfeldt disease, 307
Javid shunt, 8
jejunectomy, 82
jejunojejunostomy, 82

jejunum, 83
Jesberg esophagoscope, 83

K

kalemia, 116
Kaposi's sarcoma, 307
Karsokov's psychosis, 364
karyolysis, 307
karyorrhexis, 307
keloid, 335
keloplasty, 335
keratectasia, 223
keratinocytes, 68
keratoacanthoma, 307
keratoconjunctivitis, 223
keratohyaline, 68
keratoiritis, 223
keratoleptynsis, 223
keratometry, 223
keratopathy, 223
keratosis, 69
keratotic, 83
Kerchring's, folds of, 307
kerectomy, 223
kernicterus, 155
Kerrison's ronguer, 83
Kesselbach's area, 275
Kienbock's disease, 307
kinesioneurosis, 155
kinesthesia, 155
kinetosis, 116
Kirschner wire, 35
kleptomania, 364
Kocher forceps, 81
Kocher incision, 82
kraurosis, 429
Krukenberg's tumor, 307
Kupffer's cells, 307
kwashiorkor, 429–430
kyphoscoliosis, 241
kyphosis, 241

L

L-dopa, 155
La Force adenotome, 275
labia majora, 184
labia minora, 184
lability, 364
labiomental, 335
labyrinth, 275
labyrinthitis, 275
lactation, 183
Laennec's cirrhosis, 116
lagophthalmos, 223
Lahey forceps, 81

Lambl's excrescence, 307
lamella, 241
laminagram, 382
laminagraphy, 382
laminectomy, 241
landmark, 275
Langhans' cells, 307
laparoscopy, 184
laparotomy, 184
laryngectomy, 83
laryngitis, 275
laryngocentesis, 275
laryngoparalysis, 275
laryngopharyngectomy, 275
laryngoscopy, 275
laterognathia, 35
lateropulsion, 155
latissimus, 241
Le Fort's fracture, 35
leiomyoma, 184
Lembert's suture, 184
leMesurier technique for cleft lip
    repair, 335
lemniscus, 155
lenticular, 275
lenticulo-optic, 223
lenticulothalamic, 223
lentigines, 69
lentigo maligna, 69
leptomeninges, 155
leptomeningitis, 155
Leriche's disease, 307
lethargy, 364
Letterer-Siwe disease, 307
leucine, 307
leucine aminopeptidase, 307
leukocytosis, 116
leukocyturia, 430
leukoderma, 69
leukodystrophy, 155
leukokoria, 223
leukopenia, 116
leukoplakia, 83
leukorrhea, 184
levator palpebrae muscle, 223
Levin tube, 83
Leydig's cells, 307
libido, 364
lichen planus, 69
lichenification, 69
Lidocaine, 8
ligament of Treitz, 83
linea alba, 83
lines of Zahn, 308
lingual, 35
lingular, 83
lipase, 116

tympanomandibular, 278
tympanomastoiditis, 279
tympanomeatal, 279
tympanoplasty, 279
tympanotomy tube, 279
tympanum, 279

U

ulectomy, 225
ultrasonography, 85
ultrasound, 187
umbilicus, 187
umbo, 279
unci, 311
Unna's paste boot, 86
uranoplasty, 337
urea, 433
ureterectasis, 433
ureteritis, 433
ureteroenteric, 433
ureterolithiasis, 433
ureterolithotomy, 433
ureteropelvic, 433
ureteropyelogram, 384
ureteroureterostomy, 433
urethrovesical, 433
uricosuric, 119
uriniferous, 433
urobilinogenuria, 119
uropepsinogen, 119
urotoxia, 433
urticaria, 119
urtication, 71
utero-ovarian, 187
uterosacral ligament, 187
uterovesical, 187
uterus, 187
utriculus, 433
uvea, 225
uvula, 279

V

vagina, 188
vaginitis, 188
vagotomy, 158

vagotonia, 158
valgus, 244
vallecula, 279
valvulitis, 119
valvuloplasty, 10
Van Alyea irrigator, 279
van Gieson's stain, 311
Van Lint akinesia, 225
varicocele, 433
varicosities, 188
variegated, 311
variola, 71
varus, 244
vas, 86
vasectomy, 433
vasodilation, 384
vasopressor, 10
Vater-Pacini corpuscles, 311
Velpeau dressing, 80
vena cava, 10
venocath, 10
venotomy, 10
ventriculocaval, 158
ventriculocisternostomy, 158
ventriculogram, 10
ventriculography, 384
ventriculography catheter, 10
ventriculoseptal, 10
Verhoeff's elastic stain, 311
vermiform, 119
vermilion, 86
vermilion border, 37
vermilionectomy, 86
vernix caseosa, 311
Verocay bodies, 311
verruca, 86
verrucous, 279
vertebra, 244
verumontanum, 433
vesication, 71
vesicourethropexy, 433
vesicouterine, 188
vesicovaginal, 188
vesiculobullous, 71
vessel loop, 10
vestibule, 279
vestibuloplasty, 37

Vi Drape film and adhesive, 86
villous, 86
Vim-Silverman needle, 86
Virchow-Robin spaces, 311
visceromegaly, 10
vitiligo, 71
vitrectomy, 225
vitreous 225
volvulus, 119
vomer, 279
von Willebrand's disease, 311
vulva, 188
vulvectomy, 188

W

wallerian degeneration, 158
Weber test, 278
Weil's disease, 71
Weiss procedure, 225
Wharton's duct, 119
work-up, 366

X

xanthelasma, 225
xanthoma, 225
xanthomatosis, 119
xenograft, 337
Xenon 133, 384
xeroderma, 71
Xeroform, 86
xerophthalmia, 225
xiphoid, 86
xiphoid process, 244
xyphoid

Y

Yttrium-90, 384

Z

Z-plasty, 37
Zenker's fixation, 311
Ziehl-Neelsen's method, stain, 311
zygomaticomaxillary, 279